Unified Transfer Tax Rates

FOR GIFTS MADE AND FOR DEATHS IN 2004

If the Amount with Respect to Which the Tentative Tax to Be Computed Is:	The Tentative Tax Is:
Not over $10,000	18 percent of such amount.
Over $10,000 but not over $20,000	$1,800, plus 20 percent of the excess of such amount over $10,000.
Over $20,000 but not over $40,000	$3,800, plus 22 percent of the excess of such amount over $20,000.
Over $40,000 but not over $60,000	$8,200, plus 24 percent of the excess of such amount over $40,000.
Over $60,000 but not over $80,000	$13,000, plus 26 percent of the excess of such amount over $60,000.
Over $80,000 but not over $100,000	$18,200, plus 28 percent of the excess of such amount over $80,000.
Over $100,000 but not over $150,000	$23,800, plus 30 percent of the excess of such amount over $100,000.
Over $150,000 but not over $250,000	$38,800, plus 32 percent of the excess of such amount over $150,000.
Over $250,000 but not over $500,000	$70,800, plus 34 percent of the excess of such amount over $250,000.
Over $500,000 but not over $750,000	$155,800, plus 37 percent of the excess of such amount over $500,000.
Over $750,000 but not over $1,000,000	$248,300, plus 39 percent of the excess of such amount over $750,000.
Over $1,000,000 but not over $1,250,000	$345,800, plus 41 percent of the excess of such amount over $1,000,000.
Over $1,250,000 but not over $1,500,000	$448,300, plus 43 percent of the excess of such amount over $1,250,000.
Over $1,500,000 but not over $2,000,000	$555,800, plus 45 percent of the excess of such amount over $1,500,000.
Over $2,000,000	$780,800, plus 48 percent of the excess of such amount over $2,000,000.

Income Tax Rates—Corporations

Taxable Income	Tax Rate
Not over $50,000	15%
Over $50,000 but not over $75,000	25%
Over $75,000 but not over $100,000	34%
Over $100,000 but not over $335,000	39%*
Over $335,000 but not over $10,000,000	34%
Over $10,000,000 but not over $15,000,000	35%
Over $15,000,000 but not over $18,333,333	38%**
Over $18,333,333	35%

*Five percent of this rate represents a phaseout of the benefits of the lower tax rates on the first $75,000 of taxable income.

**Three percent of this rate represents a phaseout of the benefits of the lower tax rate (34% rather than 35%) on the first $10 million of taxable income.

Tax Formula for Unrelated Business Taxable Income

Gross unrelated business income
– Deductions
= Net unrelated business income
± Modifications
= Unrelated business taxable income

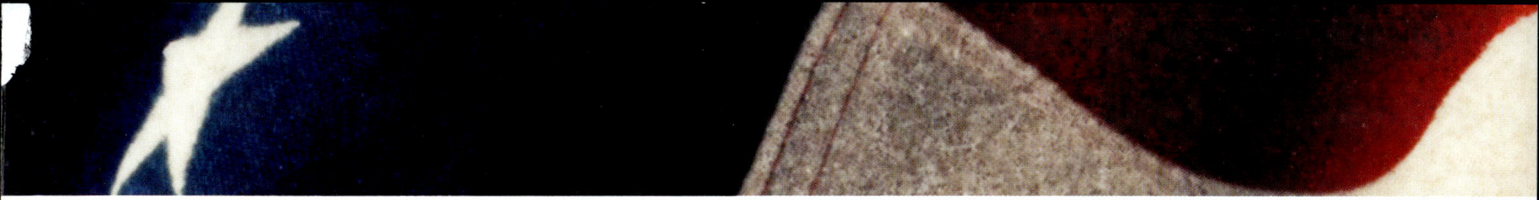

West Federal Taxation

Advanced Business Entity Taxation

2005 EDITION

General Editors

William A. Raabe
Ph.D., CPA
The Ohio State University

Eugene Willis
Ph.D., CPA
University of Illinois, Urbana-Champaign

David M. Maloney
Ph.D., CPA
University of Virginia

James E. Smith
Ph.D., CPA
College of William and Mary

THOMSON
SOUTH-WESTERN

Australia · Canada · Mexico · Singapore · Spain · United Kingdom · United States

THOMSON
SOUTH-WESTERN

West Federal Taxation: Advanced Business Entity Taxation, 2005e

William A. Raabe, Eugene Willis, David M. Maloney, James E. Smith

Contributing Authors

Gary A. McGill
Ph.D., CPA
University of Florida

Karen H. Molloy
Ph.D., CPA
University of Illinois, Urbana-Champaign

Debra L. Sanders
Ph.D., CPA
Washington State University

Thomas J. Sternburg
Ph.D., CPA
University of Illinois, Urbana-Champaign

Roby B. Sawyers
Ph.D., C.M.A., CPA
North Carolina State University

Vice President/Editorial Director:
Jack W. Calhoun

Vice President/Editor-in-Chief:
George Werthman

Acquisitions Editor:
Charles McCormick, Jr.

Senior Developmental Editor:
Craig Avery

Marketing Manager:
Chip Kislack

Production Editor:
Lora Arduser

Manager of Technology, Editorial:
Vicky True

Technology Project Editor:
Christine A. Wittmer

Manufacturing Coordinator:
Doug Wilke

Compositor:
The GTS Companies/York, PA Campus

Production House:
Litten Editing and Production, Inc.

Printer:
Thomson-West
Eagan, MN

Senior Design Project Manager:
Michelle Kunkler

Cover and Internal Designer:
Ann Small/a small design studio

Cover Image:
© William J. Hebert/Getty Images, Inc.

Printed in the United States of America
1 2 3 4 5 06 05 04

ISBN: 0-324-22094-4 (Package)
ISBN: 0-324-22093-6 (Text Only)

ISSN 1544-3582
2005 Annual Edition

For more information contact South-Western, 5191 Natorp Boulevard, Mason, Ohio. 45040.
Or you can visit our Internet site at: http://www.swlearning.com

West Federal Taxation

Preface

2005 EDITION

YOUR SUCCESS is our key goal at *West Federal Taxation.* Whether you are a student, an instructor, or a corporate or independent user of our products, we are dedicated to providing the most useful, comprehensive, and up-to-date tax texts, online materials, CDs, and learning/teaching aids available.

For over 27 years, the *West Federal Taxation (WFT)* Series has helped **more than 1.3 million users** master the ever-changing nature of Federal taxation. The 2005 Editions are no exception. Each continues to offer unparalleled comprehensive coverage in an accessible yet authoritative manner.

WFT began as a single textbook on Corporations, Partnerships, Estates, and Trusts, followed a year later by Individual taxation. Today, this unrivaled package includes five major textbooks and a selection of more than 50 outstanding ancillaries. With the 2005 Editions, *WFT* continues to build on the quality of these materials, adding innovations that enhance instruction and make learning even more engaging. As always, *WFT* strives to show its users the importance and relevance of taxation to individual taxpayers as well as to all areas of business.

Leadership, Innovation, and Service are our watchwords at *West Federal Taxation.* Read on to learn what our pledge means for *your* success.

The 2005 Edition of *WFT: Advanced Business Entity Taxation*

The Leadership You Trust

LEADERSHIP BASED ON THE MODEL TAX CURRICULUM

"[*WFT: Taxation of Business Entities*] seems to be the best textbook for the entities approach."
— *John F. Kohler, Washington University (St. Louis)*

The prescription for teaching tax courses in universities and law schools continues to evolve and change. Many instructors, academic observers, and the American Institute of Certified Public Accountants now prefer that the first two tax courses be taught with an orientation toward business entities.

A more complex, global business environment means that users of tax learning materials must demonstrate an increasingly broad array of skills upon completion of their tax courses. Besides technical tax skills, corporations, consulting firms, and others who employ tax specialists are looking for the following traits in their tax professionals:

- Dedication to learning the law, but also to employing it within a planning orientation. That is, they should have the ability to apply the tax laws and meet other goals of the taxpayer in working with the tax law and its administration.
- Integration of technical tax knowledge with skills in strategic decision making, spoken and written communications, an ethical base, and general research skills including the thorough use of Web-based and other searching tools.
- Appreciation of the "big picture"—that is, the knowledge of how tax fits in with other disciplines that are part of the education experience, such as economics, financial accounting, finance, law, and the social sciences. Part of this is an appreciation of the scope of the tax system as it works in today's economy—how many taxpayers and business entities are paying how much and what types of taxes.

The authors and editors of the acclaimed *West Federal Taxation* Series have developed the leading materials for teaching the tax law in this exciting, new environment. The result is a textbook and extensive support materials—print, electronic, and human—that offer a rich, integrated, and effective learning system.

Complementing the traditional texts of the *WFT* series, the two volumes *Taxation of Business Entities* and *Advanced Business Entity Taxation* fit the demands of the AICPA Model Tax Curriculum and of the leading tax educators in the country. In developing these two texts, we have ensured that they are characterized by the same qualities of accuracy, readability, and pedagogical design that have made the *WFT* series the most widely used tax texts on the market.

WFT: Advanced Business Entity Taxation meets the demands of today's educators, as it matches the AICPA Model Tax Curriculum's suggestions for:

- The "second tax course," in which advanced technical and technological skills are developed in entity taxation, the tax effects of multijurisdictional commerce are studied, and the advanced issues facing individual taxpayers, including retirement, estate/gift, and financial planning are explored.
- The "MBA tax course," in which tax planning and support for decision makers is prominent, and an emphasis on the tax aspects of goal setting and benchmarking is achieved.
- The entry into graduate-level tax studies, where the student is expected to demonstrate specific technical tax skills, especially in advanced business taxation, choice of entity analyses, and multijurisdictional transactions. Advanced skills with tax research materials are developed, as is an appreciation for the work ethic and professional responsibilities of the leaders of the tax profession.

"The topics covered follow our course syllabus almost to the letter. Our syllabus has been patterned based on the model tax curriculum."

— *Gregg Woodruff, Western Illinois University*

WFT: Advanced Business Entity Taxation features several critical and long-overdue advances in the pedagogy of tax education:

- **A dedication to a tax planning orientation.** Building upon the **Planning Framework** introduced and examined in detail in *WFT: Taxation of Business Entities, WFT: Advanced Business Entity Taxation* and its ancillary material continue the emphasis on developing tools and observations by which the tax professional puts in place various financial and tax planning techniques. To explain both the law and the planning behavior of the tax professional, the **Planning Strategies** feature ties together the provisions of the law with the behavior of taxpayers and advisors, so that the What and How and Why of the tax profession become clear to the reader.
- **Integration of the tax course with other disciplines that are under study by its readers.** The **Bridge Discipline** feature of this text and *WFT: Taxation of Business Entities* focuses on how the tax law follows or departs from the principles and applications of law, finance, economics, social policy, political science, and other lines of study. In addition, this text features an **entire chapter** (Chapter 2) on **how the financial accounting disclosure function of the tax expense, promulgated in controlling documents such as FAS 109, weaves together with the details of the tax law.** "Book-tax differences" of this sort must be familiar territory today for tax professionals, auditors, financial analysts, attorneys, and others who receive tax education in these pages.
- **A true focus on the tax effects of multijurisdictional transactions.** Unprecedented among tax materials, the two texts provide rich and detailed but highly useable explanations and examples of how taxpayers can use the tax law of various jurisdictions in reaching their ultimate financial goals. In Chapter 12, *WFT: Taxation of Business Entities* offers a one-chapter integrated summary of the rules and issues facing taxpayers doing business under more than one tax law regime. *WFT: Advanced Business Entity Taxation* then builds upon this foundation with **four full chapters** of text and learning support—Chapters 7, 8, 9, and 10—concerning the **taxation of entities operating in more than one country and/or more than one U.S. state.**
- **An important follow-up to the materials in the first tax course concerning the taxation of individual taxpayers.** Critical technical and planning issues are addressed with respect to the application of various tax-favored retirement provisions of the law. Also included are detailed reviews of Federal tax laws affecting the transfer of assets by gift, bequest, or trust. These topics are then integrated, with a focus on tax entities through an analysis of issues facing the owner of a family business who wants to create a tax-advantaged situation for successors to the ownership interest.

"[*WFT: Taxation of Business Entities*] was adopted in order to include course content more aligned with the AICPA recommended model tax curriculum."

— *Priscilla O'Clock, Xavier University*

Much more than an "advanced tax topics" text, *WFT: Advanced Business Entity Taxation* offers the following outstanding features:

- A rich package of learning materials.
- Critical advances in the pedagogy of tax education.
- The quality expected from the *West Federal Taxation* editor and author team.
- A 21st century approach to learning, from the features of the text to technology choices to user support.

WFT: Advanced Business Entity Taxation delivers all of the above in a fashion that is attractive to college/university, MBA, professional education, and law school users. The materials of the text can be used in chapter order, employed more selectively by using only certain chapters, or customized to meet other needs. The *WFT* Web site includes several sample syllabi illustrating these various uses; visit **http://wft-advanced.swlearning.com.**

Users of *West Federal Taxation* deserve the latest information reflecting statutory, judicial, and administrative changes in Federal tax law. For that reason, the 2005 Edition of this text and supplements incorporate the changes in tax law brought about by the **Jobs and Growth Tax Relief Reconciliation Act of 2003 (JGTRRA).** When JGTRRA became law, we at *West Federal Taxation* provided the following materials for use in the summer and fall of 2003: (1) a "WFT Transition Guide" prepared by the *WFT* Editors, which summarized the act and which was keyed to each chapter of all five *WFT* texts; (2) revised solutions to all relevant end-of-chapter items and test bank items; (3) two special reports by Deloitte outlining the legislation; and (4) a Concordance to the updated solutions. Because of the dynamic nature of tax law, we will continue to offer instant access to all relevant updates at **http://wft-advanced.swlearning.com**. In addition, *WFT* sends hard copies of major tax law changes and updates to all adopters—ensuring that important changes in Federal tax law will not be overlooked.

"It was very helpful to have the textbook page references in the update."

—Barbara J. Larew, Coe College

"[The update] was timely and well done."

—Jon S. Davis, University of Wisconsin, Madison

LEADERSHIP THAT IS MARKET TESTED

In developing *WFT: Advanced Business Entity Taxation*, we relied on our well-known texts *WFT: Individual Income Taxes* and *WFT: Corporations, Partnerships, Estates & Trusts* to serve as source material for some of the content. Where appropriate content was available in these books, it was adapted as necessary to meet our objectives for an entities text. Where material was unavailable, we created what our readers and reviewers called for. The result is an advanced entities text that meets and exceeds the high standards of the *WFT* Series.

WFT: Advanced Business Entity Taxation, 2005 Edition, prepares readers for the future with the time-tested *WFT* approach.

- **The text provides expertise** to those practicing in consulting and tax positions, preparing to attain further credentials and certifications, and demanding continuing education in tax law and policy.
- **The source material has been market tested** and widely accepted for over 27 years.
- **The organization, structure, and writing style** promote readability and comprehension.
- **The emphasis is on tax concepts and issues,** not the details of tax rules.
- **Professors can modify their approach** for the second tax course on an incremental basis rather than on a radical basis.
- **Most ancillaries have been used** and market tested for over 27 years.
- **The Deloitte Tax Cases on the product Web site** provide industry-standard support for teaching the Model Tax Curriculum.
- **Content and features,** such as the *Tax Planning Framework* discussed later, meet the high editorial standards of a *West Federal Taxation* text.

The Innovation You Expect

TECHNOLOGY FOR LEARNING

With today's mobile *WFT* users and the electronic CPA exam in mind, it's imperative that a course in Federal taxation includes the latest tax research capabilities and technology options. *WFT*'s 2005 edition of *Advanced Business Entity Taxation* offers a wealth of cutting-edge learning tools that provide unparalleled opportunities for skill-building, assessment, and course management.

SKILL-BUILDING: TECHNOLOGY TOOLS AND RESOURCES

Included with each new copy of the text are these technology tools:

Exclusive!

- **Access to RIA's Checkpoint® Online Tax Research Database, Student Edition:** Each new text contains an RIA Checkpoint® Student Edition access code, good for six months of access to content from the research database most widely used by tax professionals (12 months access included with *WFT: Comprehensive Volume*). As students use Checkpoint® to complete problems within the texts, they build research skills and familiarity with the database —valuable preparation for their professional future.
- **WebTutor™ on WebCT™ and Blackboard®:** Available in these two popular platforms, WebTutor™ extends the classroom with the power of the Internet, providing a wealth of online textbook-specific resources for both instructors and students. Visit the WebTutor™ demo at **http://wft-advanced.swlearning.com** to see the possibilities.
- **Computerized Tax Return Problems.** The 2005 Edition offers numerous tax return problems that lend themselves to computerized solutions. These problems can be solved using commercially available tax preparation software.
- **Internet Exercises.** *WFT's* online tax research capability provides ample opportunity for research. To be both flexible and comprehensive in scope, a number of *WFT's* Research Problems are designed for the exploration of tax resources on the Internet. As the basis for their answers, users are asked to review newsgroups, practitioner sites and resources, chat rooms, discussion groups, and other resources.

ASSESSMENT AND COURSE MANAGEMENT

- **WebTutor™ in WebCT™ or Blackboard® (other platforms available upon request).** This rich course management product is a specially designed extension of the classroom experience that enlivens the course by leveraging the power of the Internet with comprehensive educational content. This powerful, turnkey solution provides not only the trademark communication tools for each platform but also the following content customized for this edition:
  - **Quiz Bowl Game.** This multimedia Jeopardy!®-type game quizzes users on their understanding of tax concepts.
  - **Interactive Quizzes.** Multiple choice, true/false, and sentence completion questions, which test the knowledge of the chapter content, provide immediate feedback on the accuracy of the response. These quizzes help students assess areas needing more study.
  - **Threaded Discussion.** Threaded discussion questions, tied to the text's Tax in the News and Planning Strategies boxes, directly link each chapter's topics to open-ended discussion prompts. Students can now engage in guided discussion to further enrich course content.
  - **Flashcards.** A terminology quiz so that students have a complete understanding of the language that makes up the chapter content.
  - **Learning Objectives.** Chapter learning objectives are included for reference and study.
  - **PowerPoint® Presentation Slides.** Students can use these slides to review chapter concepts.
  - **Chapter Outlines.** The outline of topics at the beginning of each chapter is included for more organized study.
  - **Test Bank.** Access to the ExamView computerized test bank files is included. Content compatible with other course management platforms is available upon request.

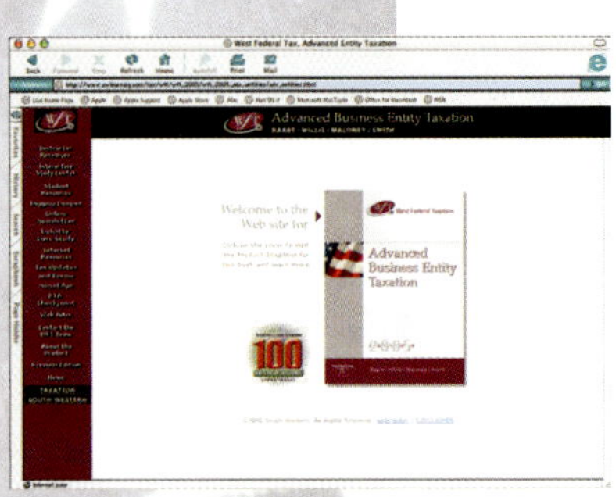

♦ **Text Web Site.** The Web site for the 2005 edition, **http://wft-advanced.swlearning.com**, continues to offer users a full range of resources for teaching and learning. Among the many elements available are:

- **Interactive Study Center.** *WFT*'s Interactive Study Center contains learning objectives, crossword puzzles, and an interactive quiz for each text chapter.
- **Deloitte Tax Case Study Competition.** These cases, available online for download, focus on business entities rather than on individual taxation. They are the same cases used in national and regional competition hosted by **Deloitte.** They may be used as team projects emphasizing issue identification, problem solving, communication, tax planning, and research. Solutions are available to instructors under password via download.
- **New!** **Online Access to TaxBrain™ Tax Preparation Software Available.** TaxBrain™ Tax Preparation Software provides students with online access to a Windows-based individual tax preparation software package that allows practice in preparing individual tax forms. Visit **http://www.taxbrain.com** today.
- **NewsEdge** delivers live tax news and company data from the world's leading news sources.
- **Links to many tax resources on the Web,** including all of the Web sites listed in the text; this provides a quick connection to key information.
- **An Online Newsletter** is posted twice each month to our Web site and can be viewed by users. Take advantage of these articles and updates to stay current in tax, or use them to generate discussion in the classroom.
- **Instructor's Resource Center.** Password protected and for instructors only, this site provides access to downloadable electronic versions of the instructor's guide, test bank, additional test items, solutions manual, practice set solutions, tax legislation updates, and PowerPoint slides. Instructors can obtain a secure password by filling out the form online at **http://wft-advanced.swlearning.com**.

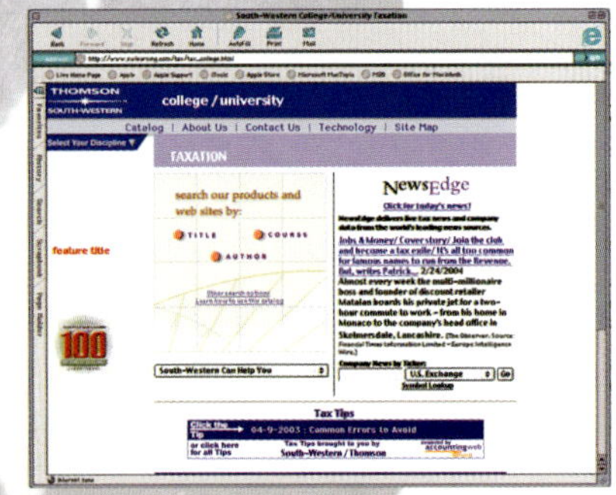

PROVEN PEDAGOGY: OPPORTUNITIES FOR LEARNING

WFT: Advanced Business Entity Taxation offers proven pedagogy that supports the Model Tax Curriculum suggested program content and fosters comprehension of presented topics. The result: users are better able to see beyond textbook examples to the real application of tax concepts and tax law. The following selection of our many pedagogical features supports this new approach:

♦ **Tax Planning Framework.** To effectively demonstrate the relevance of tax planning for business and individual taxpayers, *WFT: Advanced Business Entity Taxation* presents a unique tax planning framework. Introduced in the first chapter, this framework is then tied to the tax planning strategies incorporated throughout the remainder of the text. This feature makes it easier than ever to understand and appreciate the impact careful tax planning has in today's world. Here is how it works:

The "Tax Planning Fundamentals" section (pg. 1–3) in Chapter 1 emphasizes understanding tax planning as an important learning objective by providing specific strategies for minimizing taxes. This section then outlines a **General Framework for Income Tax Planning** using these 10 strategies, that is based on the tax formula. The framework ties terms in the formula to the 10 related tax planning strategies, which are illustrated using Examples.

> **FRAMEWORK FOCUS: DEDUCTIONS** — **TAX MINIMIZATION STRATEGIES RELATED TO DEDUCTIONS**
>
> TAX PLANNING STRATEGY ➤ **MAXIMIZE DEDUCTIBLE AMOUNTS.** A corporation that owns stock in another corporation is eligible for a *dividends received deduction (DRD).* The DRD is equal to a specified percentage of the dividends received. The percentage is based on the amount of stock that the investor corporation owns in the investee corporation (70 percent deduction for ownership of less than 20 percent, 80 percent deduction for ownership of 20 percent or more but less than 80 percent, and 100 percent deduction for ownership of 80 percent or more).
>
> EXAMPLE 3
>
> Falcon Corporation invests in bonds of Sparrow Corporation and receives interest of $20,000 in 2004. Red Hawk Corporation acquires 15% of the stock of Pheasant Corporation and receives a $20,000 dividend in 2004. Falcon's taxable income is increased by $20,000 of interest received. Red Hawk's income is increased by $20,000 in dividend income, but it is allowed a $14,000 dividends received deduction, thus increasing taxable income by only $6,000. ■

Figure 1–2 (pg. 1–5) summarizes this framework:

Tax Formula	Tax Planning Strategy	Tax Planning Examples
Income and exclusions	➤ **Avoid income recognition.**	Compensate employees with nontaxable fringe benefits (see Example 1).
	➤ **Postpone recognition of income to achieve tax deferral.**	Postpone sale of assets (see Example 2).
– Deductions	➤ **Maximize deductible amounts.**	Invest in stock of another corporation (see Example 3).
	➤ **Accelerate recognition of deductions to achieve tax deferral.**	Elect to deduct charitable contribution in year of pledge rather than in year of payment (see Example 4).

- **Planning Strategies.** This chapter feature provides topic-related examples of the 10 tax planning strategies tied to the framework by **Framework Focus** and **Strategy** references.

> PLANNING STRATEGIES — **Penalties**
>
> FRAMEWORK FOCUS: TAX CREDITS
>
> STRATEGY ➤ MAXIMIZE TAX CREDITS.
>
> Penalties are imposed upon a taxpayer's failure to file a return or pay a tax when due. These penalties can be avoided if the failure is due to reasonable cause and not
>
> Underpayment penalties may result from an individual taxpayer's failure to make quarterly estimated tax payments. If the taxpayer is an employee, he/she can request that the

This **pedagogical, framework-based approach to presenting tax planning** illustrates *WFT*'s commitment to innovation for the benefit of instructors, students, and professional users.

- **Decision Making Problems.** Whether in their future tax practice, in individual tax planning situations, within a firm's tax department, or in business contexts throughout their careers, users of *WFT: Advanced Business Entity Taxation* can model their decision making on problems at the end of every chapter that hone their analytical and decision-making skills.

> Decision Making
>
> 39. Dread Corporation operates in a high-tax state. The firm asks you for advice on a plan to outsource overhead work done in its home state to independent contractors. This work now costs the company $350,000 in wages and benefits. Dread's total payroll for the year is $2 million, of which $1.5 million is for work currently done in the home state.

- **Bridge Discipline Boxes.** These boxes throughout the text present material and concepts from other disciplines such as economics, financial accounting, and finance. They help to bridge the gap between taxation issues and issues raised in other business courses. (Bridge Discipline Questions, in the end-of-chapter material, help test these concepts.)

> BRIDGE DISCIPLINE
>
> **Bridge to Political Science**
>
> Multistate tax planning for businesses requires a multidisciplinary approach and an understanding of accounting, law, economics, business, and even politics! For example, in addition

"Pedagogically, identifying the separate strategies and how they relate to the basic tax formula is useful. Hopefully with added instructor emphasis, the students will be able to identify this formula as . . . [a] "big picture" item."

— *Gregg Woodruff, Western Illinois University*

♦ **Bridge Discipline Questions.** These questions in the end-of-chapter material give students the chance to apply concepts they've learned in the **Bridge Discipline boxes** to test their knowledge and understanding of these concepts.

BRIDGE DISCIPLINE

1. Walnut Corporation would like to acquire 100% of Acorn Corporation from its parent, Almond Corporation. Almond is very interested in selling Acorn as it is currently having cash-flow problems. The sale of Acorn could bring the cash infusion it needs to survive. Cash is so short that Almond has not paid last year's Federal consolidated

"I definitely think [*Taxation of Business Entities*'] pedagogy will fit my needs in the next three years. I believe I need to re-think my approach and I should be taking advantage of the features that are present."

—*Priscilla O'Clock, Xavier University*

♦ **Global Tax Issues.** Given today's increasing global concerns, it's critical for users to understand just how international implications influence Federal taxation. *WFT*'s Global Tax Issues feature gives insight into the ways taxation is affected by international concerns, as well as the impact of tax law across the globe.

GLOBAL TAX ISSUES

WATER'S EDGE IS NOT A DAY AT THE BEACH

As a result of pressure from the business community, the Federal government, and foreign countries, most of the states that impose an income tax on a unitary business's worldwide operations permit a multinational business to elect **water's edge** unitary reporting as an alternative to worldwide unitary filing.

The water's edge provision permits a multinational corporation to elect to limit the reach of the state's taxing jurisdiction over out-of-state affiliates to activities occurring within the boundaries of the United States. The decision to make a water's edge election may have a substantial effect on the tax liability of a multinational corporation. For instance, a water's edge election usually cannot be revoked for a number of years without permission from

♦ **Tax in the News.** Drawn from today's business and popular press, this boxed feature enlivens class discussions by presenting current issues that highlight chapter material. Tax in the News boxes can also serve as the basis for open-ended, online discussions in WebTutor.

TAX IN THE NEWS

THE IRS STRIVES TO BECOME CONSUMER-FRIENDLY

When country singer Willie Nelson was found guilty of underreporting his Federal income taxes, chiefly due to his involvement in real estate tax shelters, the total deficiency, including taxes, interest, and penalties, came to $16.7 million. The IRS intended to collect the full amount by forcing auctions of Nelson's most valuable possessions, placing claims on royalties from his recordings, encouraging him to make television commercials for fast-food outlets, and prompting him to sue his prior tax advisers for offsetting damages (to be paid

♦ **Tax Fact.** These boxes, included in each chapter, focus on fun and tax-relevant facts that enliven the chapter's topics.

TAX FACT

WHO'S ONLINE?

A total of 22,793 partnerships filed electronically for 2001, representing 4 million partners. This represents a 318 percent increase from 2000, when only 7,165 partnerships filed electronically. Partnerships with more than 100 partners are required to file electronically. Electronic filers still constituted only a small fraction of the total partnership returns filed for 2001.

♦ **Tax Talk.** These tax quotes at the beginning of each chapter tie together the chapter concepts with events in the real world, helping to make tax issues come to life.

TAX TALK

Nuclear physics is much easier than tax law. It's rational and always works the same way.

—Jerold Rochwald, Physicist

♦ **Digging Deeper.** Designed to help students go further in their knowledge of certain topics, these links within the text to deeper information can be found on the book's Web site **http://wft-advanced.swlearning.com**.

DIGGING DEEPER 1 *Find more information on this topic at our Web site:* ***http://wft-advanced.swlearning.com.***

♦ **Extender Questions.** These questions appear in the end-of-chapter material and require students to go slightly beyond the material they have covered in the chapter to solve the problem. The problems often relate to the **Digging**

Deeper items; text footnotes; or Code and Regulations material not addressed directly by the text.

> **EXTENDER** 2. What is the precedential value of rulings and regulations issued by the Multistate Tax Commission, a voluntary body with no legislative authority?

- **Suggested Further Readings.** These references point students to at least three suggestions per chapter that take students outside the text to relevant journal, newspaper, and magazine articles—providing flexibility and depth for instructors and further enrichment for individual learners.

- **Issue Identification.** A large part of understanding taxation is the ability to discern a tax issue within an individual or business situation or case. The end-of-chapter problem material includes **"Issue ID"** questions designed to help identify important tax issues. The questions are multifaceted and generally have no single right answer.

> **Issue ID** 1. Leona wants to retire and sell her shares in Puffin Corporation either to Puffin's remaining shareholders, Jacob and Ivan, or to a third party. What issues may support a preference for Puffin Corporation to redeem Leona's shares rather than for Jacob and Ivan or a third party to purchase them?

- **Research Problems.** End-of-chapter material throughout the text contains **Research Problems** that may be solved using RIA Checkpoint® Student Edition or research materials available in the library.

> **Research Problem 6.** Determine whether the income tax laws of your state, and those of two of its neighbors, allow Federal affiliated groups to file consolidated returns. How are NOL carrybacks treated by your state?

- **Ethical Problems.** Ethical problems introduce thought-provoking ethical issues related to the chapter topics. In response to the recommendations of the Accounting Education Change Commission, they also demonstrate that many issues do not have a single correct answer. The ethical problems were selected to provoke discussion and provide opportunities for debate based on the student's value system rather than provide a defensible answer.

> **Ethics** 2. Hemlock Corporation produces pharmaceuticals. It is very concerned about potential product liability for a particular drug it is developing to help individuals lose weight

- **Communication Assignments.** These end-of-chapter exercises, written in compliance with the AICPA task force recommendations, help develop essential analytical and writing skills users will need throughout their business careers.

> **Communications** 15. In a memo to the tax research file, summarize the most important positive and negative adjustments made by a parent corporation to the stock basis of its subsidiary.

- **Study Guide.** Prepared by John Everett (Virginia Commonwealth University) and Cherie O'Neil (Colorado State University), the **Study Guide** encourages learners to review the chapter's main focus, key concepts, key terms, and to brush up on homework and test-taking skills. Using the available answers and solutions to its quizzes and problems, users can prepare for tests and quizzes in their course or use the Study Guide as a self-paced quiz when preparing to take the CPA exam.

A FULL RANGE OF INDISPENSABLE REFERENCES

WFT: Advanced Business Entity Taxation contains appendices that make teaching, learning, and researching taxation easier, more flexible, and more thorough. Among the appendices are handy tax rate schedules and tables, tax forms, and a glossary, as well as research aids, indexes, tables, and present and future value tables.

"Examples are frequently used to help explain the tax concepts and laws. The examples are easily understood and the solutions, which are very in-depth and organized, immediately follow."

— *Scott Yetmar, Cleveland State University**

From Scott Yetmar, review of* **WFT: Corporations, Partnerships, Estates & Trusts, *in* Journal of the American Taxation Association *(Fall 2002), pp. 110-112. Courtesy of the American Accounting Association and Scott Yetmar. Reprinted by permission.*

The Service You Deserve

WFT: Advanced Business Entity Taxation offers the most comprehensive and easy-to-use supplements package available on the market.

Supplements for the Instructor:

- **Instructor's Resource CD-ROM with ExamView®.** Key instructor ancillaries *(Solutions Manual, Test Bank, Additional Test Bank Items and Solutions, Solutions to the Practice Sets,* and *PowerPoint® Presentation Slides)* are provided on CD-ROM—giving instructors the ultimate tool for customizing lectures and presentations. The test bank files on the CD are provided in ExamView® format and NEW in rich text format. This program is an easy-to-use test creation software compatible with Microsoft® Windows. Instructors can add or edit questions, instructions, and answers, and select questions (randomly or numerically) by previewing them on the screen. Instructors can also create and administer quizzes online, whether over the Internet, a local area network (LAN), or a wide area network (WAN).
- **WFT Online** (http://wft-advanced.swlearning.com) offers immediate access to current information as soon as it's available. Qualified adopters can log on and learn about the most recent tax information—including the Code and Regulations, case citations, new court rulings, and other newsworthy items. This information can then be transferred to word processing programs for editing, printout, and classroom use. Instructors can also access the *Solutions Manual, PowerPoint Presentation Slides, Practice Set Solutions, Test Bank,* and extra test questions.
- The **Solutions Manual** features solutions arranged in accordance with the sequence of chapter material. A matrix labels the problems by topical coverage and also denotes which problems are new, modified, or unchanged from the prior edition. This matrix also references the prior edition's problem number for the unchanged and modified problems. The solutions are referenced to the relevant pages in the text. The solutions manual is available on the *Instructor's Resource CD* and on the Web site as well.
- The **Test Bank** contains questions and solutions arranged in accordance with the sequence of chapter material. To help create an exam, a matrix labels the questions by topical coverage—reflecting which are new or modified—from the prior edition. Approximately 20 percent of the questions in the 2005 Edition are new or modified. The *Test Bank* and 10 additional multiple-choice test questions per chapter are available on the *WFT* Web site. For the convenience of our adopters, the 2005 Test Bank items are numbered in the same format as in ExamView.
- **PowerPoint Presentation Slides,** available to instructors and found in the WebTutors, allow qualified adopters to create interactive lectures and manipulate graphs, charts, and figures in the classroom. The package contains slides consisting of alternate figures, outlines, and key points.
- **Tax Subscription Service.** Adopters of the *WFT* Series may participate in this convenient service. As a subscription service member, you receive the new edition of your adopted text, plus the key print supplements you need to teach your course. The *WFT* Series Subscription Service is another way we ensure that our customers have what they need, when they need it, every time. Contact your Thomson sales representative for details.
- **Custom Solutions to Fit Your Course.** Thomson Custom Publishing gives you the opportunity to add your own personal touch to your favorite text. Custom publishing also allows you to build a text or supplement suited to your curriculum. You have the freedom to select and arrange content from Thomson's vast library of printed material and our online digital database. You can add your own notes, supplements, articles, study guide . . . you name it. You determine the length, sequence of materials, and even the cover design. In the end, you'll have a custom text of exceptional quality that is exactly what you want. Ask your Thomson sales representative, custom publisher, or customer representative for details.

"If I need anything or have any questions, the South-Western/ Thomson Learning Sales representatives are always extremely helpful."
— *Patricia Mounce, Mississippi College*

ACKNOWLEDGMENTS

We deeply appreciate the many suggestions that we have received, both in the form of reviews and in the numerous comments from adopters in feedback emails. Although many loyal users who made their thoughts known deserve our thanks, we wish to thank these reviewers in particular for their contribution to the 2005 *WFT* Editions:

Richard Alltizer, Wichita State University
Anna Marie Boulware, St. Charles Community College
Rafi Efrat, California State University, Northridge
Kenneth Hansen, University of North Dakota
Carl Keller, Indiana University—Purdue University Fort Wayne
Lorie Milam, University of Texas, San Antonio
William D. Price, Albuquerque Technical Vocational Institute
Reg Rezac, Texas Woman's University
Gregg Woodruff, Western Illinois University
James G.S. Yang, Montclair State University

We are also grateful to the following technology reviewers for their suggestions and comments:

Martin D. Rule, DePaul University
Emil A. Radosevich, Albuquerque TVI Community College
Lorraine M. Wright, North Carolina State University

Thanks go to Prof. Richard Cummings and Sean Wilson (University of Wisconsin, Whitewater) for their constructive comments.

Special thanks go to James C. Young (Northern Illinois University) for continuing to provide us with his inflation adjustments, which are available prior to the release of the official amounts by the IRS.

Our Update on the Jobs and Growth Tax Relief Reconciliation Act of 2003 was a major undertaking. We wish to thank Jim Young and Mark Persellin (St. Mary's University) for their exhaustive review of the Act and its effect on the *WFT* titles. We also wish to thank Deloitte for its kind permission to allow us to post two timely special reports on the Act for the tax community.

We would also like to thank the people who have painstakingly worked through all the problems and test questions and generally acted as problem checkers to ensure the accuracy of the *WFT* texts and ancillary packages. They are **Chris Bjornson** (Indiana University Northeast), **Sara Linton** (University of Scranton), **Dorothea Malloy** (University of Maryland University College), **John McGowan** (Saint Louis University), **Shawn Novak** (Boise State University), **Randall K. Serrett** (University of Houston, Downtown), **Julie Shapland** (University of Illinois, Urbana-Champaign), **Donald R. Trippeer** (Colorado State University, Pueblo), and **Raymond F. Wacker** (Southern Illinois University, Carbondale).

This 2005 Edition would not have been possible without the technical assistance of and manuscript review by **Bonnie Hoffman,** CPA; **Freda Mulhall,** CPA; and **Nora Smith,** M.Ed. We are indebted to them for their efforts.

Finally, this textbook would not have been possible without the support of **Charles McCormick Jr., Chip Kislack, Craig Avery,** and **Lora Arduser** at Thomson Learning/South-Western and the ongoing work of **Peggy Shelton** and **Pat Lewis.** Their editorial and development assistance is greatly appreciated.

William A. Raabe *Eugene Willis* *David M. Maloney* *James E. Smith*

June 1, 2004

Additional Offerings from the West Federal Taxation Series

To find out more about these books, go to **http://wft.swlearning.com**.

***West Federal Taxation: Individual Income Taxes*, 2005 Edition (Hoffman, Smith, Willis, editors)** continues to set the standard in introductory tax. Because it adheres to the recommendations of the Accounting Education Change Commission (AECC) and the American Institute of Certified Public Accountants' (AICPA) Model Tax Curriculum Task Force and because its authors and editors stay on top of trends in both tax law and tax education, the 2005 Edition is thoroughly up-to-date, current in its thinking, and pedagogically advanced. No other text is as effective at helping users master the ever-changing Internal Revenue Code. It provides accessible, comprehensive, and authoritative coverage of the relevant tax code and regulations as they pertain to the individual taxpayer, as well as coverage of all major developments in Federal taxation.

> "The textbook does a great job of explaining concepts, provisions, and exceptions to provisions."
>
> — *Patricia Mounce, Mississippi College*

***West Federal Taxation: Corporations, Partnerships, Estates & Trusts*, 2005 Edition (Hoffman, Raabe, Smith, Maloney, editors).** This volume maintains the tradition of excellence with its coverage of tax legislation as it impacts Corporations, Partnerships, Estates, and Trusts. The authors provide accessible, comprehensive, and authoritative coverage of relevant tax code and regulations, as well as all major developments in Federal taxation. This market-leading text is intended for students who have had a previous course in tax.

> "Highly readable. Excellent supplements for the students. Ditto for the instructor. Examples are good and relevant."
>
> — *Richard Alltizer, Wichita State University*

***West Federal Taxation: Comprehensive Volume*, 2005 Edition (Willis, Hoffman, Maloney, Raabe, editors).** Combining the number one Individual tax text with the number one Corporations text, *WFT: Comprehensive Volume*, 2005 Edition is a true winner. An edited version of the first two *WFT* textbooks, this book offers a thorough and balanced treatment of relevant tax code and regulations as applied to individuals and corporations. Ideal for undergraduate or graduate levels, this text works for either a one-semester course in which an instructor wants to integrate coverage of individual and corporate taxation or for a two-semester sequence in which the use of only one book is desired.

> "Good examples in the text, good homework exercises ...good coverage of the most important issues."
>
> — *William Whitley, Athens State University*

***West Federal Taxation: Taxation of Business Entities*, 2005 Edition (Smith, Raabe, Maloney, Willis, editors).** The 2005 Edition of *WFT: Taxation of Business Entities* provides thorough coverage of all relevant tax code sections and regulations, emphasizing the high-interest and multidisciplinary aspects of taxation. Designed with the AICPA model tax curriculum in mind, this text presents the introductory Federal taxation course from a business entity perspective. Its **Tax Planning Framework** helps users fit tax planning strategies into an innovative pedagogical framework. *WFT: Taxation of Business Entities* is an ideal fit for the program that offers only one course in taxation where users need to be exposed to corporate taxation as well as individual taxation. This text assumes no prior course in taxation has been taken.

"It seems to be the best textbook for the entities approach."

— John F. Kohler,
Washington University (St. Louis)

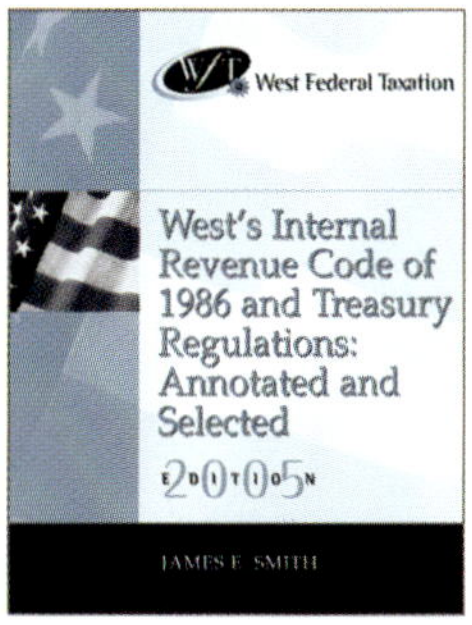

***West's Internal Revenue Code of 1986 and Treasury Regulations: Annotated and Selected*, 2005 Edition (James E. Smith, College of William and Mary).** An ideal alternative to the traditional, bulky, and expensive multivolume set of Code and Regulations, this single-volume reference book provides a useful selection of Code and Regulations sections and clear annotations in the form of editorial summaries. These concise annotations explain, analyze, and cross-reference topics to help students fully understand the intricacies of the tax Code. Smith's *Internal Revenue Code* is a perfect supplement for any *West Federal Taxation* text as well as an excellent primary text for a Federal taxation course that stresses a Code and Regulations approach.

"Its many innovative features and ease of use make it superior, for educational purposes, to the complete code and regulations."

— James E. Smith,
"Preface"

***West's Federal Tax Research*, 6e (William A. Raabe, Ohio State University; Gerald E. Whittenburg, San Diego State University; Debra Sanders, Washington State University; John Bost, San Diego State University).** *West's Federal Tax Research* is the most thorough and up-to-date tax research text available on the market. No other text can better prepare the user on tax research procedures and their multiple applications. From its tax planning orientation to the real-life cases, this is one book that conveys a true understanding of the most important elements of the Federal tax law.

"A hands-on, case-based approach to becoming a high-level tax practitioner, incorporating the latest technology and expert learning methods, supplemented with a tax planning orientation and a focus on spoken and written communication skills."

— William A. Raabe,
Co-author

About the Editors

William A. Raabe teaches tax courses in the Fisher College of Business at The Ohio State University. A graduate of Carroll College (WI) and the University of Illinois, Dr. Raabe's teaching and research interests include international and multistate taxation, technology in tax education, personal financial planning, and the economic impact of sports teams and fine arts groups. Dr. Raabe also is the author of *West's Federal Tax Research* and the *Multistate Corporate Tax Guide.* He coordinates the material on the *West Federal Taxation* Internet page, and he has written estate planning software used widely by tax professionals. Dr. Raabe has been a visiting tax faculty member for a number of public accounting firms, bar associations, and CPA societies. He has received numerous teaching awards, including the Accounting Educator of the Year award from the Wisconsin Institute of CPAs.

Eugene Willis is the Arthur Andersen Alumni Professor of Accountancy Emeritus at the University of Illinois, Urbana-Champaign. He joined the Illinois faculty in 1975 after receiving his Ph.D. from the University of Cincinnati. His articles have appeared in leading academic and professional journals, including *The Accounting Review, The Journal of the American Taxation Association, The Journal of Accountancy,* and *The Journal of Taxation.* Professor Willis is co-director of the National Tax Education Program, a continuing education program co-sponsored by the American Institute of CPAs and the University of Illinois.

David M. Maloney, Ph.D., CPA, completed his undergraduate work at the University of Richmond and his graduate work at the University of Illinois, Urbana-Champaign. He teaches courses in Federal taxation in the graduate and undergraduate programs at the University of Virginia's McIntire School of Commerce. Since joining the Virginia faculty in January 1984, Professor Maloney has been a recipient of major research grants from Ernst & Young and the KPMG Foundation. In addition, his work has been published in numerous professional journals, including *The Journal of Taxation, The Tax Adviser, Tax Notes, The Journal of Corporate Taxation, Accounting Horizons,* and *The Journal of Accountancy.* He is a member of several professional organizations, including the American Accounting Association and the American Taxation Association.

James E. Smith is the John S. Quinn Professor of Accounting at the College of William and Mary. He has been a member of the Accounting Faculty for over thirty years. He received his Ph.D. degree from the University of Arizona.

Professor Smith has served as a discussion leader for Continuing Professional Education programs for the AICPA, Federal Tax Workshops, and various state CPA societies. He has conducted programs in over 40 states for approximately 25,000 CPAs. He has been the recipient of the AICPAs' Outstanding Discussion Leader Award and the American Taxation Association/Arthur Andersen Teaching Innovation Award.

Other awards received by him include the Virginia Society of CPAs' Outstanding Accounting Educator Award and the James Madison University's Outstanding Accounting Educator Award. He was the President of the Administrators of Accounting Programs Group (AAPG) in 1991-1992. He was the faculty adviser for the William and Mary teams that received first place in the Andersen Tax Challenge in 1994, 1995, 1997, 2000, and 2001 and in the Deloitte & Touche Tax Case Study Competition in 2002.

Contents in Brief

Contents

PART THREE ADVANCED JURISDICTIONAL ISSUES

APPENDIXES

PART 1

The Tax Professional

The text begins with a review of the Tax Planning Framework that binds together this book's approach to studying the tax law. It then addresses the opportunities and challenges facing today's tax professional in working with other parties interested in the taxpayer's liabilities to the government, namely, the U.S. Treasury and financial accountants charged with disclosures to the investment markets.

CHAPTER 1

Tax Administration and Practice

LEARNING OBJECTIVES

After completing Chapter 1, you should be able to:

LO.1
Recognize tax planning opportunities and apply a general framework for tax planning.

LO.2
Describe the organization and structure of the IRS.

LO.3
Identify the various administrative pronouncements issued by the IRS and explain how they can be used in tax practice.

LO.4
Describe the audit process, including how returns are selected for audit and the various types of audits.

LO.5
Explain the taxpayer appeal process, including various settlement options available.

LO.6
Determine the amount of interest on a deficiency or a refund and when it is due.

LO.7
Discuss the various penalties that can be imposed on acts of noncompliance by taxpayers and return preparers.

LO.8
Understand the rules governing the statute of limitations on assessments and on refunds.

LO.9
Summarize the legal and ethical guidelines that apply to those engaged in tax practice.

OUTLINE

TAX TALK

If you drive a car, I'll tax the street,
If you try to sit, I'll tax your seat,
If you get too cold, I'll tax the heat,
If you take a walk, I'll tax your feet.
'Cause I'm the Taxman,
And you're working for no one but me.

—*George Harrison*

TAXMAN

Taxpayers increasingly look to professional tax advisers for guidance in dealing with the complex world of Federal, state/local, and international taxation. In this text, we address some of the most important and rewarding provisions of the tax law that face today's business enterprises. These provisions, and potential taxpayer responses to them, offer an effective blueprint for the tax professional in rendering valuable service to a client or employer.

More than half of taxpayers at all income levels engage professional tax advisers to file annual tax returns, and most businesses have at least one tax adviser on staff or retainer. In today's dynamic, multinational economy, it is critical that the taxpayer receive high-quality guidance as to how to manage the tax liability. Thus, our approach in this text is to arm the taxpayer and adviser with tools necessary to succeed in working with the tax law. Such skills include facility in:

- Dealing with issues raised by governmental agencies, in filing tax returns and guiding them through administrative and judicial challenges, and working with financial accountants and others who desire public disclosure of information about the tax expenses of a business entity.
- Working with the taxpayer undergoing capital structure changes, such as a merger or partnership liquidation, or employing the consolidated return election.

TAX FACT

WHICH TAX? ON WHOM?

For 2001 there were 130,255,234 individual tax returns filed; 104,174,654 of these returns had taxable income of $4,268,506,425,000. Of these returns, 1,120,047 incurred alternative minimum tax (AMT) of $6,756,705,000. The AMT returns included 4,649 taxpayers who reported no adjusted gross income. This group paid $94,531,000 in alternative minimum tax.

Source: IRS, *Statistics of Income Bulletin*, Fall 2003, Publication 1135 (Rev. 12–03).

- Optimizing the taxpayer's opportunities in dealing with multiple taxing jurisdictions, especially those making international investments and operating a business entity in more than one of the U.S. states.
- Using available elections and computations as to fiscal tax years and tax accounting methods, and adopting qualified retirement plans and other devices to defer income recognition.
- Assisting high-income and -wealth taxpayers in managing transfer taxes, shifting business ownership to younger generations, and using tax-exempt entities to accomplish desirable social goals.

In this chapter, we help to equip the tax professional in attaining these objectives. We will focus on:

- Bringing a Tax Planning orientation to studying the tax law and using it in the course of the demands of the taxpayer's business entity operations.
- Understanding how the Internal Revenue Service is organized and operates interactively with the taxpayer, and the choices available to the taxpayer when a dispute with the Service cannot be resolved within the agency.
- The negative sanctions that the tax administration can bring to bear on taxpayers who do not fully comply with the requirements of the law, especially in the form of interest and penalties.
- The ethical and professional constraints on the advice tax advisers can give and the actions they can take on behalf of their clients, within the context of an adversarial relationship with the IRS.

LO.1

Recognize tax planning opportunities and apply a general framework for tax planning.

Tax Planning Fundamentals

OVERVIEW OF TAX PLANNING

Minimizing taxes legally is referred to as **tax avoidance.** On the other hand, some taxpayers attempt to *evade* income taxes illegally. There is a major distinction between tax avoidance and **tax evasion.** Though eliminating or reducing taxes is also a goal of tax evasion, the term *evasion* implies the use of subterfuge and fraud as a means to this end. Tax avoidance is legal, while tax evasion subjects the taxpayer to numerous civil and criminal penalties, including prison sentences.

Clients expect tax practitioners to provide advice to help them minimize their tax costs. This part of the tax practitioner's practice is referred to as **tax planning.** To structure a sound tax minimization plan, a practitioner must have a thorough knowledge of the tax law. Tax planning skill is based on knowledge of tax-reducing provisions in the tax law, as well as provisions that contain costly pitfalls for the

■ FIGURE 1–1
Basic Formula for Federal Income Tax

Income (broadly conceived)	$xxx,xxx
Less: Exclusions (income that is not subject to tax)	(xx,xxx)
Gross income (income that is subject to tax)	$xxx,xxx
Less: Deductions	(xx,xxx)
Taxable income	$xxx,xxx
Federal income tax on taxable income (see Tax Rate Schedules inside front cover of text)	$ xx,xxx
Less: Tax credits (including Federal income tax withheld and other prepayments of Federal income taxes)	(x,xxx)
Tax owed (or refund)	$ xxx

unwary. Thorough study of the remainder of this text will provide a solid base of the knowledge required to recognize opportunities and avoid pitfalls. Tax planning requires the practitioner to have in mind both a framework for planning and an understanding of the tax planning implications of a client's situation.

TAX PLANNING FRAMEWORK

A GENERAL FRAMEWORK FOR INCOME TAX PLANNING

The primary goal of tax planning is to design a transaction so as to minimize the present value of its tax costs, while meeting the other nontax objectives of the client. Generally, this means that the client attempts to maximize the present value of its after-tax income and assets. Selecting a specific form of transaction solely for the sake of tax minimization often leads to a poor business decision. Effective tax planning requires careful consideration of the nontax issues involved in addition to the tax consequences.

Careful analysis of the tax formula (refer to Figure 1–1) reveals a series of tax minimization strategies. Through creative tax planning that also takes into consideration a client's nontax concerns, each component of the tax formula can be managed in a way that will help to minimize the client's tax liability. The General Framework for Income Tax Planning in Figure 1–2 lists each element in the income tax formula, develops tax planning strategies designed to minimize taxes, and provides brief summaries of specific examples of tax planning. The framework is followed by a discussion of the tax planning strategies, along with detailed examples of how the strategies can be applied. In Chapters 3–16 of this book, these strategies and their tax formula components provide the framework for Planning Strategies features.

FRAMEWORK FOCUS: INCOME

TAX PLANNING STRATEGY

TAX MINIMIZATION STRATEGIES RELATED TO INCOME

➤**AVOID INCOME RECOGNITION.** Section 61(a) defines gross income as "all income from whatever source derived." However, the Code has provisions that allow various types of income to be excluded from the tax base. Numerous exclusions are available for individuals, but very few are available for corporations. However, a corporation can provide excludible income for its owners at no tax cost to the corporation.

EXAMPLE 1

The average employee of Penguin Corporation pays state and Federal income taxes at a 27% marginal rate. In negotiations with the employees' union, Penguin proposes that it will increase the amount it spends on nontaxable fringe benefits by an average of $3,000 per employee in lieu of granting a $3,000 average salary increase. The average employee will be better off by $810 if the union accepts Penguin's offer.

FIGURE 1–2
General Framework for Income Tax Planning

Tax Formula	Tax Planning Strategy	Tax Planning Examples
Income and exclusions	➤ **Avoid income recognition.**	Compensate employees with nontaxable fringe benefits (see Example 1).
	➤ **Postpone recognition of income to achieve tax deferral.**	Postpone sale of assets (see Example 2).
– Deductions	➤ **Maximize deductible amounts.**	Invest in stock of another corporation (see Example 3).
	➤ **Accelerate recognition of deductions to achieve tax deferral.**	Elect to deduct charitable contribution in year of pledge rather than in year of payment (see Example 4).
= Taxable income		
× Tax rate	➤ **Shift net income from high-bracket years to low-bracket years.**	Postpone recognition of income to a low-bracket year (see Example 5).
		Postpone recognition of deductions to a high-bracket year (see Example 6).
	➤ **Shift net income from high-bracket taxpayers to low-bracket taxpayers.**	Pay children to work in the family business (see Example 7).
	➤ **Shift net income from high-tax jurisdictions to low-tax jurisdictions.**	Establish subsidiary operations in countries with low tax rates (see Examples 8 and 9).
	➤ **Control the character of income and deductions.**	Hold assets long enough to qualify for long-term capital gain rates before selling them (see Example 10).
		Invest in small business stock to obtain ordinary loss treatment under § 1244 (see Example 11).
	➤ **Avoid double taxation.**	Operate as a flow-through entity rather than a C corporation (see Example 12).
		Maximize deductible expenses paid by a C corporation to a shareholder/employee (see Example 13).
= Federal income tax		
– Tax credits	➤ **Maximize tax credits.**	Hire employees who qualify the business for the work opportunity tax credit (see Example 15).
= Tax owed (or refund)		

	Salary Increase	Fringe Benefit Increase
Value of compensation received	$3,000	$3,000
Tax on employee's compensation	810	–0–
After-tax increase in compensation	$2,190	$3,000

Although the average employee receives an $810 benefit, there is no tax cost to Penguin because both fringe benefits and salaries are deductible by the corporation. ■

TAX PLANNING STRATEGY

➤**POSTPONE RECOGNITION OF INCOME TO ACHIEVE TAX DEFERRAL.** The IRS requires that both income and expenses be reported in the proper year. If not for this requirement, taxpayers could freely shift income and expenses from year to year to take advantage of tax rate differentials or could defer tax liabilities indefinitely. Although various rules limit the shifting of income and deductions across time periods, some opportunities still exist.

EXAMPLE 2

In 1995, Turquoise Corporation acquired land for investment purposes at a cost of $500,000. In November 2004, Turquoise is negotiating to sell the land to Aqua Corporation for $800,000. Aqua insists that the transaction be completed in 2004, but Turquoise wants to delay the sale until 2005 to defer the tax on the gain. In an effort to compromise, Turquoise agrees to sell the land in November 2004 and asks Aqua to pay for the land in two installments, $400,000 in December 2004 and $400,000 in January 2005. This enables Turquoise to use the installment sale method, under which Turquoise will report $150,000 of the gain in 2004 and the remaining $150,000 in 2005. By electing the installment method, Turquoise defers the payment of tax on $150,000 of the gain for one year. If Turquoise's marginal tax rate[1] (or marginal tax bracket) is 35%, this tax deferral strategy provides $52,500 ($150,000 × 35%) of new-found cash, to be invested or used in the business for a year. ■

FRAMEWORK FOCUS: DEDUCTIONS

TAX MINIMIZATION STRATEGIES RELATED TO DEDUCTIONS

TAX PLANNING STRATEGY

➤**MAXIMIZE DEDUCTIBLE AMOUNTS.** A corporation that owns stock in another corporation is eligible for a *dividends received deduction (DRD)*. The DRD is equal to a specified percentage of the dividends received. The percentage is based on the amount of stock that the investor corporation owns in the investee corporation (70 percent deduction for ownership of less than 20 percent, 80 percent deduction for ownership of 20 percent or more but less than 80 percent, and 100 percent deduction for ownership of 80 percent or more).

EXAMPLE 3

Falcon Corporation invests in bonds of Sparrow Corporation and receives interest of $20,000 in 2004. Red Hawk Corporation acquires 15% of the stock of Pheasant Corporation and receives a $20,000 dividend in 2004. Falcon's taxable income is increased by $20,000 of interest received. Red Hawk's income is increased by $20,000 in dividend income, but it is allowed a $14,000 dividends received deduction, thus increasing taxable income by only $6,000. ■

TAX PLANNING STRATEGY

➤**ACCELERATE RECOGNITION OF DEDUCTIONS TO ACHIEVE TAX DEFERRAL.** Both corporate and noncorporate taxpayers may deduct charitable contributions if the recipient is a qualified charitable organization. Generally, a deduction is allowed only for the year in which the payment is made. However, an important exception is available for *accrual basis corporations*. They may claim the deduction in the year *preceding* payment if two requirements are met. First, the contribution must be authorized by the board of directors by the end of that year. Second, the contribution must be paid on or before the fifteenth day of the third month of the next year.

EXAMPLE 4

Blue, Inc., a calendar year, accrual basis corporation, wants to make a $10,000 donation to the Atlanta Symphony Association (a qualified charitable organization), but does not have adequate funds to make the contribution in 2004. On December 28, 2004, Blue's board of directors authorizes a $10,000 contribution to the Association. The donation is made on March 14, 2005. Because Blue is an accrual basis corporation, it may claim the $10,000 donation as a deduction for calendar year 2004, even though payment is not made until 2005. ■

[1]A taxpayer's *marginal tax rate* (or *marginal tax bracket*) is the rate that would be paid on an additional dollar of taxable income.

In the preceding example, Blue Inc., could take advantage of a tax provision and reduce taxable income for 2004 by $10,000. Assuming that Blue is in the 35 percent marginal bracket, the corporation has been able to defer payment of $3,500 in Federal income tax. The $3,500 can be invested or used in the business for a year.

FRAMEWORK FOCUS: TAX RATES

TAX MINIMIZATION STRATEGIES RELATED TO TAX RATES

TAX PLANNING STRATEGY

➤**SHIFT NET INCOME FROM HIGH-BRACKET YEARS TO LOW-BRACKET YEARS.** One objective of shifting income is to defer the payment of income tax (refer to Example 2). A second time-shifting strategy is to move *net* income from high-tax to low-tax years. This can be accomplished by shifting income from high-bracket years to low-bracket years or by shifting deductions from low-bracket years to high-bracket years.

EXAMPLE 5

Egret Corporation, a calendar year taxpayer, is in the 34% bracket in 2004, but expects to be in the 25% bracket in 2005. The corporation, which is negotiating a $10,000 service contract with a client, decides to wait until 2005 to sign the contract and perform the services. The client is indifferent as to when the contract is completed. Thus, Egret saves $900 in income tax by deferring the service contract income to 2005, when it will be taxed at the 25% rate instead of the current 34% rate. In this case, the income-shifting strategy is used to accomplish two tax planning objectives. First, shifting the income defers the payment of income tax from 2004 to 2005. Second, the shifting strategy results in the income being taxed at a rate of 25% rather than 34%. ■

EXAMPLE 6

Macaw Corporation has been sued for $125,000 damages by a customer, and the parties decided in December to settle out of court for $100,000. Macaw expects to be in the 25% bracket in 2004 and the 35% bracket in 2005. Macaw saves $10,000 in income tax if it pays the damages in January 2005 rather than December 2004 [$100,000 × (35% – 25%)]. ■

TAX PLANNING STRATEGY

➤**SHIFT NET INCOME FROM HIGH-BRACKET TAXPAYERS TO LOW-BRACKET TAXPAYERS.** Individual income tax rates (for 2004) range from 10 to 35 percent. Although several provisions in the tax law prevent shifting income from high-bracket taxpayers to low-bracket taxpayers, many opportunities to do so remain. Business entities can be effective vehicles for shifting income to low-bracket taxpayers.

EXAMPLE 7

Bill Gregory is the president and sole shareholder of Grayhawk, Inc., an S corporation. He projects that Grayhawk will earn $400,000 in 2004. Bill will be taxed on this income at a 35% marginal rate. Bill and his wife have four teenage children, all of whom are dependents. Bill decides to employ the children as part-time workers throughout 2004 and pay them $10,750 each. This reduces Bill's income from Grayhawk by $43,000 and reduces his Federal income tax by $15,050 ($43,000 × 35%). Each child reports taxable income of $5,900 ($10,750 – $4,850 standard deduction) and pays $590 of Federal income tax ($5,900 × 10% rate). As a result of this income-shifting strategy, the family unit saves $12,690 ($15,050 tax saved by Bill – $2,360 tax paid by children). ■

TAX PLANNING STRATEGY

➤**SHIFT NET INCOME FROM HIGH-TAX JURISDICTIONS TO LOW-TAX JURISDICTIONS.** The state or country where income is earned (or where a deduction is incurred) can have a large effect on an entity's overall tax liability. Hence, shifting income from high-tax jurisdictions to low-tax jurisdictions or shifting deductions from low-tax jurisdictions to high-tax jurisdictions is an important tax planning strategy.

EXAMPLE 8

Gold International owns a sales subsidiary in Texas and a manufacturing subsidiary in Ireland (which imposes a 10% tax rate on certain types of business income). The Irish subsidiary makes drill presses and sells them for $4 million to the Texas subsidiary, which then modifies them and offers them for sale to businesses in the United States for $8.4 million. The cost of manufacturing and modifying each drill press is $3 million. Of the $5.4 million of profit earned, $1 million is attributable to the Irish corporation (which is subject to a 10% tax rate), and $4.4 million is attributable to the U.S. corporation (which is subject to a 34% tax rate). Gold's total tax liability is $1,596,000 [($1,000,000 × 10%) + ($4,400,000 × 34%)]. ■

EXAMPLE 9

Assume the same facts as in the previous example, except $5 million of the profit is attributable to the Irish corporation and $400,000 is attributable to the U.S. corporation. In this case, Gold's total tax liability is $636,000 [($5,000,000 × 10%) + ($400,000 × 34%)]. Thus, by altering the amount of work done in each of the two subsidiaries and the amount of income generated by each, Gold's tax liability is decreased by $960,000 ($1,596,000 – $636,000). ■

TAX PLANNING STRATEGY

➤**CONTROL THE CHARACTER OF INCOME AND DEDUCTIONS.** For various policy reasons, Congress has chosen to treat certain categories of income and losses more favorably than others. For instance, the provisions that tax long-term capital gains at a maximum rate of 15 percent, compared to a 35 percent rate on ordinary income, were enacted to encourage individuals to make long-term investments of capital in the economy.

EXAMPLE 10

Lisa is the proprietor of Designer Enterprises. Because a proprietorship is a flow-through entity, Lisa must report all of Designer's transactions on her individual income tax return. On October 9, 2004, Lisa invested $25,000 of Designer's excess cash in Lavender Corporation stock. On October 1, 2005, the stock was worth $35,000.

Lisa, who is a 35% bracket taxpayer, has decided to sell the stock and use the cash to increase Designer's inventory. She must hold the stock until October 10, 2005, for the gain to qualify as long term (held more than a year). If she sells the stock before October 10, 2005, the gain will be short term, and she will pay 35% tax on the gain. If she sells the stock after October 9, 2005, the gain will be long term, and she will pay 15% tax on the gain. ■

To encourage investment in small businesses, Congress enacted the § 1244 provisions, which provide favorable treatment of losses incurred on the sale of qualifying small business stock. Generally, losses on the sale of stock are treated as capital losses. Individuals with capital losses in excess of capital gains are permitted to deduct only $3,000 of such losses against ordinary income in a tax year. To make small business stock more attractive as an investment, § 1244 allows up to $50,000 ($100,000 if married filing jointly) of losses on such stock to be treated as ordinary losses, thus exempting the § 1244 losses from being offset against capital gains and then from the $3,000 limit that would otherwise apply to any excess capital losses.

EXAMPLE 11

Roberto invested $80,000 in Mauve Corporation stock and sold the stock in 2004 for $40,000. He has no other capital asset transactions and does not expect to have any in future years. If the Mauve stock qualifies as § 1244 stock, Roberto may deduct the entire $40,000 loss in 2004 as an ordinary loss. If the stock does not qualify as § 1244 stock, Roberto may deduct only $3,000 as a capital loss in 2004 and must carry the remaining loss of $37,000 forward. In future years, the loss will continue to be subject to the $3,000 limitation. ■

TAX PLANNING STRATEGY

➤**AVOID DOUBLE TAXATION.** The owners of a corporation can choose between two entity forms. A C corporation, also referred to as a regular corporation, is a taxable entity that pays tax on corporate profits. Shareholders also pay tax on dividends received from a C corporation, resulting in what is commonly referred to as *double taxation*.

Shareholders can avoid double taxation by electing S status for a corporate entity. Unlike a C corporation, an S corporation is not a taxable entity. Instead, the profits and losses of the S corporation flow through to the shareholders and are reported on their tax returns.

EXAMPLE 12

Chickadee, Inc., a C corporation with net income of $100,000 in 2004, pays Carl, its sole shareholder, a $77,750 dividend. Chickadee must pay corporate income tax of $22,250 on the net income of $100,000, and Carl must pay tax on the $77,750 dividend. Sparrow, Inc., an S corporation, earns $100,000 in 2004. Sparrow is not a taxable entity, so it pays no income tax on the $100,000 net income. Sam, who is the sole shareholder of Sparrow, must include $100,000 ordinary income on his 2004 Form 1040. ■

Choosing to operate as a flow-through entity is not the only way to avoid double taxation. Double taxation can be avoided or minimized by having the corporation make payments, such as salaries, rent, and interest to the shareholders.

EXAMPLE 13

Walt is the president and sole shareholder of Meadowlark, Inc., a C corporation. Meadowlark's taxable income before any payment to Walt is $300,000. Walt, a skilled manager, is primarily responsible for the profitability of the corporation. If Meadowlark pays Walt a dividend of $200,000, the corporation pays Federal income tax on $300,000, and Walt reports a $200,000 dividend. However, if Meadowlark pays Walt a salary of $200,000, it deducts the salary and reports only $100,000 of taxable income. Walt includes the $200,000 salary in his gross income. In either case, Walt includes $200,000 in gross income. Meadowlark recognizes $200,000 less taxable income if the payment to Walt is a salary. But Walt pays a 15% tax rate on dividends, and his salary is taxed as ordinary income. ■

FRAMEWORK FOCUS: CREDITS

TAX MINIMIZATION STRATEGIES RELATED TO CREDITS

TAX PLANNING STRATEGY

➤**MAXIMIZE TAX CREDITS.** For many years, Congress has used the tax credit provisions of the Internal Revenue Code liberally in implementing tax policy. It is important to understand the difference between a credit and a deduction, both of which reduce a taxpayer's tax liability. A deduction reduces taxable income, which results in a reduction of the tax paid. The tax benefit of the deduction depends on the amount of the qualifying expenditure and the taxpayer's tax rate. A tax credit reduces the tax liability dollar for dollar and is not affected by the taxpayer's tax rate.

EXAMPLE 14

Oriole Corporation, which is in the 25% marginal bracket, has a $6,000 deduction for expenditures made to repair a machine. The deduction will reduce taxable income by $6,000 and will result in a tax liability reduction of $1,500 ($6,000 deduction × 25% marginal rate). Oriole also incurred expenditures of $6,000 to rehabilitate a building, which qualifies the corporation for a tax credit of $600 ($6,000 rehabilitation expenditures × 10% rate for the credit). The rehabilitation expenditures credit results in a $600 reduction of Oriole's tax liability. In addition, Oriole's depreciable basis for the building will increase by $5,400 ($6,000 expenditures – $600 credit). ■

One example of the use of credits to influence taxpayer behavior is the work opportunity tax credit, which was enacted to encourage employers to hire employees from several targeted and economically disadvantaged groups, including high-risk youths, summer youth employees, and military veterans. The employee is certified to be a member of a qualifying targeted group. The work opportunity tax credit is 40 percent of the first $6,000 of wages paid during the first 12 months of employment (hired before 2004).

EXAMPLE 15

Robin Corporation hired a high-risk youth for four months at a cost of $6,000. Robin will qualify for the work opportunity tax credit and will be allowed a credit of $2,400 ($6,000 wages × 40% credit rate) and a wage deduction of $3,600 ($6,000 wages – $2,400 credit). Robin is a 34% bracket taxpayer. The $3,600 deduction will reduce Robin's income tax by $1,224 ($3,600 × 34%). The total tax saving will be $3,624 ($1,224 + $2,400 credit).

If the employee does not qualify Robin for the work opportunity tax credit, Robin will be allowed a deduction of $6,000, which will result in a tax saving of $2,040 ($6,000 × 34%). Thus, hiring an employee who qualifies Robin for the work opportunity tax credit will save an additional $1,584 in tax ($3,624 – $2,040). ■

THINKING OUTSIDE THE FRAMEWORK

Although the General Framework for Income Tax Planning in Figure 1–2 is broad and covers most tax planning strategies, some strategies fall outside the framework. In addition, other planning ideas can supplement the strategies in the framework.

To engage in effective tax planning, one must be able to identify the relevant tax rate that will be applied to a transaction. There are three kinds of tax rates. A taxpayer's *marginal* tax rate (or tax bracket) is the rate that would be paid on an additional dollar of taxable income. Referring to the corporate income tax rate schedule inside the front cover of this text, a corporation's marginal tax rate on its first dollar of income is 15 percent. Similarly, the marginal tax rate faced by a corporation with $100,001 of income is 39 percent. The *average* tax rate is the ratio of taxes paid to the tax base. Thus, a corporation with $100,000 of taxable income is subject to an average tax rate of 22.25 percent ($22,250 in tax divided by $100,000 in taxable income). A third kind of tax rate, the *effective* tax rate, can be seen as either (1) the ratio of taxes paid to financial net income before tax or (2) the sum of currently payable and deferred tax expense divided by net income before tax. Of these approaches to determining a taxpayer's tax rate, the marginal tax rate is most appropriate for tax planning purposes.

EXAMPLE 16

Azure Corporation has taxable income of $80,000. Azure also has $10,000 of tax-free interest income from municipal bonds. Using the corporate tax rate schedule inside the front cover of this text, one can determine that the company's tax liability is $15,450. If Azure were to earn an additional dollar in taxable income, it would pay $0.34 in tax. Thus, the company's marginal tax rate is 34%. Azure's average tax rate is the ratio of taxes paid to taxable income or 19.3% ($15,450/$80,000). Finally, the company has an effective rate of tax of 17.2% ($15,450/$90,000), the ratio of taxes paid to financial net income before tax (here, the sum of taxable income and tax-free income). ■

The actual tax paid may not always be apparent. For example, the amount of taxes paid should include both current taxes and the present value of future taxes generated by a transaction.

EXAMPLE 17

Magenta Corporation is a publishing company that specializes in electronic media. It is a new corporation that was formed on January 1, 2001. During that year, it generated a net operating loss (NOL) of $300,000. The NOL can be carried forward to offset future years' taxable income and thereby reduce Magenta's future tax liabilities. Magenta expects to earn $100,000 of income each year over the next four years. The NOL should completely offset the company's taxable income for the first three of these years.

At the beginning of 2002, Magenta must decide whether to invest in a project that will earn an additional $40,000 of taxable income during 2002 or a project that will generate $36,000 tax-free. The company's president reasons that, since the company has an NOL carryforward, the applicable tax rate is 0%, so the taxable project should be chosen.

The president's reasoning is incorrect, because an additional $40,000 of income now will result in $40,000 of taxable income in 2004 (since there will be $40,000 less NOL available in that year).

	2002	2003	2004	2005
Alternative 1 (tax-free investment)				
Pre-NOL taxable income	$ 100,000	$ 100,000	$ 100,000	$100,000
NOL carryforward (from 2001)	(300,000)	(200,000)	(100,000)	–0–
Taxable income	$ –0–	$ –0–	$ –0–	$100,000
Alternative 2 (taxable investment)				
Pre-NOL taxable income	$ 140,000	$ 100,000	$ 100,000	$100,000
NOL carryforward (from 2001)	(300,000)	(160,000)	(60,000)	–0–
Taxable income	$ –0–	$ –0–	$ 40,000	$100,000

The tax on the $40,000 project equals the discounted value of the tax due in 2004. Assuming a 10% discount rate and a 15% corporate tax rate, the present value of taxes paid in three years is $4,508, and the discounted tax rate is 11.27%. Thus, the after-tax proceeds on the taxable project will be $35,492, or $508 *less* than the $36,000 earnings on the tax-free project. ■

Tax Administration

Few events arouse so much fear in the typical individual or corporation as the receipt of a letter from the Internal Revenue Service (IRS), notifying the taxpayer that prior years' tax returns are to be the subject of an audit. Almost immediately, calls are made to the tax adviser. Advice is sought as to what to reveal (or not reveal) in the course of the audit, how to delay or avoid the audit, and how friendly one should be with the auditor when he or she ultimately arrives.

Indeed, many tax practitioners' reputations with their clients have been made or broken by the way they are observed to behave under the pressure of an audit situation. The strategy and tactics of audits—including such seemingly unimportant issues as whether the tax adviser brings donuts or other refreshments to the audit session, the color of his or her suit and tie, and the most effective negotiation techniques—are the subject of both cocktail party banter and scholarly review.

THE IRS TODAY

The Treasury has delegated the administration and enforcement of the tax laws to its subsidiary agency, the IRS. In this process, the Service is responsible for providing adequate information, in the form of publications and forms with instructions, to taxpayers so that they can comply with the laws in an appropriate manner. The IRS also identifies delinquent tax payments and carries out assessment and collection procedures under the restrictions of due process and other constitutional guarantees.

In meeting these responsibilities, the Service conducts audits of selected tax returns. Fewer than 0.5 percent of all individual tax returns are subjected to audit in a given tax year. However, certain types of both taxpayers and income—including, for instance, high-income individuals (about 3 percent), cash-oriented businesses, real estate transactions, and estate- and gift-taxable transfers (15 to 30 percent)—are subject to much higher probabilities of audit. One's residence also

TAX IN THE NEWS

Should the IRS Be Larger?

What is the optimal size of the IRS? The IRS maintains in congressional testimony that it can produce three to four dollars of revenue for every dollar spent on its ongoing operations. Actually, the rate of return might be higher, especially for special projects that the Service itself devises and undertakes. As the agency becomes more proficient with computers and more aggressive in finding and treating nonfilers, the temptation to enlarge the Service increases as well.

Given concerns about the Federal deficit and an underground economy measured in the hundreds of billions of dollars, one might expect the number of IRS operatives to keep increasing, even though it already is one of the largest Federal agencies, with a staff of about 100,000. Yet, the last few presidents have found that pledges to cut back the size of government also apply to the IRS (i.e., the public does not apply such a rate of return test itself).

Thus, the IRS must live within its budget allocations and reallocate the resources that it now has. Can a stepped-up education campaign, further reliance on electronic filing, and an overall consumer-friendly operation produce significant revenue increases for the IRS?

affects the chances of audit, ranging from about 1.5 percent in California to under 0.2 percent in Georgia.

Recently, much of the IRS's effort has been devoted to developing statutory and administrative requirements relative to information reporting and document matching. For instance, when a taxpayer engages in a like-kind exchange or sells a personal residence, various parties to the transaction are required to report the nature and magnitude of the transaction to the IRS. Later the Treasury's computers determine whether the transaction has been reported properly by comparing the information reported by the third parties with the events included on the relevant taxpayers' returns for the year.

In addition, the IRS has been placing increasing pressure on the community of tax advisers. Severe penalties may be assessed on those who have prepared the appropriate return when the Service's interpretation of applicable law conflicts with that of the preparer.

The IRS processes over 130 million individual income tax returns every year, over 50 million of which are filed electronically. It collects more than $2 trillion in tax revenues and pays refunds to about 100 million taxpayers every year.

Current operational strategies of the IRS include the following.

- Focusing on taxpayer education.
- Developing a "customer first" orientation in working with all taxpayers.
- Adapting to the changing cultural and linguistic needs of the public.
- Accelerating the modernization of equipment and operating methods.
- Making the Regulations and tax procedures as simple and fair as possible.

The IRS believes that, under these principles, the taxpayer will benefit in a number of ways.

- Taxpayers will spend significantly less time dealing with the IRS.
- The IRS will issue refunds more rapidly.
- Taxpayers will have more filing and payment choices.
- Taxpayers will pay less interest.

TAX FACT

WHO PAYS THE INCOME TAX?

The following table is from preliminary data furnished by the IRS for individual 2001 taxpayers, as summarized by the Tax Foundation.

	Number of Returns	AGI Income Share	Federal Income Tax Share	Income Split Point
Top 1%	1,288,000	17.5%	33.9%	above $292,913
Top 5%	6,441,000	32.0%	53.3%	above $127,904
Top 10%	12,882,000	43.1%	64.9%	above $92,754
Top 25%	32,204,000	65.2%	82.9%	above $56,085
Top 50%	64,409,000	86.2%	96.1%	above $28,528
Bottom 50%	64,409,000	13.8%	3.9%	below $28,528
All Taxpayers	128,817,000			

Sources: http://www.taxfoundation.org/prtopincometable.html: Federal Individual Income Taxes by Income Class, Tax Foundation.

LO.2

Describe the organization and structure of the IRS.

ORGANIZATIONAL STRUCTURE OF THE IRS

The structure of the IRS is moving toward that illustrated in Figure 1–3. The IRS Commissioner, a presidential appointee, has organized the day-to-day operations of the agency into four divisions, conducted using regional and district offices. Table 1–1 provides estimates of the workload of each operating division. Administrative functions, such as those relating to personnel and computer issues, are organized on a shared-services model, managed from the national office. Broader functions, such as litigation, investigations, and taxpayer relations, are managed at the national level as well.

The Chief Counsel, another presidential appointee, is the head legal officer of the IRS. The Chief Counsel's office provides legal advice to the IRS and guidance to the public on matters pertaining to the administration and enforcement of the tax laws. For instance, the Chief Counsel's duties include establishing uniform nationwide interpretative positions on the law, drafting tax guide material for taxpayers and IRS personnel, issuing technical rulings to taxpayers, and providing advice and technical assistance to IRS personnel. The Chief Counsel reports to the Commissioner and represents the IRS in all litigation before the Tax Court.

LO.3

Identify the various administrative pronouncements issued by the IRS and explain how they can be used in tax practice.

PRIVATE LETTER RULINGS

When a tax issue is controversial or a transaction involves considerable tax dollars, the taxpayer often wishes to obtain either assurance or direction from the IRS as to the treatment of the event. The **letter ruling** process is an effective means of dealing directly with the IRS while in the planning stages of a large or otherwise important transaction.

■ **FIGURE 1–3**
IRS National Office Organization

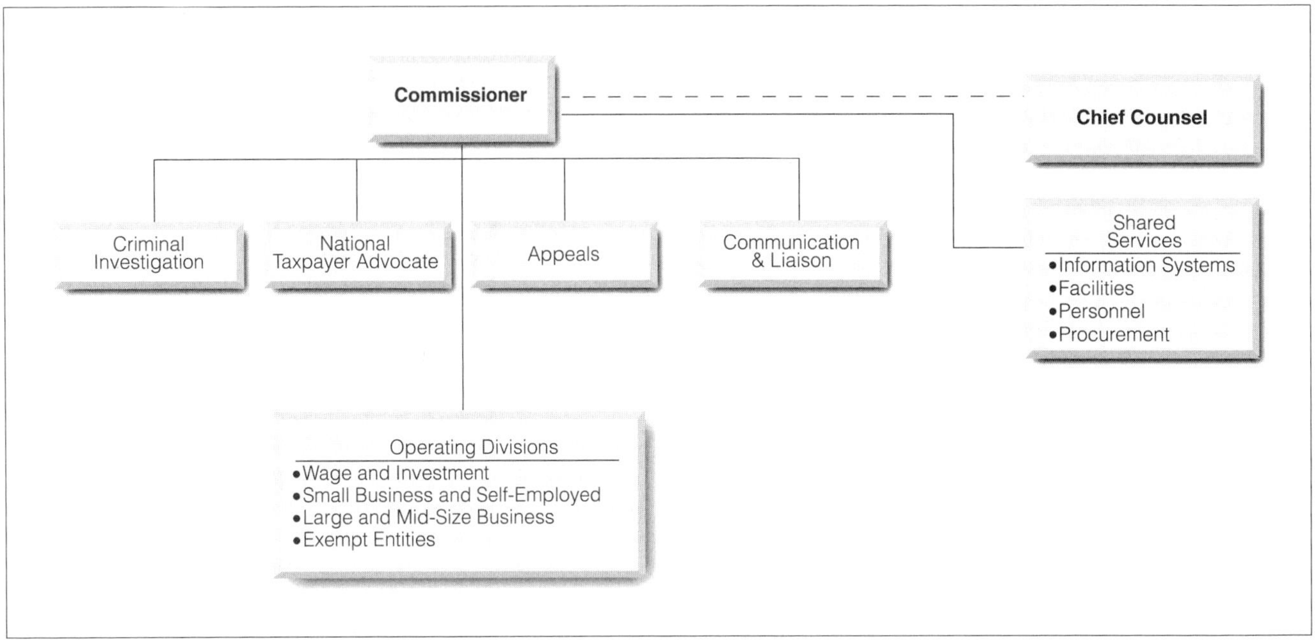

■ **TABLE 1–1**
IRS Operating Divisions: Tax Year 2000 Estimates

	Wage and Investment	**Small Business and Self-Employed**	**Large and Mid-Size Businesses (Assets > $10 Million)**	**Exempt Entities (Charities, Retirement Plans, Governments)**
Type of return filed	1040 with only wage and investment income (no Schedule C, E, F, or Form 2106)	1040 Schedules C and F, Forms 1120, 1120S, and 1065	1040 Schedules C and F, Forms 1120, 1120S, and 1065	Form 990 and various payroll forms
Number of filers	90 million, 116 million taxpayers	45 million	210,000	3 million entities, 1.9 million pay tax
Annual income tax liabilities	$265 billion	$816 billion	$466 billion	$94 billion
Payroll taxes, withholdings paid	$38 billion	$562 billion	$712 billion	$198 billion
Notes	Fewer than half use a paid tax preparer. Only 2% earn >$100,000 per year, 85% earn <$50,000, 28% earn <$10,000.	Pay in over 40% of all cash received by the IRS 4–60 annual transactions with the IRS	Further organized into industry segments to handle complex filing requirements About 10% are audited every year; some deal with IRS agents year-round.	Control about $7 trillion in assets

Rulings issued by the National Office provide a written statement of the position of the IRS concerning the tax consequences of a course of action contemplated by the taxpayer. Letter rulings do not have the force and effect of law, but they do provide guidance and support for taxpayers in similar transactions. The IRS will issue rulings only on uncompleted, actual (rather than hypothetical) transactions or on transactions that have been completed before the filing of the tax return for the year in question.

In certain circumstances, the IRS will not issue a ruling. It ordinarily will not rule in cases that essentially involve a question of fact. For example, no ruling will be issued to determine whether compensation paid to employees is reasonable in amount and therefore allowable as a deduction.[2]

A letter ruling represents the current opinion of the IRS on the tax consequences of a transaction with a given set of facts. IRS rulings are not unchangeable. They are frequently declared obsolete or are superseded by new rulings in response to tax law changes. However, revocation or modification of a ruling is usually not applied retroactively to the taxpayer who received the ruling, if it was relied on in good faith and if the facts in the ruling request were in agreement with the completed transaction. The IRS may revoke any ruling if, upon subsequent audit, the agent finds a misstatement or omission of facts or substantial discrepancies between the facts in the ruling request and the actual situation.

PLANNING STRATEGIES

Administrative Rulings

FRAMEWORK FOCUS: INCOME AND EXCLUSIONS, DEDUCTIONS

STRATEGY ➤ AVOID INCOME RECOGNITION.
➤ MAXIMIZE DEDUCTIBLE AMOUNTS.

There are many instances where it is advisable to seek an advance ruling or a determination letter from the IRS. The receipt of a favorable ruling or determination letter reduces the risk associated with the tax results of a transaction.

For example, a qualified retirement plan administrator should always request a determination letter on the exemption of the plan (see Chapter 11). There is a tremendous tax cost for a plan that is determined to be nonqualified. The employer loses the contribution deduction (although the payment then becomes additional deductible wages to the employee/beneficiary), the earnings on the trust assets are taxable as earned, and the beneficiaries of the trust cannot deduct any of their own contributions.

A corporation that is planning a tax-deferred reorganization (see Chapter 4) may want to request a private letter ruling on the tax ramifications of the proposed transaction. For example, in a spin-off ("Type D" reorganization), if the transaction does not meet the requirements of a tax-deferred reorganization, then the corporation is treated as making a taxable distribution of property, and the recipient shareholders are treated as receiving a distribution that may be taxable as a dividend.

A ruling may be relied upon only by the taxpayer who requested and received it. It must be attached to the tax return for the year in question.

Letter rulings benefit both the IRS and the taxpayer. Not only do they help promote a uniform application of the tax laws, but they may also reduce the potential for litigation or disputes with IRS agents. In addition, they make the IRS aware of significant transactions being consummated by taxpayers. A significant fee is charged for processing a ruling request.

[2]Rev.Proc. 2004–3, I.R.B. No. 1, 114.

OTHER ISSUANCES

In addition to issuing unpublished letter rulings and published rulings and procedures, the IRS issues determination letters and technical advice memoranda.

- A **determination letter** is issued by the Director in response to a taxpayer's inquiry concerning issues involving clearly established statutory authority, Regulations, rulings, or court decisions. Determination letters are summarized or published in the *Internal Revenue Bulletin*.

  Determination letters are issued to address various death, gift, income, excise, and employment tax matters.
- A **technical advice memorandum (TAM)** is issued by the National Office to a Director and/or Regional Commissioner in response to a specific request by an agent, Appellate Conferee, or Director. TAMs are issued in connection with an audit or a claim for refund.

EXAMPLE 18

True Corporation recently opened a car clinic and has employed numerous mechanics. The corporation is not certain whether its educational reimbursement plan is nondiscriminatory. True may request a determination letter from the appropriate Director. ■

EXAMPLE 19

Assume the same facts as in Example 18. True would like to establish a pension plan that qualifies for the tax advantages of § 401(k). To determine whether the plan qualifies, True should request and obtain a determination letter from the IRS. ■

EXAMPLE 20

A group of physicians plans to form an association to construct and operate a hospital. The determination letter procedure is appropriate to ascertain whether the group is subject to the Federal income tax or is tax-exempt. ■

DIGGING DEEPER 1

Find more information on this topic at our Web site: ***http://wft-advanced.swlearning.com.***

ADMINISTRATIVE POWERS OF THE IRS

The IRS has broad administrative powers to enforce the tax laws promulgated by Congress. They include the powers to:

- Examine the taxpayer's books and records.[3]
- Assess a tax deficiency and issue a demand for payment of the tax. However, no assessment or effort to collect the tax may be made until 90 days after a statutory notice of a deficiency (90-day letter) is issued.[4]
- Collect the tax when the taxpayer either neglects to pay or refuses to pay. This may be accomplished by securing a lien in favor of the IRS on all property owned by the taxpayer (tangible or intangible). This prevents the taxpayer from disposing of any property, even funds in the taxpayer's own checking account. The IRS also may seize property in satisfaction of any tax deficiency.

Generally the burden of proof is on the taxpayer in an IRS audit. However, the burden of proof shifts to the IRS during litigation when the taxpayer meets the Code's recordkeeping requirements and substantiates income and deductions properly.[5]

DIGGING DEEPER 2

Find more information on this topic at our Web site: ***http://wft-advanced.swlearning.com.***

---

[3]§ 7602.
[4]§§ 6212 and 6213.
[5]§ 7491.

BRIDGE DISCIPLINE

Bridge to Public Finance

Adam Smith developed the following four principles to help define a good tax system.

- Taxes should be *equal* or *equitable*. Taxpayers should support the government in proportion to their ability to pay, and in proportion to the income they received under the protection of a good government. This principle is the foundation of most political debates concerning tax policy. The debates always involve the questions, "Who should bear the tax burden? What is fair?"

  Our current system tries to achieve equity through the application of vertical and horizontal equity theories. The income tax system contains progressive tax rates, certain deductions are phased out for high-income earners, low-income earners are removed from the tax rolls entirely, and an alternative minimum tax was created to force higher-income earners to pay at least a minimum amount of tax. Equity is a matter of personal belief, which makes it very difficult to agree on.

- Taxes should be *certain* and not arbitrary. Taxpayers should know what the tax law is, so that they can plan their affairs. All taxpayers should be treated the same, with defined outcomes. Tax liabilities should not become a negotiating exercise at the end of an accounting period.

  The income tax law is set by Congress and administered by the IRS. A taxpayer's tax liability is fixed by law, not by a negotiation with a tax collector. A number of safeguards are built into the system to protect the taxpayer from an arbitrary enforcement of the tax law. This gives our tax system certainty. However, Congress is always changing the income tax, so there is uncertainty as to how income will be taxed in the future. From a tax planning standpoint, this is not efficient.

- Taxes should be *convenient*. The time and manner of collection should not be too burdensome to the taxpayer.

  The withholding of income tax from wages, the single largest source of income for most taxpayers, simplifies the paying of taxes. However, the overall burden of filing tax returns is not very convenient for many taxpayers.

- Taxes should be *economical*. The cost of administering the tax system should not be too high for either the taxpayer or the government.

  The Internal Revenue Service actually pays for itself. Every dollar spent on audits comes back several times. However, the cost to the taxpayer is high, as seen in the amount of time spent gathering and summarizing information, and in the cost of paying a tax professional to prepare the return.

Adapted from Harold Groves, *Tax Philosophers* (Madison: University of Wisconsin Press, 1974), p. 18.

LO.4

Describe the audit process, including how returns are selected for audit and the various types of audits.

THE AUDIT PROCESS

Selection of Returns for Audit. The IRS utilizes mathematical formulas to select tax returns that are most likely to contain errors and yield substantial amounts of additional tax revenues upon audit. The IRS does not openly disclose all of its audit selection techniques. However, some observations can be made regarding the probability of a return's selection for audit.

TAX FACT

IRS Likes the Match Game

A quotation from an internal IRS directive indicates that Schedule K–1 matching is a high-priority item.

For tax year 2001, over 23 million Schedule K–1 forms were filed reporting over $1 trillion in income to partners, shareholders and some trust beneficiaries. A matching program to ensure all Schedule K–1 income is being reported is critical to the IRS' tax administration policies.

Source: IR-2003–27 March 10, 2003.

- Certain groups of taxpayers are subject to audit more frequently than others. These groups include individuals with gross income in excess of $100,000, self-employed individuals with substantial business income and deductions, and cash businesses where the potential for tax evasion is high.

EXAMPLE 21

Tracey owns and operates a liquor store. As nearly all of her sales are for cash, Tracey might be a prime candidate for an audit by the IRS. Cash transactions are easier to conceal than those made on credit. ■

- If a taxpayer has been audited in a past year and the audit led to the assessment of a substantial deficiency, the IRS often makes a return visit.
- An audit might materialize if information returns (e.g., Form W–2, Form 1099) are not in substantial agreement with the income reported on the taxpayer's return. Obvious discrepancies do not necessitate formal audits and usually can be handled by correspondence with the taxpayer.

PLANNING STRATEGIES

Considerations in Handling an IRS Audit

Framework Focus: Income and Exclusions, Deductions

Strategy ➤ **Avoid Income Recognition.**
➤ **Maximize Deductible Amounts.**

An IRS audit can be very time consuming for a taxpayer and the tax practitioner. It is very important that information requested by the IRS be furnished in a timely and organized manner. Here are some general Do's and Don'ts when participating in an audit.

- Settle a dispute at the earliest possible point of the administrative process.
- Furnish only pertinent information requested by the IRS agent.
- Avoid making extraneous comments or furnishing extra information. This may open up new issues that the agent may not have thought of.
- Furnish all requested information promptly. The agent may be judged in part on his/her efficiency in closing or settling a case.
- If possible, conduct field audits in the practitioner's office rather than the client's office. This provides greater control over the audit investigation and facilitates the agent's review and prompt closure of the case.

DIGGING DEEPER 3 *Find more information on this topic at our Web site:* ***http://wft-advanced.swlearning.com.***

TAX IN THE NEWS

IRS Inside Information

There is nothing like turnover in the IRS Commissioner's office to produce leaks of new information about how the IRS really works. In conjunction with his recent farewell speech, outgoing Commissioner Rossotti revealed some interesting statistics, including the following.

- The IRS gets a budget of 41 cents per return to collect taxes. This is 10 percent less than it received in real terms just five years ago. In the meantime, tax planning efforts by taxpayers have accelerated, and Congress has passed almost 300 new tax laws.
- The 10 percent "cut" in IRS appropriations translates into a 28 percent decline in resources dedicated to audits, collections, and investigations.
- For some types of tax understatements, four in five "tax cheats" escape detection because of this underfunding.
- The IRS can follow up on only 20 percent of all income understatements by partners and partnerships because the document matching program is underfunded.

EXAMPLE 22

Phil reports to the police that burglars broke into his home while he was out of town and took a shoe box containing $25,000 in cash, among other things. A representative of the IRS reading the newspaper account of the burglary might wonder why Phil kept such a large amount of cash in a shoe box at home. ■

EXAMPLE 23

After 15 years, Betty is discharged by her employer, Dr. Franklin. Shortly thereafter, the IRS receives a letter from Betty stating that Franklin keeps two sets of books, one of which substantially understates his cash receipts. ■

The statistical models used by the IRS to select individual tax returns for audit come from random audits of a small number of taxpayers, who are required to document every entry that they made on the Form 1040. The latest round of these National Research Program (NPR) audits took place in 2003 and resulted in the construction of new Discriminant Information Function (DIF) scores that project the amount of revenue that the IRS will gain from pursuing tax returns with various statistical profiles. The higher the DIF score, the better the return to the IRS from pursuing the audit, and the higher the probability of selection for an examination.

These data-seeking audits have been delayed since the late 1980s as a result of taxpayer complaints to Congress about the stress that they create.[6] But the data from the older DIF models no longer match our service-based, information-powered economy. Consequently, updating the underlying models was essential.

Many individual taxpayers mistakenly assume that if they do not hear from the IRS within a few weeks after filing their return or if they have received a refund check, no audit will be forthcoming. As a practical matter, most individual returns are examined about two years from the date of filing. If not, they generally remain unaudited. All large corporations, however, are subject to annual audits.

[6] About 39,000 NRP audits required a meeting between the IRS and the taxpayer. The total audit sample constituted 49,000 returns. About 4,000 of these returns were analyzed without contacting the taxpayer, and another 2,000 taxpayers were contacted only by mail with queries about one or two items. The rest of the sample consisted largely of proprietors, partners, and farmers (i.e., those using Schedules C, E, and F). Only about 1,700 returns were subjected to "line-by-line" review.

PLANNING STRATEGIES

Preparation for the Audit

FRAMEWORK FOCUS: INCOME AND EXCLUSIONS, DEDUCTIONS

STRATEGY ➤ **AVOID INCOME RECOGNITION.**
➤ **MAXIMIZE DEDUCTIBLE AMOUNTS.**

The tax professional must prepare thoroughly for the audit or appeals process.

- Make certain that both sides agree on the issues to be resolved in the audit. The goal is to limit the number of issues raised by the auditor.
- Identify all the facts underlying the issues in dispute, including those favorable to the IRS.
- Conduct any necessary tax research for issues raised in the audit.
- Determine the degree of discretion that the IRS agent is likely to have in disposing of the case.
- Prepare a list of points supporting and contradicting the taxpayer's case. Short research memos can be useful in the discussions with the IRS agent as well as in getting points favoring the taxpayer "entered into the record."
- Prepare tax and interest computations showing the effects of points that are in dispute, so that the consequences of closing or compromising on an issue can be readily determined.
- Determine a "litigation point." This position should be based on the dollars of tax, interest, and penalty involved, the chance of prevailing in various trial-level courts, and other strategies discussed with the taxpayer.
- The tax practitioner's workpapers should include all research memoranda, and a list of resolved and unresolved issues should be continually updated during the audit.
- Avoid blanket access to working papers when possible. Workpapers should be carefully reviewed to minimize opportunities for the agent to raise new issues not otherwise apparent.
- The IRS should be furnished copies of workpapers and other documentation. The client and/or tax practitioner should retain all originals.
- If a Special Agent becomes involved in the audit process, the taxpayer should be advised to seek legal counsel to determine the extent of cooperation in providing the agent with information. A Special Agent gets involved only when there is a possibility of criminal charges.
- The tax adviser should also consult legal counsel when involved with a Special Agent.

Verification and Audit Procedures. The filed tax return is immediately reviewed for mathematical accuracy. A check is also made for deductions, exclusions, etc., that are clearly erroneous. One obvious error would be the failure to comply with the 7.5 percent limitation on the deduction for medical expenses.

Over 10 percent of all individual returns show a math error. In such cases, the Service Center merely sends the taxpayer revised computations and a bill or refund as appropriate. Taxpayers usually are able to settle such matters through a direct *correspondence audit* with the IRS without the necessity of a formal meeting.

Office audits are conducted by a representative of the Director's Office, either in the office of the IRS or through correspondence. Individual returns with few or no items of business income are usually handled through the office audit procedure. In most instances, the taxpayer is required merely to substantiate a deduction, credit, or item of income that appears on the return. The taxpayer presents documentation in the form of canceled checks, invoices, etc., for the items in question.

The *field audit* procedure is commonly used for corporate returns and for returns of individuals engaged in business or professional activities. This type of audit generally involves a more complete examination of a taxpayer's transactions.

A field audit is conducted by IRS agents at the office or home of the taxpayer or at the office of the taxpayer's representative. The agent's work may be facilitated

BRIDGE DISCIPLINE

Bridge to Public Finance

The Federal individual income tax was created by the Sixteenth Amendment to the Constitution in 1913. This amendment spawned the current income tax system. The amendment states:

> Congress shall have the power to lay and collect taxes on incomes, from whatever source derived, without apportionment among the several states, and without regard to any census of enumeration.

Since 1913 Congress has promulgated numerous laws that define what income is and indicate the rate at which that income should be taxed. The tax system has in part been constructed with several equity principles as part of its foundation.

- ***Horizontal equity*** Individuals with the same amount of economic income should pay relatively the same amount of income tax. This principle is in part why the alternative minimum tax was created.
- ***Vertical equity*** Individuals who earn more income should pay a relatively higher tax than those who make less. This principle is in part achieved by the progressive tax rate structure and the various deduction phaseout rules found in the individual income tax system.
- ***Ability to pay*** The tax burden should be apportioned to the taxpayers that have the capacity to pay the tax. This principle is very closely tied to vertical equity.

These principles are the foundation of our present tax system. For a voluntary system to work, the governed must agree that there is an equitable distribution of the tax burden. Otherwise, the citizens would no longer voluntarily comply, and a vast underground economy would be created. In the United States, there is a general consensus that voluntary compliance is desirable, and the vast majority of the taxpayers file their returns accordingly. Still, estimates of the untaxed net taxable income sheltered currently in the U.S. underground economy range from $100 to $300 billion annually.

by a review of certain tax workpapers and discussions with the taxpayer's representative about items appearing on the tax return. Table 1–2 summarizes key audit information.

Prior to or at the initial interview, the IRS must provide the taxpayer with an explanation of the audit process that is the subject of the interview and describe the taxpayer's rights under that process. If the taxpayer clearly states at any time during the interview the desire to consult with an attorney, CPA, or enrolled agent or any other person permitted to represent the taxpayer before the IRS, then the IRS representative must suspend the interview.[7]

TABLE 1–2
IRS Audit Information by Type (Individual Returns Filed in 2002)

	Conducted (Number)	Conducted (Percent)
Correspondence audit	575,000	79%
Office audit	68,000	9%
Field audit	86,000	12%

[7] § 7521(b).

Any officer or employee of the IRS must, upon advance request, allow a taxpayer to make an audio recording of any in-person interview with the officer or employee concerning the determination and collection of any tax.

Settlement with the Revenue Agent. Following an audit, the IRS agent may either accept the return as filed or recommend certain adjustments. The **Revenue Agent's Report (RAR)** is reviewed within the IRS. In most instances, the agent's proposed adjustments are approved.

Agents must adhere strictly to IRS policy as reflected in published rulings, Regulations, and other releases. The agent cannot settle an unresolved issue based upon the probability of winning the case in court. Usually, issues involving factual questions can be settled at the agent level, and it may be advantageous for both the taxpayer and the IRS to reach agreement at the earliest point in the settlement process. For example, it may be to the taxpayer's advantage to reach agreement at the agent level and avoid any further opportunity for the IRS to raise new issues.

If agreement is reached upon the proposed deficiency, the taxpayer signs Form 870 (Waiver of Restrictions on Assessment and Collection of Deficiency in Tax). One advantage to the taxpayer of signing Form 870 at this point is that interest stops accumulating on the deficiency 30 days after the form is filed.[8] When this form is signed, the taxpayer effectively waives the right to receive a statutory notice of deficiency (90-day letter) and to subsequently petition the Tax Court. In addition, it is no longer possible for the taxpayer later to go to the IRS Appeals Division. The signing of Form 870 at the agent level generally closes the case. However, the IRS is not restricted by Form 870 and may assess additional deficiencies if deemed necessary.

LO.5

Explain the taxpayer appeal process, including various settlement options available.

THE TAXPAYER APPEAL PROCESS

If agreement cannot be reached at the agent level, the taxpayer receives a copy of the Revenue Agent's Report and a **30-day letter.** The taxpayer has 30 days to request an administrative appeal. If an appeal is not requested, a **90-day letter** is issued. Figure 1–4 illustrates the taxpayer's alternatives when a disagreement with the IRS persists.

A taxpayer who wishes to appeal must make an appropriate request to the Appeals Division. The request must be accompanied by a written protest except in the following cases.

- The proposed tax deficiency does not exceed $10,000 for any of the tax periods involved in the audit.
- The deficiency resulted from a correspondence or office audit (i.e., not as a result of a field audit).

The Appeals Division is authorized to settle all tax disputes based on the hazards of litigation (the chances of winning in court). Since the Appeals Division has final settlement authority until a 90-day letter has been issued, the taxpayer may be able to negotiate a settlement. In addition, an overall favorable settlement may be reached by "trading" disputed issues. The Appeals Division occasionally may raise new issues if the grounds are substantial and of significant tax impact.

Both the Appeals Division and the taxpayer have the right to request technical advice memoranda from the National Office of the IRS. A TAM that is favorable to the taxpayer is binding on the Appeals Division. Even if the TAM is favorable to the IRS, the Appeals Division may nevertheless settle the case based on the hazards of litigation.

[8] § 6601(c).

■ **FIGURE 1–4**
Income Tax Appeal Procedure

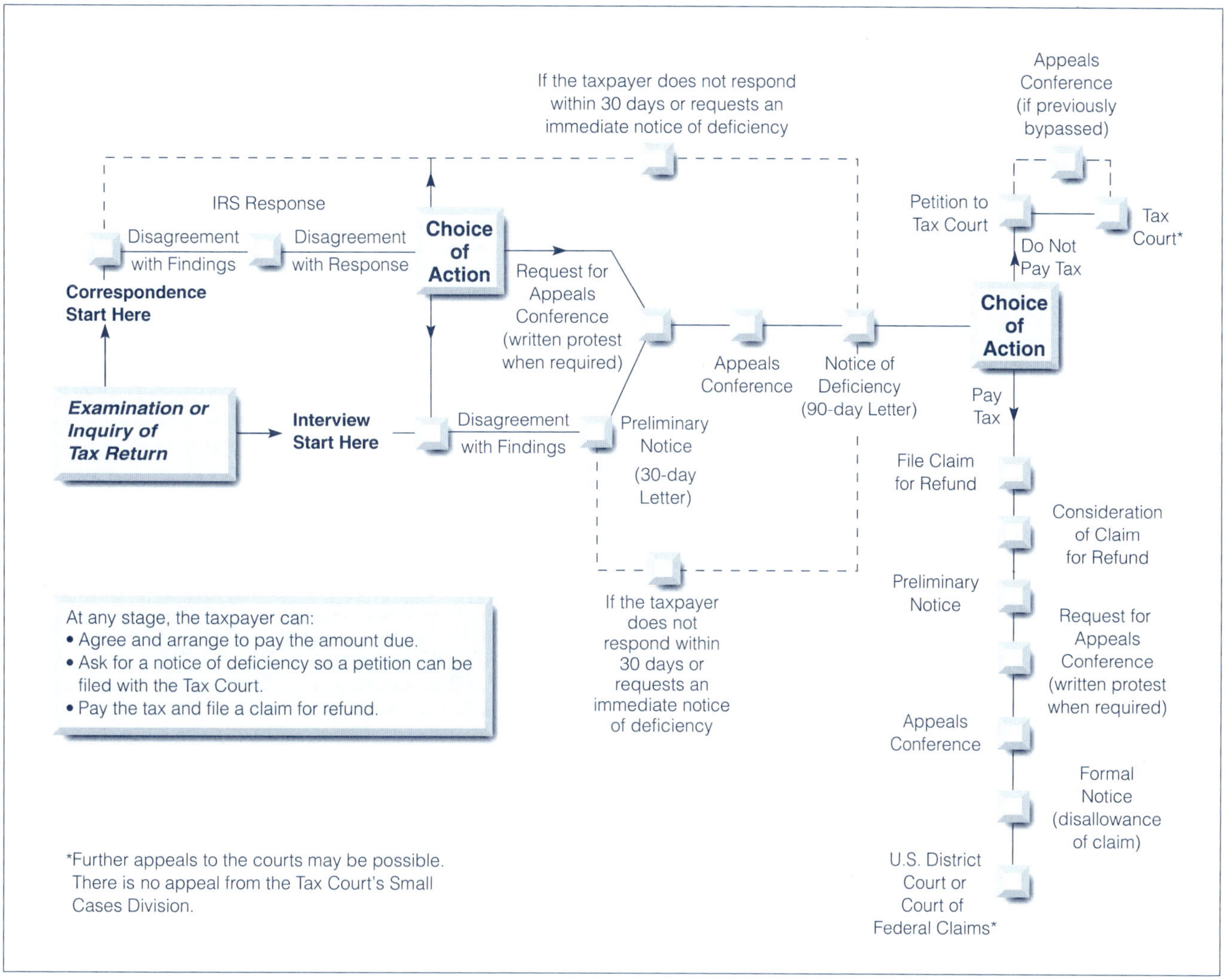

EXAMPLE 24

At the time Terri is audited, the corporation that she controls had advances outstanding to her in the amount of $80,000. The IRS field agent held that these advances were constructive dividends to her. Some facts point toward this result (e.g., the corporation is closely held, Terri has made no repayments, and the loan balance has increased over several years). Other facts, however, appear to indicate that these advances are bona fide loans (e.g., a written instrument provides for interest, Terri has the independent means of repayment, and the corporation has a good dividend-paying record).

The Appeals Division and Terri's representative assess the hazards of litigation as being 50% for each side. Thus, if Terri chooses to take the issue to court, she would have an even chance of winning or losing her case. Based on this assessment, both sides agree to treat $40,000 of the advance as a dividend and $40,000 as a bona fide loan. The agreement enables Terri to avoid $40,000 of dividend income (the loan portion) and saves her the cost of litigating the issue.

Thus, by going to the Appeals Division, Terri obtained a satisfactory settlement otherwise unobtainable from the agent. ■

PLANNING STRATEGIES

Litigation Considerations

FRAMEWORK FOCUS: INCOME AND EXCLUSIONS, DEDUCTIONS

STRATEGY ➤ AVOID INCOME RECOGNITION.
➤ MAXIMIZE DEDUCTIBLE AMOUNTS.

- Consider the probability of winning in court in comparison to the costs of litigation (legal, support, and court costs).
- The Tax Court provides the taxpayer an opportunity to litigate issues without first paying the tax on the deficiency. However, some taxpayers prefer to litigate the case in Federal District Court or the Court of Federal Claims, since the payment of tax effectively stops the running of interest on the deficiency.
- In selecting a proper judicial forum, consideration should be given to the decisions of the various courts in related cases. The Tax Court follows the decisions of Courts of Appeal if the court is one to which the taxpayer may appeal.
- If the issues involve a question of fact, then the Federal District Court is more appropriate (a jury trial is obtainable).

Taxpayers who file a petition with the U.S. Tax Court have the option of having the case heard before the more informal Small Cases Division if the amount of tax in dispute does not exceed $50,000.[9] If the Small Cases Division is used, neither party may appeal the case.

The economic costs of a settlement offer from the Appeals Division should be weighed against the costs of litigation and the probability of winning the case. The taxpayer should also consider the impact of the settlement upon the tax liability for future periods in addition to the years under audit.

If a settlement is reached with the Appeals Division, the taxpayer is required to sign Form 870–AD. Interest stops running on the deficiency when the Appeals Division accepts the Form 870–AD. According to the IRS, this settlement is binding upon both parties unless fraud, malfeasance, concealment, or misrepresentation of material fact has occurred. Nevertheless, the question of whether this settlement form prevents the taxpayer from filing a subsequent refund claim and suit for refund has been litigated with conflicting results.[10]

OFFERS IN COMPROMISE AND CLOSING AGREEMENTS

The IRS can negotiate a compromise if the taxpayer's ability to pay the tax is doubtful. If the taxpayer is financially unable to pay the total amount of the tax, a Form 656 (Offer in Compromise) is filed with the Memphis Internal Revenue Service Center or the Brookhaven Internal Revenue Service Center in Holtsville, New York, depending on the location of the taxpayer. An **offer in compromise** is appropriate in the following circumstances.[11]

[9] § 7463(a).

[10] Compare *Stair v. U.S.*, 75–1 USTC ¶9463, 35 AFTR2d 75–1515, 516 F.2d 560 (CA–2, 1975), with *Unita Livestock Corp. v. U.S.*, 66–1 USTC ¶9193, 17 AFTR2d 254, 355 F.2d 761 (CA–10, 1966).

[11] § 7122 and Reg. § 301.7122–1T(b).

- There is doubt as to the taxpayer's liability for the tax (i.e., disputed issues still exist).
- There is doubt as to the collectibility of the tax (i.e., the taxpayer's net worth and earnings capacity are low).
- Payment of the disputed amount would constitute an economic hardship for the taxpayer. For instance, the taxpayer is incapable of earning a living because of a long-term illness or disability, or liquidation of the taxpayer's assets to pay the amount due would leave the taxpayer unable to meet basic living expenses.

The IRS investigates the offer by evaluating the taxpayer's financial ability to pay the tax. In some instances, the compromise settlement includes an agreement for final settlement of the tax through payments of a specified percentage of the taxpayer's future earnings. This settlement procedure usually entails lengthy negotiations with the IRS, but the presumption is that the agency will find terms upon which to enter into a compromise with the taxpayer. The IRS is charged to use a "liberal acceptance policy" in compromising with taxpayers and to increase educational efforts so that taxpayer rights and obligations are better known.

The IRS has statutory authority to enter into a written agreement allowing taxes to be paid on an installment basis if that arrangement facilitates the tax collection. The agency encourages its employees to use installment plans, and an individual is guaranteed the right to use an installment agreement when the amount in dispute does not exceed $10,000. The taxpayer uses Form 9465 to initiate the installment plan.

The IRS provides an annual statement accounting for the status of the agreement. The agreement may later be modified or terminated because of (1) inadequate information, (2) subsequent change in financial condition, or (3) failure to pay an installment when due or to provide requested information.[12]

A **closing agreement** is binding on both the taxpayer and the IRS except upon a subsequent showing of fraud, malfeasance, or misrepresentation of a material fact.[13] The closing agreement may be used when disputed issues carry over to future years. It may also be employed to dispose of a dispute involving a specific issue for a prior year or a proposed transaction involving future years. If, for example, the IRS is willing to make substantial concessions in the valuation of assets for death tax purposes, it may require a closing agreement from the recipient of the property to establish the income tax basis of the assets.

PLANNING STRATEGIES

Offers in Compromise

FRAMEWORK FOCUS: INCOME AND EXCLUSIONS, DEDUCTIONS

STRATEGY ➤ AVOID INCOME RECOGNITION.
➤ MAXIMIZE DEDUCTIBLE AMOUNTS.

The IRS is encouraging the use of offers in compromise to a greater degree than ever before as part of its "consumer-friendly" approach to its enforcement obligations and its efforts to bring more nonfilers into compliance.

[12] § 6159.

[13] § 7121(b).

Several attributes of an offer in compromise could be detrimental to the taxpayer, however.

- Just as the IRS no longer can raise new issues as part of the audit proceedings against the taxpayer, the taxpayer cannot contest or appeal any such agreement.
- The taxpayer must disclose all relevant finances and resources.
- Both parties are bound to the filing positions established by the compromise for five tax years, a level of inflexibility that may work against a taxpayer whose circumstances change over time.

LO.6

Determine the amount of interest on a deficiency or a refund and when it is due.

INTEREST

Determination of the Interest Rate. Congress sets the interest rates applicable to Federal tax underpayments (deficiencies) and overpayments (refunds) close to the rates available in financial markets. The Code provides for the rates to be determined quarterly.[14] Thus, the rates that are determined during March are effective for the following April through June.

IRS interest is based on the Federal short-term rates published periodically by the IRS in Revenue Rulings. They are based on the average market yield on outstanding marketable obligations of the United States with remaining maturity of three years or less.

For noncorporate taxpayers, the interest rate applicable to *both* overpayments and underpayments is 5 percent for the second quarter of 2004. For most corporate taxpayers, the rate is 4 percent for overpayments and 5 percent for underpayments. Corporations with large overpayments or underpayments are subject to different rates. Interest payable to or by the U.S. Treasury is compounded on a daily basis.[15]

The amount of interest owed depends on whether it relates to a tax deficiency or a refund. Generally, interest accrues on a tax deficiency from the date the tax was required to be paid, which is usually the due date of the return, through the date of actual payment. However, the calculation of interest owed the taxpayer on a refund favors the Treasury. Generally if an overpayment is refunded within 45 days after the date the return is filed or is due, no interest is allowed.

DIGGING DEEPER 4

Find more information on this topic at our Web site: ***http://wft-advanced.swlearning.com.***

EXAMPLE 25

Naomi, a calendar year taxpayer, files her 2003 return on December 1, 2004. The return reflects an overwithholding of $2,500. On June 8, 2005, Naomi receives a refund of her 2003 overpayment. Interest on the refund began to accrue on December 1, 2004 (not April 15, 2004). If the refund is paid to Naomi on January 5, 2005, (rather than June 8, 2005), no interest is payable by the IRS, since the refund was made within 45 days of the filing of the return. ■

LO.7

Discuss the various penalties that can be imposed on acts of noncompliance by taxpayers and return preparers.

TAXPAYER PENALTIES

To promote and enforce taxpayer compliance with the U.S. voluntary self-assessment system of taxation, Congress has enacted a comprehensive array of penalties.

Tax penalties may involve both criminal and civil offenses. Criminal tax penalties are imposed only after the usual criminal process, in which the taxpayer is entitled to the same constitutional guarantees as nontax criminal defendants. Normally, a criminal penalty provides for imprisonment. Civil tax penalties are collected in the same manner as other taxes and usually provide only for monetary

[14]§ 6621.

[15]§ 6622.

TAX IN THE NEWS

The IRS Strives to Become Consumer-Friendly

When country singer Willie Nelson was found guilty of underreporting his Federal income taxes, chiefly due to his involvement in real estate tax shelters, the total deficiency, including taxes, interest, and penalties, came to $16.7 million. The IRS intended to collect the full amount by forcing auctions of Nelson's most valuable possessions, placing claims on royalties from his recordings, encouraging him to make television commercials for fast-food outlets, and prompting him to sue his prior tax advisers for offsetting damages (to be paid directly to the IRS). Three years of such collections totaled only about $4 million.

As part of a nationwide effort to expand the use of the offer in compromise program, the IRS then settled with Nelson for total collections of $9 million, to be paid over a five-year period, with no future liens or collection activities. An IRS spokesperson asserted that the broader use of the compromise powers indicated the agency was "willing to settle for something less than the entire amount . . . to be more reasonable with taxpayers" having difficulty finding the full deficiency amount. As more taxpayers are having such difficulties, the IRS seems willing to collect what it can, rather than haggle in court for years to collect the "last penny" due.

fines. Criminal and civil penalties are not mutually exclusive; therefore, both types of sanctions may be imposed on a taxpayer.

The Code characterizes tax penalties as additions to tax; thus, they cannot subsequently be deducted by the taxpayer.

Ad valorem penalties are additions to tax that are based upon a percentage of the owed tax. *Assessable penalties*, on the other hand, typically include a flat dollar amount. Assessable penalties are not subject to review by the Tax Court, but ad valorem penalties are subject to the same deficiency procedures that apply to the underlying tax.

PLANNING STRATEGIES

Penalties

FRAMEWORK FOCUS: TAX CREDITS

STRATEGY ➤ MAXIMIZE TAX CREDITS.

Penalties are imposed upon a taxpayer's failure to file a return or pay a tax when due. These penalties can be avoided if the failure is due to reasonable cause and not due to willful neglect. Reasonable cause is not well defined and should not be relied upon if possible. The taxpayer should always try to obtain a valid IRS extension of time for filing the return.

Underpayment penalties may result from an individual taxpayer's failure to make quarterly estimated tax payments. If the taxpayer is an employee, he/she can request that the employer withhold more tax from the paycheck. The additional withholding may cure the earlier underpayment, since withholding is deemed to be made pro rata during the year, even if it is all withheld in December.

DIGGING DEEPER 5 *Find more information on this topic at our Web site:* ***http://wft-advanced.swlearning.com.***

Failure to File and Failure to Pay. For a failure to file a tax return by the due date (including extensions), a penalty of 5 percent per month (up to a maximum of 25 percent) is imposed on the amount of tax shown as due on the return, with a minimum penalty amount of $100.[16] If the failure to file is attributable to fraud, the penalty becomes 15 percent per month, to a maximum of 75 percent of the tax.[17]

For a failure to pay the tax due as shown on the return, a penalty of 0.5 percent per month (up to a maximum of 25 percent) is imposed on the amount of the tax. The penalty is doubled if the taxpayer fails to pay the tax after receiving a deficiency assessment.

In all of these cases, a fraction of a month counts as a full month. These penalties relate to the net amount of the tax due.

Obtaining an extension for filing a tax return does not by itself extend the date by which the taxes due must be paid. Thus, an application for an extended due date for a tax return almost always is accompanied by a payment by the taxpayer of a good faith estimate of the taxes that will be owed with the return when it is filed by the extended due date. If the taxpayer does not make such a good faith estimate and payment, the extension itself may be voided by the IRS (e.g., when the return is filed by the extended due date with a much larger amount due than had been estimated).

EXAMPLE 26

Conchita uses an automatic four-month extension for the filing of her 2004 tax return. Thus, the return is due on August 15, 2005, not on April 15. Conchita's application for the extension includes a $5,000 check, the amount that she estimates her 2004 return will show as owing for the year when she files it in August. ■

During any month in which both the failure to file penalty and the failure to pay penalty apply, the failure to file penalty is reduced by the amount of the failure to pay penalty.

EXAMPLE 27

Jason files his tax return 10 days after the due date. Along with the return, he remits a check for $3,000, which is the balance of the tax he owes. Disregarding any interest liabilities, Jason's total penalties are as follows.

Failure to pay penalty (½% × $3,000)		$ 15
Failure to file penalty (5% × $3,000)	$150	
Less failure to pay penalty for the same period	15	
Failure to file penalty		135
Total penalties		$150

The penalties for one full month are imposed even though Jason was delinquent by only 10 days. Unlike the method used to compute interest, any part of a month is treated as a whole month. ■

Accuracy-Related Penalties. Major civil penalties relating to the accuracy of tax return data, including misstatements stemming from taxpayer negligence and improper valuation of income and deductions, are coordinated under the umbrella term **accuracy-related penalties.**[18] This consolidation of related penalties into a single levy eliminates the possibility that multiple penalties will apply to a single understatement of tax.

[16] § 6651(a).
[17] § 6651(f).
[18] § 6662.

GLOBAL TAX ISSUES

Advance Pricing Agreements Reduce International Uncertainty

Two of the more severe accuracy-related penalties involve the transfer pricing issues surrounding the IRS's application of § 482. Transfer pricing issues are particularly difficult—and important—in an international context because multiple taxing authorities are involved. Consequently, taxpayers have begun to negotiate international transfer pricing agreements in advance with the IRS and other countries. Obtaining one of these *advance pricing agreements (APAs)* can require a substantial amount of work from the taxpayer, but the certainty they bring is valuable.

Over 400 APAs have been completed with the United States. The IRS offers a simpler APA process for small businesses.

The accuracy-related penalties each amount to 20 percent of the portion of the tax underpayment that is attributable to one or more of the following infractions.

- Negligence or disregard of rules and regulations.
- Substantial understatement of tax liability.
- Substantial valuation overstatement.
- Substantial valuation understatement.

The penalties apply only where the taxpayer fails to show a reasonable basis for the position taken on the return.[19]

Substantial Understatement of Tax Liability. The understatement penalty is designed to strike at middle- and high-income taxpayers who are tempted to play the so-called audit lottery.[20] Some taxpayers take questionable and undisclosed positions on their tax returns in the hope that the return will not be selected for audit. Disclosing the positions would have called attention to the return and increased the probability of audit.

A substantial understatement of a tax liability transpires when the understatement exceeds the larger of 10 percent of the tax due or $5,000 ($10,000 for a C corporation). The understatement to which the penalty applies is the difference between the amount of tax required to be shown on the return and the amount of tax actually shown on the return.

The penalty can be avoided if the taxpayer has substantial authority for and adequately discloses the disputed tax return position.

Penalty for Overvaluation. The objective of the overvaluation penalty is to deter taxpayers from inflating values (or basis), usually of charitable contributions of property, to reduce income taxes.[21]

- The penalty is 20 percent of the additional tax that would have been paid had the correct valuation (or basis) been used.
- The penalty applies only when the valuation (or basis) used is 200 percent or more of the correct valuation (or basis). The penalty is doubled if the valuation is overstated by 400 percent or more.

[19] Temporary Regulations issued as TD 8533, 1994–1 C.B. 307. Most tax professionals measure this standard as a one-fourth probability of prevailing in court.

[20] § 6662(b)(2).

[21] §§ 6662(b)(3) and (h).

- The penalty applies only to the extent that the resulting income tax underpayment exceeds $5,000 ($10,000 for C corporations).

EXAMPLE 28

Gretchen (a calendar year taxpayer) purchased a painting for $10,000. Years later, when the painting is worth $18,000 (as later determined by the IRS), Gretchen donates the painting to an art museum. Based on the appraisal of a cousin who is an amateur artist, she deducts $40,000 for the donation. Since Gretchen was in the 30% tax bracket, overstating the deduction by $22,000 results in a tax underpayment of $6,600.

Gretchen's penalty for overvaluation is $1,320 [20% × $6,600 (the underpayment that resulted from using $40,000 instead of $18,000)]. ■

The substantial valuation overstatement penalty is avoided if the taxpayer can show reasonable cause and good faith. However, when the overvaluation involves *charitable deduction property*, the taxpayer must show two *additional* facts.

- The claimed value of the property is based on a qualified appraisal made by a qualified appraiser.
- The taxpayer made a good faith investigation of the value of the contributed property.[22]

Based on these criteria, Gretchen in Example 28 would find it difficult to avoid the penalty. A cousin who is an amateur artist does not meet the definition of a qualified appraiser. Likewise, she apparently has not made a good faith investigation of the value of the contributed property.

Penalty for Undervaluation. When attempting to minimize the income tax, it is to the benefit of taxpayers to *overvalue* deductions. When attempting to minimize transfer taxes (estate and gift taxes), however, executors and donors may be inclined to *undervalue* the assets transferred. A lower valuation reduces estate and gift taxes. An accuracy-related penalty is imposed for substantial estate or gift tax valuation understatements.[23] As with other accuracy-related penalties, reasonable cause and good faith on the part of the taxpayer are a defense.

- The penalty is 20 percent of the additional transfer tax that would have been due had the correct valuation been used on Form 706 (estate tax return) or Form 709 (gift and generation-skipping tax return).
- The penalty applies only if the value of the property claimed on the return is 50 percent or less than the amount determined to be correct. The penalty is doubled if the reported valuation was 25 percent or less than the correct determination.
- The penalty applies only to an additional transfer tax liability in excess of $5,000.

Civil Fraud Penalty. A 75 percent civil penalty is imposed on any underpayment resulting from **fraud** by the taxpayer who has filed a return.[24] For this penalty, the burden of proof *is on the IRS* to show by a preponderance of the evidence that the taxpayer had a specific intent to evade a tax.

Once the IRS has initially established that fraud has occurred, the taxpayer then bears the burden of proof to show by a preponderance of the evidence the portion of the underpayment that is not attributable to fraud.

[22]§ 6664(c)(2).
[23]§ 6662(b)(5).
[24]§ 6663. As noted later in the chapter, underpayments traceable to fraudulent acts are not subject to a statute of limitations.

Although the Code and Regulations do not provide any assistance in ascertaining what constitutes civil fraud, it is clear that mere negligence on the part of the taxpayer (however great) will not suffice. Fraud has been found in cases of manipulation of the books,[25] substantial omissions from income,[26] and erroneous deductions.[27]

EXAMPLE 29

Frank underpaid his income tax by $90,000. The IRS can prove that $60,000 of the underpayment was due to fraud. Frank responds by a preponderance of the evidence that $30,000 of the underpayment was not due to fraud. The civil fraud penalty is $45,000 (75% × $60,000). ■

If the underpayment of tax is partially attributable to negligence and partially attributable to fraud, the fraud penalty is applied first.

Criminal Penalties. In addition to civil fraud penalties, the Code contains numerous criminal sanctions that carry various monetary fines and/or imprisonment. The difference between civil and criminal fraud is often one of degree. A characteristic of criminal fraud is the presence of willfulness on the part of the taxpayer. Thus, § 7201, dealing with attempts to evade or defeat a tax, contains the following language.

> Any person who *willfully* attempts in any manner to evade or defeat any tax imposed by this title or the payment thereof shall, in addition to other penalties provided by law, be guilty of a felony and, upon conviction thereof, shall be fined not more than $100,000 ($500,000 in the case of a corporation), or imprisoned not more than five years, or both, together with the costs of prosecution. [Emphasis added.]

As to the burden of proof, the IRS must show that the taxpayer was guilty of willful evasion "beyond the shadow of any reasonable doubt."

Failure to Pay Estimated Taxes. A penalty is imposed for a failure to pay estimated income taxes. The penalty applies to individuals and corporations and is based on the rate of interest in effect for deficiency assessments.[28] The penalty also applies to trusts and certain estates that are required to make estimated tax payments. The penalty is not imposed if the tax due for the year (less amounts withheld and credits) is less than $500 for corporations, $1,000 for all others. For employees, an equal part of withholding is deemed paid on each due date.

Quarterly payments are to be made on or before the fifteenth day of the fourth month (April 15 for a calendar year taxpayer), sixth month, ninth month, and the first month of the following year. Corporations must make the last quarterly payment by the twelfth month of the same year.

An individual's underpayment of estimated tax is the difference between the estimates that were paid and the least of (1) 90 percent of the current-year tax, (2) 100 percent of the prior-year tax (the tax year must have been a full 12 months, and a return must have been filed), and (3) 90 percent of the tax that would be due on an annualized income computation for the period running through the end of the quarter. When the taxpayer's prior-year adjusted gross income (AGI) exceeds $150,000, the required payment percentage for the prior-year alternative is 110 percent.

[25]*Dogget v. Comm.*, 60–1 USTC ¶9342, 5 AFTR2d 1034, 275 F.2d 823 (CA–4, 1960).

[26]*Harvey Brodsky*, 21 TCM 578, T.C.Memo. 1962–105.

[27]*Lash v. Comm.*, 57–2 USTC ¶9725, 51 AFTR 492, 245 F.2d 20 (CA–1, 1957).

[28]§§ 6655 (corporations) and 6654 (other taxpayers). Other computations can avoid the penalty. See §§ 6654(d)(2) and (k), 6655(e) and (i).

A corporation's underpayment of estimated tax is the difference between the estimates that were paid and the least of (1) the current-year tax, (2) the prior-year tax, and (3) the tax on an annualized income computation using one of three methods of computation sanctioned by the Code. For the prior-year alternative, (1) the prior tax year must have been a full 12 months, (2) a nonzero tax amount must have been generated for that year, and (3) large corporations (taxable income of $1 million or more in any of the three immediately preceding tax years) can use the alternative only for the first installment of a year.

In computing the penalty, Form 2210 (Underpayment of Estimated Tax by Individuals) or Form 2220 (Underpayment of Estimated Tax by Corporations) is used.

Failure to Make Deposits of Taxes and Overstatements of Deposits. When business is not doing well or cash-flow problems develop, employers have a great temptation to "borrow" from Uncle Sam. One way this can be done is to fail to pay to the IRS the amounts that have been withheld from the wages of employees for FICA and income tax purposes. The IRS does not appreciate being denied the use of these funds and has a number of weapons at its disposal to discourage the practice.

LO.8

Understand the rules governing the statute of limitations on assessments and on refunds.

STATUTES OF LIMITATIONS

A **statute of limitations** defines the period of time during which one party may pursue against another party a cause of action or other suit allowed under the governing law. Failure to satisfy any requirement provides the other party with an absolute defense should the statute be invoked. Inequity would result if no limits were placed on such suits. Permitting an extended period of time to elapse between the initiation of a claim and its pursuit could place the defense at a serious disadvantage. Witnesses may have died or disappeared; records or other evidence may have been discarded or destroyed.

Assessment and the Statute of Limitations. In general, any tax that is imposed must be assessed within three years of the filing of the return (or, if later, the due date of the return).[29] Some exceptions to this three-year limitation exist.

- If no return is filed or a fraudulent return is filed, assessments can be made at any time. There is, in effect, no statute of limitations in these cases.
- If a taxpayer omits an amount of gross income in excess of 25 percent of the gross income stated on the return, the statute of limitations is increased to six years. The courts have interpreted this rule as including only items affecting income and not the omission of items affecting cost of sales.[30] In addition, gross income includes capital gains in the *gross* income amount (not reduced by capital losses).

EXAMPLE 30

During 2000, Jerry had the following income transactions (all of which were duly reported on his timely filed return).

---

[29]§§ 6501(a) and (b)(1).

[30]*The Colony, Inc. v. Comm.*, 58–2 USTC ¶9593, 1 AFTR2d 1894, 78 S.Ct. 1033 (USSC, 1958).

Gross receipts		$ 480,000
Cost of sales		(400,000)
Net business income		$ 80,000
Capital gains and losses		
Capital gain	$ 36,000	
Capital loss	(12,000)	24,000
Total income		$ 104,000

Jerry retains your services in 2005 as a tax consultant. It seems that he inadvertently omitted some income on his 2000 return and he wishes to know if he is "safe" under the statute of limitations. The six-year statute of limitations would apply, putting Jerry in a vulnerable position only if he omitted more than $129,000 on his 2000 return [($480,000 + $36,000) × 25%]. ■

- The statute of limitations may be extended by mutual consent of the IRS and the taxpayer. This extension covers a definite period and is made by signing Form 872 (Consent to Extend the Time to Assess Tax). The extension is frequently requested by the IRS when the lapse of the statutory period is imminent and the audit has not been completed. This practice is often applied to audits of corporate taxpayers and explains why many corporations have more than three "open years."

Special rules relating to assessment are applicable in the following situations.

- Taxpayers (corporations, estates, etc.) may request a prompt assessment of the tax.
- The assessment period for capital loss and net operating loss carrybacks generally relates to the determination of tax in the year of the loss or unused credit rather than in the carryback years.

If the IRS issues a statutory notice of deficiency to the taxpayer, who then files a Tax Court petition, the statute is suspended on both the deficiency assessment and the period of collection until 60 days after the decision of the Tax Court becomes final. The statute is also suspended when the taxpayer is "financially disabled"; that is, the taxpayer has been rendered unable to manage his or her financial affairs by a physical or mental impairment that is likely to last for a year or more or to cause the taxpayer's death. The statute continues to run if another party is authorized to act for the taxpayer in financial matters.[31]

Refund Claims and the Statute of Limitations. To receive a tax refund, the taxpayer is required to file a valid refund claim. The official form for filing a claim is Form 1040X for individuals and Form 1120X for corporations. If the refund claim does not meet certain procedural requirements, the IRS may reject the claim with no consideration of its merit.

- A separate claim must be filed for each taxable period.
- The grounds for the claim must be stated in sufficient detail.
- The statement of facts must be sufficient to permit the IRS to evaluate the merits of the claim.

[31] "Equitable tolling" or suspension of the statute of limitations has been allowed by the courts when attributable to a taxpayer disability or IRS misconduct. See *Brockamp v. Comm.*, 97–1 USTC ¶50,216, 79 AFTR2d 97–986, 117 S.Ct. 849 (USSC, 1997). §§ 6501(c)(4) and 6511(h).

The refund claim must be filed within three years of the filing of the tax return or within two years following the payment of the tax if this period expires on a later date.[32]

EXAMPLE 31

On March 11, 2002, Louise filed her 2001 income tax return reflecting a tax of $10,500. On July 10, 2003, she filed an amended 2001 return showing an additional $3,000 of tax that was then paid. On May 19, 2005, she filed a claim for refund of $4,500.

Assuming that Louise is correct in claiming a refund, how much tax can she recover? The answer is only $3,000. Because the claim was not filed within the three-year period, Louise is limited to the amount she actually paid during the last two years. ■

Special rules are available for claims relating to bad debts and worthless securities. A seven-year period of limitations applies in lieu of the normal three-year rule.[33] The extended period is provided in recognition of the inherent difficulty of identifying the exact year in which a bad debt or security becomes worthless.

LO.9

Summarize the legal and ethical guidelines that apply to those engaged in tax practice.

Tax Practice

THE TAX PRACTITIONER

Definition. Who is a tax practitioner? What service does the practitioner perform? To begin defining the term *tax practitioner,* one should consider whether the individual is qualified to practice before the IRS. Generally, practice before the IRS is limited to CPAs, attorneys, and persons who have been enrolled to practice before the IRS (called **enrolled agents [EAs]**). In most cases, EAs are admitted to practice only if they pass an examination administered by the IRS. CPAs and attorneys are not required to take this examination and are automatically admitted to practice if they are in good standing with the appropriate licensing board regulating their profession.

Persons other than CPAs, attorneys, and EAs may be allowed to practice before the IRS in limited situations. Circular 230 (entitled "Rules Governing the Practice of Attorneys and Agents Before the Internal Revenue Service") issued by the Treasury Department permits certain notable exceptions.

- A taxpayer may always represent himself or herself. A person may also represent a member of the immediate family if no compensation is received for such services.
- Regular full-time employees may represent their employers.
- Corporations may be represented by any of their bona fide officers.
- Partnerships may be represented by any of the partners.
- Trusts, receiverships, guardianships, or estates may be represented by their trustees, receivers, guardians, or administrators or executors.
- A taxpayer may be represented by whoever prepared the return for the year in question. However, such representation cannot proceed beyond the agent level.

EXAMPLE 32

Joel is currently undergoing audit by the IRS for tax years 2001 and 2002. He prepared the 2001 return himself but paid AddCo, a bookkeeping service, to prepare the 2002 return. AddCo may represent Joel only in matters concerning 2002. However, even for 2002, AddCo would be unable to represent Joel at an Appeals Division proceeding. Joel could, of course,

[32]§§ 6511(a) and 6513(a).

[33]§ 6511(d)(1).

represent himself, or he could retain a CPA, attorney, or EA to represent him in matters concerning both years under examination. ■

Rules Governing Tax Practice. Circular 230 further prescribes the rules governing practice before the IRS. The following are some of the most important rules imposed on CPAs, attorneys, EAs, and all others who prepare tax returns for compensation.

- A prohibition against taking a position on a tax return unless there is a *realistic possibility* of the position being sustained on its merits. Generally, the realistic possibility standard is met when a person knowledgeable in the tax law would conclude that the position has at least a one-in-three probability of prevailing in court.
- A prohibition against taking frivolous tax return positions.
- A requirement that nonfrivolous tax return positions that fail the realistic possibility standard be disclosed in the return (i.e., using Form 8275).
- A requirement to inform clients of penalties likely to apply to return positions and of ways such penalties can be avoided.
- A requirement to make known to a client any error or omission the client may have made on any return or other document submitted to the IRS.
- A duty to submit in a timely fashion records or information lawfully requested by the IRS.
- An obligation to exercise due diligence in preparing and filing tax returns accurately.
- A restriction against unreasonably delaying the prompt disposition of any matter before the IRS.
- A restriction against charging the client a contingent fee for preparing an original return. Such a fee can be charged when the tax professional deals with an audited or emended return.
- A restriction against charging the client "an unconscionable fee" for representation before the IRS.
- A restriction against representing clients with conflicting interests.

Anyone can prepare a tax return or render tax advice, regardless of his or her educational background or level of competence. Likewise, nothing prevents the "unlicensed" tax practitioner from advertising his or her specialty, directly soliciting clients, or otherwise violating any of the standards of conduct controlling CPAs, attorneys, and EAs. Nevertheless, some restraints do govern all parties engaged in rendering tax returns for the general public.

- A person who holds himself or herself out to the general public as possessing tax expertise could be liable to the client if services are performed in a negligent manner. At a minimum, the practitioner is liable for any interest and penalties the client incurs because of the practitioner's failure to exercise due care.
- If a practitioner agrees to perform a service (e.g., prepare a tax return) and subsequently fails to do so, the aggrieved party may be in a position to obtain damages for breach of contract.
- The IRS requires all persons who prepare tax returns for a fee to sign as preparer of the return.[34] Failure to comply with this requirement could result in penalty assessment against the preparer.

[34]Reg. § 1.6065–1(b)(1). Rev.Rul. 84–3, 1984–1 C.B. 264, contains a series of examples illustrating when a person is deemed to be a preparer of the return.

- The Code prescribes various penalties for the deliberate filing of false or fraudulent returns. These penalties apply to a tax practitioner who either was aware of the situation or actually perpetrated the false information or the fraud.[35]
- Penalties are prescribed for tax practitioners who disclose to third parties information they have received from clients in connection with the preparation of tax returns or the rendering of tax advice.[36]

EXAMPLE 33

Sarah operates a tax return preparation service. Her brother-in-law, Butch, has just taken a job as a life insurance salesman. To help Butch find contacts, Sarah furnishes him with a list of the names and addresses of all of her clients who report AGI of $50,000 or more. Sarah is subject to penalties. ■

- All nonattorney tax practitioners should avoid becoming engaged in activities that constitute the unauthorized practice of law. If they engage in this practice (e.g., by drafting legal documents for a third party), action could be instituted against them in the appropriate state court by the local or state bar association. What actions constitute the unauthorized practice of law is largely undefined, though, and such charges are filed only rarely today.

BRIDGE DISCIPLINE

Bridge to Public Finance/Ethics

Tax professionals occupy a unique position in the tax system. The tax professional is both an advocate for the taxpayer/client and a guardian of the tax system. This conflict is evident especially in two overlapping tax doctrines.

Form v. Substance. This judicial doctrine traces its roots back to the 1935 Supreme Court case of *Gregory v. Helvering.*[37] The Court held that the IRS can look beyond the form of the transaction and focus on its economic substance. The taxpayer tried to use a tax-favored reorganization to obtain capital gain treatment, but the Court held that the transaction in substance was a dividend.

Business Purpose. Under this doctrine, which also is based in the *Gregory* decision, a transaction must have a valid business purpose as its the principal motivation. Avoiding paying taxes is not a valid business purpose. The Supreme Court stated:

> *When* [current § 368(a)(1)(D)] *speaks of a transfer of assets by one corporation to another, it means a transfer made "in pursuance of a plan of reorganization" of corporate business; and not a transfer of assets by one corporation to another in pursuance of a plan having no relation to the business of either, as is plainly the case here. . . . Simply an operation having no business or corporate purpose. . . .*

Over the years, Congress has codified these doctrines in many parts of the Internal Revenue Code. The following are several examples of the statutory application of the doctrines.

- § 482 Allocation of Income and Deductions Among Taxpayers—transfer pricing can be voided if abusive of the tax system.
- § 446(b) General Rules for Methods of Accounting—accounting method must clearly reflect income; otherwise, the IRS may reallocate.
- § 269 Acquisitions Made to Evade or Avoid Income Tax—business purpose is required.

[35] § 7206.
[36] § 7216.

[37] *Gregory v. Helvering,* 293 U.S. 465, 35–1 USTC ¶9043, 14 AFTR 1191, 55 S. Ct. 266 (1935).

Preparer Penalties. The Code also provides for penalties to discourage improper actions by tax practitioners. Some of the most important preparer penalties include the following.

- A $250 penalty for understatements due to taking unrealistic positions.[38]
- A $1,000 penalty for willful and reckless conduct.[39]
- A $1,000 ($10,000 for corporations) penalty per return or document for aiding in the preparation of returns or other documents that the preparer knows (or has reason to believe) would result in an understatement of the tax liability of another person.[40]
- A $50 penalty for failure to sign a return or furnish the preparer's identifying number.[41]
- A $50 penalty for failure to furnish a copy of a tax return to the taxpayer.
- A $500 penalty if the preparer endorses or otherwise negotiates a check for refund of tax issued to the taxpayer.

Beyond the monetary penalties the IRS can assess, the tax preparer faces the loss of the ability to practice before the IRS. This would essentially terminate the tax preparer's professional endeavors.

Privileged Communications. Communications between an attorney and client have long been protected from disclosure to other parties (such as the IRS and the tax courts). A similar privilege of confidentiality extends to tax advice between a taxpayer and tax practitioner, as we used that term above. The privilege is not available for matters involving criminal charges or questions brought by other agencies, such as the Securities and Exchange Commission.[42] Nor is it allowed in matters involving promoting or participating in tax shelters.

A taxpayer will likely want to protect documents such as the tax adviser's research memo detailing the strengths and weaknesses of a tax return position or a conversation about an appeals strategy. The confidentiality privilege should be interpreted in the following manner.

- The privilege is often available when an attorney or CPA completes a tax return for the taxpayer. But some courts have restricted the attorney's privilege in this context on the ground that the tax professional is conducting accounting work, not offering legal advice. Others assert that the confidentiality privilege is waived when the taxpayer discloses financial data on the tax return. To the contrary, if the tax professional is providing traditional legal advice to help the client decide what to disclose on a tax return, the privilege should be available.
- The privilege for CPAs applies only to tax advice. Attorneys can still exercise the privilege concerning advice rendered as a business consultant, estate/financial planner, and so on.
- About a third of the states offer a similar confidentiality privilege for CPAs, but outside the Federal tax appeals process, protection is not yet the norm.
- The privilege is not available for tax accrual workpapers prepared as part of an independent financial audit.

Thus, the CPA needs to exercise care to ensure that the privilege of confidentiality will apply to his or her tax work. Taking the following steps can help.

[38] § 6694(a).
[39] § 6694(b).
[40] § 6701.
[41] § 6695.
[42] § 7525(a)(1).

Concept Summary 1–1

Tax Administration and Practice

1. The Internal Revenue Service (IRS) enforces the tax laws of the United States. Its size and form of organization reflect its various responsibilities relative to taxpayer interaction, litigation, and collection, as well as its internal functions.
2. The IRS issues various pronouncements, communicating its position on certain tax issues. These pronouncements promote the uniform enforcement of the tax law among taxpayers and among the internal divisions of the IRS. Taxpayers should seek such rulings and memoranda when the nature or magnitude of a pending transaction requires a high degree of certainty in the planning process.
3. Taxpayers are selected for IRS audit based on the probable net dollar return to the Treasury from the process. Offers in compromise and closing agreements can be a useful means of completing an audit without resorting to litigation.
4. Certain IRS personnel are empowered to consider the hazards of litigation in developing a settlement with the taxpayer during the audit process.
5. The IRS pays interest to taxpayers on overpaid taxes, starting essentially 45 days after the due date of the return, in amounts tied to the Federal short-term rate. Interest paid to the IRS on underpayments is similarly based on the Federal rate, starting essentially on the due date of the return. Interest for both purposes is compounded daily.
6. The Treasury assesses penalties when the taxpayer fails to file a required tax return or pay a tax. Penalties also are assessed when an inaccurate return is filed due to negligence or other disregard of IRS rules. Tax preparers are subject to penalties for assisting a taxpayer in filing an inaccurate return, failing to follow IRS rules in an appropriate manner, or mishandling taxpayer data or funds.
7. Statutes of limitations place outer boundaries on the timing and amounts of proposed amendments to completed tax returns that can be made by the taxpayer or the IRS.
8. Tax practitioners must operate under constraints imposed on them by codes of ethics or pertinent professional societies and by Treasury Circular 230. These rules also define the parties who can represent others in an IRS proceeding.
9. A limited privilege of confidentiality exists between taxpayer and tax preparer.

- Segregate the time spent and documents produced in rendering services for tax compliance from the time and documents devoted to tax advice. Doing this will protect the privilege from being waived as to the tax advice.
- Explain the extent of the privilege to the client—specify what will and will not be protected from the IRS in a dispute.
- Do not inadvertently waive the privilege, say, by telling "too much" to the IRS or to a third party who is not protected by the privilege.
- Indemnify the CPA for time spent protecting and enforcing the privilege once it is challenged.

AICPA STATEMENTS ON STANDARDS FOR TAX SERVICES

Tax practitioners who are CPAs, attorneys, or EAs must abide by the codes or canons of professional ethics applicable to their respective professions. The various codes and canons have much in common with and parallel the standards of conduct set forth in Circular 230.[43]

The AICPA has issued a series of Statements on Standards for Tax Services (SSTSs). The Statements are enforceable standards of professional practice for AICPA members working in state or Federal tax practice. The SSTSs comprise part

[43]For an additional discussion of tax ethics, see Raabe, Whittenburg, and Sanders, *West's Federal Tax Research*, 6th ed. (South-Western/Thomson Learning, 2003), especially Chapters 1 and 13.

of the AICPA's Code of Professional Conduct. Together with the provisions of Circular 230 and the penalty provisions of the Code, the SSTSs make up a set of guidelines for the conduct of the tax practitioner who is also a CPA. Other sources of descriptions of professional ethics are issued by state bar associations and CPA societies, the American Bar Association, and the associations of enrolled agents.

DIGGING DEEPER 6

Find more information on this topic at our Web site: ***http://wft-advanced.swlearning.com****.*

Suggested Further Readings

O. Chang, D. Nichols, and J. Schultz, "Taxpayer Attitude Toward Tax Audit Risk," *Journal of Economic Psychology,* 1987(8), pp. 299–309.

Andrew D. Cuccia, "The Effects of Increased Sanctions on Paid Preparers: Integrating Economic and Psychological Factors," *Journal of the American Taxation Association,* 1994, pp. 41–66.

Andrew D. Cuccia, K. Hackebrack, and M. W. Nelsen, "The Ability of Professional Standards to Mitigate Aggressive Reporting," *Accounting Review,* 1995(70), pp. 227–248.

Glenn D. Fletham and S. M. Paquette, "The Interrelationship Between Estimated Tax Payments and Taxpayer Compliance," *Journal of the American Taxation Association,* 2002 Supplement, pp. 27–45.

J. C. Gardner, B. Eide, and S. Willey, "Circular 230 Final Regs. (Part I)," *The Tax Adviser,* January 2003, pp. 26–32.

J. C. Gardner, B. Eide, and S. Willey, "Circular 230 Final Regs. (Part II)," *The Tax Adviser,* February 2003, pp. 96–99.

Lesli Laffie, ed., "From the Tax Adviser: Amnesty for Offshore Tax Evasion," *Journal of Accountancy* (online issues), April 2003 (**http://www.aicpa.org/pubs/jofa/apr2003/ftta.htm**).

J. Scott Moody and Scott A. Hodge, "America Celebrates Tax Freedom Day," *Tax Foundation Special Report,* no. 129, April 2004.

Thomas J. Purcell III and David Lifson, "Tax Services after Sarbannes-Oxley," *Journal of Accountancy* (online issues), November 2003 (**http://www.aicpa.org/pubs/jofa/nov2003/purcell.htm**).

KEY TERMS

Accuracy-related penalty, 1–28
Closing agreement, 1–25
Determination letter, 1–16
Enrolled agent (EA), 1–34
Fraud, 1–30
Letter ruling, 1–13
Ninety-day letter, 1–22
Offer in compromise, 1–24
Revenue Agent's Report (RAR), 1–22
Statute of limitations, 1–32
Tax avoidance, 1–3
Tax evasion, 1–3
Tax planning, 1–3
Technical advice memorandum (TAM), 1–16
Thirty-day letter, 1–22

PROBLEM MATERIALS

Problems

1. On February 10, 2005, Quon, a calendar year taxpayer, files her 2004 income tax return on which she claims a $1,200 refund. If Quon receives her refund check on May 2, 2005, will it include any interest? Explain.

2. Indicate whether each of the following statements is true or false.
   a. The government never pays a taxpayer interest on an overpayment of tax.
   b. The IRS can compromise on the amount of tax liability if there is doubt as to the taxpayer's ability to pay.
   c. The statute of limitations for assessing a tax never extends beyond three years from the filing of a return.
   d. A taxpayer's claim for a refund is not subject to a statute of limitations.

3. Carol takes some very aggressive positions on her tax return. She maintains, "With the downsizing of the government, my chances of getting caught are virtually zero." Is Carol's approach correct?

4. Compute the failure to pay and failure to file penalties for John, who filed his 2004 income tax return on November 10, 2005, paying the $8,000 amount due. On April 1, 2005, John had received a four-month extension of time in which to file his return. He has no reasonable cause for failing to file his return by August 15 or for failing to pay the tax that was due on April 15, 2005. John's failure to comply with the tax laws was not fraudulent.

5. Orville, a cash basis, calendar year taxpayer, filed his income tax return 70 days after the due date. Orville never extended his return, and he paid the taxes that were due when he filed the return. What penalty will Orville incur, and how much will he have to pay if his additional tax is $3,000? Disregard any interest he must pay.

6. Rhoda, a calendar year individual taxpayer, files her 2004 return on December 12, 2005. She did not obtain an extension for filing her return, and the return reflects additional income tax due of $7,000. What are Rhoda's penalties for failure to file and to pay?

7. For the completion and filing of his 2005 income tax return, Ron retains the services of a CPA. Because of a particularly hectic tax season, the CPA does not complete and file the return until June 2006. Is Ron excused from the failure to file and pay penalties under the reasonable cause exception? Would it make any difference if Ron were entitled to a refund?

8. Kim underpaid her taxes by $15,000. Of this amount, $9,500 was due to negligence on her part, as her record-keeping system is highly inadequate. Determine the amount of any negligence penalty.

9. Dana underpaid her taxes by $250,000. A portion of the underpayment was shown to be attributable to Dana's negligence ($200,000). A court found that a portion of that deficiency constituted civil fraud ($110,000). Compute the total fraud and negligence penalties incurred.

10. Olivia, a calendar year taxpayer, does not file her 2004 return until October 4, 2005. At this point, she pays the $7,000 balance due on her 2004 tax liability of $70,000. Olivia did not apply for and obtain any extension of time for filing the 2004 return. When questioned by the IRS on her delinquency, Olivia asserts: "If I was too busy to file my regular tax return, I was too busy to request an extension."
    a. Is Olivia liable for any penalties for failure to file and for failure to pay?
    b. If so, compute the penalty amounts.

11. Compute the overvaluation penalty for each of the following independent cases involving the taxpayer's reporting of the fair market value of charitable contribution property. In each case, assume a marginal income tax rate of 35%.

Taxpayer	Corrected IRS Value	Reported Valuation
a. Individual	$ 30,000	$ 50,000
b. C corporation	30,000	50,000
c. S corporation	40,000	50,000
d. Individual	150,000	250,000
e. Individual	150,000	500,000
f. C corporation	150,000	900,000

12. Compute the undervaluation penalty for each of the following independent cases involving the executor's reporting of the value of a closely held business in the decedent's gross estate. In each case, assume a marginal estate tax rate of 50%.

	Reported Value	Corrected IRS Valuation
a.	$20,000	$ 25,000
b.	80,000	150,000
c.	80,000	250,000
d.	80,000	530,000

13. Arnold made a charitable contribution of property that he valued at $70,000. He deducted this amount as an itemized deduction on his tax return. The IRS can prove that the real value of the property is $55,000. Arnold is in the 30% income tax bracket. Determine Arnold's overvaluation penalty.

EXTENDER

14. Marla owns and operates a tavern. Because she had been keeping "two sets of books," one for herself and one for the benefit of the IRS, she has been charged with civil fraud in the District Court. The IRS assesses an additional $75,000 in taxes, but Marla shows by a preponderance of the evidence that two-thirds of that amount was due to mere negligence, not to her fraudulent actions. Compute Marla's civil fraud tax penalty in this matter.

15. Moose, a former professional athlete, now supplements his income by signing autographs at collectors' shows. Unfortunately, Moose has not been conscientious about reporting all of this income on his tax return. Now the IRS has charged him with additional taxes of $80,000 due to negligence in his record keeping and $20,000 due to an intent to defraud the U.S. government of income taxes. No criminal fraud charges are brought against Moose. The District Court finds by a preponderance of the evidence that only half of the $20,000 underpayment was due to Moose's fraudulent action; the remainder was due to mere negligence. Compute the accuracy-related and civil fraud penalties in this matter.

16. Trudy's AGI last year was $170,000. Her Federal income tax came to $50,000, which she paid through a combination of withholding and estimated payments. This year, her AGI will be $270,000, with a projected tax liability of $85,000, all to be paid through estimates. Ignore the annualized income method. Compute Trudy's quarterly estimated payment schedule for this year.

17. Kold Corporation estimates that its 2004 taxable income will be $500,000. Thus, it is subject to a flat 34% income tax rate and incurs a $170,000 liability. For each of the following independent cases, compute Kold's minimum quarterly estimated tax payments that will avoid an underpayment penalty.
    a. For 2003, taxable income was ($100,000). Kold carried back all of this loss to prior years and exhausted the entire net operating loss in creating a zero 2003 liability.
    b. For 2003, taxable income was $300,000, and tax liability was $102,000.
    c. For 2002, taxable income was $2 million, and tax liability was $680,000. For 2003, taxable income was $300,000, and tax liability was $102,000.

EXTENDER
Communications

18. The Scooter Company, owned equally by Julie (chair of the board of directors) and Jeff (company president), is in very difficult financial straits. Last month, Jeff used the $100,000 withheld from employee paychecks for Federal payroll and income taxes to pay off a creditor who threatened to cut off all supplies. To keep the company afloat, Jeff used these government funds willfully for the operations of the business, but even that effort was not enough. The company missed the next two payrolls, and today other creditors took action to shut down Scooter altogether. How much will the IRS assess in taxes and penalties in this matter, and from whom? How can you as a tax professional best offer service to Julie, Jeff, and Scooter? Address these matters in a memo for the tax research file.

19. What is the applicable statute of limitations in each of the following independent situations?
    a. No return was filed by the taxpayer.
    b. The taxpayer incurred a bad debt loss that she failed to claim.
    c. A taxpayer inadvertently omitted a large amount of gross income.
    d. Same as (c), except that the omission was deliberate.
    e. A taxpayer innocently overstated her deductions by a large amount.

20. Suzanne (a calendar year taxpayer) had the following transactions, all of which were properly reported on a timely filed return.

Gross receipts		$ 960,000
Cost of sales		(800,000)
Gross profit		$ 160,000
Capital gain	$ 72,000	
Capital loss	(24,000)	48,000
Total income		$ 208,000

    a. Presuming the absence of fraud, how much of an omission from gross income is required before the six-year statute of limitations applies?
    b. Would it matter if cost of sales had been inadvertently overstated by $100,000?
    c. How does the situation change in the context of fraud by Suzanne?

21. On April 2, 2002, Mark filed his 2001 income tax return, which showed a tax due of $40,000. On June 1, 2004, he filed an amended return for 2001 that showed an additional tax of $12,000. Mark paid the additional amount. On May 18, 2005, Mark filed a claim for a refund of $18,000.
    a. If Mark's claim for a refund is correct in amount, how much tax will he recover?
    b. What is the period that interest runs with respect to Mark's claim for a refund?
    c. How would you have advised him differently?

Communications

22. Carol owed $4,000 in Federal income tax when she filed her Form 1040 for 2004. She attached a Post-It note to the 1040 saying, "My inventory computations on last year's return were wrong so I paid $1,000 too much in tax." Carol then included a check for $3,000 with the Form 1040 for 2004. Write a memo to the tax research file commenting on Carol's actions.

23. Rod's Federal income tax returns (Form 1040) for the indicated three years were prepared by the following persons.

Year	Preparer
2002	Rod
2003	Ann
2004	Cheryl

Ann is Rod's next-door neighbor and owns and operates a pharmacy. Cheryl is a licensed CPA and is engaged in private practice. In the event Rod is audited and all three returns are examined, who may represent him before the IRS at the agent level? Who may represent Rod before the Appeals Division?

24. Discuss which penalties, if any, might be imposed on the tax adviser in each of the following independent circumstances. In this regard, assume that the tax adviser:
    a. suggested to the client various means by which to acquire excludible income.
    b. suggested to the client various means by which to conceal cash receipts from gross income.
    c. suggested to the client means by which to improve her cash flow by delaying for six months or more the deposit of the employee's share of Federal employment taxes.
    d. kept in his own safe deposit box the concealed income of item (b).

e. failed, because of pressing time conflicts, to conduct the usual review of the client's tax return. The IRS later discovered that the return included fraudulent data.
f. failed, because of pressing time conflicts, to conduct the usual review of the client's tax return. The IRS later discovered a mathematical error in the computation of the personal exemption.

EXTENDER

25. Compute the preparer penalty that the IRS could assess on Gerry in each of the following independent cases.
   a. On March 21, the copy machine was not working, so Gerry gave original returns to her 30 clients that day without providing any duplicates for them. Copies for Gerry's files and for use in preparing state tax returns had been made on March 20.
   b. Because Gerry extended her vacation a few days, she missed the Annual Tax Update seminar that she usually attends. As a result, she was unaware that Congress had changed a law affecting limited partnerships. The change affected the transactions of 20 of Gerry's clients, all of whom understated their tax as a result.
   c. Gerry heard that the IRS was increasing its audits of corporations that hold assets in a foreign trust. As a result, Gerry instructed the intern who prepared the initial drafts of the returns for three corporate clients to leave blank the question about such trusts. Not wanting to lose his position, the intern, a senior accounting major at State University, complied with Gerry's instructions.

EXTENDER

26. You are the chair of the Ethics Committee of your state's CPA Licensing Commission. Interpret controlling AICPA authority in addressing the following assertions by your membership.
   a. When a CPA has reasonable grounds for not answering an applicable question on a client's return, a brief explanation of the reason for the omission should not be provided, because it would flag the return for audit by the IRS.
   b. If a CPA discovers during an IRS audit that the client has a material error in the return under examination, he should immediately withdraw from the engagement.
   c. If the client tells you that she had contributions of $500 for unsubstantiated cash donations to her church, you should deduct an odd amount on her return (e.g., $499), because an even amount ($500) would indicate to the IRS that her deduction was based on an estimate.
   d. If a CPA knows that the client has a material error in a prior year's return, he should not, without the client's consent, disclose the error to the IRS.
   e. If a CPA's client will not correct a material error in a prior year's return, the CPA should not prepare the current year's return for the client.

27. Indicate which codes, canons, and other bodies of ethical statements apply to each of the following tax practitioners.
   a. CPAs who are members of the AICPA.
   b. CPAs who are not members of the AICPA.
   c. Attorneys.
   d. Enrolled agents.
   e. Tax preparers who are not CPAs, EAs, or attorneys.

BRIDGE DISCIPLINE

EXTENDER

1. Design a tax system and explain how that system meets the equity principles of horizontal equity, vertical equity, and ability-to-pay. Explain your use of the equity principles in your design and indicate what the goals of your tax system are. Remember there is no one correct system, but you must support your design in your discussion.
   a. Are any of the equity principles a violation of the equal protection clause of the U.S. Constitution?
   b. Does our current Federal income tax system achieve the desired equity principles?

Communications

2. Joan, a tax client of yours, wants to know whether the following tax planning idea will work. Joan owns 100 acres of land. She paid $4,500 per acre in 1998. She wants to sell all of the land to her daughter for $3,800 per acre, the current fair market value. Joan

knows that if the land is sold to her daughter at a $700 per acre loss, she will not be able to deduct the loss because of the related-party rules (§ 267). Instead of a direct sale to her daughter, she proposes to sell the land to her attorney for $3,800 per acre (her attorney is unrelated to her). The attorney then will sell the land to Joan's daughter for $3,850 per acre. The $50 per acre premium essentially is the attorney's fee for doing the transaction.

Can Joan deduct the $70,000 loss, now that she is not selling the land to her daughter? Write a research memo to your supervisor detailing your analysis of the tax outcome.

Research Problems

THOMSON RIA™

*Note: Solutions to Research Problems can be prepared by using the **RIA Checkpoint® Student Edition** online research product, which is available to accompany this text. It is also possible to prepare solutions to the Research Problems by using tax research materials found in a standard tax library.*

Communications

Research Problem 1. The Bird Estate committed tax fraud when it purposely understated the value of the business created and operated by the decedent, Beverly Bird. Executor Wilma Holmes (1111 East Michigan Avenue, Charleston, WV 44333) admitted to the Tax Court that she had withheld several contracts and formulas that, had they been disclosed to the valuation experts used by the government and the estate, would have added $1 million in value to the business and over half that amount in Federal estate tax liabilities. Summary data include the following.

	Reported on Form 706	Other Amounts
Gross estate	$12 million	$1 million understatement
Deductions on original return	2 million	
Interest on estate tax deficiency, professional fees incurred during administration period		400,000

Holmes asks you for advice in computing the fraud penalty. Ignore interest amounts. She wonders whether to take the 75% civil penalty against the full $1 million understatement or against the $600,000 net amount that the taxable estate would have increased had the administrative expenses been incurred prior to the filing date of the Form 706. Write Holmes, an experienced CPA with an extensive tax practice, a letter stating your opinion.

Partial list of research aids:
§ 6663.
Estate of Emanuel Trompeter, 111 T.C. 57 (1998).

Communications

Research Problem 2. The IRS has issued a summons for the tax file held by CPA Ann Whitman for her clients, the Harberts. The file consists of paper and electronic spreadsheets in which Whitman detailed some tax computations using assumptions that the IRS would find to be "too aggressive." In addition, the file includes notes from meetings with the Harberts, income and balance sheet data as to their personal assets, and other technical correspondence, including e-mail messages. In a memo to the tax research file, summarize the current status of the law as to whether the privilege of confidentiality protects these documents from the government.

Communications

Research Problem 3. Blanche Creek (111 Elm Avenue, Patriotville, IN 40123) has engaged your firm because she has been charged with failure to file her 2003 Federal Form 1040. Blanche maintains that the "reasonable cause" exception should apply. During the entire tax filing season in 2004, she was under a great deal of stress at work and in her personal life. As a result, Blanche developed a sleep disorder, which was treated through a combination of pills and counseling.

Your firm ultimately prepared the 2003 tax return for Blanche, but it was filed far beyond the due date. Blanche is willing to pay the delinquent tax and related interest.

However, she feels that the failure to pay penalty is unfair as she was ill. Consequently, she could not be expected to keep to the usual deadlines for filing.

Write a letter to Blanche concerning these matters.

Research Problem 4. Max and Annie are roommates sharing an apartment. Although they know each other well, they have respect for each other's privacy. Thus, when Max's 2003 Form 1040 was audited by the IRS, he made no mention of the audit to Annie.

When Annie was clearing the answering machine that they shared, she heard the following message: "Max, this is Richard, the IRS auditor. My figures show that you owe the government $10,000 in taxes and another $4,500 in penalties and interest."

When Annie brought up the message during dinner conversation that night, Max was furious. How could the IRS be so careless as to broadcast this news to a stranger? Didn't he have any privacy and confidentiality rights? Max calls you to determine whether he might have a case against the IRS or Richard, the agent.

Research Problem 5. You have just rendered service for a taxpayer as an expert witness in a case heard by the U.S. Tax Court. The taxpayer is requesting reimbursement for your fees and for those amounts paid to her attorney in presenting the case. Your billing rate for this type of engagement is $200 per hour, the market rate for such services in your city, plus out-of-pocket expenses (e.g., auto mileage, computer charges). How much of your fee will the taxpayer recover?

Internet Activity

Use the tax resources of the Internet to address the following questions. Do not restrict your search to the World Wide Web, but include a review of newsgroups and general reference materials, practitioner sites and resources, primary sources of the tax law, chat rooms and discussion groups, and other opportunities.

Research Problem 6. Find an article in which a tax professional describes the confidentiality privilege available under the Code for a CPA tax adviser. Then construct a list of "Confidentiality Dos and Don'ts for the CPA."

Communications

Research Problem 7. Find an article that discusses these terms: realistic possibility, reasonable basis, frivolous return. Summarize the article in an e-mail to your professor.

Research Problem 8. Corporations with large estimated tax overpayments and underpayments are subject to special interest rates.

a. Find in the Code how these rates are determined.
b. List such rates that have been in effect for the last six calendar quarters.

Research Problem 9. Use the most recent IRS data to answer the following questions. Before you complete this assignment, make certain that you can define each of the italicized terms.

- How many *offers in compromise* did the IRS consider, and how many did it accept?
- How many taxpayers had a *lien* placed on their property by the IRS?
- How many taxpayers had property *seized* by the IRS?

Communications

Research Problem 10. Prepare a graph illustrating the trends in IRS audit activity over the past decade, and submit it to your instructor. First decide whether you are measuring audited returns, tax dollars recovered by audit, or budget resources dedicated to audit activities. Next decide which types of taxpayers and returns you will be graphing. Then find your data at **http://www.irs.gov**.

CHAPTER 2

Taxes on the Financial Statements

LEARNING OBJECTIVES

After completing Chapter 2, you should be able to:

LO.1

Recognize the difference between book and tax methods of computing income tax expense.

LO.2

Compute a corporation's book income tax expense under FAS 109.

LO.3

Describe the purpose of the valuation allowance.

LO.4

Recognize the effect of APB 23 on effective tax rates.

LO.5

Interpret the disclosure information contained in an income tax note.

LO.6

Use financial statement income tax information to benchmark a company's tax position.

http://wft.swlearning.com

OUTLINE

TAX TALK

Truth is, figuring out how much tax a company actually pays is impossible. . . . Tax disclosure is just inscrutable.

—Robert Willens

The bottom line result of the many tax planning ideas, advice, and compliance efforts provided by tax professionals to their clients is captured in a simple summary number—income tax expense. A U.S. corporation's tax expense is reported in its annual Federal tax return, its financial statements, and other regulatory filings and is often the starting point for state and local tax returns. As it turns out, however, deriving a corporation's income tax expense is not so simple.

A corporation may report millions of dollars in tax expense in its financial statements and yet pay virtually nothing to the U.S., state, or foreign governments. Alternatively, a corporation may pay substantial amounts to the U.S., state, and foreign governments and report very little income tax expense in its financial statements. Why do such differences exist? Which income tax expense is the "correct" number? How can data regarding a corporation's income tax expense provide valuable information for the corporation, its competitors, and tax professionals assisting in the planning function? This chapter addresses these questions.

LO.1

Recognize the difference between book and tax methods of computing income tax expense.

Book-Tax Differences

A significant difference may exist between a corporation's Federal income tax liability as reported on its Form 1120 (tax) and the corporation's income tax expense as reported on its financial statements (book) prepared using **generally accepted accounting principles (GAAP).** This book-tax difference is caused by any or all of the following.

- Differences in reporting entities included in the calculation.
- Different definition of taxes included in the income tax expense amount.
- Different accounting methods.

DIFFERENT REPORTING ENTITIES

A corporate group must consolidate all U.S. and foreign subsidiaries within a single financial statement for book purposes when the parent corporation controls more

TAX IN THE NEWS

HERE, THERE, AND EVERYWHERE—ENRON'S CORPORATE STRUCTURE

The collapse of Enron Corporation gave the public a peek behind the scenes of a multinational corporation's financial and tax strategies. It turned out that Enron used many sophisticated techniques—some legal and some not—to increase its reported net income and decrease its taxes.

Enron used so-called special purpose entities structured so that the income or loss of the entities was not included in Enron's financial statements. Enron had over 900 subsidiaries located in a number of tax haven countries around the world. For example, Enron had 692 subsidiaries incorporated in the Cayman Islands, 119 subsidiaries in the Turks and Caicos Islands, and 43 subsidiaries in Mauritius.

than 50 percent of the voting power of those subsidiaries.[1] In cases where the parent corporation owns between 20 and 50 percent of another corporation, the parent uses the **equity method** to account for the earnings of the subsidiary. Under the equity method, the parent currently records its share of the subsidiary's income or loss for the year.[2] Corporations that own less than 20 percent of other corporations typically use the *cost method* to account for income from these investments and include income only when actual dividends are received.

EXAMPLE 1

Fisher, Inc., a domestic corporation, owns 100% of Gator, Inc., a domestic corporation; 100% of Hurricane, Ltd., a foreign corporation; and 40% of Beach, Inc., a domestic corporation. Fisher's combined financial statement includes its own net income and the net income of both Gator and Hurricane. In addition, Fisher's financial statement includes its 40% share of Beach's net income. Fisher's financial statement includes the income of these subsidiaries regardless of whether Fisher receives any actual profit distributions from its subsidiaries. ■

For Federal tax purposes, a U.S. corporation may elect to include any *domestic* subsidiaries that are 80 percent or more owned in its consolidated U.S. tax return.[3] The income of foreign subsidiaries and less than 80 percent owned domestic subsidiaries is not included in the consolidated tax return.

EXAMPLE 2

If Fisher from Example 1 elects to include Gator as part of its consolidated Federal income tax return, Fisher's return includes its own taxable income and the taxable income generated by Gator. Hurricane's taxable income is not included in the consolidated return because it is a non-U.S. corporation. Beach, although a domestic corporation, cannot be consolidated with Fisher because Fisher owns only 40% of the stock. Income from Hurricane and Beach will be included in Fisher's U.S. taxable income only when Fisher receives actual or constructive dividends. ■

[1] *Statement of Financial Accounting Standards No. 94—Consolidation of All Majority-Owned Subsidiaries,* Financial Accounting Standards Board. Certain adjustments are made to reduce book income for the after-tax income related to minority shareholders.

[2] *Opinion No. 18—The Equity Method of Accounting for Investments in Common Stock,* Accounting Principles Board.

[3] §§ 1501–1504. The election to consolidate an 80% or more owned subsidiary can be changed only with the permission of the IRS. See Chapter 5.

DIFFERENT TAXES

The income tax expense reported on a corporation's financial statement is the combination of Federal, state, local, and foreign income taxes. Furthermore, this tax expense number includes both current and deferred tax expense amounts. The distinction between current and deferred income taxes is discussed later in this chapter.

EXAMPLE 3

For book purposes, Fisher, Gator, and Hurricane from Example 1 combine their income and expenses into a single financial statement. The book tax expense for the year includes all Federal, state, local, and foreign income taxes paid or accrued by these three corporations. In addition, the tax expense amount includes any future Federal, state, local, or foreign income tax expenses (or tax savings) on income reported in the current income statement. ■

The income tax expense computed on the Federal income tax return is the U.S. *Federal* income tax expense. This amount is based on the U.S. corporation's taxable income. State income taxes are reported on the Federal tax return, but as deductions in arriving at taxable income.

EXAMPLE 4

Fisher and Gator, from Example 1, file a consolidated Federal tax return. The tax expense reported on the Form 1120 is only the U.S. Federal income tax expense for the consolidated taxable income of Fisher and Gator. This tax expense does not include the income taxes that Fisher and its subsidiaries paid to state, local, or foreign governments. ■

DIFFERENT METHODS

Many differences exist between book and tax accounting methods. Some are simply **temporary differences,** with income and expenses appearing in both the financial statement and tax return, but in different periods (i.e., a timing difference). Others are **permanent differences,** with items appearing in the financial statement or the tax return, but not both.

Examples of temporary differences include the following.

- *Depreciation on fixed assets.* Taxpayers may use an accelerated depreciation method under the modified accelerated cost recovery system (MACRS) rules but a straight-line method for book purposes. Even if identical methods are used, the period over which the asset is depreciated may differ between book and tax.
- *Compensation-related expenses.* Several differences exist in this category. For example, under GAAP, corporations must accrue the future expenses related to providing postretirement benefits other than pensions (e.g., health insurance coverage). However, these expenses are deductible for tax purposes only when paid.
- *Accrued income and expenses.* Although most income and expense items are recognized for tax and book purposes in the same period, a number of items potentially appear in different periods. For example, warranty expenses are accrued for book purposes but are not deductible for tax purposes until incurred. Inventory write-offs are accrued for book but are not deductible for tax until incurred. On the income side, different methods applicable to the timing of income recognition may create temporary differences.
- *Net operating losses.* Operating losses from one tax year may be used to offset taxable income in another tax year. Thus, the losses incurred in one year for book purposes may be used as a deduction for tax purposes in a different year.

- *Intangible assets*. Goodwill and some other intangibles are not amortizable for book purposes. However, GAAP requires an annual determination of whether the intangible has suffered a reduction in value (i.e., impairment).[4] If an intangible has suffered an impairment, a deduction is required to reduce the intangible's book value to the lower level. For tax purposes, post-1993 intangibles are amortized over 15 years.[5]

Examples of permanent differences include the following.[6]

- *Nontaxable income*. A common example is municipal bond interest, which is income for book purposes but is not taxable.
- *Nondeductible expenses*. For example, the disallowed portion of meals and entertainment expense and certain penalties are not deductible for tax purposes but are expensed in arriving at book income.
- *Tax credits*. Credits such as the research activities credit reduce Federal income tax liability but have no corresponding book treatment.

DIGGING DEEPER 1 *Find more information on this topic at our Web site:* ***http://wft-advanced.swlearning.com.***

EXAMPLE 5

Wise, Inc., reported the following results for the current year.

Book income (before tax)	$ 685,000
Tax depreciation in excess of book	(125,000)
Nondeductible warranty expense	65,000
Municipal bond interest income	(35,000)
Taxable income (Form 1120)	$ 590,000

Wise reports net income before tax of $685,000 on its financial statement but must adjust this amount for differences between book and tax income. Tax depreciation in excess of book is a tax deduction not deducted for book purposes, and warranty expense is deductible for book purposes but not yet deductible for tax. Both these items are temporary differences because they will eventually reverse (with book depreciation eventually exceeding tax depreciation and the warranty expense ultimately deducted for tax when incurred). The municipal bond adjustment is a permanent difference because this income will never be subject to tax. ■

Figure 2–1 contains the **Schedule M–1** from Form 1120, the corporate income tax return. The purpose of Schedule M–1 is to reconcile book income to the taxable income reported on the tax return. Line 1 is the net income or loss per books, and line 2 adds back the book tax expense in order to get back to book income before tax.[7] The remainder of Schedule M–1 contains positive and negative adjustments for both temporary and permanent differences until arriving at taxable income on line 10. The income tax note of the financial statements also contains a tax

[4] *Statement of Financial Accounting Standards No. 142—Goodwill and Other Intangible Assets*, Financial Accounting Standards Board.

[5] § 197. Note that prior to 1994, goodwill and similar intangibles were not amortizable for tax purposes but were amortizable for book purposes over a maximum period of 40 years. Thus, goodwill acquired during this period triggered a permanent difference (amortizable for book but not for tax).

[6] Nonqualified stock option expenses also create a permanent difference because the corporation receives a tax deduction on the date the employee exercises the option but is not required to deduct an expense for book purposes under current GAAP. For an extended discussion of this issue, see M. Hanlon and T. Shevlin, "Accounting for Tax Benefits of Employee Stock Options and Implications for Research," *Accounting Horizons*, March 2002.

[7] Line 1, "Net income (loss) per books" is not defined in the instructions to the form, and corporations seem to use various starting points in the Schedule M–1 (e.g., only the book income from U.S. members of the group). The proposed new Schedule M–3 would expand the M–1 and provide more detail and consistency.

TAX IN THE NEWS

To Deduct or Not To Deduct—That Is the Question

In March 2004, the Financial Accounting Standards Board proposed that companies be required to report the value of options they provide to their employees as an expense on their financial statements beginning in 2005. The International Accounting Standards Board adopted a similar rule effective in 2004. Some companies fear the effect this rule might have on their share prices, with the lower net income that stock option expensing will produce. High-tech companies are particularly concerned with this proposal because they are heavy users of stock options to attract employees.

The opponents of stock option expensing are hard at work, lobbying Congress to intervene with the FASB and prevent the adoption of this rule. This is not the first time the option-expensing controversy has erupted. The FASB almost adopted a similar rule in 1994 but backed down after intervention by the U.S. Senate and the Securities and Exchange Commission. The recent history of corporate failure and fraud, combined with the push for more transparency in financial statements, makes it less likely that Congress will get involved this time around.

Expecting the rule to take effect, many companies are making changes in their stock option programs in order to minimize the impact of the new rule on net income. Not all companies disagree with the proposed rule. A number of companies have begun voluntarily expensing stock options.

reconciliation, but as discussed later, the purpose and content of this reconciliation are quite different.

Schedule M–1 is typically the starting point for IRS audits of corporations. Identifying large differences between book and taxable income may offer the IRS auditor insights into tax saving strategies (some perhaps questionable) employed by the taxpayer. Concept Summary 2–1 summarizes the book-tax differences in arriving at income tax expense.

■ **FIGURE 2–1**
Schedule M–1

Schedule M-1 Reconciliation of Income (Loss) per Books With Income per Return (see page 20 of instructions)

1	Net income (loss) per books		7	Income recorded on books this year not included on this return (itemize): Tax-exempt interest $	
2	Federal income tax per books				
3	Excess of capital losses over capital gains				
4	Income subject to tax not recorded on books this year (itemize):				
5	Expenses recorded on books this year not deducted on this return (itemize):		8	Deductions on this return not charged against book income this year (itemize):	
a	Depreciation $		a	Depreciation $	
b	Charitable contributions $		b	Charitable contributions $	
c	Travel and entertainment $				
			9	Add lines 7 and 8	
6	Add lines 1 through 5		10	Income (line 28, page 1)—line 6 less line 9	

CONCEPT SUMMARY 2–1

Book versus Tax

Financial Statement	U.S. Federal Income Tax Return
Reporting entities	**Reporting entities**
• 50% or more owned domestic and foreign subsidiaries *must* be consolidated.	• 80% or more owned domestic subsidiaries *may* be consolidated.
• Share of income from 20 to 50% owned domestic and foreign corporations included in current income.	• Share of income from other corporations reported only when actual or constructive dividends are received.
Income tax expense	**Income tax expense**
• Federal income taxes.	• Federal income taxes.
• State income taxes.	• Current only.
• Local income taxes.	
• Foreign income taxes.	
• Current and deferred.	
Methods	**Methods**
• Temporary differences.	• Temporary differences.
• Permanent differences.	• Permanent differences.
• Income tax note reconciliation.	• Schedule M–1 reconciliation.

LO.2

Compute a corporation's book income tax expense under FAS 109.

Income Taxes in the Financial Statements

FAS 109 PRINCIPLES

As pointed out earlier, a corporation's financial statements are prepared in accordance with GAAP. The purpose and objectives of these statements are quite different from the objective of the corporation's income tax return.

The **FAS 109** approach produces a total income tax expense (also called the **income tax provision**) for the income currently reported on a corporation's combined financial statement.[8] This approach follows the matching principle, where all the expenses related to earning income are reported in the same period as the income without regard to when the expenses are actually paid.

EXAMPLE 6

PanCo, Inc., earns $100,000 in book income before tax in 2004. PanCo has a single temporary difference. Tax depreciation exceeds book depreciation by $20,000 in 2004. Accordingly, PanCo's taxable income is $80,000 ($100,000 – $20,000 additional tax deduction). On its income tax return, PanCo reports total Federal tax expense of $28,000 ($80,000 × 35%). On its financial statement, PanCo reports a total tax expense of $35,000 ($100,000 × 35%). This $7,000 book-tax difference is the difference between book and taxable income times the current corporate tax rate ($7,000 = $20,000 × 35%). Although PanCo did not actually pay the $7,000 this year, in future years when the book-tax depreciation difference reverses, the

[8] *Statement of Financial Accounting Standards No. 109—Accounting for Income Taxes*, Financial Accounting Standards Board.

TAX IN THE NEWS

The Book-Tax Income Gap

The corporate financial scandals of Enron, WorldCom, and others have heightened interest in whether corporations are making appropriate disclosures (i.e., transparency) and in whether they are shouldering their fair share of the tax burden. Adding fuel to the fire is the fact that the gap between book income and taxable income seems to be growing.

According to the Citizens for Tax Justice, 41 large companies reported over $28 billion in pretax book income but paid no U.S. taxes in at least one year between 1996 and 1998. An IRS study found that the aggregate difference between book and taxable income of active corporations increased by more than 70 percent between 1996 and 1998, with corporations reporting substantially more book income than taxable income during this period.

Congress and the U.S. Treasury are concerned about the increased use of tax shelters by corporations to reduce U.S. tax and have recently issued regulations that require disclosure of certain "tax shelter" transactions. Corporations counter that the large differences in book and tax income are a function of the different rules and objectives of GAAP for financial statements and the Internal Revenue Code for tax returns.

$7,000 will eventually be paid. Hence, the *future* income tax expense related to the current book income is reported in the current year. ■

The total book tax expense under FAS 109 is made up of both current and deferred components.[9] The **current tax expense** theoretically represents the taxes actually payable to (or refund receivable from) the governmental authorities for the current period. Although an oversimplification, think of this amount as the actual check the taxpayer writes to the government (or refund received) for the current year. Keep in mind, though, that the current portion of the book income tax expense rarely matches the taxpayer's actual tax liability. A major cause of this disconnect is the tax deduction for employee stock options. The corporation receives a tax deduction at the date of employee exercise but is not required to deduct an expense for book purposes. Although this is a book-tax difference, it is not treated as a temporary or permanent difference in the FAS 109 calculation.[10] Figure 2–2 summarizes the computation of a corporation's current tax expense.

The deferred component of the book tax expense is called the **deferred tax expense** or **deferred tax benefit.** This component represents the future tax cost (or savings) connected with income reported in the current-period financial statement. Deferred tax expense or benefit is created as a result of temporary differences. More technically, FAS 109 adopts a **balance sheet approach** to measuring deferred taxes. Under this approach, the deferred tax expense or benefit is the change from one year to the next in the net **deferred tax liability** or **deferred tax asset.**

[9]Corporations also may include a "cushion" in their provision for income tax expense in order to currently account for potential tax costs in the future (e.g., deficiencies related to losing a potential IRS audit). See *Statement of Financial Accounting Standards No. 5—Accounting for Contingencies*, Financial Accounting Standards Board.

[10]See G. A. McGill and E. Outslay, "Did Enron Pay Taxes? Using Accounting Information to Decipher Tax Status," *Tax Notes*, August 19, 2002, for a discussion of issues surrounding the interpretation of the current tax payable account.

■ FIGURE 2-2
Current Tax Expense

	Pretax book income
±	Schedule M–1 adjustments
	Taxable income before NOLs
–	NOL carryforwards
	Taxable income
×	Applicable tax rate
	Current tax expense (provision) before tax credits
–	Tax credits
	Current tax expense (tax provision)

A deferred tax liability is the expected future tax liability related to current income (measured using enacted tax rates and rules).[11] A deferred tax liability is created in the following situations.

- An expense is deductible for tax in the current period but is not deductible for book until some future period.
- Income is includible currently for book purposes but is not includible in taxable income until a future period.

EXAMPLE 7

PJ Enterprises earns net income before depreciation of $500,000 in 2004 and $600,000 in 2005. Assume that PJ has a single depreciable asset acquired in 2004 for $80,000 and that for tax purposes PJ may deduct $60,000 in depreciation expense for the first year and $20,000 in depreciation expense for the second year (i.e., an accelerated method). For book purposes, assume that PJ depreciates the asset on a straight-line basis over two years ($40,000 depreciation deduction per year).

2004

	Book		Tax
Income before depreciation	$500,000		$500,000
Depreciation	(40,000)		(60,000)
Income after depreciation	460,000		440,000
Corporate tax rate	× 35%		× 35%
Income tax expense	$161,000		$154,000
Current tax expense	$154,000		
Deferred tax expense	$ 7,000		
Starting adjusted basis in depreciable asset	$ 80,000		$ 80,000
Ending adjusted basis in depreciable asset	(40,000)		(20,000)
Change in adjusted basis	$ 40,000		$ 60,000
	↘		↙
Book-tax balance sheet difference		$20,000	
Corporate tax rate		× 35%	
Deferred tax liability		$ 7,000	

[11] If the tax rate will be different in future years, the *enacted* future tax rate should be used in the computation.

In this example, it is easy to "back into" the deferred tax expense amount of $7,000 by simply taking the difference between the tax expense per the tax return ($154,000) and the book tax expense ($161,000). However, the technical computation of the deferred tax expense is based on the difference between the book and tax asset basis numbers ($20,000) at the corporate tax rate (35%).

2005	**Book**	**Tax**
Income before depreciation	$600,000	$600,000
Depreciation	(40,000)	(20,000)
Income after depreciation	560,000	580,000
Corporate tax rate	× 35%	× 35%
Income tax expense	$196,000	$203,000
Current tax expense	$203,000	
Deferred tax expense	($ 7,000)	
Starting adjusted basis in depreciable asset	$ 40,000	$ 20,000
Ending adjusted basis in depreciable asset	(–0–)	(–0–)
Change in adjusted basis	$ 40,000 ↘	$ 20,000 ↙
Book-tax balance sheet difference	($20,000)	
Corporate tax rate	× 35%	
Deferred tax liability	($ 7,000)	

In 2005, the book-tax difference in asset basis reverses, with a resulting reverse in the deferred tax liability account. ■

EXAMPLE 8

Continue with the facts in Example 7. The following journal entries record the book tax expense (provision) for each year. Notice that the book total tax expense combines the current amount (income tax payable) and the future amount (deferred tax liability).

2004 journal entry		
Income tax expense (provision)	$161,000	
Income tax payable		$154,000
Deferred tax liability		7,000
2005 journal entry		
Income tax expense (provision)	$196,000	
Deferred tax liability	7,000	
Income tax payable		$203,000

At the end of 2004, the balance sheet reflects a net deferred tax liability of $7,000. At the end of 2005, the balance sheet contains no deferred tax liability because the temporary difference that created the deferred tax liability has reversed itself. ■

A deferred tax asset is the expected future tax benefit related to current book income (measured using enacted tax rates and rules). A deferred tax asset is created in the following situations.

- An expense is deductible for book in the current period but is not deductible for tax until some future period.
- Income is includible in taxable income currently but is not includible in book income until a future period.

EXAMPLE 9

MollCo, Inc., earns net income before warranty expense of $400,000 in 2004 and $450,000 in 2005. In 2004, MollCo deducts $30,000 in warranty expense for book purposes related to expected warranty repairs. This warranty expense is not deductible for tax purposes until actually incurred. Assume the $30,000 warranty expense is actually incurred in 2005 and this is MollCo's only temporary difference.

2004

	Book	Tax
Income before warranty expense	$400,000	$400,000
Warranty expense	(30,000)	—
Income after warranty expense	$370,000	$400,000
Corporate tax rate	× 35%	× 35%
Income tax expense	$129,500	$140,000
Current tax expense	$140,000	
Deferred tax expense	($ 10,500)	
Basis in warranty expense payable	$ 30,000 ↘	$ –0– ↙
Book-tax balance sheet difference	($30,000)	
Corporate tax rate	× 35%	
Deferred tax asset	($10,500)	

In this example, it is easy to "back into" the deferred tax expense amount of $10,500 by simply taking the difference between the tax expense per the tax return ($140,000) and the book tax expense ($129,500). However, the technical computation of the deferred tax expense is based on the difference between the book and tax basis in the warranty expense payable ($30,000) at the corporate tax rate (35%).

2005

	Book	Tax
Income before warranty expense	$450,000	$450,000
Warranty expense	—	(30,000)
Income after depreciation	$450,000	$420,000
Corporate tax rate	× 35%	× 35%
Income tax expense	$157,500	$147,000
Current tax expense	$147,000	
Deferred tax expense	$ 10,500	
Basis in warranty expense payable	$ –0– ↘	$ 30,000 ↙
Book-tax balance sheet difference	$30,000	
Corporate tax rate	× 35%	
Deferred tax liability	$10,500	

In 2005, the book-tax difference in warranty expense payable reverses, with a resulting reverse in the deferred tax asset account. ■

EXAMPLE 10

Continue with the facts in Example 9. The following journal entries record the book tax expense (provision) for each year. Notice that the book total tax expense combines the current amount (income tax payable) and the future amount (deferred tax asset).

2004 journal entry		
Income tax expense (provision)	$129,500	
Deferred tax asset	10,500	
Income tax payable		$140,000
2005 journal entry		
Income tax expense (provision)	$157,500	
Deferred tax asset		$ 10,500
Income tax payable		147,000

At the end of 2004, the balance sheet reflects a net deferred tax asset of $10,500. At the end of 2005, the balance sheet contains no deferred tax asset because the temporary difference that created the deferred tax asset has reversed itself. ■

Deferred tax assets and liabilities are reported on the balance sheet just as any other asset or liability would be. However, the interpretation of these assets and liabilities is quite different. Typically, an asset is "good" because it represents a claim on something of value, and a liability is "bad" because it represents a future claim against the corporation's assets. In the case of deferred tax assets and liabilities, the interpretation is reversed. Deferred tax liabilities are "good" because they represent an amount that may be paid to the government in the future. In essence, deferred tax liabilities are like an interest-free loan from the government with a due date perhaps many years in the future. Deferred tax assets, on the other hand, are future tax benefits and thus are similar to a receivable from the government that may not received until many years in the future.

LO.3

Describe the purpose of the valuation allowance.

VALUATION ALLOWANCE

Much of GAAP is based on the **conservatism principle.** That is, accounting rules are designed to provide assurance that assets are not overstated and liabilities are not understated. Current recognition of deferred tax liabilities does not require significant professional judgment because future tax liabilities are always expected to be settled. However, under FAS 109, deferred tax assets are recognized only when it is more likely than not that the future tax benefits will be realized.

EXAMPLE 11

Warren, Inc., reported book income before tax of $2 million in 2004. Warren's taxable income is also $2 million (no temporary or permanent differences). Warren has a current U.S. income tax liability for 2004 of $700,000 before tax credits ($2 million × 35%). During 2004, Warren paid $100,000 in foreign income taxes that it is not able to use as a credit on its 2004 tax return because of the foreign tax credit (FTC) limitation (see Chapter 7). Warren's auditors believe it is more likely than not that Warren will be able to use the $100,000 in FTCs within the next five years before they expire. Consequently, the future tax benefit of the FTCs is accounted for in the current year book tax expense as follows.

	Book	Tax
Income tax expense	$600,000	$700,000
Current tax expense	$700,000	
Deferred tax expense (benefit)	($100,000)	

Warren makes the following journal entry to record the book income tax expense and deferred tax asset related to the expected use of the FTCs.

Income tax expense (provision)	$600,000	
Deferred tax asset	100,000	
Income tax payable		$700,000

Because Warren is able to record the benefit of the future FTCs, its effective tax rate is 30% ($600,000 tax expense/$2 million book income before tax).

When a deferred tax asset does not meet the *more likely than not* threshold for recognition, FAS 109 requires that a **valuation allowance** be created. The valuation allowance is a contra-asset account that offsets all or a portion of the deferred tax asset.

EXAMPLE 12

Assume that the auditors in Example 11 believe that Warren will be able to use only $40,000 of the FTCs, with the remaining $60,000 expiring. In this case, the future tax benefit recognized currently should be only $40,000 rather than the full $100,000. To implement this reduction in the deferred tax asset, Warren must record a valuation allowance of $60,000, resulting in a book tax expense of $660,000 as follows.

	Book	Tax
Income tax expense	$660,000	$700,000
Current tax expense	$700,000	
Deferred tax expense (benefit)	($ 40,000)	

Warren makes the following journal entry to record the book income tax expense and deferred tax asset related to the expected use of the FTCs.

Income tax expense (provision)	$660,000	
Deferred tax asset	100,000	
Valuation allowance		$ 60,000
Income tax payable		700,000

Warren must reduce the deferred tax asset by $60,000, which increases its effective tax rate to 33% ($660,000 tax expense/$2 million book income before tax), compared with the 30% effective tax rate in Example 11.

To determine whether a valuation allowance is required, both positive and negative evidence must be evaluated. Examples of negative evidence (i.e., evidence suggesting that the deferred tax asset will not be realized) include the following.

- History of losses.
- Expected future losses.
- Short carryback/carryforward periods.
- History of tax credits expiring unused.

Positive evidence (i.e., support for realizing the current benefit of future tax savings) includes the following.

- Strong earnings history.
- Existing contracts.
- Unrealized appreciation in assets.
- Sales backlog of profitable orders.

The valuation allowance is examined for appropriateness each year. The allowance may be increased or decreased if facts and circumstances change in the future.

PLANNING STRATEGIES

Releasing Valuation Allowances

FRAMEWORK FOCUS: DEDUCTIONS

STRATEGY ➤ **MAXIMIZE DEDUCTIBLE AMOUNTS.**

When a corporation records a valuation allowance, it loses the ability to recognize the benefit of future tax savings in the current period. However, all is not lost if the taxpayer can demonstrate that facts and circumstances have changed. For example, if a taxpayer generates a net operating loss (NOL), it records a deferred tax asset for the future tax savings related to using the NOL. However, if the evidence suggests that it is more likely than not that the NOL will expire unused, a valuation allowance must be recorded. To reduce this valuation allowance, the taxpayer must demonstrate that there will be future taxable income sufficient to absorb the NOL within the carryforward period. Sources of future taxable income include reversals of temporary differences that will produce future taxable income and other sources of future profits. Taxpayers also may demonstrate that the adoption of new tax planning strategies will allow the use of deferred tax assets.

For example, assume that Warren, Inc., from Example 12, adopts new planning strategies in 2005 that will allow it ultimately to use all $100,000 of its FTC carryforward. Warren earns $2.3 million in book income before tax and reports $2.3 million in taxable income in 2005 (i.e., no permanent or temporary differences). The current tax expense is $805,000 ($2.3 million × 35%). Based on new evidence (implementation of tax planning strategies), the auditors determine that the entire $100,000 in FTCs will be used in the future before expiration. Accordingly, the $60,000 valuation allowance from 2004 is "released," and the tax benefit of this release affects the 2005 financial results as follows.

	Book	Tax
Income tax expense	$745,000	$805,000
Current tax expense	$805,000	
Deferred tax expense	($ 60,000)	

Warren makes the following journal entry to record the book income tax expense and valuation allowance release related to the expected use of the FTCs.

Income tax expense (provision)	$745,000	
Valuation allowance	60,000	
Income tax payable		$805,000

Warren's effective tax rate for 2005 is 32.4 percent ($745,000/$2.3 million). Without the valuation allowance release, Warren's effective tax rate would have been 35 percent ($805,000/$2.3 million). Note that this tax rate benefit is realized even though the $100,000 in FTC carryforwards have yet to be actually used in Warren's tax return.

DIGGING DEEPER 2 *Find more information on this topic at our Web site:* ***http://wft-advanced.swlearning.com.***

LO.4

Recognize the effect of APB 23 on effective tax rates.

EARNINGS OF FOREIGN SUBSIDIARIES AND APB 23

As discussed earlier, a corporate group's financial statements include both domestic and foreign controlled subsidiaries. However, foreign corporations, even those controlled by U.S. shareholders, are not part of a U.S. consolidated tax return. Consequently, U.S. taxpayers can achieve deferral of current U.S. taxes on foreign income if they operate their foreign activities through foreign subsidiary corporations in jurisdictions with lower tax rates than the United States (see Chapters 7 and 8). Although the *actual* U.S. taxes on foreign corporations' profits are deferred, the reported effective tax rate for financial statement purposes may not reflect this deferral because FAS 109 requires that a corporate group report both current and deferred income tax expense.

EXAMPLE 13

USCo, a domestic corporation, operates a manufacturing facility in Singapore through a Singapore corporation. Assume that the U.S. tax rate is 35% and the Singapore tax rate is 6%. For the current year, USCo earns $600,000 in taxable income. The Singapore corporation earns $400,000 in taxable income from its operations, pays $24,000 in taxes to Singapore, and makes no distributions to its U.S. parent. The Singapore corporation is not taxed in the United States because it is not a U.S. person and has no activities in the United States. USCo is not taxed on the Singapore profits because it has not received any distributions of these profits. Accordingly, USCo has achieved deferral and reduced its worldwide cash tax costs.

However, for financial statement purposes, the USCo group must include the $400,000 in Singapore profits in its net income and report both the Singapore tax and any *potential* U.S. tax (after allowable FTCs) as its total tax expense.

U.S. Tax Return		**Potential U.S. Tax on Non-U.S. Income**	
Income	$600,000	Income	$400,000
Tax rate	× 35%	Tax rate	× 35%
U.S. tax	$210,000	Total tax	$140,000
		Foreign tax credit	(24,000)
		Net U.S. tax	$116,000

Consequently, the total tax expense for financial statement purposes is $350,000.

Current U.S. tax	$210,000
Current foreign tax	24,000
Deferred U.S. tax	116,000
Total tax expense	$350,000

The financial statement effective tax rate on global income is 35% ($350,000 total tax expense/ $1,000,000 net income). Thus, although USCo paid only $234,000 in taxes, its effective tax rate (and thus its after-tax book income) does not reflect the savings generated from operating in Singapore, a low-tax country. ■

APB 23 provides a special exception to FAS 109 for income from foreign subsidiaries.[12] If a corporation documents that it is **permanently reinvesting** the earnings of its foreign subsidiaries outside the United States, the corporation does not record as an expense any future U.S. income tax that the corporation may pay on such earnings.

EXAMPLE 14

Assume that USCo, in Example 13, uses APB 23 to avoid reporting the $116,000 in deferred taxes. Because USCo plans to reinvest indefinitely its Singapore earnings outside the United States, it is not required to include the deferred U.S. taxes as part of its total tax expense. Thus, USCo's total financial statement income remains $1 million, but its total tax expense is only $234,000 (the taxes currently paid to the United States and Singapore). The resulting financial statement effective tax rate is 23.4% ($234,000/$1,000,000), and the USCo group's after-tax book income reflects the Singapore tax savings. ■

Using APB 23 is not an "all or nothing" decision. It can be adopted in some years and not others. Even within a year it may be used for only a portion of foreign subsidiary earnings.

[12]*Opinion No. 23—Accounting for Income Taxes—Special Areas,* Accounting Principles Board.

EXAMPLE 15

Larson, Inc., a domestic corporation, has two wholly owned foreign subsidiaries, Arendt, Ltd., and Carroll, Ltd. Larson can choose to apply APB 23 to both subsidiaries in 2004 and to only Arendt in 2005. In 2006, Larson can choose to use APB 23 for 40% of Arendt's earnings and 80% of Carroll's earnings. ■

PLANNING STRATEGIES

Reducing Effective Tax Rates with APB 23 Can Backfire

FRAMEWORK FOCUS: DEDUCTIONS

STRATEGY ➤ **MAXIMIZE DEDUCTIBLE AMOUNTS.**

Because APB 23 allows for higher reported book earnings (no deferred U.S. tax expense is recorded), its use may be reflected in higher stock prices and increased shareholder wealth. Although academic studies find mixed evidence on this effect, many U.S. multinationals with foreign subsidiaries do in fact use APB 23 to avoid reporting U.S. deferred taxes on foreign earnings.

The "permanent reinvestment" exception should not be employed unless the corporation truly expects to keep its foreign earnings outside the United States. Using APB 23 and then repatriating foreign profits after all can cause extreme spikes in a corporation's effective tax rate.

For example, USCo, a domestic corporation, owns 100 percent of Shamrock, Ltd., an Irish corporation. Assume that the U.S. tax rate is 35 percent and the Irish tax rate is 10 percent. In 2004, USCo earns $100,000 in taxable income and pays $35,000 to the United States. Shamrock earns $400,000 in taxable income and pays $40,000 in taxes to Ireland. Shamrock makes no distributions to its U.S. parent and is not taxed in the United States because it is not a U.S. person and has no activities in the United States. USCo is not taxed on the Irish profits because it has not received any distributions of these profits. Furthermore, USCo uses APB 23 to avoid recording any deferred U.S. income tax expense on its financial statements. Accordingly, USCo has achieved deferral and reduced its worldwide cash tax costs and book income tax expense.

USCo's total tax expense for financial statement purposes is $75,000.

Current U.S. tax	$35,000
Current foreign tax	40,000
Total tax expense	$75,000

The financial statement effective tax rate on global income is 15 percent ($75,000 total tax expense/$500,000 net income). Thus, the USCo group has achieved higher after-tax book income and earnings per share.

In 2005, USCo earns $200,000 in taxable income and pays $70,000 to the United States. Shamrock breaks even for the year and pays no taxes to Ireland. In 2005, USCo decides to have Shamrock pay it a dividend of $360,000.

U.S. Tax Return	
U.S. income	$200,000
Foreign dividend*	400,000
Taxable income	$600,000
Tax rate	× 35%
	$210,000
FTC	(40,000)
Net U.S. tax	$170,000

*The foreign dividend is the $360,000 cash dividend grossed up by the $40,000 potential FTC (see Chapter 7).

For book purposes, USCo reports only $200,000 in net income (the $400,000 in Irish income was previously included in book income in 2004 and is not included again). The 2005 total tax expense for financial statement purposes is $170,000.

Current U.S. tax	$170,000
Current foreign tax	–0–
Total tax expense	$170,000

The financial statement effective tax rate on global income is 85 percent ($170,000 total tax expense/$200,000 net income). This extremely high effective rate is caused by the mismatching of the Irish income (reported in 2004) and the U.S. taxes on the Irish income (reported in 2005).

APB 23 is only a major issue when the foreign subsidiary is taxed at rates below the U.S. tax rate. Otherwise, there is no deferral potential. However, using APB 23 may limit the availability of creating deferred tax assets when foreign subsidiaries pay taxes at greater than the U.S. rate. Then the multinational group could use these excess foreign taxes as credits on the U.S. tax return. See Chapter 7.

EXAMPLE 16

AmeriCo, a domestic corporation, operates a manufacturing facility in the Netherlands through a Dutch corporation. Assume that the U.S. tax rate is 35% and the Netherlands tax rate is also 35%. For the current year, AmeriCo earns $400,000 in taxable income. The Netherlands corporation earns $300,000 in taxable income from its operations, pays $105,000 in taxes to the Netherlands, and makes no distributions to its U.S. parent. The Netherlands corporation is not taxed in the United States because it is not a U.S. person and has no activities in the United States. AmeriCo is not taxed on the Netherlands profits because it has not received any distributions of these profits.

For financial statement purposes, the AmeriCo group must include the $300,000 in Dutch profits in its net income and report both the Dutch tax and any *potential* U.S. tax (after allowable FTCs) as its total tax expense.

U.S. Tax Return		**Potential U.S. Tax on Foreign Income**	
Income	$400,000	Income	$ 300,000
Tax rate	× 35%	Tax rate	× 35%
U.S. tax	$140,000	Total tax	$ 105,000
		FTC	(105,000)
		Net U.S. tax	$ –0–

Consequently, the total tax expense for financial statement purposes is $245,000.

Current U.S. tax	$140,000
Current foreign tax	105,000
Total tax expense	$245,000

The financial statement effective tax rate on global income is 35% ($245,000 total tax expense/ $700,000 book net income). Even without APB 23, there is no deferred U.S. tax on the Dutch income, because AmeriCo would pay no additional U.S. tax upon repatriation of the Netherlands earnings after its use of the available FTC. ■

LO.5

Interpret the disclosure information contained in an income tax note.

TAX DISCLOSURES IN THE FINANCIAL STATEMENTS

As illustrated earlier, any temporary differences create deferred tax liabilities or deferred tax assets, and these amounts appear in the corporation's balance sheet. As with any asset or liability, these accounts must be classified as either current or noncurrent, based on the assets or liabilities that created the temporary difference. If the deferred tax liability or asset is not related to any asset, then the classification is based on the expected reversal period.

EXAMPLE 17

JenCo, Inc., has a deferred tax liability generated because tax depreciation exceeds book depreciation on manufacturing equipment. Because the equipment is classified as a noncurrent asset, the deferred tax liability is classified as noncurrent. JenCo also has a deferred tax asset related to bad debt expense deductible for book purposes but not yet deductible for tax purposes. Because the bad debt expense is related to accounts receivable, a current asset, the associated deferred tax asset is classified as current.

If JenCo incurs an NOL, a deferred tax asset is created, because of the future tax benefit provided by the NOL deduction. The NOL is not related to any specific asset or liability. Accordingly, the deferred tax asset is classified based on when the corporation expects to use the NOL. If the expected use is more than one year in the future, the deferred tax asset is classified as noncurrent. ■

A corporation may have both deferred tax assets and liabilities, current and noncurrent. The corporation reports the *net* current deferred tax assets or liabilities, and the *net* noncurrent deferred tax assets or liabilities.

EXAMPLE 18

Jordan, Inc., has the following deferred tax asset and liability accounts for the current year.

Current deferred tax assets	$50,000
Current deferred tax liabilities	72,000
Noncurrent deferred tax assets	93,000
Noncurrent deferred tax liabilities	28,000

On its balance sheet, Jordan reports a $22,000 current net deferred tax liability ($72,000 – $50,000) and a $65,000 noncurrent net deferred tax asset ($93,000 – $28,000). ■

In its income statement, a corporation reports a total income tax expense that consists of both the current tax expense (or benefit) and the deferred tax expense (or benefit). The tax expense must be allocated to income from continuing operations, discontinued operations, extraordinary items, prior-period adjustments, and the cumulative effect of accounting changes. Additional disclosures are required for tax expense allocated to income from continuing operations (e.g., current versus deferred, benefits of NOL deductions, changes in valuation allowances, etc.).

The income tax note contains a wealth of information, including the following.

- Breakdown of income between domestic and foreign.
- Detailed analysis of the provision for income tax expense.
- Detailed analysis of deferred tax assets and liabilities.
- Effective tax **rate reconciliation** (dollar amount or percentage).
- Information on use of APB 23 for the earnings of foreign subsidiaries.
- Discussion of significant tax matters.

Figure 2–3 contains selected information from Microsoft's 2003 financial statements. The balance sheet detail shows both deferred tax assets and liabilities. The income statement indicates that Microsoft's income before tax was $14,726 million, and its total income tax expense was $4,733 million. The income tax note indicates that $11,346 million of the book income was earned from domestic operations and $3,380 million from foreign operations. The $4,733 million total income tax expense reported in the income statement is further divided into $4,669 million of current tax expense ($808 million of which was paid to non-U.S. governments) and $64 million of deferred tax expense (i.e., future tax costs related to current-year activities).

The note provides detail on the cumulative deferred tax assets and liabilities. Microsoft has a net deferred tax asset of $775 million ($5,129 deferred tax assets – $4,354 deferred tax liabilities). Microsoft's auditors must believe that these deferred tax assets will be fully realized because no valuation allowance is required. Because of the way the balance sheet accounts are summarized, the deferred tax asset and liability amounts in the balance sheet do not match the amounts reported in the income tax note. This is because the deferred tax assets and liabilities are separated into current and noncurrent components in the balance sheet and may be subsumed within other balance sheet accounts (e.g., other long-term assets).

■ **FIGURE 2–3**
Microsoft, Inc., Selected 2003 Financial Statement Information (in Millions)

Balance Sheet	
Assets	
Current assets	
Cash and equivalents	$ 6,438
Short-term investments	42,610
Total cash and short-term investments	$ 49,048
Accounts receivable, net	5,196
Inventories	640
Deferred income taxes	2,506
Other	1,583
Total current assets	$ 58,973
Property and equipment, net	2,223
Equity and other investments	13,692
Goodwill	3,128
Intangible assets, net	384
Other long-term assets	1,171
Total assets	$ 79,571
Liabilities and stockholders' equity	
Current liabilities	
Accounts payable	$ 1,573
Accrued compensation	1,416
Income taxes	2,044
Short-term unearned revenue	7,225
Other	1,716
Total current liabilities	$ 13,974
Long-term unearned revenue	1,790
Deferred income taxes	1,731
Other long-term liabilities	1,056
Stockholders' equity	
Common stock and paid-in capital—shares authorized 24,000; Shares issued and outstanding 10,718 and 10,771	$ 35,344
Retained earnings, including accumulated other comprehensive income of $583 and $1,840	25,676
Total stockholders' equity	$ 61,020
Total liabilities and stockholders' equity	$ 79,571

(*continued on next page*)

Microsoft is using APB 23 to avoid currently recording a deferred tax expense for $1.64 billion of its foreign subsidiary earnings. Microsoft also reports on the status of a litigation matter with the IRS.

Microsoft's effective rate reconciliation starts with its book income before taxes at the U.S corporate tax rate ($5,154 = $14,726 × 35%). Adjustments are made for two permanent differences: (1) the tax benefits related to the reversal of accrued taxes related to a favorable Tax Court Ruling received by Microsoft [$126 or 0.9% ($126/$14,726)] and (2) other tax reducing differences [$295 or 2.0% ($295/$14,726)]. The ending tax amount is $4,733, which ties to the total income tax expense

FIGURE 2–3
(continued)

Income Statement

Revenue	$ 32,187
Operating expenses	
Cost of revenue	$ (5,686)
Research and development	(4,659)
Sales and marketing	(6,521)
General and administrative	(2,104)
Total operating expenses	$(18,970)
Operating income	$ 13,217
Losses on equity investees and other	(68)
Investment income/(loss)	1,577
Income before income taxes	$ 14,726
Provision for income taxes	4,733
Net income	$ 9,993

Income Tax Note

U.S. and international components of income before income taxes were:

U.S.	$ 11,346
International	3,380
Income before income taxes	$ 14,726

The provision for income taxes consisted of:

Current taxes	
U.S. and state	$ 3,861
International	808
Current taxes	$ 4,669
Deferred taxes	64
Provision for income taxes	$ 4,733

Deferred income taxes were:

Deferred income tax assets	
Revenue items	$ 2,556
Expense items	1,048
Impaired investments	1,525
Deferred income tax assets	$ 5,129
Deferred income tax liabilities	
Unrealized gain on investments	$ (1,584)
International earnings	(1,809)
Other	(961)
Deferred income tax liabilities	$ (4,354)

Effective Tax Rate Reconciliation

	$	%
Hypothetical income taxes at U.S. rate	$ 5,154	35.0
Reversal of previously accrued taxes related to a favorable Tax Court ruling	(126)	(0.9)
Other	(295)	(2.0)
Provision for income tax	$ 4,733	32.1

(continued on next page)

■ **FIGURE 2-3**
(concluded)

> Microsoft has not provided for U.S. deferred income taxes or foreign withholding taxes on $1.64 billion of its undistributed earnings for certain non-U.S. subsidiaries, all of which relate to fiscal 2002 and 2003 earnings, because these earnings are intended to be reinvested indefinitely. On September 15, 2000, the U.S. Tax Court issued an adverse ruling with respect to Microsoft's claim that the Internal Revenue Service (IRS) incorrectly assessed taxes for 1990 and 1991. The Company has filed an appeal with the Ninth Circuit Court of Appeals on this matter. Income taxes, except for items related to the 1990 and 1991 assessments, have been settled with the IRS for all years through 1996. The IRS is examining the Company's 1997 through 1999 U.S. income tax returns. Management believes any adjustments which may be required will not be material to the financial statements. Income taxes paid were $1.3 billion in 2001, $1.9 billion in 2002, and $2.8 billion in 2003.

reported in the income statement. This is an effective tax rate of 32.1 percent ($4,733/$14,726). Thus, Microsoft's overall effective tax rate (local, state, U.S., and foreign) on its worldwide income is less than the U.S. corporate tax rate.

The purpose of the rate reconciliation is to demonstrate how a corporation's actual book effective tax rate relates to its "hypothetical tax rate" as if the book income were taxed at the U.S. corporate rate of 35 percent. Although similar to Schedule M–1, the tax note rate reconciliation only reports differences triggered by permanent differences. As discussed in the benchmarking section later in this chapter, an analysis of the rate reconciliation can provide substantial clues as to the tax planning strategies adopted (or not adopted) by a company.

Microsoft's income tax note states that the company "paid" $2.8 billion in income taxes for 2003. Notice that this amount does not match either the total income tax expense of $4,733 million or the current income tax expense of $4,669 million. This anomaly illustrates the difficulty in interpreting the true tax position of a corporation from its financial statements. The most likely candidate for this approximately $2.2 billion difference lies in Microsoft's tax deduction related to employee stock options, which substantially reduces its current-year Federal income tax liability but does not affect its book tax expense (current or deferred).

The steps in determining a corporation's income tax expense for book purposes are summarized in Concept Summary 2–2.

EXAMPLE 19

BoxCo, Inc., a domestic corporation, owns 100% of PaperCo, Ltd., an Irish corporation. Assume that the U.S. corporate tax rate is 35% and the Irish rate is 10%. BoxCo is permanently reinvesting PaperCo's earnings outside the United States under APB 23. The corporations' book income, permanent and temporary differences, and current tax expense are as follows.

	BoxCo	PaperCo
Book income before tax	$300,000	$200,000
Permanent differences		
Meals and entertainment expense	20,000	—
Municipal bond interest income	(50,000)	—
Book income after permanent differences	$270,000	$200,000
Temporary differences		
Tax > book depreciation	(50,000)	—
Book > tax bad debt expense	10,000	—
Taxable income	$230,000	$200,000
Tax rate	× 35%	× 10%
Current tax expense	$ 80,500	$ 20,000

CONCEPT SUMMARY 2–2

Steps in Determining Book Tax Expense

Start with the corporation's book income after permanent differences.

↓

Determine the corporation's temporary differences.

↓

Compute the corporation's current tax provision.

↓

Compute the corporation's deferred tax provision.

↓

Determine if a valuation allowance is required.

↓

Prepare the income tax note disclosures.

Assume that the beginning-of-the-year difference between book and tax basis in the depreciable assets is $150,000 and the beginning-of-the-year difference between book and tax basis in the bad debt expense is $50,000. Thus, the beginning-of-the-year deferred tax liability is $35,000 [($150,000 – $50,000) × 35%]. To determine the deferred tax expense (benefit) for the current year, the change in these temporary differences from the beginning to the end of the year must be determined and then multiplied by the appropriate tax rate.

Temporary Differences	**Beginning of Year**	**Change**	**End of Year**
Depreciation	$150,000	$ 50,000	$200,000
Bad debts	(50,000)	(10,000)	(60,000)
Total temporary differences	$100,000	$ 40,000	$140,000
Tax rate	× 35%	× 35%	× 35%
	$ 35,000	$ 14,000	$ 49,000

The deferred tax liability increased by $14,000 for the year. Consequently, BoxCo's total tax expense for book purposes is $114,500.

Current tax expense:	
Domestic	$ 80,500
Foreign	20,000
Deferred tax expense:	
Domestic	14,000
Foreign	—
Total tax expense	$114,500

The journal entry to record the book income tax expense is as follows.

Income tax expense (provision)	$114,500	
Income tax payable		$100,500
Deferred tax liability		14,000

BoxCo's book income is $500,000 (the combined book income of both BoxCo and PaperCo). The effective tax rate reconciliation is based on this book income, with the dollar amounts in the table representing the tax expense (benefit) related to the item and the percentage representing the tax expense (benefit) as a percentage of book income. For example, the municipal bond interest of $50,000 reduces tax liability by $17,500 ($50,000 × 35%). This $17,500 as a percentage of the $500,000 book income is 3.5%.

	Effective Tax Rate Reconciliation	
	$	**%**
Hypothetical tax at U.S. rate	$175,000	35.0
Disallowed meals and entertainment expense	7,000	1.4
Municipal bond interest	(17,500)	(3.5)
Foreign income taxed at less than U.S. rate	(50,000)	(10.0)
Income tax expense (provision)	$114,500	22.9

Only permanent differences appear in the rate reconciliation. Temporary differences do not affect the *total* book income tax expense; they simply affect the amount of the tax expense that is current versus deferred. ■

EXAMPLE 20

Assume the same facts as Example 19, except that a new Federal income tax law is enacted before the end of the current year that will increase the corporate tax rate to 40% beginning next year. In this case, multiply the year-end total temporary differences of $140,000 by 40% rather than 35%. This results in an increase in the deferred tax liability of $21,000 as illustrated below.

Temporary Differences	**Beginning of Year**	**End of Year**	**Effect**
Depreciation	$150,000	$200,000	
Bad debts	(50,000)	(60,000)	
Total temporary differences	$100,000	$140,000	
Tax rate	× 35%	× 40%	
Deferred tax liability	$ 35,000	$ 56,000	$21,000

The current-year deferred tax liability amount is a function of both the change in temporary differences at the enacted rate ($40,000 × 40%) and the additional 5% tax on the beginning temporary differences [$100,000 × (40% – 35%)]. This example illustrates the "balance sheet" approach of FAS 109. ■

TAX FACT

Effective Tax Rates for Selected Fortune 100 Companies

The following table shows the provisions for income taxes made by selected major corporations, as a percentage of their book income before taxes.

General Electric	21.7%
General Motors	24.5
Verizon	26.3
IBM	30.0
Citigroup	31.1
Ford	31.7
ExxonMobil	34.4
Wal-Mart	35.3
ChevronTexaco	41.8

Source: 2002 or 2003 10-K Filings with Securities and Exchange Commission.

PLANNING STRATEGIES

Tax Savings Are Not Always Created Equal

FRAMEWORK FOCUS: THINKING OUTSIDE THE FRAMEWORK

Many different types of tax planning strategies can produce tax savings. Yet, even when planning ideas produce identical current cash-flow effects, some ideas may have an edge. CEOs and CFOs of public companies are very focused on the bottom line—the company's net income after tax and related earnings per share. A CFO is likely just as interested in an idea's effect on the company's bottom line income as on the cash tax savings.

For example, consider two tax planning ideas that each produce $700,000 of current tax savings. The first idea generates its $700,000 in tax savings by increasing tax depreciation relative to book depreciation by $2 million ($700,000 = $2 million × 35%). The second idea produces research activities tax credits of $700,000, thus reducing current-year tax by $700,000.

Idea 1 produces its current tax savings via a temporary difference. Accordingly, the book tax expense will not reflect the $700,000 in tax savings. Instead, this $700,000 simply moves from the current tax category into the deferred tax category. Even if the book-tax difference is not expected to reverse in the next 30 years (effectively generating "permanent" savings), the book tax expense does not reflect this savings.

In contrast, idea 2 produces its current tax savings via a permanent difference. Thus, the book tax expense also declines by $700,000. This item is a reconciling item in the income tax note rate reconciliation.

LO.6

Use financial statement income tax information to benchmark a company's tax position.

Benchmarking

As the *outcome* of the taxpayer's activities combined with the tax professional's advice, the income tax expense amount may appear to be of little interest to anyone beyond the taxpayer that makes the payment and the government agencies that collect it. The tax year is over, the transactions completed, and the final costs tallied.

■ FIGURE 2–4
Tax Rate Reconciliation for Tommy Hilfiger and Polo Ralph Lauren

	Tommy Hilfiger		Polo Ralph Lauren	
	2002	**2003**	**2002**	**2003**
Hypothetical tax (benefit) at U.S. Federal rate	35.0%	(35.0)%	35.0%	35.0%
State and local income taxes, net of Federal benefits	(6.5)	(29.1)	2.6	1.1
Non-U.S. income taxed at different rates	(22.6)	(48.2)	(2.6)	0.2
Valuation allowance	5.2	53.3	—	—
Goodwill amortization	3.7	—	—	—
Goodwill impairment	—	75.9	—	—
Other	(1.9)	3.5	2.5	0.2
Provision for income tax expense (effective tax rate)	12.9%	20.4%	37.5%	36.5%
Book income before tax (in millions)	$155	($69)	$276	$274

Source: 2002 and 2003 10-K Filings with Securities and Exchange Commission.

Still, this historical tax information may prove very valuable. A company's income tax expense is one of the single largest expense items on its income statement, and understanding the components of this expense is a critical activity for the tax professional.

Consider a typical baseball game. Two teams meet, interact following a specific set of rules, and ultimately complete the game generating a final score. Of course, the final score is of immediate interest to the teams and the fans, but once the game is over, the score and associated statistics (runs, hits, errors) are relegated to the history books. Yet these statistics are still quite useful. A team coach may use the game statistics to evaluate the strengths and weaknesses of the players to assist in improving performance. Other teams in the league may use the statistics to develop strategies for upcoming games. Players can use the statistics to benchmark themselves against their own performance in prior games or against players in other teams. In short, there is a wealth of information in these historical data.

A taxpayer's reported income tax expense is likewise a valuable source of information for the company, its tax advisers, and its competitors. The reported information provides clues about a company's operational and tax planning strategies.

Companies may benchmark their tax situation to other years' results or to other companies within the same industry. The starting point for a **benchmarking** exercise is the data from the income tax note rate reconciliation.

Figure 2–4 contains the tax rate reconciliation information from the income tax notes of Tommy Hilfiger (Tommy) and Polo Ralph Lauren (Polo). Both companies are listed on the New York Stock Exchange, are in the same industry (clothing and accessories), and operate around the world. Although the income and tax expense amounts of both companies are quite different, the tax amounts are converted to percentage of income numbers for comparability purposes. In 2002, Tommy has a very low effective tax rate at 12.9 percent, compared with Polo's 37.5 percent rate. Tommy's 2003 rate is also substantially lower than Polo's 2003 rate. What factors create this difference? Rate reconciliation information can provide clues.

BRIDGE DISCIPLINE

Financial Statement Analysis

Benchmarking a company's tax position with other companies in the same industry or against prior-year results is simply part of a more comprehensive benchmarking analysis of a company's financial results. For example, analysts often perform ratio analysis when benchmarking a company. The information gleaned from the debt-to-equity ratio, return on assets, return on equity, inventory turnover, and the like is useful in comparing the overall performance of two or more companies. Effective tax rates are simply one more bit of information for the analysts to compare and contrast.

Tax information, however, is often misunderstood by analysts, who may not understand the difference between current and deferred taxes (or that the reported current tax expense does not necessarily represent the taxes the company actually paid for the year). Add stock options, APB 23, and tax cushions under FAS 5 to the mix and the likelihood of the tax note producing a clear picture for the analyst is low. The subtle and sometimes confusing nature of accounting for income taxes creates a special demand for professionals who can demystify the income tax note.

The major difference between Tommy and Polo is in the foreign income taxed at less than the U.S. rate. In Tommy's case, this factor reduces the effective tax rate by 22.6 percentage points in 2002 and 18.2 percentage points in 2003. This factor reduces the effective tax rate by only 2.6 percentage points for Polo in 2002 and increases the rate by a slight amount in 2003. Closer examination of the financial statements provides an explanation for this difference. Tommy is incorporated in the British Virgin Islands, a tax haven (low or no tax) country, while Polo is incorporated in the United States. As discussed in Chapters 7 and 8, establishing a company offshore can generate substantial tax savings. Obviously, Tommy has used this strategy to its advantage in structuring its multinational operations.

Another difference between Tommy and Polo is the effect of state and local taxes. Tommy is actually receiving tax savings from state and local taxes (perhaps through local tax incentives and losses), while Polo is paying an effective state and local rate of 2.6 percent (2002) and 1.1 percent (2003).

If Polo could reduce its effective tax rate to 12.9 percent through tax planning or restructuring its operations, its after-tax net income in 2002 would have increased by $67.9 million [difference in tax rates (37.5% – 12.9%) × $276 million book income]. After examination of this simple benchmarking exercise, Polo might engage a tax adviser to investigate the potential of implementing state and local and international tax planning strategies. It appears that Polo has already reduced its state and local taxes (1.1 percent versus 2.6 percent).

When comparing effective tax rates, it is important to consider which components of the effective rate produce one-time effects. For example, the foreign tax rate differential for Tommy and Polo is likely a long-term structural difference in effective tax rates due to the two companies being incorporated in different jurisdictions. However, the large valuation allowance and goodwill impairment effects for Tommy may be a one-time reconciling item. Other typical one-time reconciling items are IRS tax settlements.

In addition to comparing effective tax rates, companies can compare levels of deferred tax assets and liabilities.

EXAMPLE 21

Akiko Enterprises reports a net deferred tax liability of $280,000. Asare, Inc., a company in the same industry, reports a net deferred tax liability of $860,000. Seeing deferred tax liabilities on the balance sheet indicates that these companies are both benefiting from deferring actual tax payments (essentially, an interest-free loan from the government). At first glance it may appear that Asare is doing better in this regard. However, what if Akiko holds total assets of $2.6 million and Asare's assets total $19.2 million? This information indicates that Akiko has 10.8% ($280,000/$2.6 million) of its total assets "financed" with an interest-free loan from the government, while Asare has only 4.5% ($860,000/$19.2 million) of its assets "financed" with its deferred tax liabilities. ■

A company may do a more refined benchmarking analysis of its deferred tax assets and liabilities by examining each component of its deferred tax assets and liabilities as a percentage of total assets. For example, a company can examine how the deferred tax assets or liabilities related to property, plant, and equipment compare with its competitors.

Suggested Further Readings

S. Gupta and K. Newberry, "Corporate Effective Tax Rates after the Tax Reform Act of 1986," *Tax Notes*, May 4, 1992.

G. A. McGill and E. Outslay, "Did Enron Pay Taxes? Using Accounting Information to Decipher Tax Status," *Tax Notes*, August 19, 2002.

L. K. Mills, K. Newberry, and W. B. Trautman, "Trends in Book-Tax Income and Balance Sheet Differences, *Tax Notes*, August 19, 2002.

KEY TERMS

APB 23, 2–15
Balance sheet approach, 2–8
Benchmarking, 2–25
Conservatism principle, 2–12
Current tax expense, 2–8
Deferred tax asset, 2–8
Deferred tax benefit, 2–8
Deferred tax expense, 2–8
Deferred tax liability, 2–8
Equity method, 2–3
FAS 109 (income tax provision), 2–7
Generally accepted accounting principles (GAAP), 2–2
Income tax provision, 2–7
Permanent differences, 2–4
Permanently reinvesting, 2–15
Rate reconciliation, 2–18
Schedule M–1, 2–5
Temporary differences, 2–4
Valuation allowance, 2–13

PROBLEM MATERIALS

Problems

Ethics

1. Evaluate the following statement: To avoid the appearance of tax evasion, a corporation's reported book and taxable income should be virtually identical in any given year.

2. USCo, a domestic corporation, owns 100% of ForCo, a foreign corporation, and SubCo, a domestic corporation. USCo also owns 35% of InvestCo, a domestic corporation. USCo receives no distributions from any of these corporations. Which of these entities' net income is included in USCo's income statement for current-year financial reporting purposes?

3. USCo, a domestic corporation, owns 100% of ForCo, a foreign corporation, and SubCo, a domestic corporation. USCo also owns 35% of InvestCo, a domestic corporation. USCo receives no distributions from any of these corporations. Which of these entities' taxable income is included in USCo's current-year Form 1120, U.S. income tax return? Assume USCo consolidates all eligible subsidiaries.

Communications

4. Sarah Carter, the CFO of Mac, Inc., notices that the tax expense reported on Mac's tax return differs from the tax expense reported on Mac's financial statement. Provide a letter to Sarah outlining why these two tax expense numbers differ. Mac's address is 482 Linden Road, Paris, KY 40362.

Issue ID

5. Temporary and permanent differences both cause taxable income to differ from book income. Describe how these two book-tax differences affect the gap between book and taxable income.

6. Identify two temporary differences and two permanent differences.

7. Indicate whether the following items create temporary or permanent differences.
   a. Tax depreciation in excess of book depreciation.
   b. Book depreciation in excess of tax depreciation.
   c. Municipal bond interest income.
   d. Increase in the allowance for doubtful accounts.
   e. Disallowed meals and entertainment expense for tax purposes.
   f. Deduction for legal expenses expected to be incurred to settle a lawsuit.

8. Indicate whether the following temporary differences produce deferred tax assets or deferred tax liabilities (considered independently).
   a. Tax depreciation in excess of book depreciation.
   b. Book depreciation in excess of tax depreciation.
   c. Increase in the allowance for doubtful accounts.
   d. Deduction for legal expenses expected to be incurred to settle a lawsuit.
   e. A current-year net operating loss.
   f. Foreign tax credits that are not allowed in the current year because of the foreign tax credit limitation.

9. Indicate whether the following temporary differences produce current or noncurrent deferred tax assets or deferred tax liabilities (considered independently).
   a. Tax depreciation in excess of book depreciation.
   b. Book depreciation in excess of tax depreciation.
   c. Increase in the allowance for doubtful accounts.
   d. Deduction for legal expenses expected to be incurred to settle a lawsuit.
   e. A current-year net operating loss.

10. Evaluate the following statement: The purpose of the Schedule M–1 is to report the book income tax expense to the IRS.

11. Idil, a stock analyst, wants to understand the income tax expense reported in financial statements. Briefly describe the objective of FAS 109 with regard to reporting income tax expense.

12. GlobalCo, Inc., earns book net income of $250,000 in 2004. GlobalCo acquires a depreciable asset in 2004, and first-year tax depreciation exceeds book depreciation by $25,000. GlobalCo has no other temporary or permanent differences. Assuming the U.S. tax rate is 35%, compute GlobalCo's total income tax expense, current income tax expense, and deferred income tax expense.

13. Using the facts of Problem 12, determine the 2004 end-of-year balance in GlobalCo's deferred tax asset and deferred tax liability balance sheet accounts.

14. GlobalCo, in Problem 12, reports $300,000 of book net income in 2005. GlobalCo's book depreciation exceeds tax depreciation in this year by $10,000. GlobalCo has no other temporary or permanent differences. Assuming the U.S. tax rate is 35%, compute GlobalCo's total income tax expense, current income tax expense, and deferred income tax expense.

15. Using the facts of Problem 14, determine the 2005 end-of-year balance in GlobalCo's deferred tax asset and deferred tax liability balance sheet accounts.

16. WorldCo, Inc., earns book net income of $500,000 in 2004. WorldCo deducted $60,000 in bad debt expense for book purposes. This expense is not yet deductible for tax purposes. WorldCo has no other temporary or permanent differences. Assuming the U.S. tax rate is 35%, compute WorldCo's total income tax expense, current income tax expense, and deferred income tax expense.

17. Using the facts of Problem 16, determine the 2004 end-of-year balance in WorldCo's deferred tax asset and deferred tax liability balance sheet accounts.

18. WorldCo, in Problem 16, reports $800,000 of book net income in 2005. WorldCo did not deduct any bad debt expense for book purposes but did deduct $40,000 in bad debt expense for tax purposes. WorldCo has no other temporary or permanent differences. Assuming the U.S. tax rate is 35%, compute WorldCo's total income tax expense, current income tax expense, and deferred income tax expense.

19. Using the facts of Problem 18, determine the 2005 end-of-year balance in WorldCo's deferred tax asset and deferred tax liability balance sheet accounts.

20. Zoom, Inc., hopes to report a total book tax expense of $50,000 in the current year. This $50,000 expense consists of $80,000 in current tax expense and a $30,000 tax benefit related to the expected future use of an NOL by Zoom. If the auditors determine that a valuation allowance of $20,000 must be placed against Zoom's deferred tax assets, what is Zoom's total book tax expense?

21. Describe the factors considered in evaluating the need for a valuation allowance.

22. How does the release of a valuation allowance in a future year affect the book effective tax rate for that year?

Decision Making

23. RadioCo, a domestic corporation, owns 100% of TVCo, a manufacturing facility in Ireland. TVCo has no operations or activities in the United States. The U.S. tax rate is 35%, and the Irish tax rate is 10%. For the current year, RadioCo earns $400,000 in taxable income. TVCo earns $800,000 in taxable income from its operations, pays $80,000 in taxes to Ireland, and makes no distributions to RadioCo. Determine RadioCo's effective tax rate for book purposes with and without the permanent reinvestment assumption of APB 23. Under what conditions should RadioCo adopt APB 23 for TVCo's earnings?

Issue ID

24. Shannon, the CFO of TechCo, Inc., has used APB 23 to avoid reporting any U.S. deferred tax expense on $30 million of the earnings of TechCo's foreign subsidiaries. All of these subsidiaries operate in countries with lower tax rates than the United States. Shannon wants to bring home $10 million in profits from these foreign subsidiaries in the form of dividends. How will this profit repatriation affect TechCo's book effective tax rate?

Issue ID

25. Brian, the CFO of AutoCo, Inc., has used APB 23 to avoid reporting any U.S. deferred tax expense on $60 million of the earnings of AutoCo's foreign subsidiaries. All of these subsidiaries operate in countries with higher tax rates than the ones that apply under U.S. law. Brian wants to bring home $20 million in profits from these foreign subsidiaries in the form of dividends. How will this profit repatriation affect AutoCo's book effective tax rate?

EXTENDER

26. Rufus Enterprises acquires another corporation. This acquisition created $10 million of goodwill for both book and tax purposes. The $10 million in goodwill is amortized over 15 years for tax purposes but is not deductible for book purposes unless impaired. Will this book-tax difference create a permanent or temporary difference?

Decision Making

27. Lydia is the CFO of FarmTime, Inc. FarmTime's tax advisers have recommended two tax planning ideas that will each provide $8 million of current-year cash tax savings. One idea is based on a timing difference and is expected to reverse 20 years in the future. The other idea creates a permanent difference that will never reverse. Determine whether these ideas will allow FarmTime to reduce its reported book income tax expense for the current year. Illustrate your preference for one planning strategy over the other in a spreadsheet. Which idea will you recommend to Lydia?

Communications

28. Sam Taggart, the CEO of Skate, Inc., has reviewed Skate's tax return and its financial statement. He notices that both the Schedule M–1 and the rate reconciliation in the income tax note provide a reconciliation of tax information. However, he sees very little correspondence between the two schedules. Outline the differences between these two schedules in a letter to Sam. Skate's address is 499 Lucerne Avenue, Ocala, FL 34482.

BRIDGE DISCIPLINE

1. Using publicly available Web resources, locate summary financial information for two companies in the same industry. Compare and contrast the following items across the two companies: debt-to-equity ratio, return on assets, return on equity, inventory turnover ratio, and effective tax rate.

Research Problems

Internet Activity

Use the tax resources of the Internet to address the following questions. Do not restrict your search to the World Wide Web, but include a review of newsgroups and general reference materials, practitioner sites and resources, primary sources of the tax law, chat rooms, discussion groups, and other opportunities.

Communications

Research Problem 1. Locate the Web page of Citizens for Tax Justice and find the report "Corporate Income Taxes in the 1990s." Using this report, identify the effective tax rates of three companies, as estimated in the report. Also locate the financial statements of these three companies (using the companies' Web sites or the SEC's Web site **http://www.sec.gov**). From the financial statement income tax note, identify the reported effective tax rate from the rate reconciliation for each company. Compare and contrast the financial statement effective tax rates with those estimated by the Citizens for Tax Justice report. Summarize this information in an e-mail to your instructor.

Communications

Research Problem 2. Locate the most recent financial statements of two companies in the same industry using the companies' Web sites or the SEC's Web site (**http://www.sec.gov**). Perform a benchmarking analysis of the two companies' effective tax rates, components of the effective tax rate reconciliation, levels of deferred tax assets and liabilities, and other relevant data. Summarize this information in an e-mail to your instructor.

PART 2

Advanced Entity Issues

In Part II we examine the tax effects of transactions and elections encountered only infrequently by business taxpayers. Capital changes in the stock of a corporation, the interests in a partnership, or the membership of a limited liability entity bring into play a number of issues as to the timing and recognition of gain and loss items. The election to file a consolidated return also offers the conglomerate several opportunities to manage the tax liability effectively.

CHAPTER 3

Corporations: Stock Redemptions and Liquidations

LEARNING OBJECTIVES

After completing Chapter 3, you should be able to:

LO.1
Identify the stock redemptions that qualify for sale or exchange treatment.

LO.2
Understand the tax impact of stock redemptions on the distributing corporation.

LO.3
Recognize the restrictions on sale or exchange treatment for certain redemption-like transactions.

LO.4
Understand the tax consequences of complete liquidations for both the corporation and its shareholders.

LO.5
Understand the tax consequences of a subsidiary liquidation for both the parent and the subsidiary corporations.

OUTLINE

TAX TALK

Nuclear physics is much easier than tax law. It's rational and always works the same way.

—Jerold Rochwald, Physicist

Corporate earnings are subject to taxation at the entity level and then, when distributed as dividends, at the shareholder level. Even though the maximum tax rate on dividends is only 15 percent for individuals, this second level of taxation still creates incentives for corporations and shareholders to devise methods for distributing earnings in ways other than as dividends. One method is for the shareholders to sell their stock back to the corporation. Assuming that they held the stock for more than one year, noncorporate shareholders will be taxed at the special capital gain rates on the difference between the amounts received and their basis in the stock sold. Thus, the shareholders receive the return of their basis in the stock tax-free. The liquidation of a corporation can also provide this same preferential treatment because the corporation is acquiring all of its stock and distributing all of its assets.

For corporate shareholders, however, receiving dividend distributions may be more beneficial than sale or exchange treatment. The ability to reduce the dividends by a 70, 80, or 100 percent dividends received deduction can cause the taxable portion to be less than the gain recognized from a sale or exchange. In some situations, though, such as when a shareholder has a recognized loss, a sale of stock would be preferred to dividend treatment.

The preferences of the shareholders can conflict and may vary depending on the circumstances surrounding a distribution. Consequently, tax planning for corporate distributions, either during the corporation's continuing operation or upon its liquidation, must consider the preferences of the various shareholders at the time of the transaction. This chapter addresses the tax rules related to corporate stock redemptions and liquidations.

LO.1

Identify the stock redemptions that qualify for sale or exchange treatment.

Stock Redemptions—In General

In a **stock redemption,** a corporation distributes cash or other property in exchange for a shareholder's stock in the corporation. Except for the fact that the shareholder is selling the stock back to the issuing corporation, a stock redemption resembles a sale of stock to an unrelated third party. While a sale of stock to an outsider invariably results in sale or exchange treatment, only a *qualifying* stock redemption is treated as a sale for tax purposes. A nonqualified stock redemption generally has the same effect as a dividend distribution and is taxed as such.

Stock redemptions occur for a variety of reasons. For instance, a redemption is often used to acquire the stock of a retiring or deceased shareholder. Having the corporation provide the funds to purchase the stock relieves the remaining shareholders of the need to use their own money to acquire the stock. Further, stock redemptions also occur as a result of divorce actions. Often some or all of the stock owned by a husband and/or wife must be converted to cash in order to effect the divorce property settlement. By using a stock redemption, the spouses are relieved of the need to secure funds for the property settlement.

Stock Redemptions—Sale or Exchange Treatment

Noncorporate taxpayers will generally prefer to have a stock redemption treated as a *sale or exchange* rather than as a dividend distribution. For such taxpayers, the maximum tax rate for long-term capital gains is currently 15 percent (5 percent for taxpayers in the 10 or 15 percent marginal tax bracket). The preference for qualifying stock redemption treatment is based on the fact that such transactions result in (1) the tax-free recovery of the redeemed stock's basis and (2) capital gains that can be offset by capital losses. In a nonqualified stock redemption, the *entire* distribution is taxed as dividend income [assuming adequate earnings and profits (E & P)], which, although taxed at the same rate as long-term capital gains, cannot be offset by capital losses.

EXAMPLE 1

Abby, an individual in the 35% tax bracket, acquired stock in Quail Corporation four years ago for $200,000. In the current year, Quail Corporation redeems her shares for $300,000. If the redemption qualifies for sale or exchange treatment, Abby will have a long-term capital gain of $100,000 [$300,000 (redemption amount) – $200,000 (basis)]. Her income tax liability on the $100,000 gain will be $15,000 ($100,000 × 15%). If the stock redemption does not qualify as a sale or exchange, the entire distribution will be treated as a dividend and Abby's tax liability will be $45,000 ($300,000 × 15%). Thus, Abby will save $30,000 ($45,000 – $15,000) in income taxes if the transaction is a qualifying stock redemption. ■

EXAMPLE 2

Assume that in Example 1 Abby has a capital loss carryover of $90,000 in the current tax year and no other capital transactions. If the transaction is a qualifying stock redemption, Abby can offset the entire $90,000 capital loss carryover against her $100,000 long-term capital gain. As a result, only $10,000 of the gain will be taxed, and her tax liability will be only $1,500 ($10,000 × 15%). On the other hand, if the transaction does not qualify for sale or exchange treatment, Abby will be able to deduct only $3,000 of the $90,000 capital loss carryover to offset her other (ordinary) income. ■

GLOBAL TAX ISSUES

Foreign Shareholders Prefer Sale or Exchange Treatment in Stock Redemptions

As a general rule, foreign shareholders of U.S. corporations are subject to U.S. tax on dividend income but not on capital gains. In some situations, a nonresident alien is taxed on a capital gain from the disposition of stock in a U.S. corporation, but only if the stock was effectively connected with the conduct of a U.S. trade or business of the individual. Foreign corporations are similarly taxed on gains from the sale of U.S. stock investments. Whether a stock redemption qualifies for sale or exchange treatment therefore takes on added significance for foreign shareholders. If one of the qualifying stock redemption rules can be satisfied, the foreign shareholder typically will avoid U.S. tax on the transaction. If, instead, dividend income is the result, a 30 percent withholding tax typically applies.

Corporate shareholders, however, normally receive more favorable tax treatment from a dividend distribution than from a qualifying stock redemption. The preferential tax rates applicable to dividends and long-term capital gains are not applicable to corporations. However, the dividends received deduction allows corporate shareholders to report only a small portion of the distribution as taxable income (see Chapter 2). Consequently, tax planning for stock redemptions must consider the varying preferences of corporate and noncorporate shareholders.

EXAMPLE 3

Assume that in Example 1 Abby is a corporation, that the stock represents a 40% ownership interest in Quail Corporation, and that Abby has corporate taxable income of $500,000 before the redemption transaction. If the transaction is a qualifying stock redemption, Abby has a long-term capital gain of $100,000 that will be subject to tax at 34%, or $34,000. On the other hand, if the $300,000 distribution is treated as a dividend, Abby will have a dividends received deduction of $240,000 ($300,000 × 80%), so only $60,000 of the payment will be taxed. Consequently, Abby's tax liability on the transaction will be only $20,400 ($60,000 × 34%). ■

When a loss occurs in a qualifying stock redemption, § 267 disallows recognition if the shareholder owns (directly or indirectly) more than 50 percent of the corporation's stock. The shareholder's basis in property received in any stock redemption, qualifying or not qualified, generally is the property's fair market value on the redemption date. Further, the holding period of the property begins on that date.

OVERVIEW

The Code establishes the criteria for determining whether a transaction is a qualifying stock redemption. The terminology in an agreement between the parties is not controlling, nor is state law. Currently, the following five types of stock redemptions qualify for sale or exchange treatment:

- Distributions not essentially equivalent to a dividend (not essentially equivalent redemptions).
- Distributions substantially disproportionate in terms of shareholder effect (disproportionate redemptions).
- Distributions in complete termination of a shareholder's interest (complete termination redemptions).

EXHIBIT 3–1
Stock Attribution Rules

	Deemed or Constructive Ownership
• Family	Stock owned by the spouse, children, grandchildren, and parents (not siblings or grandparents) is deemed to be owned by the individual.
• Partnership	A partner is deemed to be the owner of shares owned by a partnership to the extent of the partner's proportionate interest in the partnership.
	Stock owned by a partner is deemed to be owned in full by a partnership.
• Estate or trust	A beneficiary or heir is deemed to be the owner of shares owned by an estate or trust to the extent of the beneficiary or heir's proportionate interest in the estate or trust.
	Stock owned by a beneficiary or heir is deemed to be owned in full by an estate or trust.
• Corporation	Stock owned by a corporation is deemed to be owned proportionately by any shareholder owning 50% or more of the corporation's stock.
	Stock owned by a shareholder who owns 50% or more of a corporation is deemed to be owned in full by the corporation.

- Distributions to noncorporate shareholders in partial liquidation of a corporation (partial liquidations).
- Distributions to pay a shareholder's death taxes (redemptions to pay death taxes).

Concept Summary 3–1 at the end of this section summarizes the requirements for each of the qualifying stock redemptions.

STOCK ATTRIBUTION RULES

To qualify for sale or exchange treatment, a stock redemption generally must result in a substantial reduction in a shareholder's ownership interest in the corporation. In the absence of this reduction in ownership interest, the redemption proceeds are taxed as dividend income. In determining whether a stock redemption has sufficiently reduced a shareholder's interest, the stock owned by related parties is attributed to the redeeming shareholder.[1] Thus, the stock **attribution** rules must be considered as well as the stock redemption provisions. Under these rules, related parties are defined to include the following family members: spouses, children, grandchildren, and parents. Attribution also takes place *from* and *to* partnerships, estates, trusts, and corporations (50 percent or more ownership required in the case of regular corporations). Exhibit 3–1 summarizes the stock attribution rules.

EXAMPLE 4

Kim owns 45% of the stock in Raven Corporation, with the other 55% being held by Kim's children. For purposes of the stock attribution rules, Kim is treated as owning 100% of the stock in Raven Corporation. Kim owns 45% directly and, because of the family attribution rules, 55% indirectly. ■

[1]§ 318.

EXAMPLE 5

Chris owns 30% of the stock in Finch Corporation. The other 70% is owned by a partnership in which Chris owns a 40% interest. Chris is deemed to own 58% of Finch Corporation: 30% directly and, because of the partnership interest, 28% indirectly (40% × 70%). ■

Fortunately, the *family* attribution rules can be waived in the case of some complete termination redemptions. In addition, the stock attribution rules do not apply to partial liquidations or redemptions to pay death taxes.

NOT ESSENTIALLY EQUIVALENT REDEMPTIONS

Under § 302(b)(1), a redemption qualifies for sale or exchange treatment if it is "not essentially equivalent to a dividend." This provision applies specifically to redemptions of preferred stock because shareholders often have no control over when corporations call in such stock.[2] Since the not essentially equivalent to a dividend redemption lacks an objective test, each case must be resolved on a facts and circumstances basis.[3]

A redemption will qualify as a **not essentially equivalent redemption** only when the shareholder's interest in the redeeming corporation has been *meaningfully reduced*.[4] In determining whether a meaningful reduction has occurred, the stock attribution rules apply.

A decrease in the redeeming shareholder's voting control appears to be the most significant indicator of a meaningful reduction,[5] but reductions in the rights of redeeming shareholders to share in corporate earnings or to receive corporate assets upon liquidation are also considered.[6] The **meaningful reduction test** is applied whether common stock or preferred stock is being redeemed.

EXAMPLE 6

Sasha owns 58% of Falcon Corporation's common stock. After part of Sasha's stock is redeemed, she owns 51% of Falcon. Sasha continues to have controlling voting rights in Falcon; thus, the redemption is treated as essentially equivalent to a dividend, and Sasha has dividend income equal to the entire amount of the distribution, assuming adequate E & P. ■

EXAMPLE 7

Myna Corporation redeems 20% of its stock from Maria. Before the redemption, Maria owned 30% of Myna Corporation. In this case, the redemption may qualify as not essentially equivalent to a dividend. Maria experiences a reduction in her voting rights, her right to participate in current earnings and accumulated surplus, and her right to share in net assets upon liquidation. ■

If a redemption distribution is treated as a dividend, the basis in the stock redeemed attaches to the shareholder's remaining stock (or to stock the shareholder owns constructively).[7] This is the case in any redemption that does not satisfy the requirements of any of the qualifying stock redemption provisions.

EXAMPLE 8

Floyd and Fran, husband and wife, each own 50 shares in Grouse Corporation, representing 100% of the corporation's stock. All the stock was purchased for $50,000. Both Floyd and Fran serve as directors of the corporation. The corporation redeems Floyd's 50 shares. Floyd continues to serve as a director of the corporation. The redemption is treated as a taxable dividend (assuming adequate E & P) because Floyd constructively owns Fran's stock. Floyd's

---

[2]See S.Rept. No. 1622, 83d Cong., 2d Sess. 44 (1954).
[3]Reg. § 1.302–2(b).
[4]*U.S. v. Davis*, 70–1 USTC ¶9289, 25 AFTR2d 70–827, 90 S.Ct. 1041 (USSC, 1970).
[5]See, for example, *Jack Paparo*, 71 T.C. 692 (1979).
[6]See, for example, *Grabowski Trust*, 58 T.C. 650 (1972).
[7]Reg. § 1.302–2(c).

TAX IN THE NEWS

PUBLICLY TRADED STOCK REDEMPTIONS TYPICALLY RESULT IN SALE OR EXCHANGE TREATMENT

Publicly traded corporations often repurchase their shares in the marketplace. These stock buybacks occur for a variety of reasons. For example, Metrocall Holdings, Inc., recently announced a redemption of $20 million of its 15 percent cumulative preferred stock outstanding. The redemption, which closely followed the corporation's retirement of all its long-term debt obligations, is part of an overall plan to create more value for its common stock shareholders. Because the stock of publicly traded corporations is widely held, redemptions of such stock typically qualify for sale or exchange treatment for the shareholders, often as not essentially equivalent redemptions.

basis in the 50 shares redeemed, $25,000, attaches to Fran's stock. She then has a basis of $50,000 in the 50 shares she owns in Grouse. ■

DISPROPORTIONATE REDEMPTIONS

A stock redemption qualifies for sale or exchange treatment under § 302(b)(2) as a **disproportionate redemption** if the following conditions are met:

- The distribution is substantially disproportionate. To be substantially disproportionate, the shareholder must own, after the distribution, *less than* 80 percent of the interest owned in the corporation before the redemption. For example, if a shareholder owns a 60 percent interest in a corporation that redeems part of the stock, the redemption is substantially disproportionate only if the shareholder's ownership interest after the redemption is less than 48 percent (80 percent of 60 percent).
- The shareholder owns, after the distribution, *less than* 50 percent of the total combined voting power of all classes of stock entitled to vote.

In determining a shareholder's ownership interest before and after a redemption, the attribution rules apply.

EXAMPLE 9

Amir, Olga, and Dan, unrelated individuals, own 30 shares, 30 shares, and 40 shares, respectively, in Wren Corporation. Wren has E & P of $800,000. The corporation redeems 20 shares of Dan's stock for $60,000. Dan paid $500 a share for the stock two years ago. Dan's ownership in Wren Corporation before and after the redemption is as follows:

	Total Shares	Dan's Ownership	Ownership Percentage	80% of Original Ownership
Before redemption	100	40	40% (40 ÷ 100)	32% (80% × 40%)
After redemption	80	20	25% (20 ÷ 80)*	

*Note that the denominator of the fraction is reduced after the redemption (from 100 to 80).

Dan's 25% ownership after the redemption meets both tests of § 302(b)(2). It is less than 80% of his original ownership and less than 50% of the total voting power. The distribution therefore qualifies as a disproportionate redemption and receives sale or exchange treatment. As a result, Dan has a long-term capital gain of $50,000 [$60,000 – $10,000 (20 shares × $500)]. ■

TAX IN THE NEWS

Final Regulations Provide Clarity and Flexibility to Divorce-Related Stock Redemptions

When divorcing spouses are shareholders in a closely held corporation, the shareholder interest of one spouse (the "retiring spouse") is typically bought out, either by the other spouse (the "remaining spouse") or by the corporation. Until recently, when a stock redemption was used for the buyout, the proper tax treatment accorded the transaction was uncertain. If a stock redemption was used to satisfy a buyout obligation of the remaining spouse, the IRS might argue that the redemption constituted a constructive dividend to that spouse. The remaining spouse would counter that the redemption was a tax-free transfer incident to divorce under § 1041. Recently, final Regulations for § 1041 were issued that should clear up much of the uncertainty and provide increased flexibility for taxpayers to control the tax treatment of divorce-related stock redemptions. These Regulations allow the spouses to establish in a written agreement (e.g., divorce agreement) which spouse will be taxed on the redemption.

EXAMPLE 10

Assume that Amir and Dan are father and son. The redemption described above would not qualify for sale or exchange treatment because of the effect of the attribution rules. Dan is deemed to own Amir's stock before and after the redemption. Dan's ownership in Wren Corporation before and after the redemption is as follows:

	Total Shares	Dan's Direct Ownership	Amir's Ownership	Dan's Direct and Indirect Ownership	Ownership Percentage	80% of Original Ownership
Before redemption	100	40	30	70	70% (70 ÷ 100)	56% (80% × 70%)
After redemption	80	20	30	50	62.5% (50 ÷ 80)	

Dan's direct and indirect ownership of 62.5% fails to meet either of the tests of § 302(b)(2). After the redemption, Dan owns more than 80% of his original ownership and more than 50% of the voting stock. Thus, the redemption does not qualify for sale or exchange treatment and results in a dividend distribution of $60,000 to Dan. The basis in the 20 shares redeemed is added to Dan's basis in his remaining 20 shares. ■

Even if a redemption does not qualify as a disproportionate redemption, it may still qualify as a not essentially equivalent redemption if it meets the meaningful reduction test (see Example 7). A reduction in voting control when the shareholder does not have a majority controlling interest may qualify as a not essentially equivalent redemption. However, the stock attribution rules apply in determining whether there has been a reduction in voting control.

COMPLETE TERMINATION REDEMPTIONS

A stock redemption that terminates a shareholder's *entire* stock ownership in a corporation will qualify for sale or exchange treatment under § 302(b)(3). The attribution rules generally apply in determining whether the shareholder's stock ownership has been completely terminated. However, the *family* attribution rules do not apply to a **complete termination redemption** if the following conditions are met:

- The former shareholder has no interest, other than that of a creditor, in the corporation for at least 10 years after the redemption. An interest includes being an officer, director, or employee.
- The former shareholder files an agreement to notify the IRS of any prohibited interest acquired within the 10-year period and to retain all necessary records pertaining to the redemption during this time period. Stock acquired by bequest or inheritance will not constitute a prohibited interest.

EXAMPLE 11

Lemar owns 50% of the stock in Flicker Corporation while the remaining interest in Flicker is held as follows: 40% by Wilma (Lemar's wife) and 10% by Carmen (a key employee). Flicker redeems all of Lemar's stock for its fair market value. As a result, Wilma and Carmen are the only remaining shareholders, now owning 80% and 20%, respectively. If the requirements for the family attribution waiver are met, the transaction will qualify as a complete termination redemption and result in sale or exchange treatment. If the waiver is not allowed, Lemar will be deemed to own Wilma's (his wife's) stock, and the entire distribution will be a dividend, assuming adequate E & P. ■

EXAMPLE 12

Assume that in Example 11 Lemar qualifies for the family attribution waiver for the redemption. In the year of the redemption, Lemar treats the transaction as a sale or exchange. However, if he purchases Carmen's stock seven years after the redemption, he has acquired a prohibited interest, and the redemption distribution is reclassified as a dividend. Lemar owes additional taxes due to this revised treatment. ■

EXAMPLE 13

Assume that in Example 12 Lemar inherits Carmen's stock rather than purchasing it. Since Lemar did not have control over his acquisition of the stock through inheritance, he has not received a prohibited interest. The former redemption treatment is not affected by the inheritance. ■

PARTIAL LIQUIDATIONS

Under § 302(b)(4), a *noncorporate* shareholder is allowed sale or exchange treatment for a distribution that qualifies as a **partial liquidation.** A partial liquidation is a distribution that (1) is *not essentially equivalent to a dividend* and (2) is both pursuant to a plan and made within the plan year or within the succeeding taxable year. There is no requirement that stock actually be redeemed in a partial liquidation. If there is a redemption pursuant to a partial liquidation, the redemption may be pro rata with respect to the shareholders.

In determining whether a distribution is not essentially equivalent to a dividend, the effect of the distribution on the *corporation* is examined.[8] As a result, to qualify as a partial liquidation, the distribution must result in a *genuine contraction* of the business of the corporation.

EXAMPLE 14

Dove Corporation owned a building with seven floors. Part of the building was rented, and part was used directly in Dove's business. A fire destroyed the two top floors, and Dove received insurance proceeds in reimbursement for the damage sustained. For business reasons, Dove did not rebuild the two floors, but chose to operate on a smaller scale than before the fire. Pursuant to a plan adopted in the current year, Dove uses unreinvested insurance proceeds to redeem some stock from its shareholders. The distribution is not essentially equivalent to a dividend at the corporate level and qualifies as a partial liquidation.[9] ■

Applying the genuine contraction of a corporate business concept has proved difficult due to the lack of objective tests. The IRS has ruled that using proceeds

[8] § 302(e).

[9] See *Joseph W. Imler*, 11 T.C. 836 (1948) and Reg. § 1.346–1(a)(2).

from the sale of investments or excess inventory to redeem part of the shareholders' stock will not qualify.[10] To minimize uncertainty, the genuine contraction test should be relied upon only after obtaining a favorable ruling from the IRS.

A safe-harbor rule, the *termination of an active business* test, will satisfy the not essentially equivalent to a dividend requirement. Unlike the contraction test, the termination of an active business test has objective requirements. A distribution will qualify under the termination of an active business test if the following conditions are met:

- The corporation has two or more trades or businesses that (1) have been in existence for the five-year period ending on the date of the redemption and (2) were not acquired in taxable transactions during that period ("qualified trades or businesses").
- The corporation terminates one qualified trade or business while continuing another qualified trade or business.

The distribution can be in the form of the assets of the terminated business or the proceeds from the sale of such assets.

EXAMPLE 15

Loon Corporation owns and operates a wholesale grocery business. Since it has a substantial amount of excess cash, Loon purchases a freight-hauling concern. Six years later, Loon distributes the freight-hauling assets in kind on a pro rata basis to all its noncorporate shareholders. The distribution satisfies the requirements of the termination of an active business test. Loon conducted the freight-hauling business for at least five years and continues to conduct the wholesale grocery business. Thus, the distribution qualifies as a partial liquidation and is treated as a sale or exchange to the shareholders. ■

REDEMPTIONS TO PAY DEATH TAXES

Section 303 provides sale or exchange treatment when stock of a closely held corporation that represents a substantial portion of a decedent's gross estate is redeemed. The purpose of this provision is to provide an estate with liquidity to pay death-related expenses. Often closely held stock is not easily marketable, so a stock redemption represents the only viable option for its disposition. The redemption might not otherwise qualify for sale or exchange treatment under the § 302 redemption rules because of the stock attribution rules. The attribution of stock from individuals (the beneficiaries) to an entity (the estate) cannot be waived under the complete termination redemption rules. Fortunately, § 303 does not require the application of the attribution rules.

Generally, little to no income taxes are associated with the **redemption to pay death taxes.** The income tax basis of property owned by an estate is the property's fair market value on the date of death (or alternate valuation date if available and if elected).[11] Therefore, in a redemption to pay death taxes, the redemption price generally equals (or approximates) the basis of the stock.

Section 303 applies only to redemptions of stock where the value of that one corporation's stock in the gross estate of a decedent *exceeds* 35 percent of the value of the adjusted gross estate. (For a definition of "gross estate" and "adjusted gross estate," see the Glossary of Tax Terms in Appendix C.) The sale or exchange treatment is limited to the sum of the estate taxes, funeral costs, and administration expenses. Redemptions in excess of this sum may qualify under one of the § 302 provisions.

---

[10] Rev.Rul. 60–322, 1960–2 C.B. 118.

[11] § 1014(a).

EXAMPLE 16

Juan's adjusted gross estate is $4 million. The death taxes, funeral costs, and administration expenses of the estate total $400,000. Included in the gross estate is stock of Sparrow Corporation valued at $1.5 million. Juan had acquired the stock years ago at a cost of $500,000. Sparrow redeems $400,000 of the stock from Juan's estate. Because the value of the Sparrow stock in Juan's estate exceeds the 35% threshold ($1.5 million ÷ $4 million = 37.5%), the redemption qualifies under § 303 as a sale or exchange to Juan's estate. Assuming the value of the stock has remained unchanged since the date of Juan's death, there is no recognized gain (or loss) on the redemption [$400,000 (amount realized) – $400,000 (stock basis)]. ■

In determining whether stock value exceeds 35 percent of the adjusted gross estate, the stock of two or more corporations may be treated as the stock of a single corporation. Stock of corporations in which the decedent held a 20 percent or more interest is treated as stock of a single corporation for this purpose.[12] When this exception is used, the stock redeemed can be that of any of the 20 percent or more shareholder interests.

EXAMPLE 17

The adjusted gross estate of a decedent is $3 million. The gross estate includes stock of Owl and Robin Corporations valued at $700,000 and $650,000, respectively. Unless the two corporations are treated as a single corporation, § 303 does not apply to a redemption of the stock of either corporation. Assuming the decedent owned all the stock of Owl and 80% of the stock of Robin, § 303 applies because the decedent's estate includes a 20% or more interest in the stock of each corporation. The 35% test is met when the stock of Owl and Robin is treated as that of a single corporation [($700,000 + $650,000) ÷ $3,000,000 = 45%]. The stock of Owl or Robin (or both) can be redeemed under § 303. ■

PLANNING STRATEGIES

Stock Redemptions

FRAMEWORK FOCUS: TAX RATE

STRATEGY ➤ **CONTROL THE CHARACTER OF INCOME AND DEDUCTIONS.**

Stock redemptions offer several possibilities for tax planning:

- The alternative to a qualifying stock redemption is dividend treatment. The preferential tax rates for dividends reduce some of the negative consequences of a redemption being classified as nonqualified. Further, a nonqualified redemption may even be preferable if the distributing corporation has little or no E & P or the distributee-shareholder is another corporation. In the latter situation, dividend treatment may be preferred due to the availability of the dividends received deduction.
- Stock redemptions are particularly well suited for purchasing the interest of a retiring or deceased shareholder. Rather than the remaining shareholders buying the stock of the retiring or deceased shareholder, the corporation uses its funds to redeem the stock from the retiring shareholder or from the decedent shareholder's estate. The ability to use the corporation's funds to buy out a shareholder's interest is also advantageous in property settlements between divorcing taxpayers.
- A third party who wishes to purchase all the stock of a corporation can use a stock redemption to obtain the needed purchase money. This technique is referred to as a "bootstrap acquisition." The third party first purchases a small amount of stock from the shareholders. The corporation then redeems all of its outstanding stock except that of the third party. The third party becomes the sole shareholder of the corporation, but the corporation furnished most of the purchase money.
- A not essentially equivalent redemption provides minimal utility and generally should be relied upon only

[12] § 303(b)(2)(B).

as a last resort. Instead, the redemption should be structured to satisfy the objective tests required of one of the other qualifying redemptions. These include disproportionate redemptions, complete termination redemptions, or redemptions to pay death taxes.

- The timing and sequence of a redemption should be handled carefully, as illustrated in the following example.

EXAMPLE 18

Vulture Corporation's stock is held as follows: Alma (60 shares), Antonio (20 shares), and Ali (20 shares). Alma, Antonio, and Ali are not related to each other. The corporation redeems 24 of Alma's shares. Shortly thereafter, it redeems 5 of Antonio's shares. Does Alma's redemption qualify as a disproportionate redemption? Taken in isolation, it would appear to meet the 80% and 50% tests. Yet, if the IRS takes into account the later redemption of Antonio's shares, Alma has not satisfied the 50% test; she still owns $36/71$ of the corporation after the two redemptions. A greater time lag between the redemptions places Alma in a better position to argue against collapsing the two redemptions as parts of one integrated plan. ■

- For a family corporation in which all of the shareholders are related to each other, the only hope of achieving sale or exchange treatment may lie in the use of a redemption that completely terminates a shareholder's interest or one that follows a shareholder's death. In a complete termination redemption, it is important that the family stock attribution rules be avoided. Here, strict compliance with the requirements for the family attribution waiver (e.g., the withdrawing shareholder does not acquire a prohibited interest in the corporation within 10 years) is crucial.
- In a redemption to pay death taxes, the amount to be sheltered from dividend treatment is limited to the sum of death taxes, funeral costs, and administration expenses. However, a redemption in excess of the limitation does not destroy the applicability of § 303. Additionally, if the transaction is structured properly, the excess amount may qualify for sale or exchange treatment under one of the other redemption rules.

LO.2

Understand the tax impact of stock redemptions on the distributing corporation.

Effect on the Corporation Redeeming Its Stock

Thus far, the discussion has focused on the effect of stock redemptions on the *shareholder*. If sale or exchange treatment is allowed for the shareholder, what is the tax effect on the *corporation* redeeming its stock? Does the corporation recognize gain or loss on property other than cash distributed in the redemption? Also, what effect does the redemption have on the corporation's E & P? Furthermore, can the corporation deduct expenditures incurred in the redemption of its stock? These matters are discussed in the following paragraphs.

RECOGNITION OF GAIN OR LOSS

Section 311 provides that corporations are taxed on all nonliquidating distributions of appreciated property as if the property had been sold at its fair market value. This is the case for all stock redemptions, whether they are qualifying or not. Losses, however, are not recognized on nonliquidating distributions. When distributed property is subject to a corporate liability, the fair market value of that property is treated as not being less than the amount of the liability.

EXAMPLE 19

In a stock redemption, Blackbird Corporation transfers land (basis of $80,000, fair market value of $300,000) to a shareholder. Blackbird recognizes a $220,000 gain ($300,000 – $80,000). ■

EXAMPLE 20

Warbler Corporation makes a redemption distribution with assets having a basis of $20,000 and a fair market value of $60,000. A loan associated with the assets exists in the amount of $70,000. For gain recognition purposes, the fair market value is equal to the liability, or $70,000. Thus, Warbler has a gain of $50,000 ($70,000 – $20,000). If, instead, the basis of the assets was $90,000, no loss would be recognized. ■

CONCEPT SUMMARY 3–1

Summary of the Qualifying Stock Redemption Rules

Type of Redemption	Requirements to Qualify
Not essentially equivalent to a dividend [§ 302(b)(1)]	Meaningful reduction in shareholder's voting interest. If less than a majority interest, reduction in interest in assets and E & P also considered. Stock attribution rules apply.
Substantially disproportionate [§ 302(b)(2)]	Shareholder's interest in the corporation, after the redemption, must be less than 80% of interest before the redemption and less than 50% of total combined voting power of all classes of stock entitled to vote. Stock attribution rules apply.
Complete termination [§ 302(b)(3)]	Entire stock ownership terminated. In general, stock attribution rules apply. However, *family* stock attribution rules may be waived. Former shareholder must have no interest, other than as a creditor, in the corporation for at least 10 years and must file an agreement to notify the IRS of any prohibited interest acquired during 10-year period. Shareholder must retain all necessary records during 10-year period.
Partial liquidation [§ 302(b)(4)]	Not essentially equivalent to a dividend at corporate level. • Genuine contraction of corporation's business. • Termination of an active business. • Corporation has two or more qualified trades or businesses. • Corporation terminates one qualified trade or business while continuing another qualified trade or business. Distribution may be in form of cash or property. Redemption may be pro rata. Attribution rules do not apply.
Redemption to pay death taxes [§ 303]	Value of one corporation's stock owned by decedent exceeds 35% of value of adjusted gross estate. • Stock of two or more corporations treated as stock of a single corporation in applying the 35% test if decedent held a 20% or more interest in the stock of the corporations. Redemption limited to amount of death taxes, funeral costs, and administration expenses. Generally tax-free because tax basis of stock is FMV on date of decedent's death and value is unchanged at redemption.

Since losses are disallowed, property with a basis greater than its fair market value should not be distributed in a stock redemption. Instead, the corporation could sell the property in a taxable transaction, thereby ensuring loss recognition. It could then distribute the proceeds.

EFFECT ON EARNINGS AND PROFITS

The E & P account of a corporation is reduced by a qualifying stock redemption. The amount by which E & P is reduced cannot exceed the ratable share of the E & P attributable to the redeemed stock.[13]

[13] § 312(n)(7).

EXAMPLE 21

Jay Corporation has 100 shares of stock outstanding. It redeems 30 shares for $100,000 at a time when it has paid-in capital of $120,000 and E & P of $150,000. The charge to E & P is 30% of the amount in the E & P account ($45,000), and the remainder of the redemption price ($55,000) is a reduction of the capital account. If, instead, the 30 shares were redeemed for $40,000, the charge to E & P would be limited to $40,000, the amount paid by the corporation for the stock. ■

REDEMPTION EXPENDITURES

In redeeming its shares, a corporation may incur certain expenditures such as accounting, brokerage, legal, and loan fees. Section 162(k) specifically denies a deduction for expenditures incurred in a stock redemption.

LO.3

Recognize the restrictions on sale or exchange treatment for certain redemption-like transactions.

Stock Redemptions—Additional Limitations

Stock redemptions that do not fall under any of the qualifying stock redemption provisions are treated as dividend distributions to the extent of E & P. Resourceful taxpayers, however, devised ways to circumvent the redemption provisions. Two types of these transactions involved structuring what was, in effect, a stock redemption or a dividend distribution as a sale of the stock. The widespread use of these approaches to obtain sale or exchange treatment led to the enactment of § 306, dealing with preferred stock bailouts, and § 304, dealing with sales of stock to related corporations. The relevant loophole-closing provisions are covered next.

PREFERRED STOCK BAILOUTS

When a corporation's stock is owned entirely (or predominantly) by a few family members and/or related entities, the attribution rules severely limit the opportunities for effecting a qualifying stock redemption. Nevertheless, clever tax advisers devised a scheme called the **preferred stock bailout** in an attempt to obtain the benefits of a qualifying stock redemption without the attendant limitations.[14] Under this scheme, a corporation issues a nontaxable (nonvoting) preferred stock dividend on common stock.[15] The shareholder assigns a portion of his or her basis in the common stock to the preferred stock. The shareholder then sells the preferred stock to a third party. Unlike a sale of common shares, the sale of preferred stock does not reduce the shareholder's percentage ownership in the corporation. Since the transaction does not take the form of a stock redemption, the related limitations on sale or exchange treatment do not apply. The difference between the selling price and the shareholder's basis is a capital gain. At a later date, the corporation redeems the stock purchased by the third party in a complete termination of its interest. The result is a bailout of corporate profits as a capital gain. No diminution in control of the corporation occurs because the voting common stock remains intact.

Tax Treatment of Preferred Stock Bailouts. The tax avoidance possibilities of the preferred stock bailout led to the enactment of § 306. When § 306 stock is sold to a third party, the tax consequences are as follows:

- The shareholder has ordinary income on the sale equal to the fair market value of the preferred stock on the date of the stock dividend. However, the ordinary income amount is limited to the amount that would have been a

[14] See, e.g., *Chamberlin v. Comm.*, 53–2 USTC ¶9576, 44 AFTR 494, 207 F.2d 462 (CA–6, 1953) *cert. den.* 74 S.Ct. 516 (USSC, 1954).

[15] § 305(a).

dividend had the corporation distributed cash in lieu of stock (the "§ 306 taint").[16] If the selling price of the preferred stock exceeds the § 306 taint, the excess is an untaxed return of capital that reduces the shareholder's basis in the preferred stock. Any excess received over the § 306 taint and the preferred stock's basis is capital gain.

- The ordinary income to the shareholder is *not a dividend* and has no effect on the issuing corporation's E & P. In this respect, the statutory solution leads to a harsher result than does a taxable dividend distribution. However, the ordinary income is *treated* as a dividend for purposes of the 15 percent (or 5 percent) maximum tax rate on dividends.
- No loss is recognized on any sale of the preferred stock by the shareholder.[17] Instead, any unrecovered basis in the preferred stock sold is added to the basis of the shareholder's common stock.[18]
- Section 306 does not apply to stock sales that terminate the shareholder's entire stock interest (§ 318 attribution rules apply) or result from the complete liquidation of the corporation.[19]

EXAMPLE 22

As of January 1 of the current year, Tern Corporation has E & P of $150,000. Naomi owns all of Tern's common stock (100 shares) with a basis of $60,000. On that date, Tern declares and issues a nontaxable preferred stock dividend of 100 shares. After the dividend, the fair market value of one share of common is $2,000, and the fair market value of one share of preferred is $1,000. Two days later, Naomi sells the 100 shares of preferred stock to Emily for $100,000. Section 306 produces the following results:

- After the distribution and before the sale, the preferred stock has a basis to Naomi of $20,000 [($100,000 value of preferred ÷ $300,000 value of preferred and common) × $60,000 (the original basis of the common stock)]. At this time, the common stock has a new basis of $40,000.
- The sale of the preferred stock generates $100,000 of ordinary income to Naomi. This is the amount of dividend income Naomi would have recognized had cash been distributed instead of preferred stock (i.e., the § 306 taint). The preferential dividend tax rates apply to the $100,000.
- The $20,000 basis allocated to the preferred stock is added to the basis of the common stock; thus, the common stock basis returns to $60,000.
- Tern Corporation's E & P account is unaffected by either the stock dividend or its subsequent sale. ■

EXAMPLE 23

Assume in Example 22 that Tern Corporation's E & P is only $50,000 on the date the preferred stock is distributed. Under these circumstances, the $100,000 sale proceeds are accounted for as follows: $50,000 ordinary income (limited to the § 306 taint), $20,000 applied against the basis of the preferred stock, and $30,000 capital gain. Whether the capital gain is long term or short term depends upon the holding period of the underlying common stock. ■

DIGGING DEEPER 1

Find more information on this topic at our Web site: ***http://wft-advanced.swlearning.com.***

Definition of § 306 Stock. Section 306 stock is stock other than common that is one of the following.

- Received as a nontaxable stock dividend,
- Has a basis determined by reference to the basis of § 306 stock (e.g., such as a gift of § 306 stock), or

[16] § 306(a)(1).
[17] § 306(a)(1)(C).
[18] Reg. § 1.306–1(b)(2) (Example 2).
[19] § 306(b).

- Received tax-free in a corporate reorganization or separation to the extent that either the effect of the transaction was substantially the same as the receipt of a stock dividend or the stock was received in exchange for § 306 stock. (Corporate reorganizations are discussed in Chapter 4.)

If a corporation has no E & P on the date of distribution of a nontaxable preferred stock dividend, the stock will not be § 306 stock.[20]

PLANNING STRATEGIES

Disposing of § 306 Stock

FRAMEWORK FOCUS: TAX RATE

STRATEGY ➤ **CONTROL THE CHARACTER OF INCOME AND DEDUCTIONS.**

Distributing the preferred stock dividend at a time when the corporation has no E & P avoids the § 306 taint altogether. Otherwise, avoiding ordinary income on the disposition of § 306 stock is a difficult feat. Unless the corporation's E & P was nominal at the time of the stock dividend (in the case of a § 306 stock sale) or at the time of the redemption (in the case of a § 306 stock redemption), the disposition of § 306 stock typically produces only ordinary income. The gifting of § 306 stock does not defeat the ordinary income taint as the taint remains with the stock. Further, under § 170(e), the deduction for a charitable contribution of § 306 stock must be reduced by the ordinary income taint.

The sale of § 306 stock in a transaction that terminates the shareholder's entire stock interest in the corporation will avoid ordinary income treatment, as will a disposition in liquidation of the corporation. Similarly, a redemption of § 306 stock in a complete termination redemption or a partial liquidation avoids the ordinary income result. However, these exceptions are of limited use in the typical disposition of § 306 stock.

DIGGING DEEPER 2 DIGGING DEEPER 3

Find more information on these topics at our Web site: ***http://wft-advanced.swlearning.com.***

LO.4

Understand the tax consequences of complete liquidations for both the corporation and its shareholders.

Liquidations—In General

When a corporation makes a nonliquidating distribution, the entity typically will continue as a going concern. With a complete liquidation, however, corporate existence terminates, as does the shareholder's ownership interest. A complete liquidation, like a qualifying stock redemption, produces sale or exchange treatment to the *shareholder*. However, the tax effects of a liquidation to the *corporation* vary somewhat from those of a redemption. Sale or exchange treatment is the general rule for the liquidating corporation, although some losses are disallowed.

THE LIQUIDATION PROCESS

A **corporate liquidation** exists when a corporation ceases to be a going concern. The corporation continues solely to wind up affairs, pay debts, and distribute any remaining assets to its shareholders. Legal dissolution under state law is not required for a liquidation to be complete for tax purposes. A liquidation can exist

[20] § 306(c).

even if the corporation retains a nominal amount of assets to pay remaining debts and preserve legal status.[21]

Shareholders may decide to liquidate a corporation for one or more reasons, including the following:

- The corporate business has been unsuccessful.
- The shareholders wish to acquire the corporation's assets.
- Another person or corporation wants to purchase the corporation's assets. The purchaser may buy the shareholders' stock and then liquidate the corporation to acquire the assets. Alternatively, the purchaser may buy the assets directly from the corporation. After the assets are sold, the corporation distributes the sales proceeds to its shareholders and liquidates.

As one might expect, the different means used to liquidate a corporation produce varying tax results.

LIQUIDATIONS AND OTHER DISTRIBUTIONS COMPARED

Like a qualifying stock redemption, a complete liquidation produces sale or exchange treatment for the shareholders. Similarly, E & P has no impact on the gain or loss to be recognized by the shareholder in either type of distribution.[22] However, a complete liquidation produces different tax consequences to the liquidating corporation. With certain exceptions, a liquidating corporation recognizes gain *and* loss upon the distribution of its assets.

EXAMPLE 24

Pursuant to a plan of complete liquidation, Goose Corporation distributes equipment to Kareem who owns 20% of Goose's stock. The equipment has an adjusted basis of $80,000 and a fair market value of $50,000. Goose recognizes a $30,000 loss on the liquidating distribution. ■

In the event a corporate distribution results in a *loss* to the shareholder, an important distinction exists between qualifying stock redemptions and liquidations. Section 267 disallows recognition of losses between related parties in qualifying stock redemptions but not in complete liquidations.

EXAMPLE 25

Hawk Corporation is owned equally by Raji, Sam, and Tara Corporation. Raji is the sole shareholder of Tara and is not related to Sam. Hawk makes a distribution of $50,000 to Raji in cancellation of all of his shares. Raji's basis in his stock is $60,000. Whether Raji recognizes the $10,000 loss depends on the type of distribution he received. If it is a stock redemption in complete termination of his interest, he cannot recognize the loss because under the attribution rules he is treated as owning what Tara Corporation owns. Since Raji owns 66⅔% of the stock (actual plus constructive ownership), § 267 disallows the loss. However, if the distribution qualifies as a complete liquidation distribution, Raji may recognize the $10,000 loss because § 267 does not apply to liquidating distributions. ■

The rules governing the basis of property received from the corporation are identical for both liquidations and stock redemptions. Section 334(a) specifies that the basis of property received in a complete liquidation is its fair market value on the date of distribution.

---

[21] Reg. § 1.332–2(c).

[22] § 331.

Liquidations—Effect on the Distributing Corporation

THE GENERAL RULE

Section 336(a) provides that a corporation recognizes gain or loss on the distribution of property in a complete liquidation. The property is treated as if it were sold at its fair market value. This treatment is consistent with the notion of double taxation that is inherent in operating a business as a C corporation—once at the corporate level and again at the shareholder level.

As in the case of a nonliquidating distribution, when property distributed in a complete liquidation is subject to a liability of the liquidating corporation, the fair market value used to calculate gain or loss may not be less than the amount of the liability.

PLANNING STRATEGIES

Asset Purchase versus Stock Purchase

FRAMEWORK FOCUS: THINKING OUTSIDE THE FRAMEWORK

The acquisition of a corporation's assets generally takes one of two forms. In one form, the acquiring corporation purchases the stock of the target corporation, and then the target (subsidiary) is liquidated. In the other form, the acquiring corporation purchases the assets of the target corporation, and then the target distributes the proceeds in liquidation. Nontax considerations may affect the form of acquisition, with each form having both favorable and unfavorable aspects.

An asset purchase requires that title be transferred and that creditors be notified. Further, an asset purchase may not be feasible if valuable nontransferable trademarks, contracts, or licenses are involved. Alternatively, an asset purchase may be preferable to a stock purchase if the target's shareholders refuse to sell their stock. Additionally, an asset purchase avoids the transfer of liabilities (including unknown liabilities) generally inherent in stock acquisitions. An asset purchase also has the advantage of allowing the purchaser to avoid the acquisition of unwanted assets, whereas a stock purchase would involve all of a target's assets.

There are four exceptions to the general rule of gain and loss recognition by a liquidating corporation:

- Losses are not recognized on certain liquidating distributions to related-party shareholders.
- Losses are not recognized on certain sales and liquidating distributions of property that was contributed to the corporation with a built-in loss shortly before the adoption of a plan of liquidation.
- A subsidiary corporation does not recognize gains or losses on liquidating distributions to its parent corporation.
- A subsidiary corporation does not recognize losses on liquidating distributions to its minority shareholders.

The first two exceptions, referred to as the "antistuffing rules," are discussed in the next section and are summarized in Figure 3–1 at the end of the section. The last two exceptions, covering the liquidation of a subsidiary corporation, are also discussed in this chapter.

PLANNING STRATEGIES

Corporate Liquidations

FRAMEWORK FOCUS: DEDUCTIONS

STRATEGY ➤ **MAXIMIZE DEDUCTIBLE AMOUNTS.**

FRAMEWORK FOCUS: TAX RATE

STRATEGY ➤ **SHIFT NET INCOME FROM HIGH-BRACKET TAXPAYERS TO LOW-BRACKET TAXPAYERS.**

With the exception of parent-subsidiary liquidations, distributions in liquidation are taxed at both the corporate level and the shareholder level. When a corporation liquidates, it can, as a general rule, claim losses on assets that have depreciated in value. These assets should not be distributed in the form of a property dividend or stock redemption because losses are not recognized on nonliquidating distributions.

Shareholders faced with large prospective gains in a liquidation may consider shifting part or all of that gain to other taxpayers. One approach is to donate stock to charity. A charitable contribution of the stock produces a deduction equal to the stock's fair market value. Alternatively, the stock may be given to family members. If the family member is in the 10 or 15 percent marginal income tax bracket, some or all of the gain on the liquidation could be taxed at the 5 percent preferential long-term capital gain rate. Whether these procedures will be successful in shifting the liquidation-related gain from the taxpayer depends on the timing of the transfer. If the donee of the stock is not in a position to prevent the liquidation of the corporation, the donor may be deemed to have made an anticipatory assignment of income. In such a case, the gain is still taxed to the donor. In addition, the gift tax must be considered. Hence, advance planning of stock transfers is crucial in arriving at the desired tax result.

ANTISTUFFING RULES

A transfer of property to a corporation under § 351 or as a contribution of capital results in no gain or loss recognition to either the shareholder or the corporation. The shareholder's basis in the transferred property becomes the basis in the stock received (or, in the case of a capital contribution, is added to the shareholder's existing stock basis). Additionally, the corporation's basis in the transferred property is typically the shareholder's basis in such property. Concerned that these carryover basis rules would allow taxpayers to create artificial losses in liquidation transactions, Congress enacted two loss limitation provisions.[23]

EXAMPLE 26

Nora, the sole shareholder of Canary Corporation, transfers property (basis of $10,000, fair market value of $3,000) to the corporation in a transaction that qualifies under § 351. Nora's basis in the additional stock acquired in Canary Corporation, in exchange for the property, is $10,000. Canary Corporation's basis in the property is also $10,000. A few months after the transfer, Canary Corporation adopts a plan of complete liquidation. Upon liquidation, Canary distributes the property to Nora. If Canary were permitted a loss deduction of $7,000, there would be a double loss because Nora also recognizes a loss of $7,000 upon receipt of the property [$3,000 (fair market value of the property) – $10,000 (basis in Nora's stock)]. To prevent this doubling of losses, Canary Corporation's loss on the distribution is disallowed. ■

Related-Party Loss Limitation. Losses are disallowed on distributions to *related parties* in either of the following cases:

- The distribution is *not* pro rata, or
- The property distributed is disqualified property.

[23] § 336(d).

A corporation and a shareholder are considered related if the shareholder owns (directly or indirectly) more than 50 percent in value of the corporation's outstanding stock.[24]

A *pro rata distribution* is one where *each* shareholder receives his or her share of the corporate asset distributed. *Disqualified property* is property that is acquired by the liquidating corporation in a § 351 or contribution to capital transaction during the five-year period ending on the date of the distribution. The related-party loss limitation can apply even if the property was appreciated (fair market value greater than basis) when it was transferred to the corporation.

EXAMPLE 27

Bluebird Corporation's stock is owned by Ana and Sanjay, who are unrelated. Ana owns 80% and Sanjay owns 20% of the stock in the corporation. Bluebird has the following assets (none of which were acquired in a § 351 or contribution to capital transaction) that are distributed in complete liquidation of the corporation:

	Adjusted Basis	Fair Market Value
Cash	$600,000	$600,000
Equipment	150,000	200,000
Building	400,000	200,000

Assume Bluebird Corporation distributes the equipment to Sanjay and the cash and the building to Ana. Bluebird recognizes a gain of $50,000 on the distribution of the equipment. The loss of $200,000 on the building is disallowed because the property is distributed to a related party and the distribution is not pro rata (i.e., the building is not distributed 80% to Ana and 20% to Sanjay). ■

EXAMPLE 28

Assume in Example 27 that Bluebird Corporation distributes the cash and equipment to Ana and the building to Sanjay. Again, Bluebird recognizes the $50,000 gain on the equipment. However, it now recognizes the $200,000 loss on the building because the property is not distributed to a related party (i.e., Sanjay does not own more than 50% of the stock in Bluebird Corporation). ■

EXAMPLE 29

Crane Corporation's stock is held equally by three sisters. One year before Crane's liquidation, the shareholders transfer jointly owned property (basis of $150,000, fair market value of $200,000) to the corporation in return for stock in a § 351 transaction. In liquidation, Crane transfers the property (now worth $100,000) on a pro rata basis back to the sisters. Even though the distribution is pro rata, Crane does not recognize the $50,000 loss ($100,000 fair market value – $150,000 basis). The property is considered disqualified because it was contributed within five years of the distribution date. It is distributed to related parties as each sister is considered to own 100% of the stock through attribution. ■

Built-in Loss Limitation. The loss limitation provisions are extended to sales, exchanges, or distributions to *unrelated parties* when built-in loss property (fair market value less than basis) is transferred to a corporation shortly before the corporation is liquidated. The built-in loss limitation applies when both of the following conditions are met:

- The property was acquired by the corporation in a § 351 or contribution to capital transaction.

[24]Section 267 provides the definition of related party for purposes of this provision. The rules are similar to the stock attribution rules discussed earlier in this chapter; one exception, however, is that stock owned by a sibling is treated as owned by the taxpayer under § 267.

- Such acquisition was part of a plan whose principal purpose was to recognize a loss on that property by the liquidating corporation. A tax avoidance purpose is presumed in the case of transfers occurring within two years of the adoption of a plan of liquidation.

Only the built-in loss (the amount by which the property's basis exceeded its fair market value at the time it was acquired by the corporation) is disallowed by this provision. Any loss attributable to a decline in value that occurs after the property's contribution to the corporation is recognized (subject to the related-party loss limitation).[25]

The built-in loss limitation applies to a broader range of transactions than the related-party exception. It also applies to distributions of property to any shareholder, including an unrelated party, and to a *sale or exchange* of property by a liquidating corporation. However, the limitation is narrower than the related-party exception in that it applies only to property that had a built-in loss upon its acquisition by the corporation and only as to the amount of that built-in loss.

EXAMPLE 30

On January 2, Duck Corporation acquires property (basis of $30,000, fair market value of $5,000) in a transaction that qualifies under § 351. Later in the same year, Duck adopts a plan of liquidation on July 1 and distributes the property to an unrelated shareholder on November 10, when the property is worth $1,000. Duck Corporation can recognize a loss of $4,000, the difference between the value of the property on the date of acquisition ($5,000) and the value of the property on the date of distribution ($1,000). The built-in loss of $25,000 [$5,000 (fair market value on date of acquisition) – $30,000 (basis)] is disallowed. ■

EXAMPLE 31

Assume in Example 30 that the property was worth $32,000 on the date Duck Corporation acquired the property. If the distribution is to an unrelated shareholder, Duck Corporation will recognize the entire $29,000 loss [$1,000 (fair market value on date of distribution) – $30,000 (basis)]. However, if the distribution is to a related party, Duck cannot recognize any of the loss under the related-party loss limitation. When the distribution is to a related party, the loss is disallowed even though the entire decline in value occurred during the period the corporation held the property. ■

DIGGING DEEPER 4

Find more information on this topic at our Web site: ***http://wft-advanced.swlearning.com.***

Liquidations—Effect on the Shareholder

The tax consequences to the shareholders of a corporation in the process of liquidation are governed either by the general rule of § 331 or by the exception of § 332 relating to the liquidation of a subsidiary. The general rule is discussed in this section.

THE GENERAL RULE

In the case of a complete liquidation, § 331 provides for sale or exchange treatment for the shareholders.[26] Therefore, the difference between the fair market value of the assets received from the corporation and the adjusted basis of the stock surrendered is the shareholder's recognized gain or loss. Typically, the stock is a capital asset in the hands of the shareholder, and capital gain or loss results. The burden of proof is on the taxpayer to furnish evidence as to the adjusted basis of the stock. In the

[25] § 336(d)(2).

[26] § 331(a).

■ FIGURE 3–1
Distributions of Loss Property by a Liquidating Corporation

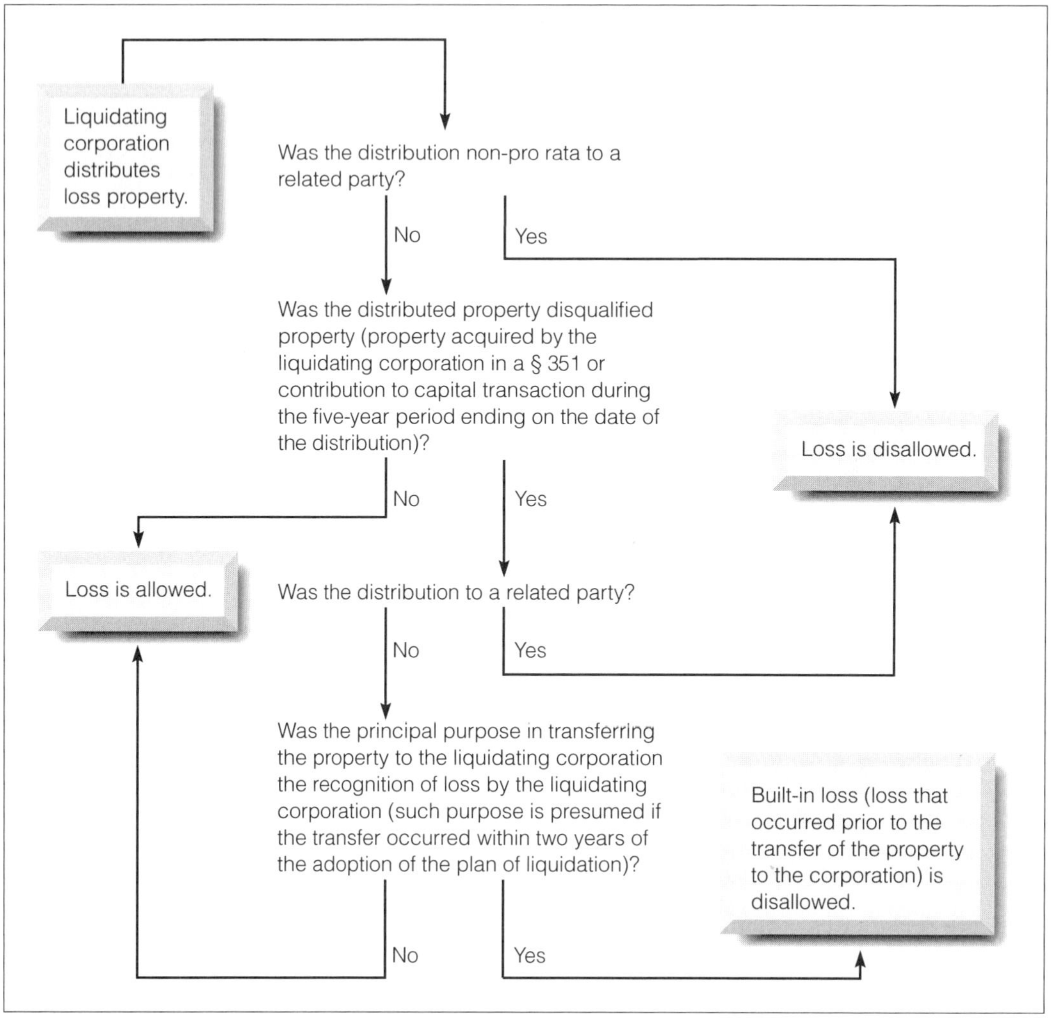

absence of such evidence, the stock is deemed to have a zero basis, and the full amount of the liquidation proceeds equals the amount of the gain recognized.[27] The basis of property received in a liquidation is the property's fair market value on the date of distribution.[28]

DIGGING DEEPER 5

Find more information on this topic at our Web site: ***http://wft-advanced.swlearning.com***.

LO.5

Understand the tax consequences of a subsidiary liquidation for both the parent and the subsidiary corporations.

Liquidations—Parent-Subsidiary Situations

Section 332, an exception to the general rule of § 331, provides that a parent corporation does *not* recognize gain or loss on a liquidation of its subsidiary. In addition, the subsidiary corporation recognizes *neither gain nor loss* on distributions of property to its parent.[29]

[27] *John Calderazzo*, 34 TCM 1, T.C.Memo. 1975–1.
[28] § 334(a).
[29] § 337(a). This is an exception to the general rule of § 336.

BRIDGE DISCIPLINE

Bridge to Finance

The usual order of payments in a liquidation is that the creditors come first, the preferred stockholders are next, and the common stockholders are last and receive whatever is left. However, a common financing tool known as liquidation preferences allows selected investors to receive a return on their investment before any of the other shareholders receive a distribution. In today's economy, a savvy venture capitalist is likely to demand these preferences. Management/shareholders should fully understand the potentially draconian consequences of granting these benefits.

In the event of a liquidation, the shareholders holding liquidation preferences receive a multiple of their original investment first. For example, a $1 million investor with a 1.5 multiple liquidation preference receives the first $1.5 million generated by a sale of the corporation's assets. This guarantee is an attractive way for the investors to limit their downside losses. But this insurance comes at the expense of preferred and common shareholders. They will have claims only on what is remaining after the preferences are fulfilled. If the liquidation proceeds are not more than the preference payments, the preferred and common shareholders will receive nothing.

There are two basic types of liquidation preferences: nonparticipating and participating. Investors holding nonparticipating preferences receive only their guaranteed multiple liquidation payment. With participating preferences, on the other hand, the selected investors are able to double-dip. They receive both their multiple preference payment and their share of the remaining proceeds based on their stock ownership. After the preference payments are made, the remaining proceeds will be distributed first to the preferred shareholders; then the common shareholders will share in any excess based on their stock ownership percentages.

The requirements for applying § 332 are as follows:

- The parent must own at least 80 percent of the voting stock of the subsidiary and at least 80 percent of the value of the subsidiary's stock.
- The subsidiary must distribute all its property in complete cancellation of all its stock within the taxable year or within three years from the close of the tax year in which the first distribution occurred.
- The subsidiary must be solvent.[30]

If these requirements are met, nonrecognition of gains and losses becomes mandatory. If the subsidiary is insolvent, the parent corporation will have an ordinary loss deduction under § 165(g).

When a series of distributions occurs in the liquidation of a subsidiary corporation, the parent corporation must own the required amount of stock (80 percent) on the date the plan of liquidation is adopted. Such ownership must continue at all times until all property has been distributed.[31] If the parent fails the control requirement at any time, the provisions for nonrecognition of gain or loss do not apply to any distribution.[32]

[30] § 332(b) and Reg. §§ 1.332–2(a) and (b).

[31] Establishing the date of the adoption of a plan of complete liquidation could be crucial in determining whether § 332 applies. See, for example, *George L. Riggs, Inc.*, 64 T.C. 474 (1975).

[32] § 332(b)(3) and Reg. § 1.332–2(a).

TAX FACT

BUSINESS TERMINATIONS AND FORMATIONS

During the year 2000, an estimated 9.7 percent of businesses in the United States failed. This means that of the approximately 5.7 million firms in existence in 2000, more than 550,000 terminated. While the most populous states, such as California and New York, had the highest number of liquidations, the state of Washington had the highest rate of failures (22 percent). Interestingly, Washington also had the highest rate of new businesses formed during 2000 (21.3 percent). Unfortunately, Washington lost ground as its percentage of formations was slightly less than its percentage of terminations. Colorado, on the other hand, had one of the highest rates for business formation (19.8 percent) and almost the lowest rate for business failures (5.9 percent).

The table below lists the states with the most terminations and the highest and lowest rates of failures; it also shows the rates of business formation for these states.

		Business Terminations		Business Formations	
State	**Number of Terminations**	**Rate**	**Rank**	**Rate**	**Rank**
California	134,500	14.8%	14	18.4%	5
New York	57,400	12.4	34	13.3	23
Texas	57,300	15.0	13	14.2	16
Washington	41,800	22.0	1	21.3	1
Utah	10,100	19.7	2	19.2	4
New Hampshire	7,300	18.8	3	12.0	30
South Dakota	1,800	8.2	49	9.7	47
Colorado	7,500	5.9	50	19.8	3
Minnesota	4,900	3.8	51	11.0	37

Source: Small Business Administration.

MINORITY SHAREHOLDER INTERESTS

A distribution of property to a minority shareholder in a liquidation otherwise governed by § 332 is treated in the same manner as a *nonliquidating* distribution. That is, the subsidiary corporation recognizes gain (but not loss) on the property distributed to the minority shareholder.[33]

EXAMPLE 32

The stock of Moa Corporation is held as follows: 80% by Mallard Corporation and 20% by Arethia. Moa is liquidated on December 10 of the current year pursuant to a plan adopted on January 10. At the time of its liquidation, Moa Corporation has assets with a basis of $100,000 and fair market value of $500,000. Moa distributes the property pro rata to Mallard Corporation and to Arethia. Moa must recognize gain of $80,000 [($500,000 fair market value – $100,000 basis) × 20% minority interest]. Since the corporate tax due in this liquidation relates entirely to the minority shareholder distribution, that amount will most likely be deducted from the $100,000 distribution ($500,000 × 20%) going to Arethia. The remaining gain of $320,000 is not recognized because it is attributable to property being distributed to Mallard, the parent corporation. ■

[33] §§ 336(a) and (d)(3).

GLOBAL TAX ISSUES

Exception to § 332 for Liquidations of U.S. Subsidiaries of Foreign Corporations

When a U.S. subsidiary is liquidated into a U.S. parent, gains (or losses) are not recognized immediately, but rather are deferred as a result of the carryover basis rule. Gains inherent in the transferred assets will be recognized upon their disposition by the parent. Foreign corporations generally are not subject to U.S. taxation, so the liquidation of a U.S. subsidiary into a foreign parent could avoid gain recognition entirely if § 332 were to apply unabated. Section 367(b) overrides § 332 when a U.S. subsidiary is liquidated into a foreign parent, however. Under § 367(b), the subsidiary will recognize gain on the transfer of certain "tainted" assets. Tainted assets include inventory, installment obligations, accounts receivable, and depreciable property (to the extent of depreciation recapture).

A minority shareholder is subject to the general rule requiring the recognition of gain or loss in a liquidation. Accordingly, the difference between the fair market value of the assets received and the basis of the minority shareholder's stock is the amount of gain or loss recognized. Further, the basis of property received by the minority shareholder is the property's fair market value on the date of distribution.[34]

INDEBTEDNESS OF THE SUBSIDIARY TO THE PARENT

If a subsidiary transfers appreciated property to its parent to satisfy a debt, it must recognize gain on the transaction unless the subsidiary is liquidating and the conditions of § 332 (discussed above) apply. When § 332 applies, the subsidiary does not recognize gain or loss upon the transfer of properties to the parent in satisfaction of indebtedness.[35]

EXAMPLE 33

Eagle Corporation owes its parent, Osprey Corporation, $20,000. It satisfies the obligation by transferring land (basis of $8,000, fair market value of $20,000). Normally, Eagle would recognize a gain of $12,000 on the transaction. However, if the transfer is made pursuant to a liquidation under § 332, Eagle does not recognize a gain. ■

DIGGING DEEPER 6

*Find more information on this topic at our Web site: **http://wft-advanced.swlearning.com**.*

BASIS OF PROPERTY RECEIVED BY THE PARENT CORPORATION—THE GENERAL RULE

Property received in the complete liquidation of a subsidiary has the same basis it had in the hands of the subsidiary.[36] Unless the parent corporation makes a § 338 election (discussed below), this carryover basis in the assets generally will differ significantly from the parent's basis in the stock of the subsidiary. Since the liquidation is a nontaxable exchange, the parent's gain or loss on the difference in basis is not recognized. Further, the parent's basis in the stock of the liquidated subsidiary disappears.

[34] § 334(a).
[35] § 337(b)(1).
[36] § 334(b)(1) and Reg. § 1.334–1(b).

TAX FACT

Liquidations by Industry

Liquidations do not occur evenly across major industries. Some industries are more likely to have liquidations than others due to the nature of their businesses. The apparel/textile industry has the highest average rate of failure whereas the personal finance and financial services industry has the lowest. The following table shows the industries with the highest and lowest average rates of business failures per 10,000 firms over the past 10 years.

Industry	Rate per 10,000 Firms
Apparel and textile	122
Furniture and fixtures	108
Transportation and utilities	107
Construction	106
Petroleum and coal	61
Services	61
Finance, insurance, and real estate	56

Source: Bureau of Census.

EXAMPLE 34

Lark Corporation purchased 85% of all classes of Heron Corporation's stock 10 years ago for $600,000. In the current year, Heron liquidates, and Lark acquires assets that are worth $500,000 and have a tax basis to Heron of $400,000. Lark takes a basis of $400,000 in the assets. Lark's $600,000 basis in Heron's stock disappears. If Lark sells the assets, it has a gain of $100,000 ($500,000 value – $400,000 basis) even though its basis in the Heron stock was $600,000. Lark's loss on its stock investment in Heron is never recognized. ■

In addition to the parent corporation taking the subsidiary's basis in its assets, the carryover rules of § 381 apply (see Chapter 4). Under that provision, the parent acquires various tax attributes of the subsidiary, including the subsidiary's net operating loss, business credit carryover, capital loss carryover, and E & P.

BASIS OF PROPERTY RECEIVED BY THE PARENT CORPORATION—§ 338 ELECTION

Background. As discussed above, the liquidation of a subsidiary generally is a nontaxable transaction, resulting in the nonrecognition of gain or loss for both the parent and the subsidiary corporation and the carryover of the subsidiary's asset bases (and other tax attributes). This treatment reflects the fact that such a liquidation often is merely a change in corporate structure and not a change in substance. This is particularly the case when the parent has owned the stock of the subsidiary since the subsidiary's inception. In such cases, the carried-over bases are comparable to what the parent would have in the subsidiary's assets if the parent, and not the subsidiary, had originally acquired the assets. However, inequities can develop when a subsidiary is liquidated shortly after its acquisition by the parent.

When a corporation acquires a controlling interest (80 percent) in another corporation over a short period of time, the acquisition cost of the stock reflects the fair market value of the subsidiary's assets (including goodwill). Generally, the

CONCEPT SUMMARY 3–2

Summary of Liquidation Rules

Effect on the Shareholder	Basis of Property Received	Effect on the Corporation
§ 331—The general rule provides for capital gain treatment on the difference between the FMV of property received and the basis of the stock in the corporation.	§ 334(a)—Basis of assets received by the shareholder will be the FMV on the date of distribution (except for installment obligations on which gain is deferred to the point of collection).	§ 336—Gain or loss is recognized for distributions in kind and for sales by the liquidating corporation. Losses are not recognized for distributions to related parties if the distribution is not pro rata or if disqualified property is distributed. Losses may be disallowed on sales and distributions of built-in loss property even if made to unrelated parties.
§ 332—In liquidation of a subsidiary, no gain or loss is recognized to the parent. Subsidiary must distribute all of its property within the taxable year or within three years from the close of the taxable year in which the first distribution occurs.	§ 334(b)(1)—Property has the same basis as it had in the hands of the subsidiary. Parent's basis in the stock disappears. Carryover rules of § 381 apply.	§ 337—No gain or loss is recognized to the subsidiary on distributions to the parent. Gain (but not loss) is recognized on distributions to minority shareholders.
	§ 338—Subsidiary need not be liquidated. If subsidiary is liquidated, parent's basis is new stepped-up (or -down) basis. Parent's basis in the stock disappears. Carryover rules of § 381 apply, but such amounts are likely to be nominal.	§ 338—Gain or loss is recognized to the subsidiary. Subsidiary is treated as a new corporation, and its basis in assets is stepped up (or down) to reflect parent's basis in subsidiary stock plus subsidiary's liabilities. New basis is allocated among various asset classes.

parent's basis in the stock of the subsidiary will vary greatly from the subsidiary's basis in its assets. Under the general rule of nonrecognition, the difference between the parent's basis in the stock and the carried-over basis in the assets is a nonrecognized gain or loss. This is the case even if the parent acquired the subsidiary stock solely to obtain the subsidiary's assets. If a parent corporation could treat the stock purchase as a purchase of the assets, it could take a basis in the assets equal to the acquisition cost of the stock. In most cases, this would mean a higher asset basis and, as a result, larger cost recovery deductions and lower gains on disposition for the parent corporation.

To obtain the stock-basis-for-asset-basis result, taxpayers successfully devised stock purchase/subsidiary liquidation transactions that fell outside the general rule.[37] Congress codified this treatment by enacting § 338, which permits the purchase of a controlling interest of stock to be treated as a purchase of the subsidiary's assets.

[37]See, e.g., *U.S. v. M.O.J. Corp.*, 60–1 USTC ¶9209, 5 AFTR2d 535, 274 F.2d 713 (CA–5, 1960). See also *Kimbell-Diamond Milling Co.*, 14 T.C. 74 (1950), *aff'd* 51–1 USTC ¶9201, 40 AFTR 328, 187 F.2d 718 (CA–5, 1951), *cert. den.* 72 S.Ct. 50 (USSC, 1951) (IRS argued stock-for-asset basis).

Requirements for Application. A corporation (the "parent") may *elect* the provisions of § 338 if it acquires stock representing at least 80 percent of the voting power and at least 80 percent of the value of another corporation (the "subsidiary") within a 12-month period (*"qualified stock purchase"*). The stock must be acquired in a taxable transaction (i.e., § 351 and other nonrecognition provisions cannot apply). An acquisition of stock by any member of an affiliated group that includes the parent corporation is considered to be an acquisition by the parent. The **§ 338 election** must be made by the fifteenth day of the ninth month beginning after the month in which a qualified stock purchase occurs. If made, the election is irrevocable.

Tax Consequences. Upon a qualified § 338 election, the subsidiary is treated as having sold its assets on the qualified stock purchase date for a value that is determined with reference to the parent's basis in the subsidiary stock plus any liabilities of the subsidiary.[38] The subsidiary is then treated as a new corporation that purchased those assets for a similarly computed amount on the day following the qualified stock purchase date.[39] The deemed sale results in gain (or loss) recognition to the subsidiary, and the deemed purchase results in a stepped-up (or -down) basis for the subsidiary's assets.[40] The subsidiary may, but need not, be liquidated. If the subsidiary is liquidated, the parent will obtain a carryover of the stepped-up (or -down) basis of the subsidiary's assets.

PLANNING STRATEGIES

Parent-Subsidiary Liquidations

FRAMEWORK FOCUS: INCOME AND EXCLUSIONS

STRATEGY ➤ AVOID INCOME RECOGNITION.

The nonrecognition provision applicable to the liquidation of a subsidiary, § 332, is not elective. Nevertheless, some flexibility may be available:

- Whether § 332 applies depends on the 80 percent stock ownership test. A parent corporation may be able to avoid § 332 by reducing its stock ownership in the subsidiary below this percentage to allow for recognition of a loss. On the other hand, the opposite approach may be desirable to avoid gain recognition. A corporate shareholder possessing less than the required 80 percent ownership may want to acquire additional stock to qualify for § 332 treatment.
- Once § 332 becomes effective, less latitude is allowed in determining the parent's basis in the subsidiary's assets. Generally, the subsidiary's existing basis in its assets carries over to the parent. If a timely § 338 election is made, the subsidiary's basis in its assets is stepped up to reflect, in part, the parent's basis in the subsidiary stock. If the subsidiary also is liquidated, the parent obtains assets with the stepped-up basis.
- An election to have the § 338 rules apply should be carefully weighed as the election can be detrimental. The tax on the subsidiary's recognized gain that results from the deemed sale of its assets is the cost under § 338 for obtaining the stepped-up basis. As a result, a § 338 election may be a viable option only when the subsidiary possesses loss and/or credit carryovers that can be used to reduce the associated tax.

[38]See §§ 338(a)(1) and (b) and Reg. § 1.338–4.

[39]See §§ 338(a)(2) and (b) and Reg. § 1.338–5.

[40]For the rules governing the allocation of the purchase price to the assets, see § 338(b)(5) and Reg. § 1.338–6.

TAX IN THE NEWS

Nature of Gain from Deemed Sale under § 338 Is a Source of Contention in State Tax Dispute

A recent decision from a Pennsylvania state court involved the nature of the gain recognized by a subsidiary corporation as a result of a § 338 election. Under Pennsylvania's Tax Code, nonbusiness income is subject to a lower corporate tax rate than business income. The taxpayer reported the fictitious gain arising from the § 338 election as nonbusiness income for purposes of its Pennsylvania corporate tax return. The Pennsylvania Department of Revenue reclassified the gain as business income and asserted a deficiency for the increased tax liability. A Department regulation clearly required the classification of § 338 gain as business income. The Commonwealth Court of Pennsylvania, however, said that the regulation was inconsistent with a decision of the Pennsylvania Supreme Court, and ruled that the gain was nonbusiness income. (See *Canteen Corp. v. Pennsylvania*, Pa. Commw. Ct., No. 856 F.R. 1997, March 6, 2003.)

A Comparison of the General Rule and the § 338 Election. Under the general rule of nonrecognition, the liquidation of a subsidiary is tax-free to both the subsidiary (except for any minority interest) and the parent corporation. Under § 338, the subsidiary recognizes gain (or loss) on the deemed disposition of its assets. The liquidation of a subsidiary remains tax-free to the parent. While a carryover basis rule applies in both cases, the subsidiary's assets generally will have a stepped-up basis as a result of the § 338 election. The liquidation of the subsidiary will result in a carryover of the stepped-up basis to the parent. Further, a liquidation of the subsidiary results in a carryover of its other tax attributes (e.g., E & P) to the parent whether or not a § 338 election is made. However, when the election is made, the subsidiary is treated as a new corporation as of the day following the qualified stock purchase date; as a result, any tax attributes acquired by the parent are likely to be nominal (or zero) in amount. The holding period of the subsidiary's assets is determined with reference to the substance of the transaction. The parent-subsidiary liquidation rules are set out in Concept Summary 3–2 as shown earlier in the chapter.

Suggested Further Readings

Richard W. Baline, "The Elucidation of the Liquidation-Reincorporation Doctrine," *Corporate Taxation*, March/April 2003, pp. 34–38.

Paul D. Carman, "The Proposed 302 Regulations: A Move to Suspended Losses from Basis Shifting," *Corporate Taxation*, January/February 2003, pp. 17–25.

B. Benjamin Haas, "Favorable Treatment for Distributions after Corporate Dispositions: Use of Partial Liquidations," *Journal of Taxation*, March 2003, pp. 142–149.

Joyce M. Robinson and Ted Waters, "Time Corporate Terminations to Achieve Desired Tax Treatment," *Practical Tax Strategies*, February 2003, pp. 77–80.

Robert Willens, "Avoiding Prohibited Retained Interests That will Subject a Redemption to Family Attribution," *Journal of Taxation*, December 2003, pp. 342–348.

KEY TERMS

Attribution, 3-5
Complete termination redemption, 3-8
Corporate liquidation, 3-16
Disproportionate redemption, 3-7
Meaningful reduction test, 3-6
Not essentially equivalent redemption, 3-6
Partial liquidation, 3-9
Preferred stock bailout, 3-14
Redemption to pay death taxes, 3-10
Section 338 election, 3-28
Stock redemption, 3-3

PROBLEM MATERIALS

Problems

Issue ID

1. Leona wants to retire and sell her shares in Puffin Corporation either to Puffin's remaining shareholders, Jacob and Ivan, or to a third party. What issues may support a preference for Puffin Corporation to redeem Leona's shares rather than for Jacob and Ivan or a third party to purchase them?

2. During the current year, Flicker, Inc., distributed $50,000 each to Kanisha and Susan in redemption of some of their Flicker stock. The two shareholders are in the 35% tax bracket, and each had a $20,000 basis in her redeemed stock. Kanisha incurred $7,720 of tax on her redemption, but Susan incurred only $4,500 on her redemption. Discuss the likely reason for the difference in their tax liabilities.

Decision Making

3. Teal Corporation, with E & P of $2.5 million, distributes property with a basis of $200,000 and a fair market value of $450,000 to Grace, one of its three shareholders. Each shareholder has a one-third interest in the corporation.
   a. What are the tax consequences to Teal Corporation and to Grace if the distribution is a property dividend?
   b. What are the tax consequences in (a) if Grace is a corporation?
   c. What are the tax consequences to Teal Corporation and to Grace if the distribution is a qualifying stock redemption? Assume that half of Grace's stock (basis of $120,000) is redeemed in the transaction.
   d. What are the tax consequences in (c) if Grace is a corporation?
   e. If the parties involved could choose from among the preceding options, which would they choose and why?

4. Julio is in the 30% tax bracket. He acquired 300 shares of stock in Grebe Corporation three years ago at a cost of $100 per share. In the current year, Julio received a payment of $120,000 from Grebe Corporation in exchange for 100 of his shares in Grebe. Grebe's E & P was $1 million at the time of the exchange. What tax liability would Julio incur on the $120,000 payment in each of the following situations? Assume that Julio has no capital losses.
   a. The payment qualifies for stock redemption (i.e., sale or exchange) treatment.
   b. The payment does not qualify for stock redemption (i.e., sale or exchange treatment is not applicable) treatment.

5. How would your answer to Problem 4 differ if Julio were a corporate shareholder (in the 34% tax bracket) rather than an individual shareholder and the stock ownership in Grebe Corporation represented a 15% interest?

Decision Making

6. Assume in Problem 4 that Julio has a capital loss carryover of $70,000 in the current tax year. Julio has no other capital gain transactions during the year. What amount of the capital loss may Julio deduct in the current year in the following situations?
   a. The $120,000 payment from Grebe Corporation is a qualifying stock redemption for tax purposes (i.e., receives sale or exchange treatment).

b. The $120,000 payment from Grebe Corporation does not qualify as a stock redemption for tax purposes (i.e., does not receive sale or exchange treatment).
c. If Julio had the flexibility to structure the transaction as described in either (a) or (b), which form would he choose?

7. Cardinal Corporation has 200 shares of common stock outstanding. Hubert owns 80 of the shares, Hubert's mother owns 50 shares, Hubert's brother owns 20 shares, and Redbird Corporation owns 20 shares. Hubert owns 80% of the stock in Redbird Corporation.
   a. Applying the § 318 stock attribution rules, how many shares does Hubert own in Cardinal Corporation?
   b. Assume Hubert owns only 25% of Redbird Corporation. How many shares does Hubert own directly and indirectly in Cardinal Corporation?
   c. Assume the same facts as in (a) above, but in addition, Hubert owns 40% of Yellow Partnership. The partnership owns 30 shares in Cardinal Corporation. How many shares does Hubert own directly and indirectly in Cardinal Corporation?

EXTENDER

8. Shonda owns 20 shares of the 200 shares of Hawk Corporation. Shonda paid $1,000 per share for the stock five years ago. The remaining stock in Hawk Corporation is owned as follows: 95 shares by Vulcan Corporation and 85 shares by several unrelated individuals. Shonda owns 100% of the stock of Vulcan Corporation. In the current year, Hawk redeems Shonda's 20 shares for $60,000 ($3,000 per share). Hawk has E & P of $200,000.
   a. How must Shonda report the $60,000?
   b. What happens to Shonda's basis in the redeemed shares?
   c. What is Hawk's E & P after the redemption?

Communications

9. Stork Corporation has 1,000 shares of common stock outstanding. The shares are owned by the following unrelated shareholders: Leo Jones, 300 shares; Lori Johnson, 400 shares; and Lana Pierce, 300 shares. The corporation redeems 200 shares of Lana's stock for $80,000. Lana paid $50 per share for her stock two years ago. Stork's E & P was $350,000 on the date of redemption. What is the tax effect to Lana of the redemption? Prepare a letter to Lana (1000 Main Street, Oldtown, MN 55166) and a memo for the file in which you explain your conclusions.

10. Thrush Corporation has 2,000 shares of common stock outstanding. The shares are owned as follows: Jacque Jones, 800 shares; Monique Jones (Jacque's daughter), 800 shares; and Enrique Jones (Jacque's brother) 400 shares. In the current year, Thrush redeems all of Jacque's shares. Determine whether the redemption can qualify for sale or exchange treatment under the complete termination redemption rules in the following independent circumstances.
    a. Jacque remains as a director of Thrush Corporation.
    b. Jacque resigns as director of Thrush Corporation; Monique becomes a director of Thrush to replace Jacque.
    c. Two years after the redemption, Jacque acquires 25 shares in Thrush Corporation as a gift from Enrique.

11. Roberta and Lori are sisters and own all the stock in Swan Corporation (E & P of $1.4 million). Each has a basis of $50,000 in her 200 shares. Roberta wants to sell her stock for $800,000, the fair market value. However, she wants to maintain her position on Swan Corporation's board of directors after the sale. Lori would like to purchase Roberta's shares and, thus, become the sole shareholder in Swan, but Lori is short of funds. What are the tax consequences to Roberta, Lori, and Swan Corporation under the following circumstances?
    a. Swan Corporation distributes cash of $800,000 to Lori, and she uses the cash to purchase Roberta's shares.
    b. Swan Corporation redeems all of Roberta's shares for $800,000.

Ethics

12. Penguin Corporation was started many years ago by Max Polar. Max is now ready to retire and turn Penguin over to his children. In a redemption qualifying as a complete termination of his interest, Max relinquishes all interest in Penguin and resigns as president. Max's CPA, Stan, treats the redemption as a sale of the stock. Six years after

the redemption, Max tells Stan that he has made some bad investment decisions and is struggling financially. He has returned to work at Penguin. Stan asks if Max is going to inform the IRS of his position at Penguin. Since Max is in financial troubles, he does not have the wherewithal to pay any additional taxes for violating the 10-year prohibition on working at Penguin, which was a condition of the sale treatment of his prior redemption. Consequently, Max is not going to report his breach of the redemption requirements. What should Stan do?

13. Sean owns all 100 shares of the outstanding stock of Crane Corporation (E & P of $800,000). Sean acquired the stock 10 years ago for $60,000. Crane has several trades or businesses that it has developed and operated for more than five years. In the current year, Crane Corporation sells one of those trades or businesses and, in a transaction qualifying as a partial liquidation [under § 302(b)(4)], redeems 20 shares of Sean's stock for $300,000. What are the tax consequences of the redemption to Sean and to Crane Corporation?

Issue ID

14. Two years ago, Jorge transferred property he had used in his sole proprietorship to Flycatcher Corporation, a newly formed corporation, for 50 shares of stock in Flycatcher. The property had an adjusted basis of $300,000 and a fair market value of $800,000. Six months later, Jorge's friend, Polly, transferred property she had used in her sole proprietorship to Flycatcher Corporation for 50 shares of the stock in Flycatcher and cash of $100,000. Her property had an adjusted basis of $150,000 and a value of $900,000. Both Jorge and Polly serve on the board of directors of Flycatcher Corporation. In addition, Polly has a contract to perform consulting services for Flycatcher. In the current year, Flycatcher Corporation redeems all of Polly's shares in Flycatcher for property with a value of $1.4 million. What are the tax issues for Polly and Flycatcher?

15. Raul's adjusted gross estate is $2 million. The estate will incur death taxes, funeral costs, and administration expenses of $900,000. Raul's gross estate includes stock of Harrier Corporation (fair market value of $1.4 million; original cost to Raul of $300,000). Raul owned 70% of the stock of Harrier Corporation at the time of his death. In the current year, Harrier Corporation (E & P of $3 million) redeems all of the estate's stock for $1.4 million. Raul named his daughter, Rachel, who has no interest in Harrier Corporation, as his sole heir. What are the tax consequences of the redemption to Raul's estate and to Harrier Corporation?

16. On January 1, 2004, Warbler Corporation has paid-in capital of $500,000 and accumulated E & P of $900,000. Warbler has no current E & P for 2004. Warbler's 450 shares outstanding are held equally by three unrelated shareholders: Tia, Jorge, and Gabriel. Each of the shareholders acquired their Warbler stock four years ago for $110,000. On September 3, 2004, Warbler Corporation redeems all of Jorge's stock for $700,000 in a transaction that qualifies as a complete termination redemption. On December 10, 2004, Warbler distributes $400,000 to Tia and $400,000 to Gabriel. What are the tax consequences of the redemption to Jorge and the distributions to Tia and Gabriel?

17. At the time of her death, Yolanda owned 20% of the outstanding stock of Violet Corporation (basis of $300,000, fair market value of $700,000). Yolanda's adjusted gross estate is $1.8 million, and the death taxes, funeral costs, and administration expenses total $350,000. Can Yolanda's estate qualify for a redemption to pay death taxes under § 303?

EXTENDER

Issue ID

18. Angie and her daughter, Ann, who are the only shareholders of Bluebird Corporation, each paid $100,000 four years ago for their shares in Bluebird. Angie also owns 20% of the stock in Redbird Corporation. The Redbird stock is worth $500,000, and Angie's basis in the stock is $50,000. Angie died in the current year leaving all her property to her husband, Gary, but Ann wants to be the sole shareholder of Bluebird Corporation. Bluebird has assets worth $2 million (basis of $700,000) and E & P of $1 million. Angie's estate is worth approximately $4 million. Angie has made gifts during her lifetime to Ann. What are the tax issues for Angie's estate, Ann, and Bluebird?

Decision Making

19. Ibis Corporation desires to transfer cash of $30,000 or property worth $30,000 to its sole shareholder, Linda, in a redemption transaction that will be treated as a dividend to Linda. If Ibis distributes property, the corporation will choose between two assets that are each worth $30,000 and are no longer needed in its business: Property A (basis of

$12,000) and Property B (basis of $36,000). Ibis is indifferent as to the form of the distribution, but Linda prefers a cash distribution. Considering the tax consequences to Ibis on the distribution to redeem Linda's shares, what should Ibis distribute?

Communications

20. Crane Corporation has 1,000 shares of stock outstanding. It redeems 150 shares for $200,000 when it has paid-in capital of $500,000 and E & P of $900,000. The redemption qualifies for sale or exchange treatment for the shareholder. Crane incurred $30,000 of accounting and legal fees in the redemption transaction. What is the effect of the distribution on Crane Corporation's E & P? Also, what is the proper tax treatment of the redemption expenditures? Prepare a letter to the president of Crane Corporation (506 Wall Street, Winona, MN 55987) and a memo for the file in which you explain your conclusions.

EXTENDER

21. Pete, a 30% shareholder in Starling Corporation, sells for a gain one-half of his preferred stock and one-half of his common stock to a third party.
    a. Is there any danger that the § 306 prohibition on preferred stock bailouts could apply to the sale of the preferred stock?
    b. If § 306 does apply, what would be the treatment of Pete's gain on the sale of the preferred stock?
    c. How would your answers to (a) and (b) change if, instead of a sale, the stock had been redeemed by Starling Corporation?

EXTENDER

22. Ahmad and Cora are the sole shareholders of Bobwhite Corporation. Ahmad and Cora each have a basis of $25,000 in their 200 shares of Bobwhite common stock. When its E & P was $900,000, Bobwhite Corporation issued a preferred stock dividend on the common shares of Ahmad and Cora, giving each 100 shares of preferred stock with a par value of $50 per share. Fair market value of one share of common was $120, and fair market value of one share of preferred was $60.
    a. What are the tax consequences of the distribution to Ahmad and Cora?
    b. What are the tax consequences to Ahmad if he later sells his preferred stock to Adam for $15,000? Adam is not related to Ahmad.
    c. What are the tax consequences to Ahmad if Bobwhite Corporation later redeems his preferred stock for $15,000 at a time when its E & P balance is $950,000?

EXTENDER

23. Bob owns 1,000 shares of stock in Goose Corporation and 500 shares of stock in Heron Corporation, representing a 100% interest in each corporation. Bob sells 200 shares of Goose stock to Heron Corporation for $30,000. The Goose stock was acquired 10 years ago; the tax basis to Bob of these 200 shares is $5,000. On the date of sale, Goose Corporation and Heron Corporation have E & P of $100,000 and $150,000, respectively. What are the tax consequences of this transaction?

24. Green Corporation acquired land in a § 351 exchange in 2001. The land had a basis of $625,000 and a fair market value of $700,000 on the date of the transfer. Green Corporation has two shareholders, Mark and Megan, who are brother and sister. During 2004, Green Corporation adopts a plan of liquidation, and when the fair market value of the land is $550,000, it is distributed pro rata to Mark and Megan. What amount of loss may Green Corporation recognize on the liquidating distribution of the land?

25. On April 12, 2003, Crow Corporation acquired land in a § 351 transaction. At that time, the land had a basis of $300,000 and a fair market value of $220,000. The land was transferred to Crow Corporation for use as security for a loan the corporation was in the process of obtaining from a local bank. The bank required the additional capital investment as a condition for making the loan. Crow Corporation adopted a plan of liquidation on October 1, 2004. On December 1, 2004, Crow Corporation distributes the land to Ali, a 40% shareholder. On the date of the distribution, the land had a fair market value of only $70,000. What amount of loss may Crow Corporation recognize on the distribution of the land?

26. On January 10, 2003, Grackle Corporation acquired equipment as a contribution to capital. At that time, the equipment had an adjusted basis of $200,000 and a fair market value of $110,000. On July 30, 2004, Grackle Corporation adopted a plan of liquidation. On November 15, 2004, Grackle sold the equipment to Chris, an unrelated party, for its current fair market value of $50,000. Grackle Corporation never used the equipment for

any business purpose during the time it owned the equipment. What amount of loss may Grackle Corporation recognize on the sale of the land?

Decision Making

27. Pheasant Corporation acquired land in a § 351 tax-free exchange in 2003. The land had a basis of $1,800,000 and a fair market value of $1,950,000 on the date of the transfer. Pheasant Corporation has two unrelated shareholders, Maria (80%) and Paul (20%). The corporation adopts a plan of liquidation in 2004. On this date the value of the land has decreased to $600,000. What is the effect of each of the following on Pheasant Corporation? Which option should be selected?
    a. Distribute all the land to Maria.
    b. Distribute all the land to Paul.
    c. Distribute 80% of the land to Maria and 20% to Paul.
    d. Distribute 50% of the land to Maria and 50% to Paul.
    e. Sell the land and distribute the proceeds of $600,000 proportionately to Maria and to Paul.

Decision Making

28. Assume in Problem 27 that the land had a fair market value of $1.5 million on the date of its transfer to Pheasant Corporation. On the date of the liquidation, the land's fair market value is still $600,000. How would your answer to Problem 27 change if:
    a. All the land is distributed to Maria?
    b. All the land is distributed to Paul?
    c. The land is distributed 80% to Maria and 20% to Paul?
    d. The land is distributed 50% to Maria and 50% to Paul?
    e. The land is sold and the proceeds of $600,000 are distributed proportionately to Maria and to Paul?

Ethics

29. In 2001, Woodpecker Corporation sold all of its assets and distributed the proceeds to its two equal shareholders in complete liquidation. The two shareholders, Dena Hall and Tony Oats, each received $100,000 in redemption of their stock. In 2004, the IRS audited Woodpecker and assessed additional taxes, penalties, and interest of $60,000. Since Woodpecker had liquidated, the IRS then assessed the entire $60,000 deficiency against Dena, based on transferee liability. The IRS did not attempt to collect any of the deficiency from Tony. Dena contacted Tony regarding the deficiency. Tony refuses to speak with Dena regarding this matter. Up to this point Dena and Tony had been friends. What should Dena do?

30. Three years ago, Cardinal Corporation acquired 100% of all classes of stock of Wren Corporation for $900,000. In the current year, Cardinal liquidates Wren Corporation and acquires assets worth $1.5 million with an adjusted basis to Wren of $1.2 million. At the time of its liquidation, Wren had E & P of $700,000 and a general business credit carryover of $20,000.
    a. How much gain (or loss) will Wren Corporation recognize as a result of its liquidation?
    b. How much gain (or loss) will Cardinal Corporation recognize as a result of Wren Corporation's liquidation?
    c. What basis does Cardinal Corporation take in the assets acquired in the liquidation?
    d. What happens to Wren Corporation's E & P and general business credit carryover?

Communications

31. Quail Corporation paid $5.4 million for all the stock of Sparrow Corporation 10 years ago. Sparrow Corporation's balance sheet currently reflects the following fair market values:

Assets		*Liabilities and Shareholders' Equity*	
Cash	$ 135,000	Accounts payable	$ 5,400,000
Inventory	405,000	Common stock	5,400,000
Machinery	270,000	Deficit	(7,560,000)
Equipment	1,080,000		
Land	1,350,000		
	$3,240,000		$ 3,240,000

What are the tax consequences to Quail Corporation if it liquidates Sparrow Corporation? Prepare a letter to your client Quail Corporation (1010 Cypress Lane, Community, MN 55166) and a memo for the file in which you explain your conclusions.

32. The stock of Thrasher Corporation is owned by Flamingo Corporation (95%) and Marta (5%). Thrasher is liquidated on September 5, 2004, pursuant to a plan of liquidation adopted earlier in the same year. In the liquidation, Thrasher distributes various assets worth $950,000 (basis of $620,000) to Flamingo (basis of $700,000 in Thrasher stock) and a parcel of land worth $50,000 (basis of $75,000) to Marta (basis of $30,000 in Thrasher stock). Assuming the § 338 election is not made, what are the tax consequences of the liquidation to Thrasher, Flamingo, and Marta?

33. Falcon Corporation is owned 90% by Canary Corporation. The parent is contemplating a liquidation of Falcon Corporation and the acquisition of its assets. Canary Corporation purchased the Falcon stock from Falcon's two individual shareholders a month ago on January 1, 2004, for $400,000. The financial statements of Falcon Corporation as of January 1, 2004, reflect the following:

	Assets	
	Basis to Falcon Corporation	**Fair Market Value**
Cash	$ 40,000	$ 40,000
Inventory	80,000	60,000
Accounts receivable	160,000	100,000
Equipment	400,000	320,000
Land	520,000	280,000
	$1,200,000	$800,000
	Liabilities and Shareholders' Equity	
Accounts payable	$ 120,000	$120,000
Mortgages payable	200,000	200,000
Common stock	1,000,000	480,000
Retained earnings	(120,000)	
	$1,200,000	$800,000

The management of Canary Corporation asks your advice on the feasibility of an election under § 338.

a. Can Canary Corporation make a § 338 election?
b. Assuming Canary can make a § 338 election, is such an election feasible?

Decision Making

34. Albatross Corporation has two equal and unrelated shareholders, Alex Solo and Glenn Lands. Albatross is at a critical point in its existence, and the shareholders cannot agree on the path to take. Alex wants Albatross to retain all of its earnings to expand its lines of business. Glenn, on the other hand, feels that the lines are fine as they are; he wants Albatross to repay the shareholder loans and start paying substantial dividends. They are at an impasse. They cannot even decide on whether Albatross should liquidate and distribute the assets to Alex and Glenn or whether either Glenn or Alex should have all of his stock redeemed. Below is the current balance sheet for Albatross. The adjusted basis and fair market value of the assets are provided.

Assets	Adjusted Basis	FMV	Liabilities and Shareholders' Equity	
Cash	$ 10,000	$ 10,000	Current liabilities	$ 15,000
Investments	40,000	50,000	Loans from shareholders	30,000
Inventory	30,000	45,000	Loans on equipment	40,000
Equipment	125,000	93,000	Accumulated earnings	200,000
Plant and land	170,000	227,000	Stockholders' equity	90,000
Total	$375,000	$425,000	Total	$375,000

a. Determine the tax consequences to Albatross and Glenn if Albatross distributes the plant and land to Glenn in a redemption of all of Glenn's stock and repays his $15,000 loan.
b. Determine the tax consequences to Albatross and the shareholders if Albatross liquidates and distributes the after-tax proceeds to Alex and Glenn. Alex and Glenn each have a $45,000 basis in their stock.
c. Which solution should Albatross select?

BRIDGE DISCIPLINE

1. Sparrow, Inc., is looking for an infusion of $2 million to develop a new medical device. Since the risk of the venture is high, few investors are interested in acquiring stock. Bank loans or bond issuances seem out of the question as the interest rates would be too high given the risk involved. Sparrow therefore turns to venture capitalists for the needed funding. The only deal Sparrow can swing for the $2 million requires Sparrow to provide nonparticipating liquidation preferences with a 1.4 multiple. This provides the funds Sparrow needs, and Sparrow issues an additional 100,000 shares of common stock to the venture capitalist. The equity structure of Sparrow is 300,000 shares of common stock ($20 par) and 3,000 shares of preferred stock with a $100 par and liquidation value.
   After two years in development, it is determined that the medical device is not viable due to the thin market for the product. Sparrow liquidates when it has net assets of $3 million. What amount will each type of shareholder receive upon Sparrow's liquidation?

2. Assume the same facts as Problem 1 except that Sparrow has $5 million in net assets prior to liquidation and the venture capitalist has a participating liquidation preference. What amount will the venture capitalist and other shareholders receive if the liquidation preference is participating?

Research Problems

THOMSON RIA

Note: Solutions to Research Problems can be prepared by using the ***RIA Checkpoint® Student Edition*** *online research product, which is available to accompany this text. It is also possible to prepare solutions to the Research Problems by using tax research materials found in a standard tax library.*

Communications

Research Problem 1. Twenty years ago, Galvin Alexander (6870 Broadway, San Antonio, TX 78209) formed Beige Corporation and became its sole shareholder (1,000 shares). Since that time, Galvin's son, Joseph, has been substantially involved in the management and operation of the corporation's businesses. Galvin has made several gifts of Beige stock to Joseph in an effort to increase his son's vested interest in the success of the corporation. By 2001, when Galvin owned 600 shares of Beige and Joseph owned the remaining 400 shares, the working and personal relationship between father and son had soured to the point that they refused to speak to each other. Recognizing that Beige's success was at risk, the parties agreed that the corporation (E & P of $3 million) would redeem all of Galvin's stock for $1 million (basis of $200,000). The redemption occurred in 2002, and

Galvin reported the transaction as a sale or exchange, resulting in a long-term capital gain of $800,000. Under the agreement between the father and son, Galvin continued to serve as a director on the board of Beige until 2006. He was compensated $20,000 annually for serving as a director. In the current year, the IRS audited Galvin's return for 2002 and assessed additional taxes (plus penalties and interest) based on the recharacterization of the redemption as a $1 million dividend distribution. Galvin has contacted you regarding whether he should contest the proposed deficiency. Prepare a letter to Galvin and a memo for the file documenting your conclusions.

Research Problem 2. Beth Thorson has owned 80% of the common stock of Green Corporation (basis of $10,000) since the corporation's formation. In 2002, when Green had E & P of $300,000, the corporation issued to Beth a nontaxable dividend of 100 shares of preferred stock (value of $80,000 on date of distribution) on her common stock interest (value of $320,000 on date of distribution). In 2003, Beth donated the 100 shares of preferred stock to her favorite charity, State University. Beth deducted $80,000, the fair market value of the stock on the date of the gift, as a charitable contribution on her 2003 income tax return. Beth's adjusted gross income for 2003 was $500,000. Two months after the contribution, Green Corporation redeemed the preferred stock from State University for $80,000. Upon an audit of Beth's 2003 tax return, the IRS disallowed the entire deduction, asserting that the preferred stock was § 306 stock and that § 170(e)(1)(A) precluded a deduction for contributions of such stock. What is the proper tax treatment for Beth's charitable contribution of the Green Corporation preferred stock?

Partial list of research aids:
Reg. § 1.170(A)–4(b)(1).
§ 306(b)(4).

Communications

Research Problem 3. Scott Davison (255 N. Bayshore Boulevard, Clearwater, FL 34619) is the president and sole shareholder of Bluebird Corporation (stock basis of $270,000). Since 1990, Bluebird has imported fine Mexican pottery and sold it to large nurseries and hardware stores across the United States. On July 1, 2002, Bluebird transferred its entire pottery inventory to Davison in a transaction described by the parties as a sale. According to Davison and corroborated by the minutes of the corporation's board of directors, the inventory was "sold" to him for the sum of $1 million, the fair market value of the inventory (Bluebird's basis, $350,000). The terms of the sale provided that Davison would pay Bluebird the $1 million at some future date. This debt obligation was not evidenced by a promissory note, and, to date, Davison has made no payments (principal or interest) on the obligation. The inventory transfer was not reported on Bluebird's 2002 tax return, either as a sale or as a distribution. After the transfer of inventory to Davison, Bluebird had no remaining assets and ceased to conduct any business. Upon an audit of Bluebird's 2002 tax return, the IRS asserted that the transfer of inventory constituted a liquidation of Bluebird and, as such, that the corporation recognized a gain on the liquidating distribution in the amount of $650,000 ($1 million value – $350,000 basis). Further, the IRS assessed a tax due from Davison for his gain recognized in the purported liquidating distribution. Davison has contacted you regarding the IRS's determination. Prepare a letter to Scott Davison and a memo for the file documenting your research.

Partial list of research aids:
Reg. § 1.332–2(c).
Kennemer v. Comm., 38–1 USTC ¶9297, 21 AFTR 103, 96 F.2d 177 (CA–5, 1938).

Research Problem 4. Four years ago, Roadrunner Corporation was completely liquidated, and all of its shareholders reported long-term capital gains as a result. One year after the liquidation, the shareholders sued a former Roadrunner Corporation CEO for large insider profits. In the current year, the shareholders' lawsuit against the former CEO was settled, and they were awarded a $3 million judgment. What is the proper tax treatment for the shareholders' judgment proceeds?

Internet Activity

Use the tax resources of the Internet to address the following questions. Do not restrict your search to the World Wide Web, but include a review of newsgroups and general reference materials, practitioner sites and resources, primary sources of the tax law, chat rooms and discussion groups, and other opportunities.

Communications

Research Problem 5. Legal forms for a variety of agreements can be found via the Internet. Although they should be used with some caution, these free legal forms provide excellent insight into the wording and clauses a particular type of agreement should incorporate. Using the Internet as your sole research source, prepare an outline highlighting the wording/clauses typically found in a stock redemption agreement.

Communications

Research Problem 6. Review the Internet sites of several public accounting firms and find discussions regarding the § 338 election. Based on your findings, prepare an outline discussing the advantages and disadvantages of the § 338 election.

CHAPTER 4

Corporations: Reorganizations

LEARNING OBJECTIVES

After completing Chapter 4, you should be able to:

LO.1
Understand the general requirements of corporate reorganizations.

LO.2
Determine the tax consequences of a corporate reorganization.

LO.3
Explain the statutory requirements for the different types of reorganizations.

LO.4
Delineate the judicial and administrative conditions for a nontaxable corporate reorganization.

LO.5
Apply the rules pertaining to the carryover of tax attributes in a corporate reorganization.

http://wft.swlearning.com

OUTLINE

TAX TALK

The fact that the incidences of income taxation may have been taken into account by arranging matters one way rather than another, so long as the way chosen was the way the law allows, does not make a transaction something else than it truly is.

—*Felix Frankfurter*

One of the tenets of U.S. tax policy is to encourage business development. To this end, the tax laws allow entities to form without taxation, assuming certain requirements are met. As an extension of this concept, certain corporate restructurings are also favored with tax-free treatment. Corporations may engage in a variety of acquisitions, combinations, consolidations, and divisions tax-free, as long as the "reorganization" requirements in the Code are met.

Courts originally concluded that even minor changes in a corporation's structure would produce taxable gains for the shareholders involved.[1] Congress, however, determined that businesses should be allowed to make necessary capital adjustments without being subject to taxation.[2] The theory for nonrecognition in certain corporate restructurings or "reorganizations" is similar to that underlying § 351 treatment and like-kind exchanges.

Given the magnitude of the dollar amounts involved in most reorganizations, tax planning strategies play an important role in corporate restructurings. Careful planning can reduce or eliminate taxation for both the corporations involved in the reorganization and their shareholders. Therefore, tax law often dictates the form of the restructuring. Corporate mergers and divisions generally are tax-free when the target corporation exchanges stock or assets for the stock of the acquiring

[1] *U.S. v. Phellis,* 1 USTC ¶54, 3 AFTR 3123, 42 S.Ct. 63 (USSC, 1921).

[2] Reg. § 1.368–1(b). See S.Rept. No. 275, 67th Cong., 1st Sess. (1921), at 1939–1 C.B. 181.

TAX FACT

The Slowing of Merger and Acquisition Activity

Mergers and acquisitions (M & A) are a popular method of increasing the economic vitality of a business. The restructuring frenzy peaked in 1999–2000 with more than 20,000 major mergers (values greater than $5 million), amounting to almost $2.7 trillion in value. The recent downturn in the global economy dramatically slowed M & A activity. Between 2000 and 2003, the yearly number of restructurings fell by more than 30 percent, and as the table shows, only one of the 10 largest M & A took place after 2000.

Largest M & A in the United States, 1998–2003

Companies	Year	Total Assets (in Billions)
Time Warner and AOL	2000	$165.9
Sprint and MCI	1999	119.0
Warner-Lambert and Pfizer	1999	82.4
Mobil and Exxon	1998	77.2
Air Touch and Vodafone	1999	62.0
Ameritech and SBC Communications	1998	61.4
Pharmacia and Pfizer	2002	58.3
Amoco and British Petroleum	1998	56.2
Media One and AT&T	1999	55.8
GTE and Bell Atlantic	1998	52.9

Source: Data are from Mergerstat.com.

corporation. If other property or cash is given by the acquiring corporation, the reorganization may be partly or fully taxable. When the reorganization is taxable to the shareholders, the gains are likely to be treated as either dividends or capital gains. For individual shareholders, both of these are subject to a maximum tax rate of 15 percent. Corporate shareholders would be allowed a dividends received deduction if the gains are categorized as dividends. However, since corporations receive no tax rate reduction for capital gains, corporate shareholders and the corporations involved in the restructuring would be taxed at their highest marginal rate on any gains classified as capital. Consequently, it may be paramount that the transaction be structured to meet the requirements for nontaxable treatment.

LO.1

Understand the general requirements of corporate reorganizations.

Reorganizations—In General

Although the term **reorganization** is commonly associated with a corporation in financial difficulty, for tax purposes the term refers to any corporate restructuring that may be tax-free under § 368. To qualify as a tax-free reorganization, a corporate restructuring transaction must meet not only the specific requirements of § 368 but also several general requirements. These requirements include the following.

1. There must be a *plan of reorganization.*
2. The reorganization must meet the *continuity of interest* and the *continuity of business enterprise* tests set out in the Regulations.
3. The restructuring must meet the judicial doctrine of having a *sound business purpose.*
4. The court-imposed *step transaction* doctrine should not apply to the reorganization.

All of these concepts are discussed in this chapter. The initial and most important consideration, however, is whether the reorganization qualifies for nonrecognition status under § 368.

SUMMARY OF THE DIFFERENT TYPES OF REORGANIZATIONS

Section 368(a) specifies seven corporate restructurings or *reorganizations* that will qualify as nontaxable exchanges. If the transaction fails to qualify as a reorganization, it will not receive the special tax-favored treatment. Therefore, a corporation considering a business reorganization must determine in advance if the proposed transaction specifically falls within one of these seven types. In situations involving substantial tax dollars, the parties should obtain a letter ruling from the IRS verifying that the proposed transaction under § 368 qualifies as a tax-free reorganization.

Section 368(a)(1) states that the term *reorganization* applies to any of the following.

A. A statutory merger or consolidation.
B. The acquisition by a corporation of another using solely stock of each corporation (voting-stock-for-stock exchange).
C. The acquisition by a corporation of substantially all of the property of another corporation in exchange for voting stock (stock-for-asset exchange).
D. The transfer of all or part of a corporation's assets to another corporation when the original corporation's shareholders are in control of the new corporation immediately after the transfer (divisive exchange, also known as a spin-off, split-off, or split-up).
E. A recapitalization.
F. A mere change in identity, form, or place of organization.
G. A transfer by a corporation of all or a part of its assets to another corporation in a bankruptcy or receivership proceeding.

These seven types of tax-free reorganizations typically are designated by their identifying letters: "Type A," "Type B," "Type C," and so on. Each will be described in more detail later in the chapter.

LO.2

Determine the tax consequences of a corporate reorganization.

SUMMARY OF TAX CONSEQUENCES IN A TAX-FREE REORGANIZATION

The tax treatment of the parties involved in a tax-free reorganization almost exactly parallels the treatment under the like-kind exchange provisions of § 1031. In the simplest like-kind exchange, neither gain nor loss is recognized on the exchange of "like-kind" property. When "boot" (defined as non-like-kind property) is involved, gain may be recognized. The four-column template of Concept Summary 4–1 can be used to compute the amount of gain recognized and the adjusted basis in the new asset received in the like-kind exchange.

Concept Summary 4–1

Gain and Basis Rules for Nontaxable Exchanges

(1) Realized Gain/Loss	(2) Recognized Gain (Not Loss)	(3) Postponed Gain/Loss	(4) Basis of New Asset
Amount realized – Adjusted basis of asset surrendered	Lesser of boot received or gain realized	Gain/loss realized (column 1) – Gain recognized (column 2)	FMV of asset (stock) received – Postponed gain (column 3) or + Postponed loss (column 3)
Gain/loss realized	Gain recognized	Gain/loss postponed	Adjusted basis in new asset (stock)

Unfortunately, the like-kind exchange provisions do not apply to the exchange of stock or securities.[3] Therefore, when an investor exchanges stock in one corporation for stock in another, the exchange is a taxable transaction. If the transaction qualifies as a reorganization under § 368, however, the exchange will be nontaxable. Thus, a § 368 reorganization, in substance, is similar to a nontaxable exchange of like-kind property, and the four-column template of Concept Summary 4–1 is useful for reorganizations as well.

EXAMPLE 1

Sam holds 1,000 shares of Lotus stock that he purchased for $10,000 several years ago. In a merger of Lotus into Blossom, Sam exchanges his 1,000 shares of Lotus for 1,000 shares of Blossom. Both investments are valued at $18 per share. Sam's realized gain on the exchange is $8,000 [($18 per share × 1,000 shares) – $10,000 basis]. Assuming this exchange qualifies for tax-free treatment under § 368, Sam's recognized gain is zero. Since his postponed gain is $8,000, Sam's basis in his new stock is $10,000 [$18,000 (FMV of new stock) – $8,000 (postponed gain)]. The exchange of Sam's stock has no tax consequences for Lotus or Blossom. ■

Gain or Loss. Corporations involved in a reorganization described by § 368 do not recognize gain or loss on the restructuring. There are exceptions to the nonrecognition rule, however. If the acquiring corporation transfers property to the target corporation along with its stock and securities, gain, but not loss, may be recognized. The target may also recognize gain, but not loss, when it fails to distribute the *other property* it receives in the restructuring or distributes its own appreciated property to its shareholders. *Other property* in this case is defined as anything received other than stock or securities.[4]

EXAMPLE 2

In a restructuring qualifying as a reorganization, Acquiring Corporation exchanges $80,000 of stock and land with a fair market value of $20,000 (basis of $15,000) for all of the assets of Target Corporation. Target's assets have a fair market value of $100,000 and a basis of $60,000. Due to the *other property* (land) Acquiring uses in the transfer, it recognizes a gain of $5,000 ($20,000 – $15,000) on the reorganization. If Target distributes the land to its shareholders, it does not recognize gain. If Target retains the land, however, it recognizes gain to the extent of the *other property* received, $20,000. ■

[3] § 1031(a)(2)(B).

[4] §§ 361(a) and (b).

TAX IN THE NEWS

Are Mergers Coming Back in Fashion?

Wall Street analysts are becoming cautiously optimistic about the mergers and acquisitions (M & A) business, which has been in a slump since 2000. The volume of M & A deals is beginning to increase, although the dollar value of these deals is not keeping pace. One problem slowing recovery is that M & A deals are now taking much longer to complete than they did in 2000. Deals that used to take four to six months are taking nine months to a year due to the increased scrutiny caused by accounting scandals and economic changes. Nevertheless, many M & A deals are currently in the pipeline and should be emerging next year.

Since M & A transactions are among the most profitable for Wall Street and investment bankers, earnings for firms in this industry are expected to increase in the near future. Not only are the fees for advising on such deals lucrative, but often M & A deals lead to corporate loans, foreign currency exchanges, restructuring advice, and a multitude of other business.

Don't expect this increased business to lead to new hiring on Wall Street in the near future. Hiring usually lags increases in activity. Therefore, the people in the M & A industry will be working harder for a while and will not be able to share their load with eager new hires for some time to come.

SOURCE: Adapted from Pradnya Joshi, "Mergers May Spell Relief; Flurry of Activity Could Help Outlook," *Newsday*, July 9, 2003.

Generally, the stockholders of the corporations involved in a tax-free reorganization do not recognize gain or loss on the exchange of their stock unless they receive cash or other property in addition to stock. The cash or other property is considered boot. The gain recognized by the stockholder is the lesser of the boot received or the realized gain. This is analogous to the treatment of boot in a like-kind exchange.

EXAMPLE 3

Kalla, the sole shareholder of Target Corporation in Example 2, has a basis in her stock of $70,000. She exchanges her Target stock for the $80,000 of Acquiring stock plus the land ($20,000) transferred by Acquiring to Target. Kalla has a realized gain of $30,000 [$80,000 (value of stock received) + $20,000 (value of land received) – $70,000 (basis of stock given)]. Receiving the land (boot) causes her to recognize a $20,000 gain. ■

Once the gain is computed, its character must be determined. The following are the possibilities for gain characterization.

- Dividend to the extent of the shareholder's proportionate share of corporate earnings and profits. The remaining gain is generally characterized as capital.
  - The distinction between dividends and long-term capital gains may be less critical now that the tax rate is the same for both. However, this distinction is still important when the taxpayer has capital losses to offset or when the capital gain would be classified as short term and therefore not subject to the special tax rates.
- If the requirements of § 302(b) can be met, the transaction will qualify for stock redemption treatment (see Chapter 3).
  - Gains from qualifying stock redemptions are treated as capital gains.

- In computing the shareholder's ownership reduction, shares actually received in the acquiring corporation are compared with the number of shares the shareholder would have received if solely stock of the acquiring corporation had been distributed in the reorganization.[5]

EXAMPLE 4

John exchanges his 10% stock interest in Target (basis $8,000) for $4,000 cash and stock in Acquiring worth $11,000. At the time of the reorganization, Target's E & P is $25,000. John has a realized gain of $7,000 ($15,000 cash and stock received – $8,000 basis of Target stock) and a recognized gain of $4,000 (the cash received). The first $2,500 ($25,000 × 10%) is taxable as a dividend, and the remaining $1,500 is treated as capital gain. Both are taxed at a maximum rate of 15%.

Suppose instead that John received 1% of Acquiring stock with a fair market value of $10,000 and $5,000 cash. If John had received solely stock, he would have received 1.5% of Acquiring stock. Since John owns less than 80% of what he would have owned (1% ÷ 1.5% is less than 80%) and less than 50% of Acquiring, he meets the qualifications for sale or exchange treatment under § 302(b)(2). Therefore, John's $5,000 recognized gain is a capital gain. ■

Debt security (debenture) holders receive treatment similar to shareholders. They recognize gain only when the principal amount of the debentures received is greater than the debt securities given up. If debentures are received and no securities are surrendered, the debenture holders also recognize gain.

EXAMPLE 5

Alejandra was a debenture holder in Hibiscus. She owned bonds with a principal value of $10,000. As part of the merger of Hibiscus with Carnation, Alejandra surrenders her Hibiscus bonds and receives long-term Carnation debentures with a principal value of $15,000. Alejandra recognizes a $5,000 capital gain on the exchange. ■

Basis. The assets transferred from the target corporation to the acquiring corporation retain their basis. This carryover basis is increased by any gain recognized by the target corporation on the reorganization. Concept Summary 4–2 shows this computation.

EXAMPLE 6

Target exchanges its assets with a fair market value of $50,000 and a basis of $30,000 for $45,000 of Acquiring stock and $5,000 of land. Target does not distribute the land to its shareholders. Target recognizes a $5,000 gain on the reorganization (due to the other property not being distributed). Acquiring's basis in the assets received from Target is $35,000 [$30,000 (Target's basis) + $5,000 (Target's gain recognized)]. ■

The tax basis of the stock and securities received by a shareholder pursuant to a tax-free reorganization generally is the same as the basis of those surrendered. This basis is decreased by the fair market value of boot received and increased by the gain and/or dividend income recognized on the transaction. Concept Summary 4–2 provides a summary of these calculations. Another way to compute the basis in the stock and securities received, using the template of Concept Summary 4–1, is to subtract the gain (or add the loss) postponed from the fair market value of the stock and securities received. This basis computation ensures that the postponed gain or loss will be recognized when the new stock or securities are disposed of in a taxable transaction.

EXAMPLE 7

Quinn exchanges all of his stock in Target Corporation for stock in Acquiring Corporation plus $3,000 cash. The exchange qualifies as a tax-free reorganization. Quinn paid $10,000 for the stock in Target two years ago. The Acquiring stock received has a fair market value

---

[5] *Comm. v. Clark*, 89–1 USTC ¶9230, 63 AFTR2d 89–860, 109 S.Ct. 1455 (USSC, 1989), and Rev.Rul. 93–61, 1993–2 C.B. 118.

CONCEPT SUMMARY 4–2

Basis Rules for a Tax-Free Reorganization

Basis to Acquiring Corporation of Property Received	
Target's basis in property transferred	$xx,xxx
Plus: Gain recognized by Target on the transaction	x,xxx
Equals: Basis of property to Acquiring Corporation	$xx,xxx

Basis to Target Shareholders of Stock and Securities Received	
Basis of stock and securities transferred	$xx,xxx
Plus: Gain and dividend income recognized	x,xxx
Minus: Money and fair market value of other property received	(x,xxx)
Equals: Basis of stock and securities received	$xx,xxx

of $12,000. Quinn has a realized gain of $5,000 [$12,000 (value of stock received) + $3,000 (cash received) – $10,000 (basis in Target stock)], which is recognized to the extent of the boot received, $3,000. Quinn's basis in the Acquiring stock is $10,000. This can be computed using the template in Concept Summary 4–1 [$12,000 (value of Acquiring stock) – $2,000 (postponed gain)] or Concept Summary 4–2 [$10,000 (basis) + $3,000 (gain) – $3,000 (cash received)].

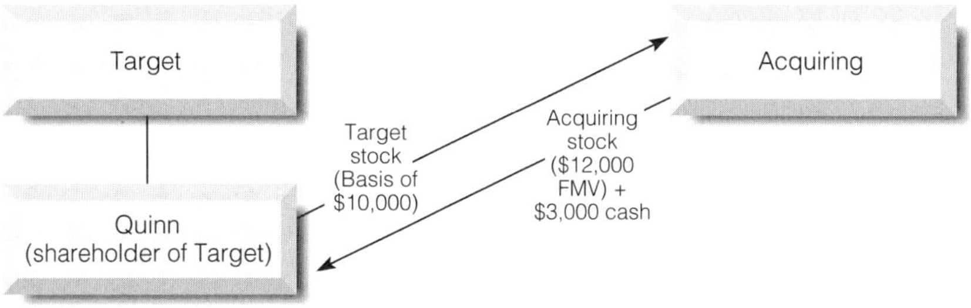

EXAMPLE 8

Assume the same facts as in Example 7, except that Quinn's basis in the Target stock was $16,000. Quinn realizes a loss of $1,000 on the exchange, none of which is recognized. His basis in the Acquiring stock is $13,000 [Concept Summary 4–1: $12,000 (value of stock received) + $1,000 (loss postponed) or Concept Summary 4–2: $16,000 (basis) – $3,000 (cash received)].

Concept Summary 4–3 furnishes a review of the tax consequences of tax-free reorganizations.

LO.3

Explain the statutory requirements for the different types of reorganizations.

Types of Tax-Free Reorganizations

TYPE A

The "Type A" reorganizations can be classified as either mergers or consolidations. A **merger** is the union of two or more corporations, with one of the corporations retaining its corporate existence and absorbing the others. The other corporations

Concept Summary 4–3

Tax Consequences of Tax-Free Reorganizations

Treatment is similar to like-kind exchanges.

- No gain or loss is recognized by the acquiring or target corporation unless other property (i.e., boot) is transferred or received by any parties to the reorganization.
- Basis in the assets received by the acquiring corporation is generally carried over from the target corporation.
- Basis in the stock received by the target corporation's shareholders takes a substituted basis, derived from the basis in their target stock.
- Gain, but not loss, may be recognized when boot is transferred by the acquiring corporation.
- Gain, but not loss, may be recognized when the target corporation receives boot and does not distribute the boot to its shareholders.
- Gain, but not loss, may be recognized when target shareholders receive anything other than stock (i.e., boot) in exchange for their target stock.

cease to exist by operation of law. A **consolidation** occurs when a new corporation is created to take the place of two or more corporations. The "Type A" reorganizations are illustrated in Figure 4–1. To qualify as a "Type A" reorganization, mergers and consolidations must comply with the requirements of state law.

EXAMPLE 9

Acquiring Corporation obtains all the assets of Target Corporation in exchange for 5,000 shares of Acquiring stock. Target is liquidated by distributing the Acquiring stock to its shareholders in exchange for their shares in Target. This transaction qualifies as a "Type A" reorganization (assuming that all other requirements of state law are met). It is a statutory merger. ■

EXAMPLE 10

White and Black Corporations are united under state law into new Gray Corporation by transferring all of their assets to Gray in exchange for all of Gray Corporation's stock. White and Black Corporations are then liquidated by distributing Gray stock to their shareholders in exchange for the shareholders' stock in White and Black. This is a "Type A" reorganization in the form of a consolidation. ■

Advantages and Disadvantages. The "Type A" reorganization allows more flexibility than the other types of reorganizations.

- Unlike both the "Type B" and the "Type C" reorganizations, the acquiring corporation's consideration need not be voting stock.
- The acquiring corporation can transfer money or other property to the target corporation without destroying the tax-free treatment for the stock also exchanged.
  - The money or other property, however, constitutes boot and may cause the recognition of gain by the acquiring corporation, the target, and/or the target's shareholders.
- When consideration other than stock is given by the acquiring corporation, care must be taken not to run afoul of the **continuity of interest test.**
  - This test, promulgated by the courts, requires that at least 50 percent of the consideration given by the acquiring corporation must be stock.
- There is no requirement that "substantially all" of the assets of the target be transferred to the acquiring corporation as in a "Type C" reorganization.
  - Thus, the target can sell or otherwise dispose of assets not desired by the acquiring corporation without affecting the tax-free nature of the restructuring.

FIGURE 4–1
"Type A" Reorganization

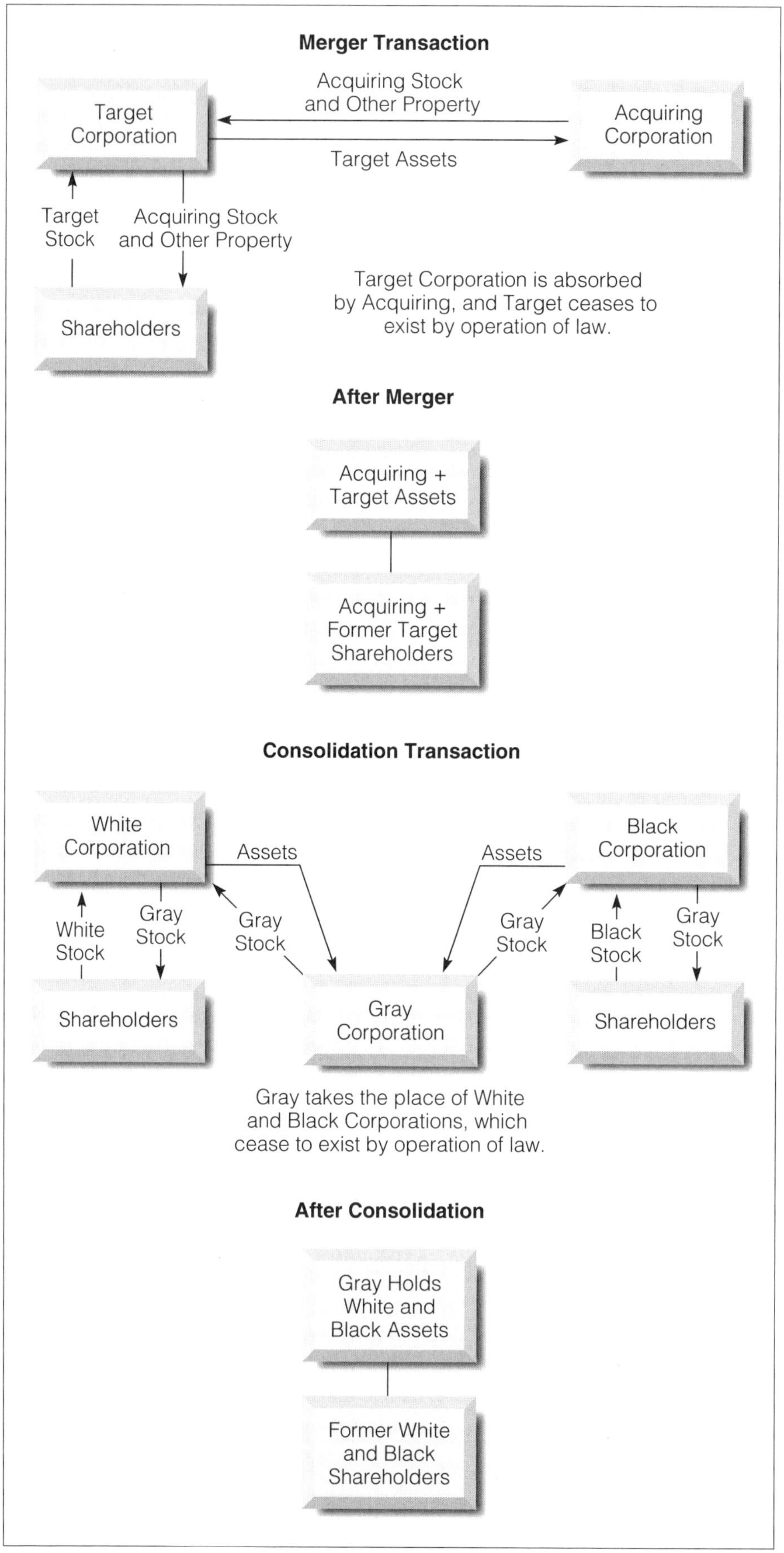

A "Type A" is not without its disadvantages.

- The majority of the shareholders of each corporation involved in the restructuring must approve the reorganization.
- In almost all states, dissenting shareholders have the right to require that their shares be appraised and purchased.
  - Meeting the demands of objecting shareholders can become so cumbersome and expensive that the parties may be forced to abandon the "Type A" reorganization.
- The acquiring corporation is required to assume *all* liabilities (including unknown and contingent liabilities) of the target corporation.
  - The surviving corporation assumes the liabilities of the target corporation as a matter of state law.

Subsidiary Used in a "Type A" Reorganization. Many of the problems with state law in the "Type A" reorganization can be reduced if a third corporation, a controlled subsidiary of the corporation desiring to acquire the target corporation, becomes the actual acquiring corporation. Using a subsidiary as the acquiring corporation allows the parent to protect its assets from the creditors of the target corporation. In this way, the acquirer can avoid any responsibility for the unknown and contingent liabilities of the target corporation.

DIGGING DEEPER 1

Find more information on this topic at our Web site: ***http://wft-advanced.swlearning.com***.

TYPE B

In a "Type B" reorganization, the acquiring corporation obtains "control" of the target corporation in an exchange involving solely stock. Thus, both corporations survive, and a parent-subsidiary relationship is created. In simple terms, this transaction is an exchange of voting stock for stock. **Control** for this purpose means that at least 80 percent of all classes of the target corporation's stock must be acquired. Voting stock must be the sole consideration given by the acquiring corporation, a requirement that is strictly construed.[6] The target's stock relinquished in the transaction may be common or preferred, voting or nonvoting. Further, the stock may be acquired from the shareholders directly or from the target corporation.

Since the "Type B" reorganization precludes the use of boot, gain is not recognized in this type of reorganization. An exception to the requirement that only voting stock be used occurs when the shareholders must receive fractional shares. The shareholders of the target corporation may receive cash rather than fractional shares in the acquiring corporation.[7] The "Type B" reorganization is illustrated in Figure 4–2.

EXAMPLE 11

Acquiring Corporation exchanges 20% of its voting stock with the Target Corporation shareholders for 80% of all classes of stock in Target Corporation. The exchange qualifies as a "Type B" reorganization. Acquiring becomes the parent of Target. ■

DIGGING DEEPER 2

Find more information on this topic at our Web site: ***http://wft-advanced.swlearning.com***.

[6] *A. S. Heverly*, 80–1 USTC ¶9322, 45 AFTR2d 80–1122, 621 F.2d 1227, and *E. S. Chapman*, 80–1 USTC ¶9330, 45 AFTR2d 80–1290, 618 F.2d 856.

[7] Rev.Rul. 66–365, 1966–2 C.B. 116.

■ **FIGURE 4–2**
"Type B" Reorganization

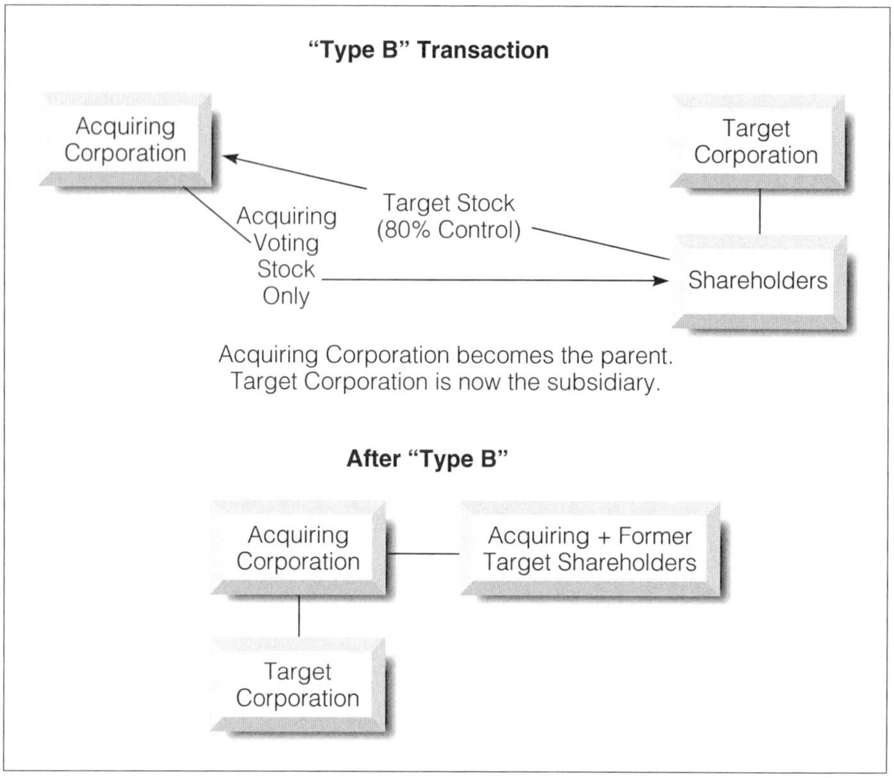

Advantages and Disadvantages. The solely voting stock consideration requirement is a substantial disadvantage of the "Type B" reorganization. Another disadvantage is that if the acquiring corporation does not obtain 100 percent control of the target corporation, problems may arise with the minority interests remaining in the target.

Nevertheless, the voting-stock-for-stock acquisition has the advantage of simplicity. Generally, the shareholders of the target corporation act individually in transferring their stock to the acquiring corporation. Thus, the target corporation itself and the shareholders of the acquiring corporation are not directly involved as long as the acquiring corporation has sufficient treasury or unissued shares to effect the transaction. Lastly, as with a "Type A" reorganization, a subsidiary of the parent can be used to facilitate the reorganization using the parent's voting stock.

DIGGING DEEPER 3 *Find more information on this topic at our Web site:* ***http://wft-advanced.swlearning.com.***

TYPE C

In the "Type C" reorganization, the acquiring corporation obtains substantially all of the target corporation's assets in exchange for voting stock and a limited amount of other property. The target corporation must distribute all assets it receives in the reorganization, as well as any of its own property retained. The target corporation then liquidates.[8] Thus, a "Type C" reorganization is essentially an exchange of

[8]Distributions may be to creditors as well as to shareholders. § 368(a)(2)(G).

■ FIGURE 4–3
"Type C" Reorganization

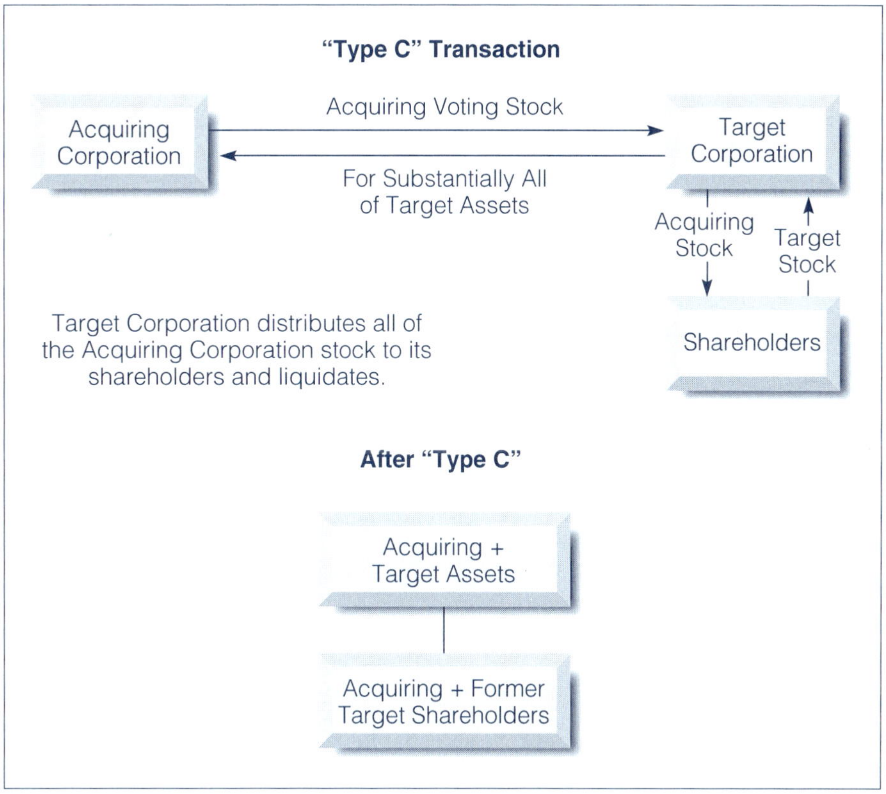

voting stock for assets followed by liquidation of the target corporation. The exchange is a taxable transaction for the shareholders to the extent that they receive assets other than stock in the acquiring corporation. The "Type C" reorganization is illustrated in Figure 4–3.

EXAMPLE 12

Acquiring Corporation transfers voting stock representing a 30% ownership interest to Target Corporation for substantially all of Target's assets. After the exchange, Target's only assets are cash and Acquiring voting stock. Target distributes the Acquiring stock and cash to its shareholders in exchange for their Target stock. The exchange qualifies as a "Type C" reorganization if Target liquidates after the distribution. The exchange is a taxable transaction for the shareholders to the extent they received cash. ■

DIGGING DEEPER 4

Find more information on this topic at our Web site: ***http://wft-advanced.swlearning.com.***

"Type A" and "Type C" Reorganizations Compared. The outcome of a "Type C" reorganization is similar to that of a "Type A" merger, as can be seen by comparing the diagrams for these reorganizations (Figure 4–3 versus Figure 4–1). However, their requirements differ. A "Type C" has more restrictions regarding the consideration that may be used by the acquiring corporation. Nevertheless, the "Type C" can be preferable to the "Type A," because in the "Type C" the acquiring corporation assumes only the liabilities of the target that it chooses. It normally is not liable for unknown or contingent liabilities. Further, in some states, only the approval of the shareholders in the target corporation is required in the "Type C" reorganization. As with a "Type A" reorganization, a subsidiary can be utilized to complete a "Type C" by using either the parent's or the subsidiary's stock but not both.

Consideration in the "Type C" Reorganization. The acquiring corporation's consideration in the "Type C" reorganization normally consists of voting stock. However, there are exceptions to this rule. Cash and other property do not destroy a "Type C" reorganization if at least 80 percent of the fair market value of the target's property is obtained with voting stock.

Although the acquiring corporation has more freedom in the consideration given in a "Type C" than in a "Type B," this freedom is not without a cost. When the acquiring corporation gives solely voting stock for the target corporation's assets, the target corporation's liabilities assumed by the acquiring corporation are not considered *other property* (i.e., boot) in the exchange. The transaction is an exchange of assets for voting stock, and the 80 percent-of-property requirement is met. However, liabilities assumed by the acquiring corporation *are* treated as *other property* if the target corporation receives any property other than voting stock in the reorganization. Liabilities assumed by the acquiring corporation are likely to exceed 20 percent of the fair market value of the assets acquired.

EXAMPLE 13

Target Corporation transfers assets with a fair market value of $200,000 to Acquiring Corporation for voting stock valued at $150,000 and assumption of $50,000 of liabilities. Target distributes the Acquiring stock to its shareholders and liquidates. The transaction qualifies as a "Type C" reorganization. The liabilities are not treated as *other property* received. Acquiring obtained 100% of Target's assets for voting stock. The liabilities assumed by Acquiring are disregarded as boot when no consideration other than stock is given.

Suppose Target had transferred its assets to Acquiring for stock valued at $140,000, cash of $10,000, and the assumption of $50,000 of liabilities. The liabilities would be considered *other property* because Target also received cash. *Other property* amounts to $60,000, which exceeds 20% of the fair market value of Target's assets ($200,000 × 20% = $40,000). The transaction does not qualify as a "Type C" reorganization.

Had Acquiring given Target its voting stock worth $170,000 and cash of $30,000, the transaction would qualify as a "Type C" reorganization. No liabilities are assumed, and the *other property* transferred is less than 20% of the fair market value of the assets ($30,000 is less than $40,000). ■

DIGGING DEEPER 5

Find more information on this topic at our Web site: ***http://wft-advanced.swlearning.com.***

Asset Transfers. The "Type C" reorganization requires that substantially all of the target corporation's assets are transferred to the acquiring corporation. However, there is no statutory definition of "substantially all." To obtain a favorable ruling from the IRS, assets representing at least 90 percent of the fair market value of the net assets and at least 70 percent of the fair market value of the gross assets held by the target corporation must be transferred.[9] Smaller percentages may still qualify. However, the parties must rely on their particular facts and circumstances to receive a favorable decision.[10]

[9]Rev.Rul. 77–37, 1977–2 C.B. 568, amplified by Rev.Proc. 86–42, 1986–2 C.B. 722.

[10]Where 70% of the assets were transferred and 30% retained to discharge the liabilities of the target prior to liquidation, the IRS found that substantially all of the assets were transferred. Rev.Rul. 57–518, 1957–2 C.B. 253.

TYPE D

The first three types of tax-free corporate reorganizations are designed for corporate combinations. The "Type D" reorganization is different; it is generally used to effect a corporate division, called a "divisive" reorganization. However, the "Type D" can also be used to carry out a corporate combination, called an "acquisitive" reorganization. "Type D" reorganizations also differ from the other restructurings in that the entity that transfers assets is the acquiring corporation rather than the target corporation.

Acquisitive "Type D" Reorganization. If a combination meets the following requirements, it will be treated as a "Type D" reorganization.

- Substantially all of the property of the acquiring corporation must be transferred to the target corporation.
- The acquiring corporation must be in control (50 percent) of the target.[11]
- Stock received by the acquiring corporation, as well as any remaining assets of the acquiring corporation, must be distributed to its shareholders.
- The acquiring corporation must liquidate.

This type of transaction may also meet the requirements of a "Type C" reorganization (from the target's viewpoint). If the transaction can be classified as both a "Type C" and a "Type D" reorganization, it is treated as a "Type D."[12] The "Type D" acquisitive reorganization is diagrammed in Figure 4–4. A comparison of Figure 4–4 with Figure 4–3 will illustrate how a "Type D" may also qualify as a "Type C" reorganization.

EXAMPLE 14

Acquiring Corporation wishes to control Target Corporation (value of $300,000), but Target holds a nontransferable license. Thus, Target must be the surviving corporation. Acquiring transfers all its assets with a value of $700,000 to Target for 70% of Target's stock. Acquiring then distributes all the Target stock to its shareholders and liquidates. The transaction qualifies as a "Type D" reorganization. ■

Divisive "Type D" Reorganization. Rather than combining, shareholders may wish to divide corporate assets and split the corporation. This might occur for many reasons including antitrust problems, differences of opinion among the shareholders, product liability concerns, or family tax planning. The more typical divisive "Type D" reorganization allows shareholders to accomplish their goals without incurring tax. In a divisive reorganization, one or more new corporations are formed to receive part or all of the assets of the original corporation. In exchange for its assets, the original corporation must receive stock.

The remaining requirements for a divisive "Type D" reorganization are as follows.

- The stock received by the original corporation must constitute control (80 percent) of the new corporation(s).
- The stock of the new corporation(s) must be distributed to the shareholders of the original corporation.
- Both the assets transferred and those retained by the original corporation must represent active businesses that have been owned and conducted by the original corporation for at least five years before the transfer.
- The distributions of stock and securities to the shareholders cannot be principally a device for distributing the earnings and profits of either the original corporation or the controlled corporation.

---

[11] No attribution of ownership is allowed in determining whether there is 50% control. §§ 368(a)(2)(H) and 304(c).

[12] Reg. § 1.368–2(d)(3).

FIGURE 4–4
Acquisitive "Type D" Reorganization

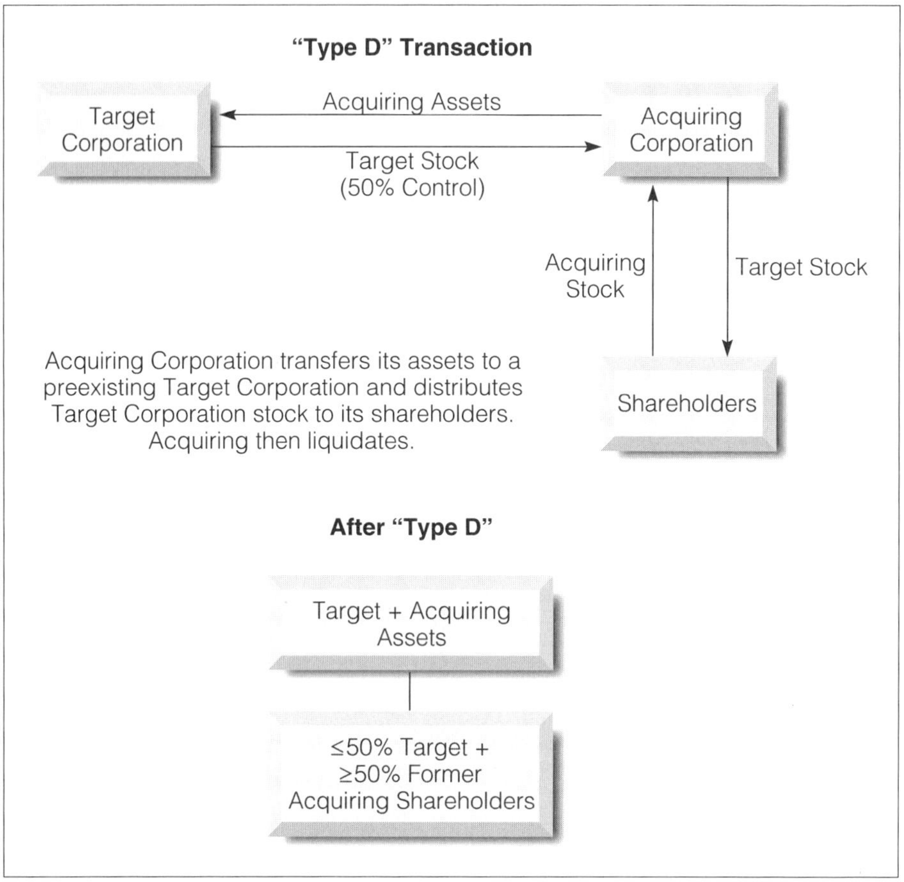

EXAMPLE 15

Bell, Inc., has been engaged in manufacturing. It also owns investment securities. Bell transfers the investment securities to a newly formed corporation and distributes the stock of the new corporation to its shareholders. The transaction does not qualify as a "Type D" reorganization. Holding investment securities does not constitute a trade or business. The shareholders of Bell, Inc., are taxed on the receipt of the stock. ■

EXAMPLE 16

Jane and Ivan are the sole shareholders of WB Corporation. WB was organized 10 years ago and has been actively engaged in manufacturing two products, widgets and bolts. Considerable friction has developed between Jane and Ivan, who now wish to divide the business. Jane wants the assets used in manufacturing widgets, and Ivan wants to continue manufacturing bolts. The separation of the business assets can be accomplished tax-free using one of the divisive "Type D" reorganizations. ■

EXAMPLE 17

CUE, Inc., has manufactured a single product at two plants for the past 10 years. It transfers one plant and related activities to a new corporation. CUE then distributes the stock of the new corporation to its shareholders. The activities of each plant constitute a trade or business. The transaction qualifies as a "Type D" reorganization. ■

Spin-Offs, Split-Offs, and Split-Ups. There are three different types of divisive "Type D" reorganizations: spin-offs, split-offs, and split-ups.

- In a **spin-off,** a new corporation is formed to receive some of the assets of the original corporation in exchange for the new corporation's stock. The stock of the new corporation is distributed to the shareholders of the original corporation. No stock of the original corporation is surrendered. The shareholders' basis in their original stock is allocated between the original and the new stock based on the relative fair market value of each.
- A **split-off** resembles a spin-off except that in a split-off the shareholders surrender stock of the original corporation in exchange for stock in the new corporation. Stock basis is computed in the same manner as for a spin-off.
- In a **split-up,** two or more new corporations are formed to receive substantially all of the assets of the original corporation. The stock of each new corporation is distributed to the shareholders of the original corporation in exchange for their original stock. The original corporation is then liquidated. The shareholders' basis in the relinquished original stock carries over as the basis of the new stock.

The spin-off and split-off are illustrated in Figure 4–5, and the split-up is illustrated in Figure 4–6.

EXAMPLE 18

Shawnee purchased 10% (500 shares) of OriginalCo eight years ago for $60,000. Before a spin-off reorganization, the total value of OriginalCo stock was $900,000, and Shawnee's stock is valued at $90,000. OriginalCo spins off 30% of its business assets into NewCo (fair market value $270,000) and distributes 10,000 shares of stock to its shareholders. Shawnee's 1,000 shares of NewCo have a $27,000 value. After the spin-off, the value of OriginalCo is reduced to $630,000, and the value of Shawnee's stock in OriginalCo, therefore, is $63,000. Shawnee's $60,000 beginning basis in OriginalCo is allocated to the two companies' stock as follows: $18,000 to NewCo stock [$60,000 × ($27,000/$90,000)] and $42,000 to OriginalCo stock [$60,000 × ($63,000/$90,000)]. ■

EXAMPLE 19

Assume the same facts as in Example 18, except that OriginalCo creates NewCo through a split-off. Shawnee is required to surrender 150 shares of OriginalCo to receive the 1,000 shares of NewCo. The fair market value of Shawnee's OriginalCo stock is now $63,000 [($90,000 ÷ 500) × (500 − 150)], and the value of the NewCo stock is $27,000 ($90,000 − $63,000). Shawnee's $60,000 beginning basis in OriginalCo is allocated to the two companies' stock as follows: $42,000 to OriginalCo stock [$60,000 × ($63,000/$90,000)] and $18,000 to NewCo stock [$60,000 × ($27,000/$90,000)]. ■

EXAMPLE 20

Gail and Gary are the sole shareholders of Publishers Corporation. Publishers was organized six years ago to publish both books and periodicals. Because of antitrust problems, Publishers wishes to divide its business. Two new corporations are formed, Books and Periodicals. All the assets relating to the book publishing business are transferred to Books. All assets relating to the publishing of periodicals are transferred to Periodicals. Gail exchanges all her stock in Publishers for the stock in Books. Gary exchanges all his stock in Publishers for the stock in Periodicals. Publishers is liquidated. The transaction qualifies as a "Type D" reorganization split-up. Neither Gail nor Gary recognizes gain on the exchange. Gail's basis in her stock in Publishers becomes the basis for her stock in Books. Gary's basis in his stock in Publishers becomes his basis for his stock in Periodicals. ■

■ **FIGURE 4–5**
"Type D" Reorganizations: Spin-Off and Split-Off

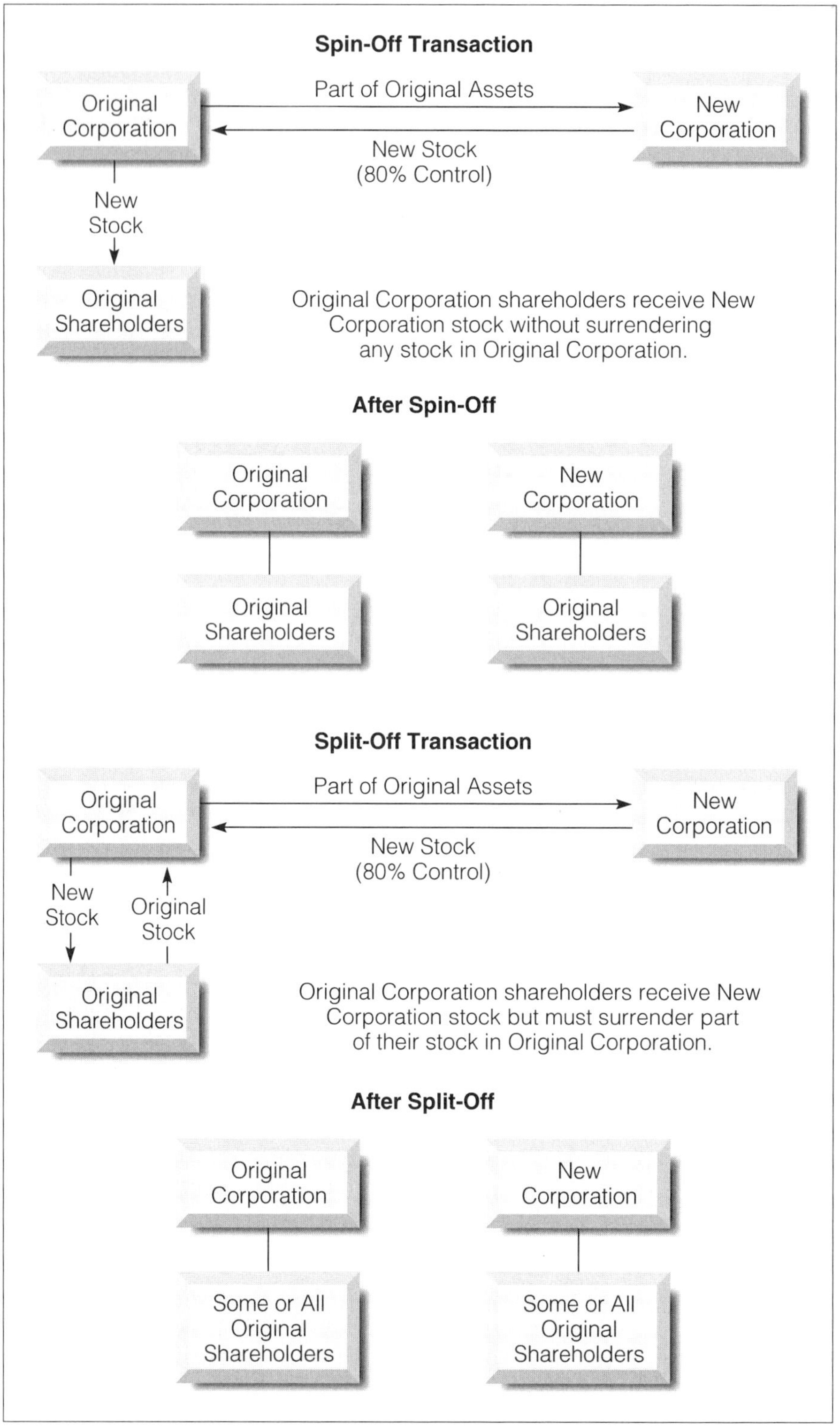

FIGURE 4–6
"Type D" Reorganization: Split-Up

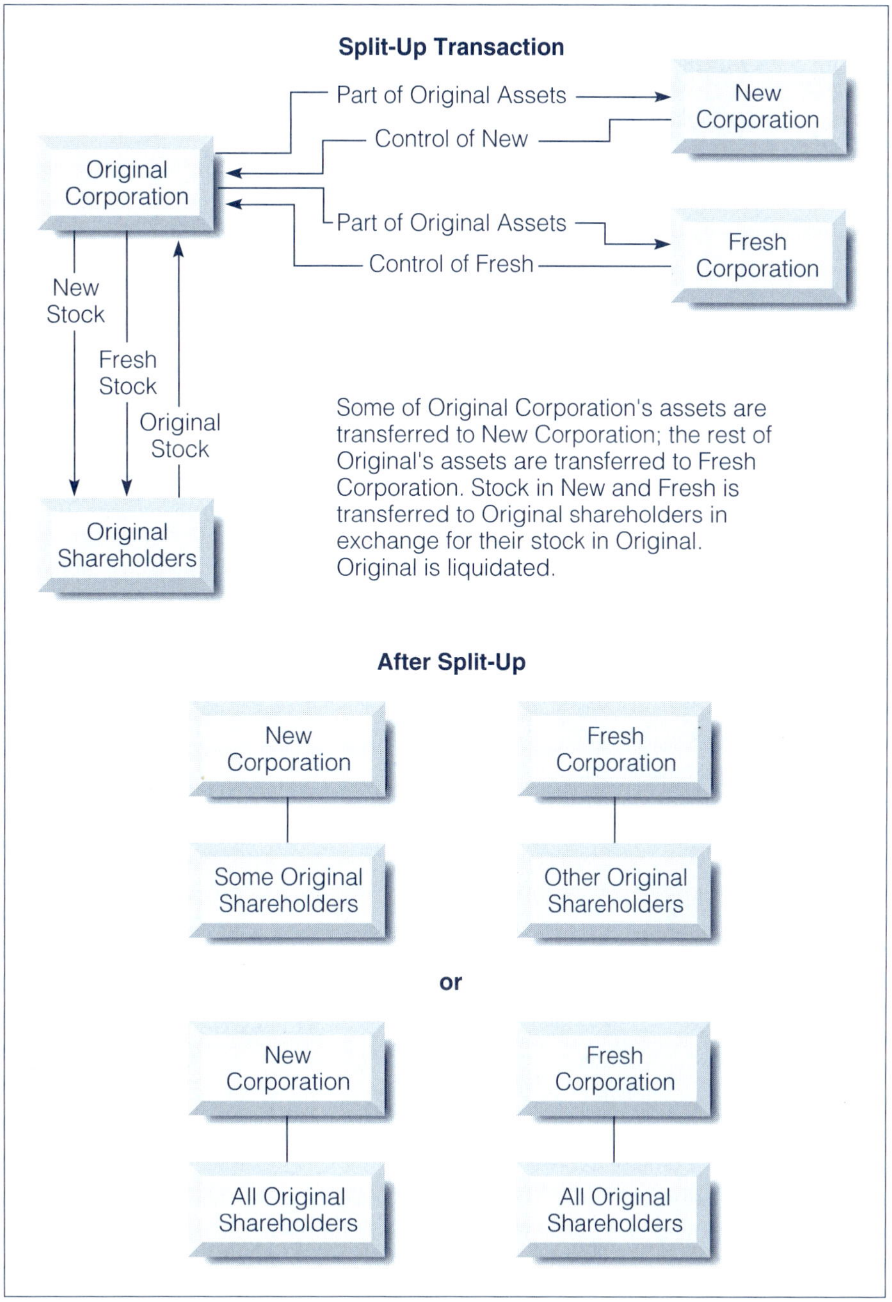

PLANNING STRATEGIES

Assessing the Possible Benefits of Restructuring Options

FRAMEWORK FOCUS: INCOME AND EXCLUSIONS

STRATEGY ➤ **AVOID INCOME RECOGNITION.**

Corporate reorganizations are valuable tools in the tax-free restructuring of corporations. However, it may not be possible to achieve the desired corporate structure by utilizing a single type of reorganization. For this reason, reorganizations should not be seen as mutually exclusive transactions; they can be combined with other tax-favored transactions into a comprehensive plan. The tax law allows a series of reorganizations to be recognized when the statutory requirements for each are met.

Suppose that Black Corporation operates two businesses, both of which have been in existence for five years. One business is a manufacturing operation; the other is a wholesale distributorship. White Corporation wishes to acquire only the manufacturing business and refuses to purchase all of Black's assets. What course of action might be advisable to transfer the manufacturing operation from Black to White with the least, if any, tax costs? Compare the following three possibilities.

1. Black Corporation transfers the manufacturing operation to White Corporation in return for some of the latter's stock.
2. Black Corporation forms Orange Corporation and transfers the wholesale distributorship to it in return for all of Orange's stock. The Orange stock is then distributed to Black's shareholders. This portion of the arrangement is a nontaxable spin-off. Black now transfers the manufacturing operation to White Corporation in exchange for some of the latter's stock.
3. After the nontaxable spin-off described in possibility 2, White acquires all of the Black stock in exchange for some of White's voting stock. Black is now a subsidiary of White.

Possibility 1 probably will not fit within the definition of a "Type C" reorganization, because Black does not transfer substantially all of the assets in return for White stock. The manufacturing operation is transferred, but the wholesale distributorship is not.

Possibility 2 suffers from these same shortcomings. If the spin-off is disregarded, the transaction becomes an unsuccessful attempt to carry out a "Type C" reorganization (possibility 1). Disregarding the spin-off is the natural result of following the step transaction doctrine (as explained later in this chapter, under this doctrine a series of interdependent transactions may be collapsed into a single step).[13]

Possibility 3 follows a different approach. It starts with the spin-off of the *unwanted* assets and concludes with White obtaining the *wanted* assets by exchanging its stock for the Black stock. Taken by itself, this last step satisfies the stock-for-stock requirement of a "Type B" reorganization. If, however, the step transaction doctrine is applied and the spin-off is disregarded, the Orange stock distributed to Black's shareholders might be considered as property *other than voting stock* in White. The IRS has not chosen to take this position and probably will recognize the nontaxability of a spin-off of *unwanted* assets followed by a "Type B" reorganization.[14] Thus, possibility 3, the "Type B" reorganization, appears to be the best choice, although there is still some risk of current taxation.

TYPE E

The "Type E" reorganization is a **recapitalization**—a major change in the character and amount of outstanding capital stock, securities, or paid-in capital of a corporation. The transaction is significant only for the stock- or bondholders who exchange their equity or securities. The corporation exchanges no property with another corporation. Thus, a "Type E" reorganization has no tax implications for the corporation. Further, transactions in a corporation's own stock or bonds are not taxable events.[15]

The following types of exchanges qualify for nonrecognition treatment as a "Type E" reorganization: bonds for stock, stock for stock, and bonds for bonds. A

[13] *Helvering v. Elkhorn Coal Co.*, 38–1 USTC ¶9238, 20 AFTR 1301, 95 F.2d 732 (CA–4, 1938), *cert. den.* 59 S.Ct. 65 (USSC, 1938).

[14] Rev.Rul. 70–434, 1970–2 C.B. 83.

[15] Reg. §§ 1.1032–1(a) and (c).

TAX IN THE NEWS

THE SARBANES-OXLEY EFFECT ON MERGERS AND ACQUISITIONS

The M & A market has been suffering from a lack of confidence, evidenced by the stock market's negative reaction to many of the recent mergers and the lower volume of deals. This lack of confidence stems from several concerns. One is that acquiring corporations may be getting more than they expect in terms of legal liabilities stemming from accounting misstatements. The Sarbanes-Oxley (S-O) Act, however, is expected to ease this anxiety and help restore some of the vigor to the M & A market. The stringent S-O requirements should enable acquirers to once again have confidence that the certified financial statements actually fairly represent the financial position of the target firm.

Even though the Securities and Exchange Commission has deferred the implementation of S-O, corporations on the market should make sure that they are currently in compliance and that their financial numbers are squeaky clean. Most sellers have not yet fully incorporated the effects of S-O into their mindset, but ignoring the importance of S-O could invoke a high price. Acquiring corporations are expecting compliance with S-O as a minimum requisite for potential acquisitions. Therefore, noncompliers could have fewer suitors, and with less competition, the offered price may be lower than desired. Any buyer not concerned about compliance with S-O or the validity of the financial numbers is likely looking for a bargain and thus will be offering only a bargain price.

Savvy corporate buyers are learning how to use S-O to their own advantage, and smart sellers always make sure that what they are marketing meets the desires of the buyers. Thus, implementing S-O will help the M & A industry in the long run by increasing buyer confidence. This in turn should stimulate the M & A market and ultimately benefit both buyers and sellers.

SOURCES: Adapted from Marilyn Much, "Declining Confidence Puts a Hold on M&As," *Investor's Business Daily*, June 5, 2003, and Martin Sikora, "Sellers Could Suffer Price Erosion for Sarbanes Slip-Ups," *Mergers and Acquisitions Journal*, September 1, 2003.

corporation can exchange its common stock for preferred stock or its preferred stock for common stock tax-free. The exchange of bonds for other bonds is tax-free when the principal amount of the debt surrendered is not less than that of the debt received.

EXAMPLE 21

Half of the stock in Spruce Corporation is owned by Wade and half by his children, Mark and Marcia. Wade wishes to retire and relinquish control of the corporation. He exchanges his common voting stock for nonvoting preferred stock. The exchange qualifies as a "Type E" reorganization. However, any difference in value between stock received and stock surrendered could be treated as compensation or as a gift. ■

EXAMPLE 22

Cedar Corporation exchanges each of its $1,000 bonds for 10 shares of common stock with a value of $100 per share. This qualifies as a "Type E" reorganization, and no gain is recognized because the value of the bonds given up is equal to the value of the stock received ($1,000 = 10 × $100). ■

TYPE F

The "Type F" reorganization is "a mere change in identity, form, or place of organization . . . however effected." Since a "Type F" is restricted to a single operating corporation, the successor corporation is the same corporation as its predecessor. Consequently, the tax characteristics of the predecessor carry over to the successor. A "Type F" reorganization does not jeopardize the status of § 1244

TAX IN THE NEWS

Type "G" Reorganizations Devastate Employee Retirement Plans

Over the last three years, more and more companies have filed for protection under the Chapter 11 bankruptcy rules ("Type G" reorganizations). The dollar amounts involved are staggering—the total assets of these companies exceed $525 billion. The largest failure was WorldCom at $103.9 billion with Enron a distant second at $63.4 billion.

Not only do shareholders, bondholders, and creditors lose in a bankruptcy, but so do employees, especially those whose pension plans are heavily invested in the company's stock. Employees of other companies whose pension plans invested in these bankrupt companies are also on the long list of losers. Both Enron and WorldCom had more than 50 percent of their pension assets invested in their own stock. According to the employees, management strongly encouraged them to invest their retirement contributions in the company's stock. Most employees chose to follow management's advice. WorldCom and Enron also matched their employees' contributions using their own stock, thereby exacerbating the concentration problem. Having the majority of a pension plan's assets in company stock is not unusual, however. The plans of General Electric and Coca-Cola, among others, have more than 75 percent of their assets in company stock. WorldCom maintains that it is not liable for its employees' losses. Pointing out that employees had 17 other options for investing their retirement contributions, WorldCom contends that the losses are due to the employees' unwillingness to diversify their retirement holdings, rather than the fault of the company.

SOURCES: Adapted from articles by Julie Earle in *The Financial Times Limited*, July 16, 2002, and July 22, 2002.

stock, nor will it terminate a valid S corporation election unless that is desired. The IRS has ruled that if a restructuring could qualify as a "Type A," "Type C," or "Type D" as well as a "Type F" reorganization, the "Type F" treatment prevails.[16]

EXAMPLE 23

Conifer Corporation changes its name to Evergreen Corporation. This is a "Type F" reorganization. ■

EXAMPLE 24

Orchard Corporation is organized as a Subchapter S corporation. Its shareholders wish to revoke its S election. Changing from an S corporation to a regular C corporation qualifies as a "Type F" reorganization. ■

TYPE G

Bankruptcy legislation introduced the "Type G" reorganization. In this type of restructuring, all or a part of the assets of a debtor corporation are transferred to an acquiring corporation in a bankruptcy or similar proceeding of a Federal or state court. The debtor corporation's creditors must receive voting stock of the acquiring corporation in exchange for debt representing 80 percent or more of the total fair market value of the debtor corporation's liabilities. Since a "Type G" reorganization must proceed according to a plan approved under a bankruptcy proceeding, tax planning for its use is limited.

A summary of the advantages and disadvantages of the various corporate reorganizations described in this chapter is found in Concept Summary 4–4.

[16]Rev.Rul. 57–276, 1957–1 C.B. 126.

Concept Summary 4-4

Corporate Reorganizations

Reorganization	Type	Advantages	Disadvantages
A	Merger or consolidation	• No requirement that consideration be voting stock. As much as 50% of consideration can be cash and property without tax consequences for the stock received (cash and other property received *are* taxed).	• All liabilities of target corporation are assumed by acquiring corporation as a matter of law. • Since state law must be followed, acquiring approval of majority shareholders, dealing with dissenters' rights, and holding required shareholder meetings may present problems.
B	Stock-for-stock exchange	• Stock may be acquired from shareholders. • Procedures to effect reorganization are not complex.	• *Only* voting stock of acquiring corporation may be used. • Must have 80% control of a target corporation. • May have minority interest remaining in target corporation.
C	Assets-for-stock exchange	• Less complex as to state law than "Type A." • Cash or property can be used as consideration for 20% or less of fair market value of property transferred. • Acquiring corporation assumes only the liabilities of the target it chooses.	• *Substantially all* assets of target corporation must be transferred. • Liabilities count as *other property* for 20% rule if any consideration other than stock and liabilities is used. • The target corporation must distribute the stock, securities, and other properties it receives in the reorganization to its shareholders.
D	Corporate division: spin-off, split-off, split-up Acquisitive	• Permits corporate division without tax consequences if no *boot* is involved. • Allows smaller target corporation to retain its existence.	
E	Recapitalization	• Allows for major change in makeup of corporation's equity.	
F	Change in identity, form, or place of organization	• Survivor is treated as same entity as predecessor; thus, tax attributes of predecessor can be carried back as well as forward.	
G	Court-approved reorganization of debtor corporation	• Creditors can exchange debts for stock tax-free. • State merger laws need not be followed.	• Tax planning for use is limited.

LO.4

Delineate the judicial and administrative conditions for a nontaxable corporate reorganization.

Judicial Doctrines

Besides the statutory requirements for reorganizations, several judicially created doctrines have become basic requirements for tax-free treatment. These doctrines include the sound business purpose, continuity of interest, and continuity of business enterprise doctrines. The courts have also formulated the step transaction

TAX FACT

Mega-Bankruptcies Are on the Rise

While the recent downturn in the global economy has dramatically slowed merger and acquisition activity, one type of restructuring has seen a surge in popularity: the "Type G" mega-bankruptcy reorganization. This increase has been fueled not only by the slow economy but also by the financial statement misstatement scandals of the past few years. As the table indicates, most of the largest bankruptcies occurring in the United States during the last 15 years took place in 2001 or 2002.

Largest Bankruptcies in the United States, 1987–2003

Companies	Year	Total Assets (in Billions)
WorldCom, Inc.	2002	$103.9
Enron Corp.	2001	63.4
Conseco	2002	61.4
Texaco, Inc.	1987	35.9
Financial Corp. of America	1988	33.9
Global Crossing, Ltd.	2002	30.2
UAL (United Airlines parent)	2002	25.2
Adelphia Communications	2002	21.5
Pacific Gas and Electric Co.	2001	21.5
Mcorp (financial services)	1989	20.2
Mirant Corp.	2003	19.4

Sources: Data are from BankruptcyData.com; New Generation Research, Inc., Boston, Mass.

doctrine to determine the tax status of a reorganization occurring through a series of related transactions. In addition, a plan of reorganization that is consistent with one of the Code reorganizations is required.[17]

SOUND BUSINESS PURPOSE

Even if the statutory requirements of a reorganization have been literally followed, a transaction will not be tax-free unless it exhibits a **business purpose.**[18] The business purpose requirement is meant to limit nonrecognition treatment to transactions that are motivated, at least in part, by the valid needs of the corporations. The transaction must have economic consequences germane to the businesses that go beyond the mere avoidance of Federal taxes. Although avoidance of taxes is not,

[17]Reg. § 1.368–1(c) and *William Hewitt,* 19 B.T.A. 771 (1930). For a definition of a plan of reorganization, see Reg. § 1.368–2(g).

[18]Reg. §§ 1.368–1(c) and 1.355–2. See also *Gregory v. Helvering,* 35–1 USTC ¶9043, 14 AFTR 1191, 55 S.Ct. 266 (USSC, 1935). The doctrine as developed in the *Gregory* case became a precedent for all transactions that might be shams devised merely for tax avoidance purposes. It brought about the principle of substance over form. All business transactions must have a sound business purpose.

by itself, considered a business purpose, the absence of a tax avoidance motive does not establish that there was the requisite business purpose.[19]

Given that a business purpose is required for tax-free treatment, whose business purpose must it be—the corporation's or the shareholders'? The Regulations indicate that the corporation's business purpose should be paramount. However, the courts have considered both corporate and shareholder purposes because it is sometimes impossible to distinguish between them.[20]

DIGGING DEEPER 6

Find more information on this topic at our Web site: ***http://wft-advanced.swlearning.com.***

CONTINUITY OF INTEREST

The *continuity of interest* requirement prevents transactions that appear to be sales from qualifying as nontaxable reorganizations. Therefore, this test provides that if a shareholder has substantially the same investment after the restructuring as before, the transaction is not a taxable event. To qualify for tax-favored status, the target corporation shareholders must receive an equity interest in the acquiring corporation.[21]

The Regulations deem the continuity of interest test to be met when the shareholders of the target corporation receive acquiring corporation stock equal to at least 50 percent of their prior stock ownership in the target. Not all shareholders of the target corporation need to receive stock in the surviving corporation. The requirement is applied to the aggregate consideration given by the acquiring corporation.

EXAMPLE 25

Target Corporation merges into Acquiring Corporation pursuant to state statutes. Under the merger plan, Target's shareholders can elect to receive either cash or stock in Acquiring. The shareholders who hold 40% of Target's outstanding stock elect to receive cash; the remaining 60% of the shareholders elect to receive Acquiring stock. This plan satisfies the continuity of interest test. The shareholders receiving cash are taxed on the transaction. Those receiving stock are not. ■

EXAMPLE 26

Juanita owns 100% of the stock of Target Corporation. Target merges into Acquiring Corporation. Juanita receives 1% of Acquiring's outstanding stock in exchange for all of her stock in Target. The continuity of interest test is met; Juanita received only stock for her interest. ■

If the continuity of interest requirement is met at the time of the reorganization, a sale of stock to an unrelated party immediately before or after the restructuring will not destroy the continuity of interest. Unrelated parties include individuals, noncorporate entities, and corporations that are not part of either the acquirer's or the target's affiliated group.[22]

[19] Reg. § 1.355–2(b) and *Marnes Wilson*, 66–1 USTC ¶9103, 16 AFTR2d 6030, 353 F.2d 184 (CA–9, 1966).

[20] *Lewis Trustee v. Comm.*, 49–2 USTC ¶9377, 38 AFTR 377, 176 F.2d 646 (CA–1, 1949); *Estate of Parshelsky v. Comm.*, 62–1 USTC ¶9460, 9 AFTR2d 1382, 303 F.2d 14 (CA–2, 1962).

[21] *Pinellas Ice & Cold Storage v. Comm.*, 3 USTC ¶1023, 11 AFTR 1112, 53 S.Ct. 257 (USSC, 1933), and *LeTulle v. Scofield*, 40–1 USTC ¶9150, 23 AFTR 789, 60 S.Ct. 313 (USSC, 1940). In *LeTulle*, a corporation transferred all its assets to another corporation for cash and bonds. The Court held that the transaction was not a tax-free reorganization if the transferor's only retained interest was that of a creditor. This concept is now in Reg. §§ 1.368–1(b) and (c).

[22] Reg. § 1.368–1(e)(3).

EXAMPLE 27

Pursuant to a preexisting contract, Juanita, in Example 26, sells all her stock in Acquiring Corporation to Ying for its fair market value. This sale occurs one week after the reorganization. Since Ying is not considered a party related to Juanita, the sale to Ying does not affect the continuity of interest test. Continuity of interest is determined at the time of the reorganization, and subsequent (or preceding) transactions between unrelated parties are disregarded. ■

CONTINUITY OF BUSINESS ENTERPRISE

The **continuity of business enterprise** test ensures that tax-free reorganization treatment is limited to situations where there is a continuing interest in the target's business. Specifically, this test requires the acquiring corporation to either (1) continue the target corporation's historic business or (2) use a significant portion of the target corporation's assets in business. The acquiring corporation's continuation of one of the target corporation's significant lines of business satisfies the continuity of business requirement. The use of a "significant" portion of the assets test is based on the relative importance of the assets to the target's former business or their net fair market value.[23] Whether these requirements are met depends on the facts of each case.

STEP TRANSACTION

The **step transaction** doctrine ensures that taxpayers cannot engage in a series of transactions for the purpose of obtaining tax benefits that would not be allowed if the transaction was accomplished in a single step. When the steps are so interdependent that the accomplishment of one step would be fruitless without the completion of the series of steps, the transactions may be collapsed into a single step.[24]

The step transaction doctrine presents problems for reorganizations when the acquiring corporation does not want all of the target's assets. For a "Type C" and acquisitive "Type D," the target (acquirer for "Type D") is required to transfer substantially all of its assets to the acquiring (target for "Type D") corporation. If the target corporation attempts to dispose of its unwanted assets before a reorganization, the step transaction doctrine could ruin the tax-favored status of the transaction. The acquiring corporation would have failed to obtain substantially all of the target corporation's assets. Without direct evidence to the contrary, the IRS generally views any transactions occurring within one year of a reorganization as part of the restructuring.[25]

LO.5

Apply the rules pertaining to the carryover of tax attributes in a corporate reorganization.

Carryover of Corporate Tax Attributes

Some tax features of the target corporation (the carryover of losses, tax credits, and E & P deficits) are welcomed by the successor corporation. Others may prove less desirable (positive E & P and assumption of liabilities). The mandatory carryover rules should be carefully considered in every corporate acquisition; they may, in fact, determine the form of the transaction.

[23]Reg. § 1.368–1(d).

[24]*American Bantam Car Co.*, 11 T.C. 397 (1948), *aff'd* in 49–2 USTC ¶9471, 38 AFTR 820, 177 F.2d 513 (CA–3, 1949), *cert. den.* 70 S.Ct. 622 (USSC, 1950). If the steps have independent economic significance, the doctrine does not apply. See *Esmark, Inc.*, 90 T.C. 171 (1988) and Rev.Rul. 79–250, 1979–2 C.B. 156.

[25]Reg. § 1.368–2(c), but in Rev.Rul. 69–48, 1969–1 C.B. 106, the IRS applied the step transaction doctrine to transactions that were 22 months apart.

BRIDGE DISCIPLINE

Bridge to Financial Accounting

The pooling-of-interests method for financial accounting is dead! Mergers and acquisitions (M & A) must now utilize the purchase method in accounting for combinations of companies. Pooling of interests was a popular financial accounting treatment for mergers because it did not affect the companies' "bottom line." Pooling permitted the companies to simply combine their assets and earnings on their financial statements in a manner similar to the tax-free reorganization treatment provided under tax law. Any merger premium (amount in excess of the value of the target's assets) was not recorded as goodwill and therefore was not written off against future earnings. By contrast, the purchase method, which is used in most of the rest of the world, requires the merger premium to be recorded as goodwill and amortized. This amortization could have a devastating effect on financial accounting income.

The death of the pooling-of-interests method was not as catastrophic for M & A as had been feared when the Financial Accounting Standards Board (FASB) first indicated its intention of issuing the new standard (Statement 141) on this issue. The reason for corporate America's turnaround was the issuance of another standard (Statement 142) eliminating the amortization of purchased goodwill. Many believe that FASB changed the treatment of goodwill to make the M & A accounting standard more acceptable to the business community. The elimination of goodwill amortization causes its treatment once again to differ for tax and financial accounting purposes. Prior to 1993, goodwill was amortized for financial accounting but not for tax purposes (permanent book-to-tax difference). With the enactment of § 197, goodwill was amortizable for both tax and financial accounting although over different periods (timing difference). Now, the tide has turned, and goodwill may be amortized for tax but not financial accounting (permanent book-to-tax difference). It will be interesting to see the future developments in the treatment of M & A for tax and financial accounting.

ASSUMPTION OF LIABILITIES

Since a corporate reorganization must result in some continuation of the business activities of the previous corporations, existing liabilities seldom are liquidated (a "Type G" reorganization is the exception). The acquiring corporation either assumes the liabilities of the target corporation or takes the target's property subject to its liabilities. These liabilities are not considered boot when determining gain recognition for the corporations involved in the restructuring. Generally, liabilities are problematic only in the "Type C" reorganization, when the acquiring corporation transfers other property to the target as well as stock. In this situation, the liabilities can cause a violation of the 80 percent-of-property for voting-stock requirement.

ALLOWANCE OF CARRYOVERS

When a corporation acquires the assets of a target corporation, the target's tax attributes are also acquired. This occurs in the "Type A," "Type C," acquisitive "Type D," "Type F," and "Type G" reorganizations. Section 381 determines which tax benefits of the target corporation can be carried over to the successor. The "Type B," divisive "Type D," and "Type E" reorganizations do not fall under the carryover rules of § 381. In a "Type B" reorganization, the target corporation merely becomes a subsidiary. The corporation remains intact and its tax attributes are retained. With the spin-off and split-off "Type D" divisions, the old distributing

GLOBAL TAX ISSUES

Europe Moves toward U.S.-Style Disclosures

The European Union (EU) has more than 20 stock exchanges and even more regulating bodies issuing different requirements for financial disclosures. For example, some countries, such as Germany, allow corporations to release earnings information only twice a year. Others, such as the United Kingdom, require quarterly reporting. As another example, if a French company wants to acquire a U.K.-listed corporation, the British rules apply. However, if a U.K. company is merging with a French corporation, the French regulations must be met. Such inconsistencies are difficult to manage and are frustrating the European security markets.

Many of the major European financial players would like to have a single set of rules covering disclosure, trading, and takeovers and a single regulating body overseeing these rules. However, a report issued recently by the so-called Committee of Wise Men—a committee of influential individuals in the securities industry selected by the European finance ministers—indicates that a single regulating agency like the U.S. Securities and Exchange Commission is not in the near future for Europe. Even if all the countries could agree on such a body, the treaty governing the EU would have to be amended to create it—a process that would take a minimum of four years.

Meanwhile, some progress is being made. The EU is considering the use of electronic disclosures, and it has proposed requiring public companies to issue quarterly reports and follow U.S.-style disclosure rules. These changes would consolidate all disclosure requirements and upgrade regular reporting requirements. Current European reporting does not meet U.S. standards, so the dissemination of financial statements in the United States is limited. Ultimately, the market will drive the changes needed for global reporting standards. As the desires to access cross-border capital increase, the private sector will demand a universal system of providing the information needed to assess the value of a firm.

corporation retains its tax attributes, and the new corporation starts fresh with regard to its tax attributes (with the exception of E & P). A split-up division, on the other hand, causes the tax attributes of the distributing corporation to disappear when it liquidates. Like a "Type B" reorganization, the "Type E" involves exchanges of stock between the corporation and shareholders, with no change in the corporation's assets. Since only one corporation is involved in the "Type E" reorganization, it retains its tax attributes.

NET OPERATING LOSS CARRYOVERS

A net operating loss (NOL) of a target corporation is one of the beneficial tax attributes that may be carried forward to the acquiring corporation. The NOL cannot be carried back to a prior acquiring corporation tax year; it can only be used prospectively. An NOL is a valuable asset of the target because it can offset future income of the combined successor corporation.

EXAMPLE 28

Target Corporation has an NOL of $3 million. In the past, Acquiring Corporation has generated annual taxable income of about $5 million. It expects about the same amount of taxable income in future years. Acquiring undoubtedly will incur a large tax liability in the future years unless it can use Target's NOL. Upon merging, Target's $3 million NOL carries over to offset Acquiring's taxable income of $5 million, reducing it to $2 million. Acquiring will benefit from a tax savings of $1,020,000 [$3 million (reduction in taxable income) × 34%]. ■

Ownership Changes. Due to the beneficial nature of NOLs, the Code limits the amount of NOL that can be utilized each year by the successor corporation in § 382. The **§ 382 limitation** applies when there has been an ownership change for the target's (loss corporation's) common shareholders of more than 50 percentage points (by value). An **ownership change** occurs on the day (called the *change date*) when there is either an *equity structure shift* or an *owner shift* in the stockholders' holdings.

- An **equity structure shift** occurs when a tax-free reorganization causes an owner shift. The change date for an equity shift is the date the reorganization takes place. The equity shift limitation is not applicable to "Type F," divisive "Type D," or "Type G" reorganizations.
- An **owner shift** is any change in the common stock ownership of shareholders owning at least 5 percent. Owner shifts can be caused by purchases, issuances of corporate stock, redemptions, recapitalizations, and transfers to controlled corporations.

Whether an ownership change has occurred is determined by examining the common stock ownership during a testing period, generally the prior three years.[26] Shareholders owning less than a 5 percent interest during the testing period are aggregated and treated as one shareholder for determining ownership changes. Thus, transfers between shareholders who own less than 5 percent do not influence the percentage-point ownership change computation.

EXAMPLE 29

Target Corporation is merged into Acquiring Corporation in a "Type A" reorganization. At the time of the merger, Target had an NOL of $100,000. Pursuant to the merger, Target's shareholders, none of whom owns a 5% interest, receive 40% of the stock of Acquiring. An equity structure shift has taken place. Since all of Target's shareholders owned less than 5%, they are aggregated in determining the owner shift. Therefore, they owned 100% of the loss corporation prior to the reorganization and only 40% of the successor corporation after the reorganization. More than a 50-percentage-point change in ownership has occurred. ■

When an ownership change has occurred, the yearly amount of NOL available to the successor corporation is limited to the value of the target loss corporation multiplied by the **long-term tax-exempt rate** (the highest adjusted Federal long-term rate for the prior three-month period). The value of the loss corporation is the fair market value of the stock (both common and preferred) immediately before the ownership change occurs.[27] The value of stock received or the price paid for the loss corporation's stock generally indicates the fair market value of the stock.

DIGGING DEEPER 7

*Find more information on this topic at our Web site: **http://wft-advanced.swlearning.com**.*

The objective of the *§ 382 limitation* is to restrict the use of NOLs to a hypothetical future income stream from the loss corporation. This future income stream is considered to be equal to the yield that would have been received if the stock was sold and the proceeds invested in long-term tax-exempt securities. Section 382 does not disallow an NOL. It merely limits the amount of NOL carryover that the

[26]The testing period is the period following the most recent ownership change if that change occurred within the past three years. Further, the testing period cannot begin before the year in which the carryforward being tested occurs. See § 382(i).

[27]The determination of value occurs immediately *after* the ownership change in the case of redemptions or other contractions that are associated with the ownership change.

surviving corporation can utilize on an annual basis. If the surviving corporation's current-year taxable income is insufficient to offset the authorized NOL deduction, the amount not utilized may be carried forward and added to the next year's § 382 limitation.

A further limitation on the ability to utilize the NOL carryforward arises in the year that the ownership change occurs (change year). The amount of NOL available to the successor corporation in the change year is limited to the percentage of days remaining in the tax year after the change day. The amount of the § 382 yearly NOL limitation is multiplied by this percentage.

Lastly, the NOL carryover is disallowed for future taxable years if the surviving corporation fails to satisfy the continuity of business enterprise requirement for at least two years following any ownership equity shift. The continuity of business enterprise test is the same as for tax-free reorganizations. That is, the significant historical line of the loss corporation's business must be continued, or the successor corporation must use a significant amount of the loss corporation's assets in its business.

EXAMPLE 30

On December 1, Minus transfers all of its assets to Plus (a calendar year corporation) in exchange for 40% of Plus's stock. At the time of the merger, Minus is valued at $900,000 and has an NOL carryover of $200,000. Assume the long-term tax-exempt rate is 5%. Since there has been an ownership change of more than 50 percentage points for Minus's shareholders, the amount of NOL available for use in the merger year is $3,699 [$900,000 × 5% = $45,000 × (30/365)]. The NOL available to reduce Plus's taxable income in the next year is $45,000. If Plus fails to continue Minus's historical business or use substantially all of its assets for a two-year period, Plus is not allowed to use any of Minus's NOL. ■

PLANNING STRATEGIES

Ownership Changes

FRAMEWORK FOCUS: DEDUCTIONS

STRATEGY ➤ **MAXIMIZE DEDUCTIBLE AMOUNTS.**

An ownership shift can have an unexpected and devastating effect on a corporation's ability to use its NOL or other carryovers. This is especially true for closely held corporations. The small number of owners make an ownership change more likely to run afoul of § 382. With proper planning, a termination of an owner's interest or a shift of ownership from one set of owners to another can take place without invoking the § 382 limitation.

Suppose that Cardinal Corporation, worth $200,000, has an NOL of $150,000. The stock in Cardinal is owned by Kevin, 55 percent, and Fran, 45 percent. Kevin wants to sell his interest in Cardinal and retire. But what happens to the NOL if Kevin sells his entire interest? There would be a more than 50-percentage-point change in the ownership of Cardinal Corporation. Therefore, the § 382 limitation would be $200,000 times the long-term tax-exempt rate. Assume the rate is 10 percent. The loss of $150,000 is now limited to $20,000 annually. Can a sale be structured so that the NOL is not limited?

An owner shift is calculated for the three-year testing period. Kevin could sell 35 percent of Cardinal stock in Year 1, 5 percent in Year 2, 5 percent in Year 3, and 10 percent in Year 4. None of the three-year testing periods has a more than 50-percentage-point change in the ownership of the corporation. Thus, there is no § 382 limitation. Cardinal can deduct the entire $150,000 NOL sooner rather than later.

EARNINGS AND PROFITS

The E & P of an acquired corporation carries over to a successor corporation.[28] However, the Supreme Court later held that a successor corporation was not permitted to apply a deficit in the acquired corporation's E & P against its own E & P.[29] The result was confusion in applying these general rules. Earnings and profits of a deficit corporation are now deemed to have been received by the acquiring corporation as of the change date. A deficit may be used only to offset E & P accumulated by the successor corporation after the change date.[30]

Consequently, the successor corporation must maintain two separate E & P accounts after the change date: one account contains the prior accumulated E & P as of the change date, and the other contains the deficit transferred and E & P accumulated since the change date. The deficit in the post-transfer account may not be used to reduce accumulated E & P in the pre-transfer account.

EXAMPLE 31

Target Corporation is merged into Acquiring Corporation on December 31, 2003. On that date, the E & P balance for Target is a negative $75,000, and for Acquiring it is a positive $400,000. In 2004, the current E & P for Acquiring is $50,000. Acquiring now has two E & P balances: pre-2004 $400,000 and post-2003 negative $25,000 ($50,000 – $75,000). ■

OTHER CARRYOVERS

The benefits to the successor corporation of capital losses and excess tax credits carried over from a loss corporation are also limited when there has been an ownership change.[31] The capital loss carryovers are characterized as short term when carried to the successor corporation. These losses are taken before the NOL carryovers in applying the § 382 limitation.

DIGGING DEEPER 8

Find more information on this topic at our Web site: ***http://wft-advanced.swlearning.com.***

The benefit from all loss corporation carryovers taken in the current year cannot, in total, exceed the calculated yearly § 382 limitation. When a corporation has several types of carryovers, the sequence in which the loss corporation carryovers are applied to the § 382 limitation is as follows.

1. Built-in capital losses.
2. Capital loss carryovers.
3. Built-in ordinary losses.
4. NOL carryovers.
5. Foreign tax credits.
6. Business credit carryovers.
7. Minimum tax credit carryovers.[32]

Besides the § 382 limitation, the year-of-transfer limitation applies to all of these carryovers.

DISALLOWANCE OF CARRYOVERS

Irrespective of the carryover rules, the IRS can utilize § 269 to disallow the carryover of tax benefits if a tax avoidance scheme is apparent. Such items are disallowed when a corporation acquires property of another corporation primarily to

[28] *Comm. v. Sansome,* 3 USTC ¶978, 11 AFTR 854, 60 F.2d 931 (CA–2, 1931), *cert. den.* 53 S.Ct. 291 (USSC, 1932).

[29] *Comm. v. Phipps,* 49–1 USTC ¶9204, 37 AFTR 827, 69 S.Ct. 616 (USSC, 1949).

[30] § 381(c)(2) and Reg. § 1.381(c)(2)–1(a)(5).

[31] § 383.

[32] Reg. § 1.383–1(d).

evade or avoid Federal income tax by securing the benefits that the acquiring corporation would not otherwise enjoy. Whether the principal purpose is the evasion or avoidance of taxes is a question of fact. If the business of the loss corporation is promptly discontinued after a corporate reorganization, the IRS may use § 269 in an attempt to disallow the loss carryover.

PLANNING STRATEGIES

Carryover Considerations

FRAMEWORK FOCUS: DEDUCTIONS

STRATEGY ➤ **MAXIMIZE DEDUCTIBLE AMOUNTS.**

Careful consideration of the forms of restructuring can enhance the preservation of desirable tax carryover attributes.

Suppose that Acquiring Corporation wants to obtain the assets of Target Corporation. These assets have a basis to Target of $300,000 and a fair market value of $200,000. Target has incurred losses in its operations during the past several years and possesses NOLs of $250,000. Acquiring plans to continue the business conducted by Target, hoping to do so on a profitable basis.

To accomplish the planned acquisition of Target's assets, Acquiring could consider the following alternatives.

1. Using cash and/or other property, Acquiring purchases the assets directly from Target. Following the purchase, Target liquidates and distributes the cash and/or property to its shareholders.
2. Acquiring purchases for cash and/or other property all of the stock in Target from its shareholders. Target becomes a subsidiary of Acquiring. Shortly thereafter, Acquiring liquidates Target.
3. Utilizing a "Type A" reorganization, Target merges into Acquiring. In exchange for their stock, the shareholders of Target receive stock in Acquiring.
4. Under a "Type C" reorganization, Target transfers all of its assets to Acquiring in return for the latter's voting stock. Target distributes the Acquiring stock to its shareholders.

A satisfactory solution must center around the preservation of Target Corporation's favorable tax attributes—the high basis in the assets and the NOL carryovers.

- *Alternative 1—highly unsatisfactory.* It will not retain Target's favorable tax attributes. The purchase price (probably $200,000) becomes the basis of the assets in the hands of Acquiring Corporation.
- *Alternative 2—a better solution but entails a major risk.* When Target, a subsidiary of Acquiring, is liquidated under § 332, Target's basis in its assets ($300,000) carries over to Acquiring Corporation. What Acquiring paid for the Target stock becomes irrelevant. Target's NOLs also carry over to Acquiring. However, § 269 could present a problem. Section 269(b) specifically applies to a liquidation within two years after the acquisition date.
- *Alternatives 3 and 4—achieve the same tax result but with less tax risk.* Presuming Acquiring can establish a business purpose for the "Type A" or "Type C" reorganization, § 269 can be avoided. The preservation of favorable tax attributes, such as the NOL carryover and any capital loss carryovers, should be considered in the context of the sale of a small corporation.

THE ROLE OF THE LETTER RULING

When feasible, the parties contemplating a corporate reorganization should apply for and obtain from the IRS a letter ruling concerning the income tax effect of the transaction(s). Assuming the parties carry out the transfers as proposed in the ruling request, a favorable ruling provides, in effect, an insurance policy. If the tax implications are significant, as they often are with corporate reorganizations, the advantage of obtaining prior IRS approval is clear.

CONCEPT SUMMARY 4–5

Summary of Carryover Rules

Tax attributes that carry over from a loss corporation to the successor corporation:

1. Loss carryovers—subject to the § 382 limitation.
   - A. Annual limitations on use of carryovers are evoked when there is an ownership change—a more than 50-percentage-point owner shift or an equity structure shift.
     - Owner shift is a change in the ownership of shareholders owning 5% or more of the corporate stock.
     - Equity shift occurs in tax-free reorganizations, other than a divisive "Type D," a "Type F," or a "Type G."
   - B. Annual carryover usage cannot exceed the value of the old loss corporation on the change date (date of transfer) multiplied by the highest long-term Federal rate for the three calendar months prior to the structure change.
   - C. Year of transfer. The loss claimed in the year of transfer is limited to the annual limitation multiplied by a percentage representing the remaining days in the year of transfer.
   - D. Loss corporation carryovers are applied to the § 382 limitation in this order: built-in capital losses, capital loss carryovers, built-in ordinary losses, NOL carryovers, foreign tax credits, business credit carryovers, and minimum tax credit carryovers.
2. Earnings and profits.
   - A. Positive E & P of an acquired corporation carries over.
   - B. If either corporation has a deficit in E & P, the surviving corporation will have two E & P accounts. One account contains the total positive accumulated E & P as of the date of the transfer. The other contains the total deficit as of the date of the transfer. Future positive E & P may be offset by the deficit E & P account.
3. Other tax attributes.
   - A. Depreciation and cost recovery methods carry over.
   - B. The installment method of reporting carries over.

Suggested Further Readings

David Madden, "Variations on a D Reorganization Theme," *The Tax Adviser*, June 2003, pp. 319–321.

Robert A. Rizzi, "Bankruptcy Reorganizations: A Primer for the Former Bubble Economy," *Corporate Taxation*, July/August 2003, pp. 26–31.

Gregory W. Walkauskas, "Using A and C Reorganizations in Restructurings," *The Tax Adviser*, October 2002, pp. 652–659.

KEY TERMS

Business purpose, 4–24
Consolidation, 4–9
Continuity of business enterprise, 4–26
Continuity of interest test, 4–9
Control, 4–11
Equity structure shift, 4–29
Long-term tax-exempt rate, 4–29
Merger, 4–8
Owner shift, 4–29
Ownership change, 4–29
Recapitalization, 4–20
Reorganization, 4–3
Section 382 limitation, 4–29
Spin-off, 4–17
Split-off, 4–17
Split-up, 4–17
Step transaction, 4–26

PROBLEM MATERIALS

Problems

Communications

1. Black Corporation is considering acquiring Blue Corporation using its stock in exchange for Blue's assets. Black is aware of the statutory requirements of § 368. Explain in a memo to Black's president, Carol Carson, the general requirements that also must be met in order for a reorganization to receive tax-free treatment.

Issue ID

2. Channel purchased 1,000 shares of Fern Corporation five years ago. This represented 20% of Fern's outstanding stock. As part of a merger agreement between Fern and Ivy Corporation, Channel receives Ivy stock with a fair market value of $100,000 and a $30,000 bond, in exchange for all of her stock in Fern. The stock represents 10% of Ivy's outstanding shares after the merger is completed. Fern Corporation is liquidated after the merger. What are the tax issues regarding this transaction?

3. Five years ago, Anatep paid $200,000 for 80% of Tecca Corporation's stock. In the current year, Tecca merges with Azza Corporation, and Anatep receives 25% of Azza's stock (worth $500,000) plus $100,000 cash. At the time of the transaction, Tecca's E & P was $75,000, and Azza's E & P was $800,000. How will Anatep treat this transaction for tax purposes?

4. Quinn purchased 20% of Redbird Corporation for $100,000 and a $50,000 bond five years ago. In a transaction qualifying as a reorganization under § 368, Redbird exchanges all of its assets valued at $1.6 million (basis of $900,000) for 395,000 shares of Bluebird Corporation stock plus a parcel of land. Redbird distributes 700 shares of Bluebird stock (valued at $280,000), a $60,000 Bluebird bond, and the land (valued at $20,000) to Quinn in exchange for his Redbird stock and bond. Redbird's current and accumulated E & P before the reorganization amount to $150,000.
   a. How will Quinn treat this transaction for tax purposes? What is Quinn's basis in the stock, bond, and land?
   b. How will Redbird treat this transaction for tax purposes? What is Bluebird's basis in the assets it receives from Redbird?

5. Rosa owns 60% of the stock of Pine Corporation (basis of $100,000), and the other 40% was recently purchased by Arvid (basis of $110,000). Rosa also holds a $50,000 Pine bond. Pine enters into a tax-free consolidation with Lodgepole Corporation, in which Rosa will receive a 12% interest in the new Lodgepole Pine Corporation and Arvid will receive a 6% interest plus assets worth $30,000. Pine's basis in these assets is $10,000. Rosa will also exchange her $50,000 Pine bond for a $55,000 Lodgepole Pine debenture. The interest rate on the new bond is lower than the rate on Rosa's Pine bond. At the time of the reorganization, Pine's value is $300,000 and Lodgepole's value is $1.2 million.
   a. What are Rosa's and Arvid's bases in their new Lodgepole Pine stock?
   b. What is the amount of gain (loss) recognized by Rosa, Arvid, Pine, and Lodgepole on the reorganization?

6. Yellow Corporation and Red Corporation are interested in merging. To indicate to the public that the transaction is not a takeover, a new entity, Orange Corporation, will be formed. Yellow and Red will transfer all of their assets to Orange in exchange for 100% of Orange's common stock worth $500,000 and $600,000 in long-term bonds. The stock and bonds are distributed to the shareholders of Yellow and Red in exchange for their stock. Yellow and Red then liquidate.
   a. Will the merger of Yellow and Red qualify as a reorganization under § 368? If so, identify its type.
   b. Same as (a), except that only Orange stock worth $1.1 million is received and exchanged with the Yellow and Red shareholders.

EXTENDER

7. Brown Corporation has a wholly owned subsidiary, Green Corporation. One of the assets that Green owns is Brown stock. Green exchanges its stock in Brown for all of the assets in Red Corporation. Red distributes the Brown stock to its shareholders in

exchange for their Red stock. Red then liquidates. Can this transaction qualify as a tax-free corporate reorganization?

Issue ID

8. Sitka Corporation has 100,000 shares outstanding valued at $5 million. Canada Corporation would like to acquire Sitka but has had a difficult time negotiating with Sitka's management. Canada makes a tender offer to the Sitka shareholders of two shares of Canada (value of $26 per share) for each share of Sitka or $50 per share. Of the Sitka shareholders, 77% exchange their stock for Canada stock, and 15% take cash. The remaining 8% of the shareholders prefer to retain their Sitka stock. Discuss the tax consequences of this transaction to Sitka, Canada, and the Sitka shareholders. Suggest changes to the transaction that would produce more favorable tax treatment. Assume that Canada is only interested in owning Sitka as a subsidiary.

Communications

9. Vine Corporation is considering the acquisition of Lawn Corporation. Lawn has assets valued at $3 million and known liabilities of $1 million. Lawn has just received a patent on a new chemical fertilizer that should revolutionize the gardening industry. The product has been tested for the past two years and appears to be safe for outdoor plants. However, there is always the possibility that individuals or pets could have an undesirable reaction to the chemical. Further, the EPA has not finished testing the product. Because of the potential for product liabilities, Vine is concerned about going through with the acquisition. Vine's president calls you for guidance in this matter. You present the merits and shortcomings of having the acquisition qualify as a "Type A," "Type B," or "Type C" reorganization. Write a memo to the tax files documenting the advice you gave to the president of Vine Corporation.

10. Gray Corporation offers to acquire White stock by exchanging two shares of its voting stock for each share of White stock issued and outstanding. Ninety percent of the White shareholders enter into the exchange with Gray. After the exchange, the White shareholders own 30% of Gray's common stock. Does this transaction qualify as a nontaxable reorganization? If not, what must Gray do to have it qualify as tax-free?

Ethics

11. Retail Corporation is a regional chain of clothing stores that has become very profitable. Mirage, Inc., has noticed this success and decides to make an unsolicited tender offer for Retail's stock. In the past, Mirage has made such offers for other small companies. Once it owns enough stock to take control of the board of directors, Mirage forces the liquidation of the company to obtain its liquid assets. Therefore, Retail is very concerned about Mirage's interest in obtaining its stock. To avoid being taken over by Mirage, Retail negotiates with KnightCo to merge the two companies. KnightCo is fully aware of the dangers faced by Retail as it was the target of an unsuccessful takeover by Mirage in the past. Mirage discovers Retail's plan to foil its hostile takeover. To sabotage Retail's merger, it offers KnightCo an exclusive contract to sell its merchandise in Mirage's national chain of stores. KnightCo's board of directors feels this contract is too good to turn down, so KnightCo abandons the merger negotiations with Retail. Retail ultimately is taken over by Mirage, all 500 employees are fired, and Retail is liquidated. What ethical issues, if any, did KnightCo's directors face in their dealings with Mirage and Retail?

EXTENDER

12. Medford transferred 40% of its voting stock to Ashland, Inc., in exchange for all of Ashland's stock. Therefore, Medford Corporation is the parent of Ashland. Medford would like to acquire all of the stock in KlamathCo using the stock that Ashland owns in Medford. The transaction proceeds with Ashland exchanging its 40% interest in Medford for all of the KlamathCo stock. Medford now owns all of Ashland's stock, and Ashland owns all of KlamathCo's stock. The former KlamathCo shareholders are now owners of Medford stock. Does this transaction qualify as a tax-free reorganization?

13. Black Corporation exchanges 40% of its voting stock for 90% of White's assets worth $900,000 and all of White's liabilities amounting to $200,000. The remaining White assets are distributed to its shareholders. The Black stock is also distributed to the White shareholders in exchange for their stock. White then terminates.
    a. Demonstrate whether this transaction qualifies as a tax-free reorganization.
    b. Same as (a), except that Black transfers 40% of its stock and $100,000 in bonds in exchange for all of White's assets.

14. Target Corporation has assets with a fair market value of $4 million (adjusted basis of $1 million) and liabilities of $500,000. It transfers assets worth $3.7 million to Acquiring Corporation in a "Type C" reorganization in exchange for Acquiring voting stock and the assumption of Target's liabilities. Target retained a building worth $300,000 (adjusted basis of $150,000). Target distributes the voting stock in Acquiring and the building to Wanda, its sole shareholder. How much gain does Target recognize on the reorganization?

15. Assume in Problem 14 that the consideration Acquiring Corporation gives for all of the assets of Target Corporation is voting stock worth $3.2 million and a building worth $300,000, basis of $150,000. Target distributes the stock and the building to its sole shareholder, Wanda. Will either Target or Acquiring recognize any gain on the reorganization?

EXTENDER

16. Red Corporation owns 90% of Pink Corporation, and Pink holds 30% of Red's voting stock. Red desires to acquire Maroon Corporation. It causes Pink to transfer all of its stock in Red for $800,000 of Maroon's assets with an adjusted basis of $600,000. Maroon's remaining assets have a fair market value of $200,000 and an adjusted basis of $150,000. These assets along with the stock of Red are distributed to Maroon's shareholders in full redemption of their stock. Maroon then liquidates. To what extent, if any, will this transaction be taxable to Maroon or its shareholders?

Communications

17. AlCo currently owns 20% of TransCo, which it acquired five years ago for cash. AlCo is now interested in acquiring the remaining assets of TransCo in a transaction qualifying as a "Type C" reorganization. TransCo currently has assets valued at $2 million, of which $250,000 are liquid. It also has outstanding liabilities of $600,000; thus, its net value is $1.4 million.

Most of the shareholders of TransCo are agreeable to exchanging their stock for voting stock of AlCo. However, 10% of the shareholders will agree to the reorganization only if their shares are purchased for cash. The chair of AlCo's board of directors, Lisa Spring, requests your advice on this matter. AlCo's address is 3443 E. Riverbank Road, Walla Walla, WA 99163. Write a letter to Ms. Spring indicating how to arrange this transaction and meet the requirements of a "Type C" reorganization.

Communications

18. Daniel Jiosa owns all the stock of DJ Corporation. DJ runs a small grocery store that has a very favorable location. Circle 7 Corporation wishes to acquire DJ and add the grocery store to its chain of convenience stores. Circle 7 has offered DJ 500 shares of its common stock for all of DJ's assets. The 500 shares would amount to a .01% ownership interest in Circle 7.

Daniel has heard of the continuity of interest requirement for corporate reorganizations and is concerned that the proposed transaction will not meet this requirement. Write a letter to Daniel Jiosa explaining the application of the continuity of interest doctrine to this proposed reorganization. Daniel's address is 5103 E. Shady Lane, Sallisaw, OK 74955.

19. The shareholders of Blue Corporation and Yellow Corporation agree to form Green Corporation. All of the assets of Blue and 60% of the assets of Yellow are transferred to Green in exchange for all of Green's common stock. Some Green stock is distributed to the shareholders of Blue in exchange for all of their Blue stock. Blue then terminates. The Yellow shareholders receive the remaining Green stock and do not have any of their Yellow stock redeemed. How will this transaction be treated for tax purposes?

20. Purple Corporation manufactures toys and plastic pots. Due to the possible product liability associated with toys, Purple wants to separate the two divisions. Purple creates two corporations, Blue and Red. It transfers the toy division assets to Blue and the plastic pot division assets to Red in exchange for all of the stock of Blue and Red. Purple then liquidates. Is this transaction a corporate reorganization under § 368? If it is, identify its type.

Issue ID

21. Home Corporation is owned by four shareholders: Alicia, Boyd, Camille, and Devon. Each shareholder contributed $100,000 10 years ago for a 25% interest in Home. Home was initially engaged in the manufacture and installation of prefabricated homes, but in the last three years it has branched into the design and service of these homes. The addition of the new lines of business has caused tension among the owners. Alicia thinks the new lines have potential for rapid growth, whereas Camille feels that Home should focus on what it does best—manufacturing and installation. Devon thinks that

design and manufacturing naturally form one business but that installation and service should each be a separate business. Boyd, on the other hand, thinks that installation and service are complementary businesses and should be one company.

After much negotiation, it is decided that Home will transfer the installation and service lines of business to a new corporation called InstaServ and the design and manufacturing lines to another new corporation called ManuSign. Boyd and Camille will receive the stock in InstaServ, and Alica and Devon will acquire ManuSign. Home will not retain any assets and will therefore liquidate. Discuss the tax consequences of the proposed transaction.

Issue ID

22. Refer to the facts of Problem 21, but now assume that the shareholders decide that Home should become three corporations: Home, Design, and Service. Home will retain the manufacturing and installation businesses, and all four shareholders will retain their interests in it. Design will be owned by Alicia and Devon, and Service will be owned by Boyd. Discuss the tax consequences of the proposed transaction.

23. Pink Corporation redeems its 20-year, 5% bonds. The bonds have a face value of $1,000. For each bond, Pink issues 10 shares of cumulative preferred stock with $100 par value. The preferred stock will pay dividends of $4 per share each June 30 and December 31 until the shares are redeemed in 15 years. What is the amount of gain or loss the bondholders will recognize on this exchange?

24. Teal Corporation has been selling and servicing computers for the last 10 years. The shareholders think that it would be wise to separate the company into two corporations for marketing purposes. Aqua Corporation is created. Teal transfers all of the service division (30% of Teal) to Aqua in exchange for all of the stock of Aqua. The stock of Aqua then is distributed to some of the Teal shareholders in exchange for their Teal stock. Not all shareholders participate in the exchange. After the transaction, 30% of the former Teal shareholders own all of the Aqua stock. How will this transaction be treated for tax purposes?

25. Yong owns all 1,000 shares of Jade Corporation's common stock. His basis is $50,000, and the fair market value of the stock is $400,000. The 200 shares of preferred stock outstanding (par value of $900 and fair market value of $1,000 a share) are owned equally by Yong's children, Hue and Mian. Their basis in the stock is equal to the par value. Now that the children have become adults, Yong wants to encourage them to participate in the management of Jade. He believes that owning common stock would provide the children an incentive to become dedicated members of management. Therefore, the corporation recalls all of the preferred stock and issues Hue and Mian each 250 shares of common. Yong receives 200 shares of preferred stock in exchange for 500 shares of common stock. What is the taxable income each shareholder must recognize on the stock exchanges? What is each shareholder's basis in the new stock received?

26. Svet owns 2,000 shares of noncumulative preferred stock (par $100 per share) of Palm Corporation. Due to the volatility of its cash flows, Palm has not always paid the 6% yearly preferred dividend. Since the preferred stock is not cumulative, Svet has lost the return on his investment in some years. Thus, Svet would prefer to be a bondholder with a guaranteed 6% interest rate on his investment. Svet exchanges his preferred stock for $200,000 of Palm bonds. What are the tax consequences of this exchange to Svet?

Issue ID

27. Green Corporation (a steel manufacturer) is interested in acquiring Yellow Corporation (a toy manufacturer) because it has a substantial capital loss carryover and assets valued below their basis of $450,000. Before the merger takes place, Green would like Yellow to sell all of its assets that Green is not interested in acquiring. Green will exchange 25% of its stock and $200,000 in cash for all of the stock in Yellow. After the merger, Green will sell most of Yellow's assets to obtain the built-in losses. As Green's tax adviser, what concerns do you have regarding the proposed merger of Green and Yellow?

28. Green Corporation made a Subchapter S election in 1995. In the current year, Brown Corporation purchases 60% of Green's stock from the shareholders. Since an S corporation cannot have a corporation as a shareholder, the transaction causes Green to violate the S corporation requirements. Green thus becomes a regular C corporation. To what extent do the events described cause Green to have taxable income?

Issue ID
Communications

29. Beach Corporation has just lost a $1.5 million product liability lawsuit. Its assets currently have a value of $2 million, and its outstanding liabilities amount to $800,000 without considering the lawsuit liability. As a result of the lawsuit, Beach's future revenue stream appears to be substantially impaired. Beach's president, Sandy Jones, asks your advice regarding the possibilities of restructuring the corporation. Write Sandy a memo explaining her choices in restructuring Beach.

30. Amber Corporation has been having financial difficulties and is not able to make the interest payments to its bondholders. Under the guidance of a state court, all of its assets are transferred to New Corporation. New Corporation's voting stock is distributed to all of Amber's bondholders as full payment for the bonds. Amber's shareholders exchange their stock for stock in New. After the transaction, the former Amber bondholders own 60% of New, and the former shareholders own the remaining 40% of New stock. Explain whether this transaction qualifies as a § 368 tax-free reorganization.

Issue ID

31. Acquiring Corporation is interested in merging with Target Corporation because Target has a large capital loss carryover that Acquiring could readily use in the next two years. Acquiring is in the computer education business, and Target is in the music CD industry. In exchange for 2% of Acquiring stock and assumption of Target's $300,000 of liabilities, Acquiring obtains all of Target's assets and tax attributes, valued at $900,000. Target distributes the Acquiring stock to its shareholders in exchange for 100% of their Target stock. Acquiring will sell all of Target's assets with the exception of its CD burning equipment. It will use this equipment to produce educational CDs for personal computer use. What are the tax issues to be considered in these transactions?

Issue ID

32. Assume the same facts as in Problem 31, except that Acquiring purchased $350,000 of Target stock three months before the reorganization. Acquiring therefore exchanged $250,000 in stock and assumed the $300,000 of liabilities to acquire Target's assets and tax attributes. Discuss the tax consequences of this transaction.

Issue ID

33. Jack and Jill are the sole shareholders of Playco, a corporation that develops and manufactures interactive games for young children. They have developed some very interesting games but have had substantial problems manufacturing and marketing their products. Due to these problems, Playco has never shown a profit. Its current NOL is $300,000. Jack and Jill cannot afford to invest any more in Playco, and the banks are not willing to increase their lines of credit.

    Sellco, a widely held corporation, is a distributor of prepackaged foods. It has approached Playco regarding a merger. Sellco has been very successful in marketing its products to children and thinks it could be successful with Playco's products. What issues need to be considered before a merger between Playco and Sellco takes place?

EXTENDER

34. Corpus Corporation enters into a merger with Christi Corporation, which has a substantial NOL carryforward. The transaction qualifies as a "Type C" reorganization. After completion of the transaction, Corpus decides to reduce losses by selling all of the assets utilized in one of Christi's minor lines. These assets have a fair market value of $300,000 and an adjusted basis of $100,000. Corpus realizes that if the transaction had not qualified as a reorganization, Christi would have recognized gain on the transaction to the extent that its adjusted basis was less than the fair market value of its assets. Given that Christi has an NOL, no taxes would be paid on the gain recognized. Corpus treats the transaction as taxable to receive a stepped-up basis in the assets. When Corpus sells the minor line, it recognizes no gain on the transaction. Upon audit, Corpus argues that it had no business purpose for acquiring Christi and therefore the transaction should be taxable. Will Corpus be successful in this defense?

35. Ruby Corporation completed a restructuring transaction with Gold Corporation on August 31 of the current year. Gold distributed 30% of Ruby's stock to its shareholders in exchange for all of its own stock. Just prior to completion of the reorganization, Gold had assets worth $500,000, liabilities of $150,000, and an NOL carryover of $300,000. The Federal long-term tax-exempt rate was 10%. What is the amount of NOL that Ruby may use in the current year? How much will it be able to utilize in the next tax year?

36. Phoenix Corporation merged into Olympus Corporation on July 15 of the current year. Phoenix had an accumulated deficit of $210,000 in its E & P account, and Olympus had

accumulated $150,000 in its E & P account. At the end of the current year, Olympus showed an operating loss and, therefore, a deficit in current E & P of $100,000. Despite this loss, Olympus distributed $80,000 to its shareholders. To what extent is this distribution taxable to the Olympus shareholders?

EXTENDER

37. Winston Corporation, a manufacturer of tires, is interested in acquiring Salem, Inc., the small company that supplies its raw rubber. Salem has a $600,000 NOL that is an attractive tax attribute for Winston to acquire since Winston is very profitable. Given that there will be an equity shift, Winston is aware that the § 382 limitation will apply. When Winston discovers that the value of Salem is $500,000 and the long-term tax-exempt rate is 5%, it determines that the NOL is not worth as much as it had hoped. To accelerate Winston's ability to use the NOL, the Salem shareholders suggest that they contribute $1.5 million to increase the value of Salem to $2 million. Will this strategy be successful in reducing the limitation imposed by § 382 and therefore increase the amount of NOL Winston can use each year?

EXTENDER

38. Tulip Corporation merged with Lilly Corporation on May 15 of last year when the applicable long-term tax-exempt rate was 5%. Tulip exchanged all of its assets, liabilities, and tax attributes (capital loss carryforward of $70,000 and excess credits of $40,000) for $3 million in Lilly stock (a 5% interest). For the current year, Lilly has taxable income before application of any carryovers of $600,000. Of this income, $50,000 is capital gains. Determine Lilly's tax liability for the current year and its carryovers to the next year.

Communications

39. Jaysa Jones, president of Sea Corporation, is negotiating the acquisition of Salt Corporation. Salt is a supplier of raw materials to Sea but has been incurring substantial losses due to poor management. It also holds tax credits that it has not been able to use due to its lack of taxable income. Ms. Jones is aware that there are some limitations on the use of Salt's losses but is unclear as to the particulars. Write a memo to Jaysa Jones explaining the application of § 382 and the order in which losses and credits are allowed each year.

Decision Making
Communications

40. Disc Corporation is contemplating the acquisition of Density Corporation. Disc is interested in Density because it has a valuable patent used in the process of manufacturing CDs. Density is a young company and has yet to show substantial profits (accumulated E & P of $28,000). However, Disc thinks it can turn Density around by replacing Density's inexperienced managers with a more mature management team. The value of Density is currently estimated at $800,000, and it has a basis in its assets of $500,000. Disc's president asks you to illustrate (with diagrams) the possible tax-free reorganizations of Disc and Density.
    a. Assume that the patent held by Density is transferable.
    b. Assume that the patent held by Density is *not* transferable.

BRIDGE DISCIPLINE

1. Caramel Corporation is merging into Chocolate Corporation on June 30 of the current year in a transaction that does not meet all of the state merger requirements. On that date, the fair market value of Chocolate's assets is $1.6 million (adjusted basis $1.2 million), its liabilities amount to $500,000, and its retained earnings balance is $800,000. It has a $50,000 capital loss carryforward with three years remaining. Chocolate has no tax carryovers. On June 30, Caramel's assets have a fair market value of $10.2 million (adjusted basis $8.9 million), liabilities of $4 million, and retained earnings of $5 million. It uses a calendar year. Caramel exchanges $1 million of voting stock and $400,000 of cash for all of Chocolate's assets. The merger premium Caramel pays is due to Chocolate's valuable reputation.
    a. How will this merger be treated for tax purposes? Assume that the long-term tax-exempt rate is 5%.
    b. How will this merger be treated for financial accounting purposes?
    c. Compare the balance sheets for tax and accounting.
    d. Determine the treatment of goodwill (if any is created) for tax and accounting purposes.

Research Problems

THOMSON RIA

Note: Solutions to Research Problems can be prepared by using the ***RIA Checkpoint® Student Edition*** *online research product, which is available to accompany this text. It is also possible to prepare solutions to the Research Problems by using tax research materials found in a standard tax library.*

Communications

Research Problem 1. Exterminator Corporation was a small, closely held business that provided pest control services to commercial businesses. Generally, Exterminator's clients purchased three- or six-month contracts with full payment due when the contracts were signed. When the contract payments were collected, they were treated as liabilities and converted to income only when the services were actually provided. This is the customary industry practice and is accepted by the IRS as proper reporting.

A few years ago, a large national corporation, Terminator, Inc., moved into Exterminator's territory and cut into its business. As a matter of fact, Exterminator accumulated a $300,000 NOL. Realizing that the only way to survive was to merge with Terminator, Exterminator shareholders exchanged 100% of their stock and received a 5% interest in Terminator in a transaction qualifying as a "Type C" reorganization. At the time of the reorganization, Exterminator had a fair market value of $600,000, service liabilities of $100,000, other liabilities of $50,000, and adjusted basis in its assets of $150,000. After the acquisition, Terminator provided all services to the Exterminator customers and converted the liabilities into income. Terminator treated the income as recognized built-in gain when computing the yearly § 382 limitation. Upon audit, the IRS disallowed this treatment. The IRS is not questioning the timing of income recognition but rather whether these prepaid pre-change amounts constituted built-in gains within the meaning of § 382. Prepare a memo for Terminator's tax file explaining your findings.

Communications

Research Problem 2. Las Vegas Corporation is in the business of developing software used exclusively by multinational corporations. Among its assets are innovative software, valuable trademarks, outstanding corporate name recognition, and a large NOL carryover. These assets make Las Vegas a very appealing takeover prospect to Santa Fe Corporation. Santa Fe is a little known corporation that distributes software products to corporate clients. It is the largest business of its kind and is quite profitable.

After entering into negotiations, Santa Fe learns that Las Vegas's trademarks are not transferable. With further planning, the combination is expected to take place on June 30 of next year.

The president of Santa Fe, Darla Threestars, has requested your expert advice on two matters. First, Ms. Threestars would like to know what type of reorganization would be most effective in acquiring Las Vegas. Second, will the § 381 NOL limitations apply after the reorganization? Santa Fe is subject to the alternative minimum tax (AMT) each year and assumes this situation will continue in the future. Does § 381 only limit the amount of NOL that can offset regular tax in the first year, or does it also apply to the AMT?

Draft a letter to Darla Threestars explaining your conclusions. Her address is 1235 Pinto Drive, Santa Fe, NM 87505.

Research Problem 3. Hawaii Corporation, which is owned equally by two brothers and their younger sister, has been in the business of growing coffee and onions for the last 10 years. Lately, the brothers have been arguing about the management, operations, and expansion of the business. A professional mediator has suggested that the only way to resolve these issues is to divide the entity. The older brother will retain the coffee business and the Hawaii name. The younger brother and sister will receive stock in a newly formed corporation, Maui Corporation, in exchange for their stock in Hawaii. Maui will continue growing onions, but also will expand into other Hawaiian products.

Hawaii is organized as an S corporation, and Maui will elect S status at the earliest possible date. The transaction will take place as follows. Hawaii will transfer the onion farming assets to Maui in exchange for all of its stock. Hawaii will then exchange all of the younger brother's and sister's stock in Hawaii for all of the stock in Maui. After the transaction, the older brother will own all of Hawaii, and the younger brother and sister will own all of Maui. Both corporations want to retain their S status. Will this division of Hawaii qualify as a "Type D" reorganization? Will this division terminate Hawaii's S election or prevent Maui from electing S status?

Research Problem 4. As part of an integrated plan, Manchester Corporation creates Bedford Corporation as a wholly owned subsidiary. Then, Manchester acquires all of Bismark Corporation by merging Bedford into Bismark. After this transaction, Bedford no longer exists, and Manchester owns all of the Bismark stock valued at $1 million. Bismark shareholders received Manchester stock valued at $700,000 and $300,000 of cash for their shares of Bismark. Lastly, Bismark merges into Manchester in a statutory merger.

Thus, Manchester owns all of the assets of Bismark, and 70% of the Bismark shareholders are now Manchester shareholders. Explain whether this step transaction restructuring qualifies as a tax-free reorganization. Support your position with citations to primary tax sources.

Internet Activity

Use the tax resources of the Internet to address the following questions. Do not restrict your search to the World Wide Web, but include a review of newsgroups and general reference materials, practitioner sites and resources, primary sources of the tax law, chat rooms and discussion groups, and other opportunities.

Communications

Research Problem 5. Select one of the mergers listed in the Tax Fact earlier in the chapter and, using the Internet, research the facts surrounding the merger. Write a two-page summary of the restructuring that provides all of the essential details. Be sure to describe the structuring of the merger and try to classify it as to type (e.g., A, B, C).

Communications

Research Problem 6. Select one of the bankruptcies listed in the Tax Fact earlier in the chapter and, using the Internet, research the facts surrounding the bankruptcy. Write a two-page summary of the bankruptcy that provides all of the essential details. Indicate when the corporation emerged or is expected to emerge from the protection of the bankruptcy court.

Communications

Research Problem 7. Using an Internet tax service or other Internet source, select a recent court case that pertains to mergers, acquisitions, or the bankruptcy area of the tax law. Write a one-page case brief for the case.

CHAPTER 5

Consolidated Tax Returns

LEARNING OBJECTIVES

After completing Chapter 5, you should be able to:

LO.1
Apply the fundamental concepts of consolidated tax returns.

LO.2
Identify the sources of the rules for consolidated taxable income.

LO.3
Recognize the major advantages and disadvantages of filing consolidated tax returns.

LO.4
Describe the corporations that are eligible to file on a consolidated basis.

LO.5
Explain the compliance aspects of consolidated returns.

LO.6
Compute a parent's investment basis in a subsidiary.

LO.7
Account for intercompany transactions of a consolidated group.

LO.8
Identify limitations that restrict the use of losses and credits of group members derived in separate return years.

LO.9
Derive deductions and credits on a consolidated basis.

http://wft.swlearning.com

OUTLINE

TAX TALK

We have from time-to-time complained about the complexity of our revenue laws and the almost impossible challenge they present to taxpayers or their representatives . . . . Our complaints have obviously fallen upon deaf ears.

—Arnold Raum, Senior U.S. Tax Court Judge

Context of the Consolidated Return Rules

Through acquisitions and mergers, multigroup corporations, called **conglomerates,** are created. These conglomerates are present in every aspect of life. The local dairy or bakery is likely to be owned by General Mills or General Foods. Oil and insurance companies own movie-making corporations. Professional sports teams are corporate cousins of the newspapers and television/radio stations that carry their games. The same corporate group that produces night lights for a child's nursery may manufacture control equipment for bombers and other elements of the Defense Department's arsenal.

LO.1

Apply the fundamental concepts of consolidated tax returns.

MOTIVATIONS TO CONSOLIDATE

What brings together these sometimes strange corporate bedfellows? As Chapter 4 indicated, nontax motivations provide the strongest incentives for creating multiple corporation groups. Although these nontax concerns are important, tax incentives may also play a role. To a large extent, these incentives can be found in the rules that control the filing of **consolidated returns.** In general terms, certain corporate groups can be treated as a single entity for Federal income tax purposes. This enables the group to use available tax exemptions and brackets optimally among its members and to shelter the income of profitable members with the losses of other members. Thus, through the consolidated return rules, corporate taxpayers have an opportunity to manage the combined tax liability of the members of the group.

TAX FACT

Consolidated Returns

Consolidated returns represent only about 1 percent of the total number of corporate returns filed, yet they generate a significant amount of the total reported taxable income. Consolidated filers own a high percentage of the total corporate assets. Corporations filing consolidated returns are concentrated in the manufacturing wholesale, retail, and finance/insurance industries. These industries account for almost 50 percent of the consolidated returns filed.

Consolidated Returns versus Total Corporate Returns, Tax Year 2000

	Consolidated Returns	Total Corporate Returns
Number of returns filed	57,000	5,045,000
Total assets	$ 32.7 trillion	$ 47.0 trillion
Total receipts	13.3 trillion	20.6 trillion
Net income subject to tax	655.4 billion	760.4 billion
Income tax after credits	173.5 billion	204.0 billion

The consolidated return rules apply to a taxpayer as a result of various business decisions.

- A consolidated return may result from a merger, acquisition, or other corporate combination (discussed in Chapter 4).

EXAMPLE 1

When Maple Corporation acquires all of the stock of Wood Corporation, a new corporate group, Maple Wood Corporation, is formed. The two group members can elect to file their tax return on a consolidated basis. ■

- A group of business taxpayers may be restructured to comply with changes in regulatory requirements, meet the demands of a competitive environment, or gain economies of scale and operate more efficiently in a larger arrangement. Consequently, the election to file a consolidated return becomes available.

EXAMPLE 2

Fruit Corporation, a retailer, acquires Tree Corporation, a producer, in an effort to control its flow of inventory in unstable economic times. The two group members can elect to file their tax returns on a consolidated basis. ■

- Corporations may seek to protect their assets from potential liabilities by isolating the assets of one line of business in a separate corporation.

EXAMPLE 3

Palm Corporation manufactures two lines of products: toys and spatulas. Palm spins off the toy business into the Coconut Corporation. This restructuring isolates possible product liability from the manufacturing of toys to the assets held by Coconut. Palm's assets are protected from possible lawsuits involving the toy products. ■

TAX IN THE NEWS

Do Conglomerates Create Conflicts of Interest?

One part of what is now the entertainment giant Time Warner started not long ago as a small UHF station in Atlanta, eventually named WTBS. The Turner Broadcasting System was a small station with a weak signal and no "software" (i.e., programming to fill the broadcast schedule) other than dated reruns of network programs like *The Andy Griffith Show* and low-budget syndicated fare like *Hee Haw*.

With the advent of cable and then satellite television and the demand for all-day news and sports programming, the media company began to emerge from its humble beginnings. Another boost came when Ted Turner became the owner of local professional sports teams—the Braves and the Hawks—and began broadcasting their games. The games filled large blocks of airtime and attracted an audience of great import to advertisers.

But can the disparate members of a conglomerate resist the temptation to act in concert for the good of the entire group? Charges of "soft reporting" among corporate cousins often arise when critical reporting seems lacking. How will a CNN reporter address the Braves infielder whose error cost the team the World Series? Now that General Electric owns NBC, will we ever see a *Dateline* segment about how GE works to obtain Defense Department contracts? Can ABC and ESPN critics comment negatively on a movie from Disney, the corporate parent?

- The taxpayers may be seeking to gain tax and other financial advantages that are more readily available to corporate combinations.

EXAMPLE 4

Over the next three years, Elm Corporation will be selling a number of its business assets at a loss. If Birch Corporation acquires all of Elm's stock and the group elects to file its tax returns on a consolidated basis, Birch will be able to combine its gains from the sale of business property with Elm's losses in computing the group's consolidated § 1231 gain/loss for the year. ■

LO.2

Identify the sources of the rules for consolidated taxable income.

SOURCE OF CONSOLIDATED RETURN RULES

Congress has delegated most of its legislative authority involving consolidated returns to the Treasury. As a result, the majority of the rules that affect consolidated groups are found in the Regulations. The Code provisions addressing consolidated returns are strictly definitional in nature and broad in scope.[1] The related Regulations dictate the computational and compliance requirements for consolidated returns.[2]

Keep in mind that **legislative Regulations** of this sort carry the full force and effect of law. Challenges to the content of these Regulations seldom are supported by the courts. Consequently, taxpayers generally participate actively in the hearings process in an effort to have their interpretations included in the final Regulations.

The length and detail of these Regulations make the consolidated return rules among the most complex in the entire Federal income tax law. For the most part, the underlying objective of the rules remains one of organizational neutrality; that

[1] §§ 1501–1505.

[2] Reg. §§ 1.1501–1, 1.1502–0 through 1.1502–100, 1.1503–1 through 1.1503–2T, and 1.1504–1.

is, a group of closely related corporations should have neither a tax advantage nor a disadvantage relative to taxpayers who file separate corporate returns.

The derivation of a set of consolidated financial statements for a conglomerate and the computation of its consolidated taxable income correspond only slightly. The equity approach followed for financial accounting purposes has a role in the consolidated return rules, but exceptions to accounting conventions are both critical and numerous. Thus, a knowledge of financial accounting consolidation procedures is not necessarily of great assistance in computing consolidated taxable income, nor is a lack of familiarity with accounting conventions a hindrance.

EXAMPLE 5

Dividends paid by Sapling Corporation to its 100% owner, Oak Corporation, are eliminated from the separate taxable income computations of both group members in deriving consolidated taxable income. This treatment parallels the eliminating entry that is made in developing the group's consolidated financial statements.

Later, Sapling sells an asset to Oak Corporation, at a tax and accounting gain of $100,000. The asset appreciates by another $20,000 before Oak sells it to an unrelated party, Outsider Corporation.

No tax or accounting gain is reported by the group members until the ultimate sale by Oak to Outsider. In constructing the consolidated financial statements, Oak realizes a $120,000 gain. For tax purposes, however, Sapling is assigned $100,000 of the gain, and Oak recognizes only "its" $20,000. ■

LO.3

Recognize the major advantages and disadvantages of filing consolidated tax returns.

Assessing Consolidated Return Status

Before making an election to file consolidated tax returns, affiliated taxpayers must weigh the relative advantages and disadvantages. The following are factors to consider when making a consolidated return election.

- The election is binding on all subsequent tax years of the consolidated group, unless either the makeup of the affiliated group changes or the IRS consents to revoke the election.
- All members of the consolidated group must have the same year-end. This can cause short tax years when members join the affiliated group.
- The parent corporation's return elections (e.g., to claim a § 901 credit for foreign tax payments rather than a deduction) are binding on all members of the group.
- Capital and operating losses of one member of the affiliated group are applied against the corresponding income of the other members. This netting of gains and losses occurs even when assigning the losses to separate return years would produce a greater tax benefit.
- Recognition of income and losses from certain intercompany transactions is deferred.
- Intercompany dividends are eliminated from income. To the extent these distributions are made from earnings and profits, they reduce the parent's tax basis in the subsidiary's stock.
- Consolidated limits must be used in computing certain deductions and credits.
- The tax basis in the subsidiary's stock is increased (decreased) by the amount of income (loss) the subsidiary contributes to the consolidated return.
- The alternative minimum tax (AMT) attributes of all group members can be used in deriving consolidated alternative minimum taxable income (AMTI). This can reduce the adjusted current earnings (ACE) adjustment and optimize other AMT preferences and adjustments.

- The share holdings of all group members can be used in meeting other statutory requirements.[3]
- Additional administrative costs may be incurred in complying with the consolidated return Regulations.

PLANNING STRATEGIES

Choosing Consolidated Return Partners

FRAMEWORK FOCUS: TAX RATE

STRATEGY ➤ SHIFT NET INCOME FROM HIGH-BRACKET TAXPAYERS TO LOW-BRACKET TAXPAYERS.

Taxpayers should optimize their overall tax benefits when choosing consolidated return partners. Within the limitations of the rules discussed in the next section, attributes of potential target corporations might include some of the following.

- Loss and credit carryovers.
- Passive activity income, loss, or credits.
- Gains that can be deferred through intercompany sales.
- Contributions to consolidated ACE adjustments.
- Excess limitation amounts (e.g., with respect to charitable contributions).
- Section 1231 gains, losses, and lookback profiles.

Electing Consolidated Return Status

A corporation can join in a consolidated tax return if it meets three requirements, as shown in Concept Summary 5–1.

- It must be a member of an affiliated group.[4]
- It cannot be ineligible to file on a consolidated basis.[5]
- It must meet the initial and ongoing compliance requirements specified in the Code and Regulations.[6]

A Federal election to form a consolidated group may not be binding for state income tax purposes. Some states allow only separate return filing, and others may define the members of an electing group or tax their income differently than the Federal rules. See Chapter 9 for additional discussion of the multistate taxation of related corporations.

AFFILIATED GROUP

An affiliated group is similar but not identical to a *parent-subsidiary controlled group*. A parent-subsidiary controlled group exists when one corporation owns at least 80 percent of the voting power *or* stock value of another corporation on the *last day* of the tax year.[7] Multiple tiers of subsidiaries and chains of ownership are allowed, as long as the group has an identifiable parent corporation.

[3]E.g., for purposes of the § 165(g)(3) ordinary deduction for losses from worthlessness of securities. For the 80% corporate control requirement of § 351, see the discussion in Chapter 3.

[4]§§ 1504(a)(1) and (2).

[5]This is a negative definition, rooted in §§ 1504(b) through (f).

[6]See especially Reg. §§ 1.1502–75, –76, and –77.

[7]§ 1563(a)(1). For this purpose, stock attribution rules apply. In addition, all stock options are considered to be exercised by their holders. §§ 1563(d)(1) and (e)(1) through (3).

TAX FACT

Some States Don't Allow Consolidation

Some states have been hesitant to allow a corporate conglomerate doing business within their boundaries to make a consolidation election when computing state taxable income. There is no real consensus among the states as to how to tax a group consolidated for Federal tax purposes. Some states require the group to make a separate election to file on a consolidated basis. Others reserve the right to force the consolidation treatment on a Federal group for state purposes. The diversity that exists is evident in the following table showing a sample of state rules applicable to consolidated returns.

State	Consolidation Allowed?
Alabama	A Federal electing group can make a separate election to file on a consolidated basis for state purposes. With no such election, all must file separate returns.
Alaska	If the group files consolidated returns for Federal purposes, it must do so for state purposes.
Arizona	A Federal electing group can elect to file on a consolidated basis in the state. The state can require a consolidated return to protect its revenues.
Arkansas	A Federal electing group can elect to file a consolidated return in the state so long as it shows some Arkansas taxable income.
Connecticut	A Federal electing group can elect to file a consolidated return in the state, but it is called a "combined return."
Delaware	No consolidation allowed.
District of Columbia	Consolidation allowed only with prior approval of the revenue department.
Louisiana	The state can require a consolidated return, but the taxpayer cannot elect to file one.
Mississippi	The state can require a consolidated return. The taxpayer can elect to file a consolidated return only with respect to affiliates whose income is generated solely within the state.

Concept Summary 5-1

The Consolidated Return Election

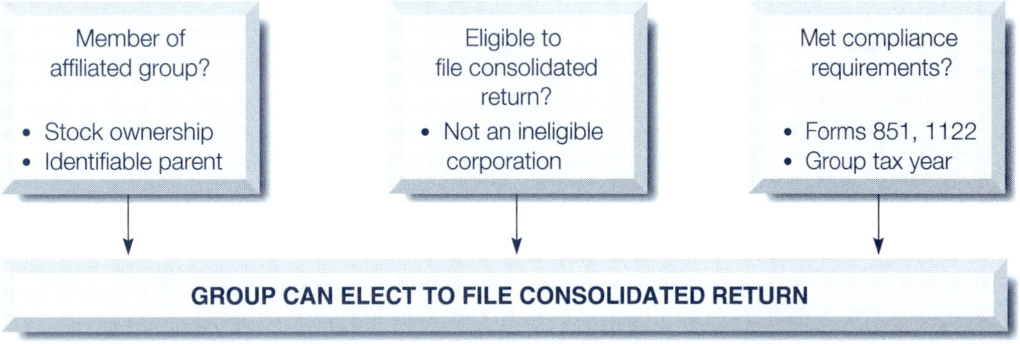

Advantages

- Taxable income computations allow the taxpayer to offset losses of one group member against income of others.
- Deferred income recognition from certain intercompany sales.
- Group computation of alternative minimum tax, credits, and deductions can reduce overall taxes by fully utilizing statutory floors and ceilings.

Disadvantages

- Deriving group taxable income may prevent the use of some members' losses or credits.
- Binding election with additional compliance requirements.
- Deferred loss recognition from certain intercompany sales.
- Certain Code limitations are applied on a group basis (e.g., tax brackets and exemptions).

An **affiliated group** exists when one corporation owns at least 80 percent of the voting power *and* stock value of another corporation.[8] This stock ownership test must be met on *every day* of the tax year. Multiple tiers and chains of corporations are also allowed as long as the group has an identifiable parent corporation (i.e., at least 80 percent of one corporation must be owned by another).

EXAMPLE 6

Two corporate group structures are illustrated below. Both meet the 80% stock ownership test, but the structure on the right is not an affiliated group because there is no identifiable parent entity.

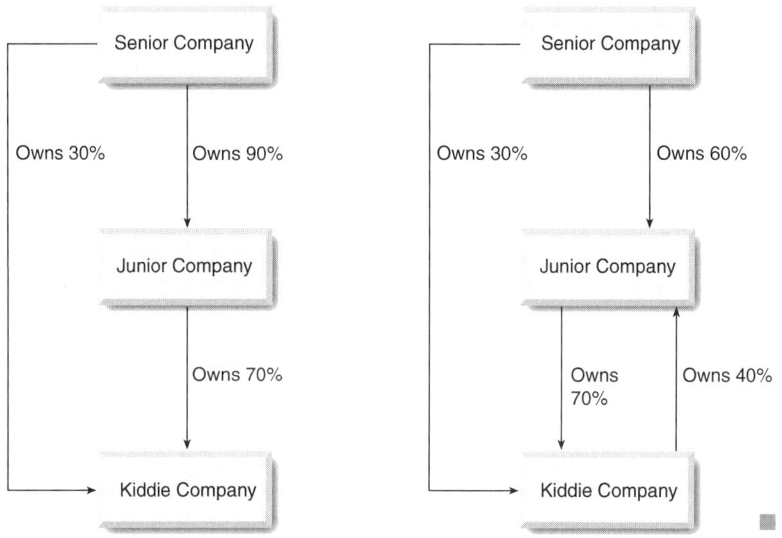

Members of an affiliated group can file tax returns in either of two ways.

- File a separate tax return for each member of the group and claim a 100 percent dividends received deduction for payments passing among them.
- Elect to file income tax returns on a consolidated basis. No 100 percent dividends received deduction is allowed for payments among group members. Rather, the dividends are eliminated from income.

Table 5–1 provides additional details as to the tax effects of making a consolidated return election.

Members of a controlled group are required to share a number of tax benefits, including the following.

- Discounted marginal tax rates on the first $75,000 of taxable income.[9]
- The $150,000 or $250,000 accumulated earnings credit.[10]
- The $40,000 exemption in computing the alternative minimum tax liability.[11]

In addition, members of a controlled group must defer the recognition of any realized loss on intercompany sales until a sale is made at a gain to a nongroup

[8]§§ 1504(a)(1) and (2).
[9]§§ 11(b)(1) and 1561(a)(1).
[10]§§ 535(c)(2) and 1561(a)(2).
[11]§§ 55(d)(2) and 1561(a)(3).

■ **TABLE 5–1**
Comparison of Tax Effects Available to Affiliated Group

Attribute	Treatment If Consolidated Returns Are Filed	Treatment If Separate Returns Are Filed
Tax year	All companies use the parent's tax year.	Companies use various tax years.
Change to common tax year	Required, no IRS permission needed.	Requires IRS permission.
Returns of acquired companies	Separate returns through date of consolidation, then join in consolidated return.	Continue filing for each company's tax year. No extra returns needed.
Intercompany dividend	Eliminated, not taxed.	Include in taxable income, then claim dividends received deduction.
Lower tax brackets	Share one set of rates among the group.	Share one set of rates among the group.
Accumulated earnings credit, $150,000/$250,000 floor	Share one floor among the group.	Share one floor among the group.
Liability for tax	Each company liable for the entire consolidated tax liability.	Each company liable only for its own tax.
Statute of limitations	Extension for one company applies to all in the group.	Each company retains its own statute of limitations.
Accounting methods	Need not conform to parent.	Need not conform to parent.
NOLs, capital gains/losses, § 1231 gains/losses, charitable contribution deductions, dividends received deductions, foreign tax credit payments and baskets, etc.	Computed on a consolidated basis.	Computed separately for each company.
Gain/loss on intercompany transactions	Deferred.	Gains not deferred; losses deferred between related parties.
Basis of parent's investment	Changes due to subsidiary operating gain/loss, taxes, and distributions.	No adjustments.

member.[12] Similarly, any gain on the sale of depreciable property between members of a controlled group is recognized as ordinary income.[13]

The tax effects brought about by electing to file on a consolidated basis include all of the benefit-sharing effects of controlled group membership. In addition, membership in a consolidated group leads to a much more complex set of controlling tax rules, as discussed in the remainder of this chapter.

EXAMPLE 7

ParentCo owns all of the stock of SubCo, and TopCo owns all of the stock of BottomCo. Both pairs of corporations constitute affiliated groups, as well as controlled groups. ParentCo and SubCo elect to file Federal income tax returns on a consolidated basis. TopCo and BottomCo do not so elect. Consequently, they file separate Federal income tax returns.

Both groups share the lower tax rates on the first $75,000 of combined taxable income—ParentCo and SubCo because they file a combined tax return, and TopCo and BottomCo because of the controlled group rules. Neither group can deduct a loss realized on an

[12] §§ 267(a)(1), (b)(3), and (f).

[13] §§ 1239(a) and (c).

intercompany sale. But accounting for the taxable income of the consolidated group is much more complex, as indicated by the rules summarized in Table 5–1. ■

DIGGING DEEPER 1

Find more information on this topic at our Web site: ***http://wft-advanced.swlearning.com.***

LO.4

Describe the corporations that are eligible to file on a consolidated basis.

ELIGIBILITY FOR THE CONSOLIDATION ELECTION

The Code lists a number of corporations that may *not* use a consolidated return to report their taxable income.[14] Thus, these corporations cannot be used to meet the stock ownership tests, and their taxable incomes cannot be included in a consolidated return. Some of the most frequently encountered entities that are **ineligible** for consolidated return status include:

- Corporations established outside the United States or in a U.S. possession.
- Tax-exempt (charitable) corporations.[15]
- Insurance companies.
- Partnerships, trusts, estates, limited liability entities, and any other noncorporate entities.

EXAMPLE 8

In the first ownership structure in the accompanying figure, Ash, Beech, Cedar, and Dogwood form an affiliated group, with Ash as the parent, under the stock ownership rules. Dogwood, a life insurance company, cannot be included in a consolidated return, however, so the consolidation election is available only to Ash, Beech, and Cedar. In the second structure, Ash, Beech, and Cedar form an affiliated group, and all of them can be included in a properly executed consolidated return. Ash is the identifiable parent of the group. Beech and Cedar essentially form a brother-sister group below Ash.

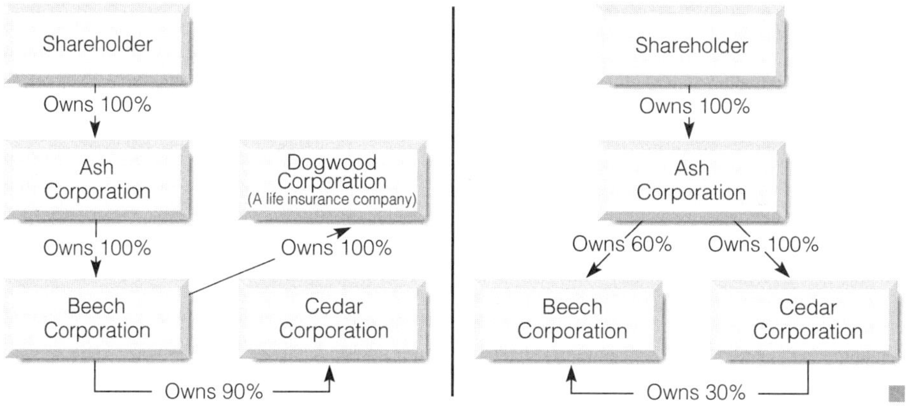

■

LO.5

Explain the compliance aspects of consolidated returns.

COMPLIANCE REQUIREMENTS

An eligible entity that meets the stock ownership test can be included in a consolidated group if several **compliance requirements** are met.

[14] § 1504(b).

[15] This includes any entity that is exempt from tax under § 501. See Chapter 13 for a discussion of the qualification of organizations for exempt status.

The Initial Consolidated Return. The first consolidated tax return must meet the following requirements.

- The Form 1120 for the tax year of the consolidated group should include the taxable results of the operations of all of the members of the consolidated group. This return is filed in lieu of the separate returns of the group members.[16] The identified group then continues to file on a consolidated basis until an eligible group no longer exists or an election to "de-consolidate" is made.[17]
- A Form 1122 should be attached to the first consolidated tax return for each of the subsidiaries included in the group.[18] This form represents a consent by the affiliate to be included in the consolidated group.

The election must be made no later than the extended due date of the parent's return for the year. Only in the case of an inadvertent error can the election to consolidate be rescinded once this extended due date passes.

EXAMPLE 9

Douglas Corporation owns 100% of the stock of Fir. Both corporations use calendar tax years and file separate returns. The entities wish to file on a consolidated basis starting with the tax return for 2004. Douglas Corporation does not file to obtain an extended due date for its 2004 return.

If the consolidation election is to be effective, Douglas must file a Form 1120 that includes the taxable income of the two corporations by March 15, 2005. Fir must execute a Form 1122 and attach it to the consolidated Form 1120.

Now assume that Douglas Corporation files a complete consolidated Form 1120 on March 3, 2005. On March 7, 2005, the Supreme Court issues a decision that will have a considerable adverse effect on the group's 2006–2009 taxable incomes. If Douglas and Fir file separate 2004 returns by March 15, 2005 (or by some later date if an extension to file is obtained in a timely fashion), the IRS will ignore the consolidation election.

If Douglas and Fir fail to file separate returns in this manner, the election to consolidate is in force for all future years, or until the IRS approves Douglas's application to revoke it. ■

An application to terminate the consolidation election must be filed at least 90 days prior to the extended due date of the consolidated return.[19] Generally, when a subsidiary leaves an ongoing consolidated group, it must wait five years before it can reenter the group.[20]

Subsequent Consolidated Returns. Each consolidated tax return must include Form 851, Affiliations Schedule. This report identifies all of the corporations in the electing group, summarizes pertinent shareholdings and stock ownership changes that occurred during the tax year, and lists the estimated tax payments made by the group members for the year. Affiliates joining an existing consolidated group need not file a Form 1122, though.

Consolidated tax returns are due on the fifteenth day of the third month following the close of the group's tax year (this is March 15 for a calendar year taxpayer). A six-month extension to file the return can be obtained by executing Form 7004, but an estimated payment of the remaining tax liability for the group must accompany the extension application.

[16] Reg. § 1.1502–75(a)(1).

[17] Reg. § 1.1502–75(c). The IRS permits such an election only rarely, on the parent's assertion of (1) a good-cause reason to disengage from consolidated status or (2) a substantial change in the tax law that adversely affects the consolidated tax liability.

[18] Reg. § 1.1502–75(b).

[19] Reg. § 1.1502–75(c)(1)(i).

[20] § 1504(a)(3); Rev.Proc. 2002–32, 2002–1 C.B. 959.

Liability for Taxes. Group members are jointly and severally liable for the entire consolidated tax liability.[21] This rule applies to interest and penalties imposed as a result of audits as well as to tax liabilities. Furthermore, the IRS is not bound to follow internal agreements among group members in apportioning the liability.[22]

EXAMPLE 10

Olive Corporation, a calendar year taxpayer, acquired 100% of the stock of calendar year Pine on December 20, 2002. The group filed on a consolidated basis from that date until December 31, 2004, when all of the Pine stock was sold to Foreign Corporation.

An IRS audit determined that Olive owed an additional $10 million in Federal income taxes, relating to a sale it made on December 30, 2002. By mid-2005, however, Olive's cash-flow difficulties had brought it close to bankruptcy and forced it to cease activities.

Due to the consolidation election, the IRS can assess the delinquent taxes from Pine (and Foreign Corporation) in 2004. Pine is liable for the full amount of any consolidated tax liability, even when it is not the source of the income that led to the tax. ■

Regular tax liability is computed applying the graduated tax rates to consolidated taxable income, following the requirements of controlled group status. In this regard, contributions to the actual payment of the tax liability often are arranged to correspond to contributions to consolidated taxable income.

PLANNING STRATEGIES

Protecting Group Members

FRAMEWORK FOCUS: TAX RATE

STRATEGY ➤ AVOID DOUBLE TAXATION.

Since all group members are responsible for consolidated tax liabilities, interest, and penalties, target subsidiaries and their (present and potential) shareholders should take measures to protect their separate interests.

Examine the facts of Example 10. Exposure by Pine and its successive shareholders to tax (and all other) liabilities of Olive Corporation should be minimized by including appropriate clauses in purchase contracts and related documents. For instance, (1) Foreign Corporation could alter its negotiating position so that it pays less to acquire the Pine stock, or (2) Pine might attempt to recover any Olive taxes that it pays through courts other than the Tax Court.

Benefits accruing from the graduated corporate tax rates are apportioned equally among the group members unless all members consent to some other method through an annual election. The most commonly used tax-sharing agreements are the *relative taxable income* and *relative tax liability* methods. Under the **relative taxable income method,**[23] the consolidated tax liability is allocated among the members based on their relative amounts of separate taxable income. When the **relative tax liability method** is used,[24] the consolidated tax liability is allocated based on the relative hypothetical separate tax liabilities of the members. IRS permission is required for the group to change from one allocation method to another.

DIGGING DEEPER 2

Find more information on this topic at our Web site: ***http://wft-advanced.swlearning.com.***

[21]Reg. § 1.1502–6(a).
[22]Reg. § 1.1502–6(c).
[23]§ 1552(a)(1); Reg. § 1.1552–1(a)(1).
[24]§ 1552(a)(2); Reg. § 1.1552–1(a)(2).

BRIDGE DISCIPLINE

Bridge to Corporate Law

When corporations file consolidated returns, Regulation § 1502–6(a) makes each member of the consolidated group jointly and severally liable for the entire consolidated tax liability. Holding a subsidiary liable for the consolidated tax liability is, in essence, the reverse of piercing the corporate veil. While not a common legal situation, lawyers must consider the risks to corporate clients who are acquiring subsidiaries from a parent corporation, especially if the parent is having financial difficulties. Even though the subsidiary has been sold out of the affiliated group, it is still legally liable for any tax liability imposed for prior years in which it was part of the consolidated group.

One method to avoid this potential tax liability is to purchase the assets of the subsidiary rather than its stock. The subsidiary would cease to exist for legal purposes and, consequently, so would the potential liability for the taxes. There can be two problems with this solution, however. First, purchasing the assets may be legally impractical. For example, suppose the subsidiary is in the lumber industry and holds thousands of road easements filed in hundreds of jurisdictions. Treating each easement as being sold separately and thus requiring the recording of the new owner for each easement would be a monumental legal task and likely to be cost prohibitive. Secondly, there are avenues under the jurisdictional concepts of bulk sales and fraudulent transfers that could allow the purchaser of the subsidiary's assets to be legally liable for the consolidated tax liability.

A more practical solution may be to require the selling parent to indemnify the buyer for any consolidated liability that might be imposed in the future. When the former parent is experiencing financial problems, hold-backs, liens on the parent's assets, or escrows may be more effective solutions to the potential liability problems.

Tax Accounting Periods and Methods. All the members of a consolidating group must use the parent's tax year.[25] As a result, the group may be required to file a short-year return for the first year a subsidiary is included in the consolidated return, so that the parent's year-end can be adopted.

When a mid-year acquisition occurs, both short years are used in tracking the carryforward period of unused losses and credits. Short-year income and deductions are apportioned between the pre- and post-acquisition periods. The apportionment may be done either on a daily basis or as the items are recorded for financial accounting purposes, at the election of the corporation being acquired.[26]

EXAMPLE 11

All of the stock of calendar year Alder is acquired by Hazel Corporation on July 15, 2004. The corporations elect to file a consolidated return immediately upon the acquisition.

Alder had generated a long-term capital loss in its 2001 tax year. As of January 1, 2005, only one year remains in the five-year carryforward period for the capital loss.

According to Alder's financial accounting records, $400,000 of its $1 million accounting and taxable income for the year was generated in 2004 after the acquisition. At Alder's election, either $400,000 (the "books" apportionment method) or $464,481 [(170 postacquisition days/366 days) × $1 million income] (the "daily" method) can be included in the first consolidated return. ■

[25] Reg. § 1.1502–76(a)(1).

[26] Reg. § 1.1502–76(b)(4).

Members of a consolidated group can continue to use the tax accounting methods that were in place prior to the consolidation election.[27] Thus, the members of a consolidated group may use different accounting methods.

PLANNING STRATEGIES

Short Years

FRAMEWORK FOCUS: TAX RATE

STRATEGY ➤ **SHIFT NET INCOME FROM HIGH-BRACKET YEARS TO LOW-BRACKET YEARS.**

A short tax year may be created when a member with a nonmatching tax year joins or leaves the group. When this occurs, the group should consider measures to limit the ensuing negative tax consequences. For instance, additional income can be accelerated into the short year of acquisition. This will reduce any loss carryforwards when the carryover period is effectively shortened due to the takeover. The group should also make suitable income-allocation elections in assigning income to the short year. Finally, group estimated tax payments should be computed using both consolidated and separate liability amounts to determine the more beneficial method. In this way, only the minimum quarterly tax payments are made, and the benefits of the time value of money are maximized.

LO.6

Compute a parent's investment basis in a subsidiary.

Stock Basis of Subsidiary

Upon acquiring a subsidiary, the parent corporation records a stock basis on its tax balance sheet equal to the acquisition price. At the end of every consolidated return year, the parent records one or more adjustments to this stock basis, as in the financial accounting "equity" method. This treatment prevents double taxation of gain (or deduction of loss) upon the ultimate disposal of the subsidiary's shares.

In this regard, positive adjustments to stock basis include:

- An allocable share of consolidated taxable income for the year.
- An allocable share of the consolidated operating or capital loss of a subsidiary that could not utilize the loss through a carryback to a prior year.

Negative adjustments to stock basis include:

- An allocable share of a consolidated taxable loss for the year.
- An allocable share of any carryover operating or capital losses that are deducted on the consolidated return and have not previously reduced stock basis.
- Dividends paid by the subsidiary to the parent out of the subsidiary's E & P.

EXAMPLE 12

Sequoia Corporation acquired all of the stock of Redwood on January 1, 2002, for $1 million. The parties immediately elected to file consolidated tax returns. Redwood had a taxable loss of $100,000 in 2002, but it generated $40,000 taxable income in 2003 and $65,000 in 2004. Redwood paid a $10,000 dividend in mid-2004.

Sequoia has the following stock bases in Redwood on the last day of each of the indicated years.

2002 $900,000 **2003** $940,000 **2004** $995,000 ■

[27] Reg. § 1.1502–17(a).

PLANNING STRATEGIES

Electing to Postpone Recognition of the Excess Loss Account

FRAMEWORK FOCUS: INCOME AND EXCLUSIONS

STRATEGY ➤ **POSTPONE RECOGNITION OF INCOME TO ACHIEVE TAX DEFERRAL.**

An election to reduce the investment basis of remaining subsidiary stock and debt (i.e., upon disposition of shares when an excess loss account exists) may be attractive when the remaining shares are not likely to be sold in the near future. In that case, the present value of the tax on any resulting increased gain will be low. The election may also be used to offset any recognition of the postponed gain upon debt repayments or stock sales when future operating losses are anticipated. The election generally is not attractive when operating loss carryforwards are available in the current year. These can be used to shelter the gain recognized on recovery of the excess loss account.

EXAMPLE 13

Parent Corporation owns preferred stock of SubCo with a basis of $10,000. Parent's basis in its common stock investment in SubCo has been eliminated through SubCo's operating losses; in fact, Parent holds a $6,000 excess loss account for SubCo.

Parent sells the SubCo common for $9,000. Thus, it must recognize a $15,000 capital gain on the sale. Alternatively, Parent can elect to recognize only a $9,000 gain on the sale and to reduce its basis in the SubCo preferred to $4,000. ■

When accumulated postacquisition taxable losses of the subsidiary exceed the acquisition price, an **excess loss account** is created.[28] This account (1) allows the consolidated return to recognize the losses of the subsidiary in the current year and (2) enables the group to avoid the need to reflect a negative stock basis on its tax-basis balance sheet. If the subsidiary stock is redeemed or sold to a nongroup member while an excess loss account exists, the seller recognizes the balance of the account as capital gain income.[29]

EXAMPLE 14

Juniper Corporation acquired all of the stock of Sumac early in Year 1, for $100,000. As a result of Sumac's operations, the group records the amounts listed.

Year	Operating Gain/(Loss)	Stock Basis	Excess Loss Account
1	($ 40,000)	$60,000	$ -0-
2	(80,000)	-0-	20,000
3	30,000	10,000	-0-

If Juniper sells the Sumac stock for $50,000 at the end of Year 2, Juniper recognizes a $70,000 capital gain ($50,000 amount realized − $0 adjusted basis in stock + $20,000 recovery of excess loss account). If the sale takes place at the end of Year 3, the capital gain is $40,000. ■

In a chain of more than one tier of subsidiaries, the computation of the stock basis amounts starts with the lowest-level subsidiary, then proceeds up the ownership structure to the parent's holdings. In this regard, there is no such concept as consolidated E & P. Rather, each entity accounts for its own share of consolidated

[28]Reg. § 1.1502–19.

[29]Reg. §§ 1.1502–19(a)(1) and (2).

■ FIGURE 5–1
Computing Consolidated Taxable Income

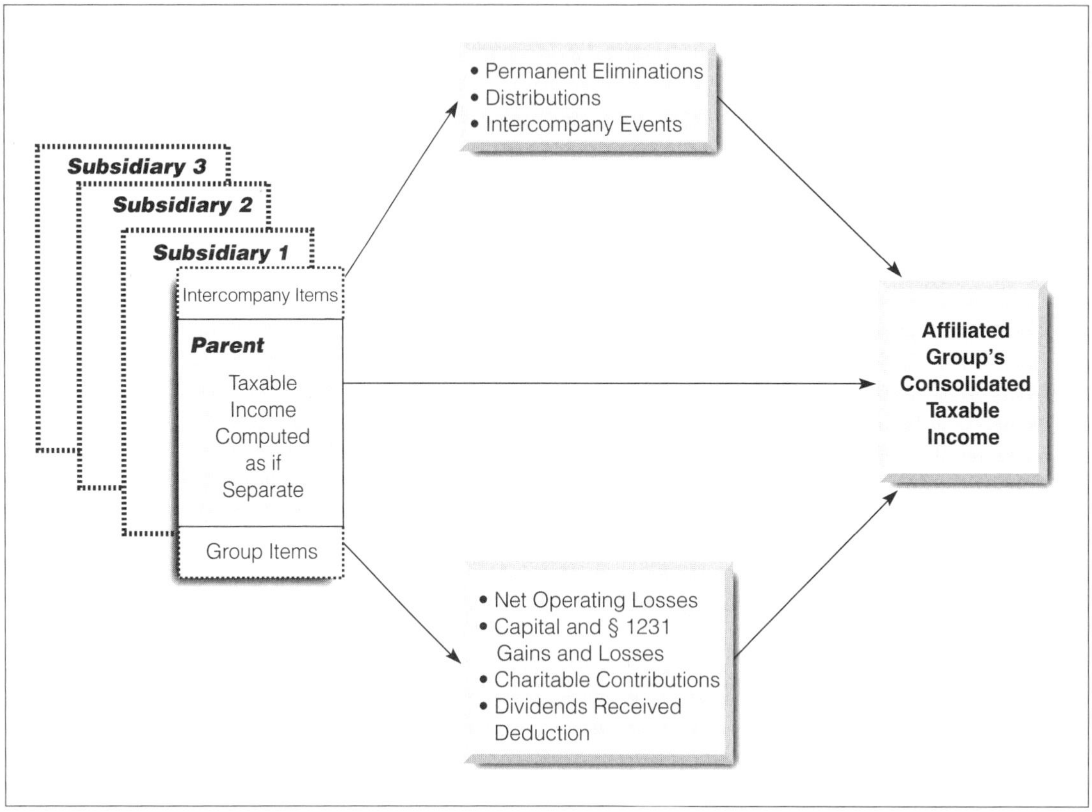

taxable income on an annual basis, immediately recognizing within E & P any gain or loss on intercompany transactions and reducing E & P by an allocable share of the consolidated tax liability.[30]

Computing Consolidated Taxable Income

When an affiliated group computes its taxable income for the year, it does not simply add together the separate taxable income amounts of its members. Two groups of transactions are removed from the members' tax returns and receive special treatment. Then the special items are recombined with the remaining items of members' taxable incomes to obtain the group's consolidated taxable income for the year. Figure 5–1 illustrates how consolidated taxable income is constructed using this sequential approach.

1. Taxable income is computed for each member on a separate basis.
2. "Group items" and "intercompany items" are isolated and receive special treatment.
3. The remaining separate incomes are combined with the group and intercompany items, resulting in consolidated taxable income.

[30]Reg. § 1.1502–33(d). In the absence of an election to use some other allocation method, the consolidated tax liability is allocated to each group member according to the relative taxable income method.

FIGURE 5–2
Consolidated Taxable Income Worksheet

	Separate Taxable Income	Adjustments	Post-adjustment Amounts
Parent information	______	______	______
Subsidiary information	______	______	______
Group-basis transactions	______	______	______
Intercompany events	______	______	______
Consolidated taxable income			______

*Permanent eliminations. **Group-basis transaction. †Matching rule.

The Code requires this computational procedure to accomplish several goals.

- Certain transactions are accounted for on a consolidated basis (e.g., charitable contributions and capital gains and losses). This requires that the transactions be isolated from the separate tax returns and computed on a groupwide basis.
- Gains and losses from certain intercompany transactions are deferred until a later tax year. Consequently, they are removed from the tax returns of the members that generated them.
- A few intercompany transactions (e.g., dividend payments) are removed from the taxable income calculation altogether, never to appear in a consolidated return.

COMPUTATIONAL PROCEDURE

Figure 5–2 presents a skeleton worksheet for the computational procedure to be used in examples throughout the remainder of this chapter. Additional information is added to the worksheet for every additional subsidiary. In each case, the starting point for this procedure is the separate taxable incomes of all the group members. Adjustments then are made for group and intercompany items, as indicated in the footnotes to the worksheet.

LO.7

Account for intercompany transactions of a consolidated group.

TYPICAL INTERCOMPANY TRANSACTIONS

General Rules. When one member of a consolidated group engages in a transaction with another member of the group, an **intercompany transaction** occurs. In contrast to the financial accounting treatment of such transactions, the most commonly encountered items *remain in* the members' separate taxable incomes and therefore cancel each other out on a consolidated basis. For instance, when one group member performs services for another member during the year, the purchaser of the services incurs a deductible expenditure, while the service provider generates includible income. The net result is a zero addition to consolidated taxable income.[31]

This two-step procedure prevents the group from recognizing any related-party losses. Furthermore, when the members involved in the transaction are using different tax accounting methods, the payor's deduction for the expenditure is deferred until the year in which the recipient recognizes the related gross income.[32]

EXAMPLE 15

In the current year, Parent Corporation provided consulting services to its 100%-owned subsidiary, SubCo, under a contract that requires no payments to Parent until next year.

[31] Reg. §§ 1.1502–13(a)(1)(i) and (b)(1).

[32] §§ 267(a)(2) and (b)(3); Reg. § 1.1502–13(b)(2).

Both parties use the accrual method of tax accounting. The services that Parent rendered are valued at $100,000. In addition, Parent purchased $15,000 of supplies from SubCo.

Including these transactions, Parent's taxable income for the year amounted to $500,000. SubCo reported $150,000 of separate taxable income. The group is not required to make any eliminating adjustments. The members' deductions incurred offset the income included by the other party to the intercompany transaction. The consolidated taxable income includes both Parent's $15,000 deduction for supplies and SubCo's $15,000 gross receipts from the sale, so the consolidated taxable income computation *de facto* results in an elimination similar to the kind made in financial accounting. No further adjustment is needed.

	Separate Taxable Income	Adjustments	Post-adjustment Amounts
Parent information	$500,000	______	$500,000
SubCo information	150,000	______	150,000
Group-basis transactions	______	______	______
Intercompany events	______	______	______
Consolidated taxable income			$650,000

*Permanent eliminations. **Group-basis transaction. †Matching rule.

EXAMPLE 16

Continue with the facts of the previous example, except that Parent is a cash basis taxpayer. Since Parent will not recognize the $100,000 of service income earned in the current year until the next tax period, SubCo's related deduction also is deferred until the following year. Thus, the intercompany item—SubCo's deduction—must be eliminated from consolidated taxable income. Additional record keeping is required to keep track of this intercompany transaction (and all others like it), so that the deduction is claimed in the appropriate year.

	Separate Taxable Income	Adjustments	Post-adjustment Amounts
Parent information	$400,000	______	$400,000
SubCo information	150,000	+ $100,000 due to use of different tax accounting methods	250,000
Group-basis transactions	______	______	______
Intercompany events	______	______	______
Consolidated taxable income			$650,000

*Permanent eliminations. **Group-basis transaction. †Matching rule.

Several other rules also apply to intercompany transactions. Dividends received from other group members are eliminated from the recipients' separate taxable incomes; therefore, no dividends received deduction is allowed. When the distribution consists of noncash assets, the subsidiary payor realizes (but defers recognition of) any gain on the distributed property until the asset leaves the group, and the (eliminated) dividend amount equals the fair market value of the asset.[33]

[33]§§ 301(b)(1) and (d); 311(b)(1); Reg. §§ 1.1502–14(c)(1) and –14T; Ltr.Rul. 8922096.

EXAMPLE 17

Parent Corporation received a $50,000 cash dividend from 100%-owned SubCo in the current year. Including this item, Parent's separate taxable income amounted to $200,000, and SubCo reported $240,000 separate taxable income.

Since the dividend is eliminated in computing consolidated taxable income, Parent cannot claim a dividends received deduction for this payment. No elimination is required for SubCo, as dividend payments are nondeductible.

	Separate Taxable Income	Adjustments	Post-adjustment Amounts
Parent information	$200,000	– $50,000 dividend received from SubCo*	$150,000
SubCo information	240,000	______	240,000
Group-basis transactions	______	______	______
Intercompany events	______	______	______
Consolidated taxable income			$390,000

*Permanent eliminations. **Group-basis transaction. †Matching rule.

LO.8

Identify limitations that restrict the use of losses and credits of group members derived in separate return years.

Members' Net Operating Losses. Most often, the election to file consolidated returns is motivated by the parent corporation's desire to use the positive tax attributes of the subsidiary corporation, especially its NOLs. A number of provisions, however, discourage corporate acquisitions that are solely tax motivated.[34]

The usual corporate NOL computations are available for the losses of the consolidated group. Excess losses are carried back 2 years and then forward 20 years, although the parent may elect to forgo the carryback deductions for all members of the group. The NOL is derived after removing any consolidated charitable contribution deduction and capital gain or loss from consolidated taxable income. These items are removed because they have their own carryover periods and rules. The consolidated dividends received deduction remains a part of the consolidated NOL.[35]

EXAMPLE 18

Parent Corporation and SubCo have filed consolidated returns since both entities were incorporated in 2002. Neither group member incurred any capital gain or loss transactions during 2002–2005, nor did they make any charitable contributions. Taxable income computations for the members include the following.

Year	Parent's Taxable Income	SubCo's Taxable Income	Consolidated Taxable Income
2002	$100,000	$ 40,000	$140,000
2003	100,000	(40,000)	60,000
2004	100,000	(140,000)	?
2005	100,000	210,000	?

[34]See Chapter 4 and §§ 269, 381, 382, and 482.

[35]Reg. § 1.1502–21(f).

■ **FIGURE 5–3**
Limitations on Use of Net Operating Losses

Year of Loss	Year Reported	Applicable Rules
Consolidated	Consolidated	• Carry back 2 years, forward 20; parent can elect to carry forward only. • § 382 limitations apply if ownership change occurs.
Consolidated	Separate	• Carry back/forward only the member's apportioned loss to its separate return. • Offspring rule may allow carryback of apportioned loss to year/return prior to member's existence. • Departing group member takes apportioned loss with it.
Separate	Consolidated	• Group's deduction of member's loss carryforward is limited to member's current-year or cumulative contribution to consolidated taxable income. This limit does not apply to a group's parent. • § 382 limitations apply if ownership change occurs.

The 2004 consolidated loss of $40,000 can be carried back to offset 2002 consolidated taxable income. Alternatively, Parent can elect to carry the loss forward to 2005, forgoing any carryback computation. This might be appropriate given an increase in statutory tax rates effective for 2005 or an application of the AMT in 2002 and 2003. ■

Complications arise, however, when the corporations enter or depart from a consolidated group, so that members' operating losses are either incurred in a "separate return year" and deducted in a "consolidated return year," or vice versa. A variety of restrictions limit the availability of such deductions to discourage profitable corporations from acquiring unprofitable entities simply to file immediate refund claims based on loss and credit carryforwards. Figure 5–3 summarizes the applicable limitations.

In any case where the members of a consolidated group change over time, the taxpayer must apportion the consolidated NOL among the group members. When more than one group member generates a loss for the consolidated year, the following formula is used to apportion the loss among the electing group's members.

$$\frac{\text{Member's separate NOL}}{\text{Members' aggregate NOLs}} \times \text{Consolidated NOL} = \text{Member's apportioned NOL}$$

EXAMPLE 19

Parent Corporation and SubCo have filed consolidated returns since 2003. Both entities were incorporated in 2002. Neither group member incurred any capital gain or loss transactions during 2002–2005, nor did they make any charitable contributions. Taxable income computations for the members are listed below.

Year	Parent's Taxable Income	SubCo's Taxable Income	Consolidated Taxable Income
2002*	$100,000	$ 40,000	N/A
2003**	100,000	(40,000)	$60,000
2004**	100,000	(140,000)	?
2005**	100,000	210,000	?

*Separate return year. **Consolidated return year.

In 2004, SubCo can carry back the entire $40,000 consolidated NOL to its separate 2002 tax year, because it is solely responsible for generating the loss. SubCo files for the refund of taxes that result from the carryback, and it alone receives the refund.[36]

Alternatively, Parent could elect to forgo the carryback of the 2004 consolidated loss, thereby preserving the loss deduction for the group's subsequent years. In that case, the 2005 tax reduction from the $40,000 NOL deduction would be claimed merely by filing the 2005 consolidated tax return, and Parent would receive the refund on behalf of the group. ■

In years when a group member files a separate return, only the apportioned NOL may be carried over.

EXAMPLE 20

Parent Corporation, SubOne, and SubTwo have filed consolidated returns since 2003. All of the entities were incorporated in 2002. None of the group members incurred any capital gain or loss transactions during 2002–2005, nor did they make any charitable contributions. Taxable income computations for the members are listed below.

Year	Parent's Taxable Income	SubOne's Taxable Income	SubTwo's Taxable Income	Consolidated Taxable Income
2002*	$100,000	$ 100,000	$ 40,000	N/A
2003**	100,000	100,000	(40,000)	$160,000
2004**	100,000	(60,000)	(120,000)	?
2005**	100,000	100,000	210,000	?

*Separate return year. **Consolidated return year.

If Parent does not elect to forgo the carryback of the 2004 consolidated NOL of $80,000, both subsidiaries can carry losses back to their 2002 separate return years and receive separate refunds. SubOne can carry back a $26,667 loss [(SubOne's NOL $60,000/aggregate NOLs $180,000) × consolidated NOL $80,000], and SubTwo can carry back a $53,333 loss. ■

Under the so-called **offspring rule,** the consolidated group can use a carryback loss that is apportioned to a member of the electing group, even though that member was not in existence in the carryback year.[37] If the member joined the group immediately upon its incorporation, but cannot use an apportioned loss in the carryback period because it was not in existence, that loss is still available to the group.[38]

EXAMPLE 21

Parent Corporation, SubOne, and SubTwo have filed consolidated returns since 2003. The first two entities were incorporated and consolidated in 2002, and SubTwo came into existence in 2003 through an asset spin-off from Parent. None of the group members incurred any

[36]Reg. §§ 1.1502–78(b)(1) and (c), Example 4.

[37]Reg. § 1.1502–79(a)(2).

[38]Prop.Reg. § 1.1502–21(b)(2)(ii)(B) restricts the use of this loss to the parent, if the carryback year is a separate return year for the parties.

GLOBAL TAX ISSUES

Consolidated Returns and NOLs

Very few countries besides the United States allow the use of consolidated returns. In the view of most countries, tax deductions for operating losses should be used only by those who generated them, not by some sister or other related corporation. This is as much a social principle (the sanctity of the corporate entity) as a revenue-raising provision (NOL deductions mean lower tax collections).

The way European business is conducted makes this result more understandable, as the tax laws of the various countries must ensure that operating losses generated in Tedesco, for instance, are not shifted to Cadenza and converted to deductions there.

This restrictive approach to the trading of operating loss deductions is found in U.S. multistate tax law as well, where tax-oriented border incentives can be especially important. Some states (like Pennsylvania) have, over a specified time period, disallowed the use of loss carryovers of any sort, whereas others (like Ohio) require the taxpayer to deduct only losses assigned to the taxpayer's in-state operations.

capital gain or loss transactions during 2002–2005, nor did they make any charitable contributions. Taxable income computations for the members are listed below.

Year	Parent's Taxable Income	SubOne's Taxable Income	SubTwo's Taxable Income	Consolidated Taxable Income
2002*	$100,000	$ 40,000	—	$140,000
2003*	100,000	100,000	($ 40,000)	160,000
2004*	100,000	(60,000)	(120,000)	?
2005*	100,000	100,000	210,000	?

*Consolidated return year.

If Parent does not elect to forgo the carryback of the 2004 consolidated NOL of $80,000, SubOne can carry its $26,667 loss back to 2002. SubTwo's $53,333 share of the loss can also be carried back to 2002 and used by members of the consolidated group. Under the offspring rule, SubTwo is treated as being a member of the group for the entire *group* carryback period because its existence is rooted in Parent's assets. ■

When a corporation leaves a consolidated group, it takes with it any apportioned share of any unused loss carryforwards, to be used on its subsequent separate returns.

EXAMPLE 22

Parent Corporation, SubOne, and SubTwo have filed consolidated returns since 2002, the year in which all of the entities were incorporated. None of the group members incurred any capital gain or loss transactions during 2002–2005, nor did they make any charitable contributions. Taxable income computations for the members are listed below.

Year	Parent's Taxable Income	SubOne's Taxable Income	SubTwo's Taxable Income	Consolidated Taxable Income
2002*	$100,000	$100,000	$ 40,000	$240,000
2003*	100,000	100,000	(40,000)	160,000
2004*	100,000	(60,000)	(120,000)	?
2005**	100,000	100,000	210,000	N/A

*Consolidated return year. **Separate return year.

Parent elects to forgo any loss carryback for the group's 2004 operations. On the first day of the 2005 tax year, a non-U.S. investor purchases all of the stock of SubTwo. On its 2005 separate return, SubTwo can deduct its $53,333 share of the 2004 NOL carryforward. ■

When an NOL is carried forward from a separate return year onto a consolidated return, another set of limitations, known as the **separate return limitation year (SRLY)** rules, applies.[39] The consolidated return can include an NOL carryforward from the member's SRLY period only to the extent of the lesser of its (1) current-year income or (2) cumulative positive contribution to current-year consolidated income.[40] The SRLY limitations never apply to the electing group's identifiable parent.[41]

EXAMPLE 23

Parent Corporation and SubCo have filed consolidated returns since 2003. Both entities were incorporated in 2002. Neither group member incurred any capital gain or loss transactions during 2002–2005, nor did they make any charitable contributions. Taxable income computations for the members are listed below.

Year	Parent's Taxable Income	SubCo's Taxable Income	Consolidated Taxable Income
2002*	$100,000	($40,000)	N/A
2003**	100,000	(10,000)	$90,000
2004**	100,000	15,000	?
2005**	100,000	70,000	?

*Separate return year. **Consolidated return year.

The thrust of the SRLY rules is to limit Parent's deduction of SubCo's losses from a separate return year against consolidated income. Accordingly, none of SubCo's separate return loss from 2002 can be deducted in computing 2003 consolidated taxable income; the deduction is limited to the lesser of SubCo's current-year taxable income (zero) or cumulative (zero) contribution to consolidated taxable income.

In computing 2004 consolidated taxable income, the SubCo SRLY loss deduction is limited to $5,000, the lesser of SubCo's current-year ($15,000) or cumulative ($5,000) contribution to consolidated taxable income. The remaining SRLY deduction reduces consolidated taxable income in 2005. ■

When both the SRLY rules and a § 382 limitation apply because an ownership change has occurred (see Chapter 4), the § 382 provisions override the SRLY limits.[42]

EXAMPLE 24

The Parent consolidated group includes SubTwo, which was acquired as part of a § 382 ownership change. SubTwo brought to the group a $180,000 NOL carryforward, $125,000 of which is available this year under the SRLY rules due to SubTwo's positive contribution to the group's taxable income. The § 382 limitation with respect to SubTwo is $100,000. Accordingly, only $100,000 of the SubTwo NOL can be used to reduce consolidated taxable income this year.

If the § 382 limitation had been $200,000 instead, the full $180,000 NOL deduction would have been allowed. The § 382 rules prevail even with respect to SRLY losses that overlap with the same tax year. ■

[39] Reg. § 1.1502–21(c). The SRLY rules apply to capital loss and credit carryforwards as well.

[40] Prop.Reg. § 1.1502–21(c).

[41] Reg. § 1.1502–1(f)(2)(i), known as the "lonely parent" rule.

[42] Reg. §§ 1.1502–15(g) and –21(g).

PLANNING STRATEGIES

Consolidation versus 100 Percent Dividends Received Deduction

FRAMEWORK FOCUS: INCOME AND EXCLUSIONS

STRATEGY ➤ AVOID INCOME RECOGNITION.

When adequate ownership is held, a 100 percent dividends received deduction is available for payments received from subsidiaries with whom a consolidated return is *not* filed. Thus, this tax benefit is still available when the taxpayer wishes to affiliate with an insurance company, foreign entity, or other ineligible corporation. A taxpayer that cannot find potential group partners with the desired level of complementary tax attributes may also take advantage of this benefit.

LO.9

Derive deductions and credits on a consolidated basis.

COMPUTATION OF GROUP ITEMS

Several income and deduction items are derived on a consolidated-group basis. Therefore, statutory limitations and allowances are applied to the group as though it were a single corporation. This computational convention allows group members to match various types of gains and losses and to increase specific limitations, required by the Code, in a manner that optimizes the overall tax benefit.

Specifically, the following items are computed on a group basis with the usual C corporation tax effects applied to the combined group amounts.

- Net capital gain/loss.
- Section 1231 gain/loss.
- Casualty/theft gain/loss.
- Charitable contributions.
- Dividends received deduction.
- Net operating loss.

Following the computational procedure of Figures 5–1 and 5–2, all of the group-basis items are removed from each member's separate taxable income. Then, using the consolidated taxable income figure to that point, statutory limitations are applied to determine group-basis gains, losses, income, and deductions.

EXAMPLE 25

Parent Corporation's current-year taxable income included $300,000 net income from operations and a $50,000 net long-term capital gain. Parent also made a $40,000 contribution to State University. Accordingly, its separate taxable income amounted to $315,000.

Income from operations	$300,000
Capital gain income	+50,000
Charitable contribution (maximum)	–35,000
Separate taxable income	$315,000

SubCo generated $170,000 income from operations and incurred a $45,000 short-term capital loss. Thus, its separate taxable income was $170,000, and aggregate separate taxable income for the group amounted to $485,000.

Upon consolidation, a larger amount of Parent's charitable contribution is deductible, and its capital gain is almost fully sheltered from current-year tax.

	Separate Taxable Income	Adjustments	Post-adjustment Amounts
Parent information	$315,000	– $50,000 capital gain income** + $35,000 charitable contribution deduction**	$300,000
SubCo information	170,000	$45,000 short-term capital loss**	170,000
Group-basis transactions		+ $5,000 net long-term capital gain – $40,000 charitable contribution deduction (maximum for group is $47,500)	–35,000
Consolidated taxable income			$435,000

*Permanent eliminations. **Group-basis transaction. †Matching rule.

Computing these items on a group basis does not always result in a reduction of aggregate group taxable income. Nevertheless, the possibility of using the group-basis computations may affect transactions by group members late in the tax year when it becomes apparent that planning opportunities may be available. It may also encourage the taxpayer to seek out fellow group members that bring complementary tax attributes to the consolidated return.

EXAMPLE 26

Parent Corporation owns 15% of the stock of Outsider Corporation throughout the year. Outsider paid a $150,000 dividend to Parent during the year. Parent also generated $400,000 of taxable operating income and sold a § 1231 asset at a $10,000 gain. Parent's separate taxable income is computed below.

Operating income	$ 400,000
Dividend income	+150,000
§ 1231 gain	+10,000
Dividends received deduction (70%)	–105,000
Separate taxable income	$ 455,000

A 10% owner of Outsider, SubCo also received a $100,000 dividend. SubCo's operations produced a $20,000 net taxable loss for the year, and it sold a § 1231 asset at a $4,000 loss. Thus, SubCo's separate taxable income is computed as follows.

Operating income	($ 20,000)
Dividend income	+100,000
§ 1231 loss	–4,000
Dividends received deduction	–53,200
Separate taxable income	$ 22,800

Notice that the dividends received deduction is limited to 70% of taxable income.[43]

[43] § 246(b)(1).

A consolidated return increases the group's dividends received deduction by eliminating the taxable income limitation. However, the Regulations do not permit an increase in the dividend received deduction percentage from 70% to 80%, even though the aggregate ownership of Outsider is greater than 20%.[44] Filing a consolidated return wastes the opportunity to claim SubCo's § 1231 loss as an ordinary deduction.

	Separate Taxable Income	Adjustments	Post-adjustment Amounts
Parent information	$455,000	– $150,000 dividend received from Outsider**	$400,000
		– $10,000 § 1231 gain**	
		+ $105,000 dividends received deduction**	
SubCo information	22,800	– $100,000 dividend received from Outsider**	(20,000)
		+ $4,000 § 1231 loss	
		+ $53,200 dividends received deduction	
Group-basis transactions		+ $250,000 dividend received from Outsider	+81,000
		– $175,000 dividends received deduction (70% × $250,000)	
		+ $6,000 § 1231 gain	
Consolidated taxable income			$461,000

*Permanent eliminations. **Group-basis transaction. †Matching rule.

Other items computed on a consolidated basis include all elements of the general business and research credits, any recapture of those credits, the foreign tax credit, the percentage depletion deduction, and all elements of AMTI.

THE MATCHING RULE

A special class of intercompany transactions receives deferral treatment under the Regulations.[45] The gain or loss realized on these transactions is removed from consolidated taxable income until the assets involved in the transaction leave the affiliated group. The purpose of this "**matching rule**" is to prevent group members from accelerating transaction results that relate to sales of assets within the group. Therefore, for purposes of these intercompany transactions, the group is treated as a single corporation with multiple divisions rather than a conglomerate of separate corporations.

The matching rule applies to all sales of assets or the performance of services among group members. For sales, the entire deferred gain or loss enters the consolidated taxable income computation when the asset is transferred outside the group through a subsequent transaction. Full gain or loss recognition can also be triggered under the "acceleration rule" when the seller of the property leaves the

[44]Reg. § 1.1502–26(a)(1)(i).

[45]Reg. §§ 1.1502–13(c) through (h) and –13T.

group or the consolidation election is terminated. The acceleration rule applies when it is no longer possible to produce a proper result under the matching rule.

Generally, when gain or loss on the sale is ultimately recognized, it is in the same manner as it would have been on the initial sale.[46]

EXAMPLE 27

Mulbury Corporation sold a plot of land to its 100%-owned subsidiary, CherryCo, in the current year for $100,000. Mulbury had acquired the land 10 years ago for $40,000. The consolidated return also reflects the operating results of the parties: Mulbury generated $10,000 income, and CherryCo produced a $100,000 gain.

This intercompany transaction triggers the matching rule. Mulbury's $60,000 realized gain is deferred through an elimination in the computation of consolidated taxable income. CherryCo's basis in the land is $100,000. The $60,000 gain is recognized by the group when CherryCo later sells the land to Outsider Corporation.

	Separate Taxable Income	**Adjustments**	**Post-adjustment Amounts**
Mulbury information	$ 70,000	______	$ 70,000
CherryCo information	100,000	______	100,000
Group-basis transactions			
Intercompany events		– $60,000 gain on intercompany sale to CherryCo†	–60,000
Consolidated taxable income			$110,000
*Permanent eliminations.	**Group-basis transaction.		†Matching rule.

CherryCo sold the land to Outsider for $110,000 in a year in which its operating income totaled $60,000 (exclusive of the sale of the land), and Mulbury's operating income amounted to $170,000.

	Separate Taxable Income	**Adjustments**	**Post-adjustment Amounts**
Mulbury information	$170,000	______	$170,000
CherryCo information	70,000	______	70,000
Group-basis transactions			
Intercompany events		+ $60,000 restored gain on Mulbury's sale to CherryCo†	+60,000
Consolidated taxable income			$300,000
*Permanent eliminations.	**Group-basis transaction.		†Matching rule.

The matching rule is attractive to an affiliated group when intercompany sales take place at a gain. When such sales generate losses, however, the mandatory nature of the rules may become burdensome.

[46] Sections 267 and 1239 may convert other types of gain into ordinary income. See especially Reg. §§ 1.267(f)–1 and 1.1239–1(a) and (b)(3).

Concept Summary 5–2

The Consolidated Tax Return

1. Groups of corporations form for a variety of tax and nontax reasons. The election to file Federal income tax returns on a consolidated basis allows certain group members to use their positive tax attributes (e.g., loss or credit carryovers) to offset negative tax attributes (e.g., positive taxable income) of other members.
2. Consolidated tax returns are limited to eligible corporations that satisfy stock ownership tests and meet various compliance requirements. For instance, all group members must conform their tax years to that of the parent of the group. Group members may use different tax accounting methods, however.
3. Group members are jointly and severally liable for the overall tax liability of the group. For the most part, computations of estimated tax liabilities must be made on a consolidated basis.
4. The stock basis of a subsidiary is derived from the acquisition price of the stock, increased by the taxable income (or decreased by the losses) of the subsidiary, and decreased by dividend distributions. An excess loss account is created when aggregate losses of the subsidiary exceed both the purchase price and ensuing income amounts. The excess loss account is recaptured as capital gain when the subsidiary stock is disposed of.
5. Under the § 382 or SRLY rules, NOL carryforwards may be deferred when they relate to subsidiaries acquired by the group. When both restrictions apply, the § 382 rules prevail.
6. In computing consolidated taxable income, certain items, such as charitable contributions and § 1231 gains and losses, are computed on a consolidated basis, while other gains and losses are deferred until later tax periods. The group is subject to severe restrictions in using any operating losses of a subsidiary that has been acquired or disposed of.

Suggested Further Readings

Jeremy B. Blank, Gary T. Weaver, Jared H. Gordon, and Edward A. Sair, "Applying Attribute Reduction under Sec.108(B) in a Consolidated Group," *The Tax Adviser*, March 2003, pp. 128–132.

Bryan P. Collins and Darin A. Zywan, "Rite Aid—The Final Word on Loss Duplication within a Consolidated Group," *Journal of Corporate Taxation*, March/April 2002, pp. 5–12.

Karyn Bybee Friske and Darlene Pulliam Smith, "IRS Again Revises Duplicated Loss Regs. to Curb Double Benefit," *Practical Tax Strategies*, May 2003, pp. 288–295.

KEY TERMS

Affiliated group, 5–8
Compliance requirements, 5–10
Conglomerates, 5–2
Consolidated return, 5–2
Excess loss account, 5–15
Ineligible entities, 5–10
Intercompany transaction, 5–17
Legislative Regulations, 5–4
Matching rule, 5–26
Offspring rule, 5–21
Relative taxable income method, 5–12
Relative tax liability method, 5–12
Separate return limitation year (SRLY), 5–23

PROBLEM MATERIALS

Problems

1. The decision to file consolidated returns may be the result of a variety of business decisions. List possible nontax business decisions that can lead to filing consolidated returns.

Ethics

2. Hemlock Corporation produces pharmaceuticals. It is very concerned about potential product liability for a particular drug it is developing to help individuals lose weight

quickly. It spins off only those assets essential for the development and production of this product into a new corporation, Weight-off. The new corporation retains a low level of working capital and liquid assets by paying large dividends to its parent. When the drug is found to have severe negative side effects for a small portion of the population, large losses result. Hemlock uses these losses through filing consolidated returns. When numerous lawsuits are brought, Weight-off files for bankruptcy and, given its low level of assets, owns little with which to compensate the injured individuals. Evaluate Hemlock's actions from both a business and an ethical perspective.

Communications

3. You are the tax member of a consulting team that is presenting ideas for a possible restructuring to a client. The client has heard that filing consolidated tax returns can produce savings. Prepare for the client an outline on the pros and cons of filing a consolidated return.

Issue ID

4. Black, Brown, and Red Corporations are considering a corporate restructuring that would allow them to file Federal income tax returns on a consolidated basis. Black holds significant NOL carryforwards from several years ago. Brown has always been profitable and is projected to remain so. Red has been successful, but its product cycles are mature and operating losses are likely to begin three years from now and last for a decade. What tax issues should the corporations consider before electing to file on a consolidated basis?

Issue ID

5. Continue with the facts presented in Problem 4. In addition, assume that for the last four years Brown Corporation has had capital losses on the sale of its investments that it was unable to utilize. To try to curb the operating losses predicted for Red, a new product line will be developed over the next three years. Significant development costs will be incurred, and it is likely that one of Red's plants and adjacent land will need to be sold. A new plant will be opened closer to Red's customers. Modify your list of tax issues to include these considerations.

6. Determine which of the following corporations can file consolidated returns. All entities described are U.S. corporations.
   a. Hazel owns 40% of Branch. Trunk owns 90% of Nut, 15% of Hazel, and 50% of Branch. Nut owns 70% of Hazel. Twig owns 10% of Hazel, Nut, and Branch.
   b. Paloverde owns 75% of Mesquite. The other 25% is owned by Saguaro. Paloverde also owns 60% of Saguaro, and Mesquite owns the remaining 40% of Saguaro.
   c. Magnolia owns 20% of Blossom with Mint, owning 40% and Leaf owning the remaining 40%. Magnolia also owns 85% of Mint, with 15% owned by individuals. Mint owns 70% of Leaf, and individuals own the remaining 30%.

EXTENDER

7. The requirements to be considered part of a parent-subsidiary controlled group are different from those for being part of an affiliated group that can file a consolidated return. In each of the following situations, determine whether the corporations form an affiliated group or a parent-subsidiary controlled group.
   a. Cypress, Inc., owns 95% of the voting power of MossCo for nine months of the year. Enrique owns all of the nonvoting preferred stock of MossCo. The preferred stock's value is 50% of the common stock's value.
   b. CrabTree Corporation owns 100% of all voting and nonvoting classes of Apple's stock for the last six months of the year. It purchased all the stock from Jasmine.
   c. Cottonwood, Inc., owns 90% of the voting common stock and 60% of the nonvoting preferred stock of GrownCo for the entire year. The preferred stock's value is 50% of the common stock's value.

Decision Making

8. Lavender and Azure began filing a calendar year consolidated return for tax year 2003. The group never extends the due date of its tax returns. Lavender acquires all of the stock of Rose on January 1, 2004, and immediately joins the filing election. All of the Rose stock is sold to another investor at the end of 2006. Explain the significance of the following dates. Which of your answers can change if the taxpayers so elect?
   a. March 15, 2004.
   b. January 1, 2005.
   c. March 15, 2005.
   d. January 1, 2012.

9. Apply the controlled and affiliated group rules to determine whether a parent-subsidiary controlled group or an affiliated group exists in each of the following independent situations. Circle Y for yes and N for no.

Situation	Parent-Subsidiary Controlled Group?	Affiliated Group?
a. Throughout the year, Parent owns 85% of the voting and 75% of the non-voting stock of SubCo, which is 81% of SubCo's stock value.	Y N	Y N
b. Throughout the year, Parent owns 90% of the voting and 5% of the non-voting stock of SubCo, which is 75% of SubCo's stock value.	Y N	Y N
c. For 11 months, Parent owns 75% of all stock of SubCo. For the last month of the tax year, Parent owns 100% of all SubCo stock.	Y N	Y N

Decision Making

10. Senior Corporation owns all of the stock of Junior, Ltd., a corporation that has been declared bankrupt and has no net assets. Junior still owes $1 million to Wholesale, Inc., one of its suppliers, and $2.5 million to the IRS for unpaid Federal income taxes. Senior and Junior have always filed Federal income tax returns on a consolidated basis. What is Senior's exposure concerning Junior's outstanding liabilities?

11. Apricot Corporation owns 100% of the stock of Peach Corporation. The entities wish to file on a consolidated basis starting with the tax return for 2004. Apricot and Peach are both calendar year taxpayers.
    a. What must Apricot and Peach do and by what dates if the consolidation election is to be effective?
    b. Assume that Apricot Corporation files a complete consolidated Form 1120 one month before the due date of the return. Five days before the return's due date, Peach comes under investigation for tax fraud. Apricot would now prefer not to file a consolidated return with Peach. Can Apricot or Peach do anything to void the filing on a consolidated basis?

EXTENDER

12. The Parent consolidated group reports the following results for the tax year. Determine each member's share of the consolidated tax liability, assuming that the members all have consented to use the relative taxable income method. Assume a 35% marginal tax rate.

	Parent	SubOne	SubTwo	SubThree	Consolidated
Ordinary income	$700	$200	$ 20	($30)	$ 890
Capital gain/loss	-0-	-0-	40	(25)	15
§ 1231 gain/loss	150	-0-	(55)	-0-	95
Separate taxable incomes	$850	$200	$ 5	($30) with a $25 capital loss carryover	
Consolidated taxable income					$1,000
Consolidated tax liability					$ 350
Energy tax credit, from SubOne					(44)
Net tax due					$ 306

EXTENDER

13. Assume the same facts as in Problem 12, except that the group members have adopted the relative tax liability tax-sharing method.

Issue ID

14. Parent Corporation and its wholly owned subsidiary, Child Corporation, file Federal tax returns on a separate basis. Parent manufactures postage meters, and Child provides mail-order services to a cross section of clients in the state.

    Parent uses a calendar tax year, while Child files using an April 30 year-end. Parent's gross receipts for the year total $10 million, and Child's are $2.5 million. Identify some tax issues as to accounting periods and methods that the group would face if the corporations elect to consolidate.

Communications

15. In a memo to the tax research file, summarize the most important positive and negative adjustments made by a parent corporation to the stock basis of its subsidiary.

16. Senior, Ltd., acquires all of the stock of JuniorCo for $20 million at the beginning of 2003. The group immediately elects to file income tax returns on a consolidated basis. Senior's operations generate a $50 million profit every year. In 2004, JuniorCo pays its parent a $3 million dividend. Operating results for JuniorCo are as follows.

2003	$4 million
2004	1 million
2005	10 million

    a. Compute Senior's basis in the JuniorCo stock as of the end of 2003, 2004, and 2005.
    b. Same as (a), except that the 2004 tax year produced a $6 million NOL.
    c. Same as (a), except that the 2004 tax year produced a $40 million NOL.

17. Orange Corporation owns all of Seed Corporation's stock. Orange and Seed had the following transactions for the current tax year.

    - Orange purchased machinery from Seed at a gain to Seed of $20,000.
    - Seed declared and distributed a $15,000 dividend to Orange.
    - Ordinary income for Orange was $300,000 and for Seed was $200,000.
    - Orange sold land to an unrelated party for a $50,000 gain.
    - Seed purchased inventory from Orange for $300,000. At the end of the year $50,000 of the inventory remained on hand. Orange's profit percentage is 10%.
    - Seed sold equipment to an unrelated party for a $10,000 loss.
    - Charitable contributions were made by Orange ($45,000) and by Seed ($5,000).

    Indicate how each of these transactions is treated on the consolidated return filed by Orange and Seed.

Issue ID

18. In December 2005, Parent Corporation renders services worth $250,000 to its wholly owned subsidiary, Child Corporation. Both entities use calendar tax years. Parent uses accrual tax accounting, while Child employs the cash method of accounting. The entities have been filing on a consolidated basis since Child was incorporated many years ago.

    Parent's operations for 2005 resulted in a $2 million loss. Parent sends Child an invoice for the services in December 2005, and Child pays it in January 2006. What tax consequences are the parties trying to accomplish?

19. Compute consolidated taxable income for the calendar year Teak Group, which elected consolidated status immediately upon creation of the two member corporations in January 2003. All recognized income relates to the consulting services of the firms. No intercompany transactions were completed during the indicated years.

Year	Teak Corporation	Koa Corporation
2003	$250,000	$ 10,000
2004	250,000	(200,000)
2005	250,000	(600,000)
2006	250,000	10,000

20. Compute consolidated taxable income for the calendar year Juniper Group, which elected consolidated status immediately upon the creation of the two member corporations on January 1, 2003. All recognized income is ordinary in nature, and no intercompany transactions were completed during the indicated years.

Year	Juniper Corporation	Ash Corporation
2003	$50,000	($ 90,000)
2004	50,000	(80,000)
2005	50,000	10,000
2006	50,000	25,000

21. Maple, Oak, and Alder Corporations have filed on a consolidated, calendar year basis for many years. At the beginning of the 2004 tax year, the group elects to de-consolidate. The group's $4 million NOL carryforward can be traced in the following manner: one-half to Maple's operations and one-quarter each to Oak's and Alder's. How will Alder treat the NOL on its 2004 separate tax return?

22. Child Corporation joined the Thrust consolidated group in 2003. At the time it joined the group, Child held a $400,000 NOL carryforward. On a consolidated basis, the members of Thrust generated significant profits for many years.

    Child's operating results during the first few consolidated return years were as follows.

2003	($200,000)
2004	90,000
2005	115,000

The § 382 rules do not apply to the group.

How will Child's NOLs affect consolidated taxable income for these years? Is any refund available with respect to the NOL that Child brought into the group?

23. SubOne Corporation brought a $2 million NOL carryforward into a group of corporations that elected to file on a consolidated basis as of the beginning of this year. Combined results for the year generated $10 million taxable income, $500,000 of which was attributed to SubOne's activities for the year. Has SubOne been a good consolidation partner?

Decision Making

24. Parent and Child Corporations have filed on a consolidated basis since the mid-1970s. Junior Corporation was formed at the beginning of this year through an asset split-off from Parent. Operations this year resulted in a $2 million operating loss, one-fourth of which can be traced to Junior. Should Junior join the consolidated group this year? Will the group be able to carry back and claim a refund for the $500,000 NOL that is attributable to Junior?

25. Birch owned all of the stock of Elm when the two corporations were formed a decade ago. The group immediately elected to file on a consolidated basis. The management team of Elm now has purchased the company from the parent and intends to carry on and expand the business into new markets. When Elm left the Birch consolidated group, the group held a $3 million NOL carryforward, $800,000 of which was attributable to Elm operations under formulas used by all of the parties. Elm will generate $300,000 on each of its first five years' worth of separate returns.

    Advise Elm as to who "owns" the carryforwards after the corporate division.

26. In the current year, Citrus Corporation's taxable income before the dividends received deduction and charitable contributions deduction is $100,000. Included in Citrus's taxable income are the dividends it received from other corporations. Its charitable contributions for the year are $20,000. The following presents the dividend amounts and percentages Citrus owns of each corporation, the corporation's charitable contributions, and its taxable income before charitable contributions.

	Citrus Corporation's			
Name	**Dividend**	**% Owned**	**Charitable Contribution**	**Taxable Income**
Lemon	$40,000	100%	$ 5,000	$200,000
Lime	60,000	40%	40,000	500,000
Orange	30,000	15%	15,000	300,000

Lemon, Lime, and Orange do not own stock in Citrus or in each other.

a. What is Citrus' taxable income if it does not file a consolidated return?

b. Assume that the above information is based on Citrus Corporation filing a consolidated return with its affiliated corporations. What is the consolidated taxable income for the affiliated group?

EXTENDER

27. Cherry and Pit are corporations that have operations in several states, one of which is State A. State A requires all corporations to file separate returns based on income apportioned to the state. It follows Federal carryover NOL rules. In 2003, Cherry acquired 100% of Pit and elected to file consolidated returns for Federal purposes. The total income and losses for three years as well as those amounts assigned to State A are listed below.

Year	Total Cherry	Total Pit	State A Cherry	State A Pit
2002	$ 45,000	$ 30,000	$ 18,000	$ 15,000
2003	40,000	(60,000)	16,000	(30,000)
2004	(55,000)	15,000	(20,000)	7,000

a. What is the Federal consolidated taxable income (loss) for each year?

b. What is the State A taxable income (loss) for Cherry and Pit for each year?

28. The Parent consolidated group includes SubTwo, which was acquired as part of a § 382 ownership change. SubTwo brought with it to the group a large NOL carryforward, $500,000 of which is available this year under the SRLY rules due to SubTwo's positive contribution to the group's taxable income. The § 382 limitation with respect to SubTwo is $400,000. How much of SubTwo's NOL can be used this year to reduce consolidated taxable income?

Communications

29. Junior was a member of the Rice consolidated group for many years. It left the group effective for the 2004 tax year. In 2001, Junior sold a plot of land to Parent at a $600,000 realized loss. Recognition of that loss by the group was deferred under the intercompany sale rule. As a departing group member, does Junior have any right to take the loss with it to be used on its subsequent separate returns? Prepare a memo for the tax research file, outlining the arguments both in Junior's favor and in the remaining group's favor.

30. Parent Corporation sold a plot of undeveloped land to SubCo this year for $100,000. Parent had acquired the land several years ago for $20,000. The consolidated return also reflects the operating results of the parties: Parent generated $130,000 income from operations, and SubCo produced a $20,000 operating loss.

a. Use the computational worksheet of Figure 5–2 to derive the group members' separate taxable incomes and the group's consolidated taxable income.

b. Same as (a), except that SubCo sold the land to Outsider Corporation for $110,000 in a subsequent year, when its operating income totaled $30,000 (exclusive of the sale of the land), and Parent's operating income amounted to $90,000.

31. SubCo sold an asset to Parent at a tax and accounting gain of $300,000. The asset appreciated by another $20,000 before Parent sold it to an unrelated party, Outsiders, Inc.

a. Compute the realized financial accounting and recognized taxable income of the group members for these transactions, indicating the date upon which the gain is triggered and the member that includes the gain.

b. Same as (a), except that the asset declines in value by $20,000 while it is in Parent's hands.

Decision Making

32. Chestnut Corporation is considering whether to elect filing a consolidated return. It owns 100% of Cashew Corporation and 10% of Pistachio Corporation. Cashew owns 15% of Pistachio and 5% of Pinyon Corporation. Chestnut and Cashew have the following income and expenses for the current year.

	Chestnut	Cashew
Operating income	$ 550,000	$ 25,000
Operating expenses	200,000	80,000
Dividends:		
Cashew	40,000	
Pistachio	10,000	15,000
Pinyon		20,000
Capital gain (loss)	(50,000)	40,000
§ 1231 gain (loss)	20,000	(10,000)
Charitable contributions	30,000	5,000

Determine whether Chestnut should elect to file a consolidated return.

BRIDGE DISCIPLINE

1. Walnut Corporation would like to acquire 100% of Acorn Corporation from its parent, Almond Corporation. Almond is very interested in selling Acorn as it is currently having cash-flow problems. The sale of Acorn could bring the cash infusion it needs to survive. Cash is so short that Almond has not paid last year's Federal consolidated income taxes. As a consultant to Walnut, what suggestions would you make regarding the structure of the acquisition of Acorn?

Research Problems

THOMSON RIA

*Note: Solutions to Research Problems can be prepared by using the **RIA Checkpoint® Student Edition** online research product, which is available to accompany this text. It is also possible to prepare solutions to the Research Problems by using tax research materials found in a standard tax library.*

Communications

Research Problem 1. Kite is the parent of a group of corporations that files on a consolidated basis. The other group members are Lite and Mite. The group claimed an NOL carryback deduction based solely on expenses incurred to carry out the members' product liability programs. Kite could deduct all of its separate product liability expenses (PLEs), but separately Lite and Mite could not, because of a lack of sufficient other net taxable income.

Member	Separate Taxable Income before PLEs	PLE for Tax Year	Separate Deduction for PLE
Kite	$1,000,000	$ 350,000	$ 350,000
Lite	2,000,000	3,000,000	2,000,000
Mite	4,000,000	7,000,000	4,000,000
Totals	$7,000,000	$10,350,000	$6,350,000

The group wants to deduct the full $10,350,000 in PLE deductions for the year so that it can create a $3,350,000 consolidated NOL carryback to a prior tax year and receive an immediate tax refund. This result would seem to follow from the consolidated tax return rules. The IRS wants to limit the deduction to the aggregate of the separate company amounts, $6,350,000. Kite is incorporated in the jurisdiction of the First Circuit Court of Appeals.

Kite's tax director, Clara Trask, asks your opinion as to whether the $10,350,000 deduction will hold up under audit. Respond to her in the form of a letter. Kite's address is 600 Bearpath Road, Falmouth, ME 04105.

Research Problem 2. The calendar year Thor Group files its Federal income tax returns on a consolidated basis. The group's members elected to file on a consolidated basis because some of them were generating income, while others were generating losses. To utilize the deductions for the losses, the group began filing a consolidated return.

Now market conditions have changed. Currently, group members are all producing positive Federal taxable incomes. Various groups of shareholders desire to purchase the affiliates of the now-profitable group. If this occurs, the group will no longer meet the ownership requirements for consolidation starting in tax year 2004.

Is it possible to effect a de-consolidation of the group for tax year 2003? Why not just file separate returns for each member of the group for that year? The parent would claim the 100% dividends received deduction on its own return, and this should void the election.

The breakup of the group will take place by the end of June 2004, so no consolidated group will exist for that calendar tax year. But, by using the suggested strategy, the de-consolidation can be effective all the way back to January 2003. Do you agree?

Communications

Research Problem 3. The Cardinal Group had filed on a consolidated basis for several years. Parent Cardinal, Ltd., had a wholly owned subsidiary, Swallow, Inc. The group used a calendar tax year.

On January 25, 2002, Heron acquired all of the stock of Cardinal, including its ownership in Swallow, an important supplier for Heron's manufacturing process. All parties in the new group intended to file on a consolidated basis immediately and, indeed, used consolidated amounts in filing the 2002 Heron Group return on September 10, 2003.

During the audit of Heron Group's 2002 tax return, the IRS disallowed the use of the consolidated method because no Form 1122s had ever been filed for the affiliates in the new group. In a memo to the tax research file, summarize the possibilities for the Heron Group to be granted an extension to elect consolidated return status.

Internet Activity

Use the tax resources of the Internet to address the following questions. Do not restrict your search to the World Wide Web, but include a review of newsgroups and general reference materials, practitioner sites and resources, primary sources of the tax law, chat rooms and discussion groups, and other opportunities.

Communications

Research Problem 4. The Rite Aid case (88 AFTR2d 2001–5058; U.S. Court of Appeals, Federal Circuit) has received considerable attention in the popular press. Find two news articles (not articles in tax journals) regarding the findings in the Rite Aid case. Prepare a summary of the articles and e-mail the summary to your professor. Make sure to include proper citations of the articles.

Research Problem 5. Look at the financial statements of a conglomerate with several affiliates. Use the footnotes to the statements to determine the tax savings produced by the election to consolidate.

Research Problem 6. Determine whether the income tax laws of your state, and those of two of its neighbors, allow Federal affiliated groups to file consolidated returns. How are NOL carrybacks treated by your state?

CHAPTER 6

Partnerships and LLCs: Distributions, Ownership Changes

LEARNING OBJECTIVES

After completing Chapter 6, you should be able to:

LO.1

Determine the tax treatment of proportionate nonliquidating distributions from a partnership to a partner.

LO.2

Determine the tax treatment of proportionate distributions that liquidate a partnership.

LO.3

Describe the tax treatment that applies to distributions treated as disguised sales and distributions of marketable securities and precontribution gain property.

LO.4

Determine the tax treatment of payments from a partnership to a retiring or deceased partner.

LO.5

Calculate the selling partner's amount and character of gain or loss on the sale or exchange of a partnership interest.

LO.6

Describe tax issues related to other dispositions of partnership interests.

LO.7

Calculate the optional adjustments to basis under § 754.

LO.8

Outline the methods of terminating a partnership.

LO.9

Describe the special considerations of a family partnership.

OUTLINE

TAX TALK

There are two systems of taxation in our country: one for the informed and one for the uninformed.

—Judge Learned Hand

Partnership taxation is unique in that there are two competing economic theories running through the tax law. The aggregate theory, which dominates, posits that a partner owns an undivided interest in all of the partnership's assets and liabilities. This accounts for the flow-through treatment of partnership income, gains, expenses, and losses to the partners. At the same time, a partnership is a separate legal entity in which the partner owns an interest—a relationship similar to that between a shareholder and a corporation. Consequently, the entity theory also applies.

Much of the complexity found in the partnership tax law occurs as a result of the interaction between these two theories. The Code and the Regulations have been drafted so as to prevent shifting of tax items among partners without an economic price being paid for the allocation. The partnership agreement is merely a contract between partners enumerating how everything is to be divided.

EXAMPLE 1

The Rock Ltd., a general partnership owned equally by Mark and John, has inventory as its only asset. The inventory has a fair market value of $500,000 and a tax basis of $100,000. If the partnership sold the inventory, $400,000 of ordinary income would result.

John wants to sell his half-interest to Jill for $250,000. John thinks the sale will trigger a capital gain, because an interest in a partnership is a capital asset. This would be the proper treatment if the entity theory applied. However, this is not an equitable result, because the only asset of value inside the partnership produces ordinary income. The aggregate theory applies to this sale, so any gain on the sale of the partnership interest is reclassified as ordinary. (See the later discussion of § 751 "hot assets.") ■

TAX FACT

WHO'S ONLINE?

A total of 22,793 partnerships filed electronically for 2001, representing 4 million partners. This represents a 318 percent increase from 2000, when only 7,165 partnerships filed electronically. Partnerships with more than 100 partners are required to file electronically. Electronic filers still constituted only a small fraction of the total partnership returns filed for 2001.

Distributions from a Partnership

Distributions from a partnership are viewed as a return of partner capital, reducing the partner's basis in the partnership interest (commonly referred to as outside basis), and therefore generally are not taxable. This is in keeping with the aggregate theory of partnership taxation. Because this flexibility lends itself to taxpayer abuse, certain types of distributions may result in gain being recognized, including:

- Distributions of precontribution gain property within seven years of its contribution.[1]
- Distributions of marketable securities.[2]
- Disproportionate distributions.[3]
- Distributions that are really part of a disguised sale of assets to the partnership.[4]

EXAMPLE 2

Bill is a partner in the BB Partnership. The basis in his partnership interest is $10,000. The partnership distributes $3,000 cash to Bill at the end of the year. Bill does not recognize any gain on the distribution and reduces his basis by $3,000 (the amount of the distribution) to $7,000. Bill's basis in the cash he received is $3,000, and the partnership's inside basis for its assets is reduced by the $3,000 cash distributed. ■

The result in Example 2 arises whether or not a similar distribution is made to other partners. In a partnership, it is not critical that all partners receive a distribution at the same time, as long as capital account balances are maintained appropriately, and final distributions are in accordance with ending capital account balances. Capital account maintenance requirements ensure that each partner eventually receives the proper amount, even though current distributions are not in accordance with ownership percentages.

A distribution from the partnership to a partner may consist of cash or partnership property. All distributions, cash and property, fall into two distinct categories.

- Liquidating distributions.
- Nonliquidating distributions.

Whether a distribution is a **liquidating** or **nonliquidating distribution** depends solely on whether the partner remains a partner in the partnership after the distribution is made. A *liquidating* distribution occurs either (1) when a partnership itself

[1] §§ 704(c) and 737.
[2] § 731(c).
[3] § 751(b).
[4] § 707.

liquidates and distributes all of its property to its partners or (2) when an ongoing partnership redeems the interest of one of its partners. This second type of liquidating distribution occurs, for example, when a partner retires from a partnership, or when a deceased partner's interest is liquidated. The two types of liquidating distributions receive differing tax treatment, as later sections of the chapter will explain.

A *nonliquidating* distribution is any distribution from a continuing partnership to a continuing partner—that is, any distribution that is not a liquidating distribution. Nonliquidating distributions are of two types: draws or partial liquidations. A *draw* is a distribution of a partner's share of current or accumulated partnership profits that have been taxed to the partner in current or prior taxable years of the partnership. A *partial liquidation* is a distribution that reduces the partner's interest in partnership capital but does not liquidate the partner's entire interest in the partnership. The distinction between the two types of nonliquidating distributions is largely semantic, since the basic tax treatment typically does not differ.

EXAMPLE 3

Kay joins the calendar year KLM Partnership on January 1, 2004, by contributing $40,000 cash to the partnership in exchange for a one-third interest in partnership capital, profits, and losses. Her distributive share of partnership income for the year is $25,000. If the partnership distributes $65,000 ($25,000 share of partnership profits + $40,000 initial capital contribution) to Kay on December 31, 2004, the distribution is a nonliquidating distribution as long as Kay continues to be a partner in the partnership. This is true even though Kay receives her share of profits plus her entire investment in the partnership. In this case, $25,000 is considered a draw, and the remaining $40,000 is a partial liquidation of Kay's interest. If, instead, the partnership is liquidated or Kay ceases to be a partner in the ongoing partnership, the $65,000 distribution is a liquidating distribution. ■

A payment from a partnership to a partner is not necessarily treated as a distribution. For example, a partnership may pay interest or rent to a partner for use of the partner's capital or property, make a guaranteed payment to a partner, or purchase property from a partner.

Finally, a distribution may be either proportionate or disproportionate. In a **proportionate distribution**, a partner receives the appropriate share of certain ordinary income-producing assets of the partnership. A **disproportionate distribution** occurs when the distribution increases or decreases the distributee partner's interest in certain ordinary income-producing assets.

COMPARISON OF DISTRIBUTION: PARTNERSHIPS VERSUS CORPORATIONS

There is a distinct difference between the treatment of the distributions from partnerships and corporations. The difference stems from the two competing theories, aggregate versus entity. Under the tax law, a corporation is viewed as a separate legal entity apart from its owners, the shareholders. Distributions received by a shareholder are treated as:

- dividend income[5] to the extent they come from earnings and profits,
- payment for the shareholder's stock if the stock is being redeemed,[6] or
- payment for the shareholder's stock if the corporation is liquidated.[7]

[5]§ 301(c).
[6]§ 302(b).
[7]§ 331.

Under the aggregate theory, a partner receiving a distribution from a partnership is considered to be receiving:

- income that has been previously taxed to the partner, or
- the partner's share of partnership assets.

LO.1

Determine the tax treatment of proportionate nonliquidating distributions from a partnership to a partner.

PROPORTIONATE NONLIQUIDATING DISTRIBUTIONS

In general, neither the partner nor the partnership recognizes gain or loss when a proportionate nonliquidating distribution occurs.[8] The partner usually takes a carryover basis for the assets distributed.[9] The distributee partner's outside basis is reduced (but not below zero) by the amount of cash and the adjusted basis of property distributed to the partner by the partnership.[10] The details of the taxation of such distributions are discussed below and are summarized in Concept Summary 6–1. The following examples illustrate the situation and show that a distribution does not change a partner's overall economic position.

EXAMPLE 4

Jay is a one-fourth partner in the SP Partnership. His basis in his partnership interest is $40,000 on December 31, 2004. The fair market value of the interest is $70,000. The partnership distributes $25,000 cash to him on that date. The distribution is not taxable to Jay or the partnership. The distribution reduces Jay's adjusted basis in the partnership to $15,000 ($40,000 – $25,000), and the fair market value of his partnership interest is, arguably, reduced to $45,000 ($70,000 – $25,000). ■

EXAMPLE 5

Assume the same facts as in Example 4, except that, in addition to the $25,000 cash, the partnership distributes land with an adjusted basis to the partnership of $13,000 and a fair market value of $30,000 on the date of distribution. The distribution is not taxable to Jay or the partnership. Jay reduces his basis in the partnership to $2,000 [$40,000 – ($25,000 + $13,000)] and takes a carryover basis of $13,000 in the land. The fair market value of Jay's remaining interest in the partnership is, arguably, reduced to $15,000 [$70,000 – ($25,000 + $30,000)].

If Jay had sold his partnership interest for $70,000 rather than receiving the distributions, he would have realized and recognized gain of $30,000 ($70,000 selling price – $40,000 outside basis). Because he has not recognized any gain or loss on the distribution of cash and land, he should still have the $30,000 of deferred gain to recognize at some point in the future. This is exactly what will happen. If Jay sells the cash, land, and remaining partnership interest on January 1, 2005, the day after the distribution, he realizes and recognizes gains of $17,000 ($30,000 – $13,000) on the land and $13,000 ($15,000 – $2,000) on the partnership interest. These gains total $30,000, which is the amount of the original deferred gain. ■

Gain Recognition. A partner recognizes gain from a proportionate nonliquidating distribution to the extent that the money received exceeds the outside basis of the partner's interest in the partnership.[11]

EXAMPLE 6

Samantha is a one-third partner in the SMP Partnership. Her basis in this ownership interest is $50,000 on December 31, 2004, after accounting for the calendar year partnership's 2004 operations and for Samantha's 2004 capital contributions. On December 31, 2004, the partnership distributes $60,000 cash to Samantha. She recognizes a $10,000 gain from this distribution

[8] §§ 731(a) and (b).
[9] § 732(a)(1).
[10] § 733.
[11] § 731(a)(1).

($60,000 cash received – $50,000 basis in her partnership interest). Most likely, this gain is taxed as a capital gain.[12] ■

A reduction of a partner's share of partnership debt is treated as a distribution of money from the partnership to the partner and therefore reduces the partner's basis in the partnership interest. Any reduction of a share of debt in excess of a partner's basis in the partnership is taxable to the partner as a gain.

EXAMPLE 7

Returning to the facts of Example 6, assume that Samantha's $50,000 basis in her partnership interest included a $60,000 share of partnership liabilities. If the partnership repays all of its liabilities, Samantha is treated as receiving a $60,000 distribution from the partnership. The first $50,000 of this distribution reduces her basis to $0. The last $10,000 distributed creates a taxable gain to her of $10,000. ■

A distribution of marketable securities can also be treated as a distribution of money. Determining the treatment of such distributions is complicated, though, since several exceptions may apply and the basis in the distributed stock must be calculated. Such distributions are discussed later under Property Distributions with Special Tax Treatment: Marketable Securities.

Loss Recognition. The distributee partner cannot recognize a loss on a proportionate nonliquidating distribution. This loss is deferred because tax law typically does not permit losses to be recognized until the loss is certain to occur and the amount is known. After the nonliquidating distribution, the partner still owns the partnership interest, which has an indeterminate future value. Only when a final liquidating distribution is received is the loss certain and known in amount—and potentially deductible.

EXAMPLE 8

Henry has a $50,000 basis in his partnership interest. Assume that on December 31 he receives a distribution of $10,000 cash. As a result of the distribution, his basis in the partnership interest is reduced to $40,000.

Henry knows the partnership has fallen on hard times and that future distributions will probably not amount to more than a few hundred dollars. He does not recognize a loss, even though a loss probably exists. The amount of the loss is not fixed and determinable since he still owns the partnership interest. ■

Property Distributions. In general, a distributee partner does not recognize gain or loss from a property distribution. The partner takes a substituted basis in the property received and reduces the outside interest basis.

EXAMPLE 9

Mary has a $50,000 basis in her partnership interest. The partnership distributes land it owns with a basis and a fair market value of $60,000. Mary does not recognize any gain on this distribution because it is a distribution of property. However, Mary should not be allowed to take a carryover basis of $60,000 in the land, when her basis in her partnership interest is only $50,000. Therefore, the Code provides that Mary takes a substituted basis of $50,000 in the land. Her basis in her partnership interest is reduced by the basis she takes in the asset received, or $50,000. Therefore, Mary has a $50,000 basis in the land and a $0 basis in her partnership interest, and she recognizes no gain on this distribution. ■

[12] § 731(a). If the partnership holds any "hot assets," however, Samantha probably recognizes some ordinary income. See § 751(b) and the related discussion of ordinary income ("hot") assets later in this chapter.

The rule that no gain or loss is recognized on a property distribution from a partnership has several exceptions. These situations may arise for either a current or a liquidating distribution, so discussion of these exceptions is deferred until all the general rules are discussed (see Property Distributions with Special Tax Treatment later in the chapter).

Ordering Rules. When the inside basis of the distributed assets exceeds the distributee partner's outside basis, the assets are deemed distributed in the following order.

- Money is distributed first. (See the later discussion of marketable securities.)
- Unrealized receivables and inventory are distributed second.
- All other assets are distributed last.

Unrealized receivables are receivables that have a value to the partnership, but for which the related income has not yet been realized or recognized under the partnership's method of accounting. The term *unrealized receivables* applies only to amounts that will ultimately be realized and recognized as ordinary income. If the partnership uses the cash method of accounting, trade receivables from services or sales are unrealized receivables. If the partnership uses the accrual method, they are not. Unrealized receivables include receivables from the sales of ordinary income property and rights to payments for services. For some purposes, unrealized receivables also include ordinary recapture income that would arise if the partnership sold its depreciable assets. Installment gains are unrealized receivables if the gain will be taxed as ordinary income when realized.

Inventory, for purposes of these ordering rules, includes any partnership assets except cash, capital, or § 1231 assets. For example, all accounts receivable are considered to be inventory, although only cash basis receivables are "unrealized receivables."

Since the partner typically does not recognize a gain from a *property* distribution, the Code provides that the partner's basis for property received cannot exceed the partner's basis in the partnership interest immediately before the distribution. For each level of asset distribution, the relevant adjustments are made to the partner's basis in the interest. In other words, after a cash distribution, the partner's basis in the interest is recomputed before determining the effect of a distribution of unrealized receivables or inventory. The basis is again recomputed before determining the effect of a distribution of other assets. If the remaining outside basis at the end of any step is insufficient to cover the entire inside basis of the assets in the next step, that remaining outside basis is allocated among the assets within that class.[13]

EXAMPLE 10

Sally has a $48,000 basis in her partnership interest. On September 10, 2004, the partnership distributes to her cash of $12,000, cash basis receivables with an inside basis of $0 and a fair market value of $10,000, and a parcel of land with a basis to the partnership of $60,000 and a fair market value of $100,000. Sally has a realized gain on the distribution of $74,000 ($12,000 + $10,000 + $100,000 – $48,000). None of that gain is recognized, however, since the $12,000 cash distribution does not exceed her $48,000 adjusted basis for her partnership interest. In determining the basis effects of the distribution, the cash is treated as being distributed first, reducing Sally's adjusted basis to $36,000 ($48,000 – $12,000). The receivables are distributed next, taking a $0 carryover basis to Sally. Her adjusted basis remains at $36,000. The land is distributed last, taking a substituted basis of $36,000 and reducing her adjusted basis for her partnership interest to $0. ■

[13] § 732.

When more than one asset in a particular class is distributed, special rules apply. For most proportionate nonliquidating distributions, if the partner's remaining adjusted basis for the partnership interest is less than the partnership's adjusted basis for the distributed assets in the particular class, the partner's adjusted basis for each distributed asset is computed by following three steps.

Step 1 Each distributed asset within the class initially takes a carryover basis.

Step 2 Then, this carryover basis for each of these assets is reduced in proportion to their respective amounts of unrealized depreciation (amount that carryover basis is greater than fair market value). Under no circumstances, however, can the basis of any asset be reduced below its fair market value in step 2.

Step 3 Any remaining decrease in basis is allocated among all the distributed assets in the class in proportion to their respective adjusted bases (as determined in step 2).

EXAMPLE 11

Assume the same facts as in Example 10, except that Sally receives two parcels of land, rather than a single parcel. The partnership's basis for the parcels is $15,000 for Parcel 1 and $45,000 for Parcel 2. Each parcel has a fair market value of $30,000. Sally has a realized gain on the distribution of $34,000 ($12,000 + $10,000 + $60,000 – $48,000). None of that gain is recognized, however, because the $12,000 cash distribution does not exceed her $48,000 adjusted basis.

As in Example 10, Sally takes a $12,000 basis for the cash and a $0 carryover basis for the receivables and has a $36,000 adjusted basis for her partnership interest after these two items are distributed. Because two parcels of land are distributed, and because Sally's remaining $36,000 adjusted basis for her partnership interest is less than the partnership's $60,000 total basis for the two parcels of land, Sally's adjusted basis for each parcel of land is computed by following these steps.

Step 1 She initially takes a carryover basis of $15,000 for Parcel 1 and $45,000 for Parcel 2.

Step 2 She reduces the basis of Parcel 2 to its lower fair market value of $30,000. The basis for Parcel 1 is not adjusted in this step because Parcel 1 has a fair market value greater than its basis.

Step 3 The remaining $9,000 difference between her $36,000 basis for the partnership interest and the $45,000 ($15,000 + $30,000) basis for the land parcels after step 2 is allocated to the two parcels in proportion to their respective bases (as computed in step 2). Therefore, the amount of the step 3 basis reduction allocated to Parcel 1 is:

$$\$9,000 \times \frac{\$15,000}{\$45,000} = \$3,000$$

Sally's basis for Parcel 1 is $12,000 ($15,000 – $3,000). The amount of the step 3 basis reduction allocated to Parcel 2 is:

$$\$9,000 \times \frac{\$30,000}{\$45,000} = \$6,000$$

Sally's basis for Parcel 2 is $24,000 ($30,000 – $6,000). ■

EXAMPLE 12

Assume the same facts as in Example 11, and that Sally sells both parcels of land early in 2005 for their fair market values, receiving proceeds of $60,000 ($30,000 + $30,000). She also collects $10,000 from the cash basis receivables. Now she recognizes all of the $34,000 gain that she deferred upon receiving the property from the partnership [$60,000 amount realized – $36,000 basis for the two parcels ($12,000 + $24,000) + $10,000 collected – $0 basis for the receivables]. ■

Concept Summary 6–1

Proportionate Nonliquidating Distributions (General Rules)

1. Neither the distributee partner nor the partnership recognizes any gain or loss on a proportionate nonliquidating distribution. However, if cash distributed exceeds the distributee partner's outside basis, gain is recognized. Property distributions generally do not result in gain recognition.
2. The distributee partner usually takes the same basis in the distributed property that the property had to the partnership (carryover basis). However, where the inside basis of distributed property exceeds the partner's outside basis, the basis assigned to the distributed property cannot exceed that outside basis (substituted basis).
3. Gain recognized by the distributee partner on a proportionate nonliquidating distribution is capital in nature.
4. Loss is never recognized on a proportionate nonliquidating distribution.

Calculations

1.	Partner's outside basis.	________
2.	Less: Cash distributed to partner.	________
3.	Gain recognized by partner (excess of Line 2 over Line 1).	________
4.	Partner's remaining outside basis (Line 1 – Line 2). If less than $0, enter $0.	________
5.	Partner's basis in unrealized receivables and inventory distributed (enter lesser of Line 4 or the partnership's inside basis in the unrealized receivables and inventory).	________
6.	Basis available to allocate to other property distributed (Line 4 – Line 5).	________
7.	Partnership's inside basis of other property distributed.	________
8.	Basis to partner of other property distributed (enter lesser of Line 6 or Line 7).	________
9.	Partner's remaining outside basis (Line 6 – Line 8).	________

Review the tax results of Examples 10 and 11. Although Sally does not recognize any of the gain she realizes from the distribution, she has a zero outside basis for her partnership interest. If Sally expects the partnership to generate net losses in the near future, she will *not* find this zero basis attractive. She may be unable to deduct her share of these future losses when they flow through to her on the last day of the partnership's subsequent tax year.

The low basis that Sally has assigned to the parcels of land is of no significant detriment to her if she does not intend to sell the land in the near future. Since land does not generate cost recovery deductions, the substituted basis is used only to determine Sally's gain or loss upon her disposition of the land in a taxable sale or exchange.

LO.2

Determine the tax treatment of proportionate distributions that liquidate a partnership.

PROPORTIONATE LIQUIDATING DISTRIBUTIONS

Proportionate liquidating distributions consist of a single distribution or a series of distributions that result in the termination of the partner's entire interest in the partnership. If the partnership continues in existence after the partner's interest is liquidated, the rules of § 736 govern the classification of the liquidating payments. These rules are discussed later in the chapter. Other rules apply, however, if the partner's interest is liquidated because the partnership is also liquidating. This section examines the latter type of liquidating distribution.

The partnership itself does not recognize either gain or loss on a proportionate liquidating distribution. The following discussion outlines rules for allocation of basis and possible gain/loss recognition by partners.

Gain Recognition and Ordering Rules. When a partnership liquidates, the liquidating distributions to a partner usually consist of an interest in several or all of the partnership assets. The gain recognition and ordering rules parallel those for nonliquidating distributions, except that the partner's *entire* basis in the partnership interest is allocated to the assets received in the liquidating distribution, unless the partner is required to recognize a loss. A loss may be recognized when *only* cash, unrealized receivables, or inventory is received in the distribution. As a result of the ordering rules, the basis of some assets may be adjusted upward or downward to absorb the partner's remaining outside basis. Unrealized receivables or inventory are never "stepped up," although they may be "stepped down."

The general ordering and gain recognition rules for a proportionate liquidating distribution are summarized as follows.

- Cash is distributed first and results in a capital gain if the amount distributed exceeds the partner's basis in the partnership interest. The cash distributed reduces the liquidated partner's outside basis dollar for dollar. The partner's basis cannot be reduced below zero.
- The partner's remaining outside basis is then allocated to unrealized receivables and inventory up to an amount equal to the partnership's adjusted bases in those properties. If the partnership's bases in the unrealized receivables and inventory exceed the partner's remaining outside basis, the remaining outside basis is allocated to the unrealized receivables and inventory.
- Finally, if the liquidating partner has any outside basis left, that basis is allocated to the other assets received.[14]

EXAMPLE 13

When Tara's basis in her partnership interest is $70,000, she receives cash of $15,000, a proportionate share of inventory, and a building in a distribution that liquidates both the partnership and her entire partnership interest. The inventory has a basis to the partnership of $20,000 and a fair market value of $30,000. The building's basis is $8,000, and the fair market value is $12,000. The building is not subject to depreciation recapture. Under these circumstances, Tara recognizes no gain or loss. After reducing Tara's $70,000 basis by the $15,000 cash received, the remaining $55,000 is allocated first to the inventory and then to the building. The basis of the inventory in Tara's hands is $20,000, and the basis of the building is $35,000. ■

When more than one asset in a particular class is distributed in a proportionate liquidating distribution, special rules may apply. If the partner's remaining basis for the partnership interest is less than the partnership's basis for the distributed assets in the particular class, the partner's basis for each distributed asset is computed as illustrated previously in Example 11. If, however, the partner's remaining basis for the partnership interest is greater than the partnership's basis for the distributed assets in the "other assets" class, the partner's basis for each remaining distributed asset is computed by following three steps.

Step 1 Each distributed asset within the "other assets" class initially takes a carryover basis.

Step 2 Then, this carryover basis for each of these assets is increased in proportion to their respective amounts of unrealized appreciation (amount that fair market value is greater than carryover basis). Under no circumstances, however, can the basis of any asset be increased above its fair market value in step 2.

[14] §§ 731 and 732.

Step 3 Any remaining increase in basis is allocated among all the distributed assets in the "other assets" class in proportion to their respective fair market values.

EXAMPLE 14

Assume the same facts as in Example 13, except that Tara receives two parcels of land, rather than a building. The partnership's basis for the parcels is $2,000 for Parcel 1 and $6,000 for Parcel 2. Each parcel has a fair market value of $6,000.

Tara takes a $15,000 basis for the cash and a $20,000 carryover basis for the inventory. She has a $35,000 basis for her partnership interest after these two items are distributed. Because two parcels of land are distributed, and because Tara's remaining $35,000 basis for her partnership interest exceeds the partnership's $8,000 basis for the two parcels of land, Tara's basis for each parcel of land is computed by following these steps.

Step 1 She initially takes a carryover basis of $2,000 for Parcel 1 and $6,000 for Parcel 2.

Step 2 She increases the basis of Parcel 1 by $4,000 to its fair market value of $6,000. The basis for Parcel 2 is not affected in this step because Parcel 2 has a fair market value equal to its basis.

Step 3 Tara's $23,000 ($35,000 – $6,000 – $6,000) remaining basis for her partnership interest is allocated to each land parcel in proportion to each parcel's respective $6,000 fair market value. Therefore, $11,500 [($6,000/$12,000) × $23,000] is allocated to each parcel. Tara's basis in Parcel 1 is $17,500 ($2,000 + $4,000 + $11,500). Her basis in Parcel 2 is $17,500 ($6,000 + $11,500). ■

Loss Recognition. The distributee partner may also recognize a *loss* on a liquidating distribution. The partner recognizes a loss if both of the following are true.

1. The partner receives *only* cash, unrealized receivables, or inventory.
2. The partner's outside basis in the partnership interest exceeds the partnership's inside basis for the assets distributed. This excess amount is the loss recognized by the distributee partner.[15]

The word "only" is important. A distribution of any other property precludes recognition of the loss.

EXAMPLE 15

When Ramon's outside basis is $40,000, he receives a liquidating distribution of $7,000 cash and a proportionate share of inventory having a partnership basis of $3,000 and a fair market value of $10,000. Ramon is not allowed to "step up" the basis in the inventory, so it is allocated a $3,000 carryover basis. Ramon's unutilized outside basis is $30,000 ($40,000 – $7,000 – $3,000). Since he received a liquidating distribution of *only* cash and inventory, he recognizes a capital loss of $30,000 on the liquidation.

Now assume that, in addition to the cash and inventory, Ramon receives the desk he used in the partnership. The desk has an adjusted basis of $100 to the partnership. Applying the rules outlined above to this revised fact situation produces the following results.

Step 1 Cash of $7,000 is distributed to Ramon and reduces his outside basis to $33,000.

Step 2 Inventory is distributed to Ramon. He takes a $3,000 carryover basis in the inventory and reduces his outside basis in the partnership to $30,000.

Step 3 The desk is distributed to Ramon. Since the desk is a § 1231 asset and not cash, an unrealized receivable, or inventory, he cannot recognize a loss. Therefore, Ramon's remaining basis in his partnership interest is allocated to the desk. He takes a $30,000 basis for the desk. ■

[15] § 731(a)(2).

TAX FACT

The Partnership Economy, Tax Year 2001

Partnerships and LLCs make up a significant portion of the U.S. economy. The income figures are net of deductible losses, but they do not account for suspended passive losses.

	Number of Partnerships	Number of Partners	Total Net Income
Domestic general partnerships	815,525	3,263,549	$ 83,647,778,000
Domestic limited partnerships	369,150	7,023,431	100,696,007,000
Domestic LLCs	808,692	3,231,921	47,055,843,000

Source: IRS, *Statistics of Income Bulletin*, Fall 2003, Publication 1136 (rev. 12–2003).

What can Ramon do with a $30,000 desk? If he continues to use it in a trade or business, he can depreciate it. Once he has established his business use of the desk, he could sell it and recognize a large § 1231 loss. If the loss is isolated in the year of the sale, it is an ordinary loss. Thus, with proper planning, no liquidated partner should be forced to recognize a capital loss instead of an ordinary loss.

Gain recognized by the withdrawing partner on the subsequent disposition of inventory is always ordinary income, unless the disposition occurs more than five years after the distribution.[16] The withdrawing partner's holding period for all other property received in a liquidating distribution includes the partnership's related holding period.

PLANNING STRATEGIES

Losses on Liquidating Distributions

FRAMEWORK FOCUS: DEDUCTIONS

STRATEGY ➤ MAXIMIZE DEDUCTIBLE AMOUNTS.

When a partner is to receive a liquidating distribution and the full basis of the interest will not be recovered, the partner's capital loss can be ensured by providing that the only assets received by the partner are cash, unrealized receivables and inventory. If a capital loss is undesirable, however, the partnership should also distribute a capital or §1231 asset that will take the partner's remaining basis in the interest. This may result in a more desirable ordinary deduction or loss in the future. Careful attention must be paid to what the partner does with the asset after receipt. If the partner converts the asset to personal use, a loss on its disposition is disallowed.

[16] § 735(a)(2).

Concept Summary 6–2

Proportionate Liquidating Distributions When the Partnership Also Liquidates (General Rules)

1. Generally, neither the distributee partner nor the partnership recognizes gain or loss when a partnership liquidates. However, a partner recognizes gain if the cash received exceeds the partner's outside basis. A partner recognizes loss when (a) the partner receives only cash, unrealized receivables, or inventory and (b) the partner's outside basis is greater than the partnership's inside basis of the assets distributed.
2. A partner's basis in distributed assets must be determined in a certain order. Cash is distributed first, inventory and unrealized receivables second, and all other assets last. Assets in the last category take a substituted basis equal to the distributee partner's remaining outside basis.
3. Gain or loss recognized by a distributee partner in a distribution that liquidates a partnership is usually capital in nature.

Calculations

1. Partner's outside basis.	________
2. Less: Cash distributed to partner.	________
3. Gain recognized by partner (excess of Line 2 over Line 1).	________
4. Partner's remaining outside basis (Line 1 – Line 2). If less than \$0, enter \$0.	________
5. Partner's basis in unrealized receivables and inventory distributed (enter lesser of Line 4 or the inside basis in the unrealized receivables and inventory).	________
6. Basis to partner of other property distributed (Line 4 – Line 5).	________
7. Loss recognized by partner (if no other property was distributed, enter amount from Line 6).	________
8. Partner's remaining outside basis.	$0

LO.3

Describe the tax treatment that applies to distributions treated as disguised sales and distributions of marketable securities and precontribution gain property.

PROPERTY DISTRIBUTIONS WITH SPECIAL TAX TREATMENT

Recall that a distribution from a partnership to a partner usually does not result in taxable gain. This section discusses three exceptions in which a proportionate distribution, either liquidating or nonliquidating, may result in gain to the partner.

Disguised Sales. A disguised sale is a transaction in which a partner contributes appreciated property to a partnership and soon thereafter receives a distribution of cash or property from the partnership. If the IRS determines the payment is part of a "purchase" of the property, rather than a distribution from the partnership, the usual sale or exchange rules apply. The partner is treated as having sold the property and must report a gain on the sale. The partnership takes a cost basis in the property purchased.

DIGGING DEEPER 1

Find more information on this topic at our Web site: ***http://wft-advanced.swlearning.com.***

Marketable Securities. The fair market value of a marketable security distributed to a partner is generally treated as a cash distribution.[17] Some or all of the value of the security over the partner's outside basis prior to the distribution is a taxable gain. The partner must assign a basis to the security received in the distribution, so the distribution ordering rules must be taken into account.

The primary purpose of this rule is to stop the tax avoidance that otherwise would occur if a partnership purchased marketable securities with the intent of immediately distributing them to the partner. A partnership can purchase property

[17] § 731(c).

TAX FACT

Number of Partnership and S Corporation Tax Returns Filed

Over 5 million businesses operate in the United States using the partnership or S corporation tax form. The IRS projects continued growth in the number of these entities through the end of the decade.

Calendar Year	Number of Partnerships	Growth Rate	Number of S Corporations	Growth Rate
1999	1,974,700		2,767,000	
2000	2,066,800	4.66%	2,887,100	4.34%
2001	2,165,000	4.75%	3,022,600	4.69%
2002	2,271,800	4.93%	3,191,100	5.57%

"Number of Partnerships" consists of entities filing Form 1065 and includes domestic general partnerships, limited partnerships, limited liability partnerships, limited liability companies, and other domestic entities.

Source: IRS, *Statistics of Income Bulletin,* Summer 2003, Publication 1136 (rev. 09–2003).

desired by a partner, distribute that property to the partner, and allow the partner to defer tax on any appreciation inherent in the partnership interest. Section 731(c) was enacted to prevent a partnership from arranging such a transaction with marketable securities. Unless otherwise indicated, the remaining examples in this chapter assume the partnership is not distributing marketable securities.

DIGGING DEEPER 2 *Find more information on this topic at our Web site:* ***http://wft-advanced.swlearning.com.***

DISTRIBUTIONS INVOLVING PRECONTRIBUTION GAIN OR LOSS PROPERTY

Generally, the distribution of property to a partner does not result in the recognition of gains or losses. However, in the presence of precontribution gain or loss property, the contributing partner may be required to recognize the precontribution gain or loss under two circumstances.

1. When the contributed appreciated (depreciated) property is distributed to another partner within seven years of the contribution date, the contributing partner recognizes the remaining precontribution gain (loss).[18]

DIGGING DEEPER 3 *Find more information on this topic at our Web site:* ***http://wft-advanced.swlearning.com.***

2. When the partnership distributes any property other than cash to a partner within seven years after that partner contributes appreciated property to the partnership, the contributing partner recognizes the lesser of (a) the remaining net precontribution gain, or (b) the excess of the fair market value of the property distributed over the partner's outside basis before the distribution.[19]

DIGGING DEEPER 4 *Find more information on this topic at our Web site:* ***http://wft-advanced.swlearning.com.***

[18] § 704(c)(1)(B).

[19] § 737.

TAX IN THE NEWS

Simplifying Partnership Taxation—A Losing Battle?

Partnership taxation has become increasingly complex over the past decade. The tax treatment of a distribution differs depending on the type of property being distributed, the appreciation inherent in the property, who the property is distributed to, and how the partnership originally acquired the property. And the "substantial economic effect" rules include numerous pages of guidelines on when and how to allocate income and loss among the partners.

Various parties, including the Joint Committee on Taxation, several members of Congress, and the American Bar Association, have called for simplification of the rules. Yet none of the tax legislation enacted recently has simplified partnership taxation. Also, the IRS is currently considering additional changes in the Regulations that will add considerable complexity to this already difficult area. Pundits speculate that simplification in the partnership area will be slow in coming because most necessary changes would result in a net revenue loss to the government.

DISPROPORTIONATE DISTRIBUTIONS

The general nonrecognition of gain or loss rule does not apply to a distribution of cash or property that results in a change in a partner's share of partnership unrealized receivables or substantially appreciated inventory, called "hot assets." This type of distribution is commonly referred to as a "disproportionate distribution" and results in the transaction being characterized as part distribution and part sale.[20] The partner and partnership both recognize gain or loss as a result of this type of distribution. The rules were drafted to prevent the shifting of ordinary income (or loss) to capital gain (or loss).

DIGGING DEEPER 5

Find more information on this topic at our Web site: ***http://wft-advanced.swlearning.com.***

PLANNING STRATEGIES

Preparing for Distributions

FRAMEWORK FOCUS: INCOME AND EXCLUSIONS

STRATEGY ➤ AVOID INCOME RECOGNITION.

When the partnership agreement is drafted, consider including provisions that govern liquidating distributions of partnership income and property. The specifics of the agreement generally will be followed by the IRS if these and other relevant points are addressed early in the life of the entity.

Both the IRS and the courts usually consider the value of a partner's interest or any partnership assets agreed upon by all partners to be correct. Thus, when planning the sale or liquidation of a partnership interest, the results of the bargaining process should be documented. To avoid valuation problems on liquidation, include a formula or agreed-upon valuation procedure in the partnership agreement or in a related buy-sell agreement.

[20] § 751(b).

BRIDGE DISCIPLINE

Bridge to Financial Accounting

A partnership is a contract that delineates how income, gains, expenses, and losses shall be allocated among the partners. This agreement must take into account that each partner essentially owns an undivided interest in partnership assets (the aggregate theory of partnership taxation), and that there may be a book-tax difference in an asset's basis caused by the difference between fair market value and tax basis at the time of the partnership's formation (precontribution gain or loss). When a partnership is formed, two sets of books are established.

- One set is maintained under the Regulations that is used to make economic allocations and resembles "book" generally accepted accounting principles (GAAP).
- A second set is based on the tax basis of the partnership's assets.

EXAMPLE 16

The JK Partnership is formed with two equal partners. Jack contributes land with a $50,000 fair market value and a $25,000 tax basis. Kathy contributes $50,000 cash. The initial balance sheet includes:

	Book	Tax	
Cash	$ 50,000	$50,000	
Land	50,000	25,000	precontribution gain $25,000
	$100,000	$75,000	
Capital, Jack	$ 50,000	$25,000	
Capital, Kathy	50,000	50,000	
	$100,000	$75,000	

(*continued on next page*)

LO.4

Determine the tax treatment of payments from a partnership to a retiring or deceased partner.

Liquidating Distributions to Retiring or Deceased Partners

Payments made by an ongoing partnership in complete liquidation of a retiring partner's interest are classified as either *income* or *property* payments by § 736. Payments made to a successor to the interest of a deceased partner are similarly classified by § 736.[21] It is critical to observe that § 736 only classifies the payments. Other Code sections provide the rules for computing the tax effects of these payments. Although these payments can be made in cash, property, or both cash and property, this discussion assumes that all payments are made in cash.

From a practical standpoint, the partnership and the retiring partner negotiate a total buyout package. The retiring partner expects compensation for the partner's proportionate share of the fair market value of each partnership asset. The partner also expects to be compensated for a share of the partnership's going-concern value.

[21]A successor is typically the estate of the deceased or the party who inherits the decedent's interest.

(*Bridge Discipline concluded*)

Jack's capital account reflects the economic fact that he contributed an asset with a precontribution gain of $25,000 to the partnership. Under the aggregate theory of partnership taxation, if JK disposes of this property, the first $25,000 of tax gain is allocated to Jack [§ 704(c)]. If the property increases in value while held by the partnership, both partners share in this increase.

	Jack		Kathy	
	Book	**Tax**	**Book**	**Tax**
Beginning capital	$50,000	$25,000	$50,000	$50,000

After the property has increased in value to $60,000, the partnership distributes the land to Kathy. Now an adjustment is required for the economic gain of $10,000. This book gain is equally divided between Jack and Kathy, since it happened while the property was jointly owned by the partnership and is reflected in the book capital. This is not a taxable gain, but an economic accounting gain.

	Jack		Kathy	
	Book	**Tax**	**Book**	**Tax**
Beginning capital	$50,000	$25,000	$ 50,000	$ 50,000
Book-up gain	5,000		5,000	–0–
Tax gain § 704(c)(1)(B)		25,000		–0–
Distribution			(60,000)	(50,000)
Ending capital	$55,000	$50,000	$ (5,000)	$ –0–

Since the property was disposed of within seven years, Jack is required to recognize the $25,000 precontribution gain. ■

Property payments [called § 736(b) payments] represent the former type of buyout provision, and *income* payments [§ 736(a) payments] typically represent the latter. Once the total buyout price is determined, § 736 provides rules for determining the allocation between income and property payments, but leaves some room for negotiation between the partner and the partnership over which component of the buyout represents each type of payment.

PLANNING STRATEGIES Hot Assets Can Burn

FRAMEWORK FOCUS: INCOME AND EXCLUSIONS

STRATEGY ➤ **AVOID INCOME RECOGNITION.**

Current and liquidating distributions may result in ordinary income recognition for either the receiving partner or the partnership if hot assets are present. When such income is undesirable, consider making a distribution of hot assets pro rata to the receiving partner.

These paragraphs and Example 17 describe only the general effects of § 736 and do not cover all the nuances of the provision. In general, property payments [§ 736(b) payments] are cash distributions paid by the partnership to the partner in exchange for the partner's interest in partnership assets. The partnership may not deduct these amounts. If the partnership owns no hot assets, the property payment is treated under the normal proportionate distribution rules. If the partnership owns certain hot assets (e.g., depreciation recapture or substantially appreciated inventory), and the retiring partner receives only cash, the distribution is not proportionate. In this case, the property payments to the partner are allocated between cash payments for the partner's share of (1) hot assets and (2) other assets. The hot asset portion is treated as if it were a proportionate distribution of the partner's share of all hot assets and then a sale of these back to the partnership. The income recognized in the hot asset sale is ordinary income, and the gain or loss recognized on the rest of the property payments is capital gain or loss.

Income payments [§ 736(a) payments] are treated as a partner's distributive share of partnership income or, alternatively, as a guaranteed payment to the retiring partner and treated as ordinary income. Depending on whether the amount is a distributive share or a guaranteed payment, either (1) the remaining partners report a lesser share of partnership income (distributive share), or (2) the partnership deducts the guaranteed payment.

EXAMPLE 17

Pamela receives cash of $15,000 in liquidation of her partnership interest, in which she has a basis of $10,000. The partnership owns no hot assets. After following all the classification requirements of § 736, $12,000 of this amount is classified as a property payment, and $3,000 is classified as a guaranteed payment. The $12,000 property payment is treated as a distribution from the partnership in exchange for her partnership interest, so Pamela recognizes a $2,000 capital gain on this part of her liquidation proceeds ($12,000 property payment – $10,000 basis in interest). She recognizes $3,000 ordinary income for the guaranteed payment, and the partnership deducts the same amount. ■

PROPERTY PAYMENTS

Cash payments made for the partner's pro rata share of the fair market value of each partnership asset are classified as § 736(b) payments. The following items are not treated as § 736(b) payments, however, if (1) the partnership is primarily a service provider (i.e., "capital is not a material income-producing factor for the partnership") and (2) the retiring or deceased partner was a general partner in the partnership.

- Payments made for the partner's pro rata share of unrealized receivables. For purposes of this rule, unrealized receivables do not include potential depreciation recapture.
- Payments made for the partner's pro rata share of the partnership goodwill, unless the partnership agreement states that the payments are for goodwill. This exception applies only to payments for goodwill that exceed the partner's pro rata share of the partnership's inside basis for goodwill.
- Certain annuities and lump-sum payments made to retiring partners or deceased partner's successors.

If such payments are made by a service-oriented partnership to a general partner, they are classified as § 736(a) payments.

Section 736(b) payments for "nonhot" assets are treated first as a return of the partner's outside basis in the partnership.[22] Once the entire basis is returned, any additional amounts are taxed to the partner as capital gain. If the cash distributions are not sufficient to return the partner's entire outside basis, the shortfall is taxed to the partner as a capital loss.[23]

[22] §§ 736(b) and 731(a)(1).

[23] § 731(a)(2).

EXAMPLE 18

The ABC Partnership has the following balance sheet at the end of the current tax year.

	Basis	FMV		Basis	FMV
Cash	$36,000	$36,000	Anne, capital	$15,000	$27,000
Unrealized receivables	–0–	18,000	Bonnie, capital	15,000	27,000
Land	9,000	27,000	Cindy, capital	15,000	27,000
Total	$45,000	$81,000	Total	$45,000	$81,000

Partner Anne is a general partner retiring from the service-oriented partnership. She receives $36,000 cash, none of which is stated to be for goodwill. Since the fair market value of Anne's share of the three recorded assets is only $27,000 (⅓ × $81,000), the $9,000 excess payment is for unstated goodwill.

The payment Anne receives for her interest in the cash and land is a § 736(b) property payment. This payment is $21,000, consisting of $12,000 paid for the cash (⅓ × $36,000) and $9,000 paid for Anne's share of the fair market value of the land (⅓ × $27,000). The remaining cash of $15,000 is for her $6,000 interest in the unrealized receivables and for $9,000 unstated goodwill and is a § 736(a) payment.

The property payment of $21,000 cash includes amounts for Anne's share of land and cash only, neither of which is a hot asset. If Anne's outside basis is $15,000, she recognizes capital gain of $6,000 [($12,000 + $9,000) – $15,000] on the distribution. However, if Anne's outside basis is $25,000, she recognizes a $4,000 capital loss on the distribution [($12,000 + $9,000) – $25,000]. The partnership cannot deduct any part of the $21,000 property payment. ■

DIGGING DEEPER 6

Find more information on this topic at our Web site: ***http://wft-advanced.swlearning.com.***

INCOME PAYMENTS

All payments that are not classified as § 736(b) property payments are categorized as § 736(a) income payments. These income payments are further classified into two categories. Payments that are *not* determined by reference to partnership income are treated as guaranteed payments. They are fully taxable as ordinary income to the distributee partner and are fully deductible by the continuing partnership.

Section 736(a) income payments that are determined by reference to partnership income are treated as distributive shares of that income (i.e., an allocation of partnership income for the year). They are taxed to the distributee partner according to their character to the partnership. Thus, for example, they may be taxed as capital gain as well as ordinary income.[24] Since this capital gain and ordinary income are allocated to the liquidated partner, the payments reduce the amount of partnership capital gain and ordinary income allocated to the remaining partners.[25]

EXAMPLE 19

Continue with the same facts as in Example 18 where the partnership is service oriented. The $6,000 cash payment ($18,000 × ⅓) for Anne's pro rata share of the unrealized receivables is classified as a § 736(a) income payment, as is the $9,000 payment for unstated goodwill.

Because the $15,000 § 736(a) income payment ($6,000 + $9,000) is not determined by reference to partnership income, the payment is classified as a guaranteed payment. It is included as ordinary income on Anne's tax return and is deductible by the partnership. ■

[24] § 702(b).

[25] Reg. § 1.736–1(a)(4).

CONCEPT SUMMARY 6–3

Liquidating Distributions of Cash When the Partnership Continues

1. Payments made by an ongoing partnership to a liquidating partner are classified as § 736(a) income payments or as § 736(b) property payments.
2. Section 736(b) property payments are payments made for the liquidated partner's share of partnership assets.
3. If the partnership is a service provider and the partner is a general partner, payments made for the liquidated partner's share of certain unrealized receivables, certain goodwill that is not provided for in the partnership agreement, and certain annuity payments are classified as § 736(a) income payments.
4. Section 736(a) income payments are the payments mentioned in Item 3 above and any other payments that are not classified as § 736(b) property payments.
5. To the extent the § 736(b) property payment is for the partner's share of partnership hot assets, the partner is deemed to have received and sold his or her share of such assets to the partnership. The partner reports ordinary income on this transaction, and the partnership will have a cost basis in the hot asset. (See Digging Deeper 6.)
6. To the extent the § 736(b) property payments are classified as a payment for the partner's share of the partnership's "nonhot" assets, the payment is taxed as a return of the partner's outside basis. Any excess cash received over the partner's outside basis is taxed as capital gain.
7. Section 736(a) income payments are further classified as either guaranteed payments or distributive shares. Guaranteed payments are taxable as ordinary income to the partner and are deductible by the partnership. Distributive shares retain the same tax character to the partner as they had to the partnership. Distributive shares paid to the liquidated partner are excludible from the continuing partners' tax returns.

The following table summarizes the results of Examples 18 and 19. In both cases, Anne's basis in her partnership interest was $15,000 before the distribution.

	Tax Character to Anne		Deduction to ABC
Service-oriented partnership:			
§ 736(b) (Example 18)	$ 6,000	capital gain	None
§ 736(a) (Example 19)	15,000	ordinary income	$15,000
Total gain	$21,000		

DIGGING DEEPER 7 *Find more information on this topic at our Web site:* ***http://wft-advanced.swlearning.com.***

LO.5

Calculate the selling partner's amount and character of gain or loss on the sale or exchange of a partnership interest.

Sale of a Partnership Interest

A partner can sell or exchange a partnership interest, in whole or in part. The transaction can be between the partner and a third party; in this case, it is similar in concept to a sale of corporate stock. Or, as described in the last section, the transaction can be between the partner and the partnership, in which case it is similar in concept to a redemption of corporate stock by the entity. The transfer of a partnership interest produces different results from the transfer of corporate stock because both the entity and aggregate concepts apply to the partnership situation, whereas only the entity concept applies to a sale of stock. The effect of the different rules is that gain or loss resulting from a sale of a partnership interest may be divided into capital gain or loss and ordinary income or loss.

GENERAL RULES

Generally, the sale or exchange of a partnership interest results in gain or loss, measured by the difference between the amount realized and the selling partner's adjusted basis in the partnership interest.[26]

Liabilities. In computing the amount realized and the adjusted basis of the interest sold, the selling partner's share of partnership liabilities must be determined. The purchasing partner includes any assumed indebtedness as a part of the consideration paid for the partnership interest.[27]

EXAMPLE 20

Cole originally contributed $50,000 in cash for a one-third interest in the CDE Partnership. During the time Cole was a partner, his share of partnership income was $90,000, and he withdrew $60,000 cash. Cole's capital account balance is now $80,000, and partnership liabilities are $45,000, of which Cole's share is $15,000. Cole's outside basis is $95,000 ($50,000 contribution + $90,000 allocated income – $60,000 distribution + $15,000 share of partnership debts).

Cole sells his partnership interest to Stephanie for $110,000 cash, with Stephanie assuming Cole's share of partnership liabilities. The total amount realized by Cole is $125,000 ($110,000 cash received + $15,000 of partnership debts transferred to Stephanie). Cole's gain on the sale is $30,000 ($125,000 realized – adjusted basis of $95,000).

Stephanie's adjusted basis for her partnership interest is the purchase price of $125,000 ($110,000 cash paid + $15,000 assumed partnership debt). ■

Income Allocation. When a partner sells an entire interest in the partnership:

- income for the partnership interest for the tax year is allocated between the buying partner and the selling partner, and
- the partnership's tax year "closes" with respect to the selling partner.

The closing of the tax year causes the selling partner to report the share of income on the sale date rather than at the end of the partnership's tax year.

The selling partner's basis is adjusted for the allocated income or loss before the partner calculates the gain or loss on the sale of the interest.

EXAMPLE 21

On September 30, 2004, Erica sells her 20% interest in the Evergreen Partnership to Jason for $25,000. Erica is a calendar year taxpayer. Evergreen owns no hot assets, and its tax year ends on June 30.

Before the sale, Erica's basis in the partnership interest is $8,000. Her share of partnership income is $10,000 for the period she owned the partnership interest. Since the partnership's tax year closes with respect to Erica, she must report $10,000 of income on her 2004 tax return. Her basis in the partnership interest is increased to $18,000, and she recognizes a $7,000 capital gain on the sale.

Note that Erica will also report income from Evergreen's tax year ending on June 30, 2004, on her 2004 tax return. ■

DIGGING DEEPER 8

Find more information on this topic at our Web site: ***http://wft-advanced.swlearning.com.***

[26] § 741.

[27] § 742.

If the partnership uses the cash method for certain items such as interest, taxes, rent, or other amounts that accrue over time, it must allocate these items to each day in the tax year over which they economically accrue and use the interim closing method for these items in determining the amount allocated to a selling partner.[28]

The partnership is not required to issue a Schedule K–1 to the selling partner until the normal filing of its tax return. The partner, though, is required to include the share of partnership income as of the sale date. Consequently, the partner may have to obtain an extension for filing his or her personal return until the partnership provides a Schedule K–1. If the partnership uses an IRS-approved fiscal year and the partner uses a calendar year, income bunching may occur, as described in Example 21.

Tax Reporting. Partners who sell or exchange a partnership interest must promptly notify the partnership of the transfers. After notification is received, the partnership may be required to file an information statement with the IRS for the calendar year in which the transfers took place. The statement lists the names and addresses of the transferors and transferees. The partnership provides all parties with a copy of the statement.

§ 751—"HOT ASSETS"

A major exception to capital gain or loss treatment on the sale or exchange of a partnership interest arises when a partnership has § 751 assets, or, as they are more commonly called, "hot assets." **Hot assets** comprise *unrealized receivables* and *inventory items*, assets that, when collected or disposed of by the partnership, would cause it to recognize ordinary income. When a partner sells the interest in a partnership, it is as if the partnership had sold its hot assets and allocated to the selling partner the partner's proportionate share of the ordinary income or loss created by the sale. The primary purpose of this rule is to prevent a partner from converting ordinary income into capital gain through the sale of a partnership interest.

Unrealized Receivables. Unrealized receivables include the accounts receivable of a cash basis partnership and, for sale or exchange purposes, depreciation recapture potential.[29]

EXAMPLE 22

The cash basis Thrush Partnership owns only a $10,000 receivable for rendering health care advice. Its basis in the receivable is zero because no income has been recognized. This item is a hot asset because ordinary income is not generated until Thrush collects on the account.

Jacob, a 50% partner, sells his interest to Mark for $5,000. If Jacob's basis in his partnership interest is $0, his total gain is $5,000. The entire gain is attributable to Jacob's share of the unrealized receivable, so his gain is taxed as ordinary income. ■

Depreciation recapture represents ordinary income the partnership would recognize if it sold depreciable property. Under the aggregate theory, the selling partner's share of depreciation recapture potential is treated as an unrealized receivable and is taxed to the selling partner as ordinary income, rather than capital gain. (Recall that depreciation recapture is *not* treated as an unrealized receivable for § 736 purposes, discussed previously.)

[28] § 706(d)(2).

[29] § 751(a)(1).

EXAMPLE 23

Andrew sells his 40% interest in the accrual basis Wren Partnership. The partnership has a depreciable business asset that it originally purchased for $25,000. The asset now has an adjusted basis of $15,000 and a market value of $30,000. Depreciation recapture potential is $10,000 ($25,000 – $15,000). In this case, Wren holds a $10,000 unrealized receivable with a zero basis and a $20,000 ($30,000 – $10,000) nonhot asset with an adjusted basis of $15,000. If Wren sold the asset for $30,000, it would recognize $10,000 of ordinary income and $5,000 of § 1231 gain. Therefore, Andrew recognizes $4,000 ($10,000 × 40%) of ordinary income when he sells his partnership interest. ■

The effect of the hot asset rule is that a partner selling an interest in a partnership with hot assets must usually recognize both ordinary income (loss) and capital gain (loss).

EXAMPLE 24

Ahmad sells his interest in the equal ABC Partnership to Dave for $17,000 cash. On the sale date, the partnership's cash basis balance sheet reflects the following.

	Basis	FMV		Basis	FMV
Cash	$10,000	$10,000	Liabilities	$ 9,000	$ 9,000
Accounts receivable (for services)	-0-	30,000	Capital accounts		
Nonhot assets	14,000	20,000	Ahmad	5,000	17,000
			Beth	5,000	17,000
			Chris	5,000	17,000
Total	$24,000	$60,000	Total	$24,000	$60,000

The total amount realized by Ahmad is $20,000 ($17,000 cash price + $3,000 of debt assumed by Dave). Since Ahmad's basis for his partnership interest is $8,000 ($5,000 capital account + $3,000 debt share), the total gain recognized on the sale is $12,000 ($20,000 – $8,000).

Because the partnership has an unrealized receivable, the hot asset rule applies. If ABC sold the accounts receivable for $30,000, Ahmad's proportionate share of the ordinary income recognized on this sale would be $10,000 ($30,000 × ⅓). Consequently, $10,000 of the $12,000 recognized gain on the sale relates to Ahmad's interest in the unrealized receivables and is taxed to him as ordinary income. The remaining gain of $2,000 is taxed to him as a capital gain.

Note that under the hot asset rule, Ahmad still reports $12,000 of income or gain; the hot asset rule merely reclassifies part of the gain as ordinary income. The effect of the rule is that the partnership's inherent ordinary income is allocated to the partner who earned it. ■

EXAMPLE 25

Assume the same facts as in Example 24, except that Ahmad's basis in his partnership interest is $10,000. Under these circumstances, Ahmad's capital gain or loss is zero. Ahmad still has $10,000 of ordinary income because of the unrealized receivables.

If Ahmad's basis in the partnership interest is $11,000 (instead of $10,000), an unusual result occurs. Ahmad has a $9,000 overall gain ($20,000 amount realized – $11,000 basis). The receivables generate $10,000 of ordinary income, and Ahmad recognizes a capital *loss* of $1,000 on the rest of the sale. ■

Inventory Items. For a sale or exchange of a partnership interest, the term *inventory items* includes all partnership property except money, capital assets, and § 1231 assets. Receivables of an accrual basis partnership are included in the definition of inventory, since they are neither capital assets nor § 1231 assets.[30] This definition also is broad enough to include all items considered to be unrealized receivables.

[30] § 751(d).

CONCEPT SUMMARY 6–4

Sale of a Partnership Interest

1. A partnership interest is a capital asset and generally results in capital gain or loss on disposal.
2. The outside bases of the selling and buying partners, as well as the pertinent selling price and purchase price, include an appropriate share of partnership debt.
3. Partnership income or loss for the interest is allocated between the selling and buying partners. The selling partner's basis is adjusted before the gain or loss on the sale is calculated.
4. The partnership's tax year closes with respect to the selling partner on the sale date; the seller reports partnership income at that time, and income "bunching" may occur.
5. When hot assets are present, the selling partner's overall gain or loss is reclassified into a capital gain or loss portion and an ordinary income or loss amount related to the partnership's underlying hot assets.
6. Hot assets consist of unrealized receivables and inventory items.
7. Unrealized receivables include amounts earned by a cash basis taxpayer from services rendered. They also include depreciation recapture potential that would result if an asset were sold at a gain.
8. Inventory items include all partnership property except cash, capital assets, and § 1231 assets. Inventory items also include unrealized receivables.

EXAMPLE 26

Jan sells her one-third interest in the JKL Partnership to Matt for $20,000 cash. On the sale date, the partnership balance sheet reflects the following.

	Basis	FMV		Basis	FMV
Cash	$10,000	$10,000	Jan, capital	$15,000	$20,000
Inventory	21,000	30,000	Kelly, capital	15,000	20,000
Nonhot assets	14,000	20,000	Lynn, capital	15,000	20,000
Total	$45,000	$60,000	Total	$45,000	$60,000

The overall gain on the sale is $5,000 ($20,000 – $15,000). Jan's share of the appreciation in the inventory is $3,000 [($30,000 – $21,000) × ⅓]. Therefore, she recognizes $3,000 of ordinary income because of the inventory and $2,000 of capital gain from the rest of the sale. ■

PLANNING STRATEGIES

Payments for Goodwill

FRAMEWORK FOCUS: DEDUCTIONS

STRATEGY ➤ **MAXIMIZE DEDUCTIBLE AMOUNTS.**

The partner who purchases a partnership interest often pays an amount that can be attributed, in part, to partnership goodwill. Purchased goodwill is included in a purchasing partner's outside basis. For the partner to get any deductible benefit, the partnership must make a § 754 election. The partnership then amortizes the goodwill over 15 years as an intangible asset (§ 197).

Payments for goodwill can also materialize when liquidation payments are made under § 736. Amounts paid by a service partnership for a general partner's share of partnership goodwill can be treated as a § 736(a) payment, resulting in either a deductible guaranteed payment for the partnership or an allocation of partnership income. In either case, the § 736(a) payment reduces the allocated income to the other partners.

BRIDGE DISCIPLINE

Bridge to Financial Accounting

The addition of a new partner may be a good time for the partnership to revalue its assets and adjust the existing partners' book capital accounts for any appreciation or depreciation in asset values. This is an elective adjustment[31] and does not create any taxable income or loss. The election makes accounting for precontribution gains and losses easier and more clearly reflects the partners' economic relationship.

EXAMPLE 27

Art and Betty form the AB Partnership in 2001 by each contributing $100,000 cash. The partnership immediately buys 10 acres of land as an investment, paying $200,000 for it. In 2003, when the land is worth $400,000, Chris joins the partnership as an equal partner with the contribution of five acres of land valued at $200,000. Chris purchased the land in 2000 for $75,000. The partnership's balance sheet just prior to Chris's contribution:

	Book & Tax Basis	Fair Market Value
Land	$200,000	$400,000
	$200,000	$400,000
Capital, Art	$100,000	$200,000
Capital, Betty	100,000	200,000
	$200,000	$400,000

Without a revaluation the balance sheet after Chris's contribution does not give an accurate economic picture of the partners' economic relationship as equal one-third owners.

	Book Basis	Fair Market Value	Tax Basis
Land, 10 acres	$200,000	$400,000	$200,000
Land, 5 acres	200,000	200,000	75,000
	$400,000	$600,000	$275,000
Capital, Art	$100,000	$200,000	$100,000
Capital, Betty	100,000	200,000	100,000
Capital, Chris	200,000	200,000	75,000
	$400,000	$600,000	$275,000

The book capital accounts do not indicate an equal partnership. This is because Art's and Betty's capital accounts do not include the appreciation in the 10 acres owned by the partnership prior to Chris's admittance. Art and Betty hold a precontribution gain of $200,000 in the original 10 acres. When that land is sold, Art and Betty are allocated the first $200,000 of gain just as Chris would be allocated the first $125,000 of gain upon the sale of "his" land.

(continued on next page)

[31]Reg. § 1.704–1(b)(2)(iv)(f).

The partners' economic relationship is presented more accurately when the original 10 acres are revalued, resulting in a book gain being allocated to Art and Betty. The book gain represents the appreciation in the property prior to Chris's entry. Now the book capital accounts indicate equal ownership.

Adjusting entry due to tax election	Land, 10 acres	$200,000	
	Capital, Art		$100,000
	Capital, Betty		$100,000

		Book Basis	Fair Market Value	Tax Basis
Balance sheet after tax election	Land, 10 acres	$400,000	$400,000	$200,000
	Land, 5 acres	200,000	200,000	75,000
		$600,000	$600,000	$275,000
	Capital, Art	$200,000	$200,000	$100,000
	Capital, Betty	200,000	200,000	100,000
	Capital, Chris	200,000	200,000	75,000
		$600,000	$600,000	$275,000

LO.6

Describe tax issues related to other dispositions of partnership interests.

Other Dispositions of Partnership Interests

There are a number of ways a partnership interest might be disposed of, some taxable and some nontaxable. The following is a short list of some possible partnership dispositions.

1. The partnership interest, as property, could be transferred to a controlled corporation as part of a § 351 transfer. The transferor would not recognize any gain unless property other than stock was received in the exchange.
2. The partnership itself could roll up into a corporation, transferring all of its assets and liabilities in exchange for corporate stock under § 351. This would then be followed by a liquidation of the partnership, distributing the stock in the new corporation to all of the partners in exchange for the partnership interests.
3. The partnership interest could be exchanged for other property. This would be a taxable exchange, since a partnership interest by definition cannot be like-kind property.
4. The partner could give the partnership interest away. The gift of the interest is nontaxable, but the donor recognizes items of partnership income, loss, deduction, or credit attributable to the period during the year the donor owned the interest.

DIGGING DEEPER 9

Find more information on this topic at our Web site: ***http://wft-advanced.swlearning.com.***

LO.7

Calculate the optional adjustments to basis under § 754.

Optional Adjustments to Property Basis

When a partner purchases a partnership interest, the purchase price reflects what the acquiring partner believes the interest in the partnership is worth. This price reflects, to a large extent, the value the partner placed on the partnership assets. Because the value of the assets probably differs from their inside bases, a discrepancy exists between the purchasing partner's outside basis and that partner's share of the inside basis of partnership assets.

If the partnership makes an **optional adjustment election (§ 754 election),** the inside basis of the partnership property can be adjusted to reflect the purchase price paid by the partner. If the election is not made, the statute produces some inequitable results.

EXAMPLE 28

A partnership owns a building with an adjusted basis of $450,000 and a fair market value of $900,000. George buys a one-third interest in the partnership for $300,000 (an amount equal to one-third of the value of the building). The partnership does not make an election under § 754. Although the price George paid for the interest was based on fair market value, the building's depreciation continues to be determined on the partnership's related adjusted basis of $450,000, of which George's share is only $150,000.

In contrast, assume that the building had an adjusted basis of $600,000 and a fair market value of $300,000. Assume also that George purchased the one-third interest for $100,000 (an amount equal to one-third of the value of the building). Although the purchase price was based on fair market value, George obtains the benefit of *double* depreciation deductions since these deductions are calculated on the adjusted basis of the depreciable property ($600,000), which is twice the property's market value. ■

A result similar to that in Example 28 can take place when a partnership purchases a retiring partner's interest with a cash payment that is greater than that partner's outside basis for the partnership interest. Without a § 754 election, the partnership cannot increase the adjusted basis of its assets for the excess cash paid to the retiring partner.[32]

An optional adjustment-to-basis election can be made for any year in which a transfer or distribution occurs by attaching a statement to a timely filed partnership return (including extensions).[33] An election is binding for the year for which it is made and for all subsequent years, unless the IRS consents to its revocation. Permission to revoke is granted for business reasons, such as a substantial change in the nature of the business or a significant increase in the frequency of interest transfers. Permission is not granted if it appears the primary purpose is to avoid downward adjustments to basis otherwise required under the election.

PLANNING STRATEGIES

Protect Your Cost Recovery

FRAMEWORK FOCUS: DEDUCTIONS

STRATEGY ➤ MAXIMIZE DEDUCTIBLE AMOUNTS.

If a partnership interest is acquired by purchase, the purchaser may want to condition the acquisition on the partnership's promise to make an election to adjust the basis of partnership assets. Making the election under § 754 results in the basis in the partner's ratable share of partnership assets being adjusted to reflect the purchase price. Failure to do so could result in the loss of future depreciation deductions or could convert ordinary losses into capital losses.

[32]§§ 743(a) and 734(a), respectively.

[33]§ 754.

ADJUSTMENT: SALE OR EXCHANGE OF AN INTEREST

If the § 754 optional adjustment-to-basis election is in effect and a partner's interest is sold to or exchanged with a third party, or a partner dies, the partnership adjusts the basis of its assets as illustrated in the following calculation.[34]

Transferee's outside basis in the partnership	$ xxx
Less: Transferee's share of the inside basis of all partnership property	(xxx)
Adjustment	$ xxx

If the amount calculated is positive, the partnership increases the adjusted basis of its assets. If the amount is negative, the basis of the assets is decreased. In either case, the adjustment affects the basis of partnership property with respect to the transferee partner only. When a portion of the optional adjustment results in a step-up of depreciable property, the step-up amount is depreciated as if it were a newly acquired asset. The transferee partner, therefore, shares in the depreciation taken by the partnership on the original asset and, in addition, reports all of the depreciation taken on the basis created by the optional adjustment.

The partner's basis in each property item for which an optional adjustment has been made equals the partner's share of the inside basis for the property item plus or minus the partner's optional basis adjustment that is allocated to that property.

EXAMPLE 29

Keith is a member of the KLM Partnership, and all partners have equal interests in capital and profits. The partnership has made an optional adjustment-to-basis election. Keith's interest is sold to Shawn for $76,000. The balance sheet of the partnership immediately before the sale shows the following.

	Basis	FMV		Basis	FMV
Cash	$ 15,000	$ 15,000	Capital accounts		
Depreciable assets	150,000	213,000	Keith	$ 55,000	$ 76,000
			Leif	55,000	76,000
			Marta	55,000	76,000
Total	$165,000	$228,000	Total	$165,000	$228,000

The adjustment is the difference between the basis of Shawn's interest in the partnership and his share of the adjusted basis of partnership property. The basis of Shawn's interest is his purchase price, or $76,000. His one-third share of the adjusted basis of partnership property is $55,000 ($165,000 × ⅓). The optional adjustment that is added to the basis of partnership property is $21,000.

Transferee's outside basis in partnership	$ 76,000
Less: Transferee's share of inside basis of all partnership property	(55,000)
Increase	$ 21,000

The $21,000 basis increase is treated as a new depreciable asset. Depreciation on this asset is allocated to Shawn. If the partnership later sells all the underlying assets, Shawn's share of the gain takes into account the remaining (undepreciated) balance of the $21,000 step-up. ■

[34]§ 743(b).

ADJUSTMENT: PARTNERSHIP DISTRIBUTIONS

Optional adjustments to basis are also available to the partnership when property is distributed to a partner. If a § 754 optional adjustment-to-basis election is in effect, the basis of partnership property is *increased* by the following.[35]

- Any gain recognized by a distributee partner.
- The excess of the partnership's adjusted basis for any distributed property over the adjusted basis of that property in the hands of the distributee partner.

Conversely, the basis of partnership property is *decreased* by the following:

- Any loss recognized by a distributee partner.
- In the case of a liquidating distribution, the excess of the distributee partner's adjusted basis of any distributed property over the basis of that property to the partnership.

EXAMPLE 30

Rena has a basis of $50,000 in her partnership interest and receives a building with an adjusted basis to the partnership of $120,000 in termination of her interest. (The partnership has no hot assets.) The building's basis in Rena's hands is $50,000 under the proportionate liquidating distribution rules. If an optional adjustment-to-basis election is in effect, the partnership increases the basis of its remaining property by $70,000.

Partnership's adjusted basis in distributed property	$120,000
Less: Distributee's basis in distributed property	(50,000)
Increase	$ 70,000

EXAMPLE 31

Assume the same facts as in Example 30, except the partnership's basis in the building was $40,000. Rena's basis in the building is still $50,000, and the partnership reduces the basis of its remaining property by $10,000.

Distributee's basis in distributed property	$ 50,000
Less: Partnership's adjusted basis in distributed property	(40,000)
Decrease	$ 10,000

Although these rules may seem confusing at first reading, understanding the theory on which they are based helps to clarify the situation. Section 734(b) assumes that the inside basis for all partnership assets equals the outside basis for all of the partners' interests immediately before the distribution. When this equality exists both before and after a distribution, no adjustment to the basis of partnership property is necessary. However, when the equality does not exist after the distribution, an adjustment can bring the inside and outside bases back into equality. This is the adjustment that is made by the two increases and the two decreases described in the bulleted lists above.

EXAMPLE 32

The Cardinal Partnership has an inside basis of $12,000 for its assets, which have a fair market value of $15,000. Aaron, Bill, and Carmen each have outside bases of $4,000 for their partnership interests. If the partnership liquidates partner Aaron's interest with a $5,000 cash distribution, the resulting balance sheet is unbalanced as follows.

[35] § 734(b).

	Inside (Assets)		Outside (Capital)
Before	$12,000	=	$12,000
Distribution	(5,000)	≠	(4,000)
After	$ 7,000	≠	$ 8,000

This unbalanced situation can be eliminated by adding $1,000 to the inside basis of the formula. Note that this is the same amount as the gain that Aaron recognizes on the distribution ($5,000 cash – $4,000 outside basis = $1,000 gain). Therefore, by adding the amount of Aaron's gain to the inside basis of the partnership assets, the inside basis = outside basis formula is back in balance.

Inside (Assets)		Outside (Capital)
$7,000	≠	$8,000
+1,000		
$8,000	=	$8,000

If the partnership liquidates Aaron's interest with a distribution of land having a $5,000 inside basis, the same unbalanced situation occurs. Although this transaction does not create any recognized gain for Aaron, the $1,000 optional adjustment is the excess of the $5,000 inside basis of the distributed property over the $4,000 substituted basis of that property to Aaron. ■

LO.8

Outline the methods of terminating a partnership.

Termination of a Partnership

When does a partnership's final tax year end? Technically, it ends when the partnership terminates, which occurs on either of the following events.

- No part of the business continues to be carried on by any of the partners in a partnership.
- Within a 12-month period, there is a sale or exchange of 50 percent or more of the partnership's capital and profits.[36]

The partnership terminates and its tax year closes when the partnership incorporates or when one partner in a two-party partnership buys out the other partner, thereby creating a sole proprietorship. A termination also occurs when the partnership ceases operations and liquidates.

The partnership taxable year usually does not close upon the death of a partner or upon the liquidation of a partner's interest, unless the liquidation of the interest of one partner in a two-partner partnership effectively terminates the partnership on the liquidation date. However, the partnership year will close in respect to the deceased or liquidated partner.[37] The deceased or liquidated partner's share of partnership income or loss is computed to the date of death or liquidation and reported on the partner's tax return for the year in which the death or liquidation occurs.

The partnership year does not close upon the entry of a new partner to the partnership. It also does not close upon the sale or exchange of an existing partnership

[36] § 708(b)(1).

[37] § 706(c)(2)(A).

interest unless the transaction results in 50 percent or more of the interests in the partnership capital and profits being sold within a 12-month period.

EXAMPLE 33

Partner Olaf, who held a one-third interest in the Oriole Partnership, died on November 20, 2004. The partnership uses an approved fiscal year ending September 30. Olaf used a calendar year. The partnership agreement does not contain a buy-sell provision that is triggered upon the death of a partner. The partnership's tax year does not close with Olaf's death. The partnership tax year does close, however, with respect to Olaf. His share of partnership income or loss for the period from October 1, 2004, to November 20, 2004, is reported on his final Form 1040. The partnership income or loss from November 21, 2004, to September 30, 2005, is taxed to Olaf's estate or other successor. Income from the fiscal year ending September 30, 2004, is reported on Olaf's final income tax return, which covers the period from January 1 to November 20, 2004.

A **technical termination of a partnership** occurs when the partnership business operations continue but the partnership terminates because there has been a sale or exchange of the requisite 50 percent capital and profits interests within 12 months. If the same interest (less than 50 percent) is sold more than once, only one sale is considered in determining whether more than 50 percent has been sold within 12 months. The terminated partnership is deemed to liquidate by transferring its assets and liabilities to a newly formed partnership, which continues its business operations.[38] A technical termination may have numerous consequences, such as changing the taxable year of the new partnership or modifying the cost recovery methods to be used by the new partnership.

LO.9

Describe the special considerations of a family partnership.

Other Issues

FAMILY PARTNERSHIPS

Family partnerships are owned and controlled primarily by members of the same family. Such partnerships may be established for a variety of reasons. A daughter may have a particular expertise that, coupled with her parents' abilities, allows them to establish a successful business. Often, however, the primary reason for establishing a family partnership is the desire to save taxes. If the parents are in higher marginal tax brackets than the children, family tax dollars are saved by funneling some of the partnership's income to the children.

[38]Reg. § 1.708–1(b).

TAX IN THE NEWS

Family Limited Partnerships as an Estate Planning Device

One of the most widely used estate planning tools in recent times has been the family limited partnership. The parents form a partnership with business or other assets and then give their children or grandchildren an interest in the partnership equivalent to the unified credit. Additional tax-free gifts of $11,000 per donee can also be made annually ($22,000 if the parents elect gift splitting).

The appeal of the family partnership has increased considerably in recent years since the IRS stated that a minority discount could be applied to gifts made by family members. A minority discount allows the nominal fair market value of a business interest to be reduced to account for the fact that the owner would have difficulty selling it for the cash value of the underlying assets since the purchaser would not have management control over these assets. With a minority discount of 30 percent, for example, a gift with a nominal fair market value of $15,714 could be eligible for the full $11,000 annual exclusion. With such a minority discount, a $1 million interest in a partnership could be transferred by a married couple to three children in only about two-thirds of the time it would take to transfer it without the discount. This strategy is particularly useful for assets that are expected to appreciate in value.

Nevertheless, valid family partnerships are difficult to establish for tax purposes. A basic tenet of tax law is that income must be taxed to the person who performs the services or owns the capital that generates the income. A parent, therefore, cannot transfer only a profits interest to a child and expect the transfer to be recognized for tax purposes.

Capital versus Services. Because of the concern that family partnerships are established primarily for tax avoidance purposes, a family member is recognized as a partner only in the following cases.

- Capital is a material income-producing factor in the partnership, and the family member's capital interest is acquired in a bona fide transaction (even if by gift or purchase from another family member) in which ownership and control are received.
- Capital is not a material income-producing factor, but the family member contributes substantial or vital services.[39]

If a partnership derives a substantial portion of its gross income from the use of capital, such as inventories or investments in plant, machinery, or equipment, the capital is considered to be a material income-producing factor. Ordinarily, capital is not a material income-producing factor if the partnership's income consists principally of fees, commissions, or other compensation for personal services performed by partners or employees.

Children as Partners. When capital is a material income-producing factor and a partnership interest is transferred by gift or sale to a child who is under age 14, the kiddie tax may apply. Under the kiddie tax, some of the dependent child's distributive share of partnership income may be taxed at the parent's tax rate,

[39] § 704(e).

BRIDGE DISCIPLINE

Bridge to Family Financial Planning

A family limited partnership can be used as a device to:

- transfer wealth to other family members,
- maintain control of the assets and keep them in the family,
- protect the assets from legal risk of loss, and
- allocate income to other family members.

Creation. A family limited partnership is generally created by the transfer of real estate or other investment property into a limited partnership in exchange for a small general partnership interest (the controlling interest) and a limited partnership interest representing the balance (the investment interest). The transferors retain the general partnership interest, maintaining control of the partnership, and then proceed to transfer the limited interests to other family members over time.

Wealth Transfer. The limited partnership interests are valued at a discount to the underlying value of the partnership assets. This is allowed because of the lack of marketability of the interests and the limits on transferability. Since the value of the limited interests is reduced, the overall gift tax incurred by the transferor is reduced.

The transfer of the limited interests also reduces the transferor's estate and therefore reduces the future estate tax at death.

Asset Protection. A creditor of a partner cannot reach the assets of the partnership to satisfy a claim against the partner. The creditor essentially must wait for the partnership to make a distribution. This means that the underlying assets of the family limited partnership are safe from direct forfeiture for claims against a partner.

Allocation of Income. The transfer of the limited interests allows for the allocation of income to other family members. In this way, income can be shifted to children who are in a much lower tax bracket than their parents.

Adapted from Thomas Brinker, "Utilizing Family Limited Partnerships in Financial & Asset Protection Planning: A Strategy for Income, Estate, and Gift Tax Savings," *Financial Services Advisor*, November/December 2002, pp. 12–14.

unless the income share constitutes earned income. Regardless of age, if the child provides bona fide services to a partnership and the income share constitutes earned income, the parent-partner's tax rate is avoided.

EXAMPLE 34

Karen operates a first-floor-window-washing business in a summer lakeside resort city. Relatively small amounts of capital are required to operate the sole proprietorship (buckets, sponges, squeegees, etc.). During the summer, Karen normally hires middle and high school students to wash windows. Her 13-year-old daughter and 12-year-old son want to work in the business during the summer to earn money for spending and for college. Each obtains the necessary summer work permit. Karen creates the KDS Partnership and gives each child a 5% interest.

Karen figures that if her children were paid an hourly rate, about 5% of KDS's profits would be distributed to them as wages. Karen believes that an ownership interest will help the children learn what running a profitable business entails and prepare them for an active business life after their education is completed.

BRIDGE DISCIPLINE

Bridge to Business Law

A number of different types of legal entities can obtain tax status as a partnership. The overriding difference between these legal forms is the sharing of liabilities between the partnership and the partners/members.

General Partnership. The partners take unlimited exposure in satisfying partnership liabilities.

Limited Partnership. The general partner(s) take unlimited liability, but the exposure of the limited partner(s) usually is limited to the amount invested.

Limited Liability Partnership. The partner's share of liability varies by the state of organization and operation, but the partner's liability may be limited as to acts committed by other partners.

Limited Liability Company. The member's liability is limited to the amount invested unless otherwise agreed.

Since capital is not a material income-producing factor in the business, and the children's profit percentages approximate what they would earn if they were paid an hourly rate, all of the income is classified as earned income. Thus, the kiddie tax is avoided. ■

Gift of Capital Interest. If a family member acquires a capital interest by gift in a family partnership in which capital is a material income-producing factor, only part of the income may be allocated to this interest. First, the donor of the interest is allocated an amount of partnership income that represents reasonable compensation for services to the partnership. Then, the remaining income is divided among the partners in accordance with their capital interests in the partnership. An interest purchased by one family member from another is considered to be created by gift for this purpose.[40]

EXAMPLE 35

A partnership in which a parent transferred a 50% interest by gift to a child generated a profit of $90,000. Capital is a material income-producing factor. The parent performed services valued at $20,000. The child performed no services. Under these circumstances, $20,000 is allocated to the parent as compensation. Of the remaining $70,000 of income attributable to capital, at least 50%, or $35,000, is allocated to the parent. ■

LIMITED LIABILITY PARTNERSHIPS

Despite the similarity in names, a limited liability partnership (LLP) is quite different from a limited partnership. In 1991, Texas became the first state to allow professionals to organize their practices as registered LLPs. Since then, other states have adopted similar legislation. The difference between a general partnership and an LLP is small, but very significant. Recall that general partners are jointly and severally liable for all partnership debts. In some states, partners in a registered LLP are jointly and severally liable for contractual liability (i.e., they are treated as

[40] § 704(e)(3).

general partners for commercial debt). They are also always personally liable for their own malpractice or other torts. They are not, however, personally liable for the malpractice and torts of their partners. As a result, the exposure of their personal assets to lawsuits filed against other partners and the partnership is considerably reduced.

An LLP must have formal documents of organization and register with the state. Because the LLP is a general partnership in other respects, it does not pay any state franchise taxes on its operations—an important difference between LLPs and limited liability companies (LLCs) in states that impose franchise taxes on LLCs. LLPs are taxed as partnerships under Federal tax statutes.

ANTI-ABUSE REGULATIONS

The IRS has issued Regulations that allow it to disregard the form of a partnership transaction when it believes that the transaction (or series of transactions) is abusive.[41] Under the Regulation, a transaction is abusive if it satisfies two tests. First, it must have a principal purpose of substantially reducing the present value of the partners' aggregate Federal tax liability. In addition, the potential tax reduction must be inconsistent with the intent of Subchapter K. If the IRS disregards the form of a transaction, it will recast the transaction in a manner that reflects the transaction's underlying economic arrangement.

Suggested Further Readings

Sheldon Banoff and Richard Lipton, "CA-8 Weighs in on Inconsistent Tax Reporting by Feuding Partners," *Journal of Taxation,* September 2003, pp. 187–189.

Hughlene A. Burton, "Partners & Partnerships: Current Developments," *The Tax Adviser,* February 2004, pp. 100–104.

Terence Floyd Cuff, "Drafting Partnership Allocations," *Business Entities,* March/April 2003, pp. 22–33 and 62–64.

Lisa M. Loychik, "Structuring Partnership Payments to a Retiring Partner," *The Tax Adviser*, August 2002, pp. 516–518.

Jerry Riles and Beanna Whitlock, "The ABCs of LLCs," *National Public Accountant,* August 2003, pp. 16–19.

Janet W. Tillinger, "Computing Capital Gains on Sales of Partnership and S Corporation Interests," *The Tax Adviser*, January 2002, pp. 28–40.

KEY TERMS

Disproportionate distribution, 6–4
Hot assets, 6–22
Inventory, 6–7
Liquidating distribution, 6–3
Nonliquidating distribution, 6–3
Optional adjustment election, 6–27
Proportionate distribution, 6–4
Section 754 election, 6–27
Technical termination of partnership, 6–31
Unrealized receivables, 6–7

[41]Reg. § 1.701–2.

PROBLEM MATERIALS

West Federal Taxation

Problems

Issue ID

1. The SueBart Partnership distributes the following assets to partner Bart.
   - $10,000 cash.
   - An account receivable with a $10,000 value and a $0 basis to the partnership.
   - A parcel of land with a $10,000 value and a $2,000 basis to the partnership.

   What issues must be considered in determining the tax treatment of the distribution?

2. Andrew's outside basis in his interest in the ABC Partnership is $100,000. In a proportionate nonliquidating distribution, the partnership distributes to him cash of $25,000, inventory (fair market value of $30,000, basis to the partnership of $20,000), and land (fair market value of $60,000, basis to the partnership of $30,000). The partnership continues in existence.
   a. Does the partnership recognize any gain or loss as a result of this distribution?
   b. Does Andrew recognize any gain or loss as a result of this distribution?
   c. Calculate Andrew's basis in the land, in the inventory, and in his partnership interest immediately following the distribution.

3. When Peggy's outside basis in the PQR Partnership is $25,000, the partnership distributes to her $10,000 cash, an account receivable (fair market value of $70,000, inside basis to the partnership of $0), and a parcel of land (fair market value of $30,000, inside basis to the partnership of $20,000). Peggy remains a partner in the partnership, and the distribution is proportionate to the partners.
   a. Determine the recognized gain or loss to the partnership as a result of this distribution.
   b. Determine the recognized gain or loss to Peggy as a result of the distribution.
   c. Determine Peggy's basis in the land, account receivable, and PQR Partnership after the distribution.

4. In each of the following independent cases in which the partnership owns no hot assets, indicate:
   - Whether the partner recognizes gain or loss.
   - Whether the partnership recognizes gain or loss.
   - The partner's adjusted basis for the property distributed.
   - The partner's outside basis in the partnership after the distribution.

   a. Mona receives $35,000 cash in partial liquidation of her interest in the partnership. Mona's outside basis for her partnership interest immediately before the distribution is $20,000.
   b. Mark receives $15,000 cash and land with an inside basis to the partnership of $6,000 (value $4,000) in partial liquidation of his interest. Mark's outside basis for his partnership interest immediately before the distribution is $20,000.
   c. Assume the same facts as in (b), except that Mark's outside basis for his partnership interest immediately before the distribution is $15,000.
   d. Brad receives $10,000 cash and an account receivable with a basis of $0 and a fair market value of $12,000 in partial liquidation of his partnership interest. His basis was $6,000 before the distribution. All partners received proportionate distributions.

Decision Making

5. Assume the facts of Problem 4. In each independent case, are additional planning opportunities available to the partnership to maximize its inside basis in its assets? If so, by how much can the basis be increased? What is the effect of any basis increase to the distributee partner or the other partners?

6. Tom's basis in his partnership interest is $41,000. In a proportionate nonliquidating distribution, Tom receives $20,000 cash and two inventory items with bases of $20,000 each to the partnership. The values of the inventory items are $30,000 and $10,000.
   a. How much gain or loss, if any, must Tom recognize on the distribution?
   b. What basis will Tom take in each inventory item?

Communications

7. Sam Stevens is a 40% partner in the calendar year Stevens-Stuart Partnership. On January 1, 2004, his basis in his partnership interest is $25,000, including his $13,000 share of partnership liabilities. The partnership has no taxable income or loss for the current year. Stevens-Stuart repays all liabilities before the end of 2004 from cash on hand. In a nonliquidating distribution, the partnership distributes $15,000 cash on December 15. It also distributes inventory proportionately to all partners. Sam receives inventory with a basis of $8,000 and a fair market value of $6,000. In January 2005, Sam, your client, asks your advice regarding treatment of 2004 operations and distributions. Using the format (1) facts, (2) issues, and (3) conclusion and analysis, draft a letter to Sam at the Stevens-Stuart Partnership (1622 E. Henry Street, St. Paul, MN 55163) that addresses the following points:
   a. How much gain or loss does the partnership recognize as a result of 2004 activities?
   b. How much gain or loss must Sam recognize in 2004?
   c. What is Sam's basis in inventory received?
   d. What is Sam's basis in his partnership interest at the end of 2004?

8. Describe, in general terms, two types of assets considered "hot assets." When is characterization as a "hot asset" relevant?

EXTENDER

Issue ID

9. Walden is a 40% partner in the WXY Partnership. He became a partner three years ago when he contributed land with a value of $40,000 and a basis of $20,000 (current value is $90,000). Xavier and Yolanda each contributed $30,000 cash for a 30% interest. Walden's basis in his partnership interest is currently $40,000; the other partners' bases are each $30,000. The partnership has the following assets.

	Basis	**FMV**
Cash	$ 60,000	$ 60,000
Accounts receivable	–0–	80,000
Marketable securities	20,000	70,000
Land	20,000	90,000
Total	$100,000	$300,000

The partnership will make a distribution of $150,000 in value to the partners before the end of the current year, but the type of property that will be distributed has not been determined. Describe the tax effects on the partners in each of the following independent distribution alternatives.
   a. WXY distributes a $45,000 interest in the land each to Yolanda and Xavier and $60,000 of accounts receivable to Walden.
   b. WXY distributes $60,000 cash to Walden, $45,000 of marketable securities to Yolanda, and $45,000 of accounts receivable to Xavier.
   c. WXY distributes a $36,000 interest in the land and $24,000 of accounts receivable to Walden and $27,000 of cash and $18,000 of accounts receivable each to Xavier and Yolanda.

EXTENDER

Issue ID

10. Use the assets and partners' bases from Problem 9. Assume the partnership distributes all its assets in a liquidating distribution. In deciding the allocation of assets, what issues should the partnership consider to minimize each partner's taxable gains?

11. In each of the following independent liquidating distributions in which the partnership also liquidates, determine the amount and character of any gain or loss to be recognized by each partner and the basis of each asset (other than cash) received. In each case, assume distributions of hot assets are proportionate to the partners.

a. Rachel has a $9,000 partnership basis and receives a $15,000 cash distribution.
b. Sara has a $20,000 partnership basis and receives $9,000 cash and a capital asset with a basis to the partnership of $4,000. The asset's fair market value is $12,000.
c. Tim has a $16,000 partnership basis and receives $4,000 cash, inventory with a basis to the partnership of $10,000, and a capital asset with a partnership basis of $6,000. The inventory and capital asset have fair market values of $9,000 and $7,000, respectively.
d. Suzy has a partnership basis of $50,000 and receives a distribution of $30,000 cash and an account receivable with a basis of $0 to the partnership (value is $60,000).

Decision Making

12. The basis of Lee's partnership interest is $75,000. Lee receives a pro rata liquidating distribution consisting of $42,000 cash and his proportionate share of inventory with a basis of $45,000 to the partnership and a fair market value of $52,000. Assume the partnership also liquidates.
    a. How much gain or loss, if any, must Lee recognize as a result of the distribution?
    b. What basis will Lee take in the inventory?
    c. If the inventory is sold two years later for $48,000, what are the tax consequences to Lee?
    d. What are the tax consequences to the partnership as a result of the liquidating distribution?
    e. Is any planning technique available to the partnership to avoid any "lost basis" results?
    f. Would your answer to (b) change if this had been a nonliquidating distribution?

Decision Making

13. Assume the same facts as in Problem 12, except that Lee's basis in the partnership is $130,000 instead of $75,000.
    a. How much gain or loss, if any, must Lee recognize on the distribution?
    b. What basis will Lee take in the inventory?
    c. What are the tax consequences to the partnership?
    d. Can you recommend an alternative distribution?
    e. Would your answer to (a) or (b) change if this had been a nonliquidating distribution?

14. Dave's basis in his partnership interest is $24,000. In a proportionate distribution in liquidation of the partnership, Dave receives $3,000 cash and two parcels of land with bases of $10,000 and $5,000 each to the partnership. The partnership holds both parcels of land for investment, and each parcel has a fair market value of $8,000.
    a. How much gain or loss, if any, must Dave recognize on the distribution?
    b. What basis does Dave take in each parcel?
    c. If the land had been held as inventory by the partnership, what effect, if any, would it have on your responses to (a) and (b)?

Decision Making

15. Assume the same facts as in Problem 14, except that Dave receives $3,000 cash and an old truck having a basis of $430 to the partnership and a fair market value of $2,000.
    a. How much loss, if any, may Dave recognize on the distribution?
    b. What basis does Dave take in the truck?
    c. Suppose Dave's 15-year-old son uses the truck for his personal use for one year before Dave sells it for $100. How much loss may Dave recognize on the sale of the truck? What tax planning procedures could have prevented this result?

16. Use the approach introduced in Concept Summary 6–2 to derive the realized and recognized gain or loss for the two owners of the dissolving GH Partnership and the bases of the distributed assets, given the following facts.

	Partner George (⅔)	Partner Hazel (⅓)
Basis in interest	$100,000	$15,000
Cash received	40,000	20,000
Inventory received		
Market value	12,000	6,000
Basis to GH	6,000	3,000

	Partner George (⅔)	Partner Hazel (⅓)
Building and equipment received		
Market value	$180,000	$90,000
Basis to GH	144,000	72,000
Depreciation recapture potential		
Amount	16,000	8,000
Basis to GH	–0–	–0–

EXTENDER

17. In 2001, Gabriella contributed land with a basis of $16,000 and a fair market value of $25,000 to the Meadowlark Partnership in exchange for a 25% interest in capital and profits. In 2004, the partnership distributes this property to Juanita, also a 25% partner, in a nonliquidating distribution. The fair market value has increased to $30,000 at the time the property is distributed. Juanita's and Gabriella's bases in their partnership interests are each $40,000 at the time of the distribution.
    a. How much gain or loss, if any, does Gabriella recognize on the distribution to Juanita? What is Gabriella's basis in her partnership interest following the distribution?
    b. What is Juanita's basis in the land she received in the distribution?
    c. How much gain or loss, if any, does Juanita recognize on the distribution? What is Juanita's basis in her partnership interest following the distribution?
    d. How much gain or loss would Juanita recognize if she later sells the land for its $30,000 fair market value? Is this result equitable?
    e. Would your answers to (a) and (b) change if Gabriella originally contributed the property to the partnership in 1994?

EXTENDER

18. Winston contributed a tract of undeveloped land to the Nightingale Partnership in 2001. He originally paid $20,000 for the property in 1990, but its value was $70,000 at the date of the contribution. In 2004, the partnership distributes another parcel of land to Winston; the land has a basis to the partnership of $30,000. The fair market value of the distributed property is $100,000 in 2004. Winston's basis in his partnership interest is $60,000 immediately before the distribution.
    a. How much gain or loss, if any, does Winston recognize on the distribution?
    b. What is Winston's basis in his partnership interest following the distribution?
    c. What is Winston's basis in the property he receives in the distribution?
    d. After the distribution, what is the partnership's basis in the property originally contributed by Winston?
    e. Would your answers to (b), (c), and (d) change if Winston originally contributed the property to the partnership in 1995?

Issue ID

19. Jim is retiring from the JSU general services partnership. He is trying to decide whether to sell his 51% interest in the partnership to the other partners or to the partnership. Under either scenario, payments would be paid to Jim over several years and would include amounts in exchange for Jim's share of partnership goodwill. Explain why the method selected may make a difference for tax purposes to Jim, JSU, and the other partners.

EXTENDER

20. The FABB Partnership distributes a marketable security to 25% partner Fred in complete liquidation of his interest in the partnership. Use the following facts to answer the questions that follow.
    - The partnership's basis in the security is $10,000, and its value is $20,000. The partnership did not own any of this particular security following the distribution.
    - Fred's basis in the partnership interest is $7,500 immediately prior to the distribution.
    - Fred is a general partner, and capital is a material income-producing factor to the partnership.
    - The partnership owns no hot assets.

a. How is the security classified under § 736?
b. What is the amount of the security distribution that is treated as a cash distribution?
c. How much gain does Fred report on the distribution?
d. What is Fred's basis in the security he receives in the distribution?

Decision Making

21. Maurice is a 10% general partner in the Chartreuse Partnership, which provides consulting services. The partnership distributes $100,000 cash to Maurice in complete liquidation of his partnership interest. Maurice's share of partnership unrealized receivables immediately before the distribution is $40,000. The partnership has no other hot assets. Assume none of the cash payment is for goodwill. Maurice's basis for his partnership interest immediately before the distribution is $50,000.
    a. How is the cash payment treated under § 736?
    b. How much gain or loss must Maurice recognize on the distribution, and what is the character of these amounts?
    c. How does the partnership treat the distribution to Maurice?
    d. What planning opportunities might the partnership wish to consider?
    e. How would your answers to the above questions change if Maurice were a limited partner?

22. ALF Partnership has three equal partners. One of them, Art, sells his interest to his partner, Lou, for $65,000 cash and the assumption of Art's share of partnership liabilities. On the sale date, the partnership's cash basis balance sheet reflects the following. Assume that capital accounts reflect the partners' bases in their partnership interests, excluding liabilities.

	Basis	FMV		Basis	FMV
Cash	$120,000	$120,000	Note payable	$ 15,000	$ 15,000
Accounts receivable	–0–	60,000	Capital accounts		
Capital assets	15,000	30,000	Art	40,000	65,000
			Lou	40,000	65,000
			Fran	40,000	65,000
Total	$135,000	$210,000	Total	$135,000	$210,000

    a. What is the total amount realized by Art on the sale?
    b. How much, if any, ordinary income must Art recognize on the sale?
    c. How much capital gain must Art report?
    d. What is Lou's basis in the partnership interest acquired?
    e. If the partnership makes an election to adjust the bases of the partnership assets to reflect the sale, what adjustment is made?

23. Assume in Problem 22 that Art's partnership interest is not sold to another partner. Instead, the partnership makes a liquidating distribution of $65,000 cash to Art, and the remaining partners assume his share of the liabilities. How much gain or loss must Art recognize and how is it characterized? Assume Art is a general partner and capital is not a material income-producing factor to the partnership.

Issue ID
Communications

24. Dad is the owner of a 60% general partner interest in the Consulting Services Partnership, in which capital is *not* a material income-producing factor. Two unrelated partners each own 20% partnership interests. Dad's basis in his partnership interest is $300,000.

    Dad's son, Dean, worked for the partnership on a part-time basis while he was in college and has shown a strong aptitude for the business. Dad would like to retire and allow Dean to take over the business, but he needs to dispose of his partnership interest for its $600,000 value to do so. The partnership has adequate liquidity to make this distribution.

    Dad's share of the partnership's unrealized receivables from services (no depreciation recapture, $0 basis) is $225,000. The partnership has a favorable tax year-end, so the other partners want to make sure the partnership does not terminate. Dean is the beneficiary of a trust fund established by his grandmother. He now receives about

$60,000 a year and will control the $750,000 principal amount in four years, when he reaches age 30.

Dad is considering two courses of action.

- Dad can sell his interest to Dean on an installment basis with a balloon payment of the $600,000 principal balance at the end of four years. Dean would pay Dad adequate interest (for purposes of OID and imputed interest rules) on the deferred balance each year. Under this arrangement, the entire 60% interest is deemed to be sold for tax purposes at the time the installment contract is consummated, although gain is deferred until payments are made.
- Dad can allow the partnership to redeem his partnership interest immediately. To structure a transition to the son, the partnership would enter into an employment arrangement with Dean, whereby Dean vests in a 10% interest in the partnership each year for six years in exchange for services rendered to the partnership.

Draft a letter to Dad Thomas (1329 Mesquite Boulevard, Amarillo, TX 79109) addressing the consequences of each proposed alternative. Consider the impact to Dad, the partnership, and Dean.

25. At the end of last year, Ben, a 40% partner in the four-person BBJR Partnership, has an outside basis of $50,000 in the partnership, including a $40,000 share of partnership debt. Ben's share of the partnership's § 1245 recapture potential is $25,000. All parties use the calendar year. Describe the income tax consequences to Ben in each of the following independent situations that take place in the current year.
    a. On the first day of the tax year, Ben sells his partnership interest to Marilyn for $80,000 cash and the assumption by Marilyn of the appropriate share of partnership liabilities.
    b. Ben dies after a lengthy illness on April 1 of the current year. Ben's brother immediately takes Ben's place in the partnership.

26. Briefly discuss how your responses in Problem 25 would change if the BBJR Partnership had $200,000 of unrealized receivables at the end of the current year, including the § 1245 recapture potential.

27. Daryl, a partner in the cash basis DLL Partnership, has a 30% interest in partnership profits and losses. The partnership's balance sheet at the end of the current year is as follows.

	Basis	FMV		Basis	FMV
Cash	$ 25,000	$ 25,000	Daryl, capital	$ 54,000	$135,000
Receivables	-0-	240,000	Larry, capital	63,000	157,500
Land	155,000	185,000	Lewis, capital	63,000	157,500
Total	$180,000	$450,000	Total	$180,000	$450,000

Daryl sells his interest in the DLL Partnership to Arnold at the end of the current year for cash of $135,000.

a. How much income must Daryl report on his tax return for the current year from the sale, and what is its nature?
b. If the partnership does not make an optional adjustment-to-basis election, what are the type and amount of income that Arnold must report in the next year when the receivables are collected?
c. If the partnership did make an optional adjustment-to-basis election, what are the type and amount of income that Arnold must report in the next year when the receivables are collected (assuming no other transactions in the next year)? If the land (which is used in the DLL Partnership's business) is sold for $225,000?

28. For each of the following independent fact patterns, indicate whether a termination of the partnership has occurred for tax purposes. Assume no other partnership interests are sold either one year before or one year after the transactions described.

a. Polly sells her interest in capital and profits of the MPQ Partnership. She owns a 68% interest in capital and a 48% interest in the partnership profits.
b. Rick and Ron are equal partners in the R & R Partnership. Ron dies on January 15, 2004. Rick purchases Ron's interest from his estate on March 15, 2004. Answer for January 15, 2004.
c. Answer (b), for March 15, 2004.
d. Fred, a 58% partner in the profitable F & D Partnership, gives his entire interest to his son on July 1, 2004.
e. Carol, Cora, and Chris are equal partners in the Canary Partnership. On January 22, 2004, Cora sells her entire interest to Ted. On December 29, 2004, Carol sells a 15% interest to Earl. On January 25, 2005, Chris sells his interest to Frank.

EXTENDER

29. Peggy and Cindy, parent and child, operate a local apparel shop as a partnership. The PC Partnership earned a profit of $80,000 in the current year. Cindy's equal partnership interest was acquired by gift from Peggy. Assume that capital is a material income-producing factor and that Peggy manages the day-to-day operations of the shop without any help from Cindy. Reasonable compensation for Peggy's services is $30,000.
a. How much of the partnership income is allocated to Peggy?
b. What is the maximum amount of partnership income that can be allocated to Cindy?
c. Assuming that Cindy is five years old, has no other income, and is claimed as a dependent by Peggy, how is Cindy's income from the partnership taxed?

BRIDGE DISCIPLINE

1. On July 1, 2004, José, Mark, and Hong formed JMH Real Estate Ltd., a general partnership, as equal partners. The following contributions were made.

- José contributed land with a fair market value of $150,000, nonrecourse debt of $50,000, and a tax basis of $85,000.
- Mark contributed a commercial building and land with a fair market value of $450,000 (building $375,000 and land $75,000) and nonrecourse debt of $350,000. The tax basis of the building was $200,000, and the basis of the land was $50,000. The commercial building has 20 years remaining in its class life.
- Hong contributed cash of $100,000.

a. Create the initial balance sheet for book and tax purposes.
b. Calculate each partner's initial outside basis.
c. On December 31, 2004, the partnership distributed one-sixth of the land contributed by José to Hong, but retained the entire nonrecourse debt as a partnership debt. The one-sixth interest was valued at $25,000 on the date of the distribution. What are the effects of this distribution on the partners' capital accounts? Do any of the partners recognize a gain for tax purposes?

2. On October 14, 2004, Janet and Margo admitted Justin as a one-fifth partner to the JM Gold general partnership. The partnership's balance sheet just before Justin's admittance was as follows.

	Book, Tax Basis	Fair Market Value
Cash	$ 50,000	$ 50,000
Inventory	100,000	175,000
Accounts receivable	85,000	83,000
Land	150,000	300,000
	$385,000	$608,000
Capital, Janet	$192,500	$304,000
Capital, Margo	192,500	304,000
	$385,000	$608,000

Janet and Margo formed the equal partnership three years ago when they each contributed $10,000 cash. Justin will contribute inventory with a $112,000 fair market value (adjusted basis $75,000) and $40,000 cash.

a. Create the balance sheet for book and tax purposes after Justin's admittance, assuming that the partnership does not elect to revalue its assets.

b. Create the balance sheet for book and tax purposes after Justin's admittance, assuming that the partnership elects to revalue its assets. Why does this balance sheet more clearly reflect the partners' economic interests?

c. On November 10, 2004, the partnership sold the land for $300,000. How is the tax gain allocated?

Research Problems

THOMSON RIA™

Note: Solutions to Research Problems can be prepared by using the ***RIA Checkpoint® Student Edition*** *online research product, which is available to accompany this text. It is also possible to prepare solutions to the Research Problems by using tax research materials found in a standard tax library.*

Decision Making

Research Problem 1. Your client, Paul, is a one-third general partner in the service-oriented Magpie Partnership. He would like to retire from the partnership at the end of the current year and asks your help in structuring the buyout transaction.

Based on interim financial data and revenue projections for the remainder of the year, the partnership's balance sheet is expected to approximate the following at year-end.

	Basis	FMV		Basis	FMV
Cash	$ 60,000	$ 60,000	Maggie, capital	$ 60,000	$150,000
Accounts receivable	-0-	180,000	Paul, capital	60,000	150,000
Land (capital asset)	120,000	210,000	Iris, capital	60,000	150,000
Total assets	$180,000	$450,000	Total capital	$180,000	$450,000

Although the partnership has some cash on hand, the amount is not adequate to purchase Paul's entire interest in the current year. The partnership has proposed to pay Paul, in liquidation of his partnership interest, $50,000 each at the end of this year and the next two.

Paul has agreed to the above payment schedule, but the parties are not sure of the tax consequences of the buyout and have temporarily halted negotiations to consult with their tax advisers. Paul has come to you to discuss the possible income tax ramifications of the buyout and to make sure he negotiates the most advantageous position possible.

a. If the buyout agreement between Paul and Magpie is silent as to the treatment of each payment, how will each payment be treated by Paul and the partnership?

b. As Paul's adviser, what payment schedule do you recommend that Paul negotiate to minimize his current tax liability?

c. Now assume you are the tax adviser for the partnership. What payment schedule would you propose to ensure that the remaining partners receive the earliest possible deductions?

d. What additional planning opportunity might you recommend to the partnership?

Research Problem 2. The accrual basis JB Partnership had a § 754 election in effect when partner Jill sold her 40% interest to Krista for $200,000. Krista's share of the inside basis of partnership assets was $120,000 following the acquisition. The total step-up, then, is $80,000. The basis and fair market value of JB's assets are shown below. If the partnership sold the equipment, the entire $20,000 gain would be § 1245 recapture. Using the basis allocation rules of § 755 and the Regulations thereunder, calculate the amount of the total adjustment to be allocated to each of the partnership's assets.

Item	FMV	Basis before § 754 Adjustment
Cash	$ 80,000	$ 80,000
Receivable	80,000	–0–
Equipment	120,000	100,000
Land	220,000	120,000
Total assets	$500,000	$300,000

Communications

Research Problem 3. The Western States Partnership is a cash basis general partnership that reports on a calendar year. The partnership was formed in 1996 and consists of 19 partners. Sarah has a 10% capital and profits interest in the partnership, and each of the other partners owns a 5% capital and profits interest.

During an audit of Jason, a 5% partner, in November 2004, the IRS disagrees with the handling of a $200 charitable deduction that was claimed on his 2002 tax return. This amount was reported by Western States on the charitable deduction line of Jason's Schedule K–1. On a schedule attached to each partner's K–1 for 2002, Western States indicated that it made a $4,000 deductible contribution to a foreign charity and reported that amount on the charitable deduction line of the partnership's Schedule K. The IRS properly contends that contributions to foreign-based charities are not deductible. It seeks to adjust the returns of Jason and any other partners who claimed a deduction for this contribution. Address the following points in a memo to the tax research file.

a. Can the IRS adjust Jason's tax return for this item? Must the IRS audit each of the other partners' returns to determine which partners claimed the incorrect deduction?
b. Assume the partnership has not designated a Tax Matters Partner (TMP). Which partner, if any, must fulfill this role?
c. When is the latest date that the IRS can bring a proceeding on this issue with Jason? Assume the partnership filed the 2002 Form 1065 on April 10, 2003.
d. Assume Jason recognized that the contribution was made to a foreign charity and did not deduct it on his return. What should Jason have done when filing his 2002 tax return to indicate his disagreement with the tax treatment of the item on the Schedule K–1?

Internet Activity

Use the tax resources of the Internet to address the following questions. Do not restrict your search to the World Wide Web, but include a review of newsgroups and general reference materials, practitioner sites and resources, primary sources of the tax law, chat rooms and discussion groups, and other opportunities.

Communications

Research Problem 4. Find an article written by a tax professional discussing the merits of the family limited partnership. Write a memo to your instructor discussing one of the following issues.

a. The effects of Revenue Ruling 93–12 on the use of the entity.
b. The effects of § 704(e) on income computations for the entity.
c. The accuracy of the computations made by the author in the article.

Your memo should include a summary of the findings presented in the article and a summary and discussion of your thoughts. For example, you may wish to address situations in which family limited partnerships may be beneficial or pitfalls in structuring such an entity.

Research Problem 5. On what form or attachment does a partnership report that it has made a § 754 election? Prepare such a form using the facts of Example 28 in the text.

Communications

Research Problem 6. Find a recent Tax Court case that addresses the income allocation issue illustrated in Example 35. Summarize the case in an e-mail to your instructor.

PART 3

Advanced Jurisdictional Issues

Taxpayers today operate in a multinational economy, and they offer their services and products in many of the U.S. states. Thus, their income, property, and sales can be subjected to thousands of different taxing jurisdictions, each with its own definitions, tax formulas, and operating regulations. Part III brings to the taxpayer a review of the most common of these sets of tax rules and numerous planning ideas that can be considered.

CHAPTER 7

International Tax Principles

LEARNING OBJECTIVES

After completing Chapter 7, you should be able to:

LO.1
Describe the framework underlying the U.S. taxation of cross-border transactions.

LO.2
Apply income tax treaty provisions when determining tax consequences.

LO.3
Determine the sourcing of income and deductions.

LO.4
Explain the foreign tax credit mechanism.

LO.5
Describe the tax implications of using different currencies.

LO.6
Determine the allowed foreign earned income exclusion for U.S. workers abroad.

http://wft.swlearning.com

OUTLINE

TAX TALK

I wouldn't mind paying taxes—if I knew they were going to a friendly country.

—Dick Gregory

LO.1

Describe the framework underlying the U.S. taxation of cross-border transactions.

Overview of U.S. Taxation of Cross-Border Transactions

The global nature of the economy creates both difficulties and opportunities for taxpayers. A U.S. company may be based in the United States but have customers and distribution centers in Europe and South America, manufacturing plants in Ireland and Singapore, a research and development facility in Bermuda, and a financing operation in Switzerland. In addition to these physical locations, the company's Web-based transactions take place in a "virtual" jurisdiction claimed either by no country or by multiple countries. Consequently, the company generates revenue, incurs expenses, borrows, and lends in different currencies and pays taxes to multiple governments. Operating across multiple jurisdictions certainly creates complexity for the taxpayer. At the same time, the existence of multiple taxing jurisdictions with differing tax systems presents opportunities for the company to arrange its affairs so as to keep its worldwide tax burden to a minimum.

Cross-border transactions create the need for special tax considerations for both the United States and its trading partners. From a U.S. perspective, international tax laws should promote the global competitiveness of U.S. enterprises and at the same time protect the tax revenue base of the United States. These two objectives sometimes conflict, however. The need to deal with both objectives contributes to the complexity of the rules governing the U.S. taxation of cross-border transactions.

TAX FACT

U.S. INTERNATIONAL TRANSACTIONS, 2003

During 2003, U.S. exports and imports together amounted to more than $2.5 trillion. The following table summarizes export and import data (in millions of dollars) for that year.

Exports	
Goods	$ 713,788
Services	304,932
Total exports	$1,018,720
Imports	
Goods	$1,262,945
Services	245,687
Total imports	$1,508,632

Source: U.S. International Transactions Account Data, Bureau of Economic Analysis, U.S. Department of Commerce, March 10, 2004.

EXAMPLE 1

U.S. persons engage in activities outside the United States for many different reasons. Consider two U.S. corporations that have established sales subsidiaries in foreign countries. Gelati, Inc., operates in Italy, a high-tax country, because customers demand local attention from sales agents. Cones, Inc., operates in Barbados, a tax haven country, simply to shift income outside the United States. U.S. tax law must fairly address both situations with the same law. ■

U.S. international tax provisions are concerned primarily with two types of potential taxpayers: U.S. persons earning income from outside the United States and foreign persons earning income from inside the United States.[1] U.S. persons earning income only from inside the United States do not create any international tax issues and are taxed under the purely domestic provisions of the Internal Revenue Code. Foreign persons earning income from outside the United States are not within the U.S. taxing jurisdiction (unless this income is somehow directly connected to U.S. operations).

The U.S. taxation of international transactions can be organized in terms of "outbound" and "inbound" taxation. **Outbound taxation** refers to the U.S. taxation of foreign-source income earned by U.S. taxpayers. **Inbound taxation** refers to the U.S. taxation of U.S.-source income earned by foreign taxpayers. Figure 7–1 summarizes these concepts.

[1] The term "person" includes an individual, corporation, partnership, trust, estate, or association. § 7701(a)(1). The terms "domestic" and "foreign" are defined in §§ 7701(a)(4) and (5).

■ FIGURE 7-1
Outbound versus Inbound Taxation

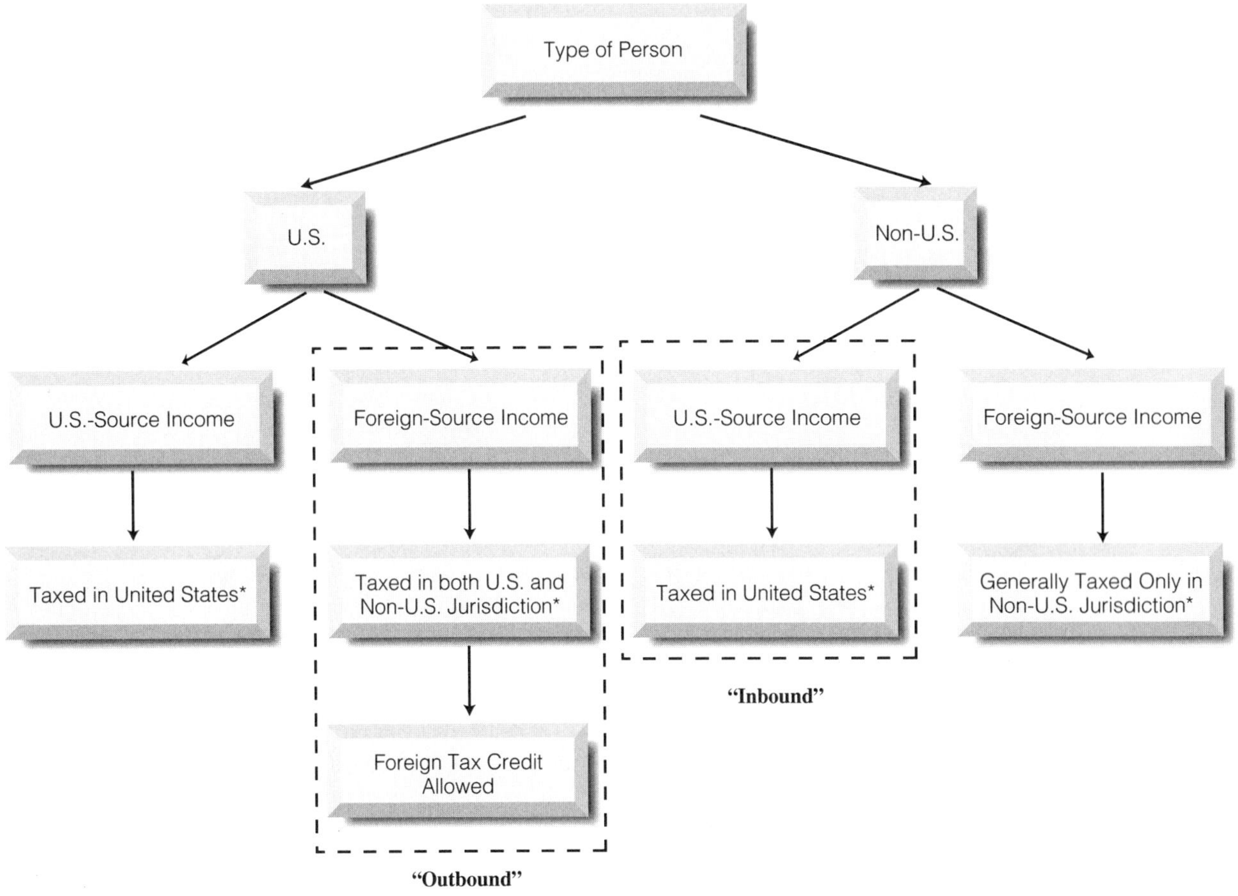

*Income may or may not be subject to tax in the non-U.S. jurisdiction, depending on local country tax law. Some U.S.-source income is exempt from tax in the United States for both U.S. and non-U.S. persons.

The United States taxes the worldwide income of U.S. taxpayers.[2] The United States claims the right to tax all of a U.S. person's income because of the protection of U.S. law provided to a person connected to the United States through citizenship, residency, or place of organization. Host-country governments also may tax some of this income if it is earned within those countries' borders, so U.S. taxpayers may be subjected to double taxation.

Two methods are available to mitigate this potential double taxation. Under the "territorial" approach, the income derived from sources outside the United

[2]Gross income for a U.S. person includes all income from whatever source derived. "Source" in this context means not only type of income (e.g., wages or interest) but geographic source as well (e.g., United States or Belgium). § 61.

States can simply be exempted from tax. The United States has adopted this approach only with regard to certain foreign earned income of U.S. citizens or residents.[3] Some countries, however, have adopted the territorial approach to the taxation of their own taxpayers.[4] A second approach, and the one adopted by the United States, is to provide a **foreign tax credit (FTC)** against U.S. taxes for income taxes paid to other countries on the foreign-source income included on the U.S. tax return. The availability of the FTC is subject to various limitations. Consequently, double taxation is not always eliminated through the credit mechanism.

EXAMPLE 2

Forrest, Inc., a U.S. corporation, provides professional engineering services to clients in London through an unincorporated branch. This branch income is taxed in the United States as part of Forrest's worldwide income, but it is also taxed in the United Kingdom. Without the availability of an FTC to mitigate this double taxation, Forrest would suffer an excessive tax burden and could not compete with local U.K. companies. ■

The United States does adopt the territorial approach in taxing foreign persons. The United States taxes such "inbound" taxpayers only on the income they earn that is connected to U.S. income-producing activities, whether the activities involve passive investments or an active trade or business. Whether foreign persons are also subject to potential tax in their home countries on their U.S. income is a function of their own local tax law. Such "inbound" taxpayers generally are subject to tax only on income earned within U.S. borders. This can be seen as a form of territorial taxation by the United States.

EXAMPLE 3

Mersy Beat, Ltd., a corporation organized in the United Kingdom, operates a branch in the United States. Although not a U.S. person, Mersy Beat is taxed in the United States on its U.S.-source business income. If Mersy Beat, Ltd., could operate free of U.S. tax, its U.S.-based competitors might face a competitive disadvantage. ■

PLANNING STRATEGIES

Form of Doing Business—Branch versus Subsidiary

FRAMEWORK FOCUS: TAX RATE

STRATEGY ➤ AVOID DOUBLE TAXATION.

U.S. taxpayers are subject to U.S. tax on their worldwide income. Non-U.S. corporations, even those controlled by U.S. shareholders, are not part of a U.S. consolidated group and therefore are not directly subject to U.S. taxation. Thus, if a U.S. corporation owns an overseas corporation, the non-U.S. corporation's income is generally not subject to U.S. taxation unless the profits are paid to the U.S. owner. Consequently, U.S. taxpayers can achieve deferral of U.S. taxes on offshore income by operating their foreign activities through subsidiary corporations organized outside the country. Note that the financial statement treatment of non-U.S. subsidiaries is quite different (see Chapter 2).

Consider the following example. USCo, a domestic corporation, operates an unincorporated manufacturing facility in Ireland. Assume that the U.S. tax rate is 35 percent and the Irish tax rate is 10 percent. USCo earns $200,000 in taxable income from its Irish operations and pays $20,000 in taxes to Ireland. Because USCo is taxed on its worldwide income,

[3]See § 911 and the related discussion later in this chapter.

[4]In some cases, countries allow the territorial exemption from home-country taxation only if the income has been subject to tax in another country. Other countries, however, exempt such income even if no source-country tax is imposed.

it must include the $200,000 on its U.S. tax return without regard to whether it brings these profits back to the home office in the United States. USCo pays an additional $50,000 in U.S. taxes on the Irish income, as illustrated below.

Income	$200,000
U.S. tax rate	× 35%
	$ 70,000
Foreign tax credit	(20,000)
Net U.S. tax	$ 50,000

Thus, USCo pays a total of $70,000 in taxes on the Irish income ($20,000 to Ireland + $50,000 in U.S. tax). Although USCo eliminates any double taxation on the $200,000 of Irish income with the use of the credit, the company has lost the benefit of the low Irish tax rate because of the residual U.S. tax. This result may be fair from a U.S. perspective. If USCo had earned this income within the United States, the total tax burden also would have been $70,000 ($200,000 × 35%). However, USCo may have difficulty competing with Irish companies that pay only 10 percent of their income in taxes.

If instead USCo operates in Ireland through a wholly owned Irish subsidiary, the Irish profits are not subject to U.S. taxation until repatriated back to the United States (for example, through dividend payments). Consequently, the potential $50,000 in residual U.S. tax is deferred until a future date.

DIGGING DEEPER 1 *Find more information on this topic at our Web site:* ***http://wft-advanced.swlearning.com.***

LO.2

Apply income tax treaty provisions when determining tax consequences.

Income Tax Treaties

It is difficult for the United States (or any country) to craft local tax laws that equitably address all the potential issues that arise when two countries attempt to tax the same income. Local law provisions such as the foreign tax credit may not fully mitigate double taxation. Furthermore, any uncertainty as to tax consequences can be an impediment to global business investment. Consequently, countries enter into **income tax treaties** with each other to provide more certainty to taxpayers.

The U.S. tax rules governing cross-border transactions are based on both the Internal Revenue Code and tax treaties. Tax treaties are bilateral agreements between countries that provide tax relief for those persons covered by the treaties. Tax treaties have equal standing with U.S. domestic tax law under the U.S. Constitution, but in most cases treaty provisions override the treatment otherwise called for under the Internal Revenue Code or foreign tax statutes.[5] More than 50 income tax treaties between the United States and other countries are in effect.

Tax treaties are the result of specific negotiations with each treaty partner, so each treaty is unique. Nevertheless, all tax treaties are organized in the same way and address similar issues. For example, all treaties include provisions regarding the taxation of investment income, business profits from a **permanent establishment (PE),** and personal services income. They provide exceptions to the general rules of the treaty for certain persons (e.g., athletes, entertainers, students, and teachers).

[5]See §§ 894(a) and 7852(d) regarding treaty and statute overlap. When a conflict exists between a treaty and a statute, the one adopted last in time will control unless it is clear that this outcome was not intended. Congress does sometimes pass laws that override existing tax treaties.

TAX FACT

The Income Tax Treaty Making Process

Income tax treaties come about through a three-step process.

Step 1. Negotiation.

- The United States starts its negotiations with the 1996 U.S. Model Income Tax Treaty. Other model treaties also exist (for example, the Organization for Economic Cooperation and Development Model Income Tax Treaty).
- Negotiations on the U.S. side are handled by the Treasury Department's Office of International Tax Counsel with help from the IRS.
- The negotiations take three or more years.
- After the negotiators agree upon the treaty language, the Secretary of State or U.S. Ambassador to that country (and counterparts from the other country) sign the treaty. Once the treaty is signed, the two countries are obligated to seek its ratification. At this point, the text of the proposed treaty is made public.
- The State Department forwards the proposed treaty to the President, who forwards it to the U.S. Senate.

Step 2. Advice and consent.

- The Senate refers the treaty to the Foreign Relations Committee.
- The Foreign Relations Committee holds a public hearing on the proposed treaty.
- After the public hearing, the Committee votes on the treaty, with four possible outcomes.
  - The Committee approves the treaty and sends a report and resolution recommending that the full Senate give its approval.
  - The Committee approves the treaty subject to specific reservations or understandings and forwards the treaty to the full Senate.
  - The Committee does not recommend ratification, and the treaty is withdrawn from consideration.
  - The treaty remains in the Senate indefinitely without action.
- Approval by the full Senate requires a two-thirds vote.

Step 3. Ratification.

- If the treaty is approved, the Senate sends it back to the President along with any added conditions.
- The President signs "instruments of ratification."
- If and when the other country completes its own ratification process, instruments of ratification are exchanged.
- The treaty usually enters into force on the date the instruments are exchanged.
- Treaties usually become effective on the first day of January following their entry into force; often portions of the treaty have different effective dates.
- Treaties are in force indefinitely if they are not explicitly terminated. Treaties are often amended following a similar ratification process.

GLOBAL TAX ISSUES

Why the Treaty Process Stalls

The United States has negotiated several income tax treaties that have never been signed or ratified (e.g., with Argentina, Bangladesh, and Brazil). The treaty process sometimes stalls for several reasons. One is the desire on the part of some less developed countries for a "tax-sparing" provision in the treaty. In other words, these countries want the United States to allow a foreign tax credit against U.S. taxes even though U.S. companies operating there actually pay no foreign taxes due to local tax reduction agreements (i.e., tax holidays). Another reason for a delay can be the exchange of information provision of the treaty. Some countries, for example, have anonymity-protecting bank rules that would preclude the exchange of information. In September 1996, the Parliament of Kazakhstan voted on a provision to eliminate secret bank accounts so that the United States–Kazakhstan income tax treaty could be ratified.

Tax treaties generally address three broad classes of income.

- Income that may be taxed without limitation in the country where earned (for example, real property income, employment income, and business profits from a permanent establishment).
- Income that may be subjected to only limited taxation in the country where earned (for example, interest, dividends, and royalties).
- Income that is taxable only in the taxpayer's home country (for example, gains from the sale of publicly traded stock).

EXAMPLE 4

Asare, Inc., a domestic corporation, is equally owned by IslandCo, a Bermuda corporation, and NordicCo, a Swedish corporation. The United States has a tax treaty with Sweden that reduces the withholding rate on dividends to 5%, but it has no tax treaty with Bermuda. Consequently, when Asare pays dividends to its owners, the payment to NordicCo is subject to only a 5% withholding tax, but the dividend payment to IslandCo is subject to the full 30% statutory withholding rate. ■

EXAMPLE 5

Anna, Ltd., is a corporation resident in the United Kingdom. Anna earns $50,000 from the sale of shares in a publicly held U.S. company. The stock sale takes place on the New York Stock Exchange and is not connected with any business activities carried on in the United States by Anna. The United States–United Kingdom tax treaty gives the United Kingdom the exclusive right to tax this income. ■

The important concept of *permanent establishment* is defined in all income tax treaties. A person has a PE within a country when its activities within that country rise beyond a minimal level. Tax treaties outline the activities that create a PE, such as maintaining an office, plant, or other fixed place of business. Treaties also specify specific activities that do not create a PE (e.g., storing goods in a warehouse or engaging in a temporary construction project). Once a person has a PE within a country, the business profits associated with the PE become subject to tax in that country.

EXAMPLE 6

Lassaline, Inc., a U.S. corporation, sells pet supplies to customers in the United States and Mexico. Lassaline has no assets or employees in Mexico. All Mexican sales transactions are conducted via the Internet or telephone from Lassaline's Texas office. Because Lassaline does not have any assets in Mexico or conduct any activities within Mexico, it does not have a Mexican PE. Consequently, Mexico does not impose an income tax on the profit

TAX FACT

U.S. Income Tax Treaties in Force

The United States has income tax treaties in force with the following countries.

Australia	France	Korea	Romania
Austria	Germany	Latvia	Russia
Barbados	Greece	Lithuania	Slovak Republic
Belgium	Hungary	Luxembourg	South Africa
Canada	Iceland	Mexico	Spain
China	India	Morocco	Sweden
Commonwealth of Independent States*	Indonesia	Netherlands	Switzerland
	Ireland	New Zealand	Thailand
Cyprus	Israel	Norway	Trinidad and Tobago
Czech Republic	Italy	Pakistan	Tunisia
Denmark	Jamaica	Philippines	Turkey
Egypt	Japan	Poland	United Kingdom
Estonia	Kazakhstan	Portugal	Venezuela
Finland			

*The income tax treaty between the United States and the former Soviet Union applies to the countries of Armenia, Azerbaijan, Belarus, Georgia, Kyrgyzstan, Moldova, Tajikistan, Turkmenistan, Ukraine, and Uzbekistan. The Commonwealth of Independent States is an association of many of the former constituent republics of the Soviet Union.

associated with Lassaline's Mexican sales. However, if Lassaline opens a sales office in Mexico, a PE will exist, and Mexico will tax the profits associated with the PE. ■

Taxpayers must be residents of a treaty country to claim treaty benefits. The residency article of the treaty typically defines a resident to include an individual, company, partnership, estate, or trust. This party is liable to tax within the country by reason of domicile, residence, place of management, or place of incorporation. In some cases, a person may appear to be a resident of multiple countries, so treaties contain "tie breaker" tests to determine a single residence for treaty purposes.

Even when a taxpayer is a bona fide resident of a treaty country, the **limitation on benefits** article of the treaty may restrict the taxpayer's ability to use the treaty to reduce taxation.[6] Many countries, including the United States, are concerned that persons who meet the technical residency tests under a treaty but are not truly residents may engage in **treaty shopping** and improperly use a treaty to avoid taxes. The limitation on benefits article generally restricts the ability to use the treaty to entities that are publicly traded or meet certain ownership or participation tests (i.e., the owners of the entity are eligible for treaty benefits if a significant portion of the entity's income is paid to persons who are eligible for treaty benefits).

EXAMPLE 7

Madison, Inc., a domestic corporation, operates Miles, Ltd., a subsidiary incorporated in Bermuda. Any U.S-source royalty payments Madison makes to Miles are subject to a 30%

[6] The United States also provides certain statutory or regulatory limitations on the use of treaty benefits. For example, see § 894(c) regarding the use of treaties for payments to or from hybrid entities and Reg. § 1.881–3 regarding the use of intermediate entities in a series of payments.

BRIDGE DISCIPLINE

Bridge to International Law

Income tax treaties are simply one sort of international "contract" that the United States enters into with other countries. Treaties also exist for nonincome tax concerns, intercountry trade, shipping, aviation, information exchange, and military armaments. The following are examples of the types of treaties the United States has entered.

- Friendship, navigation and commerce treaties.
- Bilateral investment treaties.
- Multilateral trade agreements.
- Regional free trade agreements.
- Treaties on the nonproliferation of nuclear weapons.
- Estate and gift tax treaties.
- Tax information exchange agreements.
- International shipping and aviation agreements.
- International Social Security totalization agreements.

withholding tax in the United States because no treaty exists between the United States and Bermuda. Instead of owning Miles directly, Madison creates BethCo in the Netherlands, which in turn owns Miles. Madison pays the U.S.-source royalties to BethCo. Because BethCo is a resident of the Netherlands, the United States–Netherlands treaty exempts the payment from any withholding tax. However, if BethCo does not meet the treaty's limitation on benefits tests, the treaty will not apply, and the full 30% withholding tax will be imposed on the royalty payments. For example, if BethCo pays all its income to Miles, the limitation on benefits test will not be met. ■

LO.3

Determine the sourcing of income and deductions.

Sourcing of Income and Deductions

The sourcing of income and deductions inside or outside the United States has a direct bearing on a number of tax provisions affecting both U.S. and non-U.S. taxpayers. For example, non-U.S. taxpayers generally are taxed only on income sourced inside the United States, and U.S. taxpayers receive relief from double taxation under the foreign tax credit rules based on their foreign-source income. Accordingly, an examination of sourcing rules is a good starting point in addressing international tax issues.

GROSS INCOME

A number of specific provisions contained in §§ 861 through 865 address the income-sourcing rules for all types of gross income. Although sometimes complex and subject to various exceptions, these sourcing rules generally assign income to a source based on the location where the economic activity producing the income took place. In some cases, this relationship is clear, but in others the connection is more obscure.

EXAMPLE 8

Snowball, Inc., a U.S. corporation, provides golf lessons to customers in Florida and in Australia. These services are sourced based on the place where the activity is performed. The services performed in Florida create U.S.-source income, and those performed in Australia produce foreign-source income. Because Snowball, Inc., is a U.S. person, all the income, U.S. and foreign source, is subject to U.S. taxation. But the foreign-source portion is important in determining any available foreign tax credits for Snowball. ■

EXAMPLE 9

JenCo, Inc., a U.S. corporation, receives interest income from LeeCo, a foreign corporation, based on LeeCo bonds owned by JenCo. JenCo purchased the bonds in the United States and receives all payments in the United States. At first glance, it appears that all the activities related to earning the interest income take place in the United States. Nevertheless, the interest income is treated as foreign source because it is presumed that LeeCo, as a non-U.S. person, earned the income with which to pay the interest from its business activities, all of which are presumed to take place outside the United States. ■

The determination of the source of income depends on the type of income realized (e.g., income from the sale of property versus income for the use of property). This makes the classification of income an important consideration. Section 861 contains source rules for most types of income. Other rules pertaining to the source of income are found in §§ 862–865.

Interest. Interest income received from the U.S. government, from the District of Columbia, and from noncorporate U.S. residents or domestic corporations is sourced to the United States. There are a few exceptions to this rule. Certain interest received from a U.S. corporation that earned 80 percent or more of its active business income from foreign sources over the prior three-year period is treated as foreign-source income. Interest received on amounts deposited with a foreign branch of a U.S. corporation is treated as foreign-source income if the branch is engaged in the commercial banking business.

EXAMPLE 10

Bob holds a bond issued by BoxCo, a domestic corporation. For the immediately preceding three tax years, 87% of BoxCo's gross income has been active foreign business income. The interest income that Bob receives for the current tax year from BoxCo is foreign-source income. ■

Dividends. Dividends received from domestic corporations are sourced to the United States. Generally, dividends paid by a non-U.S. corporation create foreign-source income. An exception to this rule applies, however, if 25 percent or more of the payor corporation's gross income for the three tax years immediately preceding the current tax year was effectively connected with the conduct of a U.S. trade or business. In this case, a portion of the dividends received in the tax year is U.S.-source income. This portion is equal to the proportion of gross income effectively connected with the conduct of a U.S. trade or business for the immediately preceding three-year period.

EXAMPLE 11

Laura receives dividend income from the following corporations for the current tax year.

Dividend Amount	Corporation	Effectively Connected U.S. Income for Past 3 Years	U.S.-Source Income
$500	Green (domestic)	85%	$500
600	Brown (domestic)	13%	600
300	Orange (foreign)	92%	276

Because Green Corporation and Brown Corporation are domestic corporations, the dividends they pay are U.S.-source income. Orange Corporation meets the 25% test. Specifically, 92% of Orange's business income over the prior three years was effectively connected with a U.S. trade or business. Thus, 92% of the dividend from Orange is U.S.-source income. ■

Personal Services Income. The source of income from personal services is determined by the location where the services are performed (inside or outside the United States). A limited commercial traveler exception is available. Under this exception, personal services income must meet all the following requirements to avoid being classified as U.S.-source income.

- The services must be performed by a nonresident alien who is in the United States for 90 days or less during the taxable year.
- The compensation for the services performed in the United States may not exceed $3,000 in total.
- The services must be performed on behalf of:
  - a nonresident alien, a foreign partnership, or a foreign corporation that is not engaged in a U.S. trade or business, or
  - an office or place of business maintained offshore by an individual who is a citizen or resident of the United States, a domestic partnership, or a domestic corporation.

Income tax treaties often modify this exception to allow an unlimited amount of income and presence in the United States for up to 183 days.

EXAMPLE 12

Mark, a nonresident alien, is an engineer employed by a foreign oil company. He spent four weeks in the United States arranging the purchase of field equipment for his company. His salary for the four weeks was $3,500. Even though the oil company is not engaged in a U.S. trade or business, and Mark was in the United States for less than 90 days during the taxable year, the income is U.S.-source income because it exceeds $3,000. If Mark is a resident of a treaty country that provides for an unlimited amount of income, the $3,500 is exempt from U.S. income taxation. ■

The issue of whether income is derived from the performance of personal services is important in determining the income's source. The courts have held that a corporation can perform personal services.[7] If payment is received for services performed partly inside and partly outside the United States, the income must be allocated for source purposes on some reasonable basis that clearly reflects income under the facts and circumstances.[8] The number of days worked in each country is generally acceptable.

Rents and Royalties. The source of income received for the use of tangible property is the country in which the property is located. The source of income received for the use of intangible property (e.g., patents, copyrights, secret processes, and formulas) is the country in which the property is used.

Sale or Exchange of Property. Generally, the location of real property determines the source of any income derived from the property. Income from the disposition of U.S. real property interests is U.S.-source income. The source of income from the sale of personal property (assets other than real property) depends on several factors, including the following.

[7]See *British Timken Ltd.,* 12 T.C. 880 (1949); Rev.Rul. 60–55, 1960–1 C.B. 270.

[8]Reg. § 1.861–4(b). See *Stemkowski,* 76 T.C. 252 (1981).

- Whether the property was produced by the seller.
- The type of property sold (e.g., inventory or a capital asset).
- The residence of the seller.

Generally, income, gain, or profit from the sale of personal property is sourced according to the residence of the seller. Income from the sale of purchased inventory, however, is sourced in the country in which the sale takes place.[9]

When the seller has produced the inventory property, the income must be apportioned between the country of production and the country of sale. Gross income is sourced under a 50–50 allocation method unless the taxpayer elects to use the independent factory price (IFP) method or the separate books and records method. The IFP method may be elected only where an IFP exists.[10] If the manufacturer or producer regularly sells to wholly independent distributors, this can establish an independent factory or production price.

Under § 865, income from the sale of personal property other than inventory is sourced at the residence of the seller unless one of the following exceptions applies.

- Gain on the sale of depreciable personal property is sourced according to prior depreciation, to the extent of the deductions. Any excess gain is sourced the same as the sale of inventory.
- Gain on the sale of intangibles is sourced according to prior amortization, to the extent of the deductions. Contingent payments, however, are sourced as royalty income.
- Gain attributable to an office or fixed place of business maintained outside the United States by a U.S. resident is foreign-source income.
- Income or gain attributable to an office or fixed place of business maintained in the United States by a nonresident is U.S.-source income.

The sourcing of losses is complicated and depends on the nature of the property. Different rules exist for the disposition of stock versus other personal property.[11]

PLANNING STRATEGIES

Sourcing Income from Inventory

FRAMEWORK FOCUS: TAX RATE

STRATEGY ➤ CONTROL THE CHARACTER OF INCOME AND DEDUCTIONS.

Generally, income from the sale of personal property is sourced according to the residence of the seller under § 865. Several important exceptions exist for inventory. Under the **title passage rule,** income from the sale of purchased inventory is sourced in the country in which the sale takes place. This rule provides the taxpayer with flexibility regarding tax sourcing and allows the creation of zero-taxed foreign-source income.

Assume that USCo, a domestic corporation, purchases inventory for resale from unrelated parties and sells the inventory to customers in the United States and Brazil. If title on the Brazilian sales passes in the United States (i.e., risks of loss shift to the Brazilian customers at the shipping point), the inventory income is U.S. source. If title passes outside the United States (e.g., at the customer's warehouse in Brazil), the inventory income is foreign source.

[9] §§ 861(a)(6) and 865. The sale is deemed to take place where title passes. See Reg. § 1.861–7(c) regarding title passage. There has been considerable conflict in this area of tax law. See, for example, *Liggett Group, Inc.*, 58 TCM 1167, T.C.Memo. 1990–18.

[10] § 863(b)(2), Reg. § 1.863–3, and Notice 89–10, 1989–1 C.B. 631.

[11] See Reg. § 1.861–8(e)(7) and Temp.Reg. § 1.865–1T(a)(1). See Reg. §§ 1.865–(2)(a)(1) and (2) regarding the source of losses on the disposition of stock.

Although the Code identifies the income item as foreign source, this income is likely not subject to any Brazilian tax because USCo has no employees, assets, or activities in Brazil. Although the income is subject to U.S. tax, when title passes outside the United States, USCo has generated foreign-source income with no corresponding foreign income tax. This will prove useful in managing USCo's ability to use foreign tax credits, as discussed later in this chapter.

When a taxpayer both produces and sells inventory, the income must be apportioned between the country of production and the country of sale. As allowed by § 863(b), taxpayers often use a 50–50 allocation method that assigns 50 percent of the profits from the sale to the location of the production assets and 50 percent to the location where title passes.

Assume USCo manufactures inventory in its Texas plant and sells the inventory to customers in Mexico. Regardless of the actual economic profit relationship between the manufacturing and selling activities, 50 percent of the profit on the Mexican sales can be assigned to foreign-source income simply by passing title outside the United States.

Transportation and Communication Income. Income from transportation beginning *and* ending in the United States is U.S.-source income. Fifty percent of the income from transportation beginning *or* ending in the United States is U.S.-source income, unless the U.S. point is only an intermediate stop. Income from space and ocean activities conducted outside the jurisdiction of any country is sourced according to the residence of the person conducting the activity.

International communication income derived by a U.S. person is sourced 50 percent in the United States when transmission is between the United States and a foreign country. International communication income derived by foreign persons is foreign-source income unless it is attributable to an office or other fixed place of business in the United States. In that case, it is U.S.-source income.

Software Income. Income from the sale or license of software is sourced depending on how the income is classified. Under Regulation § 1.861–18, a transfer of software is classified as either:

- the transfer of a copyright (e.g., the right to the computer program itself), to be sourced using the royalty rules,
- the transfer of a copyrighted article (the right to use a copy of the computer program), to be sourced using the personal property sales rules, or
- the lease of a copyrighted article, to be sourced using the rental income rules.

ALLOCATION AND APPORTIONMENT OF DEDUCTIONS

In addition to sourcing income, the U.S. rules require taxpayers to assign deductions to U.S.- or foreign-source categories. Deductions that are directly related to an activity or property first are allocated to the classes of income to which they directly relate. This is followed by an apportionment between the U.S. and foreign groupings using some reasonable basis (e.g., revenue, gross profit, assets, units sold, time spent). If a deduction is not definitely related to any class of gross income, the deduction is first assigned to all classes of gross income and then apportioned between U.S.- and foreign-source income.

EXAMPLE 13

PJ, Inc., a domestic corporation, has $2 million gross income and a $50,000 expense, all related to real estate sales and rental activities. The expense is allocated and apportioned using gross income as a basis.

TAX IN THE NEWS

Sourcing Income in Cyberspace

The use of the Internet in more consumer and business transactions is posing problems for the taxing authorities. Consumers purchase books, music, clothing, and food from Internet retailers. Businesses negotiate with suppliers via online auctions of products and services. Consultants provide services to their clients over the Web. Almost all transactions have a counterpart that takes place in cyberspace. The current income-sourcing rules were developed long before the existence of the Internet, and taxing authorities are finding it challenging to apply these rules to Internet transactions.

Where does a sale take place when the Web server is in the Cayman Islands, the seller is in Singapore, and the customer is in Texas? Where is a service performed when all activities take place over the Web? These questions and more will have to be answered by the United States and its trading partners as the Internet economy grows in size and importance.

	Gross Income			Apportionment	
	Foreign	U.S.	Allocation	Foreign	U.S.
Sales	$1,000,000	$500,000	$37,500*	$25,000	$12,500**
Rentals	400,000	100,000	12,500	10,000	2,500†
			$50,000	$35,000	$15,000

*$50,000 × ($1,500,000/$2,000,000).
**$37,500 × ($500,000/$1,500,000).
†$12,500 × ($100,000/$500,000).

If PJ could show that $45,000 of the expense was directly related to sales income, the $45,000 would be allocated directly to that class of gross income, with the remainder allocated and apportioned between U.S. and foreign source ratably based on gross income. ■

Many deductions may be allocated and apportioned based on any reasonable method the taxpayer chooses.[12] However, the U.S. tax rules impose a specific method for certain types of deductions, including interest, research and development (R & D) expenses, certain stewardship expenses, legal and accounting fees, state income taxes, and losses.

Interest expense is allocated and apportioned based on the theory that money is fungible. For example, if a taxpayer borrows to support its manufacturing activity, this frees up other funds for use to support its investment activities. Accordingly, the tax rules require that interest expense be allocated and apportioned to all the activities and property of the taxpayer, regardless of the specific purpose for incurring the debt on which the interest is paid. Taxpayers must allocate and apportion interest expense on the basis of assets, using either the fair market value or the tax book value of the assets.[13]

EXAMPLE 14

Wilco, Inc., a domestic corporation, generates both U.S.-source and foreign-source gross income for the current year. Wilco's assets (tax book value) are as follows.

[12] Reg. § 1.861–8.

[13] Reg. § 1.861–9T.

Assets generating U.S.-source income	$18,000,000
Assets generating foreign-source income	5,000,000
	$23,000,000

Wilco incurs interest expense of $800,000 for the current year. Using the tax book value method, the interest expense is apportioned to foreign-source income as follows.

$$\frac{\$5{,}000{,}000 \text{ (foreign assets)}}{\$23{,}000{,}000 \text{ (total assets)}} \times \$800{,}000 \text{ (interest expense)} = \$173{,}913.$$

Although U.S. companies incur about 90 percent of their R & D expenditures at U.S. facilities, several billion dollars are spent on overseas R & D each year. A portion of a U.S. company's R & D expenditures must be treated as foreign-source expense if the R & D relates to foreign-source product sales.

TRANSFER PRICING CONSIDERATIONS

Taxpayers may be tempted to manipulate the source of income and the allocation of deductions arbitrarily, to minimize taxation. This manipulation is more easily accomplished between or among related persons. The IRS uses § 482 to counter such uses of **transfer pricing.** That provision gives the IRS the power to reallocate gross income, deductions, credits, or allowances between or among organizations or businesses owned or controlled directly or indirectly by the same interests. This can be done whenever the IRS determines that reallocation is necessary to prevent the evasion of taxes or to reflect income more clearly. Section 482 is a "one-edged sword" available only to the IRS. The taxpayer typically cannot invoke it to reallocate income and expenses.[14]

The reach of § 482 is quite broad. The IRS takes the position that a corporation and its sole shareholder who works full-time for the corporation can be treated as two separate businesses for purposes of § 482.[15] Two unrelated shareholders who each owned 50 percent of a corporation were held to be acting in concert for their common good and, thus, together controlled the corporation.[16] In applying § 482, an **arm's length price** must be determined to assign the correct profits to related entities. Several alternative methods can be used in determining an arm's length price on the sale of tangible or intangible property. The major problem with most pricing methods is that uncontrolled comparable transactions are needed as a benchmark.

An accuracy-related penalty of 20 percent is provided by § 6662 for net § 482 transfer price adjustments (changes in profit allocations by the IRS) for a taxable year that exceed the lesser of $5 million or 10 percent of the taxpayer's gross receipts. In addition, there is a 40 percent penalty for "gross misstatements" of taxable income traceable to transfer pricing.

LO.4

Explain the foreign tax credit mechanism.

The Foreign Tax Credit

As discussed earlier, the United States retains the right to tax its citizens and residents on their worldwide taxable income. This approach can result in double taxation, presenting a potential problem to U.S. persons who operate abroad. To

[14]Reg. § 1.482–1(a)(3).

[15]Rev.Rul. 88–38, 1988–1 C.B. 246. But see *Foglesong v. Comm.*, 82–2 USTC ¶9650, 50 AFTR2d 82–6016, 691 F.2d 848 (CA–7, 1982), *rev'g* 77 T.C. 1102 (1981).

[16]See *B. Forman Co. v. Comm.*, 72–1 USTC ¶9182, 29 AFTR2d 72–403, 453 F.2d 1144 (CA–2, 1972).

GLOBAL TAX ISSUES

APAs Reduce Uncertainty in Pricing Disputes

As an aid to reducing transfer pricing disputes, the IRS initiated the Advance Pricing Agreement (APA) program whereby the taxpayer can propose a transfer pricing method for certain international transactions. The taxpayer provides relevant data, which are then evaluated by the IRS. If accepted, the APA provides a safe-harbor transfer pricing method for the taxpayer.

The first APA (for Apple Computer) was approved in January 1991. The IRS reports that 492 APAs have been approved and 229 others are in negotiation. The taxpayers participating in the APA program come from many different industries. The five most represented industries are financial institutions, computer equipment and software, chemicals, transportation equipment, and electrical equipment.

Only 10 percent of the largest taxpayers involved in international transactions have participated in the APA process. However, the volume of intercompany transactions represented by these taxpayers constitutes 42 percent of the total dollar value of international intercompany transactions.

The APA process is not simple or quick. The IRS reports that the average time to complete an APA is over 32 months.

SOURCES: IRS's Advance Pricing Agreement Program, General Accounting Office Report, August 2000 and Announcement 2004–26, 2004–15 I.R.B.

reduce the possibility of double taxation, Congress enacted the foreign tax credit (FTC) provisions. Under these provisions, a qualified taxpayer is allowed a tax credit for foreign income taxes paid or accrued. The credit is a dollar-for-dollar reduction of U.S. income tax liability.

EXAMPLE 15

Warren, Inc., a U.S. corporation, has a branch operation in Mexico from which it earns taxable income of $750,000 for the current year. Warren pays income tax of $150,000 on these earnings to the Mexican tax authorities. Warren must also include the $750,000 in gross income for U.S. tax purposes. Before considering the FTC, Warren owes $255,000 in U.S. income taxes on this foreign-source income. Thus, total taxes on the $750,000 could equal $405,000 ($150,000 + $255,000), a 54% effective rate. But Warren takes an FTC of $150,000 against its U.S. tax liability on the foreign-source income. Warren's total taxes on the $750,000 now are $255,000 ($150,000 + $105,000), a 34% effective rate. ■

The FTC is elective for any particular tax year. If the taxpayer does not "choose" to take the FTC, § 164 allows a deduction for foreign taxes paid or incurred. A taxpayer cannot take a credit and a deduction for the same foreign income taxes, and in most situations the FTC is more valuable to the taxpayer.

THE DIRECT CREDIT

U.S. taxpayers may claim FTCs for foreign taxes they pay directly or through withholding as so-called direct credits.[17] If a U.S. taxpayer operates in a foreign country through a branch, the direct credit is available for foreign taxes paid.

[17]§§ 901 and 903.

TAX FACT

INCOME SUBJECT TO U.S. TAX, FOREIGN-SOURCE TAXABLE INCOME, CURRENT-YEAR FOREIGN TAXES, AND FOREIGN TAX CREDIT, TAX YEARS 1993–1998

The money amounts in the following table are in millions of dollars.

			U.S. Income Tax before Credits		Foreign-Source Taxable Income (Less Loss)		Current-Year Foreign Taxes		Foreign Tax Credit Claimed	
Tax Year	Number of U.S. Corporation Returns	Income Subject to U.S. Tax	Amount	As a Percentage of Income Subject to U.S. Tax	Amount	As a Percentage of Income Subject to U.S. Tax	Amount	As a Percentage of Foreign-Source Taxable Income	Amount	As a Percentage of U.S. Income Tax before Credits
1993	6,322	$228,688	$ 81,913	35.8%	$ 94,687	41.4%	$23,716	25.0%	$22,895	28.0%
1994	7,199	255,439	90,786	35.5	101,521	39.7	26,470	26.1	25,419	28.0
1995	6,710	303,308	107,996	35.6	120,518	39.7	30,930	25.7	30,416	28.2
1996	6,100	370,049	130,748	35.3	150,826	40.8	41,177	27.3	40,255	30.8
1997	6,569	410,126	144,779	35.3	157,989	38.5	45,080	28.5	42,223	29.2
1998	5,927	377,129	132,740	35.2	147,129	35.9	47,576	32.3	37,338	28.1

Source: IRS, *Statistics of Income Bulletin*, Fall 2002. Publication 1136 (Rev. 12–2002), Figure A.

EXAMPLE 16

Scott, Inc., a domestic corporation, operates a branch in Norway. Scott pays income tax to Norway based on the income earned within the branch. Because the branch is a part of Scott, Inc., and not a separate legal entity, the Norwegian taxes paid on the branch income are considered directly imposed on Scott, Inc. Scott also receives dividends from a 5% ownership in a German corporation. Germany requires that 15% of the dividends be withheld at the source by the German corporation. Although Scott, Inc., does not directly pay the withholding tax, the tax is a direct tax because it is ultimately imposed directly on Scott's dividend income. ■

THE INDIRECT CREDIT

If a U.S. corporation operates in a foreign country through a foreign subsidiary, the direct credit is not available for foreign taxes paid by the foreign corporation. An indirect or **deemed-paid credit** is available under § 902 to U.S. corporate taxpayers that receive actual or constructive dividends from non-U.S. corporations that have paid foreign income taxes. These foreign taxes are deemed paid by the corporate shareholders in the same proportion as the dividends actually or constructively received bear to the foreign corporation's post-1986 undistributed earnings and profits (E & P).

$$\text{§ 902 Deemed-paid credit} = \frac{\text{Actual or constructive dividend}}{\text{Post-1986 undistributed E \& P}} \times \begin{matrix}\text{Post-1986}\\ \text{foreign income taxes}\end{matrix}$$

If a U.S. taxpayer claims a deemed-paid credit, § 78 requires the corporation to *gross up* (add to gross income) the dividend income by the amount of deemed-paid credit.

■ FIGURE 7–2
Deemed-Paid Foreign Tax Credit Ownership Requirements

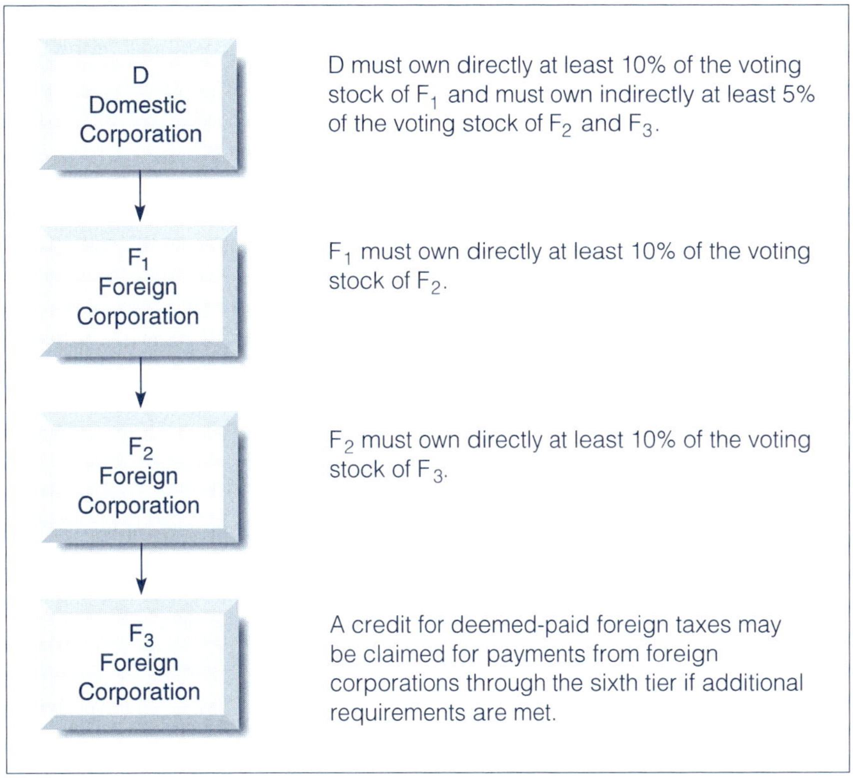

EXAMPLE 17

Lawn, Inc., a domestic corporation, owns 50% of Tree, Inc., a foreign corporation. Lawn receives a dividend of $120,000 from Tree. Tree paid foreign taxes of $500,000 on post-1986 E & P. Tree's post-1986 E & P totals $1.2 million. Lawn's deemed-paid foreign taxes for FTC purposes are $50,000.

Cash dividend from Tree	$120,000
Deemed-paid foreign taxes [($120,000/$1,200,000) × $500,000]	50,000
Gross income to Lawn	$170,000

Lawn includes $170,000 in gross income for the year. As a result of the dividend received, Lawn can claim a credit for the $50,000 in deemed foreign taxes paid. ■

Certain ownership requirements must be met before the indirect credit is available to a domestic corporation. The domestic corporation must own 10 percent or more of the voting stock of the foreign corporation. The credit is also available for deemed-paid foreign taxes of second- and third-tier foreign corporations if the 10 percent ownership requirement is met at the second- and third-tier level. A 5 percent indirect ownership requirement must also be met. The indirect credit is also available for foreign taxes paid by fourth- through sixth-tier foreign corporations if additional requirements are met, including the requirement that these corporations be **controlled foreign corporations (CFCs).**[18] The § 902 ownership requirements are summarized in Figure 7–2.

[18]See Chapter 8 for a discussion of CFCs.

The deemed-paid foreign tax credit is available only to corporate taxpayers (with limited exceptions for certain deemed dividends received by individual shareholders of a CFC). Deemed-paid foreign tax credits are available only for use as credits; in contrast to direct credits, there is no deduction option.

FOREIGN TAX CREDIT LIMITATION

The United States does not automatically grant an FTC for all foreign taxes paid, and there are limits on the amount of foreign taxes that can be taken as a credit. First, for a foreign levy to qualify for the FTC, it must be a tax, and its predominant character must be that of an income tax in the U.S. sense.[19] A levy is a tax if it is a compulsory payment, rather than a payment for a specific economic benefit such as the right to extract oil. A tax's predominant character is that of an income tax in the U.S. sense if it reaches realized net gain. A tax that is levied *in lieu of* an income tax is also creditable.[20]

EXAMPLE 18

KeenCo, a domestic corporation, generates $2 million of taxable income from operations in Gatorvakia, a foreign country. Gatorvakia law levies a tax on the gross bank deposits generated in Gatorvakia by foreign residents, plus one-half percent of the resident's net assets located in Gatorvakia. KeenCo is not allowed an FTC for taxes paid to Gatorvakia, because the foreign tax is not enough like an income tax. ■

EXAMPLE 19

LyleCo, a domestic corporation, is engaged in the oil extraction business in a foreign country where all oil reserves are owned by the government. The country imposes a tax on LyleCo equal to $5 per barrel of oil removed from any well. This tax does not meet the definition of an income tax in the U.S. sense because LyleCo receives a direct economic benefit from its payments (i.e., the right to extract and sell the oil). The tax will be treated as a royalty payment for the oil, and LyleCo will receive a deduction for the payments rather than an FTC. ■

For purposes of the FTC, foreign taxes are attributable to the year in which they are paid or accrued. Under § 905, taxpayers using the cash method of accounting for tax purposes may elect to take the FTC in the year in which the foreign taxes accrue. The election is binding on the taxpayer for the year in which it is made and for all subsequent years.

A second and more critical limitation is that the allowed FTC in any tax year is limited to the U.S. tax imposed on the foreign-source income included on the U.S. tax return.[21] Thus, taxpayers are allowed a credit for the lesser of the foreign income taxes paid or accrued, or the following limitation.

$$\text{FTC limit} = \frac{\text{Foreign-source taxable income}}{\text{Worldwide taxable income}} \times \text{U.S. tax liability before FTC}$$

Worldwide taxable income is the total taxable income reported on the taxpayer's U.S. tax return, not the total worldwide income of a group of related domestic and foreign entities. Any potential FTCs disallowed because of the FTC limitation may be carried back two years or forward five years, subject to the FTC limits in those tax years.

EXAMPLE 20

RoyCo, Inc., a domestic corporation, invests in the bonds of non-U.S. corporations. RoyCo's worldwide taxable income for the tax year is $1.2 million, consisting of $1 million U.S. sales

[19] Reg. § 1.901–2.

[20] § 903 and Reg. § 1.903–1.

[21] §§ 901, 902, and 903 provide definitions of creditable foreign taxes. Section 904 contains the FTC limitation rules.

profits and $200,000 of interest income from foreign sources. Foreign taxes of $90,000 were withheld by tax authorities on these interest payments. RoyCo's U.S. tax before the FTC is $420,000. Its FTC is limited to $70,000 [$420,000 × ($200,000/$1,200,000)]. Thus, RoyCo's net U.S. tax liability is $350,000 after allowing the $70,000 FTC. The remaining $20,000 of foreign taxes may be carried back or forward. ■

PLANNING STRATEGIES

Overcoming the FTC Limitation

FRAMEWORK FOCUS: TAX CREDITS

STRATEGY ➤ MAXIMIZE TAX CREDITS.

The FTC limitation can prevent the total amount of foreign taxes paid in high-tax jurisdictions from being credited. Taxpayers may be able to overcome this problem by generating additional foreign-source income that is subject to no, or low, foreign taxation. A U.S. taxpayer's ability to use FTCs is directly related to its level of foreign-source income relative to total taxable income. To the extent that a U.S. taxpayer can keep the average tax rate on its foreign-source income at or below the U.S. tax rate on such income, the foreign taxes are fully creditable. Consequently, combining high- and low-taxed foreign-source income is an important planning objective.

Compare the two situations below where a U.S. corporation's FTC limitation differs depending on the corporation's mix of high- and low-taxed income. In the first scenario, the corporation has only $500,000 of high-taxed foreign-source income. In the second scenario, the corporation also has $100,000 of low-taxed foreign-source interest income.

	Only High-Taxed Income	**With Low-Taxed Interest Income**
Foreign-source income	$500,000	$600,000
Foreign taxes	275,000	280,000
U.S.-source income	700,000	700,000
U.S. taxes (35%)	420,000	455,000
FTC limitation	175,000*	210,000**

*$420,000 × ($500,000/$1,200,000).
**$455,000 × ($600,000/$1,300,000).

The corporation's actual foreign taxes increase by only $5,000 ($280,000 versus $275,000), but its FTC limitation increases by $35,000 (from $175,000 to $210,000). The ability to "cross-credit" high- and low-taxed foreign-source income is available only when the foreign-source income is all classified within the same category.

To limit the ability of U.S. taxpayers to cross-credit foreign taxes, the FTC rules provide for several **separate foreign tax credit limitation categories** (or baskets). In any tax year, taxpayers are allowed to credit the lesser of foreign income taxes paid or accrued or the FTC limit *within each separate basket*. The separate FTC limitation categories for different types of income each use this same basic FTC limitation formula. The separate limitation categories affect the amount of FTC that can be taken by generally segregating income subject to a high level of foreign tax from lower-taxed foreign income.

Section 904(d) provides separate limitation baskets for the following categories of income.

- Passive income.
- High withholding tax interest.
- Financial services income.
- Shipping income.
- 10/50 company dividends (dividends from a foreign corporation owned at least 10 percent but not more than 50 percent). A look-through rule applies

to dividends paid by 10/50 companies from E & P accumulated in tax years beginning after 2002. The dividends are allocated among the separate baskets based on the ratio of the 10/50 company's post-2002 E & P in that basket to the company's total post-2002 E & P. Dividends paid by 10/50 companies out of E & P accumulated in taxable years beginning before 2003 are assigned to a single 10/50 company basket that applies to all 10/50 companies.
- Dividends from a domestic international sales corporation (DISC) or former DISC to the extent they are treated as foreign-source income.
- Taxable income attributable to foreign trade income under § 923(b).
- Distributions from a foreign sales corporation (FSC) or former FSC out of E & P attributable to foreign trade income or qualified interest and carrying charges under § 263(c).

Any income that does not fit into one of the specific categories falls into the general (or residual) category. The general limitation basket is where most active income is classified and provides the best opportunity for combining high- and low-taxed foreign-source income. The separate limitation baskets are diagrammed in Concept Summary 7–1.

EXAMPLE 21

DavidCo, Inc., a U.S. corporation, has a foreign branch in Germany that earns taxable income of $1,500,000 from manufacturing operations and $600,000 from shipping activities. DavidCo also earns German-source high withholding tax interest of $100,000. DavidCo pays foreign taxes of $600,000 (40%), $300,000 (50%), and $15,000 (15%), respectively, on this foreign-source income. The corporation also earns $4,000,000 of U.S.-source taxable income, resulting in worldwide taxable income of $6,200,000. DavidCo's U.S. taxes before the FTC are $2,170,000 (at 35%). The following tabulation illustrates the effect of the separate limitation baskets on cross-crediting.

Separate Foreign Income Category	Net Taxable Amount	Foreign Taxes	U.S. Tax before FTC at 35%	FTC Allowed with Separate Limits
Manufacturing	$1,500,000	$600,000	$525,000	$525,000
Shipping	600,000	300,000	210,000	210,000
High withholding tax interest	100,000	15,000	35,000	15,000
Total	$2,200,000	$915,000	$770,000	$750,000

Without the separate limitation provisions, the FTC would be the lesser of (1) $915,000 foreign taxes paid or accrued or (2) $770,000 [$2,170,000 × ($2,200,000/$6,200,000)]. The separate limitation provisions reduce the total FTC by $20,000, to $750,000. The effect of the separate limitation rules is that the foreign-source income taxed at the foreign tax rates of 40% and 50% cannot be aggregated with foreign-source income taxed at only 15%. ■

In the case of a CFC, the look-through rules classify any dividend (actual or deemed), interest, rent, or royalty income received from the CFC into separate limitation baskets as if such income were earned directly by the U.S. shareholders of the CFC. A partner's distributive share of partnership income is also generally categorized in separate limitation baskets based on the character of the partnership's income. Additionally, interest, rent, or royalty payments to certain partners are eligible for look-through treatment.

The FTC limitations can result in unused (noncredited) foreign taxes for the tax year. A two-year carryback and a five-year carryforward of excess foreign taxes

Concept Summary 7–1

Foreign Tax Credit: Separate Income Limitations

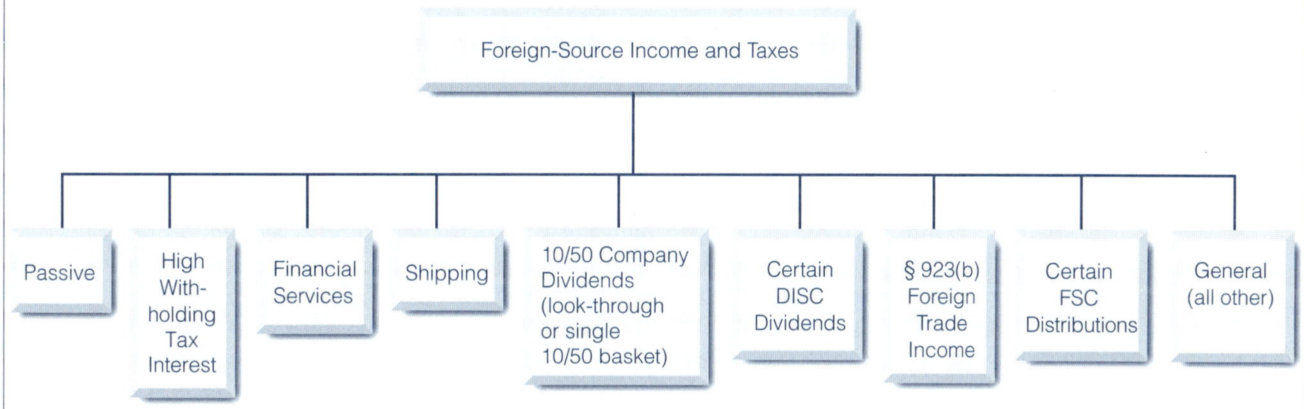

are allowed. The taxes can be credited in years when the formula limitation for that year exceeds the foreign taxes attributable to the same tax year. The carryover provisions are available only within a specific basket. In other words, excess foreign taxes in one basket cannot be carried over unless there is an excess limitation in the same basket for the carryover year.

LOSSES AND THE FTC

U.S. taxpayers that hold foreign investments or operations directly (e.g., through a branch operation) or through a conduit entity (e.g., a partnership) have the opportunity to offset foreign losses against U.S.-source income, thereby reducing the U.S. income tax due on U.S.-source income. If the net foreign-source income of a U.S. person is negative, this creates an **overall foreign loss (OFL)** under § 904(f). If the foreign country in which the loss is generated (sourced) taxes subsequent income from these foreign operations, the FTC could reduce or eliminate any future U.S. tax on the foreign-source income.

To prevent this loss of tax revenue to the United States, the Code provides that the overall foreign losses should be recaptured as U.S.-source income for FTC purposes. This is accomplished by reducing the numerator of the FTC limitation formula. Foreign-source taxable income is reduced by the lesser of (1) the remaining unrecaptured overall foreign loss or (2) 50 percent of foreign-source taxable income for the taxable year (unless the taxpayer elects to recapture a greater percentage). Unrecaptured foreign losses are carried over indefinitely until recaptured.

EXAMPLE 22

Shannon, Inc., a domestic corporation, operates a branch in Japan. The earnings record of the branch is as follows.

Year	Taxable Income (Loss)	Foreign Taxes Paid
2001	($ 15,000)	–0–
2002	(20,000)	–0–
2003	(20,000)	–0–
2004	40,000	$20,000

For 2001–2004, Shannon has U.S.-source taxable income of $300,000 each year. Shannon's 2004 U.S. tax liability before the FTC is $119,000. Its overall foreign loss is $55,000 for 2001–2003. The FTC limitation for 2004 is $7,000 {$119,000 × [$40,000 – (50% × $40,000)]/$340,000}. The remaining OFL is $35,000 and will be recaptured in the future. Without the overall foreign loss recapture rule, Shannon's FTC limit would have been $14,000. ■

A situation may arise in which overall foreign losses have been incurred and the U.S. taxpayer disposes of trade or business property used predominantly outside the United States before any or all of the loss is recaptured. The provisions described above will not necessarily reach such a situation. The statutory solution to this problem is that the U.S. taxpayer generates U.S.-source income upon disposal. The amount of income generated is the lesser of (1) the fair market value of the property less its adjusted basis or (2) the remaining amount of unrecaptured overall foreign losses.[22]

When a taxpayer has a loss for the tax year in one or more foreign-source categories (baskets), the loss must be apportioned pro rata to foreign-source categories with income for the tax year. If there is an overall foreign loss (i.e., foreign losses exceed foreign income in all categories), the overall foreign loss then reduces U.S.-source income. A U.S. loss for the tax year is apportioned pro rata to foreign-source income in each category, but only after the apportionment of any foreign losses to those income categories.

EXAMPLE 23

During 2003, Bloom, Inc., a U.S. corporation, incurred a $10,000 loss in its manufacturing activities, $20,000 in shipping income, and $5,000 in high withholding tax interest. The loss in the manufacturing basket is apportioned to the baskets with income as follows:

Foreign Income Category	Income or Loss	Foreign-Source Taxable Income
Manufacturing	($10,000)	$ –0–
Shipping	20,000	12,000*
High withholding tax interest	5,000	3,000**
Total	$15,000	$15,000

*$20,000 – [$10,000 × ($20,000/$25,000)].
**$5,000 – [$10,000 × ($5,000/$25,000)].

In 2004, Bloom earns $25,000 in manufacturing income, $18,000 in shipping income, and $6,000 in high withholding tax interest, so the previously apportioned loss must be reallocated back to the affected baskets as follows:

Foreign Income Category	Income or Loss	Previously Apportioned Loss	Foreign-Source Taxable Income
Manufacturing	$25,000	($10,000)	$15,000
Shipping	18,000	8,000	26,000
High withholding tax interest	6,000	2,000	8,000
Total	$49,000		$49,000

■

DIGGING DEEPER 2 *Find more information on this topic at our Web site:* ***http://wft-advanced.swlearning.com***.

[22]§ 904(f)(3).

THE ALTERNATIVE MINIMUM TAX FTC

For purposes of the alternative minimum tax (AMT), the FTC is limited to the lesser of (1) the credit for regular tax purposes or (2) 90 percent of the tentative minimum tax before the credit. The 10 percent cutback is calculated on the tentative minimum tax without regard to the alternative tax NOL deduction. The FTC limitation is calculated by using foreign-source alternative minimum taxable income (AMTI) in the numerator and worldwide AMTI in the denominator of the formula and the tentative minimum tax rather than the regular tax.

$$\text{AMT FTC limitation} = \frac{\text{Foreign-source AMTI}}{\text{Worldwide AMTI}} \times \text{Tentative minimum tax}$$

The taxpayer may elect to use regular foreign-source taxable income in the numerator if it does not exceed total AMTI. The AMT FTC limit is determined on a basket-by-basket basis.

LO.5

Describe the tax implications of using different currencies.

Foreign Currency

All the examples in this chapter have used the U.S. dollar currency for simplicity. Of course, cross-border transactions are denominated in a number of world currencies. The relative value of a foreign currency and the U.S. dollar is described by the foreign exchange rate. Changes in this rate affect the dollar value of foreign property held by the taxpayer, the dollar value of foreign debts, and the dollar amount of gain or loss on a transaction denominated in a foreign currency. Almost every international tax issue requires consideration of currency exchange implications.

EXAMPLE 24

Dress, Inc., a domestic corporation, purchases merchandise for resale from Fiesta, Inc., a foreign corporation, for 50,000K (a foreign currency). On the date of purchase, 1K is equal to $1 U.S. (1K:$1). At this time, the account payable is $50,000. On the date of payment by Dress (the foreign exchange date), the exchange rate is 1.25K:$1. In other words, the foreign currency has been devalued in relation to the U.S. dollar, and Dress will pay Fiesta 50,000K, which will cost Dress only $40,000. Dress must record the purchase of the merchandise at $50,000 and recognize a foreign currency gain of $10,000 ($50,000 – $40,000). ■

In recent years, U.S. currency abroad has amounted to more than 50 percent of the U.S. currency in circulation. Taxpayers may find it necessary to translate amounts denominated in foreign currency into U.S. dollars for any of the following purposes.

- Purchase of goods, services, and property.
- Sale of goods, services, and property.
- Collection of foreign receivables.
- Payment of foreign payables.
- Foreign tax credit calculations.
- Recognition of income or loss from foreign branch activities.

The foreign currency exchange rates, however, have no effect on the transactions of a U.S. person that arranges all international transactions in U.S. dollars.

EXAMPLE 25

Sellers, Inc., a domestic corporation, purchases goods from Rose, Ltd., a foreign corporation, and pays for these goods in U.S. dollars. Rose then exchanges the U.S. dollars for the currency

Concept Summary 7–2

Recognition of Foreign Exchange Gain or Loss

Transaction	Date of Recognition
Purchase or sale of inventory or business asset	Date of disposition of foreign currency
Foreign branch profits	Remittance of branch profits
Deemed dividend from CFC (Subpart F income)	Receipt of previously taxed income (accumulated E & P)
Dividend from current E & P or untaxed accumulated E & P	No exchange gain or loss to recipient

of the country in which it operates. Sellers has no foreign exchange considerations with which to contend. If instead Rose required Sellers to pay for the goods in a foreign currency, Sellers would have to exchange U.S. dollars to obtain the foreign currency to make payment. If the exchange rate changed from the date of purchase to the date of payment, Sellers would have a foreign currency gain or loss on the currency exchange. ■

The following concepts are important when dealing with the tax aspects of foreign exchange.

- Foreign currency is treated as property other than money.
- Gain or loss on the exchange of foreign currency is considered separately from the underlying transaction (e.g., the purchase or sale of goods).
- No gain or loss is recognized until a transaction is closed.

TAX ISSUES

The following major tax issues must be considered when dealing with foreign currency exchange.

- The date of recognition of any gain or loss (see Concept Summary 7–2).
- The source (U.S. or foreign) of the foreign currency gain or loss.
- The character of the gain or loss (ordinary or capital).

FUNCTIONAL CURRENCY

The Code generally adopted the approach of FAS 52, the Financial Accounting Standards Board standard on foreign currency translation. FAS 52 introduced the functional currency approach. Under this approach, the currency of the economic environment in which the foreign entity operates generally is to be used as the monetary unit to measure gains and losses.

Under § 985, all income tax determinations are to be made in the taxpayer's **functional currency.** Generally, a taxpayer's default functional currency is the U.S. dollar. In most cases, a **qualified business unit (QBU)** operating in a foreign country uses that country's currency as its functional currency. A QBU is a separate and clearly identified unit of a taxpayer's trade or business (e.g., a foreign branch). An individual is not a QBU; however, a trade or business conducted by an individual may be a QBU.[23]

[23]Reg. § 1.989(a)–1(b).

BRANCH OPERATIONS

When a foreign branch (QBU) uses a foreign currency as its functional currency, profit or loss is computed in the foreign currency each year and translated into U.S. dollars for tax purposes. The entire amount of profit or loss, not taking remittances into account, is translated using the average exchange rate for the taxable year. Exchange gain or loss is recognized on remittances from the QBU. The U.S. dollar amount of the remittance at the exchange rate in effect on the date of remittance is compared with the U.S. dollar value (basis pool) of the equity pool of the branch. The equity pool comprises the branch's initial capitalization plus contributions to the branch plus undistributed profits minus remittances and losses—all measured in the QBU's functional currency.[24] This exchange gain or loss is ordinary, and it is sourced according to the income to which the remittance is attributable.

DISTRIBUTIONS FROM FOREIGN CORPORATIONS

An actual distribution of E & P from a non-U.S. corporation is included in income by the U.S. recipient at the exchange rate in effect on the date of distribution. Thus, no exchange gain or loss is recognized. Deemed dividend distributions from a CFC under Subpart F (discussed in Chapter 8) are translated at the average exchange rate for the corporation's tax year to which the deemed distribution is attributable. Exchange gain or loss can result when an actual distribution of this previously taxed income is made.

FOREIGN TAXES

For purposes of the FTC, foreign taxes accrued are translated at the average exchange rate for the tax year to which the taxes relate. Under exceptions to this rule, foreign taxes must be translated at the exchange rate in effect when the foreign taxes were paid.[25] If foreign taxes are paid within two years of accrual, and if they differ from the accrued amount merely because of currency exchange fluctuation, no redetermination is required, even though the actual dollar value paid may differ from the accrued amount. In other cases, when the taxes paid differ from the amount accrued, a redetermination is required.

EXAMPLE 26

Music, Inc., a domestic corporation, has a foreign branch. Foreign taxes attributable to branch income amount to 5,000K (a foreign currency). The taxes are paid within two years of being accrued. The average foreign exchange rate for the tax year to which the foreign taxes relate is .5K:$1. On the date the taxes are paid, the rate is .6K:$1. No redetermination is required, and Music has foreign taxes of $10,000 for purposes of the FTC. ■

SECTION 988 TRANSACTIONS

The disposition of a nonfunctional currency can result in a foreign currency gain or loss under § 988. Section 988 transactions include those in which gain or loss is determined with regard to the value of a nonfunctional currency, such as the following.

- Acquiring (or becoming an obligor under) a debt instrument.
- Accruing (or otherwise taking into account) any item of expense or gross income or receipts that is to be paid or received at a later date.

[24] Prop.Reg. § 1.987–2.

[25] §§ 986(a)(1)(B) and (C).

- Entering into or acquiring almost any forward contract, futures contract, option, or similar investment position.
- Disposing of nonfunctional currency.

Section 988 generally treats exchange gain or loss falling within its provisions as ordinary income or loss. Capital gain or loss treatment may be elected with regard to forward contracts, futures contracts, and options that constitute capital assets in the hands of the taxpayer. A closed or completed transaction is required. The residence of the taxpayer generally determines the source of a § 988 foreign exchange gain or loss.

LO.6

Determine the allowed foreign earned income exclusion for U.S. workers abroad.

Expatriates and the Foreign Earned Income Exclusion

As discussed earlier, U.S. citizens and permanent residents are subject to U.S. tax on their worldwide income. The FTC and tax treaties help mitigate the potential double taxation problem this system creates. Another tool provided to combat double taxation is the **foreign earned income exclusion** offered by § 911. This rule provides an exclusion from U.S. gross income for a certain amount of qualified foreign earned income. This exclusion allows multinational entities to employ U.S. citizens and residents for foreign operations without having to pay them a wage or salary far in excess of that paid to nationals of the particular foreign country or countries. The tax burden on a U.S. taxpayer working abroad could be much greater than that on a native of the foreign country. The foreign earned income exclusion reduces this problem.

Section 911 allows a foreign earned income exclusion for (1) a qualified **housing cost amount** and (2) foreign earned income not in excess of $80,000.[26] The exclusion is elective and is made by filing Form 2555 with the income tax return, or with an amended return, for the first taxable year for which the election is to be effective. An election once made remains in effect for that year and for all subsequent years, unless revoked. If the election is revoked for any taxable year, the taxpayer may not make the election again (without consent of the IRS) until the sixth taxable year following the taxable year for which revocation was first effective.[27]

QUALIFIED INDIVIDUALS

The exclusion is available to an individual whose tax home is in a foreign country and who is either (1) a U.S. citizen and bona fide resident of a foreign country or countries or (2) a citizen or resident of the United States who, during any 12 consecutive months, is physically present in a foreign country or countries for at least 330 full days. "Tax home" has the same meaning as for U.S. cases relating to travel expenses while away from home.[28] The issue of whether a stay abroad is temporary can be troublesome. If the stay abroad is deemed to be temporary, the taxpayer's tax home has not shifted to the foreign country. A stay that exceeds one year is not temporary. Only whole days count for the physical presence test. The taxpayer has some flexibility in choosing the 12-month period.

[26]This $80,000 exclusion amount will be adjusted for inflation beginning in 2008.

[27]Reg. § 1.911–7.

[28]§ 162(a)(2).

TAX FACT

TOTAL WAGES AND SALARIES AND § 911 EXCLUSION AMOUNTS, 1996–2000

As the following table shows, the amount of foreign earned income excluded under § 911 increased each year from 1996 through 2000.

	1996	1997	1998	1999	2000
Total reported salaries and wages (in thousands)	$3,376,871,545	$3,613,918,456	$3,879,762,259	$4,132,473,459	$4,456,167,438
Total foreign earned income exclusion (in thousands)	11,982,578	13,170,179	13,455,924	14,136,544	15,239,672

Source: Internal Revenue Service, *Statistics of Income, Individual Income Tax Returns,* April 2003.

EXAMPLE 27

Carla, a U.S. citizen, arrived in Ireland from Boston at 3 P.M. on March 28, 2004. She remained in Ireland until 8 A.M. on March 1, 2005, when she departed for the United States. Among other possible 12-month periods, Carla was present in a foreign country an aggregate of 331 full days during each of the following 12-month periods: March 1, 2004, through February 28, 2005, and March 29, 2004, through March 28, 2005.[29] ■

THE GENERAL EXCLUSION

The foreign earned income (general) exclusion is available for foreign earned income and is limited to the lesser of (1) $80,000 or (2) foreign earned income less the housing cost exclusion amount. The exclusion is available for the tax year in which the income would be recognized. The limitation, however, is determined for each tax year in which services were performed. Income received after the close of the taxable year following the taxable year in which the services were performed does not qualify for the exclusion.

EXAMPLE 28

Tom, a U.S. resident, is present in a foreign country for all of 2004. He earns $100,000 from the performance of personal services. On January 1, 2005, he returns to the United States and remains there. Of the $100,000 foreign earned income, Tom receives $60,000 in 2004 and $40,000 in 2005. Tom can take a foreign earned income exclusion of $60,000 for 2004 and $20,000 for 2005 ($80,000 statutory limit for 2004 less the $60,000 excluded for 2004). If Tom did not receive the $40,000 until 2006, no exclusion would be allowed for 2006 because the $40,000 was received after the close of the taxable year following the taxable year in which the services were performed. ■

The statutory amount is prorated on a daily basis where the taxpayer does not qualify for the exclusion for the full tax year. If Tom in Example 28 qualified for

[29]Reg. § 1.911–2(d).

TAX IN THE NEWS

U.S. Workers Abroad—Gone But Not Forgotten

During the tax cut debates of 2003, the Senate floated the idea of axing the foreign earned income exclusion for U.S. citizens and residents working abroad. The Senate estimated that eliminating the § 911 benefit would raise an additional $32 billion in taxes. Senator John Breaux (D-Louisiana) pointed out that such a change would be a severe blow to the rank and file oil workers in his state, many of whom work on extended foreign assignments.

only 11 months of the year, the $80,000 statutory amount would be $73,206 [$80,000 (334 days/365 days)].

THE HOUSING COST AMOUNT

The housing cost amount is equal to the qualified housing expenses of an individual for the tax year less a base amount. The base amount is 16 percent of the salary of an employee of the United States for Step 1 Grade GS–14. The base amount is determined on a daily basis. The base amount for a full year is $11,233 for 2003. For a qualified individual employed overseas for 250 days of the year, the applicable base amount for 2003 would be $7,694 [$11,233 × (250 days/365 days)]. The housing cost amount exclusion is limited to foreign earned income. A self-employed individual is not eligible to exclude housing expenses, but he or she can elect to deduct them.

EXAMPLE 29

Charles, a U.S. citizen, works as an engineer for a U.S. multinational company in Bahrain. He is a bona fide resident of Bahrain for the entire calendar and tax year (2003) and earns a salary of $95,000. In addition, his employer provides $16,000 in housing costs. If the base amount is $11,233 and Charles elects both exclusions, the housing cost amount exclusion is $4,767 ($16,000 – $11,233), and the foreign earned income exclusion is $80,000 (the lesser of $111,000 foreign earned income less $4,767 housing cost amount, or the $80,000 statutory limit). Charles's gross income includes $26,233 of foreign earned income ($95,000 + $16,000 – $4,767 – $80,000). ■

Suggested Further Readings

Warren Crowdus, "The Interaction of Treaty and Code Source Rules," *Journal of International Taxation*, April 2002.

Edsel Doran and Edwin Van Schajik, "Taxation of E-Commerce: Threat or Opportunity?" *Journal of International Taxation*, February 2002.

Alan Fischl, Lewis Greenwald, and Nelson Suit, "Foreign Tax Credit Limitation Final Regs. under Sections 864(E) and 904(D), Proposed Regs. under Sections 902 and 904," *Journal of International Taxation*, October 2001.

Cym H. Lowell, "Sarbanes-Oxley Act of 2002: Impact on International Tax Planning," *Journal of International Taxation*, December 2002.

KEY TERMS

Arm's length price, 7–16
Controlled foreign corporation (CFC), 7–19
Deemed-paid credit, 7–18
Foreign earned income exclusion, 7–28
Foreign tax credit (FTC), 7–5
Functional currency, 7–26
Housing cost amount, 7–28
Inbound taxation, 7–3
Income tax treaties, 7–6
Limitation on benefits, 7–9
Outbound taxation, 7–3
Overall foreign loss, 7–23
Permanent establishment (PE), 7–6
Qualified business unit (QBU), 7–26
Separate foreign tax credit limitation categories, 7–21
Title passage rule, 7–13
Transfer pricing, 7–16
Treaty shopping, 7–9

PROBLEM MATERIALS

West Federal Taxation

Problems

1. Evaluate this statement: The U.S. FTC system provides unwarranted tax benefits to U.S. persons with foreign-source income to the detriment of other U.S. taxpayers.

EXTENDER

2. Describe a "check-the-box" entity and indicate the difference between a hybrid entity and a reverse hybrid entity.

Communications

3. Write a memo to a U.S. client explaining how operating its foreign business through a foreign corporation may be considered a tax shelter for U.S. tax purposes.

Ethics

4. Some U.S. multinational corporations generate income through wholly owned foreign corporations and do not currently pay U.S. tax on these earnings. Do you believe this is appropriate behavior on the part of such corporations? Why or why not?

5. Define the term *permanent establishment* and indicate why the existence of a permanent establishment matters to a U.S. person with foreign activities.

6. Evaluate this statement: Income tax treaties may provide for higher or lower withholding tax rates on investment income earned by a nonresident of the treaty country than the rate imposed by local country tax law.

7. Miles, a U.S. resident, received the following income items for the current tax year. Identify the source of each income item as either U.S. or foreign.
   a. $1,200 dividend from U.S. Power Company, a U.S. corporation that operates solely in the western United States.
   b. $2,600 dividend from Star Trading Corporation, a U.S. corporation that had total gross income of $2 million from the active conduct of a foreign trade or business for the immediately preceding three tax years. Star's worldwide gross income for the same period was $2.6 million.
   c. $750 dividend from International Consolidated, Inc., a foreign corporation that had gross income of $1.7 million effectively connected with the conduct of a U.S. trade or business for the immediately preceding three tax years. International's worldwide gross income for the same period was $3 million.
   d. $300 interest from a savings account at a Houston bank.
   e. $2,500 interest on Rolan Corporation bonds. Rolan is a U.S. corporation that derived $3 million of its gross income for the immediately preceding three tax years from operation of an active foreign business. Rolan's worldwide gross income for this same period was $3.6 million.

8. Determine whether the source of income for the following sales is U.S. or foreign.
   a. Kwaku, a non-U.S. resident, sells stock in Home Depot, a domestic corporation, through a broker in New York.
   b. Chris sells stock in IBM, a domestic corporation, to his brother, Rich. Both Chris and Rich are non-U.S. residents, and the sale takes place outside the United States.
   c. Crows, Inc., a domestic corporation, sells inventory produced in the United States to customers in Europe. Title passes in the international waters of the Atlantic Ocean.
   d. Jordan, Inc., a domestic corporation, manufactures equipment in Taiwan and sells the equipment to customers in the United States.

Communications

9. Monika Cashoulli, a citizen and resident of Albania, is a professional golfer. She played in 7 tournaments in the United States in the current year and earned $200,000 in prizes from these tournaments. She deposited the winnings in a bank account she opened in Albania after her first tournament win. Monika played a total of 30 tournaments for the year and earned $800,000 in total prize money. She spent 40 days in the United States, 60 days in Germany, 20 days in Ireland, and the rest of the time in Albania. Write a letter to Monika explaining how much U.S.-source income she will generate, if any, from her participation in these tournaments. Monika's address is Seventh Avenue 42, Kruja, Albania.

Decision Making

10. Blum, Inc., a domestic corporation, produces inventory in its foreign manufacturing plants for sale in the United States. Its foreign manufacturing assets have a tax book value of $6 million and a fair market value of $16 million. Its assets related to the sales activity have a tax book value of $800,000 and a fair market value of $200,000. Blum's interest expense totaled $100,000 for the current year.
    a. What amount of interest expense is allocated and apportioned to foreign-source income using the tax book value method? What amount of interest expense is allocated and apportioned to foreign-source income using the fair market value method?
    b. If Blum, Inc., wishes to maximize its FTC, which method should it use?

11. Describe the purpose § 482 and provide two examples of transactions to which the IRS might apply such an adjustment.

12. Erin, Inc., a domestic corporation, operates in both Japan and the United States. This year, the business generated taxable income of $300,000 from foreign sources and $100,000 from U.S. sources. All of Erin's foreign-source income is in the general limitation basket. The company's total worldwide taxable income is $400,000. Erin pays Japanese taxes of $130,000. What is Erin's allowed FTC for the tax year? Assume a 35% U.S. tax rate.

Decision Making

13. Griffith, Inc., a domestic corporation, earned $1 million from foreign manufacturing activities on which it paid $300,000 of foreign income taxes. Griffith's foreign sales income is taxed at a 45% foreign tax rate. Both sales and manufacturing income are assigned to the general limitation basket. What amount of foreign sales income can Griffith earn without generating any excess FTCs for the current year? Assume a 35% U.S. rate.

14. USCo, Inc., a domestic corporation, owns 70% of the stock of ForCo, Ltd., a foreign corporation. For the current year, USCo receives a dividend of $100,000 from ForCo. ForCo's post-1986 E & P (after taxes) and foreign taxes are $8 million and $600,000, respectively. What is USCo's total gross income from receipt of this dividend if it elects to claim the FTC for deemed-paid foreign taxes?

15. FLACo, Inc., a U.S. corporation, has foreign-source income and pays foreign taxes as follows.

	Income	Taxes
Shipping category	$ 200,000	$ 40,000
Passive category	400,000	12,000
General category	1,200,000	600,000

FLACo's worldwide taxable income is $2.4 million, and U.S. taxes before the FTC are $840,000 (assume a 35% rate). What is FLACo's U.S. tax liability after any allowable FTC?

16. MollCo, Inc., a domestic corporation, operates a branch in Slovakia. The earnings record of the branch is as follows.

Year	Taxable Income (Loss)	Foreign Taxes Paid
2002	($ 50,000)	–0–
2003	(80,000)	–0–
2004	(20,000)	–0–
2005	240,000	$80,000

For 2002–2005, MollCo has U.S.-source taxable income of $1 million each year. What is the allowed FTC for 2005? Assume a 35% U.S. tax rate. All income is in the general limitation basket.

Issue ID

17. Describe how the FTC calculation process changes if the taxpayer is in an alternative minimum tax position for the tax year.

EXTENDER

18. Describe the purpose of the possessions tax credit allowed by § 936. What feature of the § 936 credit differs most from the regular FTC?

19. Weight, Inc., a domestic corporation, purchases weight-lifting equipment for resale from HiDisu, a Japanese corporation, for 75 million yen. On the date of purchase, 150 yen is equal to $1 U.S. (¥150:$1). The purchase is made on December 15, 2004, with payment due in 60 days. Weight is a calendar year taxpayer. On December 31, 2004, the foreign exchange rate is ¥140:$1. What amount of foreign currency gain or loss, if any, must Weight recognize for 2004 as a result of this transaction?

Communications

20. Carroll Manufacturing, Inc., a calendar year domestic corporation, operates a branch in Ireland. In the current year, the branch generated 750,000 euros in net profit. On December 31 of the current year, one euro equaled 83 cents. The average exchange rate for the current year between the euro and the dollar was 91 cents. Write a memo to the controller of Carroll explaining (1) how and when the Irish profits will be taxed to Carroll in the United States and (2) under what conditions a foreign currency gain or loss will be recognized.

21. Forrest, Inc., a foreign corporation, pays a dividend to its shareholders on October 31. Harold, Inc., a U.S. corporation and 9% shareholder in Forrest, receives a dividend of 10,000K (a foreign currency). Pertinent exchange rates are as follows.

October 31	.8K:$1
Average for year	.6K:$1
December 31	1K:$1

What is the dollar amount of the dividend received by Harold, Inc., and does Harold have a foreign exchange gain or loss on receipt of the dividend?

22. Emily, a U.S. citizen, works as a tax consultant for a U.S.-based accounting firm. She is spending a three-year rotation working full time in the firm's London office. Emily is a bona fide resident of the United Kingdom the entire 2004 calendar and tax year and earns a salary of $103,000. In addition, her employer provides $47,000 in housing cost reimbursement. Assume the housing cost base amount for 2004 is $11,500. Compute the total foreign earned income exclusion for Emily for the 2004 tax year.

BRIDGE DISCIPLINE

1. Locate three types of treaties the United States has with Canada other than an income tax treaty.

Research Problems

Internet Activity

Use the tax resources of the Internet to address the following questions. Do not restrict your search to the World Wide Web, but include a review of newsgroups and general reference materials, practitioner sites and resources, primary sources of the tax law, chat rooms, discussion groups, and other opportunities.

Communications

Research Problem 1. Locate the most recent financial statements of two different U.S. corporations. Using the income tax footnote information, determine (1) the portion of the company's net income earned from foreign activities and (2) whether the foreign earnings are taxed at a higher or lower rate than the hypothetical 35% U.S. corporate rate (hint: examine the rate reconciliation table). Summarize this information in an e-mail sent to your instructor.

Research Problem 2. Both **http://www.taxsites.com** and **http://www.irs.gov** contain many useful links to publications, tax forms and instructions, and tax revenue statistics. Locate Web pages for at least three other countries' taxing authorities. Indicate the Web address for each of these pages and describe how these Web pages compare with the IRS's page in terms of content and ease of use.

CHAPTER 8

Capital Changes and International Tax Law

LEARNING OBJECTIVES

After completing Chapter 8, you should be able to:

LO.1
Outline the tax effects of a U.S. taxpayer's increasing international activities.

LO.2
Describe the export tax incentives offered by the United States.

LO.3
Recognize the U.S. tax effects triggered by cross-border tax-deferred transactions.

LO.4
Work with the rules concerning operations through foreign corporations.

LO.5
Describe the tax effects related to the U.S. operations of a foreign taxpayer.

OUTLINE

TAX TALK

The question where an income is earned is always a matter of doubt when the business is begun in one country and ended in another.

—William Howard Taft

LO.1

Outline the tax effects of a U.S. taxpayer's increasing international activities.

Life Cycle of Global Operations

U.S. taxpayers often take their business operations global over time in a gradual process.[1] A U.S. business may operate on a strictly domestic basis for several years, then explore foreign markets by exporting its products abroad, and later license its products to a foreign manufacturer, enter into a partnership with a foreign partner, or establish a foreign presence with employees in a local office. Some of these activities will create an overseas business presence sufficient to trigger a non-U.S. income tax, although U.S. taxpayers may mitigate this additional tax with the foreign tax credit. The profits and losses generated by all of these activities are currently subject to U.S. taxation because they are earned directly by the U.S. taxpayer.

If the forays into foreign markets are successful, the U.S. taxpayer ultimately may create a separate overseas subsidiary corporation and move a portion of its operations abroad by establishing a distribution or manufacturing facility. The profits and losses generated by a foreign corporation from its activities outside the United States are not subject to U.S. taxation. The U.S. owners will be taxed only when the profits are repatriated back to the United States in the form of dividends or other taxable payments. Nevertheless, ownership of a domestically controlled foreign corporation can have significant U.S. tax consequences for the U.S. owner. These range from increased reporting requirements to current taxation of a **deemed dividend** from the foreign corporation. Figure 8–1 summarizes the potential timeline of global activities.

[1]Foreign businesses likewise enter the U.S. market in stages. In either case, each step generates increasingly significant international tax consequences.

■ **FIGURE 8–1**
Global Activities Timeline

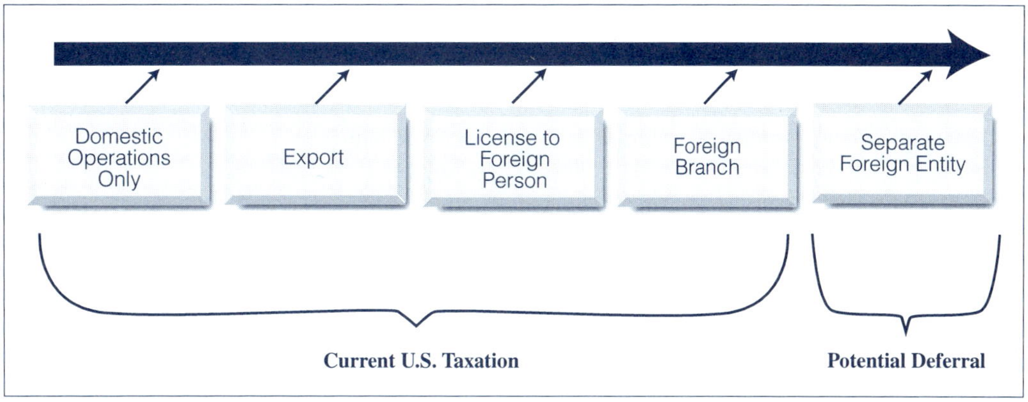

EXAMPLE 1

VoiceCo, a domestic corporation, designs, manufactures, and sells specialty microphones for use in theaters. All of its activities take place in Florida, although it ships products to customers all over the United States. When VoiceCo receives inquiries regarding its products from foreign customers, it tests the markets abroad by placing ads in overseas trade journals and begins taking orders from non-U.S. customers. Title to the microphones passes upon delivery, so all of VoiceCo's offshore sales produce foreign-source income. Because VoiceCo has no assets or employees in the other jurisdictions, it incurs no foreign income tax on these sales (although it may incur certain customs duties). Consequently, although VoiceCo is now involved in international commerce, it has not significantly changed its global tax position or its capital structure. Because VoiceCo is taxed on its worldwide income, all profits from the foreign sales are included on its U.S. tax return on a current basis. ■

EXAMPLE 2

VoiceCo's European sales become a substantial part of its total revenues. Because shipping costs are high and customers demand quick turnaround on product orders, VoiceCo decides to license its design and manufacturing process to a local European musical instruments company for sales in Europe. The European company pays VoiceCo a royalty equal to 25% of the sales price on all its sales of the VoiceCo-designed microphone. The royalty income is foreign-source income (as the underlying intangible property is exploited outside the United States). However, because VoiceCo is taxed on worldwide income, the royalties are currently taxed to VoiceCo in the United States. Again, VoiceCo has not significantly changed its global tax position or capital structure. ■

EXAMPLE 3

In a few years, VoiceCo decides to significantly expand its customer base overseas. It opens a branch sales office staffed with VoiceCo employees. This presence triggers foreign income tax expense for VoiceCo, but the company uses the foreign tax credit to offset the U.S. tax on the income of the branch abroad. VoiceCo now has multiple tax filing requirements and a more complicated U.S. tax return due to the foreign tax credit. However, its capital structure is little changed. ■

EXAMPLE 4

In time, VoiceCo expands its manufacturing facilities to include a plant in Ireland to service the European demand for its product. VoiceCo incorporates the Irish operation as VoiceCo-Ireland, a corporation organized in Ireland. Ireland imposes only a 12.5% tax on VoiceCo-Ireland's profits. So long as VoiceCo-Ireland does not distribute profits to VoiceCo, the foreign profits are not subject to tax in the United States. Consequently, VoiceCo has achieved **deferral** of U.S. tax on these foreign profits. At the same time, VoiceCo's capital structure has changed, and as discussed later in the chapter, it must carefully navigate the complex rules regarding ownership of a **controlled foreign corporation (CFC).** ■

BRIDGE DISCIPLINE

Bridge to Financial Reporting

U.S. taxpayers are subject to U.S. tax on their worldwide income. However, foreign corporations, even those controlled by U.S. shareholders, are not part of a U.S. consolidated group and therefore are not directly subject to U.S. taxation. Consequently, U.S. taxpayers can achieve deferral of U.S. taxes on foreign income if they operate their foreign activities through foreign subsidiary corporations. Although the *actual* U.S. taxes on the foreign corporation's profits are deferred, the reported **effective tax rate** for financial statement purposes may not reflect this deferral. As discussed in Chapter 2, FAS 109 requires that a corporate group report both the current and the deferred income tax expense. Furthermore, the corporate group for financial reporting purposes includes controlled foreign subsidiaries.

Consider the following example. USCo, a domestic corporation, operates a manufacturing facility in Singapore though a Singapore corporation. Assume that the U.S. tax rate is 35 percent and the Singapore tax rate is 6 percent. For the current year, USCo earns $600,000 in taxable income. The Singapore corporation earns $400,000 in taxable income from its operations, pays $24,000 in taxes to Singapore, and makes no distributions to its U.S. parent. The Singapore corporation is not taxed in the United States because it is not a U.S. person and has no activities in the United States. USCo is not taxed on the Singapore profits because it has not received any distributions of these profits. Accordingly, USCo has achieved deferral and reduced its worldwide tax costs.

For financial statement purposes, however, the USCo group must include the $400,000 in Singapore profits in its net income and report both the Singapore tax and any *potential* U.S. tax (after allowable foreign tax credits) as its total tax expense.

U.S. Tax Return		**Potential U.S. Tax on Foreign Income**	
Income	$600,000	Income	$400,000
	× 35%		× 35%
U.S. tax	$210,000	Total tax	$140,000
		Foreign tax credit	(24,000)
		Net U.S. tax	$116,000

Consequently, the total tax expense for financial statement purposes is determined as follows.

Current U.S. tax	$210,000
Current foreign tax	24,000
Deferred U.S. tax	116,000
Total tax expense	$350,000

The financial statement effective tax rate on USCo's global income is 35 percent ($350,000 total tax expense/$1,000,000 net income). Thus, although USCo paid only $234,000 in taxes, its effective tax rate (and thus its after-tax book income) does not reflect the savings generated from operating in Singapore, a low-tax country.

(*continued on next page*)

(Bridge Discipline concluded)

However, USCo may be able to use APB 23 to avoid reporting the $116,000 in deferred taxes (see Chapter 2). If USCo plans to indefinitely reinvest its Singapore earnings outside the United States, it is not required to include the deferred U.S. taxes as part of its total tax expense. Thus, USCo's total financial statement income would remain $1 million, but its total tax expense would be only $234,000 (the taxes currently paid to the United States and Singapore). The resulting financial statement effective tax rate is 23.4 percent ($234,000/$1,000,000), and the USCo group's after-tax book income reflects the Singapore tax savings.

To the extent that higher book earnings are reflected in stock prices, the use of APB 23 may increase shareholder wealth. Although academic studies find mixed evidence on this effect, many U.S. multinationals with foreign subsidiaries do in fact use APB 23 to avoid reporting deferred taxes on foreign earnings.

LO.2

Describe the export tax incentives offered by the United States.

Export Tax Incentives

HISTORY AND PURPOSE

The easiest way for a U.S. enterprise to engage in global commerce is simply to sell U.S.-produced goods and services abroad. These sales can be conducted with little or no foreign presence and allow the business to explore offshore markets without making costly financial commitments to overseas operations. The U.S. tax consequences of simple export sales are straightforward. All such income is taxed in the United States to the U.S. taxpayer. Whether foreign taxes must be paid on this export income depends on the laws of the importing jurisdiction and whether the U.S. taxpayer is deemed to have a business presence there (i.e., carrying on a trade or business or maintaining a permanent establishment when a tax treaty exists). In many cases, such export income is not taxed by the importing jurisdiction.

To improve the U.S. balance of trade, Congress has enacted various export tax incentives to encourage exports of U.S.-produced property. In the late 1970s, Congress created the domestic international sales corporation (DISC) provisions that allowed a DISC to defer the tax on a portion of its export income until actual repatriation of the earnings. After the General Agreement on Tariffs and Trade (GATT) charged that the DISC provisions were a prohibited export subsidy, the provisions were curtailed. As an alternative, in 1984 the foreign sales corporation (FSC) provisions (§§ 921–927) were enacted to provide similar tax incentives to U.S. exporters while appeasing the GATT members. FSCs were not allowed to defer the tax on export income. Instead, a certain percentage of export income was permanently exempt from U.S. taxation.

In 2000, the United States was forced to repeal the FSC provisions because of a finding by the World Trade Organization (WTO) that the FSC benefits constituted an illegal export subsidy. Congress replaced the FSC with a benefit that excludes extraterritorial income from U.S. taxation.[2] The **extraterritorial income (ETI)** regime preserves the basic incentives provided by the FSC rules. Consequently, it is not surprising that the WTO has found that the ETI provisions also violate its rules.

[2] FSC Repeal and Extraterritorial Income Exclusion Act of 2000, Public Law 106–519, and new § 114.

As of March 2004, the United States has yet to repeal the ETI provisions, but the European Union was applying trade sanctions, and some U.S. action seemed likely.

The various export tax incentive regimes have faced opposition from within the United States as well. For example, in a single year Caterpillar, Inc., used FSC benefits to reduce its taxes by $41 million. Some policy makers argue that these tax savings are simply a "giveaway" to corporations for doing what they would otherwise be doing. Others point out that the existence of large export tax savings, such as Caterpillar's, proves that the incentive works.

EXTRATERRITORIAL INCOME EXCLUSION

Under the ETI exclusion of § 114, qualifying foreign trade income is permanently exempt from U.S. taxation. Qualifying foreign trade income is a specified percentage of foreign trading gross receipts. Such receipts are generated from the sale of qualifying foreign trade property, which includes property that meets all three of the following requirements.

- The property is held for sale or lease for direct use, consumption, or disposition outside the United States in the ordinary course of business.
- No more than 50 percent of the property's value may be attributable to the combined market value of components manufactured abroad plus foreign direct labor costs.
- The property must be manufactured, produced, grown, or extracted by the taxpayer, and in the case of property that is manufactured outside the United States, the taxpayer must be a domestic corporation, a U.S. citizen or resident, a foreign corporation that elects to be treated as a domestic corporation, or a partnership with eligible partners.

Qualifying property does not include oil and gas products, intangibles (other than certain qualifying computer software licensed for reproduction outside the United States), and other specified items.[3] The key factors are that the property must be exported, a large portion of the value of the property must be attributable to U.S. components and labor, and the taxpayer must be subject to taxation in the United States.

To qualify for ETI benefits, the taxpayer must meet certain economic process requirements outlined in § 942. These include participating outside the United States in soliciting, negotiating, or making the sales contract relating to the transaction. In addition, the foreign direct costs attributable to the transaction must equal or exceed 50 percent of the total direct costs. Small exporters with annual foreign trading gross receipts of $5 million or less need not meet these requirements.

Different pricing methods are provided for determining exempt qualifying foreign trade income. The taxpayer may use whichever of the three following methods maximizes its exempt taxable income.

- 15 percent of foreign trade income (FTI).
- 1.2 percent of foreign trading gross receipts (FTGR) (not exceeding 30 percent of FTI).
- 30 percent of foreign sale and leasing income (FSALI). FSALI is defined in § 941(c) as FTI that is properly allocable to the taxpayer's foreign activities or income from renting foreign trade property for use outside the United States.

The ETI exclusion from gross income is the exempt taxable income plus the ratable share of any disallowed expenses related to the exempt income.

[3] § 943(a).

EXAMPLE 5

Murphy, Inc., a domestic corporation, manufactures recreational boats. For the current year, it reported the following operating results before consideration of any ETI benefits.

	U.S. Sales	Foreign Sales	Total Sales
Gross receipts	$ 5,000	$ 500	$ 5,500
Cost of goods sold	(4,200)	(360)	(4,560)
Gross income	$ 800	$ 140	$ 940
Overhead expenses	(120)	(20)	(140)
Taxable income	$ 680	$ 120	$ 800

Murphy's FTGR are $500 and its FTI is $120. Assume Murphy's FSALI is $50. Murphy is allowed to reduce its taxable income by the greater of the following three amounts.

- $18 ($120 FTI × 15%).
- $6 ($500 FTGR × 1.2%).
- $15 ($50 FSALI × 30%).

The $3 in overhead expenses attributable to the excluded taxable income is not deductible [$3 = $20 × ($18/$120)]. Thus, the exclusion from gross income under § 114 is $21 [$18 (reduction in taxable income) + $3 (disallowed overhead expenses)].

Murphy, Inc.'s taxable income after consideration of the ETI exclusion is calculated as follows.

Gross receipts	$ 5,500
Cost of goods sold	(4,560)
Gross income before exclusion	$ 940
ETI exclusion	(21)
Overhead expenses (before disallowed expenses)	(140)
Disallowed overhead expenses	3
Taxable income	$ 782

■

LO.3

Recognize the U.S. tax effects triggered by cross-border tax-deferred transactions.

Acquisition, Reorganization, and Disposition of Foreign Corporations

Several options are available for a U.S. taxpayer that decides to operate offshore through a corporation organized outside the United States. The U.S. taxpayer may acquire an existing non-U.S. entity through a stock purchase, or it can create a new foreign corporation by transferring assets to the entity in exchange for shares.

EXAMPLE 6

Henricks, Inc., a domestic corporation based in Texas, expands its operations to Mexico by purchasing all the shares of an existing Mexican corporation. The purchase does not trigger any current U.S. tax consequences to Henricks. Henricks now owns shares in a foreign corporation that have an adjusted basis equal to the purchase price. Going forward, Henricks must deal with any issues related to owning a CFC. Unless Henricks makes a § 338 election, the basis of the assets inside the Mexican corporation does not change. ■

BRIDGE DISCIPLINE

Bridge to Overseas Trade Management

The United States often uses tax law to encourage (or discourage) certain activities. For example, allowing deductions for charitable contributions and mortgage interest encourages charitable giving and home ownership. Similarly, providing tax benefits to companies that produce goods for export encourages exports.

The export tax incentives historically offered by the United States are only one tool the government uses to manage trade. Although the rhetoric of the United States and its trading partners is steeped in passionate arguments for free trade, all countries use many tools to manage trade levels. Governments take two types of actions to support their own country's producers.

- Imposing barriers that discourage trade (e.g., high import tariffs on products the government wishes to protect).
- Providing subsidies that encourage domestic production (e.g., payments or price supports to domestic producers).

Historically, the United States has enacted trade barriers that protect domestically produced farm goods, steel, and textiles. The United States also has provided price supports for farm products. At the other end of the spectrum, the United States has entered into a number of free trade agreements with trading partners (e.g., the North American Free Trade Agreement).

EXAMPLE 7

Shane, Inc., a domestic corporation in Maine, expands its operations to Canada by transferring machinery, equipment, inventory, and patents to a newly formed Canadian corporation in exchange for 100% of the Canadian corporation's shares. In a purely domestic context, this exchange would qualify for gain or loss deferral under § 351. However, because the assets are leaving the U.S. tax jurisdiction, the transaction may trigger a current tax cost under § 367. ■

Later on, the U.S. owner of a foreign corporation may reorganize the ownership structure or eventually liquidate the entity, bringing its assets back into the U.S. enterprise.

EXAMPLE 8

Johnson, Inc., a domestic corporation, owns 100% of Cardinal, Ltd., a foreign corporation. Johnson exchanges all the shares of Cardinal for 20% of Nimitz, Ltd., a larger foreign corporation. This exchange qualifies as a "Type B" stock-for-stock tax-deferred exchange. However, because a foreign corporation is involved, § 367 implications must be addressed to determine whether the transaction is ultimately free from U.S. tax. If, instead of the stock swap, Johnson simply liquidated Cardinal, the potentially tax-deferred § 332/§ 337 parent-subsidiary liquidation would also fall under the purview of § 367. ■

Figure 8–2 summarizes the otherwise tax-deferred capital transactions potentially taxed under § 367.

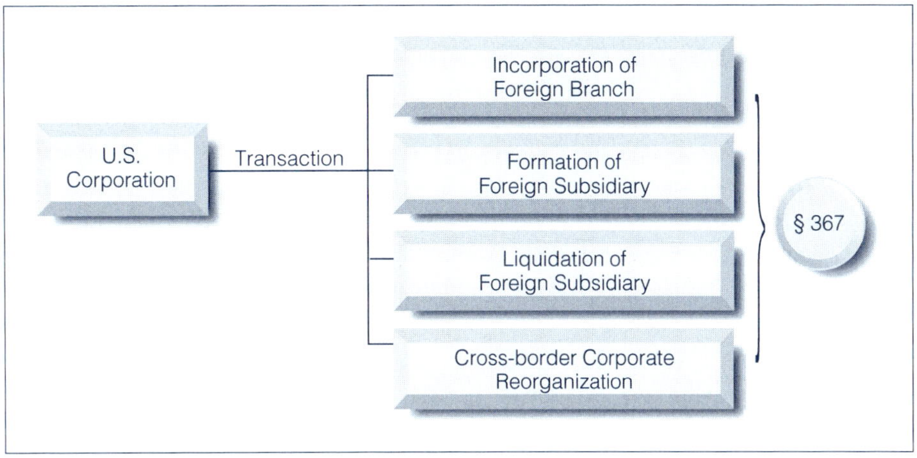

■ **FIGURE 8–2**
Cross-Border Capital Transactions Potentially Taxed under § 367

PLANNING STRATEGIES

Taxable Share Purchases and § 338

FRAMEWORK FOCUS: TAX RATE

STRATEGY ➤ **SHIFT NET INCOME FROM HIGH-BRACKET TAXPAYERS TO LOW-BRACKET TAXPAYERS.**

A taxpayer's purchase of the shares of a corporation constitutes a taxable transaction. The seller realizes and recognizes gain on the disposition of the shares, and the purchaser takes a basis in the shares equal to the purchase price. However, the basis of the assets *inside* the corporation is unchanged.

Making a § 338 election may be advantageous in this situation. Under a regular § 338(g) election, a taxpayer purchasing shares in a corporation may get a step-up in basis on the assets inside the corporation as if the assets had been purchased for their fair market value. This step-up in basis does come at a cost. To generate the step-up in basis, the acquired corporation is treated as essentially selling the assets to itself for their fair market value, and this tax fiction triggers a gain or loss depending on the difference between the adjusted basis of the assets and the deemed selling price. In a domestic context, this gain or loss is recognized on the final U.S. tax return of the "old" corporation (after the election, the acquired corporation is treated as a "new" corporation).

Consider the following example. USCo acquires 100 percent of ForCo stock for $500 million. ForCo's tangible assets are worth $100 million, and its goodwill is worth $400 million. USCo expects that ForCo will generate earnings before interest and taxes of $100 million per year. USCo pays a 35 percent tax rate, and ForCo pays a 20 percent tax rate.

Upon making the election, ForCo is deemed to have sold its assets to itself for their fair market value. Assuming that the basis in the tangible assets is $100 million and the basis in the goodwill is zero, the election triggers a $400 million gain to "old" ForCo. However, ForCo is a foreign corporation and is not subject to U.S. taxation. Consequently, there is no U.S. tax cost to making the election. From the foreign government's perspective, the § 338 election has no effect.

ForCo's E & P is determined as follows.

	No § 338(g) Election	**With the § 338(g) Election**
ForCo taxable income	$100	$100
Foreign tax	(20)	(20)
Net income	$ 80	$ 80
Goodwill adjustment	—	(27)
E & P	$ 80	$ 53

Notice that the § 338 election does not change the foreign country's tax treatment of ForCo. The host government does not recognize the step-up in basis in the goodwill. The § 338 election is only relevant for U.S. tax purposes, including the E & P calculation. In this case, the § 338 election creates a basis of $400 million in the goodwill. Under § 197, ForCo is allowed to amortize this goodwill over a 15-year period. Consequently, for purposes of determining its E & P (a U.S. concept), ForCo has a goodwill amortization deduction of $27 million ($400 million/15 years).

ForCo distributes its entire $80 net income to USCo as a dividend at the end of the year. The consequences are quite different depending on whether the election was made.

	No § 338(g) Election	With the § 338(g) Election
ForCo dividend income	$ 80	$ 53
§ 78 gross-up	20	20
Gross income	$ 100	$ 73
U.S. tax	× 35%	× 35%
	$ 35	$ 26
Foreign tax credit	(20)	(20)
Net U.S. tax	$ 15	$ 6

Without the § 338 election, USCo receives $80 million and, after the foreign tax credit calculations (see Chapter 7), pays an additional $15 million in U.S. taxes. With the election, USCo receives the same $80 million, but only $53 million is treated as a dividend because of the E & P limitation. Because ForCo has distributed all of its E & P, the entire $20 million in foreign taxes is treated as a deemed-paid credit to USCo. In this case, the residual U.S. tax is only $6 million. In summary, making the § 338 election saved USCo $9 million in taxes on the dividend distribution from ForCo.

A § 338 election is not always advantageous in a foreign stock acquisition, however. For example, if the value of the corporation's assets has declined, their basis will be stepped down. The "new" foreign corporation loses all its existing tax attributes, including E & P. Some of this E & P might be previously taxed income that could have been received in the United States tax-free (see the CFC discussion later in this chapter).

OUTBOUND ASSET TRANSFERS

Any time a U.S. person transfers assets to a foreign corporation, the potential exists to shift income outside the U.S. taxing jurisdiction. The U.S. tax implications of transferring property to a corporation organized outside the United States depend on the nature of the exchange, the assets involved, the income potential of the property, and the character of the property in the hands of the transferor or transferee.

When assets are exchanged for corporate stock in a domestic transaction, realized gain or loss may be deferred rather than recognized. Similarly, deferral treatment may be available when the following "outbound" capital changes occur (i.e., when corporate business is moved across country borders and outside the United States).

- A U.S. corporation starts up a new corporation outside the United States (§ 351).
- A U.S. corporation liquidates a U.S. subsidiary into an existing foreign corporation (§ 332).
- A U.S. corporation incorporates a non-U.S. branch of a U.S. corporation, forming a new foreign corporation (§ 351).
- A foreign corporation uses a stock swap to acquire a U.S. corporation ("Type B" reorganization).
- A foreign corporation acquires substantially all of a U.S. corporation's net assets ("Type C" or "Type D" reorganization).

These otherwise tax-deferred transactions may trigger current taxation when foreign corporations are involved. Under § 367(a), the general rule is that gain deferral is not allowed when assets are leaving the U.S. taxing jurisdiction. However, a major exception allows continued tax deferral for assets transferred to a foreign corporation to be used in a trade or business carried on outside the United States.

The trade or business exception does not apply to certain "tainted" assets, and the transfer of these assets outside the United States triggers immediate gain (but not loss) recognition. The following are "tainted" assets under § 367.

- Inventory (raw goods, work-in-progress, and finished goods).
- Installment obligations and accounts receivable.
- Foreign currency.
- Property leased by the transferor unless the transferee is the lessee.

These tainted assets are likely to turn over quickly once the asset transfer is completed, and any appreciation is likely to be recognized outside the U.S. taxing jurisdiction. Consequently, § 367 requires recognition of this gain upon transfer of the asset outside the United States.

EXAMPLE 9

Amelia, Inc., a domestic corporation, incorporates its profitable Irish manufacturing branch and creates a new wholly owned foreign corporation, St. George, Ltd., to engage in manufacturing activities in Ireland. The transfer qualifies as tax deferred under § 351. The branch assets have always been used in Ireland. Amelia transfers the following branch assets to St. George upon its creation.

Asset	Tax Basis	Market Value	Built-in Gain/(Loss)
Raw materials inventory	$100	$ 400	$ 300
Accounts receivable	200	250	50
Manufacturing equipment	450	925	475
Furniture and fixtures	150	50	(100)
Total	$900	$1,625	$ 725

Although the $725 in realized gain is deferred under § 351, the gain is potentially taxable under § 367 because the assets are leaving the U.S. taxing jurisdiction. The general rule of § 367 is that all of the realized gain is recognized by Amelia on an asset-by-asset basis with no offset for losses. Thus, the recognized gain would be $825, with no offset for the $100 loss on the furniture and fixtures. However, because St. George will use the transferred assets in the active conduct of a foreign trade or business, the realized gain remains potentially deferred. But, because the inventory and accounts receivable are "tainted assets," Amelia must recognize $350 of gain upon the transfer ($300 gain attributable to inventory and $50 gain from the accounts receivable). ■

In addition to gain on the tainted assets listed above, any U.S. depreciation (§§ 1245 and 1250) and other types of recapture potential (e.g., §§ 617, 1252, and 1254) in the assets transferred are recognized to the extent of gain realized. This provision applies only to appreciated assets for which the depreciation or other deduction has resulted in a tax benefit. The U.S. depreciation is the portion of the depreciation attributable to use of the property in the United States. Prior branch losses are also recaptured to the extent that they are not recaptured under the § 904(f) provisions.

The transfer of intangibles is treated separately under § 367(d) as a transfer pursuant to a sale for contingent payments. These amounts are treated as though received by the transferor over the life of the intangible (not to exceed 20 years) and are ordinary income. They are recognized by the transferor and must be commensurate with the income attributable to the intangible.

EXAMPLE 10

TechCo, a domestic corporation, transfers a patent to a wholly owned foreign subsidiary in a transaction qualifying for nonrecognition under § 351. The patent has a fair market value of $1 million and a useful life of 10 years. TechCo's adjusted basis in the patent is zero. Assume that an arm's length royalty payment for the use of the patent would be $150,000 per year. TechCo does not recognize any gain under § 367 as a result of the transfer. However, TechCo must report deemed royalty income of $150,000 per year for the next 10 years. The royalty income is ordinary income and is foreign source if the patent is used outside the United States.

Assume that four years after the initial transfer the patent becomes more valuable because a new technology developed by an unrelated company uses the patent knowledge for one of its components. The arm's length royalty payment based on the new value would now be $500,000 per year. Although neither TechCo nor its foreign subsidiary performed any activities that caused the patent to become more valuable, TechCo must begin reporting the higher $500,000 per year royalty amount in order to recognize income commensurate with the patent's value. ■

PLANNING STRATEGIES

Transferring Intangible Assets Offshore

FRAMEWORK FOCUS: TAX RATE

STRATEGY ➤ AVOID DOUBLE TAXATION.

In many industries, a company's intangible assets, such as licenses and patents, produce a relatively large share of total income. For example, the license to use a software program is much more valuable than the actual disk the customer purchases; thus, a large part of the profit from the sale of software accrues to the license holder. Unlike manufacturing plants, intangible assets can easily be transferred to related entities outside the United States. Congress recognized this potential, and § 367 requires gain to be recognized via deemed royalty income if intangibles are transferred outside the United States in a tax-deferred transaction.

To avoid this § 367 "toll charge," companies should consider creating their intangibles offshore so that no subsequent transfer is required. Companies may choose to perform their research and development activities within subsidiaries located in tax haven countries in order to create and keep their valuable intangibles in low-tax jurisdictions. If the intangible property has already been created in the United States, the company may want to transfer the intangible to a foreign subsidiary in a *taxable* transaction in order to avoid the deemed royalty provisions of § 367(d). Although this usually triggers a current gain to the U.S. transferor, any future increases in value of the intangible accrue to the new foreign owner, and any related profits remain with the foreign corporation where they are protected from U.S. taxation until such time as any profits are repatriated back to the United States.

Keep in mind that U.S. transfer pricing rules require that any sales price for the intangibles be based on arm's length principles.

INBOUND ASSET TRANSFERS AND OFFSHORE TRANSFERS

A second major objective of § 367 is to prevent E & P that has accumulated in U.S.-owned foreign corporations from escaping U.S. taxation. Section 367(b) covers the tax treatment of inbound and offshore transfers. Examples of inbound transactions include the following.

- The liquidation of a foreign corporation into a domestic parent under § 332.
- The acquisition of the assets of a foreign corporation by a domestic corporation in a "Type C" or "Type D" reorganization.

Examples of offshore transfers include the following.

- An offshore corporate subsidiary acquiring another non-U.S. corporation in a "Type B," "Type C," or "Type D" tax-deferred reorganization.
- The shareholders of a U.S. corporation exchanging the shares of the corporation for the shares of a non-U.S. corporation in a "Type B" reorganization (an "inversion").
- The liquidation of a lower-tier foreign corporation into a higher-tier non-U.S. subsidiary under § 332.

Section 367(b) ensures that any E & P that has been generated by a foreign corporation owned by U.S. persons is ultimately subject to U.S. taxation at the shareholder level. The rules accomplish this by triggering a dividend to the U.S. shareholders as a "toll charge" for certain transactions.

EXAMPLE 11

JaneCo, Inc., a domestic corporation, owns 100% of YiiCo, a foreign corporation. YiiCo has been in existence for 15 years and at all times has been owned by JaneCo. During this 15 years, YiiCo has generated $250,000 of E & P and paid no dividends to JaneCo. YiiCo has assets currently valued at $1.5 million with an aggregate adjusted basis of $300,000. If YiiCo liquidates into JaneCo, §§ 332 and 337 would allow tax-deferred treatment, with JaneCo stepping into YiiCo's shoes with regard to the adjusted basis in the assets. In a typical tax-deferred liquidation, the E & P of the subsidiary is simply added to the E & P of the parent corporation. In this case, however, because YiiCo's E & P has not yet been taxed in the United States, it is not possible to combine this E & P with JaneCo's E & P. Consequently, § 367(b) requires that YiiCo's $250,000 in E & P be treated as a dividend to JaneCo as a result of the liquidation, which otherwise remains tax deferred. Then, because YiiCo's E & P has now been taxed by the United States, it is combined with JaneCo's E & P. Because the $250,000 is treated as a dividend, any foreign income taxes YiiCo has paid to earn this $250,000 are available as a § 902 deemed-paid foreign tax credit to JaneCo. ■

EXAMPLE 12

Warren, Inc., a domestic corporation, owns 100% of Amrit, Ltd., a foreign corporation. Amrit has significant E & P that has not yet been taxed to Warren in the United States. In an exchange qualifying for deferral as a "Type B" reorganization, Warren exchanges all of the shares of Amrit for 3% of the shares of Ocala, Ltd., a much larger publicly held offshore corporation. Before the exchange, Amrit was a CFC. As discussed later in this chapter, the United States can currently tax U.S. shareholders of CFCs on certain E & P, even when no actual dividends are paid. After the exchange, Warren now owns shares of Ocala, which is not a CFC. Because Warren has exchanged a CFC for a non-CFC, Amrit's E & P is treated as a dividend to Warren on the day of the exchange. Any foreign taxes related to this E & P are available to Warren as a deemed-paid credit. Other than this dividend, the remainder of the transaction qualifies for nonrecognition.[4] ■

[4]Several reporting requirements must be met to obtain tax deferral in a § 367 transaction, and in some cases a gain recognition agreement must be filed with the IRS.

GLOBAL TAX ISSUES

A Move to the Beach for U.S. Corporations Seeking a Vacation from U.S. Tax Rules

A number of U.S.-based companies have decided to cast their lot on the golden shores of Bermuda, reincorporating as Bermuda companies and enjoying Bermuda's low-tax environment. Recent examples include such well-known companies as Fruit of the Loom, Cooper Industries, Foster Wheeler, and Ingersoll Rand. Even Accenture, formerly Andersen Consulting, established itself in Bermuda. Many of these companies argue that U.S. international tax policy creates an environment that damages their ability to compete in the global marketplace. The stock market often rewarded these so-called inversion transactions (i.e., conversion from U.S. to foreign based) with increased stock prices.

Although an inversion transaction often entailed a current tax cost, the long-term tax benefits were considered more important. For example, with a Bermuda parent company rather than a U.S. parent company, many of the lower-tier foreign subsidiaries would not constitute CFCs. Many other companies were preparing to invert in 2002 when Congress began developing anti-inversion legislation and the public began reacting negatively to these corporate expatriates. During the summer of 2002, toolmaker Stanley Works called off its previously announced, and very controversial, inversion plans, and 2003 saw very few inversions of U.S. companies.

TAX HAVENS

Many outbound transfers of assets to foreign corporations are to countries with tax rates higher than or equal to the U.S. rate. Thus, tax avoidance is not the motive for such transfers. Some U.S. corporations, however, make their investment abroad in (or through) a tax haven. A **tax haven** is a country where either locally sourced income or residents are subject to no or low internal taxation. One method of potentially avoiding taxation is to invest through a corporation incorporated in a tax haven. Because the non-U.S. corporation is a resident of the tax haven, the income it earns is subject to no or low internal taxes.

Tax haven countries may also have provisions limiting the exchange of financial and commercial information. A tax haven can, in effect, be created by an income tax treaty. For example, under an income tax treaty between Country A and Country B, residents of A are subject to a withholding tax of only 5 percent on dividend and interest income sourced in B. The United States and A have a similar treaty. The United States does not have a treaty with B, which imposes a withholding tax of 30 percent.

A U.S. corporation can create a foreign subsidiary in A and use that subsidiary to make investments in B. This practice is referred to as *treaty shopping*. If the B investment income had been earned directly by the U.S. corporation, it would be subject to a 30 percent withholding tax. As a result of investing through the foreign subsidiary created in A, the U.S. parent pays only 10 percent in foreign taxes on the income earned, that is, 5 percent to B and 5 percent to A.

In recent years, many countries have included *treaty shopping* provisions in their tax treaties. Under the provisions, treaty benefits are not available to a resident corporation unless certain tests are met. The most controversial article in the U.S. Model Treaty is Article 22, Limitation on Benefits, which is meant to prevent treaty shopping. Article 22 disallows treaty benefits to an entity unless more than 50 percent of the beneficial interest in the entity is owned, directly or indirectly, by one or more residents of the treaty country in which the entity is resident, or a

TAX FACT

The OECD's Tax Haven Blacklist

In 2000, the Organization for Economic Cooperation and Development (OECD) identified the following jurisdictions as tax havens that had not cooperated with its campaign to stop harmful global tax practices. As of 2003, only the countries marked with an asterisk remained on the list.

Andorra*	Guernsey	Panama
Anguilla	Isle of Man	Samoa
Antigua and Barbuda	Jersey	Seychelles
Aruba	Liberia*	St. Christopher and Nevis
Bahamas	Liechtenstein*	St. Lucia
Bahrain	Maldives	St. Vincent and the Grenadines
Barbados	Marshall Islands*	Tonga
Belize	Monaco*	Turks and Caicos Islands
British Virgin Islands	Montserrat	U.S. Virgin Islands
Cook Island	Nauru*	Vanuatu
Dominica	Netherlands Antilles	
Gibraltar	Niue	
Grenada		

Sources: Organization for Economic Cooperation and Development, *Towards Global Tax Cooperation: Progress in Identifying and Eliminating Harmful Tax Practices,* 2000; OECD News Release, April 18, 2002; OECD News Release, May 20, 2003.

substantial portion of the entity's income is paid to persons eligible for treaty benefits. Other U.S. statutory limitations on treaty shopping are contained in § 894(c) dealing with payments to hybrid entities and Regulation § 1.881–3 dealing with payments through intermediate entities.

DIGGING DEEPER 1

Find more information on this topic at our Web site: ***http://wft-advanced.swlearning.com***.

LO.4

Work with the rules concerning operations through foreign corporations.

Operations through Foreign Corporations

CONTROLLED FOREIGN CORPORATIONS

As discussed earlier, foreign corporations—even those controlled by U.S. shareholders—generally are not included in a U.S. consolidated income tax return. Consequently, in the absence of any other provision, the income of a foreign corporation is included in the U.S. shareholder's U.S. income tax return only when dividend income (or other taxable payment) is received. To minimize current U.S. tax liability, taxpayers often attempt to defer the recognition of taxable income. One way to do this is to shift the income-generating activity to a foreign entity where the income earned will not be subject to U.S. tax until repatriated.

For example, a U.S. person can create a foreign holding company to own the stock of foreign operating affiliates or intangible assets, such as patents and trademarks. The income generated by these foreign holdings would escape current

TAX IN THE NEWS

Foreign Income Deferral and the 2004 Presidential Campaign

The deferral allowed U.S. companies with foreign subsidiaries took on an important position in Senator John Kerry's (D-MA) bid for the presidency. During the campaign he attacked the availability of such deferrals, and he suggested a major revision of U.S. taxation of foreign subsidiary profits, ending most deferral opportunities. Such a change hearkens back to another senator from Massachusetts who sought the presidency. John F. Kennedy's administration presided over the creation of the original Subpart F rules in 1962.

U.S. taxation. A non-U.S. corporation also can be used to accumulate income from sales or service activities by acting as an intermediary between the U.S. corporation and an offshore customer. The foreign subsidiary corporation would be used to purchase goods from the U.S. parent or domestic affiliates and then resell the goods to foreign customers or to provide services on behalf of the U.S. parent or affiliates.

In some cases, the use of intermediate foreign subsidiaries is based on a substantive business purpose. In other cases, they are employed only to reduce tax costs. Because of this potential for abuse, Congress has enacted various provisions to limit the availability of deferral.

Subpart F, §§ 951–964 of the Code, provides that certain types of income generated by CFCs are currently included in gross income by the U.S. shareholders without regard to actual distributions. For Subpart F to apply, the foreign corporation must have been a CFC for an uninterrupted period of 30 days or more during the taxable year. When this is the case, U.S. shareholders must include in gross income their pro rata share of Subpart F income and increase in earnings that the CFC has invested in U.S. property for the tax year. This rule applies to U.S. shareholders who own stock in the corporation on the last day of the tax year or on the last day the foreign corporation is a CFC. The gross income inclusion must be made for their taxable year in which the taxable year of the CFC ends.

EXAMPLE 13

Gray, Inc., a calendar year corporation, is a CFC for the entire tax year. Chance Company, a U.S. corporation, owns 60% of Gray's one class of stock for the entire year. Subpart F income is $100,000, and no distributions have been made during the year. Chance, a calendar year taxpayer, includes $60,000 in gross income as a constructive dividend for the tax year. To the extent Gray has paid any foreign income taxes, Chance may claim a deemed-paid credit for the portion of the foreign taxes related to the $60,000 constructive dividend. ■

EXAMPLE 14

Gray, Inc., is a CFC until July 1 of the tax year (a calendar year) and earns $100,000 in Subpart F income. Terry, a U.S. citizen, owns 30% of its one class of stock for the entire year. She includes $14,877 [$100,000 × 30% × (181 days/365 days)] in gross income as a constructive dividend for the tax year. ■

A CFC is any foreign corporation in which more than 50 percent of the total combined voting power of all classes of stock entitled to vote or the total value of the stock of the corporation is owned by U.S. shareholders on any day during the taxable year of the foreign corporation. The foreign subsidiaries of most multinational U.S. parent corporations are CFCs.

For purposes of determining if a foreign corporation is a CFC, a **U.S. shareholder** is defined as a U.S. person who owns, or is considered to own, 10 percent

TAX FACT

WHO ARE THESE CFCS?

The 7,500 largest CFCs accounted for $2.7 trillion of the assets and more than $1.7 trillion of the gross receipts of all CFCs during the latest year for which complete data are available. These CFCs were engaged primarily in manufacturing (39 percent) or finance, insurance, or real estate (30 percent). Although these 7,500 CFCs were incorporated in over 100 different countries, CFCs in the United Kingdom, Canada, Germany, the Netherlands, France, and Japan accounted for over 60 percent of the gross receipts. The number of U.S. multinational corporations with CFCs increased 22 percent from 1990 to 1996. In 1996, CFCs distributed $69 billion of profits to their U.S. parents and other shareholders. A "large" CFC is one having $500 million or more in assets.

Source: *Statistics of Income Bulletin*, Spring 2001.

or more of the total combined voting power of all classes of voting stock of the foreign corporation. Stock owned directly, indirectly, and constructively is counted. Indirect ownership involves stock held through a foreign entity, such as a foreign corporation, foreign partnership, or foreign trust. This stock is considered to be actually owned proportionately by the shareholders, partners, or beneficiaries. Constructive ownership rules, with certain modifications, apply in determining if a U.S. person is a U.S. shareholder, in determining whether a foreign corporation is a CFC, and for certain related-party provisions of Subpart F.[5]

EXAMPLE 15

Shareholders of Foreign Corporation	Voting Power and Value	Classification
Alan	30%	U.S. person
Bill	9%	U.S. person
Carla	40%	Foreign person
Dora	20%	U.S. person
Ed	1%	U.S. person

Bill is Alan's son. Alan, Bill, and Dora are U.S. shareholders. Alan owns 39%, 30% directly and 9% constructively through Bill. Bill also owns 39%, 9% directly and 30% constructively through Alan. Thus, Bill is a U.S. shareholder. Dora owns 20% directly. The corporation is a CFC because U.S. shareholders own 59% of the voting power. Ed, a U.S. person, owns 1% and is not related to any of the other shareholders. Thus, Ed is not a U.S. shareholder and will not include any of the Subpart F income in gross income. If Bill were not related to Alan or to any other U.S. persons who were shareholders, Bill would not be a U.S. shareholder, and the corporation would not be a CFC. ■

U.S. shareholders must include their pro rata share of the applicable income in their gross income only to the extent of their actual ownership. Stock held indirectly (but not constructively) is considered actually owned for this purpose.

EXAMPLE 16

Bill, in Example 15, recognizes only 9% of the Subpart F income as a constructive dividend. Alan recognizes 30%, and Dora recognizes 20%. If instead Bill were a foreign corporation wholly owned by Alan, Alan would recognize 39% as a constructive dividend. ■

[5]§§ 958 and 318(a).

Subpart F Income. A U.S. shareholder of a CFC does not necessarily lose the ability to defer U.S. taxation of income earned by the CFC. Only certain income earned by the CFC triggers immediate U.S. taxation as a constructive dividend. This tainted income, referred to as **Subpart F income,** can be characterized as income with little or no economic connection with the CFC's country of incorporation. Subpart F income consists of the following.

- Insurance income (§ 953).
- Foreign base company income (§ 954).
- International boycott factor income (§ 999).
- Illegal bribes.
- Income derived from a § 901(j) foreign country.

Insurance Income. Income attributable to insuring risk of loss outside the country in which the CFC is organized is Subpart F income. This rule precludes U.S. corporations from setting up offshore insurance companies in tax havens to convert expenditures for self-insurance into a deductible insurance premium.

Foreign Base Company Income. Foreign base company income (FBCI) provisions target transactions where a CFC earns income that lacks any economic connection to its country of organization. There are five categories of FBCI.

- Foreign personal holding company income.
- Foreign base company sales income.
- Foreign base company services income.
- Foreign base company shipping income.
- Foreign base company oil-related income.

Foreign personal holding company (FPHC) income consists of the following.

- Dividends, interest, royalties, rents, and annuities.
- Excess gains over losses from the sale or exchange of property that gives rise to FPHC income.
- Excess of foreign currency gains over foreign currency losses (other than any transaction directly related to the business needs of the CFC).
- Income from notional principal contracts.
- Certain payments in lieu of dividends.

Certain FPHC income does not trigger a Subpart F inclusion under exceptions for same-country payments and active rent and royalty income.

Foreign base company (FBC) sales income is income derived by a CFC where the CFC has very little connection with the process that generates the income and a related party is involved. If the CFC earns income from the sale of property to customers outside the CFC's country of incorporation, and either the supplier or the customer is related to the CFC, such income is FBC sales income.

EXAMPLE 17

Ulysses, Ltd., is a CFC organized in the United Kingdom and owned 100% by Joyce, Inc., a U.S. corporation. Ulysses purchases finished inventory from Joyce and sells the inventory to customers in Hong Kong. This sales income constitutes FBC sales income. ■

An exception applies to property that is manufactured, produced, grown, or extracted in the country in which the CFC was organized or created and also to property sold for use, consumption, or disposition within that country. In both these situations, the CFC has participated in the economic process that generates the income.

EXAMPLE 18

If Ulysses, from Example 17, purchases raw materials from Joyce and performs substantial manufacturing activity in the United Kingdom before selling the inventory to customers in Hong Kong, the income is not FBC sales income. Even without the manufacturing activity, sales to customers within the United Kingdom would not produce FBC sales income. ■

Certain income derived by a branch of the CFC in another country can be deemed FBC sales income. This is the case when the effect of using the branch is the same as if the branch were a wholly owned subsidiary and the tax rate in the sales jurisdiction is less than that in the manufacturing jurisdiction.[6]

Unfortunately, the mechanistic application required by the Subpart F provisions sometimes catches active foreign corporations within the Subpart F system.

EXAMPLE 19

Harrell, Inc., a U.S. corporation owns all of PokerCo, Ltd., an Irish manufacturing corporation, and ChipCo, a Belgium distribution corporation. Both PokerCo and ChipCo are CFCs. PokerCo sells its inventory production to ChipCo. ChipCo sells the inventory to unrelated customers located in Switzerland, Italy, and Germany. Because ChipCo does not manufacture the inventory and acquires it from a related supplier, any sales to customers outside Belgium will produce Subpart F income and a constructive dividend to Harrell, Inc. This is true even though ChipCo is engaged in an active business and is not merely a "paper" corporation. To avoid Subpart F treatment, Harrell should create a distribution company within each country where it operates that sells to customers only within that country. ■

FBC services income is income derived from the performance of services for or on behalf of a related person and performed outside the country in which the CFC was created or organized. Income from services performed in connection with the sale of property by a CFC that has manufactured, produced, grown, or extracted such property is not FBC services income.

FBC shipping income includes the following.

- Dividends and interest received from a foreign corporation, to the extent that income is attributable to, or is derived from or in connection with, the shipping activity.
- Income attributable to the use of any aircraft or vessel in foreign commerce.
- Income attributable to the performance of services directly related to the use of that aircraft or vessel.
- Income attributable to the sale or exchange of any such aircraft or vessel.

FBC oil-related income is income, other than extraction income, derived in a foreign country by large oil producers in connection with the sale of oil and gas products and sold by the CFC or a related person for use or consumption outside the country in which the oil or gas was extracted.

Subpart F Income Exceptions. A *de minimis* rule provides that if the total amount of a foreign corporation's FBCI and gross insurance income for the taxable year is less than the lesser of 5 percent of gross income or $1 million, none of its gross income is treated as FBCI for the tax year. At the other extreme, if a foreign corporation's FBCI and gross insurance income exceed 70 percent of total gross income, all of the corporation's gross income for the tax year is treated as Subpart F income.

FBCI and insurance income subject to high foreign taxes are not included under Subpart F if the taxpayer establishes that the income was subject to an effective

[6]§ 954(d)(2).

rate, imposed by a foreign country, of more than 90 percent of the maximum corporate rate under § 11. For example, the rate must be greater than 31.5 percent (90% × 35%), where 35 percent represents the highest U.S. corporate rate.

Subpart F income inclusions are limited to current-year E & P. Consequently, even when a CFC earns Subpart F income during the taxable year, the constructive dividend to the U.S. shareholders will never exceed the CFC's current-year E & P.[7]

Investment in U.S. Property. In addition to Subpart F income, U.S. shareholders must include in gross income their pro rata share of the CFC's increase in investment in U.S. property for the taxable year.[8] U.S. property generally includes U.S. real property, debt obligations of U.S. persons, and stock in certain related domestic corporations.

EXAMPLE 20

Fleming, Ltd., a CFC, earned no Subpart F income for the taxable year. If Fleming lends $100,000 to Lynn, its sole U.S. shareholder, this debt is considered an investment in U.S. property by Fleming because it now owns a U.S. note receivable. Holding the note triggers a constructive dividend of $100,000 to Lynn. ■

PLANNING STRATEGIES

Using Subpart F Exceptions

FRAMEWORK FOCUS: INCOME AND EXCLUSIONS

STRATEGY ➤ **AVOID INCOME RECOGNITION.**

The *de minimis* rule allows a CFC to avoid the classification of income as FBCI or insurance income and prevents the U.S. shareholder from having to include it in gross income as a constructive dividend. Thus, a CFC with total FBCI and insurance income in an amount close to the 5 percent or $1 million level should monitor income realization to assure that the *de minimis* rule applies for the tax year. At least as important is avoiding the classification of all the gross income of the CFC as FBCI or insurance income. This happens when the sum of the FBCI and gross insurance income for the taxable year exceeds 70 percent of total gross income.

Careful timing of increases in investment in U.S. property can reduce the potential for constructive dividend income to U.S. shareholders. The gross income of U.S. shareholders attributable to increases in investment in U.S. property is limited to the E & P of the CFC. E & P that is attributable to amounts that have been included in gross income as Subpart F income in either the current year or a prior tax year is not taxed again when invested in U.S. property.

Distributions of Previously Taxed Income. Distributions from a CFC are treated as being first from E & P attributable to investment in U.S. property previously taxed as a constructive dividend, second from E & P attributable to previously taxed Subpart F income, and last from other E & P. Thus, distributions of previously taxed income are not taxed again as a dividend but reduce E & P. Any increase in investment in U.S. property is considered attributable first to Subpart F income and thus is not taxed twice.

[7]However, in future years when additional E & P is generated, this prior Subpart F income may be recaptured (treated as a constructive dividend in the future year).

[8]§ 956.

Concept Summary 8–1

Income of a CFC That Is Included in Gross Income of a U.S. Shareholder

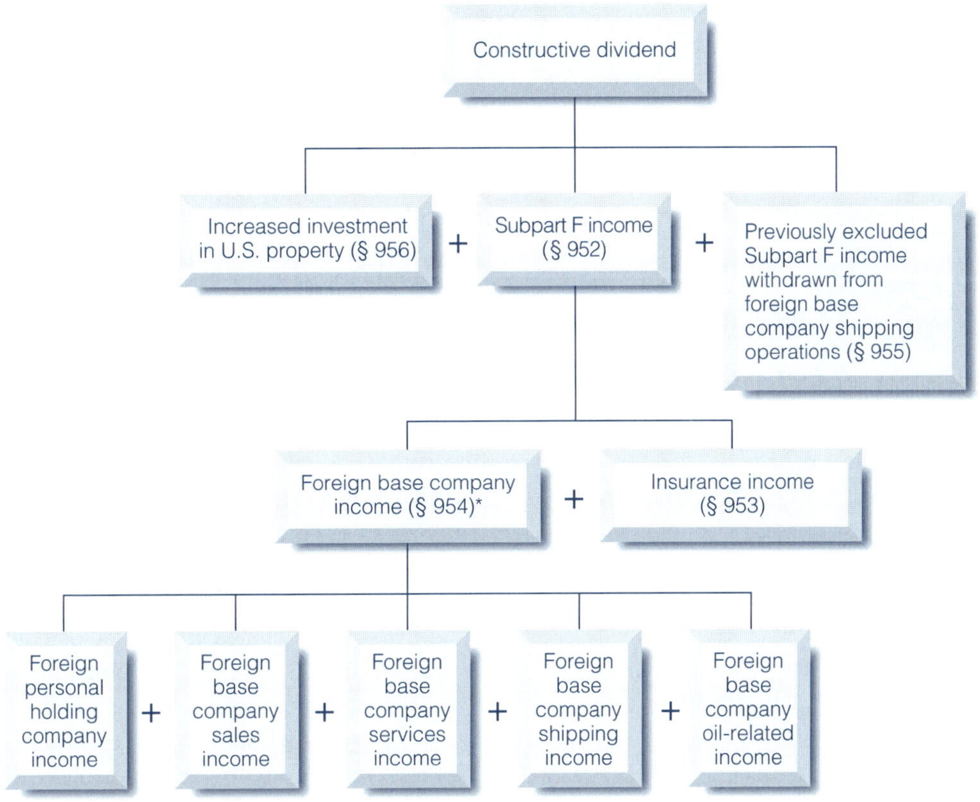

*Plus all other income, when foreign base company and insurance income exceeds 70% of gross income.

EXAMPLE 21

In the current year, Jet, Inc., a U.S. shareholder, owns 100% of a CFC, from which Jet receives a $100,000 distribution. The CFC's E & P is composed of the following amounts.

- $50,000 attributable to previously taxed increases in investment in U.S. property.
- $30,000 attributable to previously taxed Subpart F income.
- $40,000 attributable to other E & P.

Jet has a taxable dividend of only $20,000, all attributable to other E & P. The remaining $80,000 is previously taxed income. The CFC's E & P is reduced by $100,000. The remaining $20,000 E & P is all attributable to other E & P. ■

A U.S. shareholder's basis in CFC stock is increased by constructive dividends and decreased by subsequent distributions of previously taxed income. U.S. corporate shareholders who own at least 10 percent of the voting stock of a foreign corporation are allowed an indirect foreign tax credit for foreign taxes deemed paid on constructive dividends included in gross income under Subpart F. The indirect credit also is available for Subpart F income attributable to certain lower-tier foreign corporations. See the foreign tax credit discussion in Chapter 7. The various constructive dividend possibilities for CFC income appear in Concept Summary 8–1.

Dispositions of Stock of a CFC. Under the Subpart F provisions, Subpart F income of a CFC is currently taxed to U.S. shareholders to the extent of their pro rata share. This rule, however, does not reach the earnings of the CFC that are not included in the taxable income of the shareholders under Subpart F (e.g., active trade or business income not involving related persons). Section 1248 prevents the gain from the disposition of CFC stock from escaping taxation as ordinary income. This provision requires that gain on the sale or other disposition of stock of a CFC by a U.S. shareholder be treated as dividend income to the extent of the transferor's share of undistributed nonpreviously taxed E & P of the corporation.

PLANNING STRATEGIES

Using Check-the-Box Entities to Avoid Subpart F

FRAMEWORK FOCUS: INCOME AND EXCLUSIONS

STRATEGY ➤ POSTPONE RECOGNITION OF INCOME TO ACHIEVE TAX DEFERRAL.

To defer U.S. taxes on offshore income, U.S. taxpayers often create separate non-U.S. subsidiaries to hold their overseas operations. This approach is successful so long as the foreign subsidiaries do not pay dividends to the U.S. owners, and the foreign subsidiaries do not earn Subpart F income that creates constructive dividends. U.S. companies often set up foreign holding companies in tax-favorable jurisdictions to hold the foreign operating subsidiaries.

Consider the following example. A U.S. parent creates a CFC holding company in a low-tax country to hold its two operating subsidiaries located in high-tax countries. The CFC holding company owns the foreign rights to valuable patents and licenses these rights to the lower-tier subsidiaries, which both pay royalties for the right to use the patents and licenses. The royalty payments are deductible by the operating subsidiaries at a high tax rate (providing tax savings in those countries) and are taxed to the holding company at a relatively low tax rate. This approach provides a net tax savings to the foreign group. However, the royalty payments to the holding company may constitute Subpart F income and trigger a constructive dividend back to the U.S. parent. If so, the tax savings related to the intercompany licensing are offset by the U.S. taxes on the Subpart F income.

Fortunately, a mechanism exists that allows the holding company to avoid Subpart F treatment for the royalty payments. The **check-the-box** Regulations under § 7701 provide a great deal of flexibility for U.S.-based multinational corporations. For example, corporations are allowed to elect (i.e., check the box on a form) to treat certain foreign subsidiaries as unincorporated branches for U.S. purposes rather than as separate legal entities. This election does not change the treatment of the entities under local tax law.

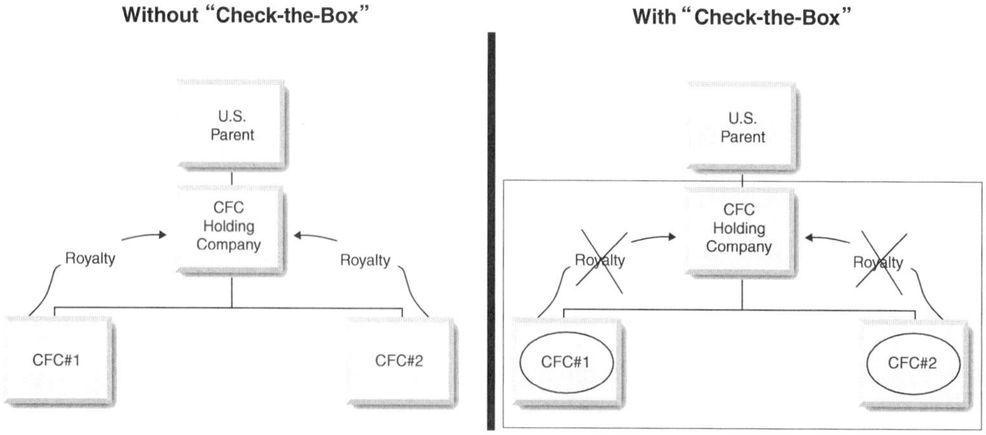

Continuing with the example, the U.S. parent can use the check-the-box rules and elect to treat its foreign subsidiaries, CFC#1 and CFC#2, as branches for U.S. purposes. In this case, the two foreign subsidiaries are treated as mere divisions of the holding company. Accordingly, the intercompany license agreements do not exist from a U.S. perspective, and there is no royalty income because the royalty payments are treated simply as transfers of funds within a single corporation. Without the royalty income, there is no Subpart F income and thus no constructive dividends. However, the foreign tax savings are still available because the royalty payments do exist from a foreign tax perspective and continue to provide royalty deductions at the CFC#1 and CFC#2 level.

INVESTMENTS THROUGH FOREIGN CORPORATIONS

A U.S. person may own shares in a non-U.S. corporation that is not considered a CFC (or the U.S. person is not a U.S. shareholder of the CFC because of less than 10 percent ownership). If that entity earns significant investment income, the U.S. owner seemingly escapes the anti-deferral rules of Subpart F. However, Congress has enacted two other provisions to limit the deferral benefits associated with earning investment income through a foreign corporation. Both the foreign personal holding company (FPHC) and the passive foreign investment company (PFIC) rules can trigger constructive dividends to U.S. persons.

A foreign corporation is an FPHC if it meets two requirements.

- Sixty percent or more of its gross income for the taxable year must be FPHC income, as defined for purposes of Subpart F income. This percentage drops to 50 percent or more after the 60 percent requirement has been met for a tax year. The percentage remains at 50 percent until the foreign corporation does not meet the 50 percent test for three consecutive years or does not meet the stock ownership requirement for an entire tax year.
- More than 50 percent of the total combined voting power or the total value of the stock of the corporation must be owned, directly or indirectly, at any time during the taxable year by five or fewer individuals who are U.S. persons.[9]

The major distinction between the FPHC tax and the domestic personal holding company (PHC) tax is that the FPHC tax is levied on the U.S. shareholders of an FPHC rather than on the corporation. A pro rata share of the undistributed FPHC income (limited to current E & P) is included in the gross income of U.S. persons who are shareholders of the FPHC. The amount taxable as a constructive dividend to a U.S. shareholder is treated as a contribution to the capital of the corporation and increases the shareholder's basis in the corporation's stock. Dividends paid can reduce the amount taxable as undistributed FPHC income. In addition, certain income otherwise qualifying as FPHC income is ignored if it is received from a related corporation. U.S. shareholders of a CFC that is also an FPHC are not taxed on the same income under Subpart F and the FPHC provisions. Income falling within both provisions is taxed only under Subpart F.[10]

A PFIC is similar in theory to an FPHC, but the rules are more restrictive. Any level of ownership can subject a U.S. person to taxation under the PFIC provisions if the foreign corporation earns substantial levels of investment income.[11] Offshore mutual funds are often PFICs to their U.S. owners. Similar to FPHCs, income falling under both Subpart F and the PFIC provisions is taxed only under Subpart F.

[9] § 552.

[10] § 951(d).

[11] § 1297.

LO.5

Describe the tax effects related to the U.S. operations of a foreign taxpayer.

U.S. Taxation of Foreign Persons

Generally, only the U.S.-source income of **nonresident alien** individuals and foreign corporations is subject to U.S. taxation. This reflects the reach of the U.S. tax jurisdiction. The constraint, however, does not prevent the United States from also taxing the foreign-source income of nonresident alien individuals and foreign corporations when that income is effectively connected with the conduct of a U.S. trade or business.[12] Concept Summary 8–2 at the end of this section summarizes these tax rules.

RESIDENCY

Individuals. A nonresident alien (NRA) individual is an individual who is not a citizen or resident of the United States. For example, Queen Elizabeth is an NRA, because she is not a citizen or resident of the United States. Citizenship is determined under the immigration and naturalization laws of the United States.[13] Citizenship statutes are broken down into two categories: nationality at birth or through naturalization.

Under § 7701(b), a person is a resident of the United States for income tax purposes if he or she meets either the green card test or the substantial presence test. If either of these tests is met for the calendar year, the individual is deemed a U.S. resident for the year.

A foreign person issued a green card is considered a U.S. resident on the first day he or she is physically present in the United States after issuance. Status as a U.S. resident remains in effect until the green card has been revoked or the individual has abandoned lawful permanent resident status.

The substantial presence test is applied to an alien without a green card. It is a mathematical test involving physical presence in the United States. An individual who is physically present in the United States for at least 183 days during the calendar year is a U.S. resident for income tax purposes. This 183-day requirement can also be met over a three-year period that includes the two immediately preceding years and the current year, as long as the individual is present in the United States at least 31 days during the current year.[14] For this purpose, each day of the current calendar year is counted as a full day, each day of the first preceding year as one-third day, and each day of the second preceding year as one-sixth day.

EXAMPLE 22

Li, a foreign citizen, was present in the United States for 90 days in 2002, 180 days in 2003, and 110 days in 2004. For Federal income tax purposes, Li is a U.S. resident for 2004, because she was physically present for 185 days [(90 days × ⅙) + (180 days × ⅓) + (110 days × 1)] during the three-year period. ■

Under the substantial presence test, residence begins the first day the individual is physically present in the United States and ends the last day of physical presence for the calendar year (assuming the substantial presence test is not satisfied for the next calendar year). Nominal presence of 10 days or less can be ignored in determining whether the substantial presence test is met.

The substantial presence test allows for several exceptions. Commuters from Mexico and Canada who are employed in the United States but return home each

[12] §§ 871, 881, and 882.

[13] Title 8, Aliens and Nationality, United States Code.

[14] § 7701(b)(3)(A).

day are excepted. Individuals who are prevented from leaving the United States by medical conditions that arose while they were in the United States do not accumulate U.S. presence. Some individuals are exempt from the substantial presence test, including foreign government-related individuals (e.g., diplomats), qualified teachers, trainees and students, and certain professional athletes.

Foreign Corporations. Ascertaining whether an entity is classified as a foreign corporation for U.S. tax purposes is an important factor in determining whether the entity is subject to U.S. tax.[15] Section 7701(a)(5) defines a foreign corporation as one that is not domestic. A domestic corporation is defined as a corporation that is created or organized in the United States. Thus, though McDonald's is, in reality, a global corporation, it is considered a domestic corporation for U.S. tax purposes, solely because it was organized in the United States. Some other countries define residency based on the location of management and control rather than the more formal place of organization approach used by the United States.

U.S. INVESTMENT ACTIVITIES

Certain U.S.-source income that is not effectively connected with the conduct of a U.S. trade or business is subject to a flat 30 percent tax. This income includes dividends, interest, rents, royalties, certain compensation, premiums, annuities, and other fixed, determinable, annual or periodic (FDAP) income.

This tax generally is levied by a withholding mechanism that requires the payors of the income to withhold 30 percent of gross amounts.[16] This method eliminates the problems of assuring payment by nonresidents, determining allowable deductions, and, in most instances, the filing of tax returns by nonresidents. In recent years, U.S. payors withheld taxes of $3 billion annually from payments to foreign persons. Japanese recipients received the most U.S.-source income, with recipients from the United Kingdom ranked second. As explained in Chapter 7, income tax treaties with other countries provide for reduced withholding on certain types of FDAP income.

Interest received from certain portfolio debt investments, even though U.S.-sourced, is exempt from taxation. Interest earned on deposits with banking institutions is also exempt as long as it is not effectively connected with the conduct of a U.S. trade or business. Capital gains of an NRA that are not effectively connected with the conduct of a U.S. trade or business are exempt from tax, as long as the NRA individual was not present in the United States for 183 days or more during the taxable year. Capital gains of a foreign corporation are not subject to tax in the United States unless effectively connected with a U.S. trade or business.

U.S. TRADE OR BUSINESS ACTIVITIES

Two important definitions determine the U.S. tax consequences to foreign corporations and NRAs with U.S.-source income: "the conduct of a **U.S. trade or business**" and "**effectively connected income.**" Specifically, for a foreign person's noninvestment income to be subject to U.S. taxation, the foreign person must be considered engaged in a U.S. trade or business and must earn income effectively connected with that business.

[15]Section 7701 also provides definitions of foreign partnerships, estates, and trusts. When these entities are treated as flow-through entities for U.S. tax purposes, the nature of the partners or beneficiaries is the key factor in determining any U.S. tax consequences.

[16]§§ 871, 881, and 1441.

TAX FACT

Selected Tax Treaty Withholding Rates

The United States has negotiated income tax treaties with various countries that allow for reduced withholding rates on certain types of investment income. The following table shows some examples.

	Interest	Dividends in General	Dividends Paid by U.S. Subsidiary to a Foreign Parent Corporation
Australia	10%	15%	15%
Canada	10	15	5
Ireland	0	15	5
Japan	10	15	10
Mexico	15	15	5
Philippines	15	25	20

Source: IRS Publication 901, *U.S. Tax Treaties.*

General criteria for determining if a U.S. trade or business exists include the location of production activities, management, distribution activities, and other business functions. Trading in commodities and securities ordinarily does not constitute a trade or business. Dealers, however, need to avoid maintaining a U.S. trading office and trading for their own accounts. Corporations (other than certain personal holding companies) that are not dealers can trade for their own accounts. There are no restrictions on individuals who are not dealers.

The Code does not explicitly define a U.S. trade or business, but case law has defined the concept as activities carried on in the United States that are regular, substantial, and continuous.[17] Once a foreign person is considered engaged in a U.S. trade or business, all U.S.-source income other than FDAP and capital gain income is considered effectively connected to that trade or business and is therefore subject to U.S. taxation. This is known as the **force of attraction** rule.

EXAMPLE 23

Vito, an NRA, produces wine in a foreign country for export to the United States. During the current year, Vito earns $500,000 from exporting wine to unrelated wholesalers in the United States. The title to the wine passes to the U.S. wholesalers in New York. Vito has no offices or employees in the United States The income from wine sales is U.S.-source income, but because Vito is not engaged in a U.S. trade or business, the income is not subject to taxation in the United States.

Vito begins operating a hot dog cart in New York City. This activity constitutes a U.S. trade or business. Consequently, all U.S.-source income other than FDAP or capital gain income is taxed in the United States as income effectively connected with a U.S. trade or business. Thus, both the hot dog cart profits and the $500,000 in wine income are taxed in the United States. ■

[17] See, for example, *Higgins v. Comm.*, 312 U.S. 212 (1941), and *Continental Trading, Inc. v. Comm.*, 265 F.2d 40 (1959).

If a foreign person qualifies for tax treaty benefits, the force of attraction rule is not applicable. Under a treaty, the concept of "engaged in a U.S. trade or business" is replaced by **permanent establishment,** and "effectively connected income" is replaced by **business profits.** The terms "permanent establishment" and "business profits" are defined in every income tax treaty (see Chapter 7).

EXAMPLE 24

Assume that Vito, in Example 23, is resident in a country with an income tax treaty with the United States. The wine export activity is not considered to be a permanent establishment in the United States because this activity has no assets, employees, or fixed place of business in the United States. However, the hot dog cart does constitute a permanent establishment. Consequently, the business profits associated with the hot dog cart are subject to U.S. tax. But because the treaty replaces the force of attraction rule with the more specific concept of business profits, the profits related to the wine sales are not considered business profits associated with the hot dog cart (the U.S. permanent establishment) and are not subject to U.S. taxation. ■

FDAP and capital gain income may be considered effectively connected income if the assets that generate this income are used in, or held for use in, the trade or business (the asset-use test) or if the activities of the trade or business are a material factor in the production of the income (the business-activities test).[18] As long as FDAP and capital gain income are not effectively connected with a U.S. trade or business, the tax treatment of these income items is the same regardless of whether the foreign persons are engaged in a U.S. trade or business.

EXAMPLE 25

Ingrid, an NRA, operates a U.S. business. During the year, cash funds accumulate. Ingrid invests these funds on a short-term basis so that they remain available to meet her business needs. Under the asset-use test, any income earned from these investments is effectively connected income. ■

Effectively connected income is taxed at the same rates that apply to U.S. citizens, residents, and corporations. Deductions for expenses attributable to that income are allowed. Foreign persons with effectively connected income are also allowed a deduction for casualty and theft losses related to property located within the United States, a deduction for qualified charitable contributions, and one personal exemption (in the case of NRAs). Foreign persons with income effectively connected with the conduct of a U.S. trade or business may also be subject to the alternative minimum tax.

SPECIAL U.S. TAX ISSUES AFFECTING FOREIGN PERSONS

Limitations on Interest Deductibility. Foreign corporations with U.S. subsidiaries often plan to reduce those subsidiaries' taxable income by making loans to the subsidiaries, with the resulting interest payments reducing U.S. taxable income.

EXAMPLE 26

Hemelt, Ltd., a corporation based in the United Kingdom, owns 100% of Stinnett, Inc., a U.S. corporation. Hemelt loans money to Stinnett, and Stinnett makes interest payments of $100,000 per year to Hemelt. Stinnett reduces its U.S. taxable income by $100,000 because of the interest deduction and saves $35,000 in U.S. taxes ($100,000 × 35% U.S. tax rate). The interest payments to Hemelt would normally be subject to a 30% U.S. withholding tax when paid (resulting in a $30,000 U.S. tax cost), but the U.K. income tax treaty reduces the

[18] § 864(c).

■ FIGURE 8–3
Section 163(j) Interest Limitation Calculation of Adjusted Taxable Income

	Taxable income
+	Net interest expense
+	Net operating loss
+	Depreciation, amortization, and depletion expenses
+	Tax-exempt interest income
+	Dividends received deduction
+/–	Other adjustments [Reg. § 1.163(j)–2(f)]
=	Adjusted taxable income

withholding tax to zero. Consequently, the Hemelt group has a net reduction of $35,000 in its worldwide tax cost. ■

Concern over the ability of foreign corporations to strip earnings from the United States in this tax-efficient way led Congress to enact the so-called **earnings stripping rules** of § 163(j). These rules limit the ability of a U.S. corporation to deduct interest payments under the following conditions.

- The U.S. payor's debt-to-equity ratio exceeds 1.5 to 1.
- The related foreign recipient is not fully subject to U.S. tax on the interest payment.
- The payor's net interest expense exceeds 50 percent of its **adjusted taxable income.**

Adjusted taxable income is an attempt to convert taxable income to a cash-flow amount. Figure 8–3 summarizes the adjusted taxable income determination.

If all of these conditions are met, the lesser of the excess interest expense (net interest expense less 50 percent of adjusted taxable income) or any disqualified interest of the U.S. payor (interest paid to a related foreign person that is not fully subject to U.S. taxation) is disallowed as a deduction in the current year. Any disallowed interest deduction is carried forward indefinitely and may be used in any year when the adjusted taxable income limitation is not binding.

EXAMPLE 27

Assume that Stinnett, Inc., in Example 26, pays only the $100,000 interest to Hemelt and earns no interest income for the year. Thus, Stinnett's net interest expense for the year is $100,000. Disqualified interest is also $100,000 (interest payments to Hemelt where Hemelt is a related party and not subject to withholding tax on the interest payment). Stinnett's adjusted taxable income is $40,000, and its disallowed interest deduction is $80,000.

Disqualified interest expense	$100,000
Net interest expense	$100,000
50% of adjusted taxable income	(20,000)
Excess interest expense	$ 80,000
Disallowed interest deduction (lesser of disqualified interest or the excess interest expense)	$ 80,000

Thus, Stinnett loses the current deduction for $80,000 and the associated $28,000 in U.S. tax savings. The $80,000 may be carried forward and deducted in a future year subject to the same § 163(j) limitations in that year. ■

PLANNING STRATEGIES

Avoiding the § 163(j) Earnings Stripping Rules

FRAMEWORK FOCUS: DEDUCTIONS

STRATEGY ➤ **MAXIMIZE DEDUCTIBLE AMOUNTS.**

The earnings stripping rules of § 163(j) may limit the ability of a foreign-owned U.S. corporation to make fully deductible interest payments to its foreign owners. The disallowance of this deduction increases the group's worldwide tax costs.

As an alternative to receiving interest payments, a foreign parent corporation may consider other types of intercompany payments that are not subject to the § 163(j) rules. For example, rather than injecting debt into the U.S. subsidiary so as to receive interest payments, the foreign parent may instead license a manufacturing process or trademark to the U.S. corporation in exchange for royalty payments. Such royalty payments are deductible for U.S. purposes. Under many treaties, royalty payments are not subject to a U.S. withholding tax.

As another alternative, the foreign parent could charge the U.S. subsidiary for certain management services. These management fees are deductible in the United States and in many cases are not subject to U.S. withholding tax.

In summary, replacing interest payments subject to limitation under §163(j) with other types of payments may preserve the otherwise disallowed U.S. tax benefits. Keep in mind, though, that any royalty payments or management fees must pass muster under the transfer pricing rules of § 482. That is, these amounts must be based on some reasonable method and generally must meet the arm's length price test.

Branch-Level Taxes. The objective of the branch-level taxes imposed by § 884 is to afford equal U.S. tax treatment to income generated by a domestic corporation controlled by a foreign corporation and to income generated by other nonincorporated U.S. operations (i.e., branches) controlled by foreign corporations. If the foreign corporation operates through a U.S. subsidiary (a domestic corporation), the income of the subsidiary is taxable by the United States when earned and is also subject to a withholding tax when repatriated (returned as dividends to the foreign parent). Before the branch profits tax was enacted, a non-U.S. corporation with a branch in the United States paid only the initial tax on its U.S. earnings; remittances were not taxed.

To resolve this discrepancy in tax treatment between subsidiaries and branches, a **branch profits tax** equal to 30 percent of the **dividend equivalent amount (DEA)** for the taxable year is imposed on any foreign corporation with effectively connected income (in addition to the regular income tax imposed under § 882 on effectively connected income of a foreign corporation). The DEA is the foreign corporation's effectively connected earnings for the taxable year, adjusted for increases and decreases in the corporation's U.S. net equity (investment in the U.S. operations). The DEA is limited to current E & P and post-1986 accumulated E & P that is effectively connected with the conduct of a U.S. trade or business. U.S. net equity is the sum of money and the aggregate adjusted basis of assets and liabilities directly connected to U.S. operations that generate effectively connected income.

EXAMPLE 28

Robin, Inc., a foreign corporation, has a U.S. branch operation with the following tax results and other information for the year.

Pretax earnings effectively connected with a U.S. trade or business	$2,000,000
U.S. corporate tax (at 35%)	700,000
Remittance to home office	1,000,000
Increase in U.S. net equity	300,000

Robin's DEA and branch profits tax are computed as follows.

E & P effectively connected with a U.S. trade or business ($2,000,000 – $700,000)	$1,300,000
Less: Increase in U.S. net equity	(300,000)
Dividend equivalent amount	$1,000,000
Branch profits tax rate	× 30%
Branch profits tax	$ 300,000

■

The 30 percent rate of the branch profits tax may be reduced or eliminated by a treaty provision. If a foreign corporation is subject to the branch profits tax, no other U.S. tax is levied on any U.S.-source portion of dividends actually paid by the foreign corporation during the taxable year.

In addition to the branch profits tax, § 884 also imposes certain branch-level interest taxes. These taxes attempt to treat interest paid by foreign corporations that is connected with their U.S. branches the same as if the payments were made directly by a U.S. corporation and thus subject to the U.S. withholding tax.

The Foreign Investment in Real Property Tax Act. Prior to 1980, NRAs and foreign corporations could avoid U.S. taxation on gains from the sale of U.S. real estate if the gains were treated as capital gains and were not effectively connected with the conduct of a U.S. trade or business. In the mid-1970s, midwestern farmers pressured Congress to eliminate what they saw as a tax advantage that would allow nonresidents to bid up the price of farmland. This and other concerns about foreign ownership of U.S. real estate led to the enactment of the Foreign Investment in Real Property Tax Act **(FIRPTA)** of 1980.

Under FIRPTA, gains and losses realized by NRAs and foreign corporations from the sale or other disposition of U.S. real property interests are treated as effectively connected with the conduct of a U.S. trade or business even when those individuals or corporations are not actually so engaged. NRA individuals must pay a tax equal to the lesser of two amounts: (1) 26 (or 28) percent of their alternative minimum taxable income or (2) regular U.S. rates on the net U.S. real property gain for the taxable year.[19] For purposes of this provision, losses are taken into account only to the extent they are deductible as business losses, losses on transactions entered into for profit, or losses from casualties and thefts.

U.S. Real Property Interest (USRPI). Any direct interest in real property situated in the United States and any interest in a domestic corporation (other than solely as a creditor) are **U.S. real property interests (USRPIs).** This definition applies unless the taxpayer can establish that a domestic corporation was not a U.S. real property holding corporation (USRPHC) during the shorter of two periods: (1) the period during which the taxpayer held an interest in the corporation or (2) the five-year period ending on the date on which the interest was disposed of (the base period). A domestic corporation is not a USRPHC if it holds no USRPIs on the date of disposition of its stock and if any USRPIs held by the corporation during the base period were disposed of in a transaction in which gain, if any, was fully recognized.

EXAMPLE 29

From January 1, 1999, through January 1, 2004, Francis (a foreign investor) held shares in Door, Inc., a U.S. corporation. During this period, Door held two parcels of U.S. real estate and stock of Sash, Inc., another U.S. corporation. Sash also owned U.S. real estate. The two

[19]§ 897.

parcels of real estate held directly by Door were disposed of on December 15, 2000, in a nontaxable transaction. Sash disposed of its U.S. real estate in a taxable transaction on January 1, 2004.

An interest in Door is treated as a USRPI because Door did not recognize gain on the December 15, 2000 disposition of the USRPIs. If Door's ownership of U.S. real estate had been limited to its indirect ownership through Sash, an interest in Door would not have constituted a USRPI as of January 2, 2004. This result would occur because Sash disposed of its USRPIs in a taxable transaction in which gain was fully recognized. ■

A USRPHC is any corporation (whether foreign or domestic) where the fair market value of the corporation's USRPIs equals or exceeds 50 percent of the aggregate of fair market value of certain specified assets. These assets are the corporation's USRPIs, its interests in real property located outside the United States, and any other of its assets that are used or held for use in a trade or business. Stock regularly traded on an established securities market is not treated as a USRPI if a person holds no more than 5 percent of the stock. Gain on a disposition of stock of a foreign real property holding corporation is not subject to tax under FIRPTA. However, gain on a disposition of a USRPI by such a foreign corporation is subject to FIRPTA.

Withholding Provisions. The FIRPTA withholding provisions require any purchaser or agent acquiring a USRPI from a foreign person to withhold 10 percent of the amount realized on the disposition.[20] A domestic partnership, trust, or estate with a foreign partner, foreign grantor treated as owner, or foreign beneficiary must withhold 35 percent (or 20 percent where allowed by the IRS) of the gain allocable to that person on a disposition of a USRPI. Foreign corporations are also subject to withholding provisions on certain distributions. Without this withholding, NRAs could sell USRPIs, receiving the sales proceeds outside the United States, and jurisdictional issues could make it difficult for the U.S. tax authorities to collect any U.S. tax that might be due on gains. Certain exceptions to FIRPTA withholding are allowed.

Failure to withhold can subject the purchaser or the purchaser's agent to interest on any unpaid amount.[21] A civil penalty of 100 percent of the amount required to be withheld and a criminal penalty of up to $10,000 or five years in prison can be imposed for willful failure to withhold.[22]

PLANNING STRATEGIES

The Foreign Corporation As a Tax Shelter

FRAMEWORK FOCUS: INCOME AND EXCLUSIONS

STRATEGY ➤ CONTROL THE CHARACTER OF INCOME AND DEDUCTIONS.

An NRA who is able to hold U.S. investments through an offshore corporation can accomplish much in the way of avoiding U.S. taxation. Capital gains (other than dispositions of U.S. real property interests) are not subject to U.S. taxation. This assumes that they are not effectively connected with a U.S. trade or business. The NRA can dispose of the stock of a foreign corporation that holds U.S. real property and not be subject to taxation under § 897 (FIRPTA). Furthermore,

[20] § 1445.

[21] §§ 6601, 6621, and 6651.

[22] §§ 6672 and 7202.

the stock of a foreign corporation is not included in the U.S. gross estate of a deceased NRA, even if all of the assets of the foreign corporation are located in the United States.

Caution is advised when the foreign corporation may generate income effectively connected with the conduct of a U.S. trade or business. The income may be taxed at a higher rate than if the NRA individually generated the income. The tradeoff between a higher U.S. tax on this income and protection from the U.S. estate tax and § 897 must be weighed.

Expatriation to Avoid U.S. Taxation. Section 877 provides for U.S. taxation of U.S.-source income earned by persons who relinquished their U.S. citizenship within 10 years of deriving that income if they gave up their citizenship to avoid U.S. taxation. Furthermore, NRAs who lost U.S. citizenship within a 10-year period immediately preceding the close of the tax year must pay taxes on their U.S.-source income as though they were still U.S. citizens. This provision applies only if the expatriation had as one of its principal purposes the avoidance of U.S. taxes. For 2004, individuals are presumed to have a tax avoidance purpose if they meet either of the following criteria.[23]

- Average annual net income tax for the five taxable years ending before the date of loss of U.S. citizenship is more than $124,000.
- Net worth as of that date is $622,000 or more.

These provisions also apply to "long-term lawful permanent residents" who cease to be taxed as U.S. residents. A long-term permanent resident is an individual (other than a citizen of the United States) who is a lawful permanent resident of the United States in at least 8 taxable years during the 15-year period ending with the taxable year in which the individual either ceases to be a lawful permanent resident of the United States or begins to be treated as a resident of another country under an income tax treaty between the United States and the other country (and does not waive the benefits of the treaty to residents of that country).

Concept Summary 8–2

U.S. Tax Treatment of Non-U.S. Person's Income

Type of Income	Tax Rate
U.S.-source fixed, determinable, annual or periodic income (not effectively connected with a U.S. business)	Generally 30% withholding on gross amount (or lower treaty rate) with certain limited exceptions.
U.S.-source income effectively connected with a U.S. business	Regular individual or corporate rates applied against net income (after deductions).
Gain on U.S. real property (direct or indirect interest)	Taxed as if effectively connected with a U.S. trade or business.
Capital gains (other than on U.S. real property) not effectively connected with a U.S. business	• Corporation: Not subject to U.S. tax. • Individual: Generally not taxed but may be subject to a 30% U.S. tax if taxpayer physically present in the United States ≥ 183 days.
Foreign-source business income	Generally not subject to U.S. taxation unless attributable to a U.S. office or fixed place of business.

[23]The dollar amounts are adjusted for inflation, using a variation of § 1(f)(3).

TAX FACT

Filing Deadlines When You're Overseas

What if you are situated outside the United States when you file a tax return? Working with a non-U.S. postal service can be challenging even on a good day. The established rule still seems to be that the date of the non-U.S. postmark determines whether the return is filed in a timely manner or whether a failure to file penalty will be assessed (Rev.Rul. 80–218).

The IRS seems to be having some trouble digesting this rule, though. In *Pekar*, 113 TC 158, where the non-U.S. postmark indicated that the return had been mailed before its due date, the IRS seemed to be taking a date-received position with the Tax Court. But the Service admitted its mistake in ITA 2000121085, where the reliance-on-postmark test was applied as expected.

No ruling to date has specifically addressed the use of a private express delivery service like UPS, but neither the Code nor rulings restrict the when-delivered-to-the-carrier rule to domestic shipments, either. Thus, if a U.S. taxpayer living overseas uses a private delivery service, some form of date stamping is a good idea.

An exception applies to certain individuals with dual citizenship. Special source rules also apply for purposes of expatriate taxation. The expatriate tax will not apply if U.S. taxation of the NRA under the normal provisions applicable to NRAs results in a greater tax liability. Certain expatriate provisions also apply for estate and gift tax purposes.

Suggested Further Readings

B. Anthony Billings, Gary A. McGill, and Mbodja Mougoué, "The Effect of Export Tax Incentives on Export Volume: The DISC/FSC Evidence," *Advances in Taxation*, 2003.

Edward D. Brown and Eric R. Kaplan, "Incorporating Offshore: Taxation and Asset Protection," *Journal of International Taxation*, June 2003.

Joseph M. Calianno and J. Michael Cornett, "Outbound Section 351 Transfers—How International Provisions Alter the General Rules," *Journal of International Taxation*, January 2002.

Michael J. A. Karlin, "Coming to America—When Does Tax Residence Begin?" *Journal of International Taxation*, December 2002.

Lowell D. Yoder and Rachel Laro Waimon, "*Seagate*: Tax Court Holds Restricted Stock Gains Are Subpart F Income," *Journal of International Taxation*, April 2001.

KEY TERMS

Adjusted taxable income, 8–28
Branch profits tax, 8–29
Business profits, 8–27
Check-the-box, 8–22
Controlled foreign corporation (CFC), 8–3
Deemed dividend, 8–2
Deferral, 8–3
Dividend equivalent amount, 8–29
Earnings stripping rules, 8–28
Effective tax rate, 8–4

PROBLEM MATERIALS

Problems

1. A U.S. multinational owns subsidiaries in several foreign countries. Discuss why the actual U.S. and foreign income taxes incurred by this multinational may differ from the tax expense reported on its financial statement.

Communications

2. Write a memo to a U.S. client explaining why stock of a foreign corporation that it holds may be considered a tax shelter for U.S. tax purposes.

3. Correy, Inc., a domestic corporation, produces automotive repair equipment. In 2003, it reported the following operating results before consideration of any extraterritorial income (ETI) exclusion benefits.

	U.S. Sales	Foreign Sales	Total Sales
Gross receipts	$10,000	$1,000	$11,000
Cost of goods sold	(8,400)	(720)	(9,120)
Gross income	$ 1,600	$ 280	$ 1,880
Overhead expenses	(240)	(40)	(280)
Taxable income	$ 1,360	$ 240	$ 1,600

Calculate Correy's taxable income for 2003 assuming it meets the foreign economic process requirements and maximizes its ETI exclusion. Assume Correy's foreign sales and leasing income (FSALI) is $100.

4. Evaluate this statement: If a U.S. corporation acquires the stock of a non-U.S. corporation and makes a § 338 election to step up the basis of the assets inside the entity, the foreign corporation can reduce its foreign income tax expense through the increased amortization and depreciation deductions.

Ethics

5. The shareholders of a publicly held U.S. corporation exchange their shares in the corporation for shares of a Bermuda corporation. After the transaction, the Bermuda corporation now owns the U.S. corporation (i.e., an "inversion" has occurred). Under § 367(b), this transaction is taxable to the shareholders. However, going forward, the Bermuda corporate group can reduce its worldwide tax costs by shifting certain profit-generating activities outside the U.S. taxing jurisdiction. In addition, the Bermuda group no longer has to deal with the CFC rules. The U.S. Congress believes these "inversion" transactions are inappropriate behavior and should be stopped. U.S. multinationals argue that they must consider this type of transaction in order to compete globally with foreign businesses and that the CFC rules severely restrict a U.S. multinational's ability to operate abroad. What do you think and why?

Issue ID

6. WorldCo, a domestic corporation, is planning to incorporate a branch that it has been operating in a foreign country. WorldCo's branch has a large amount of inventory. Discuss the tax results of transferring this inventory to a newly formed foreign corporation.

Issue ID
Communications

7. Warren, Inc., a domestic corporation, operates a branch in Mexico. Over the last 10 years, this branch has generated $80 million in losses. For the last 3 years, however, the branch has been profitable and has earned enough income to entirely offset the prior losses. Most of the assets are fully depreciated, and a net gain would be recognized if the assets were sold. The CFO believes that Warren should incorporate the branch now so that this potential gain can be transferred to a foreign corporation, thereby avoiding U.S. tax and, as an added benefit, avoiding U.S. taxes on future income. Draft an outline of a memo to the CFO addressing the tax issues involved in the proposed transaction.

Issue ID

8. Describe the policy reasons for the special "deemed royalty" tax treatment for transfers of intangible property to a foreign corporation in a tax-deferred transaction.

EXTENDER

9. ForCo is a foreign corporation located in Bermuda. ForCo owns 100% of USCo, a domestic corporation. ForCo partially funded USCo with debt and receives $200,000 in interest payments from USCo each year. The U.S. withholding tax on this payment is $60,000 ($200,000 × 30%) because Bermuda does not have a tax treaty with the United States. ForCo is considering making a deposit with a London bank equal to the USCo loan amount and having USCo borrow its money from the London bank instead of from ForCo. Under the treaty with the United Kingdom, the $200,000 interest payment would not be subject to U.S. withholding tax. Will this strategy work? Why or why not?

10. Eleven unrelated U.S. persons are considering forming a foreign corporation. Will they have to be concerned with the CFC provisions?

Issue ID

11. Joanna owns 5% of Axel, a foreign corporation. Joanna's son, Fred, is considering acquiring 15% of Axel from an NRA. The remainder of Axel is owned 27% by unrelated U.S. persons and 53% by unrelated NRAs. Currently, Fred operates (as a sole proprietorship) a manufacturing business that sells goods to Axel for resale outside the United States and outside Axel's country of residence. Joanna is not concerned about the concentration of investment because she expects to sell her stock in Axel in three years at a significant capital gain. Are there tax issues that Joanna and Fred, both U.S. citizens, need to address?

12. Knechel Enterprises, a domestic corporation, owns 100% of AnnaCo, Ltd., a Slovakian corporation. Determine Knechel's Subpart F income for the current year (before any expenses) from the following transactions.
    a. AnnaCo earned $600,000 from sales of products purchased from Knechel and sold to customers outside Slovakia.
    b. AnnaCo earned $1 million from sales of products purchased from Knechel and sold to customers in Slovakia.
    c. AnnaCo earned $400,000 from sales of products purchased from unrelated suppliers and sold to customers in Poland.
    d. AnnaCo purchased raw materials from Knechel, used these materials to manufacture finished goods, and sold these goods to customers in Austria. AnnaCo earned $200,000 from these sales.
    e. AnnaCo earned $120,000 for the performance of warranty services on behalf of Knechel. These services were performed in Belgium for customers located in Belgium.
    f. AnnaCo earned $30,000 in dividend income from investments.

13. Fisher, Inc., a U.S. corporation, owns 40% of the only class of stock of Gerson, Inc., a CFC. Gerson is a CFC until June 1 of the current tax year. Fisher has held the stock since Gerson was organized and continues to hold it for the entire year. Fisher and Gerson are both calendar year taxpayers. Gerson's Subpart F income for the tax year is $300,000, current E & P is $250,000, and no distributions have been made for the tax year. What amount, if any, must Fisher include in gross income under Subpart F for the tax year?

Communications

14. Karen Talham, a U.S. citizen, has placed all her investments in a Cayman Island corporation owned 9% by Karen, 42% by another U.S. individual, and 49% by a foreign individual. The Cayman Islands does not impose any income tax on the income earned by this

corporation. Outline a letter informing Karen of the U.S. tax consequences of her foreign investments. Her address is 1847 Main Street, Ocala, FL 32712.

15. Describe the difference between regular E & P of a foreign corporation and E & P treated as previously taxed income.

16. IrishCo, a manufacturing corporation resident in Ireland, distributes products through a U.S. office. Current-year taxable income from such sales in the United States is $12 million. IrishCo's U.S. office deposits working capital funds short term in certificates of deposit with U.S. banks. Current-year income from these deposits is $100,000. IrishCo also invests in U.S. securities traded on the New York Stock Exchange. This investing is done by the home office. For the current year, IrishCo has realized capital gains of $200,000 and dividend income of $60,000 from these stock investments. Compute IrishCo's U.S. tax liability, assuming that the U.S.-Ireland income tax treaty reduces withholding on dividends to 15% and on interest to 5%. Assume a 34% U.S. tax rate.

Issue ID

17. Cianci, Ltd., an Italian corporation, owns 100% of Stuart, Inc., a domestic corporation. Stuart earns significant profits in the United States. Cianci would like to reduce Stuart's income tax costs and decides to loan money to Stuart so that Cianci can extract large interest payments from Stuart. Under what conditions will this strategy work?

Issue ID
Communications

18. BritCo, Ltd., a foreign corporation, operates a trade or business in the United States. BritCo's U.S.-source income effectively connected with this trade or business is $400,000 for the current year. BritCo's current-year E & P is $900,000. BritCo's net U.S. equity was $4.2 million at the beginning of the year and $4.4 million at year-end. BritCo is a resident in a country that has no income tax treaty with the United States. Briefly outline a memo to BritCo's Tax VP reporting BritCo's branch profits tax liability for the current year, along with a planning idea for reducing the branch profits tax.

19. Carlos, an NRA, is interested in acquiring U.S. real property as an investment. He knows that he will be taxed in the United States on any gains from the disposition of such property if he holds it directly. Will the result be any different if he acquires the real property within a U.S. corporation?

20. Idil, an NRA individual, owns 30% of the stock of JasonCo, Inc., a U.S. corporation. JasonCo's balance sheet on the last day of the taxable year is as follows.

		Adjusted Basis	Fair Market Value
Cash (used as working capital)		$ 200,000	$ 200,000
Investment in foreign land		300,000	800,000
Investment in U.S. real estate:			
Land		150,000	400,000
Buildings	$2,300,000		
Less: Depreciation	(300,000)	2,000,000	5,000,000
		$2,650,000	$6,400,000
Accounts payable		$ 300,000	$ 300,000
Notes payable		500,000	500,000
Capital stock		400,000	4,150,000
Retained earnings		1,450,000	1,450,000
		$2,650,000	$6,400,000

Idil was in the United States only 40 days in the tax year. She sold all of her stock in JasonCo on the last day of the tax year for $6.4 million. Idil's adjusted basis in the stock sold was $500,000. She sold the stock for cash. What are the U.S. tax consequences, if any, to Idil?

21. In Problem 20, what are the U.S. tax consequences, if any, to Idil if JasonCo, Inc., is a foreign corporation instead of a domestic corporation?

Communications

22. Bob Warren is single, an attorney, and a U.S. citizen. He recently attended a seminar where he learned he could give up his U.S. citizenship, move to the Bahamas (where he would pay no income tax), and operate his law practice long distance via the Internet and phone with no U.S. tax consequences. Outline a letter informing Bob of the tax consequences of his proposed actions. His address is 403 NE 6th Avenue, Gainesville, GA 32812.

BRIDGE DISCIPLINE

1. Describe the role of U.S. export tax incentives within the broader context of U.S. policies concerning trade with other nations.

Research Problems

THOMSON RIA™

Note: Solutions to Research Problems can be prepared by using the ***RIA Checkpoint® Student Edition*** *online research product, which is available to accompany this text. It is also possible to prepare solutions to the Research Problems by using tax research materials found in a standard tax library.*

Communications

Research Problem 1. Guy Van Zant is the CFO of Custom Guitars, Inc., a Tennessee corporation. He has come to you regarding a potential restructuring of business operations to meet the growing international demand. Custom Guitars has long manufactured its guitars in plants in Tennessee and North Carolina. Recently, Custom Guitars has explored the possibility of setting up a manufacturing subsidiary in Ireland, where manufacturing profits are taxed at 12.5%. Guy sees this as a great idea, given that the alternative is to continue all manufacturing in the United States, where profits are taxed at 35%. Custom Guitars plans to continue all the design, fabrication of guitar parts, and hand crafting of the pearl inlays on the guitar neck in its U.S. plants. This material will be shipped to Ireland for final assembly, with the finished product shipped to retail outlets all over Europe and Asia. Your initial concern is whether the income generated by the Irish subsidiary will be considered foreign base company income. Address this issue in a research memo, along with any planning suggestions.

Partial list of research aids:
§ 954(d).
Reg. § 1.954-3(a).
Bausch & Lomb, 71 TCM 2031, T.C.Memo. 1996–57.

Decision Making

Research Problem 2. EcoScooters, Ltd., a foreign corporation based in Brazil, produces electric scooters. EcoScooters are very popular in South America because they are cheap to operate, easy to park, and good for the environment. EcoScooters is beginning to seek customers in the United States. Currently, it has no sales personnel or assets located in the United States, but it makes a few sales to U.S. customers based on orders from catalogs and its Web site. EcoScooters is considering sending a few sales agents to the United States to set up sales offices in large cities. The offices will have no inventory and will merely provide a place for the sales agents to meet with interested customers. Brazil has no income tax treaty with the United States. How would you advise EcoScooters on the tax consequences of its proposed U.S. venture?

Partial list of research aids:
§ 882(a)(1).
Higgins v. Comm., 41–1 USTC ¶9233, 25 AFTR 1160, 61 S.Ct. 475 (USSC, 1941).
Continental Trading, Inc. v. Comm., 59–1 USTC ¶9316, 3 AFTR2d 923, 265 F.2d 40 (CA–9, 1959).

Internet Activity

Use the tax resources of the Internet to address the following questions. Do not restrict your search to the World Wide Web, but include a review of newsgroups and general reference materials, practitioner sites and resources, primary sources of the tax law, chat rooms, and discussion groups, and other opportunities.

Research Problem 3. Locate the Web page of the Organization for Economic Cooperation and Development (OECD). Find the original 2000 report on tax haven countries considered by the OECD to be engaged in harmful tax practices. Using the most recent information available on this Web site, determine which of these countries have agreed to changes in tax policies so as to be removed from the harmful tax haven list.

Communications

Research Problem 4. Select an industry, like apparal retailing or steel processing. Find the financial statements of five corporations in that industry. Make a table of the companies' effective tax rates, both domestic and foreign. Send the table with your comments in an e-mail to your instructor.

CHAPTER 9

Multistate Income Taxation

LEARNING OBJECTIVES

After completing Chapter 9, you should be able to:

LO.1
Illustrate the computation of a multistate corporation's state tax liability.

LO.2
Define nexus and explain its role in state income taxation.

LO.3
Distinguish between allocation and apportionment of a multistate corporation's taxable income.

LO.4
Describe the nature and treatment of business and nonbusiness income.

LO.5
Discuss the sales, payroll, and property apportionment factors.

LO.6
Apply the unitary method of state income taxation.

LO.7
Discuss the states' income tax treatment of S corporations.

LO.8
Describe the state audit process.

LO.9
Describe other commonly encountered state and local taxes on businesses.

http://wft.swlearning.com

OUTLINE

TAX TALK

A state must not play favorites in the operation of its taxing system between business confined within its borders and the common interests of the nation expressed through business conducted across state lines.

—*Felix Frankfurter*

As demonstrated by the many tax forms required for the computation of a taxpayer's annual tax liability, a variety of tax bases apply to most business taxpayers. For instance, a multinational corporation may be subject to tax in a number of different countries (see Chapter 7). Similarly, the taxpayer may be subject to a state sales or use tax on many of its asset purchases (see Chapter 10) and to a state and local income or franchise tax on its net income or on the privilege of doing business in the taxing jurisdiction. Indeed, estimates are that about 40 percent of the tax dollars paid by business taxpayers go to state and local authorities.

Businesses operate in a multistate environment for a variety of reasons. For the most part, nontax motivations drive such location decisions as where to build new plants or distribution centers or whether to move communications and data processing facilities and corporate headquarters. For instance, a business typically wants to be close to its largest markets and to operate in a positive private- and public-sector business climate, where it has access to well-trained and reasonably priced labor, suppliers and support operations, sources of natural resources and well-educated personnel, and highway and airport facilities.

Many location decisions, though, are motivated by multistate tax considerations.

- The taxpayer's manufacturing, wholesaling, sales, retailing, and credit operations each may be centered in a different state to take advantage of various economic development incentives created by politicians.

TAX FACT

STATE TAX RECEIPTS

Although about 40 percent of businesses' tax liabilities are paid to state and local governments, the corporate income tax accounts for a relatively small amount of total state tax collections. In 2002, about $25.89 billion of corporate income taxes were paid to state governments, compared to $185.03 billion of individual income taxes, $178.94 billion of general sales and gross receipts taxes, and $82.02 billion of selective sales taxes on alcoholic beverages, motor fuels, tobacco, and the like.

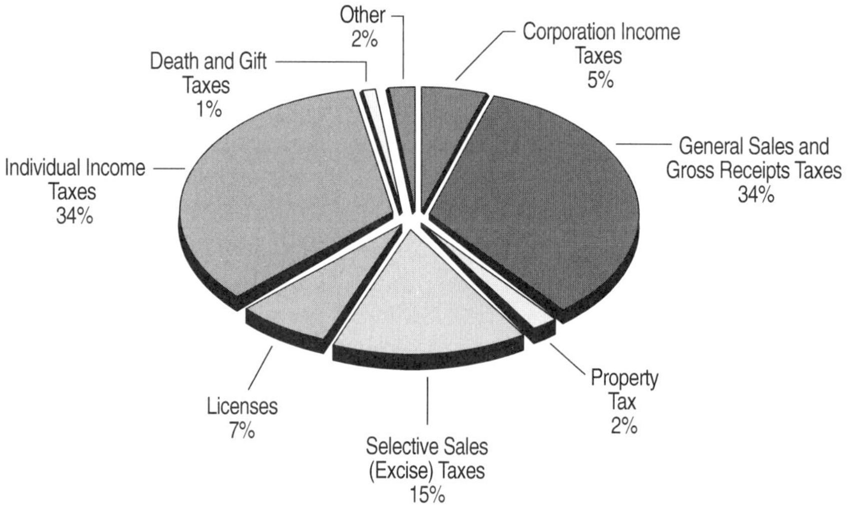

- In addition to flying over virtually the entire country, the major airlines depart from and land in the majority of the states. Which state's income tax should apply to the ticket income? Should income tax apply to sales of movies or liquor while the plane is airborne?
- Local political concerns lead to a multiplicity of tax rules as politicians attempt to serve their constituents by introducing a variety of special tax incentives. This variety can be confusing, however. Taxpayers may have difficulty determining whether they qualify for energy or enterprise zone credits, S corporation status, exemptions from income tax withholding, or passive loss relief at the local level.
- Politicians have a strong incentive to impose new tax burdens on visitors and others who have no direct say in their reelection. Thus, it is increasingly common to see tourist and hotel-bed taxes on convention delegates, city payroll taxes on commuters, and the use of obscure tax formulas that otherwise discriminate against those with limited contact with the area.
- Each jurisdiction in which the entity is subject to tax represents a geometrical increase in compliance responsibilities. For instance, how many tax returns must be filed by a three-shareholder S corporation operating in 15 states?
- Various states and localities have adopted revenue-raising statutes that vary in sophistication and operate on different time schedules. For instance, only a few states have adopted an alternative minimum tax, and states that impose the tax have tended to select different bases. In addition, the aggressiveness with which departments of revenue enforce their tax statutes varies greatly

BRIDGE DISCIPLINE

Bridge to Political Science

Multistate tax planning for businesses requires a multidisciplinary approach and an understanding of accounting, law, economics, business, and even politics! For example, in addition to considering nexus rules, apportionment rules, and the types and amounts of taxes assessed by a state government, a company considering relocating from one state to another or expanding to another state must consider the location of its current and potential customers, the extent and type of competitors in the new location, the availability of qualified trained employees, economic incentives offered by the local or state government, the types and amounts of taxes assessed by local governments, and the general political atmosphere. For example, are the governor and legislative leaders in the state and local government generally considered to be pro-business? Are the state leaders under pressure to increase taxes due to a budget shortfall?

from state to state, even in a context of ongoing pressure to enhance revenues. Accordingly, the taxpayer must deal with a patchwork of germane taxing and enforcement provisions in an environment that is often uncertain.

- The extent of a taxpayer's business operations in a state, including the location of employees, property, plant, and equipment and even the method of shipping products, may be changed in an effort to reduce the amount of state income taxes paid by the business.

This chapter reviews the basic tax concepts that are predominant among most states that impose a tax based on net income and discusses the major areas in which tax planning can reduce a corporation's overall state tax burden.

Most of this chapter is devoted to a discussion of state taxes that are based on income. Not all of the states that impose a tax on corporate income call the tax an "income tax." Rather, some states refer to their tax on corporate income as a franchise tax,[1] a business tax, a license tax, or a business profits tax.

Overview of Corporate State Income Taxation

Forty-six states and the District of Columbia impose a tax based on a corporation's taxable income. Since each state is free to create its own tax provisions, the tax practitioner could be faced with 47 entirely different state tax provisions.[2] Fortunately, however, to simplify the filing of tax returns and increase compliance with

[1]Although a franchise tax in some states is a business privilege tax based on a corporation's capital stock or net worth, several states use that term for the tax that they impose on a corporation's net income.

[2]Although the District of Columbia is not a state, it operates in much the same manner as a state and imposes a tax based on income. Four states impose no corporate income tax at all: Nevada, South Dakota, Washington, and Wyoming. Corporations, however, are subject to a business and occupation tax in Washington. Several states base the tax on gross receipts, and Michigan uses a form of value added tax.

TAX IN THE NEWS

Piggybacking—It's No Free Ride

Because most states piggyback onto the Federal income tax base, when the President and Congress make changes affecting the calculation of Federal taxable income, states also are affected. For example, increases in the bonus depreciation and increased first-year expensing for small businesses included in the 2003 tax changes are expected to cost the states almost $3 billion of revenue over the next two years.

state tax laws, the majority of states "piggyback" onto the Federal income tax base. This means they have adopted *en masse* part or all of the Federal provisions governing the definition of income and the allowance of various exemptions, exclusions, and deductions. None of the states, however, has piggybacked its tax collections with the IRS.

LO.1

Illustrate the computation of a multistate corporation's state tax liability.

COMPUTING STATE TAXABLE INCOME

In more than 40 of the states that impose a corporate income tax, the starting point in computing the tax base is taxable income as reflected on the Federal corporate income tax return (Form 1120). These states typically use either taxable income before the net operating loss and special deductions (line 28) or taxable income itself (line 30). Those states whose computation of state taxable income is not coupled to the Federal tax return have their own state-specific definitions of gross and taxable income. Nonetheless, even these states typically adopt most Federal income and deduction provisions.

Although Federal tax law plays a significant role in the computation of state taxable income, there is a wide disparity in both the methods used to determine a state's taxable income and the tax rates imposed on that income. Accordingly, increasing the number of states in which a corporation is subject to tax causes the complexity of determining the corporation's state income tax liability to rise exponentially.

The formula used by a multistate corporation to determine its tax liability in a typical state is illustrated in Figure 9–1.

OPERATIONAL IMPLICATIONS

Generally, the accounting period and methods used by a corporation for state tax purposes must be consistent with those used on the Federal return. States often apply different rules, however, in identifying the members of a group filing a consolidated return and the income of each group member that is subject to tax.

As the starting point for computing state taxable income often is directly related to the Federal taxable income amount, most states also piggyback onto the IRS's audit process. Consequently, virtually all of the states that levy an income tax require notification of the final settlement of a Federal income tax audit. State authorities then adjust the originally calculated state tax liability appropriately.

FIGURE 9–1
Computing Corporate State Income Tax Liability

	Starting point in computing taxable income*
±	State modification items
	State tax base
±	Total net allocable income/(loss) (nonbusiness income)
	Total apportionable income/(loss) (business income)
×	State's apportionment percentage
	Income apportioned to the state
±	Income/(loss) allocated to the state
	State taxable income/(loss)
×	State tax rate
	Gross income tax liability for state
−	State's tax credits
	Net income tax liability for the state

*Most states use either line 28 or line 30 of the Federal corporate income tax return (Form 1120). In other states, the corporation is required to identify and report each element of income and deduction on the state return.

STATE MODIFICATIONS

Federal taxable income generally is used as the starting point in computing the state's income tax base, but numerous state adjustments or modifications are often made to Federal taxable income to:

- Reflect differences between state and Federal tax statutes.
- Remove income that a state is constitutionally prohibited from taxing.

The required modifications to Federal taxable income vary significantly among the states. Accordingly, this discussion is limited to the most common additions and subtractions that the states require. Exhibit 9–1 lists the most frequently encountered modifications. In computing the taxable income for a given state, only a selected number of these modifications may be applicable.

EXAMPLE 1

Blue Corporation is subject to tax only in State A. The starting point in computing A taxable income is Federal taxable income. Modifications then are made to reflect, among other provisions, the exempt status of interest on A obligations, all dividends received from in-state corporations, and the disallowance of a deduction for state income taxes. Blue generated the following income and deductions this year.

Sales	$1,500,000
Interest on Federal obligations	50,000
Interest on municipal obligations of State B	100,000
Dividends received from 50%-owned State A corporations	200,000
Total income	$1,850,000
Expenses related to Federal obligations	$ 1,000
Expenses related to municipal obligations	5,000
State income tax expense	50,000
Depreciation allowed for Federal tax purposes (the deduction allowed for state purposes is $300,000)	400,000
Other allowable deductions	1,000,000
Total deductions	$1,456,000

■ **EXHIBIT 9–1**
Common State Modifications

Addition Modifications

* Interest income received on state and municipal obligations and any other interest income that is exempt from Federal income tax. For this purpose, some states exempt interest earned on their own obligations.
* Expenses deducted in computing Federal taxable income that are directly or indirectly related to U.S. obligations.
* Income-based franchise and income taxes imposed by any state and the District of Columbia that were deducted in computing Federal taxable income.
* The amount by which the Federal deductions for depreciation, amortization, or depletion exceed those permitted by the state.
* The amount by which the state gain or loss from the disposal of assets differs from the Federal gain or loss. Due to the difference in permitted depreciation methods and other adjustments, a corporation's assets may have different Federal and state tax bases. This adjustment is not necessary if the state and Federal basis provisions are identical.

Adjustments required as a result of different elections being made for state and Federal purposes. Examples of such elections include the methods under which income from installment sales or long-term contracts is determined.

Federal net operating loss deduction. This modification is not required by states in which the starting point in the computation of taxable income is Federal income before special deductions.

Subtraction Modifications

* Interest on U.S. obligations or obligations of Federal agencies to the extent included in Federal taxable income but exempt from state income taxes under U.S. law.
* Expenses that are directly or indirectly related to the state and municipal interest that is taxable for state purposes.
* Refunds of franchise and income taxes imposed by any state and the District of Columbia, to the extent included in Federal taxable income.
* The amount by which the state deductions for depreciation, amortization, or depletion exceed the deductions permitted for Federal tax purposes.

Adjustments required as a result of different elections being made for state and Federal purposes, as above.

Dividends received from certain out-of-state corporations, to the extent included in Federal taxable income.

Net operating loss deduction as determined for state tax purposes.

Deduction for Federal income tax paid. (a limited deduction is allowed in five states)

*Required by most states.

Blue's taxable income for Federal and state purposes is $139,000 and $295,000, respectively.

Federal Taxable Income	
Sales	$1,500,000
Interest on Federal obligations	50,000
Dividends received from domestic corporations	200,000
Total income	$1,750,000
Expenses related to Federal obligations	$ 1,000
State income tax expense	50,000
Depreciation	400,000
Other allowable deductions	1,000,000
Total deductions	$1,451,000
Taxable income before special deductions	$ 299,000
Less: Dividends received deduction (80% × $200,000)	160,000
Federal taxable income	$ 139,000

State A Taxable Income	
Federal taxable income	$139,000
Addition Modifications	
Interest on State B obligations	100,000
State income tax expense	50,000
Excess depreciation deduction allowed for Federal purposes ($400,000 – $300,000)	100,000
Expenses related to Federal obligations	1,000
Subtraction Modifications	
Expenses related to State B obligations	(5,000)
Dividends from in-state corporations included in Federal taxable income ($200,000 – $160,000)	(40,000)
Interest on Federal obligations	(50,000)
State A taxable income	$295,000

LO.2

Define nexus and explain its role in state income taxation.

JURISDICTION TO IMPOSE TAX: NEXUS AND PUBLIC LAW 86–272

The state in which a business is incorporated has the jurisdiction to tax the corporation, regardless of the volume of its business activity within the state. Whether a state can tax the income of a business that is incorporated in another state usually depends on the relationship between the state and the corporation.

Nexus describes the degree of business activity that must be present before a taxing jurisdiction has the right to impose a tax on an out-of-state entity's income. State law defines the measure of the relationship that is necessary to create nexus. Typically, sufficient nexus is present when a corporation derives income from sources within the state, owns or leases property in the state, employs personnel in the state, or has physical or financial capital there. However, all states are limited

TAX IN THE NEWS

WHERE WILL WE BEE TAXED?

Nexus definitions remain the most controversial aspect of state and local taxation today. In a service-based economy that depends upon electronic and other paperless transfers of information, it may be difficult for a taxing jurisdiction to find and measure nexus. For instance, assume that a toy retailer uses Billy the Bee as its national mascot. Billy appears in all of the chain's print and television advertisements, and his image has become synonymous with the retailer's operations. The retailer has a store in State A, but all of its bank accounts, inventory, and intangible assets (including the copyrights on Billy the Bee) are in another state. Does the toy chain have any tax exposure in A? Specifically, does the presence of an intangible asset (Billy's image), a financial asset (the flow of receivables in and out of the state), or an electronic presence (the flow of orders and inventory management to headquarters over the Internet) create nexus?

Or suppose that the Do It Yourself Partnership operates a retail hardware store chain, as well as the in-store credit card operations for the chain. The credit card operations are limited to State Q, but the stores are located in nearly every state. Is the income from the credit card operations subject to tax outside Q because of its relationship with the multistate partnership?

by (1) state and U.S. constitutional principles, (2) judicial doctrine, and (3) other Federal law.

DIGGING DEEPER 1

*Find more information on this topic at our Web site: **http://wft-advanced.swlearning.com**.*

Public Law 86–272 limits the states' right to impose an income tax on interstate activities.[3] This Federal law prohibits a state from taxing a business whose only connection with the state is to solicit orders for sales of tangible personal property that is sent outside the state for approval or rejection. If approved, the orders must be filled and shipped by the business from a point outside the state.

Only the sales of tangible personal property are immune from taxation under the law, however. Leases, rentals, and other dispositions of tangible personal property are not protected activities. Moreover, dispositions of real property and intangible property, as well as sales of services, are not protected by Public Law 86–272.[4] In this regard, each state constructs its own definition of tangible and intangible property. Thus, since property ownership is not a protected activity, providing company-owned fax, copy, or computer equipment to an out-of-state salesperson may create nexus with a state, even though the salesperson merely solicits sales orders there.

An activity that consists merely of solicitation is immune from taxation. The statute does not define the term *solicitation*, but the Supreme Court has held that *solicitation of orders* includes any explicit verbal request for orders and any speech or conduct that implicitly invites an order.[5] The Court also created a *de minimis* rule, allowing immunity from nexus where a limited amount of solicitation occurs.

[3] 15 U.S.C. 381–385.

[4] Public Law 86–272's protections do not extend to true franchise taxes imposed by a state for the privilege of doing business in the state.

[5] *Wisconsin Department of Revenue v. William Wrigley, Jr., Co.*, 505 U.S. 214, 120 L.Ed. 174, 112 S.Ct. 2447 (1992).

Independent Contractors. Public Law 86–272 extends immunity to certain in-state activities conducted by an independent contractor that would not be permitted if performed directly by the taxpayer. Generally, an independent contractor may engage in the following limited activities without establishing nexus for the principal: (1) soliciting sales, (2) making sales, and (3) maintaining a sales office.

THE MULTISTATE TAX COMMISSION AND THE UDITPA

The **Multistate Tax Commission (MTC)** has issued guidance under Public Law 86–272 providing a list of activities that it considers protected and a list of unprotected activities that will result in the creation of nexus (see Exhibit 9–2). The MTC is an agency of state governments established to help make state tax systems fair, effective, and efficient and to encourage states to adopt uniform tax laws and regulations as they relate to interstate and international commerce. Forty-five states currently participate in the Commission, although only 21 are members. When a new MTC rule or regulation is created, member states propose its adoption to their respective legislatures.

The majority of member states (and other participating states) adopt the regulations with no exceptions or only minor changes. Many states also structure their laws after the **Uniform Division of Income for Tax Purposes Act (UDITPA).** The UDITPA's goal is to provide a standardized model relating to the assignment of income among the states for multistate corporations.

LO.3

Distinguish between allocation and apportionment of a multistate corporation's taxable income.

Allocation and Apportionment of Income

A corporation that conducts business activities in more than one state must determine the portion of its net income that is subject to tax by each state. A corporation that has established sufficient nexus with another state generally must both **allocate** and **apportion** its income.

LO.4

Describe the nature and treatment of business and nonbusiness income.

APPORTIONMENT OF BUSINESS INCOME

Apportionment is a means by which a corporation's business income is divided among the states in which it conducts its business. Business income arises from the taxpayer's regular course of business or constitutes an integral part of the taxpayer's regular business.[6] In determining whether an item of income is apportionable business income, state courts have developed a variety of approaches to determine what constitutes a taxpayer's regular course of business.[7]

Under an apportionment procedure, a corporation determines allowable income and deductions for the company as a whole and then apportions some of its net income to a given state, using a state-mandated apportionment formula.

Apportionment assumes that the production of business income is linked to business activity. The laws of each state define a number of factors believed to indicate the amount of corporate activity conducted within the state. Typical apportionment factors include sales, property, and payroll.

[6]MTC Reg. IV.1.(a).

[7]*Atlantic Richfield Co. v. State of Colorado and Joseph F. Dolan*, 601 P.2d 628 (Colo.S.Ct., 1979); *Appeal of A. Epstein and Sons, Inc.* (Cal. State Bd. of Equalization, 1984).

EXHIBIT 9–2
Common Nexus Definitions under Public Law 86–272

General rule: P.L. 86–272 immunity applies where the sales representative's activities are ancillary to the order-solicitation process.

Activities That Usually Do Not Create Nexus under P.L. 86–272

- Advertising campaigns.
- Carrying free samples only for display or distribution.
- Owning or furnishing automobiles to salespersons.
- Passing inquiries or complaints on to the home office.
- Checking customers' inventories for reorder.
- Maintaining a sample or display room for two weeks or less during the year.

Activities Usually Sufficient to Establish Nexus

- Making repairs or providing maintenance.
- Collecting delinquent accounts; investigating creditworthiness.
- Installation or supervision of installation.
- Conducting training classes, seminars, or lectures for persons other than sales personnel.
- Approving or accepting orders.
- Picking up or replacing damaged or returned property.
- Hiring, training, or supervising personnel other than sales employees.
- Providing shipping information and coordinating deliveries.
- Carrying samples for sale, exchange, or distribution in any manner for consideration or other value.
- Owning, leasing, maintaining, or otherwise using any of the following facilities or property in the state: real estate; repair shop; parts department; employment office; purchasing office; warehouse; meeting place for directors, officers, or employees; stock of goods; telephone answering service; or mobile stores (i.e., trucks with driver-salespersons).
- Maintaining an office for an employee, including an office in the home.

ALLOCATION OF NONBUSINESS INCOME

Allocation is a method under which specific components of a corporation's nonbusiness income, net of related expenses, are directly assigned to a certain state. Allocable nonbusiness income generally is defined as "all income other than business income."[8] In general, nonbusiness income includes:

- Passive or portfolio income such as dividends and interest,[9]
- Gains or losses derived from the sale of nonbusiness real or tangible property, and
- Income or losses derived from rentals and royalties from nonbusiness real or tangible personal property.

[8] UDITPA § 1(e).

[9] However, passive or portfolio income may be classified as business income when the acquisition, management, and disposition of the underlying property constitute an integral part of the taxpayer's regular business operations.

Nonbusiness income is allocated to the state in which the asset generating the income or loss is located. For example, income derived from the rental of nonbusiness real property generally is allocated to the state in which the property is located. It is not always easy to determine if income should be classified as business or nonbusiness income. In a number of states including Connecticut, Maine, Maryland, Michigan, New Hampshire, Rhode Island, and Vermont, all income is treated as business income and is subject to apportionment.

DIGGING DEEPER 2

Find more information on this topic at our Web site: ***http://wft-advanced.swlearning.com.***

THE APPORTIONMENT AND ALLOCATION PROCESS

As Figure 9–1 indicated, total allocable (nonapportionable) income or loss typically is removed from corporate net income before the state's apportionment percentage is applied. The nonapportionable income or loss assigned to a state then is combined with the income apportionable to that state to arrive at total income subject to tax in the state.

EXAMPLE 2

Green Corporation conducts business in States N, O, P, and Q. Green's $900,000 taxable income is comprised of $800,000 apportionable income and $100,000 allocable income generated from transactions conducted in State Q. Green's sales, property, and payroll are evenly divided among the four states, and the states all employ an identical apportionment formula. Accordingly, $200,000 of Green's income is taxable in each of States N, O, and P. Green is subject to income tax on $300,000 of income in State Q.

Apportionable income	$800,000
Apportionment percentage (apportionable income is divided equally among the four states)	× 25%
Income apportioned to each state	$200,000

	State N	State O	State P	State Q
Income apportioned	$200,000	$200,000	$200,000	$200,000
Income allocated	–0–	–0–	–0–	100,000
Taxable income	$200,000	$200,000	$200,000	$300,000

The process of apportionment and allocation often does not provide a uniform division of an organization's income based on its business activity. Each state may define business and nonbusiness income differently, and each state is free to choose the type and number of factors that it believes are indicative of the business activity conducted within its borders. Therefore, a corporation may be subject to state income tax on more or less than 100 percent of its income.

EXAMPLE 3

TNT Corporation, a manufacturer of explosive devices, is a multistate taxpayer that has nexus with States P and Q. During the taxable year, TNT's net sales of explosive devices were $900,000; $600,000 of these sales were made in P and $300,000 were made in Q. The corporation also received $90,000 from the rental of nonbusiness real property located in P.

Both states employ a single-factor apportionment formula in which sales is the only factor. However, the states do not agree on the definition of apportionable income. Under P's tax provisions, nonbusiness rent income is allocable and business income is apportionable, while Q requires a corporation to apportion all of its (business and nonbusiness) income.

The sales factor (the ratio of in-state sales to total sales) for each of the states is computed as follows.

$$\text{State P: } \frac{\$600{,}000 \text{ (sales in State P)}}{\$900{,}000 \text{ (total sales)}} = 66.67\%$$

$$\text{State Q: } \frac{\$300{,}000 \text{ (sales in State Q)}}{\$990{,}000 \text{ (total sales)*}} = 30.30\%$$

*Since rent income is treated as business income, rents are included in the denominator of the sales factor. ■

EXAMPLE 4

Continue with the facts of Example 3, except that the rent income was generated from property located in Q, rather than from property located in P. Although the sales factor for P remains the same, the sales factor for Q changes.

$$\text{State P: } \frac{\$600{,}000 \text{ (sales in State P)}}{\$900{,}000 \text{ (total sales)}} = 66.67\%$$

$$\text{State Q: } \frac{\$390{,}000 \text{ (sales in State Q)}}{\$990{,}000 \text{ (total sales)}} = 39.39\%$$

Due to the composition of the sales factor in the two states, TNT's income never is perfectly apportioned: the aggregate of the sales factors is either more or less than 100%. ■

EXAMPLE 5

Scarlet Corporation is subject to income tax in several states. Scarlet earned $2.5 million from the sales of its products and $1 million from the sale of assets that were unrelated to its regular business operations.

In the states that distinguish between business and nonbusiness income, $2.5 million of Scarlet's income is apportioned to the state according to the state's apportionment formula. The gain on the sale of the nonbusiness assets is allocated to the state in which the assets were located. In the states that subject a corporation's entire income to apportionment, $3.5 million ($2,500,000 + $1,000,000) is apportioned to the states in which the taxpayer conducts business. ■

LO.5

Discuss the sales, payroll, and property apportionment factors.

APPORTIONMENT FACTORS: ELEMENTS AND PLANNING

Business income is apportioned among the states by determining the appropriate apportionment percentage for each state that has a right to tax the entity. To determine the apportionment percentage for each state, a ratio is established for each of the factors included in the state's apportionment formula. Each ratio is calculated by comparing the level of a specific business activity within a state to the total corporate activity of that type. The ratios then are summed, averaged, and appropriately weighted (if required) to determine the corporation's apportionment percentage for a specific state.

Although apportionment formulas vary among jurisdictions, the traditional three-factor formula equally weights sales, property, and payroll.[10] However, most of the states use a modified three-factor formula, where the sales factor receives more than a one-third weight. The use of a higher-weighted sales factor tends to pull a larger percentage of an out-of-state corporation's income into the taxing jurisdiction of the state, because the corporation's major activity within the

[10]Certain industries, such as financial institutions, insurance companies, air and motor carriers, pipeline companies, and public utilities, typically are required to use special apportionment formulas.

state—sales of its products—is weighted more heavily than are its payroll and property activities. Overweighting the sales factor, however, provides tax relief for corporations that are domiciled in the state. Those corporations generally own significantly more property and incur more payroll costs (factors that are given less weight in the apportionment formula) within the state than do out-of-state corporations.

EXAMPLE 6

Musk Corporation realized $500,000 of taxable income from the sales of its products in States A and B. Musk's activities in both states establish nexus for income tax purposes. Musk's sales, payroll, and property in the states include the following.

	State A	State B	Total
Sales	$1,250,000	$750,000	$2,000,000
Property	2,500,000	–0–	2,500,000
Payroll	1,500,000	–0–	1,500,000

If State B uses an equally weighted three-factor apportionment formula, $62,500 of Musk's taxable income is apportioned to B.

Sales ($750,000/$2,000,000)	=	37.5%
Property ($0/$2,500,000)	=	–0–
Payroll ($0/$1,500,000)	=	–0–
Sum of apportionment factors		37.5%
Average	÷	3
Apportionment factor for State B		12.5%
Taxable income	×	$500,000
Income apportioned to State B		$ 62,500

If State B uses a double-weighted sales factor in its three-factor apportionment formula, $93,750 of Musk's taxable income is apportioned to B.

Sales ($750,000/$2,000,000)	=	37.5% × 2	=	75%
Property ($0/$2,500,000)	=			–0–
Payroll ($0/$1,500,000)	=			–0–
Sum of apportionment factors				75%
Average			÷	4
Apportionment factor for State B				18.75%
Taxable income			×	$500,000
Income apportioned to State B				$ 93,750

When a state uses a double-weighted sales factor, typically a larger percentage of an out-of-state corporation's income is subject to tax in the state. Here, an additional $31,250 ($93,750 – $62,500) of Musk's income is subject to tax in B. ■

A single-factor apportionment formula consisting solely of a sales factor is even more detrimental to an out-of-state corporation than an apportionment factor that double weights the sales factor. Currently, Illinois, Iowa, Nebraska, and Texas require the use of a single-factor apportionment formula.

TAX FACT

Apportionment Factor Weights

Although UDITPA calls for a three-factor apportionment formula with sales, property, and payroll equally weighted, only 11 states currently use an evenly weighted three-factor formula while 20 states utilize a three-factor formula with sales double-weighted, 2 states utilize a three-factor formula with sales tripled-weighted, and 4 states utilize a one-factor sales formula. Other states allow companies to choose among formulas or require different formulas, depending on the type of company involved.

THE SALES FACTOR

The **sales factor** is a fraction, whose numerator is the corporation's total sales in the state during the tax period. The denominator is the corporation's total sales everywhere during the tax period. Gross sales for this purpose generally are net of returns, allowances, and discounts. Moreover, interest income, service charges, and carrying charges are included in the sales factor. Federal and state excise taxes and state sales taxes are included in the factor, if these taxes are either passed on to the buyer or included in the selling price of the goods.

Since the sales factor is a component in the formula used to apportion a corporation's business income to a state, only sales that generate business income are includible in the fraction. The "sales" factor actually resembles a "receipts" factor since it also generally includes business income from the sale of inventory or services, interest, dividends, rentals, royalties, sales of assets, and other business income. Income on Federal obligations, however, is not included in the sales factor.

When the sale involves capital assets, some states require that the gross proceeds, rather than the net gain or loss, be included in the fraction. Most states allow incidental or occasional asset sales and sales of certain intangible assets to be excluded from gross receipts.[11]

In determining the numerator of the sales factor, most states follow the UDITPA's "ultimate destination concept," under which tangible asset sales are assumed to take place at the point of delivery, not at the location at which the shipment originates.

EXAMPLE 7

Olive Corporation, whose only manufacturing plant is located in State A, sells its products to residents of A through its local retail store. Olive also ships its products to customers in States B and C. The products that are sold to residents of A are assigned to A, while the products that are delivered to B and C are assigned to B and C, respectively. ■

Sales of Services. Under the UDITPA, sales of services and intangibles are generally sourced to the production state instead of the destination state. If services are performed in several states, the services are usually attributed to the state providing the majority of services as measured by the cost of performance.

This approach can cause inequities in the case of sales of computer software. Computer software that is distributed on CDs will be sourced to the destination

[11]MTC Reg. IV.18.(c).

state as a sale of tangible personal property. However, digital downloads of the same software may be treated as a sale of either tangible personal property or a service (depending on the state). In most states, sales of computer programs resident on a seller's server will be sourced to the state of production. Several states have revised their sourcing rules for services to adopt a destination-based approach.

Dock Sales. **Dock sales** occur where a purchaser uses its owned or rented vehicles, or a common carrier with which it has made arrangements, to take delivery of the product at the seller's shipping dock. Most states apply the destination test to dock sales in the same manner as it is applied to other sales. Thus, if the seller makes dock sales to a purchaser that has an out-of-state location to which it returns with the product, the sale is assigned to the purchaser's state.

Throwback Rule. Out-of-state sales that are not subject to tax in the destination state are pulled back into the origination state if that state has adopted a **throwback rule**. This rule is an exception to the destination test. The rule provides that, when a corporation is not subject to tax in the destination state or the purchaser is the U.S. government, the sales are treated as in-state sales of the origination state, and the actual destination of the product is disregarded. Consequently, when the seller is immune from tax in the destination state under Public Law 86–272, the sales are considered to be in-state sales of the origination state if that state has a throwback provision.

The throwback rule seems inappropriate when the sale is made to a purchaser in a foreign country, where the transaction is subject to a gross-receipts tax (but no income tax). In these cases, the taxpayer truly is subject to double taxation, as state taxes increase but no Federal foreign tax credit is available. Nonetheless, most of the throwback states fail to distinguish between U.S. and foreign throwback sales.

EXAMPLE 8

Braun Corporation's entire operations are located in State A. Seventy percent ($700,000) of Braun's sales are made in A, and the remaining 30% ($300,000) are made in State B. Braun's solicitation of sales in B is limited to mailing a monthly catalog to its customers in that state. However, Braun employees do pick up and replace damaged merchandise in State B.

The pickup and replacement of damaged goods establish nexus with A. Braun's activities in B are sufficient (as determined by A's law) to subject Braun to a positive tax, based on its income. Therefore, Braun is permitted to apportion its income between A and B. However, B's interpretation of activities necessary to create nexus is less strict than that imposed by A; in B, the mere pickup and replacement of damaged goods do not subject a corporation's income to tax.

Braun's taxable income is $900,000. Both A and B impose a 10% corporate income tax and include only the sales factor in their apportionment formulas. If A has not adopted a throwback rule, Braun's effective state income tax rate is 7%.

	Apportionment Factors	Net Income	Tax Rate	Tax
State A	70%	$900,000	10%	$63,000
State B	*	900,000	10%	–0–
Total tax liability				$63,000
Effective state income tax rate: $63,000/$900,000 =				7%

*As determined under B's laws, Braun's income is not apportionable to State B, because insufficient nexus is present.

If A has adopted a throwback rule, Braun does not benefit from its lack of nexus with B, because the sales in B are considered to be in-state sales of A. Thus, Braun's effective tax rate is 10%.

	Apportionment Factors	Net Income	Tax Rate	Tax
State A	100%	$900,000	10%	$90,000
State B	–0–	900,000	10%	–0–
Total tax liability				$90,000
Effective state income tax rate: $90,000/$900,000 =				10%
Tax increase due to throwback provision ($90,000 – $63,000)				$27,000

THE PAYROLL FACTOR

The **payroll factor** is determined by comparing the compensation paid for services rendered within a state to the total compensation paid by the corporation. Generally, the payroll factor is a fraction, whose numerator is the total amount that a corporation paid or accrued for compensation in a state during the tax period. The denominator is the total amount paid or accrued by the corporation for compensation during the tax period. For purposes of the payroll factor, compensation includes wages, salaries, commissions, and any other form of remuneration paid or accrued to employees for personal services. Compensation may also include the value of board, rent, housing, lodging, and other benefits or services furnished to employees by the taxpayer in return for personal services, if these amounts constitute Federal gross income.

Payments made to an independent contractor or any other person who is not properly classifiable as an employee generally are excluded from the numerator and denominator of the payroll factor. Some states exclude from the payroll factor the compensation paid to corporate officers.

Several states provide that earnings paid to a cash or deferred compensation plan, excluded from Federal gross income under § 401(k), are to be included in the numerator and the denominator of the payroll factor. Accordingly, the total compensation that is included in the denominator of a corporation's payroll factor may vary among the states in which the corporation's income is apportioned.

EXAMPLE 9

Mice Corporation's sales office and manufacturing plant are located in State A. Mice also maintains a manufacturing plant and sales office in State C. For purposes of apportionment, A defines payroll as all compensation paid to employees, including contributions to § 401(k) deferred compensation plans. Under the statutes of C, neither compensation paid to officers nor contributions to § 401(k) plans are included in the payroll factor. Mice incurred the following personnel costs.

	State A	State C	Total
Wages and salaries for employees other than officers	$350,000	$250,000	$600,000
Salaries for officers	150,000	100,000	250,000
Contributions to § 401(k) plans	30,000	20,000	50,000
Total	$530,000	$370,000	$900,000

The payroll factor for State A is computed as follows.

$$\frac{\$530{,}000}{\$900{,}000} = 58.89\%$$

Since C excludes from the payroll factor any compensation paid to officers and contributions to § 401(k) plans, C's factor is computed as follows.

$$\frac{\$250{,}000}{\$600{,}000} = 41.67\%$$

The aggregate of Mice's payroll factors is 100.56% (58.89% + 41.67%). In certain cases, the sum of a corporation's payroll factors may be significantly more or less than 100%. ■

The compensation of an employee normally is not split between two or more states during the year, unless he or she is transferred or changes positions during the year. Instead, each employee's compensation is allocated to only one state. Under the UDITPA, compensation is treated as paid in the state (it is included in the numerator of the payroll factor) in which the services are primarily performed.

When an employee's services are performed in more than one state, his or her compensation is attributed to the employee's base of operations or, if there is no base of operations in any state in which some part of the service is performed, to the place from which the services are directed or controlled. When no services are performed in the state that serves as the base of operations or the place from which the services are directed, the employee's compensation is attributed to his or her state of residency.[12]

EXAMPLE 10

Geese Corporation has its headquarters and a manufacturing plant in State A. Reggie, a resident of State Y, works at the A manufacturing plant. His compensation is included in the numerator of A's payroll factor, as the service is performed entirely in A. ■

Only compensation that is related to the production of apportionable income is included in the payroll factor. Accordingly, in those states that distinguish between business and nonbusiness income, compensation related to the operation, maintenance, protection, or supervision of nonbusiness income is not includible in the payroll factor. Compensation related to both business and nonbusiness income generally is prorated between the two.

EXAMPLE 11

Dog Corporation, a manufacturer of automobile parts, is subject to tax in States X and Y. Dog incurred the following payroll costs.

	State X	State Y	Total
Wages and salaries for officers and personnel of manufacturing facilities	$450,000	$350,000	$800,000
Wages and salaries for personnel involved in nonbusiness rental activities	50,000	–0–	50,000

If both states distinguish between business and nonbusiness income in determining apportionable income and include officers' compensation in the payroll factor, Dog's payroll factors are computed as follows.

Payroll factor for State X: $450,000/$800,000 = 56.25%

Payroll factor for State Y: $350,000/$800,000 = 43.75% ■

[12]UDITPA § 14.

EXAMPLE 12

Continue with the facts of Example 11, but assume that Y defines apportionable income as the corporation's total income (business and nonbusiness income). Dog's payroll factor for X remains unchanged, but its payroll factor for Y is reduced.

Payroll factor for State X: $450,000/$800,000 = 56.25%

Payroll factor for State Y: $350,000/$850,000* = 41.18%

*$800,000 (compensation related to business income) + $50,000 (compensation related to nonbusiness income).

DIGGING DEEPER 3

Find more information on this topic at our Web site: ***http://wft-advanced.swlearning.com.***

THE PROPERTY FACTOR

The **property factor** generally is a fraction, whose numerator is the average value of the corporation's real property and its tangible personal property owned and used or rented and used in the state during the taxable year. The denominator is the average value of all of the corporation's real property and its tangible personal property owned or rented and used during the taxable year, wherever it is located. In this manner, a state's property factor reflects the extent of total property usage by the taxpayer in the state.

For this purpose, property includes land, buildings, machinery, inventory, equipment, and other real and tangible personal property, other than coins or currency.[13] Other types of property that may be included in the factor are construction in progress (even though it does not yet contribute to the production of income), offshore property, outer space property (satellites), and partnership property.

In the case of property that is in transit between locations of the taxpayer or between a buyer and seller, the assets are included in the numerator of the destination state. With respect to mobile or movable property, such as construction equipment, trucks, and leased equipment, which is both in- and outside the state during the tax period, the numerator of a state's property factor generally is determined on the basis of the total time that the property was within the state.

Space satellites used in the communication industry generally are included in the numerator of the property factor based on the ratio of earth stations serviced. For example, if a satellite is being serviced by earth stations located in San Francisco, Chicago, New York, and Houston, 25 percent of the cost of the satellite is included in the numerator of the property factor for each of the four corresponding states.

Property owned by the corporation typically is valued at its average original or historical cost plus the cost of additions and improvements, but without adjusting for depreciation. Some states allow property to be included at net book value or adjusted tax basis. The value of the property usually is determined by averaging the values at the beginning and end of the tax period. Alternatively, some states allow or require the amount to be calculated on a monthly basis if annual computation results in or requires substantial distortions.

Leased property, when included in the property factor, is valued at eight times its annual rental. Annual rentals may include payments, such as real estate taxes and insurance, made by the lessee in lieu of rent.

Only property that is used in the production of apportionable income is includible in the numerator and denominator of the property factor. In this regard, idle property and property that is used in producing nonapportionable income generally are excluded. However, property that is only temporarily idle or unused generally remains in the property factor.

[13]MTC Reg. IV.10.(a).

EXAMPLE 13

Blond Corporation, a calendar year taxpayer, owns property in States A and B. Both A and B require that the average value of assets be included in the property factor. A requires that the property be valued at its historical cost, and B requires that the property be included in the property factor at its net book value.

Account Balances at January 1

	State A	State B	Total
Inventories	$ 150,000	$ 100,000	$ 250,000
Building and machinery (cost)	200,000	400,000	600,000
Accumulated depreciation for building and machinery	(150,000)	(50,000)	(200,000)
Land	50,000	100,000	150,000
Total	$ 250,000	$ 550,000	$ 800,000

Account Balances at December 31

	State A	State B	Total
Inventories	$ 250,000	$ 200,000	$ 450,000
Building and machinery (cost)	200,000	400,000	600,000
Accumulated depreciation for building and machinery	(175,000)	(100,000)	(275,000)
Land	50,000	100,000	150,000
Total	$ 325,000	$ 600,000	$ 925,000

State A Property Factor

Historical Cost	January 1	December 31	Average
Property in State A	$ 400,000*	$ 500,000**	$ 450,000
Total property	1,000,000†	1,200,000††	1,100,000

* $150,000 + $200,000 + $50,000.
** $250,000 + $200,000 + $50,000.
† $250,000 + $600,000 + $150,000.
†† $450,000 + $600,000 + $150,000.

$$\text{Property factor for State A: } \frac{\$450{,}000}{\$1{,}100{,}000} = 40.91\%$$

State B Property Factor

Net Book Value	January 1	December 31	Average
Property in State B	$550,000	$600,000	$575,000
Total property	800,000	925,000	862,500

$$\text{Property factor for State B: } \frac{\$575{,}000}{\$862{,}500} = 66.67\%$$

Due to the variations in the property factors, the aggregate of Blond's property factors equals 107.58%. ■

DIGGING DEEPER 4

*Find more information on this topic at our Web site: **http://wft-advanced.swlearning.com**.*

PLANNING STRATEGIES

Planning with Apportionment Factors

FRAMEWORK FOCUS: TAX RATE

STRATEGY ➤ SHIFT NET INCOME FROM HIGH-TAX JURISDICTIONS TO LOW-TAX JURISDICTIONS.

SALES FACTOR

The sales factor often yields the greatest planning opportunities for a multistate corporation. In-state sales include those to purchasers with a destination point in that state; sales delivered to out-of-state purchasers are included in the numerator of the sales factor of the destination state. However, to be permitted to exclude out-of-state sales from the sales factor of the origination state, the seller generally must substantiate the shipment of goods to an out-of-state location. Therefore, the destinations of sales that a corporation makes and the means by which the goods are shipped must be carefully reviewed. The corporation's overall state tax can possibly be reduced by establishing a better record-keeping system or by manipulating the numerator of the sales factor by changing the delivery location or method.

For example, a corporation may substantially reduce its state tax if the delivery location of its sales is changed from a state in which the company is taxed to one in which it is not. This technique may not benefit the corporation if the state in which the sales originate has adopted the throwback rule.

PROPERTY FACTOR

Because most fixed assets are physically stationary in nature, the property factor is not so easily manipulated. Nonetheless, significant tax savings can be realized by establishing a leasing subsidiary in a low- or no-tax state. If the property is located in a state that does not include leased assets in the property factor, the establishment of a subsidiary from which to lease the property eliminates the assets from the property factor in the parent's state.

Permanently idle property generally is excluded from the property factor. Accordingly, a corporation should identify and remove such assets from the property factor to ensure that the factor is not distorted. It is equally important to identify and remove nonbusiness assets from the property factor in states that distinguish between business and nonbusiness income.

EXAMPLE 14

Quake Corporation's property holdings are as follows.

	State A	Total
Equipment (average historical cost)	$1,200,000	$2,000,000
Accumulated depreciation (average)	800,000	1,000,000

Twenty percent of the equipment in State A is fully depreciated and is idle. Assuming that A includes property in the factor at historical cost, Quake's property factor is 54.55% [($1,200,000 – $240,000 idle property)/($2,000,000 – $240,000)]. If the idle property is not removed from the property factor, Quake's property factor in A is incorrectly computed as 60% ($1,200,000/$2,000,000). ■

PAYROLL FACTOR

The payroll factor provides planning potential where several corporate employees spend substantial periods of time outside their state of employment, or the corporation is able to relocate highly paid employees to low- or no-tax states. Use of an independent contractor who works for more than one principal, however, can be beneficial under certain circumstances. Since the commissions paid to independent contractors are excluded from the payroll factor, the taxpayer may reduce its payroll factor in a high-tax state.

EXAMPLE 15

Yellow Corporation's total payroll costs are $1.4 million. Of this amount, $1 million was attributable to State A, a high-tax state. Yellow's payroll factor in A is 71.43% ($1,000,000/$1,400,000).

Assuming that $200,000 of the A compensation had been paid to sales representatives and that Yellow replaced its sales force with independent contractors, Yellow's payroll factor in A would be reduced to 66.67% [($1,000,000 – $200,000)/($1,400,000 – $200,000)]. ■

LO.6

Apply the unitary method of state income taxation.

The Unitary Theory

The **unitary theory** developed in response to the early problems that states faced in attributing the income of a multistate business among the states in which the business was conducted. Originally, this theory was applied to justify apportionment of the income of multiple operating divisions within a single company. Over the years, however, the concept has been extended to require the combined reporting of certain affiliated corporations, including those outside the United States.

When two affiliated corporations are subject to tax in different states, each entity must file a return and report its income in the state in which it conducts business. Each entity reports its income separately from that of its affiliated corporations. In an effort to minimize overall state income tax, multistate entities have attempted to separate the parts of the business that are carried on in the various states.

EXAMPLE 16

Arts Corporation owns a chain of retail stores located in several states. To enable each store to file and report the income earned only in that state, each store was organized as a separate subsidiary in the state in which it did business. In this manner, each store is separately subject to tax only in the state in which it is located. ■

Since most states attempt to allocate as much income to in-state sources as possible, several states have adopted the *unitary* approach to computing state taxable income. Under this method, a corporation is required to file a "combined return" that includes the results from all of the operations of the related corporations, not just from those that transacted business in the state. In this manner, the unitary method allows a state to apply formula apportionment to a firm's nationwide or worldwide unitary income. To include the activities of the corporation's subsidiaries in the apportionment formula, the state must determine that the subsidiaries' activities are an integral part of a unitary business and, as a result, are subject to apportionment.

WHAT IS A UNITARY BUSINESS?

A unitary business operates as a unit and cannot be segregated into independently operating divisions. The operations are integrated, and each division depends on or contributes to the operation of the business as a whole. It is not necessary that each unit operating within a state contribute to the activities of all divisions outside the state. The unitary theory ignores the separate legal existence of the entities and focuses instead on practical business realities. Accordingly, the separate entities are treated as a single business for state income tax purposes, and the apportionment formula is applied to the combined income of the unitary business.

DIGGING DEEPER 5

Find more information on this topic at our Web site: ***http://wft-advanced.swlearning.com***.

EXAMPLE 17

Continue with the facts of Example 16. Arts manufactured no goods, but conducted central management, purchasing, distributing, advertising, and administrative activities. The subsidiaries carried on a purely intrastate business, and they paid for the goods and services received at the parent company's cost, plus overhead. Arts and the subsidiaries constitute a unitary business due to their unitary operations (purchasing, distributing, advertising, and administrative functions). Accordingly, in states that have adopted the unitary method, the income and apportionment factors of the entire unitary group are combined and apportioned to the states in which at least one member of the group has nexus. ■

EXAMPLE 18

Crafts Corporation organized its departments as separate corporations on the basis of function: mining copper ore, refining the ore, and fabricating the refined copper into consumer products. Even though the various steps in the process are operated substantially independently of each other with only general supervision from Crafts's executive offices, Crafts is engaged in a single unitary business. Its various divisions are part of a large, vertically structured enterprise, in which each business segment needs the products or raw materials provided by another. The flow of products between the affiliates also provides evidence of functional integration, which generally requires some form of central decision or policy making, another characteristic of a unitary business. ■

Notice that the application of the unitary theory is based on a series of subjective observations about the organization and operation of the taxpayer's businesses, whereas the availability of Federal controlled and affiliated group status is based on objective, mechanical ownership tests. About half of the states require or allow unitary reporting, a somewhat smaller number than in the early 1980s.

TAX EFFECTS OF THE UNITARY THEORY

Use of the unitary approach by a state eliminates several of the planning techniques that could be used to shift income between corporate segments to avoid or minimize state taxes. In addition, the unitary approach usually results in a larger portion of the corporation's income being taxable in states where the compensation, property values, and sales prices are high relative to other states. This occurs because the larger in-state costs (numerators in the apportionment formula) include in the tax base a larger portion of the taxable income within the state's taxing jurisdiction. This has an adverse effect upon the corporation's overall state tax burden if the states in which the larger portions are allocated impose a high tax rate relative to the other states in which the business is conducted.

The presence of a unitary business is favorable when losses of unprofitable affiliates may be offset against the earnings of profitable affiliates. It also is favorable when income earned in a high-tax state may be shifted to low-tax states due to the use of combined apportionment factors.

EXAMPLE 19

Rita Corporation owns two subsidiaries, Arts and Crafts. Arts, located in State K, generated taxable income of $700,000. During this same period, Crafts, located in State M, generated a loss of $400,000. If the subsidiaries are independent corporations, Arts is required to pay K tax on $700,000 of income. However, if the corporations constitute a unitary business, the incomes, as well as the apportionment factors, of the two entities are combined. As a result, the combined income of $300,000 ($700,000 – $400,000) is apportioned to unitary states K and M. ■

EXAMPLE 20

Everett Corporation, a wholly owned subsidiary of Dan Corporation, generated $1 million taxable income. Everett's activities and sales are restricted to State P, which imposes a 10% income tax. Dan's income for the taxable period is $1.5 million. Dan's activities and sales are restricted to State Q, which imposes a 5% income tax. Both states use a three-factor

GLOBAL TAX ISSUES

WATER'S EDGE IS NOT A DAY AT THE BEACH

As a result of pressure from the business community, the Federal government, and foreign countries, most of the states that impose an income tax on a unitary business's worldwide operations permit a multinational business to elect **water's edge** unitary reporting as an alternative to worldwide unitary filing.

The water's edge provision permits a multinational corporation to elect to limit the reach of the state's taxing jurisdiction over out-of-state affiliates to activities occurring within the boundaries of the United States. The decision to make a water's edge election may have a substantial effect on the tax liability of a multinational corporation. For instance, a water's edge election usually cannot be revoked for a number of years without permission from the appropriate tax authority. Moreover, corporations making this election may be assessed an additional tax for the privilege of excluding out-of-state entities from the combined report.

apportionment formula that equally weights sales, payroll, and property. Sales, payroll, and average property for each of the corporations are as follows.

	Everett Corporation	Dan Corporation	Total
Sales	$3,000,000	$7,000,000	$10,000,000
Payroll	2,000,000	3,500,000	5,500,000
Property	2,500,000	4,500,000	7,000,000

If the corporations are independent entities, the overall state income tax liability is $175,000.

State P (10% × $1,000,000)	=	$100,000
State Q (5% × $1,500,000)	=	75,000
Total state income tax		$175,000

If the corporations are members of a unitary business, the income and apportionment factors are combined in determining the income tax liability in unitary states P and Q. As a result of the combined reporting, the overall state income tax liability is reduced.

State P Income Tax				
Total apportionable income			$2,500,000	
Apportionment formula				
Sales ($3,000,000/$10,000,000)	=	30.00%		
Payroll ($2,000,000/$5,500,000)	=	36.36%		
Property ($2,500,000/$7,000,000)	=	35.71%		
Total		102.07%		
Average (102.07% ÷ 3)			× 34.02%	
State P taxable income			$ 850,500	
Tax rate			× 10%	
State P tax liability				$ 85,050

Concept Summary 9–1

Principles of Multistate Corporate Taxation

1. Taxability of an organization's income in a state other than the one in which it is incorporated depends on the laws, regulations, and judicial interpretations of the other state; the nature and level of the corporation's activity in, or contacts with, that state; and, to a limited extent, the application of P.L. 86–272.
2. Each state has adopted its own multistate income tax laws, regulations, methods, and judicial interpretations; consequently, the nonuniformity of state income taxing provisions provides a multitude of planning techniques that allow a multistate corporation to reduce its overall state tax liability legally.
3. The apportionment procedure is used to assign the income of a multistate taxpayer to the various states in which business is conducted. Generally, nonbusiness income is allocated, rather than apportioned, directly to the state in which the nonbusiness income-generating assets are located.
4. The various state apportionment formulas offer planning opportunities in that more or less than 100% of the taxpayer's income may be subjected to state income tax.
5. Most states use a three-factor apportionment formula. However, some states equally weight the factors, while others double or triple the weight of the sales factor. A few states use only the sales factor to apportion multistate taxable income. Generally, the greater the relative weight of the sales factor, the greater the tax burden on out-of-state taxpayers.
6. The sales factor is based upon the destination concept except where a throwback rule applies. The payroll factor generally includes compensation that is included in Federal gross income, but some states include excludible fringe benefits. An employee's compensation usually is not divided among states. The property factor is derived using the average undepreciated historical costs for the assets and eight times the rental value of the asset.
7. The unitary theory may require the taxpayer to include worldwide activities and holdings in the apportionment factors. A water's edge election can limit these amounts to U.S. transactions.

State Q Income Tax

Total apportionable income			$2,500,000	
Apportionment formula				
Sales ($7,000,000/$10,000,000)	=	70.00%		
Payroll ($3,500,000/$5,500,000)	=	63.64%		
Property ($4,500,000/$7,000,000)	=	64.29%		
Total		197.93%		
Average (197.93% ÷ 3)			× 65.98%	
State Q taxable income			$1,649,500	
Tax rate			× 5%	
State Q tax liability				82,475
Total state income tax, if unitary				$167,525
Total state income tax, if nonunitary				175,000
Tax reduction from unitary combined reporting				$ 7,475

The results of unitary reporting would have been detrimental if Q had imposed a higher rate of tax than P, because a larger percentage of the corporation's income is attributable to Q when the apportionment factors are combined. ■

TAX FACT

Variations in Income Tax Rates

Corporate income tax rates imposed by states often vary a great deal—even among neighboring states. For example, while Nevada does not have a corporate income tax, its neighboring states have corporate rates ranging from Utah's 5 percent to California's 8.84 percent.

Likewise, while South Dakota and Wyoming do not have a corporate income tax, Montana has a flat rate of 6.75 percent, Minnesota has a flat rate of 9.8 percent, North Dakota has a progressive rate structure ranging from 3 percent on the first $3,000 of taxable income to 10.5 percent on income over $50,000, Iowa has a progressive rate structure topping out at 12 percent of taxable income over $250,000, and Nebraska has a progressive rate structure topping out at 7.81 percent of taxable income over $50,000.

By identifying the states that have adopted the unitary method and the criteria under which a particular state defines a unitary business, a taxpayer may reduce its overall state tax by restructuring its corporate relationships to create or guard against a unitary relationship. For instance, an independent business enterprise can be made unitary by exercising day-to-day operational control and by centralizing functions, such as marketing, financing, accounting, and legal services.

CONSOLIDATED AND COMBINED RETURNS

As discussed in Chapter 5, an affiliated group of corporations may file a consolidated return if all members of the group consent. Once such a return has been filed, the group must continue to file on a consolidated basis as long as it remains in existence, or until permission to file separate returns has been obtained. The consolidated return essentially treats the controlled corporations as a single taxable entity. Thus, the affiliated group pays only one tax, based upon the combined income of its members after certain adjustments (e.g., net operating losses) and eliminations (e.g., intercompany dividends and inventory profits).

Several states permit affiliated corporations to file a consolidated return if such a return has been filed for Federal purposes. The filing of a consolidated return is mandatory in only a few states.

Usually, only corporations that are subject to tax in the state can be included in a consolidated return unless specific requirements are met or the state permits the inclusion of corporations without nexus.

Do not confuse elective consolidated returns with required combined returns in unitary states. A **combined return** is filed in every unitary state in which one or more unitary members have nexus. The computations reflect apportioned and allocated income of the unitary members, resulting in a summary of the taxable income of the entities in each state. The combined method chiefly permits the unitary taxpayer to develop the summary of assigned taxable incomes, which is accepted by (and disclosed to) all of the states.

PLANNING STRATEGIES

Multistate Taxation Techniques

FRAMEWORK FOCUS: TAX RATE

STRATEGY ➤ SHIFT NET INCOME FROM HIGH-TAX JURISDICTIONS TO LOW-TAX JURISDICTIONS.

The inconsistencies in the tax laws and rates among the states not only complicate state tax planning, but also provide the nucleus of pertinent planning opportunities. Although several tax planning devices are available to a corporation that does business in only one state, most planning techniques are directed toward corporations that do business or maintain property in more than one state. All suggested tax planning strategies should be reviewed in light of practical business considerations and the additional administrative and other costs that may be incurred, because simply minimizing state taxes may not be prudent from a business perspective.

SELECTING THE OPTIMAL STATE IN WHICH TO OPERATE

Because the states employ different definitions of the amount and type of activity necessary to establish nexus, a company has some latitude in selecting the states by which it will be taxed. When a corporation has only a limited connection with a high-tax state, it may abandon that activity by electing an alternative means of accomplishing the same result. For example, if providing a sales representative with a company-owned computer constitutes nexus in an undesired state, the company could eliminate its connection with that state by reimbursing sales personnel for equipment expenses, instead of providing a company computer. Similarly, when nexus is caused by conducting customer training sessions or seminars in the state, the corporation could bypass this connection. This can be done by sending the personnel to a nearby state in which nexus clearly has been established or in which the activity would not constitute nexus.

In addition, when sufficient activity originates from the repair and maintenance of the corporation's products or the activities performed by the sales representatives within the state, the organization could incorporate the service or sales divisions. This would invalidate a nonunitary state's right to tax the parent corporation's income; only the income of the service or sales divisions would be subject to tax. However, this technique will be successful only if the incorporated division is a *bona fide* business operation. Therefore, the pricing of any sales or services between the new subsidiary and the parent corporation must be at arm's length, and the operations of the new corporation preferably should result in a profit.

Although most planning techniques are employed to disconnect a corporation's activities from an undesirable state, they can also be utilized to create nexus in a desirable state. For example, when the presence of a company-owned computer creates nexus in a desirable state, the corporation could provide its sales representatives in that state with company-owned equipment, rather than reimbursing or providing increased compensation for equipment costs.

Establishing nexus in a state is advantageous, for instance, when that state has a lower tax rate than the state in which the income currently is taxed, or when losses or credits become available to reduce tax liabilities in the state.

EXAMPLE 21

Bird Corporation generates $500,000 of taxable income from selling goods; specifically, 40% of its product is sold in State A and 60% in State B. Both states levy a corporate income tax and include only the sales factor in their apportionment formulas. The tax rate in A is 10%; B's rate is only 3%. Bird's manufacturing operation is located in A; therefore, the corporation's income is subject to tax in that state. Currently, Bird is immune from tax under Public Law 86–272 in B. Since A has adopted a throwback provision, Bird incurs $50,000 of state income taxes.

	Apportionment Formula	Net Income	Tax Rate	Tax
State A	100/100	$500,000	10%	$50,000
State B	0/100	500,000	3%	-0-
Total tax liability				$50,000

Because B imposes a lower tax rate than A, Bird substantially reduces its state tax liability if sufficient nexus is created with B.

	Apportionment Formula	Net Income	Tax Rate	Tax
State A	40/100	$500,000	10%	$20,000
State B	60/100	500,000	3%	9,000
Total tax liability				$29,000

Locating Inventory. A corporation may benefit by storing inventory in a low- or no-tax state because the average property value in the state in which the manufacturing operation is located is reduced significantly. When the manufacturing operation is located in a high-tax state, the establishment of a distribution center in a low- or no-tax state may reduce the overall state tax liability.

EXAMPLE 22

Trill Corporation realized $200,000 of taxable income from selling its product in States A and B. Trill's manufacturing plant, product distribution center, and warehouses are located in A. The corporation's activities within the two states are as follows:

	State A	State B	Total
Sales	$500,000	$200,000	$700,000
Property	300,000	50,000	350,000
Payroll	100,000	10,000	110,000

Trill is subject to tax in A and B. Both states utilize a three-factor apportionment formula that equally weights sales, property, and payroll; however, A imposes a 10% corporate income tax, while B levies a 3% tax. Trill incurs a total income tax liability of $17,575.

Apportionment Formulas

	State A			State B		
Sales	$500,000/$700,000	=	71.43%	$200,000/$700,000	=	28.57%
Property	$300,000/$350,000	=	85.71%	$50,000/$350,000	=	14.29%
Payroll	$100,000/$110,000	=	90.91%	$10,000/$110,000	=	9.09%
Total			248.05%			51.95%
Apportionment factor (totals/3)			82.68%			17.32%
Income apportioned to the state ($200,000 × apportionment factor)			$165,360			$34,640
Tax rate			× 10%			× 3%
Tax liability			$ 16,536			$ 1,039
Total tax liability			$ 17,575			

EXAMPLE 23

Continue with the facts of Example 22, and further assume that Trill's product distribution center and warehouse operations were acquired for $200,000 and the payroll of these operations is $20,000. Ignoring all nontax considerations, Trill could reduce its tax liability by $3,514 (a 20% reduction) by moving its distribution center, warehouses, and applicable personnel to B.

	State A	State B	Total
Sales	$500,000	$200,000	$700,000
Property	100,000	250,000	350,000
Payroll	80,000	30,000	110,000

	Apportionment Formulas						
	State A			**State B**			
Sales	$500,000/$700,000	=	71.43%	$200,000/$700,000	=	28.57%
Property	$100,000/$350,000	=	28.57%	$250,000/$350,000	=	71.43%
Payroll	$80,000/$110,000	=	72.73%	$30,000/$110,000	=	27.27%
Total			172.73%			127.27%
Apportionment factor (totals/3)			57.58%			42.42%
Income apportioned to the state ($200,000 × apportionment factor)			$115,160			$84,840
Tax rate			× 10%			× 3%
Tax liability			$ 11,516			$ 2,545
Total tax liability						$14,061
Tax imposed before move to State B						17,575
Tax reduction due to move						$ 3,514

RESTRUCTURING CORPORATE ENTITIES

One of the major objectives of state tax planning is to design the proper mix of corporate entities. An optimal mix of entities often generates the lowest combined state income tax for the corporation. Ideally, the income from all of the entities will be subject to a low tax rate or no tax at all. However, this generally is not possible. Consequently, the goal of designing a good corporate combination often is to situate the highly profitable entities in states that impose a low (or no) income tax.

Matching Tax Rates and Corporate Income. When the corporation must operate in a high-tax state, divisions that generate losses should also be located there. Alternatively, unprofitable or less profitable operations can be merged into profitable operations to reduce the overall income subject to tax in the state. An ideal candidate for this type of merger may be a research and development subsidiary that is only marginally profitable, but is vital to the parent corporation's strategic goals. By using computer simulation models, a variety of different combinations can be tested to determine the optimal corporate structure.

Passive Investment Companies. The creation of a **passive investment company** is another restructuring technique utilized to minimize a corporation's state tax burden. Nonbusiness or passive income generally is allocated to the state in which the income-producing asset is located, rather than apportioned among the states in which the corporation does business. Therefore, significant tax savings may be realized when nonbusiness assets are located in a state that either does not levy an income tax or provides favorable tax treatment for passive income. The corporation need not be domiciled in the state to benefit from these favorable provisions. Instead, the tax savings can be realized by forming a passive investment subsidiary to hold the intangible assets and handle the corporation's investment activities. The passive investment subsidiary technique usually produces the desired result in any no-tax state. Delaware, however, often is selected for this purpose due to its other corporate statutory provisions and favorable political, business, and legal climate.

Delaware does not impose an income tax upon a corporation whose only activity within the state is the maintenance and management of intangible investments and the collection and distribution of income from such investments or from tangible property physically located in another state. Consequently, trademarks, patents, stock, and other intangible property can be transferred to a Delaware corporation whose activity is limited to collecting passive income. The assets can be transferred to the subsidiary without incurring a Federal income tax under § 351.

However, to receive the desired preferential state tax treatment, the holding company's activities within the state must be sufficient to establish nexus in the state. The passive investment company should avoid performing any activity outside the state that may result in establishing nexus with another state. In addition, the formation of the subsidiary must be properly implemented to assure the legal substance of the operation. The passive investment company must have a physical office, and it must function as an independent operation. Ensuring nexus and proper formation is not difficult since numerous consulting organizations are available to furnish new passive investment companies with all of the elements necessary to fulfill these requirements.

Because the subsidiary's activities are confined to Delaware (or some other no- or low-tax state), and its operations generate only passive income, its income will not be taxed in any nonunitary state. Moreover, most states exclude dividends from taxation or otherwise treat them favorably; therefore, the earnings of a passive investment subsidiary can be distributed as a dividend to the parent at a minimal tax cost. If the state in which the parent is located does not levy the full income tax on dividends received, the entire measure of passive income may escape taxation.

Formation of a passive investment subsidiary also may favorably affect the parent corporation's apportionment formula in nonunitary states because the passive income earned by the subsidiary is excluded from the numerator of its sales factor.

EXAMPLE 24

Purple Corporation generates $800,000 of taxable income; $600,000 is income from its manufacturing operations, and $200,000 is dividend income from passive investments. All of Purple's sales are made, and assets are kept, in State A, which imposes a 10% corporate income tax and permits a 100% deduction for dividends received from subsidiaries. The corporation is not subject to tax in any other state. Consequently, Purple incurs $80,000 of income tax (tax base $800,000 × tax rate 10%).

If Purple creates a passive investment subsidiary in State B, which does not impose an income tax upon a corporation whose only activity within the state is the maintenance and management of passive investments, Purple's tax liability is reduced by $20,000 (a 25% decrease). Since passive income is nonbusiness income (which is allocated for state tax purposes to the state in which it is located), the income earned from its passive investments is not subject to tax in A.

	State A (Purple Corporation)	State B (Passive Investment Company)
Taxable income	$600,000	$200,000
Tax rate	× 10%	× -0-*
Tax liability	$ 60,000	$ -0-
Total tax liability		$ 60,000
Tax imposed without restructuring		80,000
Tax reduction due to use of subsidiary		$ 20,000

*B does not impose an income tax on a passive investment corporation.

The income earned by the subsidiary from its passive investments can be distributed to Purple as a dividend without incurring a tax liability because A allows a 100% deduction for dividends that are received from subsidiary corporations. ■

These desired results, however, will not be fully available in states that view the entire corporate operation as being unitary. Since those states require combined reporting, the income earned by the passive investment subsidiary is included in the corporation's apportionable or allocable income. In addition, a number of states have begun attacking the arrangements in the courts, arguing that the licensing of intangibles creates sufficient nexus with the taxing state to subject the passive investment company to tax.

Decisions surrounding these cases have been both favorable and unfavorable for taxpayers, even within the same jurisdiction. Structures such as these are very fact-specific, and those companies that are able to provide appropriate documentation and can demonstrate actual operations are most likely to be successful and survive these challenges.

SUBJECTING THE CORPORATION'S INCOME TO APPORTIONMENT

When a multistate organization is domiciled in a high-tax state, some of its apportionable income is eliminated from the tax base in that state. In light of the high tax rate, this may result in significant tax savings. Apportioning income will be especially effective where the income that is attributed to the other states is not subject to income tax. The income removed from the taxing jurisdiction of the domicile state entirely escapes state income taxation when the state to which the income is attributed (1) does not levy a corporate income tax; (2) requires a higher level of activity necessary to subject an out-of-state company to taxation than that adopted by the state of domicile; or (3) is prohibited under Public Law 86–272 from taxing the income (assuming that the domicile state has not adopted a throwback provision). Thus, the right to apportion income may provide substantial benefits because the out-of-state sales are excluded from the numerator of the sales factor and may not be taxed in another state.

However, to acquire the right to apportion its income, the organization must have sufficient activities in, or contacts with, one or more other states. Whether the type and amount of activities and/or contacts are considered adequate is determined by the domicile state's nexus rules. Therefore, a corporation should analyze its current activities in, and contacts with, other states to determine which, if any, activities or contacts could be redirected so that the corporation gains the right to apportion its income.

TAX IN THE NEWS

Holding Companies Make Other States Angry

A tax dollar saved in one state is a tax dollar lost in another. That's how some state tax administrators and observers view the use of the passive investment holding company. According to a spokesman for the Multistate Tax Commission, the average state income tax rate paid by larger conglomerates fell from about 9.6 percent in 1980 to about 5.2 percent currently. That isn't fair, says the Secretary of Revenue in North Carolina, who points out that as corporate income tax revenue declines, income and sales/use taxes on individuals must be increased to make up the difference.

The Delaware version of the investment holding company is the culprit largely responsible. By locating intangible assets such as trademarks and income-generating investment assets in tax-friendly states like Delaware, corporations can achieve major tax savings. The list of companies taking advantage of the Delaware holding company provisions includes such familiar names as Kmart, Home Depot, Circuit City, Staples, The Gap, Limited, and Burger King.

Although many state authorities are working hard to have the courts or Congress scale back the use of these shelters, passive investment companies remain a viable course of action.

LO.7

Discuss the states' income tax treatment of S corporations.

Taxation of S Corporations

The majority of the 46 states that impose a corporate income tax have special provisions, similar to the Federal law, that govern the taxation of S corporations. As of 2004, only a few states—including Michigan, New Hampshire, and Tennessee—and the District of Columbia do not provide special (no corporate-level tax) treatment for Federal S corporations. In addition, Massachusetts imposes a corporate-level tax on S corporations that have gross receipts in excess of $6 million. New Jersey and California apply a corporate-level tax, at special rates, on an S corporation.

In the non-S election states, a Federal S corporation generally is subject to tax in the same manner as a regular C corporation. Accordingly, if a multistate S corporation operates in any of these states, it is subject to state income tax and does not realize one of the primary benefits of S status—the avoidance of double taxation. Other potential tax-related benefits of the S election, including the pass-through of net operating losses and the reduction in the rate of tax imposed on individual and corporate taxpayers, may be curtailed.

BRIDGE DISCIPLINE

Bridge to Human Resources Management

The relocation of employees and corporate offices, with the accompanying corporate officers and directors, and the use of independent contractors instead of employees may offer planning opportunities with respect to the payroll apportionment factor.

For example, a company may relocate highly paid employees to low-tax or no-tax states to reduce the payroll factor in the high-tax jurisdiction and correspondingly increase the payroll factor in the low- or no-tax jurisdiction. Likewise, a company may locate its home office in a state that does not include officer compensation in its definition of payroll for apportionment purposes. The use of an independent contractor who works for more than one company can also be beneficial in certain circumstances. Since the commissions paid to independent contractors are excluded from the payroll factor, the taxpayer may reduce its payroll factor in a high-tax state.

Making personnel decisions based only on tax savings can be problematic, however, because it can result in a decline in morale and possibly make it more difficult to retain current employees and recruit new employees. For example, should a company with offices in Washington, D.C., and Virginia refuse to allow employees living in Maryland to telecommute from their homes for fear of creating nexus in Maryland? Such tax-smart moves may not be people-smart and may arouse resentment and animosity among employees.

EXAMPLE 25

Bryan, an S corporation, has established nexus in States A and B. A recognizes S status, while B does not. Bryan generated $600,000 of ordinary business income and $100,000 of dividends that were received from corporations in which Bryan owns 50% of the stock. Bryan's State B apportionment percentage is 50%.

For B tax purposes, Bryan must first compute its income as though it were a regular corporation and then apportion the resulting income to B. Assuming that B has adopted the Federal provisions governing the dividends received deduction, Bryan's income, determined as though it were a C corporation, is $620,000 [$600,000 + (100% – 80%) × $100,000]. Accordingly, Bryan is subject to corporate income tax in B on $310,000 ($620,000 × 50% apportionment percentage) of taxable income. ■

ELIGIBILITY

All of the states that recognize S status permit a corporation to be treated as an S corporation for state purposes only if the corporation has a valid Federal S election in place. Generally, the filing of a Federal S election is sufficient to render the corporation an S corporation for state tax purposes. In most states, an entity that is an S corporation for Federal tax purposes automatically is treated as an S corporation for state tax purposes. A few states permit the entity to *elect out* of its S status for state purposes.

CORPORATE-LEVEL TAX

A few states deviate from the Federal S corporation provisions and provide that an S corporation is entirely exempt from state income tax only if all of its shareholders are residents of the state. In these states, an S corporation is taxed on the portion of its income that is attributable to nonresident shareholders. Some of these states permit the S corporation to escape corporate-level tax on this income if its nonresident shareholders sign a form, agreeing to pay state tax on their share of the corporation's income. Moreover, about half of the states require the corporation to withhold taxes on the nonresident shareholders' portions of the entity's income.

EXAMPLE 26

ARGO, an S corporation, is subject to income tax only in Vermont. On the last day of its taxable year, 40% of ARGO's stock is held by nonresident shareholders. To the extent that ARGO's stock is held by resident shareholders, the corporation is not subject to income tax. Accordingly, ARGO is not subject to tax on 60% of its income.

The corporation *is* subject to tax on the remaining 40% of its income. ARGO may be able to avoid this corporate-level tax by withholding Vermont income tax for its nonresident shareholders. ■

COMPOSITE TAX RETURN

In an effort to decrease compliance burdens and simplify the filing process for nonresident shareholders of S corporations, several states allow an S corporation to file a single income tax return and pay the resulting tax on behalf of some or all of its nonresident shareholders. State requirements for the filing of a **composite return** vary substantially.

LO.8

Describe the state audit process.

The State Audit Process

Like the Federal income tax, state income tax systems generally are based on an assumption of voluntary compliance and self-assessment. However, this voluntary system is enforced through the audit process.

STATE INCOME TAX AUDITS

With many states facing budget crises, the audit function of the respective Departments of Revenue has become an increasingly important source of procuring tax revenue.

Since the starting point for most states is Federal taxable income (either before or after special deductions and net operating loss), state auditors ordinarily do not examine specific items of income and expense. Rather, they scrutinize state-specific adjustments made to arrive at apportionable income, and the manner in which that income is apportioned to their respective state. State auditors often look to tie the sales, payroll, and property amounts used in the apportionment formulas of their respective states to financial statements and/or Federal income tax returns.

To be more efficient, some states utilize limited-scope audits in which auditors focus on common issues and transactions for which state adjustments are most likely. In addition, some states share information with other jurisdictions, to identify taxpayers' positions taken on returns that the jurisdictions believe are subject to challenge.

The state typically contacts the taxpayer with a request for information (sometimes called an Information Document Request or IDR) and provides the taxpayer with a deadline for responding. If the statute of limitations is about to expire, the state may request an extension. The taxpayer may be able to negotiate the scope of the audit as a concession to extending the statute of limitations.

After the IDR is reviewed by the state, the state provides preliminary work papers and proposed adjustments for the taxpayer to review. The state may schedule an on-site audit visit if additional information is needed. The state processes the workpapers and issues a "Notice of Proposed Audit Adjustment/Notice of Tax Deficiency" to the taxpayer, and the taxpayer is typically given 30 to 60 days to respond before the Notice becomes final.

TAX FACT

Can You Multiply That?

The compliance burden of dealing with multiple taxing jurisdictions and multiple taxes can create multiple headaches for large multinational and multistate businesses. In a recent year, one large corporation dealt with 65 state and local income tax jurisdictions and 350 sales and use tax jurisdictions, filed or managed over 3,000 state tax returns, and was involved in over 50 audits.

After the state issues a "Final Notice," the taxpayer is given another 30 to 60 days to pay the additional taxes (plus any interest and penalties) or protest and request a hearing/conference with a State Appeals Office. The taxpayer may reach a settlement at the appeals level or take the matter to court (some states have a separate Tax Court, others do not). Decisions may be appealed to the appropriate State Supreme Court. As with audits at the Federal level, how far a taxpayer is willing to appeal an issue through the state's appeals process depends on the expected costs and benefits, and the tax dollars at risk.

In extremely rare cases, the U.S. Supreme Court has heard state tax cases, but generally it has left matters of state and local income taxation to the jurisdictions themselves. Even landmark state income tax court cases, such as the *Geoffrey* decision in South Carolina,[14] have been denied writ of *certiorari* by the U.S. Supreme Court.

FEDERAL AUDIT ADJUSTMENTS

Large corporate taxpayers routinely are audited by the IRS. Depending upon the nature and complexity of items that may be in dispute between the taxpayer and the IRS, an audit may not be resolved for several years.

The Revenue Agent's Report (RAR) summarizes and provides details of the adjustments made to the Federal return. A taxpayer must report any changes to Federal taxable income to all of the states in which the taxpayer filed a return for the period in question.

The time required to report RAR adjustments and to file amended returns at the state and local levels varies by jurisdiction and can be as little as 30 days or as long as two years. An amended return must be filed, even if the tax year for which the changes are being reported is beyond the state's statute of limitations.

This can be problematic for taxpayers, since some states allow their Departments of Revenue to examine all issues in these amended returns even when the tax year is beyond the statute of limitations.

LO.9

Describe other commonly encountered state and local taxes on businesses.

Other State and Local Taxes

In addition to sales and use taxes and property taxes (see Chapter 10), state and local jurisdictions may impose a variety of other taxes on corporations, including incorporation or entrance fees or taxes; gross receipt taxes; stock transfer taxes;

[14] *Geoffrey, Inc. v. South Carolina Tax Comm.*, 437 S.E.2d 13 (1993), *cert. denied* 510 U.S. 992 (1993).

TAX IN THE NEWS

Tax Amnesties

Tax amnesties typically allow delinquent taxpayers and other nonfilers to submit outstanding returns with "no questions asked." Often penalties for late payment are waived, and occasionally interest is waived as well.

Since 1982, 40 states have enacted temporary tax amnesties, with over half of these states offering amnesty more than once. In 2003 alone, Arizona, Colorado, Florida, Illinois, Kansas, Maine, Massachusetts, Missouri, New York, North Dakota, and Virginia either began or ended amnesty programs. The amount of tax collected ranged from less than $25 million in Colorado, Kansas, and Missouri, to over $500 million in Illinois and New York. In Illinois, about two-thirds of the revenue collected came from corporate taxpayers.

From the government's perspective, the objective is to collect unpaid taxes and to enter into the database those who have come forward to claim the amnesty. "Hunting down" those who do not file tax returns can be quite costly, in terms of audit staff and computer resources. Thus, the government is seeking the annuity of taxes that will come its way from future tax returns, once the errant taxpayer has been identified.

realty transfer and mortgage recording taxes; license taxes; and franchise taxes based on net worth or capital stock outstanding.

An *incorporation tax* is an excise tax for the corporate privilege conferred on the business. At the time the business is incorporated, the state generally imposes a fee or tax for the privilege of conducting business within the state as a corporation. Similarly, an out-of-state corporation usually must pay an entrance fee or tax before it can transact business in a state other than its state of incorporation.

Some states base the incorporation tax on the par value of the authorized stock. To prevent tax evasion, a few of these states impose a similar fee or tax on subsequent increases in the corporation's authorized stock. Where the incorporation fee or tax is based on the amount of authorized stock, the tax may be based on the total amount of the stock, even though the corporation conducts business in several states.

A *license tax* is an excise tax on the privilege of engaging in a certain business, occupation, or profession. A state may impose business, occupational, or professional license taxes as a means of generating revenue or regulating the activities of the business, occupation, or profession for the public welfare.

Stock and realty transfer and mortgage recording taxes are nonrecurring taxes that are imposed at the time of recording or transfer. *Stock transfer taxes* are imposed on the transfer of shares or certificates of stock of domestic and foreign corporations. The tax typically is based on the number of shares transferred and the par or market value of the stock. Generally, the following stock transfers are exempt from the transfer tax: original issues, deposits of stock as security for a loan, and transfers to a broker for sale or purchase.

The base of the *realty transfer tax* usually is measured by the consideration paid or to be paid for the realty. The *mortgage recording tax* may be based on the actual consideration given, the value of the property, or the debt to be secured by the instrument.

Typically, a *capital stock tax* is an excise tax imposed on a domestic corporation for the privilege of existing as a corporation or imposed on an out-of-state corporation, either for the privilege of doing business or for the actual transaction of business within the state. This annual tax usually is based on the book value of the corporation's net worth, including capital, surplus, and retained earnings. In a few states, a corporation is subject to a *franchise tax* only to the extent that the tax exceeds the corporate income tax, but in the majority of states, the entity is subject to both taxes.

The majority of capital stock taxes are apportioned if the corporation does business or maintains an office in another state. In some states, however, the tax is levied on the entire authorized or issued capital stock of a domestic corporation, even though the corporation may be engaged in business in other states. For corporations based in other states, the tax is imposed only on the capital that is employed in the state as determined by an apportionment formula.

EXAMPLE 27

The balance sheet of Bull, a domestic corporation of State A, at the end of its taxable year is as follows.

Cash	$100,000
Equipment (net of $50,000 accumulated depreciation)	150,000
Building (net of $75,000 accumulated depreciation)	225,000
Land	125,000
Total assets	$600,000
Accounts payable and other short-term liabilities	$100,000
Long-term liabilities	200,000
Capital stock	50,000
Paid-in capital in excess of par value	50,000
Retained earnings	200,000
Total liabilities and equity	$600,000

A imposes a 2% franchise tax based on the entire net worth of a domestic corporation. Bull is subject to a franchise tax in A of $6,000 ($600,000 assets – $300,000 liabilities = $300,000 net worth × 2% rate). ■

EXAMPLE 28

Continue with the facts of Example 27, except that A subjects a domestic corporation to tax only on the capital that is employed in the state. Bull properly determines its A apportionment percentage as 20%. In this case, Bull's A franchise tax liability is $1,200 ($300,000 net worth × 20% apportionment percentage = $60,000 capital employed in A × 2% rate). ■

PLANNING STRATEGIES

Capital Stock Taxation

FRAMEWORK FOCUS: DEDUCTIONS

STRATEGY ➤ **MAXIMIZE DEDUCTIBLE AMOUNTS.**

Capital stock tax liabilities can be significant for capital-intensive taxpayers to the extent that they reinvest a large portion of retained earnings (the tax base) in productive assets. If all nontax factors are equal, a taxpayer with sizable exposure to a capital stock tax should consider the following techniques.

- Funding expansion with debt, rather than retained earnings.
- Funding subsidiary operations with debt, rather than direct capital contributions.
- Regularly paying dividends to parent companies that are domiciled in tax-favored states, such as Delaware.

Suggested Further Readings

Karen J. Boucher and Shona Ponda, "Current Corporate Income Tax Developments (Part I)," *The Tax Adviser*, March 2004, pp. 156–163.

Robert Cline, William Fox, Tom Neubig, and Andrew Phillips, "Total State and Local Business Taxes: A 50-State Study of the Taxes Paid by Business in Fiscal 2003," *State Tax Notes*, March 1, 2004, pp. 737–750.

Peter L. Faber, "Intangible Holding Companies Set Back in Maryland and New York," *State Tax Notes*, July 21, 2003, pp. 225–231.

Sanjay Gupta and Lillian Mills, "Corporate Multistate Tax Planning: Benefits of Multiple Jurisdictions," *Journal of Accounting and Economics*, Vol. 33, No. 1, February 2002, pp. 117–139.

David K. Hoffman, "State Income Taxation of Nonresident Professional Athletes," *Tax Notes*, November 25, 2002, pp. 1083–1091.

Bruce Howard, "The Surprising Benefits of Nexus," *Journal of Accountancy*, November 2002, pp. 85–88.

Michael W. McLoughlin and Walter Hellerstein, "State Apportionment Issues for Corporate Owners of Passthrough Entities," *State Tax Notes*, July 28, 2003, pp. 287–291.

John A. Swain, "State Income Tax Jurisdiction: A Jurisprudential and Policy Perspective," *State Tax Notes*, February 2, 2004, pp. 341–369.

KEY TERMS

Allocate, 9–10
Apportion, 9–10
Combined return, 9–26
Composite return, 9–33
Dock sales, 9–16
Multistate Tax Commission (MTC), 9–10
Nexus, 9–8
Passive investment company, 9–29
Payroll factor, 9–17
Property factor, 9–19
Public Law 86–272, 9–9
Sales factor, 9–15
Throwback rule, 9–16
Uniform Division of Income for Tax Purposes Act (UDITPA), 9–10
Unitary theory, 9–22
Water's edge election, 9–24

PROBLEM MATERIALS

West Federal Taxation

Discussion Questions

Ethics

1. The intent of much of today's multistate income tax planning is to create so-called nowhere sales, so that the income from the transaction is not subject to tax in any state. Suppose, for instance, that a sale is made from Georgia (a state with no throwback rule) into Nevada (the place of ultimate destination, but a state with no income tax). No state-level income tax liability is generated. Is it ethical for a tax adviser to suggest such a strategy? Could you propose the establishment of a sales office in a nonthrowback state, thereby avoiding state income tax on a transaction that is fully taxable under Federal rules?

EXTENDER

2. What is the precedential value of rulings and regulations issued by the Multistate Tax Commission, a voluntary body with no legislative authority?

EXTENDER

3. List the principles by which one state gains authority under its own constitution and under the U.S. Constitution to tax the in-state activities of a conglomerate doing business in a number of jurisdictions.

4. Sales representative Jones is based in Utah, where the operating plants and corporate headquarters of her employer also are located. She visits customers in Colorado for a day, soliciting orders for the seashells that she sells. The orders are approved in Utah, and the shells are shipped from Oregon within a week. Are these sales subject to the Colorado corporate income tax?

Issue ID

5. Continue with the facts of Question 4. In processing her orders, Jones regularly reviews the credit standing of the customer and decides whether the order should be billed on company credit or sent COD (cash on delivery). Are these sales subject to the Colorado corporate income tax?

6. Evaluate the following comment: The unitary concept is similar to the idea of the Federal consolidated return.

7. Name two states that do not allow single-level corporate taxation for Federal S corporations.

8. Comment on special compliance concerns for Federal S corporations in dealing with state income tax systems.

9. Describe two approaches that the states use concerning out-of-state S corporation shareholders.

10. In the context of a state income tax on S corporations, what is a composite or block return?

Communications

11. Your client, Ecru Limited, is considering an expansion of its sales operations, but it fears adverse resulting tax consequences. Write a memo for the tax research file identifying the planning opportunities presented by the ability of a corporation to terminate or create nexus. Be certain to discuss the *Wrigley* case in your analysis.

Communications

12. Your client, Royal Corporation, generates significant interest income from its working capital liquid investments. Write a memo for the tax research file discussing the planning opportunities presented by establishing a passive investment company. Support your memo with a diagram of the resulting flow of assets and income.

Issue ID
Decision Making

13. Mollusk Corporation generates $70 million taxable income per year, all in State F, where its marginal state tax rate is 8%. The taxable income includes $20 million in interest income from Treasury bills. How might Mollusk reduce its state tax liability? Suggest three alternatives Mollusk should consider. Ignore any nontax considerations.

EXTENDER

14. Small companies with all of their payroll and property in one state but sales in multiple states (in which they have no physical presence) generally lobby their home state for the use of a single sales factor for apportionment, along with a repeal of the state's throwback rule. Why are these companies opposed to the throwback rule?

Ethics

15. A company in North Carolina is considering expanding its sales force into neighboring states in which it currently does not do business. As an alternative to serving customers in the neighboring states with the current sales force or hiring new employees, the company is considering outsourcing the sales function by using independent contractors who would be responsible for all sales in the neighboring states. The company's CPA has indicated that using independent contractors offers multiple benefits: the company will not have to pay health insurance premiums, retirement benefits, and payroll taxes for the independent contractors, and the use of independent contractors will not establish nexus in the surrounding states. What tax and nontax issues should the company consider in deciding whether to outsource?

Problems

16. For each of the following independent cases, indicate whether the circumstances call for an addition modification (*A*), a subtraction modification (*S*), or no modification (*N*) in computing state taxable income. Then indicate the amount of any modification. The starting point in computing State Q taxable income is the year's Federal taxable income.
    a. Q income taxes, deducted on the Federal return as a business expense = $10,000.
    b. State R income taxes, deducted on the Federal return as a business expense = $10,000.
    c. Federal income taxes paid = $30,000.
    d. Refund received from last year's Q income taxes = $3,000.
    e. Local property taxes, deducted on the Federal return as a business expense = $7,000.
    f. Federal cost recovery = $10,000, and Q cost recovery = $15,000.
    g. Federal cost recovery = $15,000, and Q cost recovery = $10,000.
    h. An asset was sold for $18,000; its purchase price was $20,000. Accumulated Federal cost recovery = $11,000, and accumulated Q cost recovery = $8,000.
    i. Federal investment tax credit = $0, and Q investment tax credit = $5,000.
    j. Dividend income received from State R corporation = $10,000, subject to a Federal dividends received deduction of 70%.

17. Perk Corporation is subject to tax only in State A. Perk generated the following income and deductions.

Federal taxable income	$200,000
State A income tax expense	15,000
Refund of State A income tax	13,000
Depreciation allowed for Federal tax purposes	200,000
Depreciation allowed for state tax purposes	180,000

    Federal taxable income is the starting point in computing A taxable income. State income taxes are not deductible for A tax purposes. Determine Perk's A taxable income.

18. Flip Corporation is subject to tax only in State X. Flip generated the following income and deductions. State income taxes are not deductible for X income tax purposes.

Sales	$4,000,000
Cost of sales	2,250,000
State X income tax expense	110,000
Depreciation allowed for Federal tax purposes	300,000
Depreciation allowed for state tax purposes	250,000
Interest on Federal obligations	20,000
Interest on X obligations	50,000
Expenses related to X obligations	7,000

    a. The starting point in computing the X income tax base is Federal taxable income. Derive this amount.
    b. Determine Flip's X taxable income, assuming that interest on X obligations is exempt from X income tax.
    c. Determine Flip's taxable income, assuming that interest on X obligations is subject to X income tax.

19. Jest Corporation owns and operates two facilities that manufacture paper products. One of the facilities is located in State D, and the other is located in State E. Jest generated $2.5 million of taxable income, comprised of $2 million of income from its manufacturing facilities and a $500,000 gain from the sale of nonbusiness property, located in E. E

does not distinguish between business and nonbusiness income, but D apportions only business income. Jest's activities within the two states are outlined below.

	State D	State E	Total
Sales of paper products	$4,500,000	$5,800,000	$10,300,000
Property	600,000	1,500,000	2,100,000
Payroll	1,200,000	1,900,000	3,100,000

Both D and E utilize a three-factor apportionment formula, under which sales, property, and payroll are equally weighted. Determine the amount of Jest's income that is subject to income tax by each state.

20. Assume the same facts as Problem 19, except that, under the statutes of both D and E, only business income is subject to apportionment.

21. Millie Corporation has nexus in States A and B. Millie's activities for the year are summarized as follows.

	State A	State B	Total
Sales	$1,200,000	$ 300,000	$1,500,000
Property			
Average cost	500,000	300,000	800,000
Average accumulated depreciation	(300,000)	(100,000)	(400,000)
Payroll	2,400,000	100,000	2,500,000
Rent expense	10,000	25,000	35,000

Determine the apportionment factors for A and B, assuming that A uses a three-factor apportionment formula under which sales, property (net depreciated basis), and payroll are equally weighted, and B employs a single-factor formula that consists solely of sales. State A has adopted the UDITPA with respect to the inclusion of rent payments in the property factor.

22. Assume the facts of Problem 21, except that A uses a single-factor apportionment formula that consists solely of sales, and B uses a three-factor apportionment formula that equally weights sales, property (at historical cost), and payroll. State B does not include rent payments in the property factor.

23. Assume the facts of Problem 21, except that both states employ a three-factor formula, under which sales are double weighted. The basis of the property factor in A is historical cost, while the basis of this factor in B is the net depreciated basis. Neither A nor B includes rent payments in the property factor.

24. Falcon Corporation operates in two states, as indicated below. This year's operations generated $300,000 of apportionable income.

	State A	State B	Total
Sales	$500,000	$400,000	$900,000
Property	300,000	50,000	350,000
Payroll	100,000	10,000	110,000

Compute Falcon's State A taxable income, assuming that State A apportions income based on a:

a. Three-factor formula.
b. Double-weighted sales factor.
c. Sales factor only.

25. Tootie Corporation operates in two states, as indicated below. All goods are manufactured in State A. Determine the sales to be assigned to both states in computing Tootie's sales factor for the year. Both states follow the UDITPA and the MTC regulations in this regard.

Sales shipped to A locations	$200,000
Sales shipped to B locations	190,000
Interest income from Tootie's B checking accounts	3,000
Rent income from excess space in A warehouse	13,000
Interest income from Treasury bills in Tootie's B brokerage account, holding only idle cash from operations	15,000
One-time sale of display equipment to B purchaser	45,000
Royalty received from holding patent, licensed to B user	70,000

26. State E applies a throwback rule to sales, while State F does not. State G has not adopted an income tax to date. Orange Corporation, headquartered in E, reported the following sales for the year. All of the goods were shipped from Orange's E manufacturing facilities. Orange's degree of operations is sufficient to establish nexus only in E and F. Determine its sales factor in those states.

Customer	Customer's Location	This Year's Sales
ShellTell, Inc.	E	$ 64,000,000
Tourists, Ltd.	F	40,000,000
PageToo Corp.	G	30,000,000
U.S. Department of Interior	All 50 states	18,000,000
Total		$152,000,000

27. Aqua Corporation is subject to tax in States G, H, and I. Aqua's compensation expense includes the following.

	State G	State H	State I	Total
Salaries and wages for nonofficers	$200,000	$400,000	$100,000	$700,000
Officers' salaries	–0–	–0–	250,000	250,000
Total				$950,000

Officers' salaries are included in the payroll factor for G and I, but not for H. Compute Aqua's payroll factors for G, H, and I.

28. Judy, a regional sales manager, has her office in State U. Her region includes several states, as indicated in the sales report below. Judy is compensated through straight commissions on the sales in her region and a fully excludible cafeteria plan conveying various fringe benefits to her. Determine how much of Judy's $150,000 commissions and $40,000 fringe benefit package is assigned to the payroll factor of State U.

State	Sales Generated	Judy's Time Spent There
U	$3,000,000	20%
V	4,000,000	55%
X	5,000,000	25%

29. Justine Corporation operates manufacturing facilities in State G and State H. In addition, the corporation owns nonbusiness rental property in H. Justine incurred the following compensation expenses.

	State G	State H	Total
Manufacturing wages	$475,000	$200,000	$675,000
Administrative wages	95,000	65,000	160,000
Officers' salaries	180,000	80,000	260,000

Thirty percent of the time spent by the administrative staff located in H and 15% of the time spent by officers located in H are devoted to the operation, maintenance, and supervision of the rental property. G includes all income in the definition of apportionable income, while H excludes nonbusiness income from apportionable income. Only G includes officers' compensation in the payroll factor. Determine Justine's payroll factors for G and H.

30. Kim Corporation, a calendar year taxpayer, has manufacturing facilities in States A and B. A summary of Kim's property holdings follows.

	Beginning of Year		
	State A	State B	Total
Inventory	$ 300,000	$ 200,000	$ 500,000
Plant and equipment	2,500,000	1,500,000	4,000,000
Accumulated depreciation: plant and equipment	(1,200,000)	(500,000)	(1,700,000)
Land	600,000	600,000	1,200,000
Rental property*	900,000	300,000	1,200,000
Accumulated depreciation: rental property	(200,000)	(50,000)	(250,000)

	End of Year		
	State A	State B	Total
Inventory	$ 400,000	$ 150,000	$ 550,000
Plant and equipment	2,500,000	1,200,000	3,700,000
Accumulated depreciation: plant and equipment	(1,500,000)	(450,000)	(1,950,000)
Land	600,000	400,000	1,000,000
Rental property*	950,000	300,000	1,250,000
Accumulated depreciation: rental property	(300,000)	(100,000)	(400,000)

*Unrelated to Kim's regular business operations.

Determine Kim's property factors for the two states, assuming that the statutes of both A and B provide that average historical cost of business property is to be included in the property factor.

31. Assume the facts of Problem 30, except that nonbusiness income is apportionable in B.

Decision Making

32. Crate Corporation, a calendar year taxpayer, has established nexus with numerous states. On December 3, Crate sold one of its two facilities in State X. The cost of this facility was $800,000.

On January 1, Crate owned property with a cost of $3 million, $1.5 million of which was located in X. On December 31, Crate owned property with a cost of $2.2 million, $600,000 of which was located in X.

X law allows the use of average annual or monthly amounts in determining the property factor. If Crate wants to minimize the property factor in X, which method should be used to determine the property factor there?

Decision Making
Communications

33. True Corporation, a wholly owned subsidiary of Trumaine Corporation, generated a $500,000 taxable loss in its first year of operations. True's activities and sales are restricted to State A, which imposes an 8% income tax. Trumaine's income for the taxable period is $1 million. Trumaine's activities and sales are restricted to State B, which imposes an 11% income tax. Both states use a three-factor apportionment formula that equally weights sales, payroll, and property, and both require a unitary group to file on a combined basis. Sales, payroll, and average property for each corporation are as follows.

	True Corporation	Trumaine Corporation	Total
Sales	$2,500,000	$4,000,000	$6,500,000
Property	1,000,000	2,500,000	3,500,000
Payroll	800,000	1,200,000	2,000,000

True and Trumaine have been found to be members of a unitary business.

a. Determine the overall state income tax for the unitary group.
b. Determine aggregate state income tax for the entities if they were nonunitary.
c. Incorporate this analysis in a letter to Trumaine's board of directors. Corporate offices are located at 1234 Mulberry Lane, Chartown, AL 35298.

34. Gerald Corporation is part of a three-corporation unitary business. The group has a water's edge election in effect with respect to unitary State Q. State B does not apply the unitary concept with respect to its corporate income tax laws. Nor does Despina, a European country to which Geraldine paid a $4 million value added tax this year.

Geraldine was organized in Despina and conducts all of its business there. Given the summary of operations that follows, determine Gerald's and Elena's sales factors in B and Q.

Corporation	Customer's Location	Sales
Gerald	B	$10,000,000
	Q	15,000,000
Elena	Q	20,000,000
Geraldine	Despina	25,000,000

Ethics

35. Bud and Rose's Nursery is based in a high-tax state (State A with a tax rate of 8%), but it has significant sales of plants and shrubs in a neighboring state (State B) with a lower tax rate of 4%. Sales in State A total $1 million, while sales in State B total $500,000. Apportionable income for the year is $300,000.

Currently, Bud and Rose's Nursery has not established nexus in B, but the company is contemplating renting a small office in the state to establish nexus and source the sales in the lower-tax jurisdiction. The office would be unstaffed most of the time, but the company would utilize an independent contractor for approximately two hours each week to check phone messages, pick up mail, and send unopened mail back to the corporate offices in A.

Assuming that both A and B use a single sales factor to apportion income and A has a throwback rule, what is the effect of establishing nexus in B on the company's total state tax liability? Is this legitimate tax planning?

Decision Making

36. Battery, Inc., is a manufacturer of batteries used in lawn mowers and small tractors. Battery is incorporated in State A, which uses an equally weighted three-factor apportionment formula. All of the company's manufacturing facilities and administrative offices are located in A. The company warehouses inventory in six states across the country (A, D, I, N, S, and W). State A distinguishes between business and nonbusiness income, has a throwback rule, excludes compensation paid to executive officers from the payroll factor, and follows UDITPA rules with respect to other issues.

Last year's corporate tax return for A was prepared by another CPA, and you have been asked to review it. The return reported allocable income of $500,000 and apportionable income of $6 million (before apportionment). The following values were used by the CPA to determine A's apportionment factor. Property values are based on the original cost of the property and do not include leased assets.

Sales in A	$40,000,000
Sales everywhere	60,000,000
Payroll in A	8,000,000
Payroll everywhere	10,000,000
Property in A (beginning of year)	10,000,000
Property everywhere (beginning of year)	12,000,000
Property in A (end of year)	13,000,000
Property everywhere (end of year)	16,000,000

Your review of Battery's records reveals the following.

a. Allocable income includes $400,000 of interest income; $200,000 of the interest is related to Battery's business operations, and $200,000 is unrelated to the company's business operations (derived from a long-term investment portfolio). None of the interest income has been included in Battery's sales factor.
b. Battery shipped $300,000 of inventory from A to a warehouse in B two days before the end of the year. The inventory was in transit at the end of the year and was included as A property at the end of the year.
c. Battery leases a warehouse in A for $6,000 per month ($72,000 per year).
d. Laura, a sales representative in State Q (in which Battery has not established nexus), earns a $40,000 annual salary. Her salary was excluded from the numerator of the payroll factor for A.
e. The payroll factor (numerator and denominator) for A includes $400,000 of executive compensation.
f. The numerator of the sales factor for A excludes $600,000 of sales made to customers in States B and C, with which Battery does not have nexus.
g. The numerator of the sales factor for A excludes a $800,000 sale to a customer in State G, where Battery is subject to income tax. The customer sent its own truck to A to pick up the items.
h. The A sales factor (both the numerator and denominator) excludes $700,000 in sales to the U.S. government.
i. Battery has two employees who live and work in a foreign country. Their primary job is to solicit orders for foreign sales. Orders are sent back to A for approval and shipment. Battery is exempt from tax in the country. Sales to the country totaled $1.2 million and were included in both the numerator and denominator of the A sales factor.

Using the template provided on the text's Web site (**http://wft-advanced.swlearning.com**), construct the sales, property, and payroll factors for Battery, Inc. Then compute the apportionable and allocable income for State A and the income subject to tax in A.

Communications

37. Hernandez, which has been an S corporation since inception, is subject to tax in States Y and Z. On Schedule K of its Federal Form 1120S, Hernandez reported ordinary income of $500,000 from its business, taxable interest income of $10,000, capital loss of $30,000, and $40,000 of dividend income from a corporation in which it owns 30%.

Both states apportion income by use of a three-factor formula that equally weights sales, payroll, and the average cost of property; both states treat interest and dividends as business income. In addition, both Y and Z follow Federal provisions with respect to the determination of taxable income for a corporation. Y recognizes S status, but Z does not. Based on the following information, write a memo to the shareholders of Hernandez, detailing the amount of taxable income on which Hernandez will pay tax in Y and Z. Hernandez corporate offices are located at 5678 Alabaster Circle, Koopville, KY 47697.

	State Y	State Z
Sales	$1,000,000	$800,000
Property (average cost)	500,000	200,000
Payroll	800,000	300,000

38. Wayne Corporation is subject to State A's franchise tax. The tax is imposed at a rate of 3% of the corporation's net worth that is apportioned to the state by use of a two-factor (sales and property equally weighted) formula. The property factor includes real and tangible personal property, valued at historical cost as of the end of the taxable year.

Forty percent of Wayne's sales are attributable to A, and $300,000 of the cost of Wayne's tangible personal property is located in A.

Determine the A franchise tax payable by Wayne this year, given the following end-of-the-year balance sheet.

Cash		$ 500,000
Equipment	$1,000,000	
Accumulated depreciation	(300,000)	700,000
Furniture and fixtures	$ 200,000	
Accumulated depreciation	(50,000)	150,000
Intangible assets		350,000
Total assets		$1,700,000
Accounts and taxes payable		$ 600,000
Long-term debt		350,000
Common stock		1,000
Additional paid-in capital		249,000
Retained earnings		500,000
Total liabilities and equity		$1,700,000

Decision Making

39. Dread Corporation operates in a high-tax state. The firm asks you for advice on a plan to outsource overhead work done in its home state to independent contractors. This work now costs the company $350,000 in wages and benefits. Dread's total payroll for the year is $2 million, of which $1.5 million is for work currently done in the home state.

BRIDGE DISCIPLINE

Issue ID

1. If you were a state legislator, would you push for your state to adopt a double-weighted sales or sales-factor-only apportionment formula? Why?

Ethics

2. A number of high-profile companies including Enron have come under fire for entering into questionable transactions that artificially inflated their financial statement earnings. These same companies have been criticized for entering into questionable tax shelter transactions designed to provide Federal tax benefits with minimal or no corresponding economic benefits. In light of the controversy surrounding tax shelter transactions, should companies be concerned about planning their transactions and business operations to reduce the income tax they pay to state governments?

Research Problems

Internet Activity

Use the tax resources of the Internet to address the following questions. Do not restrict your search to the World Wide Web, but include a review of newsgroups and general reference materials, practitioner sites and resources, primary sources of the tax law, chat rooms and discussion groups, and other opportunities.

Communications

Research Problem 1. Send an e-mail message to the secretary of revenue for your home state, proposing adoption of one of the following provisions that does not currently exist in your state. Justify your proposal with a numerical example.

a. Increase the apportionment weight for the sales factor.
b. Exempt computer and communications technology from the apportionment weight for the property factor.
c. Adopt a throwback rule for the sales factor.
d. Tax the income of an investment subsidiary set up by a domestic taxpayer.
e. Add a "nexus team" to find the taxpayers operating in your state, but based in Ohio, Illinois, or Arizona.

Communications

Research Problem 2. For your state and one of its neighbors, determine the following. Place your data in a chart and e-mail your findings to your instructor.

a. To what extent does each state follow the rulings of the Multistate Tax Commission?
b. What is each state's apportionment formula, with factors and weightings?

Research Problem 3. Does your state require or allow unitary reporting? If so, does it allow a water's edge election?

Ethics

Communications

Research Problem 4. Tax amnesties are sometimes criticized as being unfair to taxpayers that have paid their taxes on time or paid past-due taxes and related interest and penalties during a period when a tax amnesty was not available. Find several news articles and announcements of state tax amnesty programs. Has your state ever offered a tax amnesty? What types of taxes were eligible for the amnesty? What are some of the pros and cons of amnesties? Are they fair? Summarize your thoughts in an e-mail to your instructor.

CHAPTER 10

Sales/Use and Property Taxes

LEARNING OBJECTIVES

After completing Chapter 10, you should be able to:

LO.1

Recognize the importance of sales taxes in the United States and describe the different types of sales taxes that currently exist.

LO.2

Explain the basic framework of the retail sales tax.

LO.3

Identify the constitutional limitations on the power of state and local governments to impose sales and use taxes.

LO.4

Understand how to compute the retail sales tax base.

LO.5

Determine the key administrative issues for taxpayers in complying with sales and use tax obligations.

LO.6

Recognize the importance of property taxes in the United States.

LO.7

Distinguish between real property and personal property.

LO.8

Identify the constitutional and Federal issues involved with property taxes.

http://wft.swlearning.com

OUTLINE

TAX TALK

There is nothing in the Constitution which requires a state to adopt the best possible system of taxation.

—*Harlan F. Stone*

LO.1

Recognize the importance of sales taxes in the United States and describe the different types of sales taxes that currently exist.

Sales Taxation

Sales taxes first came into being in the United States around the Great Depression to overcome the shortfall in revenues from income and property taxes. In 1932, Mississippi became the first state to enact a tax having most of the features of sales taxes as we know them today. Many states quickly followed Mississippi's lead and enacted sales taxes of their own. Today, 45 states and the District of Columbia have a tax that can be classified as a sales tax. The five states currently without a general retail sales tax at the state level are Alaska, Delaware, Montana, New Hampshire, and Oregon.

Although sales taxes typically are levied at the state level, many municipalities and other local subdivisions also impose sales taxes, and these taxes are being used increasingly to supplement revenues from property taxes, the traditional source of revenues for local governments. An interesting example is Alaska, which does not have a state-level sales tax but has an extensive system of sales taxes at the local level. Many cities, such as Atlanta, Chicago, Los Angeles, New York, and Phoenix, also impose sales taxes of their own, which are added on top of the state-level sales tax. From an administrative standpoint, local sales taxes usually are integrated with the state sales tax so that collection is consolidated at one point. The state then distributes the local government's share of the tax for a fee.

TYPES OF SALES TAXES

The three major types of sales taxes that currently are employed by the various states are the retail consumer tax, the seller privilege tax, and the gross receipts tax. The most prevalent of these taxes is the retail sales tax.

TAX IN THE NEWS

How Much Is That Monet?

In addition to being charged with looting Tyco International, Inc., of $600 million, former CEO Dennis Kozlowski has been charged by the state of New York with evading over $1 million of sales tax on purchases of artwork including paintings by Monet and Renoir. As reported in the *Wall Street Journal*, the scheme involved shipping empty boxes to Tyco's offices in New Hampshire (which does not have a sales tax) while actually delivering the art to Mr. Kozlowski's Manhattan apartment.

Retail Sales Tax. The most common form of sales tax, as well as the most significant in revenue terms, is the retail sales tax. This tax typically is imposed on the sale of tangible personal property at retail to the final consumer. However, the term "sales tax" refers to a broad category of levies that have different names and cover different types of transactions. In some states, each of these levies is indeed a different tax, but collectively they are referred to as sales taxes. Retail sales tax rates assessed by states generally range from about 4 percent to 7 percent. When combined with local sales taxes, the maximum combined sales tax exceeds 9 percent in a half dozen states.

Seller Privilege Tax. The seller privilege tax is imposed on a seller for the privilege of doing business in the state. The seller may or may not be able to shift the tax to the consumer, depending on state law.

Alabama, Arizona, Hawaii, Kentucky, Missouri, Nevada, and others impose a seller privilege tax. However, these states use different labels for the tax and also impose it in different ways. For example, Arizona's tax is labeled the "transaction privilege tax" and is imposed on the person engaged in the taxable business activity. In Arizona, the seller can choose to pass on the tax to the end consumer; hence, the amount of the sales tax can be used as a point of negotiation on the selling price. Further, it is optional for the seller to state the amount of the tax separately on the invoice.

In contrast, Alabama requires that its seller privilege tax be shifted to the consumer and separately stated on the invoice. Thus, the Alabama tax in reality is a retail sales tax on the consumer that the seller is required to collect, even though it is labeled a seller privilege tax. Finally, Nevada, like Alabama, requires the seller to shift the tax to the consumer but only "insofar as it can be done." Thus, the burden of the tax is not really on the consumer, and the seller is not relieved of the liability to pay the tax.

Gross Receipts Tax. A gross receipts tax has the essential elements of both the retail sales tax and the seller privilege tax. Like a retail sales tax, a gross receipts tax typically is levied on the sale of property. However, the tax base in a gross receipts tax is broader than in a retail sales tax. It usually includes sales of professional services and in some instances the sale of intangibles as well. Like a seller privilege tax, the gross receipts tax is imposed on the seller with no requirement for shifting the tax to the consumer. Hawaii and New Mexico among others employ a gross receipts tax. A gross receipts tax may be assessed regardless of whether an asset is sold at a gain or a loss.

TAX FACT

Collecting the Use Tax

Collecting the use tax can be a difficult task. However, 18 states and the District of Columbia now require taxpayers to report out-of-state purchases on their individual income tax forms. Increases in collections can be dramatic. In the first year North Carolina added a line on the individual income tax form, collections increased to almost $5 million compared to $125,000 in the previous year. In addition, some states are using U.S. Customs data to make sure taxpayers pay use tax on purchases made outside the country.

EXAMPLE 1

If a business purchases an asset for $500,000 and then later sells the asset for $400,000, the business will generally have a $100,000 deductible loss for Federal and state income tax purposes. However, if the business is in a state with a 5% gross receipts tax, the transaction may result in a $20,000 tax liability ($400,000 × .05). ■

The Use Tax. Every state that has a sales tax also imposes a use tax on the "storage, use or consumption" of tangible personal property in the state. Use taxes are intended to complement sales taxes by protecting in-state merchants from discrimination (and protecting the state itself from a loss of tax revenue) arising from the inability of the state to impose the sales tax on out-of-state purchases by in-state businesses and individuals. The use tax is imposed only in cases in which a state's sales tax is not collected. When an out-of-state purchase is subject to sales tax in the other state, consumers generally receive a credit for the out-of-state sales tax against their in-state use tax. Though out-of-state retailers may be responsible for collecting the tax when they have nexus with the state, this responsibility shifts to the consumer in many cases.

EXAMPLE 2

While vacationing in Montana (a state with no sales tax), Jim and Marcia (residents of Georgia, which has a sales tax of 4%) purchase matching diamond rings for their anniversary for $10,000. Though the Montana merchant does not charge sales tax to Jim and Marcia, on their return to Georgia they will be liable for payment of a $400 use tax ($10,000 × .04). Had Jim and Marcia purchased the rings in Colorado (with a 2.9% sales tax), the use tax owed would be $110 ($10,000 × 1.1%). On the other hand, had they purchased the rings in Idaho (with a sales tax of 5%), they would owe no use tax to Georgia, but could not claim a refund. ■

IMPORTANCE OF SALES TAXES

In the last full year reported by the U.S. Census Bureau, general sales and gross receipts taxes collected from all 50 states amounted to over $178.9 billion, 34 percent of the states' total tax collections. Only the individual income tax with total tax collected of $185 billion was more important as a source of revenue to the states.[1] Considering that sales taxes became popular only in the 1930s, their share of the total state revenues underscores the tremendous importance of this tax for state governments.

In addition to its importance at the state level, the sales tax is also becoming increasingly important at the local level. Although property taxes continue to be the largest source of tax revenue for local governments, the growing importance of local sales taxes can be gauged from the fact that currently there are over 7,500 local sales tax jurisdictions in the United States.

[1]**http://www.census.gov/govs/www/index.html**.

TAX FACT

2002 Sources of State Government Tax Collections

Transaction taxes now provide more revenue to state governments than do income taxes.

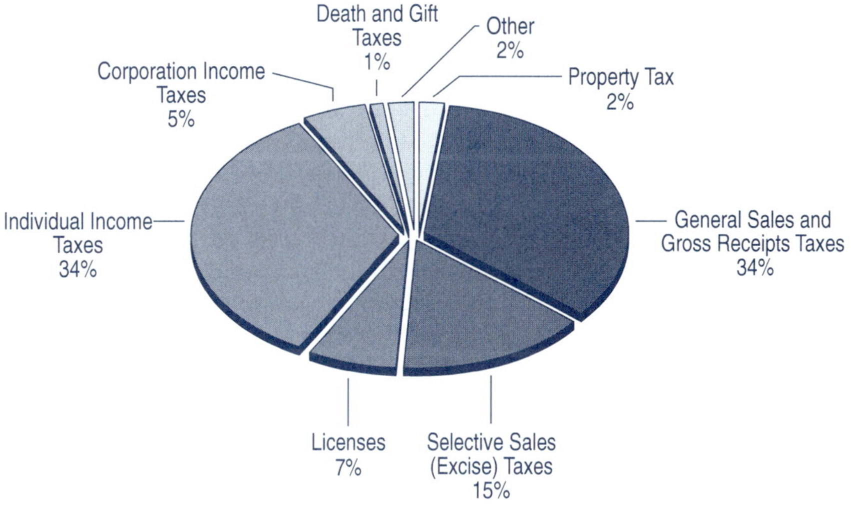

TAX FACT

2002 Local Government Tax Collections

The property tax remains the chief source of revenue for local governments.

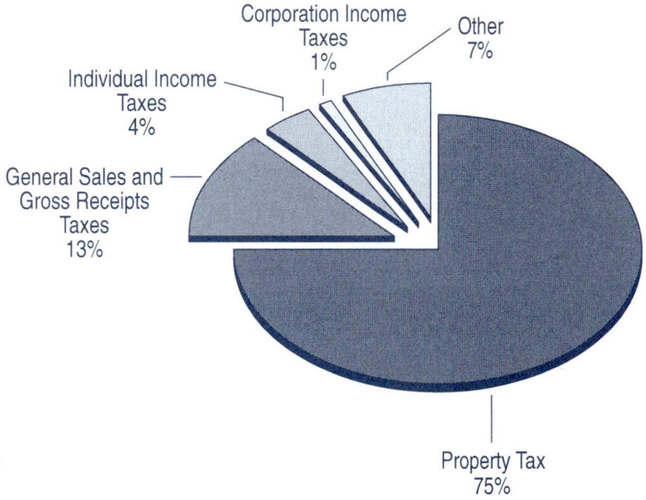

LO.2

Explain the basic framework of the retail sales tax.

The Retail Sales Tax

The general retail sales tax is the most common form of sales taxation in the country. As mentioned, this tax is imposed on the sale of tangible personal property at retail to the consumer. Certain criteria must be satisfied for this tax to apply. Specifically,

- The sale must take place within the territorial boundaries of the taxing jurisdiction; that is, the state or local jurisdiction must have power to impose the tax.
- The sale must be of tangible personal property, not services or intangible property, and the sale must be at retail.

The first criterion relates to constitutional limitations on the power of the state or local jurisdiction to impose the tax. At a very basic level, this criterion lays out the first condition that must be satisfied before the tax can be imposed—that the sale must have been consummated within the boundaries of the state or the locality seeking to impose the tax. However, a long debate of considerable importance in which the U.S. Supreme Court has weighed in on numerous occasions has addressed whether the tax can be imposed at all.

LO.3

Identify the constitutional limitations on the power of state and local governments to impose sales and use taxes.

CONSTITUTIONAL ISSUES IN IMPOSING SALES AND USE TAXES

Although sales taxes in the United States are a state- or local-level levy, the U.S. Constitution plays an overarching role in limiting the power of states to impose this tax. The specific provisions in the U.S. Constitution that do so are the Commerce Clause and the Due Process Clause. Article 1, Section 8, Clause 3 (the Commerce Clause) states that "the Congress shall have power . . . To regulate commerce with foreign nations, and among the several states." Section 1 of the Fourteenth Amendment (the Due Process Clause) states that "No state shall make or enforce any law which shall . . . deprive any person of life, liberty, or property, without due process of law." These provisions serve as a watchdog to guard against the possibility of taxpayers being subject to multiple taxation in interstate sales transactions.

The courts have interpreted these provisions as requiring a business to have some minimum connection with the state before a state has the right to tax the business. In addition, for a state tax to be constitutional, it must not discriminate against interstate commerce.

With respect to a state's sales and use tax statutes, when the entire transaction takes place within a state's borders, such as when both the buyer and the seller are located in the state and the property changes hands within the state, there is no question that the first condition is satisfied. However, the issue is not so straightforward when the transaction involves more than one state, i.e., an interstate sale. In such transactions, the question is which state has jurisdiction to impose its sales tax on the transaction. The answer depends on one word—nexus.

Nexus literally means attachment or connection. Depending on the extent of the taxpayer's presence in or proximity to the taxing jurisdiction, the taxpayer may be considered to have sufficient nexus with the jurisdiction for the purposes of its sales and use tax.

The U.S. Supreme Court's fundamental analytical framework for evaluating the constitutionality of state sales and use taxation of interstate retail sales transactions was set out in three companion cases—*McLeod v. J.E. Dilworth Co., General Trading Co. v. State Tax Commission,* and *International Harvestor Co. v. Department of Treasury.*[2]

[2]322 U.S. 327, 64 S.Ct. 1023 (1944); 322 U.S. 335, 64 S.Ct. 1028 (1944); 322 U.S. 340, 64 S.Ct. 1019 (1944), respectively.

BRIDGE DISCIPLINE

Bridge to Economics

A state tax is exportable if the burden of the tax can be shifted to residents of other states. For example, a sales tax on lodging, rental cars, and other taxes aimed at tourists and visitors often meets this criterion.

Exportability of state taxes can also be accomplished if the Federal government allows a taxpayer to deduct state and local taxes in determining Federal taxable income. By allowing state income taxes to be deducted in computing Federal income taxes, the Federal government picks up part of the cost of the state tax. For example, if a resident of a state with a 7 percent state income tax earns $100,000 of taxable income for state income tax purposes, the $7,000 of state income tax is deductible in determining Federal taxable income, reducing Federal taxable income to $93,000. If the Federal tax rate is 30 percent, the state income tax deduction saves the taxpayer $2,100 in Federal income tax ($7,000 × 30%). The out-of-pocket after-tax cost of the state income tax is $4,900 rather than $7,000.

Since 1986, the Federal government generally has not allowed individuals to deduct state and local sales taxes in determining Federal taxable income. Thus, the out-of-pocket cost of an additional dollar of state income tax is less than the out-of-pocket cost of an additional dollar of state sales tax.

In *Dilworth*, the Court considered whether Arkansas could impose its sales tax on a Tennessee corporation's sales made in Arkansas. The corporation, which had its home office and principal place of business in Memphis, solicited orders in Arkansas by mail, telephone, or by regularly sending solicitors, but accepted the orders in Tennessee and delivered the goods to a common carrier there for shipment to the purchaser in Arkansas. The Court held the Arkansas tax to be invalid because the sale was made in Tennessee. "For Arkansas to impose a tax on such transaction would be to project its powers beyond its boundaries and to tax an interstate transaction."

The *Dilworth* decision reflected the Court's early interpretation of the Commerce Clause that states could not impose a tax on interstate sales because such a tax would amount to a tax on, and thus a regulation of, interstate commerce, which only Congress was authorized to do. However, the Court stated that while the Arkansas sales tax was invalid, the state's use tax might be sustained in the same situation. The reasoning for this conclusion is that the Commerce Clause and Due Process Clause do not forbid the imposition of a use tax on property involved in an interstate sale—the tax is imposed on the use of the property, which certainly takes place within its territorial boundaries. The only question is whether the state can require the out-of-state seller to act as a vendor charged with the obligation of collecting the use tax from its in-state consumers. This has not been an easy question for the Court to answer as the following cases demonstrate.

In *Miller Brothers v. Maryland*,[3] the question was whether a Delaware department store that sold merchandise to customers residing in Maryland was liable to collect Maryland's use tax on the sales to its residents. The store delivered goods to some of the customers at its store, whereas other customers were sent goods either by common carrier or by the store's own trucks. The Court held that Maryland could not have imposed its sales tax on these sales since they were made in Delaware. Based on that reasoning, the Court's conclusion on the question of use tax collection obligation was that "[i]t would be strange law that would make appellant more vulnerable to liability for another's tax than to a tax on itself."

[3]347 U.S. 340, 74 S.Ct. 535 (1954).

In *Scripto v. Carson,*[4] the Court addressed the question of whether the presence of independent contractors in the state was a valid basis for imposing a use tax collection obligation on an out-of-state vendor. In this case, a Georgia corporation, which had no office or regular employees in Florida, employed wholesalers to solicit sales on its behalf in Florida. The Court held that, even though the wholesalers were independent contractors and not employees of the seller, these representatives gave the seller enough presence in the state to require it to collect use taxes.

In *National Bellas Hess v. Department of Revenue,*[5] the issue before the Court was whether Illinois could impose a use tax collection obligation on an out-of-state mail-order seller that had no physical presence in the state and communicated with its customers through the mail or common carrier. The Court held that the Commerce Clause and Due Process Clause precluded Illinois from making such an imposition. This decision is widely regarded as one of the Court's most important decisions on the issue of nexus in the context of taxing interstate transactions.

In *Complete Auto Transit, Inc. v. Brady,*[6] the Court set out a four-part test to determine if a state tax is valid under the Commerce Clause: the activities taxed must have a substantial nexus with the taxing state, the tax must be fairly apportioned, the tax must not discriminate against interstate commerce, and the tax must be related fairly to the services provided by the state.

In *National Geographic Society v. State Board of Equalization,*[7] the Court again dealt with an out-of-state mail-order business that had an in-state presence, although it was unrelated to the mail-order business. The taxpayer, a District of Columbia corporation, was making mail-order sales of maps, atlases, and books to customers in California. Although the corporation maintained two offices in California strictly for the purpose of soliciting advertising for its magazine, it conducted none of its mail-order business from those offices. The Court held that the taxpayer's offices and activities in California adequately established a relationship or nexus that made it valid for California to impose a use tax obligation.

In *Quill Corp. v. North Dakota,*[8] the Supreme Court reaffirmed its *Bellas Hess* decision that an out-of-state mail-order business with no physical presence in the state could not be required to collect that state's use taxes. In *Quill*, the Court categorically stated that a reason for not overturning its *Bella Hess* decision was the tremendous growth in the mail-order industry "from a relatively inconsequential market niche" to a "goliath"—a growth that was in part due to the substantial reliance placed by the industry in the *Bellas Hess* decision. However, the Court was careful to limit its holding to mail-order sales. The Court also reminded Congress that this was an area where it alone had the power under the Commerce Clause to enact legislation that could regulate such transactions.

Although legislation has been introduced in Congress that would authorize states to collect use taxes on mail-order sales, Congress has not enacted any broad-based legislation in this area. Nevertheless, many states have tried to establish their own rules under which mail-order sales are taxable.

For example, in Arizona, a mail-order business is liable for use tax if solicitations are substantial and recurring and if the retailer benefits from banking, financing, debt collection, communication systems, or marketing activities in Arizona or has authorized installation, servicing, or repair facilities in Arizona. In Indiana, liability attaches if an out-of-state retailer regularly solicits sales in Indiana. This occurs if the retailer makes at least 100 retail transactions from outside Indiana during any 12-month period or makes at least 10 retail transactions totaling more than $100,000 from outside Indiana to destinations in Indiana during a 12-month period.

---

[4]362 U.S. 207, 80 S.Ct. 619 (1960).
[5]386 U.S. 753, 87 S.Ct. 1389 (1967).
[6]430 U.S. 274 (1977).
[7]430 U.S. 551, 97 S.Ct. 1386 (1977).
[8]504 U.S. 298, 112 S.Ct. 1904 (1992).

TAX FACT

E-Commerce Cuts States' Revenues

According to a recent estimate, state sales tax revenue lost as a result of new sales made via the Internet amounted to $7 billion in 2001 and will grow to $29.2 billion by 2011. The study estimates that by 2011, states will lose anywhere from 2.6 percent to 9.2 percent of their total state tax collections as a result of e-commerce, and that sales tax rates would need to increase by between .83 and 1.72 percentage points to replace the e-commerce losses.

SALES AND USE TAX AND THE INTERNET

As the above discussion demonstrates, recent nexus cases have revolved around mail-order businesses. The nexus issue is also problematic for companies that sell goods and services via the Internet. Traditional requirements of "substantial physical presence" simply have little meaning when transactions are taking place in cyberspace.

In 1998, Congress prohibited jurisdictions from imposing new taxes on Internet service providers (ISPs), e.g., a tax of one-half cent per e-mail message received. Prior to that time, however, the income or franchise tax and sales and use taxes of each state were generally enforced on all taxpayers. Accordingly, ISPs continue to be subject to these taxes in all states that impose them.

The moratorium on new taxes also prevents state taxing authorities from asserting that a physical presence arises from certain Internet-related contacts with the state. Instead, ISPs are treated as common carriers whose contacts and agency are not considered physical contacts for nexus purposes. Another provision relates to the effect of access to a Web site on a remote vendor's liability to collect sales tax.

The moratorium on Internet access taxes expired on November 1, 2003, amid disputes in the Senate over making the moratorium permanent, defining Internet access, and expanding the moratorium to include other forms of telecommunication taxes. The Multistate Tax Commission (MTC) estimated that a permanent moratorium using a broad definition of Internet access itself would cost the states up to $9 billion annually.

EXAMPLE 3

U.S. WebCo is a California vendor of apparel. Clothing is sold from a California-based Web server owned by the company. The Web site is accessible (and orders may be placed) from all 50 states. However, the fact that the Web site may be accessed in a state cannot be used to determine if the company has nexus in any state outside California. ■

A similar rule applies when a Web site is housed on an ISP's Web server. Importantly, the provision specifically relates to a remote seller's out-of-state computer server. Nexus may exist, though, when a Web site is hosted on a server located in a state. For example, if a California company uses a Michigan ISP to host its Web site, Michigan may claim the California company has nexus for sales and use tax in Michigan.

WHAT IS "TANGIBLE PERSONAL PROPERTY"?

As noted earlier, for a sales/use tax to be applied, not only must the taxing jurisdiction have the authority to impose the tax, but the sale must meet a second criterion, which involves two fundamental questions.

- What is "tangible personal property"?
- What is a "retail sale"?

This section addresses the first question, and the next section addresses the second.

TAX IN THE NEWS

The Pros and Cons of Taxing Services

The growth of the service sector along with the serious budget shortfalls experienced by many states in the last few years has caused several states to consider expanding the sales tax base to include more services. Some argue that it is simply not fair to tax a lawn mower purchased by a homeowner who mows her own lawn while not taxing her neighbor who has a lawn service mow his lawn.

Assessing sales tax on everyday services such as photo finishing, car repairs, landscaping, house painting, and the like could increase state sales tax collections by 20 to 30 percent. Taxing a wide range of services including professional services could increase the tax base by over 100 percent.

However, taxing services is not without its problems. Very few states currently tax services. Taxing services may put service-oriented companies at a competitive disadvantage compared to similar companies located in neighboring states that do not tax services. For example, if Illinois taxes sales of accounting services and Indiana does not, Illinois residents may go across the border and hire Indiana CPAs to prepare their tax returns. Another problem is that many services such as medical care would likely require exemptions. A third problem is that many professional services such as accounting, legal, and advertising are consumed primarily by businesses. To avoid double taxation, generally only the final "retail" sale of a product or service should be taxed.

One common definition of **tangible property** describes such an asset as one that has physical form and substance and is not intangible; it may be either real or personal. Following this definition, most state tax codes define "tangible personal property" as personal property that can be seen, weighed, measured, felt or touched, or is in any other manner perceptible to the senses.

Sale of Services. Traditionally, retail sales taxes have been imposed on the sale of tangible personal property; hence, services typically have been exempt from the tax base. However, the steady growth of the service sector in the U.S. economy has prompted more and more states to add selected services to their tax bases, resulting in most states taxing at least some services. Among the services most frequently exempt from sales tax are professional services (e.g., those provided by accountants, attorneys, dentists and physicians) and personal services (e.g., hairdressing, house cleaning, lawn and landscaping, laundry, and dry-cleaning). Services that are most frequently taxed include repair and maintenance type services. Some states, such as Hawaii, New Mexico, and South Dakota, have taken this trend to the other extreme by taxing most or all services.

In some cases, distinguishing the sale of tangible personal property from the sale of services is not easy because many sales involve a mixture of both property and services.

EXAMPLE 4

A shoe-shiner provides the service of shining shoes, but in doing so uses shoe polish, cream, and other ingredients. Similarly, a hairdresser might use shampoo and conditioner in washing hair prior to performing whatever service the client might want, such as a haircut or a perm. ■

PLANNING STRATEGIES

May As Well Collect That Tax

FRAMEWORK FOCUS: TAX RATE

STRATEGY ➤ AVOID DOUBLE TAXATION.

Businesses engaged in a mixed activity, which may involve both taxable sales and nontaxable services, inevitably face some vexing decisions in the matter of sales taxes. If there is any doubt as to the sales tax liability in a given transaction, the business should collect the tax. If subsequently found liable, the business must not only bear the sales tax burden itself but also the interest and any penalties. That is, the business usually cannot go back to the buyer and collect sales taxes after the sale.

DIGGING DEEPER 1 *Find more information on this topic at our Web site:* ***http://wft-advanced.swlearning.com.***

Sale of Intangible Property. Given that retail sales taxes are imposed on tangible personal property, a key distinction that must be made is whether the property is tangible or intangible. If the property is intangible, then sales taxes generally would not be imposed on its sale. However, a comprehensive definition of this term does not appear to exist. Thus, it is not surprising that state statutes seldom define the term "intangible property," except in a negative sense as a complement to tangible property—intangible property is property other than tangible property.

Generally, **intangible property** is property that is a "right" rather than a physical object. Thus, for purposes of the tax laws, intangible property may be defined to include property that is not itself intrinsically valuable, but that derives its value from what it represents or evidences.

BRIDGE DISCIPLINE

Bridge to Economics

Sales/use taxes almost always are "flat" in that they use just one rate. But some economists criticize these taxes because they seem to be regressive in nature—that is, the average tax rate decreases as the tax base increases when total income is used as the base.

For example, assume a taxpayer earns $25,000 per year and spends all of it on items subject to a 6 percent sales tax. The taxpayer pays $1,500 in sales tax. A second taxpayer earns $30,000 per year and saves $5,000. The second taxpayer also pays $1,500 of sales tax (6 percent of the $25,000 of taxable purchases). However, the average tax rate based on wages of the second taxpayer is only 5 percent ($1,500/$30,000) compared to an average tax rate of 6 percent for the first taxpayer ($1,500/$25,000). A third taxpayer earns $100,000 per year and saves $75,000. This taxpayer also pays $1,500 of sales tax for an average tax rate of 1.5 percent. Even if the third taxpayer spends $70,000 on purchases of products and services subject to the sales tax, the average tax rate of 4.2 percent ($4,200 sales tax/$100,000 wages) is less than that of the other taxpayers.

One of the arguments for extending the sales tax to include services is that doing so would make the tax less regressive as to income (because wealthy taxpayers consume more services than less wealthy taxpayers). However, though certain types of services (estate planning) are more likely to be consumed by wealthy individuals, other types of services (automobile and appliance repairs, for example) are likely to be consumed more heavily by less wealthy individuals.

In the current business environment, the lines between tangible and intangible personal property are becoming increasingly blurred. One type of transaction that has created much consternation with regard to its taxability is the sale of computer software.

DIGGING DEEPER 2 *Find more information on this topic at our Web site:* ***http://wft-advanced.swlearning.com.***

Because of the considerable controversy surrounding the taxability of sales of computer software, states have passed specific legislation or administrative regulations to address this issue. The trend among the states has been to tax "canned" or pre-written software and exempt "custom-made" software. All states with a sales tax impose a tax on canned software, while only about one-half of those states tax modified canned software and approximately one-third tax custom software.

WHAT IS A "RETAIL SALE"?

A **sale** generally is defined as a contract or agreement by which property is transferred from the seller to the buyer for a fixed price in money, paid or agreed to be paid by the buyer. As such, legally a sale involves both an ownership transfer and consideration. Recognizing that these dual requirements would limit the scope of a sales tax, most state legislatures define the term "sale" more broadly.

Thus, depending on the specific state statute, many transactions that normally would not be considered sales may be subject to sales taxes. For example, most state sales tax statutes consider "leases" of tangible personal property to be a sale of such property and therefore subject to the sales tax.

States often give retailers the option of paying the sales tax when they first purchase the property (basically treating the property as if they were the final consumer) instead of collecting and paying the tax when they lease or rent it to customers.

Scope of a "Retail Sale." A **retail sale** usually is one made to the final consumer. Based on this principle, a retail sales tax should be structured such that it is imposed only once during the entire chain of events starting from the point when the goods are manufactured and culminating with their eventual sale to the retail customer.

EXEMPTIONS FROM THE RETAIL SALES TAX

To make their sales tax laws faithful to the basic principles of a retail sales tax, states' statutes typically provide an exemption for the following types of transactions.

- Sales for resale.
- Casual or occasional sales.
- Sales of items used in manufacturing, processing, or fabricating.
- Sales of machinery or equipment.
- Sales of certain essential items, such as food, medical devices, and prescription drugs.
- Sales to certain organizations or entities, such as governmental agencies.

Sales for Resale. Given the objective of the retail sales tax, a sale of tangible personal property that will be resold should not be included in the retail sales tax base. Indeed, this "sale-for-resale" exemption is the most common kind of exemption provided by state sales tax statutes. In fact, Hawaii is the only state that taxes sales for resale (with the exception of imports).

Under this exemption, property that will be resold, as well as property that is incorporated into another product to be resold (e.g., raw materials), is exempt. If an exemption were not allowed for these transactions, tax would be assessed with each sale, resulting in a pyramiding of the retail sales tax faced by the ultimate consumer.

Typical examples of transactions that would qualify for the sale-for-resale exemption are:

- Lumber purchased by a furniture manufacturer to make furniture.
- Feed, seed, and fertilizer sold for use in commercial agriculture.
- Food, drinks, or condiments purchased by a restaurant business.

DIGGING DEEPER 3

Find more information on this topic at our Web site: ***http://wft-advanced.swlearning.com.***

Resale Exemption Certificate. Proper documentation is required to get the sale-for-resale exemption. In most states, the buyer must provide a certificate of resale or an exemption certificate to the seller for tax not to be collected.

EXAMPLE 5

Robyn's Retail Furniture Store (located in State A) purchases $300,000 of furniture from a manufacturer located in A. The store then resells the furniture for $500,000 to consumers in States A, B, and C. Robyn's also purchases office supplies of $1,000 during the year.

While Robyn must pay sales tax on the $1,000 of office supplies as the end user of the merchandise, the company generally is not required to pay sales tax on its purchases of furniture held for resale (assuming the company has a valid resale exemption certificate). However, the company must collect and remit sales tax on the retail sales made to consumers living in A, and it may be required to collect and remit sales tax on sales made to consumers living in B and C, depending on whether the company has established nexus in those states. ■

Casual or Occasional Sales. Most states provide an exemption for occasional or casual sales that otherwise would be classified under state statutes as taxable sales. This exemption is provided primarily for administrative convenience, and to eliminate the overwhelming task of enforcing the sales tax statutes for persons who are not engaged in making taxable sales on a regular basis.

Transactions that typically are exempt under this provision include garage, yard, and tag sales, the sale of a used automobile, and the sale of a business.

The problem, of course, is in defining what constitutes a "casual" or occasional sale. Does it mean only a single sale or does it cover more than one sale? Does it matter whether the seller is engaged in the business of selling? Most states have tried to resolve this problem by setting a threshold (typically of three or more sales in a single 12-month period), which if exceeded would require compliance with the state sales tax statutes.

Business Asset Transfers. Often the state statutes concerning the casual or occasional sales exemption are written such that sales or transfers of business assets qualify under the exemption. Given the frequency with which mergers, acquisitions, and reorganizations take place, this exemption can provide practitioners with a useful planning tool. However, states usually impose strict conditions under which this exemption is available. For example, it is common for states to require that:

- The entire operating assets of the business be sold.
- The sale be made in a single transaction.
- The sale be made to a single purchaser.

Thus, even in transactions involving the sale of all of the operating assets of a business, an exemption from sales tax may not be available if the sale is structured through several transactions or if several purchasers are involved.

PLANNING STRATEGIES

Don't Acquire a Tax Liability as Well as a Business

FRAMEWORK FOCUS: TAX RATE

STRATEGY ➤ AVOID DOUBLE TAXATION.

When purchasing a business, the acquirer usually is engulfed with many important issues, such as what is the business worth, how to finance the purchase, which employees to retain, etc. One issue that does not receive such high priority is whether the seller has any unpaid sales taxes.

In most jurisdictions, the purchaser of the business steps into the shoes of the seller or succeeds the seller with regard to any unpaid sales taxes. The acquirer can protect itself by requiring the seller to obtain "good standing letters" from the appropriate departments of revenue and local governments. These letters certify that no sales or use taxes are due from the seller in those jurisdictions.

If the acquirer armed with these letters is subsequently audited and deficiencies are assessed, the department would be required to collect the sales taxes from the seller.

The occasional sales exemption also often applies when there is a transfer of all or substantially all of the property held or used in the regular course of business, if after the transfer there is no real or ultimate change in the ownership of such property. Thus, incorporation of a sole proprietorship would be exempt from sales taxes. Likewise, the transfer of assets by partners to a partnership generally would be exempt under the casual sale rule. These provisions correspond to those found in the Internal Revenue Code that exclude the gains on such transfers from being included in gross income.

PLANNING STRATEGIES

Not Completely Tax-Free

FRAMEWORK FOCUS: THINKING OUTSIDE THE FRAMEWORK

Tax advisers must be aware of the impact of sales and use taxes on a transaction that might otherwise be free of income tax. For example, although a § 351 transfer of property to a controlled corporation in exchange for its stock generally is not subject to current Federal corporate income taxes, some states provide that such transfers are subject to sales and use taxes, i.e., that the occasional sale exemption is not available or does not apply. Similarly, a corporate reorganization may be structured to avoid the current imposition of income taxes, but it still may be considered a taxable sale for sales and use tax purposes.

Items Used in Manufacturing, Processing, or Fabricating. All states imposing a sales tax provide an exemption from sales tax for purchases of materials used in the manufacturing, processing, or fabricating of tangible personal property for sale. This exemption also is referred to as the ingredient or component part exemption. The rationale underlying this exemption is similar to that for the sale-for-resale exemption—the materials purchased are in fact resold in the form of the final manufactured product, rather than being used for ultimate consumption by the purchaser. Although the rationale appears straightforward, there is much disagreement over what each of the terms—manufacturing, processing and fabricating—means.

In general, *manufacturing* refers to all stages in the production process commencing with the acquisition of raw materials and culminating with the completed

TAX IN THE NEWS

BACK TO SCHOOL? IT'S TIME FOR A SALES TAX HOLIDAY

Sales tax holidays typically last for a weekend and are held during August. They are designed to reduce the cost of back-to-school purchases. In 2003, nine states (Connecticut, Georgia, Iowa, New York, North Carolina, South Carolina, Texas, West Virginia, and Vermont) held sales tax holidays for sales of clothing (generally excluding certain types of athletic items and clothing accessories) and/or in some cases footwear, school supplies, and computers. In most cases, the maximum cost of clothing allowed to qualify for the holiday was $100, although Connecticut's limit was $300 and South Carolina had no maximum. Vermont's sales tax holiday applied to purchases of computers, with a maximum cost of $4,000. In 2002, Georgia estimated that it lost between $11 million and $14 million in sales tax revenue as a result of the holiday. After providing a sales tax holiday for several years, revenue concerns resulted in the Florida legislature ending Florida's sales tax holiday in 2003.

tangible personal property. *Processing* normally involves applying materials and labor to modify or alter the characteristics of tangible personal property. Thus, repairs or maintenance generally is not considered to be processing because typically those acts simply result in restoring the property to its original form. Finally, *fabrication* usually consists of a procedure or series of procedures whose aim is to make the property function better or differently.

Examples of processes that may not qualify as manufacturing, processing, or fabricating are those that merely reshape or repackage an item or are ancillary to the actual manufacturing process. For example, the freezing of food that has already been prepared may not be considered part of the manufacturing process. Thus, a freezer purchased for this purpose may not be exempt.

In addition, the proximity of an item to the manufacturing, processing, and fabricating process may be relevant. For example, a piece of equipment associated with preparing an item for production rather than actual production, or a piece of equipment used to test a product after it is manufactured, may not be exempt.

State statutes often contain different definitions of these terms, and various state revenue agencies and courts differ in their interpretations. It is critical that tax professionals review the statutes, administrative regulations, and court cases for a specific jurisdiction before advising clients with respect to this exemption.

Sales of Machinery or Equipment. Most states provide an exemption for machinery or equipment purchased to be used in the manufacture, production, or processing of tangible personal property that is to be sold. The rationale for this exemption is again that business inputs should be exempt to prevent the pyramiding of sales taxes. In addition to that rationale, states provide an exemption for machinery and equipment to encourage business investment and location within their boundaries. That, in turn, provides a basis for increased employment and other economic benefits.

Although the specifics of this exemption vary greatly among the states, industrial and manufacturing machinery is typically exempt. However, some states do not exempt the machinery used in manufacturing but rather tax it at a lower rate (e.g., Alabama) or provide an investment credit (e.g., New Mexico). Many states also exempt farm equipment. However, some states like Louisiana only exempt purchases of farm equipment up to $50,000. Office machinery is not exempt in any state.

An important aspect of this exemption is that states typically restrict the exemption to machinery used "directly" or "predominantly" in the manufacturing or processing of tangible personal property. So in addition to the controversy associated

CONCEPT SUMMARY 10–1

The Retail Sales Tax—The Basics

In general, on what transactions is the retail sales tax imposed?	A retail sales tax is imposed on the sales of tangible personal property at retail.
In general, what transactions are excluded from the retail sales tax?	Because the retail sales tax is imposed on the sale of tangible personal property, the following transactions typically are excluded: • Sales of services. • Sales of intangible property.

Note: Individual state statutes vary considerably in terms of how specific terms are defined and interpreted. Hence, extreme care should be exercised to ascertain whether *all* services and *all* intangible property sales are excluded from that state's sales tax statute.

with first determining whether the activity constitutes manufacturing or processing discussed above, another issue concerns whether the machinery or equipment is being used directly or predominantly in such activity.

EXAMPLE 6

A manufacturer of auto parts buys $250,000 of machinery and equipment that is directly used in the manufacturing process. It also purchases $100,000 of office equipment during the year. In most states, the company is subject to sales tax on the purchase of office equipment, but not on the purchase of the manufacturing machinery and equipment. ■

Sales of "Essential" Items. Although sales of meals by restaurants and food prepared for on-premises consumption are generally included in the tax base, many states exempt nonprepared foods purchased at grocery stores. However, certain items including alcoholic beverages, items not intended for human consumption (dog food), prepared foods (sandwiches), and, in some cases, soft drinks and candy may be excluded from the exemption. Some states including Illinois, Missouri, North Carolina, and Tennessee tax nonprepared foods, although at a lower tax rate.

Prescription drugs are exempt from sales tax in all states except Illinois. Medical devices such as wheelchairs and crutches are exempt in most states (although in most of these a prescription is required for the exemption). Nonprescription drugs are exempt in 11 states.

Though a few states (Minnesota, New Jersey, Pennsylvania, and Rhode Island) generally exempt clothing from the tax base, most states tax all sales of clothing. A few states exempt sales of specific types of clothing or clothes costing less than some stated amount, e.g., $100 or less.

TAX FACT

IS THAT DRINK TAXABLE?

In Ohio, sales of food for human consumption are exempt from sales tax. "Food" includes milk, pure fruit juices, coffee, tea, and cocoa, but not soft drinks and sodas. So bottled lemonade may be taxable while iced tea is not. However, to complicate things further, a sale technically is exempt only if the purchaser takes the item out of the store. Is that drink "for here" or "to go"?

Concept Summary 10–2

The Retail Sales Tax Base

What are the principal exemptions from the retail sales tax base?	• Sale-for-resale exemption • Casual or occasional sale exemption • Manufacturing, processing, and fabricating exemption • Machinery or equipment exemption • Exemptions on certain "essential" items (e.g., food, medical, devices, and prescription drugs) • Exemptions for certain organizations or entities, such as governmental agencies.
What amounts paid for goods and services generally are not included in the gross receipts subject to the retail sales tax?	• Cash discounts • Returns and allowances • Transportation charges separately stated if FOB origin • Trade-ins • Finance and service charges • Bad debts

Note: Individual state statutes vary considerably in terms of how specific terms are defined and interpreted. Hence, extreme care should be exercised to ascertain the exact scope of each exemption and what amounts specifically are excluded from the gross receipts subject to that state's sales tax statute.

Sales to Exempt Organizations. Most states allow the purchases of certain organizations to be exempt from sales and use tax. These organizations include:

- The United States, its unincorporated agencies and instrumentalities, and organizations fully owned by the United States.
- The State along with its counties, cities, and special districts.
- Charitable organizations.
- Educational organizations.
- Religious organizations.
- Youth athletic organizations.
- Organizations that qualify for exemption from the Federal income tax under § 501(c)(3).

In some states, exempt organizations like churches, charities, and volunteer fire departments must pay sales tax on their purchases and then periodically request a refund from the state. Thus, it becomes critical to keep track of the sales tax paid on every purchase.

LO.4

Understand how to compute the retail sales tax base.

THE RETAIL SALES TAX BASE

The measure or base of sales and use taxes generally is the consideration paid for goods and services or the gross proceeds for which the taxable item is sold, leased, or rented. The exact definition of the terms and what is included or excluded from the tax base varies by state.

As a general principle, **gross proceeds** do not include the following.

- Cash discounts allowed on the sale—some states distinguish between cash discounts and "early payment discounts," with the latter usually not excluded from the sales tax base.
- Returns and allowances—the amount charged for tangible personal property returned by a customer if the total amount charged is refunded by cash or credit.

- Actual shipping (delivery, freight, and transportation) charges, if the charges are separately stated and the goods are shipped by common carrier or if the goods are shipped FOB origin (i.e., title transfers prior to shipment and the buyer assumes liability during shipment). If the title transfers at the point of delivery (FOB destination), shipping charges are included in the tax base. Likewise, handling charges that are incurred in preparing property for shipment are generally included in the sales tax base.
- Trade-ins—many states allow trade-ins to be excluded from gross sales proceeds, thereby imposing a tax only on the net invoiced value. However, 10 states allow trade-ins to be excluded only on certain property (most frequently motor vehicles).
- Finance and service charges or interest from credit extended on sales of taxable items.
- Bad debts—some states allow gross receipts to be reduced by the amount of bad debts actually written off.

EXAMPLE 7

Daisy Janitorial Supplies sold $2.4 million of cleaning products to other companies for use in cleaning their own businesses. It also sold $600,000 of cleaning products to individual consumers. Daisy allowed a 2% cash discount on sales to other businesses, and 30% of the business clients took advantage of the discount.

Daisy charged customers $30,000 for the shipping and handling of supplies delivered by common carrier. One customer returned a $10,000 order for a cash refund.

Gross proceeds subject to sales tax are $3,005,600 [$2,400,000 + $600,000 – $14,400 cash discounts ($2,400,000 × 30% × 2% discount) + $30,000 shipping and handling – $10,000 returns]. ■

The above is by no means an exhaustive list of the issues one has to consider in determining what constitutes "gross proceeds." Some of the other questions that must be resolved in this regard include:

- Should taxes paid be included in taxable receipts for the purpose of sales taxes? Does (should) the answer depend on the type of taxes paid?
- What should be the impact of discount coupons issued by a retailer on the sales tax base?
- Are tips and service charges includible in the sales tax base?
- When should the tax be collected in an installment sale—when the goods are delivered, when the cash is collected, or when the final payment is received?

LO.5

Determine the key administrative issues for taxpayers in complying with sales and use tax obligations.

Administration of Sales and Use Taxes

Managing compliance with the sales and use tax laws is not a trivial issue, especially considering that there are over 7,500 state and local tax jurisdictions. Depending on how and where a business operates, compliance obligations arise in multiple jurisdictions. Moreover, businesses typically enter into numerous separate taxable transactions. Thus, the burden of complying with sales and local tax laws can be significant, especially if the function is not properly managed and planned. Most businesses find that their primary compliance obligations include reporting, record keeping, and preparing for and handling audits. In a recent year, one large corporation filed and/or managed 2,321 sales and use tax returns, 323 income and franchise tax returns, 225 annual reports and business license forms, and 197 property tax returns.

REPORTING OBLIGATIONS

Retailers have a fiduciary responsibility to properly collect and remit sales and use taxes. To discharge this responsibility, they must (1) register their business and (2) file tax returns.

Registration. States with sales and use taxes require all retailers engaged in the business of selling a taxable item for storage, use, or consumption to register their business with the state in which they conduct their business operations. If a retailer has multiple business locations within a state, it usually is required to register each location separately. The registration results in the taxpayer receiving an ID number.

Returns. Once registered, the taxpayer is required to file a sales and use tax return each period. In addition to filing returns, the taxpayer must also collect the taxes on a timely basis and remit those taxes to the state authorities.

- *Due dates.* Due dates for tax reports vary by state and depend on the amount of the taxpayer's tax liability.
- *Contents.* As one might expect, a sales or use tax report typically will require information about:
  - The total receipts of the seller during the reporting period (or total purchases for use tax purposes).
  - Sales to other retailers for resale.
  - Sales of exempt property.
  - Sales to the U.S. government.
  - Sales in interstate or foreign commerce.
  - Sales returns.
  - Uncollectible accounts written off.
  - Cash discounts.

  If local taxes are reported to and collected by the state, the return may also include lines to allow for that computation. Some states also allow for a vendor tax collection discount or fee to help offset the cost of collecting the tax. If allowed, the return might provide for its calculation as well. For example, Georgia allows a 3 percent discount of the first $3,000 of sales and use taxes collected and 0.5 percent of the excess. In contrast, Arizona, California, and Massachusetts are among the states that do not allow any collection discount to the seller.
- *Accounting methods.* Most states allow taxpayers a choice in the accounting method (e.g., cash or accrual basis) that they use to report their gross receipts for purposes of the sales and use tax returns. Although a choice may be allowed, some states require that taxpayers use the same method as they used for their books. Once the taxpayer chooses a method, states require consistency in its use, with changes in the method requiring a formal petition to the taxing authority.

Record Keeping. Proper documentation is of paramount importance for taxpayers to be able to support their sales and use tax liabilities. Apart from the regular books of account maintained by a business, some of the following documents can help establish the correct amount of the liability.

- Invoices to document any taxes paid or collected.
- Contracts and purchase orders to support dates of transactions.
- Bills of lading to support delivery destinations.
- Support for credits for returns and write-off of bad debts.
- Exemption and resale certificates to support exempt transactions.

BRIDGE DISCIPLINE

Public Finance

Sales taxes raise a number of important policy questions. As discussed earlier, one of the questions being addressed by states is whether the retail sales tax should be expanded to apply to sales of services in addition to sales of tangible property. In addition, at the Federal level, some politicians have proposed the enactment of a national sales tax in addition to or in lieu of our current income tax. Proponents of a national sales tax argue that the new system would be more efficient and would lower tax rates for low- and middle-income taxpayers.

For example, H.R. 25, introduced in the House of Representatives in January 2003, would repeal the income tax (both corporate and individual), payroll taxes, and estate and gift taxes and replace them with a 23 percent sales tax on the purchase of new goods and services. Low-income taxpayers with income below certain established thresholds would be eligible for rebates.

As part of the enactment of a national sales tax that would replace the income tax, the Sixteenth Amendment to the U.S. Constitution giving Congress the power to "collect taxes on incomes, from whatever source derived, without apportionment among the several States, and without regard to any census or enumeration," might need to be modified or repealed.

For more information on a national sales tax, see **http://www.salestax.org**.

AUDITS

Audits are the primary mechanism available for state tax agencies to evaluate the extent to which taxpayers are complying with the tax laws. Because the number of taxable transactions tends to be voluminous, sampling techniques are used extensively in sales tax audits to minimize costs and make the task manageable.

Sampling consists of drawing inferences about the population from a smaller set of observations. Thus, it is absolutely essential that great care be taken in identifying the procedures that would yield an appropriate sample. For example, care should be exercised to make sure that the sample captures as closely as possible the normal conditions under which the business operated during the period under audit. Typically, taxpayers have the right to be involved in developing the audit program and technique. Hence, they should ensure that the sample does not consist of unusual or nonrecurring transactions and that such transactions are identified and dealt with separately.

Generally, two types of sampling procedures are used most frequently in sales and use tax audits—block samples and random or statistical samples.

Block Samples. Under this method, the auditor first picks a block of time, such as one or more months in a year. For that block, the auditor then usually examines all transactions for compliance accuracy. Based on the error rate in the sample, the auditor extrapolates to the entire population. For example, if the auditor chooses one month in the year as the sample for examination, the errors found are multiplied by 12 to get the number of estimated errors in the population.

The biggest drawback of the block sample procedure is that the time block selected for the sample may not reflect the operations of the taxpayer in the remainder of the year. Thus, extrapolating from the sample results may lead to either over- or under-estimating the errors for the entire year.

Random or Statistical Samples. To ensure that the sampling procedure results in unbiased inferences about the population, a simple random or stratified random sample may be required. In a simple random sample, the auditor picks a sample

TAX IN THE NEWS

THE STREAMLINED SALES TAX PROJECT

The Streamlined Sales Tax Project (SSTP) was organized in March 2000 to "develop measures to design, test and implement a sales and use tax system that radically simplifies sales and use taxes." On November 12, 2002, 34 states and the District of Columbia approved the Streamlined Sales and Use Tax Agreement whose purpose is "to simplify and modernize sales and use tax administration in the member states in order to substantially reduce the burden of tax compliance." The Agreement:

- Mandates a single state and local tax based in each state.
- Mandates a single tax rate per state with the exception that a state may have a second rate on food and drugs.
- Limits states' ability to exempt specific products.
- Provides uniform sourcing rules.
- Mandates state-level administration of local sales and use taxes.
- Mandates a uniform registration system for sellers.
- Limits the use of sales tax holidays.
- Eliminates caps and thresholds on the amount of tax that is charged on a purchase.
- Provides common definitions for terms such as "clothing," "food and food ingredients," and "lease or rental" and defines "tangible personal property" as personal property that can be seen, weighed, measured, felt, or touched, or that is in any manner perceptible to the senses.
- Suggests that states avoid creating new excise or other taxes outside the general sales and use taxes.

The Agreement was to become binding after 10 states comprising at least 20 percent of the total population of states with a sales tax had enacted legislation to conform to it. This goal was met in 2003 when 20 states enacted some form of the model legislation. Ultimately, the implementing states would like Congress to give the states the authority to require remote sellers to collect and remit sales tax. The states argue that the streamlined system eliminates the burdens on interstate commerce that have been the historical legal justification for denying the states that right. Some companies already have agreed voluntarily to collect and remit over $300 million of sales tax to states participating in the SSTP.

of transactions purely at random (usually identified using a random number generator) or by employing some random sampling rule.

However, for many businesses, a simple random sample may not be appropriate; instead, the nature of the business might call for a stratified random sample. In this technique, transactions are first classified into strata or groups based on some characteristic that is suitable given the nature of the business activities. Thus, the strata might be based on the dollar amount of the sales, the geographic regions in which the taxpayer conducts business, the vendors to whom the sales are made, or some combination of these and other criteria.

Once the strata are created, then transactions are chosen at some rate from within each stratum. The sampling rate might differ for each stratum, depending on its importance or the frequency of transactions. Given the different strata and likely difference in the sampling rates within each stratum, care needs to be exercised when using this technique in drawing inferences about the population.

Managed Audits. Ten states currently allow taxpayer-initiated managed audits in some circumstances. Under a managed audit, the taxpayer or a third party hired

CONCEPT SUMMARY 10–3

Administration of Sales and Use Taxes

What are the reporting obligations of a taxpayer for sales and use taxes?	A taxpayer usually has two main reporting obligations for sales and use taxes: • Registration: Retailers in the business of selling items subject to sales or use tax are required to register their business with the appropriate authority. • Returns: Once registered, the taxpayer is required to file sales and use tax returns each period.
What are the record-keeping requirements for a taxpayer for sales and use tax purposes?	To help establish the correct amount of sales and use tax liability, taxpayers must keep the following documents: • Invoices to document taxes paid or collected. • Contracts and purchase orders to support transaction dates. • Bills of lading to support delivery destinations. • Support for credits for returns and write-off of bad debts. • Exemption and resale certificates to support exempt transactions.
In general, what procedures are used to perform an audit of a taxpayer's sales or use tax liability?	Two types of sampling procedures are used to perform sales and use tax audits: • Block sampling: This method entails selecting for audit all transactions that took place in a certain block of time. • Random or statistical sampling: This method entails selecting for audit transactions based on either a simple random sample or a stratified random sample.
In general, what is the statute of limitations for sales and use tax purposes?	Most states provide a three-year statute of limitations for sales and use taxes.

by the taxpayer performs the audit under guidelines initiated by the state. The guidelines are likely to include specific audit procedures, the audit period, and the scope of the audit.

STATUTE OF LIMITATIONS

Most states provide a three-year statute of limitations within which the audit must be performed or the claim for refund must be filed. The three-year period runs from the date the return is filed or the date the return is due, whichever is later. If the taxpayer does not file a return or files a return that is false or fraudulent, usually there is no statute of limitation; that is, the audit can be performed at any time.

LO.6

Recognize the importance of property taxes in the United States.

Property Taxation

The property tax is primarily levied and administered by local jurisdictions rather than the states. Throughout the history of the United States, this tax has contributed the lion's share of total revenues for local jurisdictions. However, as the U.S. economy has undergone significant changes, with services accounting for an increasingly larger share, the relative importance of the property tax as a source of local revenues has declined. For example, in the 1920s, property taxes constituted roughly

TAX IN THE NEWS

Cattle at Disney World?

Walt Disney World, SeaWorld Orlando, Universal Orlando, and other tourist-related companies in Florida have been accused of taking advantage of property tax exemptions for agricultural land by grazing cattle and planting pine trees on hundreds of acres of land near their theme parks and other business operations.

Anheuser Busch (which owns SeaWorld Orlando) saves more than $866,000 in property taxes each year by claiming six parcels of land (on which 100,000 pine seedlings have been planted) as agricultural land.

At Disney World, the company claims that 162 acres of land on which cattle are grazed should be valued as agricultural land worth $750,000 instead of as commercial property worth $4 million. With the property classed as agricultural land, Disney pays $12,000 in property taxes to Osceola County. If it were valued as commercial property, Disney would owe the county $66,000 in property taxes.

The companies argue that the exemptions are legitimate and note that they pay their fair share of property taxes. Disney pays $100 million each year to three local jurisdictions, while SeaWorld Orlando pays $24 million.

70 percent of the total revenue of local governments. (Total revenue includes not only tax revenue but payments from the state and Federal government and other sources.) By 2000, the share of the property tax had dropped to less than 25 percent of total revenue.

Property taxes are used to finance many types of local services, such as schools, fire stations, parks, and libraries. They are also used to provide public safety and health, transportation, and emergency services. As such, the governing body of each county, school district, city, and town levies property taxes.

LO.7

Distinguish between real property and personal property.

REAL PROPERTY VERSUS PERSONAL PROPERTY

All states allow local jurisdictions to tax the ownership of **real property** located in the jurisdiction. Real property (realty) generally includes land, buildings, and other improvements on the land. Although specific exemptions from the real property tax base vary considerably among local jurisdictions, some of the more common exemptions include the following.

- Agricultural land.
- Government property.
- Education and library property.
- Health-care property.
- Religious property.
- Cemeteries.
- Property of widows, widowers, and disabled persons.
- Observatories.
- Animal control and humane societies.
- Property of arts and science organizations.
- Volunteer fire departments.
- Property of veterans organizations.

Most states (exceptions include New Jersey, New York, and Pennsylvania) also allow local jurisdictions to tax tangible personal property used in a business. **Personal property** (personalty) usually is defined as all property that is not real property. In practice, there is often considerable controversy over classifying property as real or personal. Examples of items that might be classified as real property include wall-to-wall carpets, ceiling fans, electrical wiring, built-in furnishings, lighting fixtures, and sprinkler systems. Examples of items that are typically classified as personal property include area rugs, window air conditioners, blinds, most equipment and machinery, and movable or detachable partitions.

In most jurisdictions, different tax rates are applied to real property and personal property. Further, it is common to have multiple classes of property within these two property types, with different tax rates applied to each class.

Inventories are typically not taxed. However, a number of states including Georgia and Indiana include inventories in the tax base. In jurisdictions that do tax inventories, businesses can reduce or avoid the tax by minimizing the amount of inventory on hand at the assessment date.

In a number of states and local jurisdictions, property tax is also imposed on the value of intangible property such as stocks and bonds. For example, the state of Florida taxes intangible personal property at the rate of $1 per $1,000 of value. Taxable intangible assets include stocks, mutual funds, and bonds, but not cash, retirement plan assets, and municipal obligations issued by Florida or Florida municipalities.

VALUATION AND RATE-SETTING

The **property tax** is imposed on the value of property, which usually is defined as some measure of fair market value. In the case of real property, property values (called assessed values) are determined by qualified appraisers or assessors, who are employed by the local or state government. In many jurisdictions, assessors are elected to their office. The assessed value of real property varies greatly from 50 percent to 100 percent of fair market value. In contrast, the value of personal property is typically self-reported by the taxpayer.

DIGGING DEEPER 4

*Find more information on this topic at our Web site: **http://wft-advanced.swlearning.com**.*

Because property taxes are levied to meet projected expenditures of local jurisdictions, their amount is determined by the locality as the residual required to meet those expenses after considering the revenues from all other sources. The required property tax levy is divided by the final assessed values of the properties to compute the tax rate. Administratively, this tax rate is applied to each parcel of property on the tax rolls in proportion to its value. Statements are issued to the property owners and tax is collected usually according to a statutory schedule.

EXAMPLE 8

Chaney County's budget calls for raising $50 million in revenue from its tax on real property. Based on the most recent valuation, the assessed value of all taxable real property in Chaney County is determined to be $5.25 billion. Therefore, the county sets the tax rate at .952% ($50 million divided by $5.25 billion). ■

EXAMPLE 9

Greg and Elaine own a house in Chaney County that is valued by the tax assessor at $225,000. Their property tax bill is $2,142 ($225,000 assessed value × .952% tax rate from Example 8). Barbara also owns a house in Chaney County valued at $175,000. Her tax bill is $1,666. ■

Rather than revalue property on an annual basis, most local governments revalue or reassess property every three to eight years and when properties are sold. While the total value of all the property in the taxing jurisdiction is likely to increase over time, the value of individual properties may increase or decrease. In addition, depending on the revenue needs of the local government, tax rates may go down following revaluations. The combination of changing values and changing rates can either increase or decrease the tax liability of individual taxpayers.

TAX IN THE NEWS

Putting an Incentive Package Together

In addition to property tax exemptions, tax incentives can take the form of sales tax exemptions on the purchase of new equipment; income tax incentives including investment tax credits, job credits, and adjustments in income tax apportionment factors (see Chapter 9); and low-interest-rate financing.

For example, to keep a production facility in Toledo, Ohio, DaimlerChrysler was offered an incentive package including a 10-year exemption from property taxes and investment credits against the state's franchise tax.

Although state and local incentive plans are still very popular, they are not without their critics. For example, in Nebraska, corporate tax incentives cost the state an estimated $145 million per year in tax revenue. As states face budget deficits, many are cutting back or eliminating incentives or demanding refunds (sometimes called "clawbacks") of tax incentives for any failure to meet job creation and investment goals. In Nebraska, legislation was introduced to impose a surcharge on all corporations that have had their income tax liabilities eliminated by the state's incentive package.

In addition, the constitutionality of incentive programs is being questioned as existing businesses are questioning the legality of providing incentives to new businesses without providing the same benefits to them.

EXAMPLE 10

Chaney County assesses all property in the county every seven years. This year, Chaney County's tax assessor revalues all property in the county. The new assessed value is $6 billion. Chaney County's budget calls for $55 million of revenue from the real property tax. Therefore, the tax rate that had been .952% in Examples 8 and 9 drops to .917% ($55 million divided by $6 billion). ■

EXAMPLE 11

After revaluation, Greg and Elaine's house is valued at $250,000. Their property tax bill increases to $2,292.50. On the other hand, the value of Barbara's house increases to only $180,000. Her tax bill decreases to $1,650.60. ■

ADVANTAGES AND DISADVANTAGES OF THE PROPERTY TAX

Perhaps the most significant advantage of the tax on real property is that its base—the property on which the tax is imposed—cannot easily be relocated, reducing concerns about which locality has the jurisdiction to impose its tax. The tax base is also fairly stable. In contrast, the ability to move personal property from one jurisdiction to another and the ability to hide personal property can make the administration and collection of personal property taxes difficult.

The property tax is not without disadvantages. Its biggest advantage—the certain and determinable tax base—can turn out also to be its most significant disadvantage. Specifically, economic downturns inevitably are accompanied by declines in property values, which cause the tax base to shrink. Theoretically, the local jurisdiction can continue to raise the same amount of tax revenues by adjusting the tax rate upward, but in recessionary times such actions are of questionable economic prudence. In view of this problem, it is not surprising to see local governments seek a more diverse tax base.

ABATEMENTS AND INCENTIVES

State and local governments frequently entice new businesses to locate in their jurisdiction through the use of property tax abatements or tax exemptions. The

TAX IN THE NEWS

I Need That Money Back!

After emerging from bankruptcy in 2002, Kmart sued over 450 local governments around the country, seeking refunds of overpaid property taxes. Kmart claims that the method used by the municipalities to value its inventory and other tangible personal property overstated the value of the property and resulted in overpayments totaling $8.6 million. The refunds requested ranged from over $600,000 from Detroit to $146 from Grayson County, Texas. Kmart valued the inventory using a more sophisticated method taking into account market data, estimates of sales to other businesses, and the customer's overall financial health.

state and local governments benefit through the creation of new jobs and the positive impact on the local economy, while the business obtains a substantial tax savings (usually for a specified number of years).

ADMINISTRATIVE ISSUES

In the case of real property, the property owner generally is not required to file any reports. In contrast, taxpayers are required to file annual personal property tax returns based on values established on the annual assessment date.

After issuance of a notice of value, a certain number of days are allowed for the taxpayer to make an administrative appeal, usually to the assessor. If the meeting with the assessor does not result in a resolution of the dispute, the taxpayer must file an appeal against the proposed value shown in the notice. The State Board of Equalization (or equivalent body) usually hears this appeal. If agreement is not reached before this body, then the next stage is the courts.

LO.8

Identify the constitutional and Federal issues involved with property taxes.

CONSTITUTIONAL ISSUES

Federal Constitutional Issues. Several provisions in the U.S. Constitution have a bearing on state and local taxes. The most frequently raised challenges to state and local tax levies are based on the Due Process and the Commerce Clauses in the U.S. Constitution. With much less frequency, state and local taxes have also been challenged under the Equal Protection and the Privileges and Immunities Clauses, which have much in common with the uniformity and equality provisions in the state constitutions. The Fourteenth Amendment to the U.S. Constitution provides:

> [N]or shall any State . . . deny to any person within its jurisdiction the equal protection of the laws.

Although the Equal Protection Clause makes no mention of taxation, the context in which it has been invoked concerns whether the tax being imposed treats different "persons" equally.

To be sure, the U.S. Supreme Court's position in matters of taxation has been that state legislatures should be allowed a high degree of flexibility in classifying

TAX IN THE NEWS

Should New Owners Pay Higher Taxes?

California's Proposition 13 dealing with the state's real property tax system is perhaps one of the most widely known and controversial state tax initiatives, especially because it imposed differential tax burdens. This measure amended the state constitution to limit property taxes to 1 percent of 1975–76 valuations and to cap annual increases in valuations at 2 percent, unless the property underwent a change in ownership (e.g., sale) or was a new construction. Thus, under this system of assessing property values based on date of acquisition rather than current value, a taxpayer continuing to live in the same property might have a substantially different property tax burden from a taxpayer who newly buys a virtually identical property in the same neighborhood.

The constitutionality of Proposition 13 was challenged under the Equal Protection Clause, but the Supreme Court upheld the California scheme on the ground that the difference in treatment of newer and older owners rationally furthered a legitimate state interest of preserving and stabilizing local neighborhoods (*Nordinger v. Hahn*, 505 U.S. 1, 112 S.Ct. 2326 [1992]).

taxpayers so long as there is some reasonable basis for their position. The following statement from the decision in *Lehnhausen v. Lakeshore Auto Parts Co.*[9] is illustrative of the Court's approach when a state or local tax is attacked on equal protection grounds.

> The Equal Protection Clause does not mean that a State may not draw lines that treat one class of individuals or entities differently from the others. The test is whether the difference in treatment is an invidious discrimination. . . . Where taxation is concerned and no specific federal right, apart from equal protection, is imperiled, the States have large leeway in making classifications and drawing lines which in their judgment produce reasonable systems of taxation.

Further, the Court grants "a presumption of constitutionality" to the state's classification scheme, while placing the onus on the person raising the equal protection challenge to overcome that presumption. The Court's rationale for doing so is that it is not possible to acquire knowledge of local conditions without elaborately cataloging those conditions. The legislature is in a unique position to have intimate knowledge of such factors and must be presumed to have used that knowledge to devise its taxing scheme. So long as there is any conceivable basis for treating classes of taxpayers or members of a class differently, the taxing scheme would be able to withstand the equal protection challenge.

State Constitutional Issues. Most state constitutions contain uniformity and equality clauses that limit the state's ability to impose taxes. While these uniformity and equality clauses vary considerably among the states, they generally provide stricter tests than the Federal Constitution. However, their basic concerns are similar to that of Federal law: Can taxes be imposed at different rates on different taxpayers, property, or activities? Does providing an exemption or credit to a taxpayer, property, or activity amount to differential taxation?

[9]410 U.S. 356, 93 S.Ct. 1001 (1973).

PROPERTY TAX, EXCISE TAX, OR FEE?

Ascertaining whether a state or local levy is a property tax, excise tax, or fee is important because state equality and uniformity provisions typically apply to property taxes, but not excise taxes or fees. Thus, state and local governments may structure fee schedules and excise taxes that are not necessarily uniform or equal. Fees tend to be one-time charges imposed on the privilege of exercising some right. Examples include fees for waste disposal and recycling.

While property taxes are typically based on the value of the property, excise taxes (like sales taxes) are typically imposed on a retail sale. However, unlike a general sales tax, an excise tax is typically imposed on the sale of specific goods like gasoline, alcoholic beverages, and cigarettes. It typically is based on a quantity such as a gallon of gasoline or a package of cigarettes, rather than the dollar amount of the sale. Excise taxes vary greatly from state to state.

For instance, while the median state excise tax rate on a pack of cigarettes is 60 cents, rates range from less than 8 cents per pack in Kentucky, North Carolina, South Carolina, and Virginia, to $1.50 or higher in Connecticut, Massachusetts, New Jersey, New York, and Rhode Island. Likewise, state excise taxes on gasoline range from Georgia's 7.5 cents per gallon to Rhode Island's 31 cents per gallon.

Suggested Further Readings

Debra Callihan, Lisa Church, LeAnn Luna, and Katrina Mantzke, "Sales Tax Nexus and Remote Vendors," *State Tax Notes*, September 23, 2002, pp. 949–956.

Matthew Graham, "Evaluating Internet Sales Tax Proposals," *State Tax Notes*, September 2, 2002, pp. 721–729.

Michelle E. Hendrix and George R. Zodrow, "Sales Taxation of Services: An Economic Perspective," *State Tax Notes*, February 23, 2004, pp. 641–651.

Charles E. McLure, Jr., "The Nuttiness of State and Local Taxes—and the Nuttiness of Responses Thereto," *State Tax Notes*, September 16, 2002, pp. 841–856.

Michael Reese, "Does the Streamlined Agreement Signal the End of *Quill* in the Area of E-Commerce?" *State Tax Notes*, September 1, 2003, pp. 639–651.

Jeff Thomson and Charles Sheketoff, "Addressing the Regressivity of Sales Taxes: Hard to Overcome and Made Worse by Income Tax Cuts," *State Tax Notes*, September 22, 2003, pp. 863–866.

KEY TERMS

Audits, 10–20
Gross proceeds, 10–17
Intangible property, 10–11
Nexus, 10–6
Personal property, 10–23
Property tax, 10–24
Real property, 10–23
Retail sale, 10–12
Sale, 10–12
Tangible property, 10–10

PROBLEM MATERIALS

Discussion Questions

1. What are the different types of sales taxes currently in use in the United States? Specifically, discuss how they differ from each other.

Issue ID

2. What is the rationale, if any, for states to generally exclude services from their sales tax base?

3. What are some of the principal exemptions from the sales tax base typically found in most states' statutes? Explain the rationale of some of these exemptions.

4. What is (are) the basic principle(s) underlying a retail sales tax? How do the state statutes attempt to be faithful to these principles?

5. Define "nexus." What is the minimum nexus standard for sales and use tax purposes? After reviewing the U.S. Supreme Court cases mentioned in the chapter, do you think that the Court's opinion on the minimum nexus standard for sales tax purposes has changed over time?

6. Suppose you are advising a new client who is just starting a business in a state that imposes a sales tax. What type of records would you advise this client to keep so as to help in meeting the sales tax obligations?

7. Who remits a sales tax to the taxing state? Who remits a use tax to the taxing state?

8. Give two examples of the sales/use tax occasional sale exemption.

9. What is the Streamlined Sales Tax Project?

10. What are the advantages and disadvantages of a property tax?

11. Distinguish among a sales tax, a property tax, an excise tax, and a fee.

12. Why is a tax on real property easier to administer than a tax on personal property?

EXTENDER

13. Why do you think the excise taxes on cigarettes, alcohol, and gasoline vary so much from state to state?

Issue ID
Communications

14. Johnny's construction company owns a crane and other mobile construction equipment that is used in construction jobs in State X and State Y. What tax issues should be considered in advising Johnny with respect to his property tax liability in both states? Summarize your points in PowerPoint format.

EXTENDER
Issue ID
Communications

15. As a tax professional, you have been asked by an out-of-state company to represent them in negotiating an incentive package to locate a new manufacturing facility in Green County. In the last 10 years, Green County has typically provided a 50% reduction in property taxes for up to 10 years as well as favorable financing of new plants. The plant is expected to provide over 300 new jobs but will also put a strain on current public school facilities and water supplies and will likely cause traffic problems.

One of your current clients, a company that has been doing business in Green County for over 50 years, is adamantly opposed to the use of incentives to lure new businesses. After all, the existing business provides just as many employment opportunities for the county's workers, and the county does not offer it any incentives or provide the company with any tax reductions. Should you represent the new client? Write an editorial to your local newspaper outlining the pros and cons of incentives packages.

Problems

Ethics

16. Steve is an accounting student and lives in a state that imposes an 8% sales tax. While shopping for textbooks online, he notes that he can buy his books for $400 and that the online seller does not charge any sales tax. However, he will pay shipping charges of $29.95. The campus bookstore charges $380 for the same books before adding the 8%

sales tax. What is the total cost of purchasing the books if Steve buys the books online? What is the total cost of purchasing the books if Steve buys the books at the campus bookstore?

17. Grande Corporation operates a retail store in State C. Using the following information from the corporate books and records, determine which of the following transactions are subject to C's sales tax. In each case, also determine who pays the tax and who is responsible for remitting the tax to C.

Sales of general merchandise to consumers living in C	$700,000
Sales of crutches and other medical supplies to consumers living in C	111,000
Sales of general merchandise (via mail order) to consumers living in State D	84,000
Purchases of general merchandise from the Big Corporation, a supplier located in C	55,000

18. As a retailer, Granite Corporation sells software programs manufactured and packaged by other parties. Granite also purchases computer parts, assembles them as specified by a customer in a purchase order, and sells them as operating stand-alone computers. All of Granite's operations take place in State F, which levies a 6% sales tax. Results for the current year are as follows.

Sales of software	$1,400,000
Purchases of computer parts	1,700,000
Sales of computer systems	3,500,000
Purchases of office supplies	60,000
Purchases of packaging materials for the computer systems	7,500
Purchases of tools used by computer assemblers	52,000

a. What is Granite's own sales tax expense for the year?
b. How much F sales tax must Granite collect and pay over to the state on behalf of other taxpayers subject to the tax?

EXTENDER

19. The Johnson family has income of $45,000. Assume that the Federal tax schedule for a married couple is as follows.

Income	Rate
$0–$50,000	15%
$50,000–$75,000	25%

In addition, the Johnsons pay state income taxes at a rate of 5%. Assuming that state taxes are deductible in the calculation of Federal taxes, what is the Johnsons' total effective tax rate?

20. David is the owner of a local coffee bar located in State A with a sales tax rate of 6%. In 2003, David purchased $15,000 of coffee beans from a supplier located in a different state. In addition, he purchased $10,000 of other supplies including napkins, cups, sugar, and fresh milk and cream from the local warehouse shopping club. He also purchased a new coffee grinder for $400, an espresso machine for $5,000, and a refrigerator (to store the milk and cream) for $700. David's total sales during 2003 were $125,000.

David has a valid resale exemption certificate issued by A, and A exempts from sales tax the purchase of machinery and equipment used directly in manufacturing, processing, or fabricating. What is David's sales tax expense in 2003? How much sales tax does David collect and remit to A on behalf of other taxpayers?

21. The town of Bigville needs to raise $300 million next year from its tax on real property. If the assessed value of taxable real estate in Bigville is $10 billion, what will the tax rate be?

22. Continue your work from problem 21. The Brightlight Company owns real estate in Bigville with an assessed value of $1 million. How much property tax will the company pay next year?

23. The town of Smallville needs to raise $1 million next year from its tax on real property. If the assessed value of taxable real estate in Smallville is $25 million, what will the tax rate be?

24. A nonprofit organization that provides language training for teachers before they serve in developing countries purchases a hotel in Smallville. The assessed value of the hotel is $1.5 million. How will the purchase affect the town's property tax revenue?

25. In 2003, the County of Brownville had a real property tax rate of 3.5% and raised $10 million from the tax. What was the total assessed value of taxable real property in the County?

26. In 2004, the County of Brownville reassessed all real property in the County. The new assessed value was $350 million. If the County's budget calls for property tax revenue of $11 million, how much will the new tax rate be?

27. Company X (a manufacturer of clothing located in State Y) orders a $50,000 manufacturing loom (a piece of equipment used in the production of clothing) from a vendor located in the same state. Y applies a sales tax rate of 5%, and it exempts from the retail sales tax machinery and equipment used in the production of tangible personal property. Shipping charges (FOB destination) for the order are $500. How much sales tax will X pay? How much sales tax will X pay if the goods are shipped FOB origin?

28. Corporation X sells furniture. In 2003, the company generated sales of $800,000 but allowed a 5% early payment discount for customers paying within 10 days of placing an order. The company's total cash collections were $770,000. In addition, $20,000 of defective tables were returned by one buyer. While most of the furniture was picked up by customers at the store, shipping charges of $8,000 and handling charges of $2,000 were incurred for a large order shipped by common carrier. What are the total gross proceeds subject to the retail sales tax?

Ethics

29. Bruce and Kelly live in a state with a sales tax rate of 6%. Recently, they have been shopping for a computer for Kelly. They find a system they want for $2,000 in the local mall. While traveling in another state (with a sales tax rate of 3%), they find the same system advertised for the same price. Later while surfing the Internet, Kelly finds the system advertised for $1,900 plus shipping of $100. The Internet seller does not collect sales tax on the purchase. Which computer system should they purchase? Why?

30. W. W. Lean is a mail-order company with headquarters in Florida. The company sells fishing supplies and has retail locations in Georgia, North Carolina, and Virginia. Mail-order sales totaled $20 million. The sales by state and the corresponding sales tax rates were as follows.

State	Sales	Sales Tax Rate
Florida	$8 million	6%
Georgia	$2 million	4
South Carolina	$3 million	5
North Carolina	$4 million	4.5
Tennessee	$2 million	7
Virginia	$1 million	3.5

How much sales tax should W. W. Lean collect and remit to each state?

31. Company X (located in State Y with a sales tax of 5%) orders $50,000 of office machinery from a vendor located in the same state. Shipping charges (FOB shipping point) for the order will be $500. How much sales tax will Company X pay? How much sales tax will Company X pay if the goods are shipped FOB origin?

EXTENDER
Communications

32. Mark and Beth live in State A. Last year, their taxable income for state income tax purposes was $150,000. They paid $8,000 in state income tax and city and county property taxes of 1.3% on their personal residence (fair market value of $600,000 and an assessed value of $540,000). The couple also paid state and local sales taxes of $4,200 based on the state and local sales tax rate of 5%.

    Mark and Beth are contemplating moving to State B. While B does not have a state income tax, the state and local sales tax rate is 7%. Mark and Beth's property tax rate would be expected to increase to 3%. In addition, B assesses an intangibles tax equal to .15% of the fair market value of the intangible property (stocks and bonds) held at the end of the year. Mark and Beth's current investment portfolio is valued at approximately $900,000.

    Calculate Mark and Beth's total estimated state and local tax liability in A and B. Write a letter to the couple explaining your findings.

EXTENDER

33. John and Bill own property that qualifies as agricultural land and a reduction in valuation for property tax purposes. While the property is worth $1,000,000 as commercial property, its assessed value as agricultural land is only $200,000. If the county tax rate is 1% of the assessed value, how much does the agricultural land exemption save John and Bill?

Ethics

34. Continue with the situation described in Problem 33. Although John and Bill currently graze cattle on their land, they are discussing the sale of the property to a shopping mall developer. The developer has offered John and Bill $1.2 million for the property. Is it ethical for John and Bill to continue to claim the agricultural land exemption while they consider the offer?

Decision Making

35. Bradford Inc., a new business, is contemplating locating in either Kansas or Iowa. Kansas has a flat 4% corporate income tax rate, while Iowa has a progressive corporate rate of 6% on amounts up to $25,000, 8% on amounts between $25,000 and $100,000, 10% on amounts between $100,000 and $250,000, and 12% on amounts in excess of $250,000. However, Kansas property taxes on business machinery and equipment average 2.5% of fair market value, while Iowa does not tax business machinery and equipment.

    Bradford expects initially to invest $1 million in taxable business machinery and equipment, and it expects to earn $100,000 of annual Federal taxable income before deductions for state income tax and property tax for the next 10 years.

    a. Calculate Bradford's projected state income tax and property tax liabilities over the next 10 years, assuming the company does business in Kansas.
    b. Calculate Bradford's projected state income tax and property tax liabilities over the next 10 years, assuming the company does business in Iowa.
    c. Calculate Bradford's projected Federal income tax liabilities over the next 10 years.
    d. Calculate the net present value of the after-tax cash flow. Use a discount rate of 10%.
    e. In which state would you recommend Bradford locate its business?
    f. How would your answer change if Bradford expected to earn $450,000 Federal taxable income annually?

BRIDGE DISCIPLINE

1. Al and Jenny, age 22 and married with no children, expect to earn $60,000 taxable wages and $1,000 taxable interest income in 2004. They expect to spend about $35,000 on the purchase of restaurant food, clothing, rent, new furniture, and other items for their apartment. Assuming that the couple takes the standard deduction on their tax return, how much income tax will they owe? How much payroll tax will they pay? What is their average income tax rate? Assuming that a national sales tax of 23% would replace the current Federal income tax and payroll tax, would Al and Jenny be better off or worse off than under the current system?

Research Problems

THOMSON RIA

*Note: Solutions to Research Problems can be prepared by using the **RIA Checkpoint® Student Edition** online research product, which is available to accompany this text. It is also possible to prepare solutions to the Research Problems by using tax research materials found in a standard tax library.*

Research Problem 1. Examine the sales and use tax statutes of your home state and determine the following.

a. What type of sales tax is imposed by the state?
b. On whom is the legal imposition of the sales tax?
c. How is the sales price defined? What is included and what is excluded from this term?
d. What are the principal exemptions from the sales tax base?
e. Does the state have a machinery exemption? If so, how is machinery defined?
f. Are monies received for warranties subject to sales tax? What about extended warranties?

EXTENDER

Research Problem 2. Read the full decision of the U.S. Supreme Court in *Quill Corp. v. North Dakota*, 504 U.S. 298, 112 S.Ct. 1904 (1992).

a. Does the Court's decision imply that there is a different nexus standard for different taxes (e.g., sales tax versus income tax)?
b. In the absence of the Court's ruling in *National Bellas Hess*, would the Court have reached the same conclusion in *Quill*?
c. In your opinion, is the Court's decision limited to one industry (the mail-order industry), or does it have broad applicability to all businesses?

Research Problem 3. Research the specific food items that are exempt from sales tax in your state. Are soft drinks and candy taxed? What about prepared food like sandwiches from a deli? What about milk and bread purchased at a grocery store?

Internet Activity

Use the tax resources of the Internet to address the following questions. Do not restrict your search to the World Wide Web, but include a review of newsgroups and general reference materials, practitioner sites and resources, primary sources of the tax law, chat rooms and discussion groups, and other opportunities.

Research Problem 4. As a staff member of the governor of your state, you are charged with bringing new business into the jurisdiction and with keeping the industry and services that are already there. List some of the tax incentives that your state's Department of Revenue might provide to help meet these goals.

Communications

Research Problem 5. Write a letter to the secretary of revenue for your home state proposing adoption of one of the following provisions that does not currently exist in your state. Justify your proposal with a numerical example demonstrating the impact of the provision.

a. Subject repair and maintenance services to sales and use tax.
b. Subject professional services (accounting, legal, medical, etc.) to sales and use tax.
c. Exempt clothing under $100 from the sales tax.
d. Offer an annual "sales tax holiday" for back-to-school purchases of clothing and school supplies.

Communications

Research Problem 6. Go to **http://www.census.gov/govs/www/index.html**. How much general sales and gross receipts taxes were collected in your state during the last year reported by the U.S. Census Bureau? What percentage of the total tax collected came from general sales and gross receipts taxes? What are the three largest sources of tax revenues in your state? Summarize your findings for your instructor in graphical form.

Research Problem 7. Property tax rates may vary considerably from jurisdiction to jurisdiction. Find out the property tax rate assessed by the town or city in which you live and two or three neighboring jurisdictions. What are the tax rates in each? If they vary, why do you think they are different?

Communications

Research Problem 8. Go to **http://www.taxsites.com/state.html** or other sources on the Web and list three excise taxes collected by your state. Send this list by e-mail to your professor.

Research Problem 9. Has legislation been introduced in your state to adopt the model Streamlined Sales Tax Project? If so, when? If a vote has occurred, relate the results and effective dates.

Communications

Research Problem 10. Does Walmart.com collect sales tax when it ships an order into your state? Does Dell.com? Amazon.com? Crateandbarrel.com? SamGoody.com? If your state does not have a sales tax, answer for a neighboring state. Summarize your findings in a chart to e-mail to your instructor.

PART 4

Timing Issues

Tax planning principles dictate that the taxpayer strive to defer the recognition of income and accelerate the recognition of losses and deductions. The Code places several restrictions on the taxpayer's ability to achieve these goals, and Part IV addresses the most important of these tax accounting rules. Detailed analysis is provided with respect to qualified retirement plans and other means of deferred compensation for the executive.

Deferred Compensation

CHAPTER 11

LEARNING OBJECTIVES

After completing Chapter 11, you should be able to:

LO.1
Distinguish between qualified (defined contribution and defined benefit) and nonqualified compensation arrangements.

LO.2
Identify the qualification requirements for qualified plans.

LO.3
Discuss the tax consequences of qualified plans.

LO.4
Calculate the limitations on contributions to and benefits from qualified plans.

LO.5
Understand the qualified plan (Keogh plan) available to a self-employed person.

LO.6
Describe the benefits of the different types of Individual Retirement Accounts (IRAs).

LO.7
Understand the rationale for nonqualified deferred compensation plans and the related tax treatment.

LO.8
Explain the value of restricted property plans.

LO.9
Differentiate the tax treatment of qualified and nonqualified stock options.

http://wft.swlearning.com

OUTLINE

TAX TALK

A penny saved is a penny earned.

—Benjamin Franklin

Compensation is a very important component of any organization's cost structure, and in some cases, it is the most significant part. For example, in professional sports the product sold to the public consists entirely of the performance of the athletes who are very highly compensated compared to the average spectator in the stands. In 2003, compensation of the top 25 players averaged $14.8 million. Topping that list were the Texas Rangers' shortstop Alex Rodriguez ($22 million) [traded to the New York Yankees in 2004], the Boston Red Sox's Manny Ramirez ($20 million), and the Toronto Blue Jays' Carlos Delgado ($18.7 million).

Professional athletes are not the only employees who are being paid enormous amounts for their services. The compensation packages for Fortune 500 CEOs can be even larger when restricted stock awards and the exercise of employee stock options are combined with the paid salary and bonus. For 2003, for example, the CEO of Apple Computer, Inc., Steven Jobs, received a compensation package valued at $74.7 million, consisting entirely of restricted stock. In March, Jobs voluntarily canceled all of his outstanding options.[1]

[1]Apple Computer, Inc. SEC Definitive Proxy Statement Schedule 14A, March 11, 2004, p. 11.

Whether the employee is a professional athlete, corporate officer, or some other employee, his or her annual compensation consists of some combination of the following:

- Cash salary and bonus.
- Taxable fringe benefits.
- Interest-free loans (imputed interest).
- Nontaxable fringe benefits.
- Qualified deferred compensation.
- Qualified retirement plans.
- Incentive stock options (ISOs) and nonqualified stock options (NQSOs).
- Restricted property.
- Nonqualified deferred compensation.

Current compensation is generally taxable as ordinary income to the employee and tax deductible by the employer. The one exception is nontaxable fringe benefits. Examples of benefits that may be nontaxable include group term life insurance, medical reimbursement plans, company-supplied automobiles, and education expense reimbursement plans. Nontaxable fringe benefits are never taxable to the employee, but still are currently tax deductible to the employer. This beneficial tax treatment makes this form of compensation very desirable to employee and employer alike.

With **deferred compensation,** an employee receives compensation for services in a later period than that in which the services were performed—quite often during retirement years. The tax law encourages employers to offer deferred compensation plans to their employees to supplement the Federal Social Security retirement system.

Deferred compensation is not currently taxable to the employee and will produce a current tax deduction, a deferred tax deduction, or no deduction to the employer depending on the alternative used. Qualified deferred compensation plans receive particularly favorable tax treatment.

The contributor to a qualified retirement plan receives three major tax advantages:

- Contributions are immediately deductible by the employer.
- The employee is not taxed until these funds are made available to him or her.
- Income earned by the plan trust, which has received the contributions, is not subject to tax until made available to the employee.

Concept Summary 11–1 summarizes the general tax treatment of compensation alternatives to the employer and employee.

The employer and employee have different agendas for deferred compensation. The employer is interested in the amount and timing of any tax deduction that may be obtained and the cost of administering the deferral plan. The employee is concerned with saving for retirement or smoothing the income stream in a tax-deferred manner, the amount that can be deferred, and the current and future tax treatment of that deferral. The desirable outcome for each party is wholly dependent on current and future tax rates as well as the opportunities for investing the deferred funds. This chapter discusses the various methods available to defer the current taxation of compensation and the earnings on the deferred funds.

The type of deferred compensation plan available is contingent on the type of business entity being employed and on whether the recipient is an employee. A self-employed individual has fewer possibilities for deferring the current taxation of self-employment income and is generally limited to the use of a qualified retirement

CONCEPT SUMMARY 11–1

Tax Treatment of Compensation Alternatives

Type of Compensation	Employer	Employee
Salary, bonus, taxable fringe benefits, and imputed interest on interest-free loans	Currently deductible.	Currently taxable as ordinary income.
Nontaxable fringe benefits	Currently deductible.	Never taxable.
Qualified retirement plans	Current contribution is deductible.	Tax deferred.
Incentive stock options	Never deductible.	Tax deferred.
Nonqualified stock options	Deferred deduction.	Tax deferred.
Restricted property	Deferred deduction.	Tax deferred.
Qualified deferred compensation	Deferred deduction.	Tax deferred.
Nonqualified deferred compensation	Currently deductible or deferred deduction.	Currently taxable as ordinary income or tax deferred.

plan. However, there are many qualified retirement plans to choose from, with the same limits as employer-provided plans. This chapter discusses a number of the available plans including the following:

- Qualified pension, profit sharing, or stock bonus plans.*
- Qualified § 401(k) cash or deferred plans.
- Stock option plans.*
- Nonqualified deferred compensation plans.
- Restricted property plans.
- Various types of Individual Retirement Accounts (IRAs).
- Tax-deferred annuities.

*The stock bonus and stock option plans can be used only by corporate entities.

PLANNING STRATEGIES

Deferred Compensation

FRAMEWORK FOCUS: INCOME

STRATEGY ➤ POSTPONE RECOGNITION OF INCOME TO ACHIEVE TAX DEFERRAL.

One way for individuals to defer current taxes and save for retirement is to utilize one of the many available deferred compensation plans. The type of plan used will depend in part on the level of compensation earned and on whether the individual is a participant in a qualified plan.

Fox example, for an individual making over $205,000 per year in earned income, the amount that can be deferred in a qualified plan is limited. This individual should take advantage of one of the many nonqualified compensation arrangements such as employee stock options, restricted property, and nonqualified deferred compensation plans.

For individuals who are not participants in a qualified plan, the various types of Individual Retirement Accounts (traditional and Roth) may be appropriate choices.

TAX IN THE NEWS

Become a Millionaire

A small annual investment can grow into a $1 million balance through the annual compounding of the tax-deferred earnings. An individual who saves $3,000 annually from age 22 to 35 (total investment of $42,000) will have $1,035,643 at age 65 (assuming an annual 9 percent compounded rate of return).

The earlier you start saving, the better off you will be.

LO.1

Distinguish between qualified (defined contribution and defined benefit) and nonqualified compensation arrangements.

Qualified Pension, Profit Sharing, and Stock Bonus Plans

To ensure that retired people will not be dependent solely on government programs, the Federal government encourages private pension and profit sharing plans. Therefore, the Federal tax law provides substantial tax benefits for plans that meet certain requirements (qualified plans). The major requirement for qualification is that a plan not discriminate in favor of highly compensated employees.

TYPES OF PLANS

The tax law defines two basic types of qualified plans: defined benefit plans and defined contribution plans.

Defined Benefit Plans. A **defined benefit plan** includes a formula that defines the benefits employees are to receive.[2] Under such a plan, an employer must make annual contributions based upon actuarial computations that will be sufficient to pay the required retirement benefits. If a plan document permits, employees may make contributions to the plan. A separate account is not maintained for each participant. Benefits are generally measured by and based on such factors as years of service and employee compensation. Employer contributions under a defined benefit plan must not depend on profits. A defined benefit plan provides some sense of security for employees since the benefits may be expressed in fixed dollar amounts.

Defined Contribution Plans. **Defined contribution plans** (profit sharing, money purchase pension, and stock bonus plans) define the amount the employer is required to contribute (e.g., a flat dollar amount, an amount based on a special formula, or an amount equal to a certain percentage of compensation). A separate account must be maintained for each participant. Benefits are based solely on (1) the amount contributed and (2) income from the fund that accrues to the participant's account.[3] Consequently, actuarial calculations are not required to determine the employer's annual contribution. Upon retirement, an employee's distribution amount depends on the value of his or her account. Although it is not mandatory, a plan may require or permit employee contributions to the trust fund.

[2] § 414(j).

[3] § 414(i).

CONCEPT SUMMARY 11–2

Defined Benefit Plan and Defined Contribution Plan Compared

Defined Benefit Plan	Defined Contribution Plan
Includes a pension plan.	Includes profit sharing, stock bonus, money purchase, target benefit, qualified cash or deferred compensation, employee stock ownership plans, and some pension plans.
Determinable benefits based upon years of service and average compensation. Benefits calculated by a formula.	An account for each participant. Ultimate benefits depend upon contributions and investment performance.
Maximum annual *benefits* payable may not exceed the smaller of (1) $165,000 (in 2004)* or (2) 100% of the participant's average earnings in the three highest years of employment.	Maximum annual *contribution* to an account may not exceed the smaller of (1) $41,000** (in 2004) or (2) 100% of the participant's compensation (25% for a profit sharing plan, money purchase plan, or stock bonus plan).
Forfeitures must reduce subsequent funding costs and cannot increase the benefits any participant can receive under the plan.	Forfeitures may be allocated to the accounts of remaining participants.
Subject to minimum funding requirement in order to avoid penalties.	Exempt from funding requirements.
Greater administrative and actuarial costs and greater reporting requirements.	Costs and reporting requirements less burdensome.
Subject to plan termination insurance.	Not subject to plan termination insurance.
More favorable to employees who are older when plan is adopted since it is possible to fund higher benefits over a shorter period.	More favorable to younger employees since, over a longer period, higher benefits may result.

*This amount is subject to indexing annually in $5,000 increments.
**This amount is subject to indexing annually in $1,000 increments.

EXAMPLE 1

The qualified money purchase pension plan of Rose Company calls for both the employer and the employee to contribute annually to the pension trust an amount equal to 5% of the employee's compensation. Since the employer's rate of contribution is fixed, this pension plan is a defined contribution plan. If the plan called for contributions sufficient to provide retirement benefits equal to 30% of the employee's average salary for the last five years of employment, it would be a defined benefit plan. ■

There are a number of different types of defined contribution plans, but they all have one common characteristic. The employee's retirement benefit will depend solely on the amount of plan contributions and the earnings on those contributions. Unlike with a defined benefit plan, a poor investment performance may severely decrease (or eliminate altogether) the size of the employee's retirement benefit.

Concept Summary 11–2 compares and contrasts a defined benefit plan and a defined contribution plan.

Specific Types of Defined Benefit and Defined Contribution Plans. Among the specific types of qualified retirement plans are pension plans, profit sharing plans, stock bonus plans, and cash balance plans.

Pension Plans. Although **pension plans** usually are classified in the defined benefit category, they can also be classified in the defined contribution category.

TAX IN THE NEWS

Pension Fund Profits

Many investors may not be aware that the earnings reported by corporations include investment income earned by the company's employee pension fund. How many of IBM's shareholders, for example, were aware that in 2000 about 10 percent of the company's $11.5 billion in pretax profits came from investment income earned by its employee pension fund, not from selling computers? Furthermore, the investment income earned by a company's employee pension fund is not actual earnings, but is based on an actuarial calculation using an expected annual rate of return. During the past few years, the assumed rate of return has ranged from 9 to 10 percent. If the companies in the Standard and Poor's 500 lowered their expected annual rate of return to 6.5 percent, their earnings would be approximately $30 billion lower.

SOURCE: Adapted from Jonathan Finer, "Pension Funds' New Realities Drag Profits Down," *Washington Post*, October 23, 2002, p. E01.

The usual pension plan is a deferred compensation arrangement that provides for systematic payments of definitely determinable retirement benefits to employees who meet the requirements set forth in the plan. Benefits are generally measured by and based on such factors as years of service and employee compensation. Employer contributions under a defined benefit pension plan must not depend on profits. In addition, they must be sufficient to provide definitely determinable benefits on some actuarial basis.

A **money purchase pension plan** is a defined contribution plan that requires the employer to make annual contributions to each employee's account. The contributions are based on a fixed formula and cannot be based on profits or some similar criteria.[4] Normally, plan contributions are based on a percentage of the employee's compensation, with the amounts contributed statutorily limited. The employee's retirement benefit, as with other defined contribution plans, will be based on the value of the participant's account at the time the benefits are to begin.

Profit Sharing Plans. A **profit sharing plan** is a deferred compensation arrangement established and maintained by an employer to provide for employee participation in the company's profits. Profit sharing plans are classified in the defined contribution category. Contributions are paid from the employer's current or accumulated profits to a trustee and are commingled in a single trust fund. Thus, an employer does not have to have a profit for the current year to make a contribution (the contribution can be from accumulated profits).

In a profit sharing plan, a separate account is maintained for each participant. The plan must provide a definite, predetermined formula for allocating the contributions made to the trustee among the participants. Likewise, it must include a definite, predetermined formula for distributing the accumulated funds after a fixed number of years, on the attainment of a stated age, or on the occurrence of certain events such as illness, layoff, or retirement. A company is not required to contribute a definite, predetermined amount to the plan, although substantial and

[4]Rev.Rul. 72–302, 1972–1 C.B. 111, and Rev.Rul. 73–412, 1973–2 C.B. 125.

recurring contributions must be made to meet the permanency requirement. Forfeitures arising under this plan do not have to be used to reduce the employer's contribution. Instead, forfeitures may be used to increase the individual accounts of the remaining participants as long as these increases do not result in prohibited discrimination.[5] Since a profit sharing plan does not necessarily emphasize retirement income, benefits to employees may normally be distributed through lump-sum payouts.

Stock Bonus Plans. A **stock bonus plan** is another form of deferred compensation. Stock bonus plans are classified in the defined contribution category. The employer establishes and maintains the plan in order to contribute shares of its stock. The contributions need not be dependent on the employer's profits. A stock bonus plan is subject to the same requirements as a profit sharing plan for purposes of allocating and distributing the stock among the employees.[6] Any benefits of the plan are distributable in the form of stock of the employer company, except that distributable fractional shares may be paid in cash.

Cash Balance Plans. A **cash balance plan** is a hybrid plan that contains some characteristics of both a defined contribution plan and a defined benefit plan. These new plans are funded by the employer, and the employer bears the investment risks and rewards. Thus, the employer bears the mortality risk if an employee elects to receive benefits in the form of an annuity and lives beyond normal life expectancy. But like defined contribution plans, a cash balance plan establishes allocations to individual accounts. The payout for an employee depends on how much builds up over time in the employee's account and not on a formula based on years of service and preretirement pay.

LO.2

Identify the qualification requirements for qualified plans.

QUALIFICATION REQUIREMENTS

To be *qualified*, and thereby to receive favorable tax treatment, a plan must satisfy the following requirements:

- Exclusive benefit requirement.
- Nondiscrimination requirements.
- Participation and coverage requirements.
- Vesting requirements.
- Distribution requirements.

These qualification rules are highly technical and numerous. Thus, an employer should submit a retirement plan to the IRS for a determination letter regarding the qualified status of the plan and trust. A favorable determination letter may be expected within 6 to 12 months, indicating that the plan meets the qualification requirements and that the trust is tax-exempt. However, the continued qualification of the plan depends upon its actual operations. Therefore, the operations of the plan should be reviewed periodically.

DIGGING DEEPER 1

Find more information on this topic at our Web site: ***http://wft-advanced.swlearning.com***.

Exclusive Benefit. The qualified plan must exclusively benefit employees and plan beneficiaries. It cannot be used as a device to distribute profits to shareholders. This means that the plan cannot discriminate in favor of select groups of highly

[5] Reg. §§ 1.401–1(b) and 1.401–4(a)(1)(iii).

[6] Reg. § 1.401–1(b)(1)(iii).

BRIDGE DISCIPLINE

Bridge to Finance

Succession planning, employee ownership, tax-free capital infusion, and creation of a market for a closely held company's stock are just four of the uses of an employee stock ownership plan (ESOP).

- An ESOP is a qualified defined contribution plan that invests primarily in the stock of the sponsoring corporation. The corporation is allowed to make deductible money contributions of up to 25 percent of participant compensation. The contribution funds can then be used to purchase corporate stock from the corporation, the owner-employee, or outside shareholders.
- An ESOP is allowed to borrow money to acquire the sponsoring company's stock (leveraged ESOP). This is in sharp contrast to other qualified plans, which are not permitted to use debt finance investing without incurring taxable income.
- The amounts contributed to the ESOP to pay the interest charges on the acquisition loan are fully deductible and are not subject to the 25 percent contribution limitation.
- The realized gain on the sale of qualified stock to an ESOP can be deferred provided that the ESOP will own at least 30 percent of each class of outstanding stock immediately after the sale (§ 1042). The deferral is accomplished by the shareholder reinvesting the proceeds in qualified replacement stock. The shareholder's basis in the qualified replacement stock will equal its purchase price less any unrecognized gain.
- The employer is allowed to deduct any dividends paid to the ESOP, provided that the dividends are paid to the plan's participants no later than 90 days after the close of the plan year [§ 404(k)].

compensated employee-shareholders. To ensure this, there are a number of *prohibited transactions* restricting investments and dealings between the plan and *disqualified persons*.[7] For example, the lending of money between the plan and the employer is a prohibited transaction.

Nondiscrimination Requirements. The contributions and benefits under a plan must *not discriminate* in favor of highly compensated employees. A plan is not considered discriminatory merely because contributions and benefits are proportional to compensation.[8] For example, a pension plan that provides for the allocation of employer contributions based upon a flat 3 percent of each employee's compensation would not be discriminatory even though highly paid employees receive greater benefits.

Participation and Coverage Requirements. A qualified plan must provide, at a minimum, that all employees in the covered group who are 21 years of age are eligible to participate after completing one year of service. A year of service is generally defined as the completion of 1,000 hours of service within a measuring period of 12 consecutive months. As an alternative, where the plan provides that 100 percent of an employee's accrued benefits will be vested upon entering the plan, the employee's participation may be postponed until the later of age 21 or

[7]§ 4975(c).

[8]§§ 401(a)(4) and (5).

■ **TABLE 11–1**
Three- to Seven-Year Vesting

Years of Service	Nonforfeitable Percentage
3	20%
4	40%
5	60%
6	80%
7 or more	100%

two years from the date of employment. Once the age and service requirements are met, an employee must begin participating no later than the *earlier* of the following:

- The first day of the first plan year beginning after the date on which the requirements were satisfied.
- Six months after the date on which the requirements were satisfied.[9]

EXAMPLE 2

Coffee Corporation has a calendar year retirement plan covering its employees. The corporation adopts the most restrictive eligibility rules permitted. Wilma, age 21, is hired on January 31, 2003, and meets the service requirement over the next 12 months (completes at least 1,000 hours by January 31, 2004). Wilma must be included in this plan no later than July 31, 2004, because the 6-month limitation would be applicable. If the company had adopted the two-year participation rule, Wilma must be included in the plan no later than July 31, 2005. ■

Since a qualified plan must be primarily for the benefit of employees and be nondiscriminatory, the plan has to cover a reasonable percentage of the company employees.[10]

Vesting Requirements. The purpose of the **vesting requirements** is to protect an employee who has worked a reasonable period of time for an employer from losing employer contributions because of being fired or changing jobs. An employee's right to accrued benefits derived from his or her own contributions must be nonforfeitable from the date of contribution. The accrued benefits derived from employer contributions must be nonforfeitable in accordance with one of *two alternative minimum vesting schedules* [except for § 401(m) arrangements].

To satisfy the *first alternative*, a participant must have a nonforfeitable right to 100 percent of his or her accrued benefits derived from employer contributions upon completion of not more than five years of service (five-year or cliff vesting). The *second alternative* is satisfied if a participant has a nonforfeitable right at least equal to a percentage of the accrued benefits derived from employer contributions as depicted in Table 11–1 (graded vesting). Of the two alternatives, cliff vesting minimizes administration expenses for a company and provides more vesting for a long-term employee.

EXAMPLE 3

Mitch has six years of service completed as of February 2, 2004, his employment anniversary date. If his defined benefit plan has a five-year (cliff) vesting schedule, 100% of Mitch's accrued benefits are vested. If the plan uses the graded vesting rule, Mitch's nonforfeitable percentage is 80%. ■

[9]§§ 410(a)(1)(A) and (B) and 410(a)(4).

[10]§ 410(b).

Distribution Requirements. Uniform *minimum distribution rules* exist for all qualified defined benefit and defined contribution plans, traditional Individual Retirement Accounts (IRAs) and annuities, unfunded deferred compensation plans of state and local governments and tax-exempt employers, and tax-sheltered custodial accounts and annuities. Distributions to a participant must begin by April 1 of the calendar year *following the later* of (1) the calendar year in which the employee attains age 70½ or (2) the calendar year in which the employee retires. Thus, an employee can delay receiving distributions until retirement. However, distributions to a 5 percent owner or a traditional IRA holder must begin no later than April 1 of the calendar year *following* the year in which the 5 percent owner or the IRA holder reaches age 70½.[11] A holder of a Roth IRA does *not* have to take a distribution by April 1 of the calendar year following the calendar year in which the holder attains age 70½. That is, there is no point in time at which the holder of a Roth IRA must begin receiving distributions.

Minimum annual distributions must be made over the life of the participant or the lives of the participant and a designated individual beneficiary. The amount of the required minimum distribution for a particular year is determined by dividing the account balance as of December 31 of the prior year by the applicable life expectancy. The life expectancy of the owner and his or her beneficiary is based upon the expected return multiples in the Regulations, using ages attained within the calendar year the participant reaches age 70½.[12]

EXAMPLE 4

Beth reaches age 70½ in 2004, and she will also be age 71 in 2004. Her retirement account has a balance of $120,000 on December 31, 2003. If Beth is retired, a 5% owner, or the holder of a traditional IRA, she must withdraw $7,843 for the 2004 calendar year, assuming her multiple is 15.3 ($120,000 ÷ 15.3). This distribution need not be made until April 1, 2005, but a second distribution must be made by December 31, 2005. ■

Failure to make a minimum required distribution to a particular participant results in a *50 percent nondeductible excise tax* on the excess in any taxable year of the amount that should have been distributed over the amount that actually was distributed. The tax is imposed on the individual required to take the distribution (the payee).[13] The Secretary of the Treasury is authorized to waive the tax for a given taxpayer year if the taxpayer is able to establish that the shortfall is due to reasonable error and that reasonable steps are being taken to remedy the shortfall.

EXAMPLE 5

Assume that Beth in Example 4 withdraws only $7,000 for 2004. Because she has failed to meet the minimum distribution requirements, she will be assessed a penalty by the IRS of $422 [($7,843 – $7,000) × 50%]. ■

LO.3

Discuss the tax consequences of qualified plans.

TAX CONSEQUENCES TO THE EMPLOYEE AND EMPLOYER

In General. Although employer contributions to qualified plans are generally deductible immediately (subject to contribution and deductibility rules), these amounts are not subject to taxation until distributed to employees.[14] If benefits are paid with respect to an employee (to a creditor of the employee, a child of the employee, etc.), the benefits paid are treated as if paid to the employee. When benefits are distributed to employees, or paid with respect to an employee, the employer does not receive another deduction.

The tax benefit to the employee amounts to a substantial tax deferral and may be viewed as an interest-free loan from the government to the trust fund. Another advantage of a qualified plan is that any income earned by the trust is not taxable

[11] § 401(a)(9).
[12] Reg. § 1.72–9.
[13] § 4974(a).
[14] § 402(a)(1).

GLOBAL TAX ISSUES

Covering Expatriate Employees

Can an employer cover individuals employed outside the United States in a qualified retirement plan? This question often arises when an employee is transferred from the United States to a foreign affiliate of the employer.

The hurdle to overcome is the exclusive benefit rule in § 401(a): the qualified plan must be maintained for the exclusive benefit of the employees of the company that sponsors the plan.

If a company conducts its foreign operations through branches that are part of the U.S. entity, the employee can qualify for the plan. Likewise, all employees of all corporations that are members of a controlled group of corporations can be covered. A controlled group would include both a brother-sister group and a parent-subsidiary group.

to the trust.[15] Employees, in effect, are taxed on such earnings when they receive the retirement benefits.

The taxation of amounts received by employees in periodic or installment payments is generally subject to the annuity rules in § 72. In most situations, employee contributions have been subject to tax previously and are therefore included in the employee's *investment in the contract.* Two other alternative options are available for benefit distributions. A taxpayer may (1) receive the distribution in a lump-sum payment or (2) roll over the benefits into an IRA or another qualified employer retirement plan.

Lump-Sum Distributions from Qualified Plans. A **lump-sum distribution** occurs when an employee receives his or her entire payout from a qualified plan in a single payment rather than receiving the amount in installments. The annuity rules do not apply to a lump-sum distribution. All such payments are taxed in one year. Since lump-sum payments have been accumulated over a number of years, bunching retirement benefits into one taxable year may impose a high tax burden because of progressive rates. To overcome this bunching effect, for many years the tax law has provided favorable treatment for certain lump-sum distributions. Major changes were made in the lump-sum distribution rules by TRA of 1986. Transitional provisions allow a participant who reached age 50 before January 1, 1986 (born before 1936) to elect the pre-1987 rules on a limited basis. Otherwise, favorable treatment for lump-sum distributions is not available.

DIGGING DEEPER 2

Find more information on this topic at our Web site: ***http://wft-advanced.swlearning.com.***

Rollover Treatment. A taxpayer who receives a distribution can avoid current taxation by rolling the distribution into another qualified employer retirement plan or into an IRA.[16] The taxation of the distribution is deferred until distributions are made from the recipient qualified employer retirement plan or IRA. The rollover can be *direct* with the balance in the account going directly from a qualified employer retirement plan to another qualified employer retirement plan or an IRA. The rollover can be *indirect* with the proceeds going to the taxpayer who has 60 days to transfer the proceeds into another qualified employer retirement plan or an IRA. A benefit of the direct rollover is that it is not subject to the 20 percent withholding applicable to indirect rollovers.[17]

[15] § 501(a).
[16] § 402(c).
[17] § 3405(c).

PLANNING STRATEGIES

Qualified Plans

FRAMEWORK FOCUS: INCOME

STRATEGY ➤ **POSTPONE RECOGNITION OF INCOME TO ACHIEVE TAX DEFERRAL.**

FRAMEWORK FOCUS: DEDUCTIONS

STRATEGY ➤ **MAXIMIZE DEDUCTIBLE AMOUNTS.**

Qualified plans provide maximum tax benefits for employers because the employer receives an immediate tax deduction for contributions to such plans and the income that is earned on the contributions is not taxable to the employer. The employee is also a winner because the contributions and trust earnings are not taxable until the plan makes a distribution to the employee.

When an employee changes jobs, the employee's vested balance in the employer's qualified plan can be rolled over tax deferred into the employee's own IRA or another qualified employer retirement plan. If an employee is a participant in a nonqualified plan, however, there may be no way to defer taxation when the employee changes jobs.

Early Distributions. If a taxpayer receives an *early distribution* from a qualified retirement plan, a 10 percent penalty tax, in addition to the regular income tax, is levied on the full amount of the distribution included in gross income.[18] The penalty tax is assessed for early distributions from a qualified defined benefit plan or defined contribution plan, a tax-sheltered annuity or custodial account, or a traditional IRA. However, the following distributions will *not* be treated as early distributions:

- Distributions made on or after the date the employee attains age 59½.
- Distributions made to a beneficiary (or estate of an employee) on or after the death of the employee.
- Distributions attributable to the employee's disability.
- Distributions made as part of a scheduled series of substantially equal periodic payments (not less frequent than annually) for the life of the participant (or joint lives of the participant and the participant's beneficiary).
- Distributions made to an employee after separation from service because of early retirement under the plan after attaining age 55. This exception to early distribution treatment does not apply to a traditional IRA.
- Distributions used to pay medical expenses to the extent that the expenses are deductible under § 213 (whether or not the taxpayer itemizes deductions).
- IRA distributions used to pay qualified higher education expenses of the taxpayer, the spouse, or any child or grandchild of the taxpayer or the taxpayer's spouse.
- IRA distributions up to $10,000 that are used to pay expenses incurred by qualified first-time home buyers.

LO.4

Calculate the limitations on contributions to and benefits from qualified plans.

LIMITATIONS ON CONTRIBUTIONS TO AND BENEFITS FROM QUALIFIED PLANS

In General. Congress has imposed strict limitations on the contributions to and benefits from qualified plans (§ 415). These limits must be written into the plan document, and exceeding them will cause the plan to be terminated. Limits also exist on the tax deductibility of these contributions (§ 404). The limits are often

[18] § 72(t).

very technical, and a complete discussion is beyond the scope of this textbook. The following paragraphs cover the basic rules on both benefit and contribution limits.

Defined Contribution Plans. The employer's tax-deductible contribution to a profit sharing, money purchase, or stock bonus plan is limited to 25 percent of the compensation paid to employees participating in the plan.[19] The annual additions to an employee's account cannot exceed the smaller of $41,000[20] (in 2004) or 100 percent of the employee's compensation.[21] The annual additions for any year consist of employer contributions, employee contributions, and allocated forfeitures.

EXAMPLE 6

Cougar, Inc., maintains a qualified profit sharing plan for its employees. During 2004, Cougar paid a total of $400,000 of compensation to employees participating in the plan. Cougar's maximum tax-deductible contribution to the profit sharing plan is $100,000. ■

Defined Benefit Plans. Under a *defined benefit plan*, the annual benefit payable to an employee is limited to the smaller of $165,000 (in 2004)[22] or 100 percent of the employee's average compensation for the highest three years of employment. This benefit limit is subject to a $10,000 *de minimis* floor. The annual benefit limits are reduced if the employee has less than 10 years of participation in the plan or years of service with the employer.

The maximum deduction permitted for contributions to a defined benefit pension plan is determined actuarially. The calculation takes into consideration the stated benefit, the age of the participants, and the expected plan earnings. Essentially, the actuary is determining how much should be contributed to the plan to ensure that there will be future funds available to purchase an annuity for the employee/participant at the time of retirement.

DIGGING DEEPER 3

Find more information on this topic at our Web site: ***http://wft-advanced.swlearning.com.***

EXAMPLE 7

Adam's average compensation for the highest three years of employment is $87,000. The defined benefit plan would not qualify if the plan provides for benefits in excess of the smaller of (1) $87,000 or (2) $165,000 for Adam in 2004 (assuming normal retirement age). ■

Provisions Applicable to Both Defined Benefit Plans and Defined Contribution Plans. The amount of compensation that may be taken into account under either a defined benefit plan or a defined contribution plan is limited to $205,000 (in 2004).[23] Thus, the benefits highly compensated individuals receive may be smaller as a percentage of their pay than those received by non-highly compensated employees.

EXAMPLE 8

Swan Corporation has a defined contribution plan with a 10% contribution formula. An employee earning less than $205,000 in 2004 would not be affected by this includible compensation limitation. However, an employee earning $410,000 in 2004 would have only 5% of compensation allocated to his or her account because of the $205,000 limit on includible compensation. ■

EXAMPLE 9

In 2004, Rock, Inc., provided a defined benefit plan that used the average of the employee's three highest years of compensation in determining the annual benefit. Joan's three highest years of compensation consist of $160,000 for 2002, $300,000 for 2003, and $320,000 for 2004.

[19] § 404(a)(3).
[20] This amount is indexed for inflation [§ 415(d)(4)]. The indexed amount for 2003 was $40,000.
[21] §§ 415(c) and (d).
[22] This amount is indexed annually.
[23] §§ 401(a)(17) and 404(l). This amount is indexed in $5,000 increments. The indexed amount for 2002 was $200,000, and for 2003 it was also $200,000.

In calculating her average compensation, she is permitted to use only $200,000 of the $300,000 received in 2003 and $205,000 of the $320,000 received in 2004. Her average compensation for the benefit formula is $188,333. ■

The employer's contribution is deductible in the tax year such amounts are paid to the pension trust. However, both cash and accrual basis employers may defer the payment of contributions with respect to any tax year until the date fixed for filing the taxpayer's Federal income tax return for that year (including extensions).[24] In effect, the corporation is allowed a deduction to the extent it is compelled to make such contributions to satisfy the funding requirement.

DIGGING DEEPER 4 DIGGING DEEPER 5

Find more information on these topics at our Web site: ***http://wft-advanced.swlearning.com.***

§ 401(k) PLANS

General. A **§ 401(k) plan** allows participants to elect either to receive up to $13,000 (in 2004)[25] in cash (taxed currently) or to have a contribution made on their behalf to a profit sharing or stock bonus plan. The plan may also be in the form of a salary-reduction agreement between an eligible participant and an employer under which a contribution will be made only if the participant elects to reduce his or her compensation or to forgo an increase in compensation. Concept Summary 11–5 later in the chapter compares a § 401(k) plan with a traditional IRA.

Any pretax amount elected by the employee as a plan contribution is not includible in gross income and is 100 percent vested. Any employer contributions are tax deferred, as are earnings on contributions in the plan.

EXAMPLE 10

Sam participates in a § 401(k) plan of his employer. The plan permits the participants to choose between a full salary or a reduced salary where the reduction becomes a before-tax contribution to a retirement plan. Sam elects to contribute 10% of his annual compensation of $30,000 to the plan. Income taxes are paid on only $27,000. No income taxes are paid on the $3,000—or on any earnings—until it is distributed from the plan to Sam. The main benefit of a § 401(k) plan is that Sam can shift a portion of his income to a later taxable year. ■

The maximum employee annual elective contribution to a § 401(k) plan is $13,000 (in 2004), but that amount is reduced dollar for dollar by other salary-reduction contributions to tax-sheltered annuities and simplified employee pension plans. Elective contributions in excess of the maximum limitation are taxable in the year of deferral. These amounts may be distributed from the plan tax-free before April 15 of the following year. Excess amounts not timely distributed will be taxable in the year of distribution, even though they were included in income in the year of deferral. Annual elective contributions are also limited by complicated nondiscrimination requirements and the defined contribution plan limitations.

A person who has attained age 50 by the end of the tax year can make catch-up contributions of $1,000 for 2002, $2,000 for 2003, $3,000 for 2004, $4,000 for 2005, and $5,000 for 2006 and thereafter.[26]

EXAMPLE 11

Heather is age 53 in 2004. Heather is able to make additional catch-up elective deferrals of $1,000 for 2002 (beyond the $11,000 limit), $2,000 for 2003 (beyond the $12,000 limit), and $3,000 for 2004 (beyond the $13,000 limit). ■

---

[24] §§ 404(a)(1) and (6).

[25] §§ 402(g)(1) and (4). This amount is increased in $1,000 increments starting in 2003 until it reaches $15,000 in 2006. It will be indexed in $500 increments in years after 2006. For 2003, the amount was $12,000.

[26] The $5,000 amount will be indexed in $500 increments in 2007 and thereafter.

A 10 percent excise tax is imposed on the employer for excess contributions not withdrawn from the plan within 2½ months after the close of the plan year. The plan will lose its qualified status if these excess contributions (and any related income) are not withdrawn by the end of the plan year following the plan year in which the excess contributions were made.[27]

EXAMPLE 12

Carmen, age 36, is an employee of a manufacturing corporation. She defers $15,000 in a § 401(k) plan in 2004. The $2,000 excess over the $13,000 limit, along with the appropriate earnings, must be returned to Carmen by April 15, 2005. This $2,000 excess amount plus related income is taxable to her in 2004 and will be taxed again upon distribution (if made after April 15, 2005). There will be a 10% tax on Carmen's employer on any excess contributions not returned within 2½ months after the close of the plan year. ■

SIMPLE Plans. Employers with 100 or fewer employees who do not maintain another qualified retirement plan may establish a *savings incentive match plan for employees* (SIMPLE plan).[28] The plan can be in the form of a § 401(k) plan or an IRA. The SIMPLE plan is not subject to the nondiscrimination rules that are normally applicable to § 401(k) plans.

DIGGING DEEPER 6

Find more information on this topic at our Web site: ***http://wft-advanced.swlearning.com.***

Distributions from a SIMPLE plan generally are taxed in the same manner as an IRA.

LO.5

Understand the qualified plan (Keogh plan) available to a self-employed person.

Retirement Plans for Self-Employed Individuals

Self-employed individuals (e.g., partners and sole proprietors) and their employees are eligible to receive qualified retirement benefits under the SIMPLE plans described above or under what are known as **H.R. 10 (Keogh) plans**. The contribution and benefit limits for Keogh plans are the same as the general corporate provisions discussed previously.

COVERAGE REQUIREMENTS

Generally, the corporate coverage rules apply to Keogh plans.[29] An individual covered under a qualified corporate plan as an employee may also establish a Keogh plan for earnings from self-employment.

CONTRIBUTION LIMITATIONS

A self-employed individual's annual contribution to a *defined contribution* Keogh plan is limited to the lesser of $41,000 (in 2004) or 100 percent of earned income after adjusting for 50 percent of the self-employment tax and the Keogh deduction.[30] However, if the defined contribution plan is a profit sharing plan or a stock bonus plan, a self-employed individual's maximum deduction is limited to 25 percent of adjusted earned income,[31] with adjusted earned income limited to $205,000 for 2004.

DIGGING DEEPER 7

Find more information on this topic at our Web site: ***http://wft-advanced.swlearning.com.***

[27] § 4979(a).
[28] § 408(p).
[29] § 401(d).
[30] §§ 401(c)(1), 401(c)(2), 1402(a), 401(c)(2)(A)(v), and 415(c)(1).
[31] § 404(a)(3).

TAX FACT

COMPENSATION AND RETIREMENT PLANS

Taxpayers reported more that $4 trillion in salaries and wages for 2000 and 2001. Less that 4 percent of returns reported contributions to IRAs, and less than 2 percent reported contributions to Keogh plans.

	Tax Year 2000 (In Millions)	Tax Year 2001 (In Millions)	Percentage Increase (Decrease)
Salaries and wages	$4,456,167	$4,565,229	+2.4%
Number of returns	110.2	111.2	+.9%
Payments to IRAs	$7,477	$7,407	–.9%
Number of returns	3.51	3.45	–1.7%
Payments to Keogh plans	$12,475	$13,114	+5.1%
Number of returns	1.29	1.29	—

Source: IRS Tax Statistics.

EXAMPLE 13

Pat, a partner, has earned income of $150,000 in 2004 (after the deduction for one-half of self-employment tax). The maximum contribution Pat may make to a defined contribution Keogh plan is $41,000, the lesser of $150,000 or $41,000. ■

EXAMPLE 14

Terry, a self-employed accountant, has a profit sharing plan with a contribution rate of 15% of compensation. Terry's earned income after the deduction of one-half of self-employment tax, but before the Keogh contribution, is $250,000. Terry's contribution is limited to $26,739 ($205,000 – .15X = X), since X = $178,261 and .15 × $178,261 = $26,739. ■

Under a *defined benefit* Keogh plan, the annual benefit payable to the self-employed individual or employee is limited to the smaller of $165,000 (in 2004) or 100 percent of the average compensation for the three highest years of employment.[32] Compensation for the self-employed individual means earned income adjusted for 50 percent of the self-employment tax and the deduction to the Keogh plan.

Although a Keogh plan must be established before the end of the year in question, contributions may be made up to the normal filing date for that year.

PLANNING STRATEGIES

Self-Employed Retirement Plans

FRAMEWORK FOCUS: DEDUCTIONS

STRATEGY ➤ ACCELERATE RECOGNITION OF DEDUCTIONS TO ACHIEVE TAX DEFERRAL.

A self-employed individual has until the tax return due date, including extensions, to make a contribution to a Keogh plan for the prior year. To take advantage of this, the plan must be established by the end of the year to which the contribution is attributable.

Since the deductibility of contributions to IRAs has been restricted for many middle- and upper-income taxpayers, a Keogh or SEP IRA plan may be an attractive alternative.

[32] § 415(b)(1). This amount is indexed annually.

■ **TABLE 11–2**
Phaseout of IRA Deduction of an Active Participant in 2004

AGI Filing Status	Phaseout Begins*	Phaseout Ends
Single and head of household	$45,000	$55,000
Married, filing joint return	65,000	75,000
Married, filing separate return	–0–	10,000

*The starting point for the phaseout is increased each year through 2007 for married filing jointly and through 2005 for other filing statuses.

LO.6

Describe the benefits of the different types of Individual Retirement Accounts (IRAs).

Individual Retirement Accounts (IRAs)

GENERAL RULES

Any individual under age 70½ with earned income can establish his or her own **Individual Retirement Account (IRA).** The contribution ceiling is the smaller of $3,000 (or $6,000 for spousal IRAs) for years 2002–2004 or 100 percent of earned income.[33]

An individual who attains the age of 50 by the end of the tax year can make additional catch-up IRA contributions. The maximum contribution limit is increased by $500 for the period 2002 through 2005 and $1,000 for years after 2005.

Traditional IRAs. The tax treatment of the contribution will depend on whether the taxpayer is an active participant in a qualified plan. If the taxpayer is not an active participant, then the contribution is fully deductible within the limits described above. If the taxpayer is an active participant, then the contribution deduction is phased out proportionately between certain modified adjusted gross income (AGI) ranges, as shown in Table 11–2.[34]

DIGGING DEEPER 8

Find more information on this topic at our Web site: ***http://wft-advanced.swlearning.com.***

EXAMPLE 15

Dan, who is age 29 and single, has compensation income of $51,000 in 2004. He is an active participant in his employer's qualified retirement plan. Dan contributes $3,000 to a traditional IRA. The deductible amount is reduced from $3,000 by $1,800 because of the phaseout mechanism:

$$\frac{\$6{,}000}{\$10{,}000} \times \$3{,}000 = \$1{,}800 \text{ reduction}$$

Therefore, of the $3,000 contribution, Dan can deduct only $1,200 ($3,000 – $1,800). ■

There is a $200 floor on the IRA deduction limitation for individuals whose AGI is not above the end of the phaseout range.

EXAMPLE 16

Ben, an unmarried individual who is age 39, is an active participant in his employer's qualified retirement plan. With AGI of $54,500, he would normally have an IRA deduction limit of $150 {$3,000 – [($54,500 – $45,000)/$10,000 × $3,000]}. However, because of the special floor provision, Ben is allowed a $200 IRA deduction. ■

An individual is not considered an active participant in a qualified plan merely because the individual's spouse is an active participant in such a plan for any part of a plan year. Thus, most homemakers may take a full $3,000 deduction regardless

[33]§§ 219(b)(1) and (c)(2). The ceiling will be $4,000 for 2005–2007 and $5,000 for 2008. After 2008, the limit is adjusted annually for inflation in $500 increments.

[34]§ 219(g).

of the participation status of their spouse, unless the couple has AGI above $150,000. If their AGI is above $150,000, the phaseout of the deduction begins at $150,000 and ends at $160,000 (phaseout over the $10,000 range) rather than beginning and ending at the phaseout amounts in Table 11–2.[35]

EXAMPLE 17

Lisa, age 33, is covered by a qualified employer retirement plan at work. Her husband, Nick, is not an active participant in a qualified plan. If Lisa and Nick's combined AGI is $135,000, Lisa cannot make a deductible IRA contribution because she exceeds the income threshold for an active participant in Table 11–2. However, since Nick is not an active participant, and their combined AGI does not exceed $150,000, he can make a deductible contribution of $3,000 to an IRA. ■

To the extent that an individual is ineligible to make a deductible contribution to a traditional IRA, *nondeductible contributions* can be made to separate accounts.[36] The nondeductible contributions are subject to the same dollar limits as deductible contributions ($3,000 of earned income, $6,000 for a spousal IRA). Income in the account accumulates tax-free until distributed. Only the account earnings are taxed upon distribution because the account basis equals the contributions made by the taxpayer. A taxpayer may elect to treat deductible IRA contributions as nondeductible. If an individual has no taxable income for the year after taking into account other deductions, the election would be beneficial. The election is made on the individual's tax return for the taxable year to which the designation relates.

Roth IRAs. Introduced by Congress to encourage individual savings, a **Roth IRA** is a *nondeductible* alternative to the traditional deductible IRA. Earnings inside a Roth IRA are not taxable, and all qualified distributions from a Roth IRA are tax-free.[37] The maximum allowable annual contribution to a Roth IRA is the smaller of $3,000 ($6,000 for spousal IRAs) or 100 percent of the individual's compensation for the year. Contributions to a Roth IRA must be made by the due date (excluding extensions) of the taxpayer's tax return. Roth IRAs are not subject to the minimum distribution rules that apply to traditional IRAs.

A taxpayer can make tax-free withdrawals from a Roth IRA after an initial five-year holding period if any of the following requirements is satisfied:

- The distribution is made on or after the date on which the participant attains age 59½.
- The distribution is made to a beneficiary (or the participant's estate) on or after the participant's death.
- The participant becomes disabled.
- The distribution is used to pay for qualified first-time home buyer's expenses (statutory ceiling of $10,000).

EXAMPLE 18

Edith establishes a Roth IRA at age 42 and contributes $3,000 per year for 20 years. The account is now worth $116,400, consisting of $60,000 of nondeductible contributions and $56,400 in accumulated earnings that have not been taxed. Edith may withdraw the $116,400 tax-free from the Roth IRA because she is over age 59½ and has met the five-year holding period requirement. ■

[35]§ 219 (g)(7). However, a special rule in § 219(g)(4) allows a married person filing a separate return to avoid the phaseout rules even though the spouse is an active participant. The individual must live apart from the spouse at all times during the taxable year and must not be an active participant in another qualified plan.

[36]§ 408(o).

[37]§ 408A.

If the taxpayer receives a distribution from a Roth IRA and does not satisfy the aforementioned requirements, the distribution may be taxable. If the distribution represents a return of capital, it is not taxable. Conversely, if the distribution represents a payout of earnings, it is taxable. Under the ordering rules for Roth IRA distributions, distributions are treated as first made from contributions (return of capital).

EXAMPLE 19

Assume the same facts as in the previous example, except that Edith is only age 50 and receives a distribution of $55,000. Since her adjusted basis for the Roth IRA is $60,000 (contributions made), the distribution is tax-free, and her adjusted basis is reduced to $5,000 ($60,000 – $55,000). ■

Roth IRAs are subject to income limits. The maximum annual contribution of $3,000 is phased out beginning at AGI of $95,000 for single taxpayers and $150,000 for married couples who file a joint return. The phaseout range is $10,000 for married filing jointly and $15,000 for single taxpayers. For a married taxpayer filing separately, the phaseout begins with AGI of $0 and is phased out over a $10,000 range.

EXAMPLE 20

Bev, who is age 35 and single, would like to contribute $3,000 to her Roth IRA. However, her AGI is $105,000, so her contribution is limited to $1,000 ($3,000 – $2,000) calculated as follows:

$$\frac{\$10{,}000}{\$15{,}000} \times \$3{,}000 = \$2{,}000 \text{ reduction}$$

■

DIGGING DEEPER 9

Find information on Coverdell Education Savings Accounts (CESAs) at our Web site: ***http://wft-advanced.swlearning.com.***

PLANNING STRATEGIES

Individual Retirement Accounts

FRAMEWORK FOCUS: INCOME AND EXCLUSIONS

STRATEGY ➤ **AVOID INCOME RECOGNITION.**

Unlike a traditional IRA, which only defers taxes, a Roth IRA allows the tax-free accumulation of wealth. There is no current deduction, but plan earnings are never taxed (assuming the five-year holding period provision is satisfied). Many taxpayers are better off with this arrangement than with a traditional IRA, which allows a current tax deduction but only the deferred taxation of plan distributions.

Taxpayers should take advantage of a Roth IRA (up to $3,000 per year may be contributed) for any of their children who have earned income. The tax-free compounding of earnings can result in a substantial retirement account at age 65.

Simplified Employee Pension Plans. An employer may contribute to an IRA covering an employee an amount equal to the lesser of $41,000 (in 2004) or 25 percent of the employee's earned income. In such a plan, the employer must make contributions for *each* employee who has reached age 21, has performed service for the employer during the calendar year and at least three of the five preceding calendar years, and has received at least $450 (in 2004) in compensation from the

CONCEPT SUMMARY 11–3

Keogh Plan and SEP Compared

	Keogh	SEP
Form	Trust.	IRA.
Establishment	By end of year.	By extension due date of employer.
Type of plan	Qualified.	Qualified.
Contributions to plan	By extension due date.	By extension due date of employer.
Vesting rules	Qualified plan rules.	100% immediately.
Participants' rules	Flexible.	Stricter.
Lump-sum distributions and averaging	Yes, favorable 10-year forward averaging (if eligible).	No, ordinary income.
Deduction limitation	Varies.*	Smaller of $41,000 (in 2004) or 25% of earned income.**
Self as trustee	Yes.	No.

*For a defined contribution pension plan, the limit is the smaller of $41,000 (in 2004) or 100% of self-employment income (after one-half of self-employment tax is deducted). A defined contribution profit sharing plan has a 25% deduction limit. A defined benefit Keogh plan's limit is the smaller of $165,000 (in 2004) or 100% of the employee's average compensation for the highest three years of employment.

**Only $205,000 of income can be taken into consideration.

employer for the year.[38] Known as **simplified employee pension (SEP) plans,** these plans are subject to many of the same restrictions applicable to qualified plans (e.g., age and period-of-service requirements, and nondiscrimination limitations). Concept Summary 11–3 compares a SEP with a Keogh plan.

EXAMPLE 21

In 2004, Ryan's compensation before his employer's contribution to a SEP is $30,000. Ryan's employer may contribute and deduct up to $7,500 ($30,000 × 25%) for 2004. ■

The amounts contributed to a SEP by an employer on behalf of an employee and the elective deferrals of an employee under a SEP are excludible from gross income. Elective deferrals under a SEP are subject to a statutory ceiling of $13,000 (in 2004),[39] which is increased under the catch-up provision for employees at least 50 years of age by the end of the tax year. Only $205,000 (in 2004) in compensation may be taken into account in making the SEP computation. An employer is permitted to elect to use its taxable year rather than the calendar year for purposes of determining contributions to a SEP.[40]

SIMPLE IRA. A SIMPLE plan can be in the form of an IRA. See the earlier discussion under SIMPLE Plans.

Spousal IRA. If both spouses work, each can individually establish an IRA. Deductible IRA contributions of up to $3,000 may be made by each spouse if the combined compensation of both spouses is at least equal to the contributed amount.

[38]§§ 408(j) and (k)(2). This amount is indexed annually. For 2003, the amount was $450.

[39]Elective deferrals by an employee were repealed by the Small Business Job Protection Act of 1996 effective after December 31, 1996. However, if the employer plan was established before January 1, 1997, contributions can continue to be made under the pre-repeal provisions.

[40]§ 404(h)(1)(A). The $13,000 and $205,000 amounts are indexed annually. The $13,000 amount is increased in $1,000 annual increments until the limit reaches $15,000 and then is subject to indexing.

Thus, if each spouse has compensation of at least $3,000, they each may contribute a maximum of $3,000. Likewise, if only one spouse is employed, they each may contribute a maximum of $3,000 if the employed spouse has compensation of at least $6,000. Finally, if both spouses are employed, but one has compensation of less than $3,000, they each may contribute a maximum of $3,000 if their combined compensation is at least $6,000.

For the spousal IRA provision to apply, a joint return must be filed.[41] The spousal IRA deduction is also proportionately reduced for active participants whose AGI exceeds the target ranges in Table 11–2.

EXAMPLE 22

Tony, who is married, is eligible to establish an IRA. He received $30,000 in compensation in 2004, and his spouse does not work outside the home. Tony can contribute up to $6,000 to two IRAs, to be divided in any manner between the two spouses, except that no more than $3,000 can be allocated to either spouse. ■

EXAMPLE 23

Assume the same facts as in the previous example, except that Tony's wife has compensation income of $1,200. Without the spousal IRA provision, Tony could contribute $3,000 to his IRA, and his spouse could contribute only $1,200 to her IRA. With the spousal IRA provision, they both can contribute $3,000 to their IRAs. ■

Alimony is considered to be earned income for purposes of IRA contributions. Thus, a person whose only income is alimony can contribute to an IRA.

Timing of Contributions. Contributions (both deductible and nondeductible) can be made to an IRA anytime before the due date of the individual's tax return.[42] For example, an individual can establish and contribute to an IRA through April 15, 2005 (the return due date), and deduct this amount on his or her tax return for 2004. IRA contributions that are made during a tax return extension period do not satisfy the requirement of being made by the return due date. An employer can make contributions up until the time of the due date for filing the return (including extensions) and treat those amounts as a deduction for the prior year.[43] As noted earlier, a similar rule applies to Keogh plans. However, the Keogh plan must be established before the end of the tax year. Contributions to the Keogh plan may then be made anytime before the due date of the individual's tax return.

PENALTY TAXES FOR EXCESS CONTRIBUTIONS TO AN IRA

A cumulative, nondeductible 6 percent excise penalty tax is imposed on the smaller of (1) any excess contributions or (2) the market value of the plan assets determined as of the close of the tax year. *Excess contributions* are any contributions that exceed the maximum limitation and contributions that are made to a traditional IRA during or after the tax year in which the individual reaches age 70½.[44] Contributions can be made to a Roth IRA during or after the tax year in which the individual reaches age 70½. A taxpayer is not allowed a deduction for excess contributions. If the excess is corrected by contributing less than the deductible amount for a later year, a deduction then is allowable in the later year as a *makeup* deduction.

An excess contribution is taxable annually until returned to the taxpayer or reduced by the underutilization of the maximum contribution limitation in a subsequent year. The 6 percent penalty tax can be avoided if the excess amounts are returned.[45]

[41] § 219(c).
[42] § 219(f)(3).
[43] § 404(h)(1)(B).
[44] §§ 4973(a)(1) and (b).
[45] §§ 408(d)(4) and 4973(b)(2).

EXAMPLE 24

Nancy, age 45, establishes a traditional IRA in 2004 and contributes $3,300 in cash to the plan. She has earned income of $22,000. Nancy is allowed a $3,000 deduction *for* AGI for 2004. Assuming the market value of the plan assets is at least $300, there is a nondeductible 6% excise penalty tax of $18 ($300 × 6%). The $300 may be subject to an additional penalty tax in future years if it is not returned to Nancy or reduced by underutilization of the $3,000 maximum contribution limitation (ignoring any catch-up contributions). ■

TAXATION OF BENEFITS

A participant has a zero basis in the *deductible* contributions of a traditional IRA because the contributions were deducted.[46] Therefore, all withdrawals from a deductible IRA are taxed as ordinary income in the year of receipt.

A participant has a basis equal to the contributions made for a *nondeductible* traditional IRA. Therefore, only the earnings component of withdrawals is included in gross income.

In addition to being included in gross income, payments from IRAs made to a participant before age 59½ are subject to a nondeductible 10 percent penalty tax on such actual, or constructive, payments.[47] However, an individual may make penalty-free withdrawals to pay for medical expenses in excess of 7.5 percent of AGI, to pay for qualified higher education expenses, and to pay for qualified, first-time home buyer expenses (up to $10,000).

DIGGING DEEPER 10

Find more information on this topic at our Web site: ***http://wft-advanced.swlearning.com.***

All traditional IRAs of an individual are treated as one contract, and all distributions during a taxable year are treated as one distribution. See the earlier discussion of the special rules for distributions from Roth IRAs and traditional IRAs. If an individual who previously has made both deductible and nondeductible IRA contributions makes a withdrawal from a traditional IRA during a taxable year, the excludible amount must be calculated. The amount excludible from gross income for the taxable year is calculated by multiplying the amount withdrawn by a percentage. The percentage is calculated by dividing the individual's aggregate nondeductible traditional IRA contributions by the aggregate balance of all of his or her traditional IRAs (including rollover IRAs and SEPs).[48]

EXAMPLE 25

Carl, age 59, has a $12,000 deductible traditional IRA and a $2,000 nondeductible traditional IRA (without any earnings). Carl withdraws $1,000 from the nondeductible IRA. The excludible portion is $143 [($2,000/$14,000) × $1,000], and the includible portion is $857 [($12,000/$14,000) × $1,000]. Carl must also pay a 10% penalty tax on the prorated portion considered withdrawn from the deductible IRA and earnings in either type of IRA. Thus, the 10% penalty tax is $85.70 (10% × $857). ■

Rollovers: General Provisions. As introduced earlier, an IRA may be the recipient of a rollover from another qualified plan, including another IRA. Such a distribution from a qualified plan is not included in gross income if it is transferred within 60 days of receipt to an IRA or another qualified plan. For a series of distributions that constitute a lump-sum distribution, the 60-day period does not begin until the last distribution. Amounts received from IRAs may be rolled over tax-free only once in a 12-month period. If a person has more than one IRA, the one-year waiting period applies separately to each IRA.[49]

[46] § 408(d)(1).

[47] § 72(t). There are limited exceptions to the penalty on early distributions.

[48] § 408(d)(2).

[49] § 408(d)(3)(B) and Reg. § 1.408–4(b)(4).

EXAMPLE 26

Nonemployer stock worth $60,000 is distributed to an employee from a qualified retirement plan. Hubert, the employee, sells the stock within 60 days for $60,000 and transfers one-half of the proceeds to a traditional IRA. Hubert has $30,000 of ordinary income, which is not eligible for 10-year forward averaging or for the capital gain treatment for pre-1974 contributions. One-half of the distribution, or $30,000, does escape taxation because of the rollover. ■

Any rollover amount in a traditional IRA may later be rolled over into another qualified plan if the IRA consists of only the amounts from the original plan. The amount of nondeductible employee contributions included in a distribution may not be rolled over, but that amount is tax-free because the contributions were made with after-tax dollars. Partial rollovers are allowed, but the maximum amount that may be rolled over may not exceed the portion of the distribution that is otherwise includible in gross income. Rollovers are not available for required distributions under the minimum distribution rules once age 70½ is reached.

EXAMPLE 27

Jane withdraws $1,500 from her traditional IRA on May 2, 2004, but she redeposits it in the same IRA on June 28, 2004. Although the withdrawal and redeposit was a partial rollover and Jane may have used the funds for a limited time, this is a tax-free rollover.[50] ■

A rollover is different from a direct transfer of funds from a qualified plan to an IRA or another qualified plan by a trustee or issuer. A direct transfer is not subject to the one-year waiting period and the withholding rules.[51] Further, in many states, IRA amounts are subject to claims of creditors, which is not the case for some employer plans.

An employer must withhold 20 percent of any lump-sum distributions unless the transfer is a direct transfer to an IRA or another qualified plan.[52]

EXAMPLE 28

Kay receives a distribution from a qualified retirement plan. The amount of the distribution would have been $20,000, but Kay receives only $16,000 ($20,000 – $4,000) as a result of the 20% withholding provision. After several weeks, Kay decides to contribute $20,000 (the gross amount of the distribution) to her traditional IRA. Since she received only $16,000, she will need to contribute $4,000 from another source in order to make a $20,000 contribution. Kay will be able to claim a refund for the $4,000 that was withheld when she files her tax return for the year. ■

Concept Summary 11–4 compares traditional and Roth IRAs, and Concept Summary 11–5 compares a traditional IRA with a § 401(k) plan.

Rollovers and Conversions: Roth IRAs. A Roth IRA may be rolled over tax-free into another Roth IRA.[53]

A traditional IRA may be rolled over or converted to a Roth IRA. A conversion occurs when the taxpayer notifies the IRA trustee that the IRA is now a Roth IRA. A rollover or conversion of a traditional IRA to a Roth IRA can occur only if the following requirements are satisfied:[54]

- The participant's AGI does not exceed $100,000 (excluding the amount included in gross income resulting from the rollover or conversion).
- The participant is not married filing a separate return.
- The rollover occurs within 60 days of the IRA distribution.

[50] Ltr.Rul. 9010007.
[51] Reg. § 35.3405–1.
[52] § 3405(c).
[53] § 408A(c)(3)(B).
[54] § 408A(c)(3)(B).

CONCEPT SUMMARY 11-4

Comparison of IRAs

	Traditional		
	Deductible IRA	Nondeductible IRA	Roth IRA
Maximum contribution (per year)	$3,000*	$3,000*	$3,000*
Tax-deductible contribution	Yes	No	No
Tax-free growth of income	Yes	Yes	Yes
Beginning of AGI phaseout for active participant (2004)	$45,000 single, $65,000 joint	N/A	$95,000 single, $150,000 joint
Income tax on distributions	Yes, for entire distribution	Yes, for the earnings portion	No, if satisfy 5-year holding period**
50% excise tax: age 70½ minimum distributions	Yes	Yes	No
10% early withdrawal penalty (before age 59½)	Yes, with exceptions†	Yes, with exceptions†	Yes, with exceptions†

*The total of deductible, nondeductible, and Roth IRA contributions may not exceed $3,000 per year.
**In addition, the distribution must satisfy one of the following: after age 59½, for qualified first-time home buyer expenses, participant is disabled, or made to a beneficiary on or after the participant's death.
†Qualified education and first-time home buyer costs (up to $10,000) avoid the 10% penalty.

If a traditional IRA is rolled over or converted to a Roth IRA, the tax consequences depend on whether the traditional IRA was deductible or nondeductible. If deductible, then the basis for the IRA is zero. Thus, the entire amount of the rollover or conversion is included in gross income. If nondeductible, then the basis for the IRA is equal to the sum of the contributions. Thus, only the IRA earnings included in the rollover or conversion are included in gross income. The 10 percent penalty tax will not apply in either case.[55]

PLANNING STRATEGIES

Comparison of a § 401(k) Plan with an IRA

FRAMEWORK FOCUS: INCOME

STRATEGY ➤ POSTPONE RECOGNITION OF INCOME TO ACHIEVE TAX DEFERRAL.

Most employees will find a § 401(k) plan more attractive than an IRA. Probably the biggest limitation of an IRA is the $3,000 maximum contribution in 2004 (ignoring the catch-up provisions). Under § 401(k), employees are permitted to contribute up to $13,000 of their compensation (in 2004). In addition, the restrictions on the deductibility of IRA contributions may cause many employees to utilize § 401(k) plans more frequently.

Contributions to a § 401(k) plan are considered to be deferred compensation and therefore may reduce the employee's share of benefits that are based on current compensation, such as profit sharing payments and group term life insurance. A traditional IRA contribution does not reduce an employee's compensation, but is taken as a deduction (assuming eligibility) in arriving at AGI and therefore would not have the same effect.

[55] § 408A(d)(3)(A)(ii).

Concept Summary 11–5

Section 401(k) Plan and Traditional IRA Compared

	§ 401(k) Plan	Traditional IRA
Deduction limitation	Smaller of $13,000 (in 2004) or approximately 100% of total earnings. Limited by antidiscrimination requirements of § 401(k)(3).	$3,000 or 100% of compensation.
Distributions	Early withdrawal possible if for early retirement (55 or over) or to pay medical expenses.	10% penalty for early withdrawals, except for withdrawals to pay for certain medical expenses and health insurance, qualified education expenses, and qualified first-time home buyer expenses.
Effect on gross earnings	Gross salary reduction, which may reduce profit sharing contributions, Social Security benefits, and group life insurance.	No effect.
Employer involvement	Must keep records; monitor for compliance with antidiscrimination test.	Minimal.
Lump-sum distributions	Favorable 10-year forward averaging (if eligible).	Ordinary income.
Timing of contribution	Within 30 days of plan year-end or due date of employer's return.*	Grace period up to due date of tax return (not including extensions).
Loans from plan	Yes.	No.

*Elective contributions must be made to the plan no later than 30 days after the end of the plan year, and nonelective contributions no later than the due date of the tax return (including extensions).

LO.7

Understand the rationale for nonqualified deferred compensation plans and the related tax treatment.

Nonqualified Deferred Compensation Plans

UNDERLYING RATIONALE FOR TAX TREATMENT

Nonqualified deferred compensation (NQDC) plans provide a flexible way for taxpayers, particularly those in the 35 percent tax bracket, to defer income taxes on income payments until a possible lower tax bracket year. Where the deferred compensation is credited with annual earnings until payment, the entire deferred compensation, not the after-tax amount, is generating investment income. Also, most NQDC plans do not have to meet the discrimination, funding, coverage, and other requirements of qualified plans. In addition to these advantages for the employee, the employer may not have a current cash outflow.

The doctrine of constructive receipt is important in determining the taxability of nonqualified deferred compensation.[56] In essence, if a taxpayer irrevocably earns income but may elect to receive it now or at a later date, the income is constructively received and is immediately taxed. Income is not constructively received, however, if the taxpayer's control over the amounts earned is subject to substantial limitations or restrictions.

[56] § 451(a) and Reg. § 1.451–2.

BRIDGE DISCIPLINE

Bridge to Finance

Planning for retirement is a many faceted process, which is made increasingly complex by congressional changes to the tax laws. The easy part of the planning process is deciding how much annual retirement income the individual wants to generate. The hard part is deciding on the best course of action to get there. The following list, although not comprehensive, identifies a number of important considerations.

- *Taxable investment versus traditional IRA or § 401(k).* This choice is between (1) no current tax deduction and all earnings currently taxed and (2) a current tax deduction or exclusion, but deferral of tax until a distribution is received. The tax rates will also vary. The taxable investment may be taxed at 15 percent (if it produces qualified dividends and long-term capital gains). The traditional IRA or § 401(k) distribution will be taxed at the ordinary income rates, which are currently as high as 35 percent. Congressional changes to the tax rates would significantly alter the analysis of the two alternatives.
- *Traditional IRA versus Roth IRA.* This choice is also between a current tax deduction and no current tax deduction, but with one important distinction. The earnings inside a traditional IRA will eventually be taxed as ordinary income, but the earnings inside a Roth IRA will never be taxed.
- A Roth IRA will always be better than a taxable investment. Although neither produces a current tax deduction, the earnings from a Roth IRA will never be taxed.
- The comparison of a deductible traditional IRA or § 401(k) with a Roth IRA is more complex because of the uncertainty about future tax rates. If tax rates are expected to increase, then a Roth IRA is preferable. The following table illustrates that there is no difference between a traditional IRA and a Roth IRA if the tax rates remain constant and the other assumptions are valid.

	Available Investment	*Current Taxes**	*Investment*	*Future Value***	*Future Tax**	*Net Cash*
Traditional IRA	$3,000	—	$3,000	$39,803	$13,931	$25,872
Roth IRA	3,000	($1,050)	1,950	25,872	—	25,872

*Assume a 35% tax rate.
**Assume the investment will earn 9% compounded annually for 30 years.

Another important concept is the economic benefit theory. Although a taxpayer does not have a present right to income, the income will be taxable if a right in the form of a negotiable promissory note exists. Notes and other evidences of indebtedness received in payment for services constitute income to the extent of their fair market value at the time of the transfer.[57]

EXAMPLE 29

Eagle Corporation and Bill, a cash basis employee, enter into an employment agreement that provides an annual salary of $120,000 to Bill. Of this amount, $100,000 is to be paid in current monthly installments, and $20,000 is to be paid in 10 annual installments beginning

[57]Reg. § 1.61–2(d)(4).

GLOBAL TAX ISSUES

Moving Offshore

Large corporations are moving deferred compensation assets, especially rabbi trust assets, offshore. Deferred compensation plans use rabbi trusts as a way to place assets into an irrevocable grantor trust. Though intended for an employee, the trust is still subject to creditors' claims. By placing the trusts in "asset protection havens," the assets can be effectively moved beyond the reach of creditors. According to *The Institutional Investor*, hedge fund managers have moved billions of dollars of deferred income offshore, with some managers deferring $100 million or more.

at Bill's retirement or death. Although Eagle Corporation maintains a separate account for Bill, that account is not funded (Bill is merely an unsecured creditor of the corporation). The $20,000 is not considered constructively received and is deferred. Compensation of $100,000 is currently taxable to Bill and deductible to Eagle. The other $20,000 will be taxable and deductible when paid in future years. ■

TAX TREATMENT TO THE EMPLOYER AND EMPLOYEE

The tax treatment of an NQDC plan depends on whether it is *funded* or *unfunded* and whether it is *forfeitable* or *nonforfeitable*. In an unfunded NQDC plan, the employee relies upon the company's mere promise to make the compensation payment in the future. An unfunded, unsecured promise to pay, not represented by a negotiable note, effectively defers the recognition of income. Thus, the employee is taxed later when the compensation is actually paid or made available.[58] Similarly, the employer is allowed a deduction when the employee recognizes income.[59]

The employer can set up an escrow account to accumulate deferred payments on behalf of the employee. These funds may be invested by the escrow agent for the benefit of the employee.[60] By avoiding income recognition until the benefits from the escrow custodial account are received, the employee postpones the tax. An escrow arrangement can be appropriate for a professional athlete or entertainer whose income is earned in a few peak years.

EXAMPLE 30

Ted, a professional athlete, is to receive a bonus for signing an employment contract. An NQDC plan is established to defer the income beyond Ted's peak income years. His employer transfers the bonus to an escrow agent who invests the funds in securities, etc., which may act as a hedge against inflation. The bonus is deferred for 10 years and becomes payable gradually in years 11 through 15. The bonus is taxable to Ted and deductible by his employer when Ted receives the payments in years 11 through 15. ■

Generally, funded NQDC plans must be forfeitable to keep the compensation payments from being taxable immediately. In most instances, employees prefer to have some assurance that they will ultimately receive benefits from the NQDC (that the plan provides for nonforfeitable benefits). In such instances, the plan will have to be unfunded to prevent immediate taxation to the employee. Note that most funded NQDC plans are subject to many of the provisions that apply to qualified plans.

---

[58]Rev.Rul. 60–31, 1960–1 C.B. 174; Reg. § 1.451–2(a); *U.S. v. Basye*, 73–1 USTC ¶9250, 31 AFTR2d 73–802, 93 S.Ct. 1080 (USSC, 1973).

[59]§§ 404(a) and (d).

[60]Rev.Rul. 55–525, 1955–2 C.B. 543.

When to Use an NQDC Arrangement. As a general rule, NQDC plans are more appropriate for executives in a financially secure company. Because of the need for currently disposable income, such plans are usually not appropriate for young employees.

An NQDC plan can reduce an employee's overall tax payments by deferring the taxation of income to later years (possibly when the employee is in a lower tax bracket). In effect, these plans may produce a form of income averaging. Further, NQDC plans may discriminate in favor of shareholders, officers, specific highly compensated key employees, or a single individual.

Certain disadvantages should be noted. Nonqualified plans are usually required to be unfunded, which means that an employee is not assured that funds ultimately will be available to pay the benefits. Also, the employer's tax deduction is postponed until the employee is taxed on those payments.

PLANNING STRATEGIES

Nonqualified Deferred Compensation (NQDC) Plans

FRAMEWORK FOCUS: TAX RATE

STRATEGY ➤ SHIFT NET INCOME FROM HIGH-BRACKET YEARS TO LOW-BRACKET YEARS.

Nonqualified deferred compensation plans such as restricted property plans can be useful to attract executive talent or to provide substantial retirement benefits for executives. The plans do not face the same restrictive requirements that qualified plans must abide by. There are no dollar limits, and the terms of the plan can be negotiated for each participant.

The principal advantage of NQDC plans is that the employee can defer the recognition of compensation income to future periods when his or her income tax bracket may be lower (e.g., during retirement years). In addition, the taxpayer can defer taxation of any earnings on the deferred compensation until paid by the employer. The tax-deferred compounding of these earnings can be substantial.

The principal disadvantage of NQDC plans could be the bunching effect that takes place on the expiration of the deferral period. This could severely decrease any tax savings, especially if the tax rates go up.

Golden Parachute Arrangements. Golden parachute arrangements promise monetary benefits to key employees if they lose their jobs as a result of a change in ownership of the corporation. These payments may be unreasonable or not really for services rendered. The term **golden parachute payments,** as used in the Code, means *excess severance pay.*

These excessive severance payments to employees are penalized. The Code denies a deduction to an employer who makes a payment of cash or property to an employee or independent contractor that satisfies both of the following conditions:

- The payment is contingent on a change of ownership of a corporation through a stock or asset acquisition.
- The aggregate present value of the payment equals or exceeds three times the employee's (or independent contractor's) average annual compensation.[61]

The disallowed amount is the excess of the payment over a statutory base amount (a five-year average of taxable compensation if the taxpayer was an employee for the entire five-year period). Further, a 20 percent excise tax is imposed

[61] § 280G.

on the recipient on the receipt of these parachute payments; the tax is withheld at the time of payment.[62]

EXAMPLE 31

Irene, an executive, receives a golden parachute payment of $380,000 from her employer. Her average annual compensation for the most recent five tax years is $120,000. The corporation will be denied a deduction for $260,000 ($380,000 payment − $120,000 base amount). Irene's excise tax is $52,000 ($260,000 × 20%). ■

Golden parachute payments do not include payments to or from qualified pension, profit sharing, stock bonus, annuity, or simplified employee pension plans. Also excluded is the amount of the payment that, in fact, represents reasonable compensation for personal services actually rendered or to be rendered. Such excluded payments are not taken into account when determining whether the threshold (the aggregate present value calculation) is exceeded.

S corporations are not subject to the golden parachute rules. Generally, corporations that do not have stock that is readily tradable on an established securities market or elsewhere are also exempt.

Publicly Held Companies' Compensation Limitation. For purposes of both the regular income tax and the alternative minimum tax, the deductible compensation for the top five executives of publicly traded companies is limited to $1 million for each executive. A company is publicly held if the corporation has common stock listed on a national securities exchange.[63] This $1 million deduction limitation is decreased by any nondeductible golden parachute payments made to the employee during the same year.

This deduction limitation applies when the compensation deduction would otherwise be taken. For example, in the case of a nonqualified stock option (NQSO), which is discussed later in this chapter, the deduction is normally taken in the year the NQSO is exercised, even though the option was granted with respect to services performed in a prior year.

Certain types of compensation are *not* subject to this deduction limit and are not taken into account in determining whether other compensation exceeds $1 million:

- Compensation payable on a commission basis.
- Compensation payable solely on account of the attainment of one or more performance goals when certain requirements involving the approval of outside directors and shareholders are met.
- Payments to a tax-qualified retirement plan (including salary-reduction contributions).
- Amounts that are excludible from an executive's gross income (such as employer-provided health benefits and miscellaneous fringe benefits).

DIGGING DEEPER 11

Find more information on this topic at our Web site: ***http://wft-advanced.swlearning.com.***

LO.8

Explain the value of restricted property plans.

Restricted Property Plans

GENERAL PROVISIONS

A **restricted property plan** is an arrangement whereby an employer transfers property (e.g., stock of the employer-corporation) to an employee or other provider of services at no cost or at a bargain price. The usual purpose of a restricted stock

[62] § 4999.

[63] § 162(m).

TAX IN THE NEWS

Does High Pay Equal High Performance?

Warren Buffett said in his shareholders' letter that "executive pay seems more decoupled from performance than ever." Shareholders in Apple Computer saw their return fall by 34.6 percent in 2002, but CEO Steve Jobs was paid $78.1 million. Honeywell's return fell 27.3 percent, but CEO David Cote was paid $68.5 million.

The AICPA lost much of its power as a result of the Sarbanes-Oxley Act, yet Barry Melancon, the chief executive, received nearly $1 million, a 22 percent pay raise. By the way, the AICPA's Web portal business lost more than $80 million between its February 2001 launch and mid-2002. Melancon launched the for-profit portal, acquiring an early $100,000 stake. He later turned over his shares to an AICPA charity that funds education.

By comparison, the chairman of the Securities and Exchange Commission is paid $142,500.

SOURCES: Adapted from Jerry Useem, "Have They No Shame?" *Fortune*, April 28, 2003, pp. 57–60, 64; Cassell Bryan-Low, "AICPA CEO's Pay Rises 22% Amid Reversal," *Wall Street Journal*, June 20, 2003, p. C7.

plan is to retain the services of key employees who might otherwise leave. The employer hopes that such compensation arrangements will encourage company growth and attainment of performance objectives. Section 83 was enacted in 1969 to provide rules for the taxation of incentive compensation arrangements, which previously were governed by judicial and administrative interpretations. Although the following discussion refers to an employee as the provider of the services, the services may be performed by an independent contractor.

As a general rule, if an employee performs services and receives property (e.g., stock), the fair market value of that property in excess of any amount paid by the employee is includible in his or her gross income. The time for inclusion is the earlier of (1) the time the property is no longer subject to a substantial risk of forfeiture or (2) the time the property is transferable by the employee. The fair market value of the property is determined without regard to any restriction, except a restriction that by its terms will never lapse.[64] Since the amount of the compensation is determined at the date that the restrictions lapse or when the property is transferable, the opportunity to generate capital gain treatment on the property is denied during a period when the ordinary income element is being deferred.

EXAMPLE 32

On October 1, 2000, Blue Corporation sold 100 shares of its stock to Ahmad, an employee, for $10 per share. At the time of the sale, the fair market value of the stock was $100 per share. Under the terms of the sale, each share of stock was nontransferable and subject to a substantial risk of forfeiture (which was not to lapse until October 1, 2004). Evidence of these restrictions was stamped on the face of the stock certificates. On October 1, 2004, the fair market value of the stock was $250 per share. Since the stock was nontransferable and was subject to a substantial risk of forfeiture, Ahmad did not include any compensation in gross income during 2000 (assuming no special election was made). Instead, Ahmad was required to include $24,000 of compensation in gross income [100 shares × ($250 – $10 per share)] during 2004. If for some reason the forfeiture had occurred (e.g., the plan required

[64] § 83(a)(1); *Miriam Sakol*, 67 T.C. 986 (1977); *T. M. Horwith*, 71 T.C. 932 (1979).

TAX IN THE NEWS

Restricted Stock Shines

In July 2003, Microsoft Corporation announced that it would stop issuing employee stock options and instead give employees restricted stock. From the employees' perspective, stock options are preferable when the company's stock price is increasing rapidly, but restricted shares are less risky because they will put money in employees' pockets even if the stock declines in value. Companies tend to give only about one-third as much restricted stock as stock options, however.

Under financial accounting rules, restricted stock expenses must be expensed, but Amazon.com uses a pro forma version of earnings that backs out its restricted stock expenses. Will this subterfuge catch on?

SOURCE: Adapted from Ruth Simon, "The Employee Guide to Restricted Stock," *Wall Street Journal*, July 10, 2003, p. D1.

Ahmad to surrender the stock to the corporation if he voluntarily terminated his employment with the company before October 1, 2004) and Ahmad never received the stock certificates, he would have been allowed a capital loss of $1,000 (the extent of his investment). ■

SUBSTANTIAL RISK OF FORFEITURE

A **substantial risk of forfeiture** exists if a person's rights to full enjoyment of property are conditioned upon the future performance, or the refraining from the performance, of substantial services by that individual.[65] For example, if an employee must return the property (receiving only his or her original cost, if any) should there be a failure to complete a substantial period of service (for any reason), the property is subject to a substantial risk of forfeiture. Another such situation exists when an employer can compel an employee to return the property due to a breach of a substantial covenant not to compete. Any substantial risk of forfeiture should be stated on the face of the stock certificates. Assuming that a substantial risk of forfeiture does not exist, the property received is valued at its fair market value, ignoring any restrictions, except for one instance dealing with closely held stock.

SPECIAL ELECTION AVAILABLE

An employee may elect within 30 days after the receipt of restricted property to recognize immediately as ordinary income the fair market value in excess of the amount paid for the property. Any appreciation in the value of the property after receipt is classified as capital gain instead of ordinary income. No deduction is allowed to the employee for taxes paid on the original amount included in income if the property is subsequently forfeited.[66] The employee is permitted to take a capital loss for any amounts that were actually paid for the property. Furthermore, in such a case, the employer must repay taxes saved by any compensation deduction taken in the earlier year.[67]

Any increase in value between the time the property is received and the time it becomes either nonforfeitable or transferable is taxed as ordinary income if the

[65] § 83(c); Regulation § 1.83–3(c)(2) includes several examples of restricted property arrangements.

[66] § 83(b).

[67] Reg. §§ 1.83–6(c) and 2(a).

employee does not make this special election. However, if the employee elects to be taxed immediately on the difference between the cost and fair market value on the date of issue, any future appreciation is treated as capital gain. In determining whether the gain is long term or short term, the holding period starts when the employee is taxed on the ordinary income.[68]

EXAMPLE 33

On July 1, 1994, Sparrow Company sold 100 shares of its preferred stock, worth $15 per share, to Diane (an employee) for $5 per share. The sale was subject to Diane's agreement to resell the preferred shares to the company for $5 per share if she terminated her employment during the following 10 years. The stock had a value of $25 per share on July 1, 2004, and Diane sold the stock for $30 per share on October 10, 2004. Diane made the special election to include the original spread (between the value of $15 in 1994 and the amount paid of $5) in income for 1994. Diane was required to recognize $1,000 of compensation income in 1994 ($15 – $5 = $10 × 100 shares), at which time her holding period in her stock began. Diane's tax basis in the stock was $1,500 ($1,000 + $500). When the preferred stock was sold in 2004, Diane recognized a $1,500 long-term capital gain ($30 × 100 shares – $1,500). ■

EXAMPLE 34

Assume the same facts as in the previous example, except that Diane sells the stock in 2005 (rather than 2004). She would not recognize any gain in 2004 when the substantial risk of forfeiture lapses. Instead, Diane would recognize the $1,500 long-term capital gain in 2005. ■

This special provision is usually not elected since it results in an immediate recognition of income and adverse tax consequences result from a subsequent forfeiture. However, the special election may be attractive in the following situations:

- The bargain element is relatively small.
- Substantial appreciation is expected in the future.
- A high probability exists that the restrictions will be met.

EMPLOYER DEDUCTIONS

At the time the employee is required to include the compensation in income, the employer is allowed a tax deduction for the same amount. The employer must withhold on this amount in accordance with § 3402. In the no-election situation, the deduction is limited to the fair market value of the restricted property (without regard to the restrictions) at the time the restrictions lapse, reduced by the amount originally paid for the property by the employee.[69] When the employee elects to be taxed immediately, the corporate deduction also is accelerated and deductible in like amount. In cases of deferred income recognition, the employer can receive a sizable deduction if the property has appreciated.

EXAMPLE 35

On March 14, 2002, Gold Corporation sold to Harry, an employee, 10 shares of Gold common stock for $100 per share. Both the corporation and Harry were calendar year taxpayers. The common stock was subject to a substantial risk of forfeiture and was nontransferable; both conditions were to lapse on March 14, 2004. At the time of the sale, the fair market value of the common stock (without considering the restrictions) was $1,000 per share. On March 14, 2004, when the fair market value of the stock is $2,000 per share, the restrictions lapse. Harry did not make the special election. In 2004, Harry realizes ordinary income of $19,000 (10 shares at $2,000 per share less the $100 per share he had paid). Likewise, Gold Corporation is allowed a $19,000 compensation deduction in 2004. ■

[68] § 1223(6).

[69] Reg. § 1.83–6(a).

EXAMPLE 36

In the previous example, assume that Harry had made the special election. Since he was taxed on $9,000 in 2002, the corporation was allowed to deduct a like amount in 2002. No deduction would be available in 2004. ■

LO.9

Differentiate the tax treatment of qualified and nonqualified stock options.

Stock Options

IN GENERAL

Various equity types of stock option programs are available for an employee's compensation package. Some authorities believe that some form of *equity kicker* is needed to attract new management, convert key officers into *owners* by giving them a share of the business, and retain the services of executives who might otherwise leave. Encouraging the managers of a business to have a proprietary interest in its successful operation should provide executives with a key motive to expand the company and improve its profits. In addition, under certain conditions, stock options may fall outside the $1 million limitation on the salaries of the top five executives of publicly traded companies.

A **stock option** gives an individual the right to purchase a stated number of shares of stock from a corporation at a certain price within a specified period of time. The optionee must be under no obligation to purchase the stock, and the option may be revocable by the corporation. The option must be in writing, and its terms must be clearly expressed.[70]

There are two distinctly different stock option plans available: incentive stock options and nonqualified stock options. Concept Summary 11–6 at the end of this section summarizes the different tax treatments of the two plans.

INCENTIVE STOCK OPTIONS

An equity type of stock option called an *incentive stock option (ISO)* is available. There are no tax consequences for either the issuing corporation or the recipient when the option is granted. However, the *spread* (the excess of the fair market value of the shares at the date of exercise over the option price)[71] is a tax preference item to the recipient for purposes of the alternative minimum tax. The determination of fair market value is made without regard to any lapse restrictions (a restriction that will expire after a period of time). After the option is exercised and when the stock is sold, any gain from the sale is taxed as a long-term capital gain if certain holding period requirements are met. For a gain to qualify as a long-term capital gain, the employee must not dispose of the stock within two years after the option is granted or within one year after acquiring the stock.[72] If the employee meets the holding period requirements, none of these transactions generates any business deduction for the employer.[73] If the employee pays anything for the option and does not exercise the option, any amount paid is recognized as a capital loss.

EXAMPLE 37

Wren Corporation granted an ISO for 100 shares of its stock to Rocky, an employee, on March 18, 2001. The option price was $100, and the fair market value was $100 on the date of the grant. Rocky exercised the option on April 1, 2003, when the fair market value of the stock was $200 per share. He sells the stock on April 6, 2004, for $300 per share. Rocky did

[70]Reg. §§ 1.421–1(a)(1) and –7(a)(1).

[71]§§ 422(a), 421(a)(1), 57(a)(3), and 1234(a)(1) and (2).

[72]§ 422(a)(1).

[73]§ 421(a)(2).

not recognize any ordinary income on the date of the grant or the exercise date since the option qualified as an ISO. Wren received no compensation deduction. Rocky has a $10,000 tax preference item on the exercise date. He has a long-term capital gain of $20,000 [($300 – $100) × 100] on the sale of the stock in 2004, because the one-year and two-year holding periods and other requirements have been met. ■

As a further requirement for ISO treatment, the option holder must be an employee of the issuing corporation from the date the option is granted until 3 months (12 months if disabled) before the date of exercise. The holding period and the employee-status rules just described (the one-year, two-year, and three-month requirements) are waived in the case of the death of an employee.[74]

EXAMPLE 38

Assume the same facts as in the previous example, except that Rocky was not employed by Wren Corporation for six months before the date he exercised the options. Rocky must recognize ordinary income to the extent of the spread, assuming there was no substantial risk of forfeiture. Thus, Rocky recognizes $10,000 [($200 – $100) × 100] of ordinary income on the exercise date, because he was not an employee of Wren Corporation at all times during the period beginning on the grant date and ending three months before the exercise date. Wren is allowed a deduction at the same time that Rocky reports the ordinary income. ■

If the holding period requirements are not satisfied but all other conditions are met, the tax is still deferred to the point of the sale. However, the difference between the option price and the value of the stock at the date the option was exercised is treated as ordinary income. The difference between the amount realized for the stock and the value of the stock at the date of exercise is short-term or long-term capital gain, depending on the holding period of the stock itself. The employer is allowed a deduction equal to the amount recognized by the employee as ordinary income. The employee does not have a tax preference for alternative minimum tax purposes.

EXAMPLE 39

Assume the same facts as in Example 37, except that Rocky sells the stock on March 22, 2004, for $290 per share. Since Rocky did not hold the stock itself for more than one year, $10,000 of the gain is treated as ordinary income in 2004, and Wren Corporation is allowed a $10,000 compensation deduction in 2004. The remaining $9,000 is a short-term capital gain ($29,000 – $20,000). ■

Qualification Requirements for Incentive Stock Option Plans. An **incentive stock option (ISO)** is an option to purchase stock of a corporation granted to an individual for any reason connected with his or her employment.[75] The option is granted by the employer-corporation or by a parent or subsidiary corporation of the employer-corporation. When exercising an option, an employee can use company stock to pay for the stock without disqualifying the ISO plan. For an option to qualify as an ISO, certain statutory requirements must be satisfied.

DIGGING DEEPER 12

Find more information on this topic at our Web site: ***http://wft-advanced.swlearning.com.***

[74]§§ 422(a)(2) and (c)(3). Exceptions are made for parent and subsidiary situations, corporate reorganizations, and liquidations. Also, in certain situations involving an insolvent employee, the holding period rules are modified.

[75]§ 422(b).

An overall limitation is imposed on the amount of ISOs that can be exercised in one year by an employee. This limit is set at $100,000 per year based on the value of the stock determined at the time the option is granted.

NONQUALIFIED STOCK OPTIONS

A **nonqualified stock option (NQSO)** does not satisfy the statutory requirements for ISOs. In addition, a stock option that otherwise would qualify as an ISO will be treated as an NQSO if the terms of the stock option provide that it is not an ISO. If the NQSO has a readily ascertainable fair market value (e.g., the option is traded on an established exchange), the value of the option must be included in the employee's income at the date of grant. Thereafter, capital gain or loss is recognized only upon the disposal of the optioned stock. The employee's basis is the amount paid for the stock plus any amount reported as ordinary income. The employer obtains a corresponding tax deduction at the same time and to the extent that ordinary income is recognized by the employee.[76]

EXAMPLE 40

On February 1, 2003, Janet was granted an NQSO to purchase 100 shares of stock from her employer at $10 per share. On this date, the option was selling for $2 on an established exchange. Janet exercised the option on March 30, 2004, when the stock was worth $20 per share. On November 5, 2004, Janet sold the optioned stock for $22 per share.

- Janet must report ordinary income of $200 ($2 × 100 shares) on the date of grant (February 1, 2003), because the option has a readily ascertainable fair market value.
- Janet's adjusted basis for the stock is $1,200 ($1,000 cost + $200 recognized gain).
- Upon the sale of the stock (November 5, 2004), Janet must report a long-term capital gain of $1,000 [($22 – $12) × 100 shares].
- At the date of grant (February 1, 2003), the employer receives a tax deduction of $200, the amount of ordinary income reported by Janet. ■

If an NQSO does not have a readily ascertainable fair market value, an employee does not recognize income at the grant date. However, as a general rule, ordinary income must then be reported in the year of exercise (the difference between the fair market value of the stock at the exercise date and the option price).[77] The amount paid by the employee for the stock plus the amount reported as ordinary income becomes the basis. Any appreciation above that basis is taxed as a long-term capital gain upon disposition (assuming the stock is held for the required long-term holding period after exercise). The corporation receives a corresponding tax deduction at the same time and to the extent that ordinary income is recognized by the employee.

EXAMPLE 41

On February 3, 2002, Maria was granted an NQSO for 100 shares of common stock at $10 per share. On the date of the grant, there was no readily ascertainable fair market value for the option. Maria exercised the options on January 3, 2003, when the stock was selling for $15 per share. She sold one-half of the shares on April 15, 2003, and the other half on September 17, 2004. The sale price on both dates was $21 per share. Maria would not recognize any income on the grant date (February 3, 2002) but would recognize $500 ($1,500 – $1,000) of ordinary income on the exercise date (January 3, 2003). She would recognize a short-term capital gain of $300 on the sale of the first half in 2003 and a $300 long-term capital gain on the sale of the second batch of stock in 2004 [½($2,100 – $1,500)]. ■

[76]Reg. §§ 1.421–6(c), (d), (e), and (f); Reg. § 1.83–7.

[77]Reg. § 1.83–7(a); Reg. § 1.421–6(d).

Concept Summary 11–6

Incentive Stock Options and Nonqualified Stock Options Compared

	ISO	NQSO
Granted at any price	No	Yes
May have any duration	No	Yes
Governing Code Section	§ 422	§ 83
Spread subject to alternative minimum tax	Yes	No
Deduction to employer for spread	No	Yes
Type of gain/loss on disposal	Capital	Capital
Statutory amount ($100,000) limitation	Yes	No

The major *advantages* of NQSOs can be summarized as follows:

- A tax deduction is available to the corporation without a cash outlay.
- The employee receives capital gain treatment on any appreciation in the stock starting either at the exercise date if the option does not have a readily ascertainable fair market value or at the date of grant if the option has a readily ascertainable fair market value.
- Options can be issued at more flexible terms than under ISO plans (e.g., longer exercise period and discount on exercise price).

A major *disadvantage* is that the employee must recognize ordinary income on the exercise of the option or at the date of grant without receiving cash to pay the tax.

PLANNING STRATEGIES

Stock Options

Framework Focus: Deductions

Strategy ➤ **Maximize Deductible Amounts.**

Rather than paying compensation in the form of corporate stock, a corporation may issue options to purchase stock at a specific price to an employee. Stock option plans are used more frequently by publicly traded companies than by closely held companies. The difficulty of determining the value of the stock of a company that is not publicly traded and the dilution of ownership that would occur in a closely held company make stock options less appropriate for these companies.

Nonqualified stock options (NQSOs) are more flexible and less restrictive than incentive stock options (ISOs). For example, the option price of an NQSO may be less than the fair market value of the stock at the time the option is granted. An NQSO creates an employer deduction that lowers the cost of the NQSO to the employer. The employer may pass along this tax savings to the employee in the form of a cash payment. See Concept Summary 11–6.

The accounting for options may change in the future if publicly traded companies are required to deduct the value of the issued options from the corporation's operating income in its financial statements. Currently, this is not a requirement, although the subject is hotly debated. The debate has become even more heated since the FASB issued an exposure draft on March 31, 2004, that requires expensing.

BRIDGE DISCIPLINE

Bridge to Finance

A significant accounting controversy has developed over the treatment of employee stock option awards in the year of issuance. Currently, FAS 123 allows a company to issue employee stock options as a component of employee compensation, but the company is not required to take a charge against current earnings. The option plan is only disclosed in the corporation's footnotes.

On March 31, 2004, the FASB issued an exposure draft entitled *Share-Based Payment, an Amendment of FASB Statements No. 123 and 95* that discusses proposed changes to FAS 123. Essentially, this would require companies issuing stock options to currently expense the value of the options.

The tax treatment of employee stock options depends on the type of options issued. If the option grant consists of incentive stock options, then there is never a compensation deduction for the corporation. If the option grant consists of nonqualified stock options, in the year the option is exercised the corporation is allowed a compensation tax deduction equal to the difference between the exercise price and the fair market value of the stock. (The full exposure draft can be found at **http://www.fasb.org/draft/ed_intropg_share-based_payment.shtml**.)

Suggested Further Readings

Sharon Burnett, "Tax Matters: Bonuses and Accumulated Earnings Prove Troublesome," *Journal of Accountancy,* September 2003. (**http://www.aicpa.org/pubs/jofa/sep2003/taxcases.htm**)

William Cenker, "Tax Matters: Reasonable Compensation," *Journal of Accountancy,* November 2003. (**http://www.aicpa.org/pubs/jofa/nov2003/taxcases.htm**)

Delton Chesser, Walter Harrison Jr., and William Reichenstein, "Investment Tax Planning for Retirement," *Journal of Accountancy,* August 2003. (**http://www.aicpa.org/pubs/jofa/aug2003/chesser.htm**)

Internal Revenue Service Publication 560, Retirement Plans for Small Business (SEP, SIMPLE, and Qualified Plans), 2003.

Paul Smith, "Complexity in Retirement Savings Policy," *National Tax Journal,* September 2002, Vol. 55, Issue 3, pp. 539–554.

Paul Sweeney, "Stock Option Pitfalls and Strategies Du Jour," *Journal of Accountancy,* October 2001. (**http://www.aicpa.org/pubs/jofa/oct2001/sweeney.htm**)

Nick Wingfield, "Options Move May Be at Expense of Accounting Purists," *Wall Street Journal,* July 14, 2003, p. C1.

KEY TERMS

Cash balance plan, 11–8
Deferred compensation, 11–3
Defined benefit plan, 11–5
Defined contribution plan, 11–5
Golden parachute payments, 11–29
H.R. 10 (Keogh) plan, 11–16
Incentive stock option (ISO), 11–35
Individual Retirement Account (IRA), 11–18
Lump-sum distribution, 11–12
Money purchase pension plan, 11–7

PROBLEM MATERIALS

West Federal Taxation

Problems

EXTENDER

1. Red Corporation has a total of 1,000 employees, of whom 700 are non-highly compensated. The retirement plan covers 300 non-highly compensated employees and 200 highly compensated employees. Does this plan satisfy the minimum coverage test?

2. Which of the following would be considered a tax benefit or advantage of a qualified retirement plan?
   a. Certain lump-sum distributions may be subject to capital gain treatment.
   b. Employer contributions are deductible by the employer in the year of contribution.
   c. Employee contributions are deductible by the employee in the year of contribution.
   d. The qualified trust is tax-exempt as to all income (other than unrelated business income).
   e. In a lump-sum distribution, any capital gain tax on the portion attributable to any unrealized appreciation in the stock of the employer at the time of distribution is deferred until the time the employee disposes of the stock in a taxable transaction.
   f. Election may be made to allow a lump-sum distribution to be subject to a 10-year forward averaging technique.

3. How does a pension plan differ from a § 401(k) plan?

4. Neutral, Inc., uses the three- to seven-year graded vesting approach in its retirement plan. Calculate the nonforfeitable percentage for each of the following employees based on the years of service completed:

Participant	Years of Service
Sandy	3
Rod	4
Tony	5
Heather	8

EXTENDER

5. Squirrel, Inc., uses the two- to six-year graded vesting approach in its retirement plan. Calculate the nonforfeitable percentage for each of the following employees based on the years of service completed:

Participant	Years of Service
Sloan	2
Jacob	3
Donna	5
Ryan	7

6. Jack, age 50, is the sole remaining participant of a money purchase pension plan. The plan is terminated, and a $260,000 taxable distribution is made to Jack. Calculate the amount of the early distribution penalty tax, if any, for 2004.

EXTENDER
Decision Making
Communications

7. Yvonne Blair receives a $165,000 lump-sum distribution from a contributory pension plan in 2004; the distribution includes employer common stock with net unrealized appreciation of $30,000. Yvonne contributed $25,000 to the qualified plan while she was an active participant from February 10, 1973, to February 10, 1978. Yvonne attained age 50 before January 1, 1986. Yvonne wishes to know her tax consequences with respect to the lump-sum distribution. Write a letter to Yvonne that includes your calculations. Her address is 209 Barrett Street, Laramie, WY 82071.

8. Wade has been an active participant in a defined benefit plan for 21 years. During his last 5 years of employment, Wade earned $27,000, $42,000, $55,000, $90,000, and $100,000, respectively (representing his highest-income years).
   a. Calculate Wade's maximum allowable benefits from this qualified plan (assume there are fewer than 100 participants).
   b. Assume that Wade's average compensation for his three high years is $142,000. Calculate Wade's maximum allowable benefits.

EXTENDER

9. Determine the maximum annual benefits payable to an employee from a defined benefit plan in the following independent situations:
   a. Quincy, age 66, has been a participant for 13 years, and his highest average compensation for 3 years is $80,000.
   b. Wendy, age 67, has been a participant for 9 years (11 years of service), and her highest average compensation for 3 years is $110,000.

10. An employer with a profit sharing plan with participants earning $205,000 or more can maximize the participants' annual additions by using what percentage profit sharing contributions?

11. A money purchase plan covers three employees: Samuel (annual compensation of $250,000), Helen (annual compensation of $138,000), and Larry (annual compensation of $41,000). If the contribution rate is 20%, what amount can be contributed to these employees' accounts?

Decision Making

12. Amber's employer, Lavender, Inc., has a § 401(k) plan that permits salary deferral elections by its employees. Amber's salary is $95,000, and her marginal tax rate is 28%.
    a. What is the maximum amount Amber can elect for salary deferral treatment for 2004?
    b. If Amber elects salary deferral treatment for the amount in (a), how much can she save in taxes?
    c. What amount would you recommend that Amber elect for salary deferral treatment for 2004?

EXTENDER

13. Miguel, a single individual, participates in a SIMPLE § 401(k) plan of his employer. The plan permits participants to contribute a percentage of their salary. Miguel elects to contribute 7% of his annual compensation of $95,000 to the plan. On what amount of his salary does Miguel pay income taxes in 2004?

14. In 2004, Susan's sole proprietorship earns $210,000 of self-employment net income (after the deduction for one-half of self-employment tax).
    a. Calculate the maximum amount that Susan can deduct for contributions to a defined contribution Keogh plan.
    b. Suppose Susan contributes more than the allowable amount to the Keogh plan. What are the consequences to her?
    c. Can Susan retire and begin receiving Keogh payments at age 55 without incurring a penalty?

15. Jesse, a self-employed accountant, has a defined contribution Keogh plan. His earned income from the business (before the deduction for one-half of any self-employment tax and before any contribution to the Keogh plan) is $40,000. He has interest income of $5,000. Assuming a self-employment tax rate of 15.3% and no other earned income, calculate Jesse's maximum contribution to his Keogh plan.

EXTENDER 16. Molly is unmarried and is an active participant in a qualified retirement plan. Her modified AGI is $51,000 in 2004.

a. Calculate the amount that Molly can contribute to a traditional IRA and the amount she can deduct.

b. Assume instead that Molly is a participant in a SIMPLE IRA and that she elects to contribute 4% of her compensation to the account, while her employer contributes 3%. What amount will be contributed for 2004? What amount will be vested?

EXTENDER 17. Answer the following independent questions with respect to a deductible IRA and § 401(k) contributions for 2004:

a. Govind earns a salary of $26,000 and is not an active participant in any other qualified plan. His wife has $600 of compensation income. What is the maximum total deductible contribution to their IRAs?

b. Danos is a participant in a SIMPLE § 401(k) plan. He contributes 6% of his salary of $31,000, and his employer contributes 4%. What amount will be contributed for the year? What amount will be vested?

18. Answer the following independent questions with respect to traditional IRA contributions for 2004:

a. Juan earns a salary of $25,000 and is not an active participant in any other qualified plan. His wife, Agnes, has no earned income. What is the maximum total deductible contribution to their IRAs? Juan wishes to contribute as much as possible to his own IRA.

b. Abby has earned income of $23,000, and her husband has earned income of $1,900. They are not active participants in any other qualified plan. What is the maximum contribution to their IRAs?

c. Leo's employer makes a contribution of $3,500 to Leo's simplified employee pension plan. If Leo is single, has earned income of $32,000, and has AGI of $29,000, what amount, if any, can he contribute to an IRA?

19. Monica establishes a Roth IRA at age 40 and contributes $3,000 per year to the Roth IRA for 25 years. The account is now worth $211,000, consisting of $75,000 in contributions plus $136,000 in accumulated earnings. How much of these funds may Monica withdraw tax-free?

20. Peter has a traditional deductible IRA with an account balance of $125,000. Of this amount, $90,000 represents contributions, and $35,000 represents earnings. In 2004, he converts his traditional IRA into a Roth IRA. What amount, if any, should he include in his gross income in 2004?

21. Jane and Bill, who have been married for six years, are both active participants in qualified retirement plans. Their total AGI for 2004 is $158,000. Each is employed and earns a salary of $79,000.

a. What amount, if any, may Jane and Bill contribute to traditional IRAs?

b. What amount, if any, may Jane and Bill contribute to Roth IRAs?

EXTENDER 22. Heather is a participant in a SIMPLE IRA plan of her employer. During 2004, she contributes 9% of her $52,000 salary, and her employer contributes 3%. What amount will be vested in her account at the end of 2004?

EXTENDER 23. In 2013, Joyce receives a $4,000 distribution from her Coverdell Education Savings Account, which has a fair market value of $10,000. Total contributions to her CESA have been $7,000. Joyce's AGI is $25,000.

a. Joyce uses the entire $4,000 to pay for qualified education expenses. What amount should she include in her gross income?

b. Assume instead that Joyce uses only $2,500 of the $4,000 distribution for qualified education expenses. What amount should she include in her gross income?

24. Gene, age 34, and Beth, age 32, have been married for nine years. Gene, who is a college student, works part-time and earns $1,500. Beth is a high school teacher and earns a salary of $34,000. Their AGI is $37,000.

a. What is the maximum amount Gene can contribute to an IRA in 2004?

b. What is the maximum amount Beth can contribute to an IRA in 2004?

Decision Making

25. Samuel, age 32, loses his job in a corporate downsizing. As a result of his termination, he receives a distribution of the balance in his § 401(k) account of $20,000 ($25,000 – $5,000 withholding) on May 1, 2004. Samuel's marginal tax rate is 28%.
    a. What effect will the distribution have on Samuel's gross income and tax liability if he invests the $20,000 received in a mutual fund?
    b. Same as (a) except that Samuel invests the $20,000 received in a traditional IRA within 60 days of the distribution.
    c. Same as (a) except that Samuel invests the $20,000 received in a Roth IRA within 60 days of the distribution.
    d. How could Samuel have received better tax consequences in (b)?

Decision Making

26. Spring, Inc., an accrual method taxpayer, pays bonuses to its key employees each year. The specific employees to receive bonuses and the amount of bonus for each recipient are determined on December 1 of each year. An employee is eligible for a bonus until retirement or death. An employee electing to postpone receipt of a bonus is allowed to designate, at any time before retirement, the time and manner of the payments and to designate the persons to receive any amount payable after death. Spring does not maintain a separate account for each employee. Under this compensation plan, Heather may elect to receive her $195,000 bonus in cash, or she may elect to defer the receipt of the bonus until 2005. She must make her decision between December 1 and December 31. Recommend to Heather which alternative to accept.

27. In which of the following situations is a nonqualified deferred compensation plan taxable under the constructive receipt doctrine?
    a. The contract is funded, and there is no substantial risk of forfeiture.
    b. Same as (a), except the employee must work for three years.
    c. An agreement to defer payment is entered into after compensation is earned.
    d. An agreement to defer payment is entered into before compensation is earned.
    e. In (a), the contract is not funded.

28. Nancy is an officer of a national bank that merges with another national bank, resulting in a change of ownership. She loses her job as a result of the merger, but she receives a cash settlement of $590,000 from her employer. Her average annual compensation for the past five tax years is $200,000.
    a. What are the tax consequences to Nancy of the $590,000 payment?
    b. Assume instead that Nancy's five-year average annual compensation was $110,000, and she receives $390,000 in the settlement. What are the tax consequences to Nancy?

29. Explain the tax treatment for a restricted stock plan where the employee makes the special election under § 83(b).

Decision Making

30. On February 20, 2004, Tim (an executive of Hawk Corporation) purchased 100 shares of Hawk stock (selling at $20 a share) for $10. A condition of the transaction was that Tim must resell the stock to Hawk at cost if he voluntarily leaves the company within five years of receiving the stock (assume this represents a substantial risk of forfeiture).
    a. Assuming that no special election is made under § 83(b), what amount, if any, is taxable to Tim in 2004?
    b. Five years later when the stock is selling for $40 a share, Tim is still employed by Hawk. What amount of ordinary income, if any, is taxable to Tim?
    c. What amount, if any, is deductible by Hawk as compensation expense five years later?
    d. Should Tim make the § 83(b) special election in 2004? What amount would be taxable in 2004 if he makes the special election?
    e. In (d), what amount would be deductible by Hawk five years later?
    f. Under (d), assume Tim sold all the stock six years later for $65 per share. How much capital gain is included in his gross income?
    g. In (d), what loss is available to Tim if he voluntarily resigns in 2007 before the five-year period and does not sell the stock back to the corporation?
    h. In (g), in the year Tim resigns, what amount, if any, would be taxable to Hawk Corporation?

Decision Making

31. Would a 30-year-old corporate executive in the 35% tax bracket prefer an extra $30,000 bonus or the option to purchase $30,000 worth of securities for $13,000 from the employer under a nonqualified stock option plan in the current year?

32. On July 2, 2002, Black Corporation sold 1,000 of its common shares (worth $14 per share) to Earl, an employee, for $5 per share. The sale was subject to Earl's agreement to resell the shares to the corporation for $5 per share if his employment is terminated within the following four years. The shares had a value of $24 per share on July 2, 2006. Earl sells the shares for $31 per share on September 16, 2006. No special election under § 83(b) is made.
    a. What amount, if any, is taxed to Earl on July 2, 2002?
    b. On July 2, 2006?
    c. On September 16, 2006?
    d. What deduction, if any, will Black Corporation obtain? When?
    e. Assume the same facts, except that Earl makes an election under § 83(b). What amount, if any, will be taxed to Earl on July 2, 2002, July 2, 2006, and September 16, 2006?
    f. Will the assumption made in (e) have any effect on any deduction Black Corporation will receive? Explain.

33. Rosa exercises ISOs for 100 shares of Copper Corporation common stock at the option price of $100 per share on May 21, 2003, when the fair market value is $120 per share. She sells the 100 shares of common stock three and one-half years later for $140.
    a. Calculate the long-term capital gain and the ordinary income on the sale.
    b. Assume Rosa holds the stock only seven months and sells the shares for $140 per share. Calculate the capital gain and ordinary income on the sale.
    c. In (b), what amount can Copper Corporation deduct? When?
    d. Assume instead that Rosa holds the stock for two years and sells the shares for $115 per share. Calculate any capital gain and ordinary income on this transaction.
    e. In (a), assume the options are nonqualified stock options with a nonascertainable fair market value on the date of the grant. Calculate the long-term capital gain and ordinary income on the date of the sale.
    f. In (e), assume that each option has an ascertainable fair market value of $10 on the date of the grant and that no substantial risk of forfeiture exists. Calculate the long-term capital gain and the ordinary income on the date of the sale.

34. On November 19, 2002, Rex is granted a nonqualified stock option to purchase 100 shares of Tan Company. On that date, the stock is selling for $8 per share, and the option price is $9 per share. Rex exercises the option on August 21, 2003, when the stock is selling for $10 per share. Five months later, Rex sells the shares for $11.50 per share.
    a. What amount is taxable to Rex in 2002?
    b. What amount is taxable to Rex in 2003?
    c. What amount and type of gain are taxable to Rex in 2004?
    d. What amount, if any, is deductible by Tan Company in 2003?
    e. What amount, if any, is recognized in 2004 if the stock is sold for $9.50 per share?

Decision Making
Communications

35. Sara Reid, age 35, is the owner of a small business. She is trying to decide whether to have a § 401(k) plan or a simplified employee pension plan. She is not interested in a SIMPLE § 401(k) plan. Her salary will be approximately $42,000, and she will have no employees. She asks you to provide her with information on the advantages and disadvantages of both types of plans and your recommendation. Draft a letter to Sara that contains your response. Her address is 1000 Canal Avenue, New Orleans, LA 70148.

Decision Making

36. Lou's employer provides a qualified cafeteria plan under which he can choose cash of $9,000 or health and accident insurance premiums worth approximately $7,000. If Lou is in the 35% tax bracket, advise him of his tax alternatives.

BRIDGE DISCIPLINE

Communications

1. Eagle, Inc., is a very successful closely held corporation valued at $15 million (12,000 outstanding shares). John Harris, the founder, owns 70% of the corporation, and a group of 10 passive investors owns the remaining 30%. John is 58 years old and has substantially all of his wealth tied up in the business. Since John started the company 20 years ago, he has a very low tax basis in his stock ($25,000). He has four planning goals:

   - Diversify his investment portfolio by selling part of his stock.
   - Enable his employees to have an ownership interest in Eagle, Inc.
   - Raise $5 million of new capital.
   - Accomplish the above goals in a tax-efficient manner.

   Eagle's total annual compensation will be $5 million, with no one employee being paid more than $190,000. At this point, all of the employees are over 21 years of age and have worked at least four years for the company. Assume each share of stock will be valued at $1,250.

   Write a research memo discussing how an ESOP could be used to achieve John's goals and illustrate how the plan would work.

2. When making investment decisions for your retirement plan, one of the items you review is the reported earnings of the corporation.
   a. Describe how the current reporting of employee stock option awards affects a corporation's earnings.
   b. How does this compare to the tax treatment of employee stock options in computing the corporation's taxable income?
   c. What do you think is the proper accounting treatment for employee stock options?
   d. Are any corporations currently expensing employee stock options?

Research Problems

THOMSON RIA

Note: Solutions to Research Problems can be prepared by using the ***RIA Checkpoint® Student Edition*** *online research product, which is available to accompany this text. It is also possible to prepare solutions to the Research Problems by using tax research materials found in a standard tax library.*

Communications

Research Problem 1. Mr. Sanjay Baker and his sister owned and operated a mail-order business in corporate form. The corporation used the homes of Mr. Baker and his sister for corporate mail-order activities (assembling, storing inventory, etc.). The corporation paid Mr. Baker and the sister rent for the use of the homes. The payments were deducted as rent and reported by the two parties on their tax returns. The IRS disallowed most of the deduction, contending that the rent was excessive. Is the excessive rent deductible as compensation? Write a letter to Mr. Baker that contains your advice and prepare a memo for the tax files. His address is 63 Rose Avenue, San Francisco, CA 94117.

Partial list of research aids:
Multnomah Operating Co. v. Comm., 57–2 USTC ¶9979, 52 AFTR 672, 248 F.2d 661 (CA–9, 1957).

Research Problem 2. Shelly and Austin were divorced in 2004. Since they lived in a community property state, the judgment dissolving the marriage ordered that Austin's traditional deductible IRA be divided equally between Shelly and him. Austin accordingly withdrew $125,000 from his IRA and transferred $112,000 to Shelly. Discuss the tax consequences for Shelly and for Austin.

Partial list of research aids:
§§ 72(t), 408(d)(1), 408(d)(6), 408(g), and 6662(a).

Research Problem 3. May, Inc., maintains a money purchase pension plan (MPPP) that qualifies under § 401(a). On termination or partial termination of the plan, all of the participants will vest in 100% of their account balances. During the year, May converts the MPPP into a profit sharing plan that covers the same employees and continues the same vesting schedule. If the assets and liabilities in the profit sharing plan retain their MPPP attributes, has a partial termination occurred? Is full vesting required on the merger of an MPPP into a profit sharing plan?

Research Problem 4. Jim Raby transfers one-half of his compensatory stock options (ISOs and nonqualified stock options) to his ex-wife as part of a divorce settlement. Discuss the tax aspects of this transfer.

Research Problem 5. What is a phantom stock plan? Outline the tax treatment of such plans. Could a phantom stock payment be considered performance-based compensation for purposes of the $1 million deduction limitation on executive pay?

Internet Activity

Use the tax resources of the Internet to address the following questions. Do not restrict your search to the World Wide Web, but include a review of newsgroups and general reference materials, practitioner sites and resources, primary sources of the tax law, chat rooms and discussion groups, and other opportunities.

Research Problem 6. Locate and download an Internet retirement calculator. Use this program to help you answer the questions in Problems 13 and 14.

Research Problem 7. Search the Internet for information about cash balance plans, especially any negative information. Why are some employees so concerned about their employer's decision to convert their current retirement plan to a cash balance plan?

CHAPTER 12

Accounting Periods and Methods

LEARNING OBJECTIVES

After completing Chapter 12, you should be able to:

LO.1

Understand the relevance of the accounting period concept, the different types of accounting periods, and the limitations on their use.

LO.2

Outline the procedure for changing accounting methods.

LO.3

Determine when the installment method of accounting can be used and apply the related calculation techniques.

LO.4

Understand the alternative methods of accounting for long-term contracts (the completed contract method and the percentage of completion method).

LO.5

Recognize when accounting for inventories is required.

http://wft.swlearning.com

OUTLINE

TAX TALK

I recently heard a CPA remark that the only accounting principle which the Internal Revenue Service regards as "generally accepted" is "A bird in the hand is worth two in the bush." Although my friend overstates his case a bit—quite a bit—I cannot dismiss the thrust of his comment without some soul searching.

—Sheldon S. Cohen, former IRS Commissioner

Tax practitioners must deal with the issue of *when* particular items of income and expense are recognized as well as the basic issue of *whether* the items are includible in taxable income. Earlier chapters discussed the types of income subject to tax and allowable deductions (the *whether* issue) and explained the principal tax accounting methods available. This chapter examines in more detail the issue of the periods in which income and deductions are reported (the *when* issue). Generally, a taxpayer's income and deductions must be assigned to particular 12-month periods—calendar years or fiscal years.

Income and deductions are placed within particular years through the use of tax accounting methods. As explained in Chapters 3 and 4, the basic accounting methods are the cash method, accrual method, and hybrid method. Other special purpose methods, such as the installment method and the methods used for long-term construction contracts, are available for specific circumstances or types of transactions.

Over the long run, the accounting period used by a taxpayer will not affect the aggregate amount of reported taxable income. However, taxable income for any particular year may vary significantly due to the use of a particular reporting period. Through the choice of accounting methods or accounting periods, it is possible to accomplish one's tax goals by arranging to postpone the recognition of taxable income or accelerate an available deduction.

TAX IN THE NEWS

Changing Tax Rates Create Tax Planning Opportunities

When tax rates remain unchanged between tax years, the taxpayer will generally prefer to defer income and accelerate deductions where the opportunity exists. When tax rates will decrease in the subsequent year, however, it becomes especially important to accelerate deductions to achieve the maximum tax savings from each deduction.

The Tax Relief Reconciliation Act of 2001 created opportunities for tax planning because it provided for reductions in tax rates, to be phased in over the years 2002 through 2006. A taxpayer who accelerated deductions into 2002, rather than taking them in 2003, enjoyed an additional bonus from the Jobs and Growth Tax Relief Reconciliation Act of 2003. This legislation accelerated the reduction in tax rates, thereby reducing the tax benefits of deductions taken in 2003 compared to deductions taken in 2002.

BRIDGE DISCIPLINE

Bridge to Financial Accounting

The determination of taxable income is governed by the Federal income tax law. Conversely, the determination of financial accounting income is based on financial accounting rules (i.e., GAAP). Differences in these two amounts for a particular year may be based on permanent differences (e.g., a dividends received deduction is allowed in calculating taxable income and is not allowed in calculating financial accounting income) and on temporary differences (e.g., revenues and expenses are reported in different periods for income tax purposes and for financial reporting purposes).

The existence of these temporary differences results in substantial complexity under SFAS No. 109 in calculating the income statement tax provision and in calculating deferred taxes on the balance sheet. This complexity could be eliminated if, as some business and accounting professionals have proposed, the FASB were to modify the current financial reporting standard and base the financial accounting tax provision on the current period income tax liability on the income tax return.

The income tax liability on the Federal income tax return is calculated by applying the tax rates to the tax base (i.e., taxable income). Obviously, the tax rates used are the current income tax rates contained in the Internal Revenue Code. SFAS No. 109 provides that in calculating the tax provision and the deferred taxes, both current rates and future enacted rates (i.e., future enacted rates are used in calculating the deferred taxes) are used.

LO.1

Understand the relevance of the accounting period concept, the different types of accounting periods, and the limitations on their use.

Accounting Periods

IN GENERAL

A taxpayer who keeps adequate books and records may be allowed to elect a **fiscal year,** a 12-month period ending on the *last day* of a month other than December, for the **accounting period.** Otherwise, a *calendar year* must be used.[1] Frequently, corporations and other business entities can satisfy the record-keeping requirements

[1] § 441(g).

and elect to use a fiscal year.[2] Often the fiscal year conforms to a natural business year (e.g., a summer resort's fiscal year may end on September 30, after the close of the season). Individuals seldom use a fiscal year because they do not maintain the necessary books and records to do so, and because complications can arise as a result of changes in the tax law (e.g., often the transition rules and effective dates differ for fiscal year taxpayers).

Generally, a taxable year may not exceed 12 calendar months. However, if certain requirements are met, a taxpayer may elect to use an annual period that varies from 52 to 53 weeks.[3] In that case, the year-end must be on the same day of the week (e.g., the Tuesday falling closest to October 31 or the last Tuesday in October). The day of the week selected for ending the year will depend upon business considerations. For example, a retail business that is not open on Sundays may end its tax year on a Sunday so that it can take an inventory without interrupting business operations.

EXAMPLE 1

Wren Corporation is in the business of selling farm supplies. Its natural business year terminates at the end of October with the completion of harvesting. At the end of the fiscal year, Wren must take an inventory, which is most easily accomplished on a Tuesday. Therefore, Wren could adopt a 52–53 week tax year ending on the Tuesday closest to October 31. If Wren selects this method, the year-end date may fall in the following month if that Tuesday is closer to October 31. The tax year ending in 2004 will contain 53 weeks beginning on Wednesday, October 29, 2003, and ending on Tuesday, November 2, 2004. The tax year ending in 2005 will have 52 weeks beginning on Wednesday, November 3, 2004, and ending on Tuesday, November 1, 2005. ■

SPECIFIC PROVISIONS FOR PARTNERSHIPS, S CORPORATIONS, AND PERSONAL SERVICE CORPORATIONS

Partnerships and S Corporations. When a partner's tax year and the partnership's tax year differ, the partner will enjoy a deferral of income. This results because the partner reports his or her share of the partnership's income and deductions for the partnership's tax year ending within or with the partner's tax year.[4] For example, if the tax year of the partnership ends on January 31, a calendar year partner will not report partnership profits for the first 11 months of the partnership tax year until the following year. Therefore, partnerships are subject to special tax year requirements.

In general, the partnership tax year must be the same as the tax year of the majority interest partners. The **majority interest partners** are the partners who own a greater-than-50 percent interest in the partnership capital and profits. If there are no majority interest partners, the partnership must adopt the same tax year as its principal partners. A **principal partner** is a partner with a 5 percent or more interest in the partnership capital or profits.[5]

EXAMPLE 2

The RST Partnership is owned equally by Rose Corporation, Silver Corporation, and Tom. The partners have the following tax years.

	Partner's Tax Year Ending
Rose	June 30
Silver	June 30
Tom	December 31

The partnership's tax year must end on June 30. If Silver Corporation's as well as Tom's year ended on December 31, the partnership would be required to adopt a calendar year. ■

[2]Temp.Reg. § 1.441–1T(e)(2).
[3]§ 441(f).
[4]Reg. § 1.706–1(a).
[5]§§ 706(b)(1)(B) and (b)(3).

If the principal partners do not all have the same tax year and no majority of partners have the same tax year, the partnership must use a year that results in the *least aggregate deferral* of income.[6] Under the **least aggregate deferral method**, the different tax years of the principal partners are tested to determine which produces the least aggregate deferral. This is calculated by first multiplying the combined percentages of the principal partners with the same tax year by the months of deferral for the test year. Once this is done for each set of principal partners with the same tax year, the resulting products are summed to produce the aggregate deferral. After calculating the aggregate deferral for each of the test years, the test year with the smallest summation (the least aggregate deferral) is the tax year for the partnership.

EXAMPLE 3

The DE Partnership is owned equally by Dove Corporation and Egret, Inc. Dove's fiscal year ends on March 31, and Egret's fiscal year ends on August 31. The partnership must use the partner's fiscal year that will result in the least aggregate deferral of income. Therefore, the fiscal years ending March 31 and August 31 must both be tested.

Test for Fiscal Year Ending March 31

Partner	Year Ends	Profit %	Months of Deferral	Product
Dove	3–31	50	0	0
Egret	8–31	50	5	2.5
Aggregate deferral months				2.5

Thus, with a year ending March 31, Egret would be able to defer its half of the income for five months. That is, Egret's share of the partnership income for the fiscal year ending March 31, 2005, would not be included in its income until August 31, 2005.

Test for Fiscal Year Ending August 31

Partner	Year Ends	Profit %	Months of Deferral	Product
Dove	3–31	50	7	3.5
Egret	8–31	50	0	0
Aggregate deferral months				3.5

Thus, with a year ending August 31, Dove would be able to defer its half of the income for seven months. That is, Dove's share of the partnership income for the fiscal year ending August 31, 2005, would not be included in its income until March 31, 2006.

The year ending March 31 must be used because it results in the least aggregate deferral of income. ■

Generally, S corporations must adopt a calendar year.[7] However, partnerships and S corporations may *elect* an otherwise *impermissible year* under either of the following conditions.

- A business purpose for the year can be demonstrated.[8]
- The partnership's or S corporation's year results in a deferral of not more than three months' income, and the entity agrees to make required tax payments.[9]

[6] Temp.Reg. § 1.706–1T(a)(2).
[7] §§ 1378(a) and (b).
[8] §§ 706(b)(1)(C) and 1378(b)(2).
[9] §§ 444(b)(1) and (c)(1).

Business Purpose. The only business purpose for a fiscal year that the IRS has acknowledged is the need to conform the tax year to the *natural business year* of an entity.[10] An objective *gross receipts test* is applied to determine if the entity has a natural business year. At least 25 percent of the entity's gross receipts for the 12-month period must be realized in the final 2 months of the 12-month period for three consecutive years. Generally, only seasonal businesses qualify under this test.

EXAMPLE 4

A Virginia Beach motel had gross receipts as follows.

	2002	2003	2004
July–August receipts	$ 300,000	$250,000	$ 325,000
September 1–August 31 receipts	1,000,000	900,000	1,250,000
Receipts for 2 months divided by receipts for 12 months	30.0%	27.8%	26.0%

Since it satisfies the natural business year test, the motel will be allowed to use a fiscal year ending August 31. ■

Required Tax Payments. For S corporations and partnerships that do not wish to use a required year or a business purpose year, another year-end may be elected, as long as the resulting deferral period does not exceed three months. This election is not free of costs. In particular, the electing entity must make a *required tax payment* for any year that the election is in effect.[11] The required tax payment is a refundable, non-interest-bearing deposit (not deductible for Federal tax purposes) made to the IRS. The deposit compensates the government for the interest lost on any deferred tax liability. The required tax payment is credited against future required tax payments or returned in the following year if the entity's partners or shareholders are required to pay tax on previously deferred income.

The amount due is computed by applying the highest individual tax rate plus 1 percent to an estimate of the deferral period income. The deferral period runs from the close of the fiscal year to the end of the calendar year. Estimated income for this period is based on the average monthly earnings for the previous fiscal year. The amount due is reduced by the balance of required tax payments on deposit for the previous year.[12]

EXAMPLE 5

Brown, Inc., an S corporation, elected a fiscal year ending September 30. Bob, a calendar year taxpayer, is the only shareholder. For the fiscal year ending September 30, 2004, Brown earned $100,000. Brown is permitted to have a September 30 fiscal year, since that year-end will result in only a three-month deferral of income for Bob. An annual tax payment is also required. If required tax payments for the previous year were $5,000, the corporation must pay $4,000 by April 15, 2005.

($100,000 × 3/12 × 36%*) – $5,000 (credit from prior year) = $4,000.

*Maximum § 1 rate of 35% + 1%. ■

[10] Rev.Rul. 87–57, 1987–2 C.B. 117, and Rev.Proc. 87–32, 1987–1 C.B. 131.

[11] §§ 444(c) and 7519. No payment is required if the calculated amount is $500 or less.

[12] § 7519(b).

Personal Service Corporations. A **personal service corporation (PSC)** is a corporation whose shareholder-employees provide personal services (e.g., medical, dental, legal, accounting, engineering, actuarial, consulting, or performing arts). Generally, a PSC must use a calendar year.[13] However, a PSC can *elect* a fiscal year under either of the following conditions.

- A business purpose for the year can be demonstrated.
- The PSC year results in a deferral of not more than three months' income, the corporation pays the shareholder-employee's salary during the portion of the calendar year after the close of the fiscal year, and the salary for that period is at least proportionate to the shareholder-employee's salary received for the preceding fiscal year.[14]

DIGGING DEEPER 1

Find more information on this topic at our Web site: ***http://wft-advanced.swlearning.com***.

EXAMPLE 6

Nancy's personal service corporation paid Nancy a salary of $120,000 during its fiscal year ending September 30, 2004. The corporation cannot satisfy the business purpose test for a fiscal year. The corporation can continue to use its fiscal year without any negative tax effects, provided Nancy receives at least $30,000 [(3 months/12 months) × $120,000] as salary during the period October 1 through December 31, 2004. ■

CHOOSING A TAX YEAR

A taxpayer elects to use a calendar or fiscal year by the timely filing of the initial tax return. For all subsequent years, the taxpayer must use this same period unless approval for change is obtained from the IRS.[15]

CHANGES IN THE ACCOUNTING PERIOD

A taxpayer must obtain consent from the IRS before changing the tax year.[16] This consent requirement is significant in that it permits the IRS to issue authoritative administrative guidelines that must be met by taxpayers who wish to change their accounting period. An application for permission to change tax years must be made on Form 1128, Application for Change in Accounting Period. The application must be filed on or before the fifteenth day of the second calendar month following the close of the short period that results from the change in accounting period.[17]

EXAMPLE 7

Beginning in 2004, Gold Corporation, a calendar year taxpayer, would like to switch to a fiscal year ending March 31. The first period after the change in accounting period (January 1, 2004 through March 31, 2004) is less than a 12-month period and is referred to as a *short period*. Thus, the corporation must file Form 1128 by May 15, 2004. ■

IRS Requirements. The IRS will not grant permission for the change unless the taxpayer can establish a substantial business purpose for the request. One substantial business purpose is to change to a tax year that coincides with the *natural business year* (discussed earlier).[18]

DIGGING DEEPER 2

Find more information on this topic at our Web site: ***http://wft-advanced.swlearning.com***.

---

[13] § 441(i).

[14] §§ 444(b)(1), (c)(2), and 280H.

[15] Temp.Reg. §§ 1.441–1T(b)(3) and (4).

[16] § 442. Under certain conditions, corporations are allowed to change tax years without obtaining IRS approval. See Reg. § 1.442–1(c)(1).

[17] Reg. § 1.442–1(b)(1).

[18] Rev.Proc. 87–32, 1987–1 C.B. 131, and Rev.Rul. 87–57, 1987–2 C.B. 117.

TAX FACT

FREE TO CHOOSE?

Despite the freedom to select any fiscal tax year end, most corporations still use the calendar year.

Corporation Returns Filed Using Fiscal Tax Years, 2002 Data

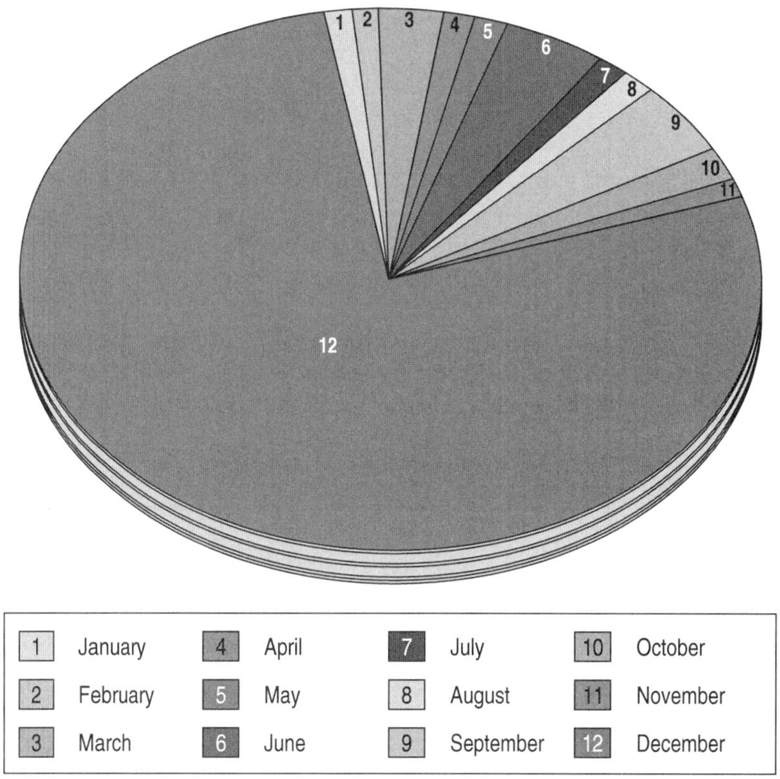

TAXABLE PERIODS OF LESS THAN ONE YEAR

A **short taxable year** (or **short period**) is a period of less than 12 calendar months. A taxpayer may have a short year for (1) the first income tax return, (2) the final income tax return, or (3) a change in the tax year. If the short period results from a change in the taxpayer's annual accounting period, the taxable income for the period must be annualized. Due to the progressive tax rate structure, taxpayers could reap benefits from a short-period return if some adjustments were not required. Thus, the taxpayer is required to complete the following.

1. Annualize the short-period income.

$$\text{Annualized income} = \text{Short-period income} \times \frac{12}{\text{Number of months in the short period}}$$

2. Compute the tax on the annualized income.
3. Convert the tax on the annualized income to a short-period tax.

$$\text{Short-period tax} = \text{Tax on annualized income} \times \frac{\text{Number of months in the short period}}{12}$$

EXAMPLE 8

Gray Corporation obtained permission to change from a calendar year to a fiscal year ending September 30, beginning in 2004. For the short period January 1 through September 30, 2004, the corporation's taxable income was $48,000. The relevant tax rates and the resultant short-period tax are computed as follows.

Amount of Taxable Income	**Tax Rates**
$0–$50,000	15% of taxable income
Over $50,000 to $75,000	$7,500 plus 25% of taxable income in excess of $50,000

Calculation of Short-Period Tax	
Annualized income ($48,000 × $^{12}/_{9}$) =	$64,000
Tax on annualized income [$7,500 + 0.25($64,000 – $50,000)] =	$11,000
Short-period tax = ($11,000 × $^{9}/_{12}$) =	$ 8,250
Annualizing the income increased the tax by $1,050:	
Tax with annualizing	$ 8,250
Tax without annualizing ($48,000 × 0.15)	(7,200)
Increase in tax from annualizing	$ 1,050

TAX YEAR RELIEF

Several provisions in the Code are designed to give the taxpayer relief from the harsh results that can be produced by the combined effects of an arbitrary accounting period and a progressive rate structure. For example, under the net operating loss carryback and carryover rules, a loss in one year can be carried back and offset against taxable income for the preceding 2 years. Unused net operating losses are then carried forward for 20 years.[19] In addition, the Code provides special relief provisions for casualty losses pursuant to a natural disaster and for the reporting of insurance proceeds from destruction of crops.[20]

DIGGING DEEPER 3

Find more information on this topic at our Web site: ***http://wft-advanced.swlearning.com.***

[19] § 172. Losses incurred in 2001 or 2002 can be carried back for 5 years.

[20] §§ 165(i) and 451(d).

TAX IN THE NEWS

Applying the All Events Test to Cooperative Advertising

Manufacturers often offer local dealers a rebate for a portion of the cost of advertising that includes the manufacturer's brand. Automobile manufacturers make extensive use of these cooperative advertising plans. Under such a plan, the dealer runs advertisements in local newspapers and applies for a rebate from the manufacturer. The tax accounting issue is when should the manufacturer take the deduction for the rebate. Is the all events test satisfied when the dealer places the advertisement or not until the dealer applies for the rebate?

The IRS has ruled that the all events test is satisfied when the advertising occurs and that the filing of a claim for a rebate is merely a ministerial act. Therefore, the manufacturer can take the deduction in the year the advertising occurs, rather than when the dealer's claim is filed.

LO.2

Outline the procedure for changing accounting methods.

Change of Accounting Methods

The Code allows taxpayers to use either the cash receipts and disbursements method, the accrual method, or some combination of the two. Taxpayers with more than one business may use a different method for each business,[21] but whichever method is used must *clearly reflect* the taxpayer's income.[22]

The two principal methods are themselves very different. The **cash method** focuses on when cash or its equivalent is received or paid. The **accrual method** reports income when it is earned as determined by legal and economic considerations. Deductions under this method are claimed when a taxpayer's liability has been established and *economic performance* has occurred.

But what happens if a taxpayer wants to change its accounting method? Some taxpayers may not change their method; for example, if inventories are a material factor

BRIDGE DISCIPLINE

Bridge to Financial Accounting

The accounting method used by an entity governs when revenues and expenses are reported. Potential methods are the cash method, the accrual method, and the hybrid method.

Generally accepted accounting principles (GAAP) utilize the accrual method, and Federal income tax reporting permits all three under particular circumstances. Recognizing the opportunities available under the cash method, the Code imposes limitations on its use.

Even when the accrual method is used for both Federal income tax purposes and financial reporting purposes, differences can occur. For financial reporting purposes, the income associated with the receipt of a cash prepayment is not recognized until it is earned. For income tax purposes, the taxpayer may be required to recognize the cash prepayment as income when it is received. An entity making a cash prepayment cannot deduct it as an expense for financial reporting purposes until the expense is incurred. For income tax purposes, the taxpayer may be able to deduct the expense when paid under the "one-year rule for prepaid expenses."

[21] § 446(d).

[22] § 446(b).

TAX IN THE NEWS

A Strict Definition of "Services" Cost American Express a Bundle

American Express charges an annual fee for the use of the credit cards it issues. Previously, the company had reported the income in the year of receipt. It attempted to change its accounting method to prorate the income over 12 months. The negative adjustment due to the change in accounting method would have reduced the company's tax bill by $200 million. The company argued that the prepaid income was for services that would be rendered over a 12-month period and therefore was eligible for amortization over the prepayment period under Revenue Procedure 71–21.

The Court of Federal Claims ruled that the customer was not prepaying for services. Rather, the customer was paying for the ability to borrow money, more akin to interest than a service, and prepaid interest is not eligible for amortization. Thus, a subtle distinction made a significant difference in American Express's cash account.

in the business (see the final section of this chapter), the accrual method is *mandatory*.[23] Similarly, the cash method may not be used by corporations that have annual gross receipts in excess of $5 million or by partnerships that have a corporation as a partner.[24] Within these limitations, however, a taxpayer can change accounting methods. This section considers the process of doing so and the adjustments that are required.

A taxpayer elects a particular accounting method when it files its initial tax return using that method. To change that method, the taxpayer must obtain the permission of the IRS. A request for change is made on Form 3115, Application for Change in Accounting Method. Generally, the form must be filed within the taxable year of the desired change.[25]

The term **accounting method** encompasses not only the overall accounting method used by the taxpayer (the cash or accrual method) but also the treatment of any material item of income or deduction.[26] Thus, a change in the method of deducting property taxes from a cash basis to an accrual basis that results in a deduction for taxes in a different year constitutes a change in an accounting method. Another example of an accounting method change is a switch in the method or basis used in the valuation of inventories.

CORRECTION OF AN ERROR

A change in accounting method must be distinguished from the *correction of an error*. A taxpayer can correct an error (by filing amended returns) without permission, and the IRS can simply adjust the taxpayer's liability if an error is discovered on audit of the return. Some examples of errors are incorrect postings, errors in the calculation of tax liability or tax credits, deductions of business expense items that are actually personal, and omissions of income and deductions.[27]

CHANGE FROM AN INCORRECT METHOD

An *incorrect accounting method* is the consistent (year-after-year) use of an incorrect rule to report an item of income or expense. An incorrect accounting method

[23]Reg. § 1.446–1(a)(4)(i).
[24]§§ 448(a) and (b)(3).
[25]Rev.Proc. 99–49, 1999–2 C.B. 725.
[26]Reg. § 1.446–1(a)(1).
[27]Reg. § 1.446–1(e)(2)(ii)(b).

generally will not affect a taxpayer's total lifetime income (unlike an error). That is, an incorrect method has a self-balancing mechanism. For example, deducting freight on inventory in the year the goods are purchased, rather than when the inventory is sold, is an incorrect accounting method. The total cost of goods sold over the life of the business is not affected, but the year-to-year income is incorrect.[28]

An incorrect method is not treated as a mechanical error that can be corrected by merely filing an amended tax return. Instead, permission must be obtained from the IRS to change to a correct method.

NET ADJUSTMENTS DUE TO CHANGE IN ACCOUNTING METHOD

In the year of a change in accounting method, some items of income and expense may have to be adjusted to prevent the change from distorting taxable income.

EXAMPLE 9

In 2004, White Corporation, with consent from the IRS, switched from the cash to the accrual basis for reporting sales and cost of goods sold. The corporation's accrual basis gross profit for the year was computed as follows.

Sales		$100,000
Beginning inventory	$ 15,000	
Plus: Purchases	60,000	
Less: Ending inventory	(10,000)	
Cost of goods sold		(65,000)
Gross profit		$ 35,000

At the end of the previous year, White Corporation had accounts receivable of $25,000 and accounts payable for merchandise of $34,000. The accounts receivable from the previous year in the amount of $25,000 were never included in gross income since White was on the cash basis and did not recognize the uncollected receivables. In the current year, the $25,000 was not included in the accrual basis sales since the sales were made in a prior year. Therefore, a $25,000 adjustment to income is required to prevent the receivables from being omitted from income.

The corollary of the failure to recognize a prior year's receivables is the failure to recognize a prior year's accounts payable. The beginning of the year's accounts payable was not included in the current or prior year's purchases. Thus, a deduction for the $34,000 was not taken in either year and is therefore included as an adjustment to income for the period of change.

An adjustment is also required to reflect the $15,000 beginning inventory that White deducted (due to the use of a cash method of accounting) in the previous year. In this instance, the cost of goods sold during the year of change was increased by the beginning inventory and resulted in a double deduction.

The net adjustment due to the change in accounting method is computed as follows.

Beginning inventory (deducted in prior and current year)	$ 15,000
Beginning accounts receivable (omitted from income)	25,000
Beginning accounts payable (omitted from deductions)	(34,000)
Net increase in taxable income	$ 6,000

[28]But see *Korn Industries v. U.S.*, 76–1 USTC ¶9354, 37 AFTR2d 76–1228, 532 F.2d 1352 (Ct.Cls., 1976).

Disposition of the Net Adjustment. If the IRS *requires* a taxpayer to change an accounting method, the net adjustment is added to gross income for the year of the change. If this adjustment exceeds $3,000, the taxpayer can elect to calculate the tax by spreading the adjustment over one or more previous years.[29] This election can be beneficial if the taxpayer's marginal tax rate was lower in those prior years than in the year of the change.

To encourage taxpayers to *voluntarily* change from incorrect methods and to facilitate changes from one correct method to another, the IRS generally allows a taxpayer to spread a positive adjustment into future years. One-fourth of the adjustment is applied to the year of the change, and one-fourth is applied to each of the next three years. A negative adjustment can be deducted in the year of the change.[30]

EXAMPLE 10

White Corporation in the preceding example voluntarily changed from an incorrect method (the cash basis was incorrect because inventories were material to the business) to a correct method. The company must add $1,500 (¼ × $6,000 positive adjustment) to its 2004, 2005, 2006, and 2007 income. ■

LO.3

Determine when the installment method of accounting can be used and apply the related calculation techniques.

Installment Method

IN GENERAL

Under the general rule for computing gain or loss from the sale of property, a taxpayer recognizes the entire amount of gain or loss upon the sale or other disposition of the property.

EXAMPLE 11

Meadowlark, Inc., sells property to Pintail Corporation for $10,000 cash plus Pintail's note (fair market value and face amount of $90,000). Meadowlark's basis for the property was $15,000. Gain or loss is computed under either the cash or accrual basis as follows.

Cash down payment	$ 10,000
Note receivable	90,000
Amount realized	$100,000
Less: Basis in the property	(15,000)
Realized gain	$ 85,000

■

In this example, the general rule for recognizing gain or loss requires Meadowlark to pay tax on the *entire* gain in the year of sale even though it received only $10,000 cash. Congress enacted the installment sales provisions to prevent this sort of hardship by allowing the taxpayer to spread the gain from installment sales over the collection period.

Eligibility. The **installment method** applies only to *gains* (not losses) from the sale of property where the seller will receive at least one payment *after* the year of

[29] § 481(b). See also Notice 98–31, 1998–2 C.B. 9.

[30] Rev.Proc. 99–49, 1999–2 C.B. 725, and Rev.Proc. 2002–19, 2002–1 C.B. 696.

sale. Even when this requirement is met, the installment method may not be used for sales of the following assets.

- Stocks or securities traded on an established market.[31]
- Property subject to *depreciation recapture,* as explained in Chapter 7.[32]
- Property held for sale in the ordinary course of business.[33]

Still, some taxpayers may use the installment method for the sale of certain residential lots, certain time-share units, and farming business property.[34]

The Nonelective Aspect. If a sale is eligible for the installment method, it *must* be reported on that basis. A special election is required to report such a sale by any method other than the installment method.

Computing the Gain for Each Year. The gain reported each year on an installment sale is computed by the following formula.

$$\frac{\text{Total gain}}{\text{Contract price}} \times \text{Payments received} = \text{Recognized gain.}$$

The taxpayer computes each variable as follows.

1. *Total gain* is the selling price reduced by selling expenses and the adjusted basis of the property, usually the taxpayer's cost. The selling price is the total amount received by the seller, including notes receivable from the buyer and any seller's liabilities that are assumed by the buyer.
2. *Contract price* is the selling price less any seller's liabilities that are assumed by the buyer. Generally, the contract price is the amount, other than interest, that the seller will eventually receive from the buyer.
3. *Payments received* are the collections on the contract price received in the tax year. This generally is the cash received less any interest income collected for the period.

DIGGING DEEPER 4

Find more information on this topic at our Web site: ***http://wft-advanced.swlearning.com.***

EXAMPLE 12

Paul accounts for his sale of some investment land as follows.

Sales price (amount realized)		
Cash down payment	$ 1,000	
Paul's mortgage assumed by buyer	3,000	
Notes payable to the seller	13,000	$ 17,000
Less: Selling expenses		(500)
Less: Paul's basis		(10,000)
Total gain		$ 6,500

The contract price is $14,000 ($17,000 sales price – $3,000 mortgage assumed). If only $1,000 is received in the year of sale, the recognized gain in that year is:

$$\frac{\$6{,}500 \text{ (total gain)}}{\$14{,}000 \text{ (contract price)}} \times \$1{,}000 = \$464.$$

[31] § 453(k)(2)(A).
[32] § 453(i).
[33] § 453(l).
[34] §§ 453(l)(2)(A) and (B).

PLANNING STRATEGIES

The Installment Method

FRAMEWORK FOCUS: INCOME

STRATEGY ➤ POSTPONE RECOGNITION OF INCOME TO ACHIEVE TAX DEFERRAL.

The installment method enables a taxpayer to defer reporting taxable gain until subsequent years. Once the method is used for a particular sale, however, that method must be continued for the duration of that transaction. While the *time value of money* generally advises deferral of tax liability, deferral is not always beneficial. A taxpayer might be in a higher tax bracket in later years due to other transactions or the expansion of that taxpayer's business. Similarly, Congress may raise tax rates in the future, and those higher rates usually apply to payments from an earlier year's installment sale, unless some special exception is created. In such circumstances, the taxpayer's increased tax liability might exceed any financial benefit obtained from deferring the tax on the original transaction, particularly if the deferral period was only a few years.

On the other hand, the installment method can be particularly useful if a taxpayer anticipates being in a *lower tax bracket* in later years. Whether due to a taxpayer's impending retirement or a significant reduction in a business's activities, this lower tax rate would mean less tax owed, in addition to the financial benefit gained by deferring taxes to a later year. Moreover, Congress also lowers tax rates from time to time, and a taxpayer might reap still further benefits from an installment sale that moves reported gain into a lower-tax rate year. The scheduled lower rates, which were accelerated into 2003 by the Jobs and Growth Tax Relief Reconciliation Act of 2003, for noncorporate taxpayers contained in the Tax Relief Reconciliation Act of 2001 support this point.

In either case, an installment sale necessarily entails the *nontax consideration* of credit risk. That is, an outright cash sale might be preferable to an installment sale if the buyer's creditworthiness is somewhat suspect. Even a creditworthy buyer, moreover, might find payment of its installment obligations difficult if general business conditions or specific industry factors cause a decline in its economic well-being. An installment sale, in other words, does not terminate a seller's exposure to the exigencies of the marketplace, and some sellers might prefer the certainty of an all-cash transaction despite its lack of deferral possibilities.

CONTINGENT SALES PRICES

Dispositions of business assets or even entire businesses sometimes employ open-ended or **contingent sales prices** to resolve disputes between the buyer and the seller about the value of the assets in question. Such transactions typically involve a portion of future receipts, profits in excess of some threshold, or some similar arrangement. Despite the absence of a specified sales price, the installment method can be used in these circumstances according to the following principles.

- If the sales contract sets forth a *maximum sales price*, that price is used.[35]
- If there is no maximum sales price but the payout is limited to a fixed number of years, divide the taxpayer's basis by that number and offset the result against the amount received each year.[36]
- If the sales agreement provides neither a maximum sales price nor a fixed payout period, use 15 years as the fixed payout term.[37]

[35]Temp.Reg. § 15A.453–1(c)(2)(i).
[36]Temp.Reg. § 15A.453–1(c)(3)(i).
[37]Temp.Reg. § 15A.453–1(c)(4).

EXAMPLE 13

Indigo, Inc., sells the rights to a newly patented blood analyzer to a major health products company for 10% of the earnings generated by this device, with a maximum sales price of $400,000. Indigo has a cost basis in this device of $100,000. In the first year after the sale, Indigo received $30,000. Since a maximum sales price is stipulated, it is used.

Maximum sales price	$ 400,000
Basis	(100,000)
Gain expected	$ 300,000

$$\frac{\text{Gain}}{\text{Contract price}} = \frac{\$300{,}000}{\$400{,}000} = 75\% \text{ (gross profit percentage).}$$

Of the $30,000 received in the first year after the sale, $22,500 ($30,000 × 75%) is reported as gain. In each subsequent year, 75% of the amount received is reported as gain. If the amount ultimately collected is less than the maximum sales price used, an appropriate adjustment will be made in the final year of the sales contract. ■

EXAMPLE 14

Assume the same facts as in the preceding example, except that no maximum sales price is provided and the payout is limited to eight years. Accordingly, the taxpayer's basis of $100,000 is divided by 8, and the result ($12,500) is then offset against the amount received each year. In the first year:

Amount received	$ 30,000
Prorated basis	(12,500)
Gain reported	$ 17,500

■

EXAMPLE 15

Assume the same facts as in the preceding examples, except that there is no fixed payout term. In this case, the taxpayer's basis of $100,000 is divided by 15 years, and the result ($6,667) offsets the amount received.

Amount received	$30,000
Prorated basis	(6,667)
Gain reported	$23,333

■

IMPUTED INTEREST

If a deferred payment contract for the sale of property with a selling price greater than $3,000 does not contain a reasonable interest rate, the tax law imputes a reasonable rate.[38] The imputing of interest effectively restates the selling price of the property to the sum of the payments at the date of the sale and the discounted present value of the future payments. The difference between the present value of a future payment and the payment's face amount is taxed as interest income, as discussed in the following paragraphs. Thus, the **imputed interest** rules prevent sellers of capital assets from increasing the selling price to reflect the equivalent of unstated interest on deferred payments and thereby converting ordinary (interest) income into long-term capital gains. In addition, the imputed interest rules affect the timing of income recognition.

[38]§§ 483 and 1274.

Generally, if the contract does not charge at least the Federal rate, interest will be imputed at the Federal rate. The Federal rate is the interest rate the Federal government pays on new borrowing and is published monthly by the IRS.

As a general rule, the buyer and seller must account for interest on the accrual basis with semiannual compounding.[39] Requiring the use of the accrual basis assures that the seller's interest income and the buyer's interest expense are reported in the same tax year.

EXAMPLE 16

Partridge & Associates, LLP, a cash basis taxpayer, sold land on January 1, 2004, for $200,000 cash and $6 million due on December 31, 2005, with 5% interest payable on December 31, 2004, and December 31, 2005. At the time of the sale, the Federal rate was 8% (compounded semiannually). Because Partridge did not charge at least the Federal rate, interest is imputed at 8% (compounded semiannually).

Date	Payment	Present Value (at 8%) on 1/1/2004	Imputed Interest
12/31/2004	$ 300,000*	$ 277,500	$ 22,500
12/31/2005	6,300,000**	5,386,500	913,500
	$6,600,000	$5,664,000	$936,000

*$6 million × 5% = $300,000 interest.
**$6 million + $300,000 interest.

Thus, the selling price is restated to $5,864,000 ($200,000 cash + $5,664,000) rather than $6,200,000 ($200,000 + $6,000,000), and Partridge recognizes interest income as follows.

	Beginning Balance	Interest Income (at 8%)*	Received	Ending Balance
2004	$5,664,000	$462,182	($ 300,000)	$5,826,182
2005	5,826,182	473,818	(6,300,000)	–0–

*Compounded semiannually.

Congress has created several exceptions regarding the rate at which interest is imputed and the method of accounting for the interest income and expense. The general rules and exceptions are summarized in Concept Summary 12–1.

RELATED-PARTY SALES

Special limitations apply when an installment sale involves related parties. These limitations prevent undue deferral of tax liability under circumstances that the taxpayers involved can presumably control. Different limitations and different definitions of *related parties* apply to sales of nondepreciable and depreciable property.

[39] §§ 1274(a), 1273(a), and 1272(a).

CONCEPT SUMMARY 12–1

Interest on Installment Sales

	Imputed Interest Rate
General rule	Federal rate
Exceptions:	
• Principal amount not over $2.8 million.[1]	Lesser of Federal rate or 9%
• Sale of land (with a calendar year ceiling of $500,000) between family members (the seller's spouse, brothers, sisters, ancestors, or lineal descendants).[2]	Lesser of Federal rate or 6%

	Method of Accounting for Interest	
	Seller's Interest Income	Buyer's Interest Expense
General rule[3]	Accrual	Accrual
Exceptions:		
• Total payments under the contract are $250,000 or less.[4]	Taxpayer's overall method	Taxpayer's overall method
• Sale of a farm (sales price of $1 million or less).[5]	Taxpayer's overall method	Taxpayer's overall method
• Sale of a principal residence.[6]	Taxpayer's overall method	Taxpayer's overall method
• Sale for a note with a principal amount of not over $2 million, the seller is on the cash basis, the property sold is not inventory, and the buyer agrees to report expense by the cash method.[7]	Cash	Cash

[1] § 1274A. This amount is adjusted annually for inflation. For 2004, the amount is $4,381,300.
[2] §§ 1274(c)(3)(F) and 483(e).
[3] §§ 1274(a) and 1272(a)(3).
[4] §§ 1274(c)(3)(C) and 483.
[5] §§ 1274(c)(3)(A) and 483.
[6] §§ 1274(c)(3)(B) and 483.
[7] § 1274A(c). This amount is adjusted annually for inflation. For 2004, the amount is $3,129,500.

Nondepreciable Property. When related parties sell nondepreciable property to one another on the installment method, § 453(e) treats the proceeds of any subsequent sale within two years as if they had been received by the first seller.

EXAMPLE 17

Joan sells some vacant land worth $100,000 to her son, Ed, with payment spread over 20 years in $5,000 annual payments. If Ed sells this property one year later for $100,000 in cash, this sum is treated as if Joan had received it, and she will report her gain accordingly. ■

Had this rule not applied, the family unit (Joan and Ed) would have the entire proceeds of $100,000 in their possession, but could continue to report Joan's gain over the remaining 19 years of her original transaction with Ed. The later sale by Ed does not produce any reportable gain, because the sales price that he received ($100,000) did not exceed the price he paid his mother for the property in the earlier transaction.

If Ed had waited two years before selling the property, the related-party sale rule would not have applied, and Joan could have reported her gain over the remaining term of her contract with Ed. During those two years, however, Ed bore the economic risk that the property might *decline in value*. His obligation to make annual payments of $5,000 to Joan is not affected by the property's subsequent value.

For this purpose, related parties include the first seller's brothers, sisters, ancestors (e.g., parents and grandparents), lineal descendants (e.g., children and grandchildren), controlled corporations, and partnerships, trusts, and estates in which the seller has an interest.[40]

Depreciable Property. The installment method cannot be used to report a gain on the sale of depreciable property to a controlled entity. The purpose of this rule is to prevent the seller from deferring gain (until collections are received) while the related purchaser is enjoying a stepped-up basis for depreciation purposes.[41]

This prohibition on the use of the installment method applies to sales between the taxpayer and a partnership or corporation in which the taxpayer holds a more-than-50 percent interest. Constructive ownership rules are used in applying the ownership test (e.g., the taxpayer is considered to own stock owned by a spouse and certain other family members).[42] However, if the taxpayer can establish that tax avoidance was not a principal purpose of the transaction, the installment method can be used to report the gain.

EXAMPLE 18

Ali purchased an apartment building from his controlled corporation, Emerald Corporation. Ali was short of cash at the time of the purchase (December 2004), but was to collect a large cash payment in January 2005. The agreement required Ali to pay the entire arm's length price in January 2005. Ali had sound business reasons for acquiring the building. Emerald Corporation should be able to convince the IRS that tax avoidance was not a principal purpose for the installment sale because the tax benefits are not overwhelming. The corporation reports all of the gain in the year following the year of sale. ■

DISPOSITION OF INSTALLMENT NOTE

Generally, a taxpayer must recognize the deferred profit from an installment sale when the note itself later is transferred to another party or is otherwise relinquished.[43] The rationale for accelerating the gain is that deferral is no longer appropriate when the taxpayer has sold the obligation and received the proceeds (under the wherewithal to pay concept).

Moreover, a gift or cancellation of an installment note is treated as a taxable disposition by the donor. The amount realized from the cancellation is the face amount of the note if the parties (obligor and obligee) are related to each other.[44]

DIGGING DEEPER 5

*Find more information on this topic at our Web site: **http://wft-advanced.swlearning.com**.*

EXAMPLE 19

Liz cancels a note issued by Tina (Liz's daughter) that arose in connection with the sale of property. At the time of the cancellation, the note had a basis to Liz of $10,000, a face amount of $25,000, and a fair market value of $20,000. Presuming the initial sale by Liz to Tina qualified as an installment sale, the cancellation results in gain of $15,000 ($25,000 – $10,000) to Liz. ■

[40] § 453(f)(1).
[41] § 453(g).
[42] §§ 1239(b) and (c).
[43] § 453B(a).
[44] § 453B(f)(2).

PLANNING STRATEGIES

Terminating the Installment Method

FRAMEWORK FOCUS: TAX RATE

STRATEGY ➤ SHIFT NET INCOME FROM HIGH-BRACKET YEARS TO LOW-BRACKET YEARS.

As suggested earlier, an installment sale might look less appealing in retrospect if a taxpayer subsequently finds itself in a higher tax bracket. Whether this predicament is due to higher legislated rates or the expansion of the taxpayer's business, the taxpayer might be inclined to *terminate the installment sale method.* Disposing of the installment obligation often accomplishes this result, because any remaining deferred gain is thereby accelerated into the current year. To be sure, the taxpayer gives up the deferral benefit obtained when the transaction was set up as an installment sale, but saving taxes that would be paid in future years at higher rates may offset the loss of deferral benefits.

Disposing of an installment obligation, however, may not be easy. Financial obligations of most private businesses or other persons can often be difficult to sell at a price equal to their present value. Intermediaries may agree to purchase such obligations only at significant discounts to their face amount. If the maker of the note (i.e., the person obligated to pay the installment obligation) is experiencing any financial difficulty at the time, the note will be even harder to sell. Thus, *nontax considerations* may effectively preclude the acceleration of taxable gain by disposing of an installment obligation.

INTEREST ON DEFERRED TAXES

With the installment method, the seller earns interest on the receivable. The receivable includes the deferred gain. In effect, the seller is earning interest on the deferred taxes. Since the installment method provides interest-free loans to those taxpayers who use it, the Code requires the taxpayers to pay interest on the deferred taxes in some situations.[45]

The taxpayer is required to pay interest on the deferred taxes only if *both* of the following requirements are met.

- The installment obligation arises from the sale of property (other than farming property) for more than $150,000.
- Such installment obligations outstanding at the close of the tax year exceed $5 million.

Interest on the deferred taxes is payable only on the portion of the taxes that relates to the installment obligations in *excess* of $5 million. The interest is calculated using the rate for underpayment of taxes and estimates.

ELECTING OUT OF THE INSTALLMENT METHOD

A taxpayer can *elect not to use* the installment method. The election is made by reporting on a timely filed return the gain computed by the taxpayer's usual method of accounting (cash or accrual).[46] The election is frequently applied to year-end sales by taxpayers who expect to be in a higher tax bracket in the following year.

DIGGING DEEPER 6 *Find more information on this topic at our Web site:* ***http://wft-advanced.swlearning.com.***

[45] § 453A.

[46] § 453(d) and Temp.Reg. § 15A.453–1(d). See also Rev.Rul. 82–227, 1982–2 C.B. 89.

EXAMPLE 20

On December 31, 2004, Blue Corporation sold land to Orange, Inc., for $20,000 (fair market value). The cash was to be paid on January 4, 2005. Blue is a cash basis taxpayer, and its basis in the land is $8,000. Blue has a large casualty loss and very little other income in 2004. Thus, its marginal tax rate in 2004 is 15%. Blue expects its rate to increase in 2005 to 34%.

The transaction constitutes an installment sale because a payment will be received in a tax year after the tax year of disposition. Orange's promise to pay Blue is an installment obligation. If Blue elects out of the installment method, it would shift $12,000 of gain ($20,000 – $8,000) from the expected higher rate of 34% in 2005 to the 15% rate in 2004. The expected tax savings based on the rate differentials may exceed the benefit of the tax deferral available with the installment method. ■

LO.4

Understand the alternative methods of accounting for long-term contracts (the completed contract method and the percentage of completion method).

Long-Term Contracts

A **long-term contract** is a building, installation, construction, or manufacturing contract that is entered into but not completed within the same tax year. However, a *manufacturing* contract is long term *only* if the contract is to manufacture (1) a unique item not normally carried in finished goods inventory or (2) items that normally require more than 12 calendar months to complete.[47] A contract to perform services (e.g., auditing or legal services) is not considered a contract for this purpose and thus cannot qualify as a long-term contract.

EXAMPLE 21

Raven & Co., Inc., a calendar year taxpayer, entered into two contracts during the year. One contract was to construct a building foundation. Work was to begin in October 2004 and be completed by June 2005. This contract is long term because it will not be entered into and completed in the same tax year. The fact that the contract requires less than 12 calendar months to complete is not relevant because the contract is not for manufacturing. The second contract was for architectural services to be performed over two years. These services will not qualify for long-term contract treatment because the taxpayer will not build, install, construct, or manufacture a product. ■

DIGGING DEEPER 7

Find more information on this topic at our Web site: ***http://wft-advanced.swlearning.com.***

Contract costs are deducted when the revenue from the contract is recognized. Generally, two methods of accounting may be used to determine when the revenue from a contract is recognized.[48]

- The completed contract method.
- The percentage of completion method.

The *completed contract method may be used* for (1) home construction contracts (contracts in which at least 80 percent of the estimated costs are for dwelling units in buildings with four or fewer units) and (2) certain other real estate construction contracts. Other real estate contracts can qualify for the completed contract method if the following requirements are satisfied.

- The contract is expected to be completed within the two-year period beginning on the commencement date of the contract.
- The contract is performed by a taxpayer whose average annual gross receipts for the three taxable years preceding the taxable year in which the contract is entered into do not exceed $10 million.

All other contractors *must* use the percentage of completion method.

[47] § 460(f) and Reg. § 1.451–3(b).

[48] § 460.

TAX IN THE NEWS

IRS Changes Its Position That the Cash Method Does Not Clearly Reflect the Income of Small Contractors

In a 1980 Tax Court decision, *Raymond Magnon,* 73 T.C. 980, the court ruled that a small contractor could use the cash method of accounting. The IRS disagreed, but was unsuccessful in a 1995 attempt to require a contractor to change from the cash method to the percentage of completion method. The IRS argued that the cash method did not clearly reflect income, but the Tax Court disagreed [*Ansley-Sheppard-Burgess Co.,*104 T.C. 367 (1995)].

In other cases, however, the IRS was successful in requiring small contractors to change from the cash method to the accrual method (*Thompson Electric Inc.,* T.C.Memo. 1995–292, and *J. P. Sheahan Associates,* T.C.Memo. 1995–239). The IRS argued that the accumulated costs for materials and labor, whether incurred by the contractor or its subcontractors, should be subject to the inventory rules. Because inventories are a material income-producing factor, the cash method does not clearly reflect income, and the IRS should be able to require the contractor to employ the accrual method.

Now, in a change of heart, the IRS has decided to let small contractors use the cash method. In Rev.Proc. 2001–10, 2001–1 C.B. 272, the IRS announced that as a matter of administrative convenience, it will permit any entity with average annual gross receipts of not more than $1 million for the most recent three-year period to use the cash method. This applies even if the taxpayer is buying and selling inventory.

Also as a matter of administrative convenience, the IRS announced in Notice 2001–76, 2001–2 C.B. 613 that it will permit certain entities whose average annual gross receipts are greater than $1 million but not more than $10 million for the most recent three-year period to use the cash method. Not eligible for this treatment are entities whose principal business activity (the activity producing the largest percentage of gross receipts) is selling goods, manufacturing, mining, and certain publishing activities. Also not eligible are the C corporations, partnerships, and tax shelters that otherwise must use the accrual method. The major beneficiaries of the $10 million exception are small construction companies and small service businesses that sell some goods in conjunction with the services provided.

COMPLETED CONTRACT METHOD

Under the **completed contract method,** no revenue from the contract is recognized or costs are deducted until the contract is completed and accepted. A taxpayer may not delay completion of a contract for the principal purpose of deferring tax.[49]

In some situations, the original contract price may be disputed, or the buyer may want additional work to be done on a long-term contract. If the disputed amount is substantial (i.e., it is not possible to determine whether a profit or loss will ultimately be realized on the contract), no income or loss is recognized until the dispute is resolved. In all other cases, the profit or loss (reduced by the amount in dispute) is recognized in the current period upon completion of the contract. However, additional work may need to be performed with respect to the disputed contract. In this case, the difference between the amount in dispute and the actual cost of the additional work is recognized in the year the work is completed, rather than in the year in which the dispute is resolved.[50]

[49]Reg. § 1.451–3(b)(2).

[50]Reg. §§ 1.451–3(d)(2)(ii)–(vii), Example (2).

EXAMPLE 22

Magenta Corporation, a calendar year taxpayer utilizing the completed contract method of accounting, constructed a building for Kingfisher Enterprises, Inc., under a long-term contract. The gross contract price was $500,000. Magenta finished construction in 2004 at a cost of $475,000. When Kingfisher examined the building, it insisted that the building be repainted or the contract price be reduced. The estimated cost of repainting is $10,000. Since under the terms of the contract, Magenta is assured of a profit of at least $15,000 [($500,000 – $475,000) – $10,000] even if the dispute is ultimately resolved in Kingfisher's favor, Magenta must include $490,000 ($500,000 – $10,000) in gross income and is allowed deductions of $475,000 for 2004.

In 2005, Magenta and Kingfisher resolve their dispute, and Magenta repaints certain portions of the building at a cost of $6,000. Magenta includes $10,000 in 2005 gross income and deducts the $6,000 expense in that year.

Now assume instead that the estimated cost of repainting the building is $50,000. Since the resolution of the dispute completely in Kingfisher's favor would mean a net loss on the contract for Magenta ($500,000 – $475,000 – $50,000 = $25,000 loss), Magenta does not recognize any income or loss until the year the dispute is resolved. ■

Frequently, a contractor receives payment at various stages of completion. For example, when a contract is 50 percent complete, the contractor may receive 50 percent of the contract price less a retainage. Generally, contractors are allowed to defer all tax effects from the advance payments until the payments are recognized as income under their method of accounting.

PERCENTAGE OF COMPLETION METHOD

The percentage of completion method must be used to account for long-term contracts unless the taxpayer qualifies for one of the two exceptions that allow the completed contract method to be used: home construction contracts and certain other real estate construction contracts. Under the **percentage of completion method,** a portion of the gross contract price is included in income during each period as the work progresses. The revenue accrued each period (except for the final period) is computed as follows.[51]

$$\frac{C}{T} \times P$$

where C = Contract costs incurred during the period,
T = Estimated total cost of the contract, and
P = Contract price.

All of the costs allocated to the contract during the period are deductible from the accrued revenue.[52] The revenue reported in the final period is simply the unreported revenue from the contract. Because T in this formula is an estimate that frequently differs from total actual costs, which are not known until the contract has been completed, the profit on a contract for a particular period may be overstated or understated.

DIGGING DEEPER 8

Find more information on this topic at our Web site: ***http://wft-advanced.swlearning.com.***

EXAMPLE 23

Tan, Inc., entered into a contract that was to take two years to complete, with an estimated cost of $2,250,000. The contract price was $3,000,000. Costs of the contract for 2004, the first

[51] § 460(b)(1)(A).

[52] Reg. § 1.451-3(c)(3).

year, totaled $1,350,000. The gross profit reported by the percentage of completion method for 2004 was $450,000 {[($1,350,000/$2,250,000) × $3,000,000 = $1,800,000] – $1,350,000}. The contract was completed at the end of 2005 at a total cost of $2,700,000. In retrospect, 2004 profit should have been $150,000 {[($1,350,000/$2,700,000) × $3,000,000 = $1,500,000] – $1,350,000}. Thus, taxes were overpaid for 2004. ■

LO.5

Recognize when accounting for inventories is required.

Inventories

Generally, tax accounting and financial accounting for inventories are much the same.

- The use of inventories is necessary to clearly reflect the income of any business engaged in the production and sale or purchase and sale of goods.[53]
- The inventories should include all finished goods, goods in process, and raw materials and supplies that will become part of the product (including containers).
- Inventory rules must give effect to the *best* accounting practice of a particular trade or business, and the taxpayer's method should be consistently followed from year to year.
- All items included in inventory should be valued at either (1) cost or (2) the lower of cost or market value.

The following are *not* acceptable methods or practices in valuing inventories.

- A reserve for anticipated price changes.
- Use of a constant price or nominal value for a so-called normal quantity of materials or goods in stock (e.g., the base stock method).
- Inclusion in inventory of stock in transit to which title is not vested in the taxpayer.
- The direct costing approach (excluding fixed indirect production costs from inventory).
- The prime costing approach (excluding all indirect production costs from inventory).

The reason for the similarities between tax and financial accounting for inventories is that § 471 sets forth what appears to be a two-prong test: "inventories shall be taken . . . on such basis . . . as conforming as nearly as may be to the *best accounting practice* in the trade or business and as most *clearly reflecting the income*." The best accounting practice is generally synonymous with generally accepted accounting principles (hereafter referred to as GAAP). However, the IRS determines whether an inventory method clearly reflects income.

In *Thor Power Tool Co. v. Comm.*,[54] there was a conflict between these two tests. The taxpayer's method of valuing obsolete parts was in conformity with GAAP. The IRS, however, successfully argued that the clear reflection of income test was not satisfied because the taxpayer's procedures for valuing its inventories were contrary to the Regulations. Under the taxpayer's method, inventories for parts in excess of estimated future sales were written off (expensed), although the parts were kept on hand and their asking prices were not reduced.

The taxpayer contended that conformity to GAAP creates a presumption that the method clearly reflects income. The Supreme Court disagreed, concluding that the clear reflection of income test was *paramount*. Moreover, it is the opinion of the IRS that controls in determining whether a method of inventory clearly reflects

[53] § 471(a) and Reg. §§ 1.471–1 and –2.

[54] 79–1 USTC ¶9139, 43 AFTR2d 79–362, 99 S.Ct. 773 (USSC, 1979).

GLOBAL TAX ISSUES

A Tax Advantage from Moving Abroad

While the United States requires producers to use the accrual method, with stringent capitalization requirements for inventories, some foreign countries allow such businesses to use the cash method. Thus, a U.S. manufacturing company experiences a tax windfall when it moves its production to a foreign subsidiary in a country where all production costs are deducted as incurred, and revenues are deferred until collected.

income. Thus, the best accounting practice test was rendered practically meaningless. A taxpayer's method of inventory must strictly conform to the Regulations, regardless of what GAAP may require.

DETERMINING INVENTORY COST

For merchandise purchased, cost is the invoice price less trade discounts plus freight and other handling charges.[55]

Uniform Capitalization. For inventory and property *produced* by a taxpayer, "(A) the direct cost of such property, and (B) such property's share of those indirect costs (including taxes) part or all of which are allocable to such property" must be capitalized. Congress wanted a set of capitalization rules that would apply to all types of businesses: contractors, manufacturers, farmers, wholesalers, and retailers.[56] Congress has labeled the resulting system the **uniform capitalization rules,** and tax practitioners refer to it as a *super-full absorption costing system.*

To value inventory under the uniform capitalization rules, a *producer* must:

- Classify all costs into three categories: (1) production, (2) general administrative expense, and (3) mixed services.
- Allocate mixed services costs to production and general administrative expenses.
- Allocate the production costs between the cost of goods sold and the ending inventory.

Mixed services costs should be allocated to production on a rational basis. For example, the costs of operating the personnel department may be allocated between production and general administration based on the number of applications processed or the number of employees. In lieu of allocating each mixed services cost, a taxpayer may elect a *simplified method* that allocates the total of all mixed services costs to production.[57]

$$\text{MSP} = \frac{\text{TP}}{\text{TC}} \times \text{TMS}$$

where MSP = Mixed services costs allocated to production,
TP = Total production costs, other than interest and mixed services,
TC = Total costs, other than interest, state, local or foreign income taxes, and mixed services costs, and
TMS = Total mixed services costs.

[55] Reg. § 1.471–3(b).

[56] H. Rep. 99–841, 99th Cong., 2nd Sess., 1986, pp. 302–309. § 263A. Reg. § 1.263A–1(a).

[57] Reg. § 1.263A–1(h)(5).

TAX IN THE NEWS

Company Capitalizes Marketing Cost on Financial Statements

Under the uniform capitalization rules, marketing costs are generally deducted in the year incurred. However, a publicly held company has gained approval from the Securities and Exchange Commission (SEC) to capitalize its television advertising costs as an intangible customer base asset. While the company was able to improve its reported earnings, other companies fear that the IRS may reason that if capitalization is good enough for the SEC, it should be used for tax purposes.

SOURCE: Adapted from "SEC Approves Unusual Accounting Method Used by Medical-Supply Company," *Knight-Ridder Tribune Business News*, September 5, 2003.

The usual cost accounting techniques (e.g., average cost per equivalent unit) can be used to allocate production costs between the cost of goods sold and the ending inventory.

Costs included in the inventory of *wholesalers and retailers* are comparable to those of the producer. However, many of these costs are captured in the price these taxpayers pay for the goods. The following additional costs must be capitalized by wholesalers and retailers.

- All storage costs for wholesalers.
- Offsite storage costs for retailers.
- Purchasing costs (e.g., buyers' wages or salaries).
- Handling, processing, assembly, and repackaging.

The uniform capitalization rules may cause some costs to be capitalized for tax purposes but not for financial accounting purposes. For example, a wholesaler's or a manufacturer's storage costs generally are expensed for financial reporting purposes, but must be capitalized for tax purposes. A taxpayer may capitalize straight-line depreciation of production equipment for financial accounting purposes, but the actual tax depreciation must be capitalized under uniform capitalization.

Lower of Cost or Market. Except for those taxpayers who use the LIFO method, inventories may be valued at the **lower of cost or market (replacement cost).**[58] Taxpayers using LIFO *must value inventory at cost*. However, the write-down of damaged or shopworn merchandise and goods that otherwise are unsalable at normal prices is not considered an application of the lower of cost or market method. Such items should be valued at bona fide selling price less direct cost of disposal.[59]

DIGGING DEEPER 9

Find more information on this topic at our Web site: ***http://wft-advanced.swlearning.com.***

In applying the lower of cost or market method, *each* item included in the inventory is valued at the lower of its cost or market value.[60]

[58] Reg. § 1.472–4.
[59] Reg. § 1.471–2(c).
[60] Reg. § 1.471–4(c).

GLOBAL TAX ISSUES

Inventory Acquired from a Foreign Subsidiary

Generally, a parent corporation and its foreign subsidiaries are treated as separate corporations. If a foreign subsidiary is producing goods in a country whose tax rates are lower than the U.S. tax rates, tax savings can accrue to the group if the foreign subsidiary's prices to the U.S. parent are as high as permissible. This will increase the income in the foreign country, but will reduce taxable income subject to the higher U.S. tax rates. Section 482 is the IRS's weapon against such income shifting. Under § 482, the prices charged on transactions between the related parties must be equal to an "arm's length price."

EXAMPLE 24

The taxpayer's ending inventory is valued as follows.

Item	Cost	Market	Lower of Cost or Market
A	$5,000	$ 4,000	$4,000
B	3,000	2,000	2,000
C	1,500	6,000	1,500
	$9,500	$12,000	$7,500

Under the lower of cost or market method, the taxpayer's inventory is valued at $7,500, not $9,500. ■

Inventory Shrinkage. Because of accidents, thefts, and recording errors, a company's inventory per physical count and its inventory according to company records may differ. This difference is called *inventory shrinkage* and is typically recorded when a company completes its physical inventory. But many companies take their physical inventories at some time other than the last day of their taxable year. As a result, they need to adjust the ending inventory, per their accounting records, for the estimated shrinkage that has occurred since the last physical inventory. A taxpayer can deduct this shrinkage on its tax return.[61]

Determining Cost—Specific Identification, FIFO, and LIFO. In some cases, it is feasible to determine the cost of the particular item sold. For example, an automobile dealer can easily determine the specific cost of each automobile that has been sold. However, in most businesses it is necessary to resort to a flow of goods assumption such as *first in, first out* (*FIFO*), *last in, first out* (*LIFO*), or an *average cost* method. A taxpayer may use any of these methods, provided the method selected is consistently applied from year to year.

During a period of rising prices, LIFO generally produces a lower ending inventory valuation and results in a higher cost of goods sold than would be obtained under the FIFO method.

EXAMPLE 25

On January 1, the taxpayer opened a retail store to sell refrigerators. At least 10 refrigerators must be carried in inventory to satisfy customer demands. The initial investment in the 10 refrigerators is $5,000 ($500 each). During the year, 10 refrigerators were sold at $750 each

[61] § 471(b).

TAX IN THE NEWS

The Dreaded LIFO Recapture

The LIFO inventory method is an obvious means of deferring income in times of rising prices. However, companies must be vigilant in avoiding the recapture of the deferred income. Thus, the LIFO user will seek to avoid a temporary year-end decline in inventory.

A special provision in the tax law requires a corporation to recapture its LIFO deferral when the corporation changes from a C corporation, whose income is subject to corporate tax, to an S corporation, whose income flows through and is taxed at the shareholder level.

In a recent Eleventh Circuit case (*Coggins Automotive Corp. v. Comm.*), a parent corporation owned several subsidiaries that used the LIFO method. The parent liquidated the subsidiaries in a nontaxable transaction and then transferred the inventories to newly formed limited liability companies that the parent controlled. Then the parent made the S election. The appellate court concluded that the inventories were owned not by the parent, but rather by the limited liability companies. Therefore, the LIFO recapture rules associated with the S election did not apply.

and were replaced at a cost of $6,000 ($600 each). Gross profit under the LIFO and FIFO methods is computed as follows.

		FIFO		LIFO
Sales (10 × $750)		$ 7,500		$ 7,500
Beginning inventory	$ 5,000		$ 5,000	
Purchases	6,000		6,000	
	$11,000		$11,000	
Ending inventory				
10 × $600	(6,000)			
10 × $500			(5,000)	
Cost of goods sold		(5,000)		(6,000)
Gross profit		$ 2,500		$ 1,500

■

Dollar-Value LIFO. In the preceding example, the taxpayer was buying and selling a single product, a particular model of a refrigerator. The taxpayer employed the *specific goods LIFO* technique. Under the specific goods approach, if identical items are not on hand at the end of the period, the LIFO inventory is depleted, and all of the deferred profit is reported. Thus, taxpayers who frequently change the items carried in inventory would realize little benefit from LIFO. However, dollar-value LIFO avoids this LIFO depletion problem.

Under **dollar-value LIFO,** each inventory item is assigned to a pool. A *pool* is a collection of similar items and is treated as a separate inventory. Determining whether items are similar involves considerable judgment. In general, however, a taxpayer would prefer broad pools so that when a particular item is sold out, it can be replaced by increases in other items in the same pool. Typically, all products manufactured at a particular plant can be treated as a pool.[62] A department store may have a separate pool for each department. An automobile dealer may have separate pools for new cars, lightweight trucks, heavy-duty trucks, and car and truck parts.

[62]Reg. § 1.472–8.

At the end of the period, the ending inventory is valued at current-year prices and then at the LIFO base period (the year LIFO was adopted) prices. The ratio of the ending inventory at current prices to the ending inventory at base period prices is the *LIFO index*. If the total current inventory at base period prices is greater than the base period inventory at base period prices, a LIFO layer must be added. The LIFO index is applied to the LIFO layer to convert it to current prices.

EXAMPLE 26

Black Company adopted LIFO effective January 1, 2004. The base LIFO inventory (from December 31, 2003) was $1,000,000. On December 31, 2004, the inventory was $1,320,000 at end-of-2004 prices and $1,200,000 at end-of-2003 (the base period) prices. Thus, Black added a 2004 layer of $200,000 ($1,200,000 – $1,000,000) at base period prices. The layer must be converted to 2004 prices.

LIFO index = $1,320,000/$1,200,000 = 1.10

2004 layer × LIFO index = $200,000 × 1.10 = $220,000

Therefore, the 2004 ending inventory is $1,000,000 + $220,000 = $1,220,000.

The inventory on December 31, 2005, is $1,325,000 using 2005 prices and $1,250,000 using base period prices. Thus, the LIFO index for 2005 is $1,325,000/$1,250,000 = 1.06. The LIFO inventory is $1,273,000.

BLACK COMPANY
LIFO Inventory
December 31, 2005

	Base Period Cost	LIFO Index	LIFO Layers
Base inventory	$1,000,000	1.00	$1,000,000
2004 layer	200,000	1.10	220,000
2005 layer	50,000	1.06	53,000
	$1,250,000		$1,273,000

THE LIFO ELECTION

A taxpayer may adopt LIFO by using the method in the tax return for the year of the change and by attaching Form 970 (Application to Use LIFO Inventory Method) to the tax return. Thus, a taxpayer need not request approval for the change. Once this election is made, it cannot be revoked. A prospective change from LIFO to any other inventory method can be made only if the consent of the IRS is obtained.[63]

DIGGING DEEPER 10

Find more information on this topic at our Web site: ***http://wft-advanced.swlearning.com.***

Once a LIFO election is made for tax purposes, the taxpayer's financial reports to owners and creditors must also be prepared on the basis of LIFO. The *conformity* of financial reports to tax reporting is specifically required by the Code and is strictly enforced by the IRS. However, the Regulations allow a taxpayer to make a footnote disclosure of the net income computed by another method of inventory valuation (e.g., FIFO).[64]

[63] Reg. §§ 1.472–3(a) and –5 and Rev.Proc. 84–74, 1984–2 C.B. 736 at 742.

[64] § 472(c), Reg. § 1.472–2(e).

PLANNING STRATEGIES

LIFO Inventory

FRAMEWORK FOCUS: TAX RATE

STRATEGY ➤ **SHIFT NET INCOME FROM HIGH-BRACKET YEARS TO LOW-BRACKET YEARS.**

During periods of anticipated cost increases, LIFO tends to reduce reported taxable income and thereby lowers current tax liabilities. This tendency reverses itself, however, if inventory *volumes* are not maintained. As older and therefore lower costs are matched against current income, a taxpayer's reported income will be *higher* under LIFO than under FIFO.

Taxpayers usually can avoid this phenomenon by ensuring that base inventory levels do not decrease. But *nontax considerations* often thwart this strategy. During periods of shortage, replacement goods may be unavailable. If interest rates are rising, a taxpayer may not want to increase its purchases and the corresponding cost of financing these purchases. If a recession is in progress, the taxpayer might be anticipating a slowdown in its sales and will resist acquiring additional inventory beyond its expected needs. As a result of these factors, inventory levels might go down, and taxable income will then increase.

In any case, the *financial statement conformity* requirement of LIFO can make this method unappealing to corporate management. While the permitted footnote disclosures can somewhat ameliorate the impact of LIFO on a company's reported earnings, such disclosures are often more effective with sophisticated creditors than with capital markets generally. Accordingly, management may wait until a general business slowdown has dampened earnings expectations before switching to LIFO and suffering from the typical drop in earnings that occurs with the switch.

Suggested Further Readings

Sharon Burnett, "IRS Approves Cash Method for More Small Businesses," *Practical Tax Strategies*, June 2002, pp. 340–350.

Dennis J. Gaffney, Richard O. Davis, Maureen H. Smith, and James E. Wheeler, "How Retailing's 'Best' Inventory Accounting Practices Produced Distorted LIFO Pools," *Journal of Taxation*, April 1999, pp. 218–227.

Dennis J. Gaffney, Richard O. Davis, Maureen H. Smith-Gaffney, and Richard P. Weber, "Advance Payments: IRS Signals Simplification, Clarity, and Opportunity," *Journal of Taxation*, April 2003, pp. 232–240.

Larry Maples, "IRS Position Restricts Percentage-of-Completion Income Deferral," *Practical Tax Strategies*, February 2003, pp. 95–98.

W. Eugene Seago and Pamela C. Smith, "Change in Accounting Method Theories: Lifetime Income, Change in Character, and Peace of Mind," *Journal of Taxation*, December 2002, pp. 339–346.

KEY TERMS

Accounting method, 12–11
Accounting period, 12–3
Accrual method, 12–10
Cash method, 12–10
Completed contract method, 12–22
Contingent sales prices, 12–15
Dollar-value LIFO, 12–28
Fiscal year, 12–3
Imputed interest, 12–16
Installment method, 12–13
Least aggregate deferral method, 12–5
Long-term contract, 12–21
Lower of cost or market (replacement cost), 12–26

PROBLEM MATERIALS

Problems

1. Red, White, and Blue are unrelated corporations engaged in real estate development. The three corporations formed a joint venture (treated as a partnership) to develop a tract of land. Assuming the venture does not have a natural business year, what tax year must the joint venture adopt under the following circumstances?

		Tax Year Ending	Interest in Joint Venture
a.	Red	March 31	60%
	White	September 30	20%
	Blue	June 30	20%
b.	Red	September 30	30%
	White	June 30	40%
	Blue	January 31	30%

Decision Making

2. The Zinnia Wholesale Company is an S corporation that began business on January 1, 2004. William, a calendar year taxpayer, owns 100% of Zinnia. He has $300,000 taxable income from other sources each year. William will work approximately 30 hours a week for the corporation. Zinnia sells swimming pool supplies, and its natural business year ends in September. Approximately 80% of Zinnia's gross receipts occur in June through September. Assume that the IRS will approve the natural business year if Zinnia so requests.
   a. What tax year should Zinnia elect, assuming that William anticipates the company will produce a net profit for all years?
   b. What tax year should Zinnia elect, assuming it will lose $10,000 a month for the first 12 months and an average of $5,000 a month for the next 12 months? In the third year and thereafter, the corporation will earn taxable income of approximately $8,000 per month.

EXTENDER

Decision Making

3. Pink Company, an architectural firm, has a bookkeeper who maintains a cash receipts and disbursements journal. At the end of the year, the company hires you to convert the cash receipts and disbursements into accrual basis revenues and expenses. The total cash receipts are summarized as follows.

Cash sales	$ 60,000
Collections on accounts receivable	300,000
Bank loan	30,000
Total cash receipts	$390,000

   The accounts receivable from customers at the end of the year are $150,000. You note that the accounts receivable at the beginning of the year were $110,000. The cash sales included $30,000 of prepayments for services to be provided over the next 36 months (i.e., 12 months of such services relate to 2004).
   a. Compute the company's accrual basis gross income for 2004.
   b. Would you recommend that Pink use the cash method or the accrual method?
   c. The company does not maintain an allowance for uncollectible accounts. Would you recommend that such an allowance be established for tax purposes?

4. Owl Corporation is in the business of sales and home deliveries of fuel oil and currently uses a calendar year for reporting its taxable income. However, Owl's natural business year ends May 31. For the short period, January 1 through May 31, 2004, the corporation earned $31,500. Assume the corporate tax rates are as follows: 15% on taxable income of $50,000 or less, 25% on taxable income over $50,000 but not over $75,000, and 34% on taxable income over $75,000.
   a. What must Owl Corporation do to change its taxable year?
   b. Compute Owl Corporation's tax for the short period.

EXTENDER

5. Which of the following businesses are permitted to use the cash method of accounting?
   a. A grocery store whose gross receipts have not exceeded $1 million in any year.
   b. A plumbing contractor whose gross receipts have never exceeded $5 million in any year.
   c. A computer consulting business that also sells computer equipment. The average annual gross receipts are $3 million from consulting and $1 million from the sales of computer equipment.
   d. A hardware store with average annual gross receipts of $6 million.

6. This year, the taxpayer was required to switch from the cash to the accrual basis of accounting for sales and cost of goods sold. Taxable income for this year computed under the cash basis was $60,000. Relevant account balances were as follows.

	Beginning of the Year	End of the Year
Accounts receivable	$56,000	$50,000
Accounts payable	29,000	28,000
Inventory	27,000	30,000

   Compute the following:
   a. The adjustment due to the change in accounting method.
   b. The accrual basis taxable income for this year.

7. Moss Company is an environmental consulting firm with average annual gross receipts of $2.5 million and $500,000 in taxable income. Approximately $800,000 of the receipts are from the sale of products that are used to remedy the client's environmental problems. The company has consistently used the cash method for the consulting services and the accrual method for the sales of products. The company recently learned that it qualified for the small business tax accounting rules and can use the cash method for the sale of products as well as for the consulting services. At the end of the previous tax year, the company had $100,000 in products on hand and accounts receivable from the sale of products of $90,000. What are the immediate tax consequences of the company changing to the cash method of accounting for the sale of products effective for the current tax year?

Ethics

8. The controller of Charcoal Construction Company has been talking to the controller of Green Building Supply Company. Charcoal qualifies to use the percentage of completion method to report its income, and Green uses the accrual method. Ordinarily, Green makes deliveries to Charcoal job sites each Friday. The Charcoal controller has suggested that no deliveries should be made on the last Friday of the year. Rather, the deliveries will be deferred until the first business day after the beginning of the new year. This will enable Charcoal not to recognize the revenues attributable to the additional costs of delivered materials that are assigned to contracts but are unused at year-end. The Charcoal controller points out that Green also will "beat the IRS" because it can defer the income from the sale of the goods until they are delivered. Is this good tax planning or an unethical business practice?

Decision Making
Communications

9. Your client, Bluebell & Associates, is negotiating a sale of investment real estate for $24 million. Bluebell believes that the buyer would pay cash of $16 million and a note for $8 million, or $6 million cash and a note for $18 million. The notes will pay interest at slightly above the market rate. Bluebell realizes that the second option involves more risks of collection, but it is willing to accept that risk if the tax benefits of the installment

sale are substantial. Write a letter advising Bluebell of the tax consequences of choosing the lower down payment and larger note option, assuming it has no other installment receivables. The company's address is 200 Jerdone, Gettysburg, PA 17325.

Ethics

10. Your new client historically has been primarily a service business, but two years ago the company began selling a few products. These sales accounted for 15% of revenues in the first year and 35% in the second year. The client consistently used the cash method of accounting for all of its income and expenses, even though it had accounts receivable from these sales and some inventory on hand at the end of each year. Accordingly, its tax returns for the two previous years may be incorrect.

    The company, however, does not want to file amended returns for those previous years and pay the resulting additional tax and interest, because it is short on cash. Nor does it want to request a change in accounting method, since such a request would require a $1,250 processing fee payable to the IRS. Instead, the company wants to use the accrual method starting this year, and then correct the effect of the previous years' errors by including beginning accounts receivable collected in this year's gross income and by treating the beginning inventory balance as zero. This approach would be the least costly for your client. What do you recommend?

Decision Making

11. Floyd, a cash basis taxpayer, has received an offer to purchase his investment land. The buyer will either pay him $100,000 at closing or pay $50,000 at closing and $52,000 one year after the date of closing. If Floyd recognizes the entire gain in the current year, his marginal tax rate will be 35% (combined Federal, state, and local rates). However, if he spreads the gain over the two years, his marginal tax rate on the gain will be only 25%. Floyd does not consider the buyer a credit risk, but he realizes that the deferred payment will, in effect, earn only 4% interest ($2,000/$50,000 = 4%). Floyd believes he can earn a 10% before-tax rate of return on his after-tax cash. Floyd's adjusted basis for the land is $25,000, the buyer is also a cash basis taxpayer, and the short-term Federal rate is 4%. Floyd has asked you to evaluate the two alternatives on an after-tax basis.

12. Jasmine & Company, a cash basis taxpayer, sold a cargo temperature detector to Peacock Manufacturing for 30% of gross sales in excess of $3 million annually, with a lifetime limit of $600,000. In the first year, Jasmine received $330,000. The cost basis of this device is $200,000. What is the profit that Jasmine must report for this year?

13. Tom, a cash basis taxpayer, sold his unincorporated accounting practice for $600,000. The basis and fair market values of the assets sold were as follows.

Assets	**Fair Market Value**	**Basis**	
Office equipment	$ 50,000	Cost	$ 120,000
		Less: Depreciation	(100,000)
Office building	180,000	Cost	220,000
		Less: Depreciation	(100,000)
Land	100,000	Cost	40,000
Goodwill	270,000	Cost	–0–
Total	$600,000	Total	$ 180,000

The buyer paid $240,000 at closing and agreed to pay the balance with interest at 8% (exceeds the Federal rate) over 10 years. The office building was depreciated using the straight-line method. Thus, there is no § 1250 gain.

a. Compute Tom's recognized gain in the year of the sale.
b. Determine the character of the gain recognized in the year of the sale.

14. On July 1, 2004, a cash basis taxpayer sold land for $800,000 due on the date of the sale and $6 million principal and $741,600 interest (6%) due on June 30, 2006. The seller's basis in the land was $1 million. The Federal short-term rate was 8%, compounded semiannually.

a. Compute the seller's interest income and gain in 2004, 2005, and 2006.
b. Same as (a), except that the amount due in two years was $2 million principal and $508,800 interest and the purchaser will use the cash method to account for interest.

15. On December 30, 2004, Father sold land to Son for $10,000 cash and a 7% installment note with a face amount of $260,000. In 2005, after paying $60,000 on the principal of the note, Son sold the land. In 2006, Son paid Father $40,000 on the note principal. Father's basis in the land was $50,000. Assuming Son sold the land for $300,000, compute Father's taxable gain in 2005.

16. George sold land to an unrelated party in 2003. His basis in the land was $40,000, and the selling price was $100,000—$25,000 payable at closing and $25,000 (plus 10% interest) due January 1, 2004, 2005, and 2006. What would be the tax consequences of the following? [Treat each part independently and assume (1) George did not elect out of the installment method and (2) the installment obligations have values equal to their face amounts.]
a. In 2004, George gave to his daughter the right to collect all future payments on the installment obligations.
b. In 2004, after collecting the payment due on January 1, George transferred the installment obligation to his 100%-controlled corporation in exchange for additional shares of stock.
c. On December 31, 2004, George received the payment due on January 1, 2005. On December 15, 2005, George died, and the remaining installment obligation was transferred to his estate. The estate collected the amount due on January 1, 2006.

17. The Heron Construction Company reports its income by the completed contract method. At the end of 2004, the company completed a contract to construct a building at a total cost of $1,980,000. The contract price was $2,200,000. However, the customer refused to accept the work and would not pay anything on the contract because he claimed the roof did not meet specifications. Heron's engineers estimated it would cost $150,000 to bring the roof up to the customer's standards. In 2005, the dispute was settled in the customer's favor; the roof was improved at a cost of $180,000, and the customer accepted the building and paid the $2,200,000.
a. What would be the effects of the above on Heron's taxable income for 2004 and 2005?
b. Same as (a), except that Heron had $2,100,000 accumulated cost under the contract at the end of 2004.

Communications

18. Daffodil Company is a real estate construction company with average annual gross receipts of $3 million. Daffodil uses the completed contract method, and the contracts require 18 months to complete. Daffodil generally builds commercial buildings under contracts with the owners and reports the income by the completed contract method. The company is considering building a series of similar stores for a retail chain. The gross profit margin would be low, but the company's gross receipts would triple. Write a letter to your client explaining the tax accounting implications of entering into these contracts. Daffodil's mailing address is P.O. Box 1000, Harrisonburg, VA 22807.

EXTENDER

19. Rust Company is a real estate construction company with average annual gross receipts of $4 million. Rust uses the completed contract method, and the contracts require 18 months to complete. Which of the following costs would be allocated to construction in progress by Rust?
a. The payroll taxes on direct labor.
b. The current services pension costs for employees whose wages are included in direct labor.
c. Accelerated depreciation on equipment used on contracts.
d. Sales tax on materials assigned to contracts.
e. The past service costs for employees whose wages are included in direct labor.
f. Bidding expenses for contracts awarded.

Issue ID

20. The Eagle Construction Company began business on April 1 this year. The company erects prefabricated steel buildings and operates as follows. After the customer selects a building model, Eagle orders the materials from the manufacturer. Eagle then erects the building on the customer's property. Eagle prices the contract at 150% of the cost of the prefabricated building. The customer pays 70% of the price at the time the materials

are ordered and the balance of the original price when the building is completed. If Eagle buys more than $1 million in materials during the year, the manufacturer will give Eagle a 2% rebate the following February. Several buildings were under construction at the end of the year. Eagle had ordered more than $1 million in materials during the year, but had paid for only about $989,000 through December. What issues involving Eagle's accounting methods are raised by these facts?

21. Indicate the accounting method that should be used to compute the income from the following contracts.
    a. A contract to build six jet aircraft.
    b. A contract to build a new home. The contractor's average annual gross receipts are $15 million.
    c. A contract to manufacture 3,000 pairs of boots for a large retail chain. The manufacturer has several contracts to produce the same boot for other retailers.
    d. A contract to pave a parking lot. The contractor's average annual gross receipts are $2 million.

Decision Making

22. Ostrich Company makes gasoline storage tanks. Everything produced is under contract (that is, the company does not produce until it gets a contract for a product). Ostrich makes three basic models. However, the tanks must be adapted to each individual customer's location and needs (e.g., the location of the valves, the quality of the materials and insulation). Discuss the following issues relative to Ostrich's operations.
    a. An examining IRS agent contends that each of the company's contracts is to produce a "unique product." What difference does it make whether the product is unique or a "shelf item"?
    b. What must Ostrich do with the costs of bidding on contracts?
    c. Ostrich frequently makes several cost estimates for a contract, using various estimates of materials costs. These costs fluctuate almost daily. Assuming Ostrich must use the percentage of completion method to report the income from the contract, what will be the consequence if the company uses the highest estimate of a contract's cost and the actual cost is closer to the lowest estimated cost?

Decision Making
Communications

23. Swallow Company is a large real estate construction company that reports its income by the percentage of completion method. In 2005, the company completed a contract at a total cost of $1,960,000. The contract price was $2,400,000. At the end of 2004, the year the contract was begun, Swallow estimated the total cost of the contract would be $2,100,000, and total accumulated costs on the contract at the end of 2004 were $1,400,000. The relevant tax rate is 34%, and the relevant Federal interest rate is 7%. Assume that all returns were filed and taxes were paid on March 15 following the close of the calendar tax year.
    a. Compute the gross profit on the contract for 2004 and 2005.
    b. Before bidding on a contract, Swallow generally makes three estimates of total contract costs: (1) optimistic, (2) pessimistic, and (3) most likely (based on a blending of optimistic and pessimistic assumptions). The company has asked you to write a letter explaining which of these estimates should be used for percentage of completion purposes. In writing your letter, you should consider the fact that Swallow is an S corporation; therefore, the income and deductions flow through to the shareholders who are all individuals in the 35% marginal tax bracket. The relevant Federal interest rate is 8%. Swallow's mailing address is 400 Front Avenue, Ashland, OR 97520.

24. Bluebird Company, a furniture retailer, is adding a new line of merchandise. In the current year, the company purchased merchandise with an invoice price of $700,000, less a 2% discount for early payment. Freight and handling charges totaled $60,000. The company had to lease additional storage space in a warehouse three blocks from the store. The lease on the storage space was $30,000 for the year. A buyer was added to handle the new line of merchandise, and her salary was $35,000 for the year. Also, as a result of the increase in inventory of goods on hand, the company's insurance increased by $5,000. The invoice cost of the goods on hand at the end of the year was $105,000. Compute the company's ending inventory under the FIFO method.

25. Flamingo Company produces small machinery. The company also produces parts used to repair the machinery. The parts may be sold for several years after the company has discontinued the product. Flamingo has on hand parts with an original cost of $600,000. The total offering price on these goods is $960,000. However, the company expects to sell only 80% of the parts on hand. The excess parts are kept in case the estimates are incorrect.
   a. Can Flamingo deduct the excess inventory under the lower of cost or market rule?
   b. Assume that Flamingo deducted the cost of the excess parts on hand. While the parts were still on hand, the company elected LIFO. What are the implications of the change in inventory method?

26. In 2004, Gail changed from the lower of cost or market FIFO method to the LIFO inventory method. The ending inventory for 2003 was computed as follows:

Item	FIFO Cost	Replacement Cost	Lower of Cost or Market
A	$21,000	$15,000	$15,000
B	50,000	66,000	50,000
C	30,000	3,000	3,000
			$68,000

Item C was damaged goods, and the replacement cost used was actually the estimated selling price of the goods. The actual cost to replace item C was $32,000.
   a. What is the correct beginning inventory for 2004 under the LIFO method?
   b. What immediate tax consequences (if any) will result from the switch to LIFO?

27. Amber Company has used the dollar-value LIFO technique for the past three years. The company has only one inventory pool. Its beginning inventory for the current year was computed as follows.

	Base Period Cost	LIFO Index	LIFO Layer
Base inventory	$1,250,000	1.0	$1,250,000
Year 1 layer	500,000	1.05	525,000
Year 2 layer	200,000	1.08	216,000
	$1,950,000		$1,991,000

The ending inventory is $1,955,000 at current period prices and $1,750,000 at base period prices. Determine the company's LIFO inventory value as of the end of the current year.

Issue ID
Communications

28. Jeffrey Boyd, the president of Eagle Furniture Company (average annual gross receipts of $4 million), has prepared the company's financial statements and income tax returns for the past 15 years. In July 2005, however, he hired you to prepare the 2004 corporate income tax return because he has not studied taxes for over 20 years and suspects the rules may have changed. Eagle uses the accrual method of accounting. Based on an initial examination of Eagle's trial balance and some account analyses, you have determined that the following items may require adjustments:

   - The company uses the FIFO inventory method, as valued at cost. However, all freight expenses on incoming merchandise have been expensed for the 15 years the company has been in business.

   - The company experiences inventory shrinkage (due to breakage and theft) of about 1% of sales each year. The shrinkage is not taken into account until the company takes a physical inventory each October, but the corporation's fiscal year ends January 31.

- The company has used an allowance for uncollectible accounts, which has a balance of $60,000. In the past, the company has been able to accurately predict its actual bad debt expense.
- The company sells a three-year service contract on its appliances. The company treats $\frac{1}{36}$ of the contract price as earned each month. At the beginning of the year, the company had $120,000 in its account for unearned revenues from the service contracts.
- The company deducts its state income tax in the year paid. Thus, the 2004 state income tax expense includes the estimated taxes paid in 2004 and the additional amount paid in 2004 on 2003 taxes.

Write a letter to Mr. Boyd explaining what adjustments will be required and how they will be implemented. The address of Eagle Furniture Company is 1000 East Maryland Street, Evansville, IL 47722.

BRIDGE DISCIPLINE

1. White Partnership is owned by the following partners who have the indicated tax years.

Partner	Percentage	Tax Year End
Robert Jones	49%	December 31
Green Partnership	11%	June 30
Bronze, Inc.	40%	June 30

Assume that White does not have a natural business year.

a. What are the tax year options for White for financial reporting purposes?
b. What are the tax year options for White for Federal income tax purposes?

2. Beige Company uses the cash method of accounting for Federal income tax purposes and the accrual method for financial reporting purposes. Beige purchases an office building and land for $750,000 on June 9, 2004, with $100,000 being allocated to the land. Beige consistently follows a policy of writing off all fixed costs as rapidly as possible for Federal income tax purposes. MACRS is used in calculating depreciation for financial reporting purposes.

a. Calculate the amount of the deduction associated with the office building for Federal income tax purposes for the current year.
b. Calculate the depreciation expense for financial reporting purposes under MACRS for the current year.
c. Calculate the amount of the book-tax differential.

3. Calico, Inc., an airplane manufacturer, uses the accrual method of accounting for both financial reporting and Federal income tax purposes. The spare parts inventory is recorded at the lower of cost or market. Some spare parts in the inventory have not been needed for several years, but Calico anticipates that it will eventually sell some of these items for repair work at the current market price (i.e., no discounts required). Based on a statistical projection, the company writes down to scrap value the spare parts that it expects it will eventually have to scrap to satisfy the external auditor. An IRS agent contends that while the writedown is in accordance with GAAP, it does not "clearly reflect income," so the writedown is disallowed.

Justify the position taken by your client in response to the external auditor, and justify the position taken by the IRS agent. Are the positions reconcilable in light of the different objectives of GAAP and the Code?

Research Problems

THOMSON RIA

Note: Solutions to Research Problems can be prepared by using the ***RIA Checkpoint® Student Edition*** *online research product, which is available to accompany this text. It is also possible to prepare solutions to the Research Problems by using tax research materials found in a standard tax library.*

Research Problem 1. Your client is an accrual basis trucking company that operates in several states. The tax year is the calendar year. Each state requires the company to pay for annual licenses and permits. The payments usually are due in December for the following calendar year. The company has consistently expensed these items, relying on the "one-year rule." The IRS agent argues that the one-year rule does not apply to an accrual basis taxpayer. Is the IRS agent correct?

Communications

Research Problem 2. Violet Company discovered that certain equipment used in its repair operations had been accounted for as inventory rather than as fixed assets. This incorrect treatment applied to all years in which the equipment had been used, and all of those years are open under the statute of limitations. Violet filed amended returns for all years affected by the incorrect treatment to obtain a refund of overpayments of taxes for the years affected. The IRS refused to accept the amended returns. The IRS reasoned that Violet was actually changing accounting methods and this can only be accomplished through a request for change in methods. In addition, the IRS concluded that an adjustment due to a voluntary change in accounting method must be taken into income for the year of the change. Is the IRS correct? Write a letter to Agnes Boyd, the president of Violet Company, that contains your advice and prepare a memo for the tax files. Violet's address is 100 Whitaker's Mill, Fargo, ND 58105.

Research Problem 3. Your client is an accrual basis taxpayer. For 2004 the company had a $600,000 net operating loss, which can be carried back to 2002. The loss can also be carried back to the 2002 state income tax return and will create a $36,000 refund of state income taxes for that year. The IRS agent insists that the state income tax refund must be included in 2004 gross income (under the tax benefit rule) and thus will reduce the 2004 Federal income tax loss available for carryback by $36,000. When does the income from the state tax refund accrue?

Research Problem 4. Your client, April Partners, is a real estate developer. Usually, April will purchase land and immediately begin development. However, for some property that it recently purchased, April has decided to wait at least one year before beginning development. April would like to know if it can deduct the costs of holding the property (insurance, taxes, and interest) while it is awaiting the appropriate time to begin development.

Partial list of research aids:
Von-Lusk, 104 T.C. 207 (1995).

Internet Activity

Use the tax resources of the Internet to address the following questions. Do not restrict your search to the World Wide Web, but include a review of newsgroups and general reference materials, practitioner sites and resources, primary sources of the tax law, chat rooms and discussion groups, and other opportunities.

Research Problem 5. Determine the current midterm "applicable Federal rate" that would be applied to impute interest on a note receivable due in four years.

Research Problem 6. Find a company that provides software for retail dollar-value LIFO inventories for grocery stores.

Research Problem 7. Join a taxpayer discussion group that is addressing issues related to the installment method. Provide statutory information concerning the method through an initial posting, then answer one or two taxpayer follow-up queries. Be sure to relate a few of the limitations on the use of the installment method to the group.

Other Taxpayers

PART 5

High-income and high-wealth individuals face a challenge in dealing with the asset-transfer taxes that face them, especially toward the end of their lives. Estate, gift, and generation-skipping transfer taxes, particularly as they apply to business owners, are reviewed in detail in Part V. In addition, the taxation of charities and other exempt entities, and the role of such organizations in society, are examined. For all of these topics, the text's planning orientation is applied.

Exempt Entities

CHAPTER 13

LEARNING OBJECTIVES

After completing Chapter 13, you should be able to:

LO.1

Identify the different types of exempt organizations.

LO.2

Enumerate the requirements for exempt status.

LO.3

Discuss the tax consequences of exempt status, including the different consequences for public charities and private foundations.

LO.4

Determine which exempt organizations are classified as private foundations.

LO.5

Recognize the taxes imposed on private foundations and calculate the related initial tax and additional tax amounts.

LO.6

Determine when an exempt organization is subject to the unrelated business income tax and calculate the amount of the tax.

LO.7

List the reports exempt organizations must file with the IRS and the related due dates.

http://wft.swlearning.com

OUTLINE

TAX TALK

Trying to understand the various exempt organization provisions of the Internal Revenue Code is as difficult as capturing a drop of mercury under your thumb.

—*Stephen J. Swift*

All business entities are ordinarily subject to the Federal income tax at one or more levels. However, entities classified as **exempt organizations** may be able to escape Federal income taxation altogether.

The availability of this exemption has spurred numerous attempts to evade tax. For example, during the 1970s and 1980s, a popular technique for attempting to avoid Federal income tax was the establishment of mail-order churches. In one typical scheme, a nurse obtained a certificate of ordination and a church charter from an organization that sold such documents.[1] The articles of incorporation stated that the church was organized exclusively for religious and charitable purposes, including a religious mission of healing the spirit, mind, emotions, and body. The nurse was the church's minister, director, and principal officer. Taking a vow of poverty, she transferred all her assets, including a house and car, to the church. The church assumed all of the nurse's liabilities, including the mortgage on her house and her credit card bills. The nurse continued to work at a hospital and deposited her salary in the church's bank account. The church provided her with a living allowance sufficient to maintain or improve her previous standard of living. She was also permitted to use the house and car for personal purposes.

The IRS declared that such organizations were shams and not bona fide churches. For a church to be tax-exempt under § 501(c)(3), none of its net earnings may be used to the benefit of any private shareholder or individual. In essence, the organization should serve a public rather than a private interest. The courts have consistently upheld this IRS position.

[1]Rev.Rul. 81–94, 1981–1 C.B. 330.

TAX IN THE NEWS

THE SOURCE OF THE MONEY

Churches qualify for tax-exempt status under § 501(c)(3). Contributions to churches are deductible under § 170(a). Lottery winnings are included in gross income under § 61(a). So what do these Code sections have in common? The answer is Andrew "Jack" Whittaker of Hurricane, West Virginia.

Jack won the Powerball lottery and an after-tax amount of $113.4 million. Jack's first announcement of his plans for the funds was to state his intention to tithe. He intends to commit $17 million ($170 million before taxes × 10%) for this purpose. His first use of his winnings was to write three checks of $334,000 each for three churches in Hurricane.

But not all of the citizens of Hurricane are pleased with the present and future infusions of Jack's lottery winnings into charitable activities in the community. Some of the citizens consider it inappropriate to use gambling winnings to support their religious institutions. As one unnamed church congregant stated, "Some churches around here are against anything like this." She added, "I don't play the lottery."

SOURCE: Adapted from Brian McGuire, "Play, Win, Give," *Wall Street Journal*, January 10, 2003, p. W11.

Although the major objective of the Federal tax law is to raise revenue, social considerations may also affect the tax law. This objective bears directly on the decision by Congress to permit exempt organization tax status. The House Report on the Revenue Act of 1938 explains:

> The exemption from taxation of money or property devoted to charitable and other purposes is based upon the theory that the Government is compensated for the loss of revenue by its relief from the financial burden which would otherwise have to be met by appropriations from public funds, and by the benefits resulting from the promotion of the general welfare.[2]

Recognizing this social objective, Subchapter F (Exempt Organizations) of the Code (§§ 501–530) provides the authority under which certain organizations are exempt from Federal income tax. It should be noted before continuing that this exemption does not guarantee that qualifying entities will completely avoid tax. Two general limitations exist. First, the nature or scope of the organization may result in it being only partially exempt from tax.[3] Second, the organization may engage in activities that are subject to special taxation.[4]

LO.1

Identify the different types of exempt organizations.

Types of Exempt Organizations

An organization qualifies for exempt status *only* if it fits into one of the categories provided in the Code. Examples of qualifying exempt organizations and the specific statutory authority for their exempt status are listed in Exhibit 13–1.[5]

[2]See 1939–1 (Part 2) C.B. 742 for reprint of H.R. No. 1860, 75th Congress, 3rd Session.

[3]See the subsequent discussion of Unrelated Business Income Tax.

[4]See the subsequent discussions of Prohibited Transactions and Taxes Imposed on Private Foundations.

[5]§ 501(a) provides for exempt status for organizations described in §§ 401 and 501. The orientation of this chapter is toward organizations that conduct business activities. Therefore, the exempt organizations described in § 401 (qualified pension, profit sharing, and stock bonus trusts) are outside the scope of the chapter and are not discussed.

■ **EXHIBIT 13–1**
Types of Exempt Organizations

Statutory Authority	Brief Description	Examples or Comments
§ 501(c)(1)	Federal and related agencies.	Commodity Credit Corporation, Federal Deposit Insurance Corporation, Federal Land Bank.
§ 501(c)(2)	Corporations holding title to property for and paying income to exempt organizations.	Corporation holding title to college fraternity house.
§ 501(c)(3)	Religious, charitable, educational, scientific, literary, etc., organizations.	Boy Scouts of America, Red Cross, Salvation Army, Episcopal Church, United Fund, University of Richmond.
§ 501(c)(4)	Civic leagues and employee unions.	Garden club, tenants' association promoting tenants' legal rights in entire community, League of Women Voters.
§ 501(c)(5)	Labor, agricultural, and horticultural organizations.	Teachers' association, organization formed to promote effective agricultural pest control, organization formed to test soil and to educate community members in soil treatment, garden club.
§ 501(c)(6)	Business leagues, chambers of commerce, real estate boards, etc.	Chambers of Commerce, American Plywood Association, National Football League, medical association peer review board, organization promoting acceptance of women in business and professions.
§ 501(c)(7)	Social clubs.	Country club, rodeo and riding club, press club, bowling club, college fraternities.
§ 501(c)(8)	Fraternal beneficiary societies.	Lodges. Must provide for the payment of life, sickness, accident, or other benefits to members or their dependents.
§ 501(c)(9)	Voluntary employees' beneficiary associations.	Provide for the payment of life, sickness, accident, or other benefits to members, their dependents, or their designated beneficiaries.
§ 501(c)(10)	Domestic fraternal societies.	Lodges. Must not provide for the payment of life, sickness, accident, or other benefits; and must devote the net earnings exclusively to religious, charitable, scientific, literary, educational, and fraternal purposes.
§ 501(c)(11)	Local teachers' retirement fund associations.	Only permitted sources of income are amounts received from (1) public taxation, (2) assessments on teaching salaries of members, and (3) income from investments.
§ 501(c)(12)	Local benevolent life insurance associations, mutual or cooperative telephone companies, etc.	Local cooperative telephone company, local mutual water company, local mutual electric company.
§ 501(c)(13)	Cemetery companies.	Must be operated exclusively for the benefit of lot owners who hold the lots for burial purposes.
§ 501(c)(14)	Credit unions.	Other than credit unions exempt under § 501(c)(1).
§ 501(c)(15)	Mutual insurance companies.	Mutual fire insurance company, mutual automobile insurance company.
§ 501(c)(16)	Corporations organized by farmers' cooperatives for financing crop operations.	Related farmers' cooperative must be exempt from tax under § 521.
§ 501(c)(19)	Armed forces members' posts or organizations.	Veterans of Foreign Wars (VFW), Reserve Officers Association.
§ 501(c)(20)	Group legal service plans.	Provided by a corporation for its employees.
§ 501(d)	Religious and apostolic organizations.	Communal organization. Members must include pro rata share of the net income of the organization in their gross income as dividends.
§ 501(e)	Cooperative hospital service organizations.	Centralized purchasing organization for exempt hospitals.
§ 501(f)	Cooperative service organization of educational institutions.	Organization formed to manage universities' endowment funds.
§ 529	Qualified tuition programs.	Prepaid tuition and educational savings programs.
§ 530	Coverdell Education Savings Accounts.	Qualified education savings accounts.

LO.2

Enumerate the requirements for exempt status.

Requirements for Exempt Status

Exempt status frequently requires more than mere classification in one of the categories of exempt organizations. Many of the organizations that qualify for exempt status share the following characteristics.

- The organization serves some type of *common good*.[6]
- The organization is *not* a *for-profit* entity.[7]
- *Net earnings* do not benefit the members of the organization.[8]
- The organization does not exert *political influence*.[9]

SERVING THE COMMON GOOD

The underlying rationale for all exempt organizations is that they serve some type of *common good*. However, depending on the type of the exempt organization, the term *common good* may be interpreted broadly or narrowly. If the test is interpreted broadly, the group being served is the general public or some large subgroup thereof. If it is interpreted narrowly, the group is the specific group referred to in the statutory language. For example, one of the factors in classifying an exempt organization as a private foundation is the size of the group it serves.[10]

NOT-FOR-PROFIT ENTITY

The organization may not be organized or operated for the purpose of making a profit. For some types of exempt organizations, the *for-profit prohibition* appears in the statutory language. For other types, the prohibition is implied.

NET EARNINGS AND MEMBERS OF THE ORGANIZATION

What uses are appropriate for the net earnings of a tax-exempt organization? The logical answer would seem to be that the earnings should be used for the exempt purpose of the organization. However, where the organization exists for the good of a specific group of members, such an open-ended interpretation could permit net earnings to benefit specific group members. Therefore, the Code specifically prohibits certain types of exempt organizations from using their earnings in this way. For example, § 501(c)(6) states that

> . . . no part of the net earnings . . . inures to the benefit of any private shareholder or individual . . .

In other instances, a statutory prohibition is unnecessary because the definition of the exempt organization in the Code effectively prevents such use. This is illustrated in the following requirement.

> . . . the net earnings of which are devoted exclusively to religious, charitable, scientific, literary, educational, and fraternal purposes . . .[11]

[6]See, for example, §§ 501(c)(3) and (4).

[7]See, for example, §§ 501(c)(3), (4), (6), (13), and (14).

[8]See, for example, §§ 501(c)(3), (6), (7), (9), (10), (11), and (19).

[9]See, for example, § 501(c)(3).

[10]Recall from the discussion of the charitable contribution deduction that special restrictions are placed on contributions to private foundations. See Chapter 15 of *West Federal Taxation: Taxation of Business Entities* for additional discussion.

[11]§ 501(c)(10).

POLITICAL INFLUENCE

Religious, charitable, educational, etc. organizations are generally prohibited from attempting to influence legislation or participate in political campaigns. Participation in political campaigns includes participation both *on behalf of* a candidate and *in opposition to* a candidate.

Only in limited circumstances are such exempt organizations permitted to attempt to influence legislation. See the subsequent discussion under Prohibited Transactions.

LO.3

Discuss the tax consequences of exempt status, including the different consequences for public charities and private foundations.

Tax Consequences of Exempt Status: General

An organization that is appropriately classified as an exempt organization is generally exempt from Federal income tax. Four exceptions to this general statement exist, however. An exempt organization that engages in a *prohibited transaction* or is a so-called *feeder organization* is subject to tax. If the organization is classified as a *private foundation*, it may be partially subject to tax. Finally, an exempt organization is subject to tax on its *unrelated business taxable income*.

In addition to being exempt from Federal income tax, an exempt organization may be eligible for other benefits, including the following.

- The organization may be exempt from state income tax, state franchise tax, sales tax, or property tax.
- The organization may receive discounts on postage rates.
- Donors of property to the organization may qualify for charitable contribution deductions on their Federal and state income tax returns. However, *not* all exempt organizations are qualified charitable contribution recipients (e.g., gifts to the National Football League, PGA Tour, and Underwriters Laboratories are not deductible).

PROHIBITED TRANSACTIONS

Prohibited transactions include lobbying, participating in political campaigns, or engaging in an activity that fails to meet the initial qualification requirements for exempt status.[12] If an exempt entity engages in a prohibited transaction, three negative results can occur. First, part or all of the organization's income may be subject to Federal income tax. Second, intermediate sanctions may be imposed on certain exempt organization insiders. Finally, the organization may forfeit its exempt status.

Failure to Continue to Qualify. Organizations initially qualify for exempt status only if they are organized as indicated in Exhibit 13–1. The initial qualification requirements then effectively become maintenance requirements. Failure to continue to meet the qualification requirements results in the loss of the entity's exempt status.

New Faith, Inc., is an excellent example of an exempt organization that failed to continue to qualify for tax exemption.[13] The stated purposes of the organization were to feed and shelter the poor. In its application for exempt status, New Faith

[12] § 503.

[13] *New Faith, Inc.*, 64 TCM 1050, T.C.Memo. 1992–601.

indicated that it would derive its financial support from donations, bingo games, and raffles. The IRS approved the exempt status.

New Faith's only source of income was the operation of several lunch trucks, which provided food to the general public in exchange for scheduled "donations." Evidence provided by the organization to the Tax Court did not show that the food from the lunch trucks was provided free of charge or at reduced prices. In addition, no evidence was presented to show that the people who received food for free or at below-cost prices were impoverished or needy. The court concluded that the primary purpose of the activity was the conduct of a trade or business. It upheld the IRS's revocation of New Faith's exempt status.

Election Not to Forfeit Exempt Status for Lobbying. Certain exempt organizations are permitted to engage in lobbying (but not political) activities on only a limited basis.[14] These organizations include educational institutions, hospitals, and medical research organizations; organizations supporting government schools; organizations publicly supported by charitable contributions; certain organizations that are publicly supported by various sources including admissions, sales, gifts, grants, contributions, or membership fees; and certain organizations that support certain types of public charities. Churches, their integrated auxiliaries, and *private foundations* are not permitted to engage in lobbying activities, however.

To participate in lobbying activities, eligible § 501(c)(3) organizations must file an election with the IRS. If the resulting lobbying expenses exceed a ceiling amount, exempt status may be lost. The ceiling amount is determined and applied independently for **lobbying expenditures** and **grass roots expenditures.**

Lobbying expenditures are made for the purpose of influencing legislation through communications with any legislator or staff member or with any government official or staff member who may participate in the formulation of legislation. Grass roots expenditures are made for the purpose of influencing legislation by attempting to affect the opinions of the general public or any segment thereof.

The statutory ceiling for lobbying expenditures and grass roots expenditures is computed as follows.

- 150% × Lobbying nontaxable amount = Lobbying expenditures ceiling.
- 150% × Grass roots nontaxable amount = Grass roots expenditures ceiling.

The *lobbying nontaxable amount* is the lesser of (1) $1 million or (2) the amount determined in Figure 13–1.[15] The *grass roots nontaxable amount* is 25 percent of the lobbying nontaxable amount.[16]

In addition to a statutory ceiling on lobbying and grass roots expenditures, tax-exempt organizations may be assessed a 25 percent tax on **excess lobbying expenditures.**[17] Excess lobbying expenditures are the greater of the following.[18]

- Excess of the lobbying expenditures for the taxable year over the lobbying nontaxable amount.
- Excess of the grass roots expenditures for the taxable year over the grass roots nontaxable amount.

[14] § 501(h).
[15] § 4911(c)(2).
[16] § 4911(c)(4).
[17] § 4911(a)(1).
[18] § 4911(b).

■ **FIGURE 13–1**
Calculation of Lobbying Nontaxable Amount

Exempt Purpose Expenditures	Lobbying Nontaxable Amount Is
Not over $500,000	20% of exempt purpose expenditures*
Over $500,000 but not over $1 million	$100,000 + 15% of the excess of exempt purpose expenditures over $500,000
Over $1 million but not over $1.5 million	$175,000 + 10% of the excess of exempt purpose expenditures over $1 million
Over $1.5 million	$225,000 + 5% of the excess of exempt purpose expenditures over $1.5 million

*Exempt purpose expenditures generally are the amounts paid or incurred for the taxable year to accomplish the following purposes: religious, charitable, scientific, literary, educational, fostering national or international amateur sports competition, or the prevention of cruelty to children or animals.

EXAMPLE 1

Tan, Inc., a qualifying § 501(c)(3) organization, incurs lobbying expenditures of $500,000 for the taxable year and grass roots expenditures of $0. Exempt purpose expenditures for the taxable year are $5,000,000. Tan elects to be eligible to make lobbying expenditures on a limited basis.

Applying the data in Figure 13–1, the lobbying nontaxable amount is $400,000 [$225,000 + 5%($5,000,000 – $1,500,000)]. The ceiling on lobbying expenditures is $600,000 (150% × $400,000). Therefore, the $500,000 of lobbying expenditures are under the permitted $600,000, so Tan can retain its exempt status. However, the election results in the imposition of tax on the excess lobbying expenditures of $100,000 ($500,000 lobbying expenditures – $400,000 lobbying nontaxable amount). The resulting tax liability is $25,000 ($100,000 × 25%). ■

A § 501(c)(3) organization that makes disqualifying lobbying expenditures is also subject to a 5 percent tax on the lobbying expenditures for the taxable year. A 5 percent tax may also be levied on the organization's management. The tax is imposed on management only if the managers knew that making the expenditures was likely to result in the organization no longer qualifying under § 501(c)(3), and if the managers' actions were willful and not due to reasonable cause. The tax does not apply to private foundations (see the subsequent discussion).[19] Concept Summary 13–1 capsulizes the rules on influencing legislation.

Intermediate Sanctions. Prior to 1996, the IRS had only two options available for dealing with exempt organizations (other than private foundations) engaging in prohibited transactions. First, it could attempt to subject part or all of the organization's income to Federal income tax. Second, it could revoke the exempt status of the organization. For private foundations, an additional option was available. The IRS could impose certain taxes on private foundations for engaging in so-called prohibited transactions (see Concept Summary 13–3 later in this chapter).

Tax legislation enacted in 1996 added another option to the IRS toolbox—**intermediate sanctions**—for so-called public charities.[20] The intermediate sanctions take the form of excise taxes imposed on disqualified persons (any individuals who are in a position to exercise substantial influence over the affairs of the organization) who engage in *excess benefit transactions* and on exempt organization

[19] § 4912.

[20] § 4958.

CONCEPT SUMMARY 13–1

Exempt Organizations and Influencing Legislation

Factor	Tax Result
Entity subject to rule	§ 501(c)(3) organization.
Effect of influencing legislation	Subject to 5% tax on lobbying expenditures under § 4912. Forfeit exempt status under § 501(c)(3). Not eligible for exempt status under § 501(c)(4).
Effect of electing to make lobbying expenditures	Permitted to make limited lobbying expenditures (up to a statutory ceiling determined separately for lobbying expenditures and grass roots expenditures). Subject to 25% tax on excess lobbying expenditures under § 4911.

managers who participate in such a transaction knowing it is improper. Such excess benefit transactions include transactions in which a disqualified person engages in a non-fair market value transaction with the exempt organization or receives unreasonable compensation.

The excise tax on the disqualified person is imposed at a rate of 25 percent of the excess benefit. For the exempt organization manager, the excise tax is imposed at a rate of 10 percent of the excess benefit (unless such participation is not willful and is due to reasonable cause) with a statutory ceiling of $10,000 for any excess benefit transaction. These excise taxes are referred to as first-level taxes.

A second-level tax is imposed on the disqualified person if the excess benefit transaction is not corrected within the taxable period. This excise tax is imposed at a rate of 200 percent of the excess benefit.

FEEDER ORGANIZATIONS

A **feeder organization** carries on a trade or business for the benefit of an exempt organization and remits its profits to the exempt organization. Such organizations are not exempt from Federal income tax. This provision is intended to prevent an entity whose primary purpose is to conduct a trade or business for profit from escaping taxation merely because all of its profits are payable to one or more exempt organizations.[21]

Some income and activities are *not* subject to the feeder organization rules.[22]

- Rent income that would be excluded from the definition of the term *rent* for purposes of the unrelated business income tax (discussed subsequently).
- A trade or business where substantially all the work is performed by volunteers.
- The trade or business of selling merchandise where substantially all the merchandise has been received as contributions or gifts.

Concept Summary 13–2 highlights the consequences of exempt status.

[21] § 502(a).

[22] § 502(b).

CONCEPT SUMMARY 13–2

Consequences of Exempt Status

General	Exempt from Federal income tax.
	Exempt from most state and local income, franchise, sales, and property taxes.
	Qualify for reductions in postage rates.
	Gifts to the organization often can be deducted by donor.
Exceptions	May be subject to Federal income tax associated with the following. • Engaging in a prohibited transaction. • Being a feeder organization. • Being a private foundation. • Generating unrelated business taxable income.

PLANNING STRATEGIES

Maintaining Exempt Status

FRAMEWORK FOCUS: INCOME AND EXCLUSIONS

STRATEGY ➤ AVOID INCOME RECOGNITION.

To maintain exempt status, the organization must satisfy both an organizational test and an operational test. The organizational test requires that the entity satisfy the statutory requirements for exempt status on paper. The operational test ensures that the entity does, in fact, satisfy the statutory requirements for exempt status.

King Shipping Consum., Inc. (Zion Coptic Church, Inc.) illustrates that it is usually much easier to satisfy the organizational test than the operational test.[23] Zion's stated purpose was to engage in activities usually and normally associated with churches. Based on this, the IRS approved Zion's exempt status as a § 501(c)(3) organization.

Zion's real intent, however, was to smuggle illegal drugs into the country and to distribute them for profit. The church's justification for the drugs was that it used marijuana in its sacrament. During a four-month period, however, the police confiscated 33 tons of marijuana from church members. The IRS calculated that, even assuming the maximum alleged church membership of several thousand, each member would have had to smoke over 33 pounds of marijuana during the four-month confiscation period.

The court concluded that Zion's real purpose was to cloak a large commercial drug smuggling operation. Since this activity was inconsistent with the religious purpose for exempt status, the court upheld the IRS's revocation of Zion's exempt status and the deficiency assessment of approximately $1.6 million.

LO.4

Determine which exempt organizations are classified as private foundations.

Private Foundations

TAX CONSEQUENCES OF PRIVATE FOUNDATION STATUS

Certain exempt organizations are classified as **private foundations.** This classification produces two negative consequences. First, the classification may have an adverse impact on the contributions received by the donee exempt organization. Contributions may decline because the tax consequences for donors may not be as

[23] 58 TCM 574, T.C.Memo. 1989–593.

TAX FACT

Compensation of Public Charities Executives

As is the case in the business community, a compensation gender gap appears to exist for public charities (i.e., compensation of males exceeds that of females).

Job Category	Gender Gap
CEO/Executive Director	40.1%
Top Development Position	15.7%
Top Education Position	16.2%
Top Financial Position	32.9%
Top Human Resources Position	28.5%
Top Legal Position	12.5%
Top Marketing Position	13.7%
Top Technology Position	20.7%

Source: Adapted from 2002 Guidestar Nonprofit Compensation Report.

favorable as if the entity were not a private foundation.[24] Second, the classification may result in taxation at the exempt organization level. The reason for this less beneficial tax treatment is that private foundations define common good more narrowly and therefore are seen as not being supported by, and operated for the good of, the public.

Definition of a Private Foundation. The following § 501(c)(3) organizations are *not* private foundations.[25]

1. Churches; educational institutions; hospitals and medical research organizations; charitable organizations receiving a major portion of their support from the general public or the United States, a state, or a political subdivision thereof that is operated for the benefit of a college or university; and governmental units (favored activities category).
2. Organizations that are broadly supported by the general public (excluding disqualified persons), by governmental units, or by organizations described in (1) above.
3. Entities organized and operated exclusively for the benefit of organizations described in (1) or (2) [a supporting organization].
4. Entities organized and operated exclusively for testing for public safety.

To meet the broadly supported requirement in (2) above, two tests (an external support test and an internal support test) must be satisfied. The *external support test* requires that the organization *normally* derive more than one-third of its support each taxable year from the three groups listed in (2) above, in the following forms.

- Gifts, grants, contributions, and membership fees.
- Gross receipts from admissions, sales of merchandise, performance of services, or the furnishing of facilities in an activity that is not an unrelated trade

[24] § 170(e)(1)(B)(ii).

[25] § 509(a).

or business for purposes of the unrelated business income tax (discussed subsequently). However, such gross receipts from any person or governmental agency in excess of the greater of $5,000 or 1 percent of the organization's support for the taxable year are not counted.

The *internal support test* limits the amount of support *normally* received from the following sources to one-third of the organization's support for the taxable year.[26]

- Gross investment income (gross income from interest, dividends, rents, and royalties).
- Unrelated business taxable income (discussed subsequently) minus the related tax.

EXAMPLE 2

Lion, Inc., a § 501(c)(3) organization, received the following support during the taxable year.

Governmental unit A for services rendered	$30,000
Governmental unit B for services rendered	20,000
General public for services rendered	20,000
Gross investment income	15,000
Contributions from individual substantial contributors (disqualified persons)	15,000

For purposes of the *external support test*, the support from A is counted only to the extent of $5,000 (greater of $5,000 or 1% of $100,000 support). Likewise, for B, only $5,000 is counted as support. Thus, the total countable support is $30,000 ($20,000 from the general public + $5,000 + $5,000), and Lion fails the test for the taxable year ($30,000/$100,000 = 30%; need more than 33.3%). The $15,000 received from disqualified persons is excluded from the numerator but is included in the denominator.

In calculating the *internal support test*, only the gross investment income of $15,000 is included in the numerator. Thus, the test is satisfied ($15,000/$100,000 = 15%; cannot be more than 33.3%) for the taxable year.

Since Lion did not satisfy both tests, it does not qualify as an organization that is broadly supported. ■

The intent of the two tests is to exclude from private foundation status those § 501(c)(3) organizations that are responsive to the general public rather than to the private interests of a limited number of donors or other persons.

Examples of § 501(c)(3) organizations that are not classified as private foundations because they receive broad public support include the United Fund, the Girl Scouts, university alumni associations, symphony orchestras, and the PTA.

LO.5

Recognize the taxes imposed on private foundations and calculate the related initial tax and additional tax amounts.

TAXES IMPOSED ON PRIVATE FOUNDATIONS

In general, a private foundation is exempt from Federal income tax. However, because a private foundation is not a broadly, publicly supported organization, it may be subject to the following taxes.[27]

- Tax based on investment income.
- Tax on self-dealing.
- Tax on failure to distribute income.
- Tax on excess business holdings.
- Tax on investments that jeopardize charitable purposes.
- Tax on taxable expenditures.

[26] Reg. § 1.509(a)–3(c) generally requires that the external and internal support tests be met in each of the four preceding tax years.

[27] §§ 4940–4945.

TAX IN THE NEWS

Who Benefits from the Charity?

Charitable foundations provide a useful benefit to society. They perform desirable functions without having the Federal government directly involved.

As one of the requirements for maintaining tax-exempt status, charitable foundations must pay out at least 5 percent of their assets annually to charitable causes. Various charitable foundations approach this requirement in different ways, with some far exceeding the 5 percent test and others barely meeting it.

An acceptable way to satisfy the 5 percent test is to include some or all of the foundation's administrative costs in calculating the 5 percent amount. According to the National Committee for Responsive Philanthropy (NCRP), the Ford Foundation included 70 percent ($98 million) of its administrative costs in satisfying the 5 percent test in 2001. The committee also reported that the Annie E. Casey Foundation included 89.9 percent ($36.4 million) and the Fannie Mae Foundation included 94 percent ($103 million) of their administrative costs in making the calculation. It should be noted that the Casey Foundation normally exceeds the 5 percent test (e.g., it expects to spend nearly 7 percent in 2003), as does the Ford Foundation (e.g., it spent 7.3 percent in 2001 and 6 percent in 2002).

Nonetheless, being able to include administrative costs in satisfying the 5 percent test, according to some, motivates foundation management to hire more staff and to pay big-dollar salaries. Representatives Roy Blunt (Missouri) and Harold Ford (Tennessee) have introduced legislation to close what they regard as an overhead loophole. Under their proposal, foundations would no longer be able to count administrative costs in satisfying the 5 percent test.

SOURCE: Adapted from Editorial, "Giving a Full 5%," *Wall Street Journal,* August 4, 2003, p. A8.

These taxes restrict the permitted activities of private foundations. Two levels of tax may be imposed on the private foundation and the foundation manager: initial taxes and additional taxes. The initial taxes (first-level), with the exception of the tax based on investment income, are imposed because the private foundation engages in so-called *prohibited transactions*. The additional taxes (second-level) are imposed only if the prohibited transactions are not corrected within a statutory time period.[28] See Concept Summary 13–3 for additional details.

As an example of the prohibited transaction taxes, consider the tax imposed for failure to distribute income. As noted, two levels of tax may be imposed on a private nonoperating foundation for failure to distribute a sufficient portion of its income. The initial tax is imposed at a rate of 15 percent on the undistributed income for the taxable year that is not distributed by the end of the following taxable year. The initial tax is imposed on such undistributed income for each year until the IRS assesses the tax. The additional tax is imposed at a rate of 100 percent on the amount of the inadequate distribution that is not distributed by the assessment date. The additional tax is effectively waived if the undistributed income is distributed within 90 days after the mailing of the deficiency notice for the additional tax. Extensions of this period may be obtained.

Undistributed income is the excess of the distributable amount (in effect, the amount that should have been distributed) over qualifying distributions made by the entity. The distributable amount is the excess of the minimum investment

[28] § 4961.

CONCEPT SUMMARY 13–3

Taxes Imposed on Private Foundations

			Private Foundation		Foundation Manager	
Type of Tax	**Code Section**	**Purpose**	**Initial Tax**	**Additional Tax**	**Initial Tax**	**Additional Tax**
On investment income	§ 4940	Audit fee to defray IRS expenses.	2%*			
On self-dealing	§ 4941	Engaging in transactions with disqualified persons.	5%**	200%**	2.5%†	50%†
On failure to distribute income	§ 4942	Failing to distribute adequate amount of income for exempt purposes.	15%	100%		
On excess business holdings	§ 4943	Investments that enable the private foundation to control unrelated businesses.	5%	200%		
On jeopardizing investments	§ 4944	Speculative investments that put the private foundation's assets at risk.	5%	25%	5%††	5%†
On taxable expenditures	§ 4945	Expenditures that should not be made by private foundations.	10%	100%	2.5%††	50%†

*May be possible to reduce the tax rate to 1%. In addition, an exempt operating foundation [see §§ 4940(d)(2) and 4942(j)(3)] is not subject to the tax.
**Imposed on the disqualified person rather than the foundation.
†Subject to a statutory ceiling of $10,000.
††Subject to a statutory ceiling of $5,000.

return over the sum of the (1) unrelated business income tax and (2) the excise tax based on net investment income.[29] The minimum investment return is 5 percent of the excess of the fair market value of the foundation's assets over the unpaid debt associated with acquiring or improving these assets. The foundation's assets employed directly in carrying on the foundation's exempt purpose are not used in making this calculation.

EXAMPLE 3

Gold, Inc., a private foundation, has undistributed income of $80,000 for its taxable year 2001. It distributes $15,000 of this amount during 2002 and an additional $45,000 during 2003. An IRS deficiency notice is mailed to Gold on August 5, 2004. The initial tax is $12,750 [($65,000 × 15%) + ($20,000 × 15%)].

At the date of the deficiency notice, no additional distributions have been made from the 2001 undistributed income. Therefore, since the remaining undistributed income of $20,000 has not been distributed by August 5, 2004, an additional tax of $20,000 ($20,000 × 100%) is imposed.

If Gold distributes the $20,000 of undistributed income for 2001 within 90 days of the deficiency notice, the additional tax is waived. Without this distribution, however, the foundation will owe $32,750 in taxes. ■

[29] § 4940.

Concept Summary 13–4

Private Foundation Status

	Exempt Organization Is	
	A Private Foundation	**Not a Private Foundation**
Reason for classification	Does not serve the common good because it lacks an approved exempt purpose or does not receive broad public financial support.	Serves the common good.
Eligible for exempt status?	Yes	Yes
Most beneficial charitable contribution deduction treatment available to donors?	Depends. No, if the private foundation is classified as a private *nonoperating* foundation.	Yes
Subject to excise taxes levied on prohibited transactions?	Yes	No
Subject to tax on unrelated business income?	Yes	Yes

PLANNING STRATEGIES Private Foundation Status

Framework Focus: Income and Exclusions; Deductions

Strategy ➤ **Avoid Income Recognition.**
➤ **Maximize Deductible Amounts.**

Exempt organizations that can qualify as public charities receive more beneficial tax treatment than do those that qualify as private foundations. In addition to the excise taxes noted above, donors to private foundations may receive less favorable tax treatment under § 170 than they would if the organization were a public charity. Thus, if possible, the organization should be structured to qualify as a public charity.

One method of avoiding private foundation status is to have a tax-exempt purpose that results in the organization not being classified as a private foundation (the *organization* approach). If this is not feasible, it may be possible to operate the organization so that it receives broad public support and thereby avoids private foundation status (the *operational* approach).

If the organization is a private foundation, care must be exercised to avoid the assessment of tax liability on prohibited transactions. This objective can best be achieved by establishing controls that prevent the private foundation from engaging in transactions that trigger the imposition of the taxes. If an initial tax is assessed, corrective actions should be implemented to avoid the assessment of an additional tax.

Finally, to protect the deductibility of donors' contributions, a private foundation should also take steps to avoid classification as a nonoperating foundation. Recall that contributions of cash and ordinary income property to such organizations are limited to 30 percent of AGI and that only the lesser of fair market value or basis of contributions of long-term capital gain property is deductible, possibly with a 20 percent-of-AGI limit. To avoid nonoperating status, private foundations should be sure to meet the conditions of § 4942(j)(3), which generally require the entity to make minimum distributions of income for use in activities related to its exempt purpose and to devote the use of a majority of its assets to exempt purpose activities. See Concept Summary 13–4.

LO.6

Determine when an exempt organization is subject to the unrelated business income tax and calculate the amount of the tax.

Unrelated Business Income Tax

As explained in the previous section, private foundations are subject to excise taxes for certain actions. One excise tax penalizes the private foundation for using the foundation to gain control of unrelated businesses (tax on excess business holdings). However, *unrelated business* has different meanings for purposes of that excise tax and for the unrelated business income tax.

The **unrelated business income tax (UBIT)** is designed to treat tax-exempt entities as if they were subject to the corporate income tax. Thus, the rates that are used are those applicable to a corporate taxpayer.[30] In general, **unrelated business income** is derived from activities not related to the exempt purpose of the exempt organization. The tax is levied because the organization engages in substantial commercial activities.[31] Without such a tax, nonexempt organizations (regular taxable business entities) would be at a substantial disadvantage when trying to compete with the exempt organization. Thus, the UBIT is intended to neutralize the exempt entity's tax advantage in the marketplace.[32]

EXAMPLE 4

Historic, Inc., is an exempt organization. Its exempt activity is to maintain a restoration of eighteenth-century colonial life (houses, public buildings, taverns, businesses, and craft demonstrations) that is visited by more than a million people each year. A fee is charged for admission to the "restored area." In addition to this "museum" activity, Historic operates two hotels and three restaurants that are available to the general public. The earnings from the hotel and restaurant business are used to defray the costs of operating the "museum" activity.

The "museum" activity is not subject to the Federal income tax. However, even though the income from the hotel and restaurant business is used for exempt purposes, that income is unrelated business income and is subject to the UBIT. ■

The UBIT applies to all organizations that are exempt from Federal income tax under § 501(c), except Federal agencies. In addition, the tax applies to state colleges and universities.[33]

UNRELATED TRADE OR BUSINESS

An exempt organization may be subject to the UBIT in the following circumstances.[34]

- The organization conducts a trade or business.
- The trade or business is not substantially related to the exempt purpose of the organization.
- The trade or business is regularly carried on by the organization.

Even if all of the above factors are present, the Code specifically exempts the following activities from classification as an unrelated trade or business.[35]

- The individuals performing substantially all the work of the trade or business do so without compensation (e.g., an orphanage operates a retail store for sales to the general public, and all the work is done by volunteers).
- The trade or business consists of selling merchandise, and substantially all of the merchandise has been received as gifts or contributions (e.g., thrift shops).
- For § 501(c)(3) organizations and for state colleges or universities, the trade or business is conducted primarily for the convenience of the organization's

[30] § 511(a)(1).
[31] § 512(a)(1).
[32] Reg. § 1.513–1(b).
[33] § 511(a)(2) and Reg. § 1.511–2(a)(2).
[34] § 513(a) and Reg. § 1.513–2(a).
[35] § 513(a).

TAX IN THE NEWS

Donate Those Old Cars

In a recent private letter ruling, a charity's arrangement with a private fund raiser to obtain cars as contributions passed muster with the IRS. That is, the proceeds the charity realized from the car donations were not classified as unrelated business income.

Under the arrangement, the private fund raiser was to solicit car donations in the name of the charity in exchange for part of the sales proceeds. The only relationship between the charity and the private fund raiser had to do with the car donation program. The fund raiser was responsible for providing appraisals and confirmation of the charitable contributions to the donors.

members, students, patients, officers, or employees (e.g., a laundry operated by the college for laundering dormitory linens and students' clothing, a college bookstore).

- For most employee unions, the trade or business consists of selling to members, at their usual place of employment, work-related clothing and equipment and items normally sold through vending machines, snack bars, or food-dispensing facilities.

Definition of Trade or Business. Trade or business, for this purpose, is broadly defined. It includes any activity conducted for the production of income through the sale of merchandise or the performance of services. An activity need not generate a profit to be treated as a trade or business. The activity may be part of a larger set of activities conducted by the organization, some of which may be related to the exempt purpose. Being included in a larger set does not cause the activity to lose its identity as an unrelated trade or business.[36]

EXAMPLE 5

Health, Inc., is an exempt hospital that operates a pharmacy. The pharmacy provides medicines and supplies to the patients in the hospital (i.e., it contributes to the conduct of the hospital's exempt purpose). In addition, the pharmacy sells medicines and supplies to the general public. Sales to the general public constitute a trade or business for purposes of the UBIT. ■

Not Substantially Related to the Exempt Purpose. Exempt organizations frequently conduct unrelated trades or businesses to provide income to help defray the costs of conducting the exempt purpose (like the hotel and restaurant business in Example 4). Providing financial support for the exempt purpose will not prevent an activity from being classified as an unrelated trade or business and thereby being subject to the UBIT.

To be related to the accomplishment of the exempt purpose, the conduct of the business activities must be causally related and contribute importantly to the exempt purpose. Whether a causal relationship exists and the degree of its importance are determined by examining the facts and circumstances. One must consider the size and extent of the activities in relation to the nature and extent of the exempt function that the activities serve.[37]

[36] Reg. § 1.513–1(b).

[37] Reg. § 1.513–1(d).

EXAMPLE 6

Art, Inc., an exempt organization, operates a school for training children in the performing arts. As an essential part of that training, the children perform for the general public. The children are paid at the minimum wage for the performances, and Art derives gross income by charging admission to the performances.

The income from admissions is not income from an unrelated trade or business, because the performances by the children contribute importantly to the accomplishment of the exempt purpose of providing training in the performing arts. ■

EXAMPLE 7

Assume the facts are the same as in Example 6, except that four performances are conducted each weekend of the year. Assume that this number of performances far exceeds that required for training the children. The income derived from admissions to the *excess* performances is income from an unrelated trade or business. ■

The trade or business may sell merchandise that has been produced as part of the accomplishment of the exempt purpose. The sale of such merchandise is normally treated as related to the exempt purpose. However, if the merchandise is not sold in substantially the same state it was in at the completion of the exempt purpose, the gross income subsequently derived from the sale of the merchandise is treated as income from an unrelated trade or business.[38]

EXAMPLE 8

Help, Inc., an exempt organization, conducts programs for the rehabilitation of the handicapped. One of the programs includes training in radio and television repair. Help derives gross income by selling the repaired items. The income is substantially related to the accomplishment of the exempt purpose. Alternatively, if Help had additional reconditioning work performed on the repaired items prior to sale, the income would be treated as unrelated business income. ■

An asset or facility used in the exempt purpose may also be used in a nonexempt purpose. Income derived from use for a nonexempt purpose is income from an unrelated trade or business.[39]

EXAMPLE 9

Civil, Inc., an exempt organization, operates a museum. As part of the exempt purpose of the museum, educational lectures are given in the museum's theater during the operating hours of the museum. In the evening, when the museum is closed, the theater is leased to an individual who operates a movie theater. The lease income received from the individual who operates the movie theater is income from an unrelated trade or business. ■

Special Rule for Corporate Sponsorship Payments. The term *unrelated trade or business* does not include the soliciting and receiving of qualified sponsorship payments.[40]

A payment qualifies as a qualified sponsorship payment if it meets the following requirements.

- There is no arrangement or expectation that the trade or business making the payment will receive any substantial benefit other than the use or acknowledgment of its name, logo, or product lines in connection with the activities of the exempt organization.

[38] Reg. § 1.513–1(d)(4)(ii).

[39] Reg. § 1.513–1(d)(4)(iii) addresses the allocation of expenses to exempt and nonexempt activities.

[40] § 513(i).

TAX IN THE NEWS

More Tax-Exempts Receiving Real Estate

Traditionally, small tax-exempt organizations received most of their charitable contributions in the form of cash, stocks, or life insurance policies. Such tax-exempts tended to shun real estate donations because real estate was considered too complex and too cumbersome. A tax-exempt that decided to operate the real estate rather than sell it would face another complexity—the unrelated business income tax. Consequently, a taxpayer wanting to donate real estate was likely to find that charities were reluctant to accept the donation and expressed a preference for more liquid assets.

Now, however, real estate gifts are welcome. According to Chase V. Magnuson, president of the National Real Estate Foundation, a San Diego organization that assists charities with real estate gifts, "charities are stretching themselves in order to accept real estate." Even tiny tax-exempts, such as the Waukesha County Historical Society and Museum, are starting to accept real estate donations; some are even hiring staff experienced in real estate dealings. A major reason for this change is that real estate values have been soaring, whereas three years of declining stock markets have eroded stock appreciation and, with it, donors' enthusiasm for gifts to charity.

SOURCE: Adapted from Kaja Whitehouse, "Charity Can Begin at Home," *Wall Street Journal*, August 13, 2003, p. D2.

- Such use or acknowledgment does not include advertising the payor's products or services.
- The payment does not include any payment that is contingent upon the level of attendance, broadcast ratings, or other factors indicating the degree of public exposure at an event.

EXAMPLE 10

Pets, Inc., a manufacturer of cat food, contributes $25,000 to Feline Care, Inc., an exempt organization that cares for abandoned cats. In return for the contributions, Feline agrees to put Pets' corporate logo in its monthly newsletter to donors. Under these circumstances, the $25,000 payment is a qualified sponsorship payment and is not subject to the UBIT. ■

EXAMPLE 11

Assume the same facts as in Example 10, except that Feline agrees to endorse Pets' cat food in its monthly newsletter by stating that it feeds only Pets' cat food to its cats. The $25,000 is not a qualified sponsorship payment and is subject to the UBIT. ■

Special Rule for Bingo Games. A special provision applies in determining whether income from bingo games is from an unrelated trade or business. Under this provision, a *qualified bingo game* is not an unrelated trade or business if both of the following requirements are satisfied.[41]

- The bingo game is legal under both state and local law.
- Commercial bingo games (conducted for a profit motive) ordinarily are not permitted in the jurisdiction.

EXAMPLE 12

Play, Inc., an exempt organization, conducts weekly bingo games. The laws of the state and municipality in which Play conducts the games expressly provide that exempt organizations may conduct bingo games, but do not permit profit-oriented entities to do so. Since both

[41] § 513(f).

of the requirements for bingo games are satisfied, the bingo games conducted by Play are not an unrelated trade or business. ■

EXAMPLE 13

Game, Inc., an exempt organization, conducts weekly bingo games in City X and City Y. State law expressly permits exempt organizations to conduct bingo games. State law also provides that profit-oriented entities may conduct bingo games in City X, which is a resort community. Several businesses regularly conduct bingo games there.

The bingo games conducted by Game in City Y are not an unrelated trade or business. However, the bingo games that Game conducts in City X are an unrelated trade or business, because commercial bingo games are regularly permitted to be conducted there. ■

DIGGING DEEPER 1

Find more information on this topic at our Web site: ***http://wft-advanced.swlearning.com.***

UNRELATED BUSINESS INCOME

Even when an exempt organization conducts an unrelated trade or business, a tax is assessed only if the exempt organization regularly conducts the activity and the business produces unrelated business income.

Regularly Carried on by the Organization. An activity is classified as unrelated business income only if it is regularly carried on by the exempt organization. This provision assures that only activities that are actually competing with taxable organizations are subject to the unrelated business income tax. Accordingly, factors to be considered in applying the *regularly carried on* test include the frequency of the activity, the continuity of the activity, and the manner in which the activity is pursued.[42]

EXAMPLE 14

Silver, Inc., an exempt organization, owns land that is located next to the state fairgrounds. During the 10 days of the state fair, Silver uses the land as a parking lot and charges individuals attending the state fair for parking there. The activity is not regularly carried on. ■

EXAMPLE 15

Black, Inc., an exempt organization, has its offices in the downtown area. It owns a parking lot adjacent to its offices on which its employees park during the week. On Saturdays, it rents the spaces in the parking lot to individuals shopping or working in the downtown area. Black is conducting a business activity on a year-round basis, even though it is only for one day per week. Thus, the activity is regularly carried on. ■

UNRELATED BUSINESS TAXABLE INCOME

General Tax Model. The formula for unrelated business taxable income (UBTI) appears in Figure 13–2. The starting point in the formula is gross income from unrelated business activities. This amount is then reduced by the deductions directly connected with the conduct of the unrelated trade or business.[43] The resulting net unrelated business income is then modified through a series of positive and negative adjustments, described below.

Positive adjustments[44]

1. Charitable contributions associated with unrelated business activities are initially deducted in full to arrive at unrelated business income. However, to the extent that charitable contributions associated with unrelated business activities exceed 10 percent of UBTI (without regard to the charitable contribution deduction), the excess is treated as a positive adjustment.

[42] § 512(a)(1) and Reg. § 1.513–1(c).
[43] § 512(a)(1).
[44] §§ 512(a)(1) and (b) and Reg. § 1.512(b)–1.

■ FIGURE 13–2
Tax Formula for Unrelated Business Taxable Income

Gross unrelated business income
– Deductions
= Net unrelated business income
+ Positive adjustments
- Charitable contributions greater than 10% of UBTI
- Net unrelated debt-financed income
- Certain net interest, annuity, royalty, and rent income from controlled organizations

– Negative adjustments
- Net income from dividends, interest, and annuities
- Net royalty income
- Certain net rent income
- Gains or losses from property dispositions (except inventory)
- Certain net research income
- Certain charitable contributions not associated with unrelated business income

= Unrelated business taxable income

EXAMPLE 16

Brown, Inc., an exempt organization, has UBTI of $100,000 (excluding any modifications associated with charitable contributions). Total charitable contributions (all associated with the unrelated trade or business) are $13,000. Assuming that the $13,000 is deducted in calculating net unrelated business income, the excess of $3,000 [$13,000 – 10%($100,000)] is a positive adjustment in calculating UBTI. ■

2. Unrelated debt-financed income net of the unrelated debt-financed deductions (see the subsequent discussion of Unrelated Debt-Financed Income).
3. Certain net interest, annuity, royalty, and rent income received by the exempt organization from an organization it controls (80 percent test). This provision overrides the negative adjustments for these types of income (see the discussion below).

Negative adjustments

1. Income from dividends, interest, and annuities net of all deductions directly related to producing such income.
2. Royalty income, regardless of whether it is measured by production, gross income, or taxable income from the property, net of all deductions directly related to producing such income.
3. Rent income from real property and from certain personal property net of all deductions directly related to producing such income. Personal property rents are included in this negative adjustment only if the personal property is leased with the real property. In addition, the personal property rent income must be incidental (it cannot exceed 10 percent of the gross rent income under the lease) to be used in computing the negative adjustment. In both of the following cases, however, *none* of the rent income is treated as a negative adjustment.
   - More than 50 percent of the rent income under the lease is from personal property.
   - Rent income is calculated using the tenant's profits.

EXAMPLE 17

Beaver, Inc., an exempt organization, leases land and a building (realty) and computers (personalty) housed in the building. Under the lease, $46,000 of the rent is for the land and building, and $4,000 is for the computers. Expenses incurred for the land and building are $10,000. The net rent income of $36,000 ($46,000 – $10,000) from the land and building and the income of $4,000 from the computers are negative adjustments. ■

EXAMPLE 18

Assume the same facts as in Example 17, except that the rent income is $35,000 from the land and building and $15,000 from the computers. Since the rent income from the computers exceeds $5,000 (10% × $50,000) and is not incidental, it is not a negative adjustment. ■

EXAMPLE 19

Assume the same facts as in Example 17, except that the rent income is $20,000 from the land and building and $30,000 from the computers. Since more than 50% of the rent income under the lease is from the computers, neither the rent income from the land and building nor that from the computers is a negative adjustment. ■

If the lessor of real property provides significant services to the lessee, such income, for this purpose, is not rent income.

4. Gains and losses from the sale, exchange, or other disposition of property *except for* inventory.

EXAMPLE 20

Beaver, the owner of the land, building, and computers in Example 17, sells these assets for $450,000. Their adjusted basis is $300,000. Beaver's recognized gain of $150,000 is a negative adjustment. ■

5. Certain research income net of all deductions directly related to producing that income.
6. A charitable contribution deduction is permitted without regard to whether the charitable contributions are associated with the unrelated trade or business. Therefore, to the extent that an exempt entity's total charitable contributions exceed those deducted in calculating net unrelated business income (see Figure 13–2), the excess is a negative adjustment in calculating UBTI. In making this calculation, be aware that the 10 percent of UBTI (without regard to the charitable contribution deduction) limit still applies (see positive adjustment 1).

EXAMPLE 21

Canine, Inc., an exempt organization, has unrelated business taxable income of $100,000 (excluding any modifications associated with charitable contributions). The total charitable contributions are $9,000, of which $7,000 (those associated with the unrelated trade or business) have been deducted in calculating net unrelated business income. Therefore, the remaining $2,000 of charitable contributions is a negative adjustment in calculating UBTI. ■

7. A specific deduction of $1,000 is permitted. This deduction effectively exempts an entity from taxation if its unrelated business income is immaterial.

EXAMPLE 22

Petit Care, Inc., an exempt organization, has net unrelated business income of $800. Since Petit will receive a specific deduction of $1,000, its UBTI is $0. Therefore, its income tax liability is $0. ■

After unrelated business taxable income is determined, it is subject to tax using regular corporate rates.

EXAMPLE 23

Patient, Inc., an exempt organization, has UBTI of $80,000. Patient's income tax liability is $15,450 [$13,750 + 0.34($80,000 – $75,000)]. ■

UNRELATED DEBT-FINANCED INCOME

In the formula for calculating unrelated business taxable income (refer to Figure 13–2), unrelated debt-financed income is a positive adjustment. Examples of debt-financed income include rent income from real estate or tangible personal property, dividends from corporate stock, and gains from the disposition of debt-financed property. Gains from unrelated business income property are also included to the extent the gains are not otherwise treated as unrelated business income.

The positive adjustment for unrelated debt-financed income in the UBTI calculation is significant. Without this provision, a tax-exempt organization could use borrowed funds to acquire unrelated business or investment property and use the untaxed (i.e., exempt) earnings from the acquisition to pay for the property.

Definition of Debt-Financed Income. **Debt-financed income** is the gross income generated from debt-financed property. *Debt-financed property* is all property of the exempt organization that is held to produce income and on which there is acquisition indebtedness, *except* for the following.[45]

- Property where substantially all (at least 85 percent) of the use is for the achievement of the exempt purpose of the exempt organization.[46] If the 85 percent test is not satisfied, only the portion of the property that is *not* used for the exempt purpose is debt-financed property.

EXAMPLE 24

Deer, Inc., an exempt organization, owns a five-story office building on which there is acquisition indebtedness. Three of the floors are used for Deer's exempt purpose. The two other floors are leased to Purple Corporation. In this case, the *substantially all* test is not satisfied. Therefore, 40% of the office building is debt-financed property, and 60% is not. ■

- Property whose gross income is otherwise treated as unrelated business income.
- Property whose gross income is from the following sources and is not otherwise treated as unrelated business income.
  - Income from research performed for the United States or a Federal governmental agency, or a state or a political subdivision thereof.
  - For a college, university, or hospital, income from research.
  - For an organization that performs fundamental (i.e., not applied) research for the benefit of the general public, income from research.
- Property used in an activity that is not an unrelated trade or business.

In addition to the above items, certain land that is acquired by an exempt organization for later exempt use is excluded from debt-financed property if the following requirements are satisfied.[47]

- The principal purpose of acquiring the land is for use (substantially all) in achieving the organization's exempt purpose.
- This use will begin within 10 years of the acquisition date.
- At the date when the land is acquired, it is located in the *neighborhood* of other property of the organization for which substantially all the use is for achieving the organization's exempt purpose.

[45] § 514(b).
[46] Reg. § 1.514(b)–1(b)(1)(ii).
[47] § 514(b)(3).

CONCEPT SUMMARY 13–5

Unrelated Business Income Tax

Purpose	To tax the entity on unrelated business income as if it were subject to the corporate income tax.
Applicable tax rates	Corporate tax rates.
Exempt organizations to which applicable	All organizations exempt under § 501(c), except Federal agencies.
Entities subject to the tax	The organization conducts a trade or business; the trade or business is not substantially related to the exempt purpose of the organization; and the trade or business is regularly carried on by the organization.
Exceptions to the tax	• All the work is performed by volunteers. • Substantially all of the merchandise being sold has been received by gift. • For § 501(c)(3) organizations, the business is conducted primarily for the benefit of the organization's members, students, patients, officers, or employees. • For most employee unions, the trade or business consists of selling to members work-related clothing and equipment and items normally sold through vending machines, snack bars, or food-dispensing facilities.
$1,000 provision	If the gross income from an unrelated trade or business is less than $1,000, it is not necessary to file a return associated with the unrelated business income tax.

Even if the third requirement is not satisfied, the land still is excluded from debt-financed property if it is converted to use for achieving the organization's exempt purpose within the 10-year period. Qualification using this conversion provision will result in a refund of taxes previously paid. If the exempt organization is a church, the 10-year period becomes a 15-year period, and the neighborhood requirement is waived.

Definition of Acquisition Indebtedness. Acquisition indebtedness is debt sustained by the exempt organization in association with the acquisition of property. More precisely, *acquisition indebtedness* consists of the unpaid amounts of the following for debt-financed property.[48]

- Debt incurred in acquiring or improving the property.
- Debt incurred before the property was acquired or improved, but which would not have been incurred without the acquisition or improvement.
- Debt incurred after the property was acquired or improved, but which would not have been incurred without the acquisition or improvement.

EXAMPLE 25

Red, Inc., an exempt organization, acquires land for $100,000. To finance the acquisition, Red mortgages the land and receives loan proceeds of $80,000. Red leases the land to Duck Corporation. The mortgage is acquisition indebtedness. ■

[48] § 514(c)(1). Educational organizations can exclude certain debt incurred for real property acquisitions from classification as acquisition indebtedness.

EXAMPLE 26

Rose, Inc., an exempt organization, makes improvements to an office building that it rents to Bird Corporation. Excess working capital funds are used to finance the improvements. To replenish working capital, Rose is later required to mortgage its laboratory building, which it uses for its exempt purpose. The mortgage is acquisition indebtedness, and the office building is debt-financed property. ■

DIGGING DEEPER 2

Find more information on this topic at our Web site: ***http://wft-advanced.swlearning.com.***

Concept Summary 13–5 presents the rules concerning the UBIT.

PLANNING STRATEGIES Unrelated Business Income Tax

FRAMEWORK FOCUS: INCOME AND EXCLUSIONS

STRATEGY ➤ **AVOID INCOME RECOGNITION.**

If the exempt organization conducts an unrelated trade or business, it may be subject to the tax on unrelated business income. Worse yet, the unrelated trade or business could result in the loss of exempt status if the IRS determines that the activity is the primary purpose of the organization. Thus, caution and planning should be used to eliminate the latter possibility and to minimize the impact of the former.

One approach that can be used to avoid the imposition of the UBIT is to establish a taxable subsidiary to conduct the unrelated trade or business. With a subsidiary, the revenues and expenses of the exempt organization can be separated from those of the unrelated trade or business. When the subsidiary remits its after-tax profits to the exempt organization in the form of dividends, the dividends will not be taxable to the exempt organization. In addition, having a taxable subsidiary conduct the unrelated trade or business avoids the possibility that the IRS will consider the unrelated business income to be an excessive percentage of the total revenues of the exempt organization. Such a view can lead to the IRS's questioning the exempt organization's right to retain its exempt status.

Another approach to avoiding the UBIT is to fail the definition of an unrelated trade or business. This is accomplished by *not* satisfying at least one of the following requirements.

- The organization conducts a trade or business.
- The trade or business is not substantially related to the exempt purpose of the organization.
- The trade or business is regularly carried on by the organization.

Even if the definitional requirements for an unrelated trade or business appear to be satisfied, the negative adjustments in calculating unrelated business taxable income (see Figure 13–2) can be used to minimize the tax liability.

Rental activities best illustrate the necessity of careful planning to avoid including the income from the activity in calculating unrelated business taxable income. The income from the rental of real property by an exempt organization is not part of unrelated business taxable income. However, leases must be drafted so as to preserve the negative adjustment and avoid the UBIT prevalent in the following circumstances.

- If personal property is leased with real property and more than 50 percent of the rent income under the lease is from personal property, all the rent income is included in calculating unrelated business taxable income.
- If rent income from real property is calculated completely, or in part, based on the profits of the lessee (unless the calculation is based on a fixed percentage of sales or receipts), the rent income is included in calculating unrelated business taxable income.
- If the lessor of real property provides significant services to the lessee, the income is not treated as rent income and thus is included in the computation of unrelated business taxable income.
- If the rent income is received from an organization that the exempt organization controls (80 percent), the income is included in calculating unrelated business taxable income.
- To the extent the rent income is classified as unrelated debt-financed income, it is included in calculating unrelated business taxable income.

BRIDGE DISCIPLINE

Bridge to Financial Disclosure

Tax-exempt entities file various reports with the IRS. In addition, they make other information directly available to the general public from whom they receive some or all of their support.

The Colonial Williamsburg Foundation, which was founded in 1928, is one such tax-exempt organization. The mission of the foundation is "to help the future learn from the past by preserving and restoring 18th century Williamsburg, and by engaging, informing, and inspiring people as they learn about this historic capital, the events that occurred here, and the diverse people who helped shape our nation." The annual report for Colonial Williamsburg included the following financial statements.

Income Statement (in 000s)

Revenues		
Contributions	$182,029	
Government grants	1,283	
Program services	51,516	
Investments	20,857	
Gross profit from sales	19,957	
Net rental income	4,357	
Other	(2,005)	$ 277,994
Expenses		
Program services	$113,143	
Administration	18,793	
Unrealized investment losses	49,924	
Fundraising	8,832	(190,692)
Net income		$ 87,302

Balance Sheet (in 000s)

Assets		
Cash and temporary cash investments	$ 26,856	
Accounts receivable	2,523	
Pledges and grants receivable	17,882	
Other receivables	1,142	
Inventory	11,206	
Prepaid expenses and deferred charges	10,106	
Investments	720,905	
Fixed assets	357,218	
Other assets	54,776	$1,202,614

Liabilities and Fund Balance		
Accounts payable	$ 20,049	
Loans and notes payable	143,302	
Tax-exempt bond liabilities	65,120	
Other	37,124	$ 265,595
Fund balance		937,019
Total liabilities and fund balance		$1,202,614

LO.7

List the reports exempt organizations must file with the IRS and the related due dates.

Reporting Requirements

OBTAINING EXEMPT ORGANIZATION STATUS

Not all exempt organizations are required to obtain IRS approval for their exempt status. Among those required by statute to do so are organizations exempt under §§ 501(c)(3), 501(c)(9), and 501(c)(20).[49] Even in these cases, exceptions are provided (e.g., churches).

Even when not required to obtain IRS approval, most exempt organizations do apply for exempt status. Typically, an organization does not want to assume that it qualifies for exempt status and describe itself in that way to the public, only to have the IRS rule later that it does not qualify. Organizations exempt under § 501(c)(3) use Form 1023 [Application for Recognition of Exemption under Section 501(c)(3)]. Form 1024 [Application for Recognition of Exemption under Section 501(a)] is used by most other types of exempt organizations.

If an organization is required to obtain IRS approval for its exempt status and does not do so, it does not qualify as an exempt organization.

ANNUAL FILING REQUIREMENTS

Most exempt organizations are required to file an annual information return.[50] The return is filed on Form 990 (Return of Organization Exempt from Income Tax). The following exempt organizations are not required to file Form 990.[51]

- Federal agencies.
- Churches.
- Organizations whose annual gross receipts do not exceed $25,000.[52]
- Private foundations.

Private foundations are required to file Form 990–PF (Return of Private Foundation). Form 990–PF requires more information than Form 990.

The due date for Form 990 or Form 990–PF is the fifteenth day of the fifth month after the end of the taxable year. These returns are filed with the appropriate IRS Service Center based on the location of the exempt organization's principal office. Requests for extensions on filing are made by filing Form 2758 (Applications for Extension of Time).

EXAMPLE 27

Green, Inc., a § 501(c)(3) organization, has a fiscal year that ends June 30, 2004. The due date for the annual return is November 15, 2004. If Green were a calendar year entity, the due date for the 2004 annual return would be May 15, 2005. ■

Exempt organizations that are subject to the UBIT may be required to file Form 990–T (Exempt Organization Business Income Tax Return). The return must be filed if the organization has gross income of at least $1,000 from an unrelated trade or business. The due date for the return is the fifteenth day of the fifth month after the end of the taxable year.

[49]§§ 505(c), 508(a), and 508(c).
[50]§ 6033(a)(1).
[51]§ 6033(a)(2).
[52]The statutory amount is $5,000. However, under its discretionary authority, the IRS has expanded the exemption amount to $25,000.

If an exempt organization is subject to any of the excise taxes imposed on private foundations, Form 4720 (Return of Certain Excise Taxes on Charities and Other Persons) must be filed. The return is filed with the private foundation's Form 990–PF.

EXAMPLE 28

During the year, the First Church of Kentwood receives parishioner contributions of $450,000. Of this amount, $125,000 is designated for the church building fund. First Church is not required to file an annual return (Form 990) because churches are exempt from doing so. In addition, it is not required to file Form 990–T because it has no unrelated business income.

Colonial, Inc., is an exempt private foundation. Gross receipts for the year total $800,000, of which 40% is from admission fees paid by members of the general public who visit Colonial's museum of eighteenth-century life. The balance is endowment income and founding donor contributions. Because Colonial is a private foundation, it must file Form 990–PF.

Orange, Inc., is an exempt organization and is not a private foundation. Gross receipts for the year are $20,000. None of this amount is unrelated business income. Orange is not required to file Form 990 because its annual gross receipts do not exceed $25,000.

Restoration, Inc., is a private foundation. Gross receipts for the year are $20,000. None of this amount is unrelated business income. Restoration must file Form 990–PF because private foundations are not eligible for the $25,000 filing exception.

During the year, the Second Church of Port Allen receives parishioner contributions of $300,000. In addition, the church has unrelated business income of $5,000. Second Church is not required to file Form 990 because churches are exempt from doing so. Form 990–T must be filed, however, because churches are not exempt from the UBIT and Second Church has exceeded the $1,000 floor. ■

DISCLOSURE REQUIREMENTS

As a result of consumer-friendly rules, exempt entities must make more information readily available to the general public.[53] Prior to the issuance of these rules, the disclosure requirements could be satisfied by making the information available for public inspection during regular business hours at the principal office of the exempt entity.

Copies of the following now must be made available to the general public.

- Form 990.
- Form 1023 (or Form 1024).

Copies of the three most recent returns of the Form 990 must be made available.

If an individual requests a copy in person, the exempt entity must provide a copy immediately. If the request is received in writing or by e-mail or fax, the copy must be provided within 30 days. The copy must be provided without charge, except for a reasonable fee for reproduction and mailing costs.

If the exempt entity has made the forms widely available to the general public, it is not required to fill individual requests. One technique for making the forms widely available is to put them on the Internet. Individual requests can also be disregarded if the exempt entity can show the request is part of a harassment campaign.

Private foundations must make Form 990–PF available for public inspection. The effective date for the disclosure requirements for private foundations is after March 12, 2000.[54]

[53]§ 6104(d), Reg. § 301.6104(d), and T.D. 8818 (April 1999).
[54]An Internet source of Forms 990 and 990–PF and other relevant materials on exempt entities is **http://www.guidestar.com**.

Suggested Further Readings

Harvey Berger, "IRS Approves Car-Donation Program," (Tax Clinic), *The Tax Adviser*, February 2003, pp. 70–72.

Pamela S. Kaufmann, "The Intermediate Sanctions Regulations Are Final—No More Excuses," *Journal of Taxation*, April 2002, pp. 240–248.

Robert A. Wexler and Stephanie L. Petit, "Two Key Revenue Rulings Provide a Road Map for Private Foundation Terminations," *Journal of Taxation*, May 2003, pp. 307–314.

LaVerne Woods, "Tax Treatment of Corporate Sponsorship Payments to Exempt Organizations: Final Regulations," *Journal of Taxation*, September 2002, pp. 174–182.

KEY TERMS

Debt-financed income, 13–23
Excess lobbying expenditure, 13–7
Exempt organization, 13–2
Feeder organization, 13–9
Grass roots expenditure, 13–7
Intermediate sanctions, 13–8
Lobbying expenditure, 13–7
Private foundation, 13–10
Unrelated business income, 13–16
Unrelated business income tax (UBIT), 13–16

PROBLEM MATERIALS

Problems

1. Match the following exempt organizations with the statutory authority under which exempt status is granted. The statutory authority may apply to more than one exempt organization.

Exempt Organizations	Statutory Authority
Girl Scouts	§ 501(c)(1)
Catholic Church	§ 501(c)(2)
National Football League (NFL)	§ 501(c)(3)
American Red Cross	§ 501(c)(4)
Salvation Army	§ 501(c)(5)
United Fund	§ 501(c)(6)
Bill and Melinda Gates Foundation	§ 501(c)(7)
University of Richmond	§ 501(c)(8)
Underwriters Laboratory (UL)	§ 501(c)(9)
PGA Tour	§ 501(c)(10)
Veterans of Foreign Wars (VFW)	§ 501(c)(11)
Dallas Rodeo Club	§ 501(c)(12)
PTA	§ 501(c)(13)
Toano Cemetery Association	§ 501(c)(14)
Alpha Chi Omega Sorority	§ 501(c)(15)
Green, Inc., Legal Services Plan	§ 501(c)(16)
National Press Club	§ 501(c)(19)
Federal Deposit Insurance Corporation (FDIC)	§ 501(c)(20)
League of Women Voters	§ 501(d)

2. Which of the following organizations qualify for exempt status?
   a. Tulane University.
   b. Virginia Qualified Tuition Program.
   c. Red Cross.
   d. Disneyland.
   e. Ford Foundation.
   f. Jacksonville Chamber of Commerce.
   g. Colonial Williamsburg Foundation.
   h. Professional Golfers Association (PGA) Tour.
   i. Green Bay Packers.
   j. Cleveland Indians.

3. Identify the statutory authority under which each of the following is exempt from Federal income tax.
   a. Kingsmill Country Club.
   b. Shady Lawn Cemetery.
   c. Amber Credit Union.
   d. Veterans of Foreign Wars.
   e. Boy Scouts of America.
   f. United Fund.
   g. Federal Deposit Insurance Corporation.
   h. Bruton Parish Episcopal Church.
   i. PTA.
   j. National Press Club.

4. Wellness, Inc., a § 501(c)(3) organization, makes lobbying expenditures of $300,000 during 2004. Exempt purpose expenditures were $900,000 for the first six months of the year and $600,000 for the last six months of the year. Determine the tax consequences to Wellness if:
   a. It does not make the § 501(h) lobbying election.
   b. It does make the § 501(h) lobbying election.

5. Choice, Inc., a § 501(c)(3) organization, pays unreasonable compensation to Monica, the treasurer of Choice. Monica's compensation is $275,000. Assume reasonable compensation would be $185,000.
   a. Determine any adverse tax consequences for Choice, Inc.
   b. Determine any adverse tax consequences for Monica.

Issue ID

6. Rex is the chief executive officer of Helping People, Inc., a § 501(c)(3) exempt organization located in Mobile, Alabama. He and the organization's board of directors are concerned about the effect that proposed legislation would have on the organization's budget and its ability to carry out its mission. They are discussing a proposal to have a law firm in Washington, D.C., aid in opposing the legislation. What tax issues are relevant to Helping People, Inc., as it makes this decision?

Decision Making
Communications

7. Roadrunner, Inc., is an exempt medical organization. Quail, Inc., a sporting goods retailer, is a wholly owned subsidiary of Roadrunner. Roadrunner inherited the Quail stock last year from a major benefactor of the medical organization. Quail's taxable income is $550,000. Quail will remit all of its earnings, net of any taxes, to Roadrunner to support the exempt purpose of the parent.
   a. Is Quail subject to Federal income tax? If so, calculate the liability.
   b. Arthur Morgan, the treasurer of Roadrunner, has contacted you regarding minimizing or eliminating Quail's tax liability. He would like to know if the tax consequences would be better if Quail were liquidated into Roadrunner. Write a letter to Morgan that contains your advice. Roadrunner's address is 500 Rouse Tower, Rochester, NY 14627.
   c. Would your answer in (a) change if Roadrunner had acquired the Quail stock by purchase or gift rather than by inheritance? Discuss.

8. Determine which of the following tax-exempt organizations are *not* private foundations.
   a. Baptist Church.
   b. Girl Scouts.

c. League of Women Voters.
d. PGA Tour.
e. American Institute of CPAs.
f. PTA.
g. American Red Cross.
h. Salvation Army.
i. Veterans of Foreign Wars.

Communications

9. Cardinal, Inc., a § 501(c)(3) organization, received support from the following sources.

Governmental unit A for services rendered	$ 6,000
Governmental unit B for services rendered	4,000
General public for services rendered	85,000
Gross investment income	37,000
Contributions from disqualified persons	24,000
Contributions from other than disqualified persons	110,000

a. Does Cardinal satisfy the test for receiving broad public support?
b. Is Cardinal a private foundation?
c. Arnold Horn, Cardinal's treasurer, has asked you to advise him on whether Cardinal is a private foundation. Write a letter to him in which you address the issue. His address is 250 Bristol Road, Charlottesville, VA 22903.

10. Gray, Inc., a private foundation, has the following items of income and deductions.

Interest income	$24,000
Rent income	60,000
Dividend income	20,000
Royalty income	10,000
Unrelated business income	75,000
Rent expenses	18,000
Unrelated business expenses	10,000

Gray is not an exempt operating foundation and is not eligible for the 1% tax rate.
a. Calculate the net investment income.
b. Calculate the tax on net investment income.
c. What is the purpose of the tax on net investment income?

11. Eagle, Inc., a private foundation, has been in existence for 10 years. During this period, Eagle has been unable to satisfy the requirements for classification as a private operating foundation. At the end of 2003, it had undistributed income of $280,000. Of this amount, $120,000 was distributed in 2004, and $160,000 was distributed during the first quarter of 2005. The IRS deficiency notice was mailed on August 1, 2006.
a. Calculate the initial tax for 2003, 2004, and 2005.
b. Calculate the additional tax for 2006.

Decision Making

12. Otis is the CEO of Rectify, Inc., a private foundation. Otis invests $500,000 (80%) of the foundation's investment portfolio in derivatives. Previously, the $500,000 had been invested in corporate bonds with an AA rating that earned 7% per annum. If the derivatives investment works as Otis's investment adviser claims, the annual earnings could be as high as 20%.
a. Determine if Rectify is subject to any of the taxes imposed on private foundations.
b. If so, calculate the amount of the initial tax.
c. If so, calculate the amount of the additional tax if the act causing the imposition of the tax is not addressed within the correction period.
d. Are Otis and the foundation better off financially if the prohibited transaction, if any, is addressed within the correction period?

13. The board of directors of Pearl, Inc., a private foundation, consists of Alice, Beth, and Carlos. They vote unanimously to provide a $100,000 grant to Doug, their business

associate. The grant is to be used for travel and education and does not qualify as a permitted grant to individuals (i.e., it is a taxable expenditure under § 4945). Each director knows that Doug was selected for the grant because he is a friend of the organization and that the grant is a taxable expenditure.

a. Calculate the initial tax imposed on the private foundation.
b. Calculate the initial tax imposed on the foundation manager (i.e., board of directors).

Issue ID

14. Welcome, Inc., a tax-exempt organization, receives 25% of its support from disqualified persons. Another disqualified person has agreed to match this support if Welcome will appoint him to the organization's board of directors. What tax issues are relevant to Welcome as it makes this decision?

Communications

15. The Open Museum is an exempt organization that operates a gift shop. The museum's annual operations budget is $2.5 million. Gift shop sales generate a profit of $750,000. Another $500,000 of endowment income is generated. Both the income from the gift shop and the endowment income are used to support the exempt purpose of the museum. The balance of $1.25 million required for annual operations is provided through admission fees. Wayne Davis, a new board member, does not understand why the museum is subject to tax at all, particularly since the profits are used in carrying out the mission of the museum. The museum's address is 250 Oak Avenue, Peoria, IL 61625.
    a. Calculate the amount of unrelated business income.
    b. Assume that the endowment income is reinvested rather than being used to support annual operations. Calculate the amount of unrelated business income.
    c. As the museum treasurer, write a letter to Wayne explaining the reason for the tax consequences. Mr. Davis's address is 45 Pine Avenue, Peoria, IL 61625.

Issue ID

16. First Church has been selling cards and small books in the church tower. A contribution box was provided in which payments were to be deposited. To increase church revenues, a task force is evaluating setting up a gift shop in the church parish house. What tax issues are relevant to the task force as it makes its decision?

Communications

17. Salmon, Inc., an exempt organization, has unrelated business taxable income of $20 million.
    a. Calculate Salmon's unrelated business income tax.
    b. Prepare an outline of a presentation you are going to give to the new members of Salmon's board on why Salmon is subject to the UBIT even though it is an exempt organization.

18. For each of the following organizations, determine the amount of the UBIT.
    a. AIDS, Inc., an exempt charitable organization that provides support for individuals with AIDS, operates a retail medical supply store open to the general public. The net income of the store, before any Federal income taxes, is $325,000.
    b. The local Episcopal Church operates a retail gift shop. The inventory consists of the typical items sold by commercial gift shops in the city. The director of the gift shop estimates that 80% of the gift shop sales are to tourists and 20% are to church members. The net income of the gift shop, before the salaries of the three gift shop employees and any Federal income taxes, is $300,000. The salaries of the employees total $80,000.
    c. Education, Inc., a private university, has vending machines in the student dormitories and academic buildings on campus. In recognition of recent tuition increases, the university has adopted a policy of merely trying to recover its costs associated with the vending machine activity. For the current year, however, the net income of the activity, before any Federal income taxes, is $75,000.
    d. Worn, Inc., an exempt organization, provides food for the homeless. It operates a thrift store that sells used clothing to the general public. The thrift shop is staffed by four salaried employees. All of the clothes it sells are received as contributions. The $100,000 profit generated for the year by the thrift shop is used in Worn's mission of providing food to the homeless.
    e. Small, Inc., an exempt organization, has unrelated business income of $900 and unrelated business expenses of $400.

Ethics

19. Matthew Sampson is the founder, and the man behind the throne, of the Church for Today television ministry. Ministry broadcasts originate from church services in California and New York and are transmitted via cable throughout the United States. Though the membership of the Church for Today is small (approximately 5,000 members), the typical member is quite wealthy. In addition to receiving contributions from its members, the church solicits and receives donations from viewers of the TV broadcasts. The church is tax-exempt under § 501(c)(3).

    The stated mission of the church is religious in nature. However, Matthew firmly believes, as do the members of the board of deacons of the church, that certain societal goals must be accomplished for the prophecies of the church to come true (i.e., their divine being expects them to be active missionaries). Among its basic beliefs, the church advocates government control and possession of all guns, the legalization of drugs, abortion on demand once approved by the appropriate government agency, the withdrawal of all U.S. troops from foreign soil and the termination of all military alliances, the abolition of capital punishment, and the availability of tuition-free university education to all U.S. citizens.

    The ministers of the Church for Today are expected to include these basic beliefs, at the subliminal level, in their sermons. Some do so more effectively and more frequently than others, but all are required to do so. Matthew and the board of deacons are dismayed that American society has not adopted many of their beliefs.

    Accordingly, Matthew proposes to the board of deacons that the church take a more proactive role. The employment contract of the ministers will now require them to include the basic beliefs in their sermons in an active manner. No longer can the beliefs just be incorporated subliminally. All the beliefs must be covered quarterly, and every sermon must present at least one of the basic beliefs. The ministers will encourage the church members and TV viewers to actively support these positions at both the state and Federal level.

    As a new member of the board of deacons, you wholeheartedly support Matthew's position. However, you are concerned about the effects of this open advocacy of positions on the tax-exempt status of the church. Matthew responds that the "church has friends in high places" and assures you that the tax-exempt status will not be endangered. What should you do?

20. Medium, Inc., an exempt organization, has unrelated business income of $3,700 and unrelated business expenses of $2,900. Calculate the amount of the UBIT.

Communications

21. Falcon Basketball League, an exempt organization, is a youth basketball league for children ages 12 through 14. The league has been in existence for 30 years. In the past, revenue for operations has been provided through community fund-raising and the sale of snacks at the games by the parents. Due to a projected revenue shortfall of approximately $5,000, the governing board has decided to charge admission to the basketball games of $1.00 for adults and $.50 for children.
    a. Will the admission charge affect Falcon's exempt status?
    b. What are the tax consequences to Falcon of the net income from snack sales and the new admission fee?
    c. As the volunteer treasurer of the Falcon League, prepare a memo for the board in which you explain the effect, if any, of the admission fee policy on Falcon's exempt status.

22. Onward, Inc., is an exempt organization that assists disabled individuals by training them in computer repair. Used computers are donated to Onward, Inc., by both organizations and individuals. Some of the donated computers are operational, but others are not. After being used in the training program, the computers, all of which are now operational, are sold to the general public. Onward's revenues and expenses for the current period are as follows.

Contributions	$ 700,000
Revenues from computer sales	3,600,000
Administrative expenses	500,000
Materials and supplies for computer repairs	800,000
Utilities	25,000
Wages paid to disabled individuals in the training program (at minimum-wage rate)	1,200,000
Rent for building and equipment	250,000

Any revenues not expended during the current period are deposited in a reserve fund to finance future activities.

a. Is the computer repair and sales activity an unrelated trade or business?
b. Calculate the net income of Onward, Inc., and the related Federal income tax liability, if any.

23. Save the Squirrels, Inc., a § 501(c)(3) organization that feeds the squirrels in municipal parks, receives a $100,000 contribution from Animal Feed, Inc., a corporation that sells animal feed. In exchange for the contribution, Save the Squirrels will identify Animal Feed as a major supporter in its monthly newsletter.
    a. If Save the Squirrels receives no other similar payments, calculate its unrelated business income tax.
    b. Calculate Save the Squirrels' unrelated business income tax if Save the Squirrels agrees to identify Animal Feed as a major supporter and to include a half-page advertisement for Animal Feed products in its monthly newsletter as a result of that contribution.

24. Faith Church is exempt from Federal income taxation under § 501(c)(3). To supplement its contribution revenue, it holds bingo games on Saturday night. It has the licenses and permits required to do so. The net income from the bingo games is $75,000. These funds are used to support the ministry of the church. Faith Church is located in a city where bingo games can only be conducted by churches and charities.
    a. Will conducting the bingo games affect the exempt status of Faith Church?
    b. Calculate the Federal tax liability, if any, associated with the bingo games.

Issue ID

25. An exempt organization is considering conducting bingo games on Thursday nights as a way of generating additional revenue to support its exempt purpose. Before doing so, however, the president of the organization has come to you for advice regarding the effect on the organization's exempt status and whether the net income from the bingo games will be taxable. Identify the relevant tax issues.

26. Bluebird, Inc., an exempt organization, has unrelated business taxable income (before any modifications associated with charitable contributions) of $200,000. Charitable contributions made by Bluebird that are associated with the unrelated trade or business are $15,000, and those made that are not associated with the unrelated trade or business are $10,000. Calculate the effect of the charitable contributions on Bluebird's unrelated business taxable income.

Decision Making

27. An exempt hospital receives as a gift from a wealthy donor all the shares of stock of Compute, Inc., a retail computer chain. Because the chain is very profitable and its CEO has offered to continue to manage it, the hospital has decided to operate the chain rather than sell the stock. All of the profits of the chain will be used in carrying out the exempt mission of the hospital. Advise the hospital on whether better tax consequences can be achieved by operating the chain as a subsidiary or as a division of the hospital corporation.

28. Comfort, Inc., an exempt hospital, is going to operate a pharmacy that will be classified as an unrelated trade or business. Comfort establishes the pharmacy as a wholly owned subsidiary. During the current year, the subsidiary generates taxable income of $200,000 and pays dividends of $125,000 to Comfort.
    a. What are the tax consequences to the subsidiary?
    b. What are the tax consequences to Comfort?

29. Rabbit, Inc., an exempt organization, has net unrelated business income of $75,000 excluding any rent income received. Rabbit owns two buildings that are leased to tenants. The net rent income on the first building is $32,000, and that on the second building is $35,000. The lessee of the first building is unrelated to Rabbit whereas the lessee of the second building is a 100%-owned for-profit subsidiary. Calculate Rabbit's unrelated business taxable income.

30. Kind, Inc., an exempt organization, leases land, a building, and factory equipment to Shirts, Inc. Shirts is a taxable entity that manufactures shirts for distribution through

its factory outlet stores. The rent income and the related expenses for Kind are as follows.

	Rent Income	Rent Expenses
Land and building	$100,000	$40,000
Factory equipment	125,000	25,000

a. Calculate the amount of Kind's unrelated business taxable income.
b. Assume instead that Kind's rent income and expenses are as follows.

	Rent Income	Rent Expenses
Land and building	$100,000	$20,000
Factory equipment	125,000	50,000

Calculate the amount of Kind's unrelated business taxable income.

31. Assistance, Inc., an exempt organization, sells the following assets during the taxable year:

Asset	Gain (Loss)	Use
Land and building	$ 80,000	In exempt purpose
Land	50,000	Leased to a taxable entity
Equipment	(20,000)	Leased to a taxable entity
Automobile	(5,000)	In exempt purpose

Determine the effect of these transactions on Assistance's unrelated business taxable income.

32. Medical, Inc., an exempt organization, has unrelated business taxable income of $400,000 (excluding any modifications associated with charitable contributions). Of total charitable contributions of $38,000 made by Medical, $31,000 are associated with its unrelated trade or business. Determine the effect of the charitable contributions on Medical's unrelated business taxable income.

EXTENDER 33. Benevolent, Inc., an exempt organization, owns the following properties.

Property	Basis	Acquisition Indebtedness	Percentage Used in Exempt Purpose
Building A	$400,000	$300,000	100%
Building B	500,000	–0–	60%
Building C	600,000	200,000	90%
Building D	700,000	500,000	70%

Calculate the adjusted basis to Benevolent of its debt-financed property.

EXTENDER 34. Fix, Inc., an exempt organization, owns a one-story building. Fix's adjusted basis for the building is $900,000. Of the building's total area of 10,000 square feet, the front portion (approximately 3,000 square feet) is used in carrying out Fix's exempt purpose. The remainder of the building is leased for $300,000 each year to Belts, Inc., a taxable entity, to use for storing its inventory. The unamortized balance of a mortgage relating to the original acquisition of the building is $600,000. Determine the portion of the adjusted basis that is treated as debt-financed property and the amount of the mortgage that is acquisition indebtedness.

EXTENDER 35. Rust, Inc., an exempt organization, acquires a building for $800,000 on September 1, 2004. The principal amount of the related mortgage on the first day of September and the following months is as follows.

September	$600,000
October	595,000
November	590,000
December	585,000

Depreciation deducted during 2004 was $7,400. Rust leases the building to Build Corporation.

a. Calculate the average acquisition indebtedness for the building.
b. Calculate the average adjusted basis for the building.
c. Calculate the debt/basis percentage.

36. Seagull, Inc., a § 501(c)(3) exempt organization, uses a tax year that ends on October 31, 2004. Seagull's gross receipts are $600,000, and related expenses are $580,000.
    a. Is Seagull required to file an annual Form 990?
    b. If so, what is the due date?

37. Education, Inc., a § 501(c)(3) organization, is a private foundation with a tax year that ends on June 30, 2004. Gross receipts for the fiscal year are $180,000, and the related expenses are $160,000.
    a. Is Education required to file an annual information return?
    b. If so, what form is used?
    c. If so, what is the due date?
    d. How would your answers in (a), (b), and (c) change if Education is an exempt organization that is not a private foundation?

38. Historic Burg is an exempt organization that operates a museum depicting eighteenth-century life. Sally gives the museum an eighteenth-century chest that she has owned for 10 years. Her adjusted basis is $55,000, and the chest's appraised value is $100,000. Sally's adjusted gross income is $300,000.
    a. Calculate Sally's charitable contribution deduction if Historic Burg is a private operating foundation.
    b. Calculate Sally's charitable contribution deduction if Historic Burg is a private nonoperating foundation.

Bridge Discipline

1. Start, Inc., a § 501(c)(3) organization, reports the following on its audited income statement.

Revenues		
Contributions	$22,000	
Admission fees	88,000	
Government grants	30,000	
Investment income	12,000	
Gross profit from sales	45,000	$ 197,000
Expenses		
Operating costs	$92,000	
Administrative expenses	45,000	
Fundraising costs	16,000	
Unrealized investment losses	13,000	(166,000)
Net income		$ 31,000

Determine the excess of revenues over expenses that would be reported in Part I of Start's Form 990.

Research Problems

THOMSON RIA

Note: Solutions to Research Problems can be prepared by using the ***RIA Checkpoint® Student Edition*** *online research product, which is available to accompany this text. It is also possible to prepare solutions to the Research Problems by using tax research materials found in a standard tax library.*

Research Problem 1. Allied Fund, a charitable organization exempt under § 501(c)(3), has branches located in each of the 50 states. Allied is not a private foundation. Rather than having each of the state units file an annual return with the IRS, Allied would like to file a single return that reports the activities of all of its branches. Is this permissible? What is the due date of the return?

Partial list of research aids:
§ 6033.
§ 6072.
Reg. § 1.6033–2(d).

Research Problem 2. City University has operated a television station since 1960. The station operates under a commercial license and is an affiliate of CBS. In addition to regular network programming, the television station broadcasts educational programming in the form of in-school classroom instruction, educational extension programming, and closed circuit educational programming. The station is also used in training students who are enrolled in degree programs as preparation for careers in the television industry.

City University maintains that the television station is substantially related to the purpose for which the university was granted exempt status under § 501(c)(3). The only purpose for operating the television station is to contribute to the achievement of the educational goals of the university.

Determine if the television station is subject to the tax on unrelated business income.

Research Problem 3. The Shark Club, an exempt organization, conducts bingo games on the weekends. Profit entities are prohibited from conducting bingo games in the state, but tax-exempt organizations are permitted to do so. Shark uses the net profits from the bingo games in carrying out its tax-exempt mission.

The bingo games are conducted by volunteers. However, the volunteers are permitted to accept tips from the players. Tipping by players is a frequent occurrence.

Determine whether Shark is subject to the unrelated business income tax on its bingo activities.

Communications

Research Problem 4. City Hospital, a tax-exempt hospital, has purchased a sports and fitness center located about three miles from the hospital. It is a state-of-the-art fitness center that includes an open fitness room with cardiovascular and strength equipment, an indoor track, exercise rooms, racquetball and tennis courts, an aquatic area with two pools, a nutrition center/juice bar, and tanning beds. The hospital's overall goals for the center are to enhance cardiovascular, physical, and psychological function, reduce morbidity and mortality, improve quality of life, and promote compliance with a lifelong prevention program.

The membership of the center will consist of three segments of the community: the general public, employees, and former rehabilitation patients. Each group will be charged a monthly fee and an initiation fee with a reduced fee provided for employees. Within each category, the fees vary depending on the member's age and restrictions on availability of the facilities during specific hours. The hospital hired a professional consulting firm to conduct a survey of the community to ensure that the fee structure would achieve its goal of making the center facilities available to an economic cross section of the community.

You have been contacted by Anne Dexter, the chief financial officer for the hospital. She is concerned that some or perhaps all of the revenue from the sports and fitness center will be classified as unrelated business income and therefore be subject to the unrelated business income tax. Write a letter to Ms. Dexter that contains your findings, and prepare a memo for the tax files. City Hospital's address is 1000 Board Street, Billings, MT 59101.

Research Problem 5. The American Accounting Association holds its regional meetings at seven locations in the spring and its national meeting in August of each year. The meetings include the formal presentation of papers, panel discussions, business sessions, and various committee meetings. In addition, textbook publishers are permitted to display their wares in a publisher's exhibit hall. The book exhibitors must pay a fee to the AAA for the right to do so. Are these fees unrelated business income?

Internet Activity

Use the tax resources of the Internet to address the following questions. Do not restrict your search to the World Wide Web, but include a review of newsgroups and general reference materials, practitioner sites and resources, primary sources of the tax law, chat rooms and discussion groups, and other opportunities.

Communications

Research Problem 6. Download an application for tax-exempt status that would be filed with the IRS. Write a one-page letter to an organization that is contemplating the filing of such an application. The letter should walk through the application and highlight the information that must be provided and the estimated time required to comply with the directives of the form.

Research Problem 7. Summarize a recent newspaper or magazine story that relates a perceived abuse of the § 501(c)(3) provisions by a business owner or politician.

Research Problem 8. Determine if the Bill and Melinda Gates Foundation is a private foundation. Print a copy of its Form 990 or Form 990–PF.

Communications

Research Problem 9. Verify the exempt status of the symphony orchestra that performs closest to your home. Who are its three highest-paid associates? Send an e-mail to your instructor explaining how you found this information.

CHAPTER 14

Federal Gift and Estate Taxes

LEARNING OBJECTIVES

After completing Chapter 14, you should be able to:

LO.1
Understand the nature of the Federal gift and estate taxes.

LO.2
Value assets for estate and gift tax purposes.

LO.3
Work with the Federal gift tax formula.

LO.4
Explain the computation of the Federal gift tax.

LO.5
Work with the Federal estate tax formula.

LO.6
Describe the components of the gross estate.

LO.7
Describe the components of the taxable estate.

LO.8
Determine the Federal estate tax liability.

LO.9
Appreciate the role of the generation skipping transfer tax.

http://wft.swlearning.com

OUTLINE

TAX TALK

In this world nothing is certain but death and taxes.

—Benjamin Franklin

Transfer Taxes—In General

Until now, this text has dealt primarily with the Federal income tax. Also important in the Federal tax structure are various excise taxes that cover transfers of property. Sometimes called transaction taxes, excise taxes are based on the value of the property transferred, not on the income derived from the property. Two such taxes—the Federal gift tax and the Federal estate tax—are the central focus of Chapters 14 and 15. Chapter 14 covers the fundamental tax laws relating to the Federal gift and estate tax. Tax planning for transfer taxes is discussed in Chapter 15 with an emphasis on the use of trusts.

The magnitude of the Federal estate tax and the importance of transfer tax planning can be shown with a simple illustration.

EXAMPLE 1

Helen's husband died several years ago leaving her all of his property. When Helen died in 2004, she had accumulated substantial wealth. Her taxable estate was valued at $3 million on the date she died. This included the family home, stocks and other investments, personal belongings, and a large life insurance policy that Helen had purchased. The Federal estate tax liability for this estate is $705,000. Thus, her heirs receive $2,295,000 instead of $3 million. Some of the estate property might have to be sold to pay the taxes. As discussed in Chapter 15, with proper planning, Helen's estate tax could have been reduced to zero. ■

LO.1

Understand the nature of the Federal gift and estate taxes.

NATURE OF THE TAXES

Before the enactment of the Tax Reform Act of 1976, Federal law imposed two distinct taxes on the gratuitous transfer of property. If the transfer occurred during the owner's life, it was subject to the Federal gift tax. If the property passed by virtue of the death of the owner, the Federal estate tax applied. The two taxes were governed by different rules including separate sets of tax rates.

TAX IN THE NEWS

An Erratic Approach to Transfer Taxes

Congressional policy toward transfer taxes has been highly erratic.

- Before the Tax Reform Act of 1976, the lower gift tax rates favored transfers by gift.
- The Tax Reform Act of 1976 took a neutral approach. It established a new unified transfer tax that applied the same tax rates to transfers by gift and transfers by death.
- The Tax Relief Reconciliation Act of 2001, once fully implemented, obviously favors transfers by death as the estate tax is to be phased out, while the gift tax is retained.

Clearly, Congress has not been consistent in its tax treatment of lifetime (i.e., gift tax) and death (i.e., estate tax) transfers.

The Tax Reform Act of 1976 significantly changed the approach to taxing gifts and estates. Much of the distinction between life and death transfers was eliminated. Instead of subjecting these transfers to two separate tax rate schedules, the Act substituted a **unified transfer tax** that covers all gratuitous transfers of wealth. Thus, gifts are subject to the same rate schedule as that applicable to transfers at death. Since these rates are progressive, the computation of the unified transfer tax requires a cumulative tracking of post-1976 transfers. This procedure will be illustrated later in the chapter. In addition, the unified transfer tax eliminates the prior exemptions allowed under each tax and replaces them with a unified tax credit. As a matter of tax policy, the unified tax credit permits all individuals to transfer during their life or at death a specific level of wealth tax-free. There is also an $11,000 per year per donee exclusion for gifts. This exclusion is a matter of administrative convenience; without it, every small birthday gift would technically be subject to the transfer tax.

The Tax Relief Reconciliation Act of 2001 made further changes. First, the top rates applicable to both taxes are lowered. Second, by scheduled increases in the unified tax credit applicable to estates, the estate tax will be eliminated by year 2010, but the gift tax is retained. For budget reasons, all changes made by the 2001 Act are eliminated after December 31, 2010 (referred to as a "sunset" provision). Thus, the estate tax is reincarnated for transfers by death after 2010.

The Federal estate tax differs from the typical **inheritance tax** imposed by many states and some local jurisdictions. The Federal estate tax is imposed on the decedent's entire estate and is a tax on the right to pass property at death. In contrast, inheritance taxes are taxes on the right to receive property at death and are therefore levied on the heirs.

DIGGING DEEPER 1

Find more information on this topic at our Web site: ***http://wft-advanced.swlearning.com.***

The Federal gift tax is imposed on the right to transfer property by one person (the donor) to another (the donee) for less than full and adequate consideration. The tax is payable by the donor.[1] If the donor fails to pay the tax when due, the donee may be held liable for the tax to the extent of the value of the property received.[2]

[1] § 2502(c).

[2] § 6324(b). Known as the doctrine of transferee liability, this rule also operates to enable the IRS to enforce the collection of other taxes (e.g., income tax, estate tax).

GLOBAL TAX ISSUES

EXPATRIATION TO AVOID U.S. TAXES

Much media attention has recently been given to wealthy individuals who renounce their U.S. citizenship and move to another country to avoid U.S. taxes. These expatriates select a country where citizenship is easily available and low, if any, income and estate taxes are imposed.

Will this so-called expatriation to avoid taxes work? One difficulty for those who voluntarily renounce U.S. citizenship is that §§ 877 and 2107 continue to apply to their income tax and estate tax for a 10-year period. The taxpayer involved may avoid the application of these provisions by showing that the giving up of citizenship did not have as one of its principal purposes the avoidance of taxes.

Thus, the expatriation procedure will not be effective for at least 10 years. But even after this period, any income may still be subject to the Federal income tax if it is sourced in the United States. Likewise, assets located in the United States will probably be subject to the estate tax at death.

Persons Subject to the Tax. The Federal gift tax is applied to all lifetime transfers of property wherever located by individuals who, at the time of the gift, were *citizens* or *residents* of the United States. The term "United States" includes only the 50 states and the District of Columbia; it does not include U.S. possessions or territories.[3] For a U.S. citizen, the place of residence at the time of the gift is irrelevant.

For individuals who are neither citizens nor residents of the United States, the Federal gift tax is applied only to gifts of property situated within the United States.[4] A gift of intangible personal property (stocks and bonds) by a nonresident alien usually is not subject to the Federal gift tax.[5]

The Federal estate tax is applied to the entire estate of a decedent who, at the time of death, was a resident or citizen of the United States. If the decedent was a U.S. citizen, the residence at death makes no difference.[6]

If the decedent was neither a resident nor a citizen of the United States at the time of death, the Federal estate tax is imposed on the value of any property located within the United States.[7] In certain instances, the tax consequences outlined in the Code may have been modified by death tax conventions (treaties) between the United States and various foreign countries. This chapter's discussion is limited to the tax treatment of decedents who were residents or citizens of the United States at the time of death.[8]

DIGGING DEEPER 2 *Find more information on this topic at our Web site:* ***http://wft-advanced.swlearning.com.***

[3]§ 7701(a)(9).
[4]§ 2511(a).
[5]§§ 2501(a)(2) and (3). But see § 2511(b) and Reg. §§ 25.2511– 3(b)(2), (3), and (4) for exceptions.
[6]§ 2001(a).
[7]Subchapter B (§§ 2101 through 2108) covers the estate tax treatment of decedents who are neither residents nor citizens. See also the Instructions to Form 706NA (U.S. Estate Tax Return of Nonresident Not a Citizen of the U.S.).
[8]Subchapter A (§§ 2001 through 2056A) covers the estate tax treatment of those who are either residents or citizens.

LO.2

Value assets for estate and gift tax purposes.

VALUATION CONCEPTS

The estate and gift taxes generally are assessed on the fair market value of the property at the date of the transfer. Regulation § 20.2031–1(b) defines fair market value as "the price at which property would change hands between a willing buyer and a willing seller, neither being under any compulsion to buy or to sell and both having reasonable knowledge of relevant facts." The same Regulation makes clear that the fair market value of property is not determined by a forced sale price. Nor is the fair market value determined by the sale price of an item in a market other than that in which the item is most commonly sold to the public. Sentiment should not play a part in the determination of value. Suppose, for example, the decedent's daughter is willing to pay $500 for a portrait of her mother. If the painting is really worth $200 (i.e., what the general public would pay), then that should be its value.

The availability of similar items to the general public must also be considered. Thus, retail sales price is deemed to be the price that would be paid by the public in a retail market.

EXAMPLE 2

At the time of his death, Don owned three automobiles. The automobiles are included in Don's gross estate at their fair market value. The fair market value of the automobiles is determined by looking to the price a member of the general public would pay for automobiles of approximately the same description, make, model, age, condition, etc. The price a dealer in used cars would pay for these automobiles is inappropriate, because an automobile is an item obtainable by the public in a retail market. ■

Similarly, if tangible personalty is sold through a classified advertisement in the newspaper and the property is of a type often sold in this manner, or if the property is sold at a public auction, the property's sale price is presumed to be its fair market value (assuming stable market conditions and sale within a reasonable period after the valuation date).[9]

Stocks and Bonds. If there is a market for stocks and bonds on a stock exchange, in an over-the-counter market, or otherwise, the mean of the highest and lowest quoted selling prices on the valuation date is the fair market value per unit. A special rule applies if no sales occurred on the valuation date but did occur on dates within a reasonable period before and after the valuation date. The fair market value is the weighted average of the means of the highest and lowest sales prices on the nearest date before and the nearest date after the valuation date. The average is weighted *inversely* by the respective number of trading days between the selling dates and the valuation date.[10]

EXAMPLE 3

Carla makes a gift to Antonio of shares of stock in Green Corporation. The transactions involving this stock that occurred closest to the date of the gift took place two trading days before the date of the gift at an average sales price of $10 and three trading days after the gift at an average sales price of $15. The $12 fair market value of each share of Green stock is determined as follows.

$$\frac{(3\text{ days} \times \$10) + (2\text{ days} \times \$15)}{5\text{ days}} = \$12$$ ■

If no transactions occurred within a reasonable period before and after the valuation date, the fair market value is determined by taking a weighted average

[9]Rev.Proc. 65–19, 1965–2 C.B. 1002.

[10]Reg. §§ 20.2031–2(b) and 25.2512–2(b).

TAX IN THE NEWS

Is There Life after Death for a Novelist?

At the time of her death, Virginia Andrews was a highly successful novelist. Her novels fit into the "children in jeopardy" genre and typically involved a child overcoming the adversities caused by adults (usually family members). As she enjoyed a very loyal readership among teenage girls and young women, every new title became an instant hit.

After Andrews's death, her publisher (Pocket Books, a division of Simon & Schuster, Inc.) contacted the estate and heirs about the possibility of sequels to existing novels. Under the proposal, several novels would be written by a ghostwriter and published under Andrews's name. An agreement was reached, and the novels were written and published. As the sequels were successful, substantial royalties were paid to the estate.

When the estate tax return was filed, it included no value for the post-death sequels. The executor contended that the post-death ventures were too speculative to possess any value to the estate. Sales would depend on the expertise of the ghostwriter and whether prospective buyers would accept the novels as the work of Virginia Andrews. In fact, if the sequels were failures, sales of earlier books would suffer.

The IRS disagreed and assigned a value of approximately $1,200,000 to the potential use of the Andrews name. In *Estate of Virginia Andrews v. U.S.*, [94–2 USTC ¶60,170, 73 AFTR2d 94–2395, 850 F.Supp. 1279 (D.Ct.Va., 1994)], a court agreed with the IRS. Because of the uncertainty, however, the gross estate value was discounted to approximately $900,000.

of the means of the bona fide bid and asked prices on the nearest trading dates before and after the valuation date. However, both dates must be within a reasonable period of time.

In many instances, there are no established market prices for securities. This lack of information is typically the case with stock in closely held corporations. The law provides that in such situations, the value shall be determined by considering, in addition to all other factors, the value of the stock or securities of corporations engaged in the same or similar line of business that are listed for sale on stock exchanges.[11]

Notes Receivable. The fair market value of notes, secured or unsecured, is the amount of unpaid principal plus interest accrued to the valuation date, unless the parties (e.g., executor, donor) establish a lower value or prove the notes are worthless. Factors such as a low interest rate and a distant maturity date are relevant in showing that a note is worth less than its face amount. Crucial elements in proving that a note is entirely or partially worthless are the financial condition of the borrower and the absence of any value for the property pledged or mortgaged as security for the obligation.[12]

EXAMPLE 4

At the time of his death, Ira held a note (face amount of $50,000) issued by his son, Kevin. Although Kevin is solvent, he is relieved of the obligation because Ira forgives the note in his will. Presuming the note is payable on demand, it is included in Ira's gross estate at $50,000 plus accrued interest. If the note is not due immediately and/or the interest provided for is under the current rate, a discount may be in order, and the fair market value of the

[11] § 2031(b).

[12] Reg. §§ 20.2031–4 and 25.2512–4.

note would be less than $50,000. The burden of proof in supporting a discount for the note is on the executor. ■

The valuation of other assets such as life estates and remainders involves more complicated calculations. Valuation problems often arise in the area of trusts and are discussed in Chapter 15.

LO.3

Work with the Federal gift tax formula.

The Federal Gift Tax

GENERAL CONCEPTS

Formula for the Gift Tax. The formula for the gift tax is summarized in Figure 14–1. As previously discussed, the beginning point in the calculation of the gift tax is the determination of the fair market value of the gift at the date of transfer. Unlimited deductions are then allowed for properties given to the donor's spouse and/or a qualified charity. An annual exclusion of up to $11,000 for each additional donee may be allowed to arrive at the current year's **taxable gifts.**

Prior-year taxable gifts, valued at the date of transfer, must then be added to the current year's taxable gifts in arriving at the tax base to which the unified transfer tax rate is applied. Otherwise, the donor would reuse the lower unified tax rates each year, circumventing the progressive rate structure.

EXAMPLE 5

Don makes taxable gifts of $1,000,000 in 1986 and $1,000,000 in 2004. Presuming no other taxable gifts and *disregarding the effect of the unified tax credit*, Don must pay a tax of $345,800 (see Appendix A) on the 1986 transfer and a tax of $780,800 on the 2004 transfer (using a tax base of $2 million). If the 1986 taxable gift had not been included in the tax base for the 2004 gift, the tax would have been $345,800. The correct tax liability of $780,800 is more than twice $345,800! ■

Because the gift tax is cumulative in effect, a credit is allowed for gift taxes paid (or deemed paid) on prior taxable gifts included in the tax base. The deemed paid credit is explained later in this chapter.

■ FIGURE 14–1
Formula for the Federal Gift Tax

Fair market value of gifts during current year		$xxx,xxx
Subtract: Marital deduction	$xx,xxx	
Subtract: Charitable deduction	xx,xxx	
Subtract: Annual $11,000 exclusion (per donee), if available	xx,xxx	xx,xxx
Taxable gifts for the current period		$ xx,xxx
Add: Taxable gifts from prior years valued at date of gift		xx,xxx
Total of current and prior taxable gifts		$ xx,xxx
Compute the gift tax on the total of current and prior taxable gifts by using the rates in Appendix A		$ x,xxx
Subtract: Gift tax paid or deemed paid on prior taxable gifts and the unified tax credit		xxx
Gift tax due on transfers during the current period		$ xxx

■ TABLE 14–1
Phase-in of Unified Tax Credit for Lifetime Transfers

Year of Gift	Amount of Credit	Amount of Exemption Equivalent
1977	$ 30,000	$ 120,667
1978	34,000	134,000
1979	38,000	147,333
1980	42,500	161,563
1981	47,000	175,625
1982	62,800	225,000
1983	79,300	275,000
1984	96,300	325,000
1985	121,800	400,000
1986	155,800	500,000
1987 through 1997	192,800	600,000
1998	202,050	625,000
1999	211,300	650,000
2000 and 2001	220,550	675,000
2002 and thereafter	345,800	1,000,000

EXAMPLE 6

Assume the same facts as in Example 5. Don will be allowed a credit of $345,800 against the gift tax of $780,800. Thus, the gift tax liability for 2004 becomes $435,000 ($780,800 – $345,800). ■

The Unified Tax Credit. Before the unified transfer tax, the gift tax allowed a $30,000 specific exemption for the lifetime of the donor. A comparable $60,000 exemption was allowed for estate tax purposes. The purpose of these exemptions was to allow donors and decedents to transfer modest amounts of wealth without being subject to the gift and estate taxes. Unfortunately, inflation took its toll, and more taxpayers became subject to these transfer taxes than Congress believed was appropriate. The congressional solution was to rescind the exemptions and replace them with the **unified tax credit.**[13] This amount was phased in gradually over a period of years; from 1987 through 1997, it was set at $192,800. Recently, new legislation has again increased the unified credit amount beginning in 1998 to partially compensate taxpayers for inflation. As shown in Table 14–1, the Tax Relief Reconciliation Act of 2001 froze the amount of the credit applicable to the gift tax at $345,800 for 2002 and succeeding years.

The **exemption equivalent** is the amount of the transfer that will pass free of the gift or estate tax by virtue of the credit. The exemption equivalent of the current $345,800 unified tax credit is $1 million of taxable transfers.

EXAMPLE 7

In 2004, Janet makes a taxable gift of $1,000,000. Presuming she has made no prior taxable gifts, Janet will not owe any gift tax. Under the tax rate schedules (see Appendix A), the tax on $1 million is $345,800, which is the exact amount of the credit allowed.[14] Since Janet has completely used the unified tax credit, she will pay tax on all future taxable gifts and on her estate. ■

Requirements for a Gift. In general, for a gift to be complete, the following elements must be present.

[13] §§ 2010 and 2505.

[14] The rate schedules are contained in § 2001(c).

- A donor competent to make the gift.
- A donee capable of receiving and possessing the property.
- Donative intent on behalf of the donor.
- Actual or constructive delivery of the property to the donee or the donee's representative.
- Acceptance of the gift by the donee.

Note that the Federal gift tax does not apply to transfers that are incomplete. Thus, if the transferor retains the right to reclaim the property or has not really parted with the possession of the property, a taxable event has not taken place. Incomplete transfers generally arise with respect to trusts and are discussed in Chapter 15.

Business versus Personal Setting. The circumstances under which the transfer is made should be considered. In a business setting, transfers generally are not deemed to be gifts because full and adequate consideration is apt to exist. The gift tax Regulations provide that "a sale, exchange, or other transfer of property made in the ordinary course of business (a transaction that is bona fide, at arm's length, and free of any donative intent) will be considered as made for an adequate and full consideration in money or money's worth."[15] If the parties are acting in a personal setting, however, a gift usually is the result.

EXAMPLE 8

Grace loans money to Debby in connection with a business venture. About a year later, Grace forgives part of the loan. Grace probably has not made a gift to Debby if she and Debby are unrelated parties.[16] ■

EXAMPLE 9

Assume the same facts as in Example 8, except that Grace and Debby are mother and daughter and no business venture is involved. If the loan itself was not actually a disguised gift, the later forgiveness is probably a gift. ■

The Regulations also hold that valuable consideration (which normally precludes gift treatment) does not include a payment or transfer based on "love and affection . . . promise of marriage, etc." Consequently, property settlements in consideration of marriage (i.e., pre- or antenuptial agreements) are regarded as gifts.

Do not conclude that the presence of *some* consideration is enough to preclude Federal gift tax consequences. Again, the answer may rest on whether the transfer occurred in a business setting.

EXAMPLE 10

Peter sells Bob some real estate for $40,000. Unknown to Peter, the property contains valuable mineral deposits and is really worth $100,000. Peter may have made a bad business deal, but he has not made a gift of $60,000 to Bob. ■

EXAMPLE 11

Assume the same facts as in Example 10, except that Peter and Bob are father and son. In addition, Peter is aware that the property is worth $100,000. Peter has made a gift of $60,000 to Bob. ■

Certain Excluded Transfers. Transfers to political organizations are exempt from the application of the Federal gift tax.[17] This provision in the Code made unnecessary the previous practice whereby candidates for public office established

[15] Reg. § 25.2512–8.

[16] The forgiveness could result in taxable income to Debby under § 61(a)(12).

[17] § 2501(a)(5).

multiple campaign committees to maximize the number of annual exclusions available to their contributors.

The Federal gift tax does not apply to tuition payments made to an educational organization (e.g., a college) on another's behalf. Nor does it apply to amounts paid on another's behalf for medical care.[18] Likewise, satisfying an obligation of support is not subject to the gift tax. Thus, no gift takes place when parents pay for their children's education because one of the obligations of parents is to educate their children. What constitutes an obligation of support is determined by applicable state law.

Lifetime versus Death Transfers. Be careful to distinguish between lifetime (inter vivos) and death (testamentary) transfers.

EXAMPLE 12

Wilber buys a U.S. savings bond, which he registers as follows: "Wilber, payable to Alice upon Wilber's death." No gift is made when Wilber buys the bond; Alice has received a mere expectancy (i.e., to obtain ownership of the bond at Wilber's death). At any time before his death, Wilber may redeem or otherwise dispose of the bond and eliminate Alice's interest. On Wilber's death, no gift is made because the bond passes to Alice by testamentary disposition. As noted later, the bond will be included in Wilber's gross estate and be subject to the estate tax as property in which the decedent had an interest (§ 2033). ■

TRANSFERS SUBJECT TO THE GIFT TAX

Whether a transfer is subject to the Federal gift tax depends upon the application of §§ 2511 through 2519 and the applicable Regulations.

Gift Loans. To understand the tax ramifications of gift loans, an illustration is helpful.

EXAMPLE 13

Before his daughter (Denise) leaves for college, Victor lends her $300,000. Denise signs a note that provides for repayment in five years. The loan contains no interest element, and neither Victor nor Denise expects any interest to be paid. Following Victor's advice, Denise invests the loan proceeds in income-producing securities. During her five years in college, she uses the income from the investments to pay for college costs and other living expenses. On the maturity date of the note, Denise repays the $300,000 she owes Victor. ■

In a gift loan arrangement, the following consequences ensue.

- Victor has made a gift to Denise of the interest element. The amount of the gift is determined by the difference between the amount of interest charged (in this case, none) and the market rate (as determined by the yield on certain U.S. government securities).
- The interest element is included in Victor's gross income and is subject to the Federal income tax.
- Denise may be allowed an income tax deduction for the interest element, but may benefit from this result only if she is in a position to itemize her deductions *from* adjusted gross income.

The Code defines a gift loan as "any below-market loan where the foregoing [sic] of interest is in the nature of a gift."[19] Unless tax avoidance was one of the principal purposes of the loan, special limitations apply if the gift loan does not

[18] § 2503(e).

[19] § 7872(f)(3).

exceed $100,000. In such a case, the interest element may not exceed the borrower's net investment income.[20] Furthermore, if the borrower's net investment income does not exceed $1,000, gift treatment is avoided. If the loan is less than $10,000, the interest element is also disregarded.

DIGGING DEEPER 3

Find more information on this topic at our Web site: ***http://wft-advanced.swlearning.com.***

Certain Property Settlements. Normally, the settlement of certain marital rights is not regarded as being for consideration and is subject to the Federal gift tax.[21] As a special exception to this general approach, Congress enacted § 2516. Under this provision, transfers of property interests made under the terms of a written agreement between spouses in settlement of their marital or property rights are deemed to be for adequate consideration. These transfers are exempt from the Federal gift tax if a final decree of divorce is obtained within the three-year period beginning on the date one year before the parties entered into the agreement. Likewise excluded are transfers to provide a reasonable allowance for the support of minor children (including legally adopted children) of a marriage. The agreement need not be approved by the divorce decree.

Disclaimers. A **disclaimer** is a refusal by a person to accept property that is designated to pass to him or her. The effect of the disclaimer is to pass the property to someone else.

EXAMPLE 14

Earl dies without a will and is survived by a son, Andy, and a grandson, Jay. At the time of his death, Earl owned real estate that, under the applicable state law, passes to the closest lineal descendant, Andy in this case. If, however, Andy disclaims his interest in the real estate, state law provides that the property passes to Jay. At the time of Earl's death, Andy has considerable property of his own, and Jay has none. ■

Why might Andy want to consider disclaiming his inheritance and have the property pass directly from Earl to Jay? By doing so, an extra transfer tax may be avoided. If the disclaimer does not take place (i.e., Andy accepts the inheritance) and the property eventually passes to Jay (either by gift or by death), the later transfer is subject to the application of either the gift tax or the estate tax.

For many years, whether a disclaimer was effective in avoiding a Federal transfer tax depended on the application of state law. To illustrate by using the facts of Example 14, if state law determined that the real estate was deemed to have passed through Andy despite his disclaimer after Earl's death, the Federal gift tax applied. In essence, Andy was treated as if he had inherited the property from Earl and then given it to Jay. As state law was not always consistent in this regard and sometimes was not even known, the application or nonapplication of Federal transfer taxes depended on where the parties lived. To remedy this situation and provide some measure of uniformity, §§ 2046 (relating to disclaimers for estate tax purposes) and 2518 (relating to disclaimers for gift tax purposes) were added to the Code.

In the case of the gift tax, when the requirements of § 2518 are met and Andy issues a timely lifetime disclaimer (refer to Example 14), the property is treated as if it goes directly from Earl to Jay. Since the property is not treated as passing through Andy (regardless of what state law holds), it is not subject to the Federal gift tax.

[20]Net investment income has the same meaning given to the term by § 163(d). Generally, net investment income is investment income (e.g., interest, dividends) less related expenses.

[21]Reg. § 25.2512–8.

To be effective, the disclaimer must be timely made. Generally, this means no later than nine months after the right to the property arose. Furthermore, the person making the disclaimer must not have accepted any benefits or interest in the property.

Jointly Owned Property. When property is transferred either by gift or by death, the form of ownership can have a direct bearing on any transfer tax consequences. Understanding the different forms of ownership is necessary for working with Federal gift and estate taxes.

Assume Dan and Vicky own an undivided but equal interest in a tract of land. Such ownership can fall into any of four categories: joint tenancy, tenancy by the entirety, tenancy in common, or community property.

If Dan and Vicky hold ownership as **joint tenants,** right of survivorship exists. This means that the last tenant to survive receives full ownership of the property. Thus, if Dan predeceases Vicky, the land belongs entirely to Vicky. In some states, a joint tenancy between husband and wife is called a **tenancy by the entirety.**

If Dan and Vicky hold ownership as **tenants in common,** unlike joint tenancies, their interests may be owned in unequal percentages. In addition, death does not defeat an owner's interest. Thus, if Dan predeceases Vicky, Dan's one-half interest in the land will pass to his estate or heirs by will or by the laws of intestate succession.

Community property interests arise from the marital relationship. Normally, all property acquired after marriage, except through gift or inheritance, by husband and wife residing in a community property state becomes part of the community. Community property is owned equally by both spouses. Like tenants in common, the decedent's share of community property does not automatically belong to the surviving spouse. At death, a spouse can transfer his or her share of community property, by will, to someone other than the spouse.

The following states have the community property system in effect: Louisiana, Texas, New Mexico, Arizona, California, Washington, Idaho, Nevada, Wisconsin, and (by election of the spouses) Alaska. All other states follow the common law system of ascertaining a spouse's rights to property acquired after marriage.

Whether a *gift* results when property is transferred into some form of joint ownership depends on the consideration furnished by each of the contributing parties for the ownership interest acquired.

EXAMPLE 15

Brenda and Sarah purchase real estate as tenants in common, each furnishing $40,000 of the $80,000 cost. If each is an equal owner in the property, no gift has occurred. ■

EXAMPLE 16

Assume in Example 15 that Brenda furnishes $60,000 and Sarah furnishes only $20,000. If each is an equal owner in the property, Brenda has made a gift to Sarah of $20,000. ■

EXAMPLE 17

Martha purchases real estate for $240,000, the title to the property being listed as follows: "Martha and David as joint tenants with the right of survivorship." If under state law the mother (Martha) and the son (David) are deemed to be equal owners in the property, Martha is treated as having made a gift of $120,000 to David, which would qualify for the annual exclusion. If Martha and David were husband and wife, the $120,000 gift would qualify for the marital deduction. ■

Several important *exceptions* exist to the general rule that gift treatment is triggered by the creation of a joint ownership with disproportionate interests resulting from unequal consideration. If the transfer involves a joint bank account, there is no gift at the time of the contribution.[22] If a gift occurs, it is when the noncontributing party withdraws the funds provided by the other joint tenant.

[22] Reg. § 25.2511–1(h)(4).

The same rule applies to the purchase of U.S. savings bonds. Again, any gift tax consequences are postponed until the noncontributing party appropriates some or all of the proceeds for his or her individual use.

EXAMPLE 18

Cynthia deposits $200,000 in a bank account under the names of Cynthia and Carla as joint tenants. Both Cynthia and Carla have the right to withdraw funds from the account without the other's consent. Cynthia has not made a gift to Carla when the account is established. ■

EXAMPLE 19

Assume the same facts as in Example 18. At some later date, Carla withdraws $50,000 from the account for her own use. At this point, Cynthia has made a gift to Carla of $50,000. ■

Other Transfers Subject to Gift Tax. Other transfers that may carry gift tax consequences (e.g., the creation of trusts) are discussed in Chapter 15.

ANNUAL EXCLUSION

In General. The first $11,000 of gifts made to any one person (except gifts of future interests in property) is excluded in determining the total amount of gifts for the year.[23] The **annual exclusion** applies to all gifts of a *present* interest made during the calendar year in the order in which they are made until the $11,000 exclusion per donee is exhausted.

A **future interest** is defined as one that will come into being (as to use, possession, or enjoyment) at some future date. A *present interest* is an unrestricted right to the immediate use, possession, or enjoyment of property or of the income.

EXAMPLE 20

During the current year, Laura makes the following cash gifts: $8,000 to Rita and $12,000 to Maureen. Laura may claim an annual exclusion of $8,000 with respect to Rita and $11,000 with respect to Maureen. ■

EXAMPLE 21

Ron buys a 7% bond that matures in 10 years. Interest is paid quarterly. He gifts it to his children, June and Albert. June is to receive the quarterly income payments, and Albert is to receive the principal on maturity in 10 years. June's interest is a present interest and qualifies for the annual exclusion. Albert's interest is a future interest and does not qualify for the annual exclusion. The valuation of each of these gifts is discussed in Chapter 15. ■

DEDUCTIONS

In arriving at taxable gifts, a deduction is allowed for transfers to certain qualified charitable organizations. On transfers between spouses, a marital deduction may be available. Since both the charitable and marital deductions also apply in determining the Federal estate tax, these deductions are discussed later in the chapter.

LO.4

Explain the computation of the Federal gift tax.

COMPUTING THE FEDERAL GIFT TAX

The Unified Transfer Tax Rate Schedule. The top rates of the unified transfer tax rate schedule originally reached as high as 70 percent (see Appendix A). Over the years, these top rates are scheduled to be reduced to 45 percent. The maximum rate for 2004 is 48 percent.[24]

[23] § 2503(b). In 1982, the annual exclusion was increased from $3,000 to $10,000 and in 2002 from $10,000 to $11,000. Effective for years after 1998, the annual exclusion is indexed to account for significant inflation.

[24] § 2001(c)(2)(B). Scheduled reductions in the maximum tax rates are as follows: 47% (2005); 46% (2006); and 45% (2007, 2008, 2009).

The Deemed Paid Adjustment. Review the formula for the gift tax in Figure 14–1, and note that the tax base for a current gift includes *all* prior taxable gifts. The effect of the inclusion is to force the current taxable gift into a higher bracket due to the progressive nature of the unified transfer tax rates (refer to Example 5). To mitigate such double taxation, the donor is allowed a credit for any gift tax previously paid or deemed paid (refer to Example 6).

Limiting the donor to a credit for the gift tax *actually paid* on pre-1977 taxable gifts would be unfair. Pre-1977 taxable gifts were subject to a lower set of rates (see Appendix A) than those in the unified transfer tax rate schedule. As a consequence, the donor is allowed a *deemed paid* credit on pre-1977 taxable gifts. This is the amount that would have been due under the unified transfer tax rate schedule had it been applicable. *Post-1976* taxable gifts *also* are subject to the deemed paid adjustment since the same rate schedule may not be involved in all gifts. Compare the variation in gift tax rates in Appendix A on gifts made before 1977 and after 1976.

EXAMPLE 22

In early 1976, Lisa made taxable gifts of $500,000, upon which a Federal gift tax of $109,275 (see Appendix A) was paid. Assume Lisa makes further taxable gifts of $1,700,000 in 2004. The unified transfer tax on the 2004 gifts is determined as follows:

Taxable gifts made in 2004		$1,700,000
Add: Taxable gifts made in 1976		500,000
Total of current and prior taxable gifts		$2,200,000
Unified transfer tax on total taxable gifts per the post-1976 gift tax rates in Appendix A [$780,800 + 48%($2,200,000 – $2,000,000)]		$ 876,800
Subtract:		
Deemed paid tax on pre-1977 taxable gifts of $500,000 per the post-1976 gift tax rates in Appendix A	$155,800	
Unified tax credit for 2004	345,800	(501,600)
Gift tax due on the 2004 taxable gift		$ 375,200

Note that the gift tax actually paid on the 1976 transfer was $109,275. Nevertheless, Lisa is allowed a deemed paid credit on the gift of $155,800, considerably more than the tax that was paid. ■

The Election to Split Gifts by Married Persons. The law allows married persons to elect to split their gifts. Under the election, each spouse is deemed to gift one-half of the fair market value of the property transferred. To understand the rationale for the gift-splitting election of § 2513, consider the following situations.

EXAMPLE 23

Dick and Margaret are husband and wife and reside in Michigan, a common law state. Dick has been the only breadwinner in the family, and Margaret has no significant property of her own. Neither has made any prior taxable gifts. In 2004, Dick makes a gift to Leslie of $2,022,000. Presuming the election to split gifts did not exist, Dick's gift tax is as follows:

Amount of gift	$2,022,000
Subtract: Annual exclusion	(11,000)
Taxable gift	$2,011,000
Gift tax on $2,011,000 per Appendix A [$780,800 + (48% × $11,000)]	$ 786,080
Subtract: Unified tax credit for 2004	(345,800)
Gift tax due on the 2004 taxable gift	$ 440,280

■

EXAMPLE 24

Assume the same facts as in Example 23, except that Dick and Margaret have always resided in California (a community property state). Even though Dick is the sole breadwinner, income from personal services generally is community property. Consequently, the gift to Leslie probably involves community property. If this is the case, the gift tax is as follows.

	Dick	Margaret
Amount of the gift (50% × $2,022,000)	$1,011,000	$1,011,000
Subtract: Annual exclusion	(11,000)	(11,000)
Taxable gifts	$1,000,000	$1,000,000
Gift tax on $1,000,000 per Appendix A	$ 345,800	$ 345,800
Subtract: Unified tax credit for 2004	(345,800)	(345,800)
Gift tax due on the 2004 taxable gifts	$ –0–	$ –0–

As the results of Examples 23 and 24 indicate, married donors residing in community property jurisdictions possessed a significant gift tax advantage over those residing in common law states. To rectify this inequity, Congress has provided that a gift made by a person to someone other than his or her spouse may be considered, for Federal gift tax purposes, as having been made one-half by each spouse. Returning to Example 23, Dick and Margaret could treat the gift passing to Leslie as being made one-half by each of them. They may do this even though the cash belonged to Dick. As a result, the parties are able to achieve the same tax consequence as in Example 24.

To split gifts, the spouses must be legally married to each other at the time of the gift. If they are divorced later in the calendar year, they may still split the gift if neither marries anyone else during that year. They both must indicate on their separate gift tax returns their consent to have all gifts made in that calendar year split between them. In addition, both must be citizens or residents of the United States on the date of the gift. A gift from one spouse to the other spouse cannot be split. Such a gift might, however, be eligible for the marital deduction.

The election to split gifts is not necessary when husband and wife jointly own the property or when the transfer involves community property. It is available, however, if the gift consists of the separate property of one of the spouses. Generally, separate property is property acquired before marriage and property acquired after marriage by gift or inheritance. Thus, the election is not limited to residents of common law states.

PROCEDURAL MATTERS

Having determined which transfers are subject to the Federal gift tax and the various deductions and exclusions available to the donor, the procedural aspects of the tax must be considered. The following sections discuss the return itself, the due dates for filing and paying the tax, and other related matters.

The Federal Gift Tax Return. For transfers by gift, a Form 709 (U.S. Gift Tax Return) must be filed whenever the gifts for any one calendar year exceed the annual exclusion or involve a gift of a future interest. A Form 709 need not be filed, however, for transfers between spouses that are offset by the unlimited marital deduction regardless of the amount of the transfer.[25]

[25] § 6019(a)(2).

CONCEPT SUMMARY 14–1

Federal Gift Tax Provisions

1. The Federal gift tax applies to all gratuitous transfers of property made by U.S. citizens or residents. In this regard, it does not matter where the property is located.
2. In the eyes of the IRS, a gratuitous transfer is one not supported by full and adequate consideration. If the parties are acting in a business setting, such consideration usually exists. If, however, purported sales are between family members, a gift element may be suspected.
3. If one party lends money to another, to the extent that the interest provided for is less than the market rate, three tax consequences result. First, a gift has taken place between the lender and the borrower as to the interest element. Second, income may result to the lender. Third, an income tax deduction may be available to the borrower. This arrangement is called a gift loan.
4. Property settlements can escape the gift tax if a divorce occurs within a prescribed time period.
5. A disclaimer is a refusal by a person to accept property designated to pass to that person. The effect of a disclaimer is to pass the property to someone else. If certain conditions are satisfied, the issuance of a disclaimer will not be subject to the Federal gift tax.
6. Except for gifts of future interests, a donor is allowed an annual exclusion of $11,000 per donee in 2004 (indexed for inflation in later years).
7. The election to split a gift enables a married couple to be treated as two donors. The election doubles the annual exclusion and the unified tax credit available.
8. The election to split gifts is not necessary when the property is jointly owned by the spouses or when community property is involved.
9. In determining the tax base for computing the gift tax, all prior taxable gifts must be added to current taxable gifts. Thus, the gift tax is cumulative in nature.
10. Gifts are reported on Form 709. The return is due on April 15 following the year of the gift.

EXAMPLE 25

In 2004, Larry makes five gifts, each in the amount of $11,000, to his five children. If the gifts do not involve future interests, a Form 709 need not be filed to report the transfers. ■

EXAMPLE 26

During 2004, Esther makes a gift of $22,000 cash of her separate property to her daughter. To double the amount of the annual exclusion allowed, Jerry (Esther's husband) is willing to split the gift. Since the § 2513 election can be made only on a gift tax return, a form must be filed even though no gift tax will be due as a result of the transfer. ■

Presuming a gift tax return is due, it must be filed on or before the fifteenth day of April following the year of the gift.[26] As is the case with other Federal taxes, when the due date falls on Saturday, Sunday, or a legal holiday, the date for filing the return is the next business day. Note that the filing requirements for Form 709 have no correlation to the accounting year used by a donor for Federal income tax purposes. Thus, a fiscal year taxpayer must follow the April 15 rule for any reportable gifts. If sufficient reason is shown, the IRS is authorized to grant reasonable extensions of time for filing the return.[27] Concept Summary 14–1 offers an overview of the Federal gift tax provisions.

[26] § 6075(b)(1).

[27] § 6081. Under § 6075(b)(2), an extension of time granted to a calendar year taxpayer for filing an income tax return automatically extends the due date of a gift tax return.

■ FIGURE 14–2
Formula for the Federal Estate Tax

Gross estate		$xxx,xxx
Subtract:		
Expenses, indebtedness, and taxes	$xx	
Losses	xx	
Charitable bequests	xx	
Marital deduction	xx	x,xxx
Taxable estate		$ xx,xxx
Add: Post-1976 taxable gifts		x,xxx
Tax base		$xxx,xxx
Tentative tax on total transfers		$ xx,xxx
Subtract:		
Unified transfer tax on post-1976 taxable gifts (gift taxes paid or deemed paid)	$xx	
Tax credits (including the unified tax credit)	xx	x,xxx
Estate tax due		$ xxx

LO.5

Work with the Federal estate tax formula.

The Federal Estate Tax

The following discussion of the estate tax coincides with the formula in Figure 14–2. The key components in the formula are the gross estate, the taxable estate, the tax base, and the credits allowed against the tentative tax.

The reason post-1976 taxable gifts are added to the taxable estate to arrive at the tax base goes back to the scheme of the unified transfer tax. Starting in 1977, all transfers, whether lifetime or by death, are treated the same. Consequently, taxable gifts made after 1976 must be accounted for upon the death of the donor. Note that the double tax effect of including these gifts is mitigated by allowing a credit against the estate tax for the gift taxes previously paid or deemed paid.

LO.6

Describe the components of the gross estate.

GROSS ESTATE

Simply stated, the **gross estate** includes the fair market value of all property subject to the Federal estate tax. This depends on the provisions of the Internal Revenue Code as supplemented by IRS pronouncements and the judicial interpretations of Federal courts.

In contrast to the gross estate, the **probate estate** is controlled by state (rather than Federal) law. The probate estate consists of all of a decedent's property subject to administration by the executor or administrator of the estate. The administration is supervised by a local court of appropriate jurisdiction (usually designated as a probate court). An executor (or executrix) is the decedent's personal representative appointed under the decedent's will. When a decedent dies without a will or fails to name an executor in the will (or that person refuses to serve), the local probate court appoints an administrator (or administratrix).

The probate estate is frequently smaller than the gross estate. It contains only property owned by the decedent at the time of death and passing to heirs under a will or under the law of intestacy (the order of distribution for those dying without a will). As discussed in Chapter 15, such items as the proceeds of many life insurance policies in which the estate is not the beneficiary become part of the gross estate but are not included in the probate estate.

All states provide for an order of distribution in the event someone dies without a will. After the surviving spouse, the preference with respect to who receives some or all of the estate is usually in the following order: down to lineal descendants (e.g., children, grandchildren), up to lineal ascendants (e.g., parents, grandparents), and out to collateral relations (e.g., brothers, sisters, aunts, and uncles).

Date of Valuation. The fair market value of the property on the date of its transfer (i.e., date of death) generally determines the amount that is included in the gross estate. Under certain conditions, however, an executor can elect to value estate assets on the **alternate valuation date.**

The alternate valuation date election was designed as a relief provision to ease the economic hardship that could result when estate assets decline in value over the six months after the date of death. If the election is made, all assets of the estate are valued six months after death *or* on the date of disposition if this occurs earlier.[28] The election covers *all* assets in the gross estate and cannot be applied to only a portion of the property.

EXAMPLE 27

Robert's gross estate consists of the following property:

	Value on Date of Death	Value Six Months Later
Land	$ 800,000	$ 840,000
Stock in Brown Corporation	900,000	700,000
Stock in Green Corporation	500,000	460,000
Total	$2,200,000	$2,000,000

If Robert's executor elects the alternate valuation date, the estate must be valued at $2,000,000. It is not permissible to value the land at its date of death value ($800,000) and choose the alternate valuation date for the rest of the gross estate. ■

EXAMPLE 28

Assume the same facts as in Example 27, except that the executor sells the stock in Green Corporation for $480,000 four months after Robert's death. If the alternate valuation date is elected, the estate must be valued at $2,020,000 ($840,000 + $700,000 + $480,000). As to the Green stock, the value on its date of disposition controls because that date occurred prior to the six months' alternate valuation date. ■

The alternate valuation date election is not available unless the estate must file a Form 706 (Estate Tax Return). When an estate is required to file a Form 706 is discussed later in this chapter.

The election of the alternate valuation date must decrease the value of the gross estate *and* decrease the estate tax liability.[29] The reason for this last requirement is that the income tax basis of property acquired from a decedent will be the value used for estate tax purposes (discussed further in Chapter 15).[30] Without a special limitation, the alternate valuation date could be elected solely to add to income tax basis.

EXAMPLE 29

Al's gross estate is comprised of assets with a date of death value of $2,000,000 and an alternate valuation date value of $2,100,000. Under Al's will, all of his property passes outright to Jean (Al's wife). Because of the marital deduction, no estate tax results regardless

[28] § 2032(a).
[29] § 2032(c).
[30] § 1014(a).

of which value is used. But if the alternate valuation date could be elected, Jean would have an income tax basis of $2,100,000 in the property acquired from Al. ■

The alternate valuation date cannot be elected in Example 29 for two reasons, either of which would suffice. First, the alternate valuation date will not decrease Al's gross estate. Second, the election will not decrease Al's estate tax liability. It will be zero in both cases. Thus, his estate must use the date of death valuation of $2 million. As a result, Jean's income tax basis in the property received from Al is $2 million.

Another valuation option available for estate tax purposes is the special use valuation method. Election of this method is limited to certain situations involving interests in closely held businesses (usually farms). Special use valuation is discussed in Chapter 16.

Property Owned by the Decedent. All property owned by the decedent at the time of death is included in the gross estate. The nature of the property or the use to which it was put during the decedent-owner's lifetime has no significance as far as the estate tax is concerned. Thus, personal effects (such as clothing), stocks, bonds, furniture, jewelry, works of art, bank accounts, and interests in businesses conducted as sole proprietorships and partnerships are all included in the deceased owner's gross estate. Retirement plan benefits from the decedent's Keogh plan, IRA, Roth IRA, and tax-deferred § 401(k) plan are invariably subject to estate tax. No distinction is made between tangible and intangible, depreciable and nondepreciable, business and personal assets. However, a deceased spouse's gross estate does not include the surviving spouse's share of community property.

EXAMPLE 30

Irma dies owning some City of Denver bonds. The fair market value of the bonds plus any interest accrued to the date of Irma's death is included in her gross estate. Although interest on municipals is normally not taxable under the Federal income tax, it is property owned by Irma at the time of death. However, any interest accrued after death is not part of Irma's gross estate. ■

EXAMPLE 31

Sharon dies on April 8, 2004, at a time when she owns stock in Robin Corporation and Wren Corporation. On March 3 of this year, both corporations authorized a cash dividend payable on May 4. Robin's dividend is payable to shareholders of record as of April 1. Wren's date of record is April 12. Sharon's gross estate includes the following: the stock in Robin Corporation, the stock in Wren Corporation, and the dividend on the Robin stock as a receivable. It does not include the dividend on the Wren stock since the date of record is after Sharon's date of death. ■

EXAMPLE 32

Ray dies holding some promissory notes issued to him by his son. In his will, Ray forgives these notes, relieving the son of the obligation to make any payments. The fair market value of these notes is included in Ray's gross estate. ■

EXAMPLE 33

At the time of his death on a business trip, Ray was a consulting engineer for Falcon Corporation. Ray's estate receives a distribution from Falcon's qualified pension plan of $1,100,000 consisting of the following:

Falcon's contributions	$450,000
Ray's contributions	350,000
Income earned by the plan	300,000

Ray's estate also receives $150,000 from Hawk Insurance Company. The payment represents the maturity value of term life insurance from a group plan Falcon maintains for its employees. As to these amounts, Ray's gross estate includes $1,250,000 ($1,100,000 +

$150,000). For income tax purposes, however, $750,000 ($450,000 + $300,000) is subject to tax, while $500,000 ($350,000 + $150,000) is not.[31] ■

Dower and Curtesy Interests. In its common law (nonstatutory) form, dower generally gives a surviving widow a life estate in a portion of her husband's estate (usually the real estate he owned) with the remainder passing to their children. Most states have modified and codified the common law rules and the resulting statutes vary among jurisdictions. In some states, for example, by statute a widow is entitled to outright ownership of a percentage of her deceased husband's real estate and personal property. Curtesy is a similar right held by the husband in his wife's property that takes effect in the event he survives her. Most states have abolished the common law curtesy concept and have, in some cases, substituted a modified statutory version.

Dower and curtesy rights are incomplete interests and may never materialize. Thus, if a wife predeceases her husband, the dower interest in her husband's property is lost.

EXAMPLE 34

Martin dies without a will, leaving an estate of $900,000. Under state law, Belinda (Martin's widow) is entitled to one-third of his property. The $300,000 Belinda receives is included in Martin's gross estate. Depending on the nature of the interest Belinda receives in the $300,000, this amount could qualify Martin's estate for a marital deduction. (This possibility is discussed at greater length later in the chapter. For the time being, however, the focus is on what is or is not included as part of the decedent's gross estate.) ■

Adjustments for Gifts Made within Three Years of Death. At one time, all taxable gifts made within three years of death were included in the donor's gross estate unless it could be shown that the gifts were not made in contemplation of death. The rule was intended to preclude tax avoidance since the gift tax and estate tax rates were separate and the former was lower than the latter. When the gift and estate tax rates were combined into the unified transfer tax, the reason for the rule for gifts in contemplation of death largely disappeared. The three-year rule has, however, been retained for the following items.

- Inclusion in the gross estate of any gift tax paid on gifts made within three years of death. Called the *gross-up* procedure, it prevents the gift tax paid from escaping the estate tax.
- Any property interests transferred by gift within three years of death that would have been included in the gross estate by virtue of the application of § 2036 (transfers with a retained life estate), § 2037 (transfers taking effect at death), § 2038 (revocable transfers), and § 2042 (proceeds of life insurance). These items are discussed in Chapter 15.

EXAMPLE 35

Before her death in 2004, Jennifer made the following taxable gifts:

Year of Gift	Nature of the Asset	Fair Market Value: Date of Gift	Fair Market Value: Date of Death	Gift Tax Paid
1992	Hawk Corporation stock	$100,000	$ 150,000	$ –0–
2002	Policy on Jennifer's life	80,000 (cash value)	1,000,000 (face value)	–0–
2003	Land	800,000	810,000	16,000

[31]If the payout is in the form of an annuity, § 2039 applies and the tax effects are the same.

Jennifer's *gross estate* includes $1,016,000 [$1,000,000 (life insurance proceeds) + $16,000 (gross-up for the gift tax on the 2003 taxable gift)] as to these transfers. Referring to the formula for the estate tax (see Figure 14–2), the other post-1976 taxable gifts of $900,000 [$100,000 (stock) + $800,000 (land)] are added to the *taxable estate* (at the fair market value on the date of the gift) in arriving at the tax base. Jennifer's estate is allowed a credit for the gift tax paid (or deemed paid) of $16,000 on the 2003 transfer. Note that since the life insurance proceeds must be included in the gross estate, the $80,000 gift value of the insurance policy is not added to the taxable estate as a post-1976 taxable gift. An addition would result in double taxation of the policy. ■

Annuities. Annuities can be divided by their origin into commercial and noncommercial contracts. Noncommercial annuities are issued by private parties and, in some cases, charitable organizations that do not regularly issue annuities. The two varieties have much in common, but noncommercial annuities present special income tax problems and are not treated further in this discussion.

Regulation § 20.2039–1(b)(1) defines an annuity as representing "one or more payments extending over any period of time." According to the Regulation, the payments may be equal or unequal, conditional or unconditional, periodic or sporadic. Annuity contracts that terminate upon the death of the person covered (i.e., annuitant) are designated as straight-life annuities. Other contracts provide for a survivorship feature (e.g., reduced payments to a surviving spouse).

In the case of a straight-life annuity, nothing is included in the gross estate of the annuitant at death. Section 2033 (property in which the decedent had an interest) does not apply because the annuitant's interest in the contract is terminated by death.

EXAMPLE 36

Arnold purchases a straight-life annuity that will pay him $6,000 a month when he reaches age 65. Arnold dies at age 70. Except for the payments he received before his death, nothing relating to this annuity affects Arnold's gross estate. ■

In the case of a survivorship annuity, the estate tax consequences under § 2039(a) are usually triggered by the death of the first annuitant. The amount included in the gross estate is the cost from the same company of a comparable annuity covering the survivor at his or her attained age on the date of the deceased annuitant's death.

EXAMPLE 37

Assume the same facts as in Example 36, except that the annuity contract provides for Veronica to be paid $3,000 a month for life as a survivorship feature. Veronica is 62 years of age when Arnold dies. Under these circumstances, Arnold's gross estate includes the cost of a comparable contract that provides an annuity of $3,000 per month for the life of a female, age 62. ■

Full inclusion of the survivorship element in the gross estate is subject to an exception under § 2039(b). The amount includible is based on the proportion of the deceased annuitant's contribution to the total cost of the contract. Note that the deceased annuitant's contribution includes payments made by the decedent's employer. This is expressed by the following formula:

$$\frac{\text{Decedent's contribution to purchase price}}{\text{Total purchase price of the annuity}} \times \text{Value of the annuity (or refund) at decedent's death} = \text{Amount includible in the deceased annuitant's gross estate}$$

EXAMPLE 38

Assume the same facts as in Example 37, except that Arnold and Veronica are husband and wife and have always lived in a community property state. The premiums on the contract were paid with community funds. Since Veronica contributed half of the cost of the contract, only half of the amount determined under Example 37 is included in Arnold's gross estate. ■

The result reached in Example 38 is not unique to community property jurisdictions. The outcome would have been the same in a noncommunity property state if Veronica had furnished half of the consideration from her own funds.

Joint Interests. Recall that joint tenancies and tenancies by the entirety are characterized by the right of survivorship. Thus, upon the death of a joint tenant, title to the property passes to the surviving tenant. None of the property is included in the *probate* estate of the deceased tenant. In the case of tenancies in common and community property, death does not defeat an ownership interest, and the deceased owner's interest is part of the probate estate.

The Federal estate tax treatment of tenancies in common or of community property follows the logical approach of taxing only the portion of the property included in the deceased owner's probate estate.

EXAMPLE 39

Homer, Wilma, and Thelma acquire a tract of land, ownership listed as tenants in common, each party furnishing $20,000 of the $60,000 purchase price. When the property is worth $90,000, Homer dies. If Homer's undivided interest in the property is 33⅓%, the gross estate *and* probate estate each include $30,000. Homer's heirs will receive the $30,000 interest. ■

Unless the parties have provided otherwise, each tenant is deemed to own an interest equal to the portion of the original consideration he or she furnished. The parties in Example 39 could have provided that Homer would receive an undivided half interest in the property although he contributed only one-third of the purchase price. In that case, Wilma and Thelma each would have made a gift of $5,000 to Homer when the tenancy was created, and Homer's gross estate as well as his probate estate would each include $45,000.

For joint tenancies with right of survivorship, the tax consequences are different. All of the property is included in the deceased co-owner's gross estate unless it can be proven that the surviving co-owners contributed to the cost of the property.[32] If a contribution can be shown, the amount to be *excluded* is calculated by the following formula.

$$\frac{\text{Surviving co-owner's contribution}}{\text{Total cost of the property}} \times \text{Fair market value of the property}$$

In computing a survivor's contribution, any funds received as a gift *from the deceased co-owner* and applied to the cost of the property cannot be counted. However, income or gain from gift assets can be counted.

If the co-owners receive the property as a gift *from another*, each co-owner is deemed to have contributed to the cost of his or her own interest. The preceding rules are illustrated below.

EXAMPLE 40

Keith and Steve (father and son) acquire a tract of land, ownership listed as joint tenancy with right of survivorship. Keith furnished $50,000 and Steve $30,000 of the $80,000 purchase price. Of the $30,000 provided by Steve, $10,000 had previously been received as a taxable gift from Keith. When the property is worth $90,000, Keith dies. Because only $20,000 of Steve's contribution can be counted (the other $10,000 was received as a gift from Keith),

[32] § 2040(a).

Steve has furnished only one-fourth ($20,000/$80,000) of the cost. Thus, Keith's gross estate must include three-fourths of $90,000, or $67,500. Keith's $10,000 taxable gift does not have to be added to the *taxable* estate because double taxation of the property would result. If Keith had not already used his annual exclusion, there would be no taxable gift.

This presumes Steve can prove that he did in fact pay $20,000 of the purchase price. In the absence of such proof, the full value of the property is included in Keith's gross estate. Keith's death makes Steve the immediate owner of the property by virtue of the right of survivorship. None of the property is part of Keith's probate estate. ■

EXAMPLE 41

Francis transfers property to Irene and Martin as a gift, listing ownership as joint tenancy with right of survivorship. Upon Irene's death, one-half of the value of the property is included in the gross estate. Since the property was received as a gift and the donees are equal owners, each is considered to have furnished half of the consideration. ■

To simplify the joint ownership rules for *married persons,* § 2040(b) provides for an automatic inclusion rule upon the death of the first joint-owner spouse to die. Regardless of the amount contributed by each spouse, one-half of the value of the property is included in the gross estate of the spouse who dies first. The special rule eliminates the need to trace the source of contributions and recognizes that any inclusion in the gross estate is neutralized by the marital deduction.

EXAMPLE 42

Ten years ago, Hank purchased real estate for $100,000 using his separate funds and listing title as "Hank and Louise, joint tenants with the right of survivorship." Hank predeceases Louise in the current year when the property is worth $300,000. If Hank and Louise are husband and wife, Hank's gross estate includes $150,000 (½ of $300,000) of the property. ■

EXAMPLE 43

Assume the same facts as in Example 42, except that Louise (instead of Hank) dies first. Presuming the value at the date of death to be $300,000, Louise's gross estate includes $150,000 of the property. In this regard, it is of no consequence that Louise did not contribute to the cost of the real estate. ■

In both Examples 42 and 43, inclusion in the gross estate of the first spouse to die is neutralized by the unlimited marital deduction allowed for estate tax purposes (see the discussion of § 2056 later in the chapter). Under the right of survivorship, the surviving joint tenant obtains full ownership of the property. The marital deduction generally is allowed for property passing from one spouse to another.

Life Insurance. Under § 2042, the gross estate includes the proceeds of life insurance on the decedent's life if (1) they are receivable by the estate, (2) they are receivable by another for the benefit of the estate, or (3) the decedent possessed an incident of ownership in the policy.

Life insurance on the life of another owned by a decedent at the time of death is included in the gross estate under § 2033 (property in which the decedent had an interest) and not under § 2042. The amount includible is the replacement value of the policy.[33] Under these circumstances, inclusion of the face amount of the policy is inappropriate as the policy has not yet matured.

EXAMPLE 44

At the time of his death, Luigi owned a life insurance policy on the life of Benito, face amount of $100,000 and replacement value of $25,000, with Sofia as the designated beneficiary. Since the policy has not matured at Luigi's death, § 2042 is inapplicable. However, § 2033 (property

[33] Reg. § 20.2031–8(a)(1).

in which the decedent had an interest) compels the inclusion of $25,000 (the replacement value) in Luigi's gross estate. If Luigi and Sofia owned the policy as community property, only $12,500 is included in Luigi's gross estate. ■

The term *life insurance* includes whole life policies, term insurance, group term life insurance, travel and accident insurance, endowment contracts (before being paid up), and death benefits paid by fraternal societies operating under the lodge system.[34]

As just noted, proceeds of insurance on the life of the decedent receivable by the executor or administrator or payable to the decedent's estate are included in the gross estate. The estate need not be specifically named as the beneficiary. Assume, for example, the proceeds of the policy are receivable by an individual beneficiary and are subject to an obligation, legally binding upon the beneficiary, to pay taxes, debts, and other charges enforceable against the estate. The proceeds are included in the decedent's gross estate to the extent of the beneficiary's obligation.

Proceeds of insurance on the life of the decedent not receivable by or for the benefit of the estate are includible if the decedent at death possessed any of the incidents of ownership in the policy. In this connection, the term *incidents of ownership* not only means the ownership of the policy in a technical legal sense but also, generally speaking, the right of the insured or his or her estate to the economic benefits of the policy. Thus, it also includes the power to change beneficiaries, revoke an assignment, pledge the policy for a loan, or surrender or cancel the policy.[35]

EXAMPLE 45

At the time of death, Broderick was the insured under a policy (face amount of $100,000) owned by Gregory with Demi as the designated beneficiary. Broderick took out the policy five years ago and immediately transferred it as a gift to Gregory. Under the assignment, Broderick transferred all rights in the policy except the right to change beneficiaries. Broderick died without having exercised this right, and the policy proceeds are paid to Demi. Under § 2042(2), Broderick's retention of an incident of ownership in the policy (i.e., the right to change beneficiaries) causes $100,000 to be included in his gross estate. ■

Assuming that the deceased-insured holds the incidents of ownership in a policy, only one-half of the policy proceeds is included in the gross estate if the insurance policy is a community asset. In determining whether a policy is *community property* or what portion of it might be so classified, state law controls. The states appear to follow one of two general approaches. Under the inception of title approach, the classification depends on when the policy was originally purchased. If purchased before marriage, the policy is separate property regardless of how many premiums were paid after marriage with community funds. However, if the noninsured spouse is not the beneficiary of the policy, he or she may be entitled to reimbursement from the deceased-insured spouse's estate for half of the premiums paid with community funds. The inception of title approach is followed in at least three states: Louisiana, Texas, and New Mexico.

Some community property jurisdictions classify a policy using the tracing approach: the nature of the funds used to pay premiums controls. Thus, a policy paid for 20 percent with separate funds and 80 percent with community funds is 20 percent separate property and 80 percent community property. The point in time when the policy was purchased makes no difference. Conceivably, a policy

[34]Reg. § 20.2042–1(a)(1). As to travel and accident insurance, see *Comm. v. Estate of Noel*, 65–1 USTC ¶12,311, 15 AFTR2d 1397, 85 S.Ct. 1238 (USSC, 1965).

[35]Reg. § 20.2042–1(c)(2).

TAX FACT

An estimated 103,982 Federal estate tax returns filed between 1998 and 2000 represented estates of individuals who died in 1998. These relatively wealthy 1998 decedents, whose gross estates totaled $195.6 billion, comprised 4.4 percent of the overall U.S. decedent population that year. However, fewer than half of these returns, 50,089, reported a tax liability, which totaled almost $22.8 billion. After debts, administration expenses, Federal estate taxes, and creditable state and foreign taxes, estate tax returns filed for 1998 decedents reported combined distributable assets of approximately $154.1 billion, of which $55.9 billion were bequeathed to a surviving spouse and $13.6 billion to charity.

Source: IRS Tax Stats.

purchased after marriage with the premiums paid exclusively from separate funds is classified entirely as separate property. The tracing approach appears to be the rule in California and Washington.

Merely purchasing a life insurance contract with someone else designated as the beneficiary does not constitute a *gift*. As long as the purchaser still owns the policy, nothing has really passed to the beneficiary. Even on the death of the insured-owner, no gift takes place because the proceeds paid to the beneficiary constitute a testamentary and not a lifetime transfer and are subject to the estate tax. But consider the following possibility.

EXAMPLE 46

Kurt purchases an insurance policy on his own life that he transfers to Olga. Kurt retains no interest in the policy (such as the power to change beneficiaries). In these circumstances, Kurt has made a gift to Olga. Furthermore, if Kurt continues to pay the premiums on the transferred policy, each payment constitutes a separate gift. ■

Under certain conditions, the death of the insured may constitute a gift to the beneficiary of part or all of the proceeds. This occurs when the owner of the policy is not the insured.

EXAMPLE 47

Randolph owns an insurance policy on the life of Frank, with Tracy as the designated beneficiary. Up until the time of Frank's death, Randolph retained the right to change the beneficiary of the policy. The proceeds paid to Tracy by the insurance company by reason of Frank's death constitute a gift from Randolph to Tracy.[36] ■

EXAMPLE 48

Hubert and Carrie live in a community property state. With community funds, Hubert purchases an insurance policy with a face amount of $100,000 on his own life and designates Ann as the revocable beneficiary. On Hubert's death, the proceeds of the policy are paid to Ann. If under state law Hubert's death makes the transfer by Carrie complete, Carrie has made a gift to Ann of $50,000. Since the policy is community property, Carrie is the owner of only one-half of the policy. Furthermore, one-half of the proceeds of the policy ($50,000) is included in Hubert's gross estate under § 2042. ■

[36] *Goodman v. Comm.*, 46–1 USTC ¶10,275, 34 AFTR 1534, 156 F.2d 218 (CA–2, 1946).

LO.7

Describe the components of the taxable estate.

TAXABLE ESTATE

After the gross estate has been determined, the next step is to determine the taxable estate. By virtue of § 2051, the **taxable estate** is the gross estate less the following: expenses, indebtedness, and taxes (§ 2053); losses (§ 2054); transfers to charities (§ 2055); and the marital deduction (§§ 2056 and 2056A). As previously noted, the charitable and marital deductions also have gift tax ramifications (§§ 2522 and 2523).

Expenses, Indebtedness, and Taxes. A deduction is allowed for funeral expenses; expenses incurred in administering property; claims against the estate; and unpaid mortgages and other charges against property, whose value is included in the gross estate (without reduction for the mortgage or other indebtedness).

Expenses incurred in administering community property are deductible only in proportion to the deceased spouse's interest in the community property.[37]

Administration expenses include commissions of the executor or administrator, attorney's fees, accountant's fees, court costs, and certain selling expenses for disposition of estate property.

Claims against the estate include property taxes accrued before the decedent's death, unpaid income taxes on income received by the decedent before he or she died, and unpaid gift taxes on gifts made by the decedent before death.

Amounts that may be deducted as claims against the estate are only for enforceable personal obligations of the decedent at the time of death. Deductions for claims founded on promises or agreements are limited to the extent that the liabilities were contracted in good faith and for adequate and full consideration. However, a pledge or subscription in favor of a public, charitable, religious, or educational organization is deductible to the extent that it would have constituted an allowable deduction had it been a bequest.[38]

Deductible funeral expenses include the cost of interment, the burial plot or vault, a gravestone, perpetual care of the grave site, and the transportation expense of the person bringing the body to the place of burial. If the decedent had, before death, acquired cemetery lots for himself or herself and family, no deduction for the cost of the lots is allowed, but the lots are not included in the decedent's gross estate under § 2033 (property in which the decedent had an interest).

Losses. Section 2054 permits an estate tax deduction for losses from casualty or theft incurred during the period when the estate is being settled. As is true with casualty or theft losses for income tax purposes, any anticipated insurance recovery must be taken into account in arriving at the amount of the deductible loss. Unlike the income tax, however, the deduction is not limited by a floor ($100) or a percentage amount (the excess of 10 percent of adjusted gross income). If the casualty occurs to property after it has been distributed to an heir, the loss belongs to the heir and not to the estate. If the casualty occurs before the decedent's death, it should be claimed on the appropriate Form 1040. The fair market value of the property (if any) on the date of death plus any insurance recovery is included in the gross estate.

As is true of certain administration expenses, a casualty or theft loss of estate property can be claimed as an income tax deduction on the fiduciary return of the estate (Form 1041). But a double deduction prohibition applies, and claiming the income tax deduction requires a waiver of the estate tax deduction.[39]

---

[37] *U.S. v. Stapf*, 63–2 USTC ¶12,192, 12 AFTR2d 6326, 84 S.Ct. 248 (USSC, 1963).

[38] § 2053(c)(1)(A) and Reg. § 20.2053–5.

[39] § 642(g).

Transfers to Charity. A deduction is allowed for the value of property in the decedent's gross estate that is transferred by the decedent through testamentary disposition to (or for the use of) any of the following.

1. The United States or any of its political subdivisions.
2. Any corporation or association organized and operated exclusively for religious, charitable, scientific, literary, or educational purposes.
3. Various veterans' organizations.

The organizations just described are identical to those that qualify for the Federal gift tax deduction under § 2522. With the following exceptions, they are also the same organizations that qualify a donee for an income tax deduction under § 170.

- Certain nonprofit cemetery associations qualify for income tax but not estate and gift tax purposes.
- Foreign charities may qualify under the estate and gift tax but not under the income tax.

No deduction is allowed unless the charitable bequest is specified by a provision in the decedent's will. Generally speaking, no charitable contribution deduction is permitted when an individual dies intestate (without a will). The amount of the bequest to charity must be mandatory and cannot be left to someone else's discretion. It is, however, permissible to allow another person—such as the executor of the estate—to choose which charity will receive the specified donation. Likewise, a bequest may be expressed as an alternative and still be effective if the noncharitable beneficiary disclaims (refuses) the intervening interest before the due date for the filing of the estate tax return (nine months after the decedent's death plus any extensions of time granted for filing).

Marital Deduction. The purpose of the **marital deduction** is to eliminate the major tax variations that exist between taxpayers residing in community property and common law states. Historically, for example, no marital deduction was allowed in a community property state because the surviving spouse already owned one-half of the community and that portion was not included in the deceased spouse's gross estate. In a common law state, however, most if not all of the assets often belonged to the breadwinner of the family. When that spouse died first, all of these assets were included in the gross estate. Recall that a dower or curtesy interest (regarding a surviving spouse's right to some of the deceased spouse's property) does not reduce the gross estate. To equalize the situation, therefore, a marital deduction is allowed upon the death of the first spouse.

Consistent with the approach taken under the income tax, the marital deduction treats spouses as a single person for transfer tax purposes. By making the marital deduction unlimited in amount, neither the gift tax nor the estate tax is imposed on outright interspousal transfers of property. The unlimited marital deduction even includes the deceased spouse's share of the community property transferred to the living spouse.

Under § 2056, the marital deduction is allowed only for property that is included in the deceased spouse's gross estate *and* that passes or has passed to the surviving spouse. Determining whether the parties are legally married is controlled by state law. Property that *passes* from the decedent to the surviving spouse includes any interest received as (1) the decedent's heir or donee; (2) the decedent's surviving tenant by the entirety or joint tenant; or (3) the beneficiary of insurance on the life of the decedent.

EXAMPLE 49

At the time of his death in the current year, Matthew owned an insurance policy on his own life (face amount of $100,000) with Minerva (his wife) as the designated beneficiary. Matthew and Minerva also owned real estate (worth $250,000) as tenants by the entirety (Matthew had furnished all of the purchase price). As to these transfers, $225,000 ($100,000 + $125,000) is included in Matthew's gross estate, and this amount represents the property that passes to Minerva for purposes of the marital deduction.[40] ■

Disclaimers can affect the amount passing to the surviving spouse. If, for example, the surviving spouse is the remainderperson under the will of the deceased spouse, a disclaimer by another heir increases the amount passing to the surviving spouse. This, in turn, will increase the amount of the marital deduction allowed to the estate of the deceased spouse.

A problem arises when a property interest passing to the surviving spouse is subject to a mortgage or other encumbrance. In this case, only the net value of the interest after reduction by the amount of the mortgage or other encumbrance qualifies for the marital deduction. To allow otherwise results in a double deduction since a decedent's liabilities are separately deductible under § 2053.

EXAMPLE 50

In his will, Oscar leaves real estate (fair market value of $200,000) to his wife. If the real estate is subject to a mortgage of $40,000 (upon which Oscar was personally liable), the marital deduction is limited to $160,000 ($200,000 – $40,000). The $40,000 mortgage is deductible under § 2053 as an obligation of the decedent (Oscar). ■

However, if the executor is required under the terms of the decedent's will or under local law to discharge the mortgage out of other assets of the estate or to reimburse the surviving spouse, the payment or reimbursement is an additional interest passing to the surviving spouse.

EXAMPLE 51

Assume the same facts as in Example 50, except that Oscar's will directs that the real estate is to pass to his wife free of any liabilities. Accordingly, Oscar's executor pays off the mortgage by using other estate assets and distributes the real estate to Oscar's wife. The marital deduction now becomes $200,000. ■

Federal estate taxes or other death taxes paid out of the surviving spouse's share of the gross estate are not included in the value of property passing to the surviving spouse. Therefore, it is usually preferable for the deceased spouse's will to provide that death taxes be paid out of the portion of the estate that does not qualify for the marital deduction.

LO.8

Determine the Federal estate tax liability.

COMPUTING THE FEDERAL ESTATE TAX

Once the taxable estate has been determined, post-1976 taxable gifts are added to arrive at the tax base. Note that pre-1977 taxable gifts do not enter into the computation of the tax base.

EXAMPLE 52

Joyce dies in 2004, leaving a taxable estate of $1,800,000. During her life, Joyce made taxable gifts as follows: $50,000 in 1975 and $100,000 in 1982. For estate tax purposes, the Federal estate tax base becomes $1,900,000 determined as follows: $1,800,000 (taxable estate) + $100,000 (taxable gift made in 1982). ■

[40]Inclusion in the gross estate falls under § 2042 (proceeds of life insurance) and § 2040 (joint interests). Although Matthew provided the full purchase price for the real estate, § 2040(b) requires inclusion of only one-half of the value of the property when one spouse predeceases the other.

TAX IN THE NEWS

WHAT ARE THE CHANCES?

Under the Tax Relief Reconciliation Act of 2001, the estate tax is scheduled to be phased out by 2010. Even more fantastic, a "sunset" provision in the Act reincarnates this tax as of January 1, 2011. (The "sunset" provision was mandated due to budget considerations.)

What are the chances that all of these provisions will take effect as scheduled? Hopefully, not very high! The sunset reincarnation is particularly absurd and makes meaningful estate planning impossible. Tax practitioners are placed in the ridiculous posture of advising clients to live at least until 2010 but to be sure and die before 2011.

Bills that would rescind the sunset provision have been introduced in Congress. If enacted, the legislation would kill the estate tax for good (as of 2010) and keep it from coming back. Such proposals, however, are not likely to succeed because of budget deficits generated by recent tax cuts and the conflict in Iraq. Perhaps an acceptable compromise would be a version that provides a generous exclusion amount and contains relief provisions to help preserve family businesses.

With the unified transfer tax rate schedule contained in § 2001(c), the tentative tax on the tax base is computed. Using the facts in Example 52, the tentative tax on $1,900,000 is $735,800 [$555,800 + (45% × $400,000)]—see Appendix A.

ESTATE TAX CREDITS

All available estate tax credits are subtracted from the tentative estate tax to arrive at the estate tax (if any) that is due.

Unified Tax Credit. Each taxpayer is entitled to one unified tax credit to offset all lifetime and death transfers. The unified tax credit must first be used to reduce gift taxes.

The amount of the unified credit is the same for lifetime and death transfers beginning in 1977 through 2003; however, the unified credit for death transfers continues to increase until 2010 when the estate tax is scheduled to be repealed as shown in Table 14–2.

Recall from previous discussion of this credit that the amount of the credit allowed depends upon the year of the transfer. Returning to Example 52, the credit allowed on the gift in 1982 was $62,800. Since the exemption equivalent of this amount is $225,000 (refer to Table 14–1), no gift tax was due on the transfer. On Joyce's death in 2004, however, the unified tax credit is $555,800, which is less than the tentative tax of $735,800 (refer to the discussion following Example 52). Disregarding the effect of any other estate tax credits, Joyce's estate owes a tax of $180,000 [$735,800 (tentative tax on a tax base of $1,900,000) – $555,800 (unified tax credit for 2004)]. Note that part of the unified tax credit offsets the $100,000 taxable gift that must be added to the taxable estate and the remaining credit reduces the tax on property included in the gross estate.

Credit for State Death Taxes. The Code allows a limited credit for the amount of any death tax actually paid to any state (or to the District of Columbia) attributable to any property included in the gross estate. This provision mitigates the harshness of subjecting the same property to multiple death taxes.

■ TABLE 14-2
Scheduled Increases in Unified Tax Credit and Exemption Amount Applicable to Estate Taxes

Year of Death	Amount of Credit	Amount of Exemption Equivalent
1977	$ 30,000	$ 120,667
1978	34,000	134,000
1979	38,000	147,333
1980	42,500	161,563
1981	47,000	175,625
1982	62,800	225,000
1983	79,300	275,000
1984	96,300	325,000
1985	121,800	400,000
1986	155,800	500,000
1987 through 1997	192,800	600,000
1998	202,050	625,000
1999	211,300	650,000
2000 and 2001	220,550	675,000
2002 and 2003	345,800	1,000,000
2004 and 2005	555,800	1,500,000
2006 through 2008	780,800	2,000,000
2009	1,455,800	3,500,000
2010	Estate tax repealed	Estate tax repealed

The credit allowed is limited to the lesser of the amount of tax actually paid or the amount provided for in a table contained in § 2011(b) (see Appendix A). The table amount is based on the adjusted taxable estate, which is defined for this purpose as the taxable estate less $60,000. No credit is allowed if the adjusted taxable estate is $40,000 or less.

EXAMPLE 53

Butch's taxable estate is $98,000, and the state of appropriate jurisdiction imposes a death tax of $1,500 on this amount. Since the adjusted taxable estate is $38,000 ($98,000 – $60,000), none of the $1,500 paid qualifies for the state death tax credit. ■

The Tax Relief Reconciliation Act of 2001 phases out § 2011 starting in 2002 at the rate of 25 percent per year. Thus, the credit allowed is 25 percent for 2004.

EXAMPLE 54

Butch's taxable estate is $200,000, and the state of appropriate jurisdiction imposes a death tax of $3,000 on this amount. Because the adjusted taxable estate is $140,000 ($200,000 – $60,000), the table amount limits the death tax credit to $1,200. For 2004, the amount allowed is $300 (25% × $1,200) (see Appendix A). ■

As Examples 53 and 54 illustrate, the credit allowed by § 2011 may be less than the amount of state death taxes paid. The reverse is possible but usually is not the case. Most states make sure that the minimum tax payable to the jurisdiction is at least equal to the credit allowed by the table. Sometimes this result is accomplished by a soak-up or sponge tax superimposed on the regular inheritance tax. Thus, if the regular inheritance tax yields $2,500, but the maximum credit allowed by the table is $3,200, a soak-up tax would impose an additional $700 in state death taxes. In other states, the state death tax liability depends entirely upon the amount allowed for Federal death tax purposes under the table. In the previous illustration, the state death tax would be an automatic $3,200.

TAX IN THE NEWS

Sorry, but We Won't Go Along

Already in dire financial straits due to the depressed economy, many states feel that they cannot afford the revenue loss that could result from the Federal tax cut of 2001. As a result, they are "decoupling" from various changes that were made. In other words, they are not adopting the changes for state tax purposes.

In the case of § 2011, many states are continuing to impose their soak-up or sponge tax despite the phaseout of the credit at the Federal level. Thus, in text Example 54, the state would require that the *full* table amount of $1,200 be paid even though the credit has been reduced from $1,200 to $300. Consequently, in such states, the amount, if any, of credit actually allowed under § 2011 for Federal estate tax purposes does not matter.

At least one state, however, is refusing to decouple. Florida is allowing its soak-up tax to "die a Federal death." As § 2011 expires, so will the state portion. Undoubtedly, this will improve Florida's retirement environment.

Credit for Tax on Prior Transfers. Suppose Nancy owns some property that she passes at death to Lisa. Shortly thereafter, Lisa dies and passes the property to Rita. Assuming both estates are subject to the Federal estate tax, the successive deaths result in a multiple effect. To mitigate the possible multiple taxation that might result, § 2013 provides relief in the form of a credit for a death tax on prior transfers. In the preceding hypothetical case, Lisa's estate may be able to claim as an estate tax credit some of the taxes paid by Nancy's estate.

The credit is limited to the lesser of the following amounts:

1. The amount of the Federal estate tax attributable to the transferred property in the transferor's estate.
2. The amount of the Federal estate tax attributable to the transferred property in the decedent's estate.

To apply the limitations, certain adjustments must be made that are not covered in this text.[41] However, it is not necessary for the transferred property to be identified in the present decedent's estate or for it to be in existence at the time of the present decedent's death. It is sufficient that the transfer of property was subjected to the Federal estate tax in the estate of the transferor and that the transferor died within a prescribed time period.

In particular, if the transferor dies within two years after or before the present decedent's death, the credit is allowed in full (subject to the preceding limitations). If the transferor died more than two years before the decedent, the credit is gradually phased out. If the transferor died within the third or fourth year preceding the decedent's death, 80 percent of the credit is allowed; if within the fifth or sixth year, 60 percent is allowed; if within the seventh or eighth year, 40 percent; if within the ninth or tenth year, 20 percent.

EXAMPLE 55

Under Nancy's will, Lisa inherits property. One year later Lisa dies. Assume the estate tax attributable to the inclusion of the property in Nancy's gross estate was $15,000 and the estate tax attributable to the inclusion of the property in Lisa's gross estate is $12,000. Under

[41] See the instructions to Form 706 and Reg. §§ 20.2013–2 and –3.

these circumstances, Lisa's estate claims a credit against the estate tax of $12,000 (refer to limitation 2). ■

EXAMPLE 56

Assume the same facts as in Example 55, except that Lisa dies three years after Nancy. The applicable credit is now 80% of $12,000, or $9,600. ■

Credit for Foreign Death Taxes. A credit is allowed against the estate tax for any estate, inheritance, legacy, or succession tax actually paid to a foreign country. For purposes of this provision, the term *foreign country* means not only states in the international sense but also possessions or political subdivisions of foreign states and possessions of the United States.

The credit is allowed for death taxes paid with respect to property (1) situated within the foreign country to which the tax is paid and (2) included in the decedent's gross estate. No credit is allowed for interest or penalties paid in connection with foreign death taxes.

The credit is limited to the lesser of the following amounts.

1. The amount of the foreign death tax attributable to the property situated in the country imposing the tax and included in the decedent's gross estate for Federal estate tax purposes.
2. The amount of the Federal estate tax attributable to particular property situated in a foreign country, subject to death tax in that country, and included in the decedent's gross estate for Federal estate tax purposes.

Both of these limitations may require certain adjustments to arrive at the amount of the allowable credit. These adjustments are illustrated in the Regulations.[42] In addition to the credit for foreign death taxes under the provisions of Federal estate tax law, similar credits are allowable under death tax conventions with a number of foreign countries.[43] If a credit is allowed under either the provisions of law or the provisions of a convention, the credit that is most beneficial to the estate should be claimed. Concept Summary 14–2 offers an overview of the Federal estate tax provisions.

PROCEDURAL MATTERS

A Federal estate tax return, if required, is due nine months after the date of the decedent's death.[44] The time limit applies to all estates regardless of the nationality or residence of the decedent. Not infrequently, an executor will request and obtain from the IRS an extension of time for filing Form 706 (estate tax return).[45]

The filing requirements parallel the exemption equivalent amounts of the unified tax credit available for each year (refer to Table 14–2). The filing requirements may be lower when the decedent has made taxable gifts after 1976.

EXAMPLE 57

Carlos dies in 2004, leaving a gross estate of $1,500,000. If Carlos did not make any post-1976 taxable gifts, his estate need not file Form 706. ■

[42] Reg. §§ 20.2014–2 and –3.

[43] At present, the United States has death tax conventions with the following countries: Australia, Austria, Canada, Denmark, Finland, France, Germany, Greece, Ireland, Italy, Japan, Netherlands, Norway, Republic of South Africa, Sweden, Switzerland, and the United Kingdom. The United States has gift tax conventions with Australia, Austria, Denmark, France, Germany, Japan, and the United Kingdom.

[44] § 6075(a).

[45] § 6081.

CONCEPT SUMMARY 14–2

Federal Estate Tax Provisions

1. The Federal gift and estate taxes are both excise taxes on the transfer of wealth.
2. The starting point for applying the Federal estate tax is to determine which assets are subject to tax. Such assets comprise a decedent's gross estate.
3. The gross estate generally will not include any gifts made by the decedent within three years of death. It does include any gift tax paid on these transfers.
4. Upon the death of a joint tenant, the full value of the property is included in the gross estate unless the survivor(s) made a contribution toward the cost of the property. Spouses are subject to a special rule that calls for automatic inclusion of half of the value of the property in the gross estate of the first tenant to die.
5. If the decedent is the insured, life insurance proceeds are included in the gross estate if either of two conditions is satisfied. First, the proceeds are paid to the estate or for the benefit of the estate. Second, the decedent possessed incidents of ownership (e.g., the right to change beneficiaries) over the policy.
6. In moving from the gross estate to the taxable estate, certain deductions are allowed. Under § 2053, deductions are permitted for various administration expenses (e.g., executor's commissions, funeral costs), debts of the decedent, and certain unpaid taxes. Casualty and theft losses incurred during the administration of an estate can be deducted in arriving at the taxable estate.
7. Charitable transfers are deductible if the designated organization holds qualified status with the IRS at the time of the gift or upon death.
8. Transfers to a spouse may qualify for the estate tax marital deduction.
9. The tax base for determining the estate tax is the taxable estate plus all post-1976 taxable gifts. All available credits are subtracted from the tax.
10. Of prime importance in the tax credit area is the unified tax credit. The unified tax credit is $555,800 (exemption equivalent of $1,500,000) for 2004.
11. Other Federal estate tax credits include credits for state death taxes, tax on prior transfers, and foreign death taxes.
12. If due, a Federal estate tax return (Form 706) must be filed within nine months of the date of the decedent's death.

EXAMPLE 58

Assume the same facts as in Example 57, except that Carlos made a taxable gift of $20,000 in 1980. Since the filing requirement now becomes $1,480,000 [$1,500,000 (the regular filing requirement for 2004) – $20,000 (the post-1976 taxable gift)], Carlos's estate must file Form 706. ■

LO.9

Appreciate the role of the generation skipping transfer tax.

The Generation Skipping Transfer Tax

In order to prevent partial avoidance of Federal gift and estate taxes on large transfers, the tax law imposes an additional generation skipping transfer tax.

THE PROBLEM

Previously, by structuring the transaction carefully, it was possible to bypass a generation of transfer taxes, as illustrated in the following example.

EXAMPLE 59

Amy gives assets to Eric (her grandson). Called a direct skip, the gift would circumvent any transfer taxes that would have resulted had the assets been channeled through Eric's parents. ■

THE SOLUTION

The generation skipping transfer tax (GSTT) is imposed when a generation is bypassed in favor of a younger generation.[46] The GSTT applies to lifetime transfers by gift and to transfers by death. The tax rate imposed is the highest rate under the gift and estate tax schedule for a given year. The GSTT rate is 48 percent for 2004. Consequently, the GSTT does not permit the use of the graduated rate structure.

In Example 59, the GSTT is imposed upon Amy when the gift is made to Eric. In this situation, not only will Amy be subject to the GSTT but the amount of the tax represents an additional gift to Eric.[47] Thus, if a gift is a direct skip (such as Example 59), the total transfer tax (the GSTT plus the gift tax) may exceed what the donee receives.

Though the GSTT seemingly yields a confiscatory result, every donor is entitled to an exemption. The exemption can be applied to whichever transfers the donor (or personal representative of the donor) chooses.

Under the Tax Relief Reconciliation Act of 2001, after 2003 the GSTT exemption becomes the exclusion amount applicable to the Federal estate tax. The exemption is $1,500,000 for 2004. Like the estate tax, the GSTT is scheduled to be phased out by 2010.

Suggested Further Readings

Jonathan G. Blattmachr and Lauren Y. Detzel, "Estate Planning Changes in the 2001 Tax Act—More Than You Can Count," *Journal of Taxation*, August 2001, pp. 74–90.

Kenneth A. Hansen, "Disclaiming Joint Marital Property to Fund a Deceased Spouse's Unified Estate Tax Credit," *Journal of Retirement Planning*, January-February 2002, pp. 31–37.

David M. Pfefferkorn and David H. Kirk, "Calculating the Lifetime Gifts Exemption: When a Million Dollars Is Not a Million Dollars," *Estate Planning*, August 2002, pp. 426–431.

KEY TERMS

Alternate valuation date, 14–18
Annual exclusion, 14–13
Community property, 14–12
Disclaimers, 14–11
Exemption equivalent, 14–8
Future interest, 14–13
Gross estate, 14–17
Inheritance tax, 14–3
Joint tenants, 14–12
Marital deduction, 14–27
Probate estate, 14–17
Taxable estate, 14–26
Taxable gift, 14–7
Tenants by the entirety, 14–12
Tenants in common, 14–12
Unified tax credit, 14–8
Unified transfer tax, 14–3

[46]The generation skipping transfer tax provisions are contained in §§ 2601–2663 of the Code.

[47]§ 2515.

PROBLEM MATERIALS

Problems

1. When Sarah died, she owned 10,000 shares of Oriole Corporation. The stock is traded in an over-the-counter market. The nearest trades before and after the date of Sarah's death are as follows.

	Per Share Mean Selling Price
Four days before Sarah's death	$210
Six days after Sarah's death	230

   Assuming the alternate valuation date is not elected, at what value should the Oriole stock be included in Sarah's gross estate?

2. In each of the following independent situations, indicate whether the transfer by Phillip is, or could be, subject to the Federal gift tax:
   a. Phillip makes a contribution to an influential political figure.
   b. In consideration of his upcoming marriage to Teri, Phillip establishes a savings account in Teri's name.
   c. Same as (b). After their marriage, Phillip establishes a joint checking account in the names of "Phillip and Teri."
   d. Same as (c). One year after the checking account is established, Teri withdraws all of the funds.
   e. Phillip enters into an agreement with Teri whereby he will transfer property to her in full satisfaction of her marital rights. One month after the agreement, the transfer occurs. Later Phillip and Teri are divorced.
   f. Phillip purchases U.S. savings bonds, listing ownership as "Phillip and Teri." Several years later, and after Phillip's death, Teri redeems the bonds.

3. In each of the following independent situations, indicate whether the transfer by Jeff is, or could be, subject to the Federal gift tax:
   a. Jeff purchases real estate and lists title as "Jeff and Chris as joint tenants." Jeff and Chris are brothers.
   b. Same as (a), except that Jeff and Chris are husband and wife.
   c. Jeff takes out an insurance policy on his life, designating Chris as the beneficiary.
   d. Same as (c). Two years later, Jeff dies and the policy proceeds are paid to Chris.
   e. Jeff takes out an insurance policy on the life of Gretchen and designates Chris as the beneficiary. Shortly thereafter, Gretchen dies and the policy proceeds are paid to Chris.
   f. Jeff pays for Chris's college tuition.

Issue ID

4. Jesse dies intestate (i.e., without a will) in May 2003. Jesse's major asset is a tract of land. Under applicable state law, Jesse's property will pass to Lorena, who is his only child. In December 2003, Lorena disclaims one-half of the property. In June 2004, Lorena disclaims the other half interest. Under state law, Lorena's disclaimer results in the property passing to Arnold (Lorena's only child). The value of the land (in its entirety) is as follows: $2 million in May 2003; $2.1 million in December 2003; and $2.2 million in June 2004. Discuss the transfer tax ramifications of these transactions.

5. In 2004, Jerold makes a gift of stock (adjusted basis of $650,000; fair market value of $1.5 million) to his daughter. Jerold has never made any prior taxable gifts. Jerold's current wife, Melanie, made a taxable gift of $750,000 in early 1976, upon which she paid a gift tax of $174,900. At the time of Melanie's gift, she was not married to Jerold. How much gift tax is due on the 2004 transfer:
   a. If the § 2513 election to split is not made?
   b. If the § 2513 election is made?

6. An estate holds the following assets.

	Fair Market Value	
	On Date of Death	Six Months Later
Land	$1,100,000	$1,150,000
Stock in Oriole Corporation	900,000	700,000
Stock in Kingfisher Corporation	800,000	750,000

The executor of the estate sells the Oriole stock for $710,000 three months after the decedent's death and sells the Kingfisher stock for $760,000 seven months after the decedent's death. Death occurred in January 2004.
   a. If the § 2032 election is made, how much is included in the gross estate?
   b. Would your answer to part (a) change if the Oriole stock was not sold but, instead, was distributed to an heir in satisfaction of a bequest in the decedent's will? Explain.
   c. What value should be included in the gross estate if the § 2032 election is not made?

7. In which, if any, of the following independent situations could the alternate valuation date *not be elected* in 2004? In all cases, assume that Bill and Nancy are husband and wife and that Nancy dies first.
   a. Nancy's will passes all of her property to Bill.
   b. Nancy's will passes all of her property to the First Baptist Church of Rome, Georgia.
   c. The election would decrease the value of Nancy's gross estate but increase her estate tax liability.
   d. The election would increase the value of Nancy's gross estate but decrease her estate tax liability.
   e. Nancy's gross estate is $1,480,000. She made a taxable gift of $40,000 in January 1976.
   f. The executor of Nancy's estate sells or otherwise disposes of all of her assets within five months of her death.

8. At the time of his death on May 12, 2004, Grover Carson held the following assets.

	Fair Market Value
Stock in Coot Corporation	$400,000
Stock in Vireo Corporation	500,000
City of Buffalo bonds	800,000
Promissory note issued by Doreen Carson	200,000

On June 1, 2004, Grover's estate received cash dividends and interest as follows: $6,000 (Coot stock), $7,500 (Vireo stock), and $12,000 (Buffalo bonds). The dividends were declared on April 9, with the record dates being May 7 for Coot and May 13 for Vireo. Of the bond interest, $1,100 had accrued since May 12. Doreen Carson is Grover's adult daughter and is a successful insurance broker. Her note was non-interest-bearing and was forgiven by Grover in his will.

As to these transactions, how much is included in Grover's gross estate?

9. Curt dies in late 2004. Previously, he was involved in the following transfers.

   - In 2002, Curt made a gift to his daughter of an insurance policy on his life. The policy has a maturity value of $80,000.
   - In 2003, Curt made a gift to his son of stock worth $340,000. The transfer resulted in a gift tax of $35,000. The stock is worth $290,000 on the date of Curt's death.
   - In 1999, Curt paid off the mortgage on his mother's personal residence. The payment resulted in a gift tax of $12,000.

   As to these transactions, how much is included in Curt's gross estate?

10. In 1998, Felix and Zoe purchased a commercial single-premium annuity. Felix furnished 70% of the cost, and his wife, Zoe, provided the 30% balance. Under the terms of the policy, Felix is to receive $120,000 per year for his life. If Zoe survives Felix, she is to receive $90,000 per year for her life.
    a. If Felix dies in 2004 when the survivorship feature is worth $800,000, how much, if any, is included in his gross estate?
    b. What is included in Zoe's estate when she dies after Felix?

11. At the time of Paul's death in 2004, he was involved in the following transactions.
    - He was an equal tenant in common with Pat in real estate worth $2 million. The property had been purchased by Paul in 1980 at a cost of $400,000.
    - Paul was a participant in his employer's contributory qualified pension plan. The plan benefit of $2.1 million was paid to Pat as the designated beneficiary and was made up as follows.

Employer's contributions	$800,000
Paul's contributions	700,000
Income earned by the plan	600,000

    - Paul was covered by his employer's group term life insurance plan for employees. His policy proceeds of $50,000 were paid to Pat, the designated beneficiary.

    Discuss the tax ramifications (including gift and income) of these transactions, based on the following assumptions.
    a. Paul and Pat are father and son.
    b. Paul and Pat are husband and wife.

12. In 1990, Bertha purchased an office building for $1.2 million listing title as "Bertha and Barney, joint tenants with the right of survivorship." In the same year, as a wedding present to Barney and his new wife, Teri, Bertha gives them her former home (worth $600,000). Title to the home is recorded as "Barney and Teri, tenants by the entirety with the right of survivorship." In 2004, Barney is killed in a skiing accident and is survived by his mother (Bertha) and wife (Teri). If at the time of Barney's death the office building has a value of $1.5 million and the residence is worth $900,000, what is included in his gross estate as to these properties? Did any gift tax consequences ensue in 1990?

13. In 1991, Gabe purchased realty for $1.4 million and listed title to the property as "Gabe and Nelda, joint tenants with right of survivorship." Nelda predeceases Gabe in 2004 when the realty is worth $2 million. Gabe and Nelda are brother and sister.
    a. What, if any, are the gift tax consequences in 1991?
    b. What, if any, are the estate tax consequences in 2004?

14. Assume the same facts as in Problem 13, except that Gabe and Nelda are husband and wife.
    a. What, if any, are the gift tax consequences in 1991?
    b. What, if any, are the estate tax consequences in 2004?

15. In each of the following independent situations, determine how much, if any, should be included in Eric's gross estate.
    a. Hope, Eric's wife, owns a policy on Eric's life (maturity value of $200,000). Upon Eric's death, the proceeds are paid to Ward, Hope's son, who is the designated beneficiary.
    b. Eric owns a policy on Hope's life (maturity value of $200,000 and current value of $40,000) with Ward, Eric's son, as the designated beneficiary.
    c. Assume the same facts as in (b) except that Eric's estate (not Ward) is the designated beneficiary.
    d. Upon Eric's death, Ward collected $200,000 on a policy he owned on Eric's life. The policy was originally taken out by Eric and was given by him to Ward two years ago.

16. Prior to his marriage to Camille, Terrence purchased an insurance policy on his life (maturity value of $200,000) with his mother as the designated beneficiary. Ten years later, Terrence predeceases Camille, and the policy proceeds are paid to his mother.

Premiums paid on the policy originated 60% from Terrence's separate property and 40% from community funds. Discuss the tax consequences of this situation if all parties live in:

a. California.
b. Texas.

17. Comment on how each of the following independent situations should be handled for estate tax purposes.
    a. At the time of his death, $18,000 of Homer's church pledge was unpaid. Homer's executor paid the pledge during the administration of the estate.
    b. At the time of her death, Saleha (a widow) owned 10 cemetery lots (each worth $5,000), which she had purchased many years before for herself and her family.
    c. At the time of his death, Stanley was delinquent in the payment of back Federal income taxes. Stanley's executor pays the taxes from assets of the estate.

18. At the time of his death in the current year, Jerome owned the following real estate.

Tract A	$1,000,000
Mortgage on tract A	(200,000)
Tract B	700,000
Mortgage on tract B	(100,000)

Under Jerome's will, both tracts of land pass to Janice (Jerome's surviving spouse). However, Jerome's will directs the executor to pay off the mortgage on tract B from the remainder interest passing to the children.

a. How much marital deduction will Jerome's estate be allowed?
b. What is the deduction for indebtedness under § 2053?

19. Determine the state death tax credit that will be allowed under § 2011 in each of the following independent situations. All deaths occur in 2004.
    a. The taxable estate is $90,000. The state death tax paid is $2,000.
    b. The adjusted taxable estate is $840,000. The state death tax paid is $32,000.
    c. The adjusted taxable estate is $1,040,000. The state death tax paid is $8,500.
    d. The adjusted taxable estate is $900,000. The state death tax is a soak-up (sponge) tax that is paid.

20. Under Martina's will, Paige (Martina's sister) inherits property. Three years later Paige dies. Determine Paige's credit for tax on prior transfers based on the following assumptions.
    a. The estate tax attributable to the inclusion of the property in Martina's gross estate is $400,000, and the estate tax attributable to the inclusion of the property in Paige's gross estate is $480,000.
    b. The estate tax attributable to the inclusion of the property in Martina's gross estate is $500,000, and the estate tax attributable to the inclusion of the property in Paige's gross estate is $450,000.

21. In each of the following independent situations, determine the decedent's final estate tax liability (net of any unified tax credit).

	Decedent			
	Homer	**Darcy**	**Gretchen**	**Kirk**
Year of death	1999	2000	2003	2004
Taxable estate	$600,000	$800,000	$1,100,000	$ 900,000
Post-1976 taxable gifts—				
Made in 1986	600,000	—	—	—
Made in 1987	—	700,000	—	—
Made in 1999	—	—	800,000	—
Made in 2003	—	—	—	1,100,000

Comprehensive Tax Return Problem

Tax Return Problem

22. During 2003, William and Margaret Rusk (Social Security numbers 010–56–0603 and 165–52–3929) resided at 432 Sunken Court, Funston, UT 84602. In their 26 years of marriage, the Rusks have always lived in common law states. William Rusk is a major partner in a local stock brokerage firm, and Margaret Rusk is a well-known plastic surgeon. Both practices have been highly successful. Over the years, the Rusks have received gifts and inheritances from various sources and have invested the funds wisely.

    In 2003, the Rusks made the following transfers (without adjustment for the annual exclusion or the marital deduction):

	William Rusk	Margaret Rusk
Cash donation to the building fund of Brigham Young University.	$ 50,000	$ 50,000
Birthday gift (Jaguar auto) from Margaret to William.	—	68,000
Payments made as a result of Joan Canby's retina operation. Joan is Margaret's aunt but does not qualify as her dependent. The payments were made directly to the care providers (e.g., hospital, surgeons).	—	19,000
Donation to the political campaign of a candidate who ran unsuccessfully for the U.S. Congress.	21,000	21,000
Cash Christmas gift to Ida Gambel who has been the Rusks' housekeeper for 10 years.	12,000	—
Equal gifts of stock in Wren Corporation valued at $600,000 to each child.	1,800,000*	—
Margaret transfers stock in Eagle Corporation to Angela.	—	550,000**

*The stock in Wren Corporation is publicly traded and was inherited by William from his mother in 1973 when it had a value of $750,000. The Rusks have three children (Angela, age 24; Arthur, age 23; and Helen, age 21).

**The stock in Eagle Corporation is publicly traded and was received by Margaret from her mother in 1983. At that time it had a value of $200,000 and a basis to Margaret's mother of $120,000.

Complete Form 709 (U.S. Federal Gift Tax Return) for gifts made by the Rusks in 2003. The election to split gifts is to be made. Assume that neither William nor Margaret has made any prior taxable gifts.

Research Problems

THOMSON RIA

*Note: Solutions to Research Problems can be prepared by using the **RIA Checkpoint® Student Edition** online research product, which is available to accompany this text. It is also possible to prepare solutions to the Research Problems by using tax research materials found in a standard tax library.*

Research Problem 1. In 2000, Mortimer made a gift of a mineral interest to his son. Mortimer had never made any prior taxable gifts. The property given was valued at $37,000. Due to the operation of the annual exclusion and the unified transfer tax credit, no gift tax was due on the transfer. However, because the gift exceeded the annual exclusion, Mortimer properly filed a Form 709 (Federal Gift Tax Return) in a timely manner.

Mortimer dies in 2004 leaving a taxable estate of $2,100,000. In arriving at the tax base, the executor adds in the 2000 taxable gift at the amount reported on Form 709. Upon audit of the estate's Form 706 (Estate Tax Return), the IRS redetermines the value of the 2000 taxable gift to be $190,000 (not $37,000). This change increases the amount of estate tax due. Mortimer's executor thinks that such an adjustment is precluded by the statute of limitations. What do you think?

Partial list of research aids:
§§ 2001(f) and 2504(c).

Research Problem 2. Jacob, a 63-year-old widower, makes a gift of land to his daughter, Emily. The gift occurs in late 2003 at a time when the land has a value of $180,000. Due to a liquidity problem on Jacob's part, he conditions the transfer on Emily's agreement to pay any gift tax that results.

The land originally cost Jacob $26,000 and has been held by him as an investment for more than 20 years. Jacob's only prior taxable gifts took place in 2002 and totaled $1 million. No gift tax resulted due to the availability of the exemption equivalent.

a. Determine Emily's gift tax under this "net gift."
b. Does Jacob have any income tax consequences as a result of the transfer? Explain.

Partial list of research aids:
Rev.Rul. 75–72, 1975–1 C.B. 310.
Diedrich v. Comm., 82–1 USTC ¶9419, 50 AFTR2d 82–5054, 102 S.Ct. 2414 (USSC, 1982).

Research Problem 3. Sal and Sally Tennant (brother and sister) purchased real estate for $100,000. They acquired title as joint tenants. They each contribute $10,000 toward the purchase price, and the balance is provided by an $80,000 mortgage signed by both Sal and Sally. Sal makes all the mortgage payments in the amount of $20,000. When he dies five years later, the mortgage is $60,000, and the value of the property is $200,000. How much is included in Sal's gross estate? With respect to the mortgage, what amount may be deducted as a debt against his gross estate?

Partial list of research aids:
§§ 2040(a) and 2053.
Rev.Rul. 79–302, 1979–2 CB 328.

Research Problem 4. Ben owns 60% of the voting stock of Mini Corporation. Mini owns a policy on Ben's life and holds all incidents of ownership. To what extent are the proceeds of the policy included in Ben's gross estate at his death if the corporation is the beneficiary? How would your answer change if the 40% minority shareholder is the beneficiary?

Partial list of research aids:
Reg. § 20.2042–1(c)(6).

Internet Activity

Use the tax resources of the Internet to address the following questions. Do not restrict your search to the World Wide Web, but include a review of newsgroups and general reference materials, practitioner sites and resources, primary sources of the tax law, chat rooms and discussion groups, and other opportunities.

Research Problem 5. The ultimate design of the Tax Relief Reconciliation Act of 2001 is to repeal the estate tax but retain the gift tax. While the Act and accompanying Conference Committee Report are silent as to why Congress intended this result, it was based on concerns raised by several legal commentators. Using the Internet, locate and comment on one (or more) of these commentaries.

Research Problem 6. Find a calculator on the World Wide Web that will estimate the Federal estate or gift tax liability. Use this device to check your answer to one of the problems that you have completed in this chapter.

CHAPTER 15

Gift and Estate Tax Planning

LEARNING OBJECTIVES

After completing Chapter 15, you should be able to:

LO.1
Plan gifts so as to minimize gift taxes and avoid estate taxes.

LO.2
Compare the income tax basis rules applying to property received by gift and by death.

LO.3
Plan gifts so as to minimize the income taxes for the family.

LO.4
Determine the types of assets that should be gifted to reduce total transfer and income taxes for the family.

LO.5
Maximize the tax benefits of giving to charities.

LO.6
Reduce probate costs in the administration of an estate.

LO.7
Recognize which types of trusts can be used to reduce the amount of the gross estate.

LO.8
Use bypass trusts to fully utilize the unified tax credits of both spouses.

LO.9
Understand how trusts can be used to provide for the needs of the surviving spouse while minimizing the transfer taxes for the family.

http://wft.swlearning.com

OUTLINE

TAX TALK

He who has the base necessities of life should pay nothing; taxation on him who has a surplus may, if need be, extend to everything beyond necessities.

—Jean Jacques Rousseau

Gift and estate tax planning involves the use of various instruments to minimize the tax consequences of transfers to one's spouse and children. Gift giving is a popular device that can be utilized to achieve both nontax and tax goals of the family unit. Trusts are also often employed to transfer income and property interests to different members of the family according to each person's specific needs.

Effective planning involves a consideration not only of estate and gift taxes but also of the income tax ramifications to both the transferor and the transferees. This chapter begins with a discussion of the advantages and disadvantages of gift giving. Next the use of trusts in effective tax planning is introduced. Finally, specific trusts designed to minimize taxes on transfers to the spouse and minors are discussed. This chapter builds on the basic principles of estate and gift taxation addressed in Chapter 14.

LO.1

Plan gifts so as to minimize gift taxes and avoid estate taxes.

Gift Planning

A systematic gift-giving program over the life of an individual can result in substantial tax savings by limiting the amount of property that will ultimately be subject to estate taxes. However, the decision to give property to one's children is also affected by nontax considerations. One major consideration when embarking on a lifelong gift program is whether parents are willing to relinquish control over the property to the children. An outright gift requires that the title of the property be transferred to the children, thereby giving them ownership rights. Although substantial tax savings may result from gift giving, parents may be reluctant to adopt such a program because of the immaturity of their children. Also, the parents may fear that they will need the assets later in life.

Although parents are sometimes hesitant to make outright gifts to children, in numerous instances such transfers are desirable. Parents may wish to help their children move into adult life. Thus, parents might make gifts to help their children finance the purchase of a home or automobile. However, to the extent that transfers to children constitute support as defined by state law, they will not be deemed to be taxable gifts. Another commonly encountered rationale for gifting is the parents' desire to motivate their children to actively participate in a family-owned business.[1] This might be facilitated by gifting stock or other ownership interests in the business to the children. In most instances, these gifts will not be included in the estate because of the annual exclusion.

When advising a client of the appropriateness of a gift-giving program, it is important to disclose both the potential tax savings and these nontax considerations. While some clients may appreciate the tax savings associated with lifetime transfers, the program will only succeed if the client is willing to relinquish some control of the assets being transferred.

MINIMIZING GIFT TAXES

Recall from Chapter 14 that the gift tax is assessed on the fair market value of the property at the date of the transfer after subtracting the annual exclusion. This exclusion is available only for present interests and does not apply to transfers made at death through the estate. Because a new annual exclusion is available each year, spacing gifts over multiple years increases the amount that can be transferred free of gift tax.

EXAMPLE 1

In 2003 and 2004, Cora makes annual gifts of $11,000 to each of her five grandchildren. During these two years, Cora will have transferred $110,000 [$11,000 (annual exclusion) × 5 (number of donees) × 2 (number of years)] with no gift tax consequences. ■

For married donors, the § 2513 election to split gifts can double the amount of a tax-free transfer.

EXAMPLE 2

Assume the same facts as in Example 1, except that Cora is married to Leon. If Leon consents to the § 2513 elections, Cora can transfer $220,000 [$22,000 (annual exclusion for two donors) × 5 (number of donees) × 2 (number of years)] with no gift tax consequences. ■

From a practical standpoint, many donors who want to take advantage of the annual exclusion do not wish to give cash or near-cash assets (e.g., marketable securities). Where the value of the gift property substantially exceeds the amount of the annual exclusion, as is often the case with real estate, gifts of a partial interest are an attractive option.

EXAMPLE 3

Seth and Kate want to give a parcel of unimproved land to their three adult children and five grandchildren as equal owners. The land has an adjusted basis of $100,000, is held in joint tenancy with right of survivorship by Seth and Kate, and has an appraised value of $352,000 as of December 20, 2004. On December 23, 2004, Seth and Kate convey a one-half undivided interest in the land to their children and grandchildren as tenants in common. This is followed by a transfer of the remaining one-half interest on January 5, 2005. Neither transfer causes gift tax, because each is fully offset by annual exclusions of $176,000 [$22,000 (annual exclusion for two donors) × 8 (number of donees)]. Thus, in a period of less than two weeks, Seth and Kate transfer $352,000 in value free of any Federal tax consequences. ■

Further examination of Example 3 leads to the following observations.

- The § 2513 election to split gifts is not necessary, because the land was held in joint tenancy. If the land had been held by one of the spouses as separate

[1]Issues relating to the transfer of a business from parents to their children are addressed in Chapter 16.

property, the election would have been necessary to generate the same $352,000 of exclusions. The annual exclusion for 2005 is assumed to remain at $11,000.

- Good tax planning generally dictates that sizable gifts of property be supported by reliable appraisals. In the case of successive gifts of partial interests in the same property, multiple appraisals should be obtained to cover each gift. This advice was not followed in Example 3 due to the short interval between gifts. Barring exceptional circumstances, the value of real estate will not change within a period of less than two weeks.

Avoiding State Transfer Taxes. Another element that may favor lifetime transfers over death transfers is the state's transfer tax system. All states impose some type of death tax, but only a few impose a gift tax. Thus, a gift may completely avoid a state transfer tax.

The states currently imposing a state gift tax include Connecticut, Louisiana, North Carolina, and Tennessee. Unfortunately, this could lead to multiple taxation of the same transfer. Unlike the *state death* tax credit (see the discussion of § 2011 in Chapter 14), the Code does not allow a credit for state gift taxes paid. In effect, the only credit allowed against the Federal gift tax is the unified transfer tax credit.

Effect of Gift Taxes Paid. When a taxable gift is made, the unified credit is applied first to offset the gift tax liability. When gifts exceed the allowable annual exclusions and the equivalent exemption amount of the unified credit, gift taxes must be paid, and the donor loses the use of this money. In effect, the donor is prepaying the transfer tax, thereby making the gift less attractive. The time value of money should be considered when making large gifts.

EXAMPLE 4

In 1999, Gail makes a gift that results in a gift tax of $100,000. She dies five years later. Presuming a 10% rate of return, the gift tax paid would have been worth $161,051 at Gail's death. Therefore, Gail has lost $61,051 by making the gift. ■

The analysis used in Example 4 requires refinement to yield a meaningful result. Variables that need to be considered include the following.

- The life expectancy of the donor at the time of the gift. Actuarial tables can provide a start, but this kind of information must be adjusted for the general health and lifestyle of the donor. In any event, accurately predicting when a specific person will die is more chance than science.
- The interest factor used. Anticipating even short-rate changes, erratic at best, becomes mere guesswork as the time interval increases.
- Any change in the value of the property from the point of gift to the date of death. Appreciation in value during this interval makes the gift look like a wise choice. The opposite is true if value declines.

Finally, a present value analysis must consider the estate tax effect of any gift tax paid. Except for gifts within three years of death (see Chapter 14), the gift tax paid itself is not subject to estate tax. Referring to Example 4, the $100,000 in gift taxes paid is not included in Gail's gross estate.

MINIMIZING ESTATE TAXES

A review of the estate tax formula in Figure 14–2 shows that *only* the fair market value as of the date of the gift on transferred property is added back to the taxable estate for post-1976 gifts. Thus, in addition to removing any gift taxes paid from the estate, lifetime transfers also remove the postgift appreciation on the transferred property from the donor's gross estate.

EXAMPLE 5

In 1986, Wilma transfers land to Karen. At the time of the transfer, the land had a fair market value of $60,000, which resulted in a taxable gift of $50,000 after subtracting the $10,000 annual exclusion. When Wilma dies in 2004, the value of the land is $250,000. By making the gift, Wilma has kept $200,000 in value from being subject to a transfer tax. ■

Besides real estate, other assets that often appreciate in value include insurance, art objects, and special collections such as rare books, coins, and stamps.

LO.2

Compare the income tax basis rules applying to property received by gift and by death.

MINIMIZING INCOME TAXES—BASIS CONSIDERATIONS

As previously mentioned, family tax planning also involves an assessment of the income tax positions of the transferor (the donor or decedent) and the transferee (the donee or heir). The following sections review the basis rules for properties acquired by gift and through the estate.

Basis of Property Acquired by Gift. The income tax basis of property acquired by gift depends on whether the donee sells the property for a gain or for a loss and, in certain cases, on when the gift occurred.

- If the gift took place after 1920 and before 1977, the donee's basis for gain is the donor's adjusted basis plus any gift tax paid on the transfer (but not to exceed the fair market value on the date of the gift). The basis for loss is the lower of the basis for gain or the fair market value of the property on the date of the gift.

EXAMPLE 6

In 1975, Norm receives stock as a gift from Lana. The stock cost Lana $20,000 and was worth $100,000 on the date of the gift. As a result of the transfer, Lana paid a gift tax of $10,000. Norm's income tax basis for gain or loss is $30,000 [$20,000 (Lana's basis) + $10,000 (gift tax paid by Lana)]. Norm does not have a different basis for loss because the fair market value of the property on the date of the gift ($100,000) is greater than the basis for gain ($30,000). ■

- If the gift took place after 1976, the donee's basis for gain is the donor's adjusted basis plus only the gift tax attributable to the appreciation of the property to the point of the gift. For this purpose, use the *taxable gift* amount (i.e., fair market value of gift less annual exclusion). The basis for loss is the lesser of the basis for gain or the fair market value of the property on the date of the gift.[2] The effect of this rule is to deny a donee any increase in basis for the gift tax attributable to the donor's adjusted basis.

EXAMPLE 7

Assume the same facts as in Example 6, except that the gift took place in 2004.

Lana's adjusted basis on the date of the gift	$20,000
Gift tax attributable to the $80,000 appreciation [($80,000/$89,000) × $10,000] rounded	9,000
Norm's income tax basis for gain	$29,000

Norm's basis for loss also is $29,000, based on the same reasoning as in Example 6. ■

[2] §§ 1015(a) and (d).

TAX IN THE NEWS

Carryover Basis—Will It Ever Happen?

Pursuant to the Tax Relief Reconciliation Act of 2001, the Federal estate tax is to be phased out by the end of 2009. If the phaseout takes place as planned, what will be the impact on the current "step-up" and "step-down" rules of § 1014? Different basis rules will come into play, and § 1014 will cease to apply.

Under new Code § 1022, scheduled to become effective in 2010, an heir will receive a carryover basis from a decedent. With certain exceptions, the basis determination rules governing property transferred by gift will also apply to transfers by death. For basis purposes, therefore, donees and heirs will be treated much the same. Whether the estate tax will ever be entirely eliminated is uncertain.

- If the gift took place at any time after 1920, and the amount realized from sale or other disposition is between the basis for loss and the basis for gain, no gain or loss is recognized.

Because the donee usually assumes the donor's basis in the property, transfers by gifts are considered carryover situations. Consistent with this approach, the donee's holding period includes that of the donor.[3]

Basis of Property Acquired by Death. Except as otherwise noted in the following sections, the income tax basis of property acquired from a decedent is the fair market value on the date of death or, if elected, on the alternate valuation date. When property has appreciated in value between acquisition and date of death, a **step-up in basis** occurs for the estate or heir of the deceased owner. A step-up in basis means that appreciation existing at death escapes the application of the Federal income tax.

EXAMPLE 8

Upon her death in 2004, Nancy owned real estate (adjusted basis of $200,000) worth $800,000 that she leaves to Jack. Assuming that the alternate valuation date is not elected, Jack's income tax basis in the property becomes $800,000. Thus, a subsequent sale of the real estate by Jack for $800,000 results in no gain or loss to him. ■

EXAMPLE 9

Assume the same facts as in Example 8, except that, shortly before her death, Nancy sells the real estate for $800,000. Nancy has a taxable gain of $600,000 for income tax purposes. ■

By contrasting Examples 8 and 9, one can see that the rules place a premium on holding appreciated property until death, to take advantage of the step-up in basis rule. The same cannot be said for property that has declined in value. In this case, death causes a **step-down in basis.** This result should be avoided if selling the property would generate a deductible income tax loss.

EXAMPLE 10

Upon his death in 2004, Wes held stock as an investment with an adjusted basis of $200,000 and a fair market value of $120,000. Because only $120,000 is included in the gross estate, the basis of the stock to the estate or heir is this amount. Had Wes sold the stock before his death, a deduction for some or all of the $80,000 loss might have been available. ■

[3]§ 1223(2).

The holding period to the estate or heir of property acquired from a decedent is automatically treated as long term.[4]

If the property does not pass through a decedent's estate, there is no step-up (or step-down) in income tax basis.

EXAMPLE 11

In 1980, Aaron and Sandra (husband and wife) purchased land for $200,000, listing title as "joint tenants with the right of survivorship." Each furnished one-half of the purchase price. In 2004, when the land is worth $600,000, Aaron dies. Under § 2040 (see Chapter 14), Aaron's estate includes $300,000 as to the land. Sandra's income tax basis in the land is $400,000, determined as follows: $100,000 (Sandra's original cost basis) + $300,000 (amount passing through Aaron's estate). ■

Community Property. Although there is usually no change in basis for property that is not part of a decedent's gross estate, a special exception applies to community property. In such situations, the surviving spouse's half of the community takes the same basis as the half included in the deceased spouse's gross estate.[5] The following example illustrates the effect of this special rule.

EXAMPLE 12

Leif and Rosa were husband and wife and lived in a community property state. At the time of Leif's death, they owned $1.6 million of assets with a basis of $200,000. If the $1.6 million of assets are community property, only one-half of this value is included in Leif's gross estate. Assuming Leif bequeaths his half of the community property to Rosa, her basis in the assets is $1.6 million. ■

Comparison of Basis Laws for Lifetime and At-Death Transfers. When considering the income tax effect of a transfer on the donee or heir, the basis rules of §§ 1014 and 1015 warrant close examination. When appreciated property is involved, receiving the property from a decedent is preferred to a lifetime transfer.

EXAMPLE 13

Keith plans to transfer unimproved real estate (basis of $100,000 and fair market value of $400,000) to his daughter, Esther. If the property passes by death, Esther's basis is $400,000. If the property passes by gift, her income tax basis (presuming no gift tax adjustment) is $100,000. The step-up effect of § 1014 provides Esther with an additional basis of $300,000. ■

EXAMPLE 14

Keith plans to transfer unimproved real estate (basis of $150,000 and fair market value of $100,000) to his daughter, Esther. If the property passes by death, Esther's basis is $100,000. If the property passes by gift, her income tax basis is $100,000 for losses and $150,000 for gains. Receiving the property as a gift, therefore, might be more advantageous to Esther than the complete step-down in basis under § 1014. ■

For Keith in Example 14 the options are not attractive. By making a gift or passing the property by death, Keith sacrifices the potential loss deduction of $50,000. Presuming he holds the land as an investment, he can use the capital loss to offset capital gains or apply it against ordinary income to the extent of $3,000 per year. Unused capital losses can be carried over indefinitely but will not survive Keith's death.

DIGGING DEEPER 1

Find more information on this topic at our Web site: ***http://wft-advanced.swlearning.com.***

Step-Up in Basis and the One-Year Rule. Section 1014(e) was enacted to prevent abuse of the step-up in basis rule, as illustrated in the following example.

---

[4] § 1223(11).

[5] § 1014(b)(6).

EXAMPLE 15

Gary and Hazel are husband and wife and reside in a common law state. When the couple learns that Hazel has a terminal illness, Gary transfers property (basis of $100,000 and fair market value of $400,000) to her as a gift. Hazel dies shortly thereafter, and under the provisions of her will, the property returns to Gary. ■

If it were not for § 1014(e), what have the parties accomplished? No gift tax occurs on the transfer from Gary to Hazel because of the application of the marital deduction. Upon Hazel's death, her bequest to Gary does not generate any estate tax because the inclusion of the property in her gross estate is offset by the marital deduction. Through the application of the general rule of § 1014, Gary ends up with the same property, with its basis stepped up to $400,000. Thus, the procedure enables Gary to get a "free" increase in income tax basis of $300,000.

When applicable, § 1014(e) forces Gary (the original donor) to assume the property with Hazel's predeath basis. Hazel's basis would have been determined under § 1015 (basis of property acquired by gift). The basis would have been $100,000 (donor's adjusted basis) plus any gift tax adjustment (none in this case) and any capital additions made by the donee (none in this case), or $100,000. If § 1014(e) applies to Example 15, Gary ends up where he started (with $100,000) in terms of income tax basis.

For § 1014(e) to be operative, both of the following conditions must be satisfied.

- The decedent must have received appreciated property as a gift during the one-year period ending with his or her death.
- The property is acquired from the decedent by the donor (or the donor's spouse).

Note that this transaction may achieve its goal of increasing the income tax basis if the time period between the date of the gift and date of death exceeds one year.

The application of § 1014(e) is not limited to transfers between spouses. The provision applies with equal effect if, for example, the donor-heir were a daughter of the donee-decedent. In such cases, the technique used in Example 15 might also be susceptible to the imposition of gift or estate taxes, because of the unavailability of the marital deduction.

Income in Respect of a Decedent. Income in respect of a decedent (IRD) is income earned by a decedent to the point of his or her death but is not reportable on the final income tax return because of the method of accounting used. IRD is most frequently applicable to cash basis decedents who have accrued income when they die. IRD also occurs when a taxpayer at the time of death held installment notes receivable on which the gain has been deferred.

IRD is included in the gross estate at its fair market value on the appropriate valuation date for estate tax purposes. However, the decedent's income tax basis transfers to the estate or heirs. IRD may not receive a basis step-up or step-down for income tax purposes.[6] Furthermore, the recipient of IRD must classify it in the same manner (e.g., ordinary income, capital gain) as the decedent would have.

EXAMPLE 16

George was a sole proprietor and reported business income using the cash method for tax purposes. When he died, he had $10,000 of accounts receivable with a basis of zero. For estate tax purposes, the gross estate must report an asset of $10,000. However, the basis in

[6] § 1014(c).

Concept Summary 15–1

Income Tax Basis Concepts

1. The income tax basis of property acquired by gift is the donor's basis with appropriate adjustment for any gift tax paid. With built-in loss situations in which the fair market value of the gift is less than the donor's basis, the income tax basis is the fair market value of the property on the date of the gift.
2. The income tax basis of property acquired through the death of the owner is its fair market value on the appropriate estate tax valuation date.
3. No step-up in basis is allowed if the property returns to the donor or donor's spouse within one year.
4. Items of income in respect of a decedent do not undergo a step-up or step-down in basis.

the accounts receivable for income tax purposes is zero. The heirs (or the estate) must report income as the receivables are collected. ■

DIGGING DEEPER 2

*Find more information on this topic at our Web site: **http://wft-advanced.swlearning.com**.*

LO.3

Plan gifts so as to minimize the income taxes for the family.

MINIMIZING INCOME TAXES THROUGH INCOME SHIFTING

One way to lower the overall tax burden on the family unit is to shift income from high-bracket taxpayers to lower-bracket family members. To accomplish this shifting, however, income-producing property must be transferred.

If a gift of property is to shift income to the donee, the transfer must be *complete*. Continued control over the property by the donor may lead the IRS to question the finality of the gift.

EXAMPLE 17

Vera, subject to a 35% marginal income tax rate, owns corporate bonds. Vera transfers the bonds by gift to her four children. The children range in age from 14 to 19 years and are all in the 10% income tax bracket. Since the children are the bondholders after the transfer, they are taxed on any interest received, and the family as a unit saves 25% on each dollar of interest income taxed to the children. ■

The new maximum rates on dividends and net long-term capital gain provide an excellent opportunity to take advantage of the 5 percent rate that normally would apply to children. The JGTRRA of 2003 set the maximum rate at 15%/5%, with the 5 percent rate being applicable to taxpayers below the 25 percent bracket (i.e., those in the 10 percent and 15 percent brackets).

EXAMPLE 18

The Stewarts have four school-age children, all age 14 or older. On June 3, 2004, they give 1,000 shares of Grey Corporation stock to each child. The stock was acquired as an investment several years ago at a cost of $4 per share. On the date of the gift, the stock has a value of $22 per share. Each child sells the stock two weeks later for $22 per share. Assuming the children have no other income, the tax consequences to each are as follows.

Sale price (1,000 shares × $22)	$22,000
Basis (1,000 shares × $4)	(4,000)
Net capital gain	$18,000
Tax rate applicable	× 5%
Tax per child	$ 900

Compare the total tax of $3,600 ($900 × 4) for the children with what would have happened if there had been no gift and the Stewarts had sold the stock.

Sale price (4,000 shares × $22)	$ 88,000
Basis (4,000 shares × $4)	(16,000)
Net capital gain	$ 72,000
Tax rate applicable	× 15%
Total tax	$ 10,800

Thus, the Stewarts save $7,200 in tax ($10,800 – $3,600) by shifting the gain to their children. (Note: In this case, the donors' holding period and basis carry over to the donees. Due to the annual exclusion, no taxable gift results.) ■

To be successful, the income-shifting technique illustrated in Examples 17 and 18 requires the donee to be in a lower tax bracket than the donor. When the donee is under age 14, however, kiddie tax treatment can neutralize the income tax effect of a gift. Under this provision, certain unearned income (e.g., interest, dividends, capital gains) received by a child is taxed at the marginal tax rate applicable to the parent.[7] In Example 17, suppose that one of Vera's children was not yet 14 years old. Giving bonds to the child would not serve the intended purpose. Even if the transfer was complete and the child recognized the interest, the applicable tax rate would be 35 percent, rather than 10 percent, on unearned income in excess of $1,600. Once the child reaches age 14, however, kiddie tax treatment no longer applies.

Income Tax Consequences to the Donor. Generally, a gift of property results in no income tax consequences to the donor. Two important exceptions, however, involve installment notes receivable and U.S. savings bonds.

A gift of an installment note receivable is a taxable disposition, and the donor is treated as if the note had been sold for its fair market value.[8] As a result, the donor recognizes the deferred profit.

EXAMPLE 19

In 2003, Adam sells real estate (basis of $200,000) to Norm (an unrelated party) for $800,000. Norm (the obligor) issues two notes of $400,000 each, one due in 2004 and one due in 2005. Adam (the obligee) does not elect out of the installment method. In 2004 and before the first note becomes due, Adam gives both notes to his son, Sam. On this date, the notes have a fair market value of $760,000. As a result of the gift to Sam, Adam recognizes a gain of $560,000 [$760,000 (fair market value of the notes) – $200,000 (Adam's unrecovered basis)]. ■

A gift of U.S. savings bonds is not effective unless the bonds are re-registered in the donee's name. This forces the donor to recognize any deferred income accrued on the bonds. The result may surprise donors who expect to postpone the recognition of interest income until the bonds are redeemed. Thus, the donor who desires to avoid income tax consequences should avoid gifts of installment notes receivable and U.S. savings bonds.

For purposes of contrasting tax results, what happens if these properties are passed by death?

- Installment notes receivable are taxed to whoever collects the notes (the estate or heirs).[9] If the notes are forgiven or canceled by the decedent's will, the income is taxed to the estate.

[7]§ 1(g). See Chapter 15 in *West's Federal Taxation: Taxation of Business Entities* for a more detailed discussion of this provision.

[8]§ 453B(a).

[9]§ 453B(c).

TAX IN THE NEWS

How to Save Taxes and Protect the Environment

What do Ted Turner, Robert Redford, Clint Eastwood, and James Baker (former secretary of state) have in common? Besides being celebrities and financially well-to-do, all have issued **conservation easements** in some or all of the real estate they own. By this means, any "scenic view" that currently exists is preserved. The owner is precluded from obstructing the view by further development of the property. Allegedly, the transfer of the easement is motivated by the owner's desire to "conserve the environment." Realistically, the transfer is largely tax motivated.

The steps involved in creating a conservation easement and the tax consequences that ensue are as follows.

- After the easement is drafted, the owner transfers it to a conservation trust. Usually, the trust is already in existence, having been created by an environmental group, and operates under the auspices of a local government agency.
- The owner obtains a generous appraisal as to the value of the easement transferred.
- The owner claims the value of the easement as an income tax deduction.
- The value of the property retained (e.g., residence, vacation home) is accordingly reduced by the value of the easement for ad valorem property tax purposes.
- Upon the owner's death, the gross estate includes the property at a discounted value due to the restrictions contained in the easement.

In summary, the conservation easement saves income, property, and estate taxes. The donor receives all of this plus the aura of being hailed as an environmentalist.

- Deferred interest income on U.S. savings bonds is taxed to whoever redeems the bonds (the estate or heirs).
- Recapture potential disappears at death.[10] The estate or heirs take the property free of any recapture potential existing at the time of the owner's death.

LO.4

Determine the types of assets that should be gifted to reduce total transfer and income taxes for the family.

TYPES OF ASSETS TO GIFT

In summary, if parents are willing to gift their property, lifetime transfers offer several tax advantages: utilization of the annual exclusion and unified credit, removal of the amount of gift tax paid and appreciation on the transferred property from the gross estate, and the opportunity to shift income to the lower tax brackets of the children. However, some disadvantages may include the prepayment of transfer taxes and the loss of the step-up in basis.

In general, if the estate will be subject to high marginal estate tax rates, it is better to gift highly appreciating assets to keep post-gift appreciation out of the estate. If the estate will not be subject to tax because of the unified credit, it would be wiser to transfer the property at the time of death so that the beneficiary will receive a higher basis.

On the other hand, if an asset is depreciating, a gift can have adverse tax consequences. First, the transfer tax will be assessed on the fair market value at the time of the gift, which will be greater than it would have been at death. Second, the donee's basis will be lower than the donor's basis if the property continues to

[10] §§ 1245(b)(1) and 1250(d)(1). Contrast this result with what happens when § 1245 or § 1250 property is transferred by gift. Here, the recapture potential carries over to the donee.

decline and the donee sells it at a loss. As a result, the decline in value during the time the donor held the property will never be recognized.

If the tax planner has the choice between gifting assets of the same value with either a low or a high basis, the decision will depend upon whether the donee plans to sell the property. If the donee plans to sell the property, all things being equal, the higher-basis property should be gifted. If the donee does not plan to sell the property, high income–producing assets should be given to donees in lower income brackets to maximize overall aftertax rates of return.

LO.5

Maximize the tax benefits of giving to charities.

GIVING TO CHARITIES

Although this discussion of transfer tax planning has concentrated thus far on the factors involved in making transfers among family members, consideration should also be given to the most effective way to transfer wealth to charities. As individuals become older, they may desire to give something back to society.

As a general guide to obtaining overall tax savings, lifetime charitable transfers are preferred over testamentary dispositions. For example, an individual who gives $10,000 to a qualified charity during his or her life secures an income tax deduction, avoids any gift tax, and reduces the gross estate by the amount of the gift. By way of contrast, if the $10,000 is willed to charity, no income tax deduction is available, and the amount of the gift is includible in the decedent's gross estate (though later deducted for estate tax purposes). The testamentary transfer merely neutralizes the effect of the inclusion of the property in the gross estate (inclusion under § 2033 and then deduction under § 2055).

To ensure that an estate tax deduction is allowed for a charitable contribution, the designated recipient must fall within the classifications set forth in § 2055. The status of the organization on the date the transfer becomes effective controls, and not the date the will authorizing the transfer was executed.

EXAMPLE 20

In 1982, Lisa drew up and executed a will in which she provided for $100,000 to pass to the Rose Academy, a nonprofit educational organization described in § 2055(a)(2) and, at that time, approved by the IRS as a qualified recipient. In 1984, the qualified status of the academy was revoked for practicing racial discrimination in the enrollment of its student body.[11] Lisa dies in 2004, and the executor of her estate, being compelled to satisfy the provisions of the will, transfers $100,000 to the academy. ■

Even though Lisa may have been unaware of the action taken by the IRS in 1984, her estate is not allowed a charitable deduction. The recipient was no longer qualified on the date of Lisa's death. It may be that Lisa, even if she had known about the probable loss of the charitable deduction, would still have wished the bequest carried out as originally conceived. If not, it is easy to see that the error was of Lisa's own making because of her failure to review her estate planning situation.

One way to circumvent the quandary posed by Example 20 (other than changing Lisa's will before her death) is to express the charitable bequest in more flexible terms. The transfer to the academy could have been conditioned on the organization's continued status as a qualified recipient at the time of Lisa's death. Alternatively, Lisa's will may grant her executor the authority to substitute a different, but comparable, charitable organization *that is qualified* in the event of the disqualification of the named group.

[11]Most of the organizations that are qualified recipients (which will permit the donor a charitable deduction) are listed in IRS Publication 78. This compilation, revised and supplemented from time to time, addresses § 170 (income tax deduction) transfers. Publication 78, with the exceptions noted in Chapter 14, also applies to § 2055 (estate tax deduction) and § 2522 (gift tax deduction) transfers.

On occasion, a charitable bequest depends on the issuance of a disclaimer by a noncharitable heir. Such a situation frequently arises with special types of property or collections, which the decedent may feel a noncharitable heir should have a choice of receiving.

EXAMPLE 21

Megan specified in her will that her valuable art collection is to pass to her son or, if the son refuses, to a designated and qualified art museum. At the time the will was drawn, Megan knew that her son was not interested in owning the collection. If, after Megan's death, the son issues a timely disclaimer, the collection passes to the museum, and Megan's estate takes a charitable deduction for its death tax value. ■

EXAMPLE 22

Dick's will specifies that one-half of his disposable estate is to pass to his wife and the remainder of his property to a specified qualified charitable organization. If the wife issues a timely disclaimer after Dick's death, all of the property passes to the charity and qualifies for the § 2055 charitable deduction. ■

Has the son in Example 21 acted wisely if he issues the disclaimer in favor of the museum? Although such a disclaimer will provide Megan's estate with a deduction for the value of the art collection, consider the income tax deduction alternative. If the son accepts the bequest, he can still dispose of the collection (and fulfill his mother's philanthropic objectives) through a lifetime donation to the museum. At the same time, he obtains an income tax deduction under § 170. Whether this saves taxes for the family depends on a comparison of the mother's estate tax bracket with the estimated income tax bracket of the son. If the value of the collection runs afoul of the percentage limitations of § 170(b)(1), the donations could be spread over more than one year. If this is done, and to protect against the contingency of the son's dying before the entire collection is donated, the son can neutralize any potential death tax consequences by providing in his will for the undonated balance to pass to the museum.

The use of a disclaimer in Example 22 would be folly. It would not reduce Dick's estate tax; it would merely substitute a charitable deduction for the marital deduction. Whether the wife issues a disclaimer or not, no estate taxes will be due. The wife should accept her bequest and, if she is so inclined, make lifetime gifts of it to a qualified charity. In so doing, she generates an income tax deduction for herself.

DIGGING DEEPER 3

Find more information on this topic at our Web site: ***http://wft-advanced.swlearning.com.***

Estate Planning

Estate planning considers the nontax and tax aspects of death. In the nontax area, trusts often are used to reduce the costs of probating an estate and secure privacy regarding the wealth of the family. In the tax area, trusts are created to reduce the size of the gross estate, maximize the marital deduction, and fully utilize the unified credit. In addition, benefits from income shifting can be obtained if the trust is properly constructed.

Trusts provide many nontax and tax advantages. When creating a trust, an estate planner must be aware of the family's nontax objectives. The planner should evaluate which trusts meet those needs and what the tax consequences are. Although only attorneys may draft the trust documents, tax accountants should be aware of how trusts fit into the overall estate plan.

TAX IN THE NEWS

HOW LONG SHOULD PROBATE TAKE?

Although Marilyn Monroe died on August 5, 1962, her estate is still in probate. Surely, a probate that has already continued for over 40 years must establish some kind of record!

The trouble stems from the wording of Marilyn's will. According to its terms, equal shares of the estate went to her psychoanalyst and her manager. The psychoanalyst then left his half to a mental health care center, while the manager's portion went to his children.

The manager's children dispute the transfer to the medical institution. They contend that Marilyn's intent was to benefit persons, not organizations.

Why all of the controversy? Perhaps it is because the estate generates annual income of more than $1 million!

LO.6

Reduce probate costs in the administration of an estate.

REDUCING PROBATE COSTS

The probate estate consists of all properties subject to disposition by an executor according to the terms of the will or by the state laws of intestate succession if there is no will. The administration is conducted under the supervision of a local court, usually called a probate court. In certain states, probate functions are performed by county courts, surrogate courts, or orphan's courts.

Probate costs include attorney fees, accountant fees, appraisal and inventory fees, court costs, expenses incident to the disposition of assets and satisfaction of liabilities, litigation costs needed to resolve will contests, and charges for the preparation of tax returns. The total amount of probate costs cannot be accurately predicted because so many variables are involved. A conservative range might be from 5 to 15 percent of the amount of the probate estate.

A number of procedures can be used to reduce the probate estate by designating the beneficiaries of the property during one's life. These procedures include use of the following instruments.

- Owning property as joint tenants (or tenants by the entirety) with right of survivorship. Upon death, the property automatically passes to the surviving tenant and generally is not subject to probate.
- Making life insurance payable to a beneficiary other than the estate.
- Establishing a trust during one's lifetime. Assets transferred to a trust pass according to the terms of the trust, thereby avoiding the probate process.

Another advantage of bypassing the probate estate is that the beneficiary can obtain immediate possession and enjoyment of the property. The probate process can become prolonged, and the heir may have to await the final settlement of the estate before getting the property.

In terms of probate costs, the ownership of out-of-state real estate can cause significant problems. Out-of-state ownership is not uncommon with decedents who have relocated after retirement or who maintain vacation homes.

EXAMPLE 23

After retirement and five years before his death, Ted moved from Nebraska to Arizona. At death, Ted still owns a rental house in Nebraska and a vacation home in Idaho. To clear title to these properties, Ted's executor must institute ancillary probate proceedings in Nebraska and Idaho. This will result in additional attorney fees and court costs. ■

The solution to the dilemma posed in Example 23 is to dispose of these properties before death by establishing joint tenancies or transferring the properties into a trust. Although this may generate some legal fees, they will be far less than the cost of ancillary probate proceedings.

In addition to avoiding probate costs, trusts are often used because of the privacy they afford to the family. Trust documents are not public documents whereas wills are open to the public for inspection. Many wealthy families use trusts to prevent the press from obtaining information about the amount and nature of the properties they own and the share passing to each beneficiary. Both of these nontax attributes make trusts a popular planning device.

LO.7

Recognize which types of trusts can be used to reduce the amount of the gross estate.

USING TRUSTS TO REDUCE THE AMOUNT OF THE GROSS ESTATE

Unlike the probate estate, the gross estate determines what property is subject to the Federal estate tax. In fact, many of the steps taken to reduce the probate estate do not have a similar effect on the gross estate.

Valuation procedures sometimes can be applied to control the amount of the gross estate. When the estate comprises assets that have declined in value shortly after death, use of the alternative valuation date under § 2032 is advised (see Chapter 14). However, one of the most important tax planning strategies to reduce both the probate and the gross estate is to gift appreciating property.

Trusts often are used as a vehicle for making gifts of property. In fact, the creation of a trust may be preferable to an outright gift of property because the trust allows the income interest in the property to be separated from the property interest itself.

EXAMPLE 24

Lesly creates a trust by transferring stocks into the title of the trust. According to the terms of the trust document, the dividend income is to be distributed annually to Mary, Lesly's sister, and when Mary dies, the stocks are to be transferred to Paul, her son. ■

In Example 24, Mary is deemed to be the **income beneficiary.** Because she is receiving the income for her life, she has a **life estate** in the property. Paul is the **remainder beneficiary** because he receives what is remaining in the trust after the income beneficiary dies. In this case, the stocks constitute the property that is left after all the dividend income has been distributed. Property held in trust is often referred to as the **corpus.**

Revocable Trusts. When a trust is created during the transferor's life, the first issue that must be addressed is whether the trust is irrevocable or revocable. If the transferor retains the power to revoke (terminate) the trust, he or she has not relinquished control over the property, and a gift has not been made at the time the trust is created. In addition, § 2038 requires that the fair market value of the trust property at the time of the transferor's death be included in his or her estate if the transferor still retains this power at death. Furthermore, the transferor is taxed on the income as it is earned in the trust and is deemed to make gifts every year when the income is distributed. The gifts of income distributions are present interests and qualify for the annual exclusion.

EXAMPLE 25

Agnes transfers $100,000 of securities into a trust during her lifetime. The income from the securities is to be paid annually to Betty for as long as Betty lives, and the remainder is to go to Cathy at Betty's death. Agnes retains the power to revoke the trust at any time. If Agnes revokes the trust, the property will revert back to Agnes.

Agnes has not created a gift when the trust is established. She must pay income taxes on the income as it is earned. Each year when the trust distributes income to Betty, Agnes has made a taxable gift equal to the amount of the distribution less the annual exclusion. If Betty dies before Agnes, then Agnes has made a gift of the property to Cathy in the year of Betty's death when the transfer actually occurs. If Betty does not die before Agnes and Agnes does not revoke the trust during her life, the fair market value of the property will be included in Agnes's gross estate. ■

The tax effects discussed in Example 25 are the same as if the trust had never been created. If Agnes owns $100,000 in securities outright, she will pay income taxes on the income. Each year, when she distributes the cash received as income, she makes a gift of a present interest to Betty. If she decides to distribute the securities to Cathy, she again makes a gift of a present interest in the year of transfer. If she does not gift the property to Cathy, then the fair market value of the securities will be includible in Agnes's gross estate. She then could transfer the property to Cathy through the terms of her will.

The question may arise as to why a family would want to create a revocable trust if no tax savings are recognized. As previously discussed, property placed in trust is not subject to the probate process and resulting costs. In addition, the privacy of the family members is respected. Thus, nontax factors motivate the creation of this type of trust, which is popularly referred to as a **living trust.**

The capacity in which the transferor retains the power to revoke or terminate the trust is immaterial. Often, the transferors will name themselves as the trustees of a living trust, and the terms of the trust will grant them the power to revoke the trust. In other cases, the transferors may initially name another person as trustee with the power to revoke but later appoint themselves as trustees. In such cases, the property is included in the transferors'gross estate. If, however, the power to revoke was held at all times solely by a person other than the transferors and the transferors did not reserve a right to assume these powers, the property is not included in their gross estate.

The Code and Regulations make it clear that a transferor cannot avoid inclusion of trust property in the gross estate under § 2038 by relinquishing a power within three years of death.[12] If the transferor converts a revocable trust into an irrevocable trust by changing the terms of the trust within three years of death, the fair market value of the trust property must still be included in the gross estate.

Irrevocable Trusts. If the transferor is willing to relinquish control over the property placed in trust, significant tax savings can be obtained. Refer to Example 25, and assume instead that Agnes creates an irrevocable trust with the terms of the trust specifying that the income is to be distributed to Betty for life and that upon Betty's death, the stocks are to be distributed to Cathy. If the trust is irrevocable, Agnes cannot terminate the trust, and unless specified otherwise, the property cannot revert back to Agnes. In this case, Agnes has made a gift of the income interest to Betty and a gift of the corpus to Cathy at the time the trust is established.

At this point, the question arises as to how the two gifts should be valued. Recall that the fair market value of the securities at the time of the transfer is $100,000. The economic concept of valuation is that the fair market value of an asset represents the present value of all expected future cash flows. Therefore, the $100,000 must be divided into the present value of the expected future income payments to Betty over her life and the present value of the property that will pass to Cathy when Betty dies. The sum of the two gifts must equal $100,000.

Since the calculation involves present value, a discount rate must be selected. The Internal Revenue Code valuation rules require the use of a current monthly discount rate that is equal to 120 percent of the applicable Federal mid-term rate, which is derived from the average market yield on U.S. Treasury obligations with

[12] § 2038(a)(1).

maturities of three to nine years. Fortunately, these rates are published by the Treasury Department and do not have to be computed. For purposes of this example, assume that the discount rate is 8.8 percent.

In addition, the calculation depends on how long Betty is expected to live. Once again, the Treasury Department has developed a table of life expectancies based on the age of an individual. The table no longer differentiates between male and female. For example, assume that at the time the trust is created, Betty is 45 years old. According to Appendix A, Table 5, the factor for the remainder interest of an individual at age 45, assuming an 8.8 percent discount rate, is 0.10792. Thus, the gift of the remainder to Cathy is valued at $10,792 ($100,000 × 0.10792). The factor for the life estate can be obtained by subtracting the remainder interest factor from 1. By multiplying the $100,000 by the factor that represents the present value of the life estate (0.89208), the gift to Betty is valued at $89,208. Note that both of these amounts represent the gifts to Betty and Cathy valued as of the date the trust is created. In addition, the gift to Betty qualifies for the annual exclusion because she is receiving a present interest in the property whereas Cathy must wait to receive her interest until Betty dies.

In summary, two completed gifts have been made when the trust is established. Agnes has retained no power over the property; therefore, the property should not be included in her gross estate at death. At the time of Agnes's death, the two taxable gifts will be added to her estate as post-1976 gifts valued as of the date of the gifts. Any appreciation on the stocks since the time the trust was established escapes transfer taxation. In addition, if the income is required to be distributed to Betty annually, Betty will be taxed on the income as it is earned each year.

A property transfer into an irrevocable trust achieves essentially the same tax consequences as an outright gift. Post-transfer appreciation is not subject to estate taxes, the annual exclusion is available for gifts of present interests, and income is shifted away from the transferor. Although the tax savings may be significant, once again the transferor must be willing to part with control over the property.

Whenever an irrevocable trust is drafted, it must be scrutinized to determine if the transferor retains any prohibited powers that may render the trust incomplete for gift tax purposes. The law addresses a number of powers that, if retained by the transferor, will cause the property to be included in the gross estate, often with disastrous results. This area becomes very complex because a transfer may be deemed to be a completed gift and yet must be included in the transferor's gross estate as illustrated in the following example.

EXAMPLE 26

Adam transfers $100,000 of securities into an irrevocable trust. The income may be distributed to Ben during the next 10 years after which time the securities and any accumulated income must be distributed to Ben. Adam retains the power to determine each year whether the income should be distributed to Ben or accumulated within the trust. ■

According to Regulation § 25.2511–2(d), Adam has made a gift of both the income and the remainder interests to Ben at the time the trust is created. Assuming a 7.8 percent interest rate and a term certain of 10 years, the income interest is valued at $52,814 ($100,000 × 0.52814) and the remainder at $47,186 ($100,000 × 0.47186) as shown in Appendix A, Table B. The income interest does not qualify for the annual exclusion because the income is not required to be distributed at least annually. Thus, a total gift of $100,000 has been made. However, according to § 2038, if Adam dies within the 10-year period and at death had the power to alter the timing of the payments to Ben, then the fair market value of the securities must be included in Adam's gross estate. If Adam must include the total value of the property in his estate, neither of the gifts must be added back as a post-1976 gift, and the estate obtains a credit for any gift taxes paid.

Irrevocable Transfers with a Retained Life Estate. An individual may want to create a trust in which he or she retains a life estate in the property for himself or herself. In this manner, the individual is assured of lifetime payments from the trust. In addition, the individual knows how the property will pass at his or her death. While these benefits make this type of trust very attractive, the tax consequences can be severe.

Code § 2036 was enacted on the premise that the estate tax can be avoided on lifetime transfers only if the decedent did not retain control over the property. The logic of this approach is somewhat difficult to dispute. One should not be able to escape the tax consequences of property transfers at death while remaining in a position to enjoy some or all of the fruits of ownership during life.

Under § 2036, the fair market value of any property transferred by the deceased during lifetime for less than adequate consideration must be included in the gross estate if the decedent retained the right to enjoy or possess the income from the property up to the time of death. "The possession or enjoyment of, or the right to the income from, the property," as it appears in § 2036(a)(1), is considered to be retained by the decedent to the extent that such income is applied toward the discharge of a legal obligation of the decedent. The term *legal obligation* includes a legal obligation of the decedent to support a dependent during the decedent's lifetime.[13]

The following examples illustrate the practical application of § 2036.

EXAMPLE 27

Carl's will passes all of his property to a trust, income to Alan for Alan's life (Alan is given a life estate). Upon Alan's death, the corpus goes to Melissa (Melissa is granted a remainder interest). On Alan's death, none of the trust property is included in his gross estate. Although Alan held a life estate, § 2036 is inapplicable because he was not the transferor of the property (Carl was). Code § 2033 (property owned by the decedent) causes any income distributions Alan was entitled to receive at the time of his death to be included in his gross estate. ■

EXAMPLE 28

By deed, Nora transfers the remainder interest in her ranch to Marcia, retaining for herself the right to continue occupying the property until death. Upon Nora's death, § 2036 requires that the fair market value of the ranch be included in her gross estate. ■

In the following example, the interaction of both the gift and estate tax consequences is examined.

EXAMPLE 29

Dan creates an irrevocable trust by transferring $200,000 of securities into the trust. Dan is 50 years old when he creates the trust and designates that the income from the trust is to be paid to himself as long as he lives. When Dan dies, the securities are to pass to Everett.

Dan has retained a life estate, and when he dies, the fair market value of the securities must be established and included in his gross estate. Dan will be taxed on the income for income tax purposes.

A gift of the remainder interest is made when the trust is created. Everett will obtain the property when Dan dies. It is a gift of a future interest. To determine the value of the gift, Everett's relationship to Dan must first be addressed. If Everett is not a family member, then the value of the remainder is determined in the normal manner, namely, $36,310 ($200,000 × 0.18155) assuming a 7.4% discount rate. Gift tax will have to be paid to the extent it exceeds the unified credit. When Dan dies, the gift will not have to be added back as a post-1976 gift because the full fair market value of the property has to be included in his gross estate. The estate is entitled to a credit for any gift taxes paid. ■

[13]Reg. § 20.2036–1(b)(2).

In Example 29, if Everett is an *applicable family member*, then § 2702 applies and the value of Dan's retained interest is automatically assigned a value of zero. Furthermore, the value of the remainder interest is equal to the total fair market value of the property on the date the trust is created. Dan is deemed to make a gift of $200,000 to Everett and must pay the gift taxes accordingly. When Dan dies, the fair market value of the property must be included in his estate, and the $200,000 gift does not have to be added back as a post-1976 gift.

The § 2702 rules apply only when the trust is a **grantor retained interest trust (GRIT).** Applicable family members include the transferor's spouse, an ancestor or descendant of the transferor or the transferor's spouse, a sibling of the transferor, and a spouse of such ancestor, descendant, or sibling. There are special ways of structuring this type of trust to avoid the automatic zero valuation of the retained interest; however, they are beyond the scope of this text. At this point, it is sufficient to be aware of the pitfalls that can arise when setting up a regular GRIT.

Section 2036 not only requires that the fair market value of trust property be included in the transferor's gross estate when he or she retains a life estate, but also includes the situation in which the transferor retains the right to designate who is entitled to receive the income in a given year.

EXAMPLE 30

Sally, age 60, creates an irrevocable trust by transferring $500,000 of income-producing property into the title of the trust. She names herself as trustee and drafts the trust document such that the trustee has the power to determine whether the income should be distributed to Mark, her son, or Lily, her daughter. When Sally dies, the property will pass to Josephine, her younger daughter. ■

Under § 2036, Sally, the transferor and original owner of the property, retains a prohibited power over the property even though she has no rights to the income herself. The mere power to determine which of the income beneficiaries (appointed in the trust document) is to receive income in a given year is a prohibited power. If the fair market value of the trust property appreciates and it is worth $700,000 when Sally dies, then her gross estate will include $700,000. In addition, at the time the trust is created, Sally has made a gift of the remainder interest valued at $500,000, since Josephine is a family member and Sally's retained interest is valued at zero. Once again, the gift will not be added back to Sally's estate as a post-1976 gift. Sally will be taxed on the income for income tax purposes, and gifts will be made subject to the annual exclusion as income is distributed annually to either Mark or Lily.

Powers of Appointment. A **power of appointment** is a power to determine who shall own or enjoy, presently or in the future, the property subject to the power.[14] It must be created by another and does not include a power created or retained by the transferor when he or she transfers his or her own property into a trust. Thus, in Example 30, Sally retains the power to determine who is to enjoy the income interest; however, she does not possess a power of appointment because she was the original owner of the property. She may set up a trust in which she gives a power of appointment to another person as illustrated in the following example.

EXAMPLE 31

Sally transfers property into an irrevocable trust. According to the terms of the trust, the trustee has the power to determine who will receive the income and who ultimately will receive the property based on a list of beneficiaries (appointees) specified in the trust document. Sally names Edward, her brother, as the trustee. If Edward dies or refuses to be the trustee, then she designates the First National Bank to be the trustee. ■

[14] § 2041.

In this example, Sally has given Edward a power of appointment. This type of trust is often called a **sprinkling trust** because the trustee has the power to sprinkle or spray income or property among the beneficiaries based on that trustee's own judgment. Powers of appointment fall into one of two classifications: *general* and *limited.* A general power of appointment is one in which the holder of the power has the right to appoint himself, his creditors, his estate, or the creditors of his estate as the beneficiary. In contrast, a limited power enables the holder to appoint to others but *not* to herself, her creditors, her estate, or the creditors of her estate.

EXAMPLE 32

Justin, Monica's father, leaves his property in trust, life estate to Monica and remainder to whichever of Monica's children she decides to appoint in her will. Monica's power is not a general power of appointment because she cannot exercise it in favor of herself. Thus, regardless of whether Monica exercises the power, none of the trust property subject to the power is included in her gross estate. ■

In Example 31, if Edward were among the list of potential appointees, then he would be a holder of a general power of appointment. As the holder of a general power of appointment, when Edward dies, the fair market value of the property subject to the power must be included in his gross estate. If he is the holder of a limited power of appointment when he dies, nothing is includible in his gross estate. In fact, no gift, income, or estate consequences are attributed to the holder of a limited power of appointment. On the other hand, the holder of a general power of appointment is deemed to own the property for income tax purposes and is taxed on the income even though he or she never exercises the power for himself or herself.

If the holder of a general power of appointment exercises the power by giving an interest in the property to a beneficiary, then the holder has made a gift and is subject to gift taxes. If the holder exercises the power in favor of himself or herself, no gift results because the holder cannot give himself or herself a gift. However, to the extent that the holder does not consume the income or property, it will be included in his or her gross estate when he or she dies.

Some complicated laws apply if the holder of a general power of appointment allows the power to lapse. The lapse of a general power of appointment is subject to gift tax only to the extent that the value of the property that could have been appointed exceeds the greater of either $5,000 or 5 percent of the aggregate value of the property out of which the appointment could have been satisfied. Thus, if the general power of appointment is over only a very small portion of the property, the lapse of the power should not trigger any estate and gift tax consequences. The $5,000 or 5 percent exclusion does not apply in the year of death for estate tax purposes.

EXAMPLE 33

Ben transfers $1,000,000 into a trust. He gives Silvia, his daughter, the annual right to withdraw up to $45,000 for her use any time during the year. To the extent that she does not withdraw this amount, the income is accumulated in the trust and will be transferred along with the corpus to Dan, her brother, when Silvia dies. Since this amount is less than $50,000 (5% × $1,000,000), if Silvia does not exercise her right during the year, she has made an irrevocable transfer to Ben, but no taxable gift has been made. However, if Silvia allows the power to lapse in the year of her death, she must include $45,000 in her gross estate. ■

One significant exception applies to the holder of a power of appointment. A power of appointment is not considered to be general if the holder has the right

BRIDGE DISCIPLINE

Bridge to Law

Asset protection is a significant part of estate planning. The estate planner should have a general background in debtor/creditor law, particularly as it relates to what assets creditors can seize and the overall vulnerability of business and personal activities that can result in exposure to creditor claims. For example, one common misconception is that assets placed in a revocable living trust are protected from creditors' claims. Knowledge of the risks involved in this arrangement may lead the client to adopt another financial planning strategy.

to consume or invade the property for his or her own benefit, as long as that right is limited to an ascertainable standard. The standard must relate to the holder's health, education, support, or maintenance. A power to use the property for the "comfort, welfare, or happiness" of the holder is not an ascertainable standard and therefore is a general power of appointment. The following example illustrates these rules.

EXAMPLE 34

Assume the same facts as in Example 32. In addition to having the testamentary power to designate the beneficiary of the remainder interest, Monica is given a power to direct the trustee to pay to her from time to time as much of the corpus as she might request "for her support." Although Monica now has a power that she can exercise in favor of herself, it is not a general power of appointment. The power is limited to an ascertainable standard. Thus, none of the property subject to these powers is included in Monica's estate at her death. ■

Trusts for Minors. As discussed in the first part of this chapter, gift giving can produce significant tax savings. When property is given to a minor, the income is taxed to the child, and the property is not included in the parents' gross estate when they die. However, many parents are reluctant to transfer property to their young children because, when an outright gift is made, legal title and all ownership rights transfer to the child. An outright gift is a gift of a present interest and qualifies for the annual exclusion.

Recognizing the social implications of gifting property outright to minors, Congress enacted § 2503(c), which allows parents to utilize the annual exclusion for transfers of property into an irrevocable trust even though the minor may not be allowed to receive any benefits from the property until age 21. In effect, § 2503(c) qualifies a future interest for the annual exclusion. For this unique exception to apply, the following conditions must be satisfied.

- Both the property and its income may be expended by or for the benefit of the minor before the minor attains the age of 21.
- Any portion of the property or its income not expended by the time the minor reaches the age of 21 shall pass to the minor at that time.
- If the minor dies before attaining the age of 21, the property and its income will be payable either to the minor's estate or as the minor may designate under a general power of appointment.

This exception allows a trustee to accumulate income on behalf of a minor beneficiary without converting the income interest to a future interest. In addition, the income is taxed at the trust's rate if it is not distributed and at the minor's rate if it is distributed. If the transferor parent is the trustee and dies before the child reaches 21, the property is included in the parent's gross estate.

EXAMPLE 35

Bret places property in trust, income payable to Billy until he reaches 21, remainder to Billy or Billy's estate. Under the terms of the trust instrument, the trustee is empowered to accumulate the trust income or apply it toward Billy's benefit. In either event, the accumulated income and principal must be paid to Billy whenever he reaches 21 years of age or to whomever Billy designates in his will if he dies before reaching that age. The conditions of § 2503(c) are satisfied, and Bret's transfer qualifies for the annual exclusion. Billy's interest is a present interest. ■

If a parent establishes a trust for a child, greater tax savings can be achieved if the parent transfers a small amount of property or cash annually to the trust instead of an initial large amount. In this way, multiple annual exclusions can be used with respect to each transfer. Through the use of gift splitting and both parents' unified credits, a substantial amount of money can escape the transfer tax if the parents have the wealth and plan early during the child's life.

DIGGING DEEPER 4

Find more information on this topic at our Web site: ***http://wft-advanced.swlearning.com***.

LO.8

Use bypass trusts to fully utilize the unified tax credits of both spouses.

USING TRUSTS TO FULLY UTILIZE THE UNIFIED CREDIT

Each parent is entitled to a unified tax credit. As previously discussed in Chapter 14, the amount sheltered by the unified credit is $1.5 million in 2004. If a couple has not utilized their unified credits by making gifts during life, a total of $3 million can be transferred tax-free through their estates in 2004. Often, however, if the family members do not plan their estates, the couple may not be able to fully utilize both credits as illustrated in the following example.

EXAMPLE 36

Dan dies in 2004 leaving his estate of $1.5 million to his wife, Dora. Because of the unlimited marital deduction, Dan's taxable estate is zero, and his estate owes no estate taxes. Dora now owns $1.5 million of property transferred by Dan to her plus her own property. Assume that when Dora dies in 2005, the fair market value of her estate is $3 million, including the property she received from Dan. Dora is not entitled to a marital deduction. Therefore, her taxable estate is $3 million, and her estate must pay estate taxes of $705,000. ■

In Example 36, the estate taxes payable at Dora's death could have been avoided if Dan had transferred his $1.5 million estate directly to the children. His estate tax liability would have been $555,800, which would be offset by the unified credit so no estate taxes would be payable. The $1.5 million of property would not have been included in Dora's estate. Her estate taxes on $1.5 million also would be offset through the use of her unified credit. In total, Dan and Dora's estates would pay no estate taxes by fully utilizing both of their unified tax credits. The property owned by Dan is said to bypass his spouse's estate.

Utilization of both unified credits can be achieved by having the first spouse to die transfer outright at death through the terms of the will an amount equal to the unified credit exemption to someone other than the surviving spouse. Usually, the beneficiaries of this amount are the children.

However, although the tax savings may be substantial, a number of couples are unwilling to bequeath assets to their children when the first spouse dies. The parents may feel that the second spouse might need the assets especially as he or she grows older and the cost of nursing homes and medical care increases. In these situations, a **bypass trust** may provide the solution.

Bypass Trust. Typically, a bypass trust is created upon the death of the first spouse and is funded with a portion of the decedent's assets up to the unified credit exemption equivalent. Since the trust is established at death, it is a testamentary trust, and the assets become part of the gross estate for estate tax purposes. The assets still have to be probated because the will must specify which assets are to be transferred into the trust. Often, the will states that the amount to be placed in the trust should equal the unified tax credit equivalency amount determined as of the date of death. After death, when the transfer occurs, the trust becomes the owner of the property.

One way to draft the terms of the trust is to designate the children as both the income and remainder beneficiaries of the trust. Clearly, in this case, the unified credit is fully utilized to offset the corresponding estate taxes. However, this case is similar to bequeathing the property outright to the children and may not achieve the nontax considerations of the family. Therefore, the bypass trust may be created in the following manner.

EXAMPLE 37

At Elsie's death in 2004, the terms of her will create an irrevocable trust by directing her executor to transfer $1,500,000 of her assets into the trust. The trust specifies that Fred, her husband, is the income beneficiary of the trust for as long as he lives. When Fred dies, the property is to pass to Gretchen and Harriet, their children. ■

By specifying the income and remainder beneficiaries in this manner, Elsie is assured that Fred will be taken care of financially as long as he lives and that her children will be the ultimate beneficiaries of the property. The question for tax purposes is whether Elsie's estate will be able to fully utilize her unified credit or whether a portion of the $1,500,000 included in her gross estate will be offset by the marital deduction.

Recall from Chapter 14 that the purpose of the marital deduction is to tax transfers from one generation to another only once; thus, interspousal transfers should not be taxed. In Example 37, the property will not be taxed in Fred's estate because his interest in the property terminates upon his death. Therefore, it must be taxed in Elsie's estate, and consequently, the marital deduction for the income interest passing to Fred is disallowed, while Elsie's unified credit is fully utilized.

Fred's interest is referred to as a **terminable interest.** A terminable interest is one that terminates or fails after the passage of time, upon the happening of some contingency, or upon the failure of some event to occur. Examples are life estates, annuities, estates for terms of years, and patents. A terminable interest does not qualify for the marital deduction if another interest in the same property will pass from the deceased spouse to some other person. By reason of the passing, that person may enjoy part of the property after the termination of the surviving spouse's interest. In Example 37, Gretchen and Harriet do indeed have an interest in the property after Fred dies, and the marital deduction is disallowed.

Similarly, if Elsie had created the trust during her life, and if the trust were irrevocable, the total value of the property at the time of transfer would be subject to gift taxes. No marital deduction would be allowed for the interest passing to Fred. Elsie would utilize the unified credit to offset her gift taxes. In addition, the property would bypass both Elsie's and Fred's estates when they died. If Elsie were willing to set up this trust during her lifetime, probate costs would be avoided at her death.

LO.9

Understand how trusts can be used to provide for the needs of the surviving spouse while minimizing the transfer taxes for the family.

USING TRUSTS TO MAXIMIZE THE MARITAL DEDUCTION

As a family's wealth increases, the estate plans become more interesting and complex. At a minimum, a family with considerable wealth should incorporate the plans discussed thus far. First, a gift-giving program should be initiated to take advantage of the gift tax annual exclusions. Appreciating property should be gifted in order to leverage the value of the annual exclusion. Second, the estate plan should be constructed to fully utilize each parent's unified credit. As previously discussed, a bypass trust is a common device for accomplishing this purpose and may be established during life or at death.

Once the annual exclusions and unified credits have been fully utilized, a common tax planning objective is to postpone estate taxation as long as possible. This strategy is known as the *deferral* approach and takes into consideration the time value of money. It involves maximizing the marital deduction at the death of the first spouse after fully utilizing the unified credit. The net effect of this approach is to pay no taxes at the time the first spouse dies.

A number of marital trusts can be used to maximize the marital deduction. The appropriate one is dependent on both the family's nontax and tax objectives. Several of the more popular ones are discussed below.

Power of Appointment Trusts. In Example 37, Elsie created a trust that she believed would accomplish the nontax financial objectives of her family; namely, income to her husband for life and remainder to their children. However, assume that Elsie has already fully utilized her unified credit during life or has established a separate testamentary bypass trust for her children. Is there any way that she can qualify the transfer of the property into the trust for the marital deduction?

One way that the terminable interest rule can be avoided is through a *power of appointment* exception. Under the exception, a property interest passing from the deceased spouse to the surviving spouse qualifies for the marital deduction (and is not considered a terminal interest) if the surviving spouse is granted a general power of appointment over the property. In Example 37, if Elsie gives Fred a general power of appointment over the property such that he can give the property to whomever is designated in the terms of the trust including himself, Elsie's estate receives a marital deduction for the fair market value of the property transferred into the trust at Elsie's death. However, since Fred possesses a general power of appointment at his death, the fair market value of the property at his death must be included in his gross estate. Thus, the property is only taxed once through Fred's estate.

Similarly, if Elsie establishes the trust during her life and makes it irrevocable, she will get a marital deduction equal to the fair market value of the property transferred into the trust at the date of the gift. The property will not be included in Elsie's gross estate when she dies. However, Fred will have to include its fair market value in his gross estate. As previously noted, the purpose of the terminable interest rule is to ensure that property not taxed to one spouse will be subject to the gift or estate tax upon disposition by the other spouse.

Qualified Terminable Interest Property (QTIP) Trusts. Consistent with the objective of the terminable interest rule, another exception offers an alternative means for using trusts to maximize the marital deduction. Under this provision, the marital deduction is allowed for transfers of **qualified terminable interest property (QTIP).** This term is defined as property that passes from one spouse to another by gift or at death and for which the transferee-spouse has a qualifying income interest for life.

TAX FACT

Qualified terminable interest property (QTIP) trusts were reported on 15,843 returns, or 34.8 percent of all returns filed for married 1998 decedents in 1998, 1999, and 2000. These trusts had a total value of almost $22.3 billion, or 75.4 percent of the nearly $29.5 billion marital deduction claimed by these estates. The percentage of estates reporting QTIP trusts as part of the marital deduction increased with the size of the gross estate. Female decedents elected to place slightly more of the marital deduction property in trust than males with gross estates of comparable size.

Source: IRS Tax Stats.

For a donee or a surviving spouse, a qualifying income interest for life exists under the following conditions.

- The person is entitled for life to all of the income from the property (or a specific portion of it), payable at annual or more frequent intervals.
- No person has a power to appoint any part of the property to any person other than the surviving spouse during his or her life.

If these conditions are met, an election can be made to claim a marital deduction with respect to the total fair market value of the QTIP. For estate tax purposes, the executor of the estate makes the election on Form 706 (the Federal estate tax return). For gift tax purposes, the donor spouse makes the election on Form 709 (the Federal gift tax return). The election is irrevocable.

If the election is made, the QTIP must be included in the gross estate of the second spouse to die to the extent that he or she has not previously gifted any of it. If no lifetime disposition takes place, the fair market value of the property on the date of death (or alternate valuation date if applicable) is included in the gross estate of the second spouse to die.

EXAMPLE 38

In 2004, Clyde dies and provides in his will that certain assets (fair market value of $400,000) are to be transferred to a trust under which Gertrude (Clyde's wife) is granted a life estate with the remainder passing to their children upon Gertrude's death. Presuming all of the preceding requirements are satisfied and Clyde's executor so elects, his estate receives a marital deduction of $400,000. ■

EXAMPLE 39

Assume the same facts as in Example 38, with the further stipulation that Gertrude dies in 2008 when the trust assets are worth $900,000. This amount is included in her gross estate. ■

Note in Example 38 that the marital deduction is equal to the full amount of the property placed in trust, not just the amount of the income interest passing to Gertrude.

The major difference between the power of appointment and the QTIP exceptions to the terminable interest rule relates to the control the surviving spouse has over the corpus of the trust. In the power of appointment situation, the surviving spouse can appoint the corpus to himself or herself (or to his or her estate). The property passes as specified in the deceased spouse's will only if this power is not exercised. In the QTIP situation, however, the surviving spouse has no such control. If the QTIP election is made, the property must pass as prescribed by the transferor

TAX IN THE NEWS

An Attempted Deferral That Backfired

A disaster involving the estate of Joe Robbie proves that Murphy's law can easily apply to estate planning. At the time of his death in January 1990, Robbie's estate had an estimated value of $70 million. His assets included Joe Robbie Stadium and the National Football League franchise the Miami Dolphins.

Apparently, Joe's plan was to place his assets in trust, life estate to his wife Elizabeth, remainder to his nine adult children. The executor of Joe's estate would make a QTIP election, with the resulting marital deduction deferring all estate taxes until Elizabeth's death. It was hoped that Elizabeth would live long enough so that only a small portion of the businesses (stadium and franchise) would be needed to satisfy her estate tax liability. Thus, controlling interests in both businesses would remain in the family.

What went wrong? First of all, Joe planted the seed of dissent by naming three of his children as trustees of the QTIP trust. This alienated the other six children. Also Elizabeth did not relish the idea of being dependent on the trust for her support. Further distress followed when the trustees dismissed their brother from his post as executive vice-president of the Dolphins. The final bombshell dropped when Elizabeth elected to take her statutory 30 percent dower share of the estate allowed under Florida law. In effect, this act eliminated the trust and nullified the QTIP marital deduction.

To pay the estate tax generated by Elizabeth's refusal to accept the QTIP trust, the Robbies sold the Dolphins and the stadium. Joe's plan for family harmony, with his heirs enjoying the fruits of his life's work, was destroyed.

(the donor in the case of a lifetime transfer or the decedent in the case of a death transfer).

DIGGING DEEPER 5 *Find more information on this topic at our Web site: **http://wft-advanced.swlearning.com**.*

Fractional QTIP Trust. Although the deferral approach to estate planning is more commonly used, another strategy is to *equalize* the estates of the two spouses. Because of the progressive nature of the transfer tax rates, clearly, for example, the estate tax on $3 million is more than double the estate tax before credits on $1.5 million [compare $1,260,800 with $1,111,600 ($555,800 × 2)].

One tool that can be used to try to equalize the estates is the QTIP election. In the preceding section, it was assumed that 100 percent of the property was QTIP'd. However, the law does permit the executor (or donor-spouse in the case of an inter vivos trust) to elect to QTIP only a certain percentage or fraction of the property. This gives the executor (or donor-spouse) flexibility to determine how much of the marital deduction should be used to achieve a certain level of taxable estate. As the QTIP fraction increases, the corresponding marital deduction increases, and the taxable estate of the first spouse to die decreases. Consequently, as the QTIP fraction increases, a greater amount must be included in the gross estate of the second spouse to die.

Algebraic equations can be developed to determine the optimal amount that should be QTIP'd to equalize the spouses' estates. However, assumptions must be made with respect to how long the surviving spouse will live and the rate of appreciation and return on the assets. In addition, the tradeoff between using the lower transfer tax rates twice and the time value of money must be incorporated into the model. The equalization approach represents a very sophisticated estate

Concept Summary 15–2

Estate and Gift Planning

1. A lifetime of giving can reduce transfer taxes by taking advantage of the annual exclusion and the election to split gifts between spouses.
2. Lifetime gifts of highly appreciating assets can reduce estate taxes by removing the post-gift appreciation from the gross estate. However, the donees will receive a lower basis in the property.
3. Gifts can relieve the income tax burden on the family unit by shifting the income from the gift property to family members who are in a lower income tax bracket. To accomplish this objective, the gift must be complete and circumvent the kiddie tax.
4. Transfers to charities during life generally result in greater tax savings because of the income tax deduction for lifetime charitable gifts.
5. Probate costs can be an important consideration in estate planning. Some procedures that reduce these costs include joint tenancies with right of survivorship, living trusts, and pre-death dispositions. Keep in mind that most of these procedures do not reduce estate taxes.
6. Irrevocable trusts established during the decedent's life can be used to keep property out of the gross estate if the donor does not retain a prohibited life interest.
7. If the trustee is given a general power of appointment over the trust property, the fair market value of the property will be included in the trustee's estate. If the trustee is given a limited power of appointment, it will not.
8. Trusts for minors can be used to maximize annual exclusions and still allow the property to be held in the trust until the minor reaches the age of 21.
9. Bypass trusts allow the income to be distributed to the surviving spouse without including the fair market value of the property in his or her estate.
10. The use of QTIPs can maximize the marital deduction for otherwise nondeductible terminable interests.

planning strategy. It is briefly discussed here to illustrate the creative and analytical abilities of the estate planner that can come into play.

Estate planners have a wealth of opportunities at their disposal. A review of the classic estate and gift planning strategies covered in this chapter appears in Concept Summary 15–2.

Suggested Further Readings

Frank S. Berall, Ellen K. Harrison, Jonathan G. Blattmachr, and Lauren Y. Detzel, "Planning for Carryover Basis That Can Be/Should Be/Must Be Done Now," *Estate Planning*, March 2002, pp. 99–112.

Thomas F. Horton, "Effective Charitable Planning Strategies After the 2001 Tax Act," *Estate Planning*, November 2002, pp. 580–586.

Martin M. Shenkman, "Planning Options to Help Families Fund a Child's Education," *Estate Planning*, January 2003, pp. 24–32.

KEY TERMS

PROBLEM MATERIALS

West Federal Taxation

Problems

1. Elsie and Garth are husband and wife with four married children and six grandchildren. Commencing in December 2004, they would like to transfer a tract of land (worth $616,000) equally to their children (including spouses) and grandchildren as quickly as possible and without making a taxable gift. What do you suggest?

2. In 2004, June gives stock to Emily when the shares have a fair market value of $100,000. June acquired the stock 10 years before the gift at a cost of $20,000 and paid a gift tax of $5,000. Determine Emily's income tax basis for gain or loss.

3. Ward gives stock to Mona in the current year when the shares have a value of $450,000. Ward acquired the stock several years ago for $500,000. As a result of the transfer, Ward incurs and pays a gift tax of $20,000. Determine Mona's gain or loss if she sells the stock for:
   a. $510,000.
   b. $440,000.
   c. $460,000.

Decision Making
Communications

4. Nat and June Duncan are married and have always lived in a community property state. Nat (age 82) suffers from numerous disorders and is frequently ill, while June (age 76) is in good health. The Duncans currently need $300,000 to meet living expenses and to pay Nat's backlog of medical expenses. They are willing to sell any one of the following assets:

	Adjusted Basis	Fair Market Value
Tern Corporation stock	$100,000	$300,000
Grebe Corporation stock	400,000	300,000
Unimproved land	450,000	300,000

   The stock investments are part of the Duncans' community property, while the land is Nat's separate property that he inherited from his mother. If the land is not sold, Nat is considering making a gift of it to June.
   a. Write a letter to the Duncans advising them on these matters. Their address is 158 Arroyo Road, Mesa Verde, NM 88003.
   b. Prepare a memo on this matter for your firm's client files.

5. In April 2003, George gives Beverly a house (basis of $50,000 and fair market value of $250,000) to be used as her personal residence. As a result of the transfer, George incurs and pays a gift tax of $15,000. Before her death in March 2004, Beverly installs a swimming pool in the backyard at a cost of $20,000. The residence is worth $270,000 on the date of Beverly's death, and her estate does not elect the alternate valuation date. Determine the income tax basis of the property to the heir, based on the following independent assumptions.
   a. Under Beverly's will, the residence passes to George.
   b. Under Beverly's will, the residence passes to Junior (Beverly's son).

Ethics

6. During the current year, Hazel sold a parcel of land for $2.5 million. Hazel inherited the land 15 years ago from her father. On the Form 706 filed for her father's estate, the property was described as pastureland and was valued at $100,000. Apparently, the executor was unaware that the property contained iron-ore deposits.

   In reporting the sale of the land, Hazel plans to use an income tax basis of $1.5 million. Based on discussions that Hazel has had with several geologists, $1.5 million was the value of the land 15 years ago had the iron-ore deposits been considered.

   Is Hazel's planned approach proper? Why or why not?

Decision Making
Communications

7. Charles Horn wants his daughter Sharon to get stock that he owns in Crimson Corporation. He acquired the stock two years ago at a cost of $800,000, and it currently has a fair market value of $650,000. Charles has made prior taxable gifts and is in poor health. He seeks your advice as to whether he should gift the stock to Sharon or pass it to her under his will. Charles has a large capital loss carryover and has no prospect for any capital gains.
   a. Write a letter to Charles regarding the tax implications of the alternatives he has suggested. His address is 648 Scenic Drive, Chattanooga, TN 37403.
   b. Prepare a memo for your firm's files on this matter.

8. Last year, Dean sold real estate (basis of $80,000) to Paul (an unrelated party) for $200,000, receiving $40,000 in cash and Paul's notes for the balance. The notes carry a 10% rate of interest and mature annually at $16,000 each year over a period of 10 years. Dean did not elect out of the installment method for reporting the gain from the sale. Before any of the notes mature and when the notes have a total fair market value of $150,000, Dean gives them to Shelley. Disregarding the interest element, what are Dean's income tax consequences as a result of the gift?

Issue ID

9. Hannah is 80 years old and very wealthy. Her taxable estate is estimated to be $10 million, and she is in the 35% income tax bracket. Hannah would like to give $500,000 to her alma mater and asks you whether she should gift the cash in the current year or transfer it through her estate. Compute the difference in the tax savings under both alternatives.

10. At the time of her death in the current year, Monica held the following assets.

	Fair Market Value
Personal residence (title listed as "Monica and Philip, tenants by the entirety with right of survivorship")	$800,000
Savings account (listed as "Monica and Rex, joint tenants with right of survivorship")	40,000
Unimproved real estate (title listed as "Monica and Rex, equal tenants in common")	300,000
Insurance policy on Monica's life, issued by Lavender Company (Monica's estate is the designated beneficiary)	200,000
Insurance policy on Monica's life, issued by Crimson Company (Rex is the designated beneficiary)	400,000
Living trust created by Monica five years ago (life estate to Philip, remainder to Rex)	700,000

Assuming Philip and Rex survive Monica, how much is included in Monica's *probate estate?*

Decision Making

11. In 1986, Irma created a revocable trust with securities worth $300,000. National Trust Company was designated as the trustee. Under the terms of the trust, her boyfriend will receive the income for as long as he lives, and the remainder will go to her children. In 2002, Irma releases the right to revoke the trust. Irma dies in 2004 when the trust assets have a fair market value of $1,200,000.
   a. What, if any, are Irma's gift tax consequences in 1986?
   b. What, if any, is included in Irma's gross estate in 2004?

12. In 2004, John creates a trust with securities worth $3 million. Under the terms of the trust, Mary (age 40) receives a life estate, while Nolan (age 15) receives the remainder interest. In the month the trust is created, the appropriate interest rate is 7.6%. Determine the value of John's gifts.

13. In 2004, Reba creates a trust with securities worth $2.5 million. Under the terms of the trust, Burl (age 12) receives the income for 15 years, remainder to Tina (age 35). In the month the trust is created, the appropriate interest rate is 7.8%. Determine the value of Reba's gifts.

14. Mona (age 65) creates an irrevocable trust with property worth $800,000. Under the terms of the trust, Mona retains a life estate with the remainder interest passing to Debby (Mona's closest friend) upon Mona's death. Mona dies in 2004 when the value of the trust is $1,100,000 and Debby is age 44. In the month the trust was created, the appropriate rate was 7.6%. Determine the taxable gift, if any, if the trust was created in 1998.

15. Assume the same facts as in Problem 14. How much, if any, of the trust is included in Mona's gross estate?

16. Assume in Problem 14 that Debby is related to Mona. Determine the amount of the taxable gift at the time the trust is created. Does Mona have to include the fair market value of the trust property in her gross estate?

17. In 1963, Frank's uncle created an irrevocable trust, income payable to Frank for life and remainder to Frank's children. Frank was named the trustee and was given the power to determine how much of the property should be distributed to each child. Does Frank have to include the fair market value of the property in his gross estate when he dies?

Decision Making
Communications

18. Mike Edwards would like to make a lifetime transfer in trust of $1,000,000 to his son, Keith, and accomplish the following objectives.
    - Avoid any death tax on the deaths of Mike, Keith, and Bette (Keith's wife).
    - Give Keith the right to determine what portion of the remainder should be allocated between Bette and their children.
    - Give Keith some additional security by allowing him to reach the principal should the need materialize.
    - Prevent Keith from squandering all of the principal to the detriment of Bette or her children.

    Write a letter to Mike recommending a course of action. Mike's address is 4320 Richmond Avenue, Syracuse, NY 13244.

19. In 1985, Brad places in trust $500,000 worth of securities. Under the terms of the trust instrument, Wanda (Brad's wife) is granted a life estate, and on Wanda's death, the remainder interest passes to Brad and Wanda's children (as Wanda determines in her will). Upon Wanda's death in 2004, the trust assets are valued at $2 million.
    a. How much, if any, marital deduction will be allowed on the gift made in 1985?
    b. How much, if any, of the trust will be included in Wanda's gross estate upon her death?

20. Assume the same facts as in Problem 19, except that Brad made the QTIP election when the trust was created. Further assume that Wanda has no choice as to which of her children will receive the remainder interest upon her death.
    a. How much, if any, marital deduction will be allowed on the gift made in 1985?
    b. How much, if any, of the trust will be included in Wanda's gross estate upon her death?

Decision Making

21. During their marriage, Brenda and Victor have operated a business together. Each has managed to accumulate approximately $1,000,000 of income-producing property. Because she is 10 years younger and in better health, Brenda is expected to survive Victor. Upon the death of the survivor, they want their property to pass to their adult children.
    Outline an estate plan for Victor that would accomplish the following objectives.
    - Give Brenda maximum income protection.
    - Avoid a concentration of wealth in Brenda's estate that would cause an estate tax liability on her later death.
    - Avoid estate taxes on Victor's prior death.

    Neither Brenda nor Victor has made any prior taxable gifts. Victor has a niece, Julia, who is a practicing attorney and is familiar with the state's trust laws. Victor has close ties with Julia as he financed her education.
    In this connection, consider Code §§ 2036 and 2041.

EXTENDER

22. Tom's mother left property to his sister, Sue, for her lifetime. When Sue dies, the property (remainder) goes to Tom. At the time of Tom's death, Sue is 55 years old and still living. The property is valued at $750,000 on the date of Tom's death. How much has to be included in Tom's gross estate?

Comprehensive Tax Return Problem

Tax Return Problem

23. Irma Winfield, age 70, a resident of Maryland, died on March 8, 2004. She was survived by her husband, Robert, age 65, and their two sons, Abe and John. Upon examining Irma's affairs, her executors found the following information:
    - Irma held the following properties solely in her name:
        a. Mutual fund and cash valued at $2,800,000.
        b. Car and personal effects valued at $50,000.
        c. Land held as investment property valued at $1,500,000.
        d. Stocks valued at $600,000 excluding dividends. Dividends of $10,000 had been declared on February 1, 2004, payable to stockholders of record on March 1, 2004, and payable on April 1, 2004.
        e. Irma was a beneficiary of a trust created by her father. Under the terms of the trust, Irma received all of the income during her lifetime; on Irma's death, the trust property was to be distributed to Irma's brother. The trust property was worth $100,000 at the time of Irma's death.
    - Irma had made the following lifetime transfers:
        a. On March 17, 1994, Irma transferred $6,000 of highly speculative stocks to a trust. The trust provided for the income to be paid to Irma's sister, Esther, for Esther's life and for the principal to be paid to Irma's son, Abe, on Esther's death. Irma retained the right to direct that the income in any year be accumulated and added to principal. The trust property was worth $50,000 at the time of Irma's death.
        b. On August 18, 1998, Irma transferred $8,000 of stocks to a trust under which the income was payable to Irma's husband for his lifetime; upon his death, the corpus is distributable to Irma's son, John. The trust property was worth $75,000 at the time of Irma's death. Assume at the time of the gift, Irma made a QTIP election.
        c. On November 10, 2003, Irma gave her son John land worth $2,511,000 (an adjusted taxable gift of $2,500,000) and paid a gift tax of $833,000. This is the only taxable gift that Irma made during her lifetime. The land was worth $5,000,000 on the date of Irma's death.
    - Other items in Irma's estate are as follows:
        a. Pursuant to a qualified pension plan funded entirely by her employer, Irma was to receive an annuity for life upon her retirement at age 65. If Irma predeceased her husband, Robert, he would receive similar payments during his life. The present value of Irma's annuity at her death was $90,000.
        b. Irma and Robert owned their personal home as joint tenants with rights of survivorship. Irma purchased the home many years ago for $100,000, using her own funds. The home was worth $500,000 at the time of Irma's death.
        c. A $100,000 life insurance policy on Irma's life named Robert as the beneficiary. Irma purchased the policy and made all of the premium payments.

    Irma's will disposed of her property in the following manner:
    - Irma left the following property to her husband, Robert:

Car and personal effects	$ 50,000
Real estate	1,500,000

    - The stocks and any accrued dividends are to be distributed to her husband.
    - Irma left $100,000 to a veterans' hospital.
    - Irma left the remainder of her estate to be divided equally between her two sons after the payment of all expenses of the estate. The expenses were as follows:

Funeral expenses	$ 30,000
State death taxes	160,000
Mortgage on investment property	250,000

    Calculate the Federal estate tax payable on Irma Winfield's estate.

Research Problems

THOMSON RIA

*Note: Solutions to Research Problems can be prepared by using the **RIA Checkpoint® Student Edition** online research product, which is available to accompany this text. It is also possible to prepare solutions to the Research Problems by using tax research materials found in a standard tax library.*

Research Problem 1. Sarah created a trust by transferring income-producing assets to a trust company. Specifics regarding the trust agreement are summarized as follows.

- Income of the trust inures to the benefit of Sarah's five minor daughters. The trustee is accorded the right to accumulate or distribute current income.
- The trust company is a corporation chartered under state law. Sarah owns none of the stock.
- Sarah retains the right to replace the trustee with another independent corporate trust company. This right is never exercised by Sarah during her lifetime.
- At the discretion of the trustee, both income and corpus may be expended on behalf of the beneficiaries before they attain the age of 21.
- At age 21, each beneficiary has the right to withdraw her share of corpus and accumulated income (if any) from the trust. If the right to distribution is not exercised, the trust is to continue until the beneficiary reaches age 35 or dies, whichever occurs first. At this point, a final liquidating distribution will be made to the beneficiary (or her estate) of her interest.
- If a beneficiary dies before attaining the age of 21, her interest in the trust is payable to her estate or as she designates under a general power of appointment.

In the year the trust was created, Sarah filed a Form 709 reflecting the gift. In computing the gift tax liability, Sarah claimed five annual exclusions.

Five years after the gift in trust was made, Sarah dies. Sarah's executor includes none of the value of the trust in the gross estate. When the estate's Form 706 is audited, the IRS determines that the trust must be included. Because of the retained right to replace trustees, Sarah's transfer was incomplete. Consequently, the IRS maintains that Code §§ 2036(a)(2) and 2038(a)(1) are applicable.

a. Was Sarah correct in claiming five annual exclusions for the gift in trust? Why or why not?
b. Is the IRS correct in including the trust in Sarah's gross estate? Why or why not?

Research Problem 2. In 1996, Anne, a 70-year-old widow, creates an irrevocable trust naming her five adult grandchildren as the beneficiaries. The assets transferred in trust consist of marketable securities (worth $600,000) and Anne's personal residence (worth $390,000). Bill, Anne's younger brother and a practicing attorney, is designated as the trustee. Other provisions of the trust are noted below.

- Bill is given the discretion to distribute the income of the trust to the beneficiaries based upon their need or to add it to corpus. He also is granted the power to terminate the trust, liquidate its assets, and distribute the proceeds to the beneficiaries.
- The trust is to last for Anne's lifetime or, if sooner, until termination by Bill.
- Upon the termination of the trust, the principal and any accumulated income are to be distributed to the beneficiaries (i.e., Anne's grandchildren).

For 1996, Anne filed a Form 709 to report the transfers in trust and paid the Federal gift tax.

After its transfer in trust and up to the time of her death, Anne continued to occupy the residence. Although she paid no rent, she maintained the property, making all necessary repairs and paying the annual property taxes. Anne never discussed the matter of her continued occupancy of the residence with either Bill or the beneficiaries of the trust.

During the existence of the trust, Bill made no distributions to the beneficiaries. All trust income was accumulated and added to corpus.

On Anne's death in 2004, the value of the trust is $2,620,000, broken down as follows: marketable securities and cash ($2,080,000) and personal residence ($540,000). Shortly thereafter, Bill liquidates the trust and distributes the proceeds to the beneficiaries.

What are the estate tax consequences of these transactions to Anne?

Partial list of research aids:
§ 2036.
Guynn v. U.S., 71–1 USTC ¶12,742, 27 AFTR2d 71–1653, 437 F.2d 1148 (CA–4, 1971).
Estate of Eleanor T. R. Trotter, 82 TCM 633, T.C.Memo. 2001–250.

Research Problem 3. In 1996, John Letts dies and is survived by his widow (Mildred) and two adult children. Under the terms of his will, most of his property passes to a trust, life estate to Mildred, remainder to their children. John designated Mildred and their children as executors of his estate.

The executors filed a Form 706 that reflected no taxes due because of the allowance of the marital deduction. On page 2 of Form 706, the executors indicated that the QTIP election of § 2056(b)(7) *was not* being made. John Letts's Form 706 was timely filed but never audited by the IRS.

In 2003, Mildred dies, and her will names her children as executors. Mildred's estate includes none of the trust created by John, as the QTIP election was not made. Mildred's life estate is not subject to inclusion under § 2036(a)(2), as she was not the grantor of the trust. The parties admit that John's estate should not have claimed a marital deduction, as what passed to Mildred was a terminable interest. The error, inadvertent as it was, cannot be corrected since the statute of limitations precludes filing an amended Form 706 for John Letts's estate.

Does the IRS have any recourse?

Partial list of research aids:
§ 2044.
Barry S. Glass, 87 T.C. 1087 (1986).
Estate of Mildred Geraldine Letts, 109 T.C. 290 (1997).

CHAPTER 16

Succession Planning for the Closely Held Business

LEARNING OBJECTIVES

After completing Chapter 16, you should be able to:

LO.1
Identify some common emotional issues encountered in succession planning from the perspectives of both the transferor and the transferee.

LO.2
Identify some common economic issues encountered in succession planning from the perspectives of the transferor, transferee, and the closely held business.

LO.3
Discuss the options available for the transfer of the closely held business interest and the relevant tax considerations.

LO.4
Understand the issues involved in the valuation of a closely held business interest.

LO.5
Understand the role that buy-sell agreements play in the context of closely held business interests.

LO.6
Describe the significance of estate freezes and the special use valuation provisions.

LO.7
Discuss the liquidity issues involved in the transfer of a closely held business and the major provisions available to ameliorate them.

OUTLINE

TAX TALK

Taxes are paid in the sweat of every man who labors. If those taxes are excessive, they are reflected in idle factories, tax-sold farms and in hordes of hungry people, tramping the streets and seeking jobs in vain.

—*Franklin D. Roosevelt*

In the realm of tax practice, succession planning offers many challenges due to the interaction of the *emotional, economic,* and *tax issues* associated with the transfer of a business from one owner to another. Some of the best tax planning strategies may be ignored because of emotional concerns and the relationships between the various parties. Thus, when preparing a succession plan, the tax practitioner's most important tool can be interpersonal skills. In addition to the emotional issues involved, the transfer of ownership of a closely held business from one generation to another also poses unique economic and tax issues. This type of estate planning can be one of the most challenging and professionally rewarding areas of tax practice.

Overview of Succession Planning

This chapter begins with a discussion of the various emotional, economic, and tax issues that tax practitioners face when planning for the succession of a closely held business from one generation to another. In the context of this chapter, a closely held business is a privately owned business. Typically, it is owned by a group of family members.

Too often, tax practitioners are tempted to prepare solutions that are innovative and exciting from a technical tax viewpoint. However satisfying such a plan may be from a professional standpoint, it will be a recipe for disaster if it does not address the emotional and economic needs of the client. To address these needs, succession planning incorporates both personal financial planning *and* retirement planning. One generation will be retiring and the other will be working to build its financial independence. There is no one-size-fits-all plan for such situations. Succession planning is *personal* in nature; no two individuals are exactly alike emotionally or economically. This is why the emotional and economic aspects of the situation must be analyzed first. Only after these needs have been properly addressed can one hope to structure a suitable succession plan. As the plan develops, tax issues can be resolved as they arise.

In a way, succession planning is like directing a three-part play. In the first act, which develops the plot, the tax professional addresses the emotional issues of both the transferor generation and the transferee generation. Here the tax professional's interpersonal skills are put to the test. Failure to meet the emotional needs of both parties may result in reluctance or refusal to implement the plan or even the outright alienation of the client. The second act unfolds as the economics of the transfer are reviewed. The tax professional must make full use of his or her financial analysis skills to assure that the proposed transaction will be economically feasible. When an ownership change occurs, certain considerations unique to a closely held business must be factored into any financial assumptions. The finale occurs when the tax professional considers the interaction of the emotional and economic factors. Here the tax issues are addressed, and a plan is prepared that appropriately resolves the emotional and economic concerns in the most tax-effective manner. In a successful succession plan, the three parts are reconciled, and all parties involved are willing to commit to it. However, failure to properly address the three types of issues may result in a tragedy instead of the desired happy ending. The outcome is determined by how well the tax professional analyzes the situation, identifies the issues, and resolves them with appropriate actions.

In this chapter, it is assumed that a willing and competent successor generation is ready to take over control of the closely held business. A reluctant or unqualified successor can spell disaster to any plan, especially if it relies upon the ongoing economic success of the business to fund any buyout.

LO.1

Identify some common emotional issues encountered in succession planning from the perspective of both the transferor and the transferee.

EMOTIONAL ISSUES IN SUCCESSION PLANNING

Emotional Issues Affecting the Transferor. To identify the emotional issues from the transferor's viewpoint, it is helpful to first examine the characteristics of successful entrepreneurs. For the most part, successful entrepreneurs are independent. They are more than willing to take charge of a situation and to accept responsibility for their decisions. The desire to be in control of a situation and the need to meet challenges are often the principal motivators for them on a day-to-day basis. Typically, they also have a strong desire to control their own financial destiny. Sometimes, they derive satisfaction and an ego boost from building up a well-recognized and financially successful business.

With these characteristics in mind, it is easy to see how the closely held business becomes part of the owner's personal identity. All businesses have a distinct culture or personality that is reflected in daily operations. How workers approach their tasks and how customers are served reflect the philosophy of the business organization. Employees are hired, trained, evaluated, and promoted in the organization based upon how well they fit and function within the culture. In this context, the business itself is a reflection of the personality of the owner. It is the owner who makes the key decisions that result in the policies governing how and when things are done. The owner's decisions determine the direction of the business, what products or services will be offered, how they will be delivered, what markets will be pursued, and, ultimately, the business's overall success or failure.

Frequently, a closely held business represents the sum total of its owner's lifework. The individual usually has spent a great portion of his or her life creating and building the business. The successful owner views the resulting enterprise with great pride and regards it as a tangible confirmation of his or her success for the rest of the world to see. For many, it represents the principal source of self-esteem. Within the business and social community, a closely held business often provides its owner with both an identity and status.

EXAMPLE 1

Fifteen years ago, Persimmon, Inc., announced that it was discontinuing the product line it manufactured in Midtown. The plant manager, Mary, loved the community and did not want to leave. In addition, she wanted the plant to remain in Midtown. Rather than accept a transfer to another plant, Mary offered to buy the product line and facilities from Persimmon, Inc. Persimmon accepted Mary's offer and assisted in the financing since many of its customers still required the product. Persimmon felt that Mary could keep customers well supplied and would continue on friendly terms with the company. Over the years, Mary succeeded in increasing the product's sales and profits. Because of Mary's success, Persimmon spun off several other product lines to her holding company, Orange Corporation. When Mary first took over, the company employed 150 people in Midtown (population 75,000). Her company now employs over 500. She has been recognized locally, statewide, and nationally by various organizations as the small business owner of the year. She is considered one of Midtown's top success stories and has been invited to serve on the board of directors of numerous charitable and civic organizations. ■

Mary's success as a business owner has led to local and national recognition and prestige, which in turn have enhanced her social status and financial rewards. Succession planning for Mary will require close attention to how her transfer of ownership affects her social status.

One of the most emotional aspects of the transfer for the owner is the decision to relinquish control. Since the business represents an integral part of his or her identity, the owner will likely place great stock in the future success of the business. Thus, the owner may have some difficulty addressing the decision to relinquish ownership and choose a successor. For this reason, some may not wish to relinquish complete control, but may choose instead to remain in some form of advisory capacity. A successor owner may not welcome such continued involvement.

EXAMPLE 2

Refer to Mary in Example 1. Since Mary's rise to public notice has been linked to her success with Orange Corporation, outsiders may view any decline in the company upon her departure as stemming from a failure on her part to provide for the continuation of the business. After all, she not only rescued 150 jobs that might have left the community but also created many additional jobs. Any drop-off in the business and related employment may be construed in the community as an attempt by Mary to "take the money and run." For this reason, Mary may desire to stay involved in the business as director or consultant upon the transfer of ownership to the next generation. In this way, she may still be able to control the business or at least be associated with any continued success. From her viewpoint, continued involvement may be necessary to retain her social status. How such involvement is greeted by Mary's successor is discussed in the next section of this chapter. ■

The next hurdle to be cleared is the transferor's emotional readiness for retirement. The psychological aspects of retirement planning must be considered here. Economic aspects of retirement will be discussed later.

Running a successful business is both time-consuming and challenging. The stress may well leave the owner feeling burned-out. Even so, upon retirement, the owner may have a great void of both time and personal challenges to fill. Some may welcome this time as an opportunity to pursue things they were too busy to do during their work years. They may find that traveling, pursuing hobbies, or becoming involved with social or charitable services will occupy their time and provide challenges without the stress of running a business. Such activities can be challenging and personally satisfying and may be accepted with great enthusiasm.

EXAMPLE 3

After 15 years of developing Orange Corporation, Mary wants to retire. The demands on her time have been considerable. She has been training her son, Gerald, to succeed her in the business. Now that she believes he is ready to take over, she is looking forward to spending more time helping some of her favorite charities. Her plans also include traveling to visit her other son on the East Coast and her daughter on the West Coast and spoiling her grandchildren. Mary wants a clean, quick departure from the business. ■

The desires of the retiring owner may not be in accord with the desires of the new owner. For example, the new owner may view some smoothing-over period for key employees and customers as critical for the ongoing success of the business. In addition, the new owner may appreciate the older generation's insights and business knowledge and wish to have access to such intangible assets during the transition of ownership. This may pose problems if the retiring owner feels burned-out and wishes to be completely removed from subsequent business operations.

EXAMPLE 4

Gerald recognizes his mother's role in the great success of Orange Corporation. Although he feels confident he can operate the business, he wants to consult with her on critical steps in the transition. Gerald feels that several key customers may need her attention during this time. Additionally, some production changes need the support of certain key personnel. Gerald would like his mother's input to help deal with these people as the changes are implemented. To guarantee he will receive the necessary support, Gerald wants Mary to serve as a paid member of the board of directors. The past policy has been to compensate only outside directors. Since she will be stepping down as CEO, he feels it is important to compensate her the same as the other outside directors. ■

As Examples 3 and 4 illustrate, the transferor and transferee may have different goals. If Mary wants a clean break, some sort of compromise will have to be reached, or their different expectations may prevent a successful plan from being implemented.

Other owners may view retirement with great trepidation. They may wonder how they will fill their time or fear that they will be bored without the daily challenges of running a business. Such individuals may have developed a comfort zone while operating the business and may not be able to see how their skills can translate into retirement opportunities. These owners may view themselves as "too old" to change or to take on the challenges of retirement. This type of person will want to work indefinitely, transferring ownership only when he or she becomes incapacitated or at death. If ownership is transferred during life, these owners will likely relinquish only partial control or involvement in the business.

EXAMPLE 5

Monty is thrilled with his success. Although his work consumes a large amount of his time, he is not ready to retire; however, he is willing to reduce the amount of time spent at the business. Additionally, Monty is not sure that his daughter, Carrie, is ready to manage the business. Monty's plan is to make Carrie the president of the company, while he works part-time and continues as the CEO and chairman of the board. ■

As in the example of Mary and Gerald, Monty's plan may not bode well with Carrie, his successor. Such a situation poses the challenge of preparing Monty to retire. This may be done by pointing out opportunities to accomplish unfulfilled dreams or by getting Monty to think about how his skills and knowledge can be challenged and satisfied outside the realm of running a business. However, this may not be achievable because some people cannot let go. In such cases, the tax professional's choice may be limited to planning for a transfer at the owner's death, even though that may not be the most economic or tax-effective way to transfer ownership.

EXAMPLE 6

Sal is convinced that his daughter, Joan, is not ready to succeed him, and he is determined to work until his death. However, he does want Joan to succeed him at death. To accomplish this, Sal grants Joan an option to acquire all of his shares at his death or incapacitation. ■

Depending on how long Sal lives and how successful the business continues to be, the value of the business may appreciate considerably. The increase in value will increase the amount of estate taxes due upon Sal's death. An earlier transfer of ownership to Joan has the potential to create significant estate tax savings. However, since Sal controls the ownership, he will have the final say in its transfer. If Joan accepts the above plan, then the tax professional needs to address the issues such an arrangement raises.

Emotional Issues Affecting the Transferee. The emotional factors that motivate the new owners are similar to those that motivated the previous owners. Once again, the opportunity to be in control of one's personal and financial destiny, the self-esteem derived from running a successful business, and the recognition of peers and others in the community are prime motivators.

For the new owner, taking over the closely held business may represent a variety of opportunities. The individual may have spent many years in the shadow of the older generation being trained for this eventual transition. Thus, the ownership transfer may provide an opportunity to fulfill family expectations that have developed over the years. On the other hand, the individual may have spent time working for other firms in the industry. In such circumstances, the new owner may enter the family business with a fresh perspective, rather than a "that's the way we've always done it" attitude.

During this period, the new owner may have developed a particular style of doing things or generated a wish list of changes to be made once the transfer of ownership takes place. The new owner may have grown tired of being in the parent's shadow or of being compared to the older generation. The younger generation may view the change in ownership as an opportunity to create an identity separate from the parents. New technologies or methodologies may be implemented. Portions of the business may need to be expanded or contracted. New markets may be emerging that change the entire operation of the business. All of these possibilities offer the new owner opportunities to transform the company to fit his or her image of what it should be.

EXAMPLE 7

Gerald worked for Persimmon, Inc., for 10 years before joining his mother's firm. For the last five years, he has been working at Orange in preparation for taking over when Mary retires. Gerald has identified several markets that he feels are lucrative and could increase profits dramatically. Mary believes these markets are both unproven and risky and therefore has not pursued them. ■

EXAMPLE 8

Mary's management style has been "hands on"; she was always involved in all the details of any new project. Gerald has a different style. He believes in providing an overall objective or vision, while allowing others to implement the details. Gerald believes that his management style will enable the business to grow much faster than it did under his mother's leadership. ■

EXAMPLE 9

During his work at Persimmon, Inc., Gerald was promoted to product line manager. He was instrumental in implementing several new manufacturing processes throughout the company. Gerald has plans to implement similar manufacturing processes at Orange. He believes that the savings from reduced quality control costs as well as reduced labor costs will pay for the modernization within three years. ■

EXAMPLE 10

From a strategic planning standpoint, Gerald's long-term goal is to take the business public. He believes that within seven years of taking control, due to modernizing production and expanding product lines, the company will be worth 10 times the amount he will have to pay to purchase it from his mother. He intends to take minimal compensation during this building period with hopes of cashing in via an initial public offering (IPO). Gerald plans to retain 25% ownership after the IPO. He believes that this level of ownership will be enough for him to remain in control of the company as chairman of the board. ■

Employees and customers may not welcome Gerald's plans. Nevertheless, the opportunity to do these things may be the driving force behind Gerald's desire to take over the closely held business. Without the freedom to do so, Gerald may feel he is being prevented from receiving the same satisfaction Mary got from being in charge and meeting the challenges of running the business. Gerald may not feel he is in control of his personal and financial destiny. Without such motivation, the continuation of the business may be highly questionable.

People have a natural resistance to change; they may view changes as threatening. The transferor (old owner) may see the changes as necessary but, at the same time, may feel uncomfortable or not competent to implement them. In such a case, both parties may agree to the transfer of ownership with enthusiasm and great expectations. They may view it as necessary to keep the business viable and growing. On the other hand, since the retiring owner may identify closely with the business, such changes might be taken personally as questioning the owner's past judgments about the company. Thus, the transferor may be hesitant to relinquish ownership, fearing that the new owner might ruin or negatively affect the business. As was discussed earlier, the transferor may view such a downturn of the business as a personal failure. After all, how could such an astute businessperson allow the ownership to fall into the hands of someone who allows the business to fail? Additionally, the transferor may fear that the changes desired by the new owner are appropriate. If the changes are extremely successful, the former owner may feel a loss in prestige.

EXAMPLE 11

Mary has considered expanding the company's product lines, but doing so would require more work than she wishes to assume so close to retirement. Gerald and Mary have discussed the possibility of expanding the product lines once Gerald takes control of the business. They agree that the changes are necessary and that Gerald is the person to implement them. ■

This discussion of emotional issues has highlighted a few of the many opportunities for conflict in succession planning. The tax practitioner will often find that the older generation wants to retain some control while the successor generation wants full control. Additionally, the desire to implement changes often leads to disagreements and reluctance to transfer any ownership. Unless a compromise that is satisfactory to both parties is achieved, any attempt to transfer ownership will be a difficult, if not impossible, proposition.

EXAMPLE 12

As indicated in Example 1, Mary founded Orange because she did not want the business and related jobs to leave town. Mary may not view Gerald's long-term objective of an IPO as desirable. Thus, Mary may be reluctant to turn over complete control of the company to her son. ■

EXAMPLE 13

Since Mary's management style has been to be very involved in all the steps of the business, she has likely developed very close personal relationships with the key production personnel. Gerald's plans to modernize the production processes may call for the elimination of these positions or a significant modification of their responsibilities. These factors may also make Mary hesitant to proceed with any succession plan. ■

EXAMPLE 14

As seen in Example 6, the older generation may not be willing to let go until death. In that case, the younger generation may not be satisfied to wait around. The potential successor may leave the company to work outside the family business if the opportunity to fulfill personal goals appears to be better there. As a result, no qualified family member may be available to take over the business when the older generation either dies or finally decides to retire. The final outcome may be a distressed sale of the business or a decline in business value due to lack of leadership. A forced sale can leave the family unit in an overall lower financial position than if an orderly succession plan had been implemented. ■

Thus, the emotional aspects of the transfer of ownership must be addressed first. If there is an unresolved conflict, one or both parties will be reluctant to follow through with the transfer, no matter how economically and tax advantageous the plan to do so might be.

LO.2

Identify some common economic issues encountered in succession planning from the perspectives of the transferor, transferee, and the closely held business.

ECONOMIC ISSUES IN SUCCESSION PLANNING

Economic Issues Affecting the Transferor. The economic issues for the transferor center on two objectives—funding retirement and funding any potential estate tax liabilities. Any succession plan must address retirement needs as well as the potential estate tax liquidity problems of the transferor.

With a closely held firm, the business interest usually represents a substantial portion of the transferor's personal net worth. As such, the transfer of ownership to the next generation may represent the only opportunity for the retiring owner to cash out the value created by decades of hard work. If the owner is counting on this as a major source of retirement funds, then the value of the transferred interest is paramount. The sale must generate sufficient funds to provide for the comfortable retirement lifestyle the owner desires.

Problems may arise, however, if the retiring owner's expectations conflict with realistic valuation of the business interest.

EXAMPLE 15

Mary has been drawing a pre-tax salary of $250,000 each year. Now she is ready to retire and turn over the business to her son. She expects that the sale to Gerald will generate sufficient funds for her retirement. Her planned retirement lifestyle requires $100,000 annually. After discussing this with her broker, she concludes that sales proceeds of $2,250,000 (after taxes) will be sufficient to generate the desired $100,000 of after-tax income. This assumes the sales proceeds are invested in low-risk municipal securities. However, the average of two independent appraisals of the business indicates that Mary will have only $1,750,000 after the sale and related capital gain taxes. ■

In this case, Mary may need to reconsider either her desired retirement lifestyle or the amount of financial risk she is willing to assume in her retirement portfolio. Her current expectations will not be satisfied based upon the fair market value of the business. Other alternatives would be for Gerald to consider:

- Keeping Mary on as a paid consultant to generate the income differential.
- Gifting annually to Mary either the income shortfall or sufficient funds to build her portfolio to the desired level.

The other aspect of the value of a closely held business is the potential for estate tax liabilities. Depending upon the other financial assets of the owner, the value of the business interest, and how well the owner has implemented effective estate planning techniques, the closely held business interest may result in significant estate taxes due upon the death of the owner. This leads to issues such as minimizing the value in the estate (which may conflict with retirement needs) and providing the liquidity to pay such taxes. Without proper succession planning, the estate may be forced to sell a significant portion of its other assets to pay the estate taxes related to the business. Even worse, it may be forced to sell a portion of the business interest at a distressed price to an outside party.

EXAMPLE 16

Jacob refused to retire or to transfer any ownership to his children during life. Upon his death, his taxable estate is $5 million, of which $4 million is attributable to stock in his business. Jacob expects that his daughter, Esther, will take over the business and his other children will have no involvement. Thus, his will stipulates that 50% of the stock is to be distributed to Esther and the remaining 50% is to be split between his two other children. Even if all other estate assets were sold, sufficient cash to pay the estate taxes would not be available. To satisfy the estate tax burden, the executor may have to sell some of the business assets or part of the business itself to outside owners. ■

Economic Issues Affecting the Transferee. One of the objectives of closely held business owners is financial independence. For the new owner, there are several related considerations. First, the added responsibility and related stress of being the final decision maker have a price. There will likely be additional demands upon the owner's time, often conflicting with other desired activities such as spending time with family.

Second, financial risks assumed with ownership must be compensated, or there will be little economic incentive to take on the business. The owner may be required to incur substantial debt to finance the acquisition. This may be in the form of second mortgages, personal loans, or personal guarantees of the business debts. Finally, the potential return on investment must be acceptable to justify ownership. With the potential for a significant portion of one's wealth to be tied up in the business, ownership must be compared to other investment alternatives.

EXAMPLE 17

In anticipation of taking over Orange Corporation in five years, Gerald quit his job at Persimmon, Inc., to begin working in the family business. As a result of the change in jobs, he took a 20% reduction in salary. When he takes over the family business, Gerald expects to receive a substantial increase in salary. He was willing to accept the temporary reduction in current income in exchange for the possibility of higher future earnings as owner of Orange. ■

EXAMPLE 18

When he purchases his mother's share of the business, Gerald will finance 10% of the price from personal savings and borrow the balance. The bulk of Gerald's savings will come from the $150,000 he rolled over to an IRA from Persimmon's 401(k) retirement plan when he left Persimmon five years ago. This premature distribution from the IRA will trigger both an income tax liability and a 10% excise tax. Gerald also will lose the benefit of tax-deferred compounding in the IRA. Thus, Gerald will have substantially less money at retirement. Any analysis of Gerald's investment in the family business should factor in the ability of the business to replace the lost retirement funds. In addition, the analysis should estimate the company's ability to generate income for repaying the debt incurred to acquire Orange ownership. ■

Most business owners say that the freedom and satisfaction of being one's own boss compensate for *part* of the lost income, but not for all of it. That is, the owner may take a slightly lower return on investment in exchange for the freedom and nonmonetary rewards of being an owner, but is unlikely to accept a zero return on investment. The business must be able to provide both a desirable current lifestyle for the new owner and potential for meeting future lifestyle expectations.

EXAMPLE 19

Refer to Example 16, but assume that the estate taxes were paid without selling any of the business assets or interests to outside parties. At this point, Esther is running a company, in which she owns only 50%, while her siblings, who do not work in the business, own the other 50%. Although Jacob may have intended her greater ownership interest to compensate her for her work in the business, this arrangement may not provide Esther with sufficient compensation for her efforts. Her siblings are entitled to one-half the profit even though they do no work to generate that profit. Depending upon Esther's ability to draw sufficient salary and her relationship with her siblings, she may not be satisfied or motivated by this arrangement. ■

Economic Issues Affecting the Business. With a change of ownership in any closely held business, two major economic concerns must be addressed. First, the business must retain the ability to survive the transition from one owner to the next. Second, the impact of any financing arrangement on current operations and the future viability of the business must be considered. An additional concern arises when there are minority ownership interests. All of these require a review (or creation) of a strategic plan for the business.

Because a closely held business is affected by the personality of its owner, a change of owners can have an impact on the future operations of the business. During the transition period, both employees and key customers' reactions to any change can greatly affect its success or failure. Changes in management style, procedures, technology, product or services offerings, or other aspects of daily operations can have an effect on employees. These changes may be for the better and enhance the profitability of the business, or they may have a detrimental effect on operations. If relations between key customers and the old owner are important to customer retention, communications with customers regarding the ownership transition are critical. Thus, the question of how to retain key customers and personnel must be addressed in any succession plan. Failure to do so may result in a fatal reduction in productivity or sales; consequently, financial obligations to the old owner may not be met, and adequate compensation may not be available to the new owner.

The ability of the business to survive the ownership transition and any related business changes is a key economic consideration. It is especially important in situations where the retiring owner provides part of the financing by taking an installment note in payment for the business interest. If future operations are not sufficient to provide for the debt repayment, the retiring owner may be left without needed retirement funds. Additionally, without sufficient compensation the new owner is unlikely to put forth the effort necessary for the business to continue its operations.

EXAMPLE 20

Refer to Examples 15 and 18. Instead of commercially financing the 90% portion of the purchase price, Mary agrees to take an installment note from Gerald. The payments on the note will be sufficient to provide her the annual retirement income she desires. The internal financing also keeps the interest paid by Gerald within the family unit. While this arrangement keeps the overall family wealth higher, it forces Mary to assume additional risk at a time when she can least afford to do so. Whether assuming this risk makes sense depends on the economic viability of the business under Gerald's direction since the business will be providing the funds for repaying the debt. ■

If the new owner plans to expand the business, any debt incurred must be analyzed for its potential impact on the future borrowing capacity of the firm. Since creditors usually view the owner and the closely held business as one, the obligations of both the owner and the business must be analyzed. Also, businesses that have seasonal inventory borrowing needs should factor them into the debt evaluation.

Another consideration is the existence of minority interests in the business. If such interests have been receiving regular profit distributions in exchange for being silent co-owners, do the economics of the transaction permit these distributions to continue? Should the new owner purchase such interests?

EXAMPLE 21

Assume that as part of the original financing package, Mary borrowed money from her brother and a close family friend. They each received preferred stock that pays an annual dividend of $20,000. Mary's brother is willing to give his shares to Gerald (his nephew) and, in turn, Orange will retire those shares. However, the family friend has come to rely upon the annual dividends from the stock and does not wish to sell. The $20,000 annual dividend on those shares may pose a cash-flow problem in the context of the financing package planned by Gerald. ■

LO.3

Discuss the options available for the transfer of the closely held business interest and the relevant tax considerations.

TRANSFER OPTIONS

A taxpayer has the option of transferring his or her interest in a closely held business either during life or at death. Transfers can occur as gifts, sales, inheritances, or a combination of these. In Chapter 15, planning considerations associated with lifetime and testamenary transfers were discussed. These include the minimization of estate taxes through lifetime giving by taking advantage of the annual gift exclusion. Use of the annual gift exclusion can ease the cost of transfer to a younger generation by reducing the value of the stock subject to transfer taxes. It can also reduce the overall estate tax burden at the older generation's death by removing the asset from the gross estate.

EXAMPLE 22

Refer to Example 17. When Gerald left Persimmon to come to work for Orange Corporation, he took an annual pay cut of $11,000. Each year Mary gives $11,000 of her Orange Corporation stock to Gerald. Had Gerald not taken a pay cut when he started working for Orange, he would have had less than $11,000 *after income taxes* to use to purchase shares from his mother. As long as the annual transfers are not part of a compensation agreement between Gerald and Mary, these transfers can help to minimize the family's overall income and estate taxes. Gerald receives the $11,000 of stock each year without having to earn *more than* $11,000 (because of income taxes) to purchase it. Additionally, Mary does not recognize any gain on the transfer to Gerald since the transfer is a gift. Since Gerald will own the stock at Mary's death, the value of his shares will not be included in Mary's gross estate. ■

Additionally, if an asset has the potential for substantial appreciation, one may wish to leverage the use of the unified credit by giving in excess of the $11,000 annual exclusion.

CONCEPT SUMMARY 16–1

Succession Planning Issues

1. Effective succession planning involves analyzing emotional, economic, and tax issues from the perspective of both the transferor and the transferee.
2. The tax professional must utilize his or her interpersonal, financial analysis, and technical tax skills to identify the issues and reconcile any differences between the transferor and the transferee.
3. Emotional issues can be the largest barrier to succession planning. The most economical and tax-advantaged plan can fail if the emotional needs of both parties are not satisfied. Unresolved emotional differences can also create resistance to implementing a plan.
4. All plans result in some trade-offs among the emotional, economic, and tax issues. Some of the best intentions can result in unwanted economic or tax consequences.
5. Addressing economic issues requires effective retirement and estate planning for the transferor, good personal financial planning for the transferee, and strategic planning for the business.
6. Resolution of the tax issues identified during the planning process focuses on the minimization of the drain on the family net worth caused by transfer (estate and gift) taxes. It also addresses the liquidity problems such taxes can create.

EXAMPLE 23

Assume Mary has sufficient retirement funds and does not need the Orange stock for her retirement. She decides to make a gift of the company to her son Gerald. The current fair market value of Orange is $550,000. If Mary were to use the $11,000 annual gift exclusion and the stock never appreciated, it would take her 50 years to give it all. If both Mary and Gerald are married, use of gift splitting could increase the annual tax-free gift to $44,000 so that only 13 years would be needed to transfer the whole business. However, if the stock goes up in value as Gerald plans in Example 10 (appreciating 10 times in seven years), Mary may never be able to transfer the entire business during her lifetime using the annual exclusion. In this case, Mary could use a portion of her unified credit by giving the entire business in one year before Gerald implements his changes and the value of the stock rapidly appreciates. This plan potentially removes millions of dollars from her gross estate since she will transfer all ownership prior to the appreciation. The downside risk is that the value of the stock could decline to zero (the company could fail) and Mary would have lost the benefit of the unified credit. In that case, the credit would have been applied to a $550,000 gift that would have had a lesser value in her gross estate had she retained ownership of it. ■

The planning issues associated with succession are reviewed in Concept Summary 16–1.

TRANSFER TAX ISSUES

As was discussed in the previous chapter, significant *tax* issues occur when transferring ownership in any asset either by gift or through the estate. First, there is the minimization of the transfer tax (gift or estate tax). Second, the income tax basis is affected by the method and timing of the transfer. The income tax basis is important for determining any taxable gain or loss upon subsequent disposition of the stock by the recipient.

Overall family tax planning attempts to minimize the reduction of family net worth caused by transfer taxes and capital gain taxes. There are trade-offs to be considered. Carryover basis as the result of a nontaxable gift results in larger capital gains on later dispositions. On the other hand, the younger generation must wait until the older generation dies to get a stepped-up basis through the estate. With

TAX FACT

Stock in the Gross Estate

Estate tax returns filed in 1998, 1999, and 2000 for 1998 decedents reported $195.6 billion in combined gross estate. Stock was the largest component of gross estate for these decedents, amounting to nearly $77.2 billion. Approximately 16 percent of the stock was comprised of closely held shares.

Source: IRS Tax Stats.

today's longer life expectancies, the children may not want to wait. Also, waiting until death may cause substantial additional appreciation to be included in the estate. A lifetime transfer can keep such appreciation out of the estate, leveraging the benefits of the annual gift exclusion and the unified credit. These issues must be factored into the analysis of any transfer of ownership in a closely held business.

Whether a gift is taxable depends on the total value of the gift as well as whether the gift is a future or present interest. The annual gift exclusion of $11,000 per recipient shelters the gift of a present interest in a closely held business. When giving shares of a closely held business, the key issue is valuation. Value is important since any increase in the value of the stock over the $11,000 threshold results in either the imposition of transfer taxes or utilization of a portion of the unified credit.

EXAMPLE 24

The book value of Quince Corporation is $110,000. Gyung intends to give his son, Tony, one-tenth of the ownership ($11,000 worth of Quince stock) each year for the next 10 years. Assuming the book value is fair market value and that book value does not increase such that the amount of the gift exceeds $11,000 per year, Gyung can transfer ownership of Quince to Tony without incurring transfer taxes. Tony's basis in the Quince stock will equal his father's basis. However, should the book value be determined to be less than the fair market value, Gyung may owe gift taxes or be forced to use a portion of his unified credit because the gifts exceed the $11,000 annual exclusion. ■

The importance of the carryover versus stepped-up basis issue depends on the intended use of the property by the recipient. If the recipient intends to retain the interest and transfer it to the next generation at death, then the stepped-up basis may not be a concern since there will be no disposition of the interest. In Example 10, however, Gerald intends to sell a portion of his interest to cash in on his efforts. Basis may become an issue since it determines how much taxable gain Gerald will have at the time of the sale. If the difference between Mary's basis and the fair market value at the date of transfer is significant, then the basis may need to be factored into the planning process.

One final point to keep in mind when dealing with the transfer of a closely held business interest by gift is to make sure that a completed transfer has taken place. Refer to the discussion of incomplete transfers in Chapter 15.

EXAMPLE 25

LuEllen is not sure which of her sons she wants to succeed her at Sage Corporation. Both have been working in the business for five years and appear equally qualified to run it. She transfers all of the Sage stock into a trust. The trust provides that income shall be paid to LuEllen for her life and that, at her death, the corpus (Sage stock) shall be distributed equally to her sons. LuEllen retains the right to modify the income beneficiary and the remainder interest beneficiaries up to her death. Under § 2036(a), the value of the trust (Sage value) will be included in her estate since by virtue of retaining the right to income and the right to change beneficiaries, she has not made a completed transfer. ■

This situation may occur when the older generation does not want to release complete control. Therefore, tax professionals must be aware of the tax implications of such situations, especially when trusts are involved in the planning for the closely held business.

LO.4

Understand the issues involved in the valuation of a closely held business interest.

Valuation Problems with a Closely Held Business

By definition, a closely held company is not a publicly traded entity. Thus, there is no easily determined market for the value of the stock. Depending on how widely held the ownership is, one may or may not be able to look to recent transactions between willing buyers and sellers to aid in determining the fair market value of the closely held business. In such cases, some reasonable method must be used to determine a fair market value of the shares transferred. Recently rejected offers from outside parties are not very useful since the owners were not willing to sell for that amount (eliminating the "willing seller" part of the definition of fair market value[1]). If the shares are not adequately valued, a financial disaster can result.

EXAMPLE 26

Mary sells her interest in Orange to Gerald for $1 million. The price is based on a book value of $100 per share. The IRS successfully challenges the use of book value since it does not reflect any goodwill created by Mary's efforts over the years or the fact that Orange's earnings are about twice the industry average. The value is adjusted up to $250 per share. As a result, Mary has sold her interest for less than fair market value and has made a taxable gift of $1,500,000 ($2,500,000 FMV – $1,000,000 sales price). Depending upon Mary's prior use of her unified credit, her net worth, and the amount of capital gain taxes paid on the sale of the Orange stock, Mary may not have the cash available to pay the gift taxes on this additional gift. This could spell financial disaster for Mary. ■

The statute of limitations with respect to the gift tax return is three years after the return is filed or the due date, whichever is later.[2] If the gift tax statute of limitations has expired, the IRS is prohibited from revaluing gifts made during life for purposes of computing the post-1976 adjusted taxable gifts on the estate tax return after the donor's death.[3] Under this law, donors have an incentive to file gift tax returns in order to freeze the value of gifts for estate taxes.

Revenue Ruling 59–60 sets forth the approach, methods, and factors to be considered in valuing the shares of closely held corporations for gift and estate tax purposes.[4] The following factors, although not all-inclusive, are fundamental and require careful analysis in each case.

- The nature of the business and the history of the enterprise from inception.
- The economic outlook in general and the condition and outlook of the specific industry in particular.
- The book value of the stock and the financial condition of the business.

[1]Regulation § 20.2031–1(b) defines fair market value as "the price at which property would change hands between a willing buyer and a willing seller, neither being under any compulsion to buy or sell and both having reasonable knowledge of relevant facts."

[2]§ 6501(a).

[3]Section 2001(f) applies to gifts made after August 5, 1997.

[4]1959–1 C.B. 237. See also Reg. § 20.2031–2(f).

- The earning capacity of the company.
- The company's dividend-paying capacity.
- Whether the enterprise has goodwill or other intangible value.
- The prices and number of shares of stock sold previously and the size of the block of stock to be valued.
- The market price of stocks issued by corporations in the same or a similar line of business and actively traded in a free and open market, either on an exchange or over-the-counter.

The effect of Revenue Ruling 59–60 is an attempt to utilize some of the same financial and business techniques used by financial analysts when valuing publicly traded companies. Securities analysts perform such analysis to develop "buy" and "sell" recommendations for their clients. Some of these factors are discussed in depth below.

GOODWILL

If a closely held corporation's record of past earnings is higher than is usual for the industry, the IRS is apt to claim the presence of goodwill as a corporate asset.

EXAMPLE 27

Gene owned 70% of the stock of Red Corporation, with the remaining 30% held by his children. Over the past five years, Red has generated average net profits of $200,000, and on the date of Gene's death, the book value of the corporation's stock was $500,000. If the IRS identifies 8% as an appropriate rate of return, one approach to the valuation of Red stock would yield the following result.

Average net profit for the past five years	$ 200,000
8% of the $500,000 book value	40,000
Excess earnings over 8%	$ 160,000
Value of goodwill (5 × $160,000)	800,000
Book value	500,000
Total value of the Red stock	$1,300,000

Thus, the IRS might contend that the stock should be included in Gene's gross estate at 70% of $1.3 million, or $910,000. If the estate wishes to argue for a lower valuation, relevant factors might include any of the following.

- The average net profit figure for the past five years ($200,000) may not be representative. Perhaps it includes some extraordinary gains that normally do not occur or are extraneous to the business conducted by the corporation. An example might be a windfall profit for a specific year because of an unusual market situation. The corporation may have recognized a large gain from an appreciated investment held for many years. The figure may also fail to take into account certain expenses that normally would be incurred but for some justifiable reason have been deferred. It is not uncommon to find an unusually low salary structure in a family business during periods of expansion and development. Profits might be considerably less if the owners/employees of the business were being paid the true worth of their services.
- The appropriate rate of return for this type of business may not be 8%. If it is higher, there would be less goodwill because the business is not as profitable as it seems.
- If Gene were a key person in Red's operations, could some or all of any goodwill developed by the business be attributed to his efforts? If so, is it not reasonable to assume that the goodwill might be seriously impaired by Gene's death? ■

MARKET DISCOUNTS

Aside from the issue of goodwill, the valuation of closely held stock must take other factors into account. For example, consider the percentage of ownership involved. If the percentage represents a **minority interest** and the corporation has a poor dividend-paying record, a substantial discount is in order.[5] The justification for the discount is the general inability of the holder of the minority interest to affect corporate policy, particularly with respect to the distribution of dividends. At the other extreme is an interest large enough to represent control, either actual or effective. Considered alone, a controlling interest calls for valuation at a premium.[6]

A controlling interest may be so large, however, that the disposition of the stock within a reasonable period of time after the valuation date could have a negative effect on the market for such shares. The **blockage rule** recognizes what might happen to per-unit value when a large block of shares is marketed at one time.[7] Most often, the rule is applied to stock that has a recognized market. The rule permits a discount from the amount at which smaller lots are selling on or about the valuation date.[8] Although the blockage rule may have a bearing on the valuation of other assets, it is more frequently applied to stocks and securities.[9]

Because most stock in closely held corporations does not trade in a recognized market, a discount for *lack of marketability* may be in order. The discount recognizes the costs that would be incurred in creating a market for such shares to effect their orderly dispositions.[10] The discount could be significant considering typical underwriting expenses and other costs involved in going public.

Closely related to the reasons that an asset's marketability might be impaired is the possibility of built-in income tax consequences. In one case, the value of stock in a holding company was significantly discounted because of the income tax that would ensue if the holding company distributed its major asset to its shareholders.[11]

Since the valuation of closely held stock is subject to so many variables, planning should be directed toward bringing about some measure of certainty.

EXAMPLE 28

Polly wants to transfer some of her stock in Brown Corporation to a trust formed for her children. She would also like to make a substantial contribution to her alma mater, State University. At present, the Brown stock is owned entirely by Polly and has never been traded on any market or otherwise sold or exchanged. Brown's past operations have proved profitable, and Brown has established a respectable record of dividend distributions. Based on the best available information and taking into account various adjustments (e.g., discount for lack of marketability), Polly feels each share of Brown stock possesses a fair market value of $120. ■

If Polly makes a gift of some of the stock to the trust set up for the children and uses the $120 per share valuation, what assurance is there that the IRS will accept this figure? If the IRS is successful in increasing the fair market value per share, Polly could end up with additional gift tax liability.

[5] See, for example, *Jack D. Carr*, 49 TCM 507, T.C.Memo. 1985–19.

[6] *Helvering v. Safe Deposit and Trust Co. of Baltimore, Exr. (Estate of H. Walters)*, 38–1 USTC ¶9240, 21 AFTR 12, 95 F.2d 806 (CA–4, 1938) *aff'g* 35 B.T.A. 259 (1937).

[7] Reg. § 20.2031–2(e).

[8] See, for example, *Estate of Robert Damon*, 49 T.C. 108 (1967).

[9] In *Estate of David Smith*, 57 T.C. 650 (1972), the estate of a now famous sculptor successfully argued for the application of the blockage rule to 425 sculptures included in the gross estate.

[10] See, for example, *Estate of Mark S. Gallo*, 50 TCM 470, T.C.Memo. 1985–363. In this case, the taxpayer also argued that a bad product image (i.e., the Thunderbird, Ripple, and Boone's Farm brands) would depress the value of the stock. Since the trend was toward better wines, association with cheaper products had a negative consumer impact. Not emphasized were the enormous profits that the sale of the cheap wines generated!

[11] *Estate of Artemus D. Davis*, 110 T.C. 530 (1998). The major asset held by the holding company was a considerable block of substantially appreciated stock in the Winn-Dixie supermarket chain.

Polly could hedge against any further gift tax liability. Concurrently with the gift of stock to the trust formed for the children, Polly could make an outright transfer of some of the shares to State University, thereby generating an income tax deduction. Polly would base the income tax deduction on the value used for gift tax purposes.[12] If the IRS later raises the value and assesses more gift tax, Polly can file an amended income tax return, claim a larger charitable contribution deduction, and obtain an offsetting income tax refund. To carry out this hedge, Polly would derive the amount of her gift of Brown stock by comparing her prevailing gift tax and income tax brackets for the year of the transfers. By virtue of the charitable deduction allowed for gift tax purposes by § 2522 (discussed in Chapter 15), no gift tax liability is incurred for the stock transferred to State University.

LO.5

Understand the role that buy-sell agreements play in the context of closely held business interests.

BUY-SELL AGREEMENTS

A **buy-sell agreement** is an essential estate-planning tool for individuals who have spent much of their lives building a business. Its main objective is to dispose of the business in an orderly manner without the risk of the interest falling into the hands of outsiders. Moreover, a buy-sell agreement can ease the problems of estate liquidity and valuation.

Two types of buy-sell agreements exist: **entity** and **cross-purchase** arrangements. Under an entity agreement, the business itself (partnership or corporation) agrees to buy out the interest of the withdrawing owner (partner or shareholder). When an owner is deceased, the estate redeems the interest and receives the proceeds from the business entity. Since the interest receives a stepped-up basis to fair market value at the date of death, the estate recognizes little or no taxable gain from the redemption. If a small amount of gain must be recognized, a corporate distribution can be treated as a sale or exchange rather than as a dividend if it qualifies under § 302(b) or § 303.

Under a cross-purchase agreement, the surviving owners (partners or shareholders) agree to buy out the withdrawing or deceased owner. As with the entity arrangement, the stock or partnership interest held by the estate receives a stepped-up basis at death, and consequently, little or no capital gain or loss is recognized on the transaction.

EXAMPLE 29

Iris, Ned, and Hal are equal and unrelated shareholders in Blue Corporation, and all three share in Blue's management. All agree to turn in their stock to the corporation for redemption at $100 per share if any one of them withdraws (by death or otherwise) from the business. Shortly thereafter, Hal dies, and the estate redeems Hal's one-third share of the Blue stock at the agreed-upon price of $100 per share. ■

EXAMPLE 30

Assume the same facts as in Example 29, except that the agreement is a cross-purchase buy-sell arrangement under which each shareholder promises to buy a portion of the withdrawing shareholder's interest. When Hal dies, the estate sells the Blue stock to Iris and Ned for $100 per share. ■

In each of these situations, the question arises as to whether the $100 price per share represents the fair market value of the business interest to be included in Hal's gross estate. Since the three shareholders are unrelated, the price of the stock

[12]The use of fair market value as the measure of the charitable contribution deduction presumes the Brown stock would yield long-term capital gain if sold by Polly. See § 170(e).

established in the agreement probably represents the fair market value because Iris and Ned would be unwilling to pay more and Hal's executor would be unwilling to accept less than its fair market value. If the shareholders are related, however, the IRS is more likely to scrutinize the motive behind the buy-sell agreement and question the use of the value established for estate tax purposes.

Assume in Example 30 that the three shareholders are related and that Iris and Ned are the persons who would otherwise inherit the stock. In this case, Iris and Ned might wish to set a very low purchase price for the stock if it could be used for purposes of valuing the business interest in the gross estate. A lower valuation would result in a lower estate tax and greater wealth passing to the decedent's beneficiaries. Because of this incentive to undervalue the business, the law now requires that the following three conditions be met before the buy-sell agreement amount can be used for valuing the business for estate tax purposes.

- The price is the result of a bona fide business agreement.
- The agreement is not a device to transfer property to family members.
- The agreement is comparable to other arrangements entered into by persons dealing at arm's length.[13]

The courts generally have accepted any reasonable method for establishing the purchase price of the stock, provided the parties demonstrate that the price was fair when the agreement was executed. Several methods may be used to establish the value of a shareholder's interest in a closely held business, including book value, capitalized earnings, or the company's ability to pay dividends. The buy-sell agreement may specify an exact dollar amount or a price to be determined by formula or appraisal. If a specific dollar amount is stipulated, provisions should be made to review the business periodically and revise this amount accordingly.

Buy-sell agreements that require the lump-sum payment of the entire contract price are usually funded by insurance. Use of insurance for funding buy-sell agreements is discussed below in the section on estate liquidity. Alternatively, the agreement may allow the survivors to pay for the business interest over time. Either way, the cash payments provide the estate with greater liquidity to meet its debt obligations. However, any installment arrangement must be carefully examined to assure that sufficient cash flow from the installments will be available to the estate to satisfy its cash-flow obligations. These include not only tax liabilities but also necessary funds for any survivors who were dependent upon the decedent. Several options exist if an estate is caught off guard by such an arrangement and is strapped for cash to make its tax payments. These include a discretionary extension of time to pay estate taxes as well as an extension of time to pay estate taxes when the estate consists largely of an interest in a closely held business. These options are discussed later in this chapter.

LO.6

Describe the significance of estate freezes and the special use valuation provisions.

ESTATE FREEZES

Corporate Estate Freezes. Over the years, owners of closely held businesses have searched for ways to transfer the major value of the business to their heirs while retaining some security interest and, oftentimes, some degree of control. In the past, a common approach with corporations has been to restructure through a tax-free recapitalization. In a typical corporate freeze, the owner controls the firm through ownership of the voting common stock prior to recapitalization. In the recapitalization, preferred stock is created and retained by the owner. Then, the

[13] § 2703.

owner gives common stock to family members, assigning a very low value to the gifts. This approach freezes the amount that would be included in the owner's gross estate to the value of the preferred stock. Any postgift appreciation in the business is attributed to the common stock and is *not* part of the owner's gross estate.

Under current law, some degree of the **estate freeze** is permitted.[14] Unfortunately, current law is designed to maximize the amount of the gift made by the donor upon the creation of the freeze. Generally, the owner's retained interest in the preferred stock is valued at zero, with the result that the *full* value of the business is subjected to the gift tax.

EXAMPLE 31

Subsequent to a recapitalization, Connor owns all of the stock in Rouge Corporation. The stock is valued as follows: $4 million *common* stock and $1 million preferred stock. The preferred stock is noncumulative, does not have a redemption date, and possesses no liquidation preference. Connor gives the common stock to his adult children and retains the preferred stock. Connor has made a gift to his children of $5 million. The $1 million worth of preferred stock Connor retained is treated as having no value. ■

Special rules apply if the preferred stock is cumulative, has a redemption date, or carries certain other preferential rights. These rules allow some value to be assigned to the preferred stock, thereby reducing the amount of the gift. However, the law now sets a minimum value in the common stock equal to at least 10 percent of the value of the entire business. The adjustments can become complex and are not discussed further in this text.

The estate freeze rules *do not apply* to transfers of the following assets.

- Retained interests for which market quotations are readily available.
- Retained interests that are the same as those transferred (e.g., common stock or a partnership interest in which all partners share equally).
- Transfers of stock to nonfamily members as defined in § 2701(e)(1).

The response of the business community to the current estate freeze rules has not been positive. Consider some of the inherent disadvantages.

- Although part or all of the value of the retained interest is deemed to be a gift, it is also included in the donor's gross estate upon death. In Example 31, therefore, the preferred stock is included in Connor's gross estate upon his subsequent death.
- The donor loses the use of any gift tax paid on the retained interest.

The estate freeze does, however, allow the owner to escape later estate taxation on any post-transfer appreciation that develops.

EXAMPLE 32

Assume the same facts as in Example 31. Connor dies 10 years after the gift when the Rouge Corporation common and preferred stock are worth $10 million and $1 million, respectively. Connor's estate includes only $1 million for the preferred stock. The $6 million appreciation on the common stock ($10 million – $4 million) has escaped transfer taxes. ■

Estate Freezes with Family Limited Partnerships. Due to the statutory limitations imposed on estate freezes using corporations, the adoption of a **family limited partnership (FLP)** to carry out an estate freeze has become popular. An FLP is an entity created under the limited partnership laws of a particular state.

[14] § 2701.

Pursuant to the Revised Uniform Limited Partnership Act, there must be at least one general partner and at least one limited partner. The general partners make the decisions regarding the partnership's management, and the limited partners are not entitled to participate in the management process.

In a common scenario, grandparents form an FLP by transferring a closely held business or other assets that can be expected to appreciate (e.g., real estate) to a limited partnership. The grandparents make themselves general partners (GP) and over a period of years make gifts of limited partnership interests to their children and grandchildren.

In valuing gifts of limited partnership interests, generous discounts (from 25 percent to 60 percent) are made for lack of marketability and minority interests. Because the grandparents are the general partners, they remain in control of the business (i.e., the FLP).

At one point, the IRS contended that a discount for a minority interest was not available as long as the business was held fully within the family unit (e.g., grandparents, children, and grandchildren). After losing on the issue in several court cases, the IRS conceded that the valuation discount is available.[15]

The overall expectation underlying the FLP approach is that a lesser value of the business can be transferred by gift than would be the case if everything is transferred at death. The key to success, however, is the acceptability of the discounts used to value the gifts. Overly generous discount percentages could result in vulnerability to the undervaluation penalty.[16] In addition, gifts of limited partnership interests satisfy the present interest requirement and qualify for the annual exclusion. Like other gift tax strategies, the FLP removes future appreciation on the gifted interest from the donor's estate, thereby reducing the estate tax liability.

Finally, there are favorable estate tax consequences under the FLP approach. The IRS has ruled that the authority of a general partner over partnership assets is not retained control within the meaning of § 2036(a)(2) and is therefore not included in the gross estate of a deceased general partner. However, in light of what happened to the estate freeze of corporate stock previously discussed, it is possible that Congress will enact statutory limitations on the use of FLPs.

REAL ESTATE AND THE SPECIAL USE VALUATION METHOD

Proper valuation principles usually require that real estate be valued at its most suitable (i.e., "best" or "highest") use. Section 2032A, however, permits an election to value certain classes of real estate used in farming or in connection with a closely held business at its "current" use, rather than the most suitable use. The major objective of the **special use value** election is to provide some limited relief to protect the heirs against the possibility of having to sell a portion of the family farm or business to pay estate taxes.

EXAMPLE 33

At the time of his death, Rex owned a dairy farm on the outskirts of a large city. For farming purposes, the property's value is $500,000 (the current use value[17]). As a potential site for a shopping center, however, the property is worth $1.2 million (the most suitable use value). The executor of Rex's estate can elect to include only $500,000 in the gross estate. ■

[15] Rev.Rul. 93–12, 1993–1 C.B. 202, rescinding Rev.Rul. 81–253, 1981–1 C.B. 187.

[16] § 6662(b)(5).

[17] Sections 2032A(e)(7) and (8) set forth the valuation methods that can be used to determine current use value.

TAX IN THE NEWS

USE OF FLPS REQUIRES CAUTION

An estate planner must exercise care when using a family limited partnership (FLP). Considering the decidedly negative attitude of the IRS, the planner must be prepared to take a defensive posture in the event of challenge. The following guidelines may be helpful.

- Avoid the appearance that tax avoidance is the only motivation for using the FLP. For example, more efficient management of the property involved is a proper business justification.
- Depending on the nature of the assets involved, temper the amount of the discount claimed. For example, taking a discount of more than 30 percent for a partnership with marketable securities is inviting IRS scrutiny.
- Be able to support the claimed discount with an appraisal.
- Avoid creating the arrangement in a "deathbed" setting.
- Allow some time to elapse between the creation of the partnership and the gifts of the limited interests.
- Try to avoid funding the partnership with personal use assets (e.g., personal residence).
- Recognize the existence of the arrangement. For example, a general partner should not claim the partnership income if it belongs to the limited partners.

For 2004, the special use valuation procedure permits a reduction of no more than $850,000 in estate tax valuation. This amount is increased for cost-of-living adjustments.

EXAMPLE 34

At the time of her death in 2004, Wanda owned a farm with a most suitable use value of $2.5 million but a current use value of $1.3 million. Assuming the property qualifies under § 2032A and the special use valuation election is made, Wanda's gross estate must include $1.65 million. Only $850,000 can be excluded under § 2032A. ■

Although the special use valuation rules are typically applied to farmland, the value of stock in a closely held business may be reduced to the extent it reflects the underlying value of real property that qualifies under § 2032A. The closely held corporation must be engaged in an active trade or business.

The special use valuation election is available if *all* of the following conditions are satisfied.

- At least 50 percent of the adjusted value of the gross estate consists of *real or personal* property devoted to a qualifying use (used for farming or in a closely held business) at the time of the owner's death.[18]
- The *real* property devoted to a qualifying use comprises at least 25 percent of the adjusted value of the gross estate.

  For purposes of satisfying both the 50 percent test (above) and the 25 percent test, the qualifying property is considered at its most suitable use value. Thus, in Example 33, the property would be treated as if it had a

[18] §§ 2032A(b)(1)(A) and (b)(2). See §§ 2032A(e)(4) and (5) for a definition of "farm" and "farming."

value of $1.2 million (not $500,000). The adjusted value of the gross estate is the gross estate less certain unpaid mortgages and other indebtedness.

- The qualifying property passes to a *qualifying heir* of the decedent. Qualifying heirs are certain family members as set forth in § 2032A(e)(2). They include the decedent's ancestors, spouse, and lineal descendants and their spouses. They also include lineal descendants of the decedent's spouse and any lineal descendants of the decedent's ancestors. Legally adopted children qualify.
- The *real* property has been owned by the decedent or the decedent's family for five out of the eight years ending on the date of the decedent's death and was devoted to a qualifying use during that period.
- The decedent or a member of the decedent's family participated materially in the operation of the farm or business during the five-year period specified above.[19] No one factor is determinative of the presence of material participation, and the practices of the particular industry must be considered.

Section 2032A(c) provides that the estate tax savings derived from the special use valuation method are recaptured from the heir, if he or she disposes of the property or ceases to use it as qualifying use property within a period of 10 years from the date of the decedent's death. Qualifying use includes the rental of the property to a family member on a net cash basis.[20]

EXAMPLE 35

Assume the same facts as in Example 34. Further assume that by electing § 2032A, Wanda's estate tax liability is reduced by $245,000. Three years after Wanda's death, Otis (the qualifying heir) sells the farm to an unrelated party. At this point, Otis must pay the $245,000 additional estate tax liability that would have been imposed had § 2032A not been utilized. ■

In the event recapture occurs, the qualifying heir may *elect* to increase the income tax basis of the property by the amount subject to the recapture. In Examples 34 and 35, Wanda's income tax basis in the farm would be stepped up to $2.5 million. If the election is made, however, interest must be paid on the additional estate tax due.[21]

To enforce compliance with the terms of § 2032A, the Code gives the IRS security by placing a special lien on the qualifying property.[22] The lien arises at the time the § 2032A special valuation is elected and continues until no further tax liability is possible.

The § 2032A election is not available for valuing transfers by gift. Nevertheless, gifts of nonqualifying property may aid in meeting the requirements of § 2032A if the family plans to make the election in the estate tax situation. Recall that one of the requirements of § 2032A is that qualified use property must constitute at least 50 percent of the adjusted value of the gross estate.

EXAMPLE 36

In 1998, Floyd's estate includes the following.

	Fair Market Value
Farm operated by Floyd with current use value of $250,000	$2,000,000
Stock in a local bank	1,400,000
Marketable securities and cash	800,000

[19]§ 2032A(b)(1)(C)(ii). "Material participation" is defined in § 2032A(e)(6).
[20]§ 2032A(c)(7)(E).
[21]§ 1016(c).
[22]§ 6324B.

CONCEPT SUMMARY 16–2

Closely Held Business Valuation Concepts

1. Fair market value is "the price at which property would change hands between a willing buyer and a willing seller, neither being under any compulsion to buy or to sell and both having reasonable knowledge of relevant facts."
2. Determining the value of the stock in a closely held corporation presents unique problems. The presence or absence of *goodwill* at the corporate level has a direct bearing on the value of the stock. A discount may be in order for any of the following: a minority interest, lack of marketability, and the application of the blockage rule. The IRS will contend that a premium attaches to an interest that represents control of the corporation.
3. A properly structured buy-sell agreement can control the value to be assigned to a deceased owner's interest in a partnership or a corporation.
4. An estate tax freeze is useful in avoiding post-transfer appreciation that develops on the partnership or corporate interest involved. However, the donor must consider the gift tax consequences that result when the freeze is created.
5. Section 2032A provides valuation relief for the estates of persons who hold real estate used in farming or in connection with a closely held business. If the requirements of the provision are met and if the executor elects, the real property can be valued at its *current use* rather than its *most suitable use*.

At this point, Floyd's estate does not qualify for the § 2032A election. The qualifying property (farm at $2,000,000) does not equal or exceed 50% of the adjusted gross estate [$2,000,000 (farm) + $1,400,000 (bank stock) + $800,000 (marketable securities and cash)]. ■

EXAMPLE 37

Continuing with the facts in Example 36, Floyd makes a gift of one-half of the bank stock in 1999. He dies in 2004 with no change in asset values. Floyd's estate now qualifies for § 2032A treatment since $2,000,000 (farm) is 50% or more of $3,500,000 [$2,000,000 (farm) + $700,000 (bank stock) + $800,000 (marketable securities and cash)]. The election enables the estate to value the farm as low as $1,150,000. As a result, the estate tax on $850,000 in value is saved. ■

Care must be taken to avoid gifts of property within three years of death. Though such gifts usually are not included in the gross estate of the donor for estate tax purposes, they are counted when testing for the percentage requirements of § 2032A.[23]

EXAMPLE 38

Assume the same facts as in Example 37, except that the gift occurs in 2002 (not 1999). Although only $700,000 of the bank stock is included in Floyd's gross estate for estate tax purposes, $1,400,000 is used for the percentage requirements of the special use valuation provisions. As a result, the estate fails to qualify for the election. ■

LO.7

Discuss the liquidity issues involved in the transfer of a closely held business and the major provisions available to ameliorate them.

Providing Estate Liquidity

Even with effective predeath family tax planning directed toward a minimization of transfer taxes, the smooth administration of an estate necessitates a certain degree of liquidity. Probate costs may be incurred and death taxes may be assessed. In

[23]§ 2035(c)(1)(B).

the meantime, the surviving spouse and dependent beneficiaries may need financial support. Without funds to satisfy these requirements, estate assets may have to be sold at distress prices, and most likely, the decedent's plan of a testamentary business transfer will be defeated.

EXAMPLE 39

At the time of Myrtle's death, her estate was made up almost entirely of a large ranch currently being operated by Jim, one of Myrtle's two sons. Because the ranch had been in the family for several generations and was a successful economic unit, Myrtle hoped that Jim would continue its operation and share the profits with Bob, her other son. Unfortunately, Bob, on learning that his mother had died without a will, demanded and obtained a partition and sale of his share of the property. Additional land was sold to pay for administration expenses and death taxes. After all of the sales had taken place, the portion remaining for Jim could not be operated profitably, and he was forced to give up the family ranch activity. ■

What type of predeath planning might have avoided the result reached in Example 39? Certainly, Myrtle should have recognized and provided for the cash needs of the estate. Life insurance payable to her estate, although it adds to the estate tax liability, could have eased or solved the problem. This presumes that Myrtle was insurable or that the cost of the insurance would not have been prohibitive. Furthermore, Myrtle made a serious error in dying without a will. A carefully drawn will could have precluded Bob's later course of action and perhaps kept much more of the ranch property intact. The ranch could have been placed in trust with a life estate to Jim and Bob and the remainder left to their children. With such an arrangement, Bob would have been unable to sell the principal (the ranch).

Being able to defer the payment of death taxes may be an invaluable option for an estate that lacks cash or near-cash assets (e.g., marketable securities). In this connection, two major possibilities exist.

- A discretionary extension of time (§ 6161).
- An extension of time when the estate consists largely of an interest in a closely held business (§ 6166).

DISCRETIONARY EXTENSION OF TIME TO PAY ESTATE TAXES

Currently, an executor or administrator may request an extension of time for paying the death tax for a period not to exceed 10 years from the date fixed for the payment. The IRS grants such requests whenever there is "reasonable cause." Reasonable cause is *not* limited to a showing of undue hardship. It includes cases in which the executor or administrator is unable to marshal liquid assets readily because they are located in several jurisdictions. It also includes situations where the estate is largely made up of assets in the form of payments to be received in the future (e.g., annuities, copyright royalties, contingent fees, or accounts receivable), or where the assets that must be liquidated to pay the estate tax must be sold at a discount or in a depressed market.

EXTENSION OF PAYMENT TIME FOR THE CLOSELY HELD BUSINESS

Congress has always been sympathetic to the plight of an estate that consists of an interest in a closely held business. The immediate imposition of the estate tax in such a situation may force the liquidation of the business at distress prices or cause the interest to be sold to outside parties.

A possible resolution of the problem is to use § 6166, which requires the IRS to accept a 15-payment procedure (5 interest-only payments, followed by 10 installment payments of the estate tax). This delay can enable the business to generate enough income to buy out the deceased owner's interest without disruption of operations or other financial sacrifice.

To meet the requirements of § 6166, the decedent's interest in a closely held business must exceed 35 percent of the adjusted gross estate.[24] The adjusted gross estate equals the gross estate less the sum allowable as deductions under § 2053 (expenses, indebtedness, and taxes) and § 2054 (casualty and theft losses during the administration of an estate).

An interest in a closely held business includes the following.[25]

- Any sole proprietorship.
- An interest in a partnership carrying on a trade or business, if 20 percent or more of the capital interest in the partnership is included in the gross estate or the partnership has 45 or fewer partners.
- Stock in a corporation carrying on a trade or business, if 20 percent or more of the value of the voting stock of the corporation is included in the gross estate or the corporation has 45 or fewer shareholders.

In meeting the preceding requirements, a decedent and his or her surviving spouse are treated as one owner (shareholder or partner) if the interest is held as community property, tenancy in common, joint tenancy with right of survivorship, or tenancy by the entirety. Attribution from family members is allowed.[26]

EXAMPLE 40

Decedent Bonnie held a 15% capital interest in the Wren Partnership. Her son holds another 10% capital interest. Wren had 46 partners including Bonnie and her son. Since the son's interest is attributed to Bonnie, her estate is deemed to hold a 25% interest, and Wren (for purposes of § 6166) has only 45 partners. ■

In satisfying the more-than-35 percent test for qualification under § 6166, interests in more than one closely held business are aggregated when the decedent's gross estate includes 20 percent or more of the value of each such business.[27]

EXAMPLE 41

Henry's estate includes stock in Green Corporation and Brown Corporation, each of which qualifies as a closely held business. If the stock held in each entity represents 20% or more of the total value outstanding, the stocks can be combined for purposes of the more-than-35% test. ■

If the conditions of § 6166 are satisfied and the provision is elected, the following results transpire.

- No payments on the estate tax attributable to the inclusion of the interest in a closely held business in the gross estate need be made with the first five payments. Then, annual installments are made over a period not longer than 10 years.
- From the outset, interest at the rate of 2 percent is paid.[28] This low rate is limited to the first $1.14 million of estate tax value for the business in excess of the unified credit exemption equivalency amount for 2004.

[24] § 6166(a)(1).
[25] § 6166(b)(1).
[26] As described in § 267(c)(4).
[27] § 6166(c).
[28] § 6601(j)(1).

- The interest rate imposed on the amount of the deferred estate tax attributable to the estate tax value of the closely held business in excess of the 2 percent portion equals 45 percent of the rate applicable to underpayments of tax.
- Acceleration of deferred payments may be triggered upon the disposition of the business or failure to make scheduled principal or interest payments.[29]

In qualifying for § 6166, certain assets that may trigger failure of the 35 percent test should be removed from the potential estate. In particular, lifetime gifts of such assets as marketable securities and life insurance should be considered.[30]

DIGGING DEEPER 1 *Find more information on this topic at our Web site:* ***http://wft-advanced.swlearning.com.***

BUY-SELL AGREEMENTS AND ESTATE LIQUIDITY PLANNING

The role of buy-sell agreements in establishing fair market values for estate and gift tax purposes was discussed previously in this chapter. These agreements also can aid in estate liquidity. First, by establishing a fair market value, it is easier to plan for the estate liquidity needs. Whether the business (entity buy-sell) or the other owners (cross-purchase buy-sell) acquire the business interest, the amount of money necessary to carry out the plan must be ascertained. Second, a properly structured buy-sell agreement ensures that the purchasers will have funds available to purchase the business from the estate and thus provide the liquidity to pay death taxes. The most common approach to funding buy-sell agreements is through the use of life insurance.

For an entity buy-sell arrangement, life insurance is purchased by the business. Then, upon the owner's death, the proceeds are used to redeem the ownership interest from the decedent's estate. The insurance premiums are not deductible for income tax purposes, but the proceeds are not included in the entity's taxable income. Any arrangement for an entity buy-sell funded with life insurance must factor in several items.

- The insurability of the owner and premium cost.
- The ability to increase coverage at a reasonable price as the value of the ownership interest increases.
- The impact on fair market value that any insurance proceeds will have. This trap can catch tax practitioners unaware if they do not specifically address how insurance proceeds are to be treated when computing book value or earnings when the purchase price is based upon either some derivative of book value or earnings history. The resulting increase in value will increase not only the need for funds but also the value of the estate.

The use of an entity buy-sell agreement is often coupled with the use of a § 303 redemption to pay death taxes when the estate qualifies. The § 303 requirements are similar to § 6166 in that the closely held business interest must be greater than 35 percent of the adjusted gross estate. The redemption is generally tax-free since the basis of the stock to the estate is fair market value at the date of death, which is normally the purchase price established by the entity buy-sell agreement.

[29]§ 6166(g).
[30]A gift within three years of death is not effective for this purpose. See § 2035(d)(4).

CONCEPT SUMMARY 16–3

Transfer Tax Planning

1. In reducing or eliminating gift taxes, one can take advantage of the annual exclusion and the election to split gifts.
2. Lifetime gifting can reduce later estate taxes. This is accomplished by giving away assets that will appreciate in value (e.g., stocks, collectibles, life insurance policies). Referred to as "leveraging," it can be done using the annual exclusion or even part of the unified credit prior to death.
3. Timely gifts can help an estate qualify for § 2032A (special use valuation method), § 6166 (15-year payment of estate taxes), and § 303 (stock redemption for the payment of death taxes). To be effective, the gift must avoid the three-year rule of § 2035.
4. Gift planning can help ease potential estate liquidity problems (see item 3 above). After death, § 6166 can be useful if the estate qualifies. The provision allows installment payments over an extended period of time.
5. A properly structured buy-sell agreement aids in liquidity planning in two ways. First, by establishing a fair market value for inclusion in the gross estate, the proper level of liquidity can be anticipated. Second, if the agreement is properly funded through savings or life insurance, the estate is assured that sufficient funds will be available for the payment of death taxes.

In a cross-purchase buy-sell agreement, the various owners take insurance policies out on the lives of their co-owners. The proceeds are payable to the policyholder. The premiums are not tax deductible, but the proceeds are received tax-free. The surviving owners then use the proceeds they received from the policy on their deceased co-owner to purchase the interest from the decedent's estate. As with entity buy-sell agreements, the ability to insure the various parties and to increase that coverage as needed is a concern. Furthermore, since the insurance proceeds are not payable to the business, they have no impact on the earnings or book value amounts used in determining the purchase price. However, a different problem arises when using insurance in a cross-purchase arrangement. Typically, the younger owners will pay higher premiums since they are insuring the lives of the older owners. This may be the case even though the older (and typically greater percentage) owner is earning more from the business than the younger owners. Also, when there are numerous owners, the number of policies that must be maintained by each owner can become quite burdensome. Thus, an entity buy-sell arrangement is often used when there are more than three or four owners.

Both entity and cross-purchase agreements may exist for the same business. In such cases, the tax professional must be sure that the pricing mechanism used for both types of agreements is consistent.

EXAMPLE 42

Refer to Example 21. Assume that instead of taking preferred stock, the uncle and family friend each took 10% of the common stock. Gerald and Orange enter into the following arrangements in connection with his acquisition of Orange. Mary grants Gerald an option to purchase the stock from her estate at a price based on a multiple of five-year trailing earnings that is consistent with publicly traded companies in Orange's industry. Gerald will fund this purchase price by taking out a policy on Mary's life. Orange enters into buy-sell agreements with the uncle and family friend to redeem their shares upon their deaths. The pricing mechanism used for this agreement should be consistent with the one used for the option on Mary's shares. Depending on how large this price is, Orange may wish to take out policies on the minority shareholders' lives or retain sufficient earnings to fund the redemption. Since the price is based on earnings and not book value, the retained earnings or life insurance proceeds should not affect the amount paid for the shares. ■

Suggested Further Readings

John A. Bogdanski, "Maximizing Discounts for 'Built-In' Corporate Taxes," *Estate Planning*, December 2002, pp. 646–653.

Scott A. Dondershine, "Planning for the Transfer of a Successful Closely Held Business," *Estate Planning*, July 2002, pp. 335–342.

Alan Gotthardt, "An Integrated Approach to Estate Planning for Employee Stock Options," *Journal of Retirement Planning*, September/October 2002, pp. 27–34.

Mark C. Tibergren, "Retirement Planning for Business Owners Brings a Fifth Dimension," *Journal of Retirement Planning*, March/April 2002, pp. 27–30.

KEY TERMS

Blockage rule, 16–16
Buy-sell agreement, 16–17
Cross-purchase buy-sell agreement, 16–17
Entity buy-sell agreement, 16–17
Estate freeze, 16–19
Family limited partnership (FLP), 16–19
Minority interest, 16–16
Special use value, 16–20

PROBLEM MATERIALS

West Federal Taxation

Problems

1. In determining the value of goodwill attributable to stock in a closely held corporation, comment on the following factors.
   a. The corporation's average profit figure includes large gains not related to the business conducted.
   b. The family members who own and run the business have not been paid adequate salaries by the corporation.
   c. The rate of return used by the IRS for this type of business is too high.
   d. The deceased owner was active in the operation of the business.

2. At the time of her death, Jean owns 55% of the stock in Gadwall Corporation, with the balance of 45% held by family members. In the past five years, Gadwall has generated average net profits of $600,000, and on the date of Jean's death, the book value of its stock was $1.5 million. An appropriate rate of return for the type of business Gadwall conducts is 8%.
   a. Presuming that some goodwill exists, what value should be included in Jean's gross estate as to the Gadwall stock?
   b. What arguments could Jean's executor make in arguing that the value determined under (a) is too high?

3. What effect, if any, will each of the following factors have on the valuation of stock in a closely held corporation?
   a. The "blockage rule."
   b. A minority interest is involved.
   c. A majority interest is involved.
   d. The cost the corporation would incur in going public.
   e. The income tax consequences upon disposition of the stock.

4. During the same year, a donor gives stock in a closely held corporation to family members and to a qualified charitable organization. In terms of tax planning, what might such a procedure accomplish?

5. Regarding buy-sell agreements, comment on the following.
   a. The difference between the entity and cross-purchase varieties.
   b. The purpose served by buy-sell agreements.

6. What conditions must be satisfied in order for a buy-sell agreement price to control value?

7. Under current law, a disadvantage of an estate freeze for a corporation is that little or no value is assigned to the newly issued preferred stock while all or most of the value is assigned to the existing common shares. If the common shares are expected to appreciate significantly before the transferor's death, is there still any advantage to using an estate freeze?

8. Caleb owns all of the stock of Swallow Corporation. The stock has a value of $3 million for the common and $750,000 for the preferred. The preferred is noncumulative, has no redemption value, and carries no preference as to liquidation. Caleb gives the common stock to his children and retains the preferred stock. What are the tax consequences?

9. Assume the same facts as in Problem 8. Five years after the gift, Caleb dies. At that time, the Swallow stock is worth $3.5 million for the common and $800,000 for the preferred. What are Caleb's tax consequences?

Issue ID

10. At the time of her death, Sally owned and operated the family farm located on the fringes of a large metropolitan area. Brad, Sally's son and sole heir, is a practicing orthopedic surgeon in the city. Brad recognizes the farm's potential for commercial development (e.g., housing subdivision, shopping center). Further, he feels that the property may double in value over the next few years. To defer estate taxes, Brad plans to continue using the property as a farm. Since he knows nothing about farming, Brad hopes to lease the property to Sally's neighbor, who is a family friend. What, if any, are the tax issues involved?

Issue ID

11. In filing his mother's estate tax return, Shawn (her sole heir) properly elects the special use valuation provision of § 2032A. Five years later, Shawn sells the property to a real estate developer. What are the tax issues confronting Shawn regarding the income tax basis of the property sold?

12. A program of lifetime gifts aids in planning for the election of the special use valuation method. Explain.

13. Regarding the special use valuation method of § 2032A, comment on the following independent statements.
    a. For purposes of meeting the requirements for making the election, the qualifying property may consist solely of personal property and need not include real property.
    b. The election of § 2032A is made by the qualifying heir.
    c. For purposes of satisfying both the 50% and the 25% tests, the qualifying property is considered at its *best use* value (rather than at its *current use* value).
    d. If the qualifying property has a most suitable use value of $2.5 million and a current use value of $2 million, the § 2032A election cannot reduce its estate tax value below $2 million.
    e. If the qualifying property has a most suitable use value of $2.5 million and a current use value of $1.4 million, the § 2032A election can reduce its estate tax value to $1.4 million.
    f. A qualifying heir can include a long-time employee who is not part of the decedent's family.

14. Regarding the recapture provisions under the special use valuation method of § 2032A, comment on each of the following independent statements.
    a. Partial recapture may occur when the qualifying use continues for more than 5 years but less than 10 years after the decedent's death.
    b. If recapture occurs, any additional estate tax liability is imposed on the estate.
    c. If recapture occurs, an income tax basis adjustment to the qualifying property may result.
    d. In the event of recapture, interest accrues on any additional estate tax that results.

e. Recapture will not occur as long as the qualifying heir continues to own the property for at least 10 years.
f. The § 2032A election should not be made if it is probable that the qualifying property will be disposed of within the 10-year recapture period.

15. At the time of her death, Hortense has an adjusted gross estate of $3.1 million. Her estate includes the family farm, with a most suitable use value of $1.6 million and a current use value of $800,000. The farm is inherited by Phil, Hortense's son, who has worked it for her since 1985. Phil plans to continue farming indefinitely.
 a. Based on the information given, is the § 2032A election available to Hortense's estate?
 b. If so, what value must be used for the farm?
 c. Suppose Hortense had made a gift of securities (fair market value of $150,000) to her cousin six months before her death. Does this fact affect your analysis? Explain.

Ethics

16. George is executor and sole heir of his father's estate. The major asset in the estate is a pecan grove located on the outskirts of a large metropolitan area. Because of suburban expansion, the grove has substantially appreciated in value over similar agricultural use property. Several of George's friends who are knowledgeable in real estate matters tell him that in five or six years the land may be worth several times its present value. George owns his own grove and will have no difficulty satisfying the qualified use requirement of § 2032A.

 George makes the special use valuation election for his father's property. Although he has no intention of keeping the property as a grove for 10 years, he reasons "why pay estate taxes today that you can put off until tomorrow." Has George acted wisely?

17. The estate of Janet (who is still living) will almost qualify for an election under § 6166. Janet is not concerned, however, because she plans on giving away her life insurance policy before her death. This, she believes, will allow her estate to meet the requirements of § 6166. How does § 2035 affect her planning with respect to the life insurance policy?

18. At the time of his death, Clint had an adjusted gross estate of $2.1 million. Included in the estate is a 15% capital interest in a partnership valued at $800,000. Except for Clint's daughter, Phoebe, none of the other 48 partners is related to him. Phoebe holds a 10% capital interest.
 a. Does Clint's estate qualify for the § 6166 election?
 b. Suppose that one year prior to his death Clint gave $200,000 cash to Phoebe. Does this change your analysis?

19. At the time of her death, Victoria had an adjusted gross estate of $1.5 million. Included in the estate were the following business interests.

	Fair Market Value
A 40% capital interest in the RH Partnership	$300,000
A 25% interest (i.e., 250 shares out of 1,000) in Olive Corporation	200,000
A catering service operated as a sole proprietorship	150,000

The RH Partnership has 42 partners while Olive Corporation has a total of 40 shareholders. None of the other partners or shareholders are related to Victoria. Can Victoria's estate qualify for an election under § 6166? Explain.

Decision Making

20. Joe is the second-generation owner of the Opus Company. He is now 65 and says he has no intentions of retiring. His only child, Beau, runs the business on a day-to-day basis, and though Joe is involved, he is enjoying his current lifestyle. He spends three months on vacation each year, has a company-provided auto, and receives an annual salary and benefits of $250,000. If he were to retire now, the company's defined benefit pension plan would pay him 80% of his salary and continue his health care benefits until his death. There are no spousal survivor benefits under the plan since he is a widower.

 Joe's will leaves all of his remaining stock in Opus to Beau, and he currently gives $11,000 of stock to Beau each year. If Joe were to die today, however, the current value of Opus would be $1.5 million. Joe's other assets in his estate equal $3 million, of which $1 million would be life insurance proceeds, $500,000 for his home and personal assets, and the balance in marketable securities. He has no debts.

Joe has approached you to discuss how his estate can plan for payment of taxes at his death and still keep the company all in Beau's hands as the third-generation owner. There have been several outside offers to buy the company, but neither Joe nor Beau wishes to sell any amount of shares to outsiders in order to raise money for the payment of death taxes.

a. What are some ways that Joe can pay his estate taxes without selling shares to outsiders?
b. What is the signficance of the potential for appreciation in value of both Opus Company stock and the marketable securities?

Research Problems

THOMSON RIA

Note: Solutions to Research Problems can be prepared by using the ***RIA Checkpoint® Student Edition*** *online research product, which is available to accompany this text. It is also possible to prepare solutions to the Research Problems by using tax research materials found in a standard tax library.*

Research Problem 1. At the time of his death in 1998, Kevin Garth owned 8,000 shares in Cimarron Corporation. Cimarron is a closely held C corporation whose stock has never been traded. Under Kevin's will, half of his stock interest (i.e., 4,000 shares) passes to his surviving spouse, Louise. In completing and filing the estate tax return (Form 706), Kevin's executor treats the 8,000 shares of Cimarron stock as a minority interest and assigns a value of $2,000 to each share.

In early 1999, Cimarron redeems all of Louise's shares for $10 million ($2,500 per share). As her basis in the stock is $8 million (4,000 × $2,000), the redemption results in a gain of $2 million ($10 million redemption amount – $8 million basis). The gain is a long-term capital gain that generates a tax of $400,000 ($2 million gain × 20% maximum long-term capital gain tax rate).

In late 1999, Louise dies, and her estate is administered. In completing her estate tax return, Louise's executor claims a $400,000 deduction under § 2053(a)(3). This reflects the claim against the estate for the income taxes resulting from the stock redemption. The executor also prepares Louise's final income tax return (Form 1040). The return reports the $2 million gain. When the return is filed, the $400,000 tax on the gain is paid to the IRS.

In 2000, Kevin's Form 706 is audited by the IRS. Among the adjustments made and agreed to by the estate is an increase in the valuation of the Cimarron stock from $2,000 to $3,000 a share. When the executor of Louise's estate learns of this change, he files an amended income tax return for tax year 1999. What was previously reported as a gain of $2 million from the redemption is now shown as a loss of $2 million ($12 million basis – $10 million redemption amount). In due course, Louise's estate receives a refund from the IRS of the income taxes previously overpaid.

In 2001, Louise's Form 706 is audited by the IRS. Among the adjustments proposed is a disallowance of the $400,000 deduction claimed under § 2053(a)(3).

On what basis can the adjustment proposed by the IRS against Louise's estate be justified? How should the estate argue against the adjustment?

Partial list of research aids:
Ithaca Trust Co. v. U.S., 1 USTC ¶386, 7 AFTR 8856, 49 S.Ct. 291 (USSC, 1929).
Estate of Smith v. Comm., 2000–1 USTC ¶50,147, 84 AFTR2d 99–7393, 198 F.3d 515 (CA–5, 1999).
Estate of Evelyn M. McMorris, 77 TCM 1552, T.C.Memo. 1999–82.

Decision Making
Communications

Research Problem 2. Dana Kerr owns all of the single-class outstanding stock of Crane Corporation. Dana transfers a 20% interest to each of her five adult children. For purposes of § 2512, is each gift to be valued as one of a minority interest? Would it not be appropriate to treat this as a gift of a controlling interest, since the ownership of Crane Corporation remains within the family group? Summarize your position in a letter to Dana. Dana's address is 1402 Milsap Avenue, Kearney, NE 68849.

Appendixes

APPENDIX A

Tax Rate Schedules and Tables

2003 Tax Rate Schedules

Single—Schedule X

If taxable income is: *Over—*	*But not over—*	The tax is:	*of the amount over—*
$0	$ 7,000	........10%	$0
7,000	28,400	$ 700.00 + 15%	7,000
28,400	68,800	3,910.00 + 25%	28,400
68,800	143,500	14,010.00 + 28%	68,800
143,500	311,950	34,926.00 + 33%	143,500
311,950	....	90,514.50 + 35%	311,950

Head of household—Schedule Z

If taxable income is: *Over—*	*But not over—*	The tax is:	*of the amount over—*
$0	$ 10,000	........10%	$0
10,000	38,050	$ 1,000.00 + 15%	10,000
38,050	98,250	5,207.50 + 25%	38,050
98,250	159,100	20,257.50 + 28%	98,250
159,100	311,950	37,295.50 + 33%	159,100
311,950	....	87,736.00 + 35%	311,950

Married filing jointly or Qualifying widow(er)—Schedule Y–1

If taxable income is: *Over—*	*But not over—*	The tax is:	*of the amount over—*
$0	$ 14,000	........10%	$0
14,000	56,800	$ 1,400.00 + 15%	14,000
56,800	114,650	7,820.00 + 25%	56,800
114,650	174,700	22,282.50 + 28%	114,650
174,700	311,950	39,096.50 + 33%	174,700
311,950	....	84,389.00 + 35%	311,950

Married filing separately—Schedule Y–2

If taxable income is: *Over—*	*But not over—*	The tax is:	*of the amount over—*
$0	$ 7,000	........10%	$0
7,000	28,400	$ 700.00 + 15%	7,000
28,400	57,325	3,910.00 + 25%	28,400
57,325	87,350	11,141.25 + 28%	57,325
87,350	155,975	19,548.25 + 33%	87,350
155,975	....	42,194.50 + 35%	155,975

2004 Tax Rate Schedules

Single—Schedule X

If taxable income is: *Over—*	*But not over—*	The tax is:	*of the amount over—*
$0	$ 7,150	........10%	$0
7,150	29,050	$ 715.00 + 15%	7,150
29,050	70,350	4,000.00 + 25%	29,050
70,350	146,750	14,325.00 + 28%	70,350
146,750	319,100	35,717.00 + 33%	146,750
319,100	....	92,592.50 + 35%	319,100

Head of household—Schedule Z

If taxable income is: *Over—*	*But not over—*	The tax is:	*of the amount over—*
$0	$ 10,200	.......10%	$0
10,200	38,900	$ 1,020.00 + 15%	10,200
38,900	100,500	5,325.00 + 25%	38,900
100,500	162,700	20,725.00 + 28%	100,500
162,700	319,100	38,141.00 + 33%	162,700
319,100	....	89,753.00 + 35%	319,100

Married filing jointly or Qualifying widow(er)—Schedule Y–1

If taxable income is: *Over—*	*But not over—*	The tax is:	*of the amount over—*
$0	$ 14,300	........10%	$0
14,300	58,100	$ 1,430.00 + 15%	14,300
58,100	117,250	8,000.00 + 25%	58,100
117,250	178,650	22,787.50 + 28%	117,250
178,650	319,100	39,979.50 + 33%	178,650
319,100	....	86,328.00 + 35%	319,100

Married filing separately—Schedule Y–2

If taxable income is: *Over—*	*But not over—*	The tax is:	*of the amount over—*
$0	$ 7,150	........10%	$0
7,150	29,050	$ 715.00 + 15%	7,150
29,050	58,625	4,000.00 + 25%	29,050
58,625	89,325	11,393.75 + 28%	58,625
89,325	159,550	19,989.75 + 33%	89,325
159,550	....	43,164.00 + 35%	159,550

Income Tax Rates—Estates and Trusts

TAX YEAR 2003

Taxable Income		The Tax Is:	
Over—	But not Over—		Of the Amount Over—
$ 0	$1,900	15%	$ 0
1,900	4,500	$ 285 + 25%	1,900
4,500	6,850	935 + 28%	4,500
6,850	9,350	1,593 + 33%	6,850
9,350	....	2,418 + 35%	9,350

TAX YEAR 2004

Taxable Income		The Tax Is:	
Over—	But not Over—		Of the Amount Over—
$ 0	$1,950	15%	$ 0
1,950	4,600	$ 292.50 + 25%	1,950
4,600	7,000	955.00 + 28%	4,600
7,000	9,550	1,627.00 + 33%	7,000
9,550	....	2,468.50 + 35%	9,550

Income Tax Rates—Corporations

Taxable Income		The Tax Is:	
Over—	But not Over—		Of the Amount Over—
$ 0	$ 50,000	15%	$ 0
50,000	75,000	$ 7,500 + 25%	50,000
75,000	100,000	13,750 + 34%	75,000
100,000	335,000	22,250 + 39%	100,000
335,000	10,000,000	113,900 + 34%	335,000
10,000,000	15,000,000	3,400,000 + 35%	10,000,000
15,000,000	18,333,333	5,150,000 + 38%	15,000,000
18,333,333	....	35%	0

Unified Transfer Tax Rates

FOR GIFTS MADE AND FOR DEATHS AFTER 1983 AND BEFORE 2002

If the Amount with Respect to Which the Tentative Tax to Be Computed Is:	The Tentative Tax Is:
Not over $10,000	18 percent of such amount.
Over $10,000 but not over $20,000	$1,800, plus 20 percent of the excess of such amount over $10,000.
Over $20,000 but not over $40,000	$3,800, plus 22 percent of the excess of such amount over $20,000.
Over $40,000 but not over $60,000	$8,200, plus 24 percent of the excess of such amount over $40,000.
Over $60,000 but not over $80,000	$13,000, plus 26 percent of the excess of such amount over $60,000.
Over $80,000 but not over $100,000	$18,200, plus 28 percent of the excess of such amount over $80,000.
Over $100,000 but not over $150,000	$23,800, plus 30 percent of the excess of such amount over $100,000.
Over $150,000 but not over $250,000	$38,800, plus 32 percent of the excess of such amount over $150,000.
Over $250,000 but not over $500,000	$70,800, plus 34 percent of the excess of such amount over $250,000.
Over $500,000 but not over $750,000	$155,800, plus 37 percent of the excess of such amount over $500,000.
Over $750,000 but not over $1,000,000	$248,300, plus 39 percent of the excess of such amount over $750,000.
Over $1,000,000 but not over $1,250,000	$345,800, plus 41 percent of the excess of such amount over $1,000,000.
Over $1,250,000 but not over $1,500,000	$448,300, plus 43 percent of the excess of such amount over $1,250,000.
Over $1,500,000 but not over $2,000,000	$555,800, plus 45 percent of the excess of such amount over $1,500,000.
Over $2,000,000 but not over $2,500,000	$780,800, plus 49 percent of the excess of such amount over $2,000,000.
Over $2,500,000 but not over $3,000,000	$1,025,800, plus 53 percent of the excess of such amount over $2,500,000.
Over $3,000,000*	$1,290,800, plus 55 percent of the excess of such amount over $3,000,000.

*For large taxable transfers (generally in excess of $10 million), there is a phaseout of the graduated rates and the unified tax credit.

Unified Transfer Tax Rates

FOR GIFTS MADE AND FOR DEATHS IN 2002

If the Amount with Respect to Which the Tentative Tax to Be Computed Is:	The Tentative Tax Is:
Not over $10,000	18 percent of such amount.
Over $10,000 but not over $20,000	$1,800, plus 20 percent of the excess of such amount over $10,000.
Over $20,000 but not over $40,000	$3,800, plus 22 percent of the excess of such amount over $20,000.
Over $40,000 but not over $60,000	$8,200, plus 24 percent of the excess of such amount over $40,000.
Over $60,000 but not over $80,000	$13,000, plus 26 percent of the excess of such amount over $60,000.
Over $80,000 but not over $100,000	$18,200, plus 28 percent of the excess of such amount over $80,000.
Over $100,000 but not over $150,000	$23,800, plus 30 percent of the excess of such amount over $100,000.
Over $150,000 but not over $250,000	$38,800, plus 32 percent of the excess of such amount over $150,000.
Over $250,000 but not over $500,000	$70,800, plus 34 percent of the excess of such amount over $250,000.
Over $500,000 but not over $750,000	$155,800, plus 37 percent of the excess of such amount over $500,000.
Over $750,000 but not over $1,000,000	$248,300, plus 39 percent of the excess of such amount over $750,000.
Over $1,000,000 but not over $1,250,000	$345,800, plus 41 percent of the excess of such amount over $1,000,000.
Over $1,250,000 but not over $1,500,000	$448,300, plus 43 percent of the excess of such amount over $1,250,000.
Over $1,500,000 but not over $2,000,000	$555,800, plus 45 percent of the excess of such amount over $1,500,000.
Over $2,000,000 but not over $2,500,000	$780,800, plus 49 percent of the excess of such amount over $2,000,000.
Over $2,500,000	$1,025,800, plus 50 percent of the excess of such amount over $2,500,000.

Unified Transfer Tax Rates

FOR GIFTS MADE AND FOR DEATHS IN 2003

If the Amount with Respect to Which the Tentative Tax to Be Computed Is:	The Tentative Tax Is:
Not over $10,000	18 percent of such amount.
Over $10,000 but not over $20,000	$1,800, plus 20 percent of the excess of such amount over $10,000.
Over $20,000 but not over $40,000	$3,800, plus 22 percent of the excess of such amount over $20,000.
Over $40,000 but not over $60,000	$8,200, plus 24 percent of the excess of such amount over $40,000.
Over $60,000 but not over $80,000	$13,000, plus 26 percent of the excess of such amount over $60,000.
Over $80,000 but not over $100,000	$18,200, plus 28 percent of the excess of such amount over $80,000.
Over $100,000 but not over $150,000	$23,800, plus 30 percent of the excess of such amount over $100,000.
Over $150,000 but not over $250,000	$38,800, plus 32 percent of the excess of such amount over $150,000.
Over $250,000 but not over $500,000	$70,800, plus 34 percent of the excess of such amount over $250,000.
Over $500,000 but not over $750,000	$155,800, plus 37 percent of the excess of such amount over $500,000.
Over $750,000 but not over $1,000,000	$248,300, plus 39 percent of the excess of such amount over $750,000.
Over $1,000,000 but not over $1,250,000	$345,800, plus 41 percent of the excess of such amount over $1,000,000.
Over $1,250,000 but not over $1,500,000	$448,300, plus 43 percent of the excess of such amount over $1,250,000.
Over $1,500,000 but not over $2,000,000	$555,800, plus 45 percent of the excess of such amount over $1,500,000.
Over $2,000,000	$780,800, plus 49 percent of the excess of such amount over $2,000,000.

Unified Transfer Tax Rates

FOR GIFTS MADE AND FOR DEATHS IN 2004

If the Amount with Respect to Which the Tentative Tax to Be Computed Is:	The Tentative Tax Is:
Not over $10,000	18 percent of such amount.
Over $10,000 but not over $20,000	$1,800, plus 20 percent of the excess of such amount over $10,000.
Over $20,000 but not over $40,000	$3,800, plus 22 percent of the excess of such amount over $20,000.
Over $40,000 but not over $60,000	$8,200, plus 24 percent of the excess of such amount over $40,000.
Over $60,000 but not over $80,000	$13,000, plus 26 percent of the excess of such amount over $60,000.
Over $80,000 but not over $100,000	$18,200, plus 28 percent of the excess of such amount over $80,000.
Over $100,000 but not over $150,000	$23,800, plus 30 percent of the excess of such amount over $100,000.
Over $150,000 but not over $250,000	$38,800, plus 32 percent of the excess of such amount over $150,000.
Over $250,000 but not over $500,000	$70,800, plus 34 percent of the excess of such amount over $250,000.
Over $500,000 but not over $750,000	$155,800, plus 37 percent of the excess of such amount over $500,000.
Over $750,000 but not over $1,000,000	$248,300, plus 39 percent of the excess of such amount over $750,000.
Over $1,000,000 but not over $1,250,000	$345,800, plus 41 percent of the excess of such amount over $1,000,000.
Over $1,250,000 but not over $1,500,000	$448,300, plus 43 percent of the excess of such amount over $1,250,000.
Over $1,500,000 but not over $2,000,000	$555,800, plus 45 percent of the excess of such amount over $1,500,000.
Over $2,000,000	$780,800, plus 48 percent of the excess of such amount over $2,000,000.

Table For Computation of Maximum Credit for State Death Taxes

(A) Adjusted Taxable Estate* Equal to or More Than	(B) Adjusted Taxable Estate* Less Than	(C) Credit on Amount in Column (A)	(D) Rate of Credit on Excess Over Amount in Column (A) (Percentage)
0	$ 40,000	0	None
$ 40,000	90,000	0	0.8
90,000	140,000	$ 400	1.6
140,000	240,000	1,200	2.4
240,000	440,000	3,600	3.2
440,000	640,000	10,000	4.0
640,000	840,000	18,000	4.8
840,000	1,040,000	27,600	5.6
1,040,000	1,540,000	38,800	6.4
1,540,000	2,040,000	70,800	7.2
2,040,000	2,540,000	106,800	8.0
2,540,000	3,040,000	146,800	8.8
3,040,000	3,540,000	190,800	9.6
3,540,000	4,040,000	238,800	10.4
4,040,000	5,040,000	290,800	11.2
5,040,000	6,040,000	402,800	12.0
6,040,000	7,040,000	522,800	12.8
7,040,000	8,040,000	650,800	13.6
8,040,000	9,040,000	786,800	14.4
9,040,000	10,040,000	930,800	15.2
10,040,000		1,082,800	16.0

*Adjusted Taxable Estate = Taxable Estate – $60,000

Scheduled phaseout:

Year	Percentage Allowed
2002	75
2003	50
2004	25
2005	0

Valuation Tables (After April 30, 1999)

TABLE S SINGLE LIFE REMAINDER FACTORS INTEREST RATE

Age	6.6%	6.8%	7.0%	7.2%	7.4%	7.6%	7.8%	8.0%
0	.02700	.02559	.02433	.02321	.02220	.02129	.02047	.01973
1	.01929	.01782	.01650	.01533	.01427	.01331	.01246	.01168
2	.01983	.01829	.01692	.01569	.01458	.01358	.01268	.01187
3	.02065	.01905	.01761	.01632	.01516	.01412	.01317	.01232
4	.02163	.01996	.01846	.01712	.01590	.01481	.01382	.01292
5	.02275	.02101	.01945	.01804	.01677	.01562	.01458	.01364
6	.02398	.02217	.02053	.01906	.01773	.01653	.01544	.01445
7	.02532	.02343	.02172	.02019	.01880	.01754	.01640	.01536
8	.02675	.02479	.02301	.02140	.01995	.01864	.01744	.01635
9	.02832	.02627	.02442	.02274	.02122	.01985	.01859	.01745
10	.03001	.02788	.02595	.02420	.02262	.02118	.01987	.01867
11	.03183	.02961	.02760	.02578	.02413	.02262	.02125	.02000
12	.03377	.03146	.02937	.02748	.02575	.02418	.02275	.02144
13	.03579	.03339	.03122	.02924	.02744	.02580	.02431	.02294
14	.03783	.03534	.03308	.03102	.02915	.02744	.02587	.02444
15	.03986	.03728	.03493	.03279	.03083	.02905	.02742	.02593
16	.04187	.03919	.03674	.03452	.03248	.03063	.02892	.02736
17	.04387	.04108	.03855	.03623	.03411	.03218	.03040	.02877
18	.04588	.04299	.04036	.03795	.03574	.03373	.03187	.03017
19	.04796	.04496	.04222	.03972	.03742	.03532	.03339	.03161
20	.05013	.04702	.04418	.04158	.03919	.03700	.03498	.03313
21	.05242	.04920	.04625	.04354	.04105	.03877	.03667	.03473
22	.05482	.05147	.04841	.04559	.04301	.04063	.03844	.03642
23	.05734	.05387	.05069	.04777	.04508	.04260	.04032	.03821
24	.06001	.05642	.05312	.05008	.04728	.04470	.04232	.04012
25	.06285	.05913	.05570	.05255	.04964	.04695	.04447	.04218
26	.06586	.06200	.05845	.05518	.05215	.04936	.04677	.04438
27	.06907	.06508	.06140	.05800	.05485	.05195	.04925	.04676
28	.07246	.06833	.06451	.06098	.05772	.05469	.05189	.04929
29	.07603	.07176	.06780	.06414	.06075	.05761	.05469	.05198
30	.07978	.07536	.07127	.06748	.06396	.06069	.05766	.05483
31	.08372	.07915	.07491	.07098	.06733	.06394	.06078	.05785
32	.08785	.08313	.07875	.07468	.07089	.06737	.06409	.06103
33	.09220	.08732	.08279	.07858	.07466	.07100	.06759	.06441
34	.09676	.09173	.08705	.08269	.07862	.07483	.07129	.06798

Valuation Tables (After April 30, 1999, *continued*)

TABLE S SINGLE LIFE REMAINDER FACTORS INTEREST RATE

Age	6.6%	6.8%	7.0%	7.2%	7.4%	7.6%	7.8%	8.0%
35	.10157	.09638	.09155	.08704	.08283	.07890	.07522	.07179
36	.10662	.10127	.09628	.09162	.08726	.08319	.07938	.07581
37	.11193	.10641	.10126	.09645	.09194	.08772	.08377	.08006
38	.11751	.11183	.10652	.10155	.09689	.09253	.08843	.08459
39	.12338	.11753	.11206	.10693	.10212	.09761	.09337	.08938
40	.12955	.12355	.11791	.11262	.10766	.10299	.09860	.09447
41	.13606	.12989	.12409	.11864	.11352	.10870	.10417	.09989
42	.14291	.13657	.13061	.12500	.11972	.11475	.11006	.10564
43	.15010	.14360	.13747	.13171	.12627	.12115	.11631	.11174
44	.15764	.15098	.14469	.13876	.13317	.12789	.12290	.11819
45	.16550	.15867	.15223	.14615	.14040	.13496	.12982	.12496
46	.17370	.16671	.16011	.15387	.14796	.14238	.13708	.13207
47	.18220	.17505	.16830	.16190	.15584	.15010	.14466	.13950
48	.19102	.18373	.17682	.17027	.16406	.15817	.15258	.14727
49	.20018	.19274	.18568	.17898	.17262	.16658	.16084	.15539
50	.20969	.20210	.19490	.18805	.18155	.17536	.16948	.16388
51	.21955	.21182	.20448	.19749	.19084	.18452	.17849	.17275
52	.22973	.22186	.21438	.20726	.20047	.19400	.18784	.18196
53	.24022	.23222	.22461	.21735	.21043	.20383	.19753	.19151
54	.25101	.24290	.23516	.22777	.22072	.21399	.20756	.20140
55	.26212	.25389	.24604	.23853	.23136	.22450	.21793	.21166
56	.27355	.26522	.25725	.24963	.24233	.23535	.22867	.22227
57	.28529	.27686	.26879	.26106	.25365	.24656	.23976	.23324
58	.29731	.28878	.28061	.27278	.26528	.25807	.25116	.24453
59	.30956	.30095	.29269	.28477	.27716	.26986	.26284	.25610
60	.32202	.31334	.30500	.29699	.28929	.28190	.27478	.26794
61	.33473	.32598	.31757	.30948	.30170	.29422	.28701	.28007
62	.34772	.33892	.33044	.32229	.31443	.30687	.29958	.29255
63	.36101	.35216	.34363	.33542	.32750	.31986	.31250	.30539
64	.37456	.36568	.35711	.34884	.34087	.33317	.32574	.31857
65	.38838	.37947	.37087	.36257	.35455	.34681	.33932	.33208
66	.40249	.39357	.38496	.37663	.36858	.36079	.35326	.34597
67	.41694	.40803	.39941	.39107	.38299	.37518	.36761	.36028
68	.43170	.42281	.41419	.40585	.39777	.38994	.38235	.37499
69	.44672	.43786	.42927	.42094	.41286	.40503	.39743	.39006

Valuation Tables (After April 30, 1999, *continued*)

TABLE S SINGLE LIFE REMAINDER FACTORS INTEREST RATE

Age	6.6%	6.8%	7.0%	7.2%	7.4%	7.6%	7.8%	8.0%
70	.46194	.45312	.44456	.43626	.42820	.42038	.41278	.40540
71	.47727	.46851	.46000	.45174	.44371	.43591	.42832	.42095
72	.49268	.48399	.47554	.46733	.45934	.45157	.44401	.43666
73	.50813	.49952	.49114	.48299	.47506	.46733	.45981	.45249
74	.52367	.51515	.50686	.49879	.49092	.48325	.47578	.46849
75	.53936	.53095	.52276	.51477	.50698	.49938	.49197	.48474
76	.55524	.54696	.53888	.53100	.52330	.51579	.50846	.50130
77	.57132	.56318	.55523	.54747	.53988	.53247	.52523	.51815
78	.58755	.57957	.57177	.56414	.55668	.54939	.54225	.53527
79	.60385	.59604	.58840	.58092	.57360	.56644	.55943	.55256
80	.62007	.61244	.60497	.59765	.59048	.58347	.57659	.56985
81	.63608	.62864	.62135	.61421	.60721	.60034	.59361	.58701
82	.65182	.64458	.63748	.63052	.62368	.61698	.61041	.60395
83	.66728	.66024	.65334	.64656	.63991	.63338	.62696	.62066
84	.68256	.67574	.66904	.66246	.65599	.64964	.64340	.63727
85	.69775	.69116	.68467	.67830	.67204	.66587	.65982	.65386
86	.71272	.70636	.70010	.69394	.68789	.68193	.67606	.67029
87	.72726	.72114	.71511	.70917	.70333	.69757	.69190	.68632
88	.74137	.73548	.72968	.72396	.71833	.71279	.70732	.70194
89	.75503	.74938	.74381	.73832	.73290	.72757	.72231	.71712
90	.76823	.76281	.75748	.75221	.74702	.74190	.73684	.73186
91	.78075	.77557	.77046	.76542	.76044	.75553	.75068	.74589
92	.79235	.78740	.78250	.77767	.77290	.76818	.76353	.75893
93	.80307	.79832	.79363	.78899	.78441	.77989	.77542	.77100
94	.81306	.80850	.80401	.79956	.79517	.79082	.78653	.78228
95	.82254	.81818	.81387	.80961	.80539	.80122	.79710	.79302
96	.83147	.82729	.82316	.81907	.81503	.81103	.80707	.80315
97	.83973	.83573	.83176	.82784	.82396	.82012	.81632	.81255
98	.84750	.84366	.83985	.83609	.83236	.82867	.82502	.82140
99	.85508	.85140	.84776	.84415	.84057	.83703	.83353	.83005
100	.86246	.85894	.85546	.85200	.84858	.84519	.84183	.83849
101	.86974	.86638	.86305	.85975	.85648	.85324	.85003	.84684
102	.87689	.87369	.87052	.86738	.86426	.86116	.85809	.85505
103	.88399	.88095	.87793	.87494	.87197	.86903	.86611	.86321
104	.89157	.88871	.88586	.88304	.88024	.87745	.87469	.87195

Valuation Tables (After April 30, 1999, *continued*)

TABLE S SINGLE LIFE REMAINDER FACTORS INTEREST RATE

Age	6.6%	6.8%	7.0%	7.2%	7.4%	7.6%	7.8%	8.0%
105	.89898	.89628	.89360	.89094	.88830	.88568	.88307	.88049
106	.90852	.90605	.90359	.90115	.89873	.89632	.89392	.89154
107	.92010	.91791	.91573	.91356	.91141	.90927	.90714	.90502
108	.93814	.93641	.93469	.93298	.93128	.92958	.92790	.92622
109	.96904	.96816	.96729	.96642	.96555	.96468	.96382	.96296

Valuation Tables (After April 30, 1989)

TABLE B TERM CERTAIN REMAINDER FACTORS INTEREST RATE

Years	7.4%	7.6%	7.8%	8.0%	8.2%	8.4%	8.6%	8.8%
1	.931099	.929368	.927644	.925926	.924214	.922509	.920810	.919118
2	.866945	.863725	.860523	.857339	.854172	.851023	.847892	.844777
3	.807211	.802718	.798259	.793832	.789438	.785077	.780747	.776450
4	.751593	.746021	.740500	.735030	.729610	.724241	.718920	.713649
5	.699808	.693328	.686920	.680583	.674316	.668119	.661989	.655927
6	.651590	.644357	.637217	.630170	.623213	.616346	.609566	.602874
7	.606694	.598845	.591111	.583490	.575982	.568585	.561295	.554112
8	.564892	.556547	.548340	.540269	.532331	.524524	.516846	.509294
9	.525971	.517237	.508664	.500249	.491988	.483879	.475917	.468101
10	.489731	.480704	.471859	.463193	.454703	.446383	.438230	.430240
11	.455987	.446750	.437717	.428883	.420243	.411792	.403526	.395441
12	.424569	.415196	.406046	.397114	.388394	.379882	.371571	.363457
13	.395316	.385870	.376666	.367698	.358960	.350445	.342147	.334060
14	.368078	.358615	.349412	.340461	.331756	.323288	.315052	.307040
15	.342717	.333285	.324130	.315242	.306613	.298236	.290103	.282206
16	.319103	.309745	.300677	.291890	.283376	.275126	.267130	.259381
17	.297117	.287867	.278921	.270269	.261901	.253806	.245976	.238401
18	.276645	.267534	.258739	.250249	.242052	.234139	.226497	.219119
19	.257584	.248638	.240018	.231712	.223708	.215995	.208561	.201396
20	.239836	.231076	.222651	.214548	.206754	.199257	.192045	.185107
21	.223311	.214755	.206541	.198656	.191085	.183817	.176837	.170135
22	.207925	.199586	.191596	.183941	.176604	.169573	.162834	.156374
23	.193598	.185489	.177733	.170315	.163220	.156432	.149939	.143726
24	.180259	.172387	.164873	.157699	.150850	.144310	.138065	.132101
25	.167839	.160211	.152943	.146018	.139418	.133128	.127132	.121416
26	.156275	.148895	.141877	.135202	.128852	.122811	.117064	.111596
27	.145507	.138379	.131611	.125187	.119087	.113295	.107794	.102570
28	.135482	.128605	.122088	.115914	.110062	.104515	.099258	.094274
29	.126147	.119521	.113255	.107328	.101721	.096416	.091398	.086649
30	.117455	.111079	.105060	.099377	.094012	.088945	.084160	.079640
31	.109362	.103233	.097458	.092016	.086887	.082053	.077495	.073199
32	.101827	.095942	.090406	.085200	.080302	.075694	.071358	.067278
33	.094811	.089165	.083865	.078889	.074216	.069829	.065708	.061837
34	.088278	.082867	.077797	.073045	.068592	.064418	.060504	.056835
35	.082196	.077014	.072168	.067635	.063394	.059426	.055713	.052238

Valuation Tables (After April 30, 1989, *continued*)

TABLE B TERM CERTAIN REMAINDER FACTORS INTEREST RATE

Years	7.4%	7.6%	7.8%	8.0%	8.2%	8.4%	8.6%	8.8%
36	.076532	.071574	.066946	.062625	.058589	.054821	.051301	.048013
37	.071259	.066519	.062102	.057986	.054149	.050573	.047239	.044130
38	.066349	.061821	.057609	.053690	.050045	.046654	.043498	.040560
39	.061778	.057454	.053440	.049713	.046253	.043039	.040053	.037280
40	.057521	.053396	.049573	.046031	.042747	.039703	.036881	.034264
41	.053558	.049625	.045987	.042621	.039508	.036627	.033961	.031493
42	.049868	.046120	.042659	.039464	.036514	.033789	.031271	.028946
43	.046432	.042862	.039572	.036541	.033746	.031170	.028795	.026605
44	.043233	.039835	.036709	.033834	.031189	.028755	.026515	.024453
45	.040254	.037021	.034053	.031328	.028825	.026527	.024415	.022475
46	.037480	.034406	.031589	.029007	.026641	.024471	.022482	.020657
47	.034898	.031976	.029303	.026859	.024622	.022575	.020701	.018986
48	.032493	.029717	.027183	.024869	.022756	.020825	.019062	.017451
49	.030255	.027618	.025216	.023027	.021031	.019212	.017552	.016039
50	.028170	.025668	.023392	.021321	.019437	.017723	.016163	.014742
51	.026229	.023855	.021699	.019742	.017964	.016350	.014833	.013550
52	.024422	.022170	.020129	.018280	.016603	.015083	.013704	.012454
53	.022739	.020604	.018673	.016925	.015345	.013914	.012619	.011446
54	.021172	.019149	.017322	.015672	.014182	.012836	.011620	.010521
55	.019714	.017796	.016068	.014511	.013107	.011841	.010699	.009670
56	.018355	.016539	.014906	.013436	.012114	.010923	.009852	.008888
57	.017091	.015371	.013827	.012441	.011196	.010077	.009072	.008169
58	.015913	.014285	.012827	.011519	.010347	.009296	.008354	.007508
59	.014817	.013276	.011899	.010666	.009563	.008576	.007692	.006901
60	.013796	.012339	.011038	.009876	.008838	.007911	.007083	.006343

APPENDIX B

Tax Forms

This Appendix includes blank forms for some of the entities and elections discussed in the text. Forms are updated at least once a year. The most current tax forms can be obtained from the IRS Web site: **http://www.irs.gov**.

IRS
Department of the Treasury
Internal Revenue Service
www.irs.gov
Form 656 (Rev. 5-2001)
Catalog Number 16728N

Form 656

Offer in Compromise

IRS RECEIVED DATE

Item 1 — **Taxpayer's Name and Home or Business Address**

Name ____________________

Name ____________________

Street Address ____________________

City State ZIP Code ____________________

Mailing Address *(if different from above)*

Street Address ____________________

City State ZIP Code ____________________

DATE RETURNED

Item 2 — **Social Security Numbers**

(a) Primary ____________________

(b) Secondary ____________________

Item 3 — **Employer Identification Number** *(included in offer)*

____

Item 4 — **Other Employer Identification Numbers** *(not included in offer)* ____________________

Item 5 — **To: Commissioner of Internal Revenue Service**

I/We (includes all types of taxpayers) submit this offer to compromise the tax liabilities plus any interest, penalties, additions to tax, and additional amounts required by law (tax liability) for the tax type and period marked below: (Please mark an "X" in the box for the correct description and fill-in the correct tax period(s), adding additional periods if needed).

❑ **1040/1120 Income Tax** — Year(s) ____________________

❑ **941 Employer's Quarterly Federal Tax Return** — Quarterly period(s) ____________________

❑ **940 Employer's Annual Federal Unemployment (FUTA) Tax Return** — Year(s) ____________________

❑ **Trust Fund Recovery Penalty** as a responsible person of (enter corporation name) ____________________, for failure to pay withholding and Federal Insurance Contributions Act Taxes (Social Security taxes), for period(s) ending ____________________.

❑ **Other Federal Tax(es)** [specify type(s) and period(s)] ____________________

Note: ***If you need more space, use another sheet titled "Attachment to Form 656 Dated ____________." Sign and date the attachment following the listing of the tax periods.***

Item 6 — **I/We submit this offer for the reason(s) checked below:**

❑ **Doubt as to Liability** — "I do not believe I owe this amount." You must include a detailed explanation of the reason(s) why you believe you do not owe the tax in Item 9.

❑ **Doubt as to Collectibility** — "I have insufficient assets and income to pay the full amount." You must include a complete Collection Information Statement, Form 433-A and/or Form 433-B.

❑ **Effective Tax Administration** — "I owe this amount and have sufficient assets to pay the full amount, but due to my exceptional circumstances, requiring full payment would cause an economic hardship or would be unfair and inequitable." You must include a complete Collection Information Statement, Form 433-A and/or Form 433B **and** complete Item 9.

Item 7

I/We offer to pay $ ____________ (must be more than zero). Complete item 10 to explain where you will obtain the funds to make this offer.

Check one of the following:

❑ **Cash Offer (Offered amount will be paid in 90 days or less.)**

Balance to be paid in: ❑ 10; ❑ 30; ❑ 60; or ❑ 90 days from written notice of acceptance of the offer.

❑ **Short-Term Deferred Payment Offer (Offered amount will be paid in MORE than 90 days but within 24 months from written notice of acceptance of the offer.)**

$____________within____________days (not more than 90 — See Instructions Section, **Determine Your Payment Terms**) from written notice of acceptance of the offer; and

beginning in the ________ month after written notice of acceptance of the offer, $____________on the ____________day of each month for a total of ____________months. (Cannot extend more than 24 months from written notice of acceptance of the offer.)

❑ **Deferred Payment Offer (Offered amount will be paid over the life of the collection statute.)**

$____________within____________days (not more than 90 — See Instructions Section, **Determine Your Payment Terms**) from written notice of acceptance of the offer; and

beginning in the first month after written notice of acceptance of the offer, $____________on the____________day of each month for a total of ____________months.

NOTE: Signature(s) of taxpayer required on last page of Form 656

Item 9 — **Explanation of Circumstances**

I am requesting an offer in compromise for the reason(s) listed below:

Note: ***If you are requesting compromise based on doubt as to liability, explain why you don't believe you owe the tax. If you believe you have special circumstances affecting your ability to fully pay the amount due, explain your situation. You may attach additional sheets if necessary.***

Item 10 — **Source of Funds**

I/we shall obtain the funds to make this offer from the following source(s):

Item 11

If I/we submit this offer on a substitute form, I/we affirm that this form is a verbatim duplicate of the official Form 656, and I/we agree to be bound by all the terms and conditions set forth in the official Form 656.

Under penalties of perjury, I declare that I have examined this offer, including accompanying schedules and statements, and to the best of my knowledge and belief, it is true, correct and complete.

11(a) Signature of Taxpayer

Date

11(b) Signature of Taxpayer

Date

For Official Use Only

I accept the waiver of the statutory period of limitations for the Internal Revenue Service.

Signature of Authorized Internal Revenue Service Official

Title

Date

NOTE: Signature(s) of taxpayer required on last page of Form 656

Form **706**

(Rev. August 2003)

Department of the Treasury
Internal Revenue Service

United States Estate (and Generation-Skipping Transfer) Tax Return

Estate of a citizen or resident of the United States (see separate instructions).
To be filed for decedents dying after December 31, 2002, and before January 1, 2004.
For Paperwork Reduction Act Notice, see the separate instructions.

OMB No. 1545-0015

Part 1.—Decedent and Executor

1a Decedent's first name and middle initial (and maiden name, if any)	1b Decedent's last name	2 Decedent's Social Security No.
3a Legal residence (domicile) at time of death (county, state, and ZIP code, or foreign country)	3b Year domicile established / 4 Date of birth	5 Date of death
6a Name of executor (see page 3 of the instructions)	6b Executor's address (number and street including apartment or suite no. or rural route; city, town, or post office; state; and ZIP code)	
6c Executor's social security number (see page 3 of the instructions)		
7a Name and location of court where will was probated or estate administered		7b Case number
8 If decedent died testate, check here ▶ ☐ and attach a certified copy of the will.	9 If Form 4768 is attached, check here ▶ ☐	
10 If Schedule R-1 is attached, check here ▶ ☐		

Part 2.—Tax Computation

1	Total gross estate less exclusion (from Part 5, Recapitulation, page 3, item 12)	1	
2	Total allowable deductions (from Part 5, Recapitulation, page 3, item 23)	2	
3	Taxable estate (subtract line 2 from line 1)	3	
4	Adjusted taxable gifts (total taxable gifts (within the meaning of section 2503) made by the decedent after December 31, 1976, other than gifts that are includible in decedent's gross estate (section 2001(b)))	4	
5	Add lines 3 and 4	5	
6	Tentative tax on the amount on line 5 from Table A on page 4 of the instructions	6	
7	Total gift tax payable with respect to gifts made by the decedent after December 31, 1976. Include gift taxes by the decedent's spouse for such spouse's share of split gifts (section 2513) only if the decedent was the donor of these gifts and they are includible in the decedent's gross estate (see instructions)	7	
8	Gross estate tax (subtract line 7 from line 6)	8	
9	Maximum unified credit (applicable credit amount) against estate tax — 9		
10	Adjustment to unified credit (applicable credit amount). (This adjustment may not exceed $6,000. See page 5 of the instructions.) — 10		
11	Allowable unified credit (applicable credit amount) (subtract line 10 from line 9)	11	
12	Subtract line 11 from line 8 (but do not enter less than zero)	12	
13	Credit for state death taxes (cannot exceed line 12). **Attach credit evidence** (see instructions). Figure the credit by using the amount on line 3 less $60,000. See Table B in the instructions. Enter the amount here from Table B ▶ .... x .50 ▶	13	
14	Subtract line 13 from line 12	14	
15	Credit for Federal gift taxes on pre-1977 gifts (section 2012) (attach computation) — 15		
16	Credit for foreign death taxes (from Schedule(s) P). (Attach Form(s) 706-CE.) — 16		
17	Credit for tax on prior transfers (from Schedule Q) — 17		
18	Total (add lines 15, 16, and 17)	18	
19	Net estate tax (subtract line 18 from line 14)	19	
20	Generation-skipping transfer taxes (from Schedule R, Part 2, line 10)	20	
21	Total transfer taxes (add lines 19 and 20)	21	
22	Prior payments. Explain in an attached statement — 22		
23	United States Treasury bonds redeemed in payment of estate tax — 23		
24	Total (add lines 22 and 23)	24	
25	Balance due (or overpayment) (subtract line 24 from line 21)	25	

Under penalties of perjury, I declare that I have examined this return, including accompanying schedules and statements, and to the best of my knowledge and belief, it is true, correct, and complete. Declaration of preparer other than the executor is based on all information of which preparer has any knowledge.

Signature(s) of executor(s) ______________________ Date ________

______________________ ________

Signature of preparer other than executor ______________ Address (and ZIP code) ______________ Date ________

Cat. No. 20548R

Form 706 (Rev. 8-2003)

Estate of:

Part 3—Elections by the Executor

Please check the "Yes" or "No" box for each question. (See instructions beginning on page 6.)		**Yes**	**No**
1 Do you elect alternate valuation?	1		
2 Do you elect special use valuation? If "Yes," you must complete and attach Schedule A-1.	2		
3 Do you elect to pay the taxes in installments as described in section 6166? If "Yes," you must attach the additional information described on page 9 of the instructions.	3		
4 Do you elect to postpone the part of the taxes attributable to a reversionary or remainder interest as described in section 6163?	4		

Part 4—General Information

(Note: *Please attach the necessary supplemental documents.* **You must attach the death certificate.)** *(See instructions on page 10.)*

Authorization to receive confidential tax information under Regs. sec. 601.504(b)(2)(i); to act as the estate's representative before the IRS; and to make written or oral presentations on behalf of the estate if return prepared by an attorney, accountant, or enrolled agent for the executor:

Name of representative (print or type)	State	Address (number, street, and room or suite no., city, state, and ZIP code)

I declare that I am the ☐ attorney/ ☐ certified public accountant/ ☐ enrolled agent (you must check the applicable box) for the executor and prepared this return for the executor. I am not under suspension or disbarment from practice before the Internal Revenue Service and am qualified to practice in the state shown above.

Signature	CAF number	Date	Telephone number

1 Death certificate number and issuing authority (attach a copy of the death certificate to this return).

2 Decedent's business or occupation. If retired, check here ▶ ☐ and state decedent's former business or occupation.

3 Marital status of the decedent at time of death:

- ☐ Married
- ☐ Widow or widower—Name, SSN, and date of death of deceased spouse ▶
- ☐ Single
- ☐ Legally separated
- ☐ Divorced—Date divorce decree became final ▶

4a Surviving spouse's name	**4b** Social security number	**4c** Amount received (see page 10 of the instructions)

5 Individuals (other than the surviving spouse), trusts, or other estates who receive benefits from the estate (do not include charitable beneficiaries shown in Schedule O) (see instructions). For Privacy Act Notice (applicable to individual beneficiaries only), see the Instructions for Form 1040.

Name of individual, trust, or estate receiving $5,000 or more	Identifying number	Relationship to decedent	Amount (see instructions)
All unascertainable beneficiaries and those who receive less than $5,000 ▶			
Total			

Please check the "Yes" or "No" box for each question.	**Yes**	**No**
6 Does the gross estate contain any section 2044 property (qualified terminable interest property (QTIP) from a prior gift or estate) (see page 11 of the instructions)?		

(continued on next page)

Form 706 (Rev. 8-2003)

Part 4—General Information *(continued)*

Please check the "Yes" or "No" box for each question.	Yes	No
7a Have Federal gift tax returns ever been filed? If "Yes," please attach copies of the returns, if available, and furnish the following information:		
7b Period(s) covered / **7c** Internal Revenue office(s) where filed		
If you answer "Yes" to any of questions 8–16, you must attach additional information as described in the instructions.		
8a Was there any insurance on the decedent's life that is not included on the return as part of the gross estate?		
b Did the decedent own any insurance on the life of another that is not included in the gross estate?		
9 Did the decedent at the time of death own any property as a joint tenant with right of survivorship in which **(a)** one or more of the other joint tenants was someone other than the decedent's spouse, and **(b)** less than the full value of the property is included on the return as part of the gross estate? If "Yes," you must complete and attach Schedule E		
10 Did the decedent, at the time of death, own any interest in a partnership or unincorporated business or any stock in an inactive or closely held corporation?		
11 Did the decedent make any transfer described in section 2035, 2036, 2037, or 2038 (see the instructions for Schedule G beginning on page 13 of the separate instructions)? If "Yes," you must complete and attach Schedule G		
12 Were there in existence at the time of the decedent's death:		
a Any trusts created by the decedent during his or her lifetime?		
b Any trusts not created by the decedent under which the decedent possessed any power, beneficial interest, or trusteeship?		
13 Did the decedent ever possess, exercise, or release any general power of appointment? If "Yes," you must complete and attach Schedule H		
14 Was the marital deduction computed under the transitional rule of Public Law 97-34, section 403(e)(3) (Economic Recovery Tax Act of 1981)?		
If "Yes," attach a separate computation of the marital deduction, enter the amount on item 20 of the Recapitulation, and note on item 20 "computation attached."		
15 Was the decedent, immediately before death, receiving an annuity described in the "General" paragraph of the instructions for Schedule I? If "Yes," you must complete and attach Schedule I		
16 Was the decedent ever the beneficiary of a trust for which a deduction was claimed by the estate of a pre-deceased spouse under section 2056(b)(7) and which is not reported on this return? If "Yes," attach an explanation.		

Part 5—Recapitulation

Item number	Gross estate		Alternate value	Value at date of death
1	Schedule A—Real Estate	1		
2	Schedule B—Stocks and Bonds	2		
3	Schedule C—Mortgages, Notes, and Cash	3		
4	Schedule D—Insurance on the Decedent's Life (attach Form(s) 712)	4		
5	Schedule E—Jointly Owned Property (attach Form(s) 712 for life insurance)	5		
6	Schedule F—Other Miscellaneous Property (attach Form(s) 712 for life insurance)	6		
7	Schedule G—Transfers During Decedent's Life (att. Form(s) 712 for life insurance)	7		
8	Schedule H—Powers of Appointment	8		
9	Schedule I—Annuities	9		
10	Total gross estate (add items 1 through 9)	10		
11	Schedule U—Qualified Conservation Easement Exclusion	11		
12	Total gross estate less exclusion (subtract item 11 from item 10). Enter here and on line 1 of Part 2—Tax Computation	12		

Item number	Deductions		Amount
13	Schedule J—Funeral Expenses and Expenses Incurred in Administering Property Subject to Claims	13	
14	Schedule K—Debts of the Decedent	14	
15	Schedule K—Mortgages and Liens	15	
16	Total of items 13 through 15	16	
17	Allowable amount of deductions from item 16 (see the instructions for item 17 of the Recapitulation)	17	
18	Schedule L—Net Losses During Administration	18	
19	Schedule L—Expenses Incurred in Administering Property Not Subject to Claims	19	
20	Schedule M—Bequests, etc., to Surviving Spouse	20	
21	Schedule O—Charitable, Public, and Similar Gifts and Bequests	21	
22	Schedule T—Qualified Family-Owned Business Interest Deduction	22	
23	Total allowable deductions (add items 17 through 22). Enter here and on line 2 of the Tax Computation	23	

Form 706 (Rev. 8-2003)

Estate of:

SCHEDULE M—Bequests, etc., to Surviving Spouse

Election To Deduct Qualified Terminable Interest Property Under Section 2056(b)(7). If a trust (or other property) meets the requirements of qualified terminable interest property under section 2056(b)(7), and

a. The trust or other property is listed on Schedule M, and

b. The value of the trust (or other property) is entered in whole or in part as a deduction on Schedule M,

then unless the executor specifically identifies the trust (all or a fractional portion or percentage) or other property to be excluded from the election, the executor shall be deemed to have made an election to have such trust (or other property) treated as qualified terminable interest property under section 2056(b)(7).

If less than the entire value of the trust (or other property) that the executor has included in the gross estate is entered as a deduction on Schedule M, the executor shall be considered to have made an election only as to a fraction of the trust (or other property). The numerator of this fraction is equal to the amount of the trust (or other property) deducted on Schedule M. The denominator is equal to the total value of the trust (or other property).

Election To Deduct Qualified Domestic Trust Property Under Section 2056A. If a trust meets the requirements of a qualified domestic trust under section 2056A(a) and this return is filed no later than 1 year after the time prescribed by law (including extensions) for filing the return, and

a. The entire value of a trust or trust property is listed on Schedule M, and

b. The entire value of the trust or trust property is entered as a deduction on Schedule M,

then unless the executor specifically identifies the trust to be excluded from the election, the executor shall be deemed to have made an election to have the entire trust treated as qualified domestic trust property.

			Yes	No
1	Did any property pass to the surviving spouse as a result of a qualified disclaimer? *If "Yes," attach a copy of the written disclaimer required by section 2518(b).*	1		
2a	In what country was the surviving spouse born? ________			
b	What is the surviving spouse's date of birth? ________			
c	Is the surviving spouse a U.S. citizen?	2c		
d	If the surviving spouse is a naturalized citizen, when did the surviving spouse acquire citizenship? ________			
e	If the surviving spouse is not a U.S. citizen, of what country is the surviving spouse a citizen? ________			
3	**Election Out of QTIP Treatment of Annuities**—Do you elect under section 2056(b)(7)(C)(ii) **not** to treat as qualified terminable interest property any joint and survivor annuities that are included in the gross estate and would otherwise be treated as qualified terminable interest property under section 2056(b)(7)(C)? (see instructions)	3		

Item number	Description of property interests passing to surviving spouse	Amount
1		
	Total from continuation schedules (or additional sheets) attached to this schedule	

4	**Total** amount of property interests listed on Schedule M			4	
5a	Federal estate taxes payable out of property interests listed on Schedule M	5a			
b	Other death taxes payable out of property interests listed on Schedule M	5b			
c	Federal and state GST taxes payable out of property interests listed on Schedule M	5c			
d	Add items 5a, b, and c			5d	
6	Net amount of property interests listed on Schedule M (subtract 5d from 4). Also enter on Part 5, Recapitulation, page 3, at item 20			6	

(If more space is needed, attach the continuation schedule from the end of this package or additional sheets of the same size.)
(See the instructions on the reverse side.)

Form 706 (Rev. 8-2003)

Estate of:

SCHEDULE O—Charitable, Public, and Similar Gifts and Bequests

		Yes	No
1a	If the transfer was made by will, has any action been instituted to have interpreted or to contest the will or any of its provisions affecting the charitable deductions claimed in this schedule? . . . . If "Yes," full details must be submitted with this schedule.		
b	According to the information and belief of the person or persons filing this return, is any such action planned? If "Yes," full details must be submitted with this schedule.		
2	Did any property pass to charity as the result of a qualified disclaimer? . . . . If "Yes," attach a copy of the written disclaimer required by section 2518(b).		

Item number	Name and address of beneficiary	Character of institution	Amount
1			
Total from continuation schedules (or additional sheets) attached to this schedule			

3	Total			3	
4a	Federal estate tax payable out of property interests listed above	4a			
b	Other death taxes payable out of property interests listed above	4b			
c	Federal and state GST taxes payable out of property interests listed above	4c			
d	Add items 4a, b, and c			4d	
5	Net value of property interests listed above (subtract 4d from 3). Also enter on Part 5, Recapitulation, page 3, at item 21			5	

(If more space is needed, attach the continuation schedule from the end of this package or additional sheets of the same size.)
(The instructions to Schedule O are in the separate instructions.)

Form 706 (Rev. 8-2003)

Estate of:

SCHEDULE P—Credit for Foreign Death Taxes

List all foreign countries to which death taxes have been paid and for which a credit is claimed on this return.

If a credit is claimed for death taxes paid to more than one foreign country, compute the credit for taxes paid to one country on this sheet and attach a separate copy of Schedule P for each of the other countries.

The credit computed on this sheet is for the ....
(Name of death tax or taxes)

.... imposed in ....
(Name of country)

Credit is computed under the ....
(Insert title of treaty or "statute")

Citizenship (nationality) of decedent at time of death

(All amounts and values must be entered in United States money.)

1 Total of estate, inheritance, legacy, and succession taxes imposed in the country named above attributable to property situated in that country, subjected to these taxes, and included in the gross estate (as defined by statute)	**1**	
2 Value of the gross estate (adjusted, if necessary, according to the instructions for item 2)	**2**	
3 Value of property situated in that country, subjected to death taxes imposed in that country, and included in the gross estate (adjusted, if necessary, according to the instructions for item 3)	**3**	
4 Tax imposed by section 2001 reduced by the total credits claimed under sections 2010, 2011, and 2012 (see instructions)	**4**	
5 Amount of Federal estate tax attributable to property specified at item 3. (Divide item 3 by item 2 and multiply the result by item 4.)	**5**	
6 Credit for death taxes imposed in the country named above (the smaller of item 1 or item 5). Also enter on line 16 of Part 2, Tax Computation	**6**	

SCHEDULE Q—Credit for Tax on Prior Transfers

Part 1—Transferor Information

	Name of transferor	Social security number	IRS office where estate tax return was filed	Date of death
A				
B				
C				

Check here ▶ ☐ if section 2013(f) (special valuation of farm, etc., real property) adjustments to the computation of the credit were made (see page 21 of the instructions).

Part 2—Computation of Credit (see instructions beginning on page 20)

Item	Transferor A	Transferor B	Transferor C	Total A, B, & C
1 Transferee's tax as apportioned (from worksheet, (line 7 ÷ line 8) × line 35 for each column) . .				
2 Transferor's tax (from each column of worksheet, line 20)				
3 Maximum amount before percentage requirement (for each column, enter amount from line 1 or 2, whichever is smaller)				
4 Percentage allowed (each column) (see instructions)	%	%	%	
5 Credit allowable (line 3 × line 4 for each column)				
6 TOTAL credit allowable (add columns A, B, and C of line 5). Enter here and on line 17 of Part 2, Tax Computation				

(The instructions to Schedules P and Q are in the separate instructions.)

Form **709**

Department of the Treasury
Internal Revenue Service

United States Gift (and Generation-Skipping Transfer) Tax Return

(For gifts made during calendar year 2003)

▶ See separate instructions.

OMB No. 1545-0020

2003

Part 1—General Information

1 Donor's first name and middle initial	2 Donor's last name	3 **Donor's social security number**
4 Address (number, street, and apartment number)		5 Legal residence (domicile) (county and state)
6 City, state, and ZIP code		7 Citizenship

		Yes	No
8	If the donor died during the year, check here ▶ ☐ and enter date of death ......, ...		
9	If you received an extension of time to file this Form 709, check here ▶ ☐ and attach the Form 4868, 2688, 2350, or extension letter		
10	Enter the total number of donees listed on Schedule A—count each person only once. ▶		
11a	Have you (the donor) previously filed a Form 709 (or 709-A) for any other year? If "No," skip line 11b		
11b	If the answer to line 11a is "Yes," has your address changed since you last filed Form 709 (or 709-A)?		
12	Gifts by husband or wife to third parties.—Do you consent to have the gifts (including generation-skipping transfers) made by you and by your spouse to third parties during the calendar year considered as made one-half by each of you? (See instructions.) (If the answer is "Yes," the following information must be furnished and your spouse must sign the consent shown below. **If the answer is "No," skip lines 13–18 and go to Schedule A.**)		
13	Name of consenting spouse — 14 SSN		
15	Were you married to one another during the entire calendar year? (see instructions)		
16	If the answer to 15 is "No," check whether ☐ married ☐ divorced or ☐ widowed, and give date (see instructions) ▶		
17	Will a gift tax return for this year be filed by your spouse? (If "Yes," mail both returns in the same envelope.)		

18 **Consent of Spouse**—I consent to have the gifts (and generation-skipping transfers) made by me and by my spouse to third parties during the calendar year considered as made one-half by each of us. We are both aware of the joint and several liability for tax created by the execution of this consent.

Consenting spouse's signature ▶ **Date ▶**

Part 2—Tax Computation

1	Enter the amount from Schedule A, Part 4, line 11	1		
2	Enter the amount from Schedule B, line 3	2		
3	Total taxable gifts (add lines 1 and 2)	3		
4	Tax computed on amount on line 3 (see Table for Computing Tax in separate instructions)	4		
5	Tax computed on amount on line 2 (see Table for Computing Tax in separate instructions)	5		
6	Balance (subtract line 5 from line 4)	6		
7	Maximum unified credit (nonresident aliens, see instructions)	7	345,800	00
8	Enter the unified credit against tax allowable for all prior periods (from Sch. B, line 1, col. C)	8		
9	Balance (subtract line 8 from line 7)	9		
10	Enter 20% (.20) of the amount allowed as a specific exemption for gifts made after September 8, 1976, and before January 1, 1977 (see instructions)	10		
11	Balance (subtract line 10 from line 9)	11		
12	Unified credit (enter the smaller of line 6 or line 11)	12		
13	Credit for foreign gift taxes (see instructions)	13		
14	Total credits (add lines 12 and 13)	14		
15	Balance (subtract line 14 from line 6) (do not enter less than zero)	15		
16	Generation-skipping transfer taxes (from Schedule C, Part 3, col. H, Total)	16		
17	Total tax (add lines 15 and 16)	17		
18	Gift and generation-skipping transfer taxes prepaid with extension of time to file	18		
19	If line 18 is less than line 17, enter **balance due** (see instructions)	19		
20	If line 18 is greater than line 17, enter **amount to be refunded**	20		

Attach check or money order here.

Sign Here

Under penalties of perjury, I declare that I have examined this return, including any accompanying schedules and statements, and to the best of my knowledge and belief, it is true, correct, and complete. Declaration of preparer (other than donor) is based on all information of which preparer has any knowledge.

▶ Signature of donor — Date

Paid Preparer's Use Only

Preparer's signature ▶ — Date — Check if self-employed ▶ ☐

Firm's name (or yours if self-employed), address, and ZIP code ▶ — Phone no. ▶ ( )

Form 709 (2003) Page 2

SCHEDULE A Computation of Taxable Gifts (Including transfers in trust) (see instructions)

A Does the value of any item listed on Schedule A reflect any valuation discount? If "Yes," see instructions . . . . Yes ☐ No ☐

B ☐ ◀ Check here if you elect under section 529(c)(2)(B) to treat any transfers made this year to a qualified state tuition program as made ratably over a 5-year period beginning this year. See instructions. Attach explanation.

Part 1—Gifts Subject Only to Gift Tax. *Gifts less political organization, medical, and educational exclusions—see instructions*

A Item number	B • Donee's name and address • Relationship to donor (if any) • Description of gift • If the gift was of securities, give CUSIP no.	C	D Donor's adjusted basis of gift	E Date of gift	F Value at date of gift	G For split gifts, enter ½ of column F	H Net transfer (subtract col. G from col. F)
1							
Gifts made by spouse—*complete **only** if you are splitting gifts with your spouse and he/she also made gifts.*							

Total of Part 1 (add amounts from Part 1, column H) . . . . ▶

Part 2—Direct skips— gifts that are direct skips and are subject to both gift tax and generation-skipping transfer tax. You must list the gifts in chronological order.

A Item number	B • Donee's name and address • Relationship to donor (if any) • Description of gift • If the gift was of securities, give CUSIP no.	C 2632(b) election out	D Donor's adjusted basis of gift	E Date of gift	F Value at date of gift	G For split gifts, enter ½ of column F	H Net transfer (subtract col. G from col. F)
1							
Gifts made by spouse—*complete **only** if you are splitting gifts with your spouse and he/she also made gifts.*							

Total of Part 2 (add amounts from Part 2, column H) . . . . ▶

Part 3—Indirect skips— gifts to trusts that are currently subject to gift tax and may later be subject to generation-skipping transfer tax. You must list these gifts in chronological order.

A Item number	B • Donee's name and address • Relationship to donor (if any) • Description of gift • If the gift was of securities, give CUSIP no.	C 2632(c) election out	D Donor's adjusted basis of gift	E Date of gift	F Value at date of gift	G For split gifts, enter ½ of column F	H Net transfer (subtract col. G from col. F)
1							
Gifts made by spouse—*complete **only** if you are splitting gifts with your spouse and he/she also made gifts.*							

Total of Part 3 (add amounts from Part 3, column H) . . . . ▶

(If more space is needed, attach additional sheets of same size.) Form **709** (2003)

Form 709 (2003) Page **3**

Part 4—Taxable Gift Reconciliation

1	Total value of gifts of donor (add totals from column H of Parts 1, 2, and 3)	1	
2	Total annual exclusions for gifts listed on line 1 (see instructions)	2	
3	Total included amount of gifts (subtract line 2 from line 1)	3	
	Deductions (see instructions)		
4	Gifts of interests to spouse for which a marital deduction will be claimed, based on items .... of Schedule A — 4		
5	Exclusions attributable to gifts on line 4 — 5		
6	Marital deduction—subtract line 5 from line 4 — 6		
7	Charitable deduction, based on items ....less exclusions — 7		
8	Total deductions—add lines 6 and 7	8	
9	Subtract line 8 from line 3	9	
10	Generation-skipping transfer taxes payable with this Form 709 (from Schedule C, Part 3, col. H, Total)	10	
11	Taxable gifts (add lines 9 and 10). Enter here and on line 1 of the Tax Computation on page 1.	11	

SCHEDULE A Computation of Taxable Gifts *(continued)*

12 Terminable Interest (QTIP) Marital Deduction. (See instructions for line 4 of Schedule A.)

If a trust (or other property) meets the requirements of qualified terminable interest property under section 2523(f), and

a. The trust (or other property) is listed on Schedule A, and

b. The value of the trust (or other property) is entered in whole or in part as a deduction on line 4, Part 4 of Schedule A,

then the donor shall be deemed to have made an election to have such trust (or other property) treated as qualified terminable interest property under section 2523(f).

If less than the entire value of the trust (or other property) that the donor has included in Parts 1 and 3 of Schedule A is entered as a deduction on line 4, the donor shall be considered to have made an election only as to a fraction of the trust (or other property). The numerator of this fraction is equal to the amount of the trust (or other property) deducted on line 6 of Part 4, Schedule A. The denominator is equal to the total value of the trust (or other property) listed in Parts 1 and 3 of Schedule A.

If you make the QTIP election (see instructions for line 4 of Schedule A), the terminable interest property involved will be included in your spouse's gross estate upon his or her death (section 2044). If your spouse disposes (by gift or otherwise) of all or part of the qualifying life income interest, he or she will be considered to have made a transfer of the entire property that is subject to the gift tax (see Transfer of Certain Life Estates on page 4 of the instructions).

13 Election Out of QTIP Treatment of Annuities

☐ ◀ Check here if you elect under section 2523(f)(6) **NOT** to treat as qualified terminable interest property any joint and survivor annuities that are reported on Schedule A and would otherwise be treated as qualified terminable interest property under section 2523(f). (See instructions.) Enter the item numbers (from Schedule A) for the annuities for which you are making this election ▶

SCHEDULE B Gifts From Prior Periods

If you answered "Yes" on line 11a of page 1, Part 1, see the instructions for completing Schedule B. If you answered "No," skip to the Tax Computation on page 1 (or Schedule C, if applicable).

A Calendar year or calendar quarter (see instructions)	B Internal Revenue office where prior return was filed	C Amount of unified credit against gift tax for periods after December 31, 1976	D Amount of specific exemption for prior periods ending before January 1, 1977	E Amount of taxable gifts
1 Totals for prior periods	1			

2	Amount, if any, by which total specific exemption, line 1, column D, is more than $30,000	2	
3	Total amount of taxable gifts for prior periods (add amount, column E, line 1, and amount, if any, on line 2). (Enter here and on line 2 of the Tax Computation on page 1.)	3	

(If more space is needed, attach additional sheets of same size.)

SCHEDULE C Computation of Generation-Skipping Transfer Tax

Note: *Inter vivos direct skips that are completely excluded by the GST exemption must still be fully reported (including value and exemptions claimed) on Schedule C.*

Part 1—Generation-Skipping Transfers

A Item No. (from Schedule A, Part 2, col. A)	B Value (from Schedule A, Part 2, col. H)	C Nontaxable portion of transfer	D Net Transfer (subtract col. C from col. B)
1			
Gifts made by spouse (for gift splitting only)			

Part 2—GST Exemption Reconciliation (Section 2631) and Section 2652(a)(3) Election

Check box ▶ ☐ if you are making a section 2652(a)(3) (special QTIP) election (see instructions)

Enter the item numbers (from Schedule A) of the gifts for which you are making this election ▶ ....

1	Maximum allowable exemption (see instructions)	1	
2	Total exemption used for periods before filing this return	2	
3	Exemption available for this return (subtract line 2 from line 1)	3	
4	Exemption claimed on this return (from Part 3, col. C total, below)	4	
5	Allocation of exemption to transfers reported on Schedule A, Part 3	5	
6	Exemption allocated to transfers not shown on line 4 or 5, above. **You must attach a Notice of Allocation.** (See instructions.)	6	
7	Add lines 4, 5, and 6	7	
8	Exemption available for future transfers (subtract line 7 from line 3)	8	

Part 3—Tax Computation

A Item No. (from Schedule C, Part 1)	B Net transfer (from Schedule C, Part 1, col. D)	C GST Exemption Allocated	D Divide col. C by col. B	E Inclusion Ratio (subtract col. D from 1.000)	F Maximum Estate Tax Rate	G Applicable Rate (multiply col. E by col. F)	H Generation-Skipping Transfer Tax (multiply col. B by col. G)
1					49% (.49)		
2					49% (.49)		
3					49% (.49)		
4					49% (.49)		
5					49% (.49)		
6					49% (.49)		
					49% (.49)		
					49% (.49)		
					49% (.49)		
					49% (.49)		
					49% (.49)		
					49% (.49)		
Total exemption claimed. Enter here and on line 4, Part 2, above. May not exceed line 3, Part 2, above			**Total generation-skipping transfer tax.** Enter here, on line 10 of Schedule A, Part 4, and on line 16 of the Tax Computation on page 1				

(If more space is needed, attach additional sheets of same size.)

Form **851** (Rev. December 2003)
Department of the Treasury
Internal Revenue Service

Affiliations Schedule

▶ **File with each consolidated income tax return.**

Tax year ending ,

OMB No. 1545-0025

Name of common parent corporation | **Employer identification number**

Number, street, and room or suite no. (If a P.O. box, see instructions.)

City or town, state, and ZIP code

Part I **Overpayment Credits, Estimated Tax Payments, and Tax Deposits** (See instructions.)

Corp. No.	Name and address of corporation	Employer identification number	Portion of overpayment credits and estimated tax payments	Portion of tax deposited with Form 7004
1	Common parent corporation			
2	Subsidiary corporations:			
3				
4				
5				
6				
7				
8				
9				
10				
	Totals (Must equal amounts shown on the consolidated tax return.) . . . . ▶			

Part II **Principal Business Activity, Voting Stock Information, Etc.** (See instructions.)

Corp. No.	Principal business activity (PBA)	PBA Code No.	Did the subsidiary make any nondividend distributions?		Stock holdings at beginning of year			
			Yes	No	Number of shares	Percent of voting power	Percent of value	Owned by corporation no.
1	Common parent corporation:							
2	Subsidiary corporations:					%	%	
3						%	%	
4						%	%	
5						%	%	
6						%	%	
7						%	%	
8						%	%	
9						%	%	
10						%	%	

Form 851 (Rev. 12-2003) Page **2**

Part III **Changes in Stock Holdings During the Tax Year**

Corp. No.	Name of corporation	Share-holder of Corpora-tion No.	Date of transaction	**(a)** Changes		**(b)** Shares held after changes described in column (a)	
				Number of shares acquired	Number of shares disposed of	Percent of voting power	Percent of value
						%	%
						%	%
						%	%
						%	%
						%	%
						%	%
						%	%
						%	%

(c) If any transaction listed above caused a deconsolidation of a group member, did the basis of any shares retained by the group exceed the value of those shares immediately before the deconsolidation? See the instructions. . . . . ☐ **Yes** ☐ **No**

(d) Is the group claiming a loss recognized on the disposition of the stock of a group member? If "Yes," see the instructions for details, including the statements that must be attached. . . . . ☐ **Yes** ☐ **No**

(e) If the equitable owners of any capital stock shown above were other than the holders of record, provide details of the changes.

(f) If additional stock was issued, or if any stock was retired during the year, list the dates and amounts of these transactions.

Form **851** (Rev. 12-2003)

Form **990-EZ**

Department of the Treasury
Internal Revenue Service

Short Form
Return of Organization Exempt From Income Tax

Under section 501(c), 527, or 4947(a)(1) of the Internal Revenue Code (except black lung benefit trust or private foundation)

▶ For organizations with gross receipts less than $100,000 and total assets less than $250,000 at the end of the year.

▶ *The organization may have to use a copy of this return to satisfy state reporting requirements.*

OMB No. 1545-1150

2003

Open to Public Inspection

A For the 2003 calendar year, or tax year beginning , 2003, and ending , 20

B Check if applicable:
☐ Address change
☐ Name change
☐ Initial return
☐ Final return
☐ Amended return
☐ Application pending

Please use IRS label or print or type. See Specific Instructions.

C Name of organization

Number and street (or P.O. box, if mail is not delivered to street address) | Room/suite

City or town, state or country, and ZIP + 4

D Employer identification number

E Telephone number ( )

F Group Exemption Number . . ▶

• ***Section 501(c)(3) organizations and 4947(a)(1) nonexempt charitable trusts must attach a completed Schedule A (Form 990 or 990-EZ).***

G Accounting method: ☐ Cash ☐ Accrual Other (specify) ▶

H Check ▶ ☐ if the organization is **not** required to attach Schedule B (Form 990, 990-EZ, or 990-PF).

I **Website:** ▶

J **Organization type** (check only one)— ☐ 501(c) ( ) ◀ (insert no.) ☐ 4947(a)(1) or ☐ 527

K Check ▶ ☐ if the organization's gross receipts are normally not more than $25,000. The organization need not file a return with the IRS; but if the organization received a Form 990 Package in the mail, it should file a return without financial data. **Some states require a complete return.**

L Add lines 5b, 6b, and 7b, to line 9 to determine gross receipts; if $100,000 or more, file Form 990 instead of Form 990-EZ. . ▶ $

Part I Revenue, Expenses, and Changes in Net Assets or Fund Balances (See page 37 of the instructions.)

	Line	Description			Line	Amount
Revenue	1	Contributions, gifts, grants, and similar amounts received			1	
	2	Program service revenue including government fees and contracts			2	
	3	Membership dues and assessments			3	
	4	Investment income			4	
	5a	Gross amount from sale of assets other than inventory	5a			
	b	Less: cost or other basis and sales expenses	5b			
	c	Gain or (loss) from sale of assets other than inventory (line 5a less line 5b) (attach schedule)			5c	
	6	Special events and activities (attach schedule). If any amount is from **gaming,** check here ▶ ☐				
	a	Gross revenue (not including $ ______ of contributions reported on line 1)	6a			
	b	Less: direct expenses other than fundraising expenses	6b			
	c	Net income or (loss) from special events and activities (line 6a less line 6b)			6c	
	7a	Gross sales of inventory, less returns and allowances	7a			
	b	Less: cost of goods sold	7b			
	c	Gross profit or (loss) from sales of inventory (line 7a less line 7b)			7c	
	8	Other revenue (describe ▶)			8	
	9	**Total revenue** (add lines 1, 2, 3, 4, 5c, 6c, 7c, and 8) ▶			9	
Expenses	10	Grants and similar amounts paid (attach schedule)			10	
	11	Benefits paid to or for members			11	
	12	Salaries, other compensation, and employee benefits			12	
	13	Professional fees and other payments to independent contractors			13	
	14	Occupancy, rent, utilities, and maintenance			14	
	15	Printing, publications, postage, and shipping			15	
	16	Other expenses (describe ▶)			16	
	17	**Total expenses** (add lines 10 through 16) ▶			17	
Net Assets	18	Excess or (deficit) for the year (line 9 less line 17)			18	
	19	Net assets or fund balances at beginning of year (from line 27, column (A)) (must agree with end-of-year figure reported on prior year's return)			19	
	20	Other changes in net assets or fund balances (attach explanation)			20	
	21	Net assets or fund balances at end of year (combine lines 18 through 20) ▶			21	

Part II Balance Sheets—If Total assets on line 25, column (B) are $250,000 or more, file Form 990 instead of Form 990-EZ.

Line	(See page 40 of the instructions.)	**(A)** Beginning of year	Line	**(B)** End of year
22	Cash, savings, and investments		22	
23	Land and buildings		23	
24	Other assets (describe ▶)		24	
25	**Total assets**		25	
26	**Total liabilities** (describe ▶)		26	
27	**Net assets or fund balances** (line 27 of column (B) **must** agree with line 21)		27	

For Paperwork Reduction Act Notice, see the separate instructions. Cat. No. 10642I Form **990-EZ** (2003)

Form 990-EZ (2003) Page **2**

Part III **Statement of Program Service Accomplishments** (See page 41 of the instructions.)

What is the organization's primary exempt purpose?

Describe what was achieved in carrying out the organization's exempt purposes. In a clear and concise manner, describe the services provided, the number of persons benefited, or other relevant information for each program title.

Expenses (Required for 501(c)(3) and (4) organizations and 4947(a)(1) trusts; optional for others.)

28	(Grants $)	28a	
29	(Grants $)	29a	
30	(Grants $)	30a	
31 Other program services (attach schedule)	(Grants $)	31a	
32 **Total program service expenses** (add lines 28a through 31a) ▶		32	

Part IV **List of Officers, Directors, Trustees, and Key Employees** (List each one even if not compensated. See page 41 of the instructions.)

(A) Name and address	**(B)** Title and average hours per week devoted to position	**(C)** Compensation **(If not paid, enter -0-.)**	**(D)** Contributions to employee benefit plans & deferred compensation	**(E)** Expense account and other allowances

Part V **Other Information** (**Note** the attachment requirement in General Instruction V, page 14.) **Yes** **No**

33 Did the organization engage in any activity not previously reported to the IRS? If "Yes," attach a detailed description of each activity

34 Were any changes made to the organizing or governing documents but not reported to the IRS? If "Yes," attach a conformed copy of the changes.

35 *If the organization had income from business activities, such as those reported on lines 2, 6, and 7 (among others), but **not** reported on Form 990-T, attach a statement explaining your reason for not reporting the income on Form 990-T.*

a Did the organization have unrelated business gross income of $1,000 or more or 6033(e) notice, reporting, and proxy tax requirements?

b If "Yes," has it filed a tax return on **Form 990-T** for this year?

36 Was there a liquidation, dissolution, termination, or substantial contraction during the year? (If "Yes," attach a statement.)

37a Enter amount of political expenditures, direct or indirect, as described in the instructions. ▶ 37a

b Did the organization file **Form 1120-POL** for this year?

38a Did the organization borrow from, or make any loans to, any officer, director, trustee, or key employee **or** were any such loans made in a prior year and still unpaid at the start of the period covered by this return?

b If "Yes," attach the schedule specified in the line 38 instructions and enter the amount involved. 38b

39 *501(c)(7) organizations.* Enter: **a** Initiation fees and capital contributions included on line 9 39a

b Gross receipts, included on line 9, for public use of club facilities 39b

40a *501(c)(3) organizations.* Enter: Amount of tax imposed on the organization during the year under:
section 4911 ▶ ______ ; section 4912 ▶ ______ ; section 4955 ▶ ______

b *501(c)(3) and (4) organizations.* Did the organization engage in any section 4958 excess benefit transaction during the year or did it become aware of an excess benefit transaction from a prior year? If "Yes," attach an explanation.

c Amount of tax imposed on organization managers or disqualified persons during the year under 4912, 4955, and 4958 ▶

d Enter: Amount of tax on line 40c, above, reimbursed by the organization ▶

41 List the states with which a copy of this return is filed. ▶

42 The books are in care of ▶ Telephone no. ▶ ( )
Located at ▶ ZIP + 4 ▶

43 *Section 4947(a)(1) nonexempt charitable trusts filing Form 990-EZ in lieu of* ***Form 1041***—Check here ▶ ☐
and enter the amount of tax-exempt interest received or accrued during the tax year ▶ 43

Please Sign Here

Under penalties of perjury, I declare that I have examined this return, including accompanying schedules and statements, and to the best of my knowledge and belief, it is true, correct, and complete. Declaration of preparer (other than officer) is based on all information of which preparer has any knowledge.

▶ Signature of officer — Date

▶ Type or print name and title.

Paid Preparer's Use Only

Preparer's signature ▶	Date	Check if self-employed ▶ ☐	Preparer's SSN or PTIN (See Gen. Inst. W)
Firm's name (or yours if self-employed), address, and ZIP + 4 ▶		EIN ▶	
		Phone no. ▶ ( )	

Form **990-T**

Department of the Treasury
Internal Revenue Service

Exempt Organization Business Income Tax Return
(and proxy tax under section 6033(e))

For calendar year 2003 or other tax year beginning ...., 2003, and ending ...., 20 ....

▶ See separate instructions.

OMB No. 1545-0687

2003

A ☐ Check box if address changed

B Exempt under section
☐ 501( )( )
☐ 408(e) ☐ 220(e)
☐ 408A ☐ 530(a)
☐ 529(a)

C Book value of all assets at end of year

Please Print or Type

Name of organization (☐ check box if name changed and see instructions)

Number, street, and room or suite no. (If a P.O. box, see page 7 of instructions.)

City or town, state, and ZIP code

D Employer identification number (Employees' trust, see instructions for Block D on page 7.)

E New unrelated bus. activity codes (See instructions for Block E on page 7.)

F Group exemption number (see instructions for Block F on page 7) ▶

G Check organization type ▶ ☐ 501(c) corporation ☐ 501(c) trust ☐ 401(a) trust ☐ Other trust

H Describe the organization's primary unrelated business activity. ▶

I During the tax year, was the corporation a subsidiary in an affiliated group or a parent-subsidiary controlled group? . . ▶ ☐ Yes ☐ No
If "Yes," enter the name and identifying number of the parent corporation. ▶

J The books are in care of ▶ Telephone number ▶ ( )

Part I Unrelated Trade or Business Income

			(A) Income	(B) Expenses	(C) Net
1a	Gross receipts or sales				
b	Less returns and allowances ______ c Balance ▶	1c			
2	Cost of goods sold (Schedule A, line 7)	2			
3	Gross profit (subtract line 2 from line 1c)	3			
4a	Capital gain net income (attach Schedule D)	4a			
b	Net gain (loss) (Form 4797, Part II, line 18) (attach Form 4797)	4b			
c	Capital loss deduction for trusts	4c			
5	Income (loss) from partnerships and S corporations (attach statement)	5			
6	Rent income (Schedule C)	6			
7	Unrelated debt-financed income (Schedule E)	7			
8	Interest, annuities, royalties, and rents from controlled organizations (Schedule F)	8			
9	Investment income of a section 501(c)(7), (9), or (17) organization (Schedule G)	9			
10	Exploited exempt activity income (Schedule I)	10			
11	Advertising income (Schedule J)	11			
12	Other income (see page 9 of the instructions—attach schedule)	12			
13	**Total** (combine lines 3 through 12)	13			

Part II Deductions Not Taken Elsewhere (See page 9 of the instructions for limitations on deductions.) (Except for contributions, deductions must be directly connected with the unrelated business income.)

14	Compensation of officers, directors, and trustees (Schedule K)	14	
15	Salaries and wages	15	
16	Repairs and maintenance	16	
17	Bad debts	17	
18	Interest (attach schedule)	18	
19	Taxes and licenses	19	
20	Charitable contributions (see page 11 of the instructions for limitation rules)	20	
21	Depreciation (attach Form 4562) ... 21		
22	Less depreciation claimed on Schedule A and elsewhere on return ... 22a	22b	
23	Depletion	23	
24	Contributions to deferred compensation plans	24	
25	Employee benefit programs	25	
26	Excess exempt expenses (Schedule I)	26	
27	Excess readership costs (Schedule J)	27	
28	Other deductions (attach schedule)	28	
29	**Total deductions** (add lines 14 through 28)	29	
30	Unrelated business taxable income before net operating loss deduction (subtract line 29 from line 13)	30	
31	Net operating loss deduction	31	
32	Unrelated business taxable income before specific deduction (subtract line 31 from line 30)	32	
33	Specific deduction (Generally $1,000, but see line 33 instructions for exceptions)	33	
34	**Unrelated business taxable income** (subtract line 33 from line 32). If line 33 is greater than line 32, enter the smaller of zero or line 32	34	

Form 990-T (2003) Page **2**

Part III Tax Computation

35 **Organizations Taxable as Corporations** (see instructions for tax computation on page 12). Controlled group members (sections 1561 and 1563)—check here ☐. **See instructions** and:		
a Enter your share of the $50,000, $25,000, and $9,925,000 taxable income brackets (in that order): **(1)** $ **(2)** $ **(3)** $		
b Enter organization's share of: **(1)** additional 5% tax (not more than $11,750) $		
(2) additional 3% tax (not more than $100,000) . . . . $		
c Income tax on the amount on line 34 . . . . ▶	35c	
36 **Trusts Taxable at Trust Rates** (see instructions for tax computation on page 13) Income tax on the amount on line 34 from: ☐ Tax rate schedule or ☐ Schedule D (Form 1041) . . . . ▶	36	
37 **Proxy tax** (see page 13 of the instructions) . . . . ▶	37	
38 Alternative minimum tax	38	
39 **Total** (add lines 37 and 38 to line 35c or 36, whichever applies)	39	

Part IV Tax and Payments

40a Foreign tax credit (corporations attach Form 1118; trusts attach Form 1116)	40a			
b Other credits (see page 13 of the instructions)	40b			
c General business credit—Check here and indicate which forms are attached: ☐ Form 3800 ☐ Form(s)(specify) ▶	40c			
d Credit for prior year minimum tax (attach Form 8801 or 8827) . . .	40d			
e **Total credits** (add lines 40a through 40d)			40e	
41 Subtract line 40e from line 39			41	
42 Other taxes. Check if from: ☐ Form 4255 ☐ Form 8611 ☐ Form 8697 ☐ Form 8866 ☐ Other (attach schedule).			42	
43 **Total tax** (add lines 41 and 42)			43	
44a Payments: A 2002 overpayment credited to 2003	44a			
b 2003 estimated tax payments	44b			
c Tax deposited with Form 8868	44c			
d Foreign organizations—Tax paid or withheld at source (see instructions)	44d			
e Backup withholding (see instructions)	44e			
f Other credits and payments (see instructions)	44f			
45 **Total payments** (add lines 44a through 44f)			45	
46 Estimated tax penalty (see page 4 of the instructions). Check ▶ ☐ if Form 2220 is attached .			46	
47 **Tax due**—If line 45 is less than the total of lines 43 and 46, enter amount owed . . . . ▶			47	
48 **Overpayment**—If line 45 is larger than the total of lines 43 and 46, enter amount overpaid . ▶			48	
49 Enter the amount of line 48 you want: **Credited to 2004 estimated tax ▶**	**Refunded ▶**		49	

Part V Statements Regarding Certain Activities and Other Information (See instructions on page 15.)

	Yes	No
1 At any time during the 2003 calendar year, did the organization have an interest in or a signature or other authority over a financial account in a foreign country (such as a bank account, securities account, or other financial account)? If "Yes," the organization may have to file Form TD F 90-22.1. If "Yes," enter the name of the foreign country here ▶		
2 During the tax year, did the organization receive a distribution from, or was it the grantor of, or transferor to, a foreign trust? If "Yes," see page 15 of the instructions for other forms the organization may have to file.		
3 Enter the amount of tax-exempt interest received or accrued during the tax year ▶ $		

Schedule A—Cost of Goods Sold — Enter method of inventory valuation ▶

1 Inventory at beginning of year	1		**6** Inventory at end of year . . .	6	
2 Purchases	2		**7** **Cost of goods sold.** Subtract line 6 from line 5. (Enter here and on line 2, Part I.)	7	
3 Cost of labor	3				
4a Additional section 263A costs (attach schedule)	4a		**8** Do the rules of section 263A (with respect to property produced or acquired for resale) apply to the organization?	Yes	No
b Other costs (attach schedule)	4b				
5 **Total**—Add lines 1 through 4b	5				

Sign Here

Under penalties of perjury, I declare that I have examined this return, including accompanying schedules and statements, and to the best of my knowledge and belief, it is true, correct, and complete. Declaration of preparer (other than taxpayer) is based on all information of which preparer has any knowledge.

▶ Signature of officer | Date | ▶ Title

May the IRS discuss this return with the preparer shown below (see instructions)? ☐ Yes ☐ No

Paid Preparer's Use Only

Preparer's signature ▶	Date	Check if self-employed ☐	Preparer's SSN or PTIN
Firm's name (or yours if self-employed), address, and ZIP code ▶		EIN	
		Phone no. ( )	

Form **1065**
Department of the Treasury
Internal Revenue Service

U.S. Return of Partnership Income

For calendar year 2003, or tax year beginning ...., 2003, and ending ...., 20.... .
▶ See separate instructions.

OMB No. 1545-0099
2003

A Principal business activity	Use the IRS label. Otherwise, print or type.	Name of partnership	D Employer identification number
B Principal product or service		Number, street, and room or suite no. If a P.O. box, see page 14 of the instructions.	E Date business started
C Business code number		City or town, state, and ZIP code	F Total assets (see page 14 of the instructions) $

G Check applicable boxes: (1) ☐ Initial return (2) ☐ Final return (3) ☐ Name change (4) ☐ Address change (5) ☐ Amended return
H Check accounting method: (1) ☐ Cash (2) ☐ Accrual (3) ☐ Other (specify) ▶..................
I Number of Schedules K-1. Attach one for each person who was a partner at any time during the tax year ▶..................

Caution: *Include **only** trade or business income and expenses on lines 1a through 22 below. See the instructions for more information.*

Income	1a	Gross receipts or sales	1a			
	b	Less returns and allowances	1b		1c	
	2	Cost of goods sold (Schedule A, line 8)			2	
	3	Gross profit. Subtract line 2 from line 1c			3	
	4	Ordinary income (loss) from other partnerships, estates, and trusts *(attach schedule)*			4	
	5	Net farm profit (loss) *(attach Schedule F (Form 1040))*			5	
	6	Net gain (loss) from Form 4797, Part II, line 18			6	
	7	Other income (loss) *(attach schedule)*			7	
	8	**Total income (loss).** Combine lines 3 through 7			8	
Deductions (see page 15 of the instructions for limitations)	9	Salaries and wages (other than to partners) (less employment credits)			9	
	10	Guaranteed payments to partners			10	
	11	Repairs and maintenance			11	
	12	Bad debts			12	
	13	Rent			13	
	14	Taxes and licenses			14	
	15	Interest			15	
	16a	Depreciation (if required, attach Form 4562)	16a			
	b	Less depreciation reported on Schedule A and elsewhere on return	16b		16c	
	17	Depletion **(Do not deduct oil and gas depletion.)**			17	
	18	Retirement plans, etc.			18	
	19	Employee benefit programs			19	
	20	Other deductions *(attach schedule)*			20	
	21	**Total deductions.** Add the amounts shown in the far right column for lines 9 through 20			21	
	22	**Ordinary income (loss)** from trade or business activities. Subtract line 21 from line 8			22	

Sign Here

Under penalties of perjury, I declare that I have examined this return, including accompanying schedules and statements, and to the best of my knowledge and belief, it is true, correct, and complete. Declaration of preparer (other than general partner or limited liability company member) is based on all information of which preparer has any knowledge.

▶ Signature of general partner or limited liability company member ▶ Date

May the IRS discuss this return with the preparer shown below (see instructions)? ☐ Yes ☐ No

Paid Preparer's Use Only

Preparer's signature	Date	Check if self-employed ▶ ☐	Preparer's SSN or PTIN
Firm's name (or yours if self-employed), address, and ZIP code ▶		EIN ▶	
		Phone no.	( )

Form 1065 (2003) Page **2**

Schedule A Cost of Goods Sold (see page 18 of the instructions)

1	Inventory at beginning of year	1	
2	Purchases less cost of items withdrawn for personal use	2	
3	Cost of labor	3	
4	Additional section 263A costs *(attach schedule)*	4	
5	Other costs *(attach schedule)*	5	
6	**Total.** Add lines 1 through 5	6	
7	Inventory at end of year	7	
8	**Cost of goods sold.** Subtract line 7 from line 6. Enter here and on page 1, line 2	8	

9a Check all methods used for valuing closing inventory:
- (i) ☐ Cost as described in Regulations section 1.471-3
- (ii) ☐ Lower of cost or market as described in Regulations section 1.471-4
- (iii) ☐ Other (specify method used and attach explanation) ▶

b Check this box if there was a writedown of "subnormal" goods as described in Regulations section 1.471-2(c) ▶ ☐

c Check this box if the LIFO inventory method was adopted this tax year for any goods *(if checked, attach Form 970)* ▶ ☐

d Do the rules of section 263A (for property produced or acquired for resale) apply to the partnership? ☐ **Yes** ☐ **No**

e Was there any change in determining quantities, cost, or valuations between opening and closing inventory? ☐ **Yes** ☐ **No**
If "Yes," attach explanation.

Schedule B Other Information

		Yes	No
1	What type of entity is filing this return? Check the applicable box: a ☐ Domestic general partnership b ☐ Domestic limited partnership c ☐ Domestic limited liability company d ☐ Domestic limited liability partnership e ☐ Foreign partnership f ☐ Other ▶		
2	Are any partners in this partnership also partnerships?		
3	During the partnership's tax year, did the partnership own any interest in another partnership or in any foreign entity that was disregarded as an entity separate from its owner under Regulations sections 301.7701-2 and 301.7701-3? If yes, see instructions for required attachment		
4	Is this partnership subject to the consolidated audit procedures of sections 6221 through 6233? If "Yes," see **Designation of Tax Matters Partner** below		
5	Does this partnership meet **all three** of the following requirements? a The partnership's total receipts for the tax year were less than $250,000; b The partnership's total assets at the end of the tax year were less than $600,000; **and** c Schedules K-1 are filed with the return and furnished to the partners on or before the due date (including extensions) for the partnership return. If "Yes," the partnership is not required to complete Schedules L, M-1, and M-2; Item F on page 1 of Form 1065; or Item J on Schedule K-1		
6	Does this partnership have any foreign partners? If "Yes," the partnership may have to file Forms 8804, 8805 and 8813. See page 20 of the instructions		
7	Is this partnership a publicly traded partnership as defined in section 469(k)(2)?		
8	Has this partnership filed, or is it required to file, **Form 8264,** Application for Registration of a Tax Shelter?		
9	At any time during calendar year 2003, did the partnership have an interest in or a signature or other authority over a financial account in a foreign country (such as a bank account, securities account, or other financial account)? See page 20 of the instructions for exceptions and filing requirements for Form TD F 90-22.1. If "Yes," enter the name of the foreign country. ▶		
10	During the tax year, did the partnership receive a distribution from, or was it the grantor of, or transferor to, a foreign trust? If "Yes," the partnership may have to file Form 3520. See page 20 of the instructions		
11	Was there a distribution of property or a transfer (e.g., by sale or death) of a partnership interest during the tax year? If "Yes," you may elect to adjust the basis of the partnership's assets under section 754 by attaching the statement described under **Elections Made By the Partnership** on page 9 of the instructions		
12	Enter the number of **Forms 8865**, Return of U.S. Persons With Respect to Certain Foreign Partnerships, attached to this return ▶		

Designation of Tax Matters Partner (see page 20 of the instructions)

Enter below the general partner designated as the tax matters partner (TMP) for the tax year of this return:

Name of designated TMP ▶ Identifying number of TMP ▶

Address of designated TMP ▶

Form **1065** (2003)

Form 1065 (2003) Page **3**

Schedule K Partners' Shares of Income, Credits, Deductions, etc.

	(a) Distributive share items		(b) Total amount
Income (Loss)	1 Ordinary income (loss) from trade or business activities (page 1, line 22)	1	
	2 Net income (loss) from rental real estate activities *(attach Form 8825)*	2	
	3a Gross income from other rental activities . . . 3a		
	b Expenses from other rental activities *(attach schedule)* . . . 3b		
	c Net income (loss) from other rental activities. Subtract line 3b from line 3a	3c	
	4 Portfolio income (loss) *(attach Schedule D (Form 1065) for lines 4d and 4e):*		
	a Interest income	4a	
	b Dividends: **(1)** Qualified dividends ▶ ________ **(2)** Total ordinary dividends ▶	4b(2)	
	c Royalty income	4c	
	d Net short-term capital gain (loss): **(1)** post-May 5, 2003 ▶ ________ **(2)** Entire year ▶	4d(2)	
	e Net long-term capital gain (loss): **(1)** post-May 5, 2003 ▶ ________ **(2)** Entire year ▶	4e(2)	
	f Other portfolio income (loss) *(attach schedule)*	4f	
	5 Guaranteed payments to partners	5	
	6a Net section 1231 gain (loss) (post-May 5, 2003) *(attach Form 4797)*	6a	
	b Net section 1231 gain (loss) (entire year) *(attach Form 4797)*	6b	
	7 Other income (loss) *(attach schedule)*	7	
Deductions	8 Charitable contributions *(attach schedule)*	8	
	9 Section 179 expense deduction *(attach Form 4562)*	9	
	10 Deductions related to portfolio income (itemize)	10	
	11 Other deductions *(attach schedule)*	11	
Credits	12a Low-income housing credit: **(1)** From partnerships to which section 42(j)(5) applies	12a(1)	
	(2) Other than on line 12a(1)	12a(2)	
	b Qualified rehabilitation expenditures related to rental real estate activities *(attach Form 3468)*	12b	
	c Credits (other than credits shown on lines 12a and 12b) related to rental real estate activities	12c	
	d Credits related to other rental activities	12d	
	13 Other credits	13	
Investment Interest	14a Interest expense on investment debts	14a	
	b **(1)** Investment income included on lines 4a, 4b(2), 4c, and 4f above	14b(1)	
	(2) Investment expenses included on line 10 above	14b(2)	
Self-Employment	15a Net earnings (loss) from self-employment	15a	
	b Gross farming or fishing income	15b	
	c Gross nonfarm income	15c	
Adjustments and Tax Preference Items	16a Depreciation adjustment on property placed in service after 1986	16a	
	b Adjusted gain or loss	16b	
	c Depletion (other than oil and gas)	16c	
	d **(1)** Gross income from oil, gas, and geothermal properties	16d(1)	
	(2) Deductions allocable to oil, gas, and geothermal properties	16d(2)	
	e Other adjustments and tax preference items *(attach schedule)*	16e	
Foreign Taxes	17a Name of foreign country or U.S. possession ▶ ________		
	b Gross income from all sources	17b	
	c Gross income sourced at partner level	17c	
	d Foreign gross income sourced at partnership level:		
	(1) Passive ▶ ________ **(2)** Listed categories *(attach schedule)* ▶ ________ **(3)** General limitation ▶	17d(3)	
	e Deductions allocated and apportioned at partner level:		
	(1) Interest expense ▶ ________ **(2)** Other ▶	17e(2)	
	f Deductions allocated and apportioned at partnership level to foreign source income:		
	(1) Passive ▶ ________ **(2)** Listed categories *(attach schedule)* ▶ ________ **(3)** General limitation ▶	17f(3)	
	g Total foreign taxes (check one): ▶ Paid ☐ Accrued ☐	17g	
	h Reduction in taxes available for credit *(attach schedule)*	17h	
Other	18 Section 59(e)(2) expenditures: **a** Type ▶ ________ **b** Amount ▶	18b	
	19 Tax-exempt interest income	19	
	20 Other tax-exempt income	20	
	21 Nondeductible expenses	21	
	22 Distributions of money (cash and marketable securities)	22	
	23 Distributions of property other than money	23	
	24 Other items and amounts required to be reported separately to partners *(attach schedule)*		

Form 1065 (2003) Page **4**

Analysis of Net Income (Loss)

1 Net income (loss). Combine Schedule K, lines 1 through 7 in column (b). From the result, subtract the sum of Schedule K, lines 8 through 11, 14a, 17g, and 18b					**1**	
2 Analysis by partner type:	**(i)** Corporate	**(ii)** Individual (active)	**(iii)** Individual (passive)	**(iv)** Partnership	**(v)** Exempt organization	**(vi)** Nominee/Other
a General partners						
b Limited partners						

Note: Schedules L, M-1 and M-2 are not required if Question 5 of Schedule B is answered "Yes."

Schedule L Balance Sheets per Books

	Beginning of tax year		End of tax year	
Assets	**(a)**	**(b)**	**(c)**	**(d)**
1 Cash				
2a Trade notes and accounts receivable				
b Less allowance for bad debts				
3 Inventories				
4 U.S. government obligations				
5 Tax-exempt securities				
6 Other current assets *(attach schedule)*				
7 Mortgage and real estate loans				
8 Other investments *(attach schedule)*				
9a Buildings and other depreciable assets				
b Less accumulated depreciation				
10a Depletable assets				
b Less accumulated depletion				
11 Land (net of any amortization)				
12a Intangible assets (amortizable only)				
b Less accumulated amortization				
13 Other assets *(attach schedule)*				
14 **Total** assets				
Liabilities and Capital				
15 Accounts payable				
16 Mortgages, notes, bonds payable in less than 1 year				
17 Other current liabilities *(attach schedule)*				
18 All nonrecourse loans				
19 Mortgages, notes, bonds payable in 1 year or more				
20 Other liabilities *(attach schedule)*				
21 Partners' capital accounts				
22 **Total** liabilities and capital				

Schedule M-1 Reconciliation of Income (Loss) per Books With Income (Loss) per Return

1 Net income (loss) per books		**6** Income recorded on books this year not included on Schedule K, lines 1 through 7 (itemize): **a** Tax-exempt interest $	
2 Income included on Schedule K, lines 1 through 4, 6b, and 7, not recorded on books this year (itemize):			
3 Guaranteed payments (other than health insurance)		**7** Deductions included on Schedule K, lines 1 through 11, 14a, 17g, and 18b, not charged against book income this year (itemize): **a** Depreciation $	
4 Expenses recorded on books this year not included on Schedule K, lines 1 through 11, 14a, 17g, and 18b (itemize): **a** Depreciation $ **b** Travel and entertainment $		**8** Add lines 6 and 7	
5 Add lines 1 through 4		**9** Income (loss) (Analysis of Net Income (Loss), line 1). Subtract line 8 from line 5	

Schedule M-2 Analysis of Partners' Capital Accounts

1 Balance at beginning of year		**6** Distributions: **a** Cash	
2 Capital contributed: **a** Cash		**b** Property	
b Property		**7** Other decreases (itemize):	
3 Net income (loss) per books			
4 Other increases (itemize):		**8** Add lines 6 and 7	
5 Add lines 1 through 4		**9** Balance at end of year. Subtract line 8 from line 5	

6511

SCHEDULE K-1 (Form 1065)
Department of the Treasury
Internal Revenue Service

Partner's Share of Income, Credits, Deductions, etc.

▶ See separate instructions.

For calendar year 2003 or tax year beginning , 2003, and ending , 20

OMB No. 1545-0099

2003

Partner's identifying number ▶

Partner's name, address, and ZIP code

Partnership's identifying number ▶

Partnership's name, address, and ZIP code

A This partner is a ☐ general partner ☐ limited partner
☐ limited liability company member
B What type of entity is this partner? ▶ ....
C Is this partner a ☐ domestic or a ☐ foreign partner?

D Enter partner's percentage of:	(i) Before change or termination	(ii) End of year
Profit sharing	%	%
Loss sharing	%	%
Ownership of capital	%	%

E IRS Center where partnership filed return:

F Partner's share of liabilities (see instructions):
Nonrecourse . . . . $ ....
Qualified nonrecourse financing . $ ....
Other . . . . $ ....

G Tax shelter registration number . ▶ ....

H Check here if this partnership is a publicly traded partnership as defined in section 469(k)(2) . . . . . ☐

I Check applicable boxes: (1) ☐ Final K-1 (2) ☐ Amended K-1

J Analysis of partner's capital account:

(a) Capital account at beginning of year	(b) Capital contributed during year	(c) Partner's share of lines 3, 4, and 7, Form 1065, Schedule M-2	(d) Withdrawals and distributions	(e) Capital account at end of year (combine columns (a) through (d))
			( )	

	(a) Distributive share item		(b) Amount	(c) 1040 filers enter the amount in column (b) on:
Income (Loss)	1 Ordinary income (loss) from trade or business activities . . .	1		See page 6 of Partner's Instructions for Schedule K-1 (Form 1065).
	2 Net income (loss) from rental real estate activities	2		
	3 Net income (loss) from other rental activities	3		
	4 Portfolio income (loss):			
	a Interest income	4a		Form 1040, line 8a
	b (1) Qualified dividends	4b(1)		Form 1040, line 9b
	(2) Total ordinary dividends	4b(2)		Form 1040, line 9a
	c Royalty income	4c		Sch. E, Part I, line 4
	d (1) Net short-term capital gain (loss) (post-May 5, 2003) . . .	4d(1)		Sch. D, line 5, col. (g)
	(2) Net short-term capital gain (loss) (entire year)	4d(2)		Sch. D, line 5, col. (f)
	e (1) Net long-term capital gain (loss) (post-May 5, 2003) . . .	4e(1)		Sch. D, line 12, col. (g)
	(2) Net long-term capital gain (loss) (entire year)	4e(2)		Sch. D, line 12, col. (f)
	f Other portfolio income (loss) *(attach schedule)*	4f		See pages 6 and 7 of Partner's Instructions for Schedule K-1 (Form 1065).
	5 Guaranteed payments to partner	5		
	6a Net section 1231 gain (loss) (post-May 5, 2003).	6a		
	b Net section 1231 gain (loss) (entire year)	6b		
	7 Other income (loss) *(attach schedule)*	7		
Deductions	8 Charitable contributions (see instructions) *(attach schedule)* . .	8		Sch. A, line 15 or 16
	9 Section 179 expense deduction	9		See page 8 of Partner's Instructions for Schedule K-1 (Form 1065).
	10 Deductions related to portfolio income *(attach schedule)* . . .	10		
	11 Other deductions *(attach schedule)*	11		
Credits	12a Low-income housing credit: (1) From section 42(j)(5) partnerships	12a(1)		Form 8586, line 5
	(2) Other than on line 12a(1)	12a(2)		
	b Qualified rehabilitation expenditures related to rental real estate activities	12b		See page 9 of Partner's Instructions for Schedule K-1 (Form 1065).
	c Credits (other than credits shown on lines 12a and 12b) related to rental real estate activities	12c		
	d Credits related to other rental activities	12d		
	13 Other credits	13		

For Paperwork Reduction Act Notice, see Instructions for Form 1065. Cat. No. 11394R **Schedule K-1 (Form 1065) 2003**

6512

Section	(a) Distributive share item		(b) Amount	(c) 1040 filers enter the amount in column (b) on:
Investment Interest	14a Interest expense on investment debts	14a		Form 4952, line 1
	b (1) Investment income included on lines 4a, 4b(2), 4c, and 4f	14b(1)		See page 9 of Partner's Instructions for Schedule K-1 (Form 1065).
	(2) Investment expenses included on line 10	14b(2)		
Self-employment	15a Net earnings (loss) from self-employment	15a		Sch. SE, Section A or B
	b Gross farming or fishing income	15b		See page 9 of Partner's Instructions for Schedule K-1 (Form 1065).
	c Gross nonfarm income	15c		
Adjustments and Tax Preference Items	16a Depreciation adjustment on property placed in service after 1986	16a		See pages 9 and 10 of Partner's Instructions for Schedule K-1 (Form 1065) and Instructions for Form 6251.
	b Adjusted gain or loss	16b		
	c Depletion (other than oil and gas)	16c		
	d (1) Gross income from oil, gas, and geothermal properties	16d(1)		
	(2) Deductions allocable to oil, gas, and geothermal properties	16d(2)		
	e Other adjustments and tax preference items *(attach schedule)*	16e		
Foreign Taxes	17a Name of foreign country or U.S. possession ▶			Form 1116, Part I
	b Gross income from all sources	17b		
	c Gross income sourced at partner level	17c		
	d Foreign gross income sourced at partnership level:			
	(1) Passive	17d(1)		
	(2) Listed categories *(attach schedule)*	17d(2)		
	(3) General limitation	17d(3)		
	e Deductions allocated and apportioned at partner level:			
	(1) Interest expense	17e(1)		
	(2) Other	17e(2)		
	f Deductions allocated and apportioned at partnership level to foreign source income:			
	(1) Passive	17f(1)		
	(2) Listed categories *(attach schedule)*	17f(2)		
	(3) General limitation	17f(3)		
	g Total foreign taxes (check one): ▶ ☐ Paid ☐ Accrued	17g		Form 1116, Part II
	h Reduction in taxes available for credit *(attach schedule)*	17h		Form 1116, line 12
Other	18 Section 59(e)(2) expenditures: **a** Type ▶			See page 10 of Partner's Instructions for Schedule K-1 (Form 1065).
	b Amount	18b		
	19 Tax-exempt interest income	19		Form 1040, line 8b
	20 Other tax-exempt income	20		See page 10 of Partner's Instructions for Schedule K-1 (Form 1065).
	21 Nondeductible expenses	21		
	22 Distributions of money (cash and marketable securities)	22		
	23 Distributions of property other than money	23		
	24 Recapture of low-income housing credit:			Form 8611, line 8
	a From section 42(j)(5) partnerships	24a		
	b Other than on line 24a	24b		

Supplemental Information

25 Supplemental information required to be reported separately to each partner *(attach additional schedules if more space is needed):*

Form **1118**
(Rev. December 2003)
Department of the Treasury
Internal Revenue Service

Foreign Tax Credit—Corporations

▶ **Attach to the corporation's tax return.**
▶ **See separate instructions.**

OMB No. 1545-0122

For calendar year 20 , or other tax year beginning , 20 , and ending , 20

Name of corporation | **Employer identification number**

Use a **separate** Form 1118 for each applicable category of income listed below. See **Categories of Income** on page 1 of instructions. Also, see **Specific Instructions** on page 5. Check only one box on each form.

- ☐ Passive Income
- ☐ High Withholding Tax Interest
- ☐ Financial Services Income
- ☐ Shipping Income
- ☐ Dividends From a DISC or Former DISC
- ☐ Taxable Income Attributable To Foreign Trade Income
- ☐ Certain Distributions From a FSC or Former FSC
- ☐ Certain Dividends From **Each** 10/50 PFIC
  Name of PFIC ▶ ______
  Country of Incorporation ▶
- ☐ Certain Dividends From 10/50 Corporations
- ☐ Section 901(j) Income: Name of Sanctioned Country ▶ ______
- ☐ Income Re-sourced by Treaty: Name of Country ▶ ______
- ☐ General Limitation Income

Schedule A Income or (Loss) Before Adjustments *(Report all amounts in U.S. dollars. See page 5 of instructions.)*

	1. Foreign Country or U.S. Possession (Enter two-letter code from list beginning on page 11 of instructions. Use a separate line for each.)*	Gross Income or (Loss) From Sources Outside the United States (*INCLUDE* Foreign Branch Gross Income here *and* on Schedule F)								
		2. Deemed Dividends (see instructions)		3. Other Dividends		4. Interest	5. Gross Rents, Royalties, and License Fees	6. Gross Income From Performance of Services	7. Other (attach schedule)	8. Total (add columns 2(a) through 7)
		(a) Exclude gross-up	(b) Gross-up (sec. 78)	(a) Exclude gross-up	(b) Gross-up (sec. 78)					
A										
B										
C										
D										
E										
F										
Totals (add lines A through F)										

* For section 863(b) income, use a single line and enter "863(b)."

	Deductions (*INCLUDE* Foreign Branch Deductions here *and* on Schedule F)							
	9. Definitely Allocable Deductions					10. Apportioned Share of Deductions Not Definitely Allocable (enter amount from applicable line of Schedule H, Part II, column (d))	11. Total Deductions (add columns 9(e) and 10)	12. Total Income or (Loss) Before Adjustments (subtract column 11 from column 8)
	Rental, Royalty, and Licensing Expenses		(c) Expenses Related to Gross Income From Performance of Services	(d) Other Definitely Allocable Deductions	(e) Total Definitely Allocable Deductions (add columns 9(a) through 9(d))			
	(a) Depreciation, Depletion, and Amortization	(b) Other Expenses						
A								
B								
C								
D								
E								
F								
Totals								

For Paperwork Reduction Act Notice, see separate instructions. Cat. No. 10900F Form **1118** (Rev. 12-2003)

Form 1118 (Rev. 12-2003) Page **2**

Schedule B **Foreign Tax Credit** *(Report all foreign tax amounts in U.S. dollars.)*

Part I—Foreign Taxes Paid, Accrued, and Deemed Paid *(see page 6 of instructions)*

	1. Credit is Claimed for Taxes:		**2.** Foreign Taxes Paid or Accrued (attach schedule showing amounts in foreign currency and conversion rate(s) used)								**3.** Tax Deemed Paid (from Schedule C—Part I, column 10, Part II, column 8(b), and Part III, column 8)
	☐ Paid	☐ Accrued	Tax Withheld at Source on:			Other Foreign Taxes Paid or Accrued on:				**(h)** Total Foreign Taxes Paid or Accrued (add columns 2(a) through 2(g))	
	Date Paid	Date Accrued	**(a)** Dividends	**(b)** Interest	**(c)** Rents, Royalties, and License Fees	**(d)** Section 863(b) Income	**(e)** Foreign Branch Income	**(f)** Services Income	**(g)** Other		
A											
B											
C											
D											
E											
F											
Totals (add lines A through F)											

Part II—Separate Foreign Tax Credit *(Complete a **separate** Part II for **each** applicable category of income.)*

1 Total foreign taxes paid or accrued (total from Part I, column 2(h))

2 Total taxes deemed paid (total from Part I, column 3)

3 Reductions of taxes paid, accrued, or deemed paid (enter total from Schedule G) ( )

4 Total carryover of foreign taxes (attach schedule showing computation in detail—see page 6 of the instructions)

5 Total foreign taxes (combine lines 1 through 4)

6 Enter the amount from the applicable column of Schedule J, Part I, line 11 (see page 6 of instructions). If Schedule J is **not** required to be completed, enter the result from the "Totals" line of column 12 of the applicable Schedule A

7a Total taxable income from all sources (enter taxable income from the corporation's tax return)

b Adjustments to line 7a (see page 6 of instructions)

c Subtract line 7b from line 7a

8 Divide line 6 by line 7c. Enter the resulting fraction as a decimal (see instructions). If line 6 is greater than line 7c, enter 1

9 Total U.S. income tax against which credit is allowed (regular tax liability (see section 26(b)) minus possessions tax credit determined under section 936 or 30A)

10 Credit limitation (multiply line 8 by line 9) (see page 6 of instructions)

11 **Separate foreign tax credit** (enter the smaller of line 5 or line 10 here and on the appropriate line of Part III)

Part III—Summary of Separate Credits (Enter amounts from Part II, line 11 for **each** applicable category of income. **Do not** include taxes on taxable income attributable to foreign trade income or taxes paid to sanctioned countries.)

1 Credit for taxes on passive income

2 Credit for taxes on high withholding tax interest

3 Credit for taxes on financial services income

4 Credit for taxes on shipping income

5 Credit for taxes on certain dividends from each 10/50 PFIC (combine all such credits on this line)

6 Credit for taxes on certain dividends from 10/50 corporations

7 Credit for taxes on dividends from a DISC or former DISC

8 Credit for taxes on certain distributions from a FSC or former FSC

9 Credit for taxes on general limitation income

10 Credit for taxes on income re-sourced by treaty (combine all such credits on this line)

11 Total (add lines 1 through 10)

12 Reduction in credit for international boycott operations (see page 6 of instructions)

13 **Total foreign tax credit** (subtract line 12 from line 11). Enter here and on the appropriate line of the corporation's tax return

Form 1118 (Rev. 12-2003) Page 3

Schedule C Tax Deemed Paid by Domestic Corporation Filing Return

Use this schedule to figure the tax deemed paid by the corporation with respect to dividends from a first-tier foreign corporation under section 902(a), and deemed inclusions of earnings from a first- or lower-tier foreign corporation under section 960(a). ***Report all amounts in U.S. dollars unless otherwise specified.***

Part I—Dividends and Deemed Inclusions From Post-1986 Undistributed Earnings

1. Name of Foreign Corporation (identify DISCs and former DISCs)	**2.** Tax Year End (Yr-Mo) (see instructions)	**3.** Country of Incorporation (enter country code from instructions)	**4.** Post-1986 Undistributed Earnings (in functional currency—attach schedule)	**5.** Opening Balance in Post-1986 Foreign Income Taxes	**6.** Foreign Taxes Paid and Deemed Paid for Tax Year Indicated		**7.** Post-1986 Foreign Income Taxes (add columns 5, 6(a), and 6(b))	**8.** Dividends and Deemed Inclusions		**9.** Divide Column 8(a) by Column 4	**10.** Tax Deemed Paid (multiply column 7 by column 9)
					(a) Taxes Paid	**(b)** Taxes Deemed Paid (from Schedule D, Part I—see instructions)		**(a)** Functional Currency	**(b)** U.S. Dollars		

Total (Add amounts in column 10. Enter the result here and include on "Totals" line of Schedule B, Part I, column 3) . . . . ▶

Part II—Dividends Paid Out of Pre-1987 Accumulated Profits

1. Name of Foreign Corporation (identify DISCs and former DISCs)	**2.** Tax Year End (Yr-Mo) (see instructions)	**3.** Country of Incorporation (enter country code from instructions)	**4.** Accumulated Profits for Tax Year Indicated (in functional currency computed under section 902) (attach schedule)	**5.** Foreign Taxes Paid and Deemed Paid on Earnings and Profits (E&P) for Tax Year Indicated (in functional currency) (see instructions)	**6.** Dividends Paid		**7.** Divide Column 6(a) by Column 4	**8.** Tax Deemed Paid (see instructions)	
					(a) Functional Currency	**(b)** U.S. Dollars		**(a)** Functional Currency	**(b)** U.S. Dollars

Total (Add amounts in column 8b. Enter the result here and include on "Totals" line of Schedule B, Part I, column 3) . . . . ▶

Part III—Deemed Inclusions From Pre-1987 Earnings and Profits

1. Name of Foreign Corporation (identify DISCs and former DISCs)	**2.** Tax Year End (Yr-Mo) (see instructions)	**3.** Country of Incorporation (enter country code from instructions)	**4.** E&P for Tax Year Indicated (in functional currency translated from U.S. dollars, computed under section 964) (attach schedule)	**5.** Foreign Taxes Paid and Deemed Paid for Tax Year Indicated (see instructions)	**6.** Deemed Inclusions		**7.** Divide Column 6(a) by Column 4	**8.** Tax Deemed Paid (multiply column 5 by column 7)
					(a) Functional Currency	**(b)** U.S. Dollars		

Total (Add amounts in column 8. Enter the result here and include on "Totals" line of Schedule B, Part I, column 3) . . . . ▶

Schedule H Apportionment of Deductions Not Definitely Allocable *(complete only once)*

Part I—Research and Development Deductions

	(a) Sales Method					(b) Gross Income Method—Check method used: ☐ Option 1 ☐ Option 2 (See page 9 of instructions.)		(c) Total R&D Deductions Not Definitely Allocable (enter all amounts from column (a)(v) or all amounts from column (b)(vii))
	Product line #1 (SIC Code:)*		Product line #2 (SIC Code:)*		(v) Total R&D Deductions Under Sales Method (add columns (ii) and (iv))			
	(i) Gross Sales	(ii) R&D Deductions	(iii) Gross Sales	(iv) R&D Deductions		(vi) Gross Income	(vii) Total R&D Deductions Under Gross Income Method	
1 Totals (see page 9 of instructions)								
2 Total to be apportioned								
3 Apportionment among statutory groupings:								
a General limitation income								
b Passive income								
c High withholding tax interest								
d Financial services income								
e Shipping income								
f Certain dividends from each 10/50 PFIC*								
g Certain dividends from 10/50 corporations								
h Taxable income attributable to foreign trade income								
i Section 901(j) income*								
j Income re-sourced by treaty*								
4 Total foreign (add lines 3a through 3j)								

Important:** See ***Computer-Generated Schedule H in instructions.

Schedule H Apportionment of Deductions Not Definitely Allocable *(continued)*

Part II—Interest Deductions, All Other Deductions, and Total Deductions

	(a) Average Value of Assets—Check method used: ☐ Fair market value ☐ Tax book value		(b) Interest Deductions		(c) All Other Deductions Not Definitely Allocable	(d) Totals (add the corresponding amounts from column (c), Part I; columns (b)(iii) and (b)(iv), Part II; and column (c), Part II). Enter each amount from lines 3a through 3l below in column 10 of the corresponding Schedule A.
	(i) Nonfinancial Corporations	(ii) Financial Corporations	(iii) Nonfinancial Corporations	(iv) Financial Corporations		
1a Totals (see page 9 of instructions)						
b Amounts specifically allocable under Temp. Regs. 1.861-10T(e)						
c Other specific allocations under Temp. Regs. 1.861-10T						
d Assets excluded from apportionment formula						
2 Total to be apportioned (subtract the sum of lines 1b, 1c, and 1d from line 1a)						
3 Apportionment among statutory groupings:						
a General limitation income						
b Passive income						
c High withholding tax interest						
d Financial services income						
e Shipping income						
f Certain dividends from each 10/50 PFIC*						
g Certain dividends from 10/50 corporations						
h Taxable income attributable to foreign trade income						
i Certain distributions from a FSC or former FSC						
j Dividends from a DISC or former DISC						
k Section 901(j) income*						
l Income re-sourced by treaty*						
4 Total foreign (add lines 3a through 3l)						

* **Important:** *See **Computer-Generated Schedule H** in instructions.*

Form **1120**

Department of the Treasury
Internal Revenue Service

U.S. Corporation Income Tax Return

For calendar year 2003 or tax year beginning ...., 2003, ending ...., 20....

▶ Instructions are separate. See page 20 for Paperwork Reduction Act Notice.

OMB No. 1545-0123

2003

A Check if a:
1 Consolidated return (attach Form 851) ☐
2 Personal holding co. (attach Sch. PH) ☐
3 Personal service corp. (as defined in Regulations sec. 1.441-3(c)— see instructions) ☐

Use IRS label. Otherwise, print or type.

Name

Number, street, and room or suite no. (If a P.O. box, see page 7 of instructions.)

City or town, state, and ZIP code

B Employer identification number

C Date incorporated

D Total assets (see page 8 of instructions)
$

E Check applicable boxes: (1) ☐ Initial return (2) ☐ Final return (3) ☐ Name change (4) ☐ Address change

Income	1a	Gross receipts or sales ______ b Less returns and allowances ______ c Bal ▶			1c	
	2	Cost of goods sold (Schedule A, line 8)			2	
	3	Gross profit. Subtract line 2 from line 1c			3	
	4	Dividends (Schedule C, line 19)			4	
	5	Interest			5	
	6	Gross rents			6	
	7	Gross royalties			7	
	8	Capital gain net income (attach Schedule D (Form 1120))			8	
	9	Net gain or (loss) from Form 4797, Part II, line 18 (attach Form 4797)			9	
	10	Other income (see page 9 of instructions—attach schedule)			10	
	11	**Total income.** Add lines 3 through 10 ▶			11	
Deductions (See instructions for limitations on deductions.)	12	Compensation of officers (Schedule E, line 4)			12	
	13	Salaries and wages (less employment credits)			13	
	14	Repairs and maintenance			14	
	15	Bad debts			15	
	16	Rents			16	
	17	Taxes and licenses			17	
	18	Interest			18	
	19	Charitable contributions (see page 11 of instructions for 10% limitation)			19	
	20	Depreciation (attach Form 4562)	20			
	21	Less depreciation claimed on Schedule A and elsewhere on return	21a		21b	
	22	Depletion			22	
	23	Advertising			23	
	24	Pension, profit-sharing, etc., plans			24	
	25	Employee benefit programs			25	
	26	Other deductions (attach schedule)			26	
	27	**Total deductions.** Add lines 12 through 26 ▶			27	
	28	Taxable income before net operating loss deduction and special deductions. Subtract line 27 from line 11			28	
	29	**Less:** a Net operating loss (NOL) deduction (see page 13 of instructions)	29a			
		b Special deductions (Schedule C, line 20)	29b		29c	
Tax and Payments	30	**Taxable income.** Subtract line 29c from line 28			30	
	31	**Total tax** (Schedule J, line 11)			31	
	32	**Payments: a** 2002 overpayment credited to 2003 — 32a				
	b	2003 estimated tax payments — 32b				
	c	Less 2003 refund applied for on Form 4466 — 32c ( ) d Bal ▶	32d			
	e	Tax deposited with Form 7004	32e			
	f	Credit for tax paid on undistributed capital gains (attach Form 2439)	32f			
	g	Credit for Federal tax on fuels (attach Form 4136). See instructions	32g		32h	
	33	Estimated tax penalty (see page 14 of instructions). Check if Form 2220 is attached ▶ ☐			33	
	34	**Tax due.** If line 32h is smaller than the total of lines 31 and 33, enter amount owed			34	
	35	**Overpayment.** If line 32h is larger than the total of lines 31 and 33, enter amount overpaid			35	
	36	Enter amount of line 35 you want: **Credited to 2004 estimated tax** ▶ **Refunded** ▶			36	

Sign Here

Under penalties of perjury, I declare that I have examined this return, including accompanying schedules and statements, and to the best of my knowledge and belief, it is true, correct, and complete. Declaration of preparer (other than taxpayer) is based on all information of which preparer has any knowledge.

Signature of officer ▶ Date ▶ Title

May the IRS discuss this return with the preparer shown below (see instructions)? ☐ **Yes** ☐ **No**

Paid Preparer's Use Only

Preparer's signature ▶	Date	Check if self-employed ☐	Preparer's SSN or PTIN
Firm's name (or yours if self-employed), address, and ZIP code ▶		EIN	
		Phone no. ( )	

Schedule A Cost of Goods Sold (see page 14 of instructions)

1	Inventory at beginning of year	1	
2	Purchases	2	
3	Cost of labor	3	
4	Additional section 263A costs (attach schedule)	4	
5	Other costs (attach schedule)	5	
6	**Total.** Add lines 1 through 5	6	
7	Inventory at end of year	7	
8	**Cost of goods sold.** Subtract line 7 from line 6. Enter here and on line 2, page 1	8	

9a Check all methods used for valuing closing inventory:

- *(i)* ☐ Cost as described in Regulations section 1.471-3
- *(ii)* ☐ Lower of cost or market as described in Regulations section 1.471-4
- *(iii)* ☐ Other (Specify method used and attach explanation.) ▶

b Check if there was a writedown of subnormal goods as described in Regulations section 1.471-2(c) ▶ ☐

c Check if the LIFO inventory method was adopted this tax year for any goods (if checked, attach Form 970) ▶ ☐

d If the LIFO inventory method was used for this tax year, enter percentage (or amounts) of closing inventory computed under LIFO **9d**

e If property is produced or acquired for resale, do the rules of section 263A apply to the corporation? ☐ Yes ☐ No

f Was there any change in determining quantities, cost, or valuations between opening and closing inventory? If "Yes," attach explanation ☐ Yes ☐ No

Schedule C Dividends and Special Deductions (see instructions beginning on page 15)

		(a) Dividends received	**(b)** %	**(c)** Special deductions **(a)** × **(b)**
1	Dividends from less-than-20%-owned domestic corporations that are subject to the 70% deduction (other than debt-financed stock)		70	
2	Dividends from 20%-or-more-owned domestic corporations that are subject to the 80% deduction (other than debt-financed stock)		80	
3	Dividends on debt-financed stock of domestic and foreign corporations (section 246A)		see instructions	
4	Dividends on certain preferred stock of less-than-20%-owned public utilities		42	
5	Dividends on certain preferred stock of 20%-or-more-owned public utilities		48	
6	Dividends from less-than-20%-owned foreign corporations and certain FSCs that are subject to the 70% deduction		70	
7	Dividends from 20%-or-more-owned foreign corporations and certain FSCs that are subject to the 80% deduction		80	
8	Dividends from wholly owned foreign subsidiaries subject to the 100% deduction (section 245(b))		100	
9	**Total.** Add lines 1 through 8. See page 16 of instructions for limitation			
10	Dividends from domestic corporations received by a small business investment company operating under the Small Business Investment Act of 1958		100	
11	Dividends from certain FSCs that are subject to the 100% deduction (section 245(c)(1))		100	
12	Dividends from affiliated group members subject to the 100% deduction (section 243(a)(3))		100	
13	Other dividends from foreign corporations not included on lines 3, 6, 7, 8, or 11			
14	Income from controlled foreign corporations under subpart F (attach Form(s) 5471)			
15	Foreign dividend gross-up (section 78)			
16	IC-DISC and former DISC dividends not included on lines 1, 2, or 3 (section 246(d))			
17	Other dividends			
18	Deduction for dividends paid on certain preferred stock of public utilities			
19	**Total dividends.** Add lines 1 through 17. Enter here and on line 4, page 1 ▶			
20	**Total special deductions.** Add lines 9, 10, 11, 12, and 18. Enter here and on line 29b, page 1 ▶			

Schedule E Compensation of Officers (see instructions for line 12, page 1, on page 10 of instructions)

Note: *Complete Schedule E only if total receipts (line 1a plus lines 4 through 10 on page 1) are $500,000 or more.*

	(a) Name of officer	**(b)** Social security number	**(c)** Percent of time devoted to business	Percent of corporation stock owned **(d)** Common	**(e)** Preferred	**(f)** Amount of compensation
1			%	%	%	
			%	%	%	
			%	%	%	
			%	%	%	
			%	%	%	

2	Total compensation of officers	
3	Compensation of officers claimed on Schedule A and elsewhere on return	
4	Subtract line 3 from line 2. Enter the result here and on line 12, page 1	

Form 1120 (2003) Page **3**

Schedule J Tax Computation (see page 17 of instructions)

1 Check if the corporation is a member of a controlled group (see sections 1561 and 1563) . . . . ▶ ☐

Important: Members of a controlled group, see instructions on page 17.

2a If the box on line 1 is checked, enter the corporation's share of the $50,000, $25,000, and $9,925,000 taxable income brackets (in that order):

(1) $ ______ **(2)** $ ______ **(3)** $ ______

b Enter the corporation's share of: **(1)** Additional 5% tax (not more than $11,750) $ ______

(2) Additional 3% tax (not more than $100,000) $ ______

3	Income tax. Check if a qualified personal service corporation under section 448(d)(2) (see page 17) . ▶ ☐	3	
4	Alternative minimum tax (attach Form 4626)	4	
5	Add lines 3 and 4	5	
6a	Foreign tax credit (attach Form 1118)	6a	
b	Possessions tax credit (attach Form 5735)	6b	
c	Check: ☐ Nonconventional source fuel credit ☐ QEV credit (attach Form 8834)	6c	
d	General business credit. Check box(es) and indicate which forms are attached. ☐ Form 3800 ☐ Form(s) (specify) ▶ ______	6d	
e	Credit for prior year minimum tax (attach Form 8827)	6e	
f	Qualified zone academy bond credit (attach Form 8860)	6f	
7	**Total credits.** Add lines 6a through 6f	7	
8	Subtract line 7 from line 5	8	
9	Personal holding company tax (attach Schedule PH (Form 1120))	9	
10	Other taxes. Check if from: ☐ Form 4255 ☐ Form 8611 ☐ Form 8697 ☐ Form 8866 ☐ Other (attach schedule)	10	
11	**Total tax.** Add lines 8 through 10. Enter here and on line 31, page 1	11	

Schedule K Other Information (see page 19 of instructions)

		Yes	No
1	Check method of accounting: **a** ☐ Cash **b** ☐ Accrual **c** ☐ Other (specify) ▶ ______		
2	See page 21 of the instructions and enter the:		
a	Business activity code no. ▶ ______		
b	Business activity ▶ ______		
c	Product or service ▶ ______		
3	At the end of the tax year, did the corporation own, directly or indirectly, 50% or more of the voting stock of a domestic corporation? (For rules of attribution, see section 267(c).)		
	If "Yes," attach a schedule showing: **(a)** name and employer identification number (EIN), **(b)** percentage owned, and **(c)** taxable income or (loss) before NOL and special deductions of such corporation for the tax year ending with or within your tax year.		
4	Is the corporation a subsidiary in an affiliated group or a parent-subsidiary controlled group?		
	If "Yes," enter name and EIN of the parent corporation ▶ ______		
5	At the end of the tax year, did any individual, partnership, corporation, estate, or trust own, directly or indirectly, 50% or more of the corporation's voting stock? (For rules of attribution, see section 267(c).)		
	If "Yes," attach a schedule showing name and identifying number. (Do not include any information already entered in **4** above.) Enter percentage owned ▶ ______		
6	During this tax year, did the corporation pay dividends (other than stock dividends and distributions in exchange for stock) in excess of the corporation's current and accumulated earnings and profits? (See sections 301 and 316.)		
	If "Yes," file **Form 5452,** Corporate Report of Nondividend Distributions.		
	If this is a consolidated return, answer here for the parent corporation and on **Form 851,** Affiliations Schedule, for each subsidiary.		
7	At any time during the tax year, did one foreign person own, directly or indirectly, at least 25% of **(a)** the total voting power of all classes of stock of the corporation entitled to vote or **(b)** the total value of all classes of stock of the corporation?		
	If "Yes," enter: **(a)** Percentage owned ▶ ______ and **(b)** Owner's country ▶ ______		
c	The corporation may have to file **Form 5472,** Information Return of a 25% Foreign-Owned U.S. Corporation or a Foreign Corporation Engaged in a U.S. Trade or Business. Enter number of Forms 5472 attached ▶ ______		
8	Check this box if the corporation issued publicly offered debt instruments with original issue discount . . ▶ ☐		
	If checked, the corporation may have to file **Form 8281,** Information Return for Publicly Offered Original Issue Discount Instruments.		
9	Enter the amount of tax-exempt interest received or accrued during the tax year ▶ $ ______		
10	Enter the number of shareholders at the end of the tax year (if 75 or fewer) ▶ ______		
11	If the corporation has an NOL for the tax year and is electing to forego the carryback period, check here ▶ ☐		
	If the corporation is filing a consolidated return, the statement required by Temporary Regulations section 1.1502-21T(b)(3)(i) or (ii) must be attached or the election will not be valid.		
12	Enter the available NOL carryover from prior tax years (Do not reduce it by any deduction on line 29a.) ▶ $ ______		
13	Are the corporation's total receipts (line 1a plus lines 4 through 10 on page 1) for the tax year **and** its total assets at the end of the tax year less than $250,000?		
	If "Yes," the corporation is not required to complete Schedules L, M-1, and M-2 on page 4. Instead, enter the total amount of cash distributions and the book value of property distributions (other than cash) made during the tax year. ▶ $ ______		

Note: *If the corporation, at any time during the tax year, had assets or operated a business in a foreign country or U.S. possession, it may be required to attach* ***Schedule N (Form 1120),*** *Foreign Operations of U.S. Corporations, to this return. See Schedule N for details.*

Form 1120 (2003) Page 4

Note: *The corporation is not required to complete Schedules L, M-1, and M-2 if Question 13 on Schedule K is answered "Yes."*

Schedule L Balance Sheets per Books

	Beginning of tax year		End of tax year	
Assets	(a)	(b)	(c)	(d)
1 Cash				
2a Trade notes and accounts receivable				
b Less allowance for bad debts	( )		( )	
3 Inventories				
4 U.S. government obligations				
5 Tax-exempt securities (see instructions)				
6 Other current assets (attach schedule)				
7 Loans to shareholders				
8 Mortgage and real estate loans				
9 Other investments (attach schedule)				
10a Buildings and other depreciable assets				
b Less accumulated depreciation	( )		( )	
11a Depletable assets				
b Less accumulated depletion	( )		( )	
12 Land (net of any amortization)				
13a Intangible assets (amortizable only)				
b Less accumulated amortization	( )		( )	
14 Other assets (attach schedule)				
15 Total assets				
Liabilities and Shareholders' Equity				
16 Accounts payable				
17 Mortgages, notes, bonds payable in less than 1 year				
18 Other current liabilities (attach schedule)				
19 Loans from shareholders				
20 Mortgages, notes, bonds payable in 1 year or more				
21 Other liabilities (attach schedule)				
22 Capital stock: **a** Preferred stock				
b Common stock				
23 Additional paid-in capital				
24 Retained earnings—Appropriated (attach schedule)				
25 Retained earnings—Unappropriated				
26 Adjustments to shareholders' equity (attach schedule)				
27 Less cost of treasury stock		( )		( )
28 Total liabilities and shareholders' equity				

Schedule M-1 Reconciliation of Income (Loss) per Books With Income per Return (see page 20 of instructions)

1 Net income (loss) per books		7 Income recorded on books this year not included on this return (itemize): Tax-exempt interest $	
2 Federal income tax per books			
3 Excess of capital losses over capital gains			
4 Income subject to tax not recorded on books this year (itemize):			
5 Expenses recorded on books this year not deducted on this return (itemize):		8 Deductions on this return not charged against book income this year (itemize):	
a Depreciation . . . . $		a Depreciation . . . . $	
b Charitable contributions $		b Charitable contributions $	
c Travel and entertainment $			
		9 Add lines 7 and 8	
6 Add lines 1 through 5		10 Income (line 28, page 1)—line 6 less line 9	

Schedule M-2 Analysis of Unappropriated Retained Earnings per Books (Line 25, Schedule L)

1 Balance at beginning of year		5 Distributions: **a** Cash	
2 Net income (loss) per books		**b** Stock	
3 Other increases (itemize):		**c** Property	
		6 Other decreases (itemize):	
		7 Add lines 5 and 6	
4 Add lines 1, 2, and 3		8 Balance at end of year (line 4 less line 7)	

Form **1120** (2003)

Form **1120S** | Department of the Treasury Internal Revenue Service

U.S. Income Tax Return for an S Corporation

▶ **Do not file this form unless the corporation has timely filed Form 2553 to elect to be an S corporation.**

▶ **See separate instructions.**

OMB No. 1545-0130

2003

For calendar year 2003, or tax year beginning , 2003, and ending , 20

A Effective date of election as an S corporation	**Use the IRS label. Other-wise, print or type.**	Name	**C Employer identification number**
B Business code number (see pages 31–33 of the Insts.)		Number, street, and room or suite no. (If a P.O. box, see page 12 of the instructions.)	**D** Date incorporated
		City or town, state, and ZIP code	**E** Total assets (see page 12 of instructions) $

F Check applicable boxes: (1) ☐ Initial return (2) ☐ Final return (3) ☐ Name change (4) ☐ Address change (5) ☐ Amended return

G Enter number of shareholders in the corporation at end of the tax year . . . . ▶

Caution: *Include **only** trade or business income and expenses on lines 1a through 21. See page 12 of the instructions for more information.*

Income	1a	Gross receipts or sales ___ **b** Less returns and allowances ___ **c** Bal ▶	1c	
	2	Cost of goods sold (Schedule A, line 8)	2	
	3	Gross profit. Subtract line 2 from line 1c	3	
	4	Net gain (loss) from Form 4797, Part II, line 18 (attach Form 4797)	4	
	5	Other income (loss) (attach schedule)	5	
	6	**Total income (loss).** Add lines 3 through 5 ▶	6	
Deductions (see page 13 of the instructions for limitations)	7	Compensation of officers	7	
	8	Salaries and wages (less employment credits)	8	
	9	Repairs and maintenance	9	
	10	Bad debts	10	
	11	Rents	11	
	12	Taxes and licenses	12	
	13	Interest	13	
	14a	Depreciation (Attach Form 4562) . . . 14a		
	b	Depreciation claimed on Schedule A and elsewhere on return . . 14b		
	c	Subtract line 14b from line 14a	14c	
	15	Depletion **(Do not deduct oil and gas depletion.)**	15	
	16	Advertising	16	
	17	Pension, profit-sharing, etc., plans	17	
	18	Employee benefit programs	18	
	19	Other deductions (attach schedule)	19	
	20	**Total deductions.** Add the amounts shown in the far right column for lines 7 through 19 ▶	20	
	21	Ordinary income (loss) from trade or business activities. Subtract line 20 from line 6	21	
Tax and Payments	22	**Tax: a** Excess net passive income tax (attach schedule) . . . 22a		
	b	Tax from Schedule D (Form 1120S) . . . 22b		
	c	Add lines 22a and 22b (see page 17 of the instructions for additional taxes)	22c	
	23	**Payments: a** 2003 estimated tax payments and amount applied from 2002 return 23a		
	b	Tax deposited with Form 7004 . . . 23b		
	c	Credit for Federal tax paid on fuels (attach Form 4136) . . . 23c		
	d	Add lines 23a through 23c	23d	
	24	Estimated tax penalty (See page 17 of instructions). Check if Form 2220 is attached ▶ ☐	24	
	25	**Tax due.** If line 23d is smaller than the total of lines 22c and 24, enter amount owed	25	
	26	**Overpayment.** If line 23d is larger than the total of lines 22c and 24, enter amount overpaid	26	
	27	Enter amount of line 26 you want: **Credited to 2004 estimated tax** ▶ **Refunded** ▶	27	

Sign Here

Under penalties of perjury, I declare that I have examined this return, including accompanying schedules and statements, and to the best of my knowledge and belief, it is true, correct, and complete. Declaration of preparer (other than taxpayer) is based on all information of which preparer has any knowledge.

▶ Signature of officer | Date | ▶ Title

May the IRS discuss this return with the preparer shown below (see instructions)? ☐ **Yes** ☐ **No**

Paid Preparer's Use Only

Preparer's signature ▶	Date	Check if self-employed ☐	Preparer's SSN or PTIN
Firm's name (or yours if self-employed), address, and ZIP code ▶		EIN	
		Phone no. ( )	

For Paperwork Reduction Act Notice, see the separate instructions. Cat. No. 11510H Form **1120S** (2003)

Schedule A Cost of Goods Sold (see page 18 of the instructions)

1	Inventory at beginning of year	1	
2	Purchases	2	
3	Cost of labor	3	
4	Additional section 263A costs (attach schedule)	4	
5	Other costs (attach schedule)	5	
6	**Total.** Add lines 1 through 5	6	
7	Inventory at end of year	7	
8	**Cost of goods sold.** Subtract line 7 from line 6. Enter here and on page 1, line 2	8	

9a Check all methods used for valuing closing inventory: *(i)* ☐ Cost as described in Regulations section 1.471-3

(ii) ☐ Lower of cost or market as described in Regulations section 1.471-4

(iii) ☐ Other (specify method used and attach explanation) ▶

b Check if there was a writedown of subnormal goods as described in Regulations section 1.471-2(c) ▶ ☐

c Check if the LIFO inventory method was adopted this tax year for any goods (if checked, attach Form 970) ▶ ☐

d If the LIFO inventory method was used for this tax year, enter percentage (or amounts) of closing inventory computed under LIFO | 9d |

e If property is produced or acquired for resale, do the rules of Section 263A apply to the corporation? ☐ Yes ☐ No

f Was there any change in determining quantities, cost, or valuations between opening and closing inventory? ☐ Yes ☐ No
If "Yes," attach explanation.

Schedule B Other Information (see page 19 of instructions)

		Yes	No
1	Check method of accounting: **(a)** ☐ Cash **(b)** ☐ Accrual **(c)** ☐ Other (specify) ▶		
2	See pages 31 through 33 of the instructions and enter the: **(a)** Business activity ▶ **(b)** Product or service ▶		
3	At the end of the tax year, did the corporation own, directly or indirectly, 50% or more of the voting stock of a domestic corporation? (For rules of attribution, see section 267(c).) If "Yes," attach a schedule showing: **(a)** name, address, and employer identification number and **(b)** percentage owned		
4	Was the corporation a member of a controlled group subject to the provisions of section 1561?		
5	Check this box if the corporation has filed or is required to file **Form 8264,** Application for Registration of a Tax Shelter ▶ ☐		
6	Check this box if the corporation issued publicly offered debt instruments with original issue discount ▶ ☐ If checked, the corporation may have to file **Form 8281,** Information Return for Publicly Offered Original Issue Discount Instruments.		
7	If the corporation: **(a)** was a C corporation before it elected to be an S corporation **or** the corporation acquired an asset with a basis determined by reference to its basis (or the basis of any other property) in the hands of a C corporation **and (b)** has net unrealized built-in gain (defined in section 1374(d)(1)) in excess of the net recognized built-in gain from prior years, enter the net unrealized built-in gain reduced by net recognized built-in gain from prior years ▶ $		
8	Check this box if the corporation had accumulated earnings and profits at the close of the tax year ▶ ☐		
9	Are the corporation's total receipts (see page 19 of the instructions) for the tax year **and** its total assets at the end of the tax year less than $250,000? If "Yes," the corporation is not required to complete Schedules L and M-1.		

Note: *If the corporation had assets or operated a business in a foreign country or U.S. possession, it may be required to attach* ***Schedule N (Form 1120),*** *Foreign Operations of U.S. Corporations, to this return. See Schedule N for details.*

Schedule K Shareholders' Shares of Income, Credits, Deductions, etc.

		(a) Pro rata share items			**(b)** Total amount
Income (Loss)	1	Ordinary income (loss) from trade or business activities (page 1, line 21)		1	
	2	Net income (loss) from rental real estate activities (attach Form 8825)		2	
	3a	Gross income from other rental activities	3a		
	b	Expenses from other rental activities (attach schedule)	3b		
	c	Net income (loss) from other rental activities. Subtract line 3b from line 3a		3c	
	4	Portfolio income (loss):			
	a	Interest income		4a	
	b	Dividends: **(1)** Qualified dividends ▶ **(2)** Total ordinary dividends ▶		4b(2)	
	c	Royalty income		4c	
	d	Net short-term capital gain (loss): **(1)** Post-May 5, 2003 ▶ **(2)** Entire year ▶		4d(2)	
	e	Net long-term capital gain (loss): **(1)** Post-May 5, 2003 ▶ **(2)** Entire year ▶		4e(2)	
	f	Other portfolio income (loss) (attach schedule)		4f	
	5	Net section 1231 gain (loss) (attach Form 4797): **(a)** Post-May 5, 2003 ▶ **(b)** Entire year ▶		5(b)	
	6	Other income (loss) (attach schedule)		6	

Form 1120S (2003) Page **3**

Schedule K **Shareholders' Shares of Income, Credits, Deductions, etc.** *(continued)*

		(a) Pro rata share items		**(b)** Total amount
Deductions	7	Charitable contributions (attach schedule)	7	
	8	Section 179 expense deduction (attach Form 4562)	8	
	9	Deductions related to portfolio income (loss) (itemize)	9	
	10	Other deductions (attach schedule)	10	
Investment Interest	11a	Interest expense on investment debts	11a	
	b (1)	Investment income included on lines 4a, 4b(2), 4c, and 4f on page 2	11b(1)	
	(2)	Investment expenses included on line 9 above	11b(2)	
Credits	12a	Credit for alcohol used as a fuel (attach Form 6478)	12a	
	b	Low-income housing credit:		
	(1)	From partnerships to which section 42(j)(5) applies	12b(1)	
	(2)	Other than on line 12b(1)	12b(2)	
	c	Qualified rehabilitation expenditures related to rental real estate activities (attach Form 3468)	12c	
	d	Credits (other than credits shown on lines 12b and 12c) related to rental real estate activities	12d	
	e	Credits related to other rental activities	12e	
	13	Other credits	13	
Adjustments and Tax Preference Items	14a	Depreciation adjustment on property placed in service after 1986	14a	
	b	Adjusted gain or loss	14b	
	c	Depletion (other than oil and gas)	14c	
	d (1)	Gross income from oil, gas, or geothermal properties	14d(1)	
	(2)	Deductions allocable to oil, gas, or geothermal properties	14d(2)	
	e	Other adjustments and tax preference items (attach schedule)	14e	
Foreign Taxes	15a	Name of foreign country or U.S. possession ▶		
	b	Gross income from all sources	15b	
	c	Gross income sourced at shareholder level	15c	
	d	Foreign gross income sourced at corporate level:		
	(1)	Passive	15d(1)	
	(2)	Listed categories (attach schedule)	15d(2)	
	(3)	General limitation	15d(3)	
	e	Deductions allocated and apportioned at shareholder level:		
	(1)	Interest expense	15e(1)	
	(2)	Other	15e(2)	
	f	Deductions allocated and apportioned at corporate level to foreign source income:		
	(1)	Passive	15f(1)	
	(2)	Listed categories (attach schedule)	15f(2)	
	(3)	General limitation	15f(3)	
	g	Total foreign taxes (check one): ▶ ☐ Paid ☐ Accrued	15g	
	h	Reduction in taxes available for credit (attach schedule)	15h	
Other	16	Section 59(e)(2) expenditures: **a** Type ▶ ______ **b** Amount ▶	16b	
	17	Tax-exempt interest income	17	
	18	Other tax-exempt income	18	
	19	Nondeductible expenses	19	
	20	Total property distributions (including cash) other than dividends reported on line 22 below	20	
	21	Other items and amounts required to be reported separately to shareholders (attach schedule)		
	22	Total dividend distributions paid from accumulated earnings and profits	22	
	23	**Income (loss).** (Required only if Schedule M-1 must be completed.) Combine lines 1 through 6 in column (b). From the result, subtract the sum of lines 7 through 11a, 15g, and 16b	23	

Form 1120S (2003) Page **4**

Note: The corporation is not required to complete Schedules L and M-1 if question 9 of Schedule B is answered "Yes."

Schedule L Balance Sheets per Books

Assets	Beginning of tax year (a)	Beginning of tax year (b)	End of tax year (c)	End of tax year (d)
1 Cash				
2a Trade notes and accounts receivable				
b Less allowance for bad debts				
3 Inventories				
4 U.S. government obligations				
5 Tax-exempt securities				
6 Other current assets (attach schedule)				
7 Loans to shareholders				
8 Mortgage and real estate loans				
9 Other investments (attach schedule)				
10a Buildings and other depreciable assets				
b Less accumulated depreciation				
11a Depletable assets				
b Less accumulated depletion				
12 Land (net of any amortization)				
13a Intangible assets (amortizable only)				
b Less accumulated amortization				
14 Other assets (attach schedule)				
15 Total assets				
Liabilities and Shareholders' Equity				
16 Accounts payable				
17 Mortgages, notes, bonds payable in less than 1 year				
18 Other current liabilities (attach schedule)				
19 Loans from shareholders				
20 Mortgages, notes, bonds payable in 1 year or more				
21 Other liabilities (attach schedule)				
22 Capital stock				
23 Additional paid-in capital				
24 Retained earnings				
25 Adjustments to shareholders' equity (attach schedule)				
26 Less cost of treasury stock		( )		( )
27 Total liabilities and shareholders' equity				

Schedule M-1 Reconciliation of Income (Loss) per Books With Income (Loss) per Return

1 Net income (loss) per books		5 Income recorded on books this year not included on Schedule K, lines 1 through 6 (itemize): a Tax-exempt interest $	
2 Income included on Schedule K, lines 1 through 6, not recorded on books this year (itemize):			
3 Expenses recorded on books this year not included on Schedule K, lines 1 through 11a, 15g, and 16b (itemize): a Depreciation $ b Travel and entertainment $		6 Deductions included on Schedule K, lines 1 through 11a, 15g, and 16b, not charged against book income this year (itemize): a Depreciation $	
		7 Add lines 5 and 6	
4 Add lines 1 through 3		8 Income (loss) (Schedule K, line 23). Line 4 less line 7	

Schedule M-2 Analysis of Accumulated Adjustments Account, Other Adjustments Account, and Shareholders' Undistributed Taxable Income Previously Taxed (see page 29 of the instructions)

	(a) Accumulated adjustments account	(b) Other adjustments account	(c) Shareholders' undistributed taxable income previously taxed
1 Balance at beginning of tax year			
2 Ordinary income from page 1, line 21			
3 Other additions			
4 Loss from page 1, line 21	( )		
5 Other reductions	( )	( )	
6 Combine lines 1 through 5			
7 Distributions other than dividend distributions			
8 Balance at end of tax year. Subtract line 7 from line 6			

6711

SCHEDULE K-1 (Form 1120S)

Department of the Treasury
Internal Revenue Service

Shareholder's Share of Income, Credits, Deductions, etc.

▶ See separate instructions.

For calendar year 2003 or tax year beginning , 2003, and ending , 20

OMB No. 1545-0130

2003

Shareholder's identifying number ▶

Shareholder's name, address, and ZIP code

Corporation's identifying number ▶

Corporation's name, address, and ZIP code

A Shareholder's percentage of stock ownership for tax year (see instructions for Schedule K-1) . . . . ▶ .... %
B Internal Revenue Service Center where corporation filed its return ▶ ....
C Tax shelter registration number (see instructions for Schedule K-1) . . . . ▶ ....
D Check applicable boxes: (1) ☐ Final K-1 (2) ☐ Amended K-1

	(a) Pro rata share items		(b) Amount	(c) Form 1040 filers enter the amount in column (b) on:
Income (Loss)	1 Ordinary income (loss) from trade or business activities	1		See page 4 of the Shareholder's Instructions for Schedule K-1 (Form 1120S).
	2 Net income (loss) from rental real estate activities	2		
	3 Net income (loss) from other rental activities	3		
	4 Portfolio income (loss):			
	a Interest income	4a		Form 1040, line 8a
	b (1) Qualified dividends	4b(1)		Form 1040, line 9b
	(2) Total ordinary dividends	4b(2)		Form 1040, line 9a
	c Royalty income	4c		Sch. E, Part I, line 4
	d (1) Net short-term capital gain (loss) (post-May 5, 2003)	4d(1)		Sch. D, line 5, col. (g)
	(2) Net short-term capital gain (loss) (entire year)	4d(2)		Sch. D, line 5, col. (f)
	e (1) Net long-term capital gain (loss) (post-May 5, 2003)	4e(1)		Sch. D, line 12, col. (g)
	(2) Net long-term capital gain (loss) (entire year)	4e(2)		Sch. D, line 12, col. (f)
	f Other portfolio income (loss) (attach schedule)	4f		(Enter on applicable line of your return.)
	5a Net section 1231 gain (loss) (post-May 5, 2003)	5a		See Shareholder's Instructions for Schedule K-1 (Form 1120S).
	b Net section 1231 gain (loss) (entire year)	5b		
	6 Other income (loss) (attach schedule)	6		(Enter on applicable line of your return.)
Deductions	7 Charitable contributions (attach schedule)	7		Sch. A, line 15 or 16
	8 Section 179 expense deduction	8		See page 5 of the Shareholder's Instructions for Schedule K-1 (Form 1120S).
	9 Deductions related to portfolio income (loss) (attach schedule)	9		
	10 Other deductions (attach schedule)	10		
Investment Interest	11a Interest expense on investment debts	11a		Form 4952, line 1
	b (1) Investment income included on lines 4a, 4b(2), 4c, and 4f above	11b(1)		See Shareholder's Instructions for Schedule K-1 (Form 1120S).
	(2) Investment expenses included on line 9 above	11b(2)		
Credits	12a Credit for alcohol used as fuel	12a		Form 6478, line 10
	b Low-income housing credit:			
	(1) From section 42(j)(5) partnerships	12b(1)		Form 8586, line 5
	(2) Other than on line 12b(1)	12b(2)		
	c Qualified rehabilitation expenditures related to rental real estate activities	12c		See pages 6 and 7 of the Shareholder's Instructions for Schedule K-1 (Form 1120S).
	d Credits (other than credits shown on lines 12b and 12c) related to rental real estate activities	12d		
	e Credits related to other rental activities	12e		
	13 Other credits	13		

For Paperwork Reduction Act Notice, see the Instructions for Form 1120S. Cat. No. 11520D **Schedule K-1 (Form 1120S) 2003**

6712

		(a) Pro rata share items		(b) Amount	(c) Form 1040 filers enter the amount in column (b) on:
Adjustments and Tax Preference Items	14a	Depreciation adjustment on property placed in service after 1986	14a		See page 6 of the Shareholder's Instructions for Schedule K-1 (Form 1120S) and Instructions for Form 6251
	b	Adjusted gain or loss	14b		
	c	Depletion (other than oil and gas)	14c		
	d	**(1)** Gross income from oil, gas, or geothermal properties	14d(1)		
		(2) Deductions allocable to oil, gas, or geothermal properties	14d(2)		
	e	Other adjustments and tax preference items (attach schedule)	14e		
Foreign Taxes	15a	Name of foreign country or U.S. possession ▶			Form 1116, Part I
	b	Gross income from all sources	15b		
	c	Gross income sourced at shareholder level	15c		
	d	Foreign gross income sourced at corporate level:			
		(1) Passive	15d(1)		
		(2) Listed categories (attach schedule)	15d(2)		
		(3) General limitation	15d(3)		
	e	Deductions allocated and apportioned at shareholder level:			
		(1) Interest expense	15e(1)		
		(2) Other	15e(2)		
	f	Deductions allocated and apportioned at corporate level to foreign source income:			
		(1) Passive	15f(1)		
		(2) Listed categories *(attach schedule)*	15f(2)		
		(3) General limitation	15f(3)		
	g	Total foreign taxes (check one): ▶ ☐ Paid ☐ Accrued	15g		Form 1116, Part II
	h	Reduction in taxes available for credit (attach schedule)	15h		See Instructions for Form 1116
Other	16	Section 59(e)(2) expenditures: **a** Type ▶			See Shareholder's Instructions for Schedule K-1 (Form 1120S).
	b	Amount	16b		
	17	Tax-exempt interest income	17		Form 1040, line 8b
	18	Other tax-exempt income	18		See page 7 of the Shareholder's Instructions for Schedule K-1 (Form 1120S).
	19	Nondeductible expenses	19		
	20	Property distributions (including cash) other than dividend distributions reported to you on Form 1099-DIV	20		
	21	Amount of loan repayments for "Loans From Shareholders"	21		
	22	Recapture of low-income housing credit:			
	a	From section 42(j)(5) partnerships	22a		Form 8611, line 8
	b	Other than on line 22a	22b		

Supplemental Information

23 Supplemental information required to be reported separately to each shareholder (attach additional schedules if more space is needed):

Form **2555**

Department of the Treasury
Internal Revenue Service (99)

Foreign Earned Income

▶ See separate instructions. ▶ Attach to Form 1040.

OMB No. 1545-0067

2003

Attachment Sequence No. **34**

For Use by U.S. Citizens and Resident Aliens Only

Name shown on Form 1040	**Your social security number**

Part I **General Information**

1 Your foreign address (including country)	2 Your occupation

3 Employer's name ▶ ....

4a Employer's U.S. address ▶ ....

b Employer's foreign address ▶ ....

5 Employer is (check any that apply): ▶ a ☐ A foreign entity b ☐ A U.S. company c ☐ Self d ☐ A foreign affiliate of a U.S. company e ☐ Other (specify) ▶ ....

6a If, after 1981, you filed Form 2555 to claim either of the exclusions or Form 2555-EZ to claim the foreign earned income exclusion, enter the last year you filed the form. ▶ ....

b If you did not file Form 2555 or 2555-EZ after 1981 to claim either of the exclusions, check here ▶ ☐ and go to line 7.

c Have you ever revoked either of the exclusions? . . . . . ☐ **Yes** ☐ **No**

d If you answered "Yes," enter the type of exclusion and the tax year for which the revocation was effective. ▶ ....

7 Of what country are you a citizen/national? ▶ ....

8a Did you maintain a separate foreign residence for your family because of adverse living conditions at your tax home? See **Second foreign household** on page 3 of the instructions . . . . . ☐ **Yes** ☐ **No**

b If "Yes," enter city and country of the separate foreign residence. Also, enter the number of days during your tax year that you maintained a second household at that address. ▶ ....

9 List your tax home(s) during your tax year and date(s) established. ▶ ....

Next, complete either Part II or Part III. If an item does not apply, enter "NA." If you do not give the information asked for, any exclusion or deduction you claim may be disallowed.

Part II **Taxpayers Qualifying Under Bona Fide Residence Test** (See page 2 of the instructions.)

10 Date bona fide residence began ▶ ...., and ended ▶ ....

11 Kind of living quarters in foreign country ▶ a ☐ Purchased house b ☐ Rented house or apartment c ☐ Rented room d ☐ Quarters furnished by employer

12a Did any of your family live with you abroad during any part of the tax year? . . . . . ☐ **Yes** ☐ **No**

b If "Yes," who and for what period? ▶ ....

13a Have you submitted a statement to the authorities of the foreign country where you claim bona fide residence that you are not a resident of that country? (See instructions.) . . . . . ☐ **Yes** ☐ **No**

b Are you required to pay income tax to the country where you claim bona fide residence? (See instructions.) ☐ **Yes** ☐ **No**

If you answered "Yes" to 13a and "No" to 13b, you do not qualify as a bona fide resident. Do not complete the rest of this part.

14 If you were present in the United States or its possessions during the tax year, complete columns **(a)–(d)** below. **Do not** include the income from column **(d)** in Part IV, but report it on Form 1040.

(a) Date arrived in U.S.	**(b)** Date left U.S.	**(c)** Number of days in U.S. on business	**(d)** Income earned in U.S. on business (attach computation)	**(a)** Date arrived in U.S.	**(b)** Date left U.S.	**(c)** Number of days in U.S. on business	**(d)** Income earned in U.S. on business (attach computation)

15a List any contractual terms or other conditions relating to the length of your employment abroad. ▶ ....

b Enter the type of visa under which you entered the foreign country. ▶ ....

c Did your visa limit the length of your stay or employment in a foreign country? If "Yes," attach explanation ☐ **Yes** ☐ **No**

d Did you maintain a home in the United States while living abroad? . . . . . ☐ **Yes** ☐ **No**

e If "Yes," enter address of your home, whether it was rented, the names of the occupants, and their relationship to you. ▶ ....

Part III **Taxpayers Qualifying Under Physical Presence Test** (See page 2 of the instructions.)

16 The physical presence test is based on the 12-month period from ▶ ____________ through ▶ ____________

17 Enter your principal country of employment during your tax year. ▶ ____________

18 If you traveled abroad during the 12-month period entered on line 16, complete columns **(a)–(f)** below. Exclude travel between foreign countries that did not involve travel on or over international waters, or in or over the United States, for 24 hours or more. If you have no travel to report during the period, enter "Physically present in a foreign country or countries for the entire 12-month period." **Do not** include the income from column **(f)** below in Part IV, but report it on Form 1040.

(a) Name of country (including U.S.)	**(b)** Date arrived	**(c)** Date left	**(d)** Full days present in country	**(e)** Number of days in U.S. on business	**(f)** Income earned in U.S. on business (attach computation)

Part IV **All Taxpayers**

Note: *Enter on lines 19 through 23 all income, including noncash income, you earned and actually or constructively received during your 2003 tax year for services you performed in a foreign country. If any of the foreign earned income received this tax year was earned in a prior tax year, or will be earned in a later tax year (such as a bonus), see the instructions.* ***Do not*** *include income from line 14, column* ***(d),*** *or line 18, column* ***(f).*** *Report amounts in U.S. dollars, using the exchange rates in effect when you actually or constructively received the income.*

If you are a cash basis taxpayer, report on Form 1040 all income you received in 2003, no matter when you performed the service.

2003 Foreign Earned Income			**Amount (in U.S. dollars)**
19 Total wages, salaries, bonuses, commissions, etc.		**19**	
20 Allowable share of income for personal services performed (see instructions):			
a In a business (including farming) or profession		**20a**	
b In a partnership. List partnership's name and address and type of income. ▶ ____________		**20b**	
21 Noncash income (market value of property or facilities furnished by employer—attach statement showing how it was determined):			
a Home (lodging)		**21a**	
b Meals		**21b**	
c Car		**21c**	
d Other property or facilities. List type and amount. ▶ ____________		**21d**	
22 Allowances, reimbursements, or expenses paid on your behalf for services you performed:			
a Cost of living and overseas differential	**22a**		
b Family	**22b**		
c Education	**22c**		
d Home leave	**22d**		
e Quarters	**22e**		
f For any other purpose. List type and amount. ▶ ____________	**22f**		
g Add lines 22a through 22f		**22g**	
23 Other foreign earned income. List type and amount. ▶ ____________		**23**	
24 Add lines 19 through 21d, line 22g, and line 23		**24**	
25 Total amount of meals and lodging included on line 24 that is excludable (see instructions)		**25**	
26 Subtract line 25 from line 24. Enter the result here and on line 27 on page 3. This is your **2003 foreign earned income** ▶		**26**	

Form 2555 (2003) Page **3**

Part V **All Taxpayers**

27	Enter the amount from line 26	27	
	Are you claiming the housing exclusion or housing deduction? ☐ **Yes.** Complete Part VI. ☐ **No.** Go to Part VII.		

Part VI **Taxpayers Claiming the Housing Exclusion and/or Deduction**

28	Qualified housing expenses for the tax year (see instructions)	28	
29	Number of days in your qualifying period that fall within your 2003 tax year (see instructions) . . . . **29** ____ days		
30	Multiply $30.77 by the number of days on line 29. If 365 is entered on line 29, enter $11,233.00 here	30	
31	Subtract line 30 from line 28. If the result is zero or less, do not complete the rest of this part or any of Part IX	31	
32	Enter employer-provided amounts (see instructions) . . . . **32** ____		
33	Divide line 32 by line 27. Enter the result as a decimal (rounded to at least three places), but do not enter more than "1.000"	33	× .
34	**Housing exclusion.** Multiply line 31 by line 33. Enter the result but do not enter more than the amount on line 32. Also, complete Part VIII . . . . ▶	34	

Note: *The housing deduction is figured in Part IX. If you choose to claim the foreign earned income exclusion, complete Parts VII and VIII before Part IX.*

Part VII **Taxpayers Claiming the Foreign Earned Income Exclusion**

35	Maximum foreign earned income exclusion	35	$80,000 00
36	• If you completed Part VI, enter the number from line 29. • All others, enter the number of days in your qualifying period that fall within your 2003 tax year (see the instructions for line 29). **36** ____ days		
37	• If line 36 and the number of days in your 2003 tax year (usually 365) are the same, enter "1.000." • Otherwise, divide line 36 by the number of days in your 2003 tax year and enter the result as a decimal (rounded to at least three places).	37	× .
38	Multiply line 35 by line 37	38	
39	Subtract line 34 from line 27	39	
40	**Foreign earned income exclusion.** Enter the **smaller** of line 38 or line 39. Also, complete Part VIII ▶	40	

Part VIII **Taxpayers Claiming the Housing Exclusion, Foreign Earned Income Exclusion, or Both**

41	Add lines 34 and 40	41	
42	Deductions allowed in figuring your adjusted gross income (Form 1040, line 34) that are allocable to the excluded income. See instructions and attach computation	42	
43	Subtract line 42 from line 41. Enter the result here and in parentheses on **Form 1040, line 21.** Next to the amount enter "Form 2555." On Form 1040, subtract this amount from your income to arrive at total income on Form 1040, line 22 . . . . ▶	43	

Part IX **Taxpayers Claiming the Housing Deduction—**Complete this part only if **(a)** line 31 is more than line 34 and **(b)** line 27 is more than line 41.

44	Subtract line 34 from line 31	44	
45	Subtract line 41 from line 27	45	
46	Enter the **smaller** of line 44 or line 45	46	
	Note: *If line 45 is* ***more than*** *line 46 and you could not deduct all of your 2002 housing deduction because of the 2002 limit, use the worksheet on page 4 of the instructions to figure the amount to enter on line 47. Otherwise, go to line 48.*		
47	Housing deduction carryover from 2002 (from worksheet on page 4 of the instructions) . . .	47	
48	**Housing deduction.** Add lines 46 and 47. Enter the total here and on Form 1040 to the left of line 33. Next to the amount on Form 1040, enter "Form 2555." Add it to the total adjustments reported on that line . . . . ▶	48	

Form **8832**
(Rev. September 2002)
Department of the Treasury
Internal Revenue Service

Entity Classification Election

OMB No. 1545-1516

Type or Print	
	Name of entity / EIN ▶
	Number, street, and room or suite no. If a P.O. box, see instructions.
	City or town, state, and ZIP code. If a foreign address, enter city, province or state, postal code and country.

1 **Type of election** (see instructions):

a ☐ Initial classification by a newly-formed entity.

b ☐ Change in current classification.

2 **Form of entity** (see instructions):

a ☐ A domestic eligible entity electing to be classified as an association taxable as a corporation.

b ☐ A domestic eligible entity electing to be classified as a partnership.

c ☐ A domestic eligible entity with a single owner electing to be disregarded as a separate entity.

d ☐ A foreign eligible entity electing to be classified as an association taxable as a corporation.

e ☐ A foreign eligible entity electing to be classified as a partnership.

f ☐ A foreign eligible entity with a single owner electing to be disregarded as a separate entity.

3 **Disregarded entity information** (see instructions):
a Name of owner ▶ ....
b Identifying number of owner ▶ ....
c Country of organization of entity electing to be disregarded (if foreign) ▶ ....

4 Election is to be effective beginning (month, day, year) (see instructions) . . . . ▶ ___/___/___

5 Name and title of person whom the IRS may call for more information

6 That person's telephone number
( )

Consent Statement and Signature(s) (see instructions)

Under penalties of perjury, I (we) declare that I (we) consent to the election of the above-named entity to be classified as indicated above, and that I (we) have examined this consent statement, and to the best of my (our) knowledge and belief, it is true, correct, and complete. If I am an officer, manager, or member signing for all members of the entity, I further declare that I am authorized to execute this consent statement on their behalf.

Signature(s)	Date	Title

APPENDIX C

Glossary of Tax Terms

The words and phrases in this glossary have been defined to reflect their conventional use in the field of taxation. The definitions may therefore be incomplete for other purposes.

A

Accelerated cost recovery system (ACRS). A method in which the cost of tangible property is recovered over a prescribed period of time. The approach disregards salvage value, imposes a period of cost recovery that depends upon the classification of the asset into one of various recovery periods, and prescribes the applicable percentage of cost that can be deducted each year. The modified system is referred to as MACRS. § 168.

Accelerated depreciation. Various methods of depreciation that yield larger deductions in the earlier years of the life of an asset than the straight-line method. Examples include the double declining-balance and the sum-of-the-years' digits methods of depreciation.

Acceleration rule. Treatment of an intercompany transaction on a *consolidated tax return,* when a sold asset leaves the group.

Accounting method. The method under which income and expenses are determined for tax purposes. Important accounting methods include the cash basis and the accrual basis. Special methods are available for the reporting of gain on installment sales, recognition of income on construction projects (the completed contract and percentage of completion methods), and the valuation of inventories (last-in, first-out and first-in, first-out). §§ 446–474. See also *accrual basis, cash basis, completed contract method*, and *percentage of completion method*.

Accounting period. The period of time, usually a year, used by a taxpayer for the determination of tax liability. Unless a fiscal year is chosen, taxpayers must determine and pay their income tax liability by using the calendar year (January 1 through December 31) as the period of measurement. An example of a fiscal year is July 1 through June 30. A change in accounting periods (e.g., from a calendar year to a fiscal year) generally requires the consent of the IRS. Some new taxpayers, such as a newly formed corporation, are free to select either an initial calendar or a fiscal year without the consent of the IRS. §§ 441–443. See also *annual accounting period concept*.

Accrual basis. A method of accounting that reflects expenses incurred and income earned for any one tax year. In contrast to the cash basis of accounting, expenses need not be paid to be deductible, nor need income be received to be taxable. Unearned income (e.g., prepaid interest and rent) generally is taxed in the year of receipt regardless of the method of accounting used by the taxpayer. § 446(c)(2). See also *accounting method, cash basis*, and *unearned income*.

Accrual method. See *accrual basis*.

Accumulated adjustments account (AAA). An account that aggregates an S corporation's post-1982 income, loss, and deductions for the tax year (including nontaxable income and nondeductible losses and expenses). After the year-end income and expense adjustments are made, the account is reduced by distributions made during the tax year.

Accumulated earnings and profits. Net undistributed tax-basis earnings of a corporation aggregated from March 1, 1913, to the end of the prior tax year. Used to determine the amount of dividend income associated with a distribution to shareholders. See also *current earnings and profits* and *earnings and profits*. § 316 and Reg. § 1.316–2.

Accumulated earnings credit. A reduction allowed in arriving at accumulated taxable income, in determining the accumulated earnings tax. See also *accumulated earnings tax* and *accumulated taxable income*.

Accumulated earnings tax (AET). A special tax imposed on corporations that accumulate (rather than distribute) their earnings beyond the reasonable needs of the business. The accumulated earnings tax and related interest are imposed on accumulated taxable income in addition to the corporate income tax. §§ 531–537.

Accumulated taxable income. The base upon which the accumulated earnings tax is imposed. Generally, it is the taxable income of the corporation as adjusted for certain items (e.g., the Federal income tax, excess charitable contributions, the dividends received deduction) less the dividends paid deduction and the accumulated earnings credit. § 535.

Accumulating trust. See *discretionary trust*.

Accuracy-related penalty. Major civil taxpayer penalties relating to the accuracy of tax return data, including misstatements stemming from taxpayer negligence and improper valuation of income and deductions, are coordinated under this umbrella term. The penalty usually equals 20 percent of the understated tax liability.

Acquiescence. Agreement by the IRS on the results reached in some of the more significant decisions involving tax issues; sometimes abbreviated *Acq.* or *A.* See also *nonacquiescence.*

Acquisition. See *corporate acquisition.*

ACRS. See *accelerated cost recovery system.*

Ad valorem tax. A tax imposed on the value of property. The most common ad valorem tax is that imposed by states, counties, and cities on real estate. Ad valorem taxes can be imposed on personal property as well. See also *personalty.*

Adjusted basis. The cost or other basis of property reduced by depreciation allowed or allowable and increased by capital improvements. Other special adjustments are provided in § 1016 and the related Regulations. See also *basis.*

Adjusted current earnings (ACE). An adjustment in computing corporate alternative minimum taxable income (AMTI), computed at 75 percent of the excess of adjusted current earnings and profits over AMTI. ACE computations reflect restrictions on the timing of certain recognition events. Exempt interest, life insurance proceeds, and other receipts that are included in earnings and profits but not in taxable income also increase the ACE adjustment. See also *alternative minimum tax* and *earnings and profits.*

Adjusted gross estate. The gross estate of a *decedent* reduced by § 2053 expenses (e.g., administration, funeral) and § 2054 losses (e.g., casualty). Necessary in testing for the extension of time for installment payment of estate taxes under § 6166. See also *gross estate.*

Adjusted gross income (AGI). A tax determination peculiar to individual taxpayers. Generally, it represents the gross income of an individual, less business expenses and less any appropriate capital gain or loss adjustment. See also *gross income.*

Adjusted ordinary gross income (AOGI). A determination peculiar to the *personal holding company tax.* In ascertaining whether a corporation is a personal holding company, personal holding company income divided by adjusted ordinary gross income must equal 60 percent or more. Adjusted ordinary gross income is the corporation's gross income less capital gains, § 1231 gains, and certain expenses. §§ 541 and 543(b)(2). See also *personal holding company income.*

Adjusted taxable estate. The taxable estate reduced by $60,000. The adjusted taxable estate is utilized only in applying § 2011 for determining the limit on the credit for state death taxes paid that will be allowed against the Federal estate tax. See also *taxable estate.*

Adjusted taxable income. An amount used in computing the limitation on related-party interest payments under the *earnings stripping rules.* Generally under § 163(j), only one-half of the taxpayer's adjusted taxable income can be eliminated through a related-party interest deduction.

Administration. The supervision and winding up of an estate. The administration of an estate runs from the date of an individual's death until all assets have been distributed and liabilities paid.

Administrator. A person appointed by the court to administer (manage or take charge of) the assets and liabilities of a decedent (the deceased). See also *executor.*

Affiliate. A member of an *affiliated group.* See also *consolidated tax return.*

Affiliated group. A parent-subsidiary group of corporations that is eligible to elect to file on a consolidated basis. Eighty percent ownership of the voting power and value of all of the corporations must be achieved on every day of the tax year, and an identifiable parent corporation must exist (i.e., it must own at least 80 percent of another group member without applying attribution rules).

AFTR. *American Federal Tax Reports* contain all of the Federal tax decisions issued by the U.S. District Courts, U.S. Court of Federal Claims, U.S. Courts of Appeals, and the U.S. Supreme Court.

AFTR2d. The second series of the *American Federal Tax Reports,* dealing with 1954 and 1986 Code case law.

Aggregate concept. The theory of partnership taxation under which, in certain cases, a partnership is treated as a mere extension of each partner.

Alimony. Alimony deductions result from the payment of a legal obligation arising from the termination of a marital relationship. Payments designated as alimony generally are included in the gross income of the recipient and are deductible *for* AGI by the payer.

Allocable share of income. Certain entities receive conduit treatment under the Federal income tax law. This means the earned income or loss is not taxed to the entity, but is allocated to the owners or beneficiaries, regardless of the magnitude or timing of corresponding distributions. The portion of the entity's income that is taxed to the owner or beneficiary is the allocable share of the entity's income or loss for the period. The allocations are determined by (1) the partnership agreement for partners, (2) a weighted-average stock ownership computation for shareholders of an S corporation, and (3) the controlling will or trust instrument for the beneficiaries of an estate or trust.

Allocate. The assignment of income for various tax purposes. A *multistate corporation*'s nonbusiness income usually is allocated to the state where the nonbusiness assets are located; it is not *apportioned* with the rest of the entity's income. The income and expense items of an estate or trust are allocated between income and corpus components. Specific items of income, expense, gain, loss, and credit can be allocated to specific partners, if a substantial economic nontax purpose for the allocation is established. See also *apportion* and *substantial economic effect.*

Alternate valuation date. Property passing from a *decedent* by death may be valued for death tax purposes as of the date of death or the alternate valuation date. The alternate valuation date is six months from the date of death or the date the property is disposed of by the estate, whichever comes first. To use the alternate valuation date, the *executor* or *administrator* of the estate must make an affirmative election. Election of the alternate valuation date is not available unless it decreases the amount of the gross estate *and* reduces the estate tax liability.

Alternative minimum tax (AMT). AMT is a fixed percentage of alternative minimum taxable income (AMTI). AMTI generally starts with the taxpayer's taxable income. To this amount, the taxpayer (1) adds designated preference items (e.g., interest income on private activity bonds), (2) makes other specified adjustments (e.g., to reflect a longer, straight-line cost recovery deduction), (3) subtracts certain AMT itemized deductions for individuals (e.g., interest incurred on housing but not taxes paid), and (4) subtracts an exemption amount (e.g., $40,000 on a C corporation's return). The taxpayer must pay the greater of the resulting AMT (reduced by only the foreign tax credit) or the regular income tax (reduced by all allowable tax credits). The AMT does not apply to certain small C corporations. AMT preferences and adjustments are assigned to partners and S corporation shareholders.

Alternative minimum taxable income (AMTI). The base for computing a taxpayer's *alternative minimum tax*. Generally, the taxable income for the year, modified for AMT adjustments, preferences, and exemptions.

Amortization. The tax deduction for the cost or other basis of an intangible asset over the asset's estimated useful life. Examples of amortizable intangibles include patents, copyrights, and leasehold interests. Most intangible assets are amortized over 15 years. § 195. For tangible assets, see *depreciation*. For natural resources, see *depletion*. See also *estimated useful life* and *goodwill*.

Amount realized. The amount received by a taxpayer upon the sale or exchange of property. Amount realized is the sum of the cash and the fair market value of any property or services received by the taxpayer, plus any related debt assumed by the buyer. Determining the amount realized is the starting point for arriving at realized gain or loss. § 1001(b). See also *realized gain or loss* and *recognized gain or loss*.

Annual accounting period concept. In determining a taxpayer's income tax liability, only transactions taking place during a specified tax year are taken into consideration. For reporting and payment purposes, therefore, the tax life of taxpayers is divided into equal annual accounting periods. See also *accounting period* and *mitigation of the annual accounting period concept*.

Annual exclusion. In computing the taxable gifts for the year, each donor excludes the first $11,000 of a gift to each donee. Usually, the annual exclusion is not available for gifts of future interests. § 2503(b). See also *future interest* and *gift splitting*.

Annuitant. The party entitled to receive payments from an annuity contract. See also *annuity*.

Annuity. A fixed sum of money payable to a person at specified times for a specified period of time or for life. If the party making the payment (i.e., the obligor) is regularly engaged in this type of business (e.g., an insurance company), the arrangement is classified as a commercial annuity. A so-called private annuity involves an obligor that is not regularly engaged in selling annuities (e.g., a charity or family member).

Anticipatory assignment of income. See *assignment of income*.

APB 23. The financial accounting standard treating the company's income tax expenses.

Appellate court. For Federal tax purposes, appellate courts include the U.S. Courts of Appeals and the U.S. Supreme Court. If the party losing in the trial (or lower) court is dissatisfied with the result, the dispute may be carried to the appropriate appellate court. See also *Court of Appeals* and *trial court*.

Apportion. The assignment of the business income of a multistate corporation to specific states for income taxation. Usually, the apportionment procedure accounts for the property, payroll, and sales activity levels of the various states, and a proportionate assignment of the entity's total income is made, using a three-factor apportionment formula. These activities indicate the commercial domicile of the corporation, relative to that income. Some states exclude nonbusiness income from the apportionment procedure; they *allocate* nonbusiness income to the states where the nonbusiness assets are located. See also *allocate, domicile, nonbusiness income, payroll factor, property factor*, and *sales factor*.

Appreciated inventory. In partnership taxation, appreciated inventory is a *hot asset*, and a partner's share of its ordinary income potential must be allocated. If a partner sells an interest in the partnership, ordinary income is recognized to the extent of the partner's share in the partnership's inventory and *unrealized receivables*. The definition of "inventory" is broad enough to include any accounts receivable, including unrealized receivables.

Arm's length price. The price at which unrelated parties would carry out a transaction. Suppose Bint Corporation sells property to its sole shareholder for $10,000. In determining whether $10,000 is an arm's length price, one would ascertain the amount for which the corporation could have sold the property to a disinterested third party.

Articles of incorporation. The legal document specifying a corporation's name, period of existence, purpose and powers, authorized number of shares, classes of stock, and other conditions for operation. The organizers of the corporation file the articles with the state of incorporation. If the articles are satisfactory and other conditions of the law are satisfied, the state will issue a charter recognizing the organization's status as a corporation.

Assessment. The process whereby the IRS imposes a tax liability. If, for example, the IRS audits a taxpayer's income tax return and finds gross income understated or deductions overstated, it will assess a deficiency in the amount of the tax that should have been paid in light of the adjustments made. See also *deficiency*.

Assignment of income. A procedure whereby a taxpayer attempts to avoid the recognition of income by assigning to another the property that generates the income. Such a procedure will not avoid the recognition of income by the taxpayer making the assignment if it can be said that the income was earned at the point of the transfer. In this case, usually referred to as an anticipatory assignment of income, the income will be taxed to the person who earns it.

Assumption of liabilities. In a corporate formation, corporate takeover, or asset purchase, the new owner often takes assets and agrees to assume preexisting debt. Such actions do not create *boot* received on the transaction for the new shareholder, unless there is no *bona fide* business purpose for the exchange, or the principal purpose of the debt assumption is the avoidance of tax liabilities. Gain is recognized to the extent that liabilities assumed exceed the aggregated bases of the transferred assets. § 357.

At-risk amount. The taxpayer has an amount at risk in a business or investment venture to the extent that personal assets have been subjected to the risks of the business. Typically, the taxpayer's at-risk amount includes (1) the amount of money or other property that the investor contributed to the venture for the investment, (2) the amount of any of the entity's liabilities for which the taxpayer personally is liable and that relate to the investment, and (3) an allocable share of nonrecourse debts incurred by the venture from third parties in arm's length transactions for real estate investments.

At-risk limitation. Generally, a taxpayer can deduct losses related to a trade or business, S corporation, partnership, or investment asset only to the extent of the at-risk amount.

Attribution. Under certain circumstances, the tax law applies attribution rules to assign to one taxpayer the ownership interest of another taxpayer. If, for example, the stock of Tree Corporation is held 60 percent by Mary and 40 percent by Sam, Mary may be deemed to own 100 percent of Tree if Sam is her son. In that case, the stock owned by Sam is attributed to Mary. Stated differently, Mary has a 60 percent direct and a 40 percent indirect interest in Tree. It can also be said that Mary is the constructive owner of Sam's interest.

Audit. Inspection and verification of a taxpayer's return or other transactions possessing tax consequences. See also *correspondence audit*, *field audit*, and *office audit*.

Automobile expenses. Automobile expenses generally are deductible only to the extent the automobile is used in business or for the production of income. Personal commuting expenses are not deductible. The taxpayer may deduct actual out-of-pocket expenses (including depreciation and insurance), or a standard mileage rate for the tax year. For 2004, per-mile deduction amounts are 37.5 cents for business use of the auto, 14 cents if in support of charity, 14 cents for medical purposes, and 14 cents for a job-related move.

B

Bailout. Various procedures whereby the owners of an entity can obtain the entity's profits with favorable tax consequences. With corporations, for example, the bailout of corporate profits might be accomplished by using *fringe benefits*, or by paying salaries or interest. The alternative of distributing the profits to the shareholders as dividends generally is less attractive since dividend payments are not deductible. See also *preferred stock bailout*.

Balance sheet approach. Under *FAS 109*, the *deferred tax expense* (benefit) is determined using the change in the balance sheet *deferred tax asset* and *deferred tax liability* accounts.

***Bardahl* formula.** A formula approved in a Tax Court memorandum decision, used in the context of the accumulated earnings tax to compute the reasonable business needs of the corporation for working capital. Most appropriate were the corporation holds inventory.

Bargain sale or purchase. A sale or purchase of property for less than fair market value. The difference between the sale or purchase price and the fair market value of the property may have tax consequences. If, for example, a corporation sells property worth $1,000 to one of its shareholders for $700, the $300 difference probably represents a constructive dividend to the shareholder. Suppose, instead, the shareholder sells the property (worth $1,000) to his or her corporation for $700. The $300 difference probably represents a contribution by the shareholder to the corporation's capital. Bargain sales and purchases among members of the same family may lead to gift tax consequences. See also *constructive dividend*.

Basis. The acquisition cost assigned to an asset for income tax purposes. For assets acquired by purchase, basis is cost (§ 1012). Special rules govern the basis of property received by virtue of another's death (§ 1014) or by gift (§ 1015), the basis of stock received on a transfer of property to a controlled corporation (§ 358), the basis of the property transferred to the corporation (§ 362), and the basis of property received upon the liquidation of a corporation (§ 334). See also *adjusted basis*.

Basis in partnership interest. The acquisition cost of the partner's ownership interest in the *partnership*. Includes purchase price and associated debt acquired from other partners and in the course of the entity's trade or business.

Benchmarking. The strategic making of comparisons of key information across two or more companies.

Beneficiary. A party who will benefit from a transfer of property or other arrangement. Examples include the beneficiary of a trust, the beneficiary of a life insurance policy, and the beneficiary of an estate.

Bequest. A transfer of personal property by will. To bequeath is to leave such property by will. See also *devise* and *personal property*.

Blockage rule. A factor to be considered in valuing a large block of stock. Application of this rule generally justifies a discount in the fair market value since the disposition of a large amount of stock at any one time may depress the value of the shares in the marketplace.

Bona fide. In good faith, or real. In tax law, this term is often used in connection with a business purpose for carrying out a transaction. Thus, was there a bona fide business purpose for a shareholder's transfer of a liability to a controlled corporation? § 357(b)(1)(B). See also *business purpose.*

Book value. The net amount of an asset after reduction by a related reserve. The book value of machinery, for example, is the amount of the machinery less the reserve for depreciation.

Boot. Cash or property of a type not included in the definition of a nontaxable exchange. The receipt of boot causes an otherwise nontaxable transfer to become taxable to the extent of the lesser of the fair market value of the boot or the realized gain on the transfer. For example, see transfers to controlled corporations under § 351(b) and like-kind exchanges under § 1031(b). See also *like-kind exchange* and *realized gain or loss.*

Branch profits tax. A tax on the effectively connected earnings and profits of the U.S. branch of a foreign corporation. The tax is levied in addition to the usual § 11 tax, in an amount equal to 30 percent of the dividend equivalent amount. Treaties can override the tax or reduce the withholding percentage. Earnings reinvested in the U.S. operations of the entity are not subject to the tax until repatriation. See also *dividend equivalent amount.*

Bribes and illegal payments. Section 162 denies a deduction for bribes or kickbacks, fines, and penalties paid to a government official or employee for violation of law, and two-thirds of the treble damage payments made to claimants for violation of the antitrust law. Denial of a deduction for bribes and illegal payments is based upon the judicially established principle that allowing such payments would be contrary to public policy.

Brother-sister controlled group. More than one corporation owned by the same shareholders. If, for example, Clara and Dan each own one-half of the stock in Top Corporation and Bottom Corporation, then Top and Bottom form a brother-sister controlled group.

B.T.A. The Board of Tax Appeals was a trial court that considered Federal tax matters. This court is now the U.S. Tax Court.

Built-in gains tax. A penalty tax designed to discourage a shift of the incidence of taxation on unrealized gains from a C corporation to its shareholders, via an S election. Under this provision, any recognized gain during the first 10 years of S status generates a corporate-level tax on a base not to exceed the aggregate untaxed built-in gains brought into the S corporation upon its election from C corporation taxable years.

Burden of proof. The requirement in a lawsuit to show the weight of evidence and thereby gain a favorable decision. In cases of tax fraud, the burden of proof in a tax case is on the IRS. See also *fraud.*

Business bad debts. A tax deduction allowed for obligations obtained in connection with a trade or business that have become either partially or completely worthless. In contrast to nonbusiness bad debts, business bad debts are deductible as business expenses. § 166. See also *nonbusiness bad debt.*

Business profits. Under the terms of an *income tax treaty,* specified business profits are protected from double taxation. See also *permanent establishment.*

Business purpose. A justifiable business reason for carrying out a transaction. Mere tax avoidance is not an acceptable business purpose. The presence of a business purpose is crucial in the area of corporate reorganizations and certain liquidations. See also *bona fide.*

Buy-sell agreement. An arrangement, particularly appropriate in the case of a closely held corporation or a partnership, whereby the surviving owners (shareholders or partners) or the entity agrees to purchase the interest of a withdrawing owner. The buy-sell agreement provides for an orderly disposition of an interest in a business and may aid in setting the value of the interest for death tax purposes. See also *cross-purchase buy-sell agreement* and *entity buy-sell agreement.*

Bypass amount. The amount that can be transferred by gift or death free of any unified transfer tax. Currently, the bypass amount is $1,500,000. See also *exemption equivalent amount.*

Bypass trust. A trust designed to contain property that bypasses the surviving spouse's estate. The bypass trust often is funded to a level of the *exemption equivalent.* Its beneficiaries should not be the spouse or a charity.

C

C corporation. A separate taxable entity, subject to the rules of Subchapter C of the Code. This business form may create a double taxation effect relative to its shareholders. The entity is subject to the regular corporate tax and a number of penalty taxes at the Federal level. §§ 301ff.

Cafeteria benefit plan. An employee benefit plan under which an employee is allowed to select from among a variety of employer-provided fringe benefits. Some of the benefits may be taxable, and some may be statutory nontaxable benefits (e.g., health and accident insurance and group term life insurance). The employee is taxed only on the taxable benefits selected. A cafeteria benefit plan is also referred to as a flexible benefit plan. § 125.

Calendar year. See *accounting period.*

Capital account. The financial accounting analog of a partner's tax basis in the entity.

Capital asset. Broadly speaking, all assets are capital except those specifically excluded by the Code. Major categories of noncapital assets include property held for resale in the normal course of business (inventory), trade accounts and notes receivable, and depreciable property and real estate used in a trade or business (§ 1231 assets). § 1221. See also *capital gain* and *capital loss.*

Capital contribution. Various means by which an owner makes additional funds available to the business entity (placed at the risk of the business). If no stock is received after a contribution to a corporation, the contributions are added to the basis of the shareholder's existing stock investment and do not generate gross income to the corporation. § 118.

Capital expenditure. An expenditure added to the basis of the property improved. For income tax purposes, this generally precludes a full deduction for the expenditure in the year paid or incurred. Any cost recovery in the form of a tax deduction comes in the form of depreciation, depletion, or amortization. § 263.

Capital gain. The gain from the sale or exchange of a capital asset. See also *capital asset.*

Capital interest. Usually, the percentage of the entity's net assets that a partner would receive on liquidation. Typically determined by the partner's capital sharing ratio.

Capital loss. The loss from the sale or exchange of a capital asset. See also *capital asset.*

Capital sharing ratio. A partner's percentage ownership of the entity's capital.

Capital stock tax. A state-level tax, usually imposed on out-of-state corporations for the privilege of doing business in the state. The tax may be based on the entity's apportionable income or payroll, or on its apportioned net worth as of a specified date.

Carryover basis. When a taxpayer exchanges one asset for another, many provisions in the tax law allow the basis assigned to the received asset to be precisely that of the traded asset. Thus, no step-up or -down of basis occurs as a result of the exchange. For instance, when an investor contributes an asset to a corporation or partnership, the entity generally takes a carryover basis in the property. § 723.

Cash balance plan. A hybrid form of pension plan similar in some aspects to a *defined benefit plan*. Such a plan is funded by the employer, and the employer bears the investment risks and rewards. But like *defined contribution plans*, a cash balance plan establishes allocations to individual employee accounts, and the payout for an employee depends on investment performance.

Cash basis. A method of accounting that reflects deductions as paid and income as received in any one tax year. However, deductions for prepaid expenses that benefit more than one tax year (e.g., prepaid rent and prepaid interest) usually must be spread over the period benefited rather than deducted in the year paid. § 446(c)(1). See also *constructive receipt of income.*

Cash method. See *cash basis.*

Cash surrender value. The amount of money that an insurance policy would yield if cashed in with the insurance company that issued the policy.

CCH. Commerce Clearing House (CCH) is the publisher of a tax service and of Federal tax decisions (USTC series).

Cert. den. By denying the Writ of Certiorari, the U.S. Supreme Court refuses to accept an appeal from a U.S. Court of Appeals. The denial of *certiorari* does not, however, mean that the U.S. Supreme Court agrees with the result reached by the lower court.

Certiorari. Appeal from a U.S. Court of Appeals to the U.S. Supreme Court is by Writ of Certiorari. The Supreme Court need not accept the appeal, and it usually does not (*cert. den.*) unless a conflict exists among the lower courts that must be resolved or a constitutional issue is involved. See also *cert. den.*

Cf. Compare.

Charitable contributions. Contributions are deductible (subject to various restrictions and ceiling limitations) if made to qualified nonprofit charitable organizations. A cash basis taxpayer is entitled to a deduction solely in the year of payment. Accrual basis corporations may accrue contributions at year-end if payment is properly authorized before the end of the year and payment is made within two and one-half months after the end of the year. § 170.

Check-the-box Regulations. A business entity can elect to be taxed as a partnership, S corporation, or C corporation by indicating its preference on the tax return. Legal structure and operations are irrelevant in this regard. Thus, by using the check-the-box rules prudently, an entity can select the most attractive tax results offered by the Code. Not available if the entity is incorporated under state law. Especially useful with multinational structures.

Civil fraud. See *fraud.*

Closely held corporation. A corporation where stock ownership is not widely dispersed. Rather, a few shareholders are in control of corporate policy and are in a position to benefit personally from that policy.

Closing agreement. In a tax dispute, the parties sign a closing agreement to spell out the terms under which the matters are settled. The agreement is binding on both the IRS and the taxpayer for the disputed year and for all future years.

Collapsing. To disregard a transaction or one of a series of steps leading to a result. See also *step transaction, substance vs. form concept,* and *telescoping.*

Combined return. Filed in every state in which a *multistate corporation* has *nexus,* if the state applies the *unitary theory.* Computations reflect the *apportioned* and *allocated* income of the entire unitary group.

Commissioner of the IRS. The head of IRS operations, a presidential appointee.

Common law state. See *community property.*

Community property. Louisiana, Texas, New Mexico, Arizona, California, Washington, Idaho, Nevada, and Wisconsin have community property systems. The rest of the states are common law property jurisdictions. Alsaka residents can elect community property status for assets. The difference between common law and community property systems centers around the property rights possessed by married persons. In a common law system, each spouse owns whatever he or she earns. Under a community property system, one-half of the earnings of each spouse is considered owned by the other spouse. Assume, for example, Hal and Wanda are husband and wife and their only income is the $50,000 annual salary Hal receives. If they live in New York (a common law state), the $50,000 salary belongs to Hal. If, however, they live in Texas (a community property state), the $50,000 salary is owned one-half each by Hal and Wanda. See also *separate property.*

Complete termination redemption. See *redemption (complete termination).*

Completed contract method. A method of reporting gain or loss on certain long-term contracts. Under this method of accounting, gross income and expenses are recognized in the tax year in which the contract is completed. Reg. § 1.451–3. See also *percentage of completion method.*

Complex trust. Not a *simple trust.* Such trusts may have charitable beneficiaries, accumulate income, and distribute corpus. §§ 661–663.

Compliance requirements. Generally, the filing requirements that must be met by a taxpayer. These include specified forms, attachments, and their due dates. Special requirements apply for the corporations that are part of an affiliated group and file a consolidated return.

Composite return. Several states allow an S corporation to file a single income tax return, reporting and paying tax on behalf of non-resident shareholders.

Concur. To agree with the result reached by another, but not necessarily with the reasoning or the logic used in reaching the result. For example, Judge Ross agrees with Judges Smith and Tanaka (all being members of the same court) that the income is taxable but for a different reason. Judge Ross would issue a concurring opinion to the majority opinion issued by Judges Smith and Tanaka.

Condemnation. The taking of property by a public authority. The taking is by legal action, and the owner of the property is compensated by the public authority.

Conduit concept. An approach assumed by the tax law in the treatment of certain entities and their owners. Permits specified tax characteristics to pass through the entity without losing their identity. For example, long-term capital losses realized by a limited liability company are passed through as such to the individual members of the entity. Varying forms of the conduit concept apply for partnerships, trusts, estates, and S corporations. See also *aggregate concept.*

Consent dividend. For purposes of avoiding or reducing the penalty tax on the unreasonable accumulation of earnings or the personal holding company tax, a corporation may declare a consent dividend. No cash or property is distributed to the shareholders, although the corporation obtains a dividends paid deduction. The consent dividend is taxed to the shareholders and increases the basis in their stock investment. § 565.

Conservation easement. An interest in real property that maintains its natural or pristine condition. Most often it restricts the development of the property. Properly structured, the grant of such an easement can generate an income tax deduction for the donor. If the grant takes place after the owner's death, a § 2055 charitable deduction results, and a portion of the property's value is excluded from the gross estate. § 2031(c).

Conservatism principle. This doctrine underlies most financial accounting principles, to ensure that assets are not overstated and liabilities are not understated.

Consolidated tax return. A procedure whereby certain affiliated corporations may file a single return, combine the tax transactions of each corporation, and arrive at a single income tax liability for the group. The election to file a consolidated return usually is binding on future years. §§ 1501–1505 and related Regulations.

Consolidation. The combination of two or more corporations into a newly created corporation. Thus, Apt Corporation and Bye Corporation combine to form Cart Corporation. A consolidation may qualify as a nontaxable reorganization if certain conditions are satisfied. §§ 354 and 368(a)(1)(A).

Constructive dividend. A taxable benefit derived by a shareholder from his or her corporation that is not actually called a dividend. Examples include unreasonable compensation, excessive rent payments, bargain purchases of corporate property, and shareholder use of corporate property. Constructive dividends generally are found in closely held corporations. See also *bargain sale or purchase, closely held corporation,* and *unreasonable compensation.*

Constructive liquidation scenario. The means by which recourse debt is shared among partners in basis determination.

Constructive ownership. See *attribution.*

Constructive receipt of income. If income is unqualifiedly available although not physically in the taxpayer's possession, it is subject to the income tax. An example is accrued interest on a savings account. Under the constructive receipt of income concept, the interest is taxed to a depositor in the year available, rather than the year actually withdrawn. The fact that the depositor uses the cash basis of accounting for tax purposes is irrelevant. See Reg. § 1.451–2. See also *cash basis.*

Contingent sales price. A sale or other disposition of property in which the aggregate selling price cannot be determined by the end of the tax year in which the sale or other disposition occurs. The term is relevant with respect to installment sales. § 453

Continuity of business enterprise. In a tax-favored reorganization, a shareholder or corporation that has substantially the same investment after an exchange as before should not be taxed on the transaction. Specifically, the transferee corporation must continue the historic business of the transferor or use a significant portion of the transferor's assets in the new business.

Continuity of interest test. In a tax-favored reorganization, a shareholder or corporation that has substantially the same investment after an exchange as before should not be taxed on the transaction. Specifically, the seller must acquire an equity interest in the purchasing corporation equal in value to at least 50 percent of all formerly outstanding stock of the acquired entity.

Continuity of life or existence. The death or other withdrawal of an owner of an entity does not terminate the existence of the entity. This is a characteristic of a corporation since the death or withdrawal of a shareholder does not affect the corporation's existence.

Contributions to the capital of a corporation. See *capital contribution.*

Contributory qualified pension or profit sharing plan. A plan funded with both employer and employee contributions. Since the employee's contributions to the plan are subject to income tax, a later distribution of the contributions to the employee generally is tax-free. See also *qualified pension or profit sharing plan.*

Control. Holding a specified level of stock ownership in a corporation. For § 351, the new shareholder(s) must hold at least 80 percent of the total combined voting power of all voting classes of stock. Other tax provisions require different levels of control to bring about desired effects, such as 50 or 100 percent.

Controlled foreign corporation (CFC). A non-U.S. corporation in which more than 50 percent of the total combined voting power of all classes of stock entitled to vote or the total value of the stock of the corporation is owned by "U.S. shareholders" on any day during the taxable year of the foreign corporation. For purposes of this definition, a U.S. shareholder is any U.S. person who owns, or is considered to own, 10 percent or more of the total combined voting power of all classes of voting stock of the foreign corporation. Stock owned directly, indirectly, and constructively is used in this measure.

Controlled group. A controlled group of corporations is required to share the lower-level corporate tax rates and various other tax benefits among the members of the group. A controlled group may be either a brother-sister or a parent-subsidiary group.

Corporate acquisition. The takeover of one corporation by another if both parties retain their legal existence after the transaction. An acquisition can be effected via a stock purchase or through a tax-free exchange of stock. See also *corporate reorganization* and *merger.*

Corporate liquidation. Occurs when a corporation distributes its net assets to its shareholders and ceases its legal existence. Generally, a shareholder recognizes capital gain or loss upon the liquidation of the entity, regardless of the corporation's balance in its earnings and profits account. However, the distributing corporation recognizes gain and loss on assets that it distributes to shareholders in kind.

Corporate reorganization. Occurs, among other instances, when one corporation acquires another in a merger or acquisition, a single corporation divides into two or more entities, a corporation makes a substantial change in its capital structure, or a corporation undertakes a change in its legal name or domicile. The exchange of stock and other securities in a corporate reorganization can be effected favorably for tax purposes if certain statutory requirements are followed strictly. Tax consequences include the nonrecognition of any gain that is realized by the shareholders except to the extent of boot received. See also *corporate acquisition* and *merger.*

Corpus. The body or principal of a trust. Suppose, for example, George transfers an apartment building into a trust, income payable to Wanda for life, remainder to Sam upon Wanda's death. Corpus of the trust is the apartment building.

Correspondence audit. An audit conducted by the IRS by mail. Typically, the IRS writes to the taxpayer requesting the verification of a particular deduction or exemption. The completion of a special form or the remittance of copies of records or other support is all that is requested of the taxpayer. See also *audit, field audit,* and *office audit.*

Court of Appeals. Any of 13 Federal courts that consider tax matters appealed from the U.S. Tax Court, a U.S. District Court, or the U.S. Court of Federal Claims. Appeal from a U.S. Court of Appeals is to the U.S. Supreme Court by *Certiorari.* See also *appellate court, Court of Federal Claims,* and *trial court.*

Court of Federal Claims. A trial court (court of original jurisdiction) that decides litigation involving Federal tax matters. Appeal is to the Court of Appeals for the Federal Circuit.

Coverdell Education Savings Account (CESA). A savings account established to pay for qualified education expenses (i.e., tuition, fees, books, supplies, related equipment, room and board if the student's course load is at least one-half of the full-time course load). The maximum annual contribution to the savings account of a beneficiary is $2,000. The maximum annual contribution is subject to phaseout beginning at $95,000 for single taxpayers and $190,000 for married couples who file a joint return. Contributions are not deductible and cannot be made to a savings account once the beneficiary attains age 18. Distributions used to pay for qualified education expenses for a designated beneficiary are tax-free. § 530.

Credit for prior transfers. The death tax credit for prior transfers applies when property is taxed in the estates of different decedents within a 10-year period. The credit is determined using a decreasing statutory percentage, with the magnitude of the credit decreasing as the length of time between the multiple deaths increases. § 2013.

Criminal fraud. See *fraud.*

Cross-purchase buy-sell agreement. Under this type of arrangement, the surviving owners of the business agree to buy out the withdrawing owner. Assume, for example, Ron and Sara are equal shareholders in Tip Corporation. Under a cross-purchase buy-sell agreement, Ron and Sara would contract to purchase the other's interest should that person decide to withdraw from the business. See also *buy-sell agreement* and *entity buy-sell agreement.*

Current earnings and profits. Net tax-basis earnings of a corporation aggregated during the current tax year. A corporate distribution is deemed to be first from the entity's current earnings and profits and then from accumulated earnings and profits. Shareholders recognize dividend income to the extent of the earnings and profits of the corporation. A dividend results to the extent of current earnings and profits, even if there is a larger negative balance in accumulated earnings and profits. § 316 and Reg. § 1.316–2.

Current tax expense. The portion of the book total tax expense that theoretically represents the taxes a company actually pays to tax authorities. However, this amount may not represent actual tax payments, due to certain book-tax differences that are not accounted for in the income tax expense calculation (e.g., stock option deductions).

Current use valuation. See *special use value.*

Curtesy. A husband's right under state law to all or part of his wife's property upon her death. See also *dower.*

D

Death benefit. A payment made by an employer to the beneficiary or beneficiaries of a deceased employee on account of the death of the employee.

Death tax. A tax imposed on property transferred by the death of the owner. See also *estate tax* and *inheritance tax.*

Debt-financed income. Included in computations of the *unrelated business income* of an *exempt organization,* the gross income generated from debt-financed property.

Decedent. An individual who has died.

Deduction. The Federal income tax is not imposed upon gross income. Rather, it is imposed upon taxable income. Congressionally identified deductions are subtracted from gross income to arrive at the tax base, taxable income.

Deductions in respect of a decedent. Deductions accrued at the moment of death but not recognizable on the final income tax return of a decedent because of the method of accounting used. Such items are allowed as deductions on the estate tax return and on the income tax return of the estate (Form 1041) or the heir (Form 1040). An example of a deduction in respect of a decedent is interest expense accrued to the date of death by a cash basis debtor.

Deemed-paid credit. A *foreign tax credit* that is allowed when an investor in a non-U.S. corporation receives a dividend distribution. The credit is allowed because the payor already had subjected to non-U.S. income taxation the profits from which the dividend was paid. The credit is computed to reflect the proportion of taxes paid from the payor's E & P.

Deferral. The use of acceptable tax accounting rules to delay the recognition of income (or deduction) until a subsequent tax year. Many *outbound* international tax strategies involve deferral of income recognition until a repatriation event.

Deferred compensation. Compensation that will be taxed when received and not when earned. An example is contributions by an employer to a qualified pension or profit sharing plan on behalf of an employee. The contributions are not taxed to the employee until they are distributed (e.g., upon retirement). See also *qualified pension or profit sharing plan.*

Deferred tax asset. Balance sheet account representing cumulative future tax benefits (tax savings) to be realized by the taxpayer.

Deferred tax benefit. The current-year reduction in book total tax expense generated by an increase in net *deferred tax assets.*

Deferred tax expense. The current-year increase in book total tax expense generated by an increase in net *deferred tax liabilities.*

Deferred tax liability. Balance sheet account representing cumulative future tax expenses to be incurred by the taxpayer.

Deficiency. Additional tax liability owed by a taxpayer and assessed by the IRS. See also *assessment* and *statutory notice of deficiency.*

Deficiency dividend. Once the IRS has established a corporation's liability for the personal holding company tax in a prior year, the tax may be reduced or avoided by the issuance of a deficiency dividend under § 547. The deficiency dividend procedure is not available in cases where the deficiency was due to fraud with intent to evade tax or to a willful failure to file the appropriate tax return [§ 547(g)]. Nor does the deficiency dividend procedure avoid the usual penalties and interest applicable for failure to file a return or pay a tax.

Deficit. A negative balance, say, in the earnings and profits account.

Defined benefit plan. A qualified retirement plan in which a formula specifies the benefits due to a participant employee. The formula usually includes compensation level and years of service. The employer makes annual deductible contributions to the plan, actuarially sufficient for the plan to meet its required distributions. See also *defined contribution pension plan* and *pension plan.*

Defined contribution pension plan. Qualified plans can be dichotomized as *defined benefit plans* and defined contribution plans. Under a defined contribution plan, a separate account is maintained for each covered employee. The employee's benefits under the plan are based solely on (1) the amount contributed and (2) income from the fund that accrues to the employee's account. The plan defines the amount the employer is required to contribute (e.g., a flat dollar amount, an amount based on a formula, or an amount equal to a certain percentage of compensation). See also *pension plan.*

Demand loan. A loan payable upon request by the creditor, rather than on a specific date.

Depletion. The process by which the cost or other basis of a natural resource (e.g., an oil or gas interest) is recovered upon extraction and sale of the resource. The two ways to determine the depletion allowance are the cost and percentage (or statutory) methods. Under cost depletion, each unit of production sold is assigned a portion of the cost or other basis of the interest. This is determined by dividing the cost or other basis by the total units expected to be recovered. Under percentage (or statutory) depletion, the tax law provides a special percentage factor for different types of minerals and other natural resources. This percentage is multiplied by the gross income from the interest to arrive at the depletion allowance. §§ 613 and 613A.

Depreciation. The deduction for the cost or other basis of a tangible asset over the asset's estimated useful life. For intangible assets, see *amortization.* For natural resources, see *depletion.* See also *estimated useful life.*

Depreciation recapture. Upon the disposition of depreciable property used in a trade or business, gain or loss is measured by the difference between the consideration received (the amount realized) and the adjusted basis of the property. The gain recognized could be § 1231 gain and qualify for long-term capital gain treatment. The recapture provisions of the Code (e.g., §§ 291, 1245, and 1250) may operate to convert some or all of the previous § 1231 gain into ordinary income. The justification for depreciation recapture is that it prevents a taxpayer from converting a dollar of ordinary deduction (in the form of depreciation) into deferred tax-favored income (§ 1231 or long-term capital gain). The depreciation recapture rules do not apply when the property is disposed of at a loss or via a gift. See also *Section 1231 gains and losses.*

Determination letter. Upon the request of a taxpayer, the IRS will comment on the tax status of a completed transaction. Determination letters frequently are used to clarify employee status, determine whether a retirement or profit sharing plan qualifies under the Code, and determine the tax-exempt status of certain nonprofit organizations.

Devise. A transfer of real estate by will. See also *bequest.*

Disclaimers. Rejections, refusals, or renunciations of claims, powers, or property. Section 2518 sets forth the conditions required to avoid gift tax consequences as the result of a disclaimer.

Discretionary trust. A trust under which the trustee or another party has the right to accumulate (rather than distribute) the income for each year. Depending on the terms of the trust instrument, the income may be accumulated for future distributions to the income beneficiaries or added to corpus for the benefit of the remainderperson. See also *corpus* and *income beneficiary.*

Disguised sale. When a partner contributes property to the entity and soon thereafter receives a distribution from the partnership, the transactions are collapsed, and the distribution is seen as a purchase of the asset by the partnership. § 707(a)(2)(B).

Disproportionate. Not pro rata or ratable. Suppose, for example, Fin Corporation has two shareholders, Cal and Dot, each of whom owns 50 percent of its stock. If Fin distributes a cash dividend of $2,000 to Cal and only $1,000 to Dot, the distribution is disproportionate. The distribution would have been proportionate if Cal and Dot had received $1,500 each.

Disproportionate distribution. A distribution from a partnership to one or more of its partners in which at least one partner's interest in partnership hot assets is increased or decreased. For example, a distribution of cash to one partner and hot assets to another changes both partners' interest in hot assets and is disproportionate. The intent of rules for taxation of disproportionate distributions is to ensure each partner eventually recognizes his or her proportionate share of partnership ordinary income.

Disproportionate redemption. See *redemption (disproportionate).*

Dissent. To disagree with the majority. If, for example, Judge Bird disagrees with the result reached by Judges Crown and Dove (all of whom are members of the same court), Judge Bird could issue a dissenting opinion.

Distributable net income (DNI). The measure that determines the nature and amount of the distributions from estates and trusts that the beneficiaries must include in income. DNI also limits the amount that estates and trusts can claim as a deduction for such distributions. § 643(a).

Distribution deduction. Used to compute an estate or trust's taxable income for the year. The lesser of the amount distributed to beneficiaries from income, or the deductible portion of distributable net income for the period.

Distributions in kind. Transfers of property "as is." If, for example, a corporation distributes land to its shareholders, a distribution in kind has taken place. A sale of land followed by a distribution of the cash proceeds would not be a distribution in kind of the land.

District Court. A Federal District Court is a trial court for purposes of litigating Federal tax matters. It is the only trial court in which a jury trial can be obtained. See also *trial court.*

Dividend. A nondeductible distribution to the shareholders of a corporation. A dividend constitutes gross income to the recipient if it is from the *current* or *accumulated earnings and profits* of the corporation.

Dividend equivalent amount (DEA). The amount subject to the *branch profits tax,* it is equal to the *effectively connected* earnings and profits of the U.S. branch of a foreign corporation, reduced/(increased) by an increase/(reduction) in U.S. net equity.

Dividends paid deduction. Relative to the *accumulated earnings* and *personal holding company taxes*, reductions in the tax base are allowed to the extent that the corporation made dividends payments during the year. Thus, this adjustment reduces *accumulated taxable income* and *personal holding company income.*

Dividends received deduction. A deduction allowed a corporate shareholder for dividends received from a domestic corporation. The deduction usually is 70 percent of the dividends received, but it could be 80 or 100 percent depending upon the ownership percentage held by the payee corporation. §§ 243–246.

Divisive reorganization. A corporate division: some of the assets of one corporation are transferred to another corporation in exchange for control of the transferee. Then, in a spin-off or split-off, stock of the transferee is distributed to the transferor's shareholders.

Dock sale. A purchaser uses its owned or rented vehicles to take possession of the product at the seller's shipping dock. In most states, the sale is apportioned to the operating state of the purchaser, rather than the seller. See also *apportion* and *sales factor.*

Dollar value LIFO. An inventory technique that focuses on the dollars invested in the inventory rather than the particular items on hand each period. Each inventory item is assigned to a pool. A pool is a collection of similar items and is treated as a separate inventory. At the end of the period, each pool is valued in terms of prices at the time LIFO was adopted (base period prices), whether or not the particular items were actually on hand in the year LIFO was adopted, to compare with current prices to determine if there has been an increase or decrease in inventories.

Domestic corporation. A corporation created or organized in the United States or under the law of the United States or any state. § 7701(a)(4). Only dividends received from domestic corporations qualify for the dividends received deduction (§ 243). See also *foreign corporation.*

Domicile. A person's legal home.

Donee. The recipient of a gift.

Donor. The maker of a gift.

Double-weighted apportionment formula. A means by which the total taxable income of a *multistate corporation* is assigned to a specific state. Usually, the payroll, property, and sales factors are equally treated, and the weighted average of these factors is used in the apportionment procedure. In some states, however, the sales factor may receive a double weight, or it may be the only factor considered. These latter formulas place a greater tax burden on the income of out-of-state corporations. See also *apportion, payroll factor, property factor, sales factor,* and *UDITPA.*

Dower. A wife's right to all or part of her deceased husband's property; unique to common law states as opposed to community property jurisdictions. See also *curtesy.*

E

Earned income. Income from personal services. Distinguished from passive, portfolio, and other unearned income (sometimes referred to as "active" income). See §§ 469, 911, and the related Regulations.

Earnings and profits (E & P). Measures the economic capacity of a corporation to make a distribution to shareholders that is not a return of capital. Such a distribution results in dividend income to the shareholders to the extent of the corporation's current and accumulated earnings and profits.

Earnings stripping rules. A means by which the U.S. Treasury defers the deduction for excessive related-party interest payments, where there is a high debt-to-equity ratio and an exclusion of some of the resulting income recognition from the payment, perhaps due to *treaty* provisions. § 163(j)

Economic effect test. Requirements that must be met before a special allocation may be used by a partnership. The premise behind the test is that each partner who receives an allocation of income or loss from a partnership bears the economic benefit or burden of the allocation.

Effective tax rate. A computation indicating the proportion of current earnings paid as a tax liability. For this purpose, "income" might be expressed as taxable income, economic income, or financial accounting income.

Effectively connected income. Income of a nonresident alien or foreign corporation that is attributable to the operations of a U.S. trade or business under either the asset-use or the business-activities test.

Electing large partnership. A partnership with 100 or more partners may elect to be subject to simplified tax reporting and audit procedures. The election allows the partnership to combine certain income and expense amounts and report net amounts to the partners. The result is fewer "pass-through" items to the partners, making the partners' tax returns easier to prepare. As an example, an electing large partnership with a long-term capital gain and a short-term capital loss would offset the two amounts and allocate the net amount among the partners.

Employee stock ownership plan (ESOP). A type of qualified profit sharing plan that invests in securities of the employer. In a noncontributory ESOP, the employer usually contributes its shares to a trust and receives a deduction for the fair market value of the stock. Generally, the employee does not recognize income until the stock is sold after its distribution to him or her upon retirement or other separation from service. See also *qualified pension or profit sharing plan.*

En banc. The case was considered by the whole court. Typically, for example, only one of the judges of the U.S. Tax Court will hear and decide on a tax controversy. However, when the issues involved are unusually novel or of wide impact, the case will be heard and decided by the full court sitting *en banc.*

Energy tax credit–business property. A 10 percent tax credit is available to businesses that invest in certain energy property. The purpose of the credit is to create incentives for conservation and to develop alternative energy sources. The credit is available on the acquisition of solar and geothermal property. §§ 46 and 48.

Enrolled agent (EA). A tax practitioner who has gained admission to practice before the IRS by passing an IRS examination.

Entity. An organization or being that possesses separate existence for tax purposes. Examples are corporations, partnerships, estates, and trusts.

Entity accounting income. Entity accounting income is not identical to the taxable income of a trust or estate, nor is it determined in the same manner as the entity's financial accounting income would be. The trust document or will determines whether certain income, expenses, gains, or losses are allocated to the corpus of the entity or to the entity's income beneficiaries. Only the items that are allocated to the income beneficiaries are included in entity accounting income.

Entity buy-sell agreement. An arrangement whereby the entity is to purchase a withdrawing owner's interest. When the entity is a corporation, the agreement generally involves a stock redemption on the part of the withdrawing shareholder. See also *buy-sell agreement* and *cross-purchase buy-sell agreement.*

Entity concept. Even in so-called flow-through entities, tax accounting elections are made (e.g., a tax year is adopted) and conventions are adopted (e.g., with respect to cost recovery methods) at the entity level. This may seem to violate the *conduit concept,* but such exceptions tend to ease the administration of such conduit taxpayers, especially in the context of a large number of shareholders/partners/members/beneficiaries.

Equity method. Financial accounting rule for determining how to report the income of corporations owned between 20 and 50 percent.

Equity structure shift. A tax-free reorganization other than a *divisive reorganization* or *recapitalization.* If there is a more than 50 percent change in the ownership of a loss corporation in an equity structure shift, § 382 limits the use of net operating loss carryovers of the loss corporation. Specifically, the annual net operating loss carryover deduction is limited to the value of the loss corporation immediately before the equity structure shift times the *long-term tax-exempt rate.*

Escrow. Money or other property placed with a third party as security for an existing or proposed obligation. Cyd, for example, agrees to purchase Don's stock in Rip Corporation but needs time to raise the necessary funds. Don places the stock with Ernie (the escrow agent), with instructions to deliver it to Cyd when the purchase price is paid.

Estate. An entity that locates, collects, distributes, and discharges the assets and liabilities of a decedent.

Estate freeze. Procedures directed toward fixing and stabilizing the value of an interest retained in a business, while transferring the growth portion to family members. In the case of a closely held corporation, the estate freeze usually involves keeping the preferred stock and giving away the common stock. The ultimate objective is to reduce estate value when the original owner-donor dies.

Estate tax. A tax imposed on the right to transfer property by death. Thus, an estate tax is levied on the decedent's estate and not on the heir receiving the property. See also *death tax* and *inheritance tax.*

Estimated useful life. The period over which an asset will be used by the taxpayer. Assets such as collectible artwork do not have an estimated useful life. The estimated useful life of an asset is essential to measuring the annual tax deduction for depreciation and amortization.

Estoppel. The process of being stopped from proving something (even if true) in court due to a prior inconsistent action. It is usually invoked as a matter of fairness to prevent one party (either the taxpayer or the IRS) from taking advantage of a prior error.

Excess lobbying expenditure. An excise tax is applied on otherwise tax-exempt organizations with respect to the excess of total lobbying expenditure over *grass roots expenditure* for the year.

Excess loss account. When a subsidiary has generated more historical losses than its parent has invested in the entity, the parent's basis in the subsidiary is zero, and the parent records additional losses in an excess loss account. This treatment allows the parent to continue to deduct losses of the subsidiary, even where no basis reduction is possible, while avoiding the need to show a negative stock basis on various financial records. If the subsidiary stock is sold while an excess loss account exists, capital gain income usually is recognized to the extent of the balance in the account.

Excise tax. A tax on the manufacture, sale, or use of goods; on the carrying on of an occupation or activity; or on the transfer of property. Thus, the Federal estate and gift taxes are, theoretically, excise taxes.

Exclusion amount. The value of assets that is equal to the credit allowed for gifts or transfers by death. Thus, if the unified transfer tax credit is $555,800, the exclusion amount is $1,500,000. Often called the *exemption equivalent amount.* See also *bypass amount.*

Executor. A person designated by a will to administer (manage or take charge of) the assets and liabilities of a decedent. See also *administrator.*

Exempt organization. An organization that is either partially or completely exempt from Federal income taxation. § 501.

Exemption. An amount by which the tax base is reduced for all qualifying taxpayers. Individuals can receive personal and dependency exemptions, and taxpayers apply an exemption in computing their alternative minimum taxable income. Often, the exemption amount is phased out as the tax base becomes sizable.

Exemption equivalent. The maximum value of assets that can be transferred to another party without incurring any Federal gift or death tax because of the application of the unified tax credit.

Exemption equivalent amount. The amount of value (currently $1,500,000) that is the equivalent of the unified transfer tax credit allowed. See also *bypass amount.*

Expenses in respect of a decedent. See *deductions in respect of a decedent.*

Extraterritorial income. A device by which the U.S. encourages outbound (export) sales, services, and leases. An exclusion from gross income is computed under § 114 for certain transactions of U.S. taxpayers.

F

Fair market value. The amount at which property would change hands between a willing buyer and a willing seller, neither being under any compulsion to buy or to sell, and both having reasonable knowledge of the relevant facts. Reg. § 20.2031–1(b).

Family limited partnership (FLP). An entity created under the limited partnership laws of a state in which there is at least one general partner and at least one limited partner. Typically, the grandparents or parents are the general partners who make gifts of limited partnership interests to their children and grandchildren.

FAS 109. Financial accounting rule for determining book tax expense, following the matching principle.

Federal Register. The first place that the rules and regulations of U.S. administrative agencies (e.g., the U.S. Treasury Department) are published.

F.3d. An abbreviation for the third series of the *Federal Reporter,* the official series in which decisions of the U.S. Court of Federal Claims and the U.S. Courts of Appeals are published. The second series is denoted F.2d.

F.Supp. The abbreviation for *Federal Supplement,* the official series in which the reported decisions of the U.S. Federal District Courts are published.

Feeder organization. An entity that carries on a trade or business for the benefit of an *exempt organization.* However, such a relationship does not result in the feeder organization itself being tax-exempt. § 502.

Fiduciary. A person who manages money or property for another and who must exercise a standard of care in the management activity imposed by law or contract. A *trustee,* for example, possesses a fiduciary responsibility to the *beneficiaries* of the *trust* to follow the terms of the trust and the requirements of applicable state law. A breach of fiduciary responsibility would make the trustee liable to the beneficiaries for any damage caused by the breach.

Field audit. An audit conducted by the IRS on the business premises of the taxpayer or in the office of the tax practitioner representing the taxpayer. See also *audit, correspondence audit,* and *office audit.*

FIRPTA. Under the Foreign Investment in Real Property Tax Act, gains or losses realized by nonresident aliens and non-U.S. corporations on the disposition of U.S. real estate create U.S.-source income and are subject to U.S. income tax.

First-in, first-out (FIFO). An accounting method for determining the cost of inventories. Under this method, the inventory on hand is deemed to be the sum of the cost of the most recently acquired units. See also *last-in, first-out (LIFO).*

Fiscal year. See *accounting period.*

Flat tax. In its pure form, a flat tax would eliminate all exclusions, deductions, and credits and impose a one-rate tax on gross income.

Foreign corporation. A corporation that is not created in the United States or organized under the laws of one of the states of the United States. § 7701(a)(5). See also *domestic corporation.*

Foreign currency transaction. An exchange that could generate a foreign currency gain or loss for a U.S. taxpayer. For instance, if Avery, Inc., contracts to purchase foreign goods, payable in a currency other than U.S. dollars, at a specified date in the future, any change in the exchange rate between the dollar and that currency will generate a foreign currency gain or loss upon completion of the contract. This gain or loss is treated as separate from the underlying transaction; it may create ordinary or capital gain or loss.

Foreign earned income exclusion. The Code allows exclusions for earned income generated outside the United States to alleviate any tax base and rate disparities among countries. In addition, the exclusion is allowed for housing expenditures incurred by the taxpayer's employer with respect to the non-U.S. assignment, and self-employed individuals can deduct foreign housing expenses incurred in a trade or business.

Foreign personal holding company (FPHC). A foreign corporation in which (1) 60 percent or more of the gross income for the taxable year is FPHC income and (2) more than 50 percent of the total combined voting power or the total value of the stock is owned, directly or indirectly, by five or fewer individuals who are U.S. persons (the U.S. group) at any time during the taxable year. The 60 percent of gross income set forth in § 2(b). This status enables the taxpayer to use a set of income tax rates that are lower than those applicable to other unmarried individuals but higher than those applicable to surviving spouses and married persons filing a joint return.

Heir. A person who inherits property from a decedent.

Highly compensated employee. The employee group is generally divided into two categories for fringe benefit purposes. These are (1) highly compensated employees and (2) non-highly compensated employees. For most fringe benefits, if the plan discriminates in favor of highly compensated employees, it will not be a qualified plan with respect to the highly compensated employees.

Hobby. An activity not engaged in for profit. The Code restricts the amount of losses that an individual can deduct for hobby activities so that these transactions cannot be used to offset income from other sources. § 183.

Holding period. The period of time during which property has been held for income tax purposes. The holding period is significant in determining whether gain or loss from the sale or exchange of a capital asset is long term or short term. § 1223.

Hot assets. Unrealized receivables and substantially appreciated inventory under § 751. When hot assets are present, the sale of a partnership interest or the disproportionate distribution of the assets can cause ordinary income to be recognized.

Housing cost amount. In conjunction with the *foreign earned income exclusion*, the expatriate U.S. employee can exclude from gross income a specified level of housing costs that are provided or reimbursed by the employer.

H.R. 10 plans. See *Keogh plans.*

I

Imputed interest. For certain long-term sales of property, the IRS can convert some of the gain from the sale into interest income if the contract does not provide for a minimum rate of interest to be paid by the purchaser. The application of this procedure has the effect of forcing the seller to recognize less long-term capital gain and more ordinary income (interest income). § 483 and the related Regulations.

In kind. See *distributions in kind.*

Inbound taxation. U.S. tax effects when a non-U.S. person begins an investment or business activity in the United States.

Incentive stock option (ISO). A type of stock option that receives favorable tax treatment. If various qualification requirements can be satisfied, there are no recognition tax consequences when the stock option is granted. However, the spread (the excess of the fair market value at the date of exercise over the option price) is a tax preference item for purposes of the alternative minimum tax. The gain on disposition of the stock resulting from the exercise of the stock option is long-term capital gain if certain holding period requirements are met (the employee must not dispose of the stock within two years after the option is granted or within one year after acquiring the stock). § 422. See also *nonqualified stock option (NQSO).*

Incident of ownership. An element of ownership or degree of control over a life insurance policy. The retention by an insured of an incident of ownership in a life insurance policy will cause the policy proceeds to be included in the insured's gross estate upon death. § 2042(2) and Reg. § 20.2042–1(c). See also *gross estate* and *insured.*

Income beneficiary. The party entitled to income from property. In a typical trust situation, Art is to receive the income for life with corpus or principal passing to Bev upon Art's death. In this case, Art is the income beneficiary of the trust.

Income in respect of a decedent (IRD). Income earned by a decedent at the time of death but not reportable on the final income tax return because of the method of accounting that appropriately is utilized. Such income is included in the gross estate and is taxed to the eventual recipient (either the estate or heirs). The recipient is, however, allowed an income tax deduction for the estate tax attributable to the income. § 691.

Income interest. The right of a beneficiary to receive distributions from the fiduciary income of a trust or estate.

Income shifting. Occurs when an individual transfers some of his or her gross income to a taxpayer who is subject to a lower tax rate, thereby reducing the total income tax liability of the group. Income shifting produces a successful assignment of income. It can be accomplished by transferring income-producing property to the lower-bracket taxpayer or to an effective trust for his or her benefit, or by transferring ownership interests in a family partnership or in a closely held corporation.

Income tax provision. A corporation's expense for Federal income taxes, relating to current-year financial accounting income.

Income tax treaty. An agreement between two countries determining how income is taxed when it is earned in one country by a citizen or resident of another, how the revenue agencies of the country interact and trade information, and at what rates various types of income are subjected to tax.

Incomplete transfer. A transfer made by a decedent during lifetime that, because of certain control or enjoyment retained by the transferor, is not considered complete for Federal estate tax purposes. Thus, some or all of the fair market value of the property transferred is included in the transferor's gross estate. §§ 2036–2038. See also *gross estate* and *revocable transfer.*

Indexation. Various components of the tax formula are adjusted periodically for the effects of inflation, so that the effects of the formula are not eroded by price level changes.

Tax rate schedules, exemption amounts, and the standard deduction, among other items, are indexed in this manner.

Individual Retirement Account (IRA). A type of retirement plan to which an individual with earned income can contribute a maximum of $3,000 ($3,000 each in the case of a married couple with a spousal IRA) per tax year for 2004. The maximum amount increases to $4,000 in 2005 and to $5,000 in 2008. IRAs can be classified as traditional IRAs or Roth IRAs. With a traditional IRA, an individual can contribute and deduct a maximum of $3,000 per tax year in 2004. The deduction is a deduction *for* AGI. However, if the individual is an active participant in another qualified retirement plan, the deduction is phased out proportionally between certain AGI ranges (note that the phaseout limits the amount of the deduction and not the amount of the contribution). With a Roth IRA, an individual can contribute a maximum of $3,000 per tax year in 2004. No deduction is permitted. However, if a five-year holding period requirement is satisfied and the distribution is a qualified distribution, the taxpayer can make tax-free withdrawals from a Roth IRA. The maximum annual contribution is phased out proportionally between certain AGI ranges. §§ 219 and 408A. See also *simplified employee pension plan.*

Ineligible entities. Corporations that cannot be included in a group filing a consolidated return. Some of the most frequently encountered ineligible entities include corporations established outside the United States, tax-exempt (charitable) corporations, insurance companies, partnerships, trusts, estates, limited liability entities, and other noncorporate entities.

Inheritance tax. A tax imposed on the right to receive property from a *decedent*. Thus, theoretically, an inheritance tax is imposed on the heir. The Federal estate tax is imposed on the estate. See also *death tax* and *estate tax.*

Inside basis. A partnership's basis in each of the assets it owns.

Installment method. A method of accounting enabling certain taxpayers to spread the recognition of gain on the sale of property over the collection period. Under this procedure, the seller arrives at the gain to be recognized by computing the gross profit percentage from the sale (the gain divided by the contract price) and applying it to each payment received. § 453.

Insured. A person whose life is the subject of an insurance policy. Upon the death of the insured, the life insurance policy matures, and the proceeds become payable to the designated beneficiary. See also *life insurance.*

Intangible property. Property that is a "right" rather than a physical object. Examples are patents, stocks and bonds, goodwill, trademarks, franchises, and copyrights. See also *amortization* and *tangible property.*

Inter vivos transfer. A transfer of property during the life of the owner. Distinguished from testamentary transfers, where the property passes at death.

Interest-free loans. Bona fide loans that carry no interest (or a below-market rate). If made in a nonbusiness setting, the imputed interest element is treated as a gift from the lender to the borrower. If made by a corporation to a shareholder, a constructive dividend could result. In either event, the lender may recognize interest income. § 7872.

Intermediate sanctions. The IRS can assess excise taxes on disqualified persons and organization managers associated with so-called public charities engaging in excess benefit transactions. An excess benefit transaction is one in which a disqualified person engages in a non-fair market value transaction with the exempt organization or receives unreasonable compensation. Prior to the idea of intermediate sanctions, the only option available to the IRS was to revoke the organization's exempt status.

Internal Revenue Code. The collected statutes that govern the taxation of income, property transfers, and other transactions in the United States and the enforcement of those provisions. Enacted by Congress, the Code is amended frequently, but it has not been reorganized since 1954. However, because of the extensive revisions to the statutes that occurred with the Tax Reform Act of 1986, Title 26 of the U.S. Code is now known as the Internal Revenue Code of 1986.

Internal Revenue Service (IRS). The Federal agency, a division of the Department of the Treasury, charged with administering the U.S. revenue enforcement and collection provisions.

Interpolated terminal reserve. The measure used in valuing insurance policies for gift and estate tax purposes when the policies are not paid up at the time of their transfer. Reg. § 20.2031–8(a)(3), Ex. (3).

Intestate. The condition when no will exists at the time of death. In such cases, state law prescribes who will receive the decedent's property. The laws of intestate succession generally favor the surviving spouse, children, and grandchildren, and then parents and grandparents and brothers and sisters.

Investment income. Consisting of virtually the same elements as portfolio income, a measure by which to justify a deduction for interest on investment indebtedness. See also *investment indebtedness* and *portfolio income.*

Investment indebtedness. Debt incurred to carry or incur investments by the taxpayer in assets that will produce portfolio income. Limitations are placed upon interest deductions that are incurred in connection with the debt (generally to the corresponding amount of investment income).

Investor losses. Losses on stock and securities. If stocks and bonds are capital assets in the hands of the holder, a capital loss materializes as of the last day of the taxable year in which the stocks or bonds become worthless. Under certain circumstances involving stocks and bonds of affiliated corporations, an ordinary loss is permitted upon worthlessness.

Involuntary conversion. The loss or destruction of property through theft, casualty, or condemnation. Any gain realized on an involuntary conversion can, at the taxpayer's election, be deferred for Federal income tax purposes if the owner reinvests the proceeds within a prescribed period of time in property that is similar or related in service or use. § 1033.

IRA. See *individual retirement account*.

Itemized deductions. Personal and employee expenditures allowed by the Code as deductions from adjusted gross income. Examples include certain medical expenses, interest on home mortgages, and charitable contributions. Itemized deductions are reported on Schedule A of Form 1040. Certain miscellaneous itemized deductions are reduced by 2 percent of the taxpayer's adjusted gross income. In addition, a taxpayer whose adjusted gross income exceeds a certain level (indexed annually) must reduce the itemized deductions by 3 percent of the excess of adjusted gross income over that level. Medical, casualty and theft, and investment interest deductions are not subject to the 3 percent reduction. The 3 percent reduction may not reduce itemized deductions that are subject to the reduction to below 20 percent of their initial amount.

J

Jeopardy assessment. If the collection of a tax appears in question, the IRS may assess and collect the tax immediately without the usual formalities. The IRS can terminate a taxpayer's taxable year before the usual date if it feels that the collection of the tax may be in peril because the taxpayer plans to leave the country. §§ 6851 and 6861–6864.

Joint and several liability. Permits the IRS to collect a tax from one or all of several taxpayers. A husband and wife who file a joint income tax return usually are collectively or individually liable for the full amount of the tax liability. The same rule applies to consolidated return partners. § 6013(d)(3).

Joint tenants. Two or more persons having undivided ownership of property with the right of survivorship. Right of survivorship gives the surviving owner full ownership of the property. Suppose Betty and Cheryl are joint tenants of a tract of land. Upon Betty's death, Cheryl becomes the sole owner of the property. For the estate tax consequences upon the death of a joint tenant, see § 2040. See also *tenants by the entirety* and *tenants in common*.

Joint venture. A one-time grouping of two or more persons in a business undertaking. Unlike a partnership, a joint venture does not entail a continuing relationship among the parties. A joint venture is treated like a partnership for Federal income tax purposes. § 7701(a)(2).

K

Keogh plans. Retirement plans available to self-employed taxpayers. They are also referred to as H.R. 10 plans. Under such plans, a taxpayer may deduct each year up to either 100 percent of net earnings from self-employment or $41,000, whichever is less. For a profit sharing plan, the percentage is 25 percent.

Kiddie tax. See *tax on unearned income of a child under age 14*.

L

Lapse. The expiration of a right either by the death of the holder or upon the expiration of a period of time. Thus, a power of appointment lapses upon the death of the holder if he or she has not exercised the power during life or at death (through a will).

Last-in, first-out (LIFO). An accounting method for valuing inventories for tax purposes. Under this method, it is assumed that the inventory on hand is valued at the cost of the earliest acquired units. § 472. See also *first-in, first-out (FIFO)*.

Leaseback. The transferor of property later leases it back. In a sale-leaseback situation, for example, Ron sells property to Sal and subsequently leases the property from Sal. Thus, Ron becomes the lessee and Sal the lessor.

Least aggregate deferral method. See *least aggregate deferral rule*.

Least aggregate deferral rule. A test applied to determine the allowable fiscal year of a *partnership*. Possible year-ends are tested, and the fiscal year allowed by the IRS is the one that offers the least amount of income deferral to the owners on an individual basis.

Legacy. A transfer of cash or other property by will.

Legal age. The age at which a person may enter into binding contracts or commit other legal acts. In most states, a minor reaches legal age or majority (comes of age) at age 18.

Legal representative. A person who oversees the legal affairs of another; for example, the executor or administrator of an estate or a court-appointed guardian of a minor or incompetent person.

Legatee. The recipient of property that is transferred under a will by the death of the owner.

Lessee. One who rents property from another. In the case of real estate, the lessee is also known as the tenant.

Lessor. One who rents property to another. In the case of real estate, the lessor is also known as the landlord.

Letter ruling. The written response of the IRS to a taxpayer's request for interpretation of the revenue laws with respect to a proposed transaction, (e.g., concerning the tax-free status of a reorganization). Not to be relied on as precedent by other than the party who requested the ruling.

LEXIS. An online database system through which a tax researcher can obtain access to the Internal Revenue Code, Regulations, administrative rulings, and court case opinions.

Liabilities in excess of basis. On the contribution of capital to a corporation, an investor recognizes gain on the exchange to the extent that contributed assets carry liabilities with a face amount in excess of the tax basis of the contributed assets. This rule keeps the investor from holding the investment asset received with a negative basis. § 357(c).

Life estate. A legal arrangement under which the beneficiary (the life tenant) is entitled to the income from the property for his or her life. Upon the death of the life tenant, the property is transferred to the holder of the remainder interest. See also *income beneficiary* and *remainder interest.*

Life insurance. A contract between the holder of a policy and an insurance company (the carrier) under which the company agrees, in return for premium payments, to pay a specified sum (the face value or maturity value of the policy) to the designated beneficiary upon the death of the insured. See also *insured.*

Like-kind exchange. An exchange of property held for productive use in a trade or business or for investment (except inventory and stocks and bonds) for other investment or trade or business property. Unless non-like-kind property (*boot*) is received, the exchange is fully nontaxable. § 1031.

Limitation on benefits. In an *income tax treaty*, the signatory countries describe the types of taxpayers who will and will not be able to avail themselves of the benefits of the treaty. Benefits sometimes are limited to discourage *treaty shopping.*

Limited liability. The liability of an entity and its owners to third parties is limited to the investment in the entity. This is a characteristic of a corporation, as shareholders generally are not responsible for the debts of the corporation and, at most, may lose the amount paid for the stock issued.

Limited liability company (LLC). A form of entity allowed by all of the states. The entity is taxed as a partnership in which all owners of the LLC are treated much like limited partners. There are no restrictions on ownership, all partners may participate in management, and none of the owners has personal liability for the entity's debts.

Limited liability partnership (LLP). A form of entity allowed by many of the states, where a general partnership registers with the state as an LLP. Owners are general partners, but a partner is not liable for any malpractice committed by other partners. The personal assets of the partners are at risk for the entity's contractual liabilities, such as accounts payable. The personal assets of a specific partner are at risk for his or her own professional malpractice and tort liability, and for malpractice and torts committed by those whom he or she supervises.

Limited partner. A partner whose liability to third-party creditors of the partnership is limited to the amount he or she has invested in the partnership. See also *general partner* and *limited partnership.*

Limited partnership. A partnership in which some of the partners are *limited partners.* At least one of the partners in a limited partnership must be a *general partner.*

Liquidating distribution. A distribution by a partnership or corporation that is in complete liquidation of the entity's trade or business activities. Typically, such distributions generate capital gain or loss to the investors without regard, for instance, to the earnings and profits of the corporation or to the partnership's basis in the distributed property. They can, however, lead to recognized gain or loss at the corporate level.

Liquidation. See *corporate liquidation.*

Living trust. A revocable trust. Often touted as a means of avoiding some probate costs.

Lobbying expenditure. An expenditure made for the purpose of influencing legislation. Such payments can result in the loss of the exempt status and the imposition of Federal income tax on an exempt organization.

Long-term capital gain or loss. Results from the sale or other taxable exchange of a capital asset that had been held by the seller for more than one year or from other transactions involving statutorily designated assets, including § 1231 property and patents.

Long-term contract. A building, installation, construction, or manufacturing contract that is entered into but not completed within the same tax year. A manufacturing contract is a long-term contract only if the contract is to manufacture (1) a unique item not normally carried in finished goods inventory or (2) items that normally require more than 12 calendar months to complete. The two available methods to account for long-term contracts are the *percentage of completion method* and the *completed contract method.* The completed contract method can be used only in limited circumstances. § 460.

Long-term tax-exempt rate. Used in deriving net operating loss limitations in the context of an equity structure shift. The highest of the Federal long-term interest rates in effect for any of the last three months. § 382.

Low-income housing credit. Beneficial treatment to owners of low-income housing is provided in the form of a tax credit. The calculated credit is claimed in the year the building is placed in service and in the following nine years. § 42. See also *general business credit.*

Lower of cost or market. An elective inventory method, whereby the taxpayer may value inventories at the lower of the taxpayer's actual cost or the current replacement cost of the goods. This method cannot be used in conjunction with the LIFO inventory method.

Lump-sum distribution. Payment of the entire amount due at one time rather than in installments. Such distributions often occur from qualified pension or profit sharing plans upon the retirement or death of a covered employee.

M

MACRS. See *accelerated cost recovery system (ACRS).*

Majority. See *legal age.*

Majority interest partners. Partners who hold in aggregate more than a 50 percent interest in partnership profits and capital, counting only those partners who have the same taxable year. The term is of significance in determining the appropriate taxable year of a partnership. § 706(b). See also *accounting period* and *principal partner*.

Malpractice. Professional misconduct; an unreasonable lack of due diligence in rendering a professional skill.

Marital deduction. A deduction allowed against the taxable estate or taxable gifts upon the transfer of property from one spouse to another.

Market value. See *fair market value*.

Matching rule. Treatment of an intercompany transaction on a *consolidated tax return*, when a sold asset remains within the group.

Meaningful reduction test. A decrease in the shareholder's voting control. Used to determine whether a redemption qualifies for sale or exchange treatment.

Merger. The absorption of one corporation by another with the corporation being absorbed losing its legal identity. Flow Corporation is merged into Jobs Corporation, and the shareholders of Flow receive stock in Jobs in exchange for their stock in Flow. After the merger, Flow ceases to exist as a separate legal entity. If a merger meets certain conditions, it is nontaxable to the parties involved. § 368(a)(1)(A). See also *corporate acquisition* and *corporate reorganization*.

Minimum credit (AET). A fixed amount, $150,000 for personal service firms and $250,000 for all others, below which the *accumulated earnings credit* cannot be derived. Assures that small and start-up corporations can generate a minimum amount of earnings before being subject to the accumulated earnings tax (AET).

Minimum tax. See *alternative minimum tax*.

Minimum tax credit (AMT). When a corporation pays an alternative minimum tax (AMT), a minimum tax credit is created on a dollar-for-dollar basis, to be applied against regular tax liabilities incurred in future years. The credit is carried forward indefinitely, but it is not carried back. The effect of the credit for corporate taxpayers alternating between the AMT and regular tax models is to make the AMT liabilities a prepayment of regular taxes. Noncorporate AMT taxpayers are allowed the credit only with respect to the elements of the AMT that reflect timing differences between the two tax models.

Minority. See *legal age*.

Minority interest. An interest in a business that is not a controlling interest in terms of voting power. Minority interest discounts often are allowed for valuing estates and gifts.

Mitigate. To make less severe. See also *mitigation of the annual accounting period concept*.

Mitigation of the annual accounting period concept. Various tax provisions that provide relief from the effect of the finality of the annual accounting period concept. For example, the net operating loss carryover provisions allow the taxpayer to apply the negative taxable income of one year against a corresponding positive amount in another tax accounting period. See also *annual accounting period concept*.

Money purchase pension plan. A type of qualified retirement plan that defines the amount the employer is required to contribute for an employee based on a fixed formula, a flat dollar amount, or a percentage of the employee's compensation. The contribution is not dependent on profits. The benefits that the employee will receive upon retirement are based on the value of the employee's account at the time the benefits begin.

Mortgagee. The party who holds the mortgage; the creditor.

Mortgagor. The party who mortgages the property; the debtor.

Most suitable use value. For gift and estate tax purposes, property that is transferred normally is valued in accordance with its most suitable or optimal use. Thus, if a farm is worth more as a potential shopping center, the value as a shopping center is used, even though the transferee (the donee or heir) continues to use the property as a farm. For an exception to this rule concerning the valuation of certain kinds of real estate transferred by death, see *special use value*.

Multistate corporation. A corporation that has operations in more than one of the states of the United States. Issues arise relative to the assignment of appropriate amounts of the entity's taxable income to the states in which it has a presence. See also *allocate, apportion, nexus,* and *UDITPA*.

Multistate Tax Commission (MTC). A regulatory body of the states that develops operating rules and regulations for the implementation of the *UDITPA* and other provisions that assign the total taxable income of a *multistate corporation* to specific states.

Multitiered partnerships. See *tiered partnerships*.

N

Necessary. Appropriate and helpful in furthering the taxpayer's business or income-producing activity. §§ 162(a) and 212. See also *ordinary*.

Negligence. Failure to exercise the reasonable or ordinary degree of care of a prudent person in a situation that results in harm or damage to another. Code § 6651 imposes a penalty on taxpayers who show negligence or intentional disregard of rules and Regulations with respect to the underpayment of certain taxes. See also *accuracy-related penalty*.

Net operating loss. To mitigate the effect of the annual accounting period concept, § 172 allows taxpayers to use an excess loss of one year as a deduction for certain past or future years. In this regard, a carryback period of 2 years and a carryforward period of 20 years currently are allowed. See also *mitigation of the annual accounting period concept*.

Net worth method. An approach used by the IRS to reconstruct the income of a taxpayer who fails to maintain adequate records. Under this method, the gross income for the year is estimated as the increase in net worth of the taxpayer (assets in excess of liabilities), with appropriate adjustment for nontaxable receipts and nondeductible expenditures. The net worth method often is used when tax fraud is suspected.

Nexus. A *multistate corporation*'s taxable income can be apportioned to a specific state only if the entity has established a sufficient presence, or nexus, with that state. State law, which often follows the *UDITPA,* specifies various activities that lead to nexus in various states.

Ninety-day letter. See *statutory notice of deficiency.*

Nonacquiescence. Disagreement by the IRS on the result reached by selected tax decisions. Sometimes abbreviated *Nonacq.* or *NA.* See also *acquiescence.*

Nonbusiness bad debt. A bad debt loss that is not incurred in connection with a creditor's trade or business. The loss is classified as a short-term capital loss and is allowed only in the year the debt becomes entirely worthless. In addition to family loans, many investor losses are nonbusiness bad debts. § 166(d). See also *business bad debts.*

Nonbusiness income. Income generated from investment assets or from the taxable disposition thereof. In some states, the nonbusiness income of a *multistate corporation* is held out of the apportionment procedure and allocated to the state in which the nonbusiness asset is located. See also *allocate* and *apportion.*

Noncontributory qualified pension or profit sharing plan. A plan funded entirely by the employer with no contributions from the covered employees. See also *qualified pension or profit sharing plan.*

Nonliquidating distribution. A payment made by a partnership or corporation to the entity's owner is a nonliquidating distribution when the entity's legal existence does not cease thereafter. If the payor is a corporation, such a distribution can result in dividend income to the shareholders. If the payor is a partnership, the partner usually assigns a basis in the distributed property that is equal to the lesser of the partner's basis in the partnership interest or the basis of the distributed asset to the partnership. In this regard, the partner first assigns basis to any cash that is received in the distribution. The partner's remaining basis, if any, is assigned to the noncash assets according to their relative bases to the partnership.

Nonqualified deferred compensation (NQDC) plans. Compensation arrangements that are frequently offered to executives. Such plans may include *stock options*, restricted stock, etc. Often, an executive may defer the recognition of taxable income. The employer, however, does not receive a tax deduction until the employee is required to include the compensation in income. See also *restricted property plan.*

Nonqualified stock option (NQSO). A type of *stock option* that does not satisfy the statutory requirements of an *incentive stock option.* If the NQSO has a readily ascertainable fair market value (e.g., the option is traded on an established exchange), the value of the option must be included in the employee's gross income at the date of the grant. Otherwise, the employee does not recognize income at the grant date. Instead, ordinary income is recognized in the year of exercise of the option.

Nonrecourse debt. Debt secured by the property that it is used to purchase. The purchaser of the property is not personally liable for the debt upon default. Rather, the creditor's recourse is to repossess the related property. Nonrecourse debt generally does not increase the purchaser's at-risk amount.

Nonresident alien. An individual who is neither a citizen nor a resident of the United States. Citizenship is determined under the immigration and naturalization laws of the United States. Residency is determined under § 7701(b) of the Internal Revenue Code.

Nonseparately stated income. The net income of a partnership or S corporation that is combined and allocated to the owners. Other items, such as capital gains and charitable contributions, that could be treated differently on the individual tax returns of the shareholders are not included in this amount but are allocated to the shareholders separately.

Not essentially equivalent redemption. See *redemption (not equivalent to a dividend).*

O

Obligee. The party to whom someone else is obligated under a contract. Thus, if Coop loans money to Dawn, Coop is the obligee and Dawn is the obligor under the loan.

Obligor. See *obligee.*

Offer in compromise. A settlement agreement offered by the IRS in a tax dispute, especially where there is doubt as to the collectibility of the full deficiency. Offers in compromise can include installment payment schedules, as well as reductions in the tax and penalties owed by the taxpayer.

Office audit. An audit conducted by the IRS in the agent's office. See also *audit, correspondence audit,* and *field audit.*

On all fours. A judicial decision exactly in point with another as to result, facts, or both.

Optimal use value. Synonym for most suitable use value.

Optional adjustment election. See *Section 754 election.*

Ordinary. Common and accepted in the general industry or type of activity in which the taxpayer is engaged. It comprises one of the tests for the deductibility of expenses incurred or paid in connection with a trade or business; for the production or collection of income; for the management, conservation, or maintenance of property held for the production of income; or in connection with the determination, collection, or refund of any tax. §§ 162(a) and 212. See also *necessary.*

Ordinary and necessary. See *necessary* and *ordinary.*

Ordinary gross income (OGI). A concept peculiar to personal holding companies and defined in § 543(b)(1). See also *adjusted ordinary gross income.*

Organizational expenditures. Items incurred early in the life of a corporate entity, qualifying for a 60-month amortization under Federal tax law. Amortizable expenditures exclude those incurred to obtain capital (underwriting fees) or assets (subject to cost recovery). Typically, amortizable expenditures include legal and accounting fees and state incorporation payments. Such items must be incurred by the end of the entity's first tax year. § 248.

Outbound taxation. U.S. tax effects when a U.S. person begins an investment or business activity outside the United States.

Outside basis. A partner's basis in his or her partnership interest.

Overall foreign loss. In computing the taxpayer's *foreign tax credit,* if the operating results in all of the *separate foreign tax credit limitation categories* net to a negative number, the aggregate foreign-source loss is used to offset *U.S.-source income.* A recapture device applies in later years, to restore the net U.S.-source income to the computation.

Owner shift. Any change in the respective ownership of stock by a 5 percent-or-more shareholder. Change is determined relative to a testing period of the prior three years. If there is a more-than-50 percent change in the ownership of a loss corporation, § 382 limitations apply to the use of net operating loss carryovers of the loss corporation.

Ownership change. An event that triggers a *Sec. 382 limitation* for the acquiring corporation.

P

Parent-subsidiary controlled group. A *controlled* or *affiliated group* of corporations, where at least one corporation is at least 80 percent owned by one or more of the others. The affiliated group definition is more difficult to meet.

Partial liquidation. A stock redemption where noncorporate shareholders are permitted sale or exchange treatment. In certain cases, an active business must have existed for at least five years. Only a portion of the outstanding stock in the entity is retired.

Partner. See *general partner* and *limited partner.*

Partnership. For income tax purposes, a partnership includes a syndicate, group, pool, or joint venture, as well as ordinary partnerships. In an ordinary partnership, two or more parties combine capital and/or services to carry on a business for profit as co-owners. § 7701(a)(2). See also *limited partnership* and *tiered partnerships.*

Passive foreign investment company (PFIC). A non-U.S. corporation that generates a substantial amount of personal holding company income. Upon receipt of an excess distribution from the entity or the sale of its shares, its U.S. shareholders are taxable on their pro rata shares of the tax that has been deferred with respect to the corporation's taxable income, plus an applicable interest charge.

Passive investment company. A means by which a *multistate corporation* can reduce the overall effective tax rate by isolating investment income in a low- or no-tax state.

Passive investment income (PII). Gross receipts from royalties, certain rents, dividends, interest, annuities, and gains from the sale or exchange of stock and securities. With certain exceptions, if the passive investment income of an *S corporation* exceeds 25 percent of the corporation's gross receipts for three consecutive years, S status is lost.

Passive loss. Any loss from (1) activities in which the taxpayer does not materially participate and (2) rental activities. Net passive losses cannot be used to offset income from nonpassive sources. Rather, they are suspended until the taxpayer either generates net passive income (and a deduction of such losses is allowed) or disposes of the underlying property (at which time the loss deductions are allowed in full). Landlords who actively participate in the rental activities can deduct up to $25,000 of passive losses annually. However, this amount is phased out when the landlord's AGI exceeds $100,000. See also *portfolio income.*

Payroll factor. The proportion of a *multistate corporation*'s total payroll that is traceable to a specific state. Used in determining the taxable income that is to be apportioned to that state. See also *apportion.*

Pecuniary bequest. A bequest of money to an heir by a decedent. See also *bequest.*

Pension plan. A type of *deferred compensation* arrangement that provides for systematic payments of definitely determinable retirement benefits to employees who meet the requirements set forth in the plan. See also *defined contribution pension plan.*

Percentage depletion. See *depletion.*

Percentage of completion method. A method of reporting gain or loss on certain long-term contracts. Under this method of accounting, the gross contract price is included in income as the contract is completed. § 460 and Reg. § 1.451–3. See also *completed contract method.*

Permanent differences. Items that will affect book income or taxable income, but not both.

Permanent establishment. A level of activity in the host country that triggers the effect of an *income tax treaty.* Usually, a PE is found to exist where an office, plant, or other fixed place of business is put in place by the taxpayer. The storage of inventory does not create a permanent establishment.

Permanently reinvesting. Use of *APB 23* to avoid reporting U.S. *deferred income tax expense* for income of foreign subsidiaries.

Personal and household effects. Items owned by a decedent at the time of death. Examples include clothing, furniture, sporting goods, jewelry, stamp and coin collections, silverware, china, crystal, cooking utensils, books, cars, televisions, radios, and sound equipment.

Personal holding company (PHC). A corporation that satisfies the requirements of § 542. Qualification as a personal holding company means a penalty tax may be imposed on the corporation's undistributed personal holding company income for the year.

Personal holding company income. Income as defined by § 543. It includes interest, dividends, certain rents and royalties, income from the use of corporate property by certain shareholders, income from certain personal service contracts, and distributions from estates and trusts. Such income is relevant in determining whether a corporation is a personal holding company and is therefore subject to the penalty tax on personal holding companies. See also *adjusted ordinary gross income.*

Personal holding company tax. A penalty tax imposed on certain closely held corporations with excessive investment income. Assessed at 15 percent on *personal holding company income,* reduced by dividends paid and other adjustments. § 541.

Personal property. Generally, all property other than real estate. It is sometimes referred to as personalty when real estate is termed realty. Personal property can also refer to property not used in a taxpayer's trade or business or held for the production or collection of income. When used in this sense, personal property can include both realty (e.g., a personal residence) and personalty (e.g., personal effects such as clothing and furniture). See also *bequest.*

Personal service corporation (PSC). An entity whose principal activity is the providing of services by owner-employees. Subject to a flat 35 percent tax rate and limited to a calendar tax year.

Personalty. All property that is not attached to real estate (realty) and is movable. Examples of personalty are machinery, automobiles, clothing, household furnishings, inventory, and personal effects. See also *ad valorem tax* and *real property.*

Portfolio income. Income from interest, dividends, rentals, royalties, capital gains, or other investment sources. Net passive losses cannot be used to offset net portfolio income. See also *passive loss* and *investment income.*

Power of appointment. A legal right granted to someone by will or other document that gives the holder the power to dispose of property or the income from property. When the holder may appoint the property to his or her own benefit, the power usually is called a general power of appointment. If the holder cannot benefit himself or herself but may only appoint to certain other persons, the power is a special power of appointment. Assume Gary places $500,000 worth of securities in trust granting Donna the right to determine each year how the trustee is to divide the income between Ann and Babs. Under these circumstances, Donna has a special power of appointment. If Donna had the further right to appoint the income to herself, she probably possesses a general power of appointment. For the estate tax and gift tax effects of powers of appointment, see §§ 2041 and 2514. See also *testamentary power of appointment.*

Precontribution gain or loss. Partnerships allow for a variety of *special allocations* of gain or loss among the partners, but gain or loss that is "built in" on an asset contributed to the partnership is assigned specifically to the contributing partner. § 704(c)(1)(A).

Preferences (AMT). See *alternative minimum tax (AMT)* and *tax preference items.*

Preferred stock bailout. A process where a shareholder used the issuance and sale, or later redemption, of a preferred stock dividend to obtain long-term capital gains, without any loss of voting control over the corporation. In effect, the shareholder received corporate profits without suffering the consequences of dividend income treatment. This procedure led Congress to enact § 306, which, if applicable, converts the prior long-term capital gain on the sale or redemption of the stock to ordinary income. See also *bailout.*

Present interest. See *future interest.*

Presumption. An inference in favor of a particular fact. If, for example, the IRS issues a notice of deficiency against a taxpayer, under certain conditions a presumption of correctness attaches to the assessment. Thus, the taxpayer has the burden of proof to show that he or she does not owe the tax listed in the deficiency notice. See also *rebuttable presumption.*

Previously taxed income (PTI). Under prior law, the undistributed taxable income of an S corporation was taxed to the shareholders as of the last day of the corporation's tax year and usually could be withdrawn by the shareholders without tax consequences at some later point in time. The role of PTI has been taken over by the *accumulated adjustments account.*

Principal. Property as opposed to income. The term is often used as a synonym for the corpus of a trust. If, for example, Gil places real estate in trust with income payable to Ann for life and the remainder to Barb upon Ann's death, the real estate is the principal, or corpus, of the trust.

Principal partner. A partner with a 5 percent or greater interest in partnership capital or profits. § 706(b)(3). See also *majority interest partners.*

Private foundation. An *exempt organization* subject to additional statutory restrictions on its activities and on contributions made to it. Excise taxes may be levied on certain prohibited transactions, and the Code places more stringent restrictions on the deductibility of contributions to private foundations. § 509.

Pro rata. Proportionately. Assume, for example, a corporation has 10 shareholders, each of whom owns 10 percent of the stock. A pro rata dividend distribution of $1,000 means that each shareholder receives $100.

Pro se. The taxpayer represents himself or herself before the court without the benefit of counsel.

Probate. The legal process by which the estate of a decedent is administered. Generally, the probate process involves collecting a decedent's assets, liquidating liabilities, paying necessary taxes, and distributing property to heirs.

Probate costs. The costs incurred in administering a decedent's estate. See also *probate estate*.

Probate court. The usual designation for the state or local court that supervises the administration (probate) of a decedent's estate.

Probate estate. The property of a decedent that is subject to administration by the executor or administrator of an estate. See also *administration*.

Profit and loss sharing ratios. Specified in the partnership agreement and used to determine each partner's allocation of ordinary taxable income and separately stated items. Profits and losses can be shared in different ratios. The ratios can be changed by amending the partnership agreement. § 704(a).

Profit sharing plan. A *deferred compensation* plan established and maintained by an employer to provide for employee participation in the company's profits. Contributions are paid from the employer's current or accumulated profits to a trustee. Separate accounts are maintained for each participant employee. The plan must provide a definite, predetermined formula for allocating the contributions among the participants. It also must include a definite, predetermined formula for distributing the accumulated funds after a fixed number of years, on the attainment of a stated age, or on the occurrence of certain events such as illness, layoff, or retirement.

Profits (loss) interest. A partner's percentage allocation of partnership operating results, determined by the *profit and loss sharing ratios*.

Property. Assets defined in the broadest legal sense. Property includes the *unrealized receivables* of a cash basis taxpayer, but not services rendered. § 351.

Property dividend. A dividend consisting of in-kind (noncash) assets of the payor, measured by the fair market value of the property on the date of distribution. The portion of the distribution representing E & P is a dividend; any excess is treated as a return of capital. Distribution of in-kind property causes the distributing corporation to recognize any underlying realized gain, but not loss.

Property factor. The proportion of a *multistate corporation*'s total property that is traceable to a specific state. Used in determining the taxable income that is to be apportioned to that state. See also *apportion*.

Property tax. An *ad valorem tax*, usually levied by a city or county government, on the value of real or personal property that the taxpayer owns on a specified date. Most states exclude intangible property and assets owned by exempt organizations from the tax base, and some exclude inventory, pollution control or manufacturing equipment, and other items to provide relocation or retention incentives for the taxpayer.

Proportionate distribution. A distribution in which each partner in a partnership receives a pro rata share of hot assets being distributed. For example, a distribution of $10,000 of hot assets equally to two 50 percent partners is a proportionate distribution.

Prop.Reg. An abbreviation for Proposed Regulation. A Regulation may first be issued in proposed form to give interested parties the opportunity for comment. When and if a Proposed Regulation is finalized, it is known as a Regulation (abbreviated Reg.).

PTI. See *previously taxed income*.

Public Law 86–272. A congressional limit on the ability of the state to force a multistate corporation to assign income to that state. Under P.L. 86–272, where orders for tangible personal property are both filled and delivered outside the state, the entity must establish more than the mere solicitation of such orders before any income can be *apportioned* to the state.

Public policy limitation. A concept developed by the courts precluding an income tax deduction for certain expenses related to activities deemed to be contrary to the public welfare. In this connection, Congress has incorporated into the Code specific disallowance provisions covering such items as illegal bribes, kickbacks, and fines and penalties. §§ 162(c) and (f).

Q

Qualified business unit (QBU). A subsidiary, branch, or other business entity that conducts business using a currency other than the U.S. dollar.

Qualified dividend. A *dividend* that is taxed to the shareholder at no more than a 15 percent rate. Generally paid by a publicly traded U.S. corporation.

Qualified nonrecourse debt. Debt issued on realty by a bank, retirement plan, or governmental agency. Included in the *at-risk amount* by the investor. § 465(b)(6).

Qualified pension or profit sharing plan. An employer-sponsored plan that meets the requirements of § 401. If these requirements are met, none of the employer's contributions to the plan will be taxed to the employee until distributed (§ 402). The employer is allowed a deduction in the year the contributions are made (§ 404). See also *contributory qualified pension or profit sharing plan, deferred compensation*, and *noncontributory qualified pension or profit sharing plan*.

Qualified small business corporation. A C corporation that has aggregate gross assets not exceeding $50 million and that is conducting an active trade or business. § 1202.

Qualified small business stock. Stock in a qualified small business corporation, purchased as part of an original issue after August 10, 1993. The shareholder may exclude from gross income 50 percent of the realized gain on the sale of the stock, if he or she held the stock for more than five years.

The exclusion creates an AMT preferrence item, though. § 1202.

Qualified terminable interest property (QTIP). Generally, the *marital deduction* (for gift and estate tax purposes) is not available if the interest transferred will terminate upon the death of the transferee spouse and pass to someone else. Thus, if Hannah places property in trust, life estate to Will, and remainder to their children upon Will's death, this is a *terminable interest* that will not provide Hannah (or her estate) with a marital deduction. If, however, the transfer in trust is treated as qualified terminable interest property (the QTIP election is made), the terminable interest restriction is waived and the marital deduction becomes available. In exchange for this deduction, the surviving spouse's gross estate must include the value of the QTIP election assets, even though he or she has no control over the ultimate disposition of the asset. Terminable interest property qualifies for this election if the donee (or heir) is the only beneficiary of the asset during his or her lifetime and receives income distributions relative to the property at least annually. For gifts, the donor spouse is the one who makes the QTIP election. As to property transferred by death, the *executor* of the estate of the deceased spouse has the right to make the election. §§ 2056(b)(7) and 2523(f).

R

RAR. A Revenue Agent's Report, which reflects any adjustments made by the agent as a result of an audit of the taxpayer. The RAR is mailed to the taxpayer along with the *30-day letter,* which outlines the appellate procedures available to the taxpayer.

Rate reconciliation. Schedule provided in the financial statement income tax footnote, to reconcile the hypothetical tax on a corporation's book income at the U.S. corporate rate and the corporation's actual total book income tax expense.

Real property. Realty. Land, buildings, and other improvements on the land. See also *personal property* and *personalty.*

Realistic possibility. A preparer penalty is assessed where a tax return includes a position that has no realistic possibility of being sustained by a court.

Realized gain or loss. The difference between the amount realized upon the sale or other disposition of property and the adjusted basis of such property. § 1001. See also *adjusted basis, amount realized, basis,* and *recognized gain or loss.*

Reasonable cause. Relief from taxpayer and preparer penalties often is allowed where there is reasonable cause for the taxpayer's actions. For instance, reasonable cause for the late filing of a tax return might be a flood that damaged the taxpayer's record-keeping systems and made difficult a timely completion of the return.

Reasonable needs of the business. A means of avoiding the penalty tax on an unreasonable accumulation of earnings. In determining the base for this tax (*accumulated taxable income*), § 535 allows a deduction for "such part of earnings and profits for the taxable year as are retained for the reasonable needs of the business." § 537.

Rebuttable presumption. A presumption that can be overturned upon the showing of sufficient proof. See also *presumption.*

Recapitalization. An E reorganization, constituting a major change in the character and amount of outstanding equity of a corporation. For instance, common stock exchanged for preferred stock can qualify for tax-free E reorganization treatment.

Recapture. To recover the tax benefit of a deduction or a credit previously taken. See also *depreciation recapture.*

Recapture potential. A measure with respect to property that, if disposed of in a taxable transaction, would result in the recapture of depreciation (§§ 1245 or 1250), deferred LIFO gain, or deferred installment method gain.

Recognized gain or loss. The portion of realized gain or loss subject to income taxation. See also *realized gain or loss.*

Recourse debt. Debt for which the lender may both foreclose on the property and assess a guarantor for any payments due under the loan, even from personal assets. A lender may also make a claim against the assets of any general partner in a partnership to which debt is issued, without regard to whether that partner has guaranteed the debt.

Redemption. See *stock redemption.*

Redemption (complete termination). Sale or exchange treatment is available relative to this type of redemption. The shareholder must retire all of his or her outstanding shares in the corporation (ignoring family attribution rules) and cannot hold an interest, other than that of a creditor, for the 10 years following the redemption. § 302(b)(3).

Redemption (disproportionate). Sale or exchange treatment is available relative to this type of redemption. After the exchange, the shareholder owns less than 80 percent of his or her pre-redemption interest in the corporation and only a minority interest in the entity. § 302(b)(2).

Redemption (not equivalent to a dividend). Sale or exchange treatment is given to this type of redemption. Although various safe-harbor tests are failed, the nature of the redemption is such that dividend treatment is avoided, because it represents a meaningful reduction in the shareholder's interest in the corporation. § 302(b)(1).

Redemption to pay death taxes. Sale or exchange treatment is available relative to this type of redemption, to the extent of the proceeds up to the total amount paid by the estate or heir for death taxes and administration expenses. The stock value must exceed 35 percent of the value of the decedent's adjusted gross estate. In meeting this test, one can combine shareholdings in corporations where the decedent held at least 20 percent of the outstanding shares.

Regular corporation. See *C corporation.*

Regulations. The U.S. Treasury Department Regulations (abbreviated Reg.) represent the position of the IRS as to how the Internal Revenue Code is to be interpreted. Their purpose is to provide taxpayers and IRS personnel with rules of general and specific application to the various provisions of the tax law. Regulations are published in the *Federal Register* and in all tax services.

Related corporations. See *controlled group.*

Related parties. Various Code sections define related parties and often include a variety of persons within this (usually detrimental) category. Generally, related parties are accorded different tax treatment from that applicable to other taxpayers who enter into similar transactions. For instance, realized losses that are generated between related parties are not recognized in the year of the loss. However, these deferred losses can be used to offset recognized gains that occur upon the subsequent sale of the asset to a nonrelated party. Other uses of a related-party definition include the conversion of gain upon the sale of a depreciable asset into all ordinary income (§ 1239) and the identification of constructive ownership of stock relative to corporate distributions, redemptions, liquidations, reorganizations, and compensation.

Remainder beneficiary. The party that is entitled to receive the property after the intervening income interest has expired. If, for example, Greg places real estate in trust with income to Ann for life and the remainder to Bill upon Ann's death, Bill is the remainder beneficiary.

Remainder interest. The property that passes to a beneficiary after the expiration of an intervening *income interest.* If, for example, Greg places real estate in trust with income to Ann for life and remainder to Bill upon Ann's death, Bill has a remainder interest. See also *life estate* and *reversionary interest.*

Remand. To send back. An appellate court may remand a case to a lower court, usually for additional fact finding. In other words, the appellate court is not in a position to decide the appeal based on the facts determined by the lower court. Remanding is abbreviated *"rem'g."*

Reorganization. See *corporate reorganization.*

Research activities credit. A tax credit whose purpose is to encourage research and development. It consists of two components: the incremental research activities credit and the basic research credit. The incremental research activities credit is equal to 20 percent of the excess qualified research expenditures over the base amount. The basic research credit is equal to 20 percent of the excess of basic research payments over the base amount. § 41. See also *general business credit.*

Residential rental property. Buildings for which at least 80 percent of the gross rents are from dwelling units (e.g., an apartment building). This type of building is distinguished from nonresidential (commercial or industrial) buildings in applying the recapture of depreciation provisions. The term also is relevant in distinguishing between buildings that are eligible for a 27.5-year life versus a 31.5- or 39-year life for MACRS purposes.

Residual method. Used to allocate the new stepped-up basis of a subsidiary's assets among its property when a § 338 election is in effect. The purchase price that exceeds the aggregate fair market values of the tangible and identifiable intangible assets is allocated to goodwill or going-concern value. § 1060.

Restricted property plan. An arrangement whereby an employer transfers property (usually stock) to an employee at a bargain price (for less than the fair market value). If the transfer is accompanied by a *substantial risk of forfeiture* and the property is not transferable, no compensation results to the employee until the restrictions disappear. An example of a substantial risk of forfeiture would be a requirement that the employee return the property if his or her employment is terminated within a specified period of time. § 83. See also *nonqualified deferred compensation (NQDC) plans.*

Retail sale. A sale made to the final consumer. See also *sale.*

Return of capital. When a taxpayer reacquires financial resources that he or she previously had invested in an entity or venture, the return of his or her capital investment itself does not increase gross income for the recovery year. A return of capital may result from an annuity or insurance contract, the sale or exchange of any asset, or a distribution from a partnership or corporation.

Revenue Agent's Report. See *RAR.*

Revenue neutrality. A change in the tax system that results in the same amount of revenue. Revenue neutral, however, does not mean that any one taxpayer will pay the same amount of tax as before. Thus, as a result of a tax law change, corporations could pay more taxes, but the excess revenue will be offset by lower taxes on individuals.

Revenue Procedure. A matter of procedural importance to both taxpayers and the IRS concerning the administration of the tax laws is issued as a Revenue Procedure (abbreviated Rev.Proc.). A Revenue Procedure is first published in an *Internal Revenue Bulletin* (I.R.B.) and later transferred to the appropriate *Cumulative Bulletin* (C.B.). Both the *Internal Revenue Bulletins* and the *Cumulative Bulletins* are published by the U.S. Government Printing Office.

Revenue Ruling. A Revenue Ruling (abbreviated Rev.Rul.) is issued by the National Office of the IRS to express an official interpretation of the tax law as applied to specific transactions. It is more limited in application than a Regulation. A Revenue Ruling is first published in an *Internal Revenue Bulletin* (I.R.B.) and later transferred to the appropriate *Cumulative Bulletin* (C.B.). Both the *Internal Revenue Bulletins* and the *Cumulative Bulletins* are published by the U.S. Government Printing Office.

Reversed (Rev'd.). An indication that a decision of one court has been reversed by a higher court in the same case.

Reversing (Rev'g.). An indication that the decision of a higher court is reversing the result reached by a lower court in the same case.

Reversionary interest. The property that reverts to the grantor after the expiration of an intervening income interest. Assume Gail places real estate in trust with income to Art for 11 years, and upon the expiration of this term, the property returns to Gail. Under these circumstances, she holds a reversionary interest in the property. A reversionary interest is the same as a *remainder interest*, except that, in the latter case, the property passes to someone other than the original owner (e.g., the grantor of a trust) upon the expiration of the intervening interest. See also *grantor trust*.

Revocable transfer. A transfer of property where the transferor retains the right to recover the property. The creation of a revocable trust is an example of a revocable transfer. § 2038. See also *incomplete transfer*.

Rev.Proc. Abbreviation for an IRS Revenue Procedure. See *Revenue Procedure*.

Rev.Rul. Abbreviation for an IRS Revenue Ruling. See *Revenue Ruling*.

Right of survivorship. See *joint tenants*.

Roth IRA. See *Individual Retirement Account (IRA)*.

S

S corporation. The designation for a small business corporation. See also *Subchapter S*.

Sale. A contract or agreement by which property is transferred from the seller to the buyer for a fixed price in money, paid or agreed to be paid by the buyer. A legal sale involves both an ownership transfer and consideration.

Sales factor. The proportion of a *multistate corporation*'s total sales that is traceable to a specific state. Used in determining the taxable income that is to be apportioned to that state. See also *apportion*.

Sales tax. A state- or local-level tax on the retail sale of specified property. Generally, the purchaser pays the tax, but the seller collects it, as an agent for the government. Various taxing jurisdictions allow exemptions for purchases of specific items, including certain food, services, and manufacturing equipment. If the purchaser and seller are in different states, a *use tax* usually applies.

Schedule M-1. On the Form 1120, a reconciliation of book net income with Federal taxable income. Accounts for timing and permanent differences in the two computations, such as depreciation differences, exempt income, and nondeductible items. On Forms 1120S and 1065, the Schedule M-1 reconciles book income with the owners' aggregate ordinary taxable income.

Schedule PH. A tax form required to be filed by corporations that are personal holding companies. The form must be filed in addition to Form 1120 (U.S. Corporation Income Tax Return).

Section 306 stock. Preferred stock issued as a nontaxable stock dividend that, if sold or redeemed, would result in ordinary income recognition. § 306(c). See also *preferred stock bailout*.

Section 306 taint. The ordinary income that would result upon the sale or other taxable disposition of § 306 stock.

Section 338 election. When a corporation acquires at least 80 percent of a subsidiary in a 12-month period, it can elect to treat the acquisition of such stock as an asset purchase. The acquiring corporation's basis in the subsidiary's assets then is the cost of the stock. The subsidiary is deemed to have sold its assets for an amount equal to the grossed-up basis in its stock.

Section 382 limitation. When one corporation acquires another, the acquiror's ability to use the loss and credit carryovers of the target may be limited, in an anti-abuse provision specified in the Code. Generally, for instance, the maximum deduction available to the acquiror is the takeover-date value of the target times the tax-exempt interest rate on that date.

Section 401(k) plan. A cash or deferred arrangement plan that allows participants to elect to receive up to $13,000 in 2004 in cash (taxed currently) or to have a contribution made on their behalf to a *profit sharing* or *stock bonus plan* (excludible from gross income). The plan may also be in the form of a salary reduction agreement between the participant and the employer.

Section 754 election. An election that may be made by a partnership to adjust the basis of partnership assets to reflect a purchasing partner's *outside basis* in the interest, or to reflect a gain, loss, or basis adjustment of a partner receiving a distribution from a partnership. The intent of the election is to maintain the equivalence between outside and *inside basis*. Once the election is made, the partnership must make basis adjustments for all future transactions, unless the IRS consents to revoke the election.

Section 1231 assets. Depreciable assets and real estate used in a trade or business and held for the appropriate holding period. Under certain circumstances, the classification also includes timber, coal, domestic iron ore, livestock (held for draft, breeding, dairy, or sporting purposes), and unharvested crops. § 1231(b). See also *Section 1231 gains and losses*.

Section 1231 gains and losses. If the combined gains and losses from the taxable dispositions of § 1231 assets plus the net gain from business involuntary conversions (of both § 1231 assets and long-term capital assets) is a gain, such gains and losses are treated as long-term capital gains and losses. In arriving at § 1231 gains, however, the depreciation recapture provisions (e.g., §§ 1245 and 1250) are first applied to produce ordinary income. If the net result of the combination is a loss, the gains and losses from § 1231 assets are treated as ordinary gains and losses. § 1231(a). See also *depreciation recapture* and *Section 1231 assets*.

Section 1244 stock. Stock issued under § 1244 by qualifying *small business corporations*. If § 1244 stock becomes worthless, the shareholders may claim an ordinary loss rather than the usual capital loss, within statutory limitations.

Section 1245 recapture. Upon a taxable disposition of § 1245 property, all depreciation claimed on such property is recaptured as ordinary income (but not to exceed recognized gain from the disposition).

Section 1250 recapture. Upon a taxable disposition of § 1250 property, some of the depreciation or cost recovery claimed on the property may be recaptured as ordinary income.

Securities. Generally, stock, debt, and other financial assets. To the extent securities other than the stock of the transferee corporation are received in a § 351 exchange, the new shareholder realizes a gain.

Separate foreign tax credit limitation categories. In computing the *foreign tax credit*, the taxpayer segregates income and deductions for purposes of sourcing and computing the credit into several Code-specified categories or "baskets." An FTC is computed within each basket, and generally the results of those separate computations cannot be combined. This approach restricts the taxpayer's ability to maximize the FTC by "cross-crediting" the profit/loss results from dissimilar operations, and from countries with widely varying tax rates.

Separate property. In a community property jurisdiction, property that belongs entirely to one of the spouses is separate property. Generally, it is property acquired before marriage or acquired after marriage by gift or inheritance. See also *community property*.

Separate return limitation year (SRLY). A series of rules limits the amount of an acquired corporation's net operating loss carryforwards that can be used by the acquiror. Generally, a *consolidated return* can include the acquiree's NOL carryforward only to the extent of the lesser of the subsidiary's (1) current-year or (2) cumulative positive contribution to consolidated taxable income. Prop.Reg. § 1.1502–21(c).

Separately stated item. Any item of a partnership or S corporation that might be taxed differently to any two owners of the entity. These amounts are not included in ordinary income of the entity, but instead are reported separately to the owners; tax consequences are determined at the owner level.

Sham. A transaction without substance that will be disregarded for tax purposes.

Short taxable year (short period). A tax year that is less than 12 months. A short taxable year may occur in the initial reporting period, in the final tax year, or when the taxpayer changes tax years.

Short-term capital gain or loss. Results from the sale or other taxable exchange of a capital asset that had been held by the seller for one year or less or from other transactions involving statutorily designated assets, including nonbusiness bad debts.

Simple trust. Simple trusts are those that are not complex trusts. Such trusts may not have a charitable beneficiary, accumulate income, or distribute corpus. See also *complex trust*.

Simplified employee pension (SEP) plan. An employer may make contributions to an employee's IRA in amounts not exceeding the lesser of 25 percent of compensation or $41,000 per individual. These employer-sponsored simplified employee pensions are permitted only if the contributions are nondiscriminatory and are made on behalf of all employees who have attained age 21 and have worked for the employer during at least three of the five preceding calendar years. § 219(b). See also *Individual Retirement Account (IRA)*.

Small business corporation. A corporation that satisfies the definition of § 1361(b), § 1244(c), or both. Satisfaction of § 1361(b) permits an S election, and satisfaction of § 1244 enables the shareholders of the corporation to claim an ordinary loss on the worthlessness of stock.

Small Cases Division of the U.S. Tax Court. Jurisdiction is limited to claims of $50,000 or less. There is no appeal from this court.

Special allocation. Any amount for which an agreement exists among the partners of a partnership outlining the method used for assigning the item among the partners.

Special power of appointment. See *power of appointment*.

Special use value. Permits the executor of an estate to value, for death tax purposes, real estate used in a farming activity or in connection with a closely held business at its current use value rather than at its most suitable or optimal use value. Under this option, a farm is valued for farming purposes even though, for example, the property might have a higher potential value as a shopping center. For the executor of an estate to elect special use valuation, the conditions of § 2032A must be satisfied. See also *most suitable use value*.

Spin-off. A type of reorganization where, for example, Ace Corporation transfers some assets to Bow Corporation in exchange for enough Bow stock to represent control. Ace then distributes the Bow stock to its shareholders.

Split-off. A type of reorganization where, for example, Arc Corporation transfers some assets to Bond Corporation in exchange for enough Bond stock to represent control. Arc then distributes the Bond stock to its shareholders in exchange for some of their Arc stock.

Split-up. A type of reorganization where, for example, Ally Corporation transfers some assets to Bar Corporation and the remainder to Zip Corporation. In return, Ally receives enough Bar and Zip stock to represent control of each corporation. Ally then distributes the Bar and Zip stock to its shareholders in return for all of their Ally stock. The result of the split-up is that Ally is liquidated, and its shareholders now have control of Bar and Zip.

Sprinkling trust. When a trustee has the discretion to either distribute or accumulate the entity accounting income of the trust and to distribute it among the trust's income beneficiaries in varying magnitudes, a sprinkling trust exists. The trustee can "sprinkle" the income of the trust.

Statute of limitations. Provisions of the law that specify the maximum period of time in which action may be taken on a past event. Code §§ 6501–6504 contain the limitation periods applicable to the IRS for additional assessments, and §§ 6511–6515 relate to refund claims by taxpayers.

Statutory depletion. See *depletion.*

Statutory notice of deficiency. Commonly referred to as the 90-day letter, this notice is sent to a taxpayer upon request, upon the expiration of the *30-day letter*, or upon exhaustion by the taxpayer of his or her administrative remedies before the IRS. The notice gives the taxpayer 90 days in which to file a petition with the U.S. Tax Court. If such a petition is not filed, the IRS will demand payment of the assessed deficiency. §§ 6211–6216. See also *deficiency.*

Step transaction. Disregarding one or more transactions to arrive at the final result. Assume that the shareholders of Clue Corporation liquidate the corporation and receive cash and operating assets. Immediately after the liquidation, the shareholders transfer the operating assets to newly formed Blue Corporation. Under these circumstances, the IRS may contend that the liquidation of Clue should be disregarded (thereby depriving the shareholders of capital gain treatment). What may really have happened is a reorganization of Clue with a distribution of boot (ordinary income) to Clue's shareholders. If so, there will be a carryover of basis in the assets transferred from Clue to Blue.

Step-down in basis. A reduction in the tax basis of property. See also *step-up in basis.*

Step-up in basis. An increase in the income tax basis of property. The classic step-up in basis occurs when a decedent dies owning appreciated property. Since the estate or heir acquires a basis in the property equal to the property's fair market value on the date of death (or *alternate valuation date* if available and elected), any appreciation is not subject to the income tax. Thus, a step-up in basis is the result, with no income tax consequences.

Stock attribution. See *attribution.*

Stock bonus plan. A type of *deferred compensation* plan in which the employer establishes and maintains the plan and contributes employer stock to the plan for the benefit of employees. The contributions need not be dependent on the employer's profits. Any benefits of the plan are distributed in the form of employer stock, except that distributable fractional shares may be paid in cash.

Stock dividend. A dividend consisting of stock of the payor. Not taxable if a pro rata distribution of stock or stock rights on common stock. However, some stock dividends are taxable. § 305.

Stock option. The right to purchase a stated number of shares of stock from a corporation at a certain price within a specified period of time. §§ 421 and 422. See also *incentive stock option (ISO)* and *nonqualified stock option (NQSO).*

Stock redemption. A corporation buys back its own stock from a specified shareholder. Typically, the corporation recognizes any realized gain on the noncash assets that it uses to effect a redemption, and the shareholder obtains a capital gain or loss upon receipt of the purchase price.

Stock rights. Assets that convey to the holder the power to purchase corporate stock at a specified price, often for a limited period of time. Stock rights received may be taxed as a distribution of earnings and profits. After the right is exercised, the basis of the acquired share includes the investor's purchase price or gross income, if any, to obtain the right. Disposition of the right also is a taxable event, with basis often assigned from the shares held prior to the issuance of the right.

Subchapter S. Sections 1361–1379 of the Internal Revenue Code. An elective provision permitting certain small business corporations (§ 1361) and their shareholders (§ 1362) to elect to be treated for income tax purposes in accordance with the operating rules of §§ 1363–1379. S corporations usually avoid the corporate income tax, and corporate losses can be claimed by the shareholders.

Subpart F. The subpart of the Code that identifies the current tax treatment of income earned by a controlled foreign corporation. Certain types of income are included in U.S. gross income by U.S. shareholders of such an entity as the income is generated, not when it is repatriated.

Substance vs. form concept. A standard used when one must ascertain the true reality of what has occurred. Suppose a father sells stock to his daughter for $1,000. If the stock is really worth $50,000 at the time of the transfer, the substance of the transaction is probably a gift to her of $49,000.

Substantial authority. Taxpayer understatement penalties are waived where substantial authority existed for the disputed position taken on the return.

Substantial economic effect. Partnerships are allowed to *allocate* items of income, expense, gain, loss, and credit in any manner that is authorized in the partnership agreement, provided that the allocation has an economic effect aside from the corresponding tax results. The necessary substantial economic effect is present, for instance, if the post-contribution appreciation in the value of an asset that was contributed to the partnership by a partner was allocated to that partner for cost recovery purposes.

Substantial risk of forfeiture. A term that is associated with a *restricted property plan.* Generally, an employee who receives property (e.g., stock of the employer-corporation) from the employer at a bargain price or at no cost must include the bargain element in gross income. However, the employee recognizes no current income until the substantial risk of forfeiture is removed. A substantial risk of forfeiture exists if a person's rights to full enjoyment of property are conditioned upon the future performance, or the refraining from the performance, of substantial services by the individual. § 83.

Substituted basis. When a taxpayer exchanges one asset for another, many provisions in the tax law allow an assignment of basis in the received asset to be that of the traded asset(s) in the hands of its former owner. Thus, no *step-up* or *-down of basis* occurs as a result of the exchange. For instance, when an investor contributes an asset to a corporation or partnership, the partner generally takes a substituted basis in the partnership interest (i.e., the interest has a basis equal to the aggregated bases of the assets contributed by that partner). § 723.

Surviving spouse. When a husband or wife predeceases the other spouse, the survivor is a surviving spouse. Under certain conditions, a surviving spouse may be entitled to use the income tax rates in § 1(a) (those applicable to married persons filing a joint return) for the two years after the year of death of his or her spouse.

Survivorship. See *joint tenants.*

Syndication costs. Incurred in promoting and marketing partnership interests for sale to investors. Examples include printing costs for prospectus and placement documents and state registration fees. These items are capitalized by the partnership as incurred, with no amortization thereof allowed.

T

Tangible property. All property that has form or substance and is not intangible. See also *intangible property.*

Tax avoidance. The minimization of one's tax liability by taking advantage of legally available tax planning opportunities. Tax avoidance can be contrasted with *tax evasion*, which entails the reduction of tax liability by illegal means. Tax avoidance also is known as *tax planning.*

Tax benefit rule. Limits the recognition of income from the recovery of an expense or loss properly deducted in a prior tax year to the amount of the deduction that generated a tax saving. Assume that last year Tom had medical expenses of $3,000 and adjusted gross income of $30,000. Because of the 7.5 percent limitation, he could deduct only $750 of these expenses [$3,000 – (7.5% × $30,000)]. If, this year, Tom is reimbursed by his insurance company for $900 of these expenses, the tax benefit rule limits the amount of income from the reimbursement to $750 (the amount previously deducted with a tax saving).

Tax Court. The U.S. Tax Court is one of four trial courts of original jurisdiction that decide litigation involving Federal income, death, or gift taxes. It is the only trial court where the taxpayer must not first pay the deficiency assessed by the IRS. The Tax Court will not have jurisdiction over a case unless a *statutory notice of deficiency* (90-day letter) has been issued by the IRS and the taxpayer files the petition for hearing within the time prescribed.

Tax evasion. The reduction of the taxpayer's tax liability through the use of illegal means. Tax evasion can be contrasted with *tax avoidance*, which entails the reduction of tax liability through the use of legal means.

Tax haven. A country in which either locally sourced income or residents of the country are subject to a low rate of taxation.

Tax on unearned income of a child under age 14. Passive income, such as interest and dividends, that is recognized by such a child is taxed *to him or her* at the rates that would have applied had the income been incurred by the child's parents, generally to the extent that the income exceeds $1,600. The additional tax is assessed regardless of the source of the income or the income's underlying property. If the child's parents are divorced, the custodial parent's rates are used. The parents' rates reflect any applicable alternative minimum tax and the phaseouts of lower tax brackets and other deductions. § 1(g).

Tax planning. Also known as *tax avoidance.* Serving a taxpayer's desire to reduce the present value of taxes paid, using a thorough knowledge of the tax law. A tax plan does not disrupt the ongoing business of the entity, and it helps to meet the nontax goals of the taxpayer as well, while avoiding planning pitfalls presented by the Code, administrative tax law, and judicial doctrines.

Tax preference items. Various items that may result in the imposition of the *alternative minimum tax.* §§ 55–58.

Tax treaty. An agreement between the U.S. State Department and another country, designed to alleviate double taxation of income and asset transfers and to share administrative information useful to tax agencies in both countries. The United States has income tax treaties with over 40 countries and transfer tax treaties with about 20.

Tax year. See *accounting period.*

Taxable estate. The *gross estate* of a *decedent* reduced by the deductions allowed by §§ 2053–2057 (e.g., administration expenses and marital and charitable deductions). The taxable estate is subject to the unified transfer tax at death. See also *adjusted taxable estate* and *gross estate.* § 2051.

Taxable gift. Amount of a gift that is subject to the unified transfer tax. Thus, a taxable gift has been adjusted by the annual exclusion and other appropriate deductions (e.g., marital and charitable). § 2503.

Taxable income. The tax base with respect to the prevailing Federal income tax. Taxable income is defined by the Internal Revenue Code, Treasury Regulations, and pertinent court cases. Currently, taxable income includes gross income from all sources except those specifically excluded by the statute. In addition, taxable income is reduced for certain allowable deductions. Deductions for business taxpayers must be related to a trade or business. Individuals can also deduct certain personal expenses in determining their taxable incomes. See also *gross income.*

Tax-free exchange. Transfers of property specifically exempted from income tax consequences by the tax law. Examples are a transfer of property to a controlled corporation under § 351(a) and a like-kind exchange under § 1031(a).

T.C. An abbreviation for the U.S. Tax Court used in citing a Regular Decision of the U.S. Tax Court.

T.C.Memo. An abbreviation used to refer to a Memorandum Decision of the U.S. Tax Court.

Technical advice memorandum. An interpretation of the tax law with respect to a disputed item, issued by the National Office of the IRS, in response to a request from an agent, appellate conferee, or Director. Often used to reconcile perceived differences in the application of the law among taxpayers or to identify an IRS position where no pertinent Regulations or rulings exist.

Technical termination of partnership. The entity is treated for tax purposes as though it has terminated, even though it continues in its activities. When there has been a sale or exchange of more than 50 percent of the capital interests of the partnership within 12 months, the partnership is deemed to have terminated when the 50 percent threshold is crossed. A new partnership immediately is formed through asset contributions by the partners. These activities can affect the entity's tax year and its bases in the assets it holds.

Telescoping. To look through one or more transactions to arrive at the final result. It is also referred to as the *step transaction* approach or the *substance vs. form concept*.

Temporary differences. Items that affect book income and taxable income, but in different tax years.

Temporary Regulation. The Treasury often issues Temporary Regulations to offer immediate guidance as to elections and other compliance matters after a change in the statute or a court ruling has been issued. Temporary Regulations carry the same precedential value as a final Regulation, and they should be followed as such for three years after issuance, after which they expire. Often a Temporary Regulation also is issued as a Proposed Regulation.

Tenants by the entirety. Essentially, a *joint tenancy* between husband and wife. See also *tenants in common*.

Tenants in common. A form of ownership where each tenant (owner) holds an undivided interest in property. Unlike a *joint tenancy* or a *tenancy by the entirety*, the interest of a tenant in common does not terminate upon that individual's death (there is no right of survivorship). Assume Brad and Connie acquire real estate as equal tenants in common, each having furnished one-half of the purchase price. Upon Brad's death, his one-half interest in the property passes to his estate or heirs, not to Connie. For a comparison of results, see *joint tenants* and *tenants by the entirety*.

Term certain. A fixed period of years used to determine the length of an income interest (i.e., prior to the termination of a trust or estate).

Terminable interest. An interest in property that terminates upon the death of the holder or upon the occurrence of some other specified event. The transfer of a terminable interest by one spouse to the other may not qualify for the *marital deduction*. §§ 2056(b) and 2523(b).

Testamentary disposition. The passing of property to another upon the death of the owner.

Testamentary power of appointment. A *power of appointment* that can be exercised only through the will (upon the death) of the holder.

Thin capitalization. When debt owed by a corporation to the shareholders becomes too large in relation to the corporation's capital structure (i.e., stock and shareholder equity), the IRS may contend that the corporation is thinly capitalized. In effect, this means that some or all of the debt is reclassified as equity. The immediate result is to disallow any interest deduction to the corporation on the reclassified debt. To the extent of the corporation's earnings and profits, interest payments and loan repayments are treated as dividends to the shareholders. § 385.

Thirty-day letter. A letter that accompanies an RAR (Revenue Agent's Report) issued as a result of an IRS audit of a taxpayer (or the rejection of a taxpayer's claim for refund). The letter outlines the taxpayer's appeal procedure before the IRS. If the taxpayer does not request any such procedures within the 30-day period, the IRS will issue a *statutory notice of deficiency* (the 90-day letter).

Three-factor apportionment formula. A means by which the total taxable income of a *multistate corporation* is assigned to a specific state. Usually, the payroll, property, and sales factors are treated equally, and the average of these factors is used in the apportionment procedure. In some states, however, the sales factor may receive a double weight, or it may be the only factor considered. These latter formulas place greater tax burden on the income of out-of-state corporations. See also *apportion, payroll factor, property factor, sales factor*, and *UDITPA*.

Throwback rule. If there is no income tax in the state to which a sale otherwise would be *apportioned*, the sale essentially is exempt from state income tax, even though the seller is *domiciled* in a state that levies an income tax. Nonetheless, if the seller's state has adopted a throwback rule, the sale is attributed to the *seller's* state, and the transaction is subjected to a state-level tax.

Tiered partnerships. An ownership arrangement wherein one partnership (the parent or first tier) is a partner in one or more partnerships (the subsidiary/subsidiaries or second tier). Frequently, the first tier is a holding partnership, and the second tier is an operating partnership.

Title passage rule. In sourcing the profits resulting from a sale of personal property, a basic provision creates *U.S.- or foreign-source income* based on the country in which title to the goods passes from seller to buyer.

Totten trust. A bank account (checking, savings, money market, CD) that designates a survivor in the event the owner predeceases. As an example, Dan purchases a $50,000 CD and lists ownership as follows: "Dan, payable on proof of Dan's death to Nancy." The transfer is incomplete and can be revoked or changed by Dan as he sees fit. Once Dan dies, however, the CD belongs to Nancy. In effect, the Totten trust arrangement carries the same tax consequences as a revocable trust. It is a simpler and cheaper way to avoid probate as no formal trust need be created. The Totten trust arrangement also can be used with most securities (i.e., stocks and bonds).

Trade or business. Any business or professional activity conducted by a taxpayer. The mere ownership of rental or other investment assets does not constitute a trade or business. Generally, a trade or business generates relatively little passive investment income.

Transfer pricing. A means by which related parties set the price for goods or services that are sold within the group. Transfer pricing is a means by which members of the group can move net taxable income from one member to another. The IRS desires that the *arm's length price* of the sold item, or an approximation thereof, be used as the transfer price, and it can reallocate the income among the group under § 482.

Transfer tax. A tax imposed upon the transfer of property. See also *unified transfer tax*.

Transferee liability. Under certain conditions, if the IRS is unable to collect taxes owed by a transferor of property, it may pursue its claim against the transferee of the property. The transferee's liability for taxes is limited to the extent of the value of the assets transferred. For example, the IRS can force a donee to pay the gift tax when such tax cannot be paid by the donor making the transfer. §§ 6901–6905.

Treasury Regulations. See *Regulations*.

Treaty shopping. An international investor attempts to use the favorable aspects of a tax treaty to his or her advantage, often elevating the form of the transaction over its substance (e.g., by establishing only a nominal presence in the country offering the favorable treaty terms).

Trial court. The court of original jurisdiction; the first court to consider litigation. In Federal tax controversies, trial courts include U.S. District Courts, the U.S. Tax Court, the U.S. Court of Federal Claims, and the Small Cases Division of the U.S. Tax Court. See also *appellate court, Court of Federal Claims, District Court, Small Cases Division of the U.S. Tax Court*, and *Tax Court*.

Trust. A legal entity created by a grantor for the benefit of designated beneficiaries under the laws of the state and the valid trust instrument. The trustee holds a fiduciary responsibility to manage the trust's corpus assets and income for the economic benefit of all of the beneficiaries.

Trustee. An individual or corporation that assumes the fiduciary responsibilities under a trust agreement.

U

UDITPA. The Uniform Division of Income for Tax Purposes Act has been adopted in some form by many of the states. The Act develops criteria by which the total taxable income of a *multistate corporation* can be assigned to specific states. See also *allocate, apportion, Multistate Tax Commission (MTC)*, and *nexus*.

Undistributed personal holding company income. The penalty tax on a *personal holding company* is imposed on the corporation's undistributed personal holding company income for the year. The adjustments necessary to convert taxable income to undistributed personal holding company income are set forth in § 545.

Unearned income. Income received but not yet earned. Normally, such income is taxed when received, even for accrual basis taxpayers.

Unified tax credit. A credit allowed against any unified transfer tax. §§ 2010 and 2505.

Unified transfer tax. Rates applicable to transfers by gift and death made after 1976. § 2001(c).

Uniform capitalization (UNICAP) rules. A set of rules that taxpayers can use to determine the items of cost (and means of allocating those costs) that must be capitalized with respect to the production of tangible property. § 263A.

Uniform Gift to Minors Act. A means of transferring property (usually stocks and bonds) to a minor. The designated custodian of the property has the legal right to act on behalf of the minor without requiring a *guardianship*. Generally, the custodian possesses the right to change investments (e.g., sell one type of stock and buy another), apply the income from the custodial property to the minor's support, and even terminate the custodianship. In this regard, however, the custodian is acting in a fiduciary capacity on behalf of the minor. During the period of the custodianship, the income from the property is taxed to the minor. The custodianship terminates when the minor reaches *legal age*.

Unitary state. A state that has adopted the *unitary theory* in its apportionment of the total taxable income of a *multistate corporation* to the state.

Unitary theory. Sales, property, and payroll of related corporations are combined for *nexus* and apportionment purposes, and the worldwide income of the unitary entity is *apportioned* to the state. Subsidiaries and other affiliated corporations found to be part of the corporation's unitary business (because they are subject to overlapping ownership, operation, or management) are included in the apportionment procedure. This approach can be limited if a *water's edge election* is in effect.

Unrealized receivables. Amounts earned by a *cash basis* taxpayer but not yet received. Because of the method of accounting used by the taxpayer, these amounts have no income tax basis. When unrealized receivables are distributed to a partner, they generally convert a transaction from nontaxable to taxable or convert otherwise capital gain to ordinary income.

Unreasonable compensation. A deduction is allowed for "reasonable" salaries or other compensation for personal services actually rendered. To the extent compensation is "excessive" ("unreasonable"), no deduction is allowed. Unreasonable compensation usually is found in closely held corporations, where the motivation is to pay out profits in some form that is deductible to the corporation. Deductible compensation therefore becomes an attractive substitute for nondeductible dividends when the shareholders also are employed by the corporation.

Unrelated business income. Income recognized by an *exempt organization* that is generated from activities not related to the exempt purpose of the entity. For instance, the pharmacy located in a hospital often generates unrelated business income. § 511.

Unrelated business income tax. Levied on the *unrelated business income* of an *exempt organization.*

U.S.-owned foreign corporation. A foreign corporation in which 50 percent or more of the total combined voting power or total value of the stock of the corporation is held directly or indirectly by U.S. persons. A U.S. corporation is treated as a U.S.-owned foreign corporation if the dividend or interest income it pays is classified as foreign source under § 861.

U.S. real property interest. Any direct interest in real property situated in the United States and any interest in a domestic corporation (other than solely as a creditor) unless the taxpayer can establish that a domestic corporation was not a U.S. real property holding corporation during the five-year period ending on the date of disposition of such interest (the base period). See *FIRPTA.*

U.S. shareholder. For purposes of classification of an entity as a *controlled foreign corporation,* a U.S. person who owns, or is considered to own, 10 percent or more of the total combined voting power of all classes of voting stock of a foreign corporation. Stock owned directly, indirectly, and constructively is counted for this purpose.

U.S.-source income. Generally, income taxed by the United States, regardless of the citizenship or residence of its creator. Examples include income from sales of U.S. real estate and dividends from U.S. corporations.

U.S. Tax Court. See *Tax Court.*

U.S. trade or business. A set of activities that is carried on in a regular, continuous, and substantial manner. A non-U.S. taxpayer is subject to U.S. tax on the taxable income that is effectively connected with a U.S. trade or business.

Use tax. A sales tax that is collectible by the seller where the purchaser is domiciled in a different state.

USSC. An abbreviation for the U.S. Supreme Court, used in citing court opinions.

USTC. Published by Commerce Clearing House, *U.S. Tax Cases* contain all of the Federal tax decisions issued by the U.S. District Courts, U.S. Court of Federal Claims, U.S. Courts of Appeals, and the U.S. Supreme Court.

V

Valuation allowance. Contra-asset account that offsets a *deferred tax asset* when the auditors determine that it is not likely that a specific future tax benefit will be realized.

Value. See *fair market value.*

Vested. Absolute and complete. If, for example, a person holds a vested interest in property, such interest cannot be taken away or otherwise defeated.

Vesting requirements. A qualified *deferred compensation* arrangement must satisfy a vesting requirement. Under this provision, an employee's right to accrued plan benefits derived from employer contributions must be nonforfeitable in accordance with one of two vesting time period schedules (or two required alternate vesting schedules for certain employer matching contributions).

Voluntary revocation. The owners of a majority of shares in an *S corporation* elect to terminate the S status of the entity, as of a specified date. The day on which the revocation is effective is the first day of the corporation's C tax year.

Voting trust. A trust that holds the voting rights to stock in a corporation. It is a useful device when a majority of the shareholders in a corporation cannot agree on corporate policy.

W

Wash sale. A loss from the sale of stock or securities that is disallowed because the taxpayer has, within 30 days before or after the sale, acquired stock or securities substantially identical to those sold. § 1091.

Water's edge election. A limitation on the worldwide scope of the *unitary theory.* If a corporate water's edge election is in effect, the state can consider only the activities that occur within the boundaries of the United States in the *apportionment* procedure.

WESTLAW. An online database system, produced by West Group, through which a tax researcher can obtain access to the Internal Revenue Code, Regulations, administrative rulings, and court case opinions.

Wherewithal to pay. A concept of tax equity that delays the recognition of gain on a transaction until the taxpayer has received means by which to pay the tax. The *installment method,* whereunder gain is taxed proportionately as installment proceeds are received, embodies the wherewithal to pay concept. See also *involuntary conversion* and *like-kind exchange.*

Writ of Certiorari. See *certiorari.*

APPENDIX D-1

Table of Code Sections Cited

[See Title 26 U.S.C.A.]

APPENDIX D-2

Table of Regulations Cited

Temporary Treasury Regulations

Treasury Regulations

Treasury Regulations

Treasury Regulations

APPENDIX D-3

Table of Revenue Procedures and Revenue Rulings Cited

Revenue Procedures

Rev.Proc.	This Work Page
65–19	14–5
71–21	12–11
84–74	12–29
86–42	4–14
87–32	12–6, 12–7
99–49	12–11, 12–13
2001–10	12–22
2002–19	12–13
2002–32	5–11
2004–3	1–15

Revenue Rulings

Rev.Rul.	This Work Page
55–525	11–28
57–276	4–22
57–518	4–14
59–60	16–14
60–31	11–28
60–55	7–12
60–322	3–10
66–365	4–11
69–48	4–26
70–434	4–20
72–302	11–7
73–412	11–7
75–72	14–40
77–37	4–14
79–250	4–26
79–302	14–40
80–218	8–33
81–94	13–2
81–253	16–20
82–227	12–20
84–3	1–35
87–57	12–6, 12–7
88–38	7–16
93–12	6–44, 16–20
93–61	4–7

APPENDIX E

Table of Cases Cited

M

N

P

Q

S

T

U

V

W

APPENDIX F

Present Value and Future Value Tables

Present Value of $1

N/R	4%	5%	6%	7%	8%	9%	10%	11%	12%	13%	14%
1	0.9615	0.9524	0.9434	0.9346	0.9259	0.9174	0.9091	0.9009	0.8929	0.8850	0.8772
2	0.9246	0.9070	0.8900	0.8734	0.8573	0.8417	0.8264	0.8116	0.7972	0.7831	0.7695
3	0.8890	0.8638	0.8396	0.8163	0.7938	0.7722	0.7513	0.7312	0.7118	0.6931	0.6750
4	0.8548	0.8227	0.7921	0.7629	0.7350	0.7084	0.6830	0.6587	0.6355	0.6133	0.5921
5	0.8219	0.7835	0.7473	0.7130	0.6806	0.6499	0.6209	0.5935	0.5674	0.5428	0.5194
6	0.7903	0.7462	0.7050	0.6663	0.6302	0.5963	0.5645	0.5346	0.5066	0.4803	0.4556
7	0.7599	0.7107	0.6651	0.6227	0.5835	0.5470	0.5132	0.4817	0.4523	0.4251	0.3996
8	0.7307	0.6768	0.6274	0.5820	0.5403	0.5019	0.4665	0.4339	0.4039	0.3762	0.3506
9	0.7026	0.6446	0.5919	0.5439	0.5002	0.4604	0.4241	0.3909	0.3606	0.3329	0.3075
10	0.6756	0.6139	0.5584	0.5083	0.4632	0.4224	0.3855	0.3522	0.3220	0.2946	0.2697
11	0.6496	0.5847	0.5268	0.4751	0.4289	0.3875	0.3505	0.3173	0.2875	0.2607	0.2366
12	0.6246	0.5568	0.4970	0.4440	0.3971	0.3555	0.3186	0.2858	0.2567	0.2307	0.2076
13	0.6006	0.5303	0.4688	0.4150	0.3677	0.3262	0.2897	0.2575	0.2292	0.2042	0.1821
14	0.5775	0.5051	0.4423	0.3878	0.3405	0.2992	0.2633	0.2320	0.2046	0.1807	0.1597
15	0.5553	0.4810	0.4173	0.3624	0.3152	0.2745	0.2394	0.2090	0.1827	0.1599	0.1401
16	0.5339	0.4581	0.3936	0.3387	0.2919	0.2519	0.2176	0.1883	0.1631	0.1415	0.1229
17	0.5134	0.4363	0.3714	0.3166	0.2703	0.2311	0.1978	0.1696	0.1456	0.1252	0.1078
18	0.4936	0.4155	0.3503	0.2959	0.2502	0.2120	0.1799	0.1528	0.1300	0.1108	0.0946
19	0.4746	0.3957	0.3305	0.2765	0.2317	0.1945	0.1635	0.1377	0.1161	0.0981	0.0829
20	0.4564	0.3769	0.3118	0.2584	0.2145	0.1784	0.1486	0.1240	0.1037	0.0868	0.0728

Present Value of an Ordinary Annuity of $1

N/R	4%	5%	6%	7%	8%	9%	10%	11%	12%	13%	14%
1	0.9615	0.9524	0.9434	0.9346	0.9259	0.9174	0.9091	0.9009	0.8929	0.8850	0.8772
2	1.8861	1.8594	1.8334	1.8080	1.7833	1.7591	1.7355	1.7125	1.6901	1.6681	1.6467
3	2.7751	2.7232	2.6730	2.6243	2.5771	2.5313	2.4869	2.4437	2.4018	2.3612	2.3216
4	3.6299	3.5460	3.4651	3.3872	3.3121	3.2397	3.1699	3.1024	3.0373	2.9745	2.9137
5	4.4518	4.3295	4.2124	4.1002	3.9927	3.8897	3.7908	3.6959	3.6048	3.5172	3.4331
6	5.2421	5.0757	4.9173	4.7665	4.6229	4.4859	4.3553	4.2305	4.1114	3.9975	3.8887
7	6.0021	5.7864	5.5824	5.3893	5.2064	5.0330	4.8684	4.7122	4.5638	4.4226	4.2883
8	6.7327	6.4632	6.2098	5.9713	5.7466	5.5348	5.3349	5.1461	4.9676	4.7988	4.6389
9	7.4353	7.1078	6.8017	6.5152	6.2469	5.9952	5.7590	5.5370	5.3282	5.1317	4.9464
10	8.1109	7.7217	7.3601	7.0236	6.7101	6.4177	6.1446	5.8892	5.6502	5.4262	5.2161
11	8.7605	8.3064	7.8869	7.4987	7.1390	6.8052	6.4951	6.2065	5.9377	5.6869	5.4527
12	9.3851	8.8633	8.3838	7.9427	7.5361	7.1607	6.8137	6.4924	6.1944	5.9176	5.6603
13	9.9856	9.3936	8.8527	8.3577	7.9038	7.4869	7.1034	6.7499	6.4235	6.1218	5.8424
14	10.5631	9.8986	9.2950	8.7455	8.2442	7.7862	7.3667	6.9819	6.6282	6.3025	6.0021
15	11.1184	10.3797	9.7122	9.1079	8.5595	8.0607	7.6061	7.1909	6.8109	6.4624	6.1422
16	11.6523	10.8378	10.1059	9.4466	8.8514	8.3126	7.8237	7.3792	6.9740	6.6039	6.2651
17	12.1657	11.2741	10.4773	9.7632	9.1216	8.5436	8.0216	7.5488	7.1196	6.7291	6.3729
18	12.6593	11.6896	10.8276	10.0591	9.3719	8.7556	8.2014	7.7016	7.2497	6.8399	6.4674
19	13.1339	12.0853	11.1581	10.3356	9.6036	8.9501	8.3649	7.8393	7.3658	6.9380	6.5504
20	13.5903	12.4622	11.4699	10.5940	9.8181	9.1285	8.5136	7.9633	7.4694	7.0248	6.6231

Future Value of $1

N/R	4%	5%	6%	7%	8%	9%	10%	11%	12%	13%	14%
1	1.0400	1.0500	1.0600	1.0700	1.0800	1.0900	1.1000	1.1100	1.1200	1.1300	1.1400
2	1.0816	1.1025	1.1236	1.1449	1.1664	1.1881	1.2100	1.2321	1.2544	1.2769	1.2996
3	1.1249	1.1576	1.1910	1.2250	1.2597	1.2950	1.3310	1.3676	1.4049	1.4429	1.4815
4	1.1699	1.2155	1.2625	1.3108	1.3605	1.4116	1.4641	1.5181	1.5735	1.6305	1.6890
5	1.2167	1.2763	1.3382	1.4026	1.4693	1.5386	1.6105	1.6851	1.7623	1.8424	1.9254
6	1.2653	1.3401	1.4185	1.5007	1.5869	1.6771	1.7716	1.8704	1.9738	2.0820	2.1950
7	1.3159	1.4071	1.5036	1.6058	1.7138	1.8280	1.9487	2.0762	2.2107	2.3526	2.5023
8	1.3686	1.4775	1.5938	1.7182	1.8509	1.9926	2.1436	2.3045	2.4760	2.6584	2.8526
9	1.4233	1.5513	1.6895	1.8385	1.9990	2.1719	2.3579	2.5580	2.7731	3.0040	3.2519
10	1.4802	1.6289	1.7908	1.9672	2.1589	2.3674	2.5937	2.8394	3.1058	3.3946	3.7072
11	1.5395	1.7103	1.8983	2.1049	2.3316	2.5804	2.8531	3.1518	3.4785	3.8359	4.2262
12	1.6010	1.7959	2.0122	2.2522	2.5182	2.8127	3.1384	3.4985	3.8960	4.3345	4.8179
13	1.6651	1.8856	2.1329	2.4098	2.7196	3.0658	3.4523	3.8833	4.3635	4.8980	5.4924
14	1.7317	1.9799	2.2609	2.5785	2.9372	3.3417	3.7975	4.3104	4.8871	5.5348	6.2613
15	1.8009	2.0789	2.3966	2.7590	3.1722	3.6425	4.1772	4.7846	5.4736	6.2543	7.1379
16	1.8730	2.1829	2.5404	2.9522	3.4259	3.9703	4.5950	5.3109	6.1304	7.0673	8.1372
17	1.9479	2.2920	2.6928	3.1588	3.7000	4.3276	5.0545	5.8951	6.8660	7.9861	9.2765
18	2.0258	2.4066	2.8543	3.3799	3.9960	4.7171	5.5599	6.5436	7.6900	9.0243	10.5752
19	2.1068	2.5270	3.0256	3.6165	4.3157	5.1417	6.1159	7.2633	8.6128	10.1974	12.0557
20	2.1911	2.6533	3.2071	3.8697	4.6610	5.6044	6.7275	8.0623	9.6463	11.5231	13.7435

Future Value of an Ordinary Annuity of $1

N/R	4%	5%	6%	7%	8%	9%	10%	11%	12%	13%	14%
1	1.0000	1.0000	1.0000	1.0000	1.0000	1.0000	1.0000	1.0000	1.0000	1.0000	1.0000
2	2.0400	2.0500	2.0600	2.0700	2.0800	2.0900	2.1000	2.1100	2.1200	2.1300	2.1400
3	3.1216	3.1525	3.1836	3.2149	3.2464	3.2781	3.3100	3.3421	3.3744	3.4069	3.4396
4	4.2465	4.3101	4.3746	4.4399	4.5061	4.5731	4.6410	4.7097	4.7793	4.8498	4.9211
5	5.4163	5.5256	5.6371	5.7507	5.8666	5.9847	6.1051	6.2278	6.3528	6.4803	6.6101
6	6.6330	6.8019	6.9753	7.1533	7.3359	7.5233	7.7156	7.9129	8.1152	8.3227	8.5355
7	7.8983	8.1420	8.3938	8.6540	8.9228	9.2004	9.4872	9.7833	10.0890	10.4047	10.7305
8	9.2142	9.5491	9.8975	10.2598	10.6366	11.0285	11.4359	11.8594	12.2997	12.7573	13.2328
9	10.5828	11.0266	11.4913	11.9780	12.4876	13.0210	13.5795	14.1640	14.7757	15.4157	16.0853
10	12.0061	12.5779	13.1808	13.8164	14.4866	15.1929	15.9374	16.7220	17.5487	18.4197	19.3373
11	13.4864	14.2068	14.9716	15.7836	16.6455	17.5603	18.5312	19.5614	20.6546	21.8143	23.0445
12	15.0258	15.9171	16.8699	17.8885	18.9771	20.1407	21.3843	22.7132	24.1331	25.6502	27.2707
13	16.6268	17.7130	18.8821	20.1406	21.4953	22.9534	24.5227	26.2116	28.0291	29.9847	32.0887
14	18.2919	19.5986	21.0151	22.5505	24.2149	26.0192	27.9750	30.0949	32.3926	34.8827	35.5811
15	20.0236	21.5786	23.2760	25.1290	27.1521	29.3609	31.7725	34.4054	37.2797	40.4175	43.8424
16	21.8245	23.6575	25.6725	27.8881	30.3243	33.0034	35.9497	39.1899	42.7533	46.6717	50.9804
17	23.6975	25.8404	28.2129	30.8402	33.7502	36.9737	40.5447	44.5008	48.8837	53.7391	59.1176
18	25.6454	28.1324	30.9057	33.9990	37.4502	41.3013	45.5992	50.3959	55.7497	61.7251	68.3941
19	27.6712	30.5390	33.7600	37.3790	41.4463	46.0185	51.1591	56.9395	63.4397	70.7494	78.9692
20	29.7781	33.0660	36.7856	40.9955	45.7620	51.1601	57.2750	64.2028	72.0524	80.9468	91.0249

Index

G

H

I

J

K

L

M

N

O

P

Q

R

S

U

V

W

AMT Formula for Individuals

Regular Taxable Income	
Plus or minus:	Adjustments
Plus:	Tax preferences
Equals:	Alternative minimum taxable income
Minus:	Exemption
Equals:	Alternative minimum tax base
Times:	26% and 28% graduated rates
Equals:	Tentative minimum tax before foreign tax credit
Minus:	Alternative minimum tax foreign tax credit
Equals:	Tentative minimum tax
Minus:	Regular income tax liability
Equals:	Alternative minimum tax (if amount is positive)

AMT Formula for Corporations

Regular Taxable Income before NOL Deduction	
Plus or minus:	Adjustments (except ACE adjustment)
Plus:	Tax preferences
Equals:	AMTI before ATNOL deduction and ACE adjustment
Plus or minus:	ACE adjustment
Equals:	Alternative minimum taxable income (AMTI) before ATNOL deduction
Minus:	ATNOL deduction (limited to 90% of AMTI before ATNOL deduction)
Equals:	Alternative minimum taxable income (AMTI)
Minus:	Exemption
Equals:	Alternative minimum tax base
Times:	20% rate
Equals:	AMT before AMT foreign tax credit
Minus:	AMT foreign tax credit (possibly limited to 90% of AMT before AMT foreign tax credit)
Equals:	Tentative minimum tax
Minus:	Regular income tax liability before credits minus regular foreign tax credit
Equals:	Alternative minimum tax (AMT) if positive

Tax Formula for Corporate Taxpayers

Income (broadly conceived)	$xxx,xxx
Less: Exclusions (income that is not subject to tax)	(xx,xxx)
Gross Income	$xxx,xxx
Less: Certain business deductions	(xx,xxx)
Taxable income	$xxx,xxx
Federal income tax (see Tax Rate Schedule inside front cover of text)	$ xx,xxx
Less: Tax credits (including Federal income tax withheld and other prepayments of Federal income taxes)	(x,xxx)
Tax owed (or refund due)	$ xx,xxx